2194 DAYS OF WAR

2194 DAYS OF WAR

An illustrated chronology of the Second World War

Compiled by Cesare Salmaggi and Alfredo Pallavisini

BARNES
&NOBLE
BOOKS
NEW YORK

PREFACE

1 September 1939—2 September 1945: just six years, 2194 days of a gigantic war, fiercer and more destructive than any in history. Fifty-five million dead, three million missing; the domination of the world at stake. Illustrated with 620 photographs and 84 maps, this work is the classified diary, day by day, front by front, of the military and political events of those years. It is a work that makes clear what happened then and much of what has happened since.

2194 Days of War presents a simultaneous, documented view of every theatre of war, from the steppes of Russia to the jungles of Malaysia and the Solomons; from the freezing cold of the northernmost fjords to the scorching sands of the Libyan desert; from the bunkers of the West Wall to the boundless wastes of the oceans. The progress and the scale of events, by relating them one to another in a more organized way, is often most enlightening. Certain gaps are filled, certain puzzling decisions now become easier to understand. To grasp the reasons, or pretexts, that motivated the many actors in this world-wide drama, the editors use a 'tracking' technique that takes in all the political, economic and strategic backgrounds to the conflicts that soaked the world in blood for six years; yet for particular events their camera zooms in for close-ups that present them in terms not of days but of hours and even minutes.

The sources drawn upon are mainly official documents – war communiques, war diaries, histories of the war published by government departments – carefully integrated with other documents less official and so often more reliable: the diaries and memoirs of the most important military and political leaders, as well as works of scholarship, both general and specialist, from world-wide sources.

Where facts, dates or figures disagree (as inevitably happens because of the propaganda to which everyone was subjected) the most reasonable synthesis has been worked out. Often, though, the conflicting versions are both recorded, to illustrate the political and psychological motives that inspired them and made them seem to follow from the most valid factors and arguments. Facts and dates which it has never been possible to confirm, which remain to this day objects of speculation and sources of assumptions, are similarly recorded here.

Beyond all, the reader will find the 'human' facts, the misery and the glory of men involved in a tragedy that brought out the worst in them, yet which sometimes inspired them to remarkable acts of nobility, chivalry and brotherhood.

Top: Chamberlain, Daladier, Hitler, Mussolini and Ciano pose for posterity in Munich, September 1938.
Above: Neville Chamberlain signs the agreement intended to avoid a new conflict in Europe.

THE BACKGROUND

29 September 1938

The Munich Pact is signed by representatives of France (Daladier), Great Britain (Chamberlain), Italy (Mussolini) and Germany (Hitler) at the end of a conference held in the Bavarian capital to solve the Sudeten problem – the question of sovereignty over German-speaking Sudetens in Bohemia who have for some time been calling for annexation to Hitler's Germany. Czechoslovakia has always opposed the demand, seeing it as a threat both to its security and to its national integrity. But violent German propaganda, a clear prelude to action, has finally driven France and Britain to seek a diplomatic solution, calling on Mussolini to intervene as a mediator. By the Munich agreement France and Britain yield to Hitler's demands almost completely, and the word 'Munich' comes to symbolize the culmination of humiliating appeasement of the German dictator. Under the agreement Germany will occupy the Sudetenland between 1 October and 10 October and the Germans renounce any further territorial aggrandizement at the expense of their neighbours. Chamberlain and Daladier are convinced that they have halted German expansionism – that they have preserved peace, or at worst won a lengthy breathing space. Seldom can illusions have been dispelled so swiftly. Deserted by France and Britain, Czechoslovakia has to cede to Germany nearly 11,500 square miles of territory with 3,500,000 inhabitants, 2,800,000 of

THE MEN OF MUNICH

Edouard DALADIER, born at Carpentras in 1884, became a Radical Socialist Deputy in 1919. He occupied several ministerial posts from 1924 onwards and was premier on two successive occasions between 1933 and 1934. He was a firm supporter of the Popular Front government of Léon Blum (1936–7) and when the left-wing coalition collapsed he was invited to form his third cabinet (10 April 1938). The precarious and unstable political and economic situation at home (in France, as in Britain, economic depression caused reductions in defence expenditure and hence insufficient military preparedness at a time when Germany was re-arming vigorously) led Daladier to yield to Hitler and, unwillingly, to sign the Munich Pact.

Arthur Neville CHAMBERLAIN was born at Edgbaston, Birmingham, in 1869 and became a Conservative Member of Parliament in 1918. After holding several important ministerial posts, he succeeded Stanley Baldwin as Prime Minister in May 1937. He tried to counter the aggressive expansionism of Hitler and Mussolini through a policy of 'appeasement'. Very few opposed this policy, though Winston Churchill, from the back benches, warned constantly against the Nazi menace, while Anthony Eden, the Foreign Secretary and champion of collective security and action, resigned in February 1938 in protest against appeasing the dictators. When he returned to London after signing the Munich Pact, Chamberlain announced 'peace in our time'.

Benito MUSSOLINI, the Fascist Duce (leader), was born at Dovia in 1883. He came to power in Italy in 1922. At first Mussolini provided Hitler with an example and an inspiration, but as Hitler's confidence and power grew, so Mussolini became increasingly distrustful and jealous.

Like Hitler for Germany, he called for 'living space' for Italy, putting forward claims to Corsica, Tunisia, Djibouti, Nice and Savoy. But in the light of the growing German power, combined with Italy's obvious intrinsic weakness, it is clear that his peace efforts as mediator at the Munich conference were sincere and genuine.

them German-speaking. But this is not the end. A second partition, on 20 November 1938, prises further territory from hapless Czechoslovakia. The Czechs are forced to surrender to Poland 650 square miles with 228,000 inhabitants and to Hungary some 7,700 square miles with 772,000 inhabitants. With these losses the economy of Czechoslovakia is deprived of a great part of its mineral resources and its industrial installations. As a sovereign nation its independence has already become little

Adolf HITLER was born at Branau, Austria, in 1889. He became Chancellor of the German Reich on 30 January 1933. Having imposed his Nazi order on Germany he set about arousing the country's traditional nationalism through an effective propaganda campaign. With a combination of astuteness and brutality he crushed all internal opposition. In March 1936 he re-occupied the demilitarized zone of the Rhineland, yet no country opposed him. And the annexation of Austria (the *Anschluss*) to Germany on 13 March 1938 was also accepted supinely by the European powers. Now success at Munich allowed him to occupy the Sudetenland as a prelude to more serious demands, demands which finally killed the discredited policy of appeasement.

more than a façade.

1 October 1938
German troops begin the occupation of the Sudetenland. The operation has been prepared in the minutest detail months before, an obvious proof that the fate of the Sudetens was sealed long before the Munich Pact was signed.

14 March 1939
Slovakia, led by the pro-German Monsignor Jozef Tiso, declares itself independent of Prague and under the protection of Germany.

15 March
German troops cross the Czech frontier. Hitler proclaims the 'Protectorate of Bohemia and Moravia' and the Czechoslovak Republic ceases to exist.
☐ Hungary annexes Sub-Carpathian Ruthenia, the extreme eastern part of the defunct Czechoslovak Republic.

17 March
Chamberlain accuses Hitler directly of having broken his pledge.

21 March
Germany renews its harsh demands on Poland, already presented three times before (the first time on 24 October 1938): (1) the restoration to Germany of Danzig; (2) agreement to the construction of a road and an extra-territorial railway allowing communication between Germany and East Prussia across the Polish Corridor; (3) long-term guarantees of the new territorial boundaries.

23 March
The Polish government reinforces the military garrisons in the Polish Corridor. At the same time, by an agreement with Lithuania after a German ultimatum, German troops occupy the territory of Memel, which adjoins East Prussia.

26 March
Poland once more refuses the German demands.

28 March
The Poles declare that any attempt by the Germans to change the status of Danzig without Polish agreement will mean war.

31 March
France and Britain announce in a joint declaration that they will guarantee the independence and territorial integrity of Poland against any possible aggressors.

6 April
The Russian Foreign Minister, Maxim Litvinov, proposes that Anglo-Russian talks should be held at ministerial level.

7 April
In order to counter-balance German expansion into Czechoslovakia, Italian troops occupy Albania.

13 April
France and Britain guarantee the independence and territorial integrity of Greece and Rumania.

15 April
President Roosevelt invites Hitler and Mussolini to give an assurance that they will not attack 29 named countries for ten years at least.
☐ The British ambassador in Moscow, Sir William Seeds, proposes to Litvinov that the USSR should join Britain and France in guarantees to Poland and Rumania.

18 April
Litvinov proposes a ten-year alliance between Great Britain, France and the USSR.

20 April
Hitler celebrates his fiftieth birthday with the most impressive military parade ever seen in Germany.

26 April
Chamberlain announces conscription to the armed forces. The first call-up is on 1 July.

28 April
Speaking in the Reichstag, Hitler denounces the ten-year non-aggression pact signed with Poland in 1934 and the agreement by which the two countries undertook to seek a peaceful solution to the Danzig question, and goes on to demand the cession of the Free City to Germany. Hitler also rejects Roosevelt's proposal of 15 April.

22 May
The Italian and German Foreign Ministers, Ciano and Ribbentrop, sign the so-called 'Pact of Steel', an indication of the identity of interests between Fascist Italy and Nazi Germany. The pact does not actually have the solidity that its title suggests. High military and political circles in Rome recognize the dangerous gamble that Hitler has embarked on in Europe; and while it may be true that Germany has accepted Italy's condition that no war shall break out for two or three years, it is no less true that Hitler wants a war of some kind and wants it immediately. The 'Polish question' will give him the opportunity.

23 May
On the 'Polish question', Hitler tells his generals: 'Gentlemen, do not expect a repetition of the affair of Czechoslovakia; this time you shall have a war.'

27 May
France and Britain try in vain to persuade the USSR to sign an alliance with Poland. In addition to mutual distrust and suspicion between East and West, the pro-Western Foreign Minister, Litvinov, has now been replaced by Molotov, a politician much readier than his predecessor to seek an agreement with Germany, if only for tactical reasons.

25 July
240 British aircraft take part in training flights over France.

23 August
Germany and the Soviet Union, represented by Ribbentrop and Molotov, sign a non-aggression pact in Moscow. Annexed is a secret protocol referring to a future (and thus taken as definite) partition of Poland. This shattering reversal of positions leaves France, Britain and the potential victims of Nazi aggression puzzled and agitated. The 'recruitment' of the USSR, which the Western powers have not been able to achieve in long months of negotiation, is accomplished by German diplomacy in a few weeks. Why? The answer is that Berlin can offer Moscow on a gold plate something that France and Britain would never have permitted: half of Poland, as well as Bessarabia and the Baltic states.
□ Poland and France call up some classes of reservists, but do not order general mobilization.

25 August
The Western powers try to conjure up some sort of reply to the brilliant German diplomatic success. Great Britain converts the unilateral guarantee given to Poland on 31 March, jointly with France, into a formal alliance. This will involve automatic intervention by either country in case of aggression by any other. The agreement is signed in the British capital.
□ Berlin, 4.30 p.m.: Hitler is told of the signing of the Anglo-Polish treaty. 7.30 p.m.: The Führer cancels an order issued to his troops at 3.00 p.m. to invade Poland.
The German newspapers and radio, orchestrated with consummate mastery by Joseph Paul Goebbels, Minister of Propaganda and Information in the Third Reich, spread false rumours about the persecution of Germans in Poland, and actually invent complete massacres; according to these sources 24 Germans have been murdered in Lodz, in central Poland, and 15 at Bielite in the south of the country.

□ The training-ship *Schleswig-Holstein* drops anchor in the port of Danzig, to the great enthusiasm of the pro-German population.

27 August
Approaches by the British and French ambassadors in Berlin, Sir Neville Henderson and Robert Coulondre, letters to Hitler from Chamberlain and Daladier, and pressure by the two statesmen to induce the Polish government to negotiate, all are of no avail.

29 August
Through the medium of the British ambassador in Berlin, Hitler issues an ultimatum. Poland must send an emissary to the German capital by 30 August to settle the questions of Danzig and the Polish Corridor on the basis of a 16-point document drawn up by Hitler and Ribbentrop.

30 August
Expecting an immediate attack, all Polish air units leave the airports on which they were dispersed and move to operational airfields.
For the same reason, the destroyers of the Polish navy are ordered to sail to Great Britain.

31 August
To give at least formal satisfaction to Mussolini, who has been pressing among other things for the calling of an international conference to avert the war, the Führer agrees to receive the Polish ambassador, Lipsky, in Berlin. But neither side is prepared to listen. The talks only last a few minutes, and then the Germans announce that their 'generous offer' has been turned down by the Poles. The meeting between Hitler and Lipsky takes place in the late afternoon, and at 9.00 p.m. Ribbentrop sends a note to the British and French ambassadors reporting that the Poles refuse to table proposals. Several hours earlier – at 12.40 p.m. – the Führer had already signed the order for the assault on Poland; zero hour is set at 4.45 a.m. on the following day, 1 September.

8.00 p.m.: The Germans manufacture a *casus belli*, which hardly seems necessary. German sources announce: 'The radio station at Gleiwitz has been attacked and briefly occupied by Polish raiders. The raiders have been driven back across the frontier. In the course of the action one of the raiders was mortally wounded.' The truth was that the 'Polish raiders' were nothing more than men of the *Sicherheitsdienst* (German security service), dressed in Polish uniforms supplied by the head of the German secret service, Admiral Wilhelm Canaris, and led by a fanatical member of the SS, Alfred Helmut Naujocks. On receipt of an order in code from the head of the SS, Reinhard Heydrich, the twelve 'raiders' simulated the attack, taking over the radio station and reading over the microphone in Polish a rambling, threatening anti-German announcement, and then running off.

Europe in March 1939 showing the territories already annexed by Hitler since he came to power in 1933 – the Rhineland re-occupied in 1936, Austria annexed by the *Anschluss* of 1938, Sudetenland also annexed in 1938 and Czechoslovakia occupied in March 1939.

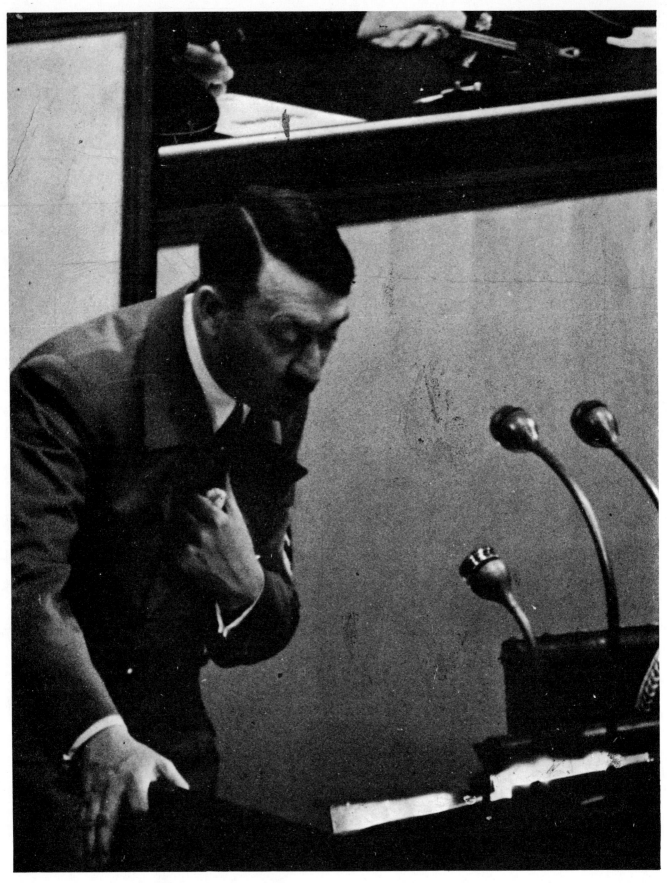

Hitler announces to the Reichstag on 1 September 1939 the entry of German troops into Poland.

1939

1939

JANUARY	
FEBRUARY	
MARCH	**15-16 March** The Czechoslovak Republic ceases to exist. The Germans occupy Bohemia-Moravia.
APRIL	**7 April** Italian troops occupy Albania. **28 April** Hitler repeals the ten-year-old non-aggression pact made with Poland in 1934.
MAY	**20 May** The Spanish civil war ends in victory for Franco. **22 May** Italian and German ministers conclude a pact of alliance.
JUNE	
JULY	
AUGUST	**23 August** Germany and the USSR sign a non-aggression pact. **25 August** Great Britain and France conclude a pact of mutual assistance.
SEPTEMBER	**1 September** At 4.45 a.m. the German army crosses the Polish frontier. War breaks out. **3 September** France and Great Britain enter the war against Germany.
OCTOBER	**6 October** The last resistance is ended and the Polish campaign is officially over. **27 October** Belgium proclaims its neutrality.
NOVEMBER	**30 November** The Russian army invades Finland.
DECEMBER	**7 December** The Fascist Grand Council reaffirms Italian non-belligerency.

Molotov signs the non-aggression pact between the USSR and Germany in the Kremlin on 23 August 1939. Behind him, from the left, are Ribbentrop, Stalin and Suslov. A secret Nazi-Soviet pact was also signed agreeing on the partition of Poland between the two countries.

Danzig, 1 September 1939: the *Schleswig Holstein*, a German armoured cruiser used as a training ship, shells the fortifications of the Westerplatte, where the arsenal of the small and vulnerable Polish navy is located.

1 September

Poland At 4.45 a.m., without any formal declaration of war, the German army crosses the Polish frontier. Operation *Fall Weiss* (White Plan) is launched. There has been no reply to the appeals of Leopold III of Belgium, made in his own name and those of six other small European countries, nor to the exhortations of the American President, Franklin Delano Roosevelt, nor to the prayers of Pope Pius XII, nor even to the proposals for mediation sent at the eleventh hour by Mussolini.

The Germans cross the frontier at several points, with 53 divisions under command of General von Brauchitsch, divided into two army groups, *Heeresgruppe Nord* commanded by General von Bock, and *Heeresgruppe Sud* under General von Rundstedt. The individual armies are commanded by Generals von Kluge, von Küchler, List, von Reichenau and Blaskowitz; the armoured formations are headed by Generals Guderian, Hoeppner and von Kleist, names which will recur again and again in the years to follow. The Polish defences are overwhelmed in a few hours, and German tanks penetrate deep into enemy territory. Simultaneously the Germans bomb several Polish cities, including Warsaw, Lodz and Krakow. In the port of Danzig the training-ship *Schleswig-Holstein*, an armoured cruiser, opens a murderous fire on the fragile defences of the Westerplatte, where the Polish navy's arsenal is situated. Danzig is annexed to the Reich (though the official act of annexation does not occur until 1 November).

The success of the invasion had been taken for granted by the Germans, and the general lines of the partition of Poland have already been laid down in the secret clauses in the Russian–German pact of 23 August. Broadly speaking, the demarcation line between Germany and the USSR is to run along the lines of the rivers Narew–Vistula–San. Lithuania is to be included in the German sphere of influence, while the Russian sphere includes Estonia, Latvia,

THE FORCES IN THE FIELD

GERMANY The quick victory over Poland probably gave an exaggerated impression of some aspects of Germany's military strength. Germany had begun rebuilding its army in 1936. Until then the conditions of the Treaty of Versailles limited the standing army to not more than 100,000 men (though in practice, with re-armament in view, many of these were officers and NCOs), with no heavy artillery and no tanks. By the end of 1939 the Wehrmacht numbered 98 divisions, 52 of them on active service and 10 others immediately available. The other 36 were largely made up of First World War veterans, and proved to be short of artillery and heavy equipment. On mobilization it would be possible in a very short time to have 16 more *Ersatz* divisions ready from support troops. The infantry were armed with the 1924 Mauser rifle, the Madsen machine-gun and the Bergmann–Schmeisser light machine-gun. It was also equipped with 81-mm mortars, 37-mm anti-tank guns, 20-mm light anti-aircraft guns and also an old 77-mm gun that dated from the Kaiser's days. The artillery, however, were well equipped, with 105-mm howitzers, 105-mm and 155-mm guns and the famous 88-mm anti-tank and anti-aircraft gun which was to become perhaps the most famous artillery weapon

of the Second World War.
However, the German Supreme Command had concentrated its efforts on the development of two arms which its strategists saw as all-important: tanks and aircraft. General Heinz Guderian, a military prophet and an indefatigable propagandist, had worked out, with Hitler's firm backing, a new strategy based on 'war of movement'. According to this tactical revolution, the tank was no longer to be auxiliary to the infantry, with artillery protection, on the traditional lines. It was to be the principal break-through weapon under its own command, followed at a distance by the infantry and protected by dive-bombers. By September 1939 the Germans could put six armoured divisions in the field, each equipped with 288 *Panzer*; of these, half were Pz Kw-1 of only 6 tons, armed with two machine-guns; their thin armour, between only 8 and 13 mm thick, gave them the nickname of 'sardine-tins'.
The really effective *Panzer* was the 20-ton Pz Kw-4, with 25-mm armour and a 75-mm gun, but there were only about 24 for each division – 144 in all. The remainder were Pz Kw-2, 9 tons, with a 20-mm gun, and Kw-3, 16 tons, with a 37-mm gun.
The aircraft industry had been rebuilt since 1935 and achieved a productive capacity of 6,000 air-

craft a year. Of the 4,800 aircraft in service, 2,695 were operational on 1 September 1939: 771 fighters, 408 fighter-bombers, 336 dive-bombers (the famous Stukas, or *Sturzkampfflugzeuge*) and 1,180 high-level bombers. They included the best types in the world – the Messerschmitt Me-109 fighters and Me-110 fighter-bombers, Junkers Ju-87 dive-bombers (Stukas), Ju-88, Dornier Do-17 and Heinkel He-111 bombers, the Ju-52 transport aircraft and the He-115 seaplane, an extremely efficient aircraft for naval reconnaissance and anti-submarine operations.
The navy was the real Cinderella of the three forces. Wholly inadequate to compete with the Western Allies' powerful fleets, it comprised the battleships *Scharnhorst* and *Gneisenau* and the 10,000-ton pocket-battleships *Deutschland*, *Scheer* and *Admiral Graf Spee* (10,000 tons was their nominal weight – in reality, they were 11,700, 12,000 and 12,100 tons). The latter were quite fast and powerfully equipped units, armed with six 280-mm cannons, eight 150-mm cannons and two anti-aircraft guns of 88-mm or 105-mm. (In December 1939, when the *Admiral Graf Spee* was scuttled, the *Deutschland* was renamed *Lützow*; it would have been a serious blow to German morale to have to risk the loss of

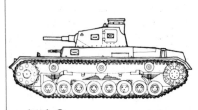

Ausf. C

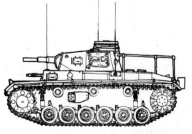

Ausf. E

Ausf. M

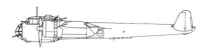

Dornier Do.17

Messerschmitt Bf.109

Heinkel He.115

Junkers Ju.88

Junkers Ju.87

Heinkel He.111

a ship bearing the name of the fatherland.) Also available were the heavy cruiser *Hipper*, the light cruisers *Emden*, *Köln*, *Königsberg*, *Leipzig*, *Nürnberg* and *Karlsruhe* (still fitting out), 21 destroyers and 12 motor torpedo boats. Still under construction were the heavy cruiser *Blücher* (commissioned towards the end of September 1939), *Prinz Eugen* (ready in August 1940), *Lützow* (handed over incomplete to the Russians at the end of 1939) and *Seydlitz*, which was never completed. Between August 1940 and February 1941 two battleships – the powerful *Bismarck* (50,900 tons) and *Tirpitz* – were commissioned, but the aircraft carrier *Graf Zeppelin* was never completed. In addition there were 159 submarines (*U-Boote*), coastal and ocean-going, and by 1 July 1943, 1,193 more had come into service.

From 19 August, twelve days before operations on the Polish

front were launched, the pocket-battleships *Deutschland* and *Admiral Graf Spee*, with 18 U-boats, took up positions in the Atlantic. Between 1 September 1939 and 30 March 1940 they sank 753,000 tons of enemy shipping, while another 317,154 tons were sunk in the Channel and North Sea by air action, destroyer and submarine attacks and mines laid by aircraft. And on 3 September 1939, the day on which France and Great Britain entered the war, many German 'auxiliary cruisers', so-called *raiders*, which were a modern version of pirate-ships, began a series of bold raids in every ocean of the world.

On the Eastern Front the Germans deployed 53 divisions, including all six armoured divisions, four motorized and four 'light' or mechanized divisions with tank contingents. Thirty-three divisions were stationed on the Western Front, largely short of

manpower, heavy equipment and artillery, and not fully trained. Only 11 of the divisions on this front were fully efficient. Hitler relied on Franco-British inertia and on the defensive Siegfried Line or West Wall, a deep fortified line which the Todt organization had started building in 1936, and which ran for 300 miles from Basel to Aachen, opposite the tremendous Maginot Line of the French. The hierarchical structure of the German armed forces was strictly centralized. At the head was the Supreme Command of the Armed Forces (*Oberkommando der Wehrmacht*, or OKW), of which Hitler and the General Staff of the Armed Forces, in the persons of Generals Jodl and Keitel, were members. Then came the high commands of the three services, of the army (*Oberkommando des Heeres*, OKH) under General Walther von Brauchitsch (Chief of Staff, General Franz Halder), of the navy (*Oberkommando der Kriegsmarine*, OKM) under Admiral Erich Raeder (Chief of Staff, Admiral Schniewind), and of the air force (*Oberkommando der Luftwaffe*, OKL), at the head of which was Field-Marshal Hermann Goering (Chief of Staff, General Hans Jeschonnek).

Panzerkampfwagen III Ausf. G-1940

Finland and Bessarabia (which is to be returned to Russia by Rumania). Britain and France demand that German forces be withdrawn from Poland. Evacuation of children from London and other vulnerable areas begins.

2 September

Poland The Germans' 'lightning war' (*Blitzkrieg*) goes ahead at full speed. The four 'border battles' (Silesia-Slovakia, Czestochowa, Pomerania, East Prussia) are all equally overwhelming victories. The forces advancing from Germany join up with those from East Prussia. Units of the 10th Army of Rundstedt's Army Group South reach the river Warta, having penetrated 50 miles into Polish territory in 36 hours. In the south General List's troops already threaten Krakow.

The Luftwaffe enjoys complete air superiority; having destroyed most of the Polish aircraft on the ground, it bombs headquarters and communications and chokes the enemy's retreat routes.

☐ Discussions take place all day between Paris and London at fever pitch. There is no question about the determination to carry out the Allies' pledges to Poland, but governments and general staffs cannot agree on when and how to intervene.

☐ Italy declares her non-belligerence, calling again for an international conference to meet on 5 September to halt the conflict.

☐ The German government declares that it will respect the territorial integrity of Norway, provided it is not threatened or attacked by other countries.

3 September

France and Great Britain enter the war against Germany. 9.00 a.m.: Sir Neville Henderson, British ambassador in Berlin, sends His Majesty's Government's ultimatum to counsellor Paul Schmidt, Hitler's interpreter. The document states that, unless by 11 a.m. – i.e. within two hours – the Germans have given definite assurances about the withdrawal of their forces from Poland, Britain will consider itself at war with Germany. France, too, finally takes action. At 12 o'clock Robert Coulondre, French ambassador in Berlin, delivers the ultimatum, to expire the following day, 4 September. But in a last desperate attempt to conciliate the German dictator the document avoids explicit use of the word 'war'. However, the sense of the two documents is identical. Hitler is astounded, for he believed that the Western powers would remain passive yet again. When Ribbentrop tells him of the new situation, he asks, surprised: 'So now what?'

11 a.m.: Great Britain is officially at war with Germany.

11.15 a.m.: Speaking from his official residence at 10 Downing Street, Chamberlain tells his countrymen the news. 'We have nothing to reproach ourselves with,' he says, and ends: 'God protect us, and defend the right.' A War Cabinet is formed; Winston Churchill becomes First Lord of the Admiralty and Anthony Eden, Secretary of State for the Dominions.

11.35 a.m.: While a Foreign Office

JOE LOUIS

On 20 September, in Detroit, the 'Black Bomber' Joe Louis successfully defended his world heavyweight boxing title by knocking out Bob Pastor in the eleventh round.

Born in Alabama in 1914, Louis turned professional in 1934. He then chalked up an astonishing sequence of victories (18 by KO), his only defeat coming against the German Max Schmeling in 1936. Next year, by beating James Braddock in Chicago, Louis became the youngest world champion in boxing history and the second coloured boxer (after the legendary Jack Johnson) to win the world championship. From then on his career was spectacular. In 1938 he got his revenge against Schmeling (who by this time had come to symbolize Nazi Germany's claim to racial superiority), knocking him out in the first round. He defended his crown another 25 times and in 1949 retired from the ring. In the following year he attempted a comeback but was beaten on points by Ezzard Charles; and in 1951, at the age of 37, he finally succumbed to the rising star Rocky Marciano.

Famed for the speed and power of his punches, Joe Louis is unanimously regarded as the greatest heavyweight in history.

Joe Louis floors J.H. Lewis.

official and the German *chargé d'affaires* are at the German embassy in London calmly arranging for the evacuation of the German diplomatic staff and their families, the sirens sound an air-raid alarm, the first of a long and terrible series. Churchill's wife remarks to her husband that one can always rely on German punctuality and precision; they go onto their roof to witness the attack, but it is a false alarm.

☐ Great Britain announces a naval blockade of Germany; all goods being carried to Germany on ships of any nation are to be confiscated.

☐ 5.00 p.m.: France declares war against the Third Reich (thus anticipating the expiry of the ultimatum, not due until the following day).

☐ India, Australia and New Zealand, the dominions most closely bound to Great Britain, declare war on Germany.

Western Front The 33 divisions of the German *Heeresgruppe C*, the army group commanded by General Ritter von Leeb, complete the garrisoning of the Siegfried Line and of the Belgian and Dutch frontiers.

Atlantic 9.00 p.m.: The German submarine U-30 sinks the British passenger ship *SS Athenia*, 13,500 tons, mistaking it for an armed merchantman; 28 American citizens are among the 112 who lose their lives. The serious episode arouses strong anti-German feeling in the USA. In Britain meanwhile consideration is given to reviving the convoy system, adopted towards the end of the First World War, to protect sea communications.

4 September

The *Völkischer Beobachter* declares that the sinking of the *SS Athenia* was arranged by Churchill to create an incident between Germany and the United States.

☐ Japan declares her neutrality and will 'concentrate her efforts on a settlement of the China affair'. Japanese troops have been fighting in China since 1931, and there has been open war since 1937.

5 September

Poland Heroism is not enough to save the Poles. The Germans force the line of the Vistula and prepare to cross the Narew and the western Bug.

☐ The United States proclaims its neutrality.

6 September

Poland The 3rd and 4th Armies of the Northern Army Group and the 8th and 10th of the Southern Group advance on Warsaw. General List's 14th Army captures Krakow and

marches towards the Rumanian frontier. The Polish supreme command gives the order for general retreat to the line of the Narew–Vistula–San. During the night the Polish government leaves Warsaw for the region of Luck–Krzemieniec, while the supreme command is moved to Brzesko on the river Bug.

☐ South Africa declares war on Germany.

7 September

Western Front French advance troops – little more than patrols –

An anti-aircraft emplacement in Paris in the Place des Invalides, during the 'phoney war'.

THE FORCES OF THE NEW COMBATANTS

FRANCE In 1939 France had the strongest army in the world, measured by the number of divisions, the establishment of artillery and, unbelievably in view of what was in store, also of tanks. In all some 110 divisions could be mobilized. There were 65 active divisions, including one armoured (still in course of formation) and two motorized; 25 more could be mobilized very quickly. Even allowing for the 13 divisions employed in the defence of vulnerable points and those guarding the Italian frontier in case of surprise attack, there were some 70 divisions facing the Germans. The French infantry were equipped with the 1886/1916 rifle, the Mas 1936 rifle, a 7.5-mm semi-automatic, St Etienne and Hotchkiss heavy machine-guns and 60-mm and 81-mm mortars. Their artillery was greatly superior to the German, even though some types dated from 1918; the 47-mm, 75-mm, 105-mm and 155-mm guns and the Hotchkiss 25-mm anti-tank gun enjoyed a considerable reputation. The 90-mm anti-aircraft gun was excellent, though only a few batteries were armed with it. Tanks, more numerous and better armoured than the German, but slower and with a smaller range, were of three types, Renault, Hotchkiss and FCM, their tonnage ranging from 6–7 tons ('armoured reconnaissance vehicles') to the 30–33 tons of the B1 and B1A. The heaviest tanks had as much as 70 mm of armour, nearly twice as much as the German Pz Kw-4; but the heavier armour reduced their speed and mobility. In all the French had

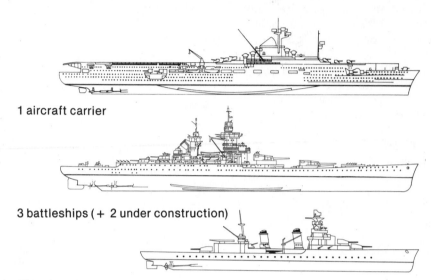

1 aircraft carrier

3 battleships (+ 2 under construction)

18 cruisers

2,475 modern and efficient tanks as well as 240 armoured cars.

The French air force was distinctly inferior to the German. France entered the war with 1,300 aircraft (a large number of them non-operational), many of them five or ten years old. The bulk of the squadrons were composed of Amiot 143, Farman 223, Bloch 174, 200 and 201; the Lioré-et-Olivier Léo-45 were really modern bombers, but only five aircraft of the type were in service on 3 September. As for fighters, the Morane-Saulnier 406 and Caudron 714 could not compete with the German Messerschmidts; the Dewoitine 520 was modern and performed well, but, again, only 90 aircraft were able to come into service before the end of 1939.

The French navy, apart from five battleships, was composed of modern and powerful units with well-trained crews. Chief of Naval Staff was Admiral François Darlan, who was later to collaborate

with the Vichy government after the fall of France. There were 8 battleships, 2 battle-cruisers, 1 aircraft carrier, 1 aircraft depot ship, 18 cruisers, 28 destroyers, 32 patrol boats, 71 submarines, 6 submersible mine-layers,, 3 motor torpedo-boats, 13 submarine hunters and other minor units.

GREAT BRITAIN Conscription was only introduced in April 1939, so that by the time war broke out on 3 September the British army was still pathetically small. In the first weeks of hostilities Great Britain was able to send five divisions to the continent, under the command of General Lord Gort; 26 more were being equipped and trained, and the intention was to bring their number up to 55 in the shortest possible time. The infantry arms were the Lee-Enfield rifle, the Bren light machine-gun, the Vickers heavy machine-gun, 2-lb and 4-lb mortars and the Boyes anti-tank rifle. The artillery was old-fashioned, apart from the new

Char B1 bis

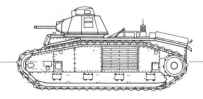

Hotchkiss H.35

Renault R.35

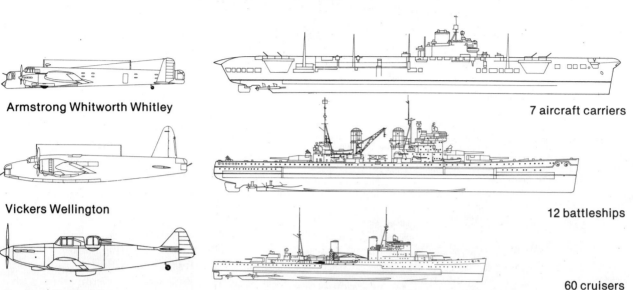

Armstrong Whitworth Whitley

Vickers Wellington

Boulton Paul Defiant

7 aircraft carriers

12 battleships

60 cruisers

25-pounders. There were few tanks; their tonnage varied between 12 and 15 tons, the biggest being the Vickers, armed with four machine-guns and a 45-mm gun.

The Royal Air Force was far from being at full operational strength (at the outbreak of war, together with the French Armée de l'Air, it was only possible to put some 950 aircraft in the air), but it was equipped largely with modern and efficient types. There were few but excellent twin-engined bombers, the Armstrong-Whitworth Whitley, Vickers Wellington and Handley-Page Hampden, as well as the lighter Bristol Blenheim. Among the fighters, besides the old Gloster Gladiator and the two-seater Boulton Paul Defiant, there were the first-class Supermarine Spitfire and the Hawker Hurricane. The big Sunderland flying-boat and the slow Swordfish were used for naval reconnaissance and bombing at sea. Chief of Air Staff was Air Chief-Marshal Sir Hugh Dowding. The main arm of the British Empire was of course the Royal

Navy, biggest in the world and also the most efficient. Besides minor units, it included 12 battleships, 3 battle-cruisers, 7 aircraft carriers, 2 depot ships for flying-boats, 15 heavy and 45 light cruisers, 184 destroyers, 58 submarines and 27 motor torpedo-boats. There was also an impressive programme of new construction: 10 battleships, 9 aircraft carriers, 23 cruisers, 32 destroyers and various other ships. The British navy had responsibilities throughout the world, yet the superiority of the Home Fleet alone over the Kriegsmarine was overwhelming, not counting the support of the not inconsiderable French navy. Many of its units, too, were equipped with the most modern scientific inventions, from Radar (*R*adio *D*etection *A*nd *R*anging, for the detection of targets by the reflection of radio waves) to Asdic

(*A*llied *S*ubmarine *D*evices *In*vestigation *C*ommittee), similar to the American Sonar, an echo-detection goniometer for locating submerged submarines – though the German navy was also equipped with this device.

In Great Britain, as in France, there was no rigid command structure as there was in Germany, but the British system was less chaotic than the French. A committee of the chiefs of staff of the three services was headed by the Chief of the Imperial General Staff, General Sir Edmund Ironside. The high command of the navy was exercised under the control of First Lord of the Admiralty, Winston Churchill.

The United Kingdom's forces were soon joined by those from various commonwealth countries (although for convenience these, as well as mixed units, are often described as 'British').

The advance of the German armies through Poland, 1–14 September 1939.

Troops of the conquering German army drawn up in a devastated Warsaw street. The capital held out heroically, but was forced to surrender on 27 September after a savage air and artillery bombardment.

cross the German frontier near Saar-louis, Saarbrücken and Zweibrücken. This is the start of what came to be called the 'phoney war', in which the armies face each other without fighting, waiting in vain for some diplomatic development.

8 September

The British revive the convoy system for their merchant ships. Three protected routes are established, two from Liverpool and from the Thames to the Atlantic, one from the Thames and the Firth of Forth.

8–11 September

Poland Fighting takes place at Radom, only some 60 miles south of Warsaw. The Germans take about 60,000 Polish prisoners.

9 September

Western Front The first units of the BEF (British Expeditionary Force) under General Lord Gort embark for France.
Poland 7.00 a.m.: The 4th *Panzer-division* launches the first attack on Warsaw, from the south-east, but is driven back to its start lines after three hours' fighting.

10 September

Western Front In reply to insistent demands by the Polish Commander-in-Chief, Marshal Smigly-Rydz, the French Chief of General Staff, General Gamelin, announces that more than half of his active divisions are in contact with the enemy on the north-east front, and that he can do no more.
☐ Canada declares war on Germany.

11 September

Poland The industrial area of Upper Silesia is completely in German hands.

12 September

Western Front The sporadic and virtually ineffective French operations against the Germans are halted. It is clear that nothing can now be done to give direct help to the Poles.

12–18 September

Poland The Polish army in the Poznan sector, the one that was to have marched on Berlin, unexpectedly turns about and attempts to take the German 8th Army in the flank. This is the start of the violent battle of the river Bzura, in which the Germans, with their greater mobility and outstanding ability to manœuvre, encircle 19 Polish divisions in the first big 'pocket' in the history of war. They take 170,000 prisoners.

13 September

The French follow Britain in setting up a War Cabinet. Edouard Daladier takes over the portfolio of Foreign Affairs in addition to that of Prime Minister.

14–15 September

Poland Warsaw is surrounded by German troops. The bulk of the Polish army, concentrated between Lvov (now in the Soviet Union) and Chelm (now on the Polish border with the USSR), comprising 38 infantry divisions, 11 cavalry brigades and 2 motorized brigades, is totally destroyed. The German generals propose to besiege Warsaw and wait until starvation drives it to surrender, but Hitler replies that the Polish capital is to be regarded as a fortress and orders the use of artillery and bombers against the city. An odd fact: the Polish general in command of the forces defending the city is called Rommel.

16 September

Poland The Germans demand the surrender of Warsaw; the demand is rejected.

17 September

Poland Molotov declares that the Polish government has ceased to exist, and the USSR gives the order for its troops to advance and occupy Eastern Poland, which is almost totally undefended.
The Germans occupy Brest-Litovsk; then, in accordance with the terms of the secret clauses of the non-aggression pact of 23 August, they evacuate some of the areas and cities they have

German troops in action in the suburbs of Warsaw. The antiquated and ill-deployed Polish forces were rapidly overwhelmed by the superior armour and mobility of the Wehrmacht, whose forces reached the outskirts of Warsaw within eight days.

SIGMUND FREUD

The father of psychoanalysis, Sigmund Freud died in exile in London on 23 September, aged 83. His legacy was the use of psychoanalysis as a cure for nervous ailments, a means of understanding the mind, thought processes and emotional life of the individual.

Born in Freiburg, Moravia, in 1856, Freud grew up in Vienna where he studied medicine and began working as a physiologist. In 1885 he went to Paris to study with the neurologist Jean Martin Charcot. His stay in France proved decisive for his career. On his return to Vienna Freud took a post as neurologist in a pediatric clinic and began to devote himself to the cure of nervous diseases. After a number of experiments in hypnotic therapy, Freud adopted the method of so-called 'free association', which sought the causes of pathological conditions by an analysis of freely associative images conjured up by the patient. It was during this fertile period that he elaborated his fundamental theories: the analysis of dreams as the key to the interpretation of mental disturbances; the existence of an unconscious life controlled by laws different from those of conscious life; the development of neuroses as the result of the repression of unconscious forces; the psychic constituents of the personality (e.g. ego, superego); the existence of repressed sexual memories in childhood (Oedipus Complex); and the conflict between fundamental instincts (love and death) as an element for the interpretation of social phenomena.

occupied, including Lvov.

The Polish president, Ignacy Mościcki, his government and the Commander-in-Chief of the Polish armed forces, Marshal Smigly-Rydz, resign and take refuge in Rumania.

☐ Off the south-west coast of Ireland the aircraft carrier *Courageous* is sunk by the U-29, commanded by Commander Schuhart; there are 500 dead. This is the first severe blow inflicted on the British fleet by the German navy, and in consequence the Admiralty determines not to employ aircraft carriers in operations against submarines.

18 September

Under pressure from the German government, Rumania interns the members of the government of Poland who had asked for asylum the previous day.

19 September

Poland The Red Army joins up with German troops at Brest-Litovsk. The Führer makes a triumphal entry into Danzig, and there makes a foreign policy speech that seems to offer conciliation with France and Britain.

For practical purposes the Polish campaign is now over. Only big mopping-up operations remain to be carried out.

Western Front The first British army corps lands in France.

27 September

Poland Warsaw, besieged and subjected to savage land and air bombardment, is forced to surrender. 160,000 men are taken prisoner.

☐ Hitler tells his principal commanders that he intends to attack France (but some of the German generals refuse to take seriously a programme apparently so far beyond the reach of German military power).

28 September

Poland In one of the last centres of Polish resistance, the ten divisions encircled since 10 September in the city of Modlin and the area of Kutno, surrender after a long and valiant defence.

TELEVISION

America's National Broadcasting Company (NBC), set up an experimental station for transmitting television programmes and at New York's World Fair carried out a series of public demonstrations that enabled thousands of visitors to get their first taste of the new medium. After some twenty years of continuous technical development, television was by now well advanced, and other companies were quick to join NBC in carrying out similar transmissions on a commercial basis. The Federal Communications Commission (FCC) therefore decided to delay operations for a while in order to introduce regulations governing both legal practices (laws against monopolies, etc.) and technical matters such as uniformity of transmitted signals.

Commercial competition in television was authorized in 1941, but America's entry into the war prevented further expansion in this field. Even so, six stations continued transmissions during the war, including NBC and CBS.

When governmental restrictions were lifted after the war, there was a rapid increase in the scope of public television transmissions and, despite the doubts of many financial experts, in the development of the industry as a whole. By 1949 there were over a million household television sets in the United States alone.

Brest-Litovsk, 21 September 1939: a Soviet officer and high-ranking officers of the Wehrmacht discuss details of the partition of Poland. Second from the right is General Guderian, the tactical genius who masterminded the use of armoured divisions as the spearhead of the new German 'war of movement'.
Above right: the partition of Poland.

29 September

In Moscow Ribbentrop and Molotov re-examine the partition of Poland and re-define the German and Russian spheres of influence. The Soviet Union is given a free hand in Lithuania, previously included in the German sphere. In exchange, the demarcation line between the Russians and Germans is moved eastwards, the Russians retiring to the line of the Narew–Bug–San, and the area between the Vistula and western Bug goes to Germany. The territory occupied by the Germans is the richest in Poland, with 22,000,000 inhabitants and something like half the total industry. The Russians annex about 77,000 square miles of Polish territory, mostly agricultural land, with 13,000,000 inhabitants.

THE 'SUMMI PONTIFICATUS' ENCYCLICAL

Elected pontiff in March 1939, when war was already imminent, Pius XII used the diplomatic channels of the Vatican and exercised his personal influence in an attempt to stop the German attack on Poland and avoid the outbreak of a general war.

On 20 October, after delivering an Easter sermon pleading for peace, Pius XII condemned the leaders of the totalitarian powers in his first encyclical, 'Summi Pontificatus', and outlined a peace formula.

□ A treaty of mutual assistance is signed between the USSR and Estonia, giving the Russians the right to occupy the country's principal naval bases.

30 September
A Polish government in exile is set up in Paris under the premiership of General Wladyslaw Sikorski; this is only the first in a long line of European governments in exile to be set up in the wake of German domination.

□ The German pocket-battleship *Admiral Graf Spee* sinks the British steamship *Clement*. The Allied forces have now lost 185,000 tons of merchant shipping. This marks the beginning of the search for the German pocket-battleships by the Royal Navy.

1 October
Poland The heroic defenders of the little garrison of the Hela Peninsula, just north of Danzig, surrender. Three destroyers and some Polish submarines succeed in escaping and making their way to British ports. Fighting ends on the Baltic and Polish coasts, and in a few days the last isolated points of resistance are overwhelmed and extinguished.

The Poles have left 694,000 prisoners in German hands and 217,000 more in the hands of the Russians. The number of Polish dead, wounded and missing is not known. The Germans have come out of the operations cheaply, with 10,572 dead, 30,322 wounded and 3,409 missing.

2 October
Delegates from 21 American countries meeting at Panama decide to set up along the coast of each nation a 'security zone', 300–600 miles deep within which any act of war would constitute a hostile act against the country concerned.

5 October
Mutual assistance treaty signed between the USSR and Latvia, granting Russia sea and air bases.

6 October
Poland The last resistance is ended and the Polish campaign can be considered over.

□ In a speech in the Reichstag, Hitler appeals for peace, proposing that the Western powers should recognize the new *status quo* in eastern Europe.

10 October
Mutual assistance treaty signed between the USSR and Lithuania; the city and area of Vilna, annexed by Poland in 1922, are restored to Lithuania, while the Russians get sea and air bases.

11 October
The French Premier, Edouard Daladier, in a broadcast to the nation, scornfully dismisses Hitler's proposals of 6 October.

12 October
Neville Chamberlain also rejects Hitler's peace proposals.

□ Negotiations between Russia and Finland for an exchange of territory are opened.

MR SMITH GOES TO WASHINGTON

On 20 October the premiere took place in New York's Radio City Music Hall of Frank Capra's *Mr Smith Goes to Washington*. The originator of sophisticated cinema comedy (*Ladies of Leisure* – 1930, *Platinum Blonde* – 1931) during the Depression years, the Italo-American director became, in the time of the New Deal, a leading spokesman for Roosevelt-style optimism and, along with Walt Disney, the most prolific creator of cultural myths during this transition period of misery to hope.

Mr Smith Goes to Washington completed a trilogy of films begun in 1936 with *Mr Deeds Goes to Town* and continued in 1938 with *You Can't Take It with You*. All three films dealt with the theme of an ordinary, honest man confronted by social wealth and corruption, fighting the evils of institutional power.

The star of this last film, which satirized the American Senate, was James Stewart, one of Capra's favourite actors.

The anchorage at Scapa Flow, the British naval base in the Orkney Islands where the German Fleet was scuttled after the First World War.

14 October

At 1.30 a.m. the German submarine U-47, commanded by Lieutenant Günther Prien, penetrates the strongly defended naval base of Scapa Flow, in the Orkney Islands, and sinks the British battleship *Royal Oak* (29,150 tons). British losses are 786 dead. The forcing of Scapa Flow, which was the graveyard of the German navy at the end of the First World War, is a serious blow to the prestige of the Royal Navy.

15 October

German-Estonian treaty signed for the transfer to the Reich of Estonians of German origin.

16 October

First air attack on British territory. German aircraft attack British ships in the Firth of Forth, damaging the cruisers *Southampton* and *Edinburgh* and the destroyer *Mohawk*.

19 October

Pact of mutual assistance between France, Great Britain and Turkey.

26 October

Monsignor Jozef Tiso becomes President of Slovakia.

☐ German-occupied Poland, apart from the areas which are shortly to be annexed to the Reich, are put under a German Governor-General, with his capital at Krakow. Hans Frank, a high Nazi official and former Reich Minister of Justice, is appointed to the post. He is installed on November 8 and begins at once the persecution of Polish intellectuals and Jews.

27 October

Belgium proclaims its neutrality.

30 October

The USSR formally annexes the occupied Polish territories.

☐ German-Latvian treaty for the evacuation of Germans from the Baltic regions.

A German mine-layer, fully laden.

31 October

The Royal Navy's hunt for the *Admiral Graf Spee* is prosecuted worldwide. Four battleships, 14 cruisers and 5 aircraft carriers are engaged.

1 November

The Free City of Danzig and the Polish Corridor are officially annexed to the Reich, together with the frontier territories ceded to Poland in 1919 under the Treaty of Versailles: eastern Upper Silesia, the area of Lodz and the district of Ciechanow.

3 November

Talks continue in Moscow between Russia and Finland on Soviet requests for an exchange of territory and the rectification of the frontier. □ The United States of America amends its law on neutrality. Despite a still strongly isolationist current of public opinion, the US government hesitantly begins to hold out a hand to the Western Allies.

7 November

Queen Wilhelmina of the Netherlands and Leopold III of the Belgians issue an appeal for peace, offering themselves as mediators between the two sides in conflict.

8 November

On secret instructions from Hitler himself, a bomb is exploded in the Bürgerbräukeller, a famous Munich beer-house and one of the shrines of the birth of Nazism. Nazi propaganda, orchestrated by Goebbels, accuses the British Intelligence Service of being responsible for the attack, naming in particular Otto Strasser, a former Nazi who opposed Hitler and fled abroad in 1933. The charge against Strasser enables Hitler to eliminate once for all one of the remaining sources of internal opposition in Germany, the left wing, notwithstanding his recent unnatural alliance with the USSR. Despite overwhelming support for the Nazi régime, enhanced still more by the success of the *Blitzkrieg* against Poland, the Führer knows that he

POMEZIA

On 29 October Pomezia, the last of the Italian 'new towns' to be built during the drainage of the Pontine Marshes, was declared open. Founded officially by Mussolini in the preceding year, Pomezia thus joined Littoria Latina, dating from 1932, Sabaudia (1934), Pontinia (1935) and Aprilia (1937). Built on the designs of the architects Petrucci, Tufaroli, Paolini and Silenzi, according to the ruralist and rationalist criteria which had governed the previous towns, Pomezia emerged as a farming community designed to accommodate 12,000 inhabitants – 3,000 of them in the urban centre – covering an overall area of 30 acres (12 hectares).

Situated almost at the gates of Rome, the new city was intended by the government to serve as a junction between the Pontine Marshes and the Roman plain, a vast territory.

Progressively and extensively transformed after the war, Pomezia has become one of Rome's major industrial satellites.

Pomezia at the time it was built.

still has some powerful enemies in Germany. Besides the more uncompromising left, there is the church, both Catholic and Protestant, and a proportion of the old military hierarchy.

12 November

Chamberlain and Daladier refuse the offer of mediation by the Netherlands and Belgium.

□ Churchill, First Lord of the Admiralty, says in a broadcast that if the British get through the winter without any serious setback, the first campaign of the war will have been won.

13 November

King Carol of Rumania offers himself as a secret mediator between the two sides.

□ The Finns break off their talks with the Russians and mobilize their forces – not exactly large, about 200,000 men – having no illusions about the outcome of the dispute. The talks began on 12 October with the arrival in Moscow of the Finnish emissary Paasikivi. The Finns were faced with a series of proposals, virtually ultimata, for an exchange of territory with the Russians. The USSR offered to cede to Finland some 2,120 square miles in the southern districts of Repola and Porajorpi in exchange for Finnish concessions in the isthmus of Karelia (between Lake Ladoga and the Gulf of Finland) and a 30-years lease of the port of Hanko. The Russians also demanded an adjustment of the boundary in the extreme north to give them the port of Petsamo (now Pechenga), the only ice-free Finnish port on the Barents Sea. The Finns were ready to meet all the Russian demands except the cession of Hanko, which would give the USSR complete control of the Gulf of Finland and the most important part of the country. But the Russians were implacable and the Finns felt they had no alternative but to leave the conference table.

14 November

Hitler rejects the mediation offered by Queen Wilhelmina and King Leopold.

16 November

The offer by King Carol of Rumania is also rejected by the belligerents.

17 November

The Supreme Allied Council meets in Paris. In case of a German attack through Belgium it is decided to defend a line from the Meuse to Antwerp. In past years Marshal Pétain had opposed extension of the Maginot Line up to the Meuse on the grounds that the terrain in the Ardennes 'would make any attempted invasion in that sector impossible'.

19 November

Churchill proposes to mine the waters of the Rhine between Strasbourg and the river Lauter, using mine-laying aircraft.

21 November

The British cruiser *Belfast* is severely damaged by a magnetic mine.

22 November

Towards evening a German aeroplane is seen to drop unidentified objects by parachute into the sea near Shoeburyness on the Essex coast. The military authorities are warned at once and send two officers of the Royal Engineers, who, when the tide goes out that night, are able

THE ROCKEFELLER CENTER

New York's Rockefeller Center, the biggest private business and amusement complex in the United States, was opened on 1 November. Begun in 1931, it was designed by a prestigious group of architectural firms (Reinhard & Hofmeister; Hoat, Godley & Fouilhouz; and Corbett, Harrison & MacMurray) and comprised space for offices, shops, gaming-rooms and entertainment halls. One of these was Radio City Music Hall, in the art deco style, opened in 1932. At the heart of Rockefeller Center is the majestic RCA Building, surrounded by thirteen smaller skyscrapers.

Opposite: an anti-magnetic mine device being installed on a British ship.

to identify the objects as submerged magnetic mines – a secret weapon which the Germans have sown in the entrances to estuaries and the approaches to British ports. The devices are de-fused and taken to an ordnance depot for further examination with a view to working out counter-measures. During September and October German magnetic mines have destroyed 56,000 tons of Allied or neutral shipping.

23 November
The British armed merchant cruiser *Rawalpindi*, on patrol between Iceland and the Faroe Islands, is sunk by the battle-cruiser *Scharnhorst*, which with her twin, the *Gneisenau*,

had gone into the Atlantic to attack the British convoys. The loss of the *Rawalpindi* is not without compensation, for the two German vessels are forced to abandon their mission and return to base, finding a way through the great number of enemy units sent out to intercept them in the North Sea. British and French ships engaged in the hunt include 15 cruisers and the battleship *Warspite*, as well as aircraft.

26 November
Russia demands the withdrawal of Finnish troops from the border.

28 November
Protesting violently that Russian

troops in the Leningrad sector have been fired on by the Finns, the Soviet government renounces the non-aggression treaty signed between the two countries in 1932. Helsinki of course denies that anything of the kind has occurred, but the Russians blow it up into their *casus belli*.

29 November
The Soviet Union breaks off diplomatic relations with Finland, ignoring the Finns' last-minute offer to withdraw their border troops unilaterally.

30 November
Finland The Soviet army invades Finland, concentrating the assault on the Karelian isthmus. Helsinki is bombed. However, the Finns stand up well to the initial assault of an enemy greatly superior to them in numbers and equipment, since the Russians, underestimating their little neighbour's capacity to resist, deploy only the major units of the Leningrad military district.

1 December
Finland Russian attacks on the Karelian isthmus continue.

2 December
Finland The Soviet news agency

Tass announces that a 'People's Government of Finland' has been formed (clearly a puppet government), under the presidency of Otto Kuusinen, a member of the Komintern for many years. But neither political and diplomatic developments nor military operations go in favour of the USSR. The Finns put up a desperate, determined and valiant defence. Moving along the narrow paths in the middle of the dense forests on bicycles or skis, they attack the big enemy units in the flank and inflict heavy losses as the Russians, of necessity, proceed along the main roads. The Finns attack the Russian tanks by hurling into their turrets a type of incendiary grenade which becomes world-famous as the 'Molotov cocktail' (basically no more than a bottle full of petrol with a lighted rag in the mouth).

Kuusinen's puppet government calls on the Finns to 'overthrow the oppressor' (meaning the legitimate government) and welcome the 'liberators' (the soldiers of the Red Army). Meanwhile Kuusinen signs a treaty with the USSR giving the Russians all they ask for, in exchange for the whole of Soviet Karelia.

☐ The *Admiral Graf Spee* sinks the British steamer *Doric Star*.

☐ The 1940 Olympic Games, which were to have been held in Finland, are cancelled.

3–12 December
Finland Finnish troops withdraw in good order under the pressure of superior enemy forces in the Karelian isthmus, and dig in on the 'Mannerheim Line', named after General Carl Gustav Mannerheim, who planned it – a national hero, founder of the Finnish Republic in 1919 and now leading the resistance against the invader. But the 'Mannerheim Line' does not really amount to very much: a modest series of wood and concrete strongpoints stretching some 25 miles across the isthmus of Karelia.

4 December
A magnetic mine damages the battle-

NYLON

The first experimental factory was set up in the United States for the industrial production of nylon, a synthetic fibre destined to revolutionize the textile industry.

In 1937, after some ten years of studies on polymers, a team of chemists led by Wallace H. Carothers produced, in the Du Pont laboratories at Nemours, a special synthetic substance composed of macromolecules belonging to the family of polyamides. In the following year Du Pont announced the discovery of this new synthetic fibre and gave it the name of nylon.

Introduced with maximum publicity to the American market as early as 1940, nylon proved an immediate success and was soon being used for making parachutes and other military materials. It served principally as a substitute for silk and helped America deal a severe blow against the economy of Japan, the world's leading producer of that natural fibre.

After the war nylon was used on a massive scale in certain sectors of industry and made its impact on the world of fashion: women's stockings manufactured from this fibre quickly brought about a virtual revolution in the clothing field, and nylon became one of the most potent symbols of that period.

Betty Grable.

ship *Nelson*. This is the last notable victim of the insidious German 'secret weapon'; English technicians have succeeded in finding a means of neutralizing the magnetic mine by 'de-magnetizing' the hull of the ships by means of an electric cable, by a method known as 'de-gaussing'.

☐ A black day for the Allied navies: two destroyers are sunk and two others and one minelayer damaged.

5 December
Finland The Russians reach the Mannerheim Line garrisoned by the II Army Corps.

6 December
Finland Heavy Russian attacks on the Mannerheim Line.

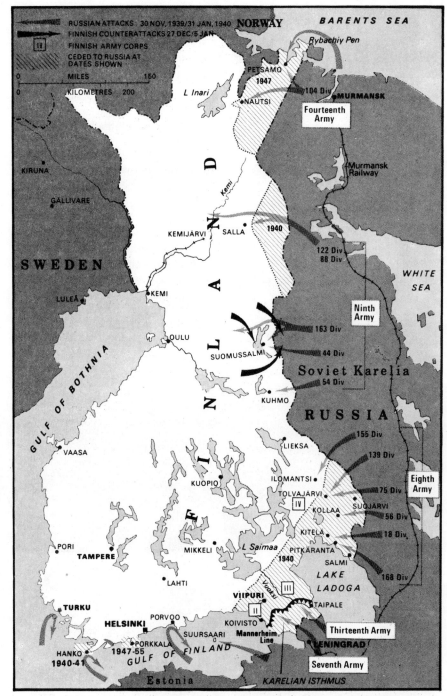

Above: the Russian campaign in Finland from 30 November 1939 to 31 January 1940.

THE FORCES IN THE FIELD

FINLAND On general mobilization the army numbered 9 divisions and 8 independent brigades, with a total of 150,000 men. Ill-equipped in all departments, the Finns were short even of uniforms and tents. The artillery was wholly inadequate; each division had 18 81-mm mortars, 36 guns, all antiquated, and 112 37-mm anti-tank guns. There was no anti-aircraft and virtually no motorized transport or radio signals. The air force consisted of about 150 aircraft, none of them modern, while the tiny navy was no more than an efficient coastal defence system.

USSR About 45 divisions took part in the war against Finland, with a total of about 800,000 men, 1,500 tanks and 1,000 aircraft. In numbers and equipment the Russians were vastly superior to the Finns, but they were ill-equipped for a winter war in northern latitudes (many of their troops were sent into action in summer uniforms, presumably on the assumption that the campaign would only last a few days), while the Finns, almost completely unprovided with war material, took advantage of the conditions magnificently and managed to surprise the powerful invader.

7 December
Finland A Russian division succeeds in breaking through to the village of Suomussalmi, on Lake Kianta.
□ The Fascist Grand Council reaffirms Italian non-belligerency.
□ Denmark, Sweden and Norway declare the strictest neutrality in the Russian-Finnish war.
Atlantic The *Admiral Graf Spee* sinks yet another British ship. This dreaded German unit has become the *bête noire* of the Allied navies. A squadron commanded by Commodore Harwood, consisting of two heavy and two light cruisers, is despatched to the estuary of the River Plate on the assumption that the German raider is bound to return to that area to attack shipping on the crowded American route based on the estuary, which includes among others the ports of Montevideo and Buenos Aires.

11 December
Hitler meets the Norwegian politician Vidkun Quisling, founder of the 'National Union', a Norwegian pro-Nazi movement.

THE SINKING OF THE *GRAF SPEE*

13 December

At 6.14 a.m. the *Admiral Graf Spee* is sighted off the estuary of the River Plate, about 150 miles from Montevideo, by the heavy cruiser *Exeter* and the two light cruisers *Ajax* and *Achilles* (the latter a ship of the New Zealand Navy); the fourth unit of the squadron, the heavy cruiser *Cumberland*, is revictualling in the Falkland Islands. The commanding officer of the *Graf Spee*, Captain Hans Langsdorff, thinking he is taking on only one cruiser (he has mistaken the *Ajax* and *Achilles* for destroyers), instead of withdrawing at full speed, opens fire on the British naval squadron. At 6.17 a.m. – three minutes later – the British squadron returns the fire. The *Graf Spee* is hit and retreats towards the River Plate under a smoke-screen. The *Exeter* and the *Ajax* are seriously damaged, but the British squadron continues to pursue the enemy, maintaining a barrage of fire. However, at 7.40 a.m. the badly damaged *Exeter* has to break off the action. The *Ajax* and *Achilles* (the latter also hit, but not so seriously) continue the pursuit. At 7.54 a.m. the action is broken off. The *Graf Spee* has a number of its guns out of action, damage to its hull and many crew-members wounded. Captain Langsdorff, though he realizes that he is entering a trap, decides to take refuge in the neutral port of Montevideo, where in accordance with international law he can stay for not more than 72 hours. The German ship enters port towards midnight. The wounded are disembarked and transferred to a German merchant ship already in the port and arrangements are made for the most urgent repairs. Although the German ambas-sador in Montevideo presses the Uruguayan government, the 72-hour term is not extended. The *Ajax* and *Achilles*, now joined by the *Cumberland*, lie in wait for their prey just outside Uruguayan territorial waters.

17 December

When the 72 hours' term conceded by the Uruguayan government expires the *Graf Spee* slowly leaves Montevideo harbour, making for the middle of the bay. Captain Langsdorff is under the impression that the British units waiting for him outside the territorial waters have been joined by the battle-cruiser *Renown* and the aircraft carrier *Ark Royal*, and has asked Berlin for permission to scuttle his ship rather than endure blockade, seizure and the internment of the crew. Berlin authorizes destruction of the battleship. At 6.15 p.m. the *Graf Spee* gets under way, watched by a vast crowd of incredulous onlookers. Most of the crew have been disembarked. At 8.50 p.m., having reached the middle of the estuary, the *Admiral Graf Spee* is scuttled; the *Renown* and the *Ark Royal*, in-

The *Graf Spee*.

direct causes of the destruction, are a thousand miles away.

So ends a hunt begun by the Royal Navy on 30 September. Together with its sister ship *Deutschland*, the *Admiral Graf Spee* was a gem of German naval architecture: 12,100 tons, with 10 cm of armour, she had six 280-mm guns and eight 150-mm; her maximum speed was 26 knots, and at her cruising speed of 19 knots she had a range of 12,000 miles. Laid down in 1934 and commissioned two years later, she was despatched to the Atlantic with the *Deutschland* in August 1939. The two ships were first in action on 26 September and in a little more than two months they sank more than 50,000 tons of Allied and neutral shipping. When news of the attacks on merchant ships reached the Admiralty they sent at least nine squadrons to seek and destroy the German battleships. The squadrons consisted of British, French and New Zealand ships – 4 battleships, 14 cruisers, 5 aircraft carriers and an appropriate number of destroyers. On 11 November the *Deutschland*, which had been watching the northern Atlantic routes, prudently returned to Germany across the Arctic Ocean and the North Sea. But the *Graf Spee* continued its operations, using 'hit-and-run' tactics in the South Atlantic and Indian Ocean. And then the German battleship encountered Commodore Harwood's squadron. Fearing the psychological damage and loss of prestige should Germany lose also a ship bearing the name *Deutschland*, Hitler orders that the sister ship should be renamed *Lützow*.

20 December
Captain Hans Langsdorff, commanding the *Graf Spee*, commits suicide, 'to prevent discredit falling on the German flag'.

17 December 1939: the *Graf Spee* leaves Montevideo harbour and makes for the centre of the bay where she is scuttled.

Clearing debris in Helsinki after a Russian bombardment.

12 December

Finland France sends Finland 5,000 1915-model machine-guns; Britain contributes a number of Brandt mortars and light machine-guns made in 1924, with some aircraft.

☐ Churchill speaks in favour of a landing in Norway. In his speech he says that 'it is humanity, and not legality, that we must look to as our judge'.

13 December

Atlantic Battle of the River Plate, *Admiral Graf Spee* damaged.

'GONE WITH THE WIND'

On 15 December the premiere took place at Atlanta's Grand Theatre, decked out for the occasion to resemble Ashley Wilkes's Twelve Oaks plantation home, of *Gone With the Wind*, probably the most famous film of all time.

Based on the highly successful novel of the same name by Margaret Mitchell, published three years previously, the film was a triumph of Hollywood's art, a synthesis of history and melodrama, brimming with emotional intensity and featuring special Technicolor effects unprecedented on the screen.

Gone With the Wind was the perfect example of a producer's film, the brainchild of David O. Selznick, one of the giants of the Hollywood scene. Having bought the rights from Margaret Mitchell, Selznick, who had just quit MGM, embarked on his enormously costly venture, continuously changing the script and the directors (he gave the job first to George Cukor, then to Sam Wood and finally to Victor Fleming), and initiating a hunt, almost literally, for the ideal actors. After innumerable screen tests, he finally came up with the inspired choices of Clark Gable (the Rhett Butler of the author's dreams) and Vivien Leigh (Scarlett O'Hara).

Apart from soaking more handkerchiefs than any other film in cinema history, *Gone With the Wind* set up a box office record for takings (80 million dollars on its original launch and more than 150 million dollars subsequently: a record unbeaten until the 1970s) and won ten Oscars.

Above: Tara, after the storm. Right: Vivien Leigh and Clark Gable.

Top: the Maginot Line; tank traps.
Above: Maurice Chevalier and Josephine Baker visiting the troops.

DDT

The Swiss chemist Paul Müller developed the formula of DDT (dichlorodiphenyl-trichloro-ethane), a very powerful synthetic insecticide, which was colourless and odourless. DDT was soon being widely used by Allied troops posted to countries infested by insects of all types.

After the war DDT was used on a massive scale until the discovery of its high level of toxicity for humans led to the gradual abandonment of the insecticide.

Division, British Expeditionary Force (BEF). This division is deployed south of Lille along a fortified line, which is extended and strengthened during the months of inactivity which Hitler allows to his troops on the Western Front, perhaps in the hope of finding a diplomatic solution. The line is reinforced with 400 new casemates and 40 miles of concreted anti-tank ditches. The BEF is only in direct contact with the enemy in the Metz sector.

16 December
Finland The main Russian assault begins. The attack takes place in the Summa sector, following intensive artillery preparation. But during the night Finnish soldiers who have been given special training put about 70 Russian tanks out of action.

17 December
The *Admiral Graf Spee* is scuttled.

22 December
Finland Despite repeated Russian attacks, the Finnish positions remain firm. This first battle has ended in a serious defeat for the Red Army.

23 December
A number of Latin American countries send a strong protest to the British, French and German governments about the recent naval action

RADIO SERIALS

The adventurous exploits of Dick Tracy and similar heroes were followed eagerly by American listeners of all ages. Equally successful were a further six daytime 'soap operas', so called because they were sponsored by leading soap and detergent manufacturers.

Probably the most popular soap opera was *Amos n' Andy*, produced by NBC. Millions of fans also tuned in regularly to the episodes of *Our Gal Sunday* (CBS).

14 December
Russia is expelled from the League of Nations following its aggression against Finland – one of the few decisive acts ever taken by this international organization which was to have guaranteed world peace. The League asks member countries to give all possible aid to Finland.
☐ Hitler orders the *Oberkommando der Wehrmacht* (OKW), the Supreme Command of the German armed forces, to prepare a preliminary study of plans for an invasion of Norway. The study later becomes the actual operational plan for invasion.

15 December
Western Front Three British infantry brigades sent to France in October are formed into the 5th

'THE GRAPES OF WRATH'

This was the year when the already celebrated writer John Steinbeck (*Tortilla Flat, Of Mice and Men*, etc.) published *The Grapes of Wrath*. The book was nominated 'novel of the year' in America and won Steinbeck the Pulitzer Prize for Literature.

A clearsighted, unsparing analysis of misery and exploitation during the Depression years, *The Grapes of Wrath* described, in terse, raw terms, the dramatic adventures of the Joad family in the Californian Dust Bowl. The book gained Steinbeck the reputation of being the mouthpiece of the American working class.

In 1940 John Ford made a film of the novel, with the same title. Although most of the original book's crude dialogue had been cut out and the ending made more optimistic, the film proved of the director's finest achievements, and with its fiery intensity of feel-

Henry Fonda in a scene from the film, directed by John Ford.

ing was hailed as the cinematic manifesto of the New Deal.

Ironically, one of the producers of *The Grapes of Wrath* was the Chase National Bank, an institution which during the Depression crisis of 1929 had played a key part in the expropriation of numerous farms, resulting in the mass exodus of thousands of farm families and labourers.

off the mouth of the River Plate. The document declares that the episode was a dangerous violation of the American 'security zone'.

□ Two German merchantmen are intercepted by British ships near the United States coast. One of them, the *Columbus*, is sunk, while the other takes refuge in territorial waters off

Florida. In an explanatory letter to Roosevelt, Churchill argues that police action by Allied fleets in the Atlantic also serves to protect US and South American merchant traffic, since German raiders have the right, after taking off the crews, to capture or sink neutral ships if they are carrying goods for the Allies.

The Maginot Line; barbed wire entanglements and fortifications.

24 December
Pope Pius XII makes a Christmas Eve appeal for peace.

25 December
Western Front Within the concrete and under the turrets of the Maginot and Siegfried Lines the armies celebrate the first Christmas of the war. The Western Front is quiet and the 'phoney war' goes on. But the Führer has prepared new plans for the coming months.
Finland The Finns have more to celebrate than the Russians, for they still manage to resist the invaders. Using intelligent and courageous guerrilla tactics in the severest conditions (they are fighting in temperatures of minus 30°C), the Finnish David has so far compelled the Soviet Goliath to mark time.

28 December
Meat rationing is introduced in Britain.

29 December
Finland The Finns succeed in their third attempt to drive the Russians back from the north bank of Lake Ladoga; the survivors of the Russian 163rd Division are driven back in a desperate retreat. The Finns capture 11 tanks, 25 guns and 150 trucks.

30 December
Hitler gives a New Year message to the German people: 'The Jewish-capitalistic world will not survive the twentieth century.'

31 December
Attacks by U-boats and surface warships, magnetic mines and air action have cost the Allies 746,000 tons of merchant shipping, one aircraft carrier, one auxiliary cruiser, and the battleship *Royal Oak*, since the opening of hostilities. On their side, the Germans have lost only about ten U-boats, the *Admiral Graf Spee* and a few tens of thousands of tons of merchant shipping. The balance is clearly in favour of the Kriegsmarine.

1940

1940

JANUARY	**30 January** In a speech at the Berlin Sportpalast, Hitler declares that the first phase of the war has been completed with the destruction of Poland.
MARCH	**12 March** A peace treaty between Finland and the Soviet Union is signed in Moscow.
APRIL	**9 April** German troops invade Denmark and Norway.
MAY	**10 May** German offensive on the Western Front: in London, Churchill forms a coalition government. **22 May** The British Parliament passes the Emergency Powers (Defence) Act, giving the government control over persons and property. **27 May** Evacuation of the British Expeditionary force from Dunkirk (Operation Dynamo).
JUNE	**10 June** Italy declares war on France and Great Britain. **18 June** General de Gaulle broadcasts his first message to the French people from London.
JULY	**16 July** Hitler issues Directive no. 16, the official 'starting-gun' for Operation Sea lion, its object the landing of 20 divisions on the south coastline of Britain.
AUGUST	**13 August** The *Adlertag* (Day of the Eagle), the code-name given to the first day of the bombing campaign by the Luftwaffe on British headquarters, airfields and aircraft factories.
SEPTEMBER	**7 September** The 'London Blitz' begins at 5.00 p.m.: 300 German bombers drop 337 tons of bombs on London. **27 September** Tripartite Pact between Germany, Italy and Japan.
OCTOBER	**28 October** At dawn Italian troops in Albania cross the Greek frontier.
NOVEMBER	**14 November** During the night 449 German aircraft bomb Coventry, centre of the British automobile industry.
DECEMBER	**9 December** In Egypt the British break through the Italian lines at Sidi Barrani. **29 December** President Roosevelt declares: 'We must be the arsenal of the democracies.'

Under constant attack by Stukas, British and Allied troops crowd the beaches at Dunkirk waiting for rescue vessels. The British abandon 2,000 guns, 60,000 vehicles, 600,000 tons of fuel and supplies, and 76,000 tons of munitions in France.

4 January

Hermann Goering takes control of all German war industries.

5 January

Russia signs a commercial treaty with Bulgaria. This is one step in a policy of growing penetration in the Balkans.

7 January

Finland Command of the Russian forces is taken over by General Semyon Konstantinovich Timoshenko.

8 January

Finland The Russian 44th Assault Division is annihilated by the Finns under General Siilasuvo in the area of Suomussalmi. The Finns capture 35 tanks, 50 guns, 25 anti-tank guns and 250 trucks.

☐ In Britain further food rationing (bacon, butter and sugar) begins.

10 January

Hitler tells the commanders of the three services, Hermann Goering (airforce), Erich Raeder (navy) and Walther von Brauchitsch (army), that he has decided to attack on the Western Front on 17 January.

A German aircraft carrying Major Reinberger and Major Hoenmans makes a forced landing near Mechelen-sur-Meuse, a Belgian agricultural town not far from the German frontier. The two officers are carrying secret documents for the commander of Army Group B, dealing with the plans for attack on the Western Front. The authorities in Brussels are thus alerted about Hitler's intention to attack their country and the Netherlands, which will be in the middle of the German thrust westward.

13 January

Hitler puts off the attack on the Western Front to 20 January because of unfavourable weather conditions.

15 January

Belgium refuses to give permission for French and British troops to cross Belgian territory.

DIRECTIVE NO. 6

According to the Führer's Directive No. 6 of 6 October 1939, a great German offensive on the Western Front should have been launched on 12 November with the objective of 'occupying enough Dutch, Belgian and French territory to permit naval and air action against Britain and to allow a security belt to be formed round the Ruhr basin' – the heart of Germany's heavy industry. (The final objective was of course the invasion of France.) The plan of attack, *Fall Gelb* (Yellow Plan), was both unpractical and out of date.

Many officers were opposed to the Yellow Plan, foremost among them General Erich von Manstein, Chief of Staff of von Rundstedt's Army Group South, who was instructed to make a study of it. Von Manstein prepared an alternative plan of his own, involving an assault by armoured divisions in the Ardennes sector. Von Manstein was relieved of his command and appointed to command the newly formed XXXVIII Army Corps. On 17 February 1940 von Manstein paid his formal visit to the Führer before taking up his new post, and he took the opportunity to discuss his plan of attack. Hitler, decided to adopt von Manstein's plan. These were its main points: two days before the Ardennes attack the Wehrmacht would invade Holland and Belgium so as to draw off as many of the Allied divisions as possible to the north. If the enemy fell into the trap a great part of the Franco–British forces would be surrounded and wiped out Having established control of the Channel coast the German army would be able to switch its attacks against Paris and the heart of France.

General Erich von Manstein.

16 January

Hitler definitely defers his offensive in the west until the spring.

☐ The French decide to raise two more armoured divisions.

☐ The Allies begin to prepare for armed intervention in the Scandinavian peninsula.

20 January

In a broadcast from London Churchill speaks of the Allied superiority at sea over the Kriegsmarine.

26 January

It is stated in London that of 734,883 children evacuated since the start of the war, 316,192 had returned to their homes by 8 January.

27 January

Although not yet fully convinced, Hitler orders preparations for the campaign against Norway and Denmark to commence. However, the Allies also have their eyes on Norway.

☐ In a speech to the Chamber of Commerce in Manchester, Churchill

WALT DISNEY

After the resounding success of *Snow White and the Seven Dwarfs* (1937), Walt Disney made two further full-length films between 1939 and 1940: *Pinocchio* and *Fantasia*.

Planned to appear in 1939, *Pinocchio's* screening was delayed because of problems related to the adaptation of Collodi's book and the implementation of the numerous special effects; so its premiere in America only took place in February 1940. The film was well received by the critics but even though the features of the puppet were reminiscent of those of the highly popular seven dwarfs, the film did not go down well with the public.

In November, New York welcomed *Fantasia*, an ambitious experiment in high-quality film animation. The collaboration between Disney and the conductor Leopold Stokowski resulted in a harmonious blend of animated cartoon and classical music, signalling the return of Mickey Mouse in the visual adaptation of *The Sorcerer's Apprentice* by Paul Dukas. Other episodes were inspired by the music of Bach, Tchaikowsky, Stravinsky, Beethoven, Ponchielli, Mussorgsky and Schubert. The visual and sound effects were extraordinary, the soundtrack being conducted by Stokowski himself. Despite all this, *Fantasia* was not the great commercial success that had been hoped for.

says he is puzzled and worried about the 'phoney war', and wonders why Britain has not been bombed yet.

29 January
Finland Secret negotiations have taken place in Stockholm on the initiative of the Russians to try and reach a diplomatic solution to the conflict. As a result of these talks the USSR sends the Swedish government a note saying: 'The Soviet Union has no objection in principle to a possible agreement with the Ryti government' (the legitimate govern-

ment of Finland). This declaration opens the way to peace, since the USSR is implicitly saying that it is ready to renounce support of Kuusinen's puppet government.

30 January
In a speech at the Berlin Sportpalast, celebrating the 7th anniversary of his Chancellorship, Hitler declares that the first phase of the war has been completed with the destruction of Poland. The second phase might perhaps start with a 'war of bombs', such as Churchill showed himself so impatient for three days before.

1 February
Finland General Timoshenko launches a large-scale attack against the Finnish line in the Summa sector. Preceded by an intensive barrage and supported by effective aerial action, the attack is carried out by tanks and infantry simultaneously.

2–3 February
Finland The Finnish army succeeds in holding the Russian attack on the Mannerheim Line.

5 February
Finland The Allied Supreme War Council approves a plan for intervention in Finland; meanwhile they send substantial help in aircraft, anti-tank and anti-aircraft guns. The expeditionary force is to comprise at least three divisions.

9 February
General von Manstein is appointed Commander-in-Chief of the newly formed XXXVIII Army Corps.

10 February
Finland At a meeting of the Finnish Defence Council attended by Prime Minister Ryti, Foreign Minister Tanner and General Mannerheim, three possible political approaches to the USSR are discussed: (1) to offer the Russians, as a peace concession, an island off Hanko, which they demanded when hostilities began; (2) to continue the war with active support from Sweden (assuming that this is forthcoming); (3) as a last resource, to accept the offer of intervention by Great Britain and France.

11 February
Finland The Soviet 7th Army breaches the Mannerheim Line. The Finns retire in good order to a second defensive line.
□ An economic agreement is signed between the Soviet Union and Germany by which Moscow will export raw materials, especially oil, and agricultural produce in exchange for manufactured goods and arms.

12 February
Finland General Mannerheim ex-

presses anxiety about the proposals for Allied intervention.

14 February

Britain announces that all her merchant ships in the North Sea are to be armed.

15 February

The German government declares that all British merchant ships will be regarded as warships.

16 February

The British destroyer *Cossack* attacks the German ship *Altmark* in Jossing fjord, in Norwegian territorial waters. The *Altmark* had been acting as a supply ship for the *Admiral Graf Spee*, and has on board 299 British prisoners, whom the *Cossack* succeeds in releasing. The Oslo government protests against British violation of Norwegian neutrality.

17 February

Finland Finnish troops complete their withdrawal from the Mannerheim Line to intermediate positions.

19 February

Hitler orders more rapid progress with Operation *Weserübung*, the code-name for the invasion of Norway and Denmark.

20 February

General Nikolaus von Falkenhorts, former commander of the XXI Army Corps, is given command of the German troops to occupy Norway and Denmark.

21 February

Finland General Timoshenko regroups his formations as a prelude to a new attack on the Finnish defensive lines.

☐ Work begins on the transformation of Auschwitz, a little town of about 12,000 people, into a German concentration camp.

23 February

Finland The Soviet government passes to Finland the final conditions for peace: Finland must surrender the Karelian isthmus and the borders of Lake Ladoga and grant a 30-year lease to the Soviet Union of the Hanko peninsula; and finally must sign a pact of mutual assistance making the Gulf of Finland strategically secure for both countries. In exchange, the Russians will evacuate the Petsamo area.

☐ Sweden announces officially that it will in no circumstances intervene in the Russian–Finnish conflict and will not allow Allied troops to cross its territory.

26 February

In view of the attack on the *Altmark*, Hitler sees Norwegian neutrality as too unreliable. Preparations for Operation *Weserübung* against Norway and Denmark are therefore accelerated and the Führer signs the first Directive to get it under way. Germany is interested in Norwegian iron ore as well as in the strategic position of the two Scandinavian countries.

27 February

Finland Towards evening General Mannerheim orders his army to evacuate the second defensive line.

28–29 February

Finland Timoshenko's troops overrun the second Finnish defensive line.

1 March

Finland The Soviet ultimatum putting peace proposals to Finland expires.

Western Front The phoney war continues with a few exchanges of artillery and a little patrol action. German air force action over the North Sea and the Orkneys.

☐ The US Secretary of State, Sumner Welles, arrives in Berlin from Rome before going on to London and Paris. His government has instructed him to offer American mediation in the search for a basis of agreement between the belligerents. But the enterprise is doomed to failure, first because it is too late, and secondly because by now none of the combatants believes that peace is possible.

2 March

The French army information services reveal German preparations for an attack on Norway and Denmark. Sweden and Norway repeat their warning that Allied troops and war material may not cross their territory.

3 March

Finland General Timoshenko launches a massive offensive in Karelia.

4 March

Finland Russian armoured troops attack the city of Viipuri (now Vyborg, in the USSR), the most important strategic point in Karelia and indeed in southern Finland. The operation is favoured by thick ice covering the waters of the Gulf of Finland.

5 March

Finland The USSR announces that it is 'once more' prepared to negotiate peace on the terms offered before, which expired on 1 March. The Finnish government, faced with a desperate military situation, accepts.

6 March

Finland A Finnish delegation led by Juho Kusti Paasikivi, an experienced politician and diplomat, arrives in Moscow. General Mannerheim, seeing it is useless to continue the one-sided struggle, has accepted that there must be talks with the Soviet Union. The Western powers still continue to offer aid, but send only small quantities of mostly out-of-date arms.

8 March

Finland The Russians take Viipuri. The USSR refuses a Finnish request for an immediate armistice.

9 March

Finland The Finnish army is no longer able to hold its positions and General Mannerheim asks the politicians to come to terms with the enemy.

The aftermath of a Russian air attack on Viipuri, the most important strategic point in southern Finland.

12 March
A peace treaty between Finland and the Soviet Union is signed in Moscow. The conditions dictated by the Soviet government and accepted by the Finns are severe; they include the cession of the Karelian isthmus, including Viipuri, of part of eastern Karelia, and of the Rybachiy peninsula in the Barents sea. The terms confirm that the Hanko peninsula must be leased to the USSR for 30 years and that Russian personnel and materials must be allowed free passage in the region of Petsamo. Stricken and humiliated, Finland still retains its independence.

CONCERTO FOR COOTIE

1940 was a particularly rewarding year for Duke Ellington, in terms of creative achievement and recording. His band, boosted by the arrival of two top-class instrumentalists in Ben Webster (tenor sax) and Jimmy Blanton (double-bass), was by this time virtually unrivalled in its field and the 'Duke' now brought out a series of extraordinary new arrangements and original compositions. Recordings which were to take their place in the annals of jazz history included 'Jack the Bear', 'Cotton Tail', 'Ko Ko' and, particularly, 'Concerto for Cootie', a piece dedicated to his trumpet soloist Charles 'Cootie' Williams. Recorded in Chicago on 15 March, 'Concerto for Cootie' remains a true masterpiece of Ellington's classic period, displaying a near-perfect balance between the orchestral and solo parts. Precise and deliberate in structure, it represents a landmark in the history of the jazz concerto.

13 March
Finland At 11.00 a.m. all hostilities cease on the Finnish front. In its war with the Soviet Union, Finland has lost some 25,000 dead, as against 200,000 lost by the Russians; the wounded number 45,000 against an unspecified, but certainly higher, number by the Russians. By the end of the operations on the Finnish front, at least 45 Russian infantry divisions, 4 cavalry divisions and 12 armoured groups have been deployed. The Finns have never been able to put more than 200,000 men altogether in the field.

18 March
Hitler and Mussolini meet at Brennero, on the Brenner Pass. The Italian dictator declares that Italy is ready to join in the war against Britain and France.

19 March
The first strong condemnation of Nazism from an official representative of the US government. The US ambassador in Canada, James Cromwell, declares that Hitler's Germany is openly trying to destroy the social and economic order on which the government of the USA is based.
□ As a reprisal for the German attack on Scapa Flow on 14 October 1939, 50 RAF bombers raid the German seaplane base at Hörnum on the island of Sylt.

20 March
Daladier's cabinet in Paris resigns. Paul Reynaud forms a war government.

21 March
The French government orders a consignment of 'heavy water' from Norway for atomic research.
□ A British delegation has a secret meeting with representatives of the Turkish government at Aleppo.

28 March
France and Britain conclude a joint undertaking that neither will make a separate peace treaty with Germany.

☐ The Allied Supreme War Council decides to mine Norwegian coastal waters and to occupy western Norwegian ports from 5 April.

31 March

German U-boats (an average of 14 craft operating at any one time) have sunk 753,803 tons of Allied shipping in the waters round Great Britain and the eastern Atlantic as far south as the Strait of Gibraltar since the start of hostilities, for a loss to the Kriegsmarine of 18 submarines. German battleships and destroyers operating in the North Sea have sunk a total of 63,098 tons of shipping, and 281,154 tons have been sunk round the coasts of Britain by mines laid by submarines, destroyers and aircraft, as well as 36,189 tons by air action.

2 April

Hitler gives orders for the start of Operation *Weserübung* against Norway and Denmark. Hostilities are timed to begin on 9 April.

3 April

Churchill is appointed Chairman of the Ministerial Defence Committee and obtains the consent of the Cabinet to the laying of minefields in Norwegian territorial waters, in line with the decision of the Allied Supreme War Council on 28 March.

5 April

For technical reasons the despatch of the first contingents of the Allied expeditionary force to Norway is postponed to 8 April.
☐ Chamberlain makes a speech in which he declares, 'Hitler has missed the bus.'

7 April

In the early hours of the morning, German warships sail with the troops who will carry out the first landings in Norway.
☐ The first contingents of the Allied expeditionary force to Norway are embarked in cruisers of the Royal Navy.
Towards evening, the British fleet leaves Scapa Flow for the Norwegian coast to intercept the German naval formation.
During the night, British destroyers lay three minefields in Norwegian territorial waters.

8 April

The Allies inform the Oslo government of the mine-laying operations in Norwegian waters.
11.50 a.m.: the German ship *Rio de Janeiro*, converted into a troop transport, is torpedoed by the Polish submarine *Orzel* off the Norwegian coast near Lillesand. The Germans are picked up by an Allied ship. Although this makes it clear that the German invasion force is already at sea, the Norwegian government still does not order general mobilization. During an evening meeting of the Council of Ministers, the Chief of Staff of the army, Colonel Rasmus Hatledal, informs the Defence Ministry that all officers of the general staff have taken up their posts. They decide on a most secret mobilization of five brigades in southern Norway.

9 April

Denmark and Norway The German invasion begins. The expeditionary force consists of seven infantry and two mountain divisions, with an air arm of over 400 fighters and bombers, 70 reconnaissance aircraft and 500 air transports. The entire German navy takes part in the operation. The army of occupation is divided into seven formations: two, commanded by General Kaupitsch, invade Denmark and take it in 48 hours (Kaupitsch's troops enter Copenhagen, the capital, within 12 hours of landing). The other five land in Norway, at Oslo, Kristiansand, Bergen, Trondheim and Narvik. In the course of the landing operations the Germans lose the heavy cruiser *Blücher* off Oslo and two light cruisers, the *Karlsruhe* at Kristiansand and the *Königsberg* off Bergen.
☐ With the news of the German attack on Denmark and Norway the British and French seek permission for their troops to enter Belgium. The request is refused by the Belgian government.

10 April

Denmark accepts the German ultimatum.
☐ King Haakon of Norway repudiates the puppet government of Vidkun Quisling.
Norway A British flotilla commanded by Captain Warburton Lee surprises ten German destroyers in Narvik fjord and sinks two, but loses two of its own ships.

11 April

Norway The Commander-in-Chief of the Norwegian army, Major-General Laake, resigns, and General Otto Ruge is appointed in his place.
☐ Belgian army leave is cancelled.

13 April

Norway Second battle of Narvik; seven German destroyers sunk.
☐ The British government gives a

KARL BOSCH

On 27 April the German chemist Karl Bosch died at Heidelberg. Born in Cologne in 1874, he studied engineering and chemistry and worked as a researcher for the Badische Anilin-und Sodafabrik (BASF). During the First World War he made a notable contribution towards the manufacture of synthetic petrol. In the 1920s Bosch obtained important results in applying Fritz Haber's process for synthesising ammonia on an industrial scale, making its use possible both in the manufacture of fertilisers and explosives.

Bosch won the Nobel Prize for Chemistry in 1931 and in 1935 became president of I.G. Farben, a post he retained until his death.

A German infantry unit protected by a light tank advances on Lillehammer.

new directive to the head of the RAF's Bomber Command, Sir Charles Portal; in the event of a German invasion of Belgium and Holland, bombing targets are to be troop concentrations and lines of communication and installations in the Ruhr; heavy bombers will operate mainly at night.

15–16 April
Norway The first Allied contingents land near Narvik.

17 April
The British cruiser *Suffolk* shells Sola airfield, near Stavanger. Attacked and severely damaged by German aircraft, the *Suffolk* manages to return to Scapa Flow.

19 April
Norway British troops land at Åndalsnes.

20 April
Norway French troops land. The Germans make contact with the Norwegian defence lines in front of Lillehammer, Rena and Aamot.

21 April
Norway The German advance continues.

22 April
Norway The Germans press northwards with two columns along the rivers Rena and Glomma.
During the afternoon German units attack in the Balbergkamp sector, a few miles north of Lillehammer.

24 April
Norway The Germans advance on all fronts. The British attempt to reach Trondheim fails.
☐ The French Premier, Paul Reynaud, urges Mussolini not to enter the war.

27 April
Hitler tells General Keitel, Commander-in-Chief of the armed forces, and General Jodl, Chief of Staff of the Supreme Command of the Wehrmacht, that he intends to launch his offensive against France in the first week in May.

28 April
Norway An attempt by the Allied XV Brigade under General Sir Bernard Paget to advance on Gudbrandsdalen from Trondheim fails. General Paget tells the Norwegian Commander-in-Chief General Otto Ruge that withdrawal from central Norway seems inevitable.

30 April
Norway The German troops advancing from Oslo and Trondheim join up at Dombås.

1 May
Norway The Germans announce the surrender of 4,000 Norwegians in the Lillehammer sector.
☐ President Roosevelt sends a personal message to Mussolini strongly urging him not to enter the war.
☐ The French military attaché in Berne sends a report to Paris: the Germans will open a major offensive between 8 and 10 May with the main thrust towards Sedan.

2 May
Norway The Germans reach Ån-

dalsnes, Allied forces embark at Namsos.

5 May

Norway The Germans advance north from Trondheim.
Norwegian Ministers arrive in London.

7 May

In a debate in the House of Commons, Chamberlain makes a statement on Norway. The government is supported by 281 votes to 200, a sufficient opposition to make Chamberlain's resignation inevitable.

8 May

The Belgian ambassador in Berlin, Jacques Davignon, reports that the Germans are drafting an ultimatum for the Belgian government. At the same time the military attaché in the Belgian embassy in Berlin tells his superiors that the German Supreme Command have sent their troops the invasion order.

9 May

The eve of the German attack in the west.

The OKW (German High Command) issues the orders for the next morning's attack. Here is the actual order issued to the German forces on the morning of 9 May:

W.FA/abt. L-Nr. 22–180/40 gk
CHEFS
The Führer, as Supreme Commander, has decided. A–Day 10/V Hour X 5.35. The code-words 'Danzig' or 'Augsburg' will be made known to the various commands of the Wehrmacht before 21.30 on 9/V. Commander-in-Chief of the Armed Forces.

Keitel

☐ 11.15 p.m.: General state of emergency in Belgium; the British and French informed.

The course of hostilities in Norway between 9 April and 8 June 1940.

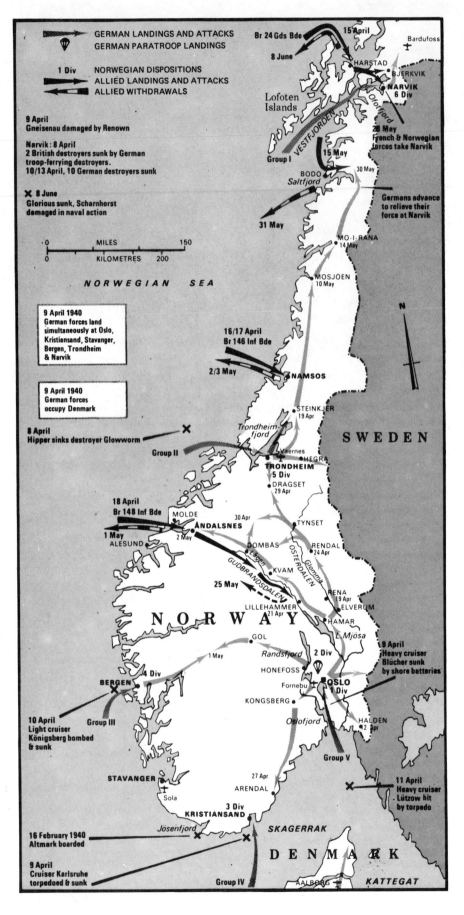

NEW YORK WORLD'S FAIR

April saw the close of the New York World's Fair, the most important international exhibition to be staged in America during the first half of the twentieth century. Although it was a financial failure and despite the difficult international situation, the Fair was an enormous success with the public, attracting a record total of almost 45 million visitors.

Even though Europe was on the brink of war, the Fair, opened in 1939 by President Roosevelt who delivered an address to 600,000 people, was formally dedicated to peace and progress (its official slogan was 'The World of Tomorrow'.

The architecture was ultra-modern, the two most central and important buildings being the Trylon, a tapering pyramid 728 ft high, and the Perisphere, a huge crystal sphere 180 ft in diameter.

The New York World's Fair attracted many foreign exhibitors: no less than 63 nations had their own pavilions, some of which were particularly outstanding. The Finnish pavilion, for example, designed by Alvar Aalto, was one of the most interesting by virtue of its modernity and boldness of conception; the Soviet pavilion featured a statue of a worker raising a red star; and a stream of water flowed through the Italian pavilion.

10 May

Western Front 5.35 a.m.: German airborne troops land on the bridges at Rotterdam, Dordrecht and Moerdijk in Holland and more parachutists drop on the fortress of Eben Emael, the key to the defence of Liège in Belgium, and the German armies of Army Groups B and A cross the frontiers of Belgium, Holland and Luxembourg.

7.30 a.m.: Advance troops of the French 7th Army and the British Expeditionary Force enter Belgium. According to the Anglo-French plan, the 'Dyle Plan', it would be possible to contain any German attack by basing the defence on Belgium and pivoting with the right flank on Sedan and the Ardennes plateau. That was the reason for the immediate advance into Belgian territory. However, the 'Dyle Plan' did not foresee that the Germans would attack across the Ardennes plateau, which was thought to be impassable, though just such an attack was the key to von Manstein's Operation Sickle. By attacking in force in the Netherlands, the Germans draw the Allies off to the northeast, breach their line on the Ardennes and quickly reach the sea near Calais. The Allied pivot at Sedan is thus destroyed at a blow, and the outcome is disastrous for the French and British.

☐ Neville Chamberlain resigns, and Winston Churchill forms a coalition government.

11 May

Western Front The Germans employ parachutists and airborne formations to take the Belgian fortress of Eben Emael (which had been thought impregnable) and surround Liège. Heavy bombing raids are carried out on many Belgian towns. Three divisions of the British Expeditionary Force take up defensive positions on the left bank of the river Dyle between Wavre and Louvain.

☐ Churchill authorizes Bomber Command to carry out raids on Germany.

☐ British War Cabinet formed.

☐ Roosevelt tells King Leopold III

of the dismay and indignation felt by Americans at the German assault.

12 May
Western Front The Belgians re-inforce their positions on the line of the Dyle.

The French 7th Army, which has entered the Netherlands, is ordered to evacuate Breda and fall back on the Schelde.

French troops dig in on the left bank of the Meuse after abandoning the right bank to the enemy. This allows the Germans to occupy Sedan, spear-headed by Guderian's 1st and 10th Armoured Divisions. Further north the 7th Armoured Division reaches the Meuse on a level with Dinant. The Luftwaffe systematically bombs the Allied lines of communication.

13 May
Western Front Guderian's armoured divisions force the crossings of the Meuse on either side of Sedan.

In Belgium the French 1st Army and Lord Gort's British divisions reach the bank of the Dyle; the British are deployed between Louvain and Wavre, the French between Wavre and Namur. Germans take Liège. The Dutch army is collapsing, and the High Command orders a general retreat to defensive positions on what is called the 'Dutch fortress', an area taking in Amsterdam, Rotterdam and Utrecht. Queen Wilhelmina and her government take refuge in London.

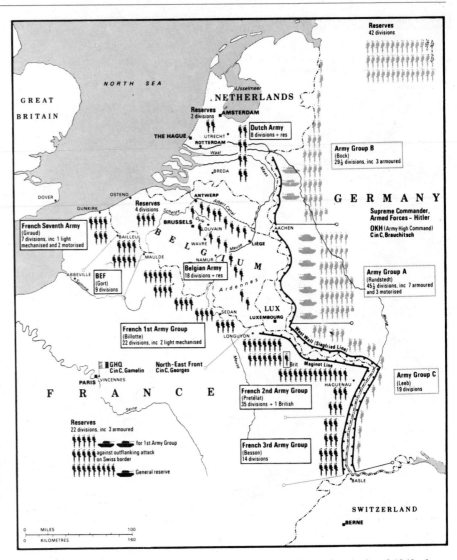

The deployment of forces along the Western Front during the early months of 1940, the period known as the 'phoney war'.

ARMIES AND DEPLOYMENT

On the German frontier, from Basel to the North Sea, millions of men and thousands of tanks faced each other. Broadly speaking, the two armies were organized as follows: German Army Group B, commanded by General Fedor von Bock and consisting of 29½ divisions, three of them armoured, was deployed from the northern tip of the Dutch frontier as far as Aachen; from Aachen to Trier was General von Rundstedt's Army Group A, with 45½ divisions, of which at least seven were armoured and three motorized; and from Trier to the Swiss border was General Leeb's Army Group C, with 19 divisions. Army Group A contained nearly half the Germans' infantry divisions and seven of the ten available armoured divisions. Reserves numbered 42 divisions. On the other side of the frontier stood at least three armies: the Dutch in the north with eight divisions (and an unknown number in reserve); the Belgians with 18 divisions deployed roughly opposite the German Army Group A; and the Anglo-French, deployed along the French frontier as follows: the French 7th Army under General Henri-Honoré Giraud, from the North Sea to Bailleul; the nine divisions of the British Expeditionary Force, commanded by General Lord Gort, from Bailleul

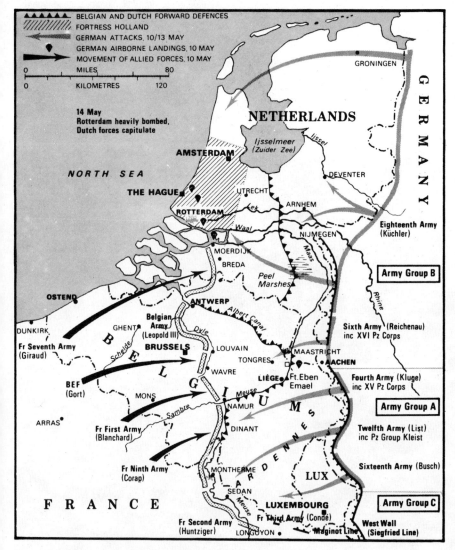

Legend:
- ▲▲▲▲▲ BELGIAN AND DUTCH FORWARD DEFENCES
- ///// FORTRESS HOLLAND
- ← GERMAN ATTACKS, 10/13 MAY
- ◆ GERMAN AIRBORNE LANDINGS, 10 MAY
- → MOVEMENT OF ALLIED FORCES, 10 MAY

0 — MILES — 80
0 — KILOMETRES — 120

14 May
Rotterdam heavily bombed,
Dutch forces capitulate

NETHERLANDS

GRONINGEN

NORTH SEA

AMSTERDAM

Ijsselmeer
(Zuider Zee)

THE HAGUE

UTRECHT

DEVENTER

ARNHEM

ROTTERDAM

NIJMEGEN

Eighteenth Army
(Küchler)

MOERDIJK

BREDA

Peel
Marshes

Army Group B

OSTEND

ANTWERP

Albert Canal

Rhine

DUNKIRK

GHENT

Belgian
Army
(Leopold III)

BRUSSELS

LOUVAIN

Sixth Army (Reichenau)
inc XVI Pz Corps

Fr Seventh Army
(Giraud)

Schelde

Dyle

WAVRE

TONGRES

MAASTRICHT

LIÈGE

Ft.Eben
Emael

AACHEN

Fourth Army (Kluge)
inc XV Pz Corps

BEF
(Gort)

MONS

Meuse

NAMUR

Army Group A

ARRAS

Sambre

Fr First Army
(Blanchard)

DINANT

Twelfth Army (List)
inc Pz Group Kleist

Fr Ninth Army
(Corap)

MONTHERME

A R D E N N E S

LUX

Sixteenth Army (Busch)

SEDAN

LUXEMBOURG

Army Group C

F R A N C E

Meuse

Fr Third Army (Condé)

West Wall
(Siegfried Line)

Fr Second Army
(Huntziger)

LONGUYON

Maginot Line

G E R M A N Y

B E L G I U M

The rapid advance of the German forces into Holland, Belgium and Luxembourg
following the assault of 10 May 1940.

A communiqué from the French headquarters admits: 'From Namur to Mézières the enemy has succeeded in establishing two small bridge-heads, one at Houx, north of Dinant, the other at Monthermé. A third, more substantial, has been established in Marfé wood, in the vicinity of Sedan.'

☐ Churchill declares to the House of Commons: 'I have nothing to offer but blood and toil and tears and sweat.'

14 May

Western Front 1.30 p.m.: Rotterdam is subjected to a savage air bombardment.

4.00 p.m.: French tanks, poised to stage a counter-attack against the German armoured formations in the area of the enemy penetration on the Meuse, are ordered to disperse over a front of 12 miles. General Corap's 9th Army retires to Rocroi.

Almost all day wave after wave of Allied bombers, numbering nearly 200, attack the German reinforcements streaming over the floating bridge thrown over the Meuse by Guderian in the area of Sedan, but with no effect. German anti-aircraft destroy 85 aircraft, 35 of them British. The Germans have opened a breach of 50 miles between Dinant and Sedan, and during the afternoon General Guderian brings almost all his tanks across the Meuse.

General Walther von Reichenau is ordered to attack the enemy posi-

to Maulde; from there to Longuyon, the French 1st Army Group with 22 divisions, including two light mechanized, under the command of General Gaston Billotte; and from Longuyon to the Swiss frontier, the French 2nd and 3rd Army Groups commanded by Generals Pretélat and Besson, and consisting respectively of 35 divisions and 14 divisions (the latter including one British division). The French

army had 22 more divisions in reserve, including three armoured divisions. Commander-in-Chief of the Allied forces was General Gamelin; the German Commander-in-Chief was Field-Marshal von Brauchitsch. In figures, the forces in the field amounted to 2,900,000 men for the Allies and 2,750,000 for the Germans. The Allies could put 2,574 modern tanks in the field and had available 2,128 aircraft,

of which 1,648 were French (219 bombers, 946 fighters and 483 reconnaissance aircraft) and 480 were British (the remaining 800 British aircraft were based on airfields in Britain). Germany could call immediately on 2,600 tanks, of more standardized types than the enemy's and allowed to operate more independently, and on 3,227 aircraft (1,120 bombers, 1,264 fighters, 501 reconnaissance aircraft and 342 Stukas).

German propaganda photograph taken on the Western Front. The caption reads: 'No force can stop our infantry.' A proud boast, but at that time, in May 1940, amply borne out by the facts.

tions between Louvain and Namur with his 6th Army. The operation is timed for the next day.

15 May

Western Front 11. a.m.: Capitulation of the Dutch Army is signed.

German 6th Armoured Division cuts off the retreat of General Corap's army, which is broken up and dispersed.

German 6th Army breaches the enemy lines between Louvian and Namur.

Although the military situation is critical, optimism still reigns at French headquarters: for example, General Georges (Commander-in-Chief of the north-east sector) declares in his official bulletins to General Gamelin (Commander-in-Chief of Land Forces: 'There is no great news ... small enemy infiltrations at Mézières-Charleville ... Closing of the breach at Sedan ... The attack seems to have been halted ... All prisoners confirm that the German troops are very tired ...' General Gamelin's daily communiqué says: 'The day of the 15th marks a lull. Our front, breached between Namur and the area west of Montmédy, is in course of gradual readjustment.'

Late in the evening it is reported that German tanks have reached Montcornet, only about 12 miles from Laon. Gamelin at once informs Daladier, Minister of National Defence, who orders an immediate counter-attack. Gamelin replies that he has no available reserves; the French army is about to collapse.

☐ RAF raids the Ruhr.

☐ The British government decides to concentrate aircraft production on a limited number of types.

16 May

Western Front Gamelin refuses to take responsibility for the defence of Paris and orders a general retreat of French forces out of Belgium.

The Belgian forces are ordered to retreat on to the Schelde. Lord Gort's

'REBECCA'

Laurence Olivier and Joan Fontaine, the stars of *Rebecca*.

A melodrama packed with mystery and suspense, *Rebecca* was the first American film made by English director Alfred Hitchcock. Based on the highly successful novel of the same name by Daphne du Maurier, the film is about a young, unsophisticated girl who marries a wealthy widower and returns to a home haunted by the memory of his first wife. Produced by David O. Selznick and shot in Monte Carlo and Cornwall, *Rebecca* (which won an Oscar for Best Film) starred Laurence Olivier, Joan Fontaine, George Sanders and Judith Anderson.

British divisions also retire. Rommel's 7th Armoured Division has penetrated 50 miles into French territory in the direction of Cambrai, capturing some 10,000 prisoners and 100 tanks.

Towards evening Guderian's armoured divisions reach a point about 60 miles east of Sedan.

☐ Churchill writes to Mussolini urging him to avoid a conflict between Britain and Italy. It could well be that the imminent threat of Italian intervention in the war could force the British to give up the Mediterranean route for the safer but longer route round the Cape of Good Hope.

☐ Roosevelt asks Congress for an extraordinary credit of 900 million dollars to strengthen the armed forces. He asks for 50,000 aircraft a year.

☐ The French Premier, Reynaud, tells Churchill by radio that the battle is lost and the road to Paris already wide open to the enemy. Early in the afternoon Churchill arrives in Paris by air. At 5.30 p.m., accompanied by Sir John Dill, Vice-Chief of the Imperial General Staff, he goes to the Quai d'Orsay (seat of the French foreign ministry) to meet Reynaud, Daladier and General Gamelin.

17 May
Western Front Instead of continuing his advance on Paris, Guderian turns north-west; by midday his advance troops reach the river Oise, south of Guise, not far from Saint-Quentin. The brave counter-attacks of Colonel de Gaulle's 4th Armoured Division (17–19 May) north of Laon can do nothing to halt the thrust of Guderian's armoured divisions; but they do earn de Gaulle promotion to the rank of general.

Troops of General von Reichenau's 6th Army enter Brussels, which is declared an 'open city'.

11 May 1940: the Belgian fortress of Eben Emael, claimed by military experts to be impregnable, is captured by German parachute troops.

Paris breathes a sigh of relief; the German avalanche is no longer threatening the capital.

☐ Reynaud recalls Marshal Pétain from the embassy in Madrid and General Weygand from his command in the Levant.

18 May

Western Front Guderian occupies Saint-Quentin. Rommel reaches Cambrai.

General Henri-Honoré Giraud and the remnants of the 9th Army (formerly under General Corap) enter Le Cateau, a small town not far from Cambrai, and are captured by the Germans, who got there some hours earlier.

The Germans take Antwerp.

☐ Encouraged by the Germans' brilliant victories, Mussolini sends a negative reply to the messages sent him by Roosevelt and Churchill.

19 May

Western Front The nine German armoured divisions which breached the French line between Sedan and Namur regroup between Cambrai and Péronne.

Rommel, who had been ordered to halt the previous day to allow his attacking troops to be regrouped, persuades his immediate superior, General Hermann Hoth (Commander of the XV Armoured Corps) that his 7th Armoured Division is in a position to advance and occupy the dominating heights at Arras, about 12 miles west of Cambrai.

☐ In Paris, Marshal Pétain is appointed Deputy Prime Minister. General Gamelin is replaced by the 73-year-old General Weygand as Commander-in-Chief of the French armed forces.

20 May

Western Front Rommel occupies the heights round Arras.

9.00 a.m.: Guderian's 1st Armoured Division takes Amiens.

7.00 p.m.: German 2nd Armoured Division occupies Abbeville.

8.00 p.m.: One of Guderian's battalions reaches the Channel at Noyelles. The German tanks have

'FOR WHOM THE BELL TOLLS'

In 1940 Ernest Hemingway published *For Whom the Bell Tolls*, his longest and for some time his most popular book. Having witnessed the Spanish civil war at first hand, Hemingway chose as the hero of his novel Robert Jordan, a young, idealistic American and member of the International Brigade who, having been given the task of blowing up a strategically important bridge, joins up with a group of Republican partisans. The book deals with ideological-political conflicts, the individuals of the group, and a love story betwen the hero and a young Spanish girl, Maria, culminating in a dramatic epilogue which sees Jordan dying as he accomplishes his mission.

A politically courageous portrayal of the civil war, the book was anathema both to fascists and, because it applauded a somewhat anarchic form of individual action, also to communists. Dedicated to his wife Martha Gellhorn, who had seen action in Spain, *For Whom the Bell Tolls* was a landmark in Hemingway's career; the blowing up of the bridge symbolised the exploding of his own past experiences, and from then on he identified his activities with those of his characters.

The film rights of the book were acquired by Paramount and in 1943 the cinema version, scripted by Dudley Nichols and directed by Sam Wood, had its premiere. The film, which did well at the box office in technicolour, was an unassuming story of love and war starring Gary Cooper, Ingrid Bergman, Akim Tamiroff and Katina Paxinou.

Gary Cooper (right) as Robert Jordan, the hero of *For Whom the Bell Tolls*.

opened a breach in the Allied line, some 20 miles wide from east to west. North of this gap is the French 1st Army, the nine divisions of the British Expeditionary Force and the Belgian army; to the south, from west to east, four French armies, the 10th, 7th, 6th and 2nd. Having reached the sea, the Germans have virtually surrounded 45 Allied divisions in Flanders and the north-east tip of France. The Führer says the armistice will be signed in the area of Réthondes (where the armistice of 11 November 1918 was signed) and that France will have to restore to Germany 'all the territory they have raped from her in the past 400 years'.

21 May
Western Front British armoured forces attack the German salient on the Arras heights, but after a favourable start they are forced back on to their start line. A similar effort is made by two divisions of the French 1st Army in the direction of Cambrai, but with a similar result.

☐ The Belgian government moves to Bruges.

☐ Grand Admiral Erich von Raeder, Commander-in-Chief of the Kriegsmarine, directs the Führer's attention to the need to plan for the invasion of Britain, which may still be necessary.

22 May
In Britain, Emergency Powers (Defence) Act passed, giving the government control over persons and property.

Western Front German forces at Noyelles now turn northwards, the 2nd Armoured Division towards Boulogne, and the 1st in the direction of Calais.

☐ At the Chateau de Vincennes on the outskirts of Paris, General Weygand explains his plan to avoid defeat to Reynaud and Churchill. Weygand proposes that the Belgians should fall back on the Iser, while the British and the French 1st Army counter-attack in force towards the south-west. At the same time the armies advancing from the south must cross the Somme and attack northwards in an attempt to join up with the Allied forces in that sector. The necessary air support would be provided by the RAF. The politicians approve Weygand's plan, but none of the planned moves can be carried out, despite an unexpected halt in the German advance from 23 to 25 May. The Belgians, particularly, are most reluctant to retire further west of the river Lys. Also, so far from attacking southwards, the British Expeditionary Force is forced to evacuate Arras during the night of 23 May. The Allied attack from the north is, therefore, put off to 26 May. But on the evening of the 25th Lord Gort has to send two of his divisions to attack in the direction of Arras, to plug a gap in the Allied line that has

Members of the British Expeditionary Force during the German bombardment of Louvain.

appeared just at the point where the British and Belgian defensive lines should have joined. Moreover, coordination between the French and British is virtually non-existent.

23 May
Western Front General von Rundstedt, Commander-in-Chief of Army Group A, orders his armoured formations to halt their advance.

24 May
Western Front The 2nd Armoured Division launches a violent attack on Boulogne; the 10th attacks Calais.

25 May
Western Front The Germans take Boulogne. They now surround the Belgian army, French forces and most of the British Expeditionary Force.
The Allies fall back on Dunkirk.
The Belgian front is breached between Geluwe and the Lys valley.

26 May
Western Front The Belgian High Command tells the British and French that its army's situation is critical. The Belgian government asks King Leopold to leave his country (as the Queen of Holland and Grand Duchess of Luxembourg have done), but the King refuses.
During the night Calais falls to the German 10th Armoured Division.
□ It is announced in London that due to enemy occupation of Holland and parts of Belgium and Northern France, children are to be evacuated from a number of towns on the east coast.

27 May
Western Front The evacuation of the British Expeditionary Force from Dunkirk (Operation Dynamo) begins. The RAF provides massive air cover.
□ Roosevelt offers to mediate in talks between Italy, France and Britain in a bid to keep Italy from entering the war.
□ 5.00 p.m.: King Leopold of the Belgians sends an envoy to the German general headquarters offering to capitulate.

10.00 p.m.: The Germans tell Leopold's emissary that the Führer demands unconditional surrender.

28 May
12.30 a.m.: King Leopold, without consulting his allies, signs his country's surrender. The Belgian Cabinet in Paris repudiates the king's action. But the fact is that the Belgian army no longer exists.
Western Front The French armies fall back on all fronts, while at Dunkirk there are some 350,000 troops waiting to be taken off by sea. So far, under 18,000 troops have been embarked, and the situation is very serious. The town and the docks of Dunkirk are heavily bombed, while those British craft that are able to leave harbour have to face the fire of German batteries at Calais and submarine attacks from the North Sea.
□ The collapse of Belgium convinces Mussolini that Italy must enter the conflict as soon as possible.

29 May
Western Front The Germans enter Ypres, Ostend and Lille.
At Dunkirk the evacuation continues under ceaseless attacks by the Luftwaffe. The German planes are under continual harassment by the RAF and a British armada of ships of all sizes brings 47,310 men across the Channel to safety.
Hitler meets the commanders of his Army Groups at Cambrai, telling them that he has decided to 'deploy the armoured forces immediately for a southwards offensive to settle accounts with the French'. The ten *Panzerdivisionen* are re-grouped to form five *Panzerkorps*, three of them under the command of von Bock, Commander of Army Group B, and two under von Rundstedt, who commands Army Group A. Von Bock moves three armies, the 4th, 6th and 9th, to the Somme to take up positions beside von Rundstedt's 2nd, 12th and 16th, already on the Aisne and the Ailette.
General Weygand, Commander in Chief of the French armed forces, plans to counter-attack on the south

Survivors of the German onslaught wander through the ruins of a small Belgian town.

side of the breach opened by the German armoured divisions, where it happens that the bulk of the French forces are concentrated. To face the *Panzerkorps* he deploys, on the left, the 10th, 7th and 6th Armies, with the 4th and 2nd in the centre and the remainder, the 3rd, 5th and 8th, on the right.
By midnight the greater part of the BEF and almost half the French 1st Army are in sight of the sea in the area of Dunkirk.

30 May
Western Front The evacuation of Allied troops from Dunkirk continues, while British artillery tries to hold the advancing German troops at bay before their ammunition runs out. The Luftwaffe sinks three destroyers and damages six, and many of the armada of ships transporting the Allied forces to British soil are sunk.
□ Mussolini decides that Italy will enter the war on 5 June.

31 May
Western Front 68,104 Allied soldiers are taken off from Dunkirk. But the Admiralty now decides to withdraw all modern destroyers from the Dunkirk area.

Leopold III, King of the Belgians, flanked by his War Minister, General Denis, inspects his slender armoured forces. The situation on the Western Front is by now desperate.

General Lord Gort hands over command of the British troops still in France to Major-General Sir Harold Alexander and embarks for Dover with General Sir Alan Francis Brooke, Commander of II Corps of the BEF.

☐ Churchill arrives in Paris with three of his closest colleagues, Clement Attlee, Lord Privy Seal, Sir John Dill, Vice-Chief of the Imperial General Staff, and General Lord Ismay, Head of the Military Wing of the War Cabinet Secretariat.

☐ Roosevelt makes yet another approach to the Italian government. If Italy enters the war against France and Britain, the President says, the USA will be compelled to give much more aid to the Western Allies.

1 June
Norway Admiral Lord Cork and Orrery, commanding the combined Allied force in Norway, tells King Haakon that his troops will have to withdraw. It is agreed that the operation can be postponed for 24 hours.
Western Front German artillery bombards the Dunkirk beaches, while the Luftwaffe launches the most violent attack since the operation began. In a few hours one

French and three British destroyers are sunk, together with two transports, one mine-sweeper and one gunboat. The British defence line is breached at Bergues, a few miles from Dunkirk, and the rearguards have to be withdrawn nearer the coast. In view of the German offensive the British Admiralty orders a short suspension of embarkation for Britain; nevertheless a further 64,229 men at least are taken off from the Dunkirk beaches before the operation is halted.

☐ Hitler asks Mussolini to postpone the date of Italy's intervention for a few days. Mussolini replies to Roosevelt's last message: he cannot undertake not to enter the war.

2 June
Western Front Operation Dynamo is concluded during the night when the last 4,000 British soldiers leave French soil.

☐ In response to Hitler's request Mussolini postpones Italian entry into the war to 10 June, at midnight.

3 June
Western Front The Germans strike a decisive blow against the defensive

perimeter at Dunkirk and the French rearguard is driven back to a line little more than 2 miles from the east mole at Dunkirk. Resistance, clearly, cannot last much longer.

☐ Paris is bombed by the Luftwaffe.

4 June
Western Front At 3.40 a.m. the destroyer *Shikari* leaves Dunkirk, the last ship to evacuate French troops. At dawn German troops reach the Dunkirk beach.

Between 27 May and the early hours of 4 June, 338,226 men have left France, including about 120,000 French and Belgian troops. The operation was directed by the senior naval officer at Dover, Admiral Sir Bertram Home Ramsey, who mobilized every available ship, including private yachts and fishing boats, big and small. In this way, against only 7,669 men embarked on the first day (27 May), 17,804 men of the BEF were embarked on 28 May, 47,310 on the 29th, 120,927 between the 30th and 31st, 64,229 on 1 June alone and another 54,000 up to the night of 3/4 June. In the course of this courageous and desperate rescue operation, some 200 ships were lost, as well as 177 aircraft (40 per cent of them bombers), against about 140 lost by the Luftwaffe. In accordance with the military principle that priority is given to men over arms and equipment, the British had to leave behind on French soil 2,000 guns, 60,000 trucks, 76,000 tons of ammunition and 600,000 tons of fuel and supplies.

☐ Britain is left practically unarmed. At the end of the Dunkirk evacuation there remain on British soil only 500 guns of all types, and some of these are museum-pieces.
Speaking in the House of Commons, Churchill declares that Britain will continue the fight from the countries of the Empire if the British Isles are ever occupied by the Germans: 'We shall fight on the beaches, we shall fight in the fields ... we shall never surrender.'

5 June
Western Front At last the 'Battle

of France' begins. The Germans unleash a fierce aerial and artillery bombardment on the line of the Somme and the Aisne and on the lines of communication of the French armies deployed between Abbeville and the Maginot Line. General Weygand issues a heartfelt appeal to his divisions: 'Let the thought of our country's sufferings inspire in you the firm resolve to resist. The fate of the nation and the future of our children depend on your determination.' The order is to defend the positions to the last man.

☐ General de Gaulle is appointed Under-Secretary of State for War.

6 June

Western Front General Hermann Hoth's XV Armoured Corps breaks through on the lower Somme between Amiens and the coast, in the French 10th Army sector. But the French 7th Army puts up a resolute resistance to von Kleist's XIV and XVI Armoured Corps between Amiens and Péronne. Further east, infantry of the German 9th Army succeed in breaking through the lines of the French 6th Army, but are driven back before Chemin-des-Dames; but the French are forced to withdraw to the south bank of the Aisne. Guderian's *Panzergruppe* (made up of two armoured corps, the XXXIX and XLI) advances southeast towards Châlons and Langres, to reach the flank of the Maginot Line and the French armies facing east, the 3rd, 5th and 8th.

7 June

Western Front The Germans occupy Montdidier, Noyon and Forges-les-Eaux, 40 miles south of the Somme and about 25 miles from Rouen, on the Seine. Nothing can now stop their advance on Rouen.

☐ King Haakon of Norway and his government embark at Tromsø on board the cruiser *Devonshire*, bound for London.

On the beach at Dúnkirk, the body of one of the many British soldiers killed during the evacuation.

8 June

The British aircraft carrier *Glorious* and the two destroyers escorting her are sunk off Narvik by the German battle-cruisers *Gneisenau* and *Scharnhorst*.

9 June

Norway The last Allied troops leave Norwegian soil and a preliminary armistice comes into force between the Germans and the military and political authorities remaining in Norway.

Western Front The Germans occupy Rouen, Dieppe, Compiègne and reach the Seine and the Marne; the battle of the Somme becomes a French rout. The left wing of the French 10th Army, left completely isolated, retires on Saint-Valéry to attempt a withdrawal by sea. Meanwhile German troops cross the Marne. General Weygand warns Reynaud that a complete collapse of the front may come at any moment; the French army is already virtually defeated.

☐ General de Gaulle pays a rapid visit to London.

10 June

Western Front The Germans cross the Seine as the French retire on to the Loire in disorder. General Weygand admits officially that the front has been breached. The French government leaves Paris for Tours, where information reaches them that Italy is about to declare war on France and Britain.

☐ 4.30 p.m.: The Italian Foreign Minister, Ciano, receives the French ambassador at the Palazzo Chigi and informs him that 'Italy considers itself in a state of war with effect from tomorrow, 11 June.'

4.45 p.m.: A similar declaration of war is sent by the Italian Foreign Minister to the British ambassador.

☐ There is bitter disagreement among the French military and political leaders. General Weygand considers that the defeat of his forces

THE JEEP

In the 1930s the American army began its plans to develop a speedy military vehicle which could be used, in place of the motorcycle, for reconnaissance work. It made its first appearance in 1940 and was immediately called 'Jeep', a name probably derived from an approximate pronunciation of the initials of the phrase 'general purpose'. Adopted by the army in 1941, the Jeep, built by the Willys Overland

Company, soon proved to be of enormous value, for it possessed great mobility even over the roughest terrain, thanks to its four driving wheels and its powerful four-cylinder petrol engine. Although the Jeep was the smallest motor vehicle operated by the US Army, its strength and manoeuvrability made it suitable for carrying troops, weapons and light loads; it could also be used as an ambulance, a fighting vehicle and a means of radio-transmission.

In 1941 an amphibious Jeep was manufactured which was designed for landing operations but because of its small size eventually proved unsuitable for this purpose.

is imminent and thinks they should surrender. But Paul Reynaud feels there should be a final stand in Brittany.

☐ Within hours of Italy's decision to enter the war President Roosevelt strongly condemns the dictatorships and promises material help to the Western Allies.

☐ During the night Italian aircraft take off from airfields in Sicily for the first air raid on Malta.

11 June

Western Front The advance into central France by the German armies continues; Rheims now falls to the invading forces.

The situation of the French army is now as follows: of the 30 divisions that still exist on paper, 11 possess more than 50 per cent of their effectives, 13 are reduced to 25 per cent, and the rest are no more than 'remnants'.

The military governor of Paris, General Hering, declares Paris an open city. This accords with the decision taken by General Weygand that Paris, already surrounded by the enemy to east and west, cannot be defended. The Germans, for their part, announce by radio that if they are to recognize Paris as an open city they require the cessation of all French military resistance north of a line Saint-Germain–Versailles–Juvisy–Saint-Maur–Meaux. The French accept this condition and the Parisians rejoice to learn that their city is to be spared.

☐ The Inter-Allied Supreme War Council meets at Briare. Reynaud, Churchill and Eden are present. The French make desperate pleas for intervention by the British air force, but Churchill refuses, fearing an offensive against Britain by the Luftwaffe.

☐ First encounters in Africa: the Italian air force bombs Port Sudan and Aden, while the RAF carries out raids on targets in Eritrea.

☐ The Italian air force carries out eight air raids on Malta.

12 June

Western Front In the morning

Guderian crosses the heights of Champagne and launches his XXXIX Armoured Corps against Châlons-sur-Marne, which falls without resistance.

General Weygand orders a general retreat. In the French Council of Ministers held near Tours, Weygand himself, supported by Pétain, presses the need for an armistice. But the proposal is firmly dismissed by the Premier, Paul Reynaud.

☐ Meeting of the Inter-Allied Supreme War Council continues at Briare.

☐ First bombing raids by the RAF on Italy. Turin and Genoa are the targets.

13 June

For the last time Churchill meets Reynaud, who still supports resistance to the enemy to the last. In a desperate message to Roosevelt, Reynaud pleads for American help; the appeal asks the American president to 'throw the weight of American power into the scales in order to save France, the advance guard of democracy'.

☐ The *Eastern Prince*, the first cargo ship with arms for Britain, sails from the USA.

☐ Spain, which had initially declared itself neutral, now adopts a position of non-belligerency.

14 June

Western Front The French 7th

THE ITALIAN ARMY

At the time when war was declared the Italian army could call on 73 divisions, comprising 106 infantry regiments, 12 regiments of *bersaglieri* (the Italian crack corps), 10 of Alpine troops, 12 of cavalry, 5 of tanks, 32 of artillery and 19 of engineers, plus a legion of Blackshirts. In practice only 19 of these 73 divisions could be manned at full strength, while 34, even though reported as efficient, were incomplete, still short of a quarter of their establishment, and the other 20 were hopelessly short. Moreover, an Italian infantry division contained only two regiments of infantry and one of artillery, whereas in all the other armies the division comprised not fewer than three infantry regiments and four or more groups of artillery. The Italian divisions were, therefore, really brigades, but without the mobility of a brigade. The infantry's weapons were inadequate to the demands of modern warfare, while the equipment of the artillery was definitely sub-standard, the best of their guns being those captured

from the Austrians in the First World War. The tanks were hopelessly inadequate, too light, insufficiently armoured and under-armed. On 10 June the Italian land forces were deployed as follows: within Italy there were 39 infantry divisions, 4 Alpine divisions, 2 motorized infantry and 3 lorry-borne divisions, 2 armoured divisions and 2 light divisions; in Albania were 3 infantry, an Alpine and an armoured division; in Libya 9 lorry-borne divisions, 3 Black-shirt divisions and 2 divisions of native troops; in Ethiopia 2 infantry divisions, and also an infantry division in the Aegean Islands.

The Italian navy had a formidable striking power: two modern battleships and four more fitting out, 19 cruisers, 132 destroyers and torpedo boats and 107 submarines. But, as time was to show, the navy lacked any operational co-ordination with the air arm (and there was an absence of any real naval air force), and in addition the Italian navy lacked fuel for more than one year of war.

Army and the Paris army retreat to the Loire.

The Maginot Line is breached south of Saarbrücken by troops of Army Group C. Meanwhile the German High Command issues new directives on the future tasks of the troops in French territory: to the south-west, towards the Loire, the XIV Armoured Corps will advance to cut off the retreat of the French troops retiring on Bordeaux; XVI Armoured Corps will move south-east towards Lyons and Dijon to enable the Italians to cross the Alpine passes and attack the French defenders in the flank; finally Guderian with his XXXIX and XLI Armoured Corps will turn east towards the Langres plateau and the Swiss border to cut off the retreat of the French armies in the Maginot.

Paris, declared an open city, is occupied by the Germans after a series of bombing raids on industrial targets in the suburbs. German soldiers lower the French tricolor on the Eiffel Tower, while radio stations are already making announcements in German. The occupation of Paris has begun.

The French government is moved from Tours to Bordeaux.

☐ Russia delivers an ultimatum to the small Baltic nation of Lithuania. The Lithuanians have no alternative but to allow the Russians to occupy their country and similar ultimata on 16 June to Estonia and Latvia bring Russian occupation of these countries also.

☐ Spanish troops occupy the international zone of Tangier.

15 June

Western Front The German war-machine seemingly invincible, Reynaud decides to sue for peace, but he is opposed by none other than General Weygand, who until now has supported an armistice.

German troops take Verdun.

☐ Roosevelt replies to Paul Reynaud's message of 13 June to the effect that the USA will increase the despatch of war materials to France and Britain, but will not become involved in hostilities.

16 June

Western Front Dijon falls and Guderian's armoured corps are on the Saône and marching on Besançon and Pontarlier. The Maginot Line is thus turned, while Army Group C crosses the Rhine at Colmar.

During a meeting of the French Council of Ministers, Pétain, the Deputy Prime Minister, calls for an armistice and threatens to resign if his cabinet colleagues refuse. The French government asks Britain for release from obligations under the Anglo-French agreement, obligations which mean that neither country would make a separate peace. Churchill replies as follows: 'On condition, and exclusively on condition, that the French fleet immediately sails for British ports during the negotiations, His Majesty's government gives its full consent to the French government to proceed with the request for armistice terms for France ...'

De Gaulle, who has been in London since the previous day, telephones Reynaud and puts before him the text prepared in Britain for an 'Anglo-French Union', in effect the fusion of the two nations into one. Reynaud himself is in favour, but he gets a poor reception when he puts the proposal to the Council of Ministers. Reynaud resigns and Pétain at once forms a new government. At 11.00 p.m. he instructs his new Foreign Minister, Paul Bau-

Soldiers from the Verdun garrison surrender their arms to the Germans.

douin, to ask the Germans and Italians for an armistice. At midnight, through the Spanish ambassador in Paris, the French government presents its request for an armistice.

☐ During the night a British ship leaves France carrying the heavy water ordered in Norway on 21 March.

17 June

Western Front Guderian's tanks are at Pontarlier, near the Swiss border. At midday the new French Premier, Marshal Pétain, broadcasts to the nation to inform his fellow countrymen that negotiations are in progress for an armistice.

☐ Churchill speaks to the British people telling them of the French step. Now that the Battle of France is ended, he declares, there must be a battle of Britain. And German naval headquarters receive the following despatch from the High Command: 'With regard to the landing in Britain, the Führer has not yet expressed any such intention, being well aware of the difficulties involved in such an operation. Up to now, therefore, the High Command of the armed forces has not carried out any preparatory work.'

☐ The speed of the German victory and the French request for an armistice compels Hitler to send new instructions to Generals Keitel and Jodl (respectively Commander-in-Chief of the Armed Forces and Chief of Staff of the OKW). The political situation and the tactical task have become more complicated. The aim is to detach France from Britain completely, because, for example, a possible transfer of the French government to North Africa could bring an inevitable psychological and political, as well as military, strengthening of Britain and would carry the war into the Mediterranean. From these considerations, the following requirements are seen to arise:

(1) The French government must survive as a sovereign power. Only in this way can the Germans be certain that the French colonial empire will not go over to Britain.

The swastika flies from the Arc de Triomphe.

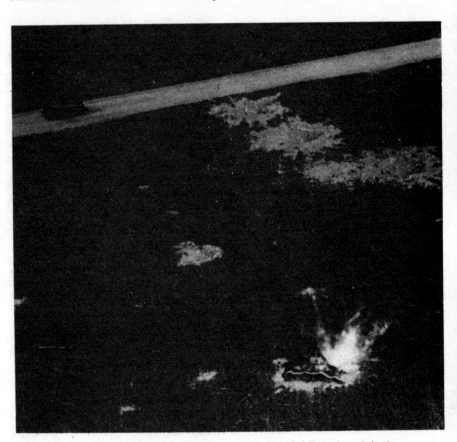

Craters made by a Stuka attack in Flanders, with a disabled French tank in the foreground.

(2) To allow the French government to survive, retaining its own sovereign sphere, it is advisable not to occupy the whole country.

(3) The French army will be required to move into the free zone and there demobilized; the retention of

some units will be permitted for maintaining public order.

(4) The French fleet must be neutralized, because if the French are required to hand it over it will probably sail overseas, possibly to Britain.

(5) Territorial questions must be

postponed during the negotiations, pending the drawing up of a peace treaty.

(6) Instructions concerning the French colonial empire can only be formulated later; to put them now would probably lead to the annexation of the colonies by the British.

18 June

Western Front The Germans take Caen, Cherbourg, Rennes, Briare, Le Mans, Nevers and Colmar.

☐ Hitler and Mussolini meet again at Munich to work out a common policy towards France.

☐ French Foreign Minister Paul Baudouin and Admiral François Darlan, French Minister of Marine, assure the American *chargé d'affaires* and the British ambassador, Sir Ronald Campbell, that the fleet will be evacuated or scuttled rather than let fall into enemy hands.

☐ 6.00 p.m.: General de Gaulle broadcasts his first message to the French nation from London. The war is by no means over, the general declares, because it is a world war in which the Battle of France represents only one episode. He, therefore, invites the French living in England to get in contact with him to continue the struggle. This appeal by the still unknown general does not arouse any great enthusiasm.

☐ The RAF bomb Hamburg and Bremen.

19 June

Western Front Brest and Nantes fall to the Germans, and so too, after a valiant defence by French military cadets, does Saumur. The Germans now advance on Lyons.

French ships in the Channel ports seek refuge, some in Great Britain, some in North Africa. Displaying remarkable skill, Captain Ronarch succeeds in sailing the battleship *Jean Bart* out of the dry dock at St. Nazaire, where she was being fitted out, and reaching Casablanca in safety.

☐ The German government 'invites' the French to despatch plenipotentiaries to negotiate armistice terms.

A French soldier surrenders to the enemy in an Amsterdam street.

☐ General de Gaulle broadcasts again to the French from London; this time his speech is political and marks his definite breach with the Pétain government.

20 June

Western Front German troops enter Lyons. Some German armoured units leave for the Alps to assist the Italians, who have opened their assault on the western Alps. Against the advice of the Italian High Command Mussolini had fixed 17 June as the date for the attack on the French frontier.

☐ France now asks Italy for an armistice.

☐ The French Foreign Minister, Paul Baudouin, sends to the Spanish ambassador to France the names of the French plenipotentiaries who will sign the armistice with the Germans. They include ambassador Léon Noël, Minister Plenipotentiary Rochard, Admiral Le Luc and

April 1940: a German sentry looks out across a Norwegian fjord. The Germans suffer heavy losses at sea during the Norwegian campaign.

Generals Parisot and Bergeret, with General Charles Huntziger as chairman. The directive given them contains a single clause: they are to break off the talks at once if the Germans ask for the French fleet to be handed over to them. At 2.00 p.m. the delegation leaves for Réthondes, in the forest of Compiegne.

The German terms include important financial concessions, such as the extension to France of *Reichskreditkassen*, banks created in wartime for the troops in occupied countries, which will issue banknotes having legal currency at par with the French currency. Another provision is the *Devisenschutzkommandos*, by which all foreign bank accounts are immediately frozen and payments to them by French citizens are blocked.

21 June

3.30 p.m.: Hitler receives the French plenipotentiaries at Réthondes in the same railway coach in which the German surrender was signed at the end of the First World War. General Keitel reads the dossier accusing the French of deceit and aggression. The French are then given the text of the armistice terms and no discussion is permitted. All the French are allowed to do is ask for clarification. 8.30 p.m.: General Huntziger obtains permission to speak to General Weygand on the telephone. Weygand is told of the severe conditions dictated by the Germans: three-fifths of French territory will be under occupation, prisoners of war will not be released, the costs of occupation will be assessed by Germany, and the French army will be reduced to 100,000 men.

22 June

6.30 p.m.: General Huntziger, head of the French delegation, and General Keitel sign the armistice.

Three French armies, the 3rd, 5th and 8th, trapped between Epinal and Belfort, near the Swiss frontier, surrender.

□ Units of the Italian 1st Army occupy Menton.

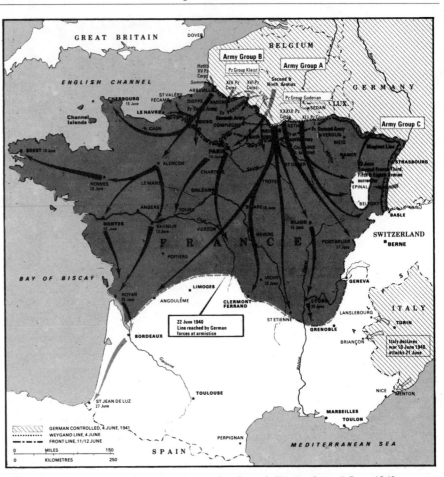

The spectacular advance of the German armies through France from 4 June 1940, following the collapse of Holland and Belgium and the British evacuation at Dunkirk. By 21 June, the French are forced to accept terms for an armistice.

23 June

De Gaulle, broadcasting from London, proposes the formation of a French National Committee.

□ The French delegation to negotiate an armistice with Italy leaves for Rome.

24 June

7.15 p.m.: At Villa Olgiata, near Rome, General Huntziger, on behalf of the French army, and General Badoglio on behalf of Italy, sign the armistice.

Western Front With the capture of Saint-Etienne and Angoulême, the Germans now occupy all territory north and west of a line Geneva–Dole–Tours–Mont-de-Marsan–Spanish border. The Channel and the entire Atlantic coast are in German hands, constituting Germany's advance posts for operations in the Atlantic and for the imminent campaign against Britain.

25 June

Western Front 1.35 a.m.: The Franco-German armistice comes into force and all hostilities on French soil cease. During the brief campaign the French have lost 92,000 men, 250,000 have been wounded and 1,500,000 taken prisoner. British losses amount to 3,500 dead and 14,000 wounded. Belgian 7,500 dead and 16,000 wounded, Dutch 2,900 dead and 7,000 wounded. German losses are 27,000 dead and 18,000 missing, with 111,000 wounded.

□ Speaking in the House of Commons, Churchill criticizes the Pétain government and declares that Britain must save herself to save the honour of France and of the world. Pétain replies that it is not for Churchill to be the judge of French honour and declares, 'Our honour is safe! Now we must concentrate our efforts on the future.

26 June
The Soviet Union demands from Rumania the cession of Bessarabia and northern Bucovina. Hitler intervenes and presses the Rumanian government to satisfy the Russians.
☐ Turkey announces its non-belligerency.

27 June
The British government takes steps to prevent French warships from returning to home ports.

28 June
General Charles de Gaulle is recognized by the United Kingdom as 'Leader of all free Frenchmen'.
☐ The Russians occupy Bessarabia and northern Bucovina. Germany has put pressure on the Rumanians to accept.
☐ Marshal Italo Balbo, Governor of Libya, dies in the air above Tobruk; the aircraft in which he is returning from a reconnaissance flight is brought down by Italian anti-aircraft fire by mistake.
☐ Channel Islands demilitarized and partly evacuated.

29 June
The French government decides to move from Bordeaux to Vichy.

30 June
The Germans land in Jersey and Guernsey.
☐ From the beginning of June up to date a dozen merchant ships have left the USA for Britain carrying guns and other arms.

1 July
Marshal Rodolfo Graziani succeeds Marshal Balbo as the new Commander-in-Chief of Italian forces in North Africa and Governor of Libya.
☐ In a note issued by the OKW to its commands, there is the first mention of Operation *Seelöwe* (Sealion), the action leading up to a landing in Britain.

2 July
Marshal Pétain's government in France moves from Bordeaux to Vichy.

3 July
A British squadron commanded by Vice-Admiral Somerville shells French naval vessels that have taken refuge at Oran and Mers-el-Kebir after the armistice at Compiegne. Several French ships are sunk or damaged, including the battleships *Provence* and *Bretagne* and the battle-cruiser *Dunkerque*; 1,300 French seamen lose their lives in the action. The other battle-cruiser in the French squadron, *Strasbourg*, the aircraft carrier *Commandant Teste* and five more destroyers succeed in escaping from the British encirclement.
French warships at anchor at Plymouth and Portsmouth are taken over.
☐ In Italian East Africa, British forces attack the defences of Metemma. The Italian air force carries out another successful attack on the air and naval base at Aden.

4 July
Towards evening the battle-cruiser *Strasbourg*, the aircraft carrier *Commandant Teste* and the five destroyers which succeeded in escaping from the British action at the port of Mers-el-Kebír, near Oran, reach port at Toulon. Winston Churchill speaks to the House of Commons on Oran: 'I leave the judgment of our actions with confidence to Parliament. I leave it to the nation and I leave it to the United States. I leave it to the world and to history.'

5 July
Following the British attack on the French fleet, Marshal Pétain's government at Vichy breaks off diplomatic relations with Britain. Operation Catapult provokes angry protests even from the French living in Great Britain.
A retaliatory action carried out by French torpedo-carrying aircraft against Gibraltar causes no damage. This is the only hostile action by the French in reply to the Mers-el-Kebir operation; the French Minister of Marine, Admiral François Darlan, has declared that British ships will only be attacked if they approach within 20 miles of the French coasts.
☐ New Rumanian Cabinet opts to join the Axis powers.

6 July
Hitler proposes a peace pact with Britain based on partition of the world.

7 July
The French Admiral Godefroy and the British Vice-Admiral Sir Andrew Cunningham agree to neutralize French vessels in the harbour of Alexandria without resort to force. The episode at Mers-el-Kebir is thus not to be repeated.

8 July
The French battleships *Richelieu* and *Jean Bart*, the one in harbour at Dakar, the other at Casablanca, are attacked by British motor torpedo boats and torpedo-carrying aircraft and seriously damaged, being put out of action for several months. A public declaration by General de Gaulle in London: the General deplores the decision taken by the British government and declares that all Frenchmen are dismayed and saddened.

9 July
First major naval encounter occurs off the coast of Calabria between a British squadron (one aircraft carrier, three battleships, five light cruisers, six destroyers) commanded by Vice-Admiral Sir Andrew Cunningham and an Italian squadron (two battleships, six heavy cruisers, twelve light cruisers and a number of destroyers) led by Admiral Campioni. Action ends when the Italian flagship, the battleship *Giulio Cesare*, is hit by the British flagship *Warspite*. Admiral Campioni manages to reach Messina. British aircraft from the aircraft carrier *Eagle* play an effective part in the battle, but the intervention of Italian aircraft is entirely ineffective. Italy claims naval victory.

10 July

First large scale attack on the United Kingdom. 70 German aircraft raid South Wales docks.

☐ The French National Assembly at Vichy gives full powers to Marshal Pétain, with 569 votes in his favour and 80 against.

11 July

Marshal Pétain is declared 'Chief of the French State', and a new government formed.

☐ Grand Admiral Erich von Raeder tries to persuade Hitler not to attack Britain from the sea – i.e. not to give orders for the carrying out of Operation Sealion. The Admiral considers that the invasion of Britain should be attempted only as a last resort.

12 July

General Jodl writes a memorandum giving his views on Operation *Seelöwe*: the practical difficulties of the action would be overcome if the invasion were treated as 'a river crossing in force on a very wide front ...' He adds that the role of the artillery in such an operation would be taken over by the Luftwaffe, which would have to overcome the RAF before landings on the British coast could be carried out.

13 July

After long discussions with his closest collaborators about the time and the manner of the attack on Britain, Hitler issues Directive No. 15, outlining the strategy to be followed by the three services in planning the invasion of Britain. The general air offensive is to begin on 5 August, and its main objective is to be the elimination of the RAF. There are 2,669 aircraft available for this purpose, divided into three 'air fleets'. No. 5, under General Stumpff, based in Scandinavia, will take on targets in the north of Britain; Kesselring's No. 2, with headquarters in Brussels, will deal with England as far as a line Portsmouth – Oxford – Manchester; and the third fleet, No. 3, will attack the western and south-western parts of the island.

14 July

'Bastille Day' in France is observed as a day of 'national mourning'. But General de Gaulle and other Free French leaders lay wreaths at the Cenotaph in London to symbolize their determination to fight on for the liberation of France

☐ General de Gaulle reviews the first Free French detachment in Whitehall, London.

☐ General elections in the Baltic republics of Estonia, Latvia and Lithuania. These three nations vote unanimously for union with the USSR.

16 July

Hitler issues Directive No. 16: 'Since Britain, despite its desperate situation, shows no sign of understanding, I have decided to prepare a landing operation against the country and to carry it out if necessary ...' This is the official 'starting-gun' for the preparation of Operation Sealion, which has as its immediate object the landing of 20 divisions on the south coastline of England. The operation will not be launched unless

the Luftwaffe has annihilated the RAF and won complete air superiority over the Channel. The land defences of Britain are in the hands of 25 infantry divisions which are ill-equipped with arms, armour and transport, and are dispersed over a very wide front. The main hope rests in the resistance of the air arm; hence the significance of the coming 'Battle of Britain'.

☐ An Italian air formation bombs the base at Haifa, in Palestine.

19 July

Speaking in Berlin to the Reichstag, Hitler addresses a last appeal to Britain. Among other things he declares: 'If the struggle continues it can only end in annihilation for one of us. Mr. Churchill thinks it will be Germany. I know it will be Britain. I am not the vanquished begging for mercy. I speak as a victor. I can see no reason why this war must go on. We should like to avert the sacrifices which must claim millions. It is possible that Mr. Churchill will once again brush aside this statement of

PAUL KLEE

The Swiss painter Paul Klee died in Locarno on 29 June of a heart attack. Having studied in Germany during the early years of the century, Klee first exhibited the Munich *Sezession* in 1906.

A teacher of painting at the Bauhaus from 1920 to 1929, Klee had to flee Germany with the advent of the Nazis, finding refuge in Switzerland. During the 1930s he produced a series of works based on the repetition of coloured squares and rectangles (each different from the next) which occupied virtually the entire surface of the canvas. An extremely prolific artist (more than 700 paintings, more than a thousand works on paper and approximately 4,000 drawings, engravings and small sculptures), Klee is regarded as one of the leading exponents of modern art.

Paul Klee.

mine by saying that it is merely born of fear and doubt of victory. In that case I shall have relieved my conscience of the things to come.'

☐ The US President Roosevelt signs the Two-Ocean Navy Expansion Act, which provides for powerful reinforcement of the American fleet within the period 1940 to 1945.

☐ General Lord Ironside is promoted Field-Marshal. General Sir Alan Brooke becomes Commander-in-Chief Home Forces.

21 July
Russia annexes the Baltic states (Estonia, Latvia and Lithuania) as autonomous republics within the USSR in accordance with decisions of July 14.

22 July
Churchill replies to Hitler's peace offer through his Foreign Minister, Lord Halifax: 'We never wanted the war; certainly no one here wants the war to go on for a day longer than is necessary. But we shall not stop fighting till freedom for ourselves and others is secure.'

☐ The British set up the SOE (Special Operations Executive) to coordinate commando operations and the clandestine struggle in countries occupied by the Germans.

23 July
Provisional Czech government under Dr Beneš is formed in London and recognized by Britain.

25 July
Italian air formations bomb the naval base at Alexandria and the base at Haifa in Palestine. Rome admits the loss of 16 submarines since war commenced.

26 July
Rumanian Prime Minister and Foreign Minister see Hitler at Berchtesgaden.

27 July
Bulgarian Prime Minister and Foreign Minister also visit Berchtesgaden for talks with Hitler.

29 July
A memorandum issued by the headquarters of the German navy states that a landing on the British coast will not be possible until the second half of September, and that even then the navy will not be able to support it from the sea. The Chief of Staff of the Kriegsmarine, Admiral Schniewind, says that 'It is impossible to accept responsibility for any such operation during the current year ... The prospect looks very doubtful.'

30 July
Demobilization of French North African and Syrian armies is announced.

31 July
Hitler calls a meeting of the top officers of the navy to discuss the situation. Admiral Raeder, the Commander-in-Chief, gives a detailed

One of the tall radar masts erected along the south coast of Britain to detect the approach of enemy aircraft.

OPERATION CATAPULT

By leaving metropolitan ports before its ships can be taken over by the Germans, the French fleet has kept its considerable power intact. What might happen to Britain, left to fight alone against Germany, should this tremendous war potential fall into enemy hands? This is the nightmare confronting Winston Churchill and the British War Cabinet following the signing of the French capitulation at Compiègne on 22 June 1940.

Hitler of course is hoping to acquire the French navy and certainly envisages such an acquisition at the time of his meeting with Mussolini at Munich on 18 June when armistice conditions to be imposed on France are discussed. Mussolini presses his ally to demand the handing over of the French fleet; the Führer, who reckons on finishing off the British quickly and who hopes, if that is not possible, to persuade the French to collaborate with him, turns out to be content with demobilization of the fleet, or alternatively with its being sent to a neutral port.

The British maintain two small fleets in the Mediterranean, one under the command of Vice-Admiral Sir Andrew Cunningham, based on Alexandria, the other, commanded by Vice-Admiral Sir James Somerville, based on Gibraltar.

On the day the Franco-German armistice is signed the British find out the whereabouts of the French warships. The ultra-modern battleships *Richelieu* (which with its 15-inch guns the First Sea Lord believes the most powerful in the world) and *Jean Bart* (the latter, only newly arrived from St. Nazaire but without its guns) have sailed, one to Dakar, the other to Casablanca.

The two battle cruisers *Dunkerque* and *Strasbourg*, the two battleships *Provence* and *Bretagne*, the aircraft carrier *Commandant Teste* and six *Terrible* class light cruisers, and a number of destroyers, submarines and other vessels, under the command of Admiral Marcel Bruno Gensoul, are concentrated in the port of Mers-el-Kebir, near Oran, in Algeria. There are seven heavy cruisers at Algiers, one battleship and four cruisers (three of them modern 8-inch-gun cruisers), under the command of Admiral Godefroy, are in harbour at Alexandria, in Egypt. Two battleships, four light cruisers, some submarines, including a very large one, the *Surcouf*, eight destroyers and some 200 smaller units are at Portsmouth and Plymouth.

What worries the British most is Admiral Gensoul's squadron at Mers-el-Kebir.

On 27 June 1940 the British War Cabinet, at Churchill's own request, decides to take surprise action to confront the French ships and neutralize their attacking power by whatever means was possible. If the ruse is not successful, recourse is to be had to force. For this purpose Force H is created, consisting of the battle-cruiser *Hood*, the battleships *Resolution* and *Valiant*, the aircraft carrier *Ark Royal*, two cruisers and eleven destroyers; the squadron assembles at Gibraltar under the command of Vice-Admiral Sir James Somerville. The code name for the operation is Catapult; it is timed to go off on 3 July.

The French ships in British ports are captured at dawn on 3 July without a shot fired, apart from one unfortunate incident aboard the submarine *Surcouf*. Due to a misunderstanding, two British

officers and a leading seaman are killed and another seaman wounded. One French seaman is also killed. The crews of the other ships, surprised in their sleep, have to surrender. The tragedy of Mers-el-Kebir takes place on the same day. In the morning Captain C. S. Holland sends the French Admiral Gensoul an ultimatum in the terms agreed between Churchill himself and the First Sea Lord on 30 June. Given that it is impossible for His Majesty's government to accept the possibility that 'the fine ships of France' should fall into German and Italian hands and be used against the Allies, the French fleet is offered several alternatives:

(1) to sail and join the British fleet and fight at its side until final victory;

(2) to sail for a British port with reduced crews;

(3) if the French fleet feels itself bound by the terms of the armistice, which prohibits the use of their ships against Italy and Germany, it would be possible to sail with a British escort to a port in the French West Indies, such as Martinique, where they would be disarmed or possibly handed over to the custody of the USA until the end of the war. In this case the crews would be repatriated.

'If you refuse these fair offers,' the text of the ultimatum goes on, 'I must with profound regret require you to sink your ships within six hours. Finally, failing the above, I bear the order from HM government to use whatever force may be necessary to prevent your ships from falling into German or Italian hands.' The document is signed by Vice-Admiral Sir James Fowness Somerville.

In the meantime the British admiral has received further instructions. If Admiral Gensoul, in command of the fleet at Mers-el-Kebir, accepts the second alternative but claims that his ships may not be used by the British during the war, Somerville is to tell him that the British will accept his request as long as the enemy respect the armistice terms. But if Gensoul refuses all the British alternatives and proposes to disarm his ships in port, that proposal, too, can be accepted on condition that the dismantling of the ships takes place within six hours under the British admiral's supervision, and is such as would make it impossible for them to be made serviceable again for at least a year. Failing any kind of agreement, the French ships at Mers-el-Kebir are to be destroyed, especially the two battle-cruisers *Dunkerque* and *Strasbourg*.

By the time Admiral Gensoul receives the British ultimatum the British ships of Somerville's squadron already have their guns trained on the French vessels. Late in the afternoon Gensoul puts a proposal of his own to the British admiral: he will disarm his ships himself and undertake that, if there is any threat from the Ita-

lians or Germans, he will have them moved to Martinique or the USA. Demobilization of the crews has already begun, says Gensoul. But the French counter-proposal arrives too late. Somerville's orders are to complete his mission before nightfall; he therefore orders his ships to open fire. The bombardment lasted some ten minutes.

When the shelling is over the battle-cruiser *Dunkerque*, the battleships *Provence* and *Bretagne* and one destroyer are severely damaged; 1,300 French seamen have been killed. The *Strasbourg*, the aircraft carrier *Commandant Teste* and the other destroyers succeed in breaking through the British blockade and make their way to Toulon.

Four days later, on 7 July, the French Admiral Godefroy and Vice-Admiral Cunningham come to an agreement about the French ships in harbour at Alexandria, by which the French ships will not be scuttled but will not try to leave port nor commit any act hostile to the British, who for their part will not try to capture the French ships. The terms will be

reconsidered in the event of the Germans or Italians taking over French ships anywhere else.

The final act of Operation Catapult on 8 July is directed against the ultra-modern battleships *Richelieu* and *Jean Bart*, in port at Dakar and Casablanca respectively. They are attacked by motor torpedo boats and torpedo-carrying aircraft and both are put out of action for several months.

Churchill's decision to attack the French fleet was not popular with some British naval chiefs, but practical considerations made it necessary. It cannot be denied that the presence of a *Richelieu* or a *Jean Bart* (to mention only the two outstanding units in the French navy) would have changed the balance of naval power decisively at a moment when Britain needed the whole of her fleet to defend her coasts against a possible enemy landing. The hostile French reaction, even to the point of a possible declaration of war, was a risk that Churchill felt it necessary to run.

In the House of Commons, on 4 July, Churchill speaks for an hour or more on what had to be done. 'I leave the judgment of our actions with confidence to Parliament. I leave it to the nation ... I leave it to the world and to history.'

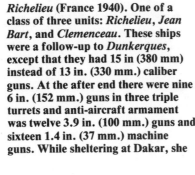

Richelieu (France 1940). One of a class of three units: *Richelieu*, *Jean Bart*, and *Clemenceau*. These ships were a follow-up to *Dunkerques*, except that they had 15 in (380 mm) instead of 13 in. (330 mm.) caliber guns. At the after end there were nine 6 in. (152 mm.) guns in three triple turrets and anti-aircraft armament was twelve 3.9 in. (100 mm.) guns and sixteen 1.4 in. (37 mm.) machine guns. While sheltering at Dakar, she

was damaged by the British fleet on July 8, 1940. In 1944, she was sent to the Far East and then took part in the Indochina War. Taken out of commission in 1956, she was broken up in 1968.

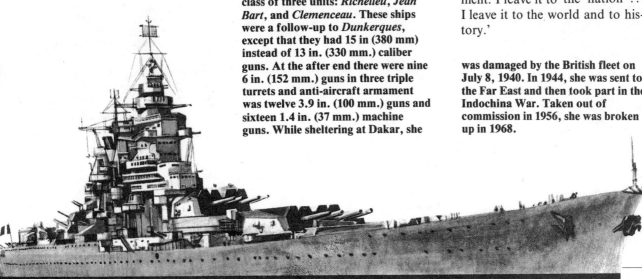

exposition of the difficulties of crossing the Channel with the means at present available to him. In his judgment it would be expedient to postpone Operation Sealion from 13 September to a date between 19 and 26 September to take advantage of favourable tides, and above all to limit the operations to the Straits of Dover; but finally he comes back to the idea he has often expressed before, that the operation should be postponed until next spring.

□ During 31 July, 15 more ships with arms and equipment sail for British ports from the USA.

□ In July civilian casualties from air raids on Britain are 258 killed and 321 injured.

1 August
Hitler issues his top secret Directive No. 17, which includes the categorical order to the Luftwaffe to 'crush the British air force by every means available'.
In the light of this order it is obvious that Operation Sealion has become subordinate to and dependent on the outcome of the air battle over Britain. The beginning of that attack is fixed for 5 August.
□ In Moscow, Foreign Minister Molotov reaffirms Russia's neutral standpoint.

2 August
Lord Beaverbrook, Minister for Aircraft Production, appointed to the War Cabinet. Other members are Churchill, Chamberlain, Lord Halifax, Attlee and Arthur Greenwood.

3 August
It is announced in London that a large contingent of Canadian troops, including some US subjects, has arrived in Britain.

4 August
In East Africa the Italian attack on British Somaliland begins.
□ Further drafts of Australian troops arrive in Britain.

5 August
Bad weather forces the Germans to postpone the start of the air offensive against Britain.

6 August
The first contingent of Southern Rhodesian airmen arrives in Britain.

7 August
It is announced that, in the week ending 28 July, 18 British ships (65,601 tons) and 2 Allied ships (7,090 tons) have been lost by enemy action.

8 August
A special 'statute', approved in London by Churchill and General de Gaulle, lays down the conditions of

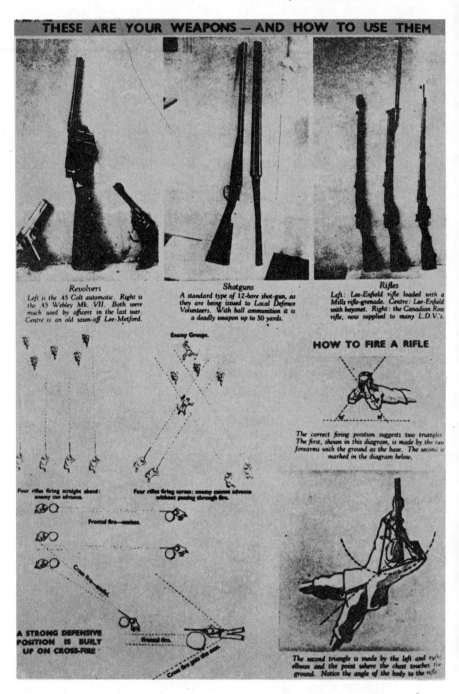

British newspapers launch a campaign to recruit a citizens' army, known as the Local Defence Volunteers and subsequently the Home Guard. Some pages from *Picture Post*

employment of the Free French volunteers.

11 August

On the eve of the German air offensive, Britain has available 704 operational fighters, of which 620 are Hurricanes and Spitfires, supported by 350 bombers. Germany can call on 2,669 aircraft, mostly bombers: normal bombers (1,015 of them Do-17, Do-217, Do-215, He-111, Ju-88), plus 346 Ju-87 single-engined dive-bombers (Stukas) and 375 twin-engined Me-110 fighter-bombers. Their fighter force comprises 933 single-engined Me-109s.

☐ Waves of German fighters and bombers carry out attacks on South-East and Channel coasts in daytime raids. Over 200 planes attack radar stations at Portland and Weymouth.

☐ RAF attacks enemy targets in France.

12 August

Heavy German air attack on Portsmouth.

13 August

This is the 'Day of the Eagle' (*Adlertag*), the code-name given to the first day of the coming weeks of full-scale bombing by the Luftwaffe of British headquarters, airfields and aircraft factories. On this first day the Germans send over 1,485 aircraft and lose 45, the RAF lose 13 fighters and seven pilots. But this initial phase of the battle already shows up the defects and shortages of the Luftwaffe. The Stukas, for instance, with a maximum speed of 190 m.p.h. and ceiling of 11,000 ft, are an easy prey for the Spitfires, which are more manœuvrable and very much faster (they can reach a speed of 375 m.p.h. and fly above 33,000 ft. Then, the Me-110 fighter-bombers are not particularly manœuvrable, and the Dornier, Heinkel and Ju-88 bombers, with a bomb-load of only 1,100 lb, have a very limited destructive capacity, allied to the risk of being brought down by enemy fighters. However, German headquarters say that four days should be enough to demolish British air defences south of a line from London to Gloucester, and four weeks sufficient to wipe out the RAF.

☐ The Italian Foreign Minister, Galeazzo Ciano, instigates a press campaign for an attack on Greece, and calls General Sebastiano Visconti Prasca, commander of the Italian troops in Albania, to Rome.

☐ The British decide to send powerful armoured forces to the Middle East.

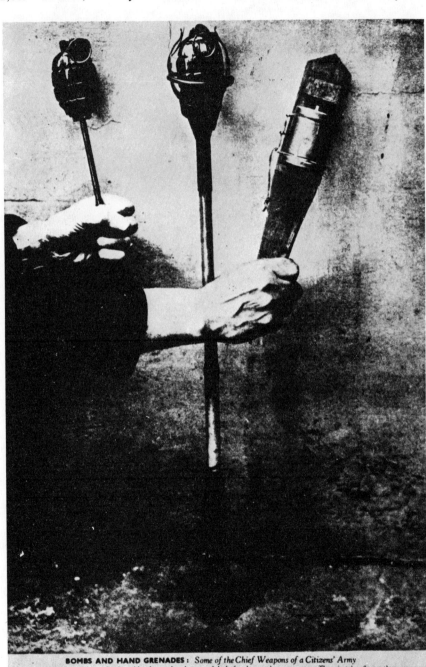

BOMBS AND HAND GRENADES : *Some of the Chief Weapons of a Citizens' Army*
Not much training is needed to use bombs and hand-grenades—but a good deal of coolness and common-sense. The principles of using them are ... *follow them carefully. Left, the Mills bomb as a rifle-grenade. When the bomb bursts, its forty sections*

for 29 June 1940. The Home Guard had only a limited usefulness, but helped to sustain British morale.

14 August

A day of bad weather; German aircraft fly only 500 missions over Britain, the targets being railway lines near the coast and RAF operational headquarters in the south of the country.

☐ The USA and Great Britain agree on the general lines of a mutual undertaking by which the Americans would give Britain 50 destroyers in exchange for the use by the American fleet of British bases in the western Atlantic.

15 August

Taking advantage of fine weather the German air force launches a large-scale assault, the biggest so far. At least seven big formations sweep over Britain; all three *Luftflotten* are employed in a series of co-ordinated attacks on targets a considerable distance apart. All the German raids, which start at 11.30 a.m. and go on until about 6.30 p.m., are tenaciously resisted by British fighters and anti-aircraft batteries; the British fighters never give the German planes a moment's respite. The Luftwaffe sends 520 bombers and 1,270 fighters into the attack, losing 75 aircraft, for the loss of 34 fighters by the RAF (the British reported 180 German planes destroyed).

16 August

More air raids on Britain. The Luftwaffe makes repeated attacks on airfields and the London docks area. HM King George VI sends the following telegram to the Secretary for War, Sir Archibald Sinclair: 'Please convey my warmest congratulations to the fighter squadrons who in recent days have been so heavily engaged in the defence of our country. I, with all their compatriots, have read with ever-increasing admiration the story of their daily victories. I wish them continued success and the best of luck.'

17 August

The Germans withdraw the Stukas from their attacking force, since they have proved too vulnerable.

☐ Hitler announces a total blockade of the British Isles.

☐ The German Foreign Minister, Joachim von Ribbentrop, brusquely

switches off the anti-Greek campaign launched three days earlier by the Italian Foreign Minister, Galeazzo Ciano. Hitler does not (for the moment) want any military involvement in the Balkans.

☐ Greek headquarters begin full-scale mobilization, calling up certain categories in the districts of Tsamuria, Epirus and western Macedonia.

☐ RAF bomb oil plants, munitions factories and other targets in France and Germany.

18 August

The Luftwaffe launches further heavy attacks at mid-day on British airfields in Kent, Surrey and Sussex, losing 71 aircraft against 27 losses by the RAF.

☐ From 8 August to date the Germans have lost at least 363 aircraft, while the British fighter squadrons have lost 211 Spitfires and Hurricanes, and 154 pilots.

19 August

The Italians occupy Berbera, capital of British Somaliland.

☐ Mussolini writes to General Rodolfo Graziani, Governor of Libya and Commander-in-Chief of Italian forces in North Africa, about future strategic objectives. Among other things he declares: 'The invasion of Great Britain is decided on; it is now in the last stages of preparation and will be successful. It may take place within a week or in about a month. Now, on the day on which the first platoon of German soldiers lands on British soil, you too will attack. As I have said to you before, there are no territorial objectives; it is not a matter of marching on Alexandria, even on Sollum. All I ask is that you attack the British troops facing you. I myself accept full responsibility for this decision.'

20 August

Churchill makes a statement on war situation, and speaking of the Battle of Britain, claims, 'Never in the field of human conflict was so much owed by so many to so few.'

Above: a formation of Spitfires on their way to intercept enemy aircraft. The superior speed and manœuvrability of the Spitfire contributed substantially to the defeat of the Luftwaffe in the Battle of Britain. Opposite: a Messerschmitt Me-109.

THE MURDER OF TROTSKY

On the evening of 20 August a stranger who claimed to be an admirer and supporter, made his way into Trotsky's office and split his skull open with an ice-pick. The great Russian revolutionary leader was rushed to hospital but in spite of medical attention died the following day. The killer, unidentified for some time, was Ramon Mercader (alias Frank Jackson, alias Jacques Mormand), almost certainly an agent of the Soviet secret police, the OGPU. The instigator of the murder, despite absence of definite proof, was hardly open to doubt, all the more since Trotsky himself had explicitly accused Stalin of having organised a previous assassination attempt in May.

Lev Trotsky was one of the most important revolutionary figures of the age. Spokesman of the Mensheviks during the 1905 Revolution, he subsequently joined the Bolsheviks and was one of the organisers, along with Lenin, of the October Revolution of 1917. Commissar for foreign affairs, he led the Soviet peace negotiations with Germany at Brest-Litovsk, and during the civil war took over the post of minister of war, virtually creating the Red Army. His rapid ascent and his particular theories on the nature of the revolutionary process earned him many enemies within the Party, and when the struggle began for the succession to Lenin, Trotsky soon found himself in a minority and was powerless to prevent Stalin's rise. Expelled from the Party in 1927 and banished to central Asia, Trotsky was soon obliged to live abroad as an exile. He eventually sought refuge in Mexico, the only country prepared to receive him. He remained intellectually and politically active, and fought until his death for the success of the Fourth International, the organisation he had founded to rally together his followers.

☐ Italian bombers raid Gibraltar.

22 August
Mussolini orders all preparations for war against Greece to be postponed *sine die*.

23 August
Nets are placed in position at entrance to main Greek harbours, in particular those on the Ionian Sea, and strict routes are specified for civil air traffic.

24 August
Heavy German air raids on North Weald and Hornchurch, two command centres of the RAF. First bombs fall on Central London; St. Giles church, Cripplegate, is damaged.

25 August
In a night retaliatory raid RAF aircraft bomb Berlin. Hermann Goering had long ago assured Hitler that such a thing could never happen.

26 August
First all-night alert in London.

28 August
Liaison officers of the army and the Royal Navy, who had been serving in Dakar, French West Africa, before the collapse of France, arrive in London.

☐ During the night many incendiary bombs are dropped on London.

29 August
South African Air Force launches raids on Italian Somaliland.
☐ Malta is attacked by Italian bombers.

30 August
Renewed German air offensive against RAF operational command centres in the south; the air base at Biggin Hill, Kent, is attacked twice. Further night incendiary raids on London and other towns. Total civilian casualties in Britain during August are 1,075 killed.

31 August
British reconnaissance reports an enormous assembly of German landing craft in ports and estuaries on the other side of the Channel.
☐ 39 aircraft are destroyed when the Luftwaffe attacks RAF operational headquarters at Debden, Biggin Hill and Hornchurch.
☐ The ships composing 'Force M' sail from Scapa Flow, Britain's principal naval base. The squadron is to support a landing at Dakar, French West Africa, by General de Gaulle and 2,700 Free French, with the object of finding new adherents to his movement and especially to detach the French colonies in equatorial Africa, and possibly also those in North Africa, from Vichy France. The plan, submitted to the British government by General de Gaulle at the beginning of August, was enthusiastically supported by Churchill. De Gaulle had managed to convince Churchill that a surprise landing at Dakar would probably meet with very little resistance. Force M con-

SIR JOSEPH JOHN THOMSON

The death occured on 30 August of the great English physicist Joseph John Thomson, renowned for his work in the fields of electricity, electronics and chemistry.

Born near Manchester in 1856, Thomson studied at Trinity College, Cambridge, and in 1884 became the first Cavendish professor of experimental physics at the university. He gathered around him a group of brilliant students (seven of whom subsequently won the Nobel Prize), and within a few years the Cavendish Laboratory became the world's major centre of research.

After prolonged study of electrical conduction through rare gases and of cathode rays, Thomson accomplished his greatest work in 1897 when he measured the ratio between the charge and mass of the particles of cathode rays, in effect discovering electrons. His principal work, *Conduction of Electricity through Gases*, appeared in 1903, and in 1906 he was awarded the Nobel Prize for Physics. During his last years he devoted himself to studies of 'positive rays' and devised a method for identifying isotopes which paved the way for the studies of F.W. Aston.

A Dornier Do-17 approaching the English coast.

sists of the battleships *Barham* and *Resolution*, the aircraft carrier *Ark Royal*, five cruisers, at least sixteen destroyers and two corvettes, plus three corvettes of the Free French navy.

1 September
Further raids by Luftwaffe aircraft on the operational centre at Biggin Hill.

2 September
Further heavy air raids on Biggin Hill and other aerodromes during daylight, and night attacks on London.

3 September
An agreement is signed between the USA and Britain by which America will supply 50 destroyers to the Royal Navy in exchange for a lease of naval bases in Jamaica, Saint Lucia, Trinidad, Antigua and British Guiana, and free bases in Newfoundland and Bermuda.
☐ The 'Vienna Award'. Under strong Axis pressure, and to accord with the decision taken by Ribbentrop

British Somaliland: a native irregular and a Fascist Blackshirt raise the Italian flag and a Fascist pennant over a newly-captured strongpoint.

and Ciano in Vienna on 30 August, the Rumanians are forced to cede to Hungary a large part of northern Transylvania, populated almost entirely by the Hungarian Székely people. But in addition to this area, and despite the opposition of King Carol II and his Prime Minister, Gigurtu, Rumania also has to surrender to the Hungarians a huge strip of territory populated by three million Rumanians and including the cities of Cluj and Oradea-Mare.

4 September
Hitler declares: 'I have tried to spare the British. They have mistaken my humanity for weakness and have replied by murdering German women and children.' (He is referring to the RAF's bombing of Berlin in the night of 25–26 August, which caused some deaths among the civil population.) 'If they attack our cities we will simply erase theirs.'
☐ Pétain terminates General Maxime Weygand's appointment as Minister of National Defence, making him general delegate of the Vichy government in Africa.
☐ During the night German aircraft drop flares over London.

5 September
London has its longest night alert so far – seven and a half hours.

6 September
German bombing raids on port installations along the south coast of Britain elicits the 'yellow' invasion alarm: 'Probable attack within three days'.
☐ RAF bombs Berlin in a two-hour night raid.
☐ In Rumania popular discontent at the territorial cessions imposed on their country increases, and the ultra-nationalist and anti-Semitic 'Iron Guard' movement provokes riots that lead to the abdication of King Carol II, who is succeeded by Crown Prince Michael. General Antonescu assumes power and proclaims himself 'Conducator' (leader) as head of a dictatorship.

7 September
Commencement of 'London Blitz'. 5.00 p.m.: 300 German bombers, escorted by 600 fighters, drop 337 tons of bombs on London, the principal targets being Woolwich Arsenal and the docks area, but also indiscriminate attacks on civilian targets. Huge fires are caused, 306 killed, 1,337 seriously injured. At 8.07 p.m. British GHQ issues the code-word 'Cromwell' to Eastern and Southern Commands, which means, 'Probable invasion of Great Britain within 24 hours'.

8 September
During the night 200 bombers of the 3rd *Luftflotte* attack electricity power stations and railway lines in London.

9 September
More German air raids on London. The Germans lose 28 aircraft during the action, the British lose 19 fighters.
☐ Italian air raids on Tel-Aviv in Palestine.

10 September
Council of War in Berlin: since RAF resistance continues and the British fighters are still so effective that it is impossible to guarantee a landing on the coasts of Britain except by surprise, the starting date of Operation Sealion is put back to the 14th. (In fact, the actual landing could not have begun before 24 September, since the German navy needed at least ten days' advance warning.) The Luftwaffe still has a few days in which to silence the RAF.
☐ Further RAF night raids on Berlin.
☐ British air raids on Massawa, Asmara and Dessye in East Africa and on targets in Cyrenaica.

11 September
Buckingham Palace damaged in air raid.
☐ The Italian offensive in Egypt begins.
☐ The ships of the British Force M are about 300 miles north-east of Dakar; at the same time it becomes known that a French squadron with three cruisers and three large destroyers has left Toulon and has entered the Atlantic through the Strait of Gibraltar, and is sailing south-west towards Dakar, with the obvious intention of resisting the landing of General de Gaulle's Free French volunteers.

12–13 September
Poor visibility considerably cuts down Luftwaffe air activity over London, and the night attacks are also reduced.

☐ Italian troops cross the Egyptian frontier on 13 September and occupy Sollum.

14 September

X–Day for Operation Sealion is postponed to 17 September, which means putting off the landing itself to 27 September, since the Kriegsmarine needs ten days to prepare and co-ordinate their action. 27 September is the last day in September on which the tides will be suitable for a landing.

15 September

German bombers fly over London in waves all day and night; the destruction is catastrophic, but does not include any essential war targets. Other Luftwaffe formations make for Southampton, seeking to hit the city's seaplane installations, but meet with violent anti-aircraft fire. Bristol, Cardiff, Liverpool and Manchester are also attacked during the night. The Germans, who have thrown 230 bombers and 700 fighters into the battle, lose 56 aircraft (original British claim 185), while the RAF lose only 23. Thus the day on which Goering had hoped to eliminate the RAF has ended in a British victory.

16 September

☐ President Roosevelt signs Conscription Bill.

☐ The Italians reach and occupy Sidi Barrani.

17 September

Operation Sealion is postponed 'until further orders'.

22 September

Between 13 August, the 'Day of the Eagle', and 22 September at least 15,000 tons of bombs have been dropped on Britain.

23 September

King George VI broadcasts to the British people. The George Cross and George Medal are instituted as civilian awards.

☐ The British ships of Force M are just off Dakar ready to launch de

Two Dornier Do-17s during a bombing raid over Greater London. On the ground can be seen smoke from the exploding bombs and, in the air, white puffs of anti-aircraft fire.

Gaulle's operation, the landing of Free French troops in French West Africa. It is hoped that the Vichy forces will offer no resistance. At 7.00 a.m. General de Gaulle broadcasts an ineffectual radio appeal to the authorities of the French colony asking permission to land with his troops. The same urgent appeal is repeated at 8.00 a.m., after five emissaries, bearers of a message from the General to governor Boisson, have been given short shrift and almost taken prisoner. Yet a third appeal remains unheard, despite the threat of the use of force. But at 10.50 a.m. it is the Dakar

coastal batteries and the ships at anchor in the port that open fire on the British ships, which return fire. Attempts by the Free French to land are quickly checked. The barrage from Dakar proves effective.

24 September

Aircraft from the British aircraft carrier *Ark Royal* try to bomb the Dakar coastal batteries and the formidable battleship *Richelieu*. But the British battleship *Barham* is hit, though not seriously.

25 September

The second battleship in the British

squadron, the *Resolution*, is also hit by French shells, and severely damaged. The defences of Dakar continue to show themselves very efficient and precise. It is realized by the British commanders and by de Gaulle himself that a landing will cost too much in men and materials, and wisely, in the morning, the British ships are ordered to withdraw to Freetown, capital of the British colony of Sierra Leone.

□ British aircraft raid the port of Tobruk, and naval forces bombard the Sidi Barrani region.

□ French air attacks on Gibraltar in reprisal for the Dakar incident.

27 September

Tripartite Pact between Germany, Italy and Japan signed in Berlin. The agreement obliges signatories to give military assistance in case of any attack by a country not already involved in the war, and recognizes the right of the Italians and Germans to establish a 'new order' in Europe and of the Japanese to impose their 'new order' in Asia.

□ 55 German planes brought down over Britain.

28 September

First US destroyers transferred to Royal Navy arrive in Britain.

29 September

British naval forces commence 'sweep' in the eastern and central Mediterranean.

30 September

Since the start of the air offensive over London on 7 September, the British have lost 247 fighters, against 433 by the Luftwaffe. British civilian casualties for September: 6,954 killed, 10,615 injured.

2 October

Night air attacks on London.

□ Arrival of New Zealand naval and air force drafts in Britain.

□ Hitler has still not lost hope of being able to carry out a landing in Britain (Operation Sealion), although the commanders of his army and navy advise him to aban-don the project rather than expose the craft gathered in European ports to British bombing.

3 October

The ships of Force M which took part in the action against Dakar from 23 to 25 September, leave Freetown, where they had taken refuge, and escort the Free French forces to Douala in the French Cameroons. They are not accompanied by the battleships *Barham* and *Resolution*, which have sailed for the Mediterranean: the *Resolution* to put into Gibraltar for repairs to the damage suffered in the action off Dakar.

□ Neville Chamberlain resigns from British Cabinet on grounds of ill-health.

4 October

Hitler and Mussolini meet at Brennero on the Brenner Pass. Hitler urges that no action be undertaken which is not 'of absolute use to the Axis'. The two Foreign Ministers, Ribbentrop and Ciano, are present, and also the German Commander-in-Chief, Keitel. The Führer offers military aid in North Africa, but the Duce declines the offer.

TOM MIX

On 12 October Tom Mix, the most popular hero of film Westerns during the 1920s, was killed in an automobile accident near Florence, Arizona. Son of an officer of the legendary Seventh Cavalry and a Red Indian woman, Mix was one of the few actors whose real life approximated that of his screen image. Born in 1880 at Clearfield, Pennsylvania, he was involved during his eventful youth in the Cuban war, the Mexican revolution and the Boxer revolt in China. He later became a cowboy, a sheriff, a Texas Ranger and a rodeo champion. In 1910, after joining a circus, he got a job in the cinema with the Selig company, serving an arduous but profitable apprenticeship by working in various capacities on seventy or so short films. In the twenties Mix, who had by then joined Fox, became a Western star, winning fame and playing an important part in popularising the genre. Although he was not a remarkable actor, Mix (and his horse, Tony, the screen's first equine star) appeared in more than seventy full-length films full of spectacle, acrobatics and moral injunction, cultivating the image of an invincible, upright hero, remorseless in his dealings with criminals, yet preferring to use the lasso and the fist in preference to firearms.

With the arrival of sound, Tom Mix's star rapidly waned and after a few disappointing attempts at a comeback, the actor decided in 1934 to retire for good from the screen.

On the spot where his fatal accident occurred, a statue of a riderless horse was set up.

5 October
Daylight air attacks on Britain by the Luftwaffe cease completely, though the night-time raids continue without respite. One-mile tunnel between Bethnal Green and Liverpool Street opened to provide underground shelter for 4,000 people.

6 October
Gales and low clouds give London its first quiet night since 7 September.

7 October
German troops enter Rumania to re-structure Rumanian armed forces. Rumanian oil wells are of vital importance to the Germans.

8 October
Britain refuses the Japanese request to close the 'Burma Road' by which Western supplies can reach the army of Chiang Kai-shek.

11 October
Marshal Pétain says 'France must free herself from all so-called traditional friendships and enmities.'

12 October
Hitler abandons work on Operation Sealion against Britain, and the invasion plan is postponed to the spring of 1941.
□ Mussolini learns that Hitler has occupied the Rumanian oil wells in order 'to protect them'. The *coup* infuriates the Fascist leader, who says angrily to Ciano: 'Hitler always presents me with a *fait accompli*, but this time I shall pay him back in his own coin. When he reads the papers he'll see that I've occupied Greece, and that will make us all square.' 'What will Badoglio [Commander-in-Chief of Italian armed forces] say?' asks Ciano. 'Badoglio doesn't know yet, but I'll soon get rid of anyone who finds any difficulty in fighting the Greeks,' replies Mussolini.

14 October
Marshal Badoglio assures Mussolini that 20 divisions will be needed to defeat Greece, and that it will take three months.

15 October
Mussolini calls a meeting at the Palazzo Venezia to discuss the occupation of Greece (as a counter to German penetration in Rumania). Talk is of a two-weeks campaign to start on 26 October (the date is later put back two days), and Foreign Minister Ciano is deputed to find a *casus belli*. The Foreign Minister says he can rely on the support of several Greek personalities who will be easy to corrupt.
□ Goering issues a directive specifying the principal objectives of the aerial *Blitzkrieg* against Britain. In order, they are: London, aircraft factories, the industrial zones of Birmingham and Coventry, and the air bases of British fighter squadrons.
□ British Admiralty reports three Italian destroyers sunk in Mediterranean operations.

16 October
RAF bomb targets in Germany, including Kiel naval base.

17 October
Eight U-boats attack convoys SC 7 and HX 79, and from 17 to 20 October sink 31 ships totalling 152,000 tons.

18 October
Anti-Semitic legislation introduced in Vichy France.
□ Malcolm MacDonald, Minister of Health, announces that 489,000 children have so far left the London area.

23 October
Hitler meets General Franco at Hendaye. Hitler promises Spain Gibraltar in return for intervention in the war.

A German heavy gun fires on Dover from an emplacement at Calais.

24 October
Meeting of Hitler and Pétain.

26 October
The ultimatum to Greece is prepared for the Italian minister in Athens, Emanuele Grazzi, to deliver at 3.00 a.m. on 28 October. The document accuses Greece of adopting a non-neutral attitude towards Italy, and the Greek government is asked to allow Italian forces to 'occupy, as a guarantee of Greek neutrality and for the duration of the present war against Britain, certain strategic points in Greek territory ... Wherever Italian troops meet with resistance, it will be crushed by force of arms, and the Greek government will be held responsible for any consequences.'

27 October
Hitler is informed of Mussolini's intention to attack Greece.

'THE GREAT DICTATOR'

'Dictators are comic. My aim is to make people laugh at them.' With this in mind, Charlie Chaplin made *The Great Dictator* while war was already raging. The film was the logical and ideal successor to *Modern Times*, Chaplin's angry satire against totalitarianism in industry, made in 1936.

The film was premiered in New York on 15 October. In spite of its hostile reception from most of the press, it was an enormous success with the public, all the more so after the US entry into the war (which had been strongly advocated in the film).

The story, veering from slapstick humour to drama, told of a Jewish barber, his love for the young girl Hannah, and his persecution in a country run by a cruel dictator. In effect, it was a savage satire against the dictatorships of Hitler and Mussolini (masterfully portrayed in the grotesque characters of Adenoid

Charlie Chaplin.

Hynkel and Napaloni).

In the sound sequences Chaplin makes Hynkel speak in a strange babble of English and German, and boldly ends the film with a six-minute speech in which the barber, who has been mistaken for the dictator and momentarily replaced him, launches a passionate appeal for peace. Summarising Chaplin's political convictions, this speech is a heartfelt plea for democracy, freedom and international accord, but also an explicit call for rebellion against oppression and a message of hope.

28 October
At 3.00 a.m., according to instructions, Grazzi presents the Italian ultimatum to the Greek Prime Minister Metaxas. Metaxas accepts it for what it is, an actual declaration of war, and consequently, with the King's agreement, he refuses it and declares that the Greeks will resist the invasion with all the forces at their command.

At dawn Italian troops in Albania cross the Greek frontier. Patras is bombed, and Britain promises help. At 11.00 a.m. Mussolini and Hitler meet at Florence, at the Santa Maria Novella station. Hitler has learned at Bologna ('from the papers', just as Mussolini wished) about the Italian action in Greece. But he is quite capable of concealing his irritation; instead, he offers his ally the assistance of his parachute divisions, which could well be necessary for the capture of the island of Crete. The two dictators look at the general situation. Hitler confirms that he will not sign any peace treaty with France that does not meet Italian demands (which he describes as 'very modest'). Spain, he says, is in a state of complete disorder, and Spanish requests for material help are too much of a burden for the Axis. As for Russia, Hitler declares: 'My distrust of Stalin is as great as Stalin's distrust of me.' But there are agreements in force that 'immobilize' Russia, and as a guarantee of that immobilization, 180 German divisions stand ready for action. He reckons to crush British resistance by aerial bombardment, and he thanks Mussolini for the help to the war effort given by Italian submarines. Mussolini says that he agrees with Hitler's appreciation of the situation, and the meeting ends with the usual 'perfect identity of views'.

☐ Laval becomes Foreign Minister in Vichy government.

29 October
Allied weekly shipping losses total 198,000 tons, the heaviest since the war started.

30 October
Admiralty announce mining of Greek waters.

☐ Pétain broadcasts to French people: Hitler's principles for collaboration accepted.

31 October
Greek–Albanian Front The Italian supreme command announces: 'Our units continue to advance into Epirus and have reached the river Kalamas at several points. Unfavourable weather conditions and action by the retreating enemy are not slowing down the movements of our troops.' But in fact the Italian offensive, carried out without conviction and without the advantage of surprise (not even for air action), under a leadership uncertain and divided by personal rivalries, is already becoming exhausted. Adverse conditions at sea make it necessary to give up a projected landing at Corfu.

☐ UK civilian casualties in October are 6,334 killed and 8,695 injured.

Of those killed 643 are children under 16.

1 November

The Battle of Britain continues. Since *Adlertag* (13 August) the British have lost 827 planes and shot down 2,409 enemy aircraft (1,505 according to official German reports).

□ Heaviest RAF raids yet on Berlin.

□ First RAF raid on Naples.

2 November

Greek–Albanian Front Greek resistance to Italians proves unexpectedly strong.

3 November

German air losses since 8 August: 2,433 planes destroyed and more than 6,000 airmen killed.

□ For the first time since September 7 no night alert in London.

4 November

Greek–Albanian Front The Greeks counter-attack, threatening to turn the whole Italian line, and reach the Korcë–Peratia road. Ciano admits: 'There has been an attack on Korcë and the enemy has made some progress, and it is true that on the eighth day of the operations the enemy hold the initiative. I do not think there is yet anything to worry too much about, though many others are beginning to think so.'

5 November

Franklin Roosevelt re-elected President of the United States.

□ Italian anti-aircraft guns frustrate a second British attempt to bomb Naples. British air raids on Lecce and Brindisi.

□ The German pocket-battleship *Scheer* attacks a British convoy and sinks the *Jervis Bay*.

7 November

RAF aircraft bomb the Krupp armaments factories at Essen in night raid.

□ Brindisi again bombed by RAF.

8 November

Greek–Albanian Front The Italian

Right: the course of hostilities in Greece and Albania from the Italian invasion on 28 October 1940 to 1 March 1941, showing the success of the Greek counter-offensive.

headquarters is forced to give the order to retire. As a result of disrupted communications the order does not reach all formations. The Julia division, or what is left of it, just succeeds in getting back over the Peratia bridge – not on the orders of the Italian command but on a decision taken by the divisional commander as a result of a report picked up on the radio from London, announcing that 'the Alpine division will be crushed by three Greek divisions'.

□/RAF bombs Munich during Hitler's *Putsch* anniversary speech.

9 November

Death of Neville Chamberlain at the age of 71.

10 November

RAF night raids on Danzig and Dresden.

11 November

Fleet Air Arm attacks Taranto. At 10.40 a.m. torpedoes from 12 British Swordfish aircraft operating from the aircraft carrier *Illustrious*, in the Ionian sea some 170 miles off the Italian coast, hit the battleships *Cavour*

(23,000 tons) and the recently-completed *Littorio* in the port of Taranto. At 11.30 a.m. a second wave of Swordfish, coming like the first from the *Illustrious*, sinks the battleship *Duilio*. This is a crippling blow to the Italian fleet, which has lost half its complement of battleships at a blow. Only two of the attacking aircraft fail to return to base.

□ During the night the British cruisers *Orion*, *Sydney* and *Ajax* and the destroyers *Nubian* and *Mohawk* sink four Italian merchant ships in the Strait of Otranto.

12 November

General Alfred Jodl, head of the operations branch at the German supreme command, and Hitler's most respected military adviser, sends the Führer a report arguing the impossibility (at any rate for the time being) of a German landing in Britain.

14 November

During the night 449 German aircraft carry out a 'carpet bombing' of Coventry, centre of the British automobile industry. Many ancient buildings in the historic city centre, including the magnificent four-

THE LASCAUX CAVE

One of the most famous painted caves in France was accidentally discovered on 1 November by a group of boys near Montignac in the Dordogne. While trying to rescue a dog which had fallen into a hole made by an uprooted tree, one of the boys slipped into the pit and after a moment of panic found himself in a cave ablaze with bright colours. Thus was revealed the Lascaux Cave, containing some of the most spectacular and beautiful examples of late Paleolithic art yet found – animal paintings and drawings which, as a result of the stable atmospheric conditions within a sealed space, had been preserved intact for thousands of years.

Above: an Italian lorry sticks in the mud.

teenth-century cathedral, are destroyed. There are 550 dead and many more wounded, and 21 factories are destroyed. Yet the city's productive capacity is still not seriously affected. After this the Germans coin the word *Coventrisieren* meaning 'annihilate, raze to the ground'.

☐ On the Greek–Albanian front the Greeks take up the offensive, while the Italian communiqué confines itself to reports of 'normal patrol and artillery activity'.

15 November

Greek–Albanian Front The Greek III Army Corps opens a breach in the area of Mount Morova in the sector of the front held by the Italian 9th Army. The Greeks continue to take many prisoners. At Menton, the French Riviera town just beyond the Italian border, posters appear saying: 'This is French territory. Greeks, do not advance further!'

☐ Heavy British air attacks on Hamburg.

16 November

The RAF creates a special unarmed Spitfire unit equipped with photo-graphic instruments so that on fine days they can photograph targets in the zones in which bombing attacks are planned, so as to reduce error and consequent waste of materials.

☐ George VI, accompanied by Herbert Morrison, visits the scenes of destruction in Coventry.

18 November

Important talks begin in Berchtesgaden, where Hitler receives the Italian Foreign Minister and the Spanish Foreign Minister. He does not conceal his anger at the failure of the Greek campaign and his anxiety about the obvious disagreement at the heart of the Italian supreme command. He argues, and repeats it in a letter to Mussolini which he hands to Ciano, that if the British acquire air bases in Greece (at Athens, Thessaloniki, Larisa and Arta) they will be able to bomb the oil wells at Ploesti. He therefore considers it necessary for Germany to intervene, though this cannot be done before 15 March in the following year. He calls on the Duce to make a radical change in his policy towards Yugoslavia, which must be attracted into the orbit of the

Axis, perhaps by promising the Yugoslavs the port of Thessaloniki when the Greeks are beaten. Mussolini must not forget that the British air bases in Greece pose a threat to Albania and the whole of southern Italy. Finally, Hitler says it is necessary to close the Mediterranean, to seek an accord with Turkey, to persuade Rumania to accept a stronger German garrison and Hungary to allow the passage of German forces, to defeat the British in North Africa, and to induce Spain to enter the war by attacking Gibraltar.

☐ Heavy fighting continues on the Greek front, especially near Koritsa.

19 November

The Spanish Foreign Minister, Serrano Suñer, on instructions from Franco and the Spanish supreme command, repeats to Hitler and Ribbentrop that Spain needs 400,000 tons of grain and two months of preparation before it can attack Gibraltar, even though Hitler has promised help by German units (Operation *Felix*). In fact, Franco has already decided to keep his country out of the conflict.

□ Heavy night raids on Birmingham.

□ RAF bombs Skoda works at Pilsen (Czechoslovakia).

20 November

The Hungarian Prime Minister and Foreign Minister (Count Teleki and Count Csaky) sign a Protocol in Vienna binding Hungary to the German-Japanese–Italian Tripartite Pact.

21 November

Greek–Albanian Front Major Greek successes reported on a broad front. Greeks enter Koritsa, capturing 2,000 men, 135 guns, and 600 machine-guns.

□ Heavy RAF attacks on Libyan bases of Benghazi, Berka, and Benina continue.

22 November

Italian communiqué admits the fall of Koritsa.

23 November

Rumania also adheres to the Tripartite Pact.

12 November 1940: the Italian naval base at Taranto after the torpedo attack by British aircraft the previous day. The three crippled battleships can be clearly seen. Only two aircraft failed to return to the carrier *Illustrious*.

☐ Heavy night bombing attack on Southampton.

24 November
Bristol suffers heavy night raid.
☐ Italian air raids on the naval base at Alexandria.
☐ Slovakia signs the Tripartite Pact.

26 November
RAF carries out heavy night raid on Cologne.

Right: the *Littorio* (43,835 tons), also damaged at Taranto, but less severely. She was in service again four months later. The attack on Taranto was a severe blow to Italian naval strength.

Below: Italian troops retreat through the mud in the face of the fierce Greek counter-offensive.

27 November
Further heavy raids on Cologne.
☐ One Italian cruiser and two destroyers damaged in action off Sardinia.

28 November
Further Greek successes reported.
☐ Liverpool attacked by large numbers of German bombers.

29 November–2 December
Greek–Albanian Front Greeks make more advances after heavy fighting.
☐ UK civilian casualties in November: 4,588 killed, 6,202 injured.

3 December
Greek–Albanion Front Greeks cross the river Kalamas and also advance along the coast, taking the village of Sarandë.

4 December
Greek-Albanian Front Greeks enter Përmet, taking over 500 prisoners.

5 December
Greek–Albanian Front The Italians, faced with an increasingly serious situation, have brought in substantial reinforcements through the port of Valona and the airfield at Tiranë including the Tridentina Alpine division, but a good number of them fall out as they march up to the line. They are extremely short of equipment; there are little or no reserves of ammunition and of woollen clothing (and in the very cold weather there are many cases of frostbite). None the less the Italian command succeeds in establishing a defensive line from Himarë (Klimara) along the coast to north of Sarandë on Lake Okhrida – largely because the Greeks, hardly motorized at all and entirely without armour, cannot exploit their successes. The pivot of the Italian line lies at the positions between Klisura (Këlcyrë) and Tepe-

Opposite: Coventry cathedral after the massive German raid on the night of 14 November.
Above: the London Blitz – among the ruins of Holland House, Kensington, visitors seem able to ignore the damage.

Colonel Charles de Gaulle, future leader of the Free French.

lenë (Tepeleni) in the Vijosë (Voiussa) valley. Klisura is lost and re-taken. Chaos reigns among the Italians. There is very heavy fighting in the Vijosë valley and at Hill 731, Monastir.

6 December
Greek–Albanian Front Greek forces occupy Sarandë.

□ Marshal Badoglio resigns as Commander-in-Chief of the Italian armed forces: General Ugo Cavalero appointed.

7 December
RAF carry out night raid on Düsseldorf.

8 December
Resignation of Admiral Cavagnari, Italian Chief of Naval Staff; replaced by Admiral Campioni.

9 December
North Africa Opening of first Western Desert offensive. In Egypt the British break through the Italian lines at Sidi Barrani. General Graziani's seven divisions cannot manage to resist the thrust of two British divisions, the 4th Indian and 7th Armoured, which the British Commander-in-Chief in the Middle East, General Sir Archibald Wavell, has sent into the attack. The Italian

troops are completely taken by surprise; despite their overwhelming numerical superiority, the Italians have done nothing since taking Sidi Barrani on 16 September but dig in instead of continuing their advance. Now the British action, as efficient as it is unexpected, puts the entire Italian force in danger; within two hours the British troops entirely surround the entrenched camp of Nibeiwa, killing among others, General Maletti, who is caught by the attackers in his pyjamas. Tummar, Maktila and Sidi Barrani fall into British hands in four days' fighting; four Italian divisions are wiped out and some 38,000 prisoners are taken, including four generals. British casualties are 624 dead, wounded and missing; and they have captured 237 guns, 73 medium and light tanks and at least 1,000 trucks.

10 December
North Africa The remnants of the Italian troops retire westwards.

11 December
North Africa Sollum is heavily shelled by ships of the Royal Navy. Italian troops resist Wavell's forces bravely at Fort Capuzzo and Sidi Omar.

12 December
North Africa The only Italian troops left on Egyptian soil, apart of course from the prisoners, are those holding

up the British advance on Sollum and the forces in the neighbourhood of Sidi Omar.

Churchill sends a telegram to General Wavell in the evening with his heartiest congratulations on his 'splendid victory' over the numerically superior Italians.

□ Heavy German night bombing raid on Sheffield.

13 December
Hitler issues his Directive 'Marita' providing for the despatch of 24 divisions to the Balkans. German troops begin moving through Hungary to Rumania.

□ Pierre Laval, Vice-President of the Vichy government, and champion of a more powerful collaboration with the Germans, is arrested on Pétain's orders two days before Napoleon's son's ashes are returned to France by the Germans.

17 December
North Africa Sidi Omar and Sollum fall into British hands. The situation has now become critical for the Italians.

□ Laval freed as a result of intervention by the German ambassador in Paris, Otto Abetz.

18 December
Hitler signs Directive No. 20, which outlines the plans for the invasion of Russia.

THE BETATRON

The American physicist D.W. Kerst, working in the laboratories of Illinois University, produced the betatron, a machine which for the first time accelerated electrons through a variable magnetic field generated by an electromagnet. The betatron is one of the so-called circular accelerators, in which the particles follow circular orbits and emerge at very high speeds. Used for research purposes in the early war years, the betatron, capable of producing highly penetrative X-rays, was subsequently used after the war both for therapeutic and industrial purposes.

The Compagnons de France sought to instil the ideas of the national revolution in the young.

THE VICHY GOVERNMENT

The French government establishes its seat at Vichy on 10th July, the chamber of deputies and the Senate voting by 468 to 80, with 20 abstentions, to give full powers to Marshal Pétain. The Vichy régime is thus initiated, marking the end of the Third Republic.

From 11th July the first three constitutional acts promulgated by the regime define the structure of what will come to be known as the 'national revolution'. Philippe Pétain proclaims himself Chief of the French State, with powers that are virtually dictatorial.

On 12th July the marshal appoints as his vice-premier Pierre Laval (later to become Admiral Darlan). In reaction to a democratic ideology responsible for a general laxity in morals, the new regime proposes to restore 'traditional moral values', defining itself as an authoritarian state founded on natural hierarchies and communities, and replacing the concept of 'liberty, equality, fraternity' with that of 'work, family, country'. Trades unions, suspected of inspiring an artificial class war, are replaced by a corporate trade organization, an institution revived from the Ancien Régime.

The land was encouraged. Freemasonry was broken up, to safeguard France against cosmopolitan contagion, and to keep it 'for the French'. Most importantly, a stringent statute on Jews instituted by the Vichy government paved the way for what was effectively state antisemitism. The Vichy regime appears as an autonomous French creation, arising from traditional intellectual and political trends. Regarding a German victory as ineluctable, it concentrates its efforts on domestic matters while offering state collaboration to the Reich in the hope that a 'renewed' France will find a place in the new European structure that will evolve at the end of the war.

The prolonged conflict, however, is soon to erode the somewhat masochistic paternalism of the summer of 1940, giving rise to contradictions within the Vichy régime.

The first phase of the régime ends in February 1941 when, under pressure from the Germans, Flandin has to give way to Darlan. The third opens in April 1942, when Pétain has to appoint Laval head of government. The final phase begins in November 1942. The 'free zone' is occupied, the armistice army disarmed, the fleet scuttled, and the Empire is in the hands of the Allies. Pétain confers on Laval the power to make laws and issue decrees. The myth of Pétain crumbles, together with the final illusions of the national revolution.

19 December

134 British Wellington bombers carry out a heavy raid on Mannheim.

20 December

British naval sweep in the Adriatic announced.

□ Further heavy night raid on Liverpool.

23 December

Churchill broadcasts to the Italians: 'One man and one man only was resolved to plunge Italy, after all these years of strain and effort, into the whirlpool of war.'

□ Italian prisoners in the Western Desert total 35,949.

24 December

President Roosevelt makes a speech in which he sharply attacks the Axis powers.

□ Rudolph Hess, deputy Nazi leader, broadcasts a Christmas message: 'Divine justice has turned against England. We are carrying on the fight in the belief in the superior value of our people. For the Almighty has also created the German people; and service for this people is thus also service in the belief in the Almighty who created it.'

25 December

George VI broadcasts Christmas Day message: 'The future will be hard, but our feet are planted on the path of victory, and with the help of God we shall make our way to justice and to peace.'

26 December

The Luftwaffe resumes the bombing of London after allowing the British capital a truce on Christmas Day.

27 December

Nauru, an Australian Protectorate in the Pacific, is shelled by a disguised German ship carrying the Japanese flag.

29 December

President Roosevelt broadcasts: 'We must be the arsenal of the democracies.'

□ Heavy incendiary raid on London. Many famous buildings, including the Guildhall, eight Wren churches and Trinity House, destroyed or severely damaged.

31 December

Hitler issues a New Year proclamation to the Nazi Party: '1941 will see the German army, navy and air force enormously strengthened and better equipped. Under their blows the last boastings of the warmongers will collapse, thus achieving the final conditions for a true understanding among the peoples.'

□ UK civilian casualties in December: 3,793 killed, 5,244 injured.

F. SCOTT FITZGERALD

Francis Scott Fitzgerald, the writer who so brilliantly captured the magical atmosphere of the Roaring Twenties, died of a heart attack on 21 December. Born in St Paul, Minnesota, in 1896, Fitzgerald displayed in his first novel *This Side of Paradise* (1920) his ability to reproduce perfectly the language and lifestyle of a frivolous, romantic 'lost generation'.

In the course of a disorderly, brilliant, desperate life, highlighted by a stormy relationship with his wife Zelda, Fitzgerald found the necessary inspiration to create two world-acclaimed masterpieces: *The Great Gatsby* (1925), a true epitome of the Jazz Age, written during his time in Europe, and *Tender Is the Night*, written in 1932.

In his last years Fitzgerald attempted to make a living, unsuccessfully, by writing film scripts. The most notable testimony to his flirtation with Hollywood is the unfinished novel *The Last Tycoon*, published posthumously in 1941.

Italian prisoners of war taken during General Wavell's first major offensive in North Africa. Two British divisions break through the Italian lines at Sidi Barrani and overwhelm no less than seven Italian divisions, taking 38,000 prisoners.

A side-car of the Afrikakorps in North Africa.

1941

1941

JANUARY	**22 January** *North Africa*: The Italian garrison at Tobruk surrenders.
FEBRUARY	
MARCH	**8 March** The US Senate passes the Lend-Lease Bill by 60 votes to 31. **28 March** Naval battle off Cape Matapan.
APRIL	**6 April** Germany invades Yugoslavia and declares war on Greece. **27 April** *Greece*: German tanks enter Athens.
MAY	**10 May** *Great Britain*: Rudolf Hess, Hitler's deputy, drops by parachute from his Messerschmitt 110 on the village of Eaglesham in Scotland. **27 May** *Atlantic*: The British Navy sinks the *Bismarck*.
JUNE	**22 June** Operation Barbarossa against the Soviet Union is initiated.
JULY	
AUGUST	**9 August** Winston Churchill meets President Roosevelt in Newfoundland.
SEPTEMBER	**23 September** *Great Britain* In London, General de Gaulle sets up the *Comité National Français*.
NOVEMBER	**7 November** The Lend-Lease Act is extended to the USSR.
DECEMBER	**7 December** Hawaii, Pearl Harbour. At 7.55 a.m. local time, with no declaration of war, Japanese aircraft mount a surprise air attack on the American air and naval base. **8 December** The United States and Great Britain officially declare war on Japan. **11 December** Mussolini and Hitler declare war on the United States.

German infantry advancing towards the Russian front.

1 January

North Africa British naval and air bombardment of Bardia, the Italian strongpoint on the Egyptian frontier.

☐ Ribbentrop meets the Bulgarian minister Filov in Vienna and makes arrangements with him for German troops to cross into Bulgarian territory.

2 January

North Africa Further attacks on Bardia

3 January

North Africa The British, reinforced by the 6th Australian Division (replacing the 4th Indian Division sent to the Sudan), resume the offensive in Cyrenaica. Bardia defences pierced by the Australians; 8,000 Italian prisoners taken on a nine-mile front.

General Wavell (Commander-in-Chief of the British forces in the Middle East) receives a request from London to begin large-scale preparations for the despatch of a British expeditionary force from Egypt to Greece. This possibly determines Wavell not to press his advantage over the Italians by pursuing them farther for the time being.

4 January

Greek–Albanian Front The Greeks launch an attack towards Valona from Berat to Klisura. Although severely stretched by the November offensive and having the equivalent of only 13 divisions against 16 Italian divisions, the Greeks are trying to achieve a decisive victory over the enemy, who are receiving continual reinforcements.

5 January

North Africa Bardia falls to the British, despite staunch resistance from General Bergonzoli's troops. The British take about 40,000 prisoners, with 462 guns, 129 light tanks and more than 700 trucks. British casualties are 456 killed and wounded. General Bergonzoli manages to withdraw from Bardia and reach Tobruk with a few thousand men.

6 January

In a long memorandum to the Chief of Staffs Committee, Churchill gives priority to aid to Greece at the risk of sacrificing any further advance in North Africa. The Prime Minister argues that help for the Greeks in their attack on Valona (in Albania), is essential in order to avoid any lessening of Greek resistance or even capitulation. A few days later, on receiving reports of German troop concentrations in preparation for large-scale action in the Balkans, Churchill tells Wavell that, once Tobruk is captured, all operations in Libya must be subordinated to the urgent needs of the Greek front.

☐ President Roosevelt's Message for Congress: weapons to be supplied to the democracies.

7 January

North Africa British and Imperial forces continue to advance from Bardia to Tobruk. The first contingents make contact with the defences in the eastern sector of Tobruk. The fall of Bardia has reduced the number of troops available to the Italian Commander-in-Chief, General Graziani, by more than half.

For the defence of Tobruk he can call on no more than 25,000 men, 220 guns and some 70-odd medium and light tanks. West of Tobruk the Sabratha division is at Derna, the 17th Regiment at Benghazi and an armoured group at Mechili.

8 January

Greek–Albanian Front The Greeks press vigorously against Klisura, which the Italian have to evacuate next day. But the Greeks do not succeed in breaking through towards Berat, and their offensive against Valona breaks down. In the fighting for Klisura the Italians suffer serious losses to their *Lupi di Toscana, Julia, Pinerolo* and *Pusteria* divisions. The engagements in this sector last until the end of the month.

☐ In the course of a British bombardment of Naples serious damage is done to the battleship *Giulio Cesare* (29,000 tons), and she has to be moved to La Spezia for lengthy repairs; the *Vittorio Veneto*, one of the latest battleships, is also hit, but not seriously.

☐ President Roosevelt orders that crews of all American warships shall

Italian trucks wrecked by an RAF attack near Bardia.

HENRY BERGSON

The French philosopher Henri Bergson died on 4 January in German-occupied Paris. Although he showed increasing sympathy in his last years towards Catholicism, Bergson, who was Jewish by birth, refused conversion in order to demonstrate his solidarity with his fellow religionists being persecuted by the Nazis.

Bergson was born in Paris in 1859. Winner of the Nobel Prize for Literature in 1928, he was to become the most important French philosopher in the first half of the twentieth century. His work, based on a form of mystical, romantic anti-intellectualism, exerted a deep influence both on the modernists and the futurists.

be gradually brought up to full wartime establishment.

10 January

Mediterranean Just after dawn, off the island of Pantelleria, two Italian torpedo boats attack a British naval squadron escorting a convoy bound for Malta. The Italian torpedo boat *Vega* is sunk. Forty German aircraft, Ju-87s and Ju-88s, then go into action, and hit the aircraft carrier *Illustrious*, which is seriously damaged, and the cruiser *Southampton*, which is sunk by the British themselves because it is impossible to recover her. The battleship *Warspite*

manages to escape the bombs, but two merchant ships in the convoy and other smaller escort vessels are hit. This is the first action by German aircraft in the Mediterranean (the bombers are part of the 10th *Fliegerkorps* stationed in Sicily).

Italian and German aircraft carry out heavy raids on Malta. Part of the 10th *Fliegerkorps* has recently been attached to the Italian air squadrons operating over the Mediterranean; it has come from bases in northern Europe and played a very important part in operations against shipping in the Norwegian campaign. The group stationed on Sicilian airfields comprises, as at 1 January 1941, 96 bombers and 25 fighters, but its full strength is a formidable 120 bombers, 150 dive-bombers, 40 fighters and 20 reconnaissance aircraft.

Greek–Albanian Front Greek troops enter Klisura.

☐ Lend-Lease Bill introduced into the American Congress.

☐ Soviet–German Pact signed in Berlin, delimiting the new frontiers between the two countries. A trade agreement is signed in Moscow.

12 January

British aircraft from Malta attack the airfield at Catania (Sicily).

13 January

Hitler 'invites' King Boris of Bulgaria to Germany. The Führer demands that Bulgaria: (1) signs the Tripartite Pact; (2) opens her borders to German troops to attack Greece; (3) takes an active part in the Axis' military operations. King Boris temporizes.

☐ Plymouth suffers three-hour bombing attack.

10 January: the attack on a British convoy bound for Malta seen from the bridge of the aircraft carrier *Illustrious*.

14–15 January

General Wavell and Air Marshal Longmore are in Athens for a review of the situation with the Greek premier Metaxas and the Commander-in-Chief of the Greek army, General Papagos. On the Albanian front the Greeks have 12 divisions and three brigades of infantry; four divisions are guarding the Bulgarian frontier, but one is to be transferred from Macedonia to Albania, where the Italians receive new reinforcements every day. It is reported that the Germans have at least 12 divisions in Rumania and that in Bulgaria German officers in civilian clothes are directing road and airport development. The Greeks, therefore, ask the British for at least nine divisions and more reliable air support. Wavell tells the Greeks that all he can give them is one regiment of artillery, one anti-tank and one anti-aircraft regiment and about 60 tanks. Later on, in the course of two or three months, Britain will be able to provide about three divisions and a stronger air contingent.

15 January

Mediterranean During the night German reconnaissance aircraft overfly Valletta (Malta) to pinpoint the aircraft carrier *Illustrious*, which put in there to repair the damage inflicted during the air attack of 10 January.

16 January

Malta About 80 Stukas, taking off from bases in Sicily, attack Valletta in an attempt to sink the aircraft carrier *Illustrious* and put the island's arsenal out of action. The carrier is hit by one bomb, but the bombers do serious damage to the port installations, several churches and a number of public and private buildings. The raid claims about 100 victims among the civil population, many of them women and children. This is the first of a long series of raids by the Germans which the Maltese refer to as the '*Illustrious* Blitz'. The operation costs the Germans ten aircraft.

An Italian S-79 bomber over the port of Valletta. Malta holds out courageously despite the prolonged and savage Axis air attacks.

17 January

Mediterranean Intensive activity by German aircraft over Malta.

18 January

Another Luftwaffe raid on Malta. This time the targets are the airfields at Luqa and Hal Far; six aircraft are destroyed on the ground and many others damaged.

☐ The Greeks accept such help as is offered by the British, but are unwilling to accept it at once for fear of giving Hitler an excuse for speeding up his intervention.

☐ Pétain receives Laval: 'misunderstandings smoothed out'.

19 January

Italian East Africa The Commander-in-Chief of British forces in the Sudan, Lieutenant-General Sir William Platt, opens an offensive against the Italian forces in Eritrea.

ROBERT BADEN-POWELL

A boy scout in uniform.

On 8 January Robert Baden-Powell, lieutenant general in the British army and founder of the Boy Scouts' movement, died in Nyeri, Kenya.

Baden-Powell was born in London in 1857, entered the army and served in India, Afghanistan and South Africa, taking part in the campaign against the Zulus and the Boer War.

When he returned to England he decided to use his considerable experience, including the training of army recruits, in developing a programme of civic and physical training for boys of all classes and creeds.

In 1907 he assembled a group of boys from different background and set up a trial camp in the woods at Brownsea Island, Dorset. His aim was to instil in the boys a strong sense of community service, a spirit of loyalty and an enthusiasm for physical fitness.

The Boy Scouts' movement successfully extended its activities worldwide and in 1910 Baden-Powell, with his sister Agnes, also founded the Girl Guides' movement (sister organization to the Girl Scouts).

He has under his command two divisions, the 4th and 5th Indian Divisions under Generals Beresford-Peirse and Heath, together with the Sudan Defence Force. The Italian troops in Eritrea, mostly concentrated in the area of Kassala and at the border strongpoints, number about 17,000 men, with light tanks and artillery, under the command of General Trusci.

Mediterranean Further very heavy attacks by the Germans on Malta; the Stukas succeed in hitting the aircraft carrier *Illustrious* again, but not seriously.

☐ Hitler and Mussolini meet at Berchtesgaden to discuss the Italians' critical situation. Mussolini asks that German reinforcements should not be sent to Albania but does not refuse some German assistance in North Africa.

20 January

North Africa Hitler has already made his own decision to send to Libya, in support of the Italian army there, the German 15th Armoured Division under the command of General Erwin Rommel, the future 'Desert Fox'.

Mediterranean The British chiefs of staff say that the presence of the Luftwaffe in Sicily makes it impossible to carry out the plan to seize the island of Pantelleria (between Sicily and the north-east coast of Tunisia) by a commando operation. Admiral Cunningham has in any case already come out against the plan (though it has Churchill's enthusiastic support); he could not accept any addition to the already immense difficulties involved in supplying the Mediterranean squadron. Malta is thus destined to remain for a long time the only British strongpoint in the central Mediterranean.

☐ In Rumania the militia of the ultra-nationalist, anti-Semitic 'Iron Guard' movement rises against the government.

21 January

Italian East Africa The British take Kassala, near the border between the Sudan and Eritrea. The Italians fall back to Agordat and on to the tiny fortress of Keren.

North Africa Australian infantry launch their attack on Tobruk. The town has already been cut off by the British 7th Armoured Division.

☐ Two urgent messages from London reach the commanders of the British land and naval forces in the Mediterranean; Admiral Cunningham is ordered to provide Malta with the air cover necessary for its defence; General Wavell is told that the capture of Benghazi is still given top priority and that he should make that his next objective. Major-General O'Connor has already ordered the Australian 4th Brigade to press on to Mechili and the 7th Armoured Brigade to continue its advance on Derna; these are two important centres in Cyrenaica.

☐ Churchill's message to Malta: 'The eyes of all Britain, and indeed of the whole Empire, are watching Malta in her struggle day by day, and we are sure that success as well as glory will reward your efforts.'

□ In Rumania General Antonescu, although it was the Fascist 'greenshirts' who put him in power, calls in the army to put down the 'Iron Guard' insurrection, and many members of the movement are arrested.

□ In Tokyo the Japanese Foreign Minister, Matsuoka, states: 'The Netherlands East Indies and French Indo-China, if only for geographical reasons, should be in intimate and inseparable friendship with our country.'

22 January

North Africa The Italian garrison at Tobruk surrenders after blowing up the port installations and the cruiser *San Giorgio*. The British take about 30,000 prisoners and capture more than 200 guns and about 70 tanks. The British themselves use only 16 Matilda tanks in this action. Allied casualties number under 500.

By evening the British 7th Armoured Brigade is about 20 miles from Derna, in Cyrenaica, while patrols from the Australian 4th Brigade are on the tracks leading west and southwest from Mechili.

Italian East Africa The British go over to the attack on the border of Italian Somaliland in the Trans-Juba region, and take Jalib. The Italian troops retire in good order.

□ Wavell is ordered to make arrangements to support the Greeks by every means available to him.

□ The chief of staff of the Bulgarian army, General Boydeff, in the name of King Boris, discusses with representatives of the German high command a plan for collaboration and co-operation between the two countries.

23 January

Mediterranean The aircraft carrier *Illustrious* is able to leave Malta for Alexandria.

24 January

North Africa One of the first tank battles of the North African war takes place near Mechili, in Cyrenaica; the British 7th Armoured Division destroys eight Italian medium tanks and captures one, losing one heavy and six light tanks.

26 January

Greek–Albanian Front The Italians launch a counter-offensive for the recapture of Klisura.

□ Matsuoka reiterates Japanese claims in the Pacific.

27 January

Italian East Africa The 4th Indian Division reaches Agordat in Eritrea.

□ The Italian Foreign Minister, Galeazzo Ciano, arrives on the Greek front to take over command of a bomber group. Other members of the government are also sent to the front. Mussolini seems to want to demonstrate either that, members of the government are not exempt from combat duty, or that Italy can be governed just as well without the ministers.

□ The United States ambassador in Tokyo reports to his government that the Japanese Imperial Staff is preparing plans to attack American air and naval bases in the Pacific. He particularly mentions Pearl Harbor.

Italian soldiers surrendering near Bardia.

29 January
North Africa Italian troops, in a bid to escape encirclement by the British 7th Armoured Division, evacuate Derna and prepare to retire from the whole of Cyrenaica and form a new, more solid defence line at El-Agheila, on the border with Tripolitania.

☐ After a brief illness the Greek Prime Minister, General Metaxas, dies at the age of 70. He is succeeded by Alexandros Korizis.

30 January
North Africa British and Empire forces occupy Derna.

1 February
North Africa The Italians abandon the Benghazi area. The Italian government is forced to ask officially for German reinforcements for the North African campaign.
First thing in the morning General O'Connor, commander of the British troops operating in Libya, sends Brigadier Eric Dorman-Smith to General Wavell's headquarters in Cairo to get his authority to cut the route of the Italian troops retreating into Tripolitania.

Italian East Africa British forces take Agordat.

☐ The United States reorganize their naval forces, re-grouping them in three fleets, Atlantic, Pacific and Asiatic.

2 February
North Africa Dorman-Smith returns from Cairo and reports to General O'Connor that Wavell authorizes the operation against the retreating enemy.

☐ The German War Council reviews Operation *Barbarossa* (invasion of the Soviet Union), based on a report on the Russian army presented by General Halder. The Soviet army is estimated to have 145 infantry and 26 cavalry divisions on the Western Front, with 40 motorized brigades – about 211 formations in all, facing the 190 of Germany and her allies. A substantial numerical superiority, concludes Halder's report, but the technical and strategic factor is firmly in favour of the Germans.

☐ In France the formation of a new pro-Nazi party, 'Rassemblement National Populaire' is announced. The party is under the aegis of Laval.

3 February
North Africa General Graziani orders retreat towards Tripolitania. The German supreme command decides to send the first contingents of the *Afrikakorps* to Libya.

Italian East Africa The battle for Keren begins.

China After a swift landing in the area of Wai Chow, Japanese units occupy Tam-shin, east of Canton.

☐ Admiral François Darlan, the French Minister of Marine and a faithful supporter of Pétain, and Pierre Laval, now Vice-President of the French Council of Ministers, second to Pétain himself, meet the German ambassador Otto Abetz in Paris. They return to Vichy with proposals for ways in which France can be fitted into Hitler's 'new order' in Europe, leading to still closer collaboration with the Germans.

January 1941: a British infantry unit outside the burning city of Tobruk.

4 February

North Africa The first British reinforcements begin to arrive at Mechili from Tobruk; the 4th Armoured Brigade can now push on westwards to cut off the Italian troops retiring from Benghazi.

☐ RAF, after fortnight's lull due to bad weather, make heavy bombing raid on Düsseldorf.

5 February

North Africa In Cyrenaica the British 4th Armoured Brigade and the armoured cars of the 11th Hussars succeed in cutting off the Italian column making for Agedabia from Benghazi.

By dusk General O'Connor's men have penetrated far westwards into southern Cyrenaica. The 4th Armoured Brigade is approaching Beda Fomm, where the Italians are hastily concentrating for what may prove to be their last stand. A 5,000-strong column – Italian gunners and civilians – surrenders south-east of Beda Fomm.

Hitler writes to Mussolini expressing his unhappiness at the way Italian commanders are conducting operations in North Africa; he offers his ally the help of an armoured division on condition that the Italians hold firm in the interim and do not withdraw as far as Tripoli.

☐ Wendell Willkie, Republican candidate in the US Presidential Election, leaves London after a visit. He broadcasts a message to Germany: 'Tell the German people that we German-Americans reject and hate the aggression and lust for power of the present German government.'

6 February

North Africa First Benghazi victory. Australian troops enter the city. More than 80 Italian tanks destroyed. Bergonzoli and six senior generals are among many thousands of prisoners taken.

In Berlin Hitler receives General Erwin Rommel, who is to command the *Afrikakorps* which is being sent to support the Italian army in Libya. Although technically under the command of General Albert Kesselring, commander of the southern operational sector which includes Italy and the Mediterranean, Rommel is to have direct access to Hitler.

7 February

North Africa In Cyrenaica the Italian 10th Army is surrounded at Beda Fomm. Agedabia, one of the last Italian strongpoints in Cyrenaica, also falls into British hands. What now remain of the Italian forces, who have lost about 20,000 men, 200 guns and 120 tanks at Beda Fomm, concentrate on the coast road from Agedabia to El-Agheila, on the border between Cyrenaica and Tripolitania. The whole of Cyrenaica is now in British hands.

☐ Vichy France – Thailand peace conference begins in Tokyo under the auspices of Japanese government.

8 February

North Africa General Rodolfo Graziani, Commander-in-Chief of the Italian armed forces in North Africa and Governor of Libya, writes a letter

JAMES JOYCE

The death occurred in Zurich on 13 January of the brilliant Irish writer James Joyce, whose works, rich in allegory and psychological symbolism, exploring the possibilities of language and meaning in a wholly innovative manner, contributed profoundly to the revitalization of modern literature.

Joyce was born in Dublin on 2 February 1882. His first work was a book of verse, *Chamber Music* (1907), followed by *Dubliners* (1914), a collection of short stories featuring typical Irish characters, and the autobiographical novel *A Portrait of the Artist as a Young Man* (1916).

Meanwhile he had left Ireland for good, working at the Berlitz School, Pola, and thereafter living in Trieste, Rome, Paris and Zurich. In 1918 he brought out his play *Exiles* and in 1922 his masterpiece *Ulysses*. Published in Paris, the book created an immediate sensation among avant-garde European and American critics who, impressed by its daring language, brilliant technique and original structure, declared it a masterpiece destined to be of lasting influence.

Many thousands of prisoners were taken during the Italian retreat from Cyrenaica.

6th February 1941: British tanks enter Benghazi. Italian armoured units are surrounded on the Benghazi–Beja road: in fierce efforts to break out, they lose 80 tanks.

to Mussolini: 'Duce, these latest events have severely depressed my nerves and my strength, so that I cannot continue to exercise command in full possession of my faculties. I therefore ask you to recall and replace me ...'

☐ The new Greek Prime Minister Korizis reopens talks with the British about aid in the event of German intervention against his country. Churchill sends him an assurance that he has ordered the formation of the nucleus of an army for speedy intervention in Greece.

☐ Germany continues to put pressure on Bulgaria and representations of the respective general staffs sign a military pact.

☐ US House of Representatives passes Lend-Lease Bill by 260 votes to 165.

9 February

North Africa British troops reach El Agheila on the border between Cyrenaica and Tripolitania.

☐ Pisa and Leghorn bombed by aircraft from the aircraft carrier *Ark Royal*. Genoa shelled by the battleships *Renown* and *Malaya* and the cruiser *Sheffield*. This surprise attack highlights the inefficiency of Italian defences; an Italian naval squadron and air reconnaissance fail to spot the British ships.

☐ Churchill in a major broadcast warns Bulgaria not to join the Axis; and tells the Americans: 'Give us the tools and we will finish the job.'

10 February

The German and Spanish governments sign a secret agreement by which Spain undertakes to resist any attack by the forces of the Western Allies.

☐ Churchill sends a telegram to Wavell, Commander-in-Chief of the British forces in the Middle East: 'The destruction of Greece', warns the British premier, 'would overshadow the victories won by British forces in Libya and our indifference to the fate of our allies might induce Turkey to change its attitude.'

Above and opposite above: Italian prisoners and lorries captured by French troops led by Colonel Leclerc and General de Larminat at Faya, after the attack on Koufra.

Arms and military equipment seized at the El Taj fort at Koufra by the Free French troops led by Colonel Leclerc (March 1941).

Colonel Leclerc at General Larminat at Faya (Chad), after the attack on Koufra.

11 February
General Rommel, Commander of the *Afrikakorps*, arrives in Rome.

12 February
General Rommel arrives in Tripoli, Libya.
North Africa General Italo Gariboldi is appointed to succeed Marshal Rodolfo Graziani in command of Italian forces in North Africa.
Churchill sends a telegram to Wavell congratulating him on the speedy capture of Benghazi, but ordering him to hold up the advance and to prepare to send all forces not absolutely indispensable to Greece. Only one squadron of fighters remains available to the British in Libya. Wavell orders O'Connor to return to Cairo, and only the lightest defences are left to cover the territory captured from the Italians.
Italian East Africa In Eritrea, Italian Alpine troops recapture the Forked Rock positions in the area of Keren, forcing the British (4th and 5th Indian Divisions) to withdraw eastwards.
☐ The British Foreign Minister, Anthony Eden, and the Chief of the Imperial General Staff, Sir John Dill, leave for Cairo. From there, together with Wavell, they visit Athens, Ankara and Belgrade for a series of talks aimed at forming a coalition against the Axis, reaching from the Aegean to the Danube. However, the Yugoslav government refuses to receive the British delegates; the Turks receive them but say they cannot go along with their proposals.
☐ Mussolini meets the Spanish head of state, General Francisco Franco, at Bordighera. The final communiqué speaks of 'identity of viewpoints' between the two rulers, but the summit meeting really achieves nothing at all.

13 February
Marshal Pétain and General Franco meet at Montpellier.
☐ Admiral Arturo Riccardi, Chief of Staff of the Italian navy, and Admiral Erich Raeder, Commander-in-Chief of the German navy, meet at Merano with their respective staffs

to arrange for closer naval collaboration.

14 February
Greek–Albanian Front The Greeks seize Hill 1178 in the Scindeli area after fierce fighting.
North Africa The first contingents of the *Afrikakorps* land at Tripoli, in Libya – a battalion of light infantry and an anti-tank battalion; these are the advance guard of the German expeditionary force, which will comprise the 15th Armoured Division and 5th Light Motorized Division.
Italian East Africa South Africa and African troops occupy Kismayu in Italian Somaliland.
☐ Hitler receives the Yugoslav Prime Minister, Dragiša Cvetković,

at Berchtesgaden and presses him strongly to get Yugoslavia to sign the Tripartite Pact.

15 February
North Africa Apart from the oases of Kufra and Jarabub, the whole of Cyrenaica is in British hands. In the battle just ended the Italians have lost 150,000 men (130,000 of them prisoners), 850 guns, 400 tanks and thousands of trucks and other motor vehicles. The British have lost 500 dead, about 1,400 wounded and 55 missing; they have advanced 500 miles employing no more than two divisions, about 31,000 men.
☐ Britain breaks off diplomatic relations with Rumania, which has

become a satellite of the Axis powers.

17 February
Under German pressure Turkey and Bulgaria sign a pact of friendship by which Turkey undertakes not to regard the passage of German troops through Bulgaria as an act of war.

19 February
Consultations at Cairo between the British Foreign Minister, Anthony Eden, the Chief of the Imperial General Staff, Sir John Dill, and General Wavell and Admiral Cunningham on the plans for sending help to Greece.
Far East Australian troops land at Singapore.

'KING BISCUIT TIME'

In 1941 Radio KFFA was founded in Helena, Arkansas. Despite the fact that its owners were white, it broadcast mainly popular black music and became the first 'blues radio' station in the United States.

Max More Interstate Grocery Company, the foodstuffs firm which manufactured 'King Biscuit' flour, bought radio time to advertise its product and put two blues singers, Rice Miller (Sonny Boy Williamson) and Robert J. Lockwood, in charge of the programme. 'King Biscuit Time', which went on the air five days a week, proved an immediate success with the public, helping to swell sales of the flour and setting a real fashion. Other foodstuffs companies and radio stations soon followed suit and launched similar shows.

Mussolini and Franco during the meeting between the two heads of state at Bordighera on 12–13 February.

22 February
A British delegation, which includes Anthony Eden, Sir John Dill, Chief of the Imperial General Staff, General Wavell, and a representative of Admiral Cunningham, commanding the British Mediterranean fleet, arrives in Athens to confer with the Greek King and his Prime Minister. They agree to the despatch of British troops as soon as possible.

23 February
Italian East Africa Free French forces land in Eritrea.
☐ The Greek Premier Korizis formally accepts the assistance offered by Britain to his country: a force of 100,000 men with 240 field guns, 32 medium guns, 192 anti-aircraft guns and 142 tanks.

24 February
Italian East Africa In Italian Somaliland the British succeed in crossing to the left bank of the lower Juba river; the Italians retire towards Mogadishu.

25 February
Italian East Africa Capture of Mogadishu by East and West African troops.
Aegean Admiralty and War Office announce capture of the island of Castelrosso (now Kastellorizon) in the Dodecanese.
☐ A pro-British plot for a *coup d'etat* in Bulgaria is thwarted. Increasing moves in Bulgaria towards full alignment with Germany.

26 February
Eden and General Dill arrive in Ankara for talks with Turkish government.
☐ General Franco sends message to Hitler: 'Entirely and decidedly at your disposal'.

27 February
North Africa First British encounter (Libya) with Germans.

South African troops inspecting Italian guns captured at Galla Sidamo in Ethiopia.

The first tanks of the *Afrikakorps* being unloaded in Tripoli harbour.

28 February

Italian East Africa British aircraft bomb the town of Asmara in Eritrea.

☐ UK civilian casualties in February: 789 killed, 1,068 injured.

Far East It is announced that eastern approaches to Singapore harbour are to be mined and closed to shipping from 3 March.

1 March

North Africa Free French troops commanded by General Jacques-Philippe Leclerc, force surrender of Italian troops defending Kufra.

☐ Bulgaria signs the Tripartite Pact.

Great concern in Yugoslavia, now virtually encircled by Axis powers.

2 March

Greek–Albanian Front Mussolini arrives in Albania to inspect the troops fighting there.

Greece In preparation for an attack on Greece, troops of the German 12th Army begin to cross the Danube into Bulgaria. Under the command of General von List, the 12th Army is made up of five army corps (IV, XI, XIV, XVIII and XXX); the 1st armoured group, consisting of three divisions (5th, 9th and 11th); under von Kleist; the 2nd armoured division, attached to XI Corps; and the 8th Airborne Corps commanded by General Wolfram von Richthofen.

☐ Germans admit their occupation of Bulgaria.

☐ Rumania passes a series of anti-Semitic measures on the lines of those in force in Germany.

☐ The British mission returns from Ankara to Athens. The talks in Turkey have not achieved an anti-Axis coalition.

3 March

Russia criticizes German occupation of Bulgaria.

4 March

Greece The first convoy of British cargo ships and warships leave Alexandria with troops and supplies for Greece. Four cruisers and four destroyers protect the convoy.

General Sir Henry Maitland Wilson, appointed on 28 February to command the British troops in Greece, arrives in Athens.

☐ Hitler receives Prince Paul, regent of Yugoslavia, at Berchtesgaden, in secret and asks him to join the Tripartite Pact powers and allow German troops to pass through Yugoslav territory; in exchange Yugoslavia will in due course be given the port of Thessaloniki and part of Greek Macedonia.

☐ Bulgaria breaks off diplomatic relations with Poland, Belgium and the Netherlands.

5 March

Britain severs diplomatic relations with Bulgaria.

6 March

German military authorities in Holland condemn to death 18 members of the underground resistance movement – the first victims of Dutch resistance to the German invaders.

☐ The Admiralty announces that German official communiqués claim to have destroyed 19 more battleships, 6 more aircraft carriers, 40 more cruisers, and 13 more submarines than the Royal Navy had at the outbreak of war.

7 March

Greece The first contingents of the British expeditionary force to Greece land at the port of Piraeus and at Volos. The land force consists of, not the 100,000 troops promised, but of four divisions (57,000 men), two of them armoured.

Atlantic The U-47 of Commander Günther Prien, the submarine that eluded the defences of Scapa Flow, is sunk by the British destroyer *Wolverine*. Its commander – 'the formidable, indomitable Prien', as Churchill described him – and his entire crew perish.

8 March

The US Senate passes the Lend-Lease Bill by 60 votes to 31. Britain and Greece to get military supplies under the Act at once.

☐ In night raids, London suffers heaviest air attack for some weeks.

9 March

Greek–Albanian Front In Mussolini's presence the Italians launch their offensive in Albania (half of which is in Greek hands) between Tomor and the Vijosë (Voiussa) river; they gain some successes in the area of Mali Arza and mount Trebescini, south-east of Berat. But by 14 March the Greeks have succeeded in halting the Italian thrust.

☐ Heavy night bombing raid on Portsmouth.

10 March

Further night raids on Portsmouth in six-hour attack.

11 March

Disorders break out in Yugoslavia, with demonstrations against Germany and Italy.

☐ Land-Lease Bill signed by President Roosevelt, becomes law.

12 March

President Roosevelt sends to Congress a request for a Lend–Lease appropriation of $7,000 million.

Winston Churchill thanks America: 'The government and people of the United States have in fact written a new Magna Carta.'

☐ Heavy night raids on Merseyside.

13 March

Greek–Albanian Front Fierce fighting continues between the attacking Italians and the defending Greeks, involving 32 Italian infantry regiments and 34 Greek regiments. The Italians are making for Klisura. They do not succeed in breaking the Greek line, and the fighting goes on to the end of the month. But the intention of the Italian command is less to gain territory than to wear down the enemy.

☐ Clydeside experiences its first heavy night attack. Further heavy attacks on Merseyside, where the raids of the last two nights have killed about 500 and seriously injured 500 more.

15 March
President Roosevelt promises aid until victory: 'The end of compromise with tyranny'.
☐ Sharp night attack on London.

16 March
East Africa British detachments arriving by sea from Aden land at Berbera, in British Somaliland, drive out the Italians who have occupied it and advance westwards towards the Ethiopian border.
☐ Bristol heavily bombed.
☐ Hitler speaks in Berlin: 'England will fall. Eternal providence does not let those be victorious who are ready to shed the blood of men merely for the attainment of their own ends.'

17 March
East Africa General Cunningham's troops (11th and 12th East African Divisions and South African 1st Division) cross the Ethiopian border from British Somaliland and reach Jijiga, recently evacuated by the Italians.

18 March
Spain annexes the Free Territory of Tangier.

19 March
London has one of its heaviest night raids since the beginning of the war.
☐ Admiral Weichold, representative of the German navy at the Italian supreme command headquarters in Rome, sends a letter to the Chief of Staff of the Italian navy. Admiral Arturo Riccardi, suggesting that the Italians should attack in force in the eastern Mediterranean; he has learnt that in the British naval base at Alexandria only one battleship, the *Valiant*, is war-ready.
☐ The Germans issue what amounts to an ultimatum to Yugoslavia, giving them only five days to decide about the demands made by Hitler to Prince Paul on 4 March.

Above: U-415, one of the new ocean-going submarines which caused such heavy losses to Atlantic convoys bringing vital supplies to Britain. (Inset the U-boat's commander, Captain H. Werner).

SHERWOOD ANDERSON

Sherwood Anderson, one of the major figures of modern American literature, died in Colón, Panama, on 8 March.

Born in 1876 into a poor family in Camden, Ohio, Anderson was continually on the move from town to town, thereby accumulating valuable experience which he later used in novels.

In his major works (*Winesburg, Ohio*, 1919, and *Poor White*, 1920), Anderson wrote with simplicity and deep conviction of farmers and townspeople who were almost always at odds with the social order, tackling themes of sexual frustration and perversion which were virtually unmentionable in what was still a profoundly puritan society.

Above: a section of Italian machine gunners attack under Greek fire in Albania. Their objective is Klisura, but they are unsuccessful.
Left: an 81-mm mortar used by Italian infantry in action in the Klisura sector.

Opposite left: the blitz continues. Every night London is devastated by countless incendiary bombs. Opposite right: an enormous crater made by a German bomb that just missed two hallowed institutions: the Stock Exchange and the Bank of England.

20 March
North Africa Capture of Jarabub by the British.

East Africa In British Somaliland, British contingents advancing from Berbera reach Hargeisa, near the Ethiopian border.

☐ Heavy and indiscriminate bombing raids on Plymouth during the night.

☐ In the course of a meeting of the Crown Council at Belgrade the regent, Prince Paul, seems inclined to agree to Hitler's requests about the Tripartite Pact and the free passage of German troops across Yugoslav territory. Four Ministers resign rather than yield to German terms.

21 March
North Africa The Italian General Gariboldi takes over as the new Governor of Libya and Commander-in-Chief of the Italian forces in North Africa, in place of General Graziani, who asked Mussolini on 8 February to replace him.

☐ Plymouth again attacked, more than 20,000 incendiaries being showered on shopping and residential areas. Mr Menzies, the Australian Prime Minister, is in Plymouth at the time and helps in rescue work.

22 March
Italian East Africa In Ethiopia the town of Harar, west of Jijiga, is declared an 'open city' by the Italians.

23 March
Observed in Britain as a National Day of Prayer at the request of the King.

☐ RAF night raid on Berlin.

24 March
North Africa In a lightning thrust, Rommel's troops reoccupy El Agheila, on the border between Tripolitania and Cyrenaica.

☐ A diplomatic note from the British government warns the Yugoslav government not to align itself with the Axis powers.

☐ USSR assures Turkey of neutrality in event of Turkey being involved in the war.

25 March
Yugoslavia signs the Tripartite Pact: agreement reached in Vienna in presence of Hitler, Ribbentrop and General Oshiona (Japanese Ambassador in Berlin). Protests take place in Belgrade when news announced.

26 March
East Africa British troops occupy Harar.

☐ *Mediterranean* Reconnaissance aircraft of the 10th *Fliegerkorps* based in Sicily warn the Italian naval command that the battleships *Barham* and *Warspite* and the aircraft carrier *Formidable* are back in the naval base at Alexandria.

☐ Demonstrations against the signing of the Tripartite Pact break out all over Yugoslavia. Protests come from trade unions, peasants, the church and the army. Mr C. S. Amery, Secretary for India and Burma, broadcasts to Yugoslavia: 'Will Yugoslavia sell her honour and liberty for a German promise?'

27 March
Italian East Africa In Eritrea, after 12 days of bitter fighting, the Italians withdraw from Keren towards Asmara. Italian resistance seems to be rapidly crumbling. The battle for Keren had lasted eight weeks and cost the British 4,000 dead and wounded, against Italian losses of 3,000.

☐ 2 a.m.: Revolution in Yugoslavia. Bloodless coup carried out by a group of air force officers led by the Chief of Staff, General Dušan Simović. Former government leaders are arrested. The Council of Regency under Prince Paul is dismissed and the prince exiled. The 17-year-old son of the murdered King Alexander takes over as King Peter II. A government of national unity is set up under General Simović, who as one of his first acts signs a non-aggression pact with Moscow.

Hitler issues his Directive No. 25, ordering the liquidation of Yugoslavia, a country which, since the military *coup d'état*, 'must be regarded as an enemy and therefore

completely crushed as soon as possible'. The OKH prepares new plans for Operation *Marita*, making it necessary to defer Operation *Barbarossa* (the invasion of the Soviet Union) from mid-May to the end of June.

☐ Consultations are finalized in Washington between representatives of the British and American General Staffs to plan strategy in the event of America being forced directly into the war.

28 March
Italian East Africa The Italians abandon Diredawa (a town in Ethiopia north-west of Harar) and withdraw towards Addis Ababa.

☐ Field Marshal Sir John Dill, Chief of the Imperial General Staff, flies to Belgrade to learn the intentions of General Dušan Simović's new government. Despite their desperate situation, it seems that the Yugoslav government will send an accredited representative for talks with the Allies about their project for a 'Balkan Alliance', from the Aegean to the Danube.

☐ UK civilian casualties to date: 28,859 killed; 40,166 seriously injured.

29 March
Italian East Africa British forces occupy Diredawa.

30 March
North Africa Beginning of enemy counter-offensive. German and Italian forces advance east from El Agheila.

Mediterranean Late in the afternoon Admiral Cunningham's British forces reach Alexandria harbour, where a religious service is held to celebrate the success at Cape Matapan, a battle in which the British lost only one aircraft.

☐ Hitler approves details of the plan to invade Yugoslavia. The Yugoslav army takes up positions on the frontier.

☐ Four countries of the American continent: the United States, Mexico, Costa Rica and Venezuela, decide to take all German, Italian

VIRGINIA WOOLF

On 28 March, Virginia Woolf, the English novelist and essayist and central figure of the celebrated Bloomsbury Group, under the renewed stress of mental illness, drowned herself.

After several works of traditional structure, Virginia Woolf, much influenced by James Joyce, wrote her masterpieces within the space of a few years: *Jacob's Room* (1922); *Mrs Dalloway* (1925); and *To the Lighthouse* (1927).

Armoured troops and infantry of the German 12th Army, under the command of General von List, crossing into Greece from Bulgaria.

and Danish ships in their harbours into protective custody.

31 March
North Africa Rommel's Italian and German forces attack Mersa Brega, north-east of El Agheila. The British are forced to withdraw, abandoning 50 armoured cars and 30 light tanks.

☐ US receives and rejects German and Italian protest notes against seizures of ships.

☐ A US scientific-military expedition arrives in Greenland to study the possibility of setting up military bases there.

☐ UK civilian casualties in March: 4,259 killed, 5,557 injured. The numbers killed include 598 children under 16.

1 April
Italian East Africa Asmara, capital of Eritrea, is taken by troops of the 4th and 5th Indian Divisions under General Platt, who have been advancing into the area from the Sudan since 19 January.

☐ The director of American naval operations points out that any initiatives taken by the Axis powers generally start on a Saturday or Sun-

day, and urges the Allies to intensify their security measures on those days.

☐ The Japanese Foreign Minister Matsuoka, on an official visit to Rome, has separate meetings with King Victor Emmanuel III and with Mussolini. He has come straight from discussions with Hitler and Ribbentrop in Berlin.

☐ In Yugoslavia the Senate is dissolved and general mobilization proclaimed. Yugoslavia already has 900,000 men deployed on its borders, and will now have 1,400,000 men under arms.

2 April
North Africa Rommel re-takes Agedabia and Zuetina.

Italian East Africa While British troops push on from Asmara towards Massawa, five Italian destroyers in harbour there put to sea and sail towards Port Sudan. But they are spotted by British reconnaissance aircraft and attacked by a squadron of torpedo-carrying aircraft; four are sunk and the fifth is scuttled by its crew.

☐ The chief of the Imperial General Staff, General Sir John Dill, is in Bel-

27 March 1941: the coup d'état in Yugoslavia. Enthusiastic demonstrators acclaim the new regime. The pro-Axis government is overthrown, Prince Paul is exiled, and Prince Peter, not yet eighteen, succeds to the throne.

grade for 'top secret' talks with the head of the Yugoslav government, General Dušan Simović. Despite his assurances General Simović will not enter into an official alliance with Britain.

☐ Reported that the RAF had dropped 75,000 tea bags over towns in Holland bearing the words: 'Holland will arise. Keep your courage up.'

3 April
North Africa British evacuate Beng-

hazi. The Axis offensive has met with considerable success, mostly owing to the boldness of General Rommel (though it should be noted that the *Afrikakorps* is still under strength) and to the relative inexperience of the British troops and commanders – the

GAUDO AND MATAPAN

27 March

Biggest naval battle of the war so far takes place off Cape Matapan, the southernmost point of Greece. 1.00 p.m.: A British Sunderland flying-boat on reconnaissance spots the Italian 3rd Naval Division, consisting of the cruisers *Trieste*, *Trento* and *Bolgano*, proceeding south-east. These are three of the ships of the Italian naval squadron that is making for the eastern Mediterranean, south of Crete, to attack British shipping supplying Greece from Alexandria. In addition to these three cruisers the squadron includes the battleship *Vittorio Veneto*, which left Naples on the night 26 March carrying the flag of Admiral Iachino, commanding the fleet at sea. The 1st Naval Division, comprising the cruisers *Zara*, *Pola* and *Fiume*, is proceeding from Taranto, and the cruisers *Duca degli Abruzzi* and *Garibaldi*, from Brindisi, with four flotillas of destroyers. The spotting of the ships by the British flying-boat not only puts the British fleet in Alexandria on the alert but also deprives the Italians of the essential element of surprise; nonetheless it is decided that the action shall continue, given the numerical superiority of the Italian naval squadron. At 7.00 p.m. Admiral Sir Andrew Cunningham, Commander-in-Chief of the British Mediterranean fleet, leaves Alexandria harbour with every ship he

has – the battleships *Valiant*, *Barham* and *Warspite*, the aircraft carrier *Formidable* and nine destroyers. The cruisers *Orion*, *Ajax*, *Perth* and *Gloucester*, with four destroyers, *Ilex*, *Hasty*, *Hereward* and *Vendetta*, under the command of Rear Admiral Henry D. Pridham-Whippell, on board the *Orion*, are ready to sail from the port of Piraeus. In order not to arouse the suspicions of the Japanese consul (who, he says, reports all the movements of British ships to the enemy) and to confuse him as to what may be happening, Admiral Cunningham has made a point of being seen at the golf club during the afternoon with a suitcase, giving the impression that he will be spending the night ashore. His ruse is successful. At about 6.40 p.m., when it is already dark, he rejoins *Warspite* and sails for Crete.

28 March

On the morning of the 28th the Italian fleet is off Gaudo, a little island south of Crete, and here the ships of the 3rd Division meet Rear Admiral Pridham-Whippell's flotilla; after an exchange of fire lasting about 40 minutes the British ships withdraw, hoping to lure the Italian ships after them towards the main British force. The sudden British retreat looks suspicious to Admiral Iachino, and he orders his cruisers to break off the pursuit and turn about. But the

British also change course, so that they are no longer pursued, but pursuing. The *Vittorio Veneto* joins in the action. but without effect; and during the afternoon the battleship is subjected to a violent aerial bombardment and is hit by an aerial torpedo. This is just after 3.00 p.m. At about 4.30 p.m. the *Vittorio Veneto* gets under way again, but at a reduced speed of 15 knots, protected by the Italian cruisers and destroyers. The engagement then shifts towards Cape Matapan, at the extreme southern tip of the Peloponnese. At sunset British aircraft attack again. In defence of the battleship the Italian ships put up a smoke-screen and open a violent anti-aircraft barrage. The cruiser *Pola*, hit by a torpedo, takes in great amounts of water and comes to a halt. Admiral Iachino sends the other two cruisers of the 1st Division, *Zara* and *Fiume*, and the IX Destroyer Flotilla (*Alfieri*, *Gioberti*, *Carducci*, *Oriani*) under Admiral Cattaneo to her help. Not expecting an enemy presence, the Italian ships have not taken the least security precautions, such as sending out an advanced screen of destroyers, a normal precaution at night in wartime. The British ships in close pursuit have already observed the cruiser *Pola* on their radar screens. At 10.30 p.m., when the stricken Italian cruiser is only about three-quarters of a mile from the British battleships *Valiant*, *Barham* and *Warspite*, which have their 15-ins guns trained on her, the British ships realize that Admiral Cattaneo's rescue ships are approaching. Within a few minutes the three British battleships bring down a hail of fire on the Italian

Zara (Italy)

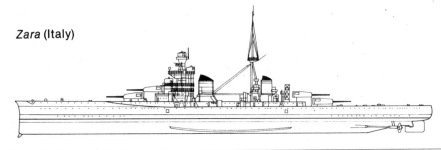

British cruisers and destroyers leave Piraeus and head towards Crete to join up with Cunningham's fleet.

cruisers and destroyers; the *Zara* and *Fiume* are sunk without being able to fire a shot. Many of their crew are killed, including Admiral Cattaneo himself. The cruiser *Pola* and the destroyers *Alfieri* and *Carducci* suffer the same fate, but the night chase fails to catch the *Vittorio Veneto*, which manages to reach the port of Taranto on the morning of the 29th. The British pick up some 900 survivors but have to break off their rescue operation and hurriedly withdraw when German reconnaissance aircraft fly over. However, as a result of signals from the aircraft, the hospital-ship *Gradisca* is sent to the spot, but only arrives on 31 March and succeeds in picking up only 160 survivors. Greek ships later pick up another 110. About 2,400 Italian sailors are lost.

The battle of Matapan was one of the most serious defeats ever suffered by the Italians at sea, clearly demonstrating the technical and tactical superiority of the British, much more experienced in the large-scale use of naval aircraft and enjoying the inestimable advantage of radar.

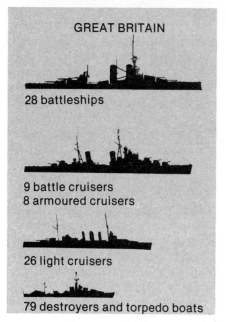

GREAT BRITAIN

28 battleships

9 battle cruisers
8 armoured cruisers

26 light cruisers

79 destroyers and torpedo boats

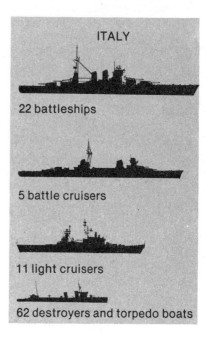

ITALY

22 battleships

5 battle cruisers

11 light cruisers

62 destroyers and torpedo boats

most experienced of them have been sent to Greece.

☐ The Hungarian Premier Count Pál Teleki commits suicide. He feels that the honour of his country has been forfeited by the decision taken by Admiral Horthy to collaborate with Germany in the invasion of Yugoslavia, a country with which Hungary had signed a non-aggression treaty less than a month before. He is succeeded by the notoriously pro-German Foreign Minister, László Bárdossy, who retains the foreign affairs portfolio.

☐ Heavy night air raid on Bristol.

4 April

North Africa From Agedabia, recaptured on 2 April, Rommel unleashes his offensive in Cyrenaica in three directions: to the north towards Benghazi, north-east to Msus and Mechili and eastwards to Ben Gama and Tengeder, thus threatening the British lines of communication. He has available the German 5th Light Motorized Division (which he sends partly in the direction of Msus and Mechili and partly, with the Italian *Ariete* Division, to Ben Gama and Tengeder) and the Italian *Trento* and *Brescia* Divisions, which he directs on Benghazi. To defend Libya the British commander, General Sir Philip Neame, has the 2nd Brigade, the 2nd Armoured Division, the Australian 9th Division and an Indian motorized brigade. General Neame has been ordered to withdraw in the event of a large-scale attack by the enemy, since there are no reinforcements. Rommel therefore meets with little or no resistance, and on the same day, 4 April, his troops enter Benghazi. In danger of being surrounded from the north, the British retire eastwards.

☐ Hitler and Matsuoka (Japanese Foreign Minister) meet in Berlin. They discuss an attack on Singapore and the possibility of war with the United States.

5 April

North Africa The swift advance of the Axis forces continues. In the north they take Barce and push on

towards Derna, and capture Tengeder in the south.

Italian East Africa The Italians evacuate the Ethiopian capital, Addis Ababa. On 3 and 4 April the Viceroy, the Duke of Aosta, dispersed the forces remaining to him in several strongpoints in the mountainous regions of the country, the 'redoubts' of Amba Alagi, Galla Sidamo and Amara.

German tank crew of the *Africakorps* putting on their khaki uniforms. Bottom: Italian troops marching towards Marada in Cyrenaica.

Opposite: a German half-track on patrol west of Marada.

LEND-LEASE ACT

Some weeks after his re-election to the White House, President Roosevelt, under pressure from his own government and military advisers, decided to launch a massive aid programme, hoping nevertheless to keep his nation out of the war.

In January the Lend-Lease Act was presented to Congress. It authorised the President, at his discretion, to send military aid and material of various kinds to countries fighting Nazism, allowing them repayment or reimbursement only when the war ended. After long and bitter debate, it won approval, and in March the Lend-Lease Act gave the American arms industry a tremendous boost in production. The Japanese bombardment of Pearl Harbor, nine months after the law was passed, brought the nation directly into the 'fighting war'.

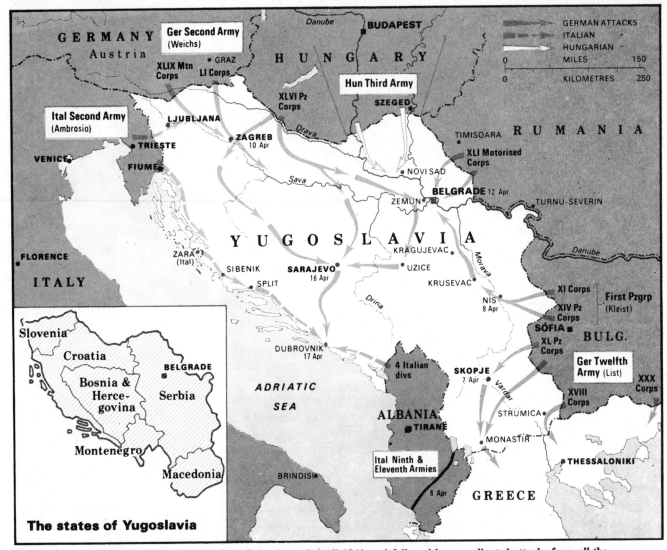

The states of Yugoslavia

The Axis invasion of Yugoslavia, launched from Bulgaria on 6 April 1941, and followed by co-ordinated attacks from all the neighbouring countries.

☐ The USSR offer Yugoslavia a treaty of friendship (but not of mutual assistance), which is immediately accepted. Signing takes place in Moscow. But this will certainly not deter Hitler.

6 April

5.15 a.m.: Germans invade Yugoslavia and Greece. 'Axis forces are on the march against Serbian treachery and the British threat,' announce the Italian and German newspapers. The Germans attack Yugoslavia without the formality of a declaration of war.

At dawn the Luftwaffe, under Goering's personal direction, launches a heavy attack (Operation *Castigo*) on Belgrade, although it has been declared an open city. A second mas-

sive raid is carried out on the following day. It is a pointless slaughter with no object but terrorism. All the airfields are also bombed and the aircraft destroyed on the ground.

The German 2nd Army (von Weichs) advances on Belgrade from Austria and Hungary. The I Armoured Group (von Kleist) advances from Bulgaria towards Nis in the north and Skopje and Monastir in the south, to prevent Yugoslav troops from joining up with the Greeks. On the very first day of hostilities they seize the Yugoslav bank of the Iron Gate, the rocky gorge through which the Danube flows along the frontier between Rumania and Yugoslavia between Oršova and Turnu-Severin. They also threaten Nis. The 12th Army (von List) attacks both in

Yugoslavia towards Strumica and in Greece against the Metaxas Line. The Luftwaffe practically destroys the port of Piraeus.

Italy declares war on Yugoslavia, and Italian troops occupy some frontier villages in Venezia Giulia. *North Africa* In Cyrenaica Axis troops occupy Mechili and Msus. The Australian 9th Division begins to withdraw from Derna; and near Derna the British Generals O'Connor and Neame are captured. *Italian East Africa* Addis Ababa is occupied by the 12th African Division under command of General Wetherall. Since 10 January, when General Cunningham's troops crossed the border into Italian Somaliland, up to the time they entered Addis Ababa, the British have

THE FORCES IN THE FIELD

Against Yugoslavia, attacking from Austria and Hungary, the Germans deployed their 2nd Army (von Weichs), with three army corps, one armoured, and the 4th *Luftflotte*. From Rumania the XLI Motorized Corps attacked towards Belgrade. The Hungarian 3rd Army was also preparing to intervene. Advancing from Bulgaria was part of the German 12th Army (von List), with five army corps and one armoured corps, von Kleist's I Armoured Group with three armoured divisions, and part of the 8th *Luftflotte* (von Richt-hofen), intended for operations against Greece. The Italians deployed their 2nd Army along the frontier with Yugoslavia, while four other divisions stood ready on the Albanian border.

In total the German forces amounted to 21 divisions, six of which were armoured and four motorized. These forces included the *SS Adolf Hitler* and *Germania* divisions and the motorized regiment *Grossdeutschland*. The Hungarians contributed six brigades to this operation. The Italians, on the Giulian frontier, provided eight infantry divisions, two motorized, one armoured and three cavalry divisions, and the four infantry divisions on the Albanian frontier. Against the aggressors, with their fifty-odd divisions, their immense armoured forces and crushing air superiority, the Yugoslavs could put no more than 28 divisions in the field, three of them armoured, and about 600 out-of-date aeroplanes. These forces were split into three groups, the first defending Croatia, from Fiume to Brod, the second protecting the Bulgarian frontier, and the third to counter any Italian attack from Albania.

covered some 1,700 miles without ever having to fight a serious battle; their total losses are only about 500 men, while the Italians have lost the bulk of their arms, equipment and supplies and tens of thousands have been taken prisoner.

7 April

Yugoslavia The German XL Armoured Corps, advancing from Bulgaria, occupies Skopje and pushes on towards Monastir. In the north of the country the 2nd Army under von Weichs advances on Zagreb. The Italian 2nd Army (General Ambrosia) crosses the Giulian frontier. The head of the Croatian separatist movement, Ante Pavelić, calls on Croatians to set up a separate state. The German 12th Army (von List) enters Greece from Bulgaria. Facing it are four Greek divisions, and at their flank, some 30 miles away, the British expeditionary force (four British divisions and a brigade of Polish volunteers), while another three and a half Greek divisions are on the Metaxas Line, a system of fortifications about 100 miles long extending from the Beles mountains to the mouth of the river Nestos. After hard fighting the Germans seize the important Rupel pass. Stukas hammer the brave defenders.
□ During the night of 6 April British bombers raid Sofia, capital of Bulgaria. It looks like nothing more than a British version of Operation *Castigo*, for, as with the German raids on Belgrade, these raids can have no other object than to sow terror among the civilian population.
North Africa Near Mechili, in Cyrenaica, Axis forces get the better of an engagement with the British 2nd Armoured Division and the 3rd Indian Brigade. Derna is occcupied. Meanwhile the British begin to strengthen the garrison of Tobruk.

8 April

Yugoslavia Faced by overwhelming German forces, the Yugoslav army shows signs of rapid disintegration. In the south the forces of I Armoured Group (von Kleist) occupy Nis and push on along the Morava valley towards Belgrade.
Italian East Africa Massawa, the last centre of Italian resistance in Eritrea, is forced to capitulate. Of the 13,000 men defending it, over 3,000 have been killed and 5,000 wounded.
□ Coventry subjected to severe bombing raid during the night.

9 April

Greece With their line turned in the west by the German 2nd Armoured Division, which entered Greece from Yugoslavia and took Thessaloniki the previous night, the Greek army of the Vardar or Axios (a river that flows into Greece from Yugoslavia and reaches the sea at Thessaloniki), commanded by General Bakopoulos, is forced, with the authority of the supreme command, to surrender. Seventy thousand men are taken prisoner. Fifteen German divisions push on towards the Aegean, where they come up against the rest of the Greek forces and the British expeditionary force.
□ Heavy night bombing attack on Birmingham.
□ UK civilian casualties to date: 29,856 killed, 40,897 injured.

10 April

Greece General Sir Henry Maitland Wilson, haunted by the spectre of a second Dunkirk, orders the British expeditionary force to retire.
Yugoslavia The defenders of Zagreb offer little resistance; it falls to Axis forces advancing south.
Croatia declares itself independent.

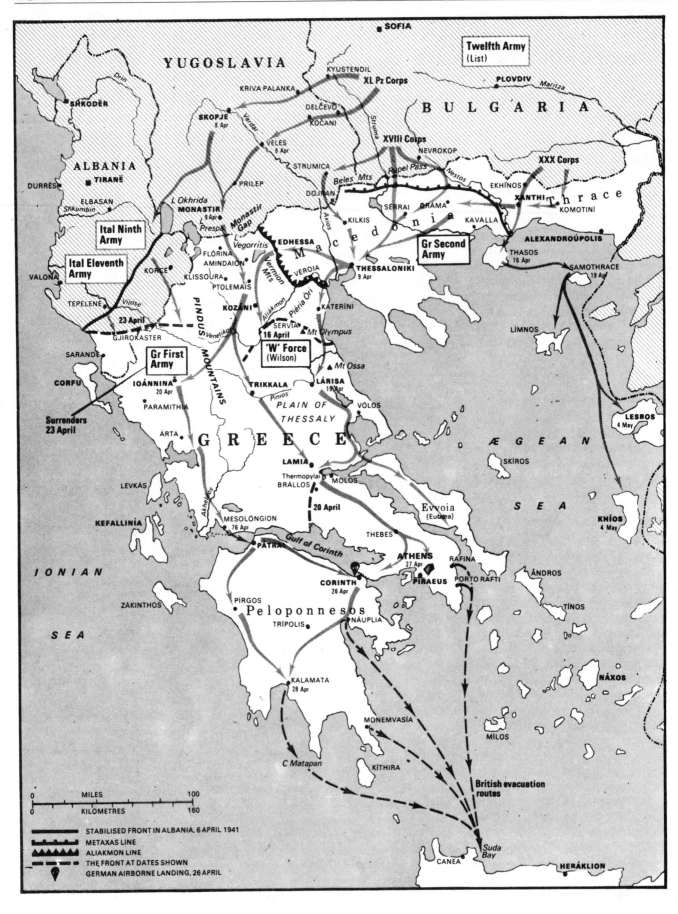

SOFIA

YUGOSLAVIA

KYUSTENDIL

XL Pz Corps

PLOVDIV

Maritza

B U L G A R I A

KRIVA PALANKA

DELČEVO

Drin

SKOPJE
8 Apr

KOČANI

SHKODËR

Vardar

VELES
6 Apr

XVIII Corps

NEVROKOP

Struma

XXX Corps

ALBANIA

TIRANË

PRILEP

STRUMICA

Rupel Pass

Nestos

EKHÍNOS

XANTHI

Thrace

KOMOTINÍ

DURRËS

ELBASAN

Shkumbin

L Okhrida

MONASTIR
9 Apr

Beles Mts

DOJRAN

SERRAI

DRAMA

KAVALLA

ALEXANDROÚPOLIS

Ital Ninth
Army

Prespa

Monastir
Gap

EDHESSA

Axios

KILKIS

Macedonia

Gr Second
Army

THASOS
16 Apr

SAMOTHRACE
19 Apr

Ital Eleventh
Army

Vegorritis

VEROIA

THESSALONIKI
9 Apr

VALONA

KORÇE

FLÓRINA
AMÍNDAION

Vermion
Mts

KLISSOURA

PTOLEMAÍS

LÍMNOS

TEPELENË

Vijose

KOZÁNI

Aliakmon

Piéria Óri

KATERÍNI

23 April

PINDUS

Venetikos

SERVIA

16 April

Mt Olympus

GJIROKASTER

SARANDE

Gr First
Army

'W' Force
(Wilson)

Mt Ossa

CORFU

IOÁNNINA
20 Apr

MOUNTAINS

TRÍKKALA

LÁRISA
19 Apr

LESBOS
4 May

Surrenders
23 April

PARAMITHIA

Pinios

PLAIN OF
THESSALY

VÓLOS

ÆGEAN

SKÍROS

ÁRTA

GREECE

SEA

LEVKÁS

Akhelóos

LAMIA

Thermopylai
BRÁLLOS

MOLOS

KEFALLINÍA

MESOLÓNGION
26 Apr

20 April

Evvoia
(Euboea)

SEA

KHÍOS
4 May

ZÁKINTHOS

Gulf of Corinth

PATRA

THEBES

ÁNDROS

ATHENS
27 Apr

RAFINA

I O N I A N

CORINTH
26 Apr

PIRAEUS

PORTO RÁFTI

TÍNOS

PÍRGOS

Peloponnesos

TRÍPOLIS

NÁUPLIA

NÁXOS

SEA

KALAMATA
28 Apr

MONEMVASÍA

MÍLOS

C Matapan

KÍTHIRA

British evacuation
routes

CANEA

Suda
Bay

HERÁKLION

STABILISED FRONT IN ALBANIA, 6 APRIL 1941
METAXAS LINE
ALIAKMON LINE
THE FRONT AT DATES SHOWN
GERMAN AIRBORNE LANDING, 26 APRIL

MILES   100

KILOMETRES   160

North Africa The Australian 9th Division withdraws to Tobruk. The Libyan strongpoint, in which the British have taken refuge under the battering of the German and Italian forces, is soon completely cut off. The Axis forces, advancing in echelon, literally besiege it. Every inch of the defensive perimeter is within range of German and Italian artillery; even working parties in the docks come under fire.

Atlantic The first hostile gesture by the Americans against Germany; during an operation to pick up survivors from a Dutch freighter sunk off Iceland the American destroyer *Niblack* drops depth-charges against the U-boat responsible for the sinking.

☐ Berlin opera house is destroyed during a British air raid.

11 April

Yugoslavia The Italian 2nd Army, advancing into Yugoslavia from Giulia, moves in two directions, inland towards Ljubljana, which is taken, and along the coast towards Split and Dubrovnik. Four more Italian divisions cross the border from Albania. The Italians employ 320 aircraft in these operations. The Hungarian 3rd Army, divided into ten brigades, now enters Yugoslavia and advances on Novi Sad.

North Africa Rommel launches a violent attack on Tobruk, using the Italian *Trento* and *Brescia* Divisions (attacking along the coast) and the German 5th Armoured Division. The beseiged garrison is ready for all eventualities, and the surprise on which Rommel had counted is therefore negated. Inside the Tobruk perimeter besides the Australian 9th Division, are an infantry brigade, an anti-aircraft regiment and a tank regiment, under the command of General Leslie Morshead. By the evening the attack by the Italians and Germans has been driven off.

☐ Further extensive night raids on Bristol.

A German submarine damaged in the Atlantic on 10 April by depth charges from a United States torpedo boat. This is America's first hostile act against Germany.

12 April

Yugoslavia Belgrade falls to the German XLI Motorized Corps advancing from Rumania. Near the capital the German troops from Hungary join up with those from Rumania.
The Italians also advance, taking a number of coastal villages and the Dalmatian island of Ugljan.

North Africa Axis forces take Bardia and advance towards the Egyptian frontier.

☐ US troops occupy Greenland.

☐ Ante Pavelic takes over as head of state of the independent Croatian state – a puppet of Mussolini.

13 April

Yugoslavia Belgrade occupied by Germans.

North Africa Rommel says he wants to follow up his advance at least to Mersa Matruh, regardless of what happens in the Tobruk sector. But from Berlin he is recommended to consolidate on a line at Sollum, on the Libyan–Egyptian frontier, and it is emphasized that he should use any possible means to eliminate the resistance of the British garrison in Tobruk.

Greek–Albanian front Powerful Italian offensive against the Greeks.

Korcë, Permet, Gjirokaster and Portë e Palermos are recaptured, and some divisions advance into the Epirus.

Malta Aircraft of the 10th *Flieger-korps* carry out heavy bombing raids on the island.

☐ In Moscow the Japanese Foreign Minister Matsuoka and the Soviet Foreign Minister Molotov sign a five-year non-aggression treaty between their two countries.

14 April

North Africa Rommel launches an attack on Tobruk from the south, using the 5th Light Motorized Division, and succeeds in breaking through the outer defences. But by the afternoon, the combined effects of a heavy artillery barrage and a strong counter-attack by British infantry, compel the German forces to withdraw. Tobruk will be a tough nut to crack. For the moment all the Italo-German forces can do is to reinforce their siege of the fortress.

16 April

Yugoslavia The Germans occupy Sarajevo. The Italians take Antivari and Danilovgrad, while a landing party of the San Marco Regiment seizes the island of Krk.

Mediterranean At 2.20 p.m., off the Tunisian coast at the latitude of the Kerkenah shoals, a British destroyer flotilla attacks an Italian convoy of five ships with a destroyer escort. All the ships in the convoy and three of the escorting destroyers (the *Tarigo*, *Lampo* and *Baleno*) are sunk. The British lose the destroyer *Mohawk*.

☐ London experiences one of the most severe and indiscriminate bombing attacks of the war so far during night raids. St Paul's Cathedral damaged.

17 April

Yugoslavia By now the Yugoslav army is destroyed. The last centres of resistance, in Bosnia, surrender. The Foreign Minister, A. Cinkar-Marković, and General Janković for Yugoslavia, General von Weichs for Germany and Colonel Bonfatti for

Italy, sign the act of surrender in Belgrade. The Axis forces have taken 334,000 prisoners. British aircraft fly King Peter II and his government to Greece, the first stage of their exile in London.

The Italians take Dubrovnik.

Greek front The Italian 9th Army advances in the Epirus.

Italian East Africa In their march to the north General Cunningham's troops reach the area of Dessie, an important centre north-east of Addis Ababa. The Italians strengthen their redoubt at Amba Alagi.

☐ Heaviest bombing raids so far by RAF on Berlin.

18 April

Greece The German XVIII Army (mountain troops) forces the passage of the river Aliakmon against the resistance of the New Zealand 2nd Division; the Germans surround Mount Olympus and take the town of Larisa. The XL Motorized Corps completes the encircling operation, pressing on Florina and Trikkala. In this way a breach is opened between the left wing of the British expeditionary force and the right wing of the Greek forces. German troops pour through the gap.

The Greek Prime Minister Alexandros Korizis commits suicide.

19 April

Greece While the Italians advance in the Epirus, the Greeks find their retreat cut off by the *SS Adolf Hitler* Division, which has attacked on the Pindo and occupied the Metsovo pass and the town of Grevenà. For the Greeks, this is the end. The rear-guards of the British expeditionary force take up positions at Thermopylai to protect the re-embarkation of the main body.

Against the orders of his superiors, General Zolakoglu, commander of the Greek army in western Macedonia, makes contact with the Germans to negotiate surrender.

In Athens, a meeting of King George II, General Papagos and the British Generals Wavell and Maitland Wilson, which agrees the evacu-

Infantry of the Italian 9th Army advancing on Epirus.

ation of the British expeditionary force from the Greek mainland. Resistance will be continued in the islands.

☐ A Luftwaffe air raid causes tremendous damage in London, with 2,300 dead.

20 April

Greece Hammered by Stukas, the British retire on Nauplia, Kalamata and Monemvasia, the points fixed for their re-embarkation. The rearguard holds firm at Thermopylai; their stand there lasts until the 24th. Greek forces in Epirus and Macedonia capitulate.

North Africa A strong British commando force tries to land at Bardia in an effort to bring relief to the defenders of Tobruk, but is driven off by the German-Italian forces. Rommel decides not to attack Tobruk again until he can use the 15th Armoured Division, which is on its way from Italy.

The commander-in-chief of the British forces, General Sir Archibald Wavell, asks Churchill for tank re-inforcements to deal with the situation in Libya.

21 April

Greece The *SS Adolf Hitler* Division takes Ioannina, on the flank of the Greek line facing the Italians.

At Larisa, the headquarters of the German 12th Army (von List), Greek plenipotentiaries sign the capitulation. Sixteen divisions lay down their arms. The news infuriates Mussolini, and on Hitler's orders the ceremony has to be repeated two days later in a villa near Thessaloniki, with an Italian representative present.

North Africa British naval forces from Malta and Alexandria shell Benghazi harbour.

☐ Further heavy night raids on Plymouth.

22 April

Greece Evacuation of Imperial forces begins.

Italian East Africa The British storm the defences of Dessie.

☐ Further heavy raids on Plymouth.

23 April

Greece In a villa near Thessaloniki the signing of the Greek surrender is repeated in the presence of an Italian representative.

Greek King and government fly to Crete in RAF plane.

☐ Plymouth again bombed during night attacks.

24 April

Greece The Germans launch attacks against the British lines at Thermopylai. The British have been reinforced by Greek detachments who refuse to surrender. The German victory is rapid and complete.

German parachutists occupy the islands of Limnos, Thasos and Samothrace in the north-eastern Aegean.

The Italian 9th Army takes the Perati bridge and joins up with the German forces.

Bulgaria invades Greek territory.

Iraq The British garrison in Iraq reinforced by the despatch of additional units.

German armoured troops advancing across the desert towards Tobruk. The Allied garrison holds out despite a series of fierce attacks launched by Rommel between 11 and 14 April.

25 April

Greece The Australians and New Zealanders, who have fallen back from Thermopylai to Thebes, are forced to continue their retreat under pressure by the Germans towards the small ports of Rafina, Magara and Porto Rafti, in mainland Greece, to re-embark.

German parachutists drop beyond the Corinth Canal at Corinth and the *SS Adolf Hitler* Division is successful in crossing the western outlet of the canal. German troops spread out over the whole of the Peloponnese.

Hitler issues Directive No. 28, Operation *Merkur* (Mercury): the invasion of Crete.

North Africa The Germans attack Halfaya Pass, the key to the eastern approach to Egypt, and succeed in driving the British back to the line Buq Buq–Sofafi.

Italian East Africa The situation grows more difficult for the Italians at Amba Alagi.

26 April

Greece The Germans continue to advance in the Peloponnese. German parachute troops capture Corinth. The re-embarkation of the British expeditionary force continues.

North Africa General von Paulus, sent by the *Oberkommando der Wehrmacht*, arrives at Tobruk to make a personal appreciation. British aircraft have bombed Benghazi during the night, causing some casualties and damage.

27 April

Greece German tanks enter Athens.

North Africa A British attempt to break through the encirclement of Tobruk is driven back.

Far East The British, Dutch and Americans meet in Singapore to draw up a common defence plan in the event of a Japanese attack in that sector.

28 April

Greece Some 43,000 British and Poles of the expeditionary force re-embark at Nauplia, Monemvasia and Kalamata. The Royal Navy

Armoured troops and infantry of the German 12th Army, under the command of General von List, crossing into Greece from Bulgaria.

sends six cruisers, 19 destroyers and a great number of small transports to carry out the evacuation.

In this disastrous campaign the expeditionary force has lost 12,712 men, including 9,000 taken prisoner by the Germans, and the whole of its heavy equipment. The evacuation (Operation *Demon*) is nevertheless successful. General Freyberg, commanding the New Zealand contingent, arrives in Crete.

Italian losses in the six months of the Greek campaign: 13,755 dead, over 50,000 wounded, 12,368 severely frostbitten and 25,067 missing. German losses in Yugoslavia and

Greece: 1,684 dead and 3,752 wounded, with 548 missing.

Greek losses: 15,700 dead and missing. About 300,000 men are taken prisoner by the Axis forces, but all except the officers are released almost at once.

North Africa Germans capture Sollum.

Malta Italian and German air formations carry out a number of raids on air and naval bases on the island.

29 April

North Africa British aircraft bomb Benghazi.

'MOTHER COURAGE AND HER CHILDREN'

On 19 April the premiere took place in Zurich of *Mother Courage and Her Children* (*Mutter Courage und ihre Kinder*) by the German playwright Bertolt Brecht. Written while in exile in 1939, *Mother Courage*, with its strong ethical content, chronicled events of the Thirty Years' War and reflected bitterly upon the causes and nature of war in general.

Italian East Africa Units of the 5th Indian Division reach the slopes of Amba Alagi from the north, while General Cunningham's troops, pushing on after the capture of Dessie, approach from the south.

Malta Another air raid on Valetta by the German air corps based in Sicily.

30 April

North Africa Rommel stages another big assault on Tobruk. The attack opens with a heavy aerial and artillery bombardment, followed up by thrusts by tanks and infantry in the western sector of the defence line. The British retaliate with incessant, violent and intensive artillery fire, but at the end of the day the attacking troops have succeeded in forming a salient some two miles deep in the defences of the western sector.

Italian East Africa The 11th African Division advances from Addis Ababa towards Shashamanna, where an Italian division is based.

Crete General Freyberg is given command of the British troops and Greek militia defending the island.

☐ UK civilian casualties in April, 6,065 killed, 6,926 injured.

1 May

North Africa Fighting in the salient won by the German-Italian troops in the western perimeter of the Tobruk defences grows fiercer; Rommel continuously sends fresh troops into the front line to widen the gap, but does not succeed in making any appreciable progress.

Italian East Africa British pressure on the Italian defences in the Amba Alagi sector is increased.

Malta Axis aircraft raid Valetta again.

Greece The Germans have failed in their intention of wiping out the entire British expeditionary force; but they now occupy the whole of the Aegean coastline.

☐ Liverpool has first of seven consecutive night raids.

2 May

North Africa The situation at Tobruk is unchanged; the British

Above: German bombers over the Acropolis in Athens.

succeed in halting the repeated efforts of the Axis troops to widen the salient in the western sector of the defensive perimeter.

Greece Allied evacuation completed.

Iraq Iraqi troops occupy Rutba and attack the British garrisons in several places near the Persian Gulf, including Basra.

☐ RAF bombs Hamburg.

3 May

Italian East Africa The last phase of the battle for Amba Alagi opens; the Italians repulse a two-pronged British attack.

Greece An imposing German-Italian parade in Athens to celebrate the Axis victory.

4 May

North Africa The attempt by General Rommel's troops to take Tobruk can be considered to have failed. Following this second failure the Axis commanders consider a plan for the reinforcement of their forces in North Africa, involving the expansion of the Italian and German forces to form an army of three army corps (two Italian and one German), with five armoured divisions (three Italian and two German), seven motorized divisions (Italian) and four non-motorized 'occupation' divisions (also Italian). For the Italians alone this project would require the transportation to Africa of 100,000 men, 14,000 trucks and 850 guns. However, the plan is never proceeded with, and the Italian-German forces were never to achieve the levels proposed in it, either in men or in equipment.

Italian East Africa The 29th Indian Brigade captures the three western peaks of the Amba Alagi redoubt and succeeds in holding them with artillery support.

☐ Robert Menzies, the Australian Prime Minister, on the eve of his departure from Britain for Australia, praises Britain's women: 'I confess myself an enthusiast about the superb women of Great Britain. In some of the great industrial cities where many hundreds of bombs had fallen, where thousands of houses had been wiped out, where vast community funerals had been held and human anguish must have been supportable only because it was so widely shared, the quickest recognition and the brightest smiles were seen on the faces of the toil-worn middle-aged women; faces transformed from homeliness to a sort of radiant beauty by sheer courage. I thank God for such people.'

☐ Hitler addresses the Reichstag: 'In this Jewish-capitalist age, the National Socialist state stands out as a solid monument to commonsense. It will survive for 1,000 years.'

5 May

Italian East Africa On the fifth anniversary of the Italian occupation of Addis Ababa, Emperor Haile Selassie of Ethiopia returns to his capital in triumph.

Crete General Freyberg appointed C-in-C Allied forces in Crete. He tells Churchill that he thinks it possible to repulse an attempted invasion of the island by sea or by parachutists provided he receives enough artillery, tanks, trucks and fighter aircraft. The RAF, after their heavy losses in Greece, are unwilling to set up permanent bases in Crete; they will provide their support from airfields in

North Africa. The Royal Navy, running the gauntlet of Luftwaffe attacks, succeeds in transporting to the island 16 light tanks and 6 armoured cars. Everyone is fully alive to the strategic importance of Crete, 600 miles from Alexandria and only a little more than 200 miles from Tobruk. The British fear is for North Africa, the German for the threat to the oil wells at Ploesti by British aircraft based on Crete.

6 May

Crete General Freyberg is told the details of Operation *Merkur*, the German plan for the invasion of Crete, by the British Secret Service.
Malta Attacks continue by German and Italian air formations on targets on the island.
Italian East Africa British pressure continues at Amba Alagi.

☐ The Praesidium of the Supreme Soviet nominates Stalin, already Party Secretary, to be President of the Council of People's Commissars.

7 May

North Africa On the Tobruk front there are exchanges of artillery fire, and British positions are bombed.

☐ Humber area suffers major night bombing raid.

8 May

North Africa A strong, swift offensive thrust by the British in an attempt to relieve the pressure on Tobruk.

☐ British bombers carry out a violent raid on Hamburg.

☐ Heavy air raids on Humberside and London by German bombers.

9 May

North Africa British air raid on Derna. Artillery activity round Tobruk, where the situation remains unchanged.
Italian East Africa British pressure increases in all sectors of the Amba Alagi front.

☐ British bombers carry out a heavy raid on Bremen.

10 May

Rudolf Hess, deputy leader of the Nazi Party, flies to Britain. Hess drops by parachute from his Messerschmitt 110 on the village of Eaglesham in Lanarkshire, not far from Dungavel House, home of the Duke of Hamilton. (Hess had met the Duke during the 1936 Berlin Olympic Games.) He is captured by the Home Guard and asks to be taken to the Duke; he tells him who he is, and that he is the bearer of a peace plan. Britain, he maintains, will never be able to win the struggle with Germany, and it is desirable and necessary to find some form of agreement between the two countries to bring the conflict to an end. Churchill is not interested in any such discussions, and in any case Hess is speaking purely for himself – Hitler has repudiated him the moment he hears of his 'desertion'. The official Nazi announcement says that Hess is suffering from 'a mental disorder'. The Nazi leader is therefore imprisoned, first in Buchanan Castle, later in the Tower of London, finally in a villa at Abergavenny in South Wales. On 10 October 1945 he is to be taken to Nuremberg to be tried with the other Nazi criminals by the Allies. Naturally the flight of Hitler's chosen deputy causes a world sensation and is taken as an indication of serious dissensions in the Nazi ranks.

☐ Another very heavy air raid by the Germans on London; among buildings damaged are the Houses of Parliament, Westminster Abbey and the British Museum. But this turns out to be the last raid until July 27.

☐ Admiral Darlan, Vice-President of the Council of Ministers and Minister for External and Internal Affairs in the Vichy French government, meets Hitler at Berchtesgaden; in exchange for some formal concessions on the part of the Germans he offers Hitler bases for the German army in Syria.

11 May

Heavy RAF night attacks on Hamburg and Bremen.

12 May

North Africa A convoy, code-named *Tiger*, of freighters carrying 238 tanks and 43 Hurricane fighter aircraft reaches Alexandria. Their despatch has been personally authorized by Churchill, in reply to the urgent message sent him by Wavell on 20 April in which he asked for reinforcements to help redress the balance on the Egyptian–Libyan border, now that the arrival of Rommel has wiped out all the British gains in Cyrenaica.

Iraq First report of German aircraft presence.

13 May

North Africa The German–Italian forces repel another British attempt to raise the siege of Tobruk.

☐ After the destruction caused by bombing attack on night of 10–11 May, House of Commons reassembles in a new home.

☐ Martin Bormann appointed successor to Hess.

14 May

Malta German and Italian aircraft bomb the island's air and naval bases. Since the first heavy German attack on the *Illustrious* on 16 January, the British fighters on Malta have shot down 62 German

aircraft and 15 Italian; the British have lost 32 Hurricanes in air combat and about the same number destroyed on the ground.

Far East Large British Army, Navy and Air Force reinforcements arrive in Singapore.

15 May

North Africa Operation *Brevity* begins. This is the code-name for the action decided on by General Wavell, Commander-in-Chief of British forces in the Middle East, to recapture Halfaya Pass on the Libyan–Egyptian frontier, which has been in German hands since 25 April. Wavell thinks this counter-attack essential if he is to organize any kind of operation to relieve the Italian–German pressure on Tobruk. Brigadier-General W. H. E. Gott is appointed to command the force that will carry out the attack (7th Armoured Brigade Group, 22nd Guards Brigade Group and Coastal Group). The attacking force makes for three different objectives: Halfaya ('Hell-fire') Pass, the town of Sollum and Fort Capuzzo. The pass is soon taken and after heavy fighting the 22nd Guards Brigade also captures Fort Capuzzo. Convinced that he is faced with an attack on a large scale, Rommel launches an im-

mediate counter-attack, carried out by three armoured regiments (the 2nd, 5th and 8th) and the 54th Infantry Regiment.

The British plan of attack was for the 7th Armoured Brigade Group to concentrate its forces in the direction of Sidi Azeiz, on the left of the front, while the 22nd Guards Brigade Group continued to hold Fort Capuzzo and tried at the same time to push eastwards in the direction of Sollum.

The next day the German counter-attack is in full swing; Rommel's armour is advancing on Fort Capuzzo and aims to get behind the British positions on Halfaya from the west. The British cannot withstand this counter-attack, and withdraw; in a short time Fort Capuzzo is in German hands again, while the recapture of Halfaya Pass is only a matter of days, depending on how long it will take Colonel Cramer's 8th Regiment to surround the pass. The manœuvre, however, was known to the English commanders and in fact General Gott ordered the 3rd Coldstream Guards defending the pass, to retreat.

Crete In accordance with Hitler's directive the Germans begin a series of aerial bombardments on Crete in preparation for a landing. The formations detailed to take part in this operation, directed by General Student, are the 7th Parachute Division and the 5th Mountain Division, supported by six infantry regiments and the VIII Air Corps (General von Richthofen), with 280 high-level bombers, 150 dive-bombers, 239 fighters and 50 reconnaissance aircraft. Transport for the first wave of the invasion is to be supplied by 500 three-engined Junkers Ju-52s and 72 gliders. The mountain troops, who are to cross to the island by sea, are provided by the Italians with an escort of two destroyers and 12 torpedo boats.

Yugoslavia Under the aegis of the Italians, the Kingdom of Croatia is constituted, which also includes the Serbian provinces of Bosnia and Herzegovina.

'CITIZEN KANE'

Orson Welles launched his cinema career as actor and director with *Citizen Kane*. Welles broke all the conventional rules of plot by involving the audience in a reconstruction of the biography of the film's central character, the wealthy newspaper proprietor Charles Foster Kane.

A reporter attempts to string together the tycoon's life story by focusing on the meaning of Kane's dying word 'rosebud', interviewing five of the people who knew him best and arriving only at the partial truth based on subjective viewpoints. Only the cinema audience eventually discovers the significance of the key word.

Orson Welles, director and star of *Citizen Kane*.

Above: Tank battle outside Tobruk.
Below: After the bombardment of the
airfields on Crete, German paratroopers
are dropped on to the island. The British
are immobilized.

Exhausted British troops on one of the rescue ships taking them to Egypt after the
evacuation of Crete.

16 May
North Africa The chief of the German general staff, Marshal Franz Halder, orders Rommel to leave the task of besieging Tobruk to the Italians and to concentrate his own troops on the operations round Sollum.
East Africa The 7,000 or more Italians garrisoning the Amba Alagi positions surrender to the British on the orders of the Viceroy of Ethiopia, the Duke of Aosta.

17 May
Crete German preparations for the attack on the island are completed in Greece. The date for the operation, fixed for 18 May, is put off to the 20th. The air offensive continues.
Iraq Italian aircraft arrive to assist in Iraq's struggle against the British.

18 May
Yugoslavia The Duke of Spoleto is proclaimed King of Croatia in Rome. He was never to visit his realm.
□ The German battleship *Bismarck* leaves the Baltic port of Gdynia at the start of her first and last adventure.

19 May
East Africa Formal surrender of Italian forces at Amba Alagi.
□ Prime Minister Churchill tells Sir John Dill, Chief of the Imperial General Staff, that the time has come for a change at the head of the British command in Africa; he intends to appoint General Sir Claude Auchinleck, Commander-in-Chief in India, to replace General Wavell, but he agrees with Dill that this is not the best moment for such a step, since important operations are under way and others are about to be launched.
Crete The six British fighters left in Crete (the Luftwaffe has destroyed 29 since the beginning of the month) are transferred to Egypt. It is felt that there is no point in sacrificing them in the light of the enemy's overwhelming superiority.

20 May
Crete 5.30 a.m.: Violent German air bombardment of the airfields at Maleme and Heraklion. At 7.15

a.m. a second air attack. The German object is to immobilize the British, and they completely succeed. After the second bombardment comes the first wave of paratroops. They look to the defending troops (about 32,000 British and Commonwealth, mainly Australian and New Zealand, with 10,000 ill-equipped Greeks; there are also 68 anti-aircraft guns, heavy and light, scattered over something like 160 miles, the whole length of the island from west to east) like 'balloons coming down from the ceiling of a dance-hall after a party'; the parachutes are of all colours, pink and violet for officers, black for NCOs and other ranks, yellow for medical supplies, white for weapons and ammunition. On landing the men have orders to regroup into units: eight men equipped with automatic rifles, two marksmen with Mauser rifles fitted with telescopic sights, and a Solothurn light

machine-gun crew of three. Special squads are armed with light anti-tank guns, flame-throwers and mortars. The paratroops are dropped from 493 three-engined Ju-52 transport aircraft and some seventy gliders. The anti-aircraft fire only manages to shoot down seven of the Ju-52s. The paratroops are dropped on Maleme and in the area of Canea, Retimo and Heraklion. They pay a high price, for they present all too easy a target for the defenders. The main concentration of the invading force is directed against the promontory of Akrotiri. In the afternoon the Germans throw in a new wave of paratroops, but this time the aircraft carrying them, instead of flying in massed formations, come over in small groups. The in-aircraft escorting the transports are forced to return to base ahead of time because the paratroop drops are late – all of which makes the defenders'

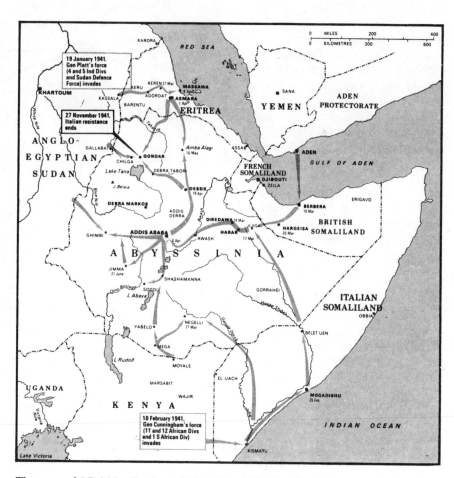

The successful British offensive in Italian East Africa between January and November 1941.

THE SINKING

OF THE *BISMARCK*

18 May

The German battleship *Bismarck* leaves the harbour of Gdynia in the Baltic at dusk, together with the heavy cruiser *Prinz Eugen*, bound for the Atlantic Ocean. The group is under the command of Admiral Günther Lütjens; captain of the *Bismarck* is Captain Ernst Lindemann, of the *Prinz Eugen*, Captain Brinckmann. The giant battleship, 50,900 tons fully laden, armed with eight 380-mm guns and 19 152 mm guns and capable of a speed of 20 knots, is on her first mission. Laid down in 1936, launched in 1939 and ready for service in the first months of 1941, the *Bismarck* is the very best that German shipyards can produce, which is why the ship's movements are so carefully watched by the British Admiralty, both by air reconnaissance and by reports sent in by spies. The news that the ship is leaving the harbour of Gdynia at once puts the British authorities on the alert; their first reaction is to intensify their aerial reconnaissance so as to keep the dreaded enemy ship under observation.

20 May

By dawn the *Bismarck* and *Prinz Eugen* have sailed a good way through the Skagerrak, the arm of the North Sea between the Norwegian and Danish coasts joining the Baltic with the North Sea.

21 May

British reconnaissance aircraft sight the two German ships in the morning in harbour at Bergen on the west coast of Norway. Their position is immediately reported to the Admiral commanding the Home Fleet at Scapa Flow, the British fleet's main base. The Home Fleet mobilizes powerful forces – the two battleships *King George V* and the brand new *Prince of Wales*, the battlecruisers *Hood*, armed with 16-in guns, carrying the flag of Vice-Admiral L. E. Holland, and *Repulse*, the aircraft carrier *Victorious*, the cruisers *Norfolk* and *Suffolk* (already patrolling the Denmark Strait) and six destroyers.

22 May

12.52 a.m.: The *Hood* and *Prince of Wales*, escorted by six destroyers, sail from Scapa Flow under the command of Vice-Admiral L. E. Holland, bound for the Denmark Strait. Their orders are to reinforce the cruisers *Norfolk* and *Suffolk*, already operating in this sector.

Reconnaissance aircraft confirm that the two German ships reported at Bergen are still there.

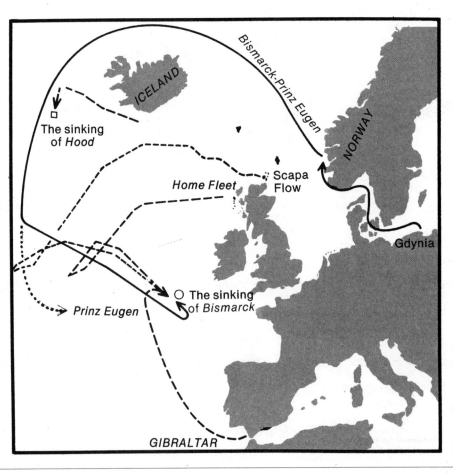

Bismarck

Prinz Eugen

The report reaches Admiral Sir John Tovey at 8.00 p.m.

10.45 p.m.: The aircraft carrier *Victorious* sails from Scapa Flow.

23 May

During the morning the battle-cruiser *Repulse* joins Tovey's squadron.

12.00 noon.: The *Bismarck* and *Prinz Eugen* enter the Denmark Strait after rounding Iceland to the north. The minefields that the British have laid along the coast of Iceland, of which the Kriegsmarine is well aware, compel the two warships to pass well out to sea, right in the middle of the channel; the sky is unusually clear.

7.22 p.m.: The two German ships are sighted by the cruiser *Suffolk*, which immediately signals to the other three ships in the British formation.

8.22 p.m.: The *Norfolk* also sights the two German ships six miles off and signals their position to the flagship.

8.30 p.m.: The *Bismarck* approaches and opens fire on the *Norfolk*, but by a miracle the

THE HOME FLEET

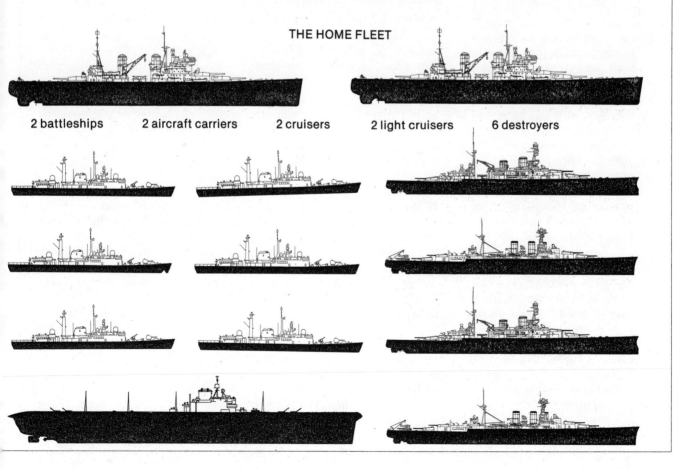

2 battleships   2 aircraft carriers   2 cruisers   2 light cruisers   6 destroyers

British cruiser manages to escape from the German battleship's broadsides.

At this point Admiral Lütjens, commanding the German ships, realizes that every little change of course and speed by his ships is observed and signalled to the British flagship; he may wonder whether he ought to abandon the plan of reaching the Atlantic and return to Germany. However, he decides to go on.

Midnight.: Vice-Admiral Holland calculates from the *Suffolk*'s signals that the *Hood* is only 120 miles from the *Bismarck*. But suddenly the *Norfolk* and *Suffolk* break off the flow of information about the enemy ships which they have been supplying; both British cruisers have lost contact with the German ships.

24 May

2.47 a.m.: The *Suffolk* 'recaptures' the image of the two German ships on her radar.

4.00 a.m.: Following her present course the German battleship should meet the *Hood* at about 5.30 a.m., just as dawn breaks.

5.35 a.m.: The *Hood* and the battleship *Prince of Wales* sight two ships to north-west. It is the quarry they are looking for. The distance is 17 miles.

5.52 a.m.: With their escort of destroyers the *Prince of Wales* and *Hood* open fire on the *Bismarck* and *Prinz Eugen*.

6.00 a.m.: A shell from the *Bismarck* passes through the light armour of the *Hood* and explodes in the stern magazine. The ship blows up and sinks almost immediately; of the 1,419 men in the ships complement (95 officers and 1.324 ratings and Royal Marines), only three are saved. Shortly afterwards the *Prince of Wales* is also hit a number of times and the captain, Captain Leach, decides to break off the action and withdraw. However, the *Bismarck* does not

try to pursue the British battleship, which is able to rejoin the *Norfolk* and *Suffolk* without more trouble. The two British cruisers continue to shadow the German battleship, which is making for the Bay of Biscay. Meanwhile the *Prinz Eugen* has broken away from the *Bismarck* and is sailing south.

During the afternoon the British Admiralty calls up the aircraft carrier *Ark Royal*, the battleships *Ramillies* and *Rodney*, the battlecruiser *Renown*, the cruiser *Sheffield* and six destroyers, all belonging to 'Force H', stationed at Gibraltar. Almost half the entire British fleet is now hunting the most powerful battleship in the world.

Eight Swordfish aircraft from the aircraft carrier *Victorious* attack the *Bismarck* with torpedoes; one hits the German ship amidships but causes no serious damage.

25 May

3.16 a.m.: The *Suffolk* loses contact with the *Bismarck*; the German ship almost seems to have evaporated.

8.10 a.m.: The Swordfish take off again from the *Victorious* in search of the enemy ship. No use; nor are the *Norfolk* and *Suffolk* any more successful in their efforts.

26 May

10.36 a.m.: A Catalina seaplane sights the *Bismarck*. The German battleship is over 700 miles west of Brest and only 130 miles from Admiral Tovey's *King George V*.

2.30 p.m.: Fifteen Swordfish torpedo-carrying aircraft take off from the aircraft carrier *Ark Royal* to try to finish off the *Bismarck*, 20 miles off, before she can seek protection under the umbrella of German bombers from bases in France. The weather is very bad, with low, dense cloud that makes observation almost im-

possible. Suddenly the British aircraft find a gap in the clouds and catch sight of a ship. They launch their torpedoes; but their target turns out to be, not the *Bismarck*, but the British cruiser *Sheffield*, which had approached the German ships without the air crews being notified. However, the *Sheffield* manages to avoid the torpedoes.

7.00 p.m.: Swordfish aircraft take off from the *Ark Royal* again.

7.50 p.m.: The torpedo-carrying aircraft from the *Ark Royal* are over the *Bismarck* and launch their missiles. One torpedo hits the German ship and seriously damages the steering-gear, causing the battleship to reduce speed considerably. During the night destroyers shadow the enemy.

27 May

8.15 a.m.: The cruiser *Norfolk* signals the exact position of the *Bismarck* to the *King George V* (the flagship) and *Rodney*, which have arrived unexpectedly.

8.47 a.m.: The *Rodney* opens fire, followed immediately afterwards by the *King George V* and, after a time, by the *Norfolk* and the *Dorsetshire*. The *Bismarck* replies with very precise salvoes, but the hail of shells now striking her steadily reduces her offensive power.

10.00 a.m.: The German superbattleship is reduced to a silent wreck.

10.15 a.m.: The cruiser *Dorsetshire* is ordered to approach the *Bismarck* and finish her off with torpedoes.

10.40 a.m.: The *Bismarck* capsizes and sinks. Of some 2,300 in her complement only 110 are picked up by the *Dorsetshire* and the destroyer *Maori*. Among the casualties are Admiral Lütjens and the captain of the ship, Captain Lindemann.

1 June

The heavy cruiser *Prinz Eugen*, skilfully avoiding the British hunt, reaches harbour at Brest.

Some phases in the battle between the *Bismarck* and the British squadron sent to hunt her down. Top left: the *Bismarck* fires on the *Hood* at the impressive rate of a salvo every 22 seconds. Top right: the *Bismarck* under fire from the *Hood* which fails to hit her. (Photo taken from the *Prince of Wales*.) Centre left: the *Bismarck* lit up by the blaze from her own guns. Centre right: the *Hood* is hit. Bottom left: the *Hood* blows up. Bottom right: the *Bismarck* opens fire on the *Prince of Wales*, which withdraws.

task easier. When evening comes the three airfields at Maleme, Retimo and Heraklion are still in British hands, and the Germans have suffered severe losses. But the British do not counter-attack during the night, and the Germans profit by this inaction to concentrate their efforts on Maleme airfield, which they capture. The first convoys of German mountain troops and reinforcements leave the ports of Piraeus and Thessaloniki for Crete escorted by Italian destroyers. The first convoy suffers heavy losses, the second is forced to turn back, but others reach Milo on the evening of the 21st. The Germans lose 297 men.

Malta German aircraft bomb the island, hitting gun and searchlight positions and causing huge fires.

21 May

Crete During the night of 20–21 May ships of the Royal Navy are sighted off the north coast of Crete. At dawn aircraft of VIII *Fliegerkorps* go into the attack, sinking the destroyer *Juno* and damaging the cruiser *Ajax*.

North Africa Exchange of artillery fire on the Tobruk front, while German and Italian aircraft bomb gun positions and supply depots.

□ The British Navy begins its hunt for the giant German battleship *Bismarck* in the seas of northern Europe.

22 May

Crete The Luftwaffe launches a series of attacks on ships of the Royal Navy, and bombs from Stukas sink the cruisers *Fiji* and *Gloucester* and four destroyers. Four other ships are damaged.

German convoys sailing for Crete with mountain troops and supplies are harassed by the Royal Navy.

North Africa British air raids on Benghazi.

East Africa British pressure on the Italian defenders is increased in the Galla Sidamo sector.

23 May

Crete Hurricane aircraft equipped with supplementary fuel tanks attack Maleme airfield. Some manage to

ZÜNDAPP

Engaged principally in producing motorcycles for the army, one of the major German automobile firms, Zündapp, began to manufacture the KS 750 specifically for war use. A powerful vehicle with four gears and a horizontal two-cylinder engine, the KS 750 was specifically made to be used with a sidecar and quickly became the most popular and successful motorcycle in the German army, more than 18,000 machines being made during the war.

German soldiers on Zündapp KS 750 motorcycles. This powerful vehicle, which had a sidecar, was used by the German army throughout the war.

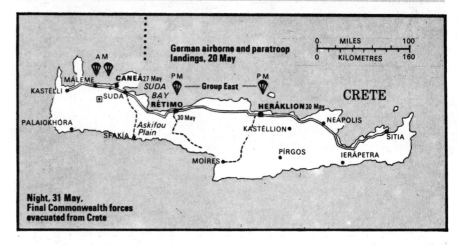

land at Heraklion, under fire by the Germans, but not for long; that same day the first German fighters succeed in landing at Maleme.

General Ringel, in command of the German operations in Crete, receives reinforcements of mountain troops and decides to clean up the whole western part of the island. The British have formed a defensive line running from the coast to the hills, in the area near Galatas. Ringel decides to split the forces in the Maleme sector in two; the paratroops are to attack along the northern coastal road while the mountain infantry move south into the rough interior to take the British in the flank. The same evening the 'western group' joins up with the 3rd Parachute Regiment at Canea.

24 May

Crete Admiral Cunningham tells London that he is no longer in a position to bar the way to the German convoys except at the risk of extremely heavy losses. London's answer is categorical: at all costs the Royal Navy and RAF must prevent the Germans from receiving reinforcements by sea.

Bitter fighting continues throughout the island, the paratroops against the British and Anzacs, the mountain troops facing the Greeks who have taken up positions in the mountains. By the evening the situation at Retimo and Heraklion is still critical; the German troops in the Heraklion sector have been reinforced by another parachute battalion during the day.

General Freyberg asks Wavell for massive intervention by the RAF in support of the ground troops. In the evening the British land two commando battalions at Suda under the command of Colonel Laycock.

25 May

Crete The Germans now really go over to the offensive. Their objectives are Alikianou, from which they can advance and cut the main road to the island south of Suda Bay, Galatas, south-west of Canea, and the village of Carceri, near Galatas. In the evening they take the position at Galatas, despite British counter-attacks with the bayonet; they lose it for a while but re-take it after savage fighting. Inland they fail to reach their objective at Alikianou, tenaciously defended by the Greek 8th Regiment.

King George of the Hellenes and his ministers escape from Crete to Egypt.

Mediterranean During the night three groups of Italian 'frogmen', under the command of a naval officer, Lieutenant Decio Cataliani, succeed in entering Gibraltar harbour in their E-boats, but their operation fails as a result of the defective working of the 'pigs' or low velocity torpedoes.

26 May

Crete Seeing how the situation has deteriorated, Freyberg tells Wavell that in his view the only course left is to evacuate the island and save at least part of the Allied force.

The British aircraft carrier *Formidable* is seriously damaged by dive-bombers and has to be sent to American dockyards for repair. Hammered by artillery and aircraft and under violent pressure by the German troops, the British have to retire eastwards to Mournies, while the Greeks withdraw inland to the south.

27 May

Crete With authority from London, General Freyberg draws up plans for the evacuation of British troops from Crete. It will be carried out over several nights on board ships provided by Admiral Cunningham, from the small ports of Ierapetra and Sfakia. The commando units and Royal Marines will protect the withdrawal and embarkation of other forces.

Meanwhile the Germans attack in the area of Pirgos. The Australians and New Zealanders are taken by surprise, but they fight back courageously and for a time succeed in driving the enemy back.

However, Freyberg has to withdraw all the forces he can in order to establish a defensive line north of the ports chosen for re-embarkation. This enables the Germans to cut off one battalion from the rest of the British forces in the area of Stilos. The forces defending Retimo and Heraklion begin to run short of ammunition.

The Germans also attack at Canea, and at the end of the day they occupy Suda Bay.

The evacuation of British troops begins.

North Africa Rommel recaptures Halfaya Pass, on the Egyptian–Libyan frontier, and fortifies it.

Atlantic The battleship *Bismarck* is sunk by British warships.

□ President Roosevelt declares: 'It is unmistakably apparent to all of us that unless the advance of Hitlerism is forcibly checked now, the western hemisphere will be within range of Nazi weapons of destruction.'

28 May

Crete General Ringel, not realizing how desperate a state the enemy is in, instead of moving all his troops to

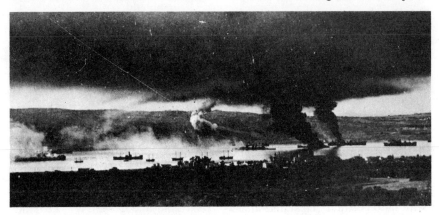

British ships in flames in Suda Bay, Crete.

the south of the island where the British are assembling for evacuation, concentrates them in the north towards Retimo and Heraklion, ordering his mountain troops to support the attacks on those two places. The embarkation of the British begins under cover of darkness and lasts until the night of 1–2 June. In the course of it the anti-aircraft cruiser *Calcutta* and the destroyers *Greyhound*, *Hereward* and *Imperial* are lost.

The Italians land at Sitia, near the north-eastern tip of the island, a contingent of 2,700 men who had left Rhodes the previous day on board thirteen small craft escorted by five destroyers and six submarines.

29 May

Crete British resistance is confined to Heraklion, Retimo and the Askifou Plain, to divert the Germans and protect the embarkation operation. Embarkation continues throughout the night; the cruisers *Phoebe*, *Perth*, *Glengyle*, *Coventry* and *Calcutta*, with three destroyers, take on board some 6,000 men at Sfakia. Crossing the Mediterranean the *Perth* is hit and seriously damaged by a Ju-88.

30 May

Crete The Germans take Retimo and Heraklion.

Two more British destroyers are hit by German aircraft on their way to the embarkation points. The evacuation proceeds; General Freyberg himself embarks. Some 9,000 troops, some of them separated from their units, still remain on the island.

North Africa A report by the Italian Supreme Command considers an attack in force on the fortress of Tobruk to be 'inadvisable': 'Unless the enemy forces receive substantial reinforcements it is felt that the situation can be regarded with calm ... Only in the event of the enemy receiving large reinforcements, with an obvious aggressive intention, and we ourselves receiving only modest reinforcements (or none at all), could the situation be reversed and become sufficiently dangerous to make it

British African troops with Fascist emblems taken from the border between Kenya and Italian Somaliland.

necessary for us to raise the siege of Tobruk.'

Iraq Pro-Axis Iraqi revolt collapses.

31 May

Crete The last detachments of British troops not separated from their units move as quickly as possible to Sfakia, but there is not room in the ships for all the men awaiting embarkation.

☐ In France Admiral Darlan makes virulent anti-British speech. The French press becomes increasingly pro-Axis.

☐ Growing German infiltration in Syria evident.

1 June

Crete The battle of Crete is virtually over, though the last embarkation of British and Anzac troops is carried out during the night. For those left isolated or abandoned, the only choice is to surrender or to move up into the hills to carry on guerrilla operations.

Iraq British troops enter Baghdad.

2 June

Crete The balance-sheet of the bloody fighting can now be drawn up. The Allied forces have lost 16,583 men (8,200 British, 3,376 Australian and 2,996 New Zealand army personnel and 2,011 men of the

Royal Navy). The Germans have lost 3,714 dead and missing and about 2,500 wounded; but these are picked men, and the High Command never again dares to employ paratroops on so large a scale.

North Africa The Vichy government grants the Axis the use of the port of Bizerta, in Tunisia; the concession applies only to the transportation of supplies of rations and clothing and excludes movements of men, war materials and ammunition.

☐ Hitler and Mussolini meet at Brennero on the Brenner Pass to discuss urgent military questions.

3 June

North Africa Axis air attacks on the Tobruk base continue.

4 June

Iraq New pro-British Cabinet announced.

5 June

Reinforcements, including Australian forces, arrive in Cyprus.

6 June

Law is passed in the United States permitting the government to requisition foreign merchant ships idle in US ports.

7 June

North Africa While Italian aircraft bomb the Tobruk base again, British squadrons carry out raids on Benghazi and Derna.

8 June

Syria 2.00 a.m.: Imperial and Free French forces enter Syria and the Lebanon and attack French garrisons loyal to the Vichy government. The Vichy forces (45,000 men under the command of General Dentz) put up a strenuous resistance to the invasion. Vichy government sends a note of protest, denying collaboration with Germans in Syria.

9 June

Syria British occupy Tyre.

10 June

Italian East Africa The British launch a strong attack on the centres of Italian resistance in the Galla Sidamo region, south-west of Addis Ababa. The Italians are commanded by General Pietro Gazzera, the

British artillery in action at Tobruk.

senior Italian commander in East Africa since the capture of the Amba Alagi and the surrender by the Duke of Aosta.

☐ Churchill answers critics on Crete operations during House of Commons debate.

☐ Mussolini announces that Italy will occupy Greece.

11 June

Sir Stafford Cripps, British ambassador in Moscow, arrives in London for consultations.

☐ RAF raids on Ruhr, Rhineland and ports in north-west Germany begin, and continue for 20 successive nights.

German tank crew advancing towards an objective hidden by a smoke screen during a British counter-offensive in Cyrenaica.

12 June

Malta Fierce air battles over the island between Italian and British fighters; the Italian war communiqué says that eight Hurricanes have been shot down for the loss of two attacking aircraft.

Italian East Africa The port of Assaḅ in southern Eritrea is occupied by an Anglo-Indian naval force; it has already been evacuated by the Italian troops.

In the area of Gondar, west of Amba Alagi, the British continue their attacks, and a heavy British artillery bombardment is directed on the troops defending Debra Tabor.

13 June

Tass news agency denies rumours of growing tension between Germany and the USSR.

14 June

North Africa During the afternoon British troops advance from Sidi Barrani to within 25 miles of the Libyan frontier. Towards evening, seeing the advance has been reinforced and is continuing, Rommel alerts his troops.

During the night Italian fighters bomb Alexandria.

East Africa British pressure continues round Gondar and Debra Tabor and in the Galla Sidamo area.

☐ President Roosevelt orders the freezing of all German and Italian assets in the USA.

15 June

North Africa The start of Operation *Battleaxe* in Cyrenaica – the operation by which General Wavell hopes to reduce the pressure of the Axis troops on Tobruk and possibly even to relieve the fortress. While the military situation at Tobruk is more or less unchanged, logistically things are growing gradually but definitely more difficult. This is what Rommel is mainly relying on, as a letter written at this time shows: 'There is a great shortage of water in Tobruk; the British troops only get half a litre [just under a pint] a day. With the

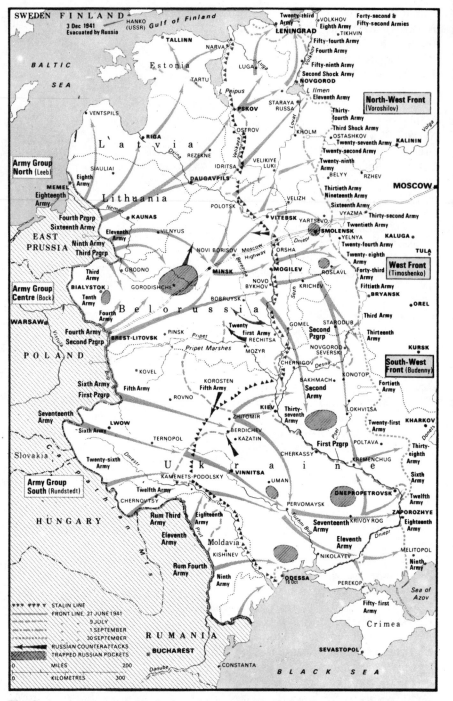

The German advance into Russia from the invasion on 22 June 1941 to 30 September.

help of our bombers I hope to be able to cut down this ration still further. The heat is getting worse every day and doesn't do anything to make you less thirsty.'

The British plan is to attack Halfaya Pass frontally, to occupy the Hafid Ridge (west of Fort Capuzzo), employing the 7th Armoured Brigade, and for the 4th Armoured Brigade and 4th Indian Division to encircle Fort Capuzzo and Sollum. By the evening the British have already taken Fort Capuzzo and the fortified position on the Hafid Ridge known as Hill 208. At Halfaya Pass the attacking forces are driven back by German artillery fire; the 88-mm anti-aircraft guns wreak havoc among the British tanks. Having received explicit orders not to attack, Rommel leaves it to troops in forti-

fied emplacements to break the British attack and moves the 5th Light Motorized Division west, then sending them south towards Sidi Omar to the west of the Hafid Ridge.
Malta The fighter aircraft on the island are reinforced by 43 Hurricanes from the aircraft carriers *Ark Royal* and *Victorious*; 64 more arrive before the end of the month, but some of these are to go on to airfields in Egypt.

16 June

North Africa As it moves southwards the German 5th Light Motorized Division is attacked all day by the British 7th Armoured Brigade; but the British brigade loses nearly all its tanks by enemy action or through mechanical failure. Meanwhile the British 4th Armoured Brigade withdraws from Fort Capuzzo to join up with the 7th Armoured Brigade to protect the left flank of the British line from being encircled by the 5th Light Motorized Division.
☐ The American State Department asks the German government to close all its consulates in the USA.

17 June

North Africa Having reached the top of Sidi Omar, the German 5th Light Motorized Division turns east towards Sidi Suleiman. Simultaneously, in the morning, Rommel throws in the 8th Armoured Regiment which has moved up to Fort Capuzzo, sending them first southwest, then east. Rommel's plan is for his armour to join up west of Halfaya Pass and then launch a joint attack on the British, who are still engaging the positions on the pass. The German manœuvre succeeds, and the British, to avoid being completely cut off, retire precipitately. By the afternoon the military situation on the Libyan–Egyptian frontier is the same as it was two days before, when Operation *Battleaxe* was launched.

18 June

North Africa German aircraft bomb the British troops retiring from Hal-

German 88-mm guns cause the British heavy losses in armoured vehicles and tanks.

faya Pass. British aircraft have again raided Benghazi.
Syria Damascus encircled. General Wilson appeals to General Dentz to evacuate Vichy forces.
☐ In Ankara the German ambassador, von Papen, signs a ten-year pact of friendship between Germany and Turkey.

19 June

German forces mass along Russian frontier.
Italian East Africa British attacks on the Italian positions at Gondar and Debra Tabor become more intensive.
☐ Italy and Germany ask the United States to close all consulates in their respective countries.

20 June

Syria Heavy fighting around Damascus.

21 June

North Africa Winston Churchill decides to replace Sir Archibald

Wavell, Commander-in-Chief of the British forces in the Middle East, by Sir Claude Auchinleck, Commander-in-Chief in India.
Italian East Africa British troops enter Jimma, south-west of Addis Ababa, and receive the surrender of the whole Italian garrison. Meanwhile the bulk of the troops under the command of General Pietro Gazzera, Commander-in-Chief of the Italian armed forces in East Africa, concentrated in the Galla Sidamo sector, are forced to evacuate their positions after holding out for three months against General Cunningham's troops. The Italians retire to the west. But Italian resistance in Ethiopia is not finished; the last detachments, dug in in the region of Lake Tana, south of Gondar, hold firm until November under the command of General Guglielmo Nasi.
Syria Free French forces occupy Damascus.

22 June

4.15 a.m., East European time:

THE RUSSIAN CAMPAIGN

GERMAN FORCES AND DISPOSITIONS

Co-ordination of the operations against the Soviet Union was entrusted to Field Marshal W. von Brauchitsch. Of the 205 divisions, 133, plus 20 held in reserve, were allocated to Operation *Barbarossa*. The remainder were deployed as follows: 38 in the west, 12 in Norway and 2 in North Africa.

Von Brauchitsch could call on 3,200,000 men, 3,580 tanks, 600,000 trucks, 600,000 horses and 7,481 guns. The land forces were supported by three *Luftflotten* comprising 1,160 bombers and fighter-bombers, 720 fighters and 120 reconnaissance aircraft. The German forces had alongside them 14 Rumanian divisions, two Hungarian and two Slovak.

The front was divided into three sectors held by three Army Groups. The northern sector, from Memel on the Baltic to the Suwalki salient in East Prussia, was taken over by the Army Group North (Field Marshal Ritter von Leeb), with 26 divisions of which three were armoured and two motorized. The group was made up of the 16th Army (Colonel-General Busch), the 18th Army (Colonel-General von Küchler) and the IV *Panzergruppe* (Colonel-General Hoeppner). Air support was provided by I *Luftflotte* (Colonel-General Keller).

The central sector, from the Suwalki salient as far as Lublin in Poland, was held by the Army Group Centre under the command of Field-Marshal Fedor von Bock, which consisted of 48 divisions, nine of them armoured, six motorized and one cavalry. From north to south, there were III *Panzergruppe* (Colonel-General Hoth), with 840 tanks, the 9th Army (General Strauss), the 4th Army (Field-Marshal von Kluge) and II *Panzergruppe* (Colonel-General Guderian) with 930 tanks. II *Luftflotte* (Field-Marshal Kesselring) was assigned to this sector. The southern sector, from Lublin down to the Black Sea, was entrusted to the Army Group South under the command of Field-Marshal Gerd von Rundstedt. This consisted of 59 divisions, of which five were armoured and three motorized, deployed from north to south as follows: between the Lublin area and the Slovak border, the 6th Army (Field-Marshal von Reichenau), I *Panzergruppe* (Colonel-General von Kleist), with 750 tanks, the 17th Army (Colonel-General von Stülpnagel) and, in Rumania, the 11th Army (Colonel-General von Schobert). Two Hungarian divisions stood ready on the Hungarian border, and in Rumania the Rumanians had 14 divisions grouped in two armies, the 3rd (General Dumitrescu) and 4th (General Ciuperca). Air support in this sector was provided by IV *Luftflotte* (Colonel-General Löhr).

RUSSIAN FORCES AND DISPOSITIONS

The Russian force was the equivalent of 158 divisions (118 infantry divisions and 40 armoured and motorized, grouped in a 'mechanized corps') – a total of 4,700,000 men, not counting reserves. However, at the time of the invasion only 2,500,000 men were actually manning the Western Front. The air force had 1,350 bombers – only 500 of them of modern design, 2,000 fighters nearly all inferior to the German fighters, and about 800 obsolete reconnaissance aircraft.

The line from the Baltic to the Black Sea was divided into five fronts, later reduced to three and put under the command of Voroshilov, Timoshenko and Budenny. At the time of the Ger-

Dornier Do.17 Z-2

Panzerkampfwagen IV

Mikoyan-Gourevitch Mig-1

T. 34/76

man attack the forces were drawn up as follows:

North Front (Latvia, east of Riga, and Leningrad) commanded by Lieutenant-General M. Popov, with four divisions. North-West Front (from Riga in Latvia as far south as Kaunas in Lithuania) under the command of Colonel-General F. I. Kuznetsov (later replaced by Sobennikov), with 24 divisions, four of them armoured, grouped into the 8th Army (Major-General Sobennikov) and 11th Army (Lieutenant-General Morosov).

West Front (from Kaunas in Lithuania to Brest-Litovsk in White Russia [Belorussia]), under the command of Lieutenant-General D. G. Pavlov (later under Timoshenko), with 38 divisions, including eight armoured divi-

sions, grouped as follows: 3rd Army (Lieutenant-General V. I. Kuznetsov), 10th Army (Major-General K. D. Golubev) and 4th Army (Major-General Korobkov). South-West Front (Brest-Litovsk to the Lower Ukraine), under the command of Colonel-General Kirponos (later under Budenny), with 56 divisions, including 16 armoured divisions, grouped as follows: 5th Army (Major-General Potapov), 6th Army (Lieutenant-General Muzychenko), 26th Army (Lieutenant-General Kostenko) and 12th Army (Major-General Ponedelin). South Front (Lower Ukraine to the Black Sea) under the command of Major-General Tyulenev, with 16 divisions, four of them armoured, grouped in the 18th Army (Lieutenant-General

Smirnov) and 9th Army (Lieutenant-General Cherevichenko). It should be observed that the Russians had some thousands of old small and medium tanks (BT-5, BT-7, T-26, etc.), however, from official documents it appears that there were in service 867 T-34 and 508 KV-1 tanks, of 28 tons and 43.5 tons respectively, armed with an excellent 76.2-mm gun plus two or three 7.6-mm machine-guns, and heavily armoured. In theory these tanks were superior to the heavy Pz-Kw IV tanks that the Germans were equipped with, both numerically and in performance, but in practice this superiority was cancelled out by the Russian commanders' mistaken strategic conception of the proper employment of armour.

A Russian air base after an attack by the Luftwaffe. A substantial proportion of the Soviet air force was destroyed on the ground during the first 24 hours of the German offensive.

A German machine-gun patrol fires on a pocket of Russian resistance in the ruins of Brest-Litovsk.

Operation *Barbarossa*, the invasion of the Soviet Union, is launched. As long ago as 21 July 1940 Hitler had ordered his generals to prepare a plan of attack against the USSR. A similar directive, No. 21, was issued by the Führer on 18 December of the same year. The plan had twice been revised. In its original form it was based on two main offensives, against Moscow and against Kiev, with a covering action in the north towards Leningrad. The second version still had Moscow as its main objective, but also provided for an advance into the Ukraine by forces based in Rumania and for a more massive thrust towards Leningrad. According to the final plan the strongest thrust would be towards Leningrad, with simultaneous pressure on Smolensk and Moscow. The Russians are completely taken by surprise by the assault; the Germans had managed to assemble their enormous army without their enemy ever recognizing the extreme danger

of his situation. The success of the invading forces, who reckon on completing their campaign before the winter, is overwhelming; the Germans break through almost all along the line.

The Führer has set up his headquarters (known as the *Wolfsschanze*, the wolf's den) in East Prussia, in a forest near Rastenburg. The German troops completely overwhelm the Russians in every sector except the south, where dogged resistance limits their advance. Not only are the Russians short of motor vehicles for rapid movement, but they are positioned, not along the border (which is a 'new' border and only lightly fortified), but in depth, in echelons anything from 65 to 325 miles deep.

The German attack should not have been unexpected; the Russian secret agent Richard Sorge, who operated in Japan, had already reported it, specifying the forces which would be employed, as early as 19 May, and on

15 June he actually notified its precise date. Confirmation of Sorge's information had come on 18 June from a German deserter who had crossed to the Russians to escape court-martial. But Stalin and Molotov, convinced that the Germans were neither able nor willing to relinquish their operations against the British, gave no credence to these informers. At 11.15 a.m. Molotov announces the German attack to the Russian people: 'At 4 o'clock this morning, with no declaration of war and no demands made on the Soviet Union, German troops have assailed our country, attacked our frontier at many points and bombed Zhitomir, Kiev, Sevastopol, Kaunas and other places. Similar attacks by bombers and artillery have also been launched from Rumanian and Finnish territory. This incredible attack on our country is an act of treachery unequalled in the history of civilized nations. It has been carried out despite the existence of a non-aggres-

sion pact between the Soviet Union and Germany ... and although the German government has never had the least cause for complaint about the way in which the Soviet Union has fulfilled its own obligations. The entire responsibility for this act of rapine must therefore fall on the Nazi rulers ... The government of the Soviet Union is deeply convinced that the whole population of our country will do its duty ... The government appeals to you, men and women, citizens of the Soviet Union, to unite more closely than ever round the glorious Bolshevist party, the Soviet government and our great leader, Comrade Stalin. Our cause is just. The enemy will be defeated. Victory will be ours.' Stalin does not speak to the people himself until eleven days later, on 3 July.

A supreme defence council, the *Stavka*, is set up urgently, and 15 million men are called up.

Italy and Rumania declare war on the USSR.

In London, at 9.00 p.m. Winston Churchill declares: 'Any state who fights Nazism will have our aid.'

North Africa General Wavell is informed by his government of their decision to relieve him of his duties as Commander-in-Chief of British Middle East forces and send him to India as Commander-in-chief of British forces there. The war in the Middle East loses a great protagonist.

23 June

Eastern Front The Germans make spectacular progress. In Army Group North's sector the 56th Armoured Corps (General Manstein) of the IV *Panzergruppe* (Hoeppner) has crossed the important Ariogala viaduct over the river Dubysa in Latvia, 50 miles from their starting point. In the central sector Guderian's tanks (XXIV Armoured Corps, General von Schweppenburg, and XLVII Armoured Corps, General Lemelsen) have stormed across the river Bug above and below Brest-Litovsk and consolidated at Kobrin and Pruzhany, 40 and 45 miles from the frontier, while those of General Hoth (LXII Armoured

Corps, General Kuntzen, and XXXIX Armoured Corps, General Schmidt) have captured Merech and Alytus, taking the bridges on the Niemen intact after an advance of 55 miles. In the southern sector, south of the river Pripet, Kleist's I *Panzergruppe* has made more modest progress; there is a strong concentration of Russian troops (56 divisions, including 16 armoured divisions) on their front.

The Luftwaffe continues to inflict tremendous damage on the enemy; 1,200 aircraft are destroyed on the ground or in combat before noon on 22 June.

Chaos reigns in the headquarters of the Russian formations, not helped by directives from the general staff that reveal a complete ignorance of the facts of the situation, such as the one sent to the headquarters of the south-western front ordering the forces there to launch a major offensive and re-take Lublin, 30 miles

behind the enemy lines, within 24 hours.

North Africa Italian and German air raids on the fortress of Tobruk continue, but without appreciable effect.

☐ Italy. British air raid on Syracuse.

24 June

Eastern Front In the northern sector the Russians launch a violent counter-attack.

North Africa British bomber squadrons attack Benghazi and Tripoli overnight.

☐ Slovakia declares war on the USSR.

☐ Recruitment of volunteers for service against the Soviet Union starts in Spain and Denmark.

25 June

Eastern Front In the southern sector the Germans occupy Dubno, an important town north-east of Lvov; the

While the British increasingly weaken Italian resistance, the Abyssinians organise themselves into armed groups.

'SPACE, TIME AND ARCHITECTURE'

The Swiss art historian Sigfried Giedion published *Space, Time and Architecture*, a book that was to prove indispensable for the study and understanding of twentieth-century architecture.

Influenced, among others, by Burckhardt and Riegl, Giedion became a keen observer of the new architectural trends thanks, too, to his post as secretary-general to the International Congresses for Modern Architecture (CIAM), an organization founded in 1928 together with the principal architects of the modern school (Gropius, Le Corbusier, etc.).

A teacher at Zurich and Harvard, Giedion was a prolific and unorthodox scholar whose principal purpose was to clarify the origins and direction of twentieth-century architecture.

A German soldier hit by Russian fire in the vicinity of Minsk.

tanks operating on the wings of the Army Group Centre, under Guderian and Hoth, reach Baranovichi, Lida and Borodechno, more than 125 miles east of Bialystok, the headquarters of Pavlov, commander of the Russian western front. The Russian 3rd, 10th and 4th Armies are in imminent danger of encirclement. On the northern front the Russians attack Finnish defence positions and counter-attack in the area of Murmansk.

The Germans bomb Odessa, Kiev, Nikolayev, Minsk and other towns.

Italian East Africa The Italian garrison of Debra Tabor, south-west of Amba Alagi, is heavily raided by British bombers.

26 June

Eastern Front In the northern sector Hoeppner's IV *Panzergruppe* spreads out into Lithuania and takes Daugavpils on the Dvina, establishing a bridgehead across the river. In the Army Group Centre sector, Guderian's and Hoth's tanks make their first contact at Slonim, between Baranovichi and Bialystok.

☐ Finland declares war on the Soviet Union.

☐ In Verona Mussolini reviews the *Torino* Division, which is being sent to the Russian front.

27 June

Eastern Front Von Bock's Army Group Centre, pressing on far beyond Brest-Litovsk, traps huge enemy forces in a pincer movement in the sector between Bialystok and Novgorod (now Novogrudok).

Von Rundstedt's Army Group South, with Kleist's I *Panzergruppe*, breaks through between the Carpathians and the Pripet marshes in the direction of Kiev and Vinnitsa (south-east of Kiev). Russian resistance is dogged and sometimes brilliant. On 2 July the Antonescu Army Group, comprising the Rumanian 3rd and 4th Armies and the German 11th Army, join the battle on the right wing in the Moldavia sector.

General Mannerheim, Finland's national hero, issues a proclamation to the Finnish people calling on them to play their part in the 'holy war' against the Russians.

Hungary declares war on the Soviet Union.

Malta Fierce air duels above the island between Axis air formations and British fighters. Raids on the port installations in Valletta are growing more and more frequent.

28 June

Eastern Front Troops of the Army Group Centre push on and threaten Minsk. Soviet troops fall back to new positions.

Albania declares war on the Soviet Union.

☐ The Japanese penetrate into Indo-China. Vichy co-operation with Japan disturbs the Americans, who are taking an increasingly pro-China stance in the Japan–China war.

29 June

Eastern Front In the central sector the armoured corps of Hoth (III *Panzergruppe*) and Guderian (II *Panzergruppe*) join up near Minsk to complete another pincer movement, cutting off the Russian forces in a huge pocket in the area of Gorodishche, a little town in White Russia south-west of Minsk, near Baranovichi. In Finland the Finns attack the Russians in Karelia, while in the extreme north German troops advancing from Norway and Finnish forces are both engaged in the area of Murmansk and Petsamo. The prizes are the only port on the Barents Sea that is ice-free all the year round, and a nickel mine of great strategic importance. The final objective of the offensive in Karelia is to link up with the German Army Group North.

30 June

Eastern Front In the central sector the Germans take Bobruisk and establish a bridgehead across the Beresina. Meanwhile they mop up the big pocket at Bialystok, destroying the remaining Russian 10th Army. The Army Group South takes Lvov and attacks the Stalin line, the fortification system built by the Russians but entirely neglected by them when they advanced to the borders of Poland. The threat to Kiev becomes increasingly imminent.

☐ Vichy France breaks off diplomatic relations with the USSR and freezes Russian assets in France.

☐ The Germans, now fully occupied with their operations against the Russians, suspend the Battle of Britain. Up to this date their air action has destroyed 116,000 buildings in London alone.

1 July

Eastern Front Riga falls to Germans.

☐ Ribbentrop urges Japan's Foreign Minister Matsuoka to press his government to declare war on the USSR. The Russians are withdrawing a large proportion of their forces from the Far East in order to despatch all possible reinforcements to the west; they have never left themselves so weak. But the Japanese refuse categorically (and the spy Sorge tells Moscow the whole story). They have already chosen the line of their expansion – towards South East Asia and the oilfields in the Dutch East Indies.

2 July

Eastern Front In the Army Group North sector the IV *Panzergruppe* under Hoeppner concentrates on the right bank of the Dvina and attacks the Russian fortifications on the border with Latvia, successfully

The devastated city of Minsk which fell only after savage fighting.

breaking through at Ostrov.
In the Army Group South sector the German 11th Army and the two Rumanian armies (3rd and 4th) come into action, considerably increasing the pressure on the Russians in Moldavia and in the direction of Vinnitsa.

☐ Night raids by RAF on Bremen and Cologne.

☐ Japan orders all its merchant ships in the Atlantic to return to home ports, calling up more than a million men.

☐ China breaks off relations with the Axis powers.

3 July

For the first time since the invasion began Stalin speaks to the Soviet people on the radio. He admits the loss of Lithuania, parts of Byelorussia and the western Ukraine. 'A grave threat hangs over our country.' But the Germans, he says, are not invincible, and he reminds his listeners of Napoleon. Then he defends the non-aggression pact of 1939 with Germany (for which the 'purists' in the party had always reproached him); it was dictated, he says, by the USSR's desire for peace. Now he urges the Russians to resist the invasion to the bitter end, leaving nothing behind them but scorched earth. Every act of cowardice will be punished. 'Military tribunals will pass summary judgment on any who fail in our defence, whether through panic or

Top: in a street in Zhitomir the crew of a German field gun prepare to open fire, while other soldiers shoot at a pocket of Russian resistance. Above: German fighter-bombers, heading for Smolensk, fly over the ruins of Vitebsk.

treachery, regardless of their position or their rank.' He announces the setting up of a national committee of defence (presided over by Stalin himself, with Molotov, Voroshilov, Malenkov and Beria), calls for partisan activities behind the enemy lines and orders the mobilization of all the country's resources. 'All the efforts of the people must be exerted to beat the enemy. On to victory!' In substance – and with great psychological acumen – Stalin appeals not so much to Communist ideals as to Russian patriotism.

The front is reorganized in three sectors: north-west, with the Baltic and Northern fleets, entrusted to Voroshilov; western, placed under the command of Timoshenko; southwestern, with the Black Sea fleet, entrusted to Budenny. Each of these commanders is given a politico-military adviser: Zhdanov, Bulganin and Khrushchev.

Battalions are also raised for service in the big cities. All men between the ages of 16 and 60 and women between 18 and 50 are called up to take part in civil defence. Positions are to be defended to the last man; the line to be held at all costs, according to the Soviet leaders, is from Smolensk to Moscow.

General Franz Halder, chief of the German general staff, notes in his *Diary* that the task given to the German armed forces may be considered fulfilled if the bulk of the enemy are driven back beyond the Dvina and the Dniepr.

Italian East Africa In the Galla Sidamo area General Pietro Gazzera is forced to surrender to the British, but his men are not required to lay down their arms.

4 July

Italian East Africa The garrison of Debra Tabor, about 6,000 men commanded by Colonel Angelini, is forced to surrender.

☐ President Roosevelt makes Independence Day broadcast: 'The US will never survive as a happy and prosperous oasis in the middle of a desert of dictatorship.'

5 July

Eastern Front In the southern sector the German 6th Army (von Reichenau) opens a breach in the Stalin line near the old Polish border east of Lvov, in the sector defended by the Russian 6th and 26th Armies. Von Kleist's I *Panzergruppe* floods through the gap making for Berdichev and Zhitomir, south-east and east of Kiev. But Hitler halts them.

6 July

Eastern Front In the southern sector Rumanian troops occupy the town of Chernovtsy, just over the Carpathians, and are given an enthusiastic welcome by the population, which is Rumanian.

In the outskirts of Vitebsk, not far from Smolensk, the 16th Army of the Army Group North makes contact with the 9th Army of the Army Group Centre. The northernmost German army, the 18th, continues its advance north, establishing a line from Lake Peipus (Cudskoje Ozero) through Tartu to Parnu, north of the Gulf of Riga.

North Africa Italian and German aircraft bomb the Tobruk fortress and the area of Sidi Barrani.

☐ British aircraft raid Palermo (Sicily).

7 July

Eastern Front German pressure continues from the Baltic to the Black Sea, while mopping-up operations liquidate the pockets in which huge Soviet forces have been trapped.

☐ In agreement with the British government and the local authorities, the Americans land their 1st Marine Brigade in Iceland, under Brigadier-General John Marston. Roosevelt justifies the operation by the necessity of defending the western hemisphere.

☐ Heavy night bombing raid on Southampton.

8 July

Eastern Front In the northern sector the IV *Panzergruppe* (Hoeppner) captures Pskov, near the southern tip of the lake of the same name, and advances north-east towards Nov-

gorod and Leningrad.

☐ Germany and Italy announce the end of the Yugoslav nation. The map of the country is redrawn as follows. Croatia is constituted an independent nation under Tomislav II (Ajmone, Duke of Spoleto, nephew of Victor Emmanuel III). The autonomous province of Ljubljana, newly created, is annexed to the Kingdom of Italy. The greater part of Dalmatia and the Adriatic islands are also assigned to Italy, together with Cattaro (Kotor). A large part of Bosnia is put under Italian protection and administration. Montenegro becomes an Italian protectorate, and it is decided to restore its monarchy, though the decision is never implemented. Croatia duly adheres to the Tripartite Pact on 12 July and the Anti-Comintern Pact on 25 November.

Lower Carinthia and part of Cariola are incorporated in Germany. Hungary receives the territory between the Sava and the Mur, the part of Barania (between the Sava and the Danube) allocated to Yugoslavia in 1918, and part of the Bachkra in Serbia.

9 July

Eastern Front Russian resistance in all the pockets not already liquidated comes to an end. Up to this time the Soviet army has lost 2,500 tanks, and 300,000 of its men have been taken prisoner. In the Bialystok sector, 40 divisions have been wiped out.

The II and III *Panzergruppen* (Guderian and Hoth), combined to form the 4th Armoured Army, advance beyond the rivers Dniepr and Dvina towards Smolensk, on the way to Moscow.

North Africa The bombardment of Tobruk by Axis aircraft and artillery continues.

☐ Night air raid on Naples by the British.

Syria General Dentz asks for armistice terms.

10 July

Eastern Front In the southern sector the Russians launch an unexpected and violent counter-attack in the area of Korosten (west of Kiev); it is checked by I *Panzergruppe* (von Kleist), but with severe losses.

Following the *Torino* Division, the rest of the Italian expeditionary force to Russia – the *Pasubio* and *Principe Amedeo Duca D'Aosta* Divisions and the *Tagliamento* Blackshirt Legion – leaves for the Eastern Front.

11 July

Eastern Front Having driven off the Soviet counter-attack at Korosten, the German armour advances to within 10 miles of Kiev, but then dogged Soviet resistance forces them to mark time.

Malta Fierce air battle in the sky over the island. According to Italian sources four British aircraft are shot down and many others destroyed on the ground.

Syria General Dentz accepts armistice terms.

12 July

Eastern Front Moscow is raided by the Luftwaffe for the first time. Germans claim to be 'before Kiev'; fall of Kiev, and also of Leningrad, said to be imminent.

Following a proposal sent to Stalin by Churchill two days before, a pact of mutual assistance is signed between Great Britain and the USSR. Both sides undertake not to sign a separate peace.

13 July

Eastern Front In the northern sector the Germans continue their advance from Pskov towards Luga, some 75 miles from Leningrad.

14 July

Eastern Front In the north the Germans reach the Luga river and now directly threaten Leningrad. Soviet resistance here is rather disorganized, by no means as brilliant as it is in other sectors of the front. The Russian leaders are well aware of the seriousness of the situation; the Commander-in-Chief of the northern front, Voroshilov, and the chief of the party organization for Leningrad, issue a general order addressed 'to all units on the north-western front' in which it says: 'Leningrad, cradle of the proletarian revolution, is directly threatened with invasion by the enemy. While the troops in the line from the Barents Sea to Tallinn and Hanko are fighting back bravely against the hordes of the Nazi and Finnish aggressors, defending every inch of our beloved Soviet ground, the troops on the central-western front (those in the Leningrad sector) often fail to stand up to the enemy attacks and abandon their positions without fighting, and by such behaviour encourage the ever-increasing arrogance of the Germans. There are cowards who not only desert the front line without orders but are spreading panic among good, brave soldiers; and in some cases officers and political leaders not only do nothing to allay the panic, but by their disgraceful conduct actually increase it, causing serious disorder at the front.' The order goes on to warn that anyone who leaves the front line without orders from a superior will be court-martialled and may be shot 'absolutely regardless of their rank or position'. It is clear that the Russians admit that the situation is critical, but that they are determined to hold firm at any cost.

Syria The armistice is accepted by Vichy and signed by the British and French. Syria is declared an independent nation.

☐ Yugoslavia and Montenegro see the start of armed resistance by 'partisans' against the occupying Italians and Germans. The resistance is led by the mysterious Tito (Josip Broz). There are many fabulous stories about his origin; some western journalists even say that he is a woman.

Italian East Africa General Smuts broadcasts on the destruction of the Italian Empire.

15 July

Eastern Front A counter-attack is launched by the Russians before Leningrad, in the southern part of the Luga line between Lake Ilmen and Solcy. The Russians keep up their efforts until 18 July, but the most they can do is to slow down the enemy advance. Their *opolcenie* divisions, civilian militia recruited in Leningrad, are eager but inexperienced; they are routed and massacred by the German tanks. Meanwhile hundreds of thousands of men and women are mobilized to build fortifications. New defence lines are constructed, one from the mouth of the Luga to Chudovo, Gatchina, Urick and Pulkovo and then along the Neva, another, the

Above: an Italian column advancing across the Libyan desert towards Jarabub.

'external' line from Peterhof to Gatchina, Pulkovo, Kolpino and Koltushi, east of the city and north of the Neva. Other lines are prepared in the immediate outskirts of the city and one in the northern suburbs facing Finland. In the end 335 miles of anti-tank ditches are dug, 400 miles of barbed wire erected, 16,000 miles of open trenches dug; 5,000 wood and concrete emplacements for guns and machine-guns are built, as well as a total of 185 miles of barriers made from felled trees.

Middle East British troops enter Beirut. Syria and Lebanon now under Allied control.

☐ The USA sets up an air base at Argentia in Newfoundland.

16 July

Eastern Front Finnish troops break through the Soviet positions north of Lake Ladoga and occupy Sortavala at the extreme north of the lake.

In the central sector of the front the troops of the Army Group Centre, continuing their advance, begin the destruction of the enormous Soviet forces trapped in a pocket in the Uman area, as well as undertaking mopping-up operations in the Dniepr basin.

The system of political commissars is re-introduced in the Red Army. The commissars are disliked by the commanders for functional reasons, and a year later they are abolished again.

☐ Hitler sends for Goering, Keitel, Larrers, Bormann and the Nazi theorist Rosenberg and at his headquarters expounds to them the Reich's objectives in the east: division of part of the occupied territories into four Reich Commission territories and direct annexation to the 'Great Reich' of the richest provinces, including the Crimea. Rosenberg is appointed head of a new ministry for eastern occupied territories. His task will be not only the exploitation of those territories for the benefit of the German economy, but also their political 'reclamation' – elimination of the Communists and deportation of the Jews.

North Africa Axis air raids continue

ARTHUR JOHN EVANS

The English historian, archaeologist and explorer, Sir Arthur John Evans, best known for his discovery of the remains of the ancient Minoan civilization on the island of Crete, died on 11 July.

Born at Nash Mills, Hertfordshire, in 1851, Evans studied modern history at Oxford and Göttingen. In 1884 he was appointed curator of the Ashmolean Museum, Oxford.

In 1893 Evans visited Crete for the first time and began the research that was later to achieve highly significant results. The excavations, which continued untile 1935, brought to light the royal palace at Knossos, magnificent testimony to a civilization that flourished from 2500 to 1200 BC and which Evans named Minoan after the mythical king Minos. Thanks to the finding of a number of clay tablets, Evans managed to identify two different types of pre-Hellenic linear script. Appointed professor extraordinary of ancient archaeology at Oxford, Evans, knighted in 1911, described his work in a monumental book entitled *The Palace of Minos at Knossos* (1921-36), a veritable encyclopedia of the Minoan civilization.

on Tobruk and British bombers raid Benghazi and Tripoli.

17 July

Eastern Front The invading forces continue their pressure all along the line. In the central sector the Germans establish a bridgehead across the Dniepr near Mogilev, east of Minsk. The Rumanians in the southern sector take Kishinev, the capital of Bessarabia. Near Vitebsk, Stalin's eldest son, Jakov Djugashvili, an artillery lieutenant in an armoured division, is taken prisoner by the Germans.

General Giovanni Messe takes over command of the Italian expeditionary force in Russia.

North Africa More Italian and German air raids on Tobruk and British air raids on Tripoli.

Malta During the night Axis aircraft bomb bases on the island, and in the morning there are fierce air battles between British and Italian fighters.

18 July

Prince Konoye forms a new government in Japan; Vice-Admiral T. Toyoda replaces Yosuke Matsuoka as Foreign Minister.

19 July

Eastern Front The OKW gives orders that, after defeating the Soviet

forces in the Smolensk sector, the II *Panzergruppe* (Guderian) and the 2nd Army are to abandon the offensive against Moscow and turn south to wipe out the Soviet 5th Army (Potapov), surround Kiev and join up with I *Panzergruppe* (von Kleist) in a pincer movement. Guderian protests against giving up the thrust against Moscow, but his objections are overruled.

North Africa Benghazi and Tripoli raided by British aircraft.

Malta The German-Italian air offensive continues.

☐ At midnight, an announcement by 'Colonel Britton' on BBC of mobilization of the 'V Army' – the dedication of oppressed peoples to victory over the Nazis. For months now the signal 'V' has been transmitted to German-occupied territory.

20 July

Stalin is named People's Commissar for defence.

☐ British aircraft bomb Naples, causing casualties and damage.

21 July

Eastern Front Russian withdrawal beyond river Dniestr announced. German night raid on Moscow.

22 July

Eastern Front Moscow has further

Top: Russian tanks disabled during the fighting near Smolensk. Above: a village near Vitebsk littered with dead horses and supply waggons following the Russian retreat.

heavy night attacks.

Malta A British supply convoy evades the Italian naval blockade to reach the island.

23 July

Eastern Front The heroic garrison of Brest-Litovsk, besieged since 22 June and ceaselessly hammered by bombers and artillery (the Germans for the first time using their giant mortar *Karl*, of 615-mm calibre and firing a projectile weighing over two tons) is finally forced to surrender.

☐ With the consent of the Vichy government Japanese forces begin the complete occupation of Indo-China, to collaborate – in the official phrase – with the French forces in its defence.

24 July

Malta The second British convoy in two days succeeds in reaching the island.

25 July

Malta During the night Italian assault vessel crews try to enter the harbour at Valletta with explosive punts and piloted torpedoes ('pigs'). They are spotted before they can line up on their targets; of the 33 men engaged in the action, 15 are killed and 18 taken prisoner.

☐ Japanese assets in UK and USA frozen.

26 July

US government puts the head-quarters of the Hawaii sector on alert. General Douglas MacArthur takes over command of American forces in the Far East and of the Philippines forces.

☐ Canada renounces its trade treaty with Japan.

☐ Japan freezes American assets.

27 July

Eastern Front The Germans take Tallinn, capital of Estonia, on the Gulf of Finland.

In the central sector the encirclement of Soviet forces at Smolensk is completed. However, the Russians manage to organize a new defensive line 25 miles east of the city, and their artillery reveals a certain superiority. In the Smolensk 'cauldron' their multiple rocket-launchers firing 320 rockets in 25 seconds (called 'Katyusha' by the Russians and 'Stalin's tools' by the Germans) make their first appearance, striking mortal terror into the Germans – and into the Russian infantry too, since they had not heard of this new weapon.

North Africa General Ettore Bastico takes over from General Gariboldi as Commander-in-Chief of Italian troops on this front.

☐ After a pause of several weeks, the Germans carry out a severe air raid on London.

28 July

Eastern Front In the central sector the Germans begin the liquidation of the Russian troops trapped in the Smolensk area.

Far East Japanese troops land in Indo-China.

29 July

Far East The Japanese complete the occupation of southern Indo-China, to which the Vichy French are forced to agree.

30 July

President Roosevelt's counsellor,

Harry Hopkins, is in Moscow to discuss the despatch of help to the USSR.

China At Chungking, the American river-gunboat *Tutuila* is bombed by Japanese aircraft. Next day the Japanese government apologizes to the Americans for the incident.

31 July

Eastern Front In the northern sector the German 16th Army reaches Lake Ilmen. When they breach the Russian positions on Lakes Ilmen and Peipus the road to Leningrad lies open, and now the city is also attacked from the south.

☐ British air raids on several places in Sicily.

☐ UK civilian casualties in July: 501 killed, 447 injured.

1 August

Eastern Front The Army Group Centre continues to attack the Soviet troops trapped in the Smolensk pocket. The Russians fight back with particular tenacity in the sector of Orsha and Vitebsk, west of Smolensk. In this same central sector, Soviet forces under Timoshenko suddenly unleash a powerful counter-offensive at Gomel, south of Mogilev, against the bridgehead established by the right wing of the Army Group Centre on the left bank of the Dniepr.

North Africa Artillery duels by both sides in the Tobruk sector.

☐ In the USA a council for economic defence is set up.

2 August

Eastern Front The advance guards of the Army Group North reach Staraya Russa, near Lake Ilmen, south of Leningrad.

In the southern sector the Italian *Pasubio* and *Torino* Divisions are sent into the line.

The first of the American aid begins to flow into the USSR.

3 August

Eastern Front In the southern sector the I *Panzergruppe* (von Kleist) joins up with the 17th Army (von Stülpnagel) after destroying big Russian

Top: a German cavalry unit entering a burning town. Centre: searching for Russian snipers near Velikiye Luki. Bottom: German infantry on Lake Ladoga.

formations west of Pervomaysk, about 100 miles north of Odessa. German night raid on Moscow.

5 August

Eastern Front The Smolensk pocket is liquidated. According to German sources there were 700,000 Russians trapped there, and 310,000 have been taken prisoner. The Russians admit the loss of nine divisions, 3,000 tanks and armoured cars and about 1,000 aircraft. The IV *Luftflotte* under General Löhr made a very substantial contribution to the operations.

☐ Further Allied reinforcements arrive in Singapore.

6 August

Eastern Front Having mopped up the few areas in Estonia where the Russians were still offering resistance, the Germans are solidly established on the coasts of the Gulf of Finland.

7 August

Eastern Front Stalin takes over as Commander-in-Chief of the Soviet armed forces.

Far East Japan denies aggressive designs against Thailand.

☐ Bruno Mussolini, second son of the Italian leader, dies in air accident near Pisa.

8 August

The Japanese ambassador in Washington, Admiral Kishisaburo Nomura, proposes that there should be direct talks between the American President and the Japanese Prime Minister to reach agreement on the differences between the two countries.

9 August

Eastern Front In the southern sector the battle of the river Bug begins, and the Soviet defence line is broken. But although they are everywhere in retreat, the Russians are by no means finished; they have some excellent tanks in the field, including the gigantic 55-ton Klim. Voroshilov. The German generals ask Hitler in vain for bigger tanks and anti-tank guns more powerful than the 37-mm and 50-mm guns they now have available to them. There are still only very few 75-mm guns.

☐ Winston Churchill and Franklin D. Roosevelt meet at Argentia, in Placentia Bay (Newfoundland). Churchill, accompanied by the Chief of the Imperial General Staff, Sir John Dill, and the First Sea Lord, Sir Dudley Pound, has arrived in the brand new battleship *Prince of Wales*; Roosevelt, with his advisers, has come in the cruiser *Augusta*. Next day, after a religious service on board the *Prince of Wales*, sees the opening of the Atlantic con-

Above: villagers in the Ukraine watching as their homes are burnt to the ground by the retreating Russians.

ference in which the principles of the Atlantic Charter are enunciated, defining the war aims of the democracies. Churchill presses the President strongly to bring America into the war, and he receives a guarantee of US intervention in the event of a Japanese attack on Malaya, Singapore and the Dutch East Indies. The two statesmen also agree on a reply to the Japanese proposals: they ask for the neutralization of Thailand and French Indo-China, and at the same time Tokyo is given a firm warning: 'Any further Japanese expansion would lead to a situation in which the government of the United States would see itself obliged to take counter-measures, even if that led to war.' The statesmen have no illusions about Japanese intentions, however. The conference goes on until 12 August.

10 August
Britain and USSR promise Turkey 'every assistance' if attacked.

☐ Night raid by Luftwaffe on Moscow.

☐ Nazi plots uncovered in Argentina, Chile and Cuba. There have been signs in several Latin American countries in recent weeks of considerable pro-Nazi agitation.

12 August
Eastern Front Hitler issues Directive No. 34 on the conduct of operations. The Army Group South is to prevent the enemy from re-occupying the eastern bank of the Dniepr, and to occupy the Crimea, the industrial district of Kharkov and the coalfields of the Donetz basin. The Army Group North is to follow up its offensive with the aim of cutting off Leningrad and joining up with the Finns.

The Army Group Centre (contrary to the precise intentions of von Brauchitsch) is to suspend the offensive against Moscow for the time being and send part of its forces to support the operations of the other two army groups.

☐ Admiral Darlan is appointed Vichy Minister of National Defence and head of the newly formed Ministry of National and Empire Defence. Marshal Pétain announces the adoption of a series of totalitarian measures, including the suppression of all political parties, the setting up of special courts, the reorganization of the economy on co-operative lines and the doubling of the police force.

RABINDRANATH TAGORE

The poet and mystic Rabindranath Tagore, leading interpreter of Indian thought to the Western world, died on 7 August in Calcutta.

Son of a noble Bengali family, Tagore was born in Calcutta on 6 May 1861; after studying for a time in England he returned home and soon displayed his considerable creative ability, composing poetry and songs inspired by popular culture and the Bengali countryside. Already during his youth, Tagore, influenced by his father Devendranath, leader of the religious sect Ādi Brāhma Samāj, sought to reconcile the principles of monotheistic religions with pantheistic doctrines, and advocated the ideals of reciprocal closeness, collaboration and integration of East and West.

In 1901, Tagore, now an educationalist and philanthropist, founded an international school, Viśva-Bhāratī, at Bolpur. The school encouraged and taught humanist, scientific, practical and creative disciplines which in Tagore's judgement were designed to broaden the feeling of unity of the spirit among the different races of mankind.

Winner of the Nobel Prize for Literature in 1913, Tagore divided his time between tecahing and travelling around the world to promote his philosophy and writings.

His political and social ideals, inextricably mingled with religion, induced him to oppose every form of nationalism and to embrace total pacifism. Although he felt deep admiration for Gandhi, he did not support the latter's political views and his rebellion against British rule. But in 1919, having been knighted by King George V four years previously, he surrendered the honour in protest against the Amritsar massacre by British troops.

Top: aerial view of Moscow during a raid by the Luftwaffe. Above: Stukas bombing a fortified island at the mouth of the Dniepr.

13 August
Eastern Front Soviet government admits evacuation of Smolensk 'some days earlier'.

14 August
3.00 p.m.: Mr Attlee broadcasts news of the Churchill–Roosevelt meeting 'at sea' and the Atlantic Charter declaration.

15 August
Stalin receives message from Churchill and Roosevelt proposing joint meeting in Moscow.

16 August
Stalin broadcasts acceptance of proposed meeting in Moscow.
☐ British air raids on Catania and Syracuse. In Catania, according to Italian sources, there are 18 killed and 25 injured.
☐ British and Soviet governments send a protest note about German infiltration of Iran.

17 August
Eastern Front In the northern sector the Germans capture the ancient city of Novgorod, north of Lake Ilmen and south-east of Leningrad.
In the southern sector they take Dniepropetrovsk, on the lower Dniepr. They are already threatening Kharkov and the Donetz basin and the Crimea. Odessa is surrounded.
☐ The US President and Secretary of State tell the Japanese ambassador the conditions that the United States consider indispensable if talks are to be resumed leading to a possible 'Pacific Conference'.

18 August
Eastern Front Russians evacuate Nikolayev.
☐ Churchill returns to England.

20 August
More British air raids on Sicily, this time on Augusta.

21 August
Eastern Front Hitler revises the instructions given in Directive No. 34

of 12 August; besides occupying the Donetz basin the German armies must also cut off the Russians from their petrol supplies from the Caucasus.

In the central sector the 6th Army and I *Panzergruppe* begin the battle for Kiev.

On the Leningrad front, in the northern sector, the defenders occupy a salient some 12 miles wide and 120 miles deep, while the Germans advance towards the Gulf of Finland south-west of the city and towards Lake Ladoga to the south-east. The Soviet commander orders his troops to withdraw from the salient to avoid being encircled. The same day the Germans capture Chudovo, cutting the main railway line between Leningrad and Moscow.

Marshal Voroshilov calls on the people of Leningrad to defend their city at all costs.

22 August
Eastern Front German sources give the losses suffered by the Russians during the first two months since the invasion as 1,250,000 prisoners, 14,000 tanks, 15,000 guns and 11,250 aircraft. The dead, according to the Germans, must number over three and a half million. Soviet sources give lower figures.

☐ A German officer is killed in Paris – the signal for the beginning of active resistance to the occupying forces and the 'collaborationist' Vichy authorities.

23 August
Eastern Front The II *Panzergruppe* and 2nd Army move south towards Gomel and Starodub, thus complying with the Führer's directive that the Army Group Centre should reinforce the Army Group South's offensive.

24 August
Eastern Front The Russians launch a counter-attack in Gomel sector.

25 August 1941: a British tank column in the Khyber Pass during the advance into Iran. Britain and Russia force the Iranian government to accept Allied protection.

25 August
Iran British and Soviet troops enter Iran.

The British and Soviet ambassadors in Teheran present an ultimatum to the Iranian government, requiring them to accept the 'protection' of the Allies. In concerted movements Soviet troops, from the north, make directly for the capital, while the British, coming up from the Persian Gulf and Iraq, occupy the Abadan oilfields. Shah Reza Pahlevi protests against the Allies' aggression. Among other things, this action by the Allies has the effect of reinforcing Turkish determination to remain neutral.

☐ An Anglo-Canadian-Norwegian commando unit lands on the Norwegian island of Spitzbergen, in the Arctic Ocean, and destroys mineral deposits and installations that are being used by the Germans.

25–29 August
Eastern Front Mussolini visits the German headquarters on the Eastern Front and spends two days in talks with Hitler and other German political and military leaders; then, accompanied by the Führer, he inspects the southern front and, together with Marshal von Rundstedt and General Messe, reviews the Italian troops engaged in recent operations.

26 August
Eastern Front In the central sector, in the area of Velikiye Luki (north of Vitebsk), the Russians launch a counter-attack. The Germans halt it within 24 hours.

Iran British troops occupy oil installations at Abadan.

27 August
Iran A new government is formed and asks for an armistice with the Allies. The treaty, by which the British and Russians will station troops at strategic points in the country, but not in the capital, is signed next day. The Allies' purpose in occupying Iran is to protect them-

selves in advance against a possible pincer movement by the Germans through Egypt and Syria.

☐ The Japanese government protests to Washington against repeated violation of Japanese territorial waters by American ships carrying aid to the Russian port Vladivostok.

☐ French patriot Paul Colette fires four shots during ceremony at Versailles, wounding Pierre Laval, Vice-President of the Council in the Vichy government, and Marcel Déat, an enthusiastic collaborator and director of the German-controlled newspaper *L'Œuvre*. Many arrests and executions of so-called 'Communists' follow.

28 August

Eastern Front In the northern sector, the Germans complete their mopping-up operations in Estonia and continue their pressure on Leningrad.

Russians destroy the great Zaporozhye dam on the Dniepr to prevent the Germans benefiting from it.

29 August

Eastern Front The Finns recapture Viipuri, which they had to cede to the Soviet Union after the earlier fighting. This brings them very close to Leningrad; but, despite German insistence, they halt on their pre-war frontier – a decision taken on political grounds. Only a few of their units enter Russian territory, pressing on

as far as the river Svir and Lake Oneg, thus cutting Russian communications between the White Sea and the Baltic.

Iran Hostilities cease.

☐ In Yugoslavia General Milan Nedić allows himself to be nominated as head of a puppet government set up by the Germans in Serbia.

30 August

Eastern Front In the northern sector the Germans capture Mga, cutting the last railway connexion between Leningrad and the rest of the country.

In the central sector the Russians launch another ineffective counter-offensive north of Gomel. The

A long column of **Russian** prisoners on the march in the Lower Ukraine.

armoured groups of Kleist and Guderian throw all their forces into the battle for Kiev, which is strenuously defended by Marshal Budenny's troops.

31 August
RAF raid on Bremen.
□ UK civilian casualties for August: 169 killed, 136 injured.

1 September
Eastern Front Northern sector. The German attacking force reaches the south shore of Lake Ladoga and takes a great part of the left bank of the Neva, though without succeeding in crossing the river. They also take Schlüsselberg (since 1944 called Petrokrepost), and Leningrad is cut off from the rest of the country except by water across Lake Ladoga. The Russian position south-west of the city is equally desperate; the Germans have established bridgeheads on the Gulf of Finland, only a few miles from Leningrad. To the south the Army Group North attacks vigorously in the Kolpino and Pulkovo sectors, 15 miles from the city. The Russians still have a major bridgehead at Oranienbaum, opposite Kronstadt and west of the point at which the Germans have established themselves on the Gulf of Finland.
□ The German government orders that all Jews over six years old must wear a badge with the Star of David sewn on their chest as 'a mark of shame'.

2 September
RAF daylight raids over Northern France, Channel, and Occupied Territory in Europe.
□ In Japan an Air Defence Bureau is formed to advise on air raid precautions throughout the country.

4 September
Eastern Front The Finns capture Beloostrov, the frontier station 20 miles from Leningrad, but are driven out again next day. In any case, for political reasons, they do not wish to advance beyond the borders of east-

Top: a German supply waggon passing through a burning village during a Russian bombardment. Centre: Russian dead in an emplacement in southern Ukraine. Above: German armoured units entering Poltava.

ern Karelia, the area they had to cede to the Russians the previous year. The Germans now begin the shelling of Leningrad. Von Leeb's troops threaten the city directly, and a long, hard siege begins.

General Jodl visits General Mannerheim and tries to persuade him to continue his offensive, but the old general refuses.

Atlantic The US destroyer *Greer* reports that she has been attacked by a German submarine 175 miles south-west of the Icelandic coast.

☐ Mr Mackenzie King, Canadian Prime Minister, speaks at the Mansion House, London: 'We in Canada cannot all share your dangers, but we are proud to share your burdens. We are determined to share them to the utmost of our strength.'

German soldiers in the Pripet marshes protect themselves against mosquitoes.

5 September

Gurkha and Scottish troops arrive in Malaya to strengthen defences.

7 September

Eastern Front Violent shelling and bombing of Leningrad. Delayed-action mines are also dropped and cause many deaths. But the greatest problem for the defenders is how to feed three million people.

Mediterranean The US merchant ship *Steel Seafarer* is sunk by German aircraft in the Gulf of Suez.

☐ Heaviest air raid on Berlin to date. Two-hour attack by strong RAF bomber force, including four-engined Stirlings and Halifaxes. Attack was made on anniversary of first German mass attack on London.

8 September

Eastern Front The Finns cut the Leningrad–Murmansk railway line at Lodeinoe Pole and threaten Petro-

Above: some of the 600,000 prisoners taken by the Germans during the battle for Kiev, assembled near Uman.

HANS SPEMANN

On 12 September the German zoologist Hans Spemann, who won the Nobel Prize for Medicine and Physiology in 1935, died in Freiburg.

Born in Stuttgart in 1869, Spemann studied natural sciences at Würzburg and became professor of zoology at Rostock University. In 1914 he was appointed director of the Kaiser Wilhelm Institute of Biology in Berlin.

His studies into the mechanics of vertebrate development were of key importance in evolving the discipline of experimental embryology.

zavodsk on Lake Oneg. USSR Supreme Council decrees removal of entire population (some 600,000) of the German Volga Republic to Asiatic Russia as a precaution against possible sabotage.

☐ Serious disturbances reported in Paris, leading to arrest of some 120 Jewish 'hostages'.

9 September
Eastern Front The *Azul* (Blue) Division, recruited from Spanish anti-Communist volunteers, is deployed in the Leningrad sector. The German bombardment of the city continues relentlessly.

☐ British air raid on Reggio Calabria and Messina. These attacks on Sicily have become almost daily occurrences, and the Italians can do little to check them.

10 September
Eastern Front The combined forces of the Army Groups Centre and South converge on Kiev, where they meet with determined Russian resistance. Von Kleist's armoured group crosses the Dniepr, and so does Guderian's, which reaches Konotop.

☐ Further anti-Nazi measures taken in Chile and Argentina.

11 September
Eastern Front Northern sector: The situation in Leningrad is desperate.

The King's African Rifles accord the honours of war to the Italian garrison at Wolkefit, near Gondar, after their surrender on 28 September. This was one of the last fortresses in Abyssinia to hold out against the Allies.

The daily bread ration, fixed on 2 September at 21 oz for workmen, 12 oz for clerical workers and 10½ oz for all others, including children, is reduced by a further 1¾ oz. And bread is made out of anything – rye, chaff, flax, soya, malt. People conceal their dead so that they can use their ration cards. There is no lighting, no heating. People are beginning to die of cold and starvation.

Voroshilov goes into the front line in the hope of finding a hero's death in the field. Then Zhukov arrives to save the city from chaos, and in the course of three days he completely reorganizes the defences. The Germans are convinced they can starve the city into submission; but Hitler does not want it to surrender – he does not want to be burdened with the task of maintaining this enormous mass of people. German troops are ordered to shoot down all who flee from the city towards their lines, but not to prevent anyone from escaping towards the east, where they will add to the prevailing chaos. Meanwhile, under Zhukov's vigorous leadership, Leningrad is fortified street by street.

☐ Following the attack on the destroyer *Greer* on 4 September, President Roosevelt gives the order 'Shoot first!' to all ships patrolling the security zone. In effect, President Roosevelt is ordering the American navy to attack any ships that threatens the free passage of US merchant ships and ships with US escorts.

12 September

Eastern Front The *Panzergruppen* of von Kleist and Guderian join up at Rovno, 105 miles east of Kiev, trapping the 5th and 38th Armies of Budenny and Timoshenko in an enormous pocket. The II *Luftflotte* has made a valuable contribution to these operations.

☐ Norway. Quisling government bans Boy Scout and other youth organizations; all boys over nine obliged to join National Socialist youth organization.

15 September

Eastern Front Northern sector: Leningrad has escaped the immediate danger of capture by the Germans, but the only hope of raising the siege is by opening a breach in the circle of steel that now completely surrounds the city except where Lake Ladoga offers a route across the water. The heroic efforts to counter-attack are in vain; the line formed by the Germans between Mga and Sinyavino is so solid that it is not breached until February 1944. At present, food reserves in the fortress are enough for one month on an average, though sugar stocks will last

Two German despatch riders rest during fighting on the Eastern Front.

'THE MALTESE FALCON'

In the late 1930s Humphrey Bogart, already forty years old and having appeared in a series of notably successful films (*The Petrified Forest*, 1936; *Dead End*, 1937; and *Roaring Twenties*, 1939) seemed destined to continue his acting career playing negative characters such as gangsters, associated with the likes of Cagney and Raft. Two classic films which appeared in 1941, Raoul Walsh's *High Sierra* and John Huston's *Maltese Falcon*, suddenly changed Bogart's future, turning him into an accomplished actor and major star.

The Maltese Falcon, the first film directed by Huston after a long apprenticeship as jack-of-all-trades and scriptwriter, was first shown in New York on 3 October and proved to be a landmark in the history fo the *film noir*. Based on the novel of the same name by Dashiell Hammett, it was a tough, fast-paced and thrilling detective

Bogart and Mary Astor in a scene from the film.

story. Bogart gave a polished, naturalistic performance as Sam Spade, the disenchanted 'private eye', cynical, unscrupulous yet basically 'straight', every line of his face expressive of romantic sadness.

two months.

16 September

Iran In contravention of the armistice terms, the Allies occupy the capital, Teheran. The Shah abdicates in protest in favour of his son, Mohammad Reza Shah, who succeeds to the throne next day.

☐ The US Marine Department announces that the Atlantic fleet will protect convoys of materials to those countries affected by the Lend-Lease Act up to the 26°W meridian.

☐ In France ten 'hostages', mainly Jewish (including a 19-year-old boy), executed in reprisal for anti-German attacks.

17 September

Eastern Front The Germans occupy the basin of the lower Dniepr and pierce the outer defences of Kiev.

18 September

President Roosevelt asks congress for additional $5,985 million for Lend-Lease supplies.

19 September

Eastern Front End of the battle of Kiev. The Germans occupy the city, (the third largest in Russia), but in so doing they lose many dead, for the Russians have left mines everywhere. They have also left much of the city in ruins.

According to German sources they captured 600,000 prisoners in the Kiev sector, and the Russians lost 2,500 guns and 1,000 tanks. Again, according to the Germans, from the start of operations up to 31 August the Wehrmacht lost on the Eastern Front 86,000 dead, 20,000 missing and 292,000 wounded. About 4,000 men were taken prisoners by the Russians.

Mediterranean An Italian raiding party landed from the submarine *Scire* sinks 30,000 tons of Allied shipping in Gibraltar harbour.

20 September

German decree imposes 9.00 p.m. to 5.00 a.m. curfew in Paris.

21 September

Eastern Front Russians admit fall of Kiev.

23 September

The *Comité National Français* is set up in London with General de Gaulle at its head.

24 September

Mediterranean A big convoy leaves Gibraltar for Malta, escorted by a powerful naval force under the command of Admiral Somerville; the escort includes three battleships (*Nelson*, *Rodney* and *Prince of Wales*), five cruisers, 18 destroyers and the aircraft carrier *Ark Royal*. The operation is code-named *Halberd*.

☐ Fifteen governments, including governments in exile, adhere to the Atlantic Charter drawn up by Churchill and Roosevelt at their conference in the waters off Newfoundland from 9 to 12 August: Australia, Belgium, Canada, Czechoslovakia, France, Great Britain, Greece, Luxembourg, Netherlands, New Zealand, Norway, Poland, South Africa, USSR and Yugoslavia.

25 September

Eastern Front German forces make dawn attack on the Crimea.

26 September

The US naval command orders the protection of all ships sailing in US 'defensive' waters and the shadowing and, where possible, sinking of every Italian and German ship found in those waters.

27 September

Eastern Front In the southern sector the Germans take Perekop. They now stand at the threshold of the Crimean peninsula. Heavy rain reported throughout whole Russian front.

Mediterranean An Italian S-84 aircraft of 36 Squadron hits the battle-

ship *Nelson* with a torpedo, but causes no serious damage. The *Nelson* is one of the ships escorting the convoy that left Gibraltar for Malta on 24 September.

☐ Unrest and repressive measures are reported from Bohemia, where Himmler's deputy, Reinhard Heydrich (the 'Aryan racist with a Jewish grandmother'), has been appointed *Reichsprotektor* in place of the less rigid von Neurath.

☐ In Baltimore naval dockyard in the USA the *Patrick Henry* is launched, the first of the 'Liberty ships', 10,000-ton merchantmen of highly standardized design, of which thousands are to be built before the end of the war.

28 September

Italian East Africa Italian garrison of Wolkefit, in Amhara, on the Adowa-Gondar road, surrenders to the British.

Malta The British convoy (Operation *Halberd*) reaches Malta almost intact and lands a total of 50,000 tons of supplies, giving the island enough provisions to hold out until May 1942.

29 September

Eastern Front In the southern sector the Germans enter the Donbas region, the important coal basin of the Don river.

A conference opens in Moscow, attended by Lord Beaverbrook for Great Britain, Averell Harriman for the USA, and Vyacheslav Molotov for the Soviet Union, to work out a plan for urgent assistance to the Russians.

☐ Stettin and Hamburg bombed in night raids by RAF.

30 September

Eastern Front Northern sector: after hard fighting Finnish units break through the Soviet positions at Petrozavodsk.

Central sector: the German forces are lined up for their offensive against Moscow.

Southern sector: the German 11th Army, supported by Italian troops, defeat a Soviet force at Petrikovska. First snowfalls in Ukraine reported. *Western Mediterranean* Two British fighters sink the Italian submarine *Adua*.

☐ UK civilian casualties for September: 217 killed, 269 injured.

1 October

End of the Moscow conference between the Soviet Union, Britain and the USA on aid to the USSR.

2 October

Eastern Front Operation *Taifun* (Typhoon), the attack on Moscow, begins. The right wing of the Army Group Centre (2nd Armoured Army, Guderian's *Panzergruppe*) smashes through the Russian defences at Glukhov and sweeps on towards Orel, then suddenly turns north towards Tula, about 125 miles from Moscow. The 2nd Army and part of Guderian's armour converge on Bryansk. The 4th Army and IV *Panzergruppe* (Hoeppner) break through the right wing of the Soviet western front (under Konev) east of Roslavl and advance on Vyazma, and the tanks of Hoth's III *Panzergruppe* converge on the same town.

In the southern sector: the start of the battle of the Sea of Azov.

3 October

Eastern Front Hitler announces that Russia 'has already been broken and will never rise again'. He tells the German people of the start, the previous day, of a great offensive on the Eastern Front. This is the attack on Moscow, regarded as decisive. But the Wehrmacht's supreme effort fails in its aim.

Northern sector: the Germans take the defences of Tsarskoe Selo (now Pushkin), near Leningrad.

Central sector: the Soviet front at Bryansk, defended by the 43rd, 3rd, 50th and 13th Armies under the command of Timoshenko, begins to crumble. Two big pockets are formed north and south of Bryansk, while further north a third pocket is forming near Vyazma.

Southern sector: the German Dne-

propetrovsk bridgehead is strengthened.

4 October

Eastern Front Central sector: exploiting the success of Hoeppner's IV *Panzergruppe*, the XL Armoured Corps (Stumme) assaults Vyazma.

6 October

Eastern Front Germans launch two-pronged assault against Moscow. German armour breaks through the line from Rzhev to Vyzama and advances on Mozhaysk, only 50 miles from Moscow. The German attack is halted by the heroic resistance put up by the Russians, but six days later the Germans surround the town, advancing south towards Kaluga.

In the southern sector the I *Panzergruppe* (von Kleist) crosses the Dniepr and the Samara and reaches Berdyansk, surrounding the Soviet 9th and 18th Armies.

7 October

Eastern Front Fierce fighting continues over whole front. Russians announce evacuation of Orel.

8 October

Eastern Front In the southern sector the Germans reach Mariupol on the Sea of Azov; seven Soviet divisions are surrounded.

In the central sector the advance of the big German mobile formations begins to be seriously held up by the rain and mud.

9 October

Eastern Front German push towards Moscow continues; fighting particularly fierce at Vyazma (140 miles west of Moscow) and Bryansk (220 miles south-west of Moscow).

10 October

Eastern Front General Zhukov takes command of a new Soviet western front (or army group) formed for the defence of Moscow.

12 October

Eastern Front Bryansk evacuated by

Russians. Women and children start being moved from Moscow. In the central sector the Germans take Kaluga, some 100 miles south-west of Moscow, an important rail centre on the Moscow–Kiev line. The Germans begin the liquidation of the Soviet troops cut off in the Vyazma and Bryansk pockets. The bulk of Timoshenko's forces are wiped out; about 660,000 men are taken prisoner.

☐ Heavy RAF bombing raid on Nuremberg.

13 October

Eastern Front Russians evacuate Vyazma. Luftwaffe makes violent raids on railway communications round Moscow. Pressure by the Army Group Centre on Moscow continues, but the Russians defend the Mozhaysk line very vigorously.

14 October

Eastern Front In the central sector German armoured forces take Kalinin, north-west of Moscow. Moscow admits the position on this front has deteriorated.

15 October

In Poland the death penalty is prescribed for all Jews found outside the ghettos.

16 October

Eastern Front In the southern sector German and Rumanian troops capture Odessa

This is the day of the *bolshoi drap*, the 'great panic', in Moscow. The people finally realize that the Germans are at their gates and, not least on account of the reports of atrocities committed by the enemy (though exaggerated for propaganda purposes), all who can, flee to the east.

☐ Heavy British air raid on Naples. Italian sources report that 'some civil buildings were hit, resulting in 12 dead and 37 wounded; incendiary bombs started fires in parts of the city, but these were soon brought under control.'

☐ Japan. Prime Minister Prince Konoye is forced to resign; he is thought too soft in his dealings with the USA. The new Prime Minister, General Hideki Tojo, is a supporter of strong methods and enjoys the trust of the military.

☐ Pétain announces sentences on Daladier, Blum, Gamelin and other French leaders accused of responsibility for France's defeat. They are to be detained in 'a fortified place'.

17 October

Eastern Front Mopping up of the Vyazma and Bryansk pockets is completed.

Atlantic The US destroyer *Kearney* is torpedoed by a U-boat north-west of Iceland.

18 October

Eastern Front Central sector: Mozhaysk, east of Moscow, one of the key points in the Soviet defence system, falls to Hoeppner's *Panzergruppe*.

19 October

Eastern Front Stalin lets it be known that he is still in Moscow. He pro-

claims state of siege, and issues Order of the Day: 'Moscow will be defended to the last.'

In the Army Group South sector the German 11th Army takes Taganrog on the Sea of Azov, near Rostov.

20 October

Eastern Front Pressure on Moscow continues without respite. The Germans advance to within 65 miles of the city. The Russians throw all available forces into the fight. All looters and black marketeers are to

The 'convoy war' rages in the Atlantic.

'TWO-FACED WOMAN'

Thanks to her success in *Ninotchka* (1939), Greta Garbo had broken away from the typecasting that had confined her to dramatic roles, and now appeared in a new comedy, *Two-faced Woman*, again alongside Melvyn Douglas. Dealing with the theme of double personality, the film, directed by George Cukor, told the story of a skiing instructor who, afraid of losing her husband, decides to turn herself into her own lively and attractive twin. Plagued by production problems and stormy scenes in the course of shooting, *Two-faced Woman* was a rather feeble and incoherent film and was savaged by the critics. Its failure did much to persuade Garbo to abandon the cinema for good at the early age of 36.

Melvyn Douglas and Greta Garbo in *Two-faced Woman*, Garbo's last film.

Below: sailors from a German 'pirate' vessel hoist the swastika on board a captured British ship. Right: Yugoslav partisans resting after an engagement with the enemy.

Top: anti-aircraft position on a Moscow rooftop.
Above: A Russian partisan being led off for execution after her capture by the SS.

be executed without trial. Up to this date the Russians have lost 600,000 square miles of territory, with a population of 65 million. According to German sources, only partly denied, the Russians have lost 3,200,000 prisoners of war besides an unknown number of dead, 19,000 tanks, 28,000 guns and 14,600 aircraft. Some of this material has been destroyed, some captured by the enemy. And still, thanks to the fresh forces brought in from beyond the Urals and the tanks they are feverishly turning out from factories in Moscow and from those transported to the other side of the Urals (plus the 'scorched earth' policy in front of the invader), the Soviet commanders are able to organize counter-attacks everywhere. The T-34 and other heavy Soviet tanks inflict heavy losses on the enemy. Their wide tracks prevent them from sinking in the mud, whereas the German tanks often get stuck.

In Moscow 500,000 people, men and women, are mobilized and in record time construct a formidable ring of fortifications, digging 5,000 miles of trenches and anti-tank ditches, putting up 185 miles of barbed wire and making barriers out of felled trees.

☐ General Tojo reports to War Office, 'Japan stands at the crossroads of its rise or fall.'

☐ Assassination of Lieutenant-Colonel Hotz, Nazi military commander of the Nantes region.

21 October

British air raid on Naples; five waves of bombers drop hundreds of incendiary and high explosive bombs, causing casualties (dead and wounded) and tremendous damage.

☐ 50 'hostages' shot at Nantes as a reprisal for the assassination of Lieutenant-Colonel Hotz.

22 October

Tokyo has first black-out, and air-defence exercises are carried out throughout Japan in the following days.

23 October

Eastern Front Marshal Timoshenko takes over command on the southern front, where von Rundstedt's forces are making spectacular progress. The German 6th and 17th Armies carry out a brilliant turning

Poster urging the people of Moscow to defend their city.

manœuvre to attack Kharkov.

Malta Yet another Italian air raid on the island, hitting Micabba airfield and the airport installations at Valletta.

North Africa British bombers raid Benghazi and Tripoli.

☐ British Parliament debates question of aid to Russia. Some members raise questions of whether Britain is giving sufficient support to her ally.

24 October

Eastern Front Southern sector: German forces take Kharkov.

I *Panzergruppe* (von Kleist) advances into the Donetz basin.

25 October

Eastern Front Moscow: bitter fighting continues amid deep snowfalls. But the first German offensive against Moscow is exhausted, partly by tenacious Soviet resistance, partly by adverse weather conditions.

26 October

Eastern Front Russia confirms evacuation of Stalino, in the Donetz basin.

☐ RAF makes heavy night attack on Hamburg.

27 October

Eastern Front Southern sector: after ten days of fierce fighting the German 11th Army occupies the whole of the Crimea except for the fortress of Sevastopol. The whole industrial area of the southern Soviet Union is now in German hands.

Moscow area: Russians launch counter-attack.

☐ Formation of a 'Jeanne d'Arc Legion' in France to fight with the Germans in Russia is reported.

28 October

Eastern Front Central sector: in a final effort to smash the defences of Moscow, Guderian's tanks launch an attack in the area between Tula and Serpukhov, south of the capital. But the combination of mud and dogged Soviet resistance paralyses them.

North-west of Moscow the Germans reach Volokolamsk, 75 miles from the Russian capital.

29 October

Eastern Front The first divisions withdrawn from Siberia go into action against the Germans in the area of Borodino.

German air attack on Moscow.

☐ During afternoon British bombers carry out raids on the provinces of Reggio Calabria and Catanzaro.

30 October

Eastern Front Southern sector: the siege of the fortress of Sevastopol begins. It is to last another eight months.

Moscow radio admits that the town of Tula is in danger.

31 October

Eastern Front The Luftwaffe carries out at least 45 air raids on Moscow in a single day.

In the extreme north of Finland, German mountain troops under General Dietl (but who come under the command of the commander-in-chief of the occupation forces in Norway, General von Falkenhorst) make a thrust towards Murmansk, but are soon firmly checked by the Russians. In central Finland there are two German divisions of XXXVI Army Corps in action, while Finnish troops are operating from the area of Salla to the Karelian isthmus, though their offensive thrust is becoming exhausted.

Atlantic The US destroyer *Reuben James* is torpedoed by a U-boat and sinks in the waters west of Iceland; there are about 100 dead. This is the first US vessel to be sunk by enemy action in the Second World War.

☐ UK civilian casualties for October: 262 killed, 361 injured.

1 November

In the United States the US coastguard is placed under the jurisdicton of the military authorities.

☐ RAF daylight offensives over Northern France, the Channel and Occupied Territory in Europe begin.

3 November

Eastern Front Southern sector: German forces take Kursk, north of Kharkov.

Northern sector: the Germans try to take the whole southern shore of Lake Ladoga, including the rail junction of Volkhov. They fail, though they do succeed in cutting the railway line from Leningrad to Vologda, and march on Tikhvin, about 110 miles east of Leningrad.

□ British air raids on Sicily continue; places between Syracuse and Licata are attacked several times.

5 November
The Japanese send Saburu Kurusu to Washington as a special representative to try to heal the breach between Japan and America. But they are only throwing dust in the Americans' eyes; all their plans are already made.

6 November
The 24th anniversary of the October Revolution is celebrated in Moscow in Mayakovsky underground railway station. Stalin speaks in reassuring tones; as is only to be expected, he minimizes the Soviet losses and exaggerates those of the enemy. In the first four months of the war, he says, the Russians have lost 350,000 dead, 378,000 missing and 1,020,000 wounded. Next day he addresses troops in Red Square, spurring them on to the defence of 'holy Russia' and declaring that the Germans have lost 4,500,000 men, killed and wounded. Also, he says, while the German reserves are exhausted (and that is to some extent true), those of the Russians are only just beginning to make their weight felt. Although ardent appeals to patriotic sentiment and to the sacred union of Russians against the invader do not please all Party 'puritans', they are necessary and effective.
Atlantic The German pirate-ship *Odenwald*, camouflaged as an American merchantman, is captured by the US navy cruiser *Omatra* and the destroyer *Somers*.

7 November
Eastern Front Central sector: during the night it freezes. No longer held up by the mud, the Germans prepare to resume their offensive against

Moscow; but soon 'General Winter' will be holding them up once more.
□ The 'Lend-Lease' Act is extended to the USSR, though in fact the USA has been sending aid to the Russians since September. Between 1 October 1941 and 31 May 1945 the USA sends 2,660 ships to the Soviet Union, with 15,239,791 tons of foodstuffs and materials – most of all trucks, but also tanks, locomotives and complete chemical plants.
□ Heavy air raid on Brindisi.
□ Night raids on Berlin, Cologne and Mannheim in the heaviest RAF offensive of the war. But 37 out of 300 planes are lost due to exceptionally adverse weather conditions.
□ In the light of the US decision to arm their merchant ships the German government gives notice that U-boats will be ordered to torpedo all armed ships.

8 November
Eastern Front In the northern sector the XXXIX Armoured Corps takes Tikhvin. The object of the advance east of Leningrad, besides the complete encirclement of the city, is to join up with the Finnish forces. But it is not achieved.
Mediterranean During the night an Italo-German convoy making for Libya is sunk by a British naval squadron 200 miles east of Malta.
□ Euphoric speech by Hitler in Munich. The Führer exaggerates the enemy's losses even more than Stalin did; since the start of the war, he says, the USSR has lost 10 million men killed, wounded and prisoners, as well as 60–75 per cent of its industrial potential and raw materials. 'However long the war may last, the last battalion in the field will be a German one ... We are deciding the fate of Europe for the next thousand years.'

9 November
Yalta occupied by the Germans.

10 November
Eastern Front Already convinced that Operation *Barbarossa* (which should have taken the Germans to the Volga) will not now be completed

within the year, Hitler lays down new objectives for his armies in Russia. In the south, von Rundstedt is to take Sevastopol and Rostov–on–Don, cross the river and take Maikop and the Kuban oilfields. In the centre von Bock will resume the attack on Moscow, which is to be taken by a broad pincer movement. In the north von Leeb must join up with the Finns so as to cut off Leningrad completely.
Mediterranean Twenty U-boats enter Mediterranean. The request to the German high command for support by German submarines was made by Rommel personally, after a number of Italo-German convoys sailing to Africa had been sunk.
Atlantic For the first time American warships escort a convoy transporting troops – 20,000 Canadians leaving Halifax (Nova Scotia) for the Far East.
□ Winston Churchill speaks in London at the Mansion House: if Japan makes war on the United States, Great Britain will support America 'within the hour'.

11 November
Eastern Front In the southern sector the Russians counter-attack powerfully. An Italian regiment (the 80th, in the *Pasubio* Division) narrowly escapes encirclement by a Soviet division.
□ Hitler and Himmler give authority for the study of the 'final solution' of the Jewish problem: genocide.

12 November
Eastern Front Final plans are laid for the culminating offensive against Moscow: the II *Panzergruppe* (Guderian), with the 2nd Army protecting its flank, is to advance from Tula towards Kolomna; 4th Army is to attack frontally in order to engage the maximum number of Soviet forces; the III *Panzergruppe* (Hoth) and IV *Panzergruppe* (Hoeppner), covered on the left flank by the 9th Army, is to cross the Moscow–Volga canal and outflank Moscow to the north, and then turn south-east to join up with Guderian's force.
The temperature is 12° below zero;

A tank hit in an engagement in the Sollum–Halfaya zone during Operation *Crusader*.

next day it falls even lower. Many Germans suffer from frostbite.

☐ The Vichy government orders the internment at Fort Portalet, in the Pyrenees, of Léon Blum and Edouard Daladier, former French Prime Ministers, and General Gamelin, lately Commander-in-Chief of the French army.

13 November
Mediterranean The German U-81, commanded by Lieutenant Guggen-berger, torpedoes and severely damages the British aircraft carrier *Ark Royal* off Gibraltar. Another submarine seriously damages the battleship *Malaya*.

14 November
Eastern Front The Germans line up for the second phase of the battle for Moscow, but they are running short of equipment. Guderian has to transform one of his armoured corps, whose establishment calls for 350

tanks, into a 'brigade' of barely 50 effective tanks.

Mediterranean 2.15 a.m.: a terrible fire breaks out in the engine-room of the *Ark Royal*, putting the pumps out of action. At about 6 o'clock the ship sinks.

☐ British air raids on Catania, Brindisi and Acireale cause casualties and damage.

☐ The USA orders the evacuation of their marines from Shanghai, Peking and Tientsin.

15 November
Eastern Front In the central sector the new offensive for the capture of Moscow is launched. South of Orel, an armed column takes Maloarchan-gelsk.

In the northern sector the Russians are forced to withdraw from Volk-hov, on the Leningrad front.

☐ Large Canadian force arrives in Hong Kong.

16 November
Eastern Front In the southern sector, while the German 11th Army besieges Sevastopol, the XLII Corps (von Sponeck) takes Kerch, at the extreme eastern point of the Crimean peninsula.

Exceptionally severe wintry conditions reported from entire front. On the Moscow front Russian ski troops go into action for the first time.

17 November
In accordance with a decision taken some time ago, the Germans set up the *Reichskommissariat Ostland* for the administration and exploitation of Estonia, Latvia, Lithuania and White Russia (Belorussia). The commissioner is Alfred Rosenberg, the Nazi Party ideologist.

North Africa British commandos raid German headquarters in Libya; Rommel absent at birthday party.

☐ Naples heavily bombed by RAF.

An anti-tank gun manned by Young Fascists from the Bir el Gubi garrison.

☐ General Chiang Kai-shek urges immediate action by the democratic nations against Japan.

18 November

North Africa British launch second Western Desert offensive in Libya. The British 8th Army, commanded by General Cunningham, launches Operation *Crusader* against the Italian and German forces surrounding Tobruk. The immediate aim of the operation is to reinforce the Tobruk bridgehead; the final objective is to recapture Cyrenaica and, if successful, to invade Tripolitania.

☐ House of Representatives in Tokyo passes resolution expressing hostility to the USA.

19 November

North Africa The British 8th Army advances without meeting any serious obstacles and reaches Sidi Rezegh. At Bir el Gubi, however, on the left flank of the British line, the Italian *Ariete* Division puts up a stout resistance, while on the right flank the IV Armoured Brigade is involved in hard fighting with contingents of the German 21st *Panzer* Division.

20 November

Eastern Front Southern sector: after an unsuccessful attempt at a flanking movement, the Germans capture Rostov-on-Don by a frontal attack. In the northern sector, there is a stalemate before Leningrad, but cold and hunger are claiming more and more victims among the population. Rations are reduced for the fifth time since the German siege began; workers and special personnel are now issued with $8\frac{3}{4}$ oz of bread per day, with other foodstuffs bringing the daily ration up to 1,667 calories; children get a ration of 644 calories, and old persons and others not engaged in productive activities 466 calories. (A normal ration in a cold climate like that of Leningrad in winter would be over 3,000 calories.) 'The people were not strong enough to dig graves in the frozen earth. The dead were left beside the cemeteries wrapped in a blanket, and generally buried in common graves excavated with dynamite. In the spring thousands of bodies were discovered that had remained covered in snow throughout the winter.'

North Africa The British move the XXII Armoured Brigade from Bir el Gubi to Gabr Saleh to meet the threat from the Germans.

☐ The Japanese envoy extraordinary to Washington, Kurusu, with ambassador Nomura, puts forward his government's final proposals for the resolution of the crisis of relations between Japan and the United States.

☐ Dismissal of General Weygand as Delegate General of Vichy France in North Africa because of his non-co-operation with Germans.

Top: The German pirate ship *Atlantis* disguised as a Japanese merchantman. Centre: the crew of the *Atlantis* after she had been sunk by the British. Above: the *Barham* explodes.

21 November
Eastern Front In the southern sector I *Panzergruppe* completes the occupation of Rostov, and the 17th Army spreads out over the industrial and mineral area of the Donetz basin.
North Africa As the British VII Armoured Brigade, starting from Gabr Saleh, approaches Tobruk, it is attacked by Rommel's armour and loses 113 of its 141 tanks.
Italian East Africa The Italian garrison of Culquaber, near Gondar, commanded by Colonel Augusto Ugolini, surrenders to the British.

22 November
North Africa Heavy fighting between the South African 5th Division and and 21st *Panzer* Division near Sidi Rezegh, with large losses on both sides.
Atlantic HMS *Devonshire* sinks the German raider *Atlantis* in the South Atlantic.

23 November
Eastern Front On the Moscow front the units designated to cross the Moscow-Volga canal capture Klin, Solnechnogorsk and Istra, the last-named only some 30 miles from the capital, to the north-west.
North Africa Engagements between British and German forces take place in the whole of the area between Bir el Gubi and Sidi Rezegh.
☐ With the consent of the Dutch government in exile in London, US forces occupy Surinam (Dutch Guiana) to protect the strategically vital bauxite mines.

24 November
North Africa German forces in Libya receive air reinforcements. General Auchinleck arrives at Libyan battle headquarters.

25 November
North Africa Off Sollum the German submarine U-331, commanded by Lieutenant von Tiesenhausen, sinks the British battleship *Barham* with four torpedoes. Loss of 868 men.
Pacific American ships off Formosa (Taiwan) sight a Japanese military

convoy presumably en route for Malaya.

☐ On the fifth anniversary of its drafting, the Anti-Comintern Pact is renewed in Berlin; the signatories are Germany, Italy, Japan, Hungary, Manchukuo (the Japanese-controlled part of Northern China previously called Manchuria), Spain and now also Bulgaria, Croatia, Denmark, Finland, Rumania, Slovakia and the puppet Chinese government at Nanking.

26 November

North Africa Major-General Ritchie replaces General Cunningham as commander of the 8th Army.

☐ In Washington the Americans put before Kurusu, the emissary from Tokyo, their requirements to solve the crisis. These are: abandonment by the Japanese of the territory they occupy in China and Indo-China, an end to the recognition of the Nanking government and withdrawal from the alliance with the Axis. Clearly these demands cannot be met. But in any case the Japanese fleet has already, in complete secrecy, left its home ports to concentrate at the points laid down in the Imperial Staff's plans.

27 November

Eastern Front In the southern sector the Soviet 37th Army and part of the 2nd Army launch a counter-attack towards Rostov and the Crimea.

☐ Admiral H. R. Stark, chief of naval operations in the US supreme command, sends a 'warning of state of war' to the commanders of the American Asian and Pacific fleets.

28 November

North Africa The defenders of Tobruk break out and join up with the forces of the 8th Army.

Italian East Africa General Guglielmo Nasi, commanding the Italian garrison of Gondar, asks the British for surrender terms.

29 November

Eastern Front While the Russians dispute every yard of the German advance on Moscow, in the south they

'SUSPICION'

A year after *Rebecca*, Alfred Hitchcock made a new film set in England, based on *Before the Fact*, a novel by Francis Iles. A young English heiress marries a penniless and amoral playboy, and is persuaded by various circumstances to conclude that her husband is planning to kill her. The cynical conclusion Hitchcock had wanted was rejected for production reasons and the happy ending is somewhat artificial, although it does not adversely affect the high quality of the film.

Suspicion marked the first collaboration between the English director and Cary Grant, already a major star in Hollywood, having appeared in successes such as *Bringing Up Baby* and *The Philadelphia Story*.

Cary Grant.

recapture Taganrog and Rostov with a violent counter-offensive, threatening to surround the enemy forces. Von Rundstedt is forced to order his troops to retire behind the line of the river Mius.

Italian East Africa The remaining Italians in Gondar lay down their arms. Italian East Africa no longer exists.

30 November

Eastern Front German pressure on Moscow takes the *Panzergruppen* of Hoeppner and Reinhardt beyond Klin to Dmitrov on the Moscow–Volga canal, and Guderian's group cuts the railway between Tula and Serpukhov.

German losses (according to German sources) from 22 June to 30 November 1941: 162,000 dead, 33,334 missing, 572,000 wounded. In beleaguered Leningrad 11,000 people have died of starvation during November. In December the figure is to rise to 52,000. At Christmas, thanks to a relative improvement in the supply position, the bread ration for workers is increased from 8 oz to

10½ oz, that for clerical and similar workers to 7 oz a day.

Malta The island has its 1,000th alert.

☐ The Japanese Prime Minister Tojo, predictably rejects the American demands for the solution of the crisis between the two countries.

Japanese fleet is reported from British North Borneo as moving southwards.

1 December

North Africa Rommel succeeds in restoring the siege conditions round Tobruk to those existing prior to 28 November. Nevertheless the first stage of Operation *Crusader* has ended in a substantial strategic success for the British forces.

Eastern Front Russians counter-attack at Tula. Von Reichenau replaces Von Rundstedt as Commander-in-Chief of the Army Group South. Von Rundstedt has resigned because Hitler tried to cancel the General's order for a withdrawal from Rostov and Taganrog.

In the central sector the Germans are only 23½ miles from Red Square, at the terminus of a bus route.

□ Off the Australian coast the German pirate ship *Kormoran* sinks the Australian cruiser *Sydney*.

□ State of emergency declared in Malaya.

□ Marshal Pétain, head of the Vichy government, meets *Reichsmarschall* Hermann Goering at Saint-Florentin to discuss the future of Franco-German relations and the integration of France in the European 'new order'.

2 December

Eastern Front Guderian, the moving spirit of the attack against Moscow, establishes his headquarters at Yasnaya Poliana, a village 4½ miles south of Tula, the site of Tolstoy's house and tomb (which Soviet propaganda says has been profaned).

In the south, the Russians attack Von Kleist's rearguard as the main German force retreats to Mariupol. The Finnish government proclaims the re-annexation of the territories ceded the previous year to the Soviet Union.

4 December

Eastern Front In the northern sector the Finns (who, as stated above, have refused to undertake any initiative against Leningrad) take Hanko, the base at the entrance to the Gulf of Finland occupied by the Russians the previous year.

In the central sector the Army Group Centre continues its pressure against Moscow, particularly in the area of Tula, south of the capital. But the next night brings the great frost, 35°C below zero. The tanks will not start, the guns will not fire and thousands of men suffer from frostbite. The Germans have made the mistake, as Zhukov observes (though some people attribute the observation to Mannerheim), of wearing the correct size of boots; over the past two centuries the Russians have learned to wear outsize boots in winter so that they can stuff them with wool and straw and protect themselves from the cold.

North Africa Rommel launches a final, abortive attack against Tobruk.

5 December

Eastern Front While the German offensive thrust exhausts itself in front of Moscow for lack of equipment combined with the terrible winter conditions, the Russians, who have built up all the human and material resources they possibly can, launch a general counter-offensive all along the front, especially on the Moscow front. Here some 88 infantry and 15 cavalry divisions, with 1,500 tanks, hurl themselves on the 67 German divisions. The intention is to break through on the wings of the Army Group Centre, to surround and wipe it out. The Soviet cavalry is mown down, but the Russian tanks are plainly superior. Guderian vainly asks Hitler to allow a defensive rectification of the front. North-west of Moscow, in the area of Krasnaya

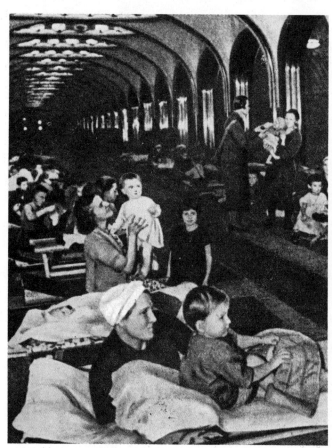 

Left: Women and children sheltering from German air attacks in the Moscow underground. Right: Russian soldiers in the streets of Moscow. Opposite: no more water in Leningrad; people melt the snow.

The war in Russia enters the inevitable winter phase. Although German armoured forces reach some of the industrial suburbs of Moscow, they are unable to take the city itself, kept at bay by the city's formidable defences, by increasingly vigorous counter-attacks by the new Soviet T-34 tank, and by harassment from partisans in the rear. Above: Russian cavalry charges the advancing enemy. Left: fighting in Mozhaysk. Below: German infantry north of Leningrad.

Polyana–Dmitrov–Kalinin, the most advanced positions of the German 9th Army and III and IV *Panzergruppen*, seven Soviet armies thrust forward. South of Moscow, in the Tula–Kashira–Mikhaylov area, three Soviet armies and a corps of Guards cavalry launch an attack against the II *Panzergruppe*. The Germans are completely taken by surprise by the violence and force of the attack.

☐ Stalin has a meeting with Eden in Moscow. The head of the Soviet government also meets General Sikorski, head of the Polish government in exile, and they sign a Russo-Polish pact of mutual assistance.

☐ Great Britain declares war on Finland, Hungary and Rumania.

☐ Japan tells America that movements of Japanese troops in Indo-China are purely precautionary.

6 December

Eastern Front In the northern sector the Russians counter-attack in the Tikhvin area east of Leningrad.
In the central sector the Russians penetrate the lines of the III *Panzergruppe*, north of Moscow, to a depth of 11 miles. South of the capital Guderian's II *Panzergruppe* resists desperately against the superior Soviet forces.

☐ Roosevelt appeals directly to the Emperor of Japan for peace.

7 December

Pearl Harbour, Hawaii At 7.55 a.m. local time, with no declaration of war, Japanese aircraft carry out a huge surprise attack on the big American air and naval base. Eight battleships are sunk or badly damaged; three cruisers, three destroyers, two auxiliary ships, one minelayer and one target-ship are sunk. 188 aircraft are destroyed or damaged on the ground. Reported casualties are 2,729 dead and 656 wounded.
The backbone of the American Pacific fleet has been eliminated from the conflict before it has even begun. It will be a long time before American industrial power can replace the

(Continued on page 182)

Pearl Harbour: a launch approaches the *West Virginia* to pick up a survivor from the water.

BACKGROUND TO THE JAPANESE–AMERICAN CONFLICT

19 September 1931
Japanese forces invaded Manchuria and during January of the next year completed its occupation.

27 March 1933
Japan, condemned by the League of Nations and the United States as an aggressor, left the League.

7 July 1937
On the pretext that Japanese soldiers had been fired upon, the Japanese occupied Peking.

26 July 1937
The Japanese opened hostilities against China without declaring war; next month they landed in Shanghai and marched from there to Tientsin. Roosevelt decided to apply 'economic quarantine' measures to the aggressor.

14 December 1937
Nanking fell to the invaders and within a short time all northern China was taken. But Chiang Kai-shek's troops, supplied with arms by the Western powers, continued to resist, and in March next year they inflicted a severe defeat on the Japanese. The Japanese set up a puppet government, the 'Central Government of the Chinese Republic', and decided to cut off Chiang completely by blocking the supply lines – the Yunnan railway (from French Tonkin), the Canton railway (British) and the Mongolia Road (Russian).

October 1938
The Japanese landed at Canton; the British and French, wedded to their 'appeasement' policy, sent only a protest note. But the British opened a new road across Burma and the Yunnan mountains to supply Chiang Kai-shek, while the Russians increased the amount of supplies sent across Mongolia. Washington also came to the aid of the Chinese with a credit of $25,000,000.

11 June 1940
The Japanese ambassador in London declared that any change of government would not bring with it an abandonment of his country's policy of neutrality in the European war.

13 June 1940
A compromise agreement reached between the British and the Japanese on the question of the British concessions at Tientsin. But only a few days later, following the collapse of France, extremists in Japan forced their government to take a tougher attitude towards the Western nations. Tokyo put forward a series of demands, foremost among them being the closing of the 'Burma Road', Chiang Kai-shek's supply line. London temporized, but fearing that Japan might take action in the east for which Britain was quite unprepared, agreed to close the Burma Road for three months. The decision took effect from 18 July, and actually the road was virtually impassable until October because of the monsoon rains. The decision was taken in agreement with the governments of Australia and New Zealand, the dominions most closely concerned.

End June 1940
The Japanese asked the Vichy government to close the frontier between Indo-China and China, and asked the Dutch for economic concessions. Roosevelt banned the export of certain goods to Japan, but the list did not include petrol.

22 July 1940
A new government came to power in Tokyo, obviously more intransigent in its relations with the West, headed by Prince Fumi-

The crew of a Japanese plane taking off to attack Pearl Harbour.

maro Konoye. The foreign ministry went to Yosuke Matsuoka. The new government, in close collaboration with the imperial staff, decided to ask for military bases in Indo-China and to demand that Britain cease all hostile activity. These requests, it was made clear with veiled threats, might be supported by force of arms. Tokyo switched its plans for expansion towards South-East Asia and the Dutch East Indies. A collision with Great Britain was foreseen sooner or later, though it was proposed if possible to avoid any conflict with the United States. On 1 August the new government declared that the object of Japanese policy was 'the setting up of a new order in greater East Asia'.

30 August 1940
The Vichy ambassador in Tokyo signed with Japanese officials an agreement by which the French gave an assurance of collaboration in the attainment of Japan's political and economic aims in Asia. They agreed to use of their territory in northern Indo-China by the Japanese for military operations against Chiang Kai-shek.

23 September 1940
After sending an ultimatum to

Saigon on the 15th, where the Vichy government seemed to be going back on its agreement, the Japanese landed troops in Tonkin. The Vichy representatives could only accept the situation.

27 September 1940
Japan joined the Tripartite Pact.

14 April 1941
A five-year non-aggression pact signed in Moscow between the Soviet Union and Japan. This strengthened the position of the 'hawks' in Tokyo, who opposed Konoye's policy towards the United States as being compliant and defeatist.

12 July 1941
The Japanese landed 50,000 men in Cochin China. The whole of Indo-China thus passed under their control.

26 July 1941
Washington's reaction to Tokyo's new expansionist move was to freeze Japanese deposits in the United States and ban the sale of aircraft fuel to Japan. Great Britain and the Netherlands followed the American example.

16 October 1941
Prince Konoye was forced to resign and was succeeded by an extremist, General Hideki Tojo. During the next weeks the feigned negotiations between Tokyo and Washington took place, as described above, until on 29 November the imperial staff decided that their attack on the United States should be launched on 7 December. (The fleet sailed to its concentration points three days before that date.) The mastermind behind the attack on Pearl Harbour was Admiral Isoruku Yamamoto, Commander-in-Chief of the Imperial Fleet, who had been given approval for his plan on 11 October.

AMERICAN COMMAND IN THE PACIFIC AT THE END OF NOVEMBER 1941

Minister of Defence: Henry Stimson (Under-Secretary, Robert P. Patterson). Minister of the Navy: Frank Knox (Under-Secretary, James V. Forrestal). The two departments collaborated through the Chief of Staffs Committee.

In the Pacific sector, under the Defence Department: the Far Eastern command with its headquarters at Manila (Philippines), Commander-in-Chief, General Douglas MacArthur, who was also Commander-in-Chief of all US forces in the Far East; the Hawaii command with headquarters at Pearl Harbour, Commander-in-Chief, General Walter C. Short.

Under the Navy Ministry there were: the staff of the Asian fleet, with headquarters at Manila, Commander-in-Chief, Admiral Thomas C. Hart; the staff of the Pacific fleet, with headquarters at Pearl Harbour, Commander-in-Chief, Admiral H. E. Kimmel.

TABLE OF THE JAPANESE COMMAND AT THE END OF NOVEMBER 1941

Prime Minister and Minister of War: General Hideki Tojo. Chief of staff of the army was General Sugiyama, and under him the area commands, regional commands and the command of the Southern Army Group under General Hisaishi Tarauchi. The army and navy worked together through the Imperial General Staff. Minister of the Navy was Admiral Shigetaro Shimada; Chief of Staff, Admiral Osami Nagano under whom was the High Fleet, commanded by Admiral Irosoku Yamamoto, in effect the director of operations.

Japanese troops at prayer before setting off for the front. Japan has 51 divisions in readiness.

Repulse Renown and *Repulse* are the only two battle cruisers to have taken part in both the First and Second World Wars. In 1934-1936 they were modernized by being fitted with a hangar and catapult for seaplanes and armed with anti-aircraft guns. During the Second World War, Repulse took part in the hunt for the *Bismarck*, and then was sent to the Indian Ocean in October 1941, where she was sunk by Japanese aircraft on December 10, 1941.

THE FORCES ON EITHER SIDE

At the time Japan entered the war, the Japanese navy consisted of: 10 battleships, 11 aircraft carriers, 18 heavy cruisers, 23 light cruisers (3 of them of out-dated design), 129 destroyers, 67 submarines and 13 gunboats, plus auxiliary craft.

When Japan entered the war the Allied navies had the following forces in the Asian–Pacific sector: 10 battleships (9 American and 1 British), 1 battle-cruiser (the *Repulse*), 3 aircraft carriers (American), 14 heavy cruisers (13 American and 1 British), 22 light cruisers (11 American, 7 British, 3 Dutch, 1 Free French), 100 destroyers (80 American, 13 British, 7 Dutch), 69 submarines (56 American, 13 Dutch), plus auxiliary craft.

It will be seen that the balance of forces between the two sides was fairly even, with the exception of aircraft carriers, (ships of decisive importance in the new type of war) where the Japanese were markedly superior. It is also worth remembering that a good half of the US fleet was engaged in the Atlantic.

Land forces:
At the beginning of the war against the USA, Britain and the Netherlands, the Japanese had 51 divisions on active service, 27 of them serving in China and 13 guarding the Mongolian frontier. In the new theatre of war they had about 400,000 men. Allied forces – British, American, Dutch, Filipino and Dutch East Indies – totalled about 340,000.

Air forces:
Here the initial superiority of the Japanese was overwhelming. Tokyo threw in 1,540 of its total strength of 2,400 warplanes. Total Allied strength in the Indian Ocean and Pacific was about 650 aircraft, fighters and bombers. And it was not only in numbers that the Japanese were superior. Their Mitsubishi A6M2 fighter (the famous Zero) was unrivalled on the Allied side for a whole year. Nor was this the only shock. Many of the Japanese ships turned out to be far superior in tonnage and fire-power than had been supposed. For instance, the *Zuikaku* class aircraft carriers, recorded in the naval year-books as between 12,000 and 15,000 tons, were actually of 30,000 tons. Like the land forces, their crews were meticulously trained, well armed, rigorously disciplined and ferocious fighters.

Zuikaku (Japan 1941). She formed a class with *Shokaku*. The flight deck was separate from the hull and supported by pillars at either end. There were two funnels, to starboard, which were angled outwards and below the flight deck. The island was small, housing just the bridge. *Zuikaku* was sunk on October 25, 1944, off Cape Engano.

DECEMBER 1941

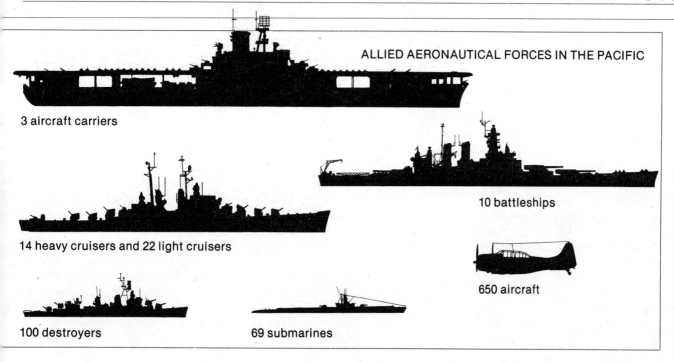

ALLIED AERONAUTICAL FORCES IN THE PACIFIC

3 aircraft carriers

14 heavy cruisers and 22 light cruisers

10 battleships

650 aircraft

100 destroyers

69 submarines

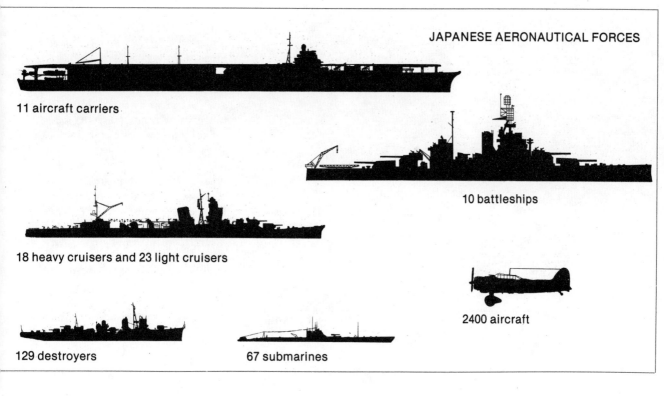

JAPANESE AERONAUTICAL FORCES

11 aircraft carriers

10 battleships

18 heavy cruisers and 23 light cruisers

2400 aircraft

129 destroyers

67 submarines

TORA! TORA! TORA!

The Japanese fleet secretly left Hikotappu Bay, at Iturup in the southern Kuriles, on 26 November, making for Hawaii by a little-used route, subject to severe storms. As an additional precaution complete radio silence was maintained.

The order to go into action reached the ships on 2 December: *Niitaka Yama Ni Nabore* (Climb Mount Niitaka), and was received with enthusiastic demonstrations by the ships' companies.

At dawn on 7 December, after the receipt of messages from secret agents sent to Hawaii in advance to the effect that everything is normal in the great American base (and also that there is no aircraft carrier in port at Pearl Harbour), the fleet takes up a position 250 miles north of the designated targets: the harbour and airfields of Hawaii. The fleet, under the command of Vice-Admiral Chuiki Nagumo, comprises the aircraft carriers *Akagi*, *Kaga*, *Shokaku*, *Zuikaku*, *Hiryu*, *Soryu* (carrying a total of 392 aircraft), the battleships *Hijei* and *Kirishima*, the two heavy cruisers *Tone* and *Chikuma* and the light cruiser *Abukuma*, nine destroyers (*Tanikaze*, *Urakaze*, *Isokaze*, *Hamakaze*, *Kasumi*, *Arage*, *Kagero*, *Shiranuhi* and *Akigumo*), three long-distance submarines (carrying midget submarines), and eight supply ships and tankers.

6.00 a.m.: The first wave of 183 attacking aircraft begins to take off from the carriers. There are 49 high-level bombers, 51 dive bombers and 40 torpedo-carrying aircraft, escorted by 43 Zero fighters (among the most outstanding aircraft of the Second World War). The Americans have been alerted since the beginning of the month, but they are less afraid

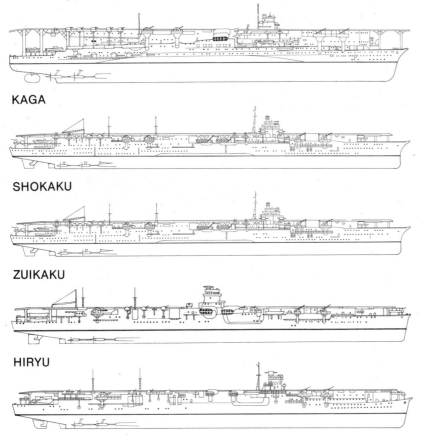

KAGA

SHOKAKU

ZUIKAKU

HIRYU

SORYU

Akagi built on the hull of an uncompleted battle cruiser, she had three flight decks with two half decks forward. She was built with two funnels instead of flues running to the stem. In 1935-1938 she was modernized and given a single full-length deck with two catapults forward and three lifts.

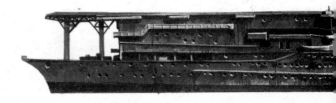

Aichi D3A1

Nakajima B5N2

of an attack from outside than of sabotage or even a rising by the 158,000 Japanese living in Hawaii. The attack takes them completely by surprise. As it happens, the two aircraft carriers based on Pearl Harbour, the *Lexington* and *Enterprise*, are at sea, escorted by three heavy cruisers and nine destroyers, the first at Midway, the second on the way to Wake Island.

7.48 a.m.: Captain Mitsuo Fuchida, commanding the first wave, gives the signal over the radio: *To, To, To*, a Japanese expression meaning 'Fight'. Then, soon after, he signals: *Tora! Tora! Tora!* ('Tiger, Tiger, Tiger'), which informs his squadrons that they have succeeded in surprising

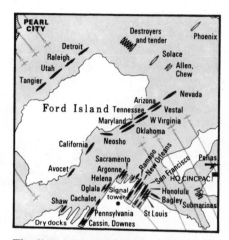

The disposition of shipping in Pearl Harbour on 7 December when the Japanese attack is launched.

the enemy. There are still 96 American vessels in Pearl Harbour.

7.55 a.m.: The whole of the seaplane base is wrecked by bombs dropped from the dive-bombers. Soon afterwards the first ship is hit, the destroyer *Monaghan*.

8.00 a.m.: Coming in like lightning, torpedo aircraft hit and seriously damage the target-ship *Utah*, the cruisers *Raleigh* and *Helena* and the minelayer *Oglala*. Next are the battleships *Arizona* and *Nevada*, then the *Oklahoma* and *West Virginia*. The battleship *California* is also hit by torpedoes. At last Admiral Kimmel issues the order to attack, emphasizing with involuntary irony: 'This is *not* an exercise!' Hickman Field airfield is destroyed; all the aircraft on it, drawn up in smart lines along the edges of the runway, burn in a fierce conflagration. Two minutes later the same fate strikes the army airfield at Wheeler Field, and after that the air base at Ewa, where 33 of the 49 aircraft are destroyed.

8.40 a.m.: The second wave, which took off from the carriers at 7.15 a.m., arrives at Hawaii – 134 bombers escorted by 36 Zero fighters.

8.54 a.m.: The aircraft attack. This time the American anti-aircraft

Mitsubishi A6M2 Reisen

Akagi

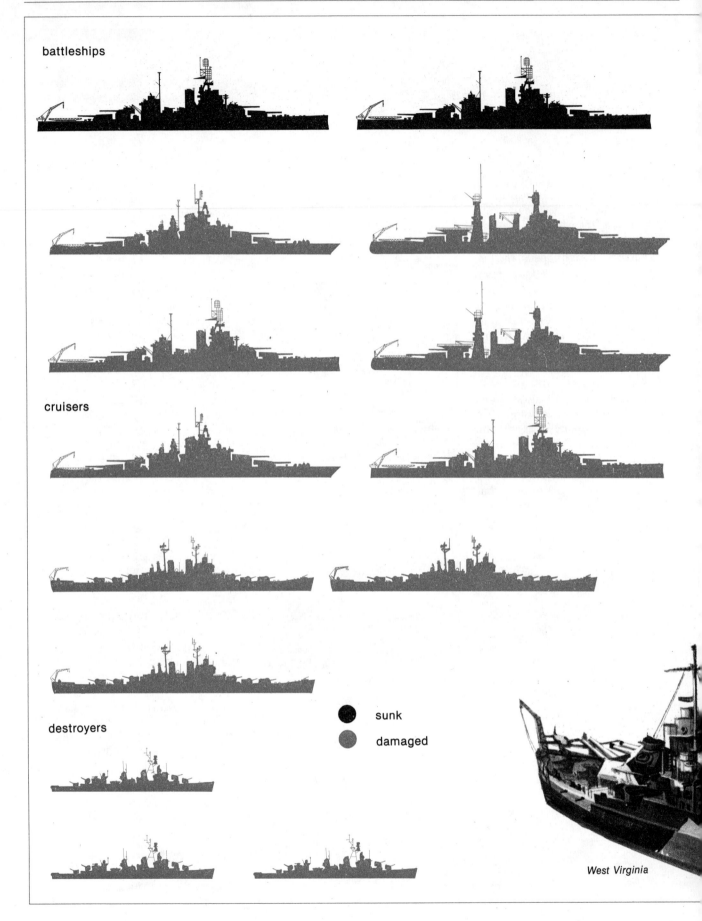

battleships

cruisers

destroyers

sunk

damaged

West Virginia

defences are not taken by surprise, and the co-ordinated fire inflicts some losses on the attackers, though without preventing them from carrying out their mission.

9.06 a.m.: The Japanese now attack the basin where the flagship, the battleship *Pennsylvania*, is moored, with the destroyers *Cassin* and *Downes*. Gigantic explosions shake the three vessels. The destroyer *Shaw*, in dry dock, is also struck. Fuel and ammunition stores explode and burn on every side.

9.45 a.m.: Aircraft of the second wave return to the ships. The naval squadron gives up the search for the two American aircraft carriers and sails for home at 1.30 p.m. Captain Fuchida argues that his aircraft can reconnoitre the sea towards the south-west in search of the carriers and their escort, but Admiral Nagumo does not want to run the risk of missing the rendezvous with the refuelling tankers, which are on the northern route. He would probably have been able to carry out the total mission assigned to him – the annihilation of the American fleet – but he is content with the remarkable results already

Aerial view of American ships at anchor in Pearl Harbour, showing the exploding bombs dropped by the first wave of Japanese aircraft.

Ford Island, in the bay of Pearl Harbour, during the Japanese air attack; in the centre of the photo, the seven battleships of 'Battleship Row'.

Planes damaged by the Japanese raid on Ford air base, Pearl Harbour.

achieved. The Japanese squadron reaches home with no enemy intervention and anchors in the Hashirajima roadstead on 23 December.

2.26 p.m. First reports of the attack reach America. The losses are severe. Ships sunk include the battleships *Arizona* and *Oklahoma*, the target-ship *Utah* and the minelayer *Oglala*. Seriously damaged – not sunk only because they were lying in shallow water – are the battleships *California*, *West Virginia* and *Nevada*; it will be a long time before they can be refloated and repaired. Also severely damaged are the battleships *Tennessee*, *Maryland* and *Pennsylvania*, the cruisers *Helena*, *Raleigh* and *Honolulu*, the destroyers *Cassin*, *Downes* and *Shaw* and the naval auxiliaries *Vestal* and *Curtiss*.

Altogether 188 aircraft are destroyed or damaged on the

Japanese pilots back from the attack on Pearl Harbour listen exultantly to the news on the American radio from Honolulu.

ground.

Japanese losses: 29 aircraft shot down or fallen in the sea in attempting to land on the aircraft carriers on their return, 5 midget submarines sunk, 64 dead or missing, one prisoner.

The US describes the 7 December as a 'Day of Shame' because of the treacherous nature of the Japanese attack. But in fact the Japanese government had sent the declaration of war to its representatives in Washington; it ought to have been handed to the Americans at the exact moment that would still allow the Japanese to take the American defences by surprise but would not lay them open to the charge of violating the first article of the Hague Convention of 1907. But there was a delay in the transcription of the message, so that it was only handed over while the attack was actually in progress.

American sailors lay wreaths on the graves of their dead comrades.

losses and achieve superiority.

When the Japanese diplomatic representatives in Washington call at the State Department to give notice of the breaking off of diplomatic relations between the two countries, the attack on Pearl Harbour has already been going on for half an hour.

Far East The Japanese II Fleet, commanded by Vice-Admiral Nobutake Kondo, escorts to the coasts of Thailand and Malaya a convoy carrying the Japanese 25th Army (General Tomoyoku Yamashita), whose task is to occupy the Malay peninsula and capture the supremely important British base of Singapore. Agana, capital of the island of Guam (the only one of the Mariana Islands administered by the USA, all the others being under Japanese administration), is bombed by Japanese aircraft.

Pacific At 11.50 a.m. Japanese aircraft bomb Wake (half way between Hawaii and eastern Asia), destroying 8 of the 12 American aircraft stationed on the island.

At 9.35 p.m. two Japanese destroyers shell Midway Island, garrisoned by a battalion of US Marines, to put the airfield out of action.

Thus, as becomes increasingly clear, the Japanese are striking everywhere. Their offensive is the fruit of a colossal effort of logistics and organization.

8 December

The USA and Great Britain formally declare war on Japan.

Far East: Malaya At 4.15 a.m. 17 Japanese bombers drop bombs on Singapore. The city is still fully lit, as in peace-time. There are 61 dead and 133 wounded, largely among the Chinese population. At 5.35 p.m. Admiral Phillips sails from Singapore with the *Prince of Wales* and *Repulse* and their destroyer escort, with the intention of intercepting the Japanese forces thought to be about to land on Singapore. In fact the Japanese have already started their landing operations at Khota Bharu, a port on the east coast of Malaya near the border with Thailand, and also at Singora (and

Chumphon), north-west of Khota Bharu, in Thai territory. The British air force can only offer the naval squadron help in reconnaissance, but no proper air cover.

Philippines The Japanese, commanded by General Masaharu Homma, launch their operations against this great archipelago, which lies along their future supply line for petrol which they wish to obtain from the East Indies. The main air base for the attack on the Philippines is Formosa (now Taiwan), where the Japanese pilots are specially trained to fly with the greatest possible economy of fuel, since they have to cover such a great distance to the Philippines. To defend the islands there are only 160 US aircraft, and 35 of those are Boeing B-17 Flying Fortress bombers, quite useless for defensive purposes. At 12.55 p.m. the Japanese make their first air attack on Luzon, the principal island of the archipelago. The Americans are caught unprepared, and lose 86 aircraft against 7 Japanese Zero fighters shot down. Besides Luzon, attacks are also made on the port of Davao in Mindanao island, causing considerable damage. The next day operations are held up by a storm. The Japanese occupy the island of Bataan, between Luzon and Formosa, without opposition.

The American Asian fleet, commanded by Rear-Admiral W. A. Glassford, leaves Iloilo in the Philippines in the direction of the Macassar Straits in the Dutch East Indies.

The crew of the US gunboat *Wake*, stranded in the port of Shanghai, fail in an attempted scuttling and surrender to the Japanese. The Japanese capture the American garrisons of Shanghai and Tientsin, and their aircraft bomb Hong Kong, Guam and Wake.

Eastern Front The Russian counter-offensive proceeds on all fronts. In the northern sector the German 16th Army has to withdraw from Tikhvin, along the metalled road between Leningrad and Vologda, captured on 8 November. The Germans only manage to avoid complete encirclement at the cost of great losses,

leaving behind vast amounts of materials, and retreating south of the Volkhov. The II Army Corps (100,000 men) still remains cut off from the rest of the army in the Demiansk area, southeast of Lake Ilmen, and has to wait, supplied by air, until 28 April 1942 before it can re-establish contact with the rest of the army.

The Germans' defensive line in the Moscow sector, held by the Army Group Centre, runs from Orel to Rzhev. To the left of this line the Soviets have succeeded in opening a dangerous breach, which the Germans are unable to close but can only contain until February 1942. The Wehrmacht holds the line Vyazma–Orel–Kursk–Kharkov with a series of strongpoints connected with one another – the system known as 'boxes'.

North Africa In Libya British forces re-take Sidi Rezegh and restore a supply corridor to Tobruk.

9 December

Far East More Japanese landings in Malaya at Khota Bharu and Singora, and also at Patani, in Thailand. Thai resistance to the Japanese ceases, and Japan is allowed to occupy the capital, Bangkok.

At 2.00 p.m. a Japanese submarine, part of Admiral Kondo's squadron, which includes the battleships *Kongo* and *Haruma*, spots the *Prince of Wales* and *Repulse* and reports to base at once, but gives the position wrongly. Some torpedo-carrying aircraft take off from the airfield at Saigon at dusk, but are unable to locate the enemy.

Pacific The Japanese land at Tarawa and Makin, in the Gilbert Islands, neutralizing the whole area by means of an air offensive.

Eastern Front Russians re-take Elets, south of Tula.

10 December

Pacific Japanese units land on the island of Guam and occupy it within a few hours.

Philippines The Japanese land at dawn on the northern tip of Luzon, near Aparri and Gonzaga, and on the island of Camiguin. American resistance is vigorous, but in vain. Powerful Japanese air attack on port installations at Cavite; one American destroyer, two submarines and a minesweeper are damaged. Two Japanese minesweepers and a submarine are sunk.

Malaya The *Prince of Wales* and *Repulse* are sunk by Japanese bombers and torpedo aircraft.

Eastern Front Russians take the offensive along whole front.

North Africa The British relieve the garrison at Tobruk.

11 December

Eastern Front The Russians announce the liberation of 400 places in the Moscow area, including Solnechnogorsk and Istra, and the destruction of 17 German divisions, including seven armoured and three motorized divisions. Rogachev and Stalinogorsk are also recaptured. This is the best day so far in the Russian counter-offensive.

Hitler announces end of winter campaign against Russia.

Far East: China The American garrison in Peking is taken prisoner by the Japanese.

The Japanese begin their operations against the British colony of Hong Kong, (which comprises the island of the same name and the so-called New Territories on the Chinese mainland). A violent air and artillery bombardment forces the 11,300 Scottish, Canadian and Indian troops in the garrison to withdraw from the mainland on to the island, leaving large amounts of arms and ammunition in enemy hands.

Pacific: Wake Island A Japanese squadron commanded by Admiral Sadamichi Kajioka, based on the Marshall Islands, and made up of the light cruiser *Yubari*, six destroyers, two patrol boats and two troop transports, arrives off Wake Island with the intention of taking it. The

Americans do not open fire or send up their aircraft until the invasion force is less than three miles off the coast. Two Japanese destroyers, the *Hayate* and the *Kisaragi*, are sunk, and Admiral Kajioka orders the force to withdraw. After this the Japanese always precede their invasion operations by heavy air raids.

Philippines Three thousand soldiers land at Aparri, in the north of Luzon, joining up with those already landed.

☐ Mussolini, from the balcony of the Palazzo Venezia, and Hitler, in the Reichstag, declare war on the United States of America.

☐ America declares war on both countries.

☐ Churchill gives review of war situation in the House of Commons: 'In Hitler's launching of the Nazi campaign on Russia we can already see, after less than six months of fighting, that he has made one of the outstanding blunders of history.'

Above: a Cossack takes cover behind his dead horse to fire on the enemy.

'TOM THUMB'S' GALLANT END

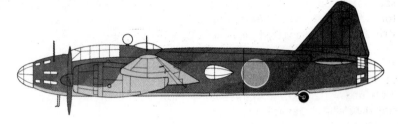

Mitsubishi G4M

On 2 December 1941 two great British ships, with an escort of four destroyers, arrive at Singapore – the so called 'arsenal of democracy', or 'Gibraltar of the East'. 'Force Z' should also have included an aircraft carrier to give air cover, but she had gone aground in shallow waters in Britain, and Churchill would brook no delay in view of the 'immense political importance' of having a strong naval squadron in the Far East. In command of the squadron is Admiral Tom Spencer Vaughan Phillips, an energetic and capable officer popular with his men, who call him 'Tom Thumb' on account of his short stature (though it was much the same as Nelson's). Phillips' force comprises the latest battleship, *Prince of Wales*, of 35,000 tons, whose main armament consists of ten 14-inch guns, the battle-cruiser *Repulse*, 32,000 tons, with six 15-in guns, and the four destroyers *Electra*, *Express*, *Tenedos* and *Vampire*. At last the great port, equipped with a dry dock big enough to take the biggest ships in the world, has a fleet. But aircraft are short: only 362 British aircraft for the whole of the Far East, 141 of them in Malaya, mostly Buffalo fighters which are no match for the brilliant Japanese Zero fighters. There are 22 airfields, but 15 of them are on grass and difficult to use in the frequent tropical rains. The land

forces consist of 88,000 men, British, Australian, Indian and Malay. The island of Singapore was strongly fortified towards the sea, where any attack was expected to come from, but completely undefended on the landward side, which was the way the Japanese planned to approach it. Five huge 15–in guns, six 9-in and 14 6-in guns were never to fire a shot.

8 December
At 5.35 p.m. Phillips sails with his squadron to meet the Japanese who are carrying out landings in the north of the Malay peninsula. Instead of observing the strategic principle of the 'fleet intact', with its consequent high deterrent value (a principle dear to Churchill), the admiral wants to join battle with the enemy. East of Singapore, but unaware of the British presence, two big Japanese warships, the *Kongo* and *Haruma*, are approaching with an escort of submarines, under the command of Admiral Kondo.

9 December
At 2.00 p.m., as described already, one of Admiral Kondo's submarines sights 'Force Z' and instantly informs the flagship, giving the position wrongly. 5.30 p.m.: Thinking they had been spotted by Japanese aircraft (which actually are giving air cover to the *Kongo* and *Haruma*

and have seen nothing) and so concluding that it would be impossible to take the enemy landing force by surprise, the British go about and sail for Singapore. At 8.15 p.m., at dusk, a formation of Japanese aircraft takes off from Saigon airport and search for the British ships for six hours, but they cannot find them because of the wrong bearings given by the submarine.

10 December
As light breaks, another Japanese submarine sights 'Force Z' and this time the precise position of the enemy is signalled to the admiral. Phillips has received a message to the effect that the Japanese will be attacking the harbour and airfield at Kuantan, on the east coast of the Malay peninsula. He decides to take the enemy by surprise. He arrives off Kuantan at 8.00 a.m. but there is no sign of the Japanese. One of his destroyers, the *Express*, enters the port and carries out an inspection, but there is nothing there. The squadron now sets a course for Singapore, maintaining radio silence so as not to attract the attention of the Japanese submarines. There is no danger of an air attack, the admiral says, since the nearest enemy air base is over 400 miles away, though in any case, on account of the radio silence, he cannot send a message to Singapore to ask for air cover.

The Japanese, however, on receipt of the new signal, have sent up several squadrons of bombers and torpedo aircraft. At 11.00 a.m. the British ships are located and the first attack comes at 11.20; the *Repulse* is hit but not severely. At 11.40 the torpedo-carrying aircraft arrive. By skilful manœuvring the *Repulse* manages to dodge 19 torpedoes, but the *Prince of Wales* is hit twice, once on the stern and once on the port side. The first torpedo damages the screws and the steering gear, bringing the ship to a halt so that it becomes an easy target. While the *Repulse* approaches the bigger ship, she is attacked by a second formation of torpedo aircraft and hit by at least five torpedoes. She sinks within six minutes, at 12.33 p.m. 513 men go down with her. Meanwhile the *Prince of Wales* has also been hit by three torpedoes. Out of control and ablaze from incendiary bombs, she sinks at 1.20 p.m., causing the deaths of 327 men, including the dauntless 'Tom Thumb', Admiral Phillips. The destroyers pick up 1,285 survivors.

This great victory has been won by the Japanese at a cost of only four aircraft. Following the virtual elimination of the American fleet at Pearl Harbour, the destruction of the two largest British ships gives the Japanese absolute mastery of the Far Eastern seas and of a great part of the Pacific barely three days after the opening of hostilities.

The crew of a Japanese aircraft carrier watch the take-off of one of the torpedo planes which sank the *Prince of Wales*.

12 December
Eastern Front Hitler replaces General von Bock, commanding German forces before Moscow, by General List.
Far East Japanese aircraft batter Hong Kong, the Philippine airfields and, particularly, Subic Bay, west of Manila. In Malaya they have carried out an average of 120 bombing missions every day since the beginning of the invasion. The airfield at Butterworth, in the north-east of the peninsula, has to be evacuated. At George Town (Penang) the raids claim 600 dead and 1,100 wounded.

The few British aircraft left, with the Dutch aircraft that have come to the Allies' help, are withdrawn southwards to defend the airfields, the harbour at Singapore and the Malayan capital Kuala Lumpur.
☐ French ships anchored in US ports are requisitioned by the Washington authorities.

13 December
Eastern Front Russian High Command reports progress on all fronts.
Hong Kong A Japanese spokesman lands on the island and hands the governor, Sir Mark Young, terms for

Mitsubishi G3M2

Map labels (reading from map):
- Isthmus of Kra, Guards Div
- SINGORA
- PATANI
- THAILAND
- KANGAR
- CHANGLUN, 12 Dec, JITRA
- ALOR STAR
- Kedah
- 11 Div, GURUN, 15 Dec
- KROH, 14 Dec
- KHOTA BHARU
- SOUTH CHINA SEA
- GONG KEDAH
- KUALA KRAI
- 9 Div
- KUALA TRENGGANU
- GEORGE TOWN, Penang, 16 Dec
- BUTTERWORTH
- Krian
- Perak
- TAIPING, 26 Dec
- IPOH, 28 Dec
- MALAYA
- KAMPAR, 2 Jan 1942
- KUALA LIPIS
- TELOK ANSON, 1 Jan 1942
- Slim
- 1 Jan
- 5 and 18 Divs
- KUANTAN, 30 Dec
- 2/3 Jan
- SERANDAH
- KUALA SELANGOR
- III Corps HQ (Percival)
- KUALA LUMPUR, 10 Jan
- 10 Jan
- PORT SWETTENHAM, 10 Jan
- Strait of
- Guards Div
- PORT DICKSON
- Malacca
- Aust 8 Div
- GEMAS
- BATU ANAM, SEGAMAT, 18 Jan
- ENDAU 16 Jan
- TAMPIN
- Sumatra
- MALACCA
- Muar
- MUAR 16 Jan
- KLUANG, 25 Jan
- DUTCH EAST INDIES
- BAKRI, PARIT SULONG
- BATU PAHAT
- 8 December 1941, Japanese 5 and 18 Divisions
- 8 December 1941, Takumi Force
- 31 January 1942, Last British and Commonwealth forces withdraw to Singapore
- JOHORE BAHRU
- SINGAPORE
- MILES 0 ... 100
- KILOMETRES 0 ... 160

surrender. The British refuse in the hope that Chiang Kai-shek's Chinese 7th Army, only some 30 miles away, can come to their help. But no such help arrives.

Borneo A detachment of Indian troops destroys the oil installations in Sarawak and Brunei, then retires to Kuching, capital of Sarawak, to defend the local airport.

Burma The British evacuate Victoria Point (on the Thai border in the southern part of the country, on the Kra isthmus), retreating north to the area of Tenasserim.

Hawaii An American squadron commanded by Rear-Admiral Fletcher sails from Pearl Harbour to bring help to Wake.

North Africa Rommel makes stand and counter-attacks in Western Desert. The battle rages for five days.

14 December

Eastern Front Russian advance continues on all fronts. Reports from Berlin admit great loss of materials through the freezing of vehicles, tanks and guns stuck in deep mud.

Thailand Japan signs a treaty of alliance with Thailand.

Malaya Japanese move into Penang and Gurun.

14–22 December

First setback for the U-boats. Using their 'wolf-pack' tactics they launch a long attack on convoy HG 76 west of Gibraltar. The Germans sink a destroyer, a tanker and three merchant ships, but lose five submarines.

15 December

Eastern Front In the northern sector the Russian forces that have crossed the Volkhov establish a bridgehead 30 miles deep on the other side of the river. In the Schlüsselburg (Petrokrepost) area the position of the Germans investing Leningrad becomes dangerous.

In the central sector, north of Moscow, the Russians capture Klin and advance on Kalinin. South of Moscow they relieve the threat to the town of Tula.

Burma A Japanese brigade enters the country across the Kra isthmus.

Malaya The Japanese open their decisive operations against Singapore. The 'impregnable fortress' is impregnable only from the sea, but not from the land.

16 December

Eastern Front After a week of intense fighting the German 9th Army is defeated and the Russians take Kalinin. In the Ukraine the Russian advance brings them to within 30 miles of Orel.

North Africa During the night Rommel begins to withdraw from the Tobruk sector. During the previous week's fighting the Axis forces have lost about 38,000 dead, against some 18,000 by the British, and have lost 300 tanks, against 278 by the enemy.

Borneo The Japanese land at Miri, in Sarawak, and at Seria, in Brunei. The 'oil road' of the Rising Sun is taking shape.

17 December

Eastern Front An official spokesman in Berlin admits the Germans have been surprised by the qualities of the Russian soldier. The Russians 'endure the severest hardships and disregard loss of life'.

Mediterranean In the Gulf of Sirte an Italian convoy bound for Libya and escorted by the entire Italian naval force (the battleships *Littorio*, *Doria*, *Cesare* and *Duilio*, five cruisers and 20 destroyers), commanded by Admiral Iachino, chances to meet a British convoy bound for Malta, with an escort under the command of Admiral Vian of six cruisers and 16 destroyers. The engagement opens at 5.40 p.m. after a prolonged 'long range observation', but it lasts only a few minutes with no damage to either side.

18 December
Hong Kong Japanese troops under cover of a heavy barrage land on Hong Kong island and occupy more than half of it within 24 hours. The garrison's position is desperate.
Borneo Off Miri the Japanese destroyer *Shinomone* strikes a mine and sinks.

19 December
Mediterranean Admiral Vian's squadron is caught in a minefield off Tripoli and loses the cruiser *Neptune* and a destroyer. At Alexandria an attack carried out by three midget submarines (the so-called 'pigs') against British ships is completely successful.
Eastern Front Hitler removes von Brauchitsch from his post and himself assumes the supreme command of the army. There is now a complete revolution among the top commanders. The Army Group Centre is entrusted to von Kluge, replacing von Bock. The Army Group North will be transferred on 15 January from von Leeb to von Küchler. And on 18 January von Bock will take command of the Army Group South, in replacement of von Reichenau, who has died of a stroke.
North Africa The Axis troops have withdrawn to Derna.

20 December
Eastern Front Goebbels broadcasts an appeal for gifts of warm clothing for German soldiers serving in Russia.
Philippines Japanese landing at Davao on the island of Mindanao. The invaders begin at once to turn the island into a vast fortified base.
□ Admiral King appointed to

Italian soldiers under British air attack in Cyrenaica fire back with an antiquated machine-gun.

supreme command of US naval forces.

21 December
North Africa In Libya British patrols enter Cirene and Apollonia, raid 150 miles inside Tripolitania.
Philippines The convoy sighted in the South China Sea by US reconnaissance aircraft on 16 December arrives at the Gulf of Lingayen, north of Manila, in the island of Luzon. Aboard the transports are 43,000 men of the Japanese 14th Army, under the command of General Masaharu Homma. The invasion has started in earnest.

22 December
Eastern Front The inexorable Russian pressure on all fronts continues.

A Russian report claims that the Red Army has recaptured 1,500 cities, towns and villages in the past 25 days.
Philippines at 1.00 a.m. the Japanese land at Bauang, Aringay and Agoo 40 miles further north than the point at which MacArthur had expected them and at which he had concentrated the bulk of his available artillery. By 11.00 a.m. the Japanese have firmly established their bridgehead and made contact with the troops landed near Aparri and Gonzaga on the 10th.
Wake 11.30 p.m.: The Japanese land on the island. This time, to avoid a new reverse, they have sent a powerful force, two aircraft carriers and two heavy cruisers with destroyer escort, under the command of

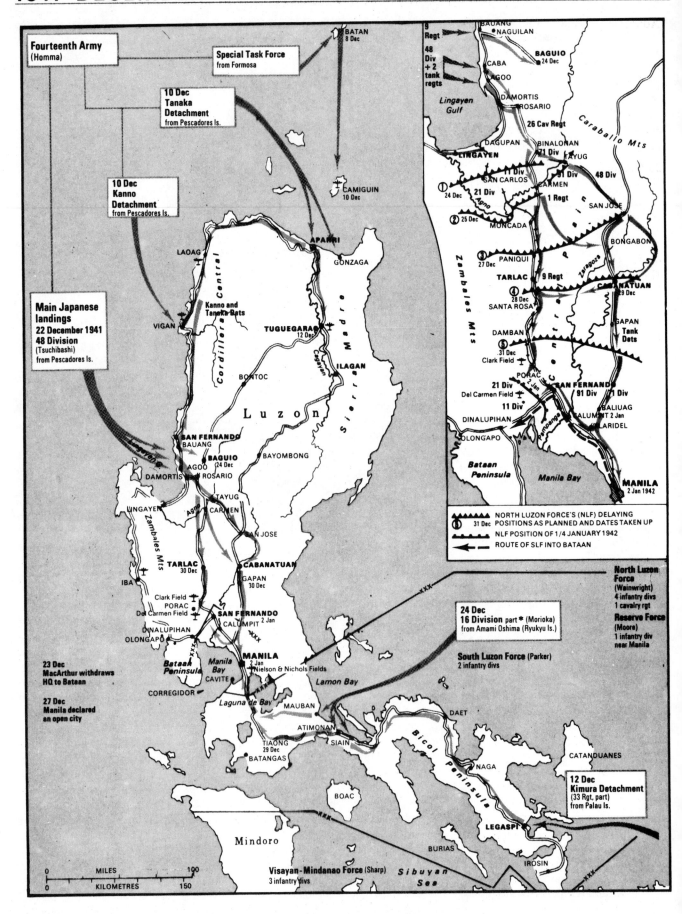

Fourteenth Army
(Homma)

Special Task Force
from Formosa

BATAN
8 Dec

10 Dec
Tanaka
Detachment
from Pescadores Is.

10 Dec
Kanno
Detachment
from Pescadores Is.

CAMIGUIN
10 Dec

Main Japanese
landings
22 December 1941
48 Division
(Tsuchibashi)
from Pescadores Is.

APARRI

LAOAG

GONZAGA

Kanno and
Tanaka Dets.

VIGAN

TUGUEGARAO
12 Dec

BONTOC

ILAGAN

Cordillera Central

Cagayan

Sierra Madre

Luzon

SAN FERNANDO
BAUANG

BAGUIO
24 Dec

BAYOMBONG

AGOO
ROSARIO
DAMORTIS

TAYUG

LINGAYEN

CARMEN

Agno

SAN JOSE

Zambales Mts

TARLAC
30 Dec

CABANATUAN

GAPAN
30 Dec

IBA

Clark Field
PORAC
Del Carmen Field

SAN FERNANDO
CALUMPIT 2 Jan

DINALUPIHAN
OLONGAPO

23 Dec
MacArthur withdraws
HQ to Bataan

27 Dec
Manila declared
an open city

Bataan
Peninsula

Manila
Bay
CAVITE

CORREGIDOR

MANILA
2 Jan
Nielson & Nichols Fields

Laguna de Bay

MAUBAN

ATIMONAN

TIAONG
29 Dec
BATANGAS

SIAIN

Lamon Bay

24 Dec
16 Division part * (Morioka)
from Amami Oshima (Ryukyu Is.)

South Luzon Force (Parker)
2 infantry divs

BOAC

Mindoro

Sibuyan Sea

Bicol Peninsula

DAET

NAGA

CATANDUANES

12 Dec
Kimura Detachment
(33 Rgt, part)
from Palau Is.

LEGASPI

BURIAS

IROSIN

Visayan-Mindanao Force (Sharp)
3 infantry divs

0 MILES 100
0 KILOMETRES 150

Inset (top right):

9 Regt

48 Div + 2 tank regts

BAUANG
NAGUILAN

BAGUIO
24 Dec

CABA

AGOO

Lingayen
Gulf

DAMORTIS
ROSARIO

Caraballo Mts

26 Cav Regt

DAGUPAN

BINALONAN
71 Div

TAYUG

LINGAYEN

SAN CARLOS
11 Div
24 Dec
21 Div

CARMEN

91 Div

48 Div

1 Regt

SAN JOSE

MONCADA
25 Dec

BONGABON

Zambales Mts

PANIQUI
27 Dec

Tarlac

TARLAC
9 Regt

CABANATUAN
29 Dec

SANTA ROSA
28 Dec

GAPAN
Tank Dets

DAMBAN

31 Dec
Clark Field

PORAC

21 Div
Del Carmen Field

11 Div

SAN FERNANDO
91 Div   71 Div

BALIUAG

CALUMPIT 2 Jan

PLARIDEL

DINALUPIHAN

OLONGAPO

Bataan
Peninsula

Manila Bay

Pampanga

MANILA
2 Jan 1942

▲▲▲▲▲ NORTH LUZON FORCE'S (NLF) DELAYING
POSITIONS AS PLANNED AND DATES TAKEN UP
① 31 Dec

NLF POSITION OF 1/4 JANUARY 1942

◄━ ━ ROUTE OF SLF INTO BATAAN

North Luzon Force
(Wainwright)
4 infantry divs
1 cavalry regt

Reserve Force
(Moore)
1 infantry div
near Manila

Admiral Kajioka. Two destroyers converted into swift troop transports land the first contingents. The battle is one-sided, and short.

☐ First Washington Conference: Roosevelt and Churchill meet for discussions on Allied co-operation. It is decided to set up a combined Anglo-American General Staff.

23 December

Wake Admiral Kajioka lands, accepts the surrender of the American garrison and officially takes possession of the island, re-naming it 'Island of Birds'. The relief fleet (Task Force 14) sent from Pearl Harbour is still 425 miles away and is diverted to Midway.

Philippines On Luzon MacArthur transfers his own headquarters to the fortified island of Corregidor, at the mouth of Manila Bay. Another 10,000 Japanese land at Lamon Bay.

Hong Kong Despite tough resistance, the Japanese cut the British positions in two.

24 December

Philippines The Japanese forces landed in Lamon Bay, in the south of the island of Luzon, take Atimonan and Siain and advance to join up with the units in the Legaspi area in the extreme south of Luzon. The forces landed in the north of the island also advance swiftly. The American and Filipino troops retire towards the Bataan peninsula, west of Manila, from both the north and the south of the island.

Japanese troops occupy the island of Jolo almost unopposed; this is the capital of the Philippine Sulu archipelago, only a short distance from Borneo. The threat to the Dutch East Indies thus draws closer.

Borneo A Japanese convoy breaks through attacks by British and Dutch aircraft and Dutch submarines to land troops in the area of Kuching, capital of Sarawak. The garrison of local troops, which has taken care to destroy the airfield, asks to be allowed to escape to Dutch Borneo, but is ordered to do everything possible to slow down the enemy advance. The Dutch withdraw their air force from Borneo to Sumatra.

Malaya The 11th Indian Division organizes a defence line in depth in the area of the river Slim and the town of Kampar, half-way down the Malay peninsula to the north of Kuala Lumpur, on the west coast.

Burma The Japanese begin a series of violent air attacks on Rangoon to assure themselves of air superiority. These attacks are continued until the end of February 1942.

25 December

Hong Kong British garrison surrenders after siege lasting 17 days. At 9.00 a.m. the Japanese present their surrender terms, proposing a three-hour cease-fire. Receiving no reply, they open fire again at midday. At 3.30 p.m., recognizing the possibility of a useless massacre, the British commander gives the order to surrender, and this is carried out at 5.30 p.m. The Chinese population of the island, with their ancient prudence, and also under the influence of Japanese propaganda heralding the 'common Asian sphere of prosperity', gives the victors a triumphant welcome, many of them waving Rising Sun flags.

China The Japanese open an offensive against Changsha, in Hunan province.

Philippines Rear-Admiral F. W. Rockwell is appointed to direct all US naval activities in the Philippines. The Japanese advance from the north of Luzon and succeed in crossing the river Agno at a point where the American line is not consolidated. The American forces defending the southern part of the island retire on to Bataan peninsula closely followed by the Japanese, who occupy Sampoloc and Pagbilao.

The Japanese complete the occupation of Jolo in the Sulu archipelago.

Borneo After bitter fighting near Kuching airport, the Indian garrison retires towards Dutch Borneo.

North Africa The British 8th Army enters Benghazi. Big Axis troop concentrations have been cut off at Sollum and Bardia.

Eastern Front The Russians begin a series of violent attacks against enemy positions in the southern sector, in particular against positions held by the Italian expeditionary force, and in the eastern Crimea. Reports continue to speak of German troops suffering from cold and frostbite.

Atlantic Free French forces commanded by Admiral Muselier occupy the islands of Saint-Pierre-et-Miquelon, between Newfoundland and Nova Scotia.

☐ General George C. Marshall, US chief of staff, proposes to the Anglo-American Washington Conference that Allied forces in the Far East should be under a unified command.

☐ King George VI broadcasts Christmas message to the Empire: 'Never did heroism shine more brightly than it does now, nor fortitude, nor sacrifice, nor sympathy, nor neighbourly kindness.'

26 December

Philippines Manila is declared an open city, but the Japanese continue to bomb it severely.

Admiral Rockwell transfers the naval defences to Corregidor. The American and Filipino land forces retire from the Agno river to the line Santa Ignacia–Guimba–San José. Those coming from the south of the island establish a defensive line west of Sariaya.

Malaya The town of Ipoh is evacuated by the 11th Indian Division; small detachments carry out rearguard actions north of Ipoh, near Kemor.

Eastern Front German armour evacuates Kaluga, south-west of Moscow.

Norway British commandos carry out swift raids on German bases on islands off the coast of Norway.

☐ The population of Saint-Pierre-et-Miquelon votes by plebiscite to recognize the change of government, from Vichy to that of de Gaulle. The decision is not welcome in Washington, which has not yet recognized Gaullist authority and still maintains diplomatic relations with Vichy.

27 December

Far East Lieutenant-General Sir Henry Pownall succeeds Air Marshall Sir Robert Brooke-Popham

PRESTON STURGES

A former scriptwriter turned director, Preston Sturges, having screened *Christmas in July* in 1940, established himself as a writer of brilliant comedies with two films that both appeared in 1941, for Paramount: *The Lady Eve* and *Sullivan's Travels*. A delightful little tale of an adventuress who turns the head of an ingenuous millionaire with a mania for snakes, *The Lady Eve* confirmed Barbara Stanwyck's talent for comedy and also featured an ironic Henry Fonda.

Sullivan's Travels was undoubtedly Sturges's masterpiece. Starring Joel McCrea and Veronica Lake, it was an original backward look at the Great Depression, seen through the eyes of a successful director who having lived for a while as a tramp discovers, through a series of dramatic adventures, the true misery of life among those whom society has forgotten.

Veronica Lake in a scene from *Sullivan's Travels*.

German patrol in the Norwegian port of Tromsö. British commandos carried out frequent raids on German bases in Norway.

in command of British forces in the Far East.

Philippines There is a pause in operations on Luzon, while the Japanese consolidate their line on the river Agno. The American and Filipino forces in northern Luzon form a line from Tarlac to Cabanatuan, on which they will be able to bring the greatest possible pressure to bear to hold up the Japanese advance. In the south of the island the Japanese follow up the retiring Americans.

Malaya The Japanese threaten Kampar on the west coast and Kuantan on the east coast of the peninsula.

Norway British commandos again attack German bases on Norwegian coastal islands. In all, some 16,000 tons of shipping destroyed.

28 December

Eastern Front Berlin reports intense Russian pressure in Ukraine sector.

Philippines The Japanese resume their large-scale offensive on Luzon. Having crossed the river Agno, they attack towards Cabanatuan. In the south of the island Filipino troops withdraw towards Manila and Bataan.

Burma General Wavell takes command of defence of Burma.

29 December

Philippines Japanese pressure in Luzon is stronger than ever. For the first time Japanese aircraft attack the fortified island of Corregidor, south of the Bataan peninsula, to which the US headquarters has been transferred.

Malaya The XII Brigade of the 11th Indian Division has to withdraw from its position at Kampar and retire to Bidor.

Borneo The Indian garrison withdrawing from Kuching reaches Sanggau in Dutch Borneo, and is placed under Dutch command.

Burma British pressure forces the Japanese back from Bokpyin into Thailand.

□ Eden meets Stalin and Molotov in Moscow to discuss co-operation both during and after the war.

30 December

Philippines Under Japanese pressure from the north the American and Filipino troops abandon the Tarlac–Cabanatuan line and retire on to the last prepared defence line in front of Bataan. The armour is concentrated to defend the Calumpit bridge over the river Pampanga, which the troops from the south of the island will have to cross to get to San Fernando and the road to the Bataan peninsula.

Malaya On the western side of the peninsula the Japanese follow up and press on towards Kampar. In the east they threaten Kuantan.

Eastern Front While the Army Group South continues its offensive against Sevastopol, Russian troops coming from the Caucasus mount an amphibious attack against the eastern Crimea, taking Kerch and Feodosia. On the central front the Germans are forced back under the pressure of the Soviet counter-offensive. The Russians occupy Kaluga.

31 December

Philippines The Americans and Filipinos complete the evacuation of Manila. Some key positions, such as the Calumpit bridge, are reinforced to hold the enemy and allow the defenders to concentrate their forces in the Bataan peninsula. At 5.45 p.m. the first Japanese enter Manila, which is in flames. MacArthur has already lost 30,000 men; he still has 80,000 (15,000 Americans and the rest Filipino).

Malaya The Indian troops still try to hold up the enemy near Kampar, on the west of the peninsula, and Kuantan on the east. But the British have already abandoned to the enemy an area that produces 38% of the world's rubber and 58% of its tin.

Eastern Front In the southern sector the Germans break off the operation against Sevastopol to check the Russian threat from Kerch and Feodosia. By mid-December the German troops fighting in the USSR are reduced to 775,000 men, slightly less than 25% of the numbers they began with.

In the central sector the Soviet counter-offensive before Moscow ends with the recapture of Kozelsk.

North Africa Rommel halts his withdrawal at El Agheila.

□ Australia. The American General Brett, from China, assumes command of American forces in Australia (USFIA). Admiral Chester W. Nimitz is appointed to command the American Asiatic Fleet.

□ The Anglo–American delegates at the Washington Conference call for the establishment of a single ABDA (Australian, British, Dutch, American) command in the Far East, to which General Wavell is appointed in overall command.

□ Hitler issues New Year message to the German people. 'He who fights for the life of a nation, for her daily bread and her future, will win, but he who, in this war, with his Jewish hate seeks to destroy whole nations will fail.'

□ UK civilian casualties in December: 34 killed, 55 injured.

Top: Near Moscow, Russian units, supported by tanks, launch a counter-attack against the Germans, who are now on the defensive.

Antitanc guns at Solloum, North Africa.

1942

1942

JANUARY	**1 January** Representatives of 26 nations sign the Atlantic Charter, the terms of which were drafted on 14 August 1941.
FEBRUARY	
MARCH	
APRIL	**18 April** *Japan*: First American air raid on Japan.
MAY	**2-8 May** Battle of the Coral Sea.
JUNE	**4-7 June** Battle of Midway. **15 June** Air-naval battle of Pantelleria.
JULY	
AUGUST	**10 August** Start of Operation *Pedestal*.
SEPTEMBER	
OCTOBER	**1-12 October** Guadalcanal. Air-naval battle of Cape Esperance.
NOVEMBER	**11 November** German troops invade Unoccupied France. **12-13 November** Battle of Guadalcanal.
DECEMBER	

A German soldier in a Panzer III surrenders to a British infantryman after El-Alamein.

1 January

Eastern Front In the Crimea the Germans forcefully counter-attack the Soviet forces that have penetrated into the peninsula around Feodosiya and Kerch.

North Africa The German and Italian forces, who have consolidated in the area of Agedabia, counterattack on the right flank, inland, to relieve the pressure exerted by the British 8th Army.

Malta Axis aircraft carry out heavy raids on the island's airfields and ports.

Philippines The American and Filipino forces on the island of Luzon fight their way back towards the Bataan peninsula.

Malaya The Japanese 25th Army under General Yamashita continues its advance south. In the eastern sector the Imperial Guard division takes Kuantan. In the west the 5th and 18th Divisions occupy Telok Anson after a brilliant amphibious operation and outflank the forces of the 11th Indian Division, which is putting up a dogged resistance to the Japanese at Kampar, north-east of Telok Anson, and along the road leading south to Kuala Lumpur and Singapore. On the island of Singapore, the first heavy Japanese air raid on Tengah airfield.

☐ Representatives of 26 nations at Washington sign the Atlantic Charter, the terms of which were drafted by Roosevelt and Churchill on 14 August 1941. The document reaffirms the principles that lie behind the struggle of the democratic countries ('to ensure life, liberty, independence and religious freedom and to preserve the rights of man and justice'). It requires the signatories to employ their full war resources against the countries of the Tripartite Pact and their allies, and not to conclude a separate peace with them. The declaration is signed by the USA, Great Britain, the USSR, China, Australia, Belgium, Canada, Czechoslovakia, Costa Rica, Cuba, El Salvador, Greece, Guatemala, Haiti, Honduras, India, Luxembourg, the Netherlands, New Zealand, Nicaragua, Norway, Panama, Poland, Santo Domingo, South Africa and Yugoslavia. Any nation that will 'contribute materially to the struggle for the achievement of victory over Hitlerism' will be able to adhere to this 'open alliance'.

☐ The Chinese government asks for help under the Lend-Lease Act to build a road from Ledo in India to Lungling in China across northern Burma, creating a real 'Burma Road' to supply the Chinese forces.

2 January

Philippines American and Filipino forces evacuate San Fernando, north of Manila, and set up strongpoints in the area of Guagua, between San Fernando and the Bataan peninsula. The Japanese occupy Baliuag and consolidate the capture of Manila and occupy the Cavite base south of the city. Their bombers begin systematic attacks against the fortified island of Corregidor.

Malaya To avoid encirclement by the Japanese, who have landed in their rear and taken Telok Anson, the Indian units defending Kampar begin in the evening to withdraw southwards to the line of the river Slim. The Japanese occupy Kampar and attempt a landing at Kuala Selangor (on the west coast, north-

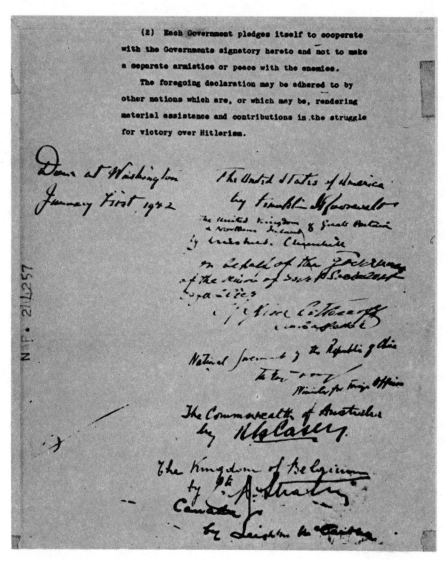

The Atlantic Charter, signed on 1 January by representatives of 26 nations. The first three signatures are those of Roosevelt, Churchill and Litvinov. The charter led directly to the formation of the United Nations.

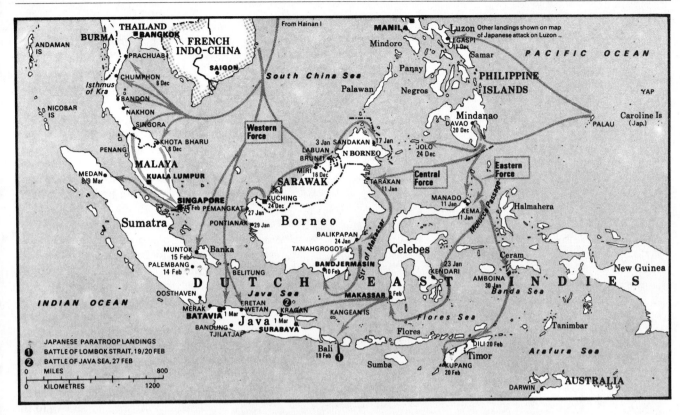

The Japanese occupation of the Dutch East Indies in early 1942.

west of Kuala Lumpur), but are held up by British artillery.
North Africa The garrison of Bardia, surrounded since the middle of December and left without supplies or ammunition, surrenders to the 2nd South African Division and the 1st Armoured Brigade, 8th Army.
Malta Axis aircraft renew their attacks on the island's air and naval bases.
☐ British aircraft raid Naples, causing severe material damage.

3 January
Allies set up unified command in South-West Pacific under General Wavell, with Major-General Brett (US) his deputy.
Philippines On Luzon, command of the American and Filipino troops cut off in the Bataan peninsula and the fortified island of Corregidor is taken over by the American General Jonathan M. Wainwright. Filipino troops succeed in containing strong Japanese attacks in the Guagua–Porac area.

Malaya On the west coast the British continue their withdrawal across the river Slim. On the east coast the forces defending Kuantan begin to retire southwards to avoid being cut off. The British headquarters would have liked to hold on

to Kuantan airport at least until 10 January.
The thin defences of Singapore are reinforced by the arrival of 51 Hurricane fighters, but only 21 pilots, who have come from Britain or the Libyan front and have no experience

Parts of a Buffalo fighter being uncrated at Singapore, one of the few supplies to reach the beleaguered garrison.

Top: a Chinese train crowded with refugees and soldiers fleeing from Kiang-si. Above: Japanese seaplane base in the Pacific.

of the conditions in which they will have to operate.

Borneo The Japanese land unopposed on the island of Labuan in the Gulf of Brunei, and from there a detachment lands on the mainland at Mempakul.

Malta Italian and German aircraft continue to attack military objectives on the island.

4 January

China Chiang Kai-shek is named Commander-in-Chief of all Allied troops operating in China. His forces hold up the advance begun by the Japanese in the area of Changsha, in Hunan province.

Philippines On Luzon, Japanese attacks continue in the area of Guagua–Porac. The Japanese capture Guagua and advance as far as Lubao, cutting the 11th Filipino Division's line of retreat towards Bataan. In the evening the defending forces break off their operations and try to establish a new defensive line between Lubao and Santa Cruz.

Malaya Japanese aircraft hammer the Indian troops in the western sector where they are preparing a defensive line along the river Slim. But the Japanese, who have landed at Kuala Selangor, are already advancing up the river Selangor in the rear of the defenders, threatening the town of Rawang, just north of Kuala Lumpur, capital of the Federated Malay States.

New Britain The Japanese open an offensive against Rabaul, a strategic base in the Bismarck Archipelago, north of New Guinea, where 1,400 British troops are guarding two airfields, at Lakunai and Vunakanu.

In these difficult conditions the Allied supreme command gives the following instructions to General Wavell: to hold the 'Malayan barrier' (the line from the Malayan peninsula through Sumatra and Java to northern Australia) and oppose any Japanese advance beyond that line; to reinforce Burma and Australia; and to re-establish contact with the Philippines across the Dutch East Indies.

5 January

Eastern Front Northern sector: fighting continues along the river Volkhov with no marked advantage to either side. At Leningrad, where cold and hunger claim hundreds of victims every day, preparations are made for a massive evacuation of the civil population across the frozen Lake Ladoga. Central sector: south of Kaluga the Russians re-take Belev, west of the river Oka. In the southern sector the Red Army lands reinforcements on the coasts of the Crimea near Evpatoriya and Sudak, in an attempt to break the siege of the fortress of Sevastopol by the Germans and Rumanians. But the Russians make little progress against stubborn German resistance.

Philippines On Luzon, the American and Filipino forces withdraw to a new defensive line at the base of the Bataan peninsula, from Dinalupihan to Hermosa. But they have to fall back from this line too at the end of

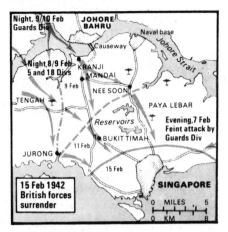

The fall of Singapore.

the day under violent Japanese pressure on the so-called 'Layac Line', where there is a bridge on which all roads leading to the Bataan peninsula converge. A little after midnight the bridge is blown up. The defenders' rations are halved. The Japanese continue their daily air offensive on Corregidor, occasionally attacking other objectives in the Manila Bay area.

Malaya On the river Slim line the 11th Indian Division repels a Japanese attack along the Penang–Singapore railway line. The headquarters of the British Far East fleet is transferred from Singapore to Batavia, in Java.

Malta Axis bombing of the island is intensified.

6 January

Philippines On Luzon there is an exchange of artillery fire in the area of Layac, at the base of the Bataan peninsula. The Japanese enter Dinalupihan, already evacuated by the Americans and Filipinos. The air offensive against Corregidor is temporarily halted, apart from some nuisance attacks.

Malaya In the western sector Indian troops are deployed to defend the Selangor river. In the east the troops that evacuated Kuantan continue to withdraw.

China Chiang Kai-shek asks Washington to name a senior American officer as chief of staff of the Allied troops (American and British) operating in China.

MOUNT RUSHMORE NATIONAL MEMORIAL

Work ended on the gigantic sculpture carved on Mount Rushmore, a granite peak in the Black Hills of South Dakota. The final touches were added by Lincoln Borglum, son of the sculptor Gutzon Borglum who in 1927 had begun carving on the north-eastern face of the mountain the heads (each about 60 ft high) of four American presidents: George Washington, Thomas Jefferson, Abraham Lincoln and Theodore Roosevelt.

Conceived as a 'shrine of democracy', Mount Rushmore National Memorial is the largest work of sculpture ever made.

From the left: Washington, Jefferson, Roosevelt and Lincoln, the United States presidents immortalized in the gigantic Mount Rushmore sculpture.

North Africa The British 1st Armoured Division, newly arrived from Britain to reinforce the 7th Armoured Division, takes up positions at Antelat in Cyrenaica. Derna harbour is reopened to traffic. The deployment of Italian and German troops along a line from El Agheila to Marada is completed.

☐ Roosevelt asks the United States Congress for an extraordinary appropriation which will allow the USA to produce, by the end of 1943, 125,000 aircraft, 75,000 tanks, 35,000 guns and 8 million tons of shipping.

7 January

Philippines The Japanese line up a big offensive against the Bataan peninsula. About 80,000 American and Filipino troops are deployed in defensive positions in depth. The Americans form new infantry battalions from the manpower available, including ground personnel of the air force, navy and US Marines.

Malaya At dawn the Japanese, with armoured support, attack the 11th Indian Division's positions on the river Slim, break through and advance swiftly towards Kuala Lumpur, reaching a point nearly two miles from the village of Slim. The Indian III Corps succeeds in forming a new defensive line further south, near Kuala Kubu.

General Wavell arrives in Singapore.

Borneo In Sarawak the Japanese reach the Sarawak–Dutch Borneo border.

Atlantic German submarines mount their first big 'hunt' along the eastern coasts of the United States. An average of 54 units are in action and in less than a month they sink 142,373 tons of enemy shipping.

North Africa XIII Corps of the British 8th Army sends advance units as far as Agedabia and finds the position abandoned by Rommel's forces. A convoy carrying supplies reaches Benghazi without loss.

Malta Axis air action continues.

8 January

Philippines The opposing forces prepare for the battle for the Bataan peninsula.

A German U-boat returns to base at Lorient from a mission off the United States coast. Opposite: the last moments of an Allied merchantman.

Malaya General Wavell visits the front and orders the Indian III Corps to withdraw into Johore state, north of Singapore, where he will try to mount the final defence of the fortress and its hinterland.

Borneo The Japanese take Jesselton in British North Borneo.

9 January

Philippines On Luzon, on the Bataan peninsula, the Japanese unleash the expected attack at 3.00 p.m. Two regiments, supported by artillery and aircraft, advance in the eastern sector of the peninsula. There are no decisive engagements. The Japanese advance is mainly opposed by demolitions carried out by the American and Filipino forces. A Japanese column from Dinalupihan reaches the area of Album.

Malaya The Indian III Corps begins its withdrawal southwards. The 11th and 9th Indian Divisions are given the task of holding up the enemy advance, covering the area Seremban, Port Dickson, Tampin and Malacca.

10 January

Eastern Front Berlin radio admits Russian penetration at various points and claims that the Germans are defending their positions in a 'wall of blood'.

Philippines General MacArthur inspects the defences of the Bataan peninsula. The Japanese drop leaflets from the air inviting the defenders to surrender. On the ground their columns keep up powerful pressure, though they are held up by thick jungle as well as by enemy resistance. They reach the river Calaguiman below the village of Samal, and in the western sector they reach the village of Olongapo.

Malaya The British abandon Port Swettenham and Kuala Lumpur, which are immediately occupied by the pursuing Japanese. Japanese aircraft, which have previously confined themselves to night attacks against the Singapore airfields, now begin to attack them by daylight.

Borneo The Japanese land on Tarakan. The Japanese 3rd Fleet, given responsibility for the Borneo operations under the command of Vice-Admiral Takahashi, consists of 2 heavy cruisers, 8 destroyers and 41 transports; they are covered by another group of 2 heavy cruisers and 7 destroyers, commanded by Rear Admiral Takagi. The land forces are commanded by General Yamashita.

11 January
Philippines On Luzon the Japanese make some progress along the east coast of the Bataan peninsula, crossing the river Calaguiman. The Americans launch a counter-attack and re-capture almost all the ground lost. At the centre of the peninsula advance elements of a Japanese column reach the river Orani after a day's fighting.

Malaya The Indian III Corps continues its withdrawal southwards. There is a pause in the ground operations, but the Japanese air attacks are intensified, especially against the area of the river Muar, south of Malacca.

Borneo General Yamashita's forces effect more landings and complete the capture of the island of Tarakan, which contain a number of oilfields.

Celebes Other Japanese units occupy Manado, at the extreme north of the island of Celebes, and nearby Kema. Naval parachutists are used in this operation. The small Dutch garrisons are quickly forced to surrender. Both the island of Tara-

kan and Manado in the Celebes are turned into air bases to support the continued Japanese drive south.

North Africa The South African 2nd Division, part of XXX Corps of the British 8th Army, attacks Sollum and takes it after 24 hours' fighting. Axis forces consolidate at El Agheila.

Eastern Front In the central sector Soviet troops continue their counter-offensive, cutting the Rzhev–Bryansk railway line. Moscow radio announces recapture of some Donetz coal-mining districts.

Malta More Axis raids.

12 January

Philippines On Luzon the Japanese press hard on the eastern sector of the Bataan peninsula, defended by the American–Filipino II Corps. The Filipino 51st Division loses ground, but succeed in counter-attacking when reinforced by reserves. On the east coast of the peninsula the Japanese re-establish the bridgehead over the river Calaguiman lost in the previous day's American counter-attack.

□ Japan declares war on Dutch East Indies, following the invasion of the Celebes and Dutch Borneo.

13 January

Philippines In the eastern sector of the Bataan peninsula the Americans, after a powerful artillery prepara-tion, counter-attack and reduce the Japanese salient south of the river Calagiuman. But on the central front the Japanese advance, forcing the Filipino 51st Division to withdraw to the river Balantay.

Malaya General Wavell visits the front again. The withdrawal of the Indian III Corps into Johore state is almost complete. A convoy carrying war materials (particularly anti-air-craft guns) and reinforcements (part of the British 18th Division) arrives at Singapore.

Eastern Front In the central sector the Red Army extends the salient it has carved out between the II and IV *Panzergruppen* south-west of Kaluga, capturing Kirov.

□ Conference, in London, of Allied

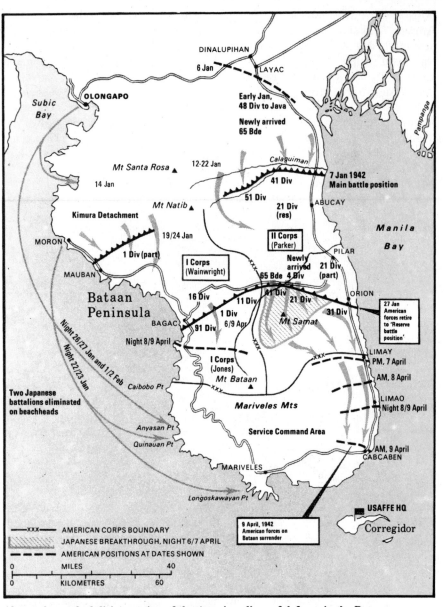

Above: the gradual disintegration of the American lines of defence in the Bataan peninsula between January and April 1942.

governments which pledge to punish Axis 'criminals' at the end of the war.

14 January

Dutch East Indies General Wavell formally assumes supreme command in Asia and arrives this day at Batavia to establish his headquarters.

Philippines On Luzon, the Japanese pressure persists against the defenders of the Bataan peninsula. In the eastern sector the 41st Division has to retire beyond the river Balan-tay. In the western sector the Japanese advance from Olongapo towards Moron in two columns, and some units land half-way between

the two places. The Americans send reinforcements to Moron.

Malaya The British forces are deployed for the defence of the southern part of the Malayan penin-sula, aiming to hold up the Japanese on a line from Muar to Segamat, then along the railway to Labis, and on to Mersing on the east coast. North of this line the British make contact with the enemy troops com-ing south from Kuantan. British patrols ambush a large number of Japanese moving south on bicycles.

Eastern Front In the central sector the Russians recapture Medyn, on the river Medynka, north-west of

Anti-aircraft gun, with Indian crew, in action during the last days before the fall of Singapore.

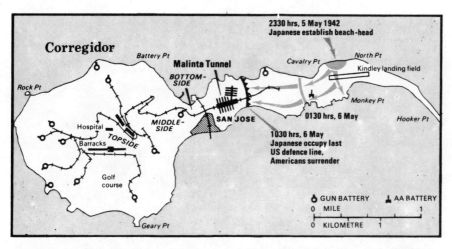

Corregidor

2330 hrs, 5 May 1942
Japanese establish beach-head

Battery Pt

Malinta Tunnel

BOTTOM-
SIDE

Cavalry Pt

North Pt

Kindley landing field

Rock Pt

MIDDLE-
SIDE

SAN JOSE

0130 hrs, 6 May

Monkey Pt

Hooker Pt

Hospital

Barracks

TOPSIDE

1030 hrs, 6 May
Japanese occupy last
US defence line,
Americans surrender

Golf
course

GUN BATTERY   AA BATTERY

0   MILE   1

Geary Pt

0   KILOMETRE   1

Kaluga.

☐ The Anglo-American *Arcadia* conference ends in Washington. The main decisions taken are: the setting up of a joint Chief of Staffs Committee to co-ordinate the Anglo-American war effort; priority in the overall operational plan is given to the campaign against Germany; the strategic importance of the occupation of French North Africa (Operation *Gymnast*) is recognized.

15 January
Philippines On Luzon the Japanese establish a bridgehead south of the river Balantay in the Bataan peninsula. The defenders' counter-attacks fail to regain the position. The

Japanese troops advancing slowly in the central sector halt to re-group. In the western sector the two Japanese columns converging on Moron are near their objective.
Malaya In the centre of the peninsula Australian units inflict heavy losses on the Japanese advance guards, but then withdraw to their assigned positions in the defence line. On the west side of the peninsula the Japanese reach the north bank of the river Muar and land small detachments between Muar and Batu Pahat, causing some confusion to the British communications in the western sector of the front.
Eastern Front Southern sector: the Russians launch a violent attack on

the sector held by the Italians.
Von Küchler replaces von Leeb in command of Army Group North, as part of the great shake-up ordered by Hitler. The Führer has been infuriated by his generals giving orders to retire without consulting him, or even withdrawing in defiance of his orders.

16 January
Eastern Front Russian High Command announces discovery of an order to German troops signed by Field Marshal von Reichenau. The order tells German troops to be 'merciless' in dealing with Russians and that food supplies for local civilians and war prisoners are 'unnecessary humanitarianism'.
Philippines In the western sector of the Bataan peninsula, on Luzon, the Filipino 51st Division counter-attacks but is driven back and put to flight by the Japanese. The Japanese column advancing in the centre over-runs enemy positions in the area of Mount Natib and proceeds south along the valley of the river Abo-Abo. In the east the Filipino 41st Division succeeds in halting the enemy advance while near Abucay the US 31st Infantry Regiment prepares a counter-attack. To the west the Japanese cross the river Batalan and attack Moron, but are driven back to the river by the Americans.
Malaya The Japanese cross the river Muar and drive the 45th Indian Brigade out of Muar village, while continuing to land troops in the area of Batu Pahat.
Burma The Japanese go over to the attack, surrounding the British forces at Myitta and threatening Tavoy.

17 January
North Africa After two months' resistance, the Axis garrisons of Sollum and Halfaya, bombarded from land, sea and air, and without water for the past three days, surrender to the British.
With the elimination of enemy resistance in Cyrenaica the first phase of the British campaign in Libya can be regarded as concluded. The Ita-

Soldiers of the British 8th Army
attack near Sollum. The garrison
finally surrenders on 17 January.

Australian prisoners of war forced to
sweep the streets by the Japanese.

lians and Germans are in position on the El-Agheila line.

Philippines Luzon: in the Bataan peninsula the troops of II Corps (General Parker), responsible for the defence of the eastern sector, carry out a counter-attack in the Abucay area, reaching the river Balantay in that sector; but they cannot profit from their success because the whole of the river line is not re-taken. In the centre the Japanese column, ready to turn east or west whenever there is a chance to surround large enemy units, continues its advance along the Abo-Abo valley towards Orion. In the west the defenders of Moron are forced to retire south and south-east.

Malaya The British send reinforcements to the Muar–Yong Peng area. The Japanese maintain their pressure on the defence, while concentrating their forces for the offensive against the southern part of the Malayan peninsula.

Borneo Japanese troops land at Sandakan, British North Borneo.

The Allied forces are too scarce on the ground to withstand the Japanese initiatives. Under Wavell are the American Admiral Hart in command of naval forces, the British Air Marshal Peirse commanding the air forces and the Dutch General ter Poorten at the head of the land forces.

Eastern Front Field Marshal von Reichenau, former commander of the German 6th Army, whose contribution was decisive in the taking of Kiev and Kharkov, dies of a stroke. On 1 December 1941 he had taken over from Field Marshal von Rundstedt, in command of the Army Group South. Next day his command is given to Field Marshal von Bock, who on 16 December, physically and mentally exhausted, had asked to be relieved of the command of Army Group Centre.

18 January

Eastern Front In the southern sector the Russians break through the enemy lines and achieve a complete penetration in the Izyum sector, west of the Donetz, in the Ukraine. Notable progress is also made in the area

of Kursk. The next ten days see significant Russian advances along the line south of Kharkov.

Philippines No change in the Bataan peninsula: the defenders' counter-attacks are ineffective in the eastern sector, while in the western pressure by the attacking forces increases slightly.

Malaya The 45th Indian Brigade repulses Japanese attacks in the Muar–Yong Peng area, but new Japanese landings immediately north of Batu Pahat put the British positions in that sector in serious danger. Towards evening the British headquarters orders these positions to be evacuated.

Apart from the 51 Hurricanes, which are not ready to go into action yet, the air force available for the defence of Malaya amounts to 75 bombers and reconnaissance aircraft and 28 fighters. The bombers are being got ready for transfer to Sumatra.

19 January

Philippines Luzon: the Japanese repulse renewed American counter-attacks. The Japanese column advancing along the Abo-Abo valley reaches the outskirts of Guitol and is engaged by the Filipino 31st Division.

Malaya Fighting continues in the Muar–Yong Peng area. The British lose Yong Peng and face the prospect of the annihilation of their forces, now cut off at Muar.

Borneo British North Borneo surrenders to the Japanese.

Burma The Japanese take Tavoy, with its airport. The British decide to withdraw the garrison at Mergui, a town the Japanese have not yet attacked, to Rangoon. A Chinese division is sent to Burma to reinforce the British.

North Africa General Auchinleck issues directives for the 8th Army. The objective is Tripoli. Defensive strategy is laid down in case the offensive in Libya has to be broken off.

Eastern Front Bitter fighting in the southern sector; the Germans retake Feodosiya in the Crimea.

20 January

Philippines Luzon: the Japanese are able to contain counter-attacks by the Filipino divisions on the left flank of the American II Corps; after fierce fighting in front of Guitol they withdraw northwards. But they continue their pressure and infiltration in the American I Corps sector.

Malaya The British counter-attack west of Yong Peng, but with no success. The forces cut off in the Muar area try to break out, but are checked.

Twenty-seven Japanese bombers attack Singapore with no fighter escort. Taken on by British Hurricanes, they lose 9 aircraft.

Bismarck Archipelago Over 100 Japanese carrier-borne bombers attack Rabaul in New Britain, causing serious damage to the airport installations. A minor attack is also carried out at Kavieng in New Ireland.

Burma Japanese forces from Thailand penetrate in force into Burma, carrying out attacks in the region of northern Tenasserim, east of Moulmein, held by 17th Indian Division.

Eastern Front Following up the counter-attack begun in the central sector, the Russians retake Mozhaysk about sixty miles west of Moscow.

21 January

North Africa The German counter-attack: Rommel launches a thrust from the El Agheila–Marada line towards Agedabia. This formidable second counter-offensive (the first was launched on 30 March, 1941) lasts until July 1.

Philippines Luzon: the Japanese concentrate their forces in preparation for a big offensive against the American and Filipino forces.

Malaya The British withdrawal from Muar and Segamat continues. The troops in the Muar sector, still cut off, have to be supplied by air. New daylight air raids on Singapore by the Japanese. This time the bombers are escorted by naval Zero fighters which prove more than a match for the Hurricanes (whose speed is reduced by the special air-inlet filters used in the Libyan desert, where these aircraft have come from). Also, the loss or destruction of the radar stations by earlier enemy action has almost eliminated the advance warning of attack, and the slow British Buffalo fighters need nearly half an hour to climb to 25,000 ft, the height at which the enemy bombers operate.

Bismarck Archipelago The Japanese resume air raids on Rabaul (New Britain) and Kavieng (New Ireland) in preparation for invasion. The only coastal battery in Rabaul is silenced.

New Guinea Japanese aircraft now open an offensive in this sector, sending 50 aircraft to attack the Lae–Salamaua area.

China US General Stilwell nominated as Chiang Kai-shek's Chief of Staff of forces operating in China.

Eastern Front In the southern sector, in the area of Izyum in the Donetz basin, the Russians succeed in breaking the front of the German

17th Army. However, within a few days three German armies, including von Kleist's 1st Armoured Army, restore the situation with a powerful and effective counter-attack.

22 January

Philippines Luzon: General MacArthur orders all American and Filipino forces to withdraw from the Mauban–Abucay line to the Bataan peninsula's final defence, behind the Pilar–Bagac road. The withdrawal is to be carried out in three days. Meanwhile Japanese attacks are held. During the night of 22–23 January the invaders begin a series of amphibious operations, carrying troops southwards from Moron to Caibobo, south of Bagac. Two Japanese lighters are sunk by US motor torpedo-boats.

Malaya The battle on the Muar front ends in complete victory for the Japanese. Despite support from air and sea, the 45th Indian Division is

wiped out. The forces defending Batu Pahat, units of the 11th Indian Division, have some skirmishes with the enemy. On the east of the peninsula a Japanese attempt to break through at Mersing is repulsed. More Indian troops arrive to reinforce Singapore. A hundred Japanese bombers attack Singapore, causing many deaths and immense damage.

North Africa Axis forces advance rapidly eastwards and re-take Agedabia. British air raids on Tripoli.

Eastern Front The mass evacuation of the civil population from Leningrad has started, buses being used to ferry the evacuees over frozen Lake Ladoga. In December alone there have been 52,000 deaths, the normal figure for a whole year. Even the rations of combatant troops are reduced, from 3,500 to 2,600 calories, while all base and line of communications troops are given rations of only 1,600 calories. By the end of January the number of deaths from starvation and cold will have passed 200,000. But still the city holds out.

23 January

Philippines In the centre of the Bataan peninsula Japanese pressure is intensified. Due to navigational errors the Japanese amphibious units embarked at Moron for Point Caibobo are landed partly near Point Quinauan and partly at Point Longoskawayan, both a long way south of their objective. American and Filipino troops sent to repel the invaders are unsuccessful.

Malaya Fighting continues in the area of Batu Pahat. The troops defending the Segamat and Muar fronts succeed in breaking off the fight and retiring southwards. The defence of Johore state, which means the defence of the Singapore base, is mainly in the hands of the Indian III Corps.

Bismarck Archipelago More Japanese troops in convoys escorted by the 4th Fleet land at Rabaul (New Britain) and Kavieng (New Ireland). The tiny garrison at Rabaul, an important base area, is quickly overcome, while Kavieng is virtually undefended.

Prisoners of war and Russian peasants are forced by the Germans to clear snow-packed roads in the central sector, January 1942.

Solomon Islands Elements of the Japanese 4th Fleet invade Kieta (Bougainville), meeting with no opposition.

Dutch East Indies Two Japanese convoys land troops at Balikpapan (Borneo) and Kendari (Celebes). Dutch aircraft attack the Japanese ships off Balikpapan, but with little success.

Burma Japanese air activity is intensified in the Rangoon area, with the object of wiping out the British air presence.

North Africa Axis forces outflank the defences of XIII Corps of the British 8th Army and take Antelat and Saunnu.

Eastern Front To the north-west of Moscow the Red Army, following up its forceful counter-attack, retakes Kholm, one of the strongpoints on the German defensive line between the North and Centre Army Groups. In the south-east another German strongpoint, Rzhev, is threatened with encirclement.

24 January

Strait of Makassar The first big naval battle since the beginning of operations in the Pacific theatre takes place off Balikpapan, between Borneo and the Celebes. Sixteen Japanese naval transports and their escort of 1 light cruiser and 9 destroyers are attacked by the American destroyers *Parrot*, *Pope*, *John D. Ford* and *Paul Jones* and a group of submarines. Four of the Japanese transports and one escort vessel are sunk. One American destroyer is damaged. The action holds up the invasion of Java for a few days, but not the occupation of the oil port of Balikpapan, which is captured on the same day.

Philippines Luzon: in the Bataan peninsula the American II Corps, defending the eastern sector, retires rapidly southwards; and the situation is no better in the western sector, where the troops of I Corps only temporarily succeed in driving back the Japanese troops landed at Point Longoskawayan, which is south of the whole American line.

Malaya Plans are made to withdraw all British forces to the island of Singapore. Hard fighting continues at Batu Pahat, and the Japanese threaten the town of Kluang. About 3,000 Australians, still not fully trained, arrive in Singapore as reinforcements.

New Guinea Allied troops evacuate Lae, the capital, and Salamaua, directly threatened by the Japanese.

Burma The Japanese approach the town of Moulmein.

North Africa A brief pause in Rommel's offensive. The British XIII Corps prepares to counter-attack. If it proves impossible to hold up the enemy, the British will withdraw to a line running from Derna to El Mechili.

Eastern Front In the southern sector, on the Donetz front, the Russians break through the German defences near Izyum and take Barvenkovo, about 40 miles east of Lozovaya, south of Kharkov. In the central sector, in the area of the Val- dai height, the Russians extend the salient between Kholm and Rzhev, coming near to Velikiye Luki, where, however, the German positions are particularly strong.

Berlin admits Russian penetration of the German defence lines at two points in the Ukraine.

25 January

New Guinea Japanese land at Lae.

Philippines On Luzon the retirement of the American and Filipino troops to the southern end of the Bataan peninsula continues. The defenders cannot manage to wipe out the enemy detachments at Point Quinauan and Point Longoskawayan.

Malaya Fighting at Batu Pahat goes on all day, but it is now clear that a Japanese victory is inevitable. On the east of the peninsula, however, enemy attacks in the Kluang area are forcefully repulsed.

Burma General Wavell visits Rangoon and orders that Moulmein

Japanese marines land a Kavieng, New Ireland, which is then converted into an air and naval base.

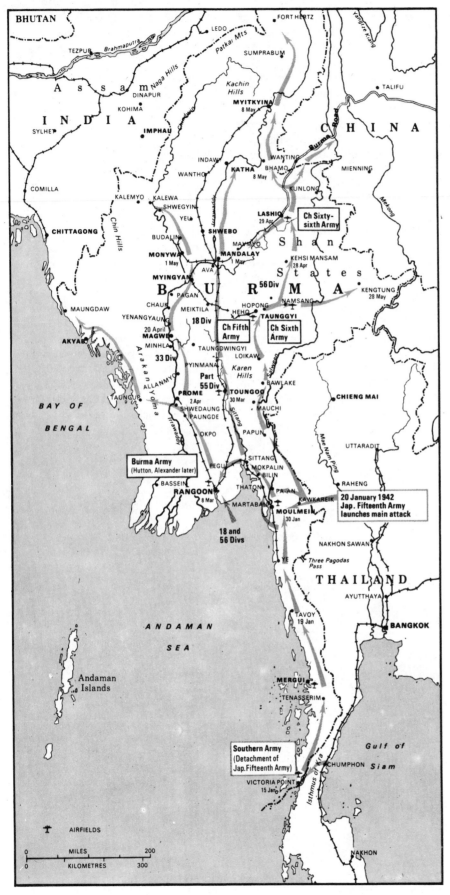

must be defended at all costs. Troops of the 17th Indian Division are deployed on the west bank of the river Salween in defence of Moulmein. The Japanese, engaged in regrouping, do not mount any substantial operations.

North Africa Axis troops occupy Msus and move on to Er Regima, east of Benghazi. The British 1st Armoured Division withdraws to El Mechili, leaving a detachment to protect the withdrawal of the 4th Indian Division from Benghazi to Barce. However, General Ritchie orders a counter-attack in the Msus area.

☐ Thailand declares war on the United States and Great Britain.

☐ Australia orders full mobilization.

26 January

Philippines Americans and Filipinos complete withdrawal to the southern tip of the Bataan peninsula, behind the line of the Pilar–Bagac road. Gaps are opened between several of the major units, hastily plugged with reserve troops. At the extreme south of the peninsula the Japanese maintain their bridgeheads at Points Quinauan and Longoskawayan. The Americans, fearing more landings, strengthen their coast defences.

Malaya Japanese amphibious units land south of Endau on the east side of the peninsula and quickly move inland. British forces in the Batu Pahat area, already outflanked by the Japanese, try to regain their lines by filtering through the jungle.

Malta More German and Italian air raids mainly against the airfields.

☐ The first contingents of American troops land in Northern Ireland. The premier of the Irish Republic, Eamon De Valera, protests strongly.

27 January

Philippines Luzon: the Japanese make a new landing at Point Anyasan, just north of Point Quinauan. After consolidating the bridgeheads in these two sectors the Japanese are ordered to advance on the town of Mariveles, at the extreme south of the Bataan peninsula. The Japanese are attacking everywhere, but the Americans and Filipinos hold out along the line running from Bagac, on the west coast, to Pilar and Orion on the east.

Malaya The commander of Allied troops in Malaya, General Percival, gets permission from General Wavell to withdraw his forces on to the island of Singapore when a suitable opportunity offers. He decides that they will move by way of Johore Bahru and the causeway linking it with Singapore, and that the movement must be completed during the night of 30–31 January. The defending troops are already fighting rearguard actions; some are being taken off by sea.

North Africa While the British XIII Corps prepares to counter-attack in the Msus area, the Italians and Germans resume their offensive with great vigour, advancing along two tracks leading to Benghazi and El Mechili.

Eastern Front In the southern sector the Russians re-take the important railway junction of Lozovaya, west of Izyum. This advance puts the Russians within 60 miles of the Dniepr river and of Dnepropetrovsk, the principal supply base of the German southern forces. The Russian general offensive by Marshal Timoshenko's armies on the Ukrainian front, begun on 18 January, has thus achieved major successes. German sources admit fierce Russian pressure on these fronts.

☐ Goering begins nine-day visit to Italy which includes talks with Mussolini. Germans need more Italian workers in view of drain on their own manpower in Russia.

☐ Winston Churchill opens three-day debate in the House of Commons on the war situation. Churchill defends government against critics, especially of the North African and Far East campaigns.

28 January
Philippines Situation unchanged in the Bataan peninsula. Americans and Filipinos continue to harass the Japanese bridgeheads at Quinauan

North Africa: British Crusader tank immobilized near Msus, east of Benghazi.

and Anyasan, but with no tangible result.

Malaya The retreat of the British forces from the mainland continues. The Japanese reach Benut in pursuit of the 11th Indian Division, which retreats in disorder, leaving the 22nd Indian Brigade uncovered on its flank and completely cut off from the main body.

North Africa Benghazi evacuated: the 4th Indian Division, holding Benghazi, is authorized to withdraw, since it will not have the promised tank support. The 7th Indian Brigade, the last to withdraw, finds the road blocked by Axis forces, but suc-

ceeds in breaking through and rejoining the 8th Army. The German 90th Light Infantry Division and Italian XX Corps occupy Er Regima, further east beyond Benghazi.

New Guinea The Japanese land on Rossel Island in the Louisiades east of New Guinea. The threat to Australia becomes increasingly grave.

☐ In Rio de Janeiro a conference of the Foreign Ministers of the American republics, begun on 15 January, to cement the unity of the continent, comes to an end.

29 January
Pacific The Chief of Staffs Com-

Burma: Japanese infantry unit in action at the Yenangyaung oilfields.
Opposite: the Japanese advance through Burma following invasion on 16 January 1942.

CAROLE LOMBARD

On 30 January a TWA Dakota heading for Los Angeles crashed in flames among the mountains of Nevada, close to Las Vegas. Among the victims was one of the most beautiful and loved Hollywood film actresses, Carole Lombard. An active worker in the propaganda campaign against the Nazis, the star was returning from Indianapolis where she had put on a show for the troops.

Born in Fort Wayne, Indiana, in 1908, Carole Lombard (Jane Alice Peters) began performing at a very young age and made her film debut in 1923 with the role of a street urchin in *A Perfect Crime*. After appearing in a number of silent movies, she emerged during the 1930s as a sophisticated comedy star in films such as *No Man of Her Own* and *My Man Godfrey*. A stylish and talented actress, she also enjoyed success in dramatic parts (*Made for Each Other* and *Vigil in the Night*), but her best performance came in a comedy, *To Be or Not to Be*, a film that she was destined never to see.

Devastated by her death, Clark Gable, whom she had married in 1939, broke his contract with MGM and enlisted in the air force.

mittee sets up the ANZAC (Australia and New Zealand Army Corps) sector; command of naval operations in the South Pacific is given to the Americans.

Fiji American troops arrive to garrison the islands.

Philippines Americans and Filipinos hold out against growing enemy pressure in the Bataan peninsula. After heavy artillery preparation they succeed in wiping out the Japanese bridgehead at Point Longoskawayan.

Malaya The British withdrawal to Singapore continues. Units of the British 18th Division arrive on the island with about ten light tanks, the only armour sent to Malaya.

Dutch East Indies The Japanese land at Bandoeng and at Mampawan in the Celebes, and in Dutch Borneo they occupy the west coast town of Pontianak.

North Africa Axis forces occupy Benghazi at first light, and send advance troops to pursue the 4th Indian Division as it retires on Derna. Hitler promises Rommel the rank of Generaloberst (Colonel-General).

Eastern Front In the central sector the Russians extend the salient splitting the German armies south-west of Kaluga, and retake Sukhinichi, inflicting heavy losses on the enemy in men and materials.

□ Great Britain and the USSR sign a treaty of alliance with Iran, by which Iran undertakes to remain neutral; British and Russian troops will be withdrawn from the country six months after the end of the war with the Axis powers. The 'Persian corridor' is to become one of the main routes by which supplies from the Western Allies reach the USSR.

30 January

Philippines In the southern part of Bataan peninsula the Japanese put pressure on the American–Filipino defensive lines and establish a bridgehead across the river Pilar. The defenders try in vain to eliminate this bridgehead as well as that at Point Quinauan.

Singapore The 22nd Indian Brigade is still cut off by the enemy advance and some of their units have to be taken to Singapore by sea. It is decided to transfer all air force units to the Dutch East Indies except for one fighter squadron, so great is the danger from enemy air attack.

Dutch East Indies The Japanese take Amboina, between Celebes and New Guinea, one of the biggest naval bases in the sector. The Dutch and Australian garrison is quickly overcome.

Burma The Japanese open a powerful onslaught on Moulmein, and capture the airport.

□ Hitler speaks on the ninth anniversary of coming to power; he calls Roosevelt a 'mad fool' and declares, 'The Jews are the ones who will be finally destroyed. This war will be fought in the true Biblical manner – an eye for an eye and a tooth for a tooth.'

31 January

Philippines Luzon: Japanese attacks

are driven off by intensive artillery fire. The Japanese units that have infiltrated behind the main American lines are still cut off from supplies; during the night they begin to evacuate their bridgehead across the river Pilar. The Japanese command sends reinforcements to the Quinauan bridgehead.

Malaya At 8.15 a.m. the last British units withdraw from the Malayan mainland to the island of Singapore. The three-quarter-mile causeway connecting the island with the mainland is blown up and the seige of Singapore begins. Lt. General A. E. Percival, GOC Malaya issues this message: 'The battle of Malaya has come to an end and the battle of Singapore has started.' The island is divided into three defensive sectors, north, south and west, under respectively Generals Heath, Simmons and Bennett, whose troops include Indians, British, Australians, Canadians and Malayans. The Japanese occupy the city of Johore Bharu, opposite the island, and at once begin shelling; the main targets now are store depots and airfields, especially that at Kalang.

Burma The garrison at Moulmein withdraws across the river Salween. The Japanese bomb and shell Martaban. A brigade of the 19th Indian Division reaches Rangoon.

North Africa Violent RAF attacks on Misurata and Tripoli. Axis troops take Barce and carry on towards Cyrene.

Malta During January Axis aircraft have carried out an average of 13 raids a day on the island.

☐ Great Britain recognizes the independence and sovereignty of Ethiopia, now liberated from Italian occupation.

1 February

Norway Puppet government set up under Quisling.

Pacific Two American navy task forces, under Vice-Admiral Halsey and Rear-Admiral Fletcher, consisting of 2 aircraft carriers, 5 cruisers and 10 destroyers, launch surprise attacks on the Japanese air bases at Kwajalein, Wotje, Roi and Mille in the Marshall Islands and Makin in the Gilbert Islands. Airport installations are severely damaged by bombs and shellfire. During the action the aircraft carrier *Enterprise* and the cruiser *Chester* are damaged, the first by a suicide bomber.

Philippines An attempted landing by the Japanese in the south of the Bataan peninsula is driven off by American motor torpedo-boats. A part of the Japanese force, which should have gone to the Point Quinauan bridgehead, manages to make a landing in the area of Anyasan. No activity of importance on the rest of the front.

North Africa General Ritchie orders the British XIII Corps, which is in danger of being surrounded by the Axis forces, to retire to the Gazala–Bir Hacheim line. The 4th Indian Division, attached to XIII Corps for operations, falls back on Derna. Having taken Cyrene, Rommel makes Derna his next objective.

Eastern Front In the southern sector the Russians reinforce their troops in the Crimea, but their efforts to relieve Sevastopol break down against the Germans' increasingly firm resistance. They also achieve no positive results from their attempts to relieve Leningrad and from other offensives that they open on several fronts, which are to last for the whole of February.

Malta Another month of severe air raids begins for the island.

2 February

Philippines In the Bataan peninsula American and Filipino forces attack the Japanese bridgehead across the river Pilar. During the night the Japanese retire across the river. However, the Americans still cannot destroy the Japanese bridgehead at Point Quinauan, though they make some progress in the Anyasan sector.

North Africa With both Barce and Cyrene in his hands, Rommel advances on Derna. General Auchinleck orders the British 8th Army to hold the Tobruk fortress at all costs as a supply base for future offensives.

3 February

Philippines American and Filipino forces retake the bridgehead over the river Pilar, evacuated by the Japanese the previous night.

Dutch East Indies The Japanese begin the air attacks that herald the invasion of Java. Their bombers, taking off from Kendari (Celebes), hit the bases at Surabaya, Madionen and Malang, severely damaging port installations and destroying on the ground all the Dutch aircraft stationed in Java.

New Guinea The Japanese begin the bombardment of Port Moresby, capital of Papua, where there is a small Australian garrison.

Burma Chiang Kai-shek sends his 5th Army and the remainder of the 6th Army to reinforce the British forces.

4 February

Singapore The Japanese demand unconditional surrender of the Imperial forces. When this is refused four days of intense bombardment follow.

Borneo A Dutch and American naval squadron with 4 cruisers and 7 destroyers, commanded by Rear-Admiral Karel W. Doorman, passes through the Strait of Madura to attack the Japanese forces landing at Balikpapan, but is spotted and attacked from the air. The mission has to be abandoned. The heavy cruiser *Houston* and the light cruiser *Marblehead*, both American, are seriously damaged.

Amboina The small garrison trying to oppose the Japanese landing is forced to surrender.

North Africa Axis forces recapture Derna. The British XIII Corps takes up positions on the line Gazala–Bir Hacheim. Axis forces are near the line Tmimi–El Mechili.

5 February

Philippines The defenders of Bataan succeed in driving the Japanese who have landed at Point Quinauan, back to the beaches. Limited activity on the rest of the front.

Singapore A convoy lands the remainder of the British 18th Division and further Indian reinforcements on the island. The slowest ship in the convoy, the *Empress of Asia*, is sunk by Japanese aircraft with considerable loss of life. Violent air raids take place on the port warehouses.

North Africa The British holding El Mechili, south-west of Derna, have to retire to avoid being surrounded. On the coast the Italians and Germans take Tmimi, only a short way from Gazala.

□ USA declares war on Thailand.

6 February

Philippines Japanese reinforcements land in the Gulf of Lingayen, Luzon. The Japanese begin shelling the fortified islands in the Gulf of Manila.

Dutch East Indies The Japanese take Samarinda, off the east coast of Borneo north of Balikpapan.

□ In Rome the Grand Mufti of Jerusalem has talks with Mussolini, who is putting himself forward as champion of the Arab cause.

7 February

Singapore General Percival, commanding Singapore, declares the city will resist to the last man.

Philippines In the Bataan peninsula the Americans attack two salients established by the Japanese in the central sector, and continue mopping up the Point Quinauan bridgehead. Japanese reinforcements trying to land in the area are driven off by artillery fire.

North Africa Rommel halts near Gazala, on the line of strongpoints and minefields that runs from Derna on the coast to Bir Hacheim inland. The Axis forces stop here, having, like the British, learned not to overstretch their supply lines.

Atlantic End of the first big 'hunt' by German submarines off the east coast of the United States, started on January 7th.

8 February

Singapore At 8.45 p.m., after powerful artillery preparation, the Japanese (units of the 5th and 18th Divisions) land on the north-west coast of the island. Despite tenacious British resistance they establish a strong bridgehead and advance towards Tengah airfield, the biggest on the island.

Philippines General Masaharu Homma, commander of the Japanese forces on Luzon, orders a general withdrawal to new positions. The Americans try to cut off the two enemy salients, and complete the annihilation of the Point Quinauan bridgehead.

New Britain The Japanese take Gasmata.

□ The German Minister of Munitions, Fritz Todt, creator of the organization named after him which planned and built Germany's great fortifications, is killed in an air accident on the Eastern Front. He is succeeded by Dr. Albert Speer.

9 February

North Africa Italian bombers attack naval and air installations at Alexandria.

Philippines In the Bataan peninsula the Filipinos and Americans continue attacks on the Japanese salients. Japanese 'suicide squads' make repeated forays.

Singapore Fierce fighting rages. Although General Percival sends reinforcements, the Japanese reach Tengah airfield. 15,000 Japanese, who have crossed in lighters and rubber boats over the arm of the sea separating the Malaya mainland from the island of Singapore, occupy the western part of the island.

10 February

Philippines The defenders continue their activity against the larger of the Japanese salients on the Bataan peninsula. In the area of Anyasan strong pressure is put on the invaders.

Singapore The British withdraw from the western part of the island to a stronger defensive line running from Kranji to Jurong. They counter-attack, but to no effect.

Dutch East Indies The Japanese continue the occupation of Borneo and the Celebes where they land in force at Makassar.

Burma The Indian troops defending the river Salween line near Martaban give way under Japanese pressure, abandon the town and carry out a fighting withdrawal to Thaton.

11 February

Philippines In the Bataan peninsula the Americans make further progress against the larger of the two Japanese salients, but the Japanese escape encirclement and retire to the north.

Singapore The Japanese advance further. General Tomoyuki Yamashita has leaflets dropped on the city giving terms for surrender. The British ignore them.

Burma The Japanese advance across the river Salween.

□ Salazar, head of the Portuguese government, and Franco, *Caudillo* of Spain, meet at Seville and make a declaration confirming the neutrality of their countries.

12 February

Singapore The Japanese attack repeatedly and forcefully. In the evening the British withdraw the gun crews from the coast defence batteries on the east and south-east of the island to reinforce the defensive perimeter round the city of Singapore. The defenders are becoming critically short of reinforcements.

English Channel The German battleships *Scharnhorst* and *Gneisenau* and the heavy cruiser *Prinz Eugen*, with 13 motor torpedo boats and 5 destroyers force the passage of the Channel guarded by the Home Fleet. The ships had been in harbour at Brest. They are attacked by British aircraft but are undamaged, and make for Norway. In their attempt to halt the German squadrons the British lose in two days 15 bombers and 17 fighters, against a small escorting force of 17 German fighters.

Eastern Front Heavy fighting continues in Leningrad sector, while in the south Berlin radio admits the Russians have broken through north of Taganrog on the Sea of Azov.

13 February

Eastern Front Vanguards of the Red Army enter the province of White Russia, but German resistance is now very strong.

Philippines In the Bataan peninsula the Americans have eliminated the larger Japanese salient and now attack the smaller. In the southern sector a Japanese landing in the area of Silaiim, near Anyasan, is wiped out.

Singapore The British defensive perimeter has to contract under incessant Japanese pressure. During the evening all ships leave the harbour. The 15-in coastal defence guns, which were to have made the island impregnable, are destroyed without a single shot being fired.

Dutch East Indies The Japanese occupy Bandjermasin, a key point in south-eastern Borneo.

14 February

Philippines In the Bataan peninsula the Filipinos and Americans reduce the Japanese salient further.

Singapore The Japanese continue to attack, mainly in the western sector of the island. Supplies of water, food and ammunition are rapidly becoming exhausted.

Dutch East Indies Japanese parachutists land at Palembang, Sumatra. The small Dutch garrison is forced to retire. An Allied task force tries to engage the enemy ships in the Banka Strait, but is heavily attacked by Japanese aircraft and has to withdraw.

North Africa Rommel renews offensive after two weeks lull.

15 February

Singapore Fall of Singapore. At 7.50 p.m. local time General Percival signs the document surrendering the city and garrison to General Tomoyuki Yamashita. The surrender is unconditional, and takes effect immediately. The Japanese take 70,000 prisoners, British, Indian, and Australian. The capture of the rich Malayan peninsula and the fortress described as the 'Gibraltar of the East' has cost the Japanese 10,000 dead, wounded and missing.

Dutch East Indies Following up the parachutists, a Japanese invasion fleet arrives off Palembang, Sumatra,

and lands substantial reinforcements in spite of attacks by British and Dutch aircraft. The Allies have to withdraw before completing the demolition of the oil refinery.

An Allied convoy sails from Darwin, in northern Australia, with reinforcements for Kupang on the island of Timor. The object of the mission is to occupy Penfoie airfield, the only airfield on Timor which aircraft can use for operations against the Japanese in Java.

Burma Indian troops abandon Thaton and begin to withdraw behind the river Bilin, pursued by the Japanese.

16 February

Dutch East Indies British aircraft and air crews leave Sumatra and cross to Java. The Allied convoy making for Timor has to change course on account of heavy Japanese air attacks.

17 February

Pacific The Americans land a battalion of Seabees, 'militarized civilians', at Bora-Bora, Society Islands, to build and equip an airfield.

Philippines Situation unchanged in the Bataan peninsula, where the Japanese continue to withdraw to more favourable positions.

North Africa General Auchinleck receives orders to despatch two divisions to the Far East. The British 70th Division leaves, but the 9th Australian Division stays in Africa. Axis aircraft bomb Tobruk fortress and an airfield near Mersa Matruh. Rommel, called to the Führer's headquarters at Rastenburg in East Prussia, asks Hitler for reinforcements, endeavouring to convince him of the importance of the African front to the war generally. But the Führer is now concentrating on the Russian front and does not want his forces dispersed, and Rommel is given no more than the 15th Parachute Brigade, which is sent to him from Greece by General Hermann Ramcke.

□ British air raid in the area of Castelvetrano, in Sicily.

19 February

Dutch East Indies The Japanese invade the island of Bali, east of Java. The British and Dutch destroy bridges and military installations. A naval engagement begins in the evening, and lasts until the next day, between the escort vessels of a Japanese convoy carrying infantry through the Strait of Lombok and an Allied squadron under the Dutch Rear-Admiral Karel Doorman. A Dutch destroyer is sunk and two Dutch cruisers and one American destroyer are damaged. The Japanese have only one destroyer damaged.

Burma The Japanese cross the River Bilin near Bilin and attack the 17th Indian Division on the flank, forcing it to retire. Mandalay is bombed.

□ Relays of aircraft taking off from carriers under the command of Admiral Noguma (the Japanese commander at Pearl Harbour) carry out successful raids on Darwin, in northern Australia, destroying port installations and sinking 12 warships, including the US destroyer *Peary*

19–23 February

North Africa Very bad weather conditions hold up any substantial activity, especially in the air.

Malta The air-pounding of the island continues without pause.

20 February

Philippines In the Bay of Manila Japanese guns pound the fortified islands off Luzon, including Corregidor. A United States submarine embarks President Quezon of the Philippines.

East Indies The Japanese land on Portuguese Timor, which for the past month has had a small Allied garrison. Australia is now directly threatened.

Burma Evacuation of Rangoon civilian population ordered within 48 hours.

Pacific An American task force consisting of the aircraft carrier *Lexington*, with cruisers and destroyers, sails for Rabaul, New Britain, to eject the Japanese, but has to turn back in the face of extremely heavy air attacks. The Japanese sacrifice many of their aircraft in repulsing this threat, and have to postpone their proposed action against New Guinea.

☐ Trial opens of 'war-guilt' prisoners, including Daladier, Blum and Gamelin, at Riom.

☐ The United States Government grants a loan of a thousand million dollars to the USSR.

21 February
Burma The 17th Indian Division retires on Mokpalin pursued by the Japanese.

Philippines The Japanese consolidate their defensive positions, withdrawing the troops still in forward positions in the area of Balanga.

22 February
Burma The Japanese launch a fierce attack against units of 17th Indian Division in the area of Mokpalin, where a bridge over the river Sittang is essential for the passage of troops.

☐ Air Marshal A. T. Harris takes command of Bomber Command, the RAF's strategic bombing force.

☐ President Roosevelt orders General MacArthur to leave the Philippines and transfer his headquarters to Australia.

23 February
Bismarck Archipelago Six American B-17 bombers take off from an Australian base and bomb Rabaul, New Britain, for the first time.

Dutch East Indies The Japanese war communiqué announces that the island of Amboina is now entirely in Japanese hands. Allied headquarters' staff leave Java, already in severe danger, for Australia.

Burma Fierce fighting round the Japanese bridgehead over the river Sittang. The Indians blow up the only bridge in the area, although many of their own units are still on the other side of the river.

North Africa General Auchinleck issues new directives on the conduct of operations: in the event of a new Axis offensive British troops should in general not try to counter-attack

Top: Japanese parachutists are dropped at Palembang, Sumatra; above: Japanese soldier honours his fallen comrades.

Bataan peninsula: an American despatch rider sleeps beside his motorcycle.

but should confine themselves to holding up the enemy advance as long as possible.

24 February
Eastern Front After a ten-day campaign on the northern front the Russians surround the II Corps of the German 16th Army south-east of Staraya Russa. In the central sector the Germans contain the Russian pressure on Smolensk, and in the south they offer firm resistance as the Russians try to break out into the great bend of the Dniepr river.
Wake An American task force commanded by Vice-Admiral W. F. Halsey, consisting of the aircraft carrier *Enterprise*, 2 cruisers and 7 destroyers, shells and bombs Japanese installations on the island.
Dutch East Indies The evacuation of Java continues.

25 February
Dutch East Indies The unified Allied ABDA command is broken up. General Wavell leaves Java and only the Dutch remain to defend it.
Burma The Japanese infiltrate through a gap opened between Nyaunglebin and Pegu, threatening the Rangoon–Mandalay railway.
Malta Axis bombers hit the naval base at Valletta and the airfields at Hal Far and Luqa.

26 February
Eastern Front Fierce fighting in the Staraya Russa area, where German 16th Army suffers heavily.
Philippines Japanese amphibious forces leave Olongapo, on the island of Luzon, for the island of Mindoro.

Indian Ocean The American flying-boat support ship *Langley*, on the way to Java, is sunk by Japanese air action with her 32 aircraft.
Burma Violent fighting between the two sides in the area of Waw, north-east of Pegu; infiltration of Japanese west of the Sittang river continues.
North Africa The British XIII Corps takes up positions defending the Gazala–Bir Hacheim line; XXX Corps prepares a defensive line along the Egyptian frontier and in the Jarabub oasis. British aircraft bomb Benghazi and Tripoli for the second day running.

27 February
Java Sea A big naval battle which ends in a Japanese victory. Near Surabaya an Allied task force commanded by Rear-Admiral Karel W.

Doorman, consisting of five cruisers and eleven destroyers, takes on the Japanese ships escorting the convoy carrying troops for the invasion of Java. Two Dutch cruisers, the *Java* and *De Ruyter*, and two British and one Dutch destroyers are sunk; one British and one American cruiser are damaged. Virtually the whole squadron is put out of action. The Japanese suffer some damage, but not enough to interfere with their invasion plans. *Philippines* The Japanese who sailed from Luzon land on the north-east coast of Mindoro and capture an airfield. The island is almost totally undefended, and the invaders have an easy task.

28 February

Java Japanese invasion force lands. After their great victory at sea Japanese troops, drawn from the 16th Army, are able to disembark without interference and now the route to the Sunda Islands lies open to them.

The four American destroyers that escaped from the battle of the Java Sea set course for the Sunda Strait.

Burma British troops fall back on Pegu, the prelude to general retirement.

☐ Subhas Chandra Bose broadcasts from Berlin on India's wish for freedom and consequent readiness to co-operate with Germany.

1 March

☐ The US War and Navy Departments announce that Major-General Walter Short and Rear-Admiral Kimmel, commanding US forces at Hawaii at the time of the Pearl Harbour attack on 7 December, are to be court-martialled on charges of dereliction of duty.

Dutch East Indies Having almost eliminated the Allied fleet and destroyed virtually all the Dutch and British aircraft on the ground, the Japanese are able to occupy Java with great speed. All Allied ships in the island's harbours leave to take refuge in Australia, but in the Sunda Strait these ships, with the remainder of Admiral Doorman's squadron, are met by superior Japanese forces. The cruisers *Houston* (US) and *Perth* (Australian), two American destroyers and one tanker are sunk

by Japanese gunfire and torpedoes, and one British and one Dutch destroyer are also lost. The Japanese lose only four transports.

Burma A Burmese division retakes Nyaunglebin, on the Rangoon–Mandalay road. The Chinese 5th Army concentrates in the area of Toungoo. The 17th Indian Division, which has by now retired from Waw, is sent back to the same area. General Wavell orders that defensive efforts must be intensified, in the expectation of the arrival of adequate reinforcements.

Eastern Front Russians launch new offensive in the Crimea and attack German positions near Kerch and Sevastopol. The Germans still cannot free the II Corps of the 16th Army from encirclement where they are cut off south-east of Staraya Russa. General Halder summarizes German losses on the Soviet front: 1,500,636 (31% of all effectives), of whom 202,257 have been killed, 725,642 wounded, 112,617 severely frostbitten, and 46,511 missing. The remainder have been taken prisoner by the enemy. Figures issued by the OKH on 16 March are much lower than these.

Malta Heavy bombing throughout the month.

2 March

Burma The Japanese continue to infiltrate between the 1st Burma Division and 17th Indian Division; by-passing Pegu, they converge on Rangoon.

Dutch East Indies The Japanese continue their occupation of Java. Their communiqués announce the capture of the capital, Batavia, which the government of the Dutch East Indies has left to move to Bandoeng.

New Guinea Japanese aircraft begin massive air raids in preparation for invasion.

☐ Australia declares war on Thailand.

☐ Two heavy air raids by British aircraft on Palermo.

3 March

Eastern Front Berlin admits that the encircled 16th Army is seriously

Below: in order to observe radio silence a reconnaissance aircraft drops a message on the flight deck of the USS *Enterprise* during the operation against Wake Island on 24 February.

short of food.

Burma Fighting continues in the Waw–Pyinbon area, north-east of Pegu. A new British brigade arrives to reinforce the defence of Rangoon.

Philippines A Japanese contingent lands at Zamboanga, in the island of Mindanao.

North Africa Axis aircraft bomb enemy installations in the Tobruk area, while the British raid Benghazi again.

☐ Japanese aircraft raid Broome, in Western Australia where most of the refugees from Java are concentrated. Many Allied aircraft are destroyed on the ground.

☐ RAF make heavy raid on the Renault works on the outskirts of Paris.

4 March

Philippines MacArthur reorganizes the forces defending the islands in readiness for his departure. General Sharp retains command of the Mindanao garrison, while General Chynoweth takes over the Central Philippines forces. Troops on Corregidor and the other fortified islands in the Bay of Manila will come under the command of General Moore, while those on Luzon will be regrouped under a general to be named.

Dutch East Indies The battle to defend Java is now lost, and the Dutch destroy all installations that can be of value to the enemy.

China General Stilwell sets up, in Chungking, the headquarters of American forces operating in China, Burma and India.

5 March

Dutch East Indies Fighting continues in Java. The Dutch announce the evacuation of Batavia.

New Britain A Japanese convoy sails from Rabaul in the direction of the Gulf of Huon in New Guinea, carrying invasion forces.

Burma General Alexander arrives at Rangoon and takes over command of the troops in Burma. He orders an immediate counter-offensive to close the gap between the 1st Burma and 17th Indian Divisions. The Japanese

Java Sea; right: the cruiser *Java*; left: the *Exeter* explodes.

attack Pegu from the west and succeed in entering the town.

Eastern Front In the central sector the Soviets recapture Yucknov, an important rail centre north-west of Kaluga.

North Africa RAF aircraft carry out heavy raids on air and naval installations at Benghazi.

Yugoslavia Patriot forces under General Mihailovitch rout Italian troops at Nikshich in Montenegro.

6 March

The 63rd Brigade of the 17th Indian Division carries out a fruitless attempt to open the Rangoon–Pegu road, blocked by the Japanese, and so relieve the garrison in Pegu, which is still cut off. In view of the serious situation General Alexander orders the evacuation of Rangoon.

7 March

Dutch East Indies Java falls to

STEFAN ZWEIG

On the morning of 25 February the Austrian writer Stefan Zweig and his wife were found dead at their house in Petropolis, near Rio de Janeiro. Forced into exile and deeply depressed by the catastrophe which had struck the world, the pair had decided to commit suicide by poison.

Born in Vienna into a well-to-do Jewish family in 1881, Zweig, after studying philosophy in Berlin and Vienna, made frequent trips abroad that brought him into contact with many stimulating aspects of European culture, which led to important friendships with leading artists and intellectuals (Gorky, Rilke, Toscanini, Rolland, Freud, etc.).

His experiences during the First World War reinforced his deep pacifist feelings, which were ever present in his works.

An extremely versatile writer, Zweig wrote essays, historical works, stories, stage scripts and opera libretti; he also translated French poetry and collections of romantic verse.

8 March 1942: Japanese infantry enter Rangoon.

Japanese. All Allied fighter aircraft have been destroyed. Radio communication with Bandoeng is cut off. The Dutch government administration has fled to Australia. The garrisons, under the command of General ter Poorten, surrender to the Japanese.

Burma Rangoon is evacuated. The British retire towards the north of the country, and from now on have to be supplied by air. The Pegu garrison, still cut off, is ordered to break out and make its way towards the north.

New Guinea During the night of 7 March the Japanese invasion convoy arrives in the Gulf of Huon and, under cover of fire from the escort vessels, lands the first contingents of troops at Salamaua and Lae, meeting with no opposition.

8 March

Burma The Japanese enter Rangoon. Indian infantry, with tank and artillery support, break through the Japanese block on the Rangoon–Prome road, along which the British are retiring.

9 March

Dutch East Indies The last Dutch units still fighting in Java surrender to the Japanese. The whole of the Dutch East Indies is now under Japanese control.

New Guinea American aircraft hit

North Africa In view of the serious supply situation in Malta, General Auchinleck orders General Ritchie to do everything possible to engage the Axis air forces, so as to make it possible to send a supply convoy to the island in conditions of maximum safety.

☐ New-style RAF air raids on Essen, the biggest city in the north Rhineland. The main target is the famous Krupp armament works. This is the first of a long series of night raids which reduce the city to a heap of ruins. A completely new technique of attack is tried out, with guide aircraft flying over the area first and dropping flares, followed by others which drop incendiary bombs to indicate the targets to the bomber squadrons.

at the Japanese troop convoy in the Gulf of Huon. The Japanese air force continues its raids on Australian and British positions on the island.

Burma The British withdrawal to the north continues.

10 March

New Guinea Another Japanese landing, at Finschhafen. A hundred and four American aircraft from the carriers *Lexington* and *Yorktown* bomb Lae and Salamaua, damaging Japanese shipping and airfields. Japanese aircraft from Rabaul (New Britain) carry out 'neutralization raids' on Port Moresby.

Solomon Islands The Japanese land on Buka.

☐ The government of the USA declares that help under the Lend–Lease Act may be extended to Iran.

11 March

Philippines General Douglas MacArthur, with his personal staff, and Rear-Admiral F. W. Rockwell, together with members of the General Staff, leave Luzon on board four motor torpedo-boats for Mindanao. Emotional but determined, the South Pacific Commander-in-Chief promises: 'I shall return!'

Burma Allied troops take up defensive positions to keep the Japanese out of the northern part of the country. The 17th Indian Division is deployed near Tharrawaddy, in the Irrawaddy valley, and the 1st Burma Division takes up positions in the upper Sittang valley. Lieutenant-General Stilwell of the US Army is appointed to command the Chinese 5th and 6th Armies; the 5th is to concentrate at Mandalay, the 6th garrisons the Shan States. Another Chinese division is deployed in the Toungoo area.

☐ Winston Churchill speaks on India. Sir Stafford Cripps is to be sent to India to prepare the way for independence.

12 March

New Caledonia 17,500 Americans commanded by General Patch land at Noumea to garrison the island and build and equip base installations.

Andaman Islands Following the fall of Rangoon the British base here is no longer defensible, and the garrison is taken off by seaplanes.

Burma Allied headquarters set up at Maymyo, near Mandalay.

☐ RAF bombers attack Kiel and other targets in north-west Germany. As the Luftwaffe is engaged more and more on the Eastern Front, the RAF is gradually winning air superiority in the West. Since the beginning of March it has been carrying out a systematic offensive against German industrial centres and submarine bases in Germany, occupied France and Italy – an offensive that is to grow steadily more powerful until 1945.

13 March

New Guinea Having now consolidated their positions around Lae and Salamaua, the Japanese replace their infantry by naval personnel.

Solomon Islands The capture of Buka and other islands in the north of the archipelago is completed. The landing operation is protected by the Japanese 4th Fleet, based on Rabaul, New Britain.

14 March

North Africa Further heavy bombing of Benghazi by the RAF.

Malta Further Axis raids on Ta Venezia and Hal Far.

Philippines General MacArthur and his staff arrive on Mindanao.

☐ The Chief of Staffs Committee decides to maintain defensive positions in the Pacific theatre and proceed with the build-up of American forces in Britain for the opening of a second front against the Axis in Europe.

15 March

Philippines In the Bay of Manila the Japanese artillery is reinforced and pounds the fortified islands day after day. This intensified fire continues until 21 March.

Burma General Stilwell officially notified that the Commander-in-Chief of operations in Burma is still the British General Wavell, Com-

General MacArthur with an ADC in a bunker on Corregidor.

mander-in-Chief of Allied forces in India (disagreement about spheres of authority had arisen).

☐ Berlin. Hitler declares that Russia will be 'annihilatingly defeated' in the coming summer. He blames the halt of the German thrust on the exceptionally early winter.

16 March

Eastern Front Although their enormous 'porcupine' defensive perimeters have held out well under constant Russian pressure, since the start of the year the Germans have been compelled to withdraw all along the line. The greatest advances have been made by the Russian horse cavalry between the northern and central sectors, in the area of Kalinin, and Kaluga and south of Lake Ilmen, where huge German forces have been trapped in pockets in the Demyansk and Kholm regions, and in the southern sector in front of Izyum. From Leningrad the front now runs to Novgorod, Staraya Russa and Velikiye Luki (the sector manned by the Army Group North, with the 18th and 16th Armies). From Velikiye Luki, in the Army Group Centre's sector, the front line is uneven on account of the Russian salients and German countersalients. It goes up to Nevel, turns east towards Velizh, near Vitebsk, Demidov and Dorogobuzh, thence north again with the Vyazma and Rzhev salient, finally turning southeast to pass through Kirov and north of Bryansk and Orel. The German 3rd Armoured Army, 9th Army, 4th Armoured Army, and 4th Army and 2nd Armoured Army are operating in this sector. The Army Group South, whose front extends from Orel to the Caucasus by way of Kursk, Kharkov, Dnepropetrovsk, Stalino, Taganrog and the centre of the Caucasus, includes the 2nd Army and 6th Army, the Kleist and Manstein Army Groups and the 11th Army, this last in the Crimea.

According to OKH statistics the Germans on the Eastern Front have lost about 240,000 men between 1 January and mid-March, including 52,000 killed and 15,000 missing. Since 22 June 1941 the Wehrmacht has lost over a million men. (General Halder's figures, reported in the entry for 1 March, speak of 1.5 mil-

Above: Japanese sappers attack a US casemate in Bataan.

lion men.) Russian losses are presumably even higher, though the data here is uncertain and controversial.

17 March

Pacific By order of President Roosevelt, General MacArthur flys from Mindanao to Darwin, in Australia, where he is to assume supreme command of Allied forces in the South-West Pacific. The territorial limits of his command have still to be worked out. However, by agreement with the Allied governments, the USA takes over responsibility for the strategic defence of the whole of the Pacific Ocean.

Malta The hammering of the island by Axis aircraft goes on without pause. Out of 25,000 tons of supplies consigned to the island during the month, only 5,000 tons get through.

18 March

New Hebrides American infantry and engineers arrive on Efate to build an airfield.

19 March

Burma The British General William Slim arrives to assume command of the British troops, now regrouped to form the I Burma Corps. In the Sittang valley the Japanese advance on Toungoo, which is defended by the Chinese 200th Division.

Eastern Front Russian pressure in the central and southern sectors continues. In the northern sector, Army Group North launches a vigorous counter-attack to relieve the II Corps of the 16th Army from encirclement in the area of Kholm and Staraya Russa.

20 March

Philippines General Wainwright is appointed to command all American forces in this theatre.

North Africa To draw away as many Axis aircraft as possible from a supply convoy en route to Malta, the RAF attacks airfields in the area of Derna and Benghazi.

21 March

Philippines General Wainwright sets

up his headquarters on the fortified island of Corregidor. His chief of staff is General Beebe, while General E. P. King takes command of American and Filipino forces on the island of Luzon.

Burma The 1st Burma Division is deployed on the Irrawaddy front, leaving a vast sector south of Toungoo open. The defence of this town and the line Toungoo–Prome is undertaken by the Chinese 5th Army in collaboration with the British. Japanese attacks on the airfields reduce further the already low strength of the Allied aircraft defending this area.

Eastern Front Breaking out from Staraya Russa, in the northern sector south of Lake Ilmen, the Germans attack with four divisions in the Demyansk sector. However, the thaw holds them up, and it is not until 21 April that these four divisions manage to re-establish contact with their army.

22 March

Burma Heavy Japanese air raids on Magwe airfield force the British and American aircraft to move to Loiwing, near the Chinese frontier, and to Akyab. The troops defending Burma are, therefore, deprived of close support from the air. In the Toungoo sector the Chinese hold out against Japanese pressure.

☐ Japanese planes bomb Darwin, in northern Australia.

☐ Sir Stafford Cripps arrives in Karachi to discuss constitutional problems.

☐ King Boris leaves Sofia for Berlin, where he will meet Hitler. The meeting, like others with leaders of vassal states, is interpreted as a demand for additional manpower for the coming German spring offensive in Russia.

23 March

Andaman Islands The Japanese occupy the islands (in the Bay of Bengal) evacuated by the British and Gurkha garrison.

24 March

Eastern Front Russian sources

GANDHI

On the outbreak of war the Indian Congress, although strongly denouncing fascism and nazism, declared its support of Britain only on condition that the principles of democracy were applied to India. The nation itself would directly express its views on the matter through a government formed from a democratically elected assembly. Although personally opposed to the war, Gandhi had agreed to act as spokesman of Congress and to put this proposal to the viceroy.

The promise made by Churchill soon after the German invasion of France to guarantee Indian independence after the war was not considered adequate by Gandhi who proceeded to promote a campaign of civil disobedience.

After the attack on Pearl Harbour and the Japanese invasion of Burma, the British government sought to come to a fresh agreement with Congress; in addition to releasing Nehru and other leaders from prison, it sent Sir Stafford Cripps to India in March 1942 in order to conduct negotiations. But the British refusal to transfer immediate military responsibility to an Indian government led to a new and violent anti-British campaign in August.

British troops dealt harshly with the disorders, bringing in repressive measures and imprisoning Gandhi and other Congress leaders.

In prison for the sixth time, the partisan of non-violence began another fast after voicing yet again the slogan, 'freedom or death'.

Mahatma Gandhi at a nationalist meeting.

is still defending parts of Toungoo. On the Irrawaddy front the Japanese concentrate forces south of Prome. With the increasing threat from the enemy, RAF aircraft are withdrawn from the Akyab base into India.
Malta The island has now suffered some 1600 bombing raids.

28 March

Philippines Luzon: the Japanese prepare to launch the final offensive against the Bataan peninsula. The supply situation of the defenders has become precarious under the incessant bombing and shelling.
Burma In response to a request by General Stilwell, General Alexander orders the I Burma Corps to attack in the Irrawaddy sector, and the Japanese are vigorously engaged at Paungde, south-east of Prome.
☐ During the night 234 aircraft of Bomber Command carry out a heavy raid on the city of Lübeck, in Schleswig-Holstein, on the Trave estuary some 10 miles from the Baltic Sea. The raid destroys many ancient buildings and monuments and gives Hitler an excuse for recalling two groups of bombers from Sicily and ordering them to carry out reprisal raids on a number of historic British cities, including Exeter, York and Canterbury.
RAF air superiority in Europe is of course by now firmly established due to the increasing demands of the Eastern Front on Luftwaffe resources.

29 March

Burma To relieve Japanese pressure on the Chinese in the Toungoo area, a special force from I Burma Corps attacks and occupies Paungde. But its position soon becomes precarious when the enemy takes up positions a little to the north of Padigon and at Shwedaung on the east bank of the Irrawaddy. The Chinese accuse the Japanese of using poison gas and bacteriological warfare.
North Africa German air raid on Tobruk.
☐ British government constitutional proposals for India published: India is to have full Dominion status after

report more than 16,000 German troops have fallen on the Leningrad front between 9 and 22 March.
Philippines On Luzon the Japanese begin a series of land and air bombardments in the Bataan peninsula. Aircraft based on the island attack Corregidor incessantly, and also begin a series of night raids.
Burma The Japanese make a surprise attack north of Toungoo and put the Chinese and Burmese defenders to flight, almost completely surrounding the town.
Papua and New Guinea Port Moresby heavily bombed.

25 March

Eastern Front Marshal Timosh-

enko's troops break into suburbs of Stalino; ferocious street fighting takes place as Germans defend their positions house by house.
Burma The I Burma Corps concentrates in the Prome–Allanmyo area.
Society Islands An American infantry regiment arrives to garrison Bora-Bora.

26 March

Burma The Japanese capture part of the town of Toungoo. A Chinese division is despatched to reinforce the 200th Division, still fighting in the town and on the outskirts.

27 March

Burma The Chinese 200th Division

OPERATION 'SAVE MALTA'
THE SECOND BATTLE OF SIRTE

20–23 March

A British convoy of four ships, the *Breconshire*, *Clan Campbell*, *Talabot* and *Pampas*, leaves Alexandria harbour at dawn bound for Malta, where the lack of supplies and incessant hammering by the Axis air forces have rendered conditions intolerable and have reduced enormously the capacity of the defending forces.

The convoy now leaving Alexandria is part of Operation 'Save Malta', an operation to get supplies to the island at all costs, without which it will be impossible for the base to remain in British hands.

The convoy is escorted by the cruisers *Dido*, *Euryalus* and *Cleopatra* (flying the flag of the commander, Admiral Philip Vian) and the light cruiser *Carlisle* and 17 destroyers. Later the squadron is joined by the destroyer *Legion* and the cruiser *Penelope*, sailing from Malta.

In accordance with instructions from the Admiralty, every warship available at the time in the Mediterranean is to be enlisted in the operation.

But the movements of the British ships do not escape the eyes and ears of enemy spies, and the Axis partners draw the conclusion that the British are mounting an operation to replenish the beleaguered island fortress.

Italian naval forces are ordered to leave port and intercept the convoy, and prevent it from reaching its destination.

21–22 March

During the night Admiral Iachino leaves Taranto, in the heel of Italy, in the battleship *Littorio* with an escort of four destroyers.

At the same time the cruisers *Gorizia*, *Trento* and *Bande Nere*, with four destroyers, sail from Messina under the command of Admiral Parona.

The Italian ships make for the Gulf of Sirte, where it is calculated they will meet up with the enemy squadron.

22 March

Italian S-79 torpedo-carrying planes attack the British formation making for Malta, but fail to scatter the convoy or hit any of the ships.

12.40 p.m.: The pilot of a reconnaissance aircraft sent up from the *Trento* reports having sighted the Allied convoy, and that it is sailing without air protection. In his account of the battle, Admiral Iachino wrote: 'For the first time, on 22 March 1942, our naval forces found themselves confronting an enemy formation which was not protected from the air, which in fact was unable to call upon any form of air–naval co-operation.'

2.40 p.m.: Admiral Parona's cruisers which are ahead of Iachino's squadron sight the British cruisers and open fire. But the convoy is well protected by a smoke-screen and escapes damage. After about a quarter of an hour the Italian admiral breaks off the engagement.

4.31 p.m.: One of the British cruisers is sighted by the *Littorio*, but weather and sea conditions are not as favourable as they were a few hours earlier.

Moreover the Allied ships have put up an effective smoke-screen behind which they have disappeared, and into which it would be both useless and dangerous for the Italian ships to venture, since they are not equipped with radar. None the less the Italian ships open fire on the enemy cruisers whenever they appear from the smoke-screen. In one such sortie, Admiral Vian's flagship, the *Cleopatra*, is hit.

6.35 p.m.: The Italian ships have reached the point at which the interception of the enemy convoy for Malta is planned to take place. Admiral Vian accepts the challenge and immediately sends in his destroyers against the *Littorio*, hoping to at least cripple the Italian battleship with torpedoes.

The Italian battleship manages to take evasive action but, fearing another attack, and because it is getting dark (it is already 7.00 p.m.), she turns away and steams north. The rest of the Italian squadron follows in the wake of the flagship.

Thus the naval battle ends. The damage caused to ships engaged in it is negligible – one hit by a shell on the *Littorio*, one shell each on the *Cleopatra*, *Euryalus* and *Kingston*. The four merchant ships are untouched. Admiral Vian can leave the merchant ships to reach harbour under cover of the dark.

23 March

Although they have proceeded at full speed throughout the night, the four merchant ships fail to reach the shelter of Malta before dawn.

At dawn they are attacked by Axis aircraft that have been lying in wait for them. The *Talabot* and *Pampas* are hit having reached port, and sink before they can be unloaded.

The *Breconshire* goes down, having also reached port, after being towed in, and the *Clan Campbell* is sunk 50 miles off Malta.

Of the 26,000 tons of petrol carried by the convoy only 5,000 tons are salvaged.

Of Operation 'Save Malta', Admiral Cunningham wrote later: 'The Axis forces had very largely achieved their object of preventing supplies from reaching the island.'

the war.

☐ At the request of King George VI this is observed as another National Day of Prayer.

30 March

Burma The Chinese 200th Division abandons Toungoo, unable to withstand Japanese pressure any longer. The special force from I Burma Corps falls back on Prome from Paungde. In the evening the Japanese attack the 63rd Indian Brigade at Prome and quickly put them to flight, so that the 17th Indian Division's flank is dangerously exposed.

Pacific The Joint Chiefs of Staff divide the Pacific theatre of operations into two zones: the Pacific Ocean Zone under the command of Admiral C. W. Nimitz, and the South-West Pacific Zone under General Douglas MacArthur (the latter includes Australia, New Guinea, the Philippines, the Bismarck Archipelago, the Solomon Islands and much of the Dutch East Indies). A conflict in attitudes to the war soon emerges, reflected in different strategic principles: Nimitz believes in 'great leaps' while MacArthur supports a policy of reconquest 'from island to island'.

A Pacific War Council, with representatives from the United States, the United Kingdom, Canada, Australia, New Zealand, the Netherlands, Philippines and China, is set up in Washington.

Indian Ocean Japanese land troops on Christmas Island, south of Java.

Ascension Island US detachment arrives on this small island, between Africa and South America.

31 March

Burma The Chinese 200th and 22nd Divisions withdraw from the Toungoo area towards Pyinmana. With the loss of Toungoo the road to Mauchi lies open to the Japanese, and the small Chinese garrison there is overwhelmed a few days later.

Indian Ocean The Allies' Indian Squadron, commanded by the British Admiral Sir James Somerville and consisting of the aircraft carriers

Indomitable, Formidable and *Hermes,* 5 old battleships, 8 cruisers (of which 2 are Dutch) and 15 destroyers, warned of an imminent Japanese attack, sail from Ceylon and take refuge at a secret base in the Maldive Islands. The Japanese fleet in pursuit of them has sailed from Kendari in the Celebes. It is under the command of Admiral Nobutake Kondo, who has under him Admiral C. Nagumo, the commander at Pearl Harbour. The Japanese fleet comprises the battleships *Kongo, Haruna, Hiei* and *Kirishima,* the aircraft carriers *Akagi, Soryu, Hiryu, Shokaku* and *Zuikaku,* the cruisers *Tone, Chikuma* and *Abukuma* and 9 destroyers. It is decided to use these greatly superior forces to destroy the Allied fleet and so eliminate a potentially serious threat to the western flank of the extended Japanese line.

1 April

Burma On the Irrawaddy front I Burma Corps is ordered to withdraw immediately from Prome to the area of Allanmyo, north of Prome, to avoid encirclement by the Japanese.

New Guinea Japanese units from the Dutch East Indies land at many places on the coast of Dutch New Guinea, from Sorong at the northwest tip of the island to Hollandia, now Djajapura. Landings continue until April 20 and are virtually unopposed.

Eastern Front The spring thaw brings a comparative lull and there is stalemate along much of the front, though there are renewed German attempts to free the II Corps of the 16th Army from the enemy's grip in the Staraya Russa area. In the south Sevastopol reaches its 150th day of siege.

Malta Two submarines sunk by Axis torpedo planes. During the coming months Axis planes drop more than 6,700 tons of bombs on Malta. The air defence of the island comprises only a few Hurricanes and Spitfires, though these do manage to check the enemy fighter-bombers and during April they shoot down at least 37 of them. But this is only one aspect of the critical situation in

which the British find themselves in the Mediterranean. They have only 4 cruisers and 15 destroyers, as against the enemy's 4 battleships, 9 cruisers, 55 torpedo-boats and more than 70 submarines. With such tremendous numerical superiority there is clearly a very real risk of an Axis invasion of Malta.

George IV sends a tribute to Malta's heroic resistance to the island's Governor, Lieutenant-General Sir William Dobbie, and announces he has accepted the Colonelcy-in-Chief of the Royal Malta Artillery.

2 April

Churchill receives a letter from Roosevelt to say that Harry Lloyd Hopkins (the President's specialist in foreign affairs) and General George Marshall, Chief of Staff of the Army, will soon be arriving in the British capital. 'They will submit to you,' writes Roosevelt, 'a plan which I hope will be received with enthusiasm by Russia.' The plan is for a second front in Europe – in France, the most sensitive point for the Germans. The plan has been drawn up by Lieutenant-Colonel Dwight David Eisenhower, and is in answer to the insistent demands of the Russians, who want a second European front to relieve German pressure on Moscow.

3 April

Burma Japanese bomb Mandalay, killing some 2,000 and setting much of the city ablaze. I Burma Corps retires from Allanmyo, not under enemy pressure but on orders from GHQ. In the Sittang valley General Stilwell's Chinese divisions take up positions in defence of Pyinmana.

Philippines The Japanese launch their big offensive in the Bataan peninsula, against troops already exhausted, ill-equipped and running out of supplies. After a five-hour-long artillery preparation the Japanese infantry go into action at 3.00 p.m., forcing the Americans and Filipinos to withdraw, often in disorder, in many sectors.

4 April

Philippines The Japanese assault on the Bataan peninsula is renewed, preceded by machine-gun fire from the air and an intensive artillery barrage to break down the defenders' morale. At nightfall the Japanese re-group for a new attack, with Mount Samat as their chief objective.

Indian Ocean A British reconnaissance aircraft sights Admiral Kondo's squadron off Colombo and manages to give the alarm before being shot down by Zero fighters.

North Africa RAF raids on Benghazi and Derna.

☐ Anglo–Italian agreement on exchange of sick and wounded prisoners of war announced.

5 April

Philippines In the Bataan peninsula, after the usual air and artillery preparation, the Japanese attack and take Mount Samat. The defending 21st Division is massacred in savage fighting.

A landing force of about 5,000 Japanese sails from the Gulf of Lingayen, Luzon, for Cebu, an

ST NAZAIRE

26 March

At 3.00 p.m. a small British force consisting of three destroyers, one gunboat and several motor-boats and motor torpedo-boats, with groups of Commandos on board, sails from Falmouth Bay (Cornwall), for the French coast. Their objective is the important German submarine base at St Nazaire, the French port situated at the mouth of the Loire estuary.

27 March

The British force is nearing St Nazaire.

11.30 p.m.: British aircraft supporting the Commando operation against St Nazaire bomb the German Atlantic naval base, but without any great result.

28 March

00.30 a.m.: The British ships enter the Loire estuary and slowly approach the port, avoiding enemy observation.

01.34 a.m.: The destroyer *Campeltown*, loaded in the bows with

The bodies of two British commandos lie on the beach at St Nazaire after the ill-fated raid.

island in the central Philippines north of Mindanao.

Indian Ocean At dawn 200 Japanese aircraft, bombers, dive-bombers and fighters, take off from aircraft-carriers 200 miles south of Ceylon. They sight and destroy 12 British torpedo planes sent to attack the Japanese ships. The Japanese planes attack Colombo, believing Admiral

several tons of explosives, intended to be detonated the next day, rams the dock gates of the naval base. The explosion causes extensive damage to the docks, and kills many Germans who had climbed on board. But this is the only substantial result of the raid, and it has been achieved at considerable loss in men and materials.

Somerville's squadron to be still at anchor there. No ships are in the harbour, but the Japanese are able to destroy the port installations. While the aircraft are regrouping a reconnaissance aircraft sent up from the cruiser *Tone* reports the presence of two British cruisers south-west of Ceylon. Eighty more dive-bombers are sent up to look for the enemy cruisers *Dorsetshire* and *Cornwall*. They are located, attacked and sunk. The Japanese squadron continues to hunt the Allied ships, which Admiral Somerville decides to disperse rather than have them attacked in mass and wiped out. His decision is approved by the Admiralty.

Malta In the course of a German air raid on Valletta harbour a British destroyer is sunk and two others seriously damaged.

6 April

Philippines Heavy Japanese attacks continue in the Bataan peninsula. The Americans and Filipinos carry out fruitless counter-attacks but are driven back by the Japanese, who have overwhelming air and artillery support. At the end of the day the defenders have had to withdraw further in the San Vicente area.

Burma The Japanese land reinforcements at Rangoon. Chiang Kai-shek visits the front and recommends that the Shan States, on the Chinese frontier, should be defended to the last man. The Chinese 96th and 200th Divisions are in defensive positions before Pyinmana, in the Sittang valley and almost half-way between Rangoon and Mandalay.

Admiralty Islands A small Japanese contingent from Truk lands at Lorengau, at the extreme north-east of Manus Island. The Admiralty Islands are part of the Bismarck Archipelago, north of New Guinea. The Japanese threat to Australia grows stronger.

☐ First Japanese bombing raids on India, at Coconada and Vizagupatam (Madras).

7 April

Philippines The Japanese advance in the Bataan peninsula continues. In

the eastern sector their divisions press on from Mount Samat, pushing the defenders back to Limay. Some sort of defence line is established from Point Caibobo on the west coast to Limao on the east. The Americans and Filipinos defend themselves more effectively in the western sector, only slowly retiring from Bagac. The submarine *Seadragon* evacuates pilots and other specialist personnel from Corregidor.

Malta The island suffers its heaviest attack to date, and also records its 2,000th alert of the war.

8 April

Philippines In the Bataan peninsula the eastern sector of the American front collapses completely under Japanese pressure, and the Japanese soon break through the emergency defence lines. The Americans and Filipinos are routed. General King decides that the Luzon force will have to surrender, and orders the destruction of all equipment during the night. Only 2,000 of the 78,000 men in the two corps on Luzon can be evacuated to Corregidor.

9 April

Philippines Luzon: at 3.30 a.m. officers sent by General King go forward with a white flag to the Japanese advance positions to begin negotiations for surrender. Unconditional surrender comes into effect at 12.30 p.m. Then follows the mopping-up operations and terrible march of the prisoners (76,000 men, including 12,000 Americans) towards San Fernando. Thousands die of starvation, exposure and dysentery during that march, which later became known as the 'march of death'. Japanese artillery sited at Cabcaben, on the south coast of the peninsula, opens fire on Corregidor, already under attack from the air. The surrender of Bataan is later approved by Roosevelt. The garrison of the island of Cebu is warned that a Japanese landing force is approaching.

Burma I Burma Corps is deployed

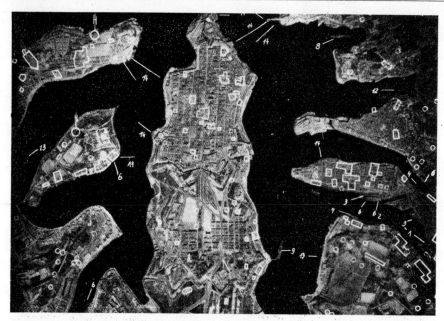

Malta: Axis reconnaissance photograph of Valletta harbour taken on 1 April 1942. Nos. 1, 2, 3, 4, 7, 8, 9, 10 and 12 mark British ships damaged or destroyed. The order numbers indicate constructions such as dockyards and emplacements.

on a front of about 37 miles between Minhla and Taungdwingyi, in the Irrawaddy basin, to defend the oil wells in the area.

Indian Ocean Japanese aircraft from Admiral Kondo's squadron make a heavy attack on the base at Trincomalee, on the east coast of the island of Ceylon, destroying naval and airfield installations. At the same time a British aircraft carrier and a destroyer are reported 70 miles south of Batticaloa, also on the island's east coast. Shortly after, the aircraft carrier *Hermes* (undefended, as its aircraft have taken off on an unsuccessful attack on the Japanese fleet) and the destroyer *Vampire* are attacked and sunk within the space of ten minutes. A 10,000-ton transport is also sunk a short way to the north of the British warships.

At the same time another Japanese fleet (6 heavy cruisers and the light aircraft carrier *Ryujo*) under Vice-Admiral Takeo Kurita enters the Bay of Bengal and sinks about 135,000 tons of shipping, almost all engaged in carrying troops and supplies to Burma. The two Japanese squadrons pass through the Strait of Malacca and return to their bases unscathed.

Eastern Front In the southern sector the Russians launch violent attacks in the area of Kerch, in the Crimea, but make virtually no progress in the face of tenacious German resistance. In the central sector the Germans are still on the defensive, fighting off Russian thrusts; in the north they advance slowly against strong Russian resistance trying to reach their forces cut off in the Kholm–Staraya Russa area.

10 April

Philippines The Japanese land at Cebu and near Toledo on Cebu Island; the garrison of 6,500 Americans and Filipinos retire inland, defending road junctions.

Burma Patrols from the I Burma Corps report that the Japanese are advancing towards the Minhla–Taungdwingyi line.

Indian Ocean In consequence of the Japanese air and naval activity south of Ceylon, the Royal Navy leaves the Indian Ocean and takes refuge in the Persian Gulf. Churchill asks the Americans if they can undertake some large-scale action in the Pacific to draw off the Japanese forces – which, surprisingly, do not exploit their successes immediately but concentrate their efforts on New Guinea and the New Hebrides in order to complete the isolation of Australia.

☐ During a night raid on Essen bombers of RAF Bomber Command drop the first aerial two-ton bomb ever used.

☐ Indian Congress Party rejects British constitutional proposals.

11 April

Philippines The Americans and Filipinos on Cebu are unable to hold up the Japanese, who advance eastwards from Toledo without check.

Burma The Japanese pass to the offensive in the central sector of the line held by the I Burma Corps.

Eastern Front In the southern sector, in the Crimea, the Russians try to land new forces at Evpatoriya but are stubbornly resisted by the Germans. No major action in the central sector. In the north, German Army Group North is still making slow progress towards their forces cut off in the Kholm–Staraya Russa area.

12 April

Philippines The defending forces on Cebu retire to the northern mountains to organize guerrilla operations. With batteries cited on the southern point of Bataan and at Cavite, the Japanese intensify the shelling of Corregidor, and continue to attack it from the air.

Burma The Chinese 38th Division, which has been responsible for the defence of Mandalay, is moved to the Irrawaddy front in support of the I Burma Corps, defending the Minhla–Taungdwingyi line. During the night the Japanese take Migyaungye, leaving the western flank of the Burmese forces undefended.

☐ Pandit Nehru speaks on the failure of the Delhi talks. He says, 'It distresses me that any Indian should talk of the Japanese liberating India'.

13 April

Philippines Cebu is now firmly in Japanese hands, though there is sporadic guerrilla action by the defenders.

Burma The Japanese break through the centre of the I Burma Corps defensive line and push on northwards, towards the oil wells. The Chinese and British reinforce the defences of

Magwe, Taunggyi, Lashio and the Thailand border. The Chinese 66th Army is ordered to concentrate south of Mandalay.

☐ Churchill announces that Lord Louis Mountbatten will be appointed Chief of Combined Operations as from 18 March.

14 April

Burma The defenders commence the destruction of the Yenangyaung oil-fields to deny them to the enemy. The Japanese begin to surround the Chinese 55th Division in the area of Mauchi–Loikaw.

☐ The British government and Chiefs of Staff accept Plan *Bolero*, submitted by General Marshall, for the preparation of a second front against Germany.

☐ Pierre Laval forms new 'collaborationist' government. Germany has been increasingly dissatisfied with its Vichy partners, and therefore exerts pressure to bring about a completely subservient régime.

15 April

Burma The Japanese push on north-wards, by-passing the 1st Burma Division.

☐ President Roosevelt's two envoys, Harry Hopkins and General Marshall, return to Washington from London taking with them the *Bolero* plan for the opening of a second front in Europe, agreed but not yet worked out in detail.

16 April

Philippines General Wainwright (US) appoints General Sharp to command the troops in the central Philippines. Having occupied Cebu, the Japanese land over 4,000 men on Panay Island, mostly near the capital, Iloilo, in the south, and at Capiz (now Roxas) in the north-east. The 7,000-strong garrison, rather than take on the invaders, withdraw inland into the mountains to operate as guerrillas.

Malta In recognition of the heroism with which it has faced up to its terrible battering by the Axis air forces, the island is awarded the George Cross by George VI.

ROBERT MUSIL

The Austrian writer Robert Musil, one of the great exponents of the modern novel, died in Geneva on 15 April.

Born in Klagenfurt in 1880, Musil was educated at a military academy and then studied engineering at the Brünn polytechnic. Around the beginning of the century he went to Berlin to study philosophy and began writing his first novel, *Die Verirrungen des Zögling Törless*, in which he evoked the ambiguous and violent atmosphere of military colleges. Having served in the First World War, he worked for a time in the war ministry in Vienna and then devoted himself entirely to writing, publishing two plays between 1921 and 1924 (*Die Schwärmer* and *Vincenz oder die Freundin bedeutender Männer*), and the collection of stories *Drei Frauen*.

Musil's fame, however, resides principally in his masterpiece, the monumental *Der Mann ohne Eigenschaften*, an unfinished novel published in three volumes (1930, 1933 and 1943, translated into English as *The Man Without Qualities*, 1953-60). With a narrative style combining poetry and scientific language, Musil created a profound and ironic work which analysed the false attitudes of an age fraught with uncertainty and unreality.

17 April

Burma On the Irrawaddy front the Japanese cut the road north and south of Pin Chaung, near Yenangyaung. The Chinese 38th Division and part of the 17th Indian Division are rushed to the area of Magwe to relieve enemy pressure on the 1st Burma Division, which is still cut off, but they are unsuccessful. On the Sittang front, following the reverses suffered by the I Burma Corps, General Stilwell's Chinese forces have to give up the defence of Pyinmana. The Japanese maintain pressure on the Chinese 55th Division in the Bawlake–Mauchi area.

☐ Admiral William D. Leahy, US ambassador in Vichy France, is called home for consultations.

18 April

Pacific The command structure in the South-West Pacific is changed. Under MacArthur, the supreme commander, are the Commander-in-Chief of Australian forces, General Sir Thomas Blamey, who will be in charge of all land operations, the American General Brett at the head of the air forces, and Admiral Leary, hitherto head of the ANZAC forces,

who will command Allied naval forces.

Burma Chinese and British troops retire in the Sittang valley. The Chinese 55th Division is wiped out by the Japanese south of Loikaw, leaving the road to Lashio wide open to the enemy. The Chinese 22nd Division withdraws north of Pyinmana.

☐ First American air raid on Japan. Sixteen B-25 bombers of XVII Bomber Group of the 8th US Air Force, commanded by Lieutenant Colonel J. H. Doolittle, take off from the aircraft carrier *Hornet* about 750 miles from Tokyo. The *Hornet* and her escort, the cruisers *Vincennes* and *Nashville* with their complement of destroyers, left on the 14th from a rendezvous north of Midway Island. Another carrier, the *Enterprise*, joins them near Japan to provide fighter escort. The B-25s arrive over their targets at 12.15 p.m., dropping bombs on Tokyo, Kobe, Yokohama, Nagoya and Yokosuka. They then fly on towards China, but owing to bad weather they either crash on landing or their crews make parachute jumps. One aircraft lands near Vladivostok and its crew is interned by the Russians. Two planes end up in

The British aircraft carrier *Hermes* sinks east of Ceylon.

The national flag and the battle flag at the masthead of a Japanese ship.
Left: American prisoners after the Luzon 'death march'.

Japanese-occupied territory where their crews are made prisoner (some being shot on 15 October 1942). The aircraft carriers and other ships taking part return unharmed. Although material results of the raid are trivial the psychological effect is profound. The heart of the Empire of the Rising Sun is not, as the Japanese have believed, invulnerable.

☐ Pierre Laval's new cabinet announced. Pétain remains head of state.

19 April

Philippines The Japanese announce the capture of the island of Cebu.

Burma There is an increasing threat to the 'Burma Road', the route by which Allied supplies are sent to China, as Japanese columns converge south of Loikaw.

20 April

Philippines The Japanese proceed with their capture of Panay Island and are now virtual masters of the central Philippines; the small garrisons on Negros, Samar, Leyte and Bohol are in no position to check them.

Burma The Chinese 38th Division retires from Yenangyaung towards Gwegyo, to the north, covering units of the 1st Burma Division escaping from the threat of enemy encirclement. Part of the Chinese 5th Army in the Sittang valley retires northwards from Pyinmana, while the Japanese are still very active in the Loikaw–Loilem area.

Malta Forty-six Spitfire fighters take off for the besieged island from the US aircraft carrier *Wasp* – a vital reinforcement for the defenders of the island, whose whole hope of survival rests on this aid.

☐ Laval makes a broadcast to the French people. The policy of 'understanding and true reconciliation with Germany must be loyally carried out'.

20–22 April

Malta Axis aircraft hammer the island ceaselessly and destroy or damage almost all the newly arrived Spitfire reinforcements on the

Retreat in Burma: American officers of Stilwell's forces refresh themselves with a footbath. By the time they reach India they will have marched 1,250 miles.

ground. It now looks as if there is nothing more that Malta can do. Axis forces can now land at will. There is actually a plan for the capture of the island, known as 'Operation C 3'. The Italian Admiral Vittorio Tur has been nominated to carry it out, and the German General Kurt Student is to throw in his parachutists (it was Student who led the capture of Crete). Mussolini is eager to occupy the Maltese islands but Hitler refuses to give the go-ahead.

21 April

Burma The Japanese make contact with the Chinese 6th Army at Hopong. Elements of the Chinese 49th Army are quickly switched west and engage the enemy in the Mong Pawn–Loilem area, near Taunggyi.

22 April

Burma General Stilwell moves the Chinese 200th Division from Meiktila to Taunggyi to counter the enemy's movements in the Loikaw–Loilem area. The Chinese 28th Division should also have moved to the Loilem area, but the order is not carried out. The Chinese 96th Division continues with its rearguard actions in the Sittang valley, while the 17th Indian Division, 7th

Armoured Brigade and Chinese 22nd Division take up positions round Meiktila and near Thazi.

23 April

Burma The Chinese 200th Division engages the enemy west of Taunggyi, while the Japanese attack Loilem. The Chinese 6th Army retreats in good order towards China.

24 April

The Luftwaffe bombs Exeter during the night. This is the start of 'terror raids' on historic towns as a reprisal for RAF attacks on Germany.

25 April

Burma General Alexander orders an immediate withdrawal from the Meiktila–Kyaukpadaung line to the north bank of the Irrawaddy. In the Meiktila sector the Chinese 22nd Division is surrounded by the Japanese. The Chinese 5th Army drives the Japanese back from Taunggyi but cannot halt their advance towards Lashio, a position of great strategic importance.

North Africa With clearer weather, air activity is resumed over the whole front. Axis formations attack Tobruk harbour, while British aircraft carry out a night raid on Benghazi.

☐ Bath is heavily bombed in night attack.

26 April

Burma Fearing that Burma is lost, General Alexander decides to concentrate all available forces on the defence of India.

Philippines A strong Japanese contingent, about 4,800 men, sails from Cebu to Mindanao, to reinforce the troops who landed there some time ago and are now engaged in combat with several Filipino battalions.

Malta German aircraft hit and silence a number of anti-aircraft positions in different parts of the island.

☐ Berlin. Hitler addresses the Reichstag. He claims that the Russian winter has been exceptionally severe, the worst for 140 years, with temperatures as low as minus 50°C; but with the coming of spring he forsees great new victories for German arms. He demands absolute powers 'to compel everyone to fulfill his duty', and says, 'I will ruthlessly eliminate everybody who does not stand up to his task.'

☐ Bath is again heavily bombed by Luftwaffe.

27 April

Norwich bombed at night as the Germans continue their reprisal raids.

28 April

Philippines The Japanese on Mindanao attack the defending forces mercilessly, to prevent them from concentrating and holding off the new landing force that is on its way.

Burma The Chinese 28th Division, at present at Mandalay, is sent urgently to Lashio, in imminent danger of capture by the Japanese. The Japanese, however, occupy Kehsi Mansam.

☐ The Luftwaffe bombs York in what are now called 'Baedeker 3-star raids', since the Germans officially claim to use this rating from the famous tourist guide as a way of selecting towns to be attacked.

29 April

Philippines On Mindanao the Japanese reinforcements from Cebu land on the west coast, at Cotabato and Parang, and capture both. One regiment and two Filipino battalions fight bravely but are unable to prevent the two bridgeheads from joining up. The Japanese, who had already landed at Davao, advance north-westwards towards Bugo. The Japanese have highly effective air support.

On Luzon the shelling and bombing of the fortified island of Corregidor is intensified.

New Guinea The Japanese, who are considering the invasion of Australia, make arrangements for the invasion of the capital of Papua, Port Moresby (the landing is code-named Operation *Mo*).

Burma The Japanese seize Lashio, the terminus of the 'Burma Road' by

18 April 1942: A B-25 bomber takes off from the American aircraft carrier *Hornet* to raid Tokyo. The raid, carried out by Colonel Doolittle's group, seriously affects Japanese morale.

which supplies are despatched to China. China is thus completely cut off and from now on can only be supplied by air. The Chinese 200th Division reaches Loilem, but then turns round and marches towards the Chinese frontier. General Alexander decides to set up a new defensive line between Kalewa, Katha, Bhamo and Hsenwi; all available troops will begin to fall back on to this line on 2 May.

Middle East General Auchinleck issues instructions on the tasks that will fall to the British 9th and 10th Armies in case of a German attack across Anatolia. There is a real fear that the Germans will carry out an enormous 'pincer movement' from Russia to the Mediterranean.

☐ Norwich has another heavy bombing attack overnight.

☐ Hitler and Mussolini meet at Salzburg. The two allies review the situation, which although not catastrophic, is hardly rosy. Hitler is obsessed with the Eastern Front. He seems quite changed, thoughtful and preoccupied, yet – as Ciano, the Italian Foreign Minister, emphasizes – he has lost none of his 'verbosity', which he demonstrates in a monologue lasting 1 hour 40 minutes.

30 April

Philippines Operations continue on

Mindanao. Troops from the contingent that landed at Parang are taken off by sea overnight and landed south of Malabang; at dawn they attack and push back the Filipino 61st Infantry Regiment some 5 miles. The Japanese who landed at Cotabato advance up the Mindanao river and reach Piket.

Burma The Japanese have now captured the whole of central Burma. British forces retire behind the Irrawaddy across the Ava bridge, which is then blown up. The Chinese 22nd Division, having covered the British withdrawal, retires from Mandalay. The Allies already have doubts about the defensive line being established on General Alexander's orders, and it seems possible that all the forces of the Chinese 5th Army may have to be withdrawn to Imphal in India.

1 May

Philippines Fighting continues on Mindanao, and so does the air and artillery offensive against Corregidor.

Burma The Japanese capture Monywa and Mandalay.

2 May

Philippines In some parts of Mindanao the Japanese offensive thrust is being held up by Filipino troops. The Japanese who landed at Cotabato advance eastwards towards Kabakan, which is reinforced with all available troops. Another convoy is sighted off the island, presumably bringing more landing forces.

Solomon Islands In the south of the archipelago, off Guadalcanal, a Japanese convoy is preparing to land troops on the small island of Tulagi. The tiny garrison, a detachment of the Australian air force, immediately destroys all the island's installations and embarks for the New Hebrides. The Americans have broken the Japanese naval code and are aware of the new landing. The officer commanding the naval squadron patrolling the Coral Sea, Rear-Admiral Frank J. Fletcher, immediately makes for Tulagi with the aircraft

carriers *Yorktown* and *Lexington* and supporting forces. Escorting the Japanese invasion force are the aircraft carriers *Shokaku* and *Zuikaku*, under Admiral Takagi, and the ships supporting them include at least one other carrier and four heavy cruisers.

Burma Three brigades of I Burma Corps attack Monywa, just captured by the Japanese, but are repulsed. They retire in disorder, while the rest of the Burma forces fall back to Shwegyin.

North Atlantic The British cruiser *Edinburgh* is sunk by a German submarine while escorting a convoy returning from the USSR.

Mediterranean British aircraft carry out overnight raids on the islands of Rhodes and Leros and, in Greece, on the Piraeus area and the outskirts of Athens.

□ Area of Townsville, in north Queensland, Australia, put on invasion alert.

3 May

Solomon Islands A small Japanese contingent lands on Tulagi, as expected, and immediately starts to convert it into a seaplane base for the support of the landing operations at Port Moresby, New Guinea, the gateway to Australia. Fletcher arrives in the area with the *Yorktown* and escorting ships, but the Japanese have already left and the Americans are only able to sink some enemy transports.

Philippines At 1.00 a.m. Japanese amphibious units from Panay land in Macajalar Bay, Mindanao, and at once begin to march south. The Filipinos are unable to hold them up. More Japanese arrive at Kabakan, and the defending troops have to retire inland into the hills.

Air and artillery activity against Corregidor, the prelude to invasion, continues without respite.

□ *Exeter* is heavily bombed by Luftwaffe.

4 May

Philippines On Mindanao the Filipinos complete their withdrawal to a new defence line in the Dalirig and Puntian sectors. A third regrouping of units defends the valley of the river

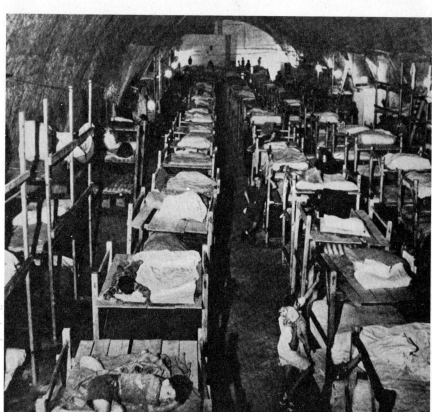

The ordeal of Malta goes on: much of the population virtually lives in air raid shelters. Axis forces could invade at any moment.

Cagayan. There is only air activity on the part of the Japanese.

Luzon. The bombardment of Corregidor rises to a climax; at least 16,000 bombs and shells land on the island.

New Britain A Japanese invasion fleet leaves Rabaul for Port Moresby.

Burma The British abandon Akyab on the Bay of Bengal. The Japanese take Bhamo and rout the Chinese 29th Division at Wanting. Chiang Kai-shek orders the Chinese 5th Army to concentrate in the Myitkyina area.

Solomon Islands The US carrier *Yorktown* rejoins the rest of the squadron in the Coral Sea.

North Africa Axis aircraft bomb Alexandria, concentrating on port and railway installations.

5 May

Madagascar A British naval squadron commanded by Rear-Admiral Syfret and consisting of the battleship *Ramillies*, the aircraft carriers *Indomitable* and *Illustrious*, the light cruiser *Hermione*, the Dutch cruiser *Van Heemskerk* and four destroyers, lands a British force at Courier Bay, on the north-east of the island, which captures the ports of Diego Suarez and Antsirene. The local garrisons, loyal to the Vichy government, offer little more than token resistance. Diego Suarez is quickly converted into a big air and naval base which is to be of considerable help against the Japanese.

US states approval of Britain's action and warns Vichy government against resistance.

Coral Sea The aircraft carriers *Lexington* and *Yorktown*, with their escort, continue their search for the Japanese squadron.

Philippines After a deadly air and artillery preparation the Japanese land on Corregidor, near North Point. On Mindanao the Filipinos organize a new defence line.

Burma General Stilwell, who is with the Chinese retiring on Myitkyina, learns at Indaw that the railway has been cut and the enemy have captured Bhamo. He therefore decides to withdraw into India instead of China.

□ Japanese Imperial General Headquarters sends orders to the Fleet to make preparations for the invasion of Midway Island and the Aleutians.

6 May

Coral Sea The battle between the American and Japanese squadrons continues.

Philippines After a whole day's negotiations General Wainwright signs the document by which all Americans and Filipinos surrender unconditionally to the Japanese general Masaharu Homma. The Japanese capture the Malinta Tunnel on Corregidor, and land new forces. On Mindanao the Japanese renew their offensive, taking Tankulan and nearing Dalirig, which they subject to artillery fire.

Burma The Chinese 200th Division, and part of the 55th, still at Taunggyi, are ordered to fall back on Myitkyina. Later they succeed in returning to China.

7 May

Philippines General Wainwright broadcasts from Manila to announce his surrender, implicitly inviting all American and Filipino units still holding out in various islands to lay down their arms. The Japanese have taken 15,000 prisoners on Corre-

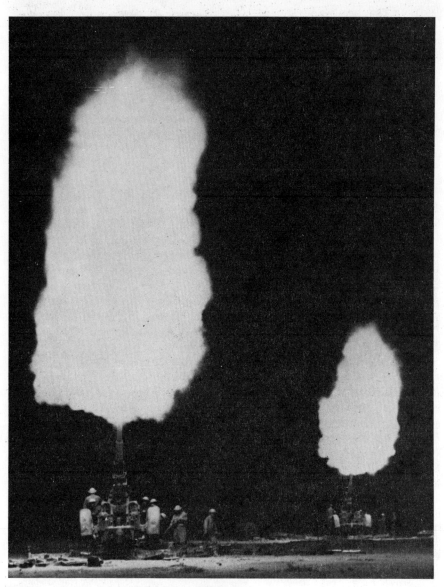

British anti-aircraft battery in action at Tobruk.

11,000 Americans and 4,000 Filipinos are taken prisoner by the Japanese on the island of Corregidor, of Luzon, the last Allied stronghold in the central Philippines.

gidor. On Mindanao they confine themselves to air and artillery activity.

8 May
Coral Sea The air–naval battle between the Americans and the Japanese comes to an end. On balance the result favours the Americans, since the Japanese are forced to put off the landing at Port Moresby.
Philippines General Wainwright gets in touch with the various military commanders authorizing them to surrender. On Mindanao the Japanese resume the offensive, wiping out an infantry regiment, and advance on Dalirig.
Burma The Japanese take Myitkyina.
Eastern Front The Germans begin a series of attacks to test the strength of the enemy forces in readiness for the large-scale offensive planned for the summer, the objective of which will be the oilfields of the Caucasus. The 11th Army, Army Group South, advances towards Kerch in the Crimea.

9 May
Philippines The Japanese take Dalirig, on Mindanao, putting the defenders to rout. The conquest of the island is virtually complete.
New Guinea The Japanese supreme command orders the suspension of the Port Moresby landing.
Malta Sixty Spitfires land on the island from the aircraft carriers *Wasp* (US) and *Eagle* (British). Having learned from previous experience, on 20 April, when a large number of aircraft that had only just landed were destroyed or damaged on the ground by an unexpected enemy attack, this time the ground crews quickly fuel the aircraft as soon as they land, and they are ready to take off again within only 35 minutes. This successful operation rekindles the hopes of the 'besieged' islanders.
Tonga The Americans land at Tongatabu.
Galapagos Islands American units land, with permission of the governor of Ecuador.

10 May
Philippines General Sharp, commanding American and Filipino forces in the central Philippines and Mindanao, orders his troops to surrender. Small groups continue to hold out both in the southern Philippines and on Luzon, but they lay down their arms during the next month.
Burma The Japanese attack in the Shwegyin sector.
Malta General Albert Kesselring, from Sicily, in his capacity as Commander-in-Chief of the southern (Mediterranean) front, reports to Berlin that Malta 'has been completely neutralized'.
☐ Churchill broadcasts a warning that if the Germans use poison gas in Russia Britain will retaliate.

11–17 May
Malta Axis aircraft continue to hammer the air and naval bases day after day, while Axis fighters are engaged in furious 'dogfights' with the British Spitfires. Both sides lose many planes.

11 May
Eastern Mediterranean Three British destroyers, *Lively*, *Kipling* and *Jackal*, sunk by Luftwaffe.
China The Japanese launch a local offensive in Chenkiang province.

12 May
Eastern Front While the German Army Group South continues its offensive against Kerch, the Russians begin a 'pincer' attack against Kharkov, northwards from the Izyum salient and south-west across the river Donetz.
Burma The Japanese cross the river Salween, making for Kengtung.

13 May
Eastern Front Withdrawal of Russian troops from Kerch peninsula ordered by the Russian High Command.
Fiji American troops replace New Zealanders in the islands' garrison.

14 May
Burma British troops withdrawing

'TO BE OR NOT TO BE'

Carole Lombard.

In occupied Warsaw a company of Polish actors, proscribed and persecuted by the Nazis, organizes a resistance group, taking as their rallying cry the opening words of Hamlet's monologue. They unmask and execute a spy, and eventually, after a series of dramatic escapades, manage to trick the Nazis and make their escape to England on a German plane.

In this delightful comedy, where fiction and reality continually merge, Ernst Lubitsch reached the pinnacle of his career, working in collaboration with two other exiles, director of photography Rudolph Maté and scriptwriter Vincent Korda. Lubitsch's switch from light comedy to treatment of a serious contemporary theme exposed him to a great deal of criticism.

from Burma reach the Indian border at Tamu, in Assam.

☐ Another American division, the 32nd, arrives in Australia.

15 May
Eastern Front After fierce fighting the Germans re-take the town and harbour of Kerch, in the Crimea. The Soviet offensive against Kharkov continues.
New Guinea Half of an Australian brigade and groups of anti-aircraft gunners leave for Port Moresby to reinforce the local defences.
India General Alexander moves his headquarters from Burma to the area of Imphal, in India. General Stilwell also arrives in India.
North Africa The British 8th Army is nearly ready to go over to the offensive, but Axis forces show every sign that they will attack first.

17 May
Eastern Front The German Army Group South counter-attacks against the Izyum salient and east of Kharkov, halting the Soviet offensive. The fighting grows more bitter.

18 May
Burma Chiang Kai-shek orders the Chinese 5th Army (already virtually reduced to the Chinese 22nd and 96th Divisions) to take up positions between Myitkyina and Fort Hertz. The survivors of the 22nd Division eventually reach the Ledo area between July and August. Later the remainder of the 96th Division return to China from Fort Hertz.
☐ London. Air Marshal A. T. Harris, head of RAF Bomber Command, submits a detailed plan for an air assault on Germany based on the assumption that it will be possible to send 1,000 bombers over Germany in a single night.

19 May
Eastern Front The Germans launch a counter-offensive 80 miles south-east of Kharkov. The battle continues until the end of June.
☐ Mannheim is heavily raided by RAF bombers in night raid.

20 May
Pacific Ocean The Americans have

broken the Japanese code and are aware that the enemy is about to invade Midway and the Aleutians; they send reinforcements urgently to these two sectors.
Burma The Japanese have now taken virtually the whole of Burma. The four divisions employed, the 18th, 33rd, 55th and 56th, now begin mopping-up operations and take up defensive positions.
The rearguards of I Burma Corps return to India and are absorbed into the IV Corps.
☐ Air Marshal Harris's plan for an air attack on Germany by the RAF receives the approval of the government and the Chiefs of Staff. In a letter sent to Coastal, Fighter and Army Co-operation Commands, Harris describes his plan and asks for the maximum possible co-operation. His directive anticipates the complete destruction of one of Germany's biggest industrial cities: Cologne, or Hamburg, must be razed to the ground in a single night.
☐ The Vice-President of the Soviet Committee of National Defence, Molotov, arrives in London. His visit sets the seal on the Anglo-Russian alliance which, among other things, requires the Soviet Union to become a member of the United Nations and not to interfere in the internal affairs of other states.

21 May
Malta Hitler decides that the invasion of Malta (now called Operation *Hercules*), put forward by the Axis commanders, should be postponed until after the capture of Egypt, for which Axis forces in North Africa are now preparing.

22 May
New Guinea Reinforcements are sent to the Wau area to defend the Bulolo valley. Native volunteers have been enrolled to fight beside the Allied – mostly Australian – troops.
☐ Mexico declares war on Germany, Japan and Italy.

23 May
Eastern Front The Army Group

THE BATTLE OF THE CORAL SEA

1 May

The US Naval Command has learned of the projected Japanese landing on Tulagi in the Solomon Islands and the much larger landing that the Japanese are preparing to carry out in New Guinea. The aircraft carriers *Yorktown* and *Lexington*, under the command of Rear-Admiral Frank J. Fletcher, with escorting ships, are therefore despatched to intercept the enemy force.

2–3 May

The *Yorktown* arrives off Tulagi, but the Japanese squadron escorting the invasion force has already disappeared. The Americans sink a number of enemy transports, then rejoin the rest of the ships concentrated in the Coral Sea. There are two task forces in action, the 17th (Rear-Admiral Fletcher) and the 44th (in support, under the British Rear-Admiral J. C. Grace). The two task forces comprise the aircraft carriers *Lexington* and *Yorktown* (with 143 aircraft), 7 heavy cruisers (*Minneapolis*, *New Orleans*, *Portland*, *Chester*, *Astoria*, *Australia* and *Chicago*), the light cruiser *Hobart*, 13 destroyers, 2 tankers and a seaplane support ship. The 4th Japanese Fleet, commanded by Vice-Admiral Shigeyoshi Inouye, with the task of covering Operation *Mo* (the landing at Port Moresby) consists of a strike force under Vice-Admiral Takeo Takagi, a support group, a cover group, a patrol group and a landing group intended partly for Tulagi and partly for Port Moresby. It comprises in all 3 aircraft carriers (*Shokaku* and *Zuikaku*, with 125 aircraft, plus the light carrier *Shoho*), 8 cruisers (*Myoko*, *Haguro*, *Tenryu*, *Tatsuta*, *Aoba*, *Kako*, *Kinugasa* and *Furutaka*), 17 destroyers, 1 seaplane transport, 7 submarines, 3 gunboats, 1 minelayer, 2 tankers, auxiliary craft and a number of troop and supply transports. The Japanese can also call on the 25th Flotilla of their air force, with 161 aircraft, fighters, bombers and reconnaissance aircraft.

4 May

At 6.30 a.m., from a point 100 miles south-west of Guadalcanal, Fletcher sends up 46 aircraft from the *Yorktown*, and off Tulagi they sink a Japanese destroyer, a minesweeper and two auxiliary vessels. Other attacks carried out during the day have no success. All day, and all the following night, the two fleets search for each other but never establish contact. Steaming full speed ahead, Fletcher with the *Yorktown* joins up with the *Lexington* group. Meanwhile Vice-Admiral Takagi with the *Zuikaku* and *Shokaku*, plus the cruisers and other escort vessels, sails past the island of San Cristobal, at the south-east tip of the Solomons, and makes for the Louisiades to protect the left flank of the Port Moresby invasion fleet.

7 May

An American reconnaissance plane reports sighting two aircraft carriers and four heavy cruisers, while a Japanese aircraft has sighted the American fleet and has had time, before being spotted and shot down, to warn the base at Rabaul. But the message is only re-transmitted to Vice-Admiral Takagi after many hours' delay and so is valueless. Meanwhile 93 aircraft have taken off from the two American carriers; at about 11.00 a.m. they reach and sink the Japanese light aircraft carrier *Shoho*. The Japanese have not yet been informed of the presence of the

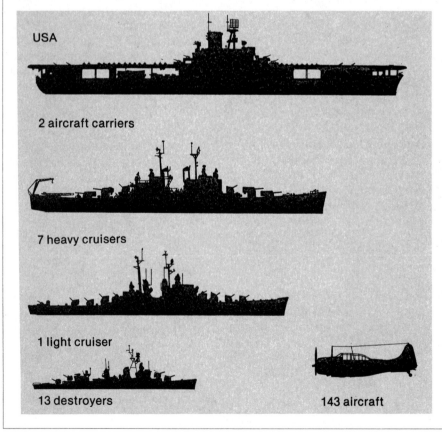

USA

2 aircraft carriers

7 heavy cruisers

1 light cruiser

13 destroyers

143 aircraft

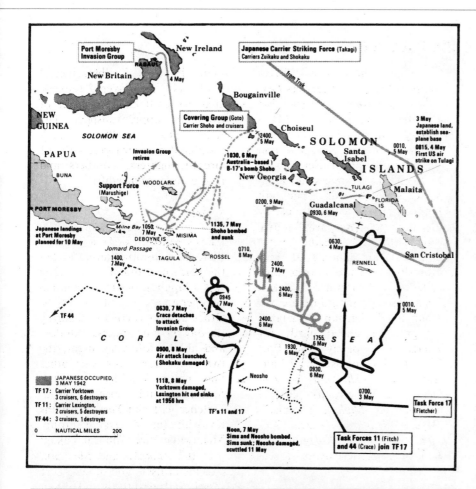

Port Moresby Invasion Group
New Ireland
Japanese Carrier Striking Force (Takagi)
Carriers Zuikaku and Shokaku

New Britain
RABAUL
4 May
from Truk

Bougainville

NEW GUINEA
SOLOMON SEA

Covering Group (Goto)
Carrier Shoho and cruisers

Choiseul
2400, 5 May
SOLOMON

3 May Japanese land, establish sea-plane base
0010, 5 May
0815, 4 May First US air strike on Tulagi

PAPUA
BUNA

Invasion Group retires

Santa Isabel
ISLANDS

1030, 6 May Australia-based B-17's bomb Shoho
New Georgia

Support Force (Marushige)
WOODLARK

TULAGI
Malaita
FLORIDA IS

PORT MORESBY

Japanese landings at Port Moresby planned for 10 May

Guadalcanal
0930, 6 May

0200, 9 May

Milne Bay 1050, 7 May
DEBOYNE IS
MISIMA

1135, 7 May Shoho bombed and sunk

0710, 8 May

0630, 4 May

Jomard Passage

1400, 7 May

2400, 7 May
2400, 6 May
2400, 6 May

RENNELL

San Cristobal

0010, 5 May

TAGULA
ROSSEL

0945, 7 May

0630, 7 May Crace detaches to attack Invasion Group

TF 44

2400, 6 May

1755, 6 May
1930, 6 May

0930, 6 May

0700, 3 May

Task Force 17 (Fletcher)

CORAL

SEA

0900, 8 May Air attack launched, (Shokaku damaged)

1118, 8 May Yorktown damaged, Lexington hit and sinks at 1956 hrs

Neosho

JAPANESE OCCUPIED, 3 MAY 1942
TF 17: Carrier Yorktown 3 cruisers, 6 destroyers
TF 11: Carrier Lexington, 2 cruisers, 5 destroyers
TF 44: 3 cruisers, 1 destroyer

0   NAUTICAL MILES   200

TF's 11 and 17

Noon, 7 May Sims and Neosho bombed. Sims sunk; Neosho damaged, scuttled 11 May

Task Forces 11 (Fitch) and 44 (Crace) join TF17

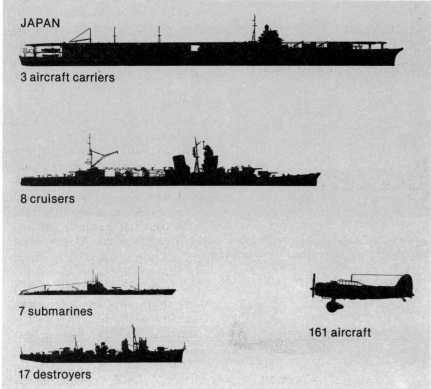

JAPAN

3 aircraft carriers

8 cruisers

7 submarines

17 destroyers

161 aircraft

American squadron, but they chance upon an American destroyer and tanker and sink both. In the afternoon Takagi sends 27 aircraft in search of the enemy. Only 6 return; the others have either been shot down or have lost their way in the bad weather and gone missing.

8 May

At 9.00 a.m. aircraft from the *Lexington* and *Yorktown* take off again in search of the enemy. The *Shokaku* is hit and badly damaged, but the *Zuikaku* and her escort manage to escape undamaged. Vice-Admiral Takagi has despatched 70 aircraft to seek and destroy the American ships. The *Yorktown* just manages to escape from a torpedo attack, and reports only slight damage. But the *Lexington* is badly hit and takes on such a list that returning aircraft cannot land on her flight-deck. The ship has to be abandoned, and before night falls, to prevent the wreck from falling into Japanese hands, she is sunk by a torpedo from an American plane. The Americans have lost 66 aircraft during the battle, the Japanese about 70.

The Japanese claim the engagement as a victory, and it is true that they have inflicted greater losses on the enemy than they have suffered themselves. But they are forced to put off the landing of a large invasion force at Port Moresby. Moreover, for the first time since the commencement of hostilities, an operation initiated by them has been met by the Americans on equal terms. The Americans are passing now from

The *Lexington* lists dangerously after being hit by aerial torpedoes at 11.27 a.m. Many of the crew jump into the sea without waiting for the order to abandon ship, although the 'Lex' stays afloat for some hours.

Shokaku

Left: american ships, some of them in flames, manœuvre to avoid the attacks of Japanese torpedo-aricraft.

Right: The *Lexington*, the beloved 'Lady Lex', sinks on the evening of 8 May.

a purely defensive strategy to a mixed defensive–offensive strategy. The Battle of the Coral Sea is the first 'air–naval' battle in history (and quite possibly the biggest); it has been fought exclusively by aircraft, without the ships ever coming into direct contact.

Lexington

South strikes hard at the Russians in the Kharkov area, cutting off part of the enemy forces in the Izyum salient, west of the Donetz.

24 May

Malta Axis air raids continue and Malta is by now completely neutralized as an air and naval base.

25 May

India Survivors from the Chinese 38th Division reach India from Burma.

26 May

North Africa Start of third German counter-offensive in Western Desert. Rommel resumes the operations broken off when he reached the Gazala line, running from Derna to Bir Hacheim. The German Commander-in-Chief has three German divisions (the 15th and 21st Armoured and 90th Light) and two Italian (*Ariete* and *Trieste*) deployed on the right wing; on the left, the Gazala sector, is General Ludwig Crüwell's group. Crüwell, a personal friend of Rommel, has under him the Italian X and XXI Corps (the *Sabratha*, *Trento*, *Brescia* and *Pavia* Divisions) and the German 15th Light Infantry Brigade. General Neil Ritchie, general officer commanding the British 8th Army, has deployed the mass of his troops opposite Crüwell, convinced that Rommel will attack along the coast so that he can make straight for Tobruk; he has XIII Corps to the north, with the 1st South African Division in the front line with the British 50th Division, flanked by the 2nd South African Division, 5th Indian Division, 9th Indian Brigade and 1st Army Tank Brigade. To the south, on the left of the British line – the sector, that is, in which Rommel's tanks will be operating – there are two armoured divisions, the 1st and 7th, together with 201st Guards Brigade, 3rd Group Indian motorized brigade and 29th Brigade of the 5th Indian Division. Bir Hacheim is held by the 1st Free French Brigade, 5,500 men commanded by General Koenig, who hold out until 11 June.

When Crüwell attacks in the Gazala sector in the early afternoon of 26 May, General Ritchie congratulates himself on having foreseen the enemy's movements precisely and deduced correctly the point at which they would try to break through the British line. But in fact Crüwell's attack is a diversion; the real, decisive assault comes in the south, carried out by Rommel's armour.

9.00 p.m.: Rommel's armoured divisions advance south-eastwards across the desert.

□ London. The orders for the 'thousand-bomber raid' are issued.

□ Molotov signs a twenty-year treaty of mutual assistance between the USSR and Britain, then leaves for Washington.

27 May

North Africa 6.00 a.m.: Rommel's tanks are south of Bir Hacheim, with the Italian *Ariete* Division; the other Italian division, the *Trieste*, moves north-east instead of south-east through some mistake, and comes up against the British 40th Brigade. The British flank in the south has been successfully turned; the intention now is to throw in the German 90th Light Division against Tobruk, to confuse the enemy's lines of communication, while the Italian *Ariete* Division deals with Bir Hacheim. The two armoured divisions of the *Afrikakorps*, the 15th and 21st, move north to surround the main body of the British 8th Army.

6.30 a.m.: Rommel sends in the German 21st Armoured Division and Italian *Ariete* Division against the positions of the 3rd Indian Brigade, south of Bir Hacheim; their troops are surprised having breakfast. Meanwhile the German 90th Light Division advances towards Tobruk, forcing the position held by the British 7th Motorized Brigade at Retma; the British manage to break away and take refuge at Bir el Gubi. The *Ariete* Division's attack on Bir Hacheim is fought off by the Free French Brigade, and the two *Panzerdivisionen* (15th and 21st) are taken in the flanks by the British 2nd Armoured Brigade from the right

and the 1st Army Tank Brigade from the left. Rommel's position has become difficult for he has lost a third of his tanks, and fuel is running short. He is thus in danger of being halted and cut off in territory controlled by the British. The 90th Light Division, too, is dangerously exposed without cover from the armoured divisions.

On the German left, in the Gazala sector, Axis troops have reached the coastal escarpment and control the 'Via Balbia', the coast road which is the only road the enemy can use to retire.

Pacific Ocean The Japanese aircraft carrier force under the command of Vice-Admiral Chuichi Nagumo sails from Japan with 21 other ships, followed at a distance of 600 miles by the bulk of the Imperial Fleet under Yamamoto, making for Midway. The other groups are commanded by Vice-Admirals Tanaka, Kurita and Kondo. Japanese transports also sail from Saipan and Guam, with an escort of cruisers and destroyers, *en route* for Midway. The American force waiting for them near Midway is under Rear-Admirals R. A. Spruance and F. J. Fletcher; it comprises three aircraft carriers (*Yorktown*, *Enterprise* and *Hornet*), 26 cruisers and destroyers, tankers and smaller ships, and 19 submarines.

□ Thunderstorms and low cloud over target force Air Marshal Harris to postpone the 'thousand-bomber raid' against one of Germany's most highly industrialized cities.

□ Sicily. Waves of British bombers attack Messina, Catania and Syracuse.

□ Czechoslovakia. Two Czech patriots, dropped by parachute from a British aircraft, attempt to assassinate the *Reichsprotektor*, Reinhard Heydrich, in Prague. The Czechs escape and Himmler's deputy dies of wounds on 4 June.

□ France. Deportations to Germany of members of the resistance movement begin.

28 May

Pacific The main body of the

Axis forces advance under enemy fire towards Gazala. But Rommel launches his main offensive of 26 May southwards.

Japanese fleet, under the command of Admiral Isoraku Yamamoto, leaves its bases to follow the advance-guards commanded by Nagumo. Rear-Admiral Spruance's squadron leaves Pearl Harbour, also making for Midway.

American troops coming from Efate land on the island of Espiritu Santo, New Hebrides, where an airfield is to be built big enough to take the bombers supporting the landing in the Solomons.

Burma The Japanese occupy Kengtung, one of the few towns in the country they have not reached.

China Under Japanese pressure the Chinese withdraw from Kinhwa, in Chekiang province.

North Africa The British 8th Army stops the Italians and Germans from reaching the coast in the rear of the Gazala positions.

Eastern Front The Kharkov battle ends in a brilliant victory for the Germans, who eliminate the enemy salient west of the Donetz in the area of Kharkov.

☐ The RAF's 'thousand-bomber raid' on Germany has to be postponed again on account of bad weather.

29 May
North Africa The Axis forces have opened a gap in the minefields defending the British 8th Army positions in the central sector and advance with tanks, despite fierce resistance by the British. Most of Rommel's tanks, temporarily on the defensive because they cannot open up a supply line, withdraw southwards under the pressure from the tanks of XXX Corps. The *Afrikakorps* is running short of fuel.

30 May
Pacific Ocean The squadron under

Rear-Admiral Fletcher's command leaves Pearl Harbour for Midway to prepare a trap for the Japanese fleet. A second Japanese squadron, with 2 aircraft carriers, 2 cruisers, 3 destroyers and 3 transports, sails from Japan for the Aleutians, with the task of landing small contingents of troops there, but most of all of carrying out a diversionary attack, to draw the Americans off from Midway and attract them into Arctic waters.

North Africa Axis forces attack the British positions with the object of consolidating the bridgehead captured beyond the British minefields, but without success. RAF activity is intensified. General Ritchie decides to counter-attack on the evening of 31 May, but at the request of his commanders in the field puts the date back 24 hours. The 1st Armoured Brigade, which has only just arrived in Libya, is detached from the other units and sent to plug the gaps.

Rommel gives up the idea of advancing northwards and goes on the defensive, moving all his armour into what is called the 'Cauldron', an area south of Sidi Muftah and west of Bir el Harmat, thus turning the flanks of the British minefields; he is expecting the British 8th Army to counter-attack at any moment, but the attack does not come.

The German General Ludwig Crüwell, in command of the Italian infantry in the Gazala area, is taken prisoner.

☐ Weather conditions over northern Germany show first signs of improvement, and all the preparations for the 'thousand-bomber raid' have been made. The aircraft are ready to take off; their destination will be Cologne.

10.30 p.m.: The operation begins. First to take off are the Stirlings of XV Group, from the airfield at Wyton in Huntingdonshire, followed one after another by the rest. The bombing of Cologne starts just after midnight. It is a terrifying experience for the city's inhabitants, hundreds of whom are unable to get out of the cellars. Raging fires devas-

Execution of a Yugoslav partisan.

tate the city centre, and the whole of Cologne is enveloped in a cloud of dense, acrid smoke. Over 2,000 tons of bombs have been dropped on the city. The damage caused is tremendous: 13,000 houses destroyed, 6,000 seriously damaged, more than 45,000 made homeless; 469 dead; more than 4,500 wounded. The British lose 39 bombers, mostly shot down by German night-fighters.

Hermann Goering wrote in his diary about the bombing of Cologne: 'Of course, the effects of aerial warfare are terrible if one looks at individual cases. But we have to accept them.'

31 May
North Africa General Neil Ritchie, commanding the British 8th Army, is convinced that Rommel's manœuvre has ground to a halt. 'Now I've got him in the hollow of my hand,' he writes to General Auchinleck, Commander-in-Chief of British armed forces in the Middle East. But Rommel is a long way from being subdued; he hurls himself on 150th Brigade of the British 50th Division, dug in between two desert tracks, the Trigh Capuzzo and the Trigh el Abd, south-west of Sidi Muftah. In the afternoon the British XXX Corps launches an ineffective counter-attack, promptly repelled.

1 June
North Africa The British 150th Brigade is wiped out by Rommel's armour; 3,000 men are taken prisoner and the Allies lose 123 guns. The *Afrikakorps* has succeeded in opening a gap for its supply columns. General Ritchie writes: 'I am sorry to have lost 150th Brigade, but the

JOHN BARRYMORE

Above: John Barrymore's famous profile. Right: Barrymore and Dolores Costello in *The Sea Beast* (1926).

John Barrymore, one of the most famous film stars of the twenties and thirties died in Hollywood, destroyed by alcohol, on 29 May.

Last member of the celebrated Barrymore (Blythe) family, John was born in Philadelphia in 1882. After a disorderly and drunken youth, he made his first stage appearance with his sister Ethel in 1902. The next year saw his cinema debut in *An American Citizen*.

Alternating work in the cinema and the theatre, Barrymore eventually went on to dramatic roles, establishing himself as a great Shakespearian actor (he played Hamlet more than a hundred times, an all-time record) and won international fame with a succession of romantic and adventure films.

Thanks to his fine voice he adapted readily to the arrival of sound and reinforced his reputation as an actor of considerable talent and personality. More popular than ever on the screen, he became known as the 'great profile'.

Towards the end of the thirties, when he had become a hopeless alcoholic, Barrymore went downhill and ended his career playing almost autobiographical parts in second-rate comedies.

situation gets better every day...'

☐ Australia. A Japanese pocket submarine makes its way into Sydney harbour and sinks a merchant ship.

☐ The RAF raids Essen and the Ruhr with 1,036 bombers.

1–2 June

North Africa A first and rather feeble attempt by British 8th Army forces to get into the 'Cauldron' fails in the face of prompt reaction by Rommel's armour.

2 June

Eastern Front In the southern sector the 11th Army of Army Group South begins a tremendous artillery barrage, lasting five days, in preparation for a German and Rumanian assault on the fortress of Sevastopol in the Crimea.

North Africa Rommel sends the *Trieste* and 90th Light Divisions, moved some days earlier into the 'Cauldron', to Bir Hacheim, defended by the Free French 1st Brigade. The two formations take over from the Italian *Ariete* Division, which has been engaged with the French brigade since 26 May.

Pacific Ocean The two task forces of Vice-Admirals Fletcher and Spruance meet about 350 miles north-east of Midway. Fletcher takes over command of the operations and moves his two squadrons to a position about 200 miles north of Midway. In the Aleutians, American reconnaissance aircraft sight two Japanese aircraft carriers 400 miles from Kiska.

3 June

Pacific Relays of American aircraft, taking off from Midway, sight and attack the transports of Admiral Yamamoto's combined fleet about 600 miles from Midway, but the attack has no conclusive result.

East Africa Half a British brigade embarks for Madagascar to relieve the troops garrisoning the island.

Malta The raids on the island generally, and particularly on Micabba airfield, continue without respite.

☐ Sardinia. British air raids on Cagliari and Sant' Antioco Island.

4 June

Pacific Ocean The decisive battle of Midway begins, a battle which will last until 7 June and see the Japanese defeated, with the loss of four aircraft carriers.

Aleutian Islands Japanese carrier-borne aircraft attack Dutch Harbour on Unalaska Island, damaging an American ship and hitting petrol tanks. American reconnaissance aircraft and bombers search all day for the Japanese fleet but without success.

North Africa The 8th Army counter-attacks at nightfall to reduce the

German tanks approach a blazing village near Kharkov.

salient made by the Axis forces in the central sector of the British line. During the night the German 15th Armoured Division digs in at Bir el Harmat, driving off British attacks. ☐ Czechoslovakia. Heydrich dies of the wounds he received in the attempt on his life on 27 May. The Germans retaliate by ordering the execution of many Czech patriots held in prison, and by massacring all the male inhabitants of Lidice while the women and children are interned in a concentration camp.

5 June

North Africa The British counter-attack, code-named *Aberdeen*, is unsuccessful. The Axis salient is not reduced and the British lose two infantry brigades and four artillery regiments. There has been a lack of co-ordination between units, and the Germans have put up a murderous barrage. Rommel launches a counter-attack in the afternoon, sending his reserve tanks eastwards. By sunset every British unit trying to get into the 'Cauldron' has been driven back. The 8th Army has lost 6,000 dead, wounded and missing. Rommel announces that he has taken 4,000 prisoners and captured 150 enemy tanks.
☐ USA declares war on Bulgaria, Rumania and Hungary.

6 June

North Africa Rommel sends the 15th *Panzerdivision* to Bir Hacheim to aid the *Trieste* and 90th Light Divisions, which have been unable to make any headway against the French under General Marie-Pierre Koenig. German and Italian troops concentrate on the area called Knightsbridge, and threaten Tobruk.
Malta Axis bombers pound the island's military installations; both sides report heavy losses in the air.
☐ During the night British aircraft carry out another heavy air raid on Messina, causing severe damage.

7 June

Eastern Front After an artillery preparation lasting five days the Germans and Rumanians launch their final assault on the fortress of Sevastopol, in the Crimea. The threat from Sevastopol has to be eliminated before they can go on to capture the Caucasus. Activity in the central and northern sectors is limited to minor rectification of the lines.
North Africa The Free French 1st Brigade still holds out at Bit Hacheim.
Aleutian Islands The Japanese land 1,800 men on the western islands Atta and Kiska.
China Continuing their offensive in Chekiang province, the Japanese take the airfield at Chuhsien.

8 June

North Africa The battle in the

Knightsbridge–Bir Hacheim area could still go either way. The Free French are defending Bir Hacheim bravely, but they have had to give ground, and their supply position is becoming precarious.

South-West Pacific Following the brilliant outcome of the Battle of Midway, General MacArthur proposes a limited offensive to re-take the positions lost in the Bismarck Archipelago.

9 June

Philippines The Japanese have already completed the conquest of the islands, though there are still isolated groups that have not yet laid down their arms. The Americans have lost a fighting force of 140,000 men.

North Africa The British make an unsuccessful attempt to bring help to the Free French surrounded at Bir Hacheim, where bitter fighting continues.

☐ *Italy.* British aircraft bomb Taranto, causing severe damage.

10 June

North Africa Assault groups of the *Afrikakorps* break into the enemy positions at Bir Hacheim. During the night French survivors escape across the German lines, leaving their wounded behind them, and succeed in rejoining the Allied forces. The British lavish praise on the French general whose courageous defence has forced Rommel to delay his final attack on Tobruk for so long. But it is still Rommel, the 'Desert Fox', who has won the day.

Eastern Front The German Army Group South makes slow progress against the Sevastopol fortifications. The fortress is defended by seven rifle divisions, one dismounted cavalry division, two brigades of infantry and three of naval riflemen, several armoured battalions and other autonomous units, ten regiments of artillery, two mortar battalions, one anti-tank regiment and forty-five groups of naval guns; altogether 101,000 men, with 600 guns and 2,000 mortars. On the German side General von Manstein commands a

force of seven divisions, plus two Rumanian divisions; they too have outstanding artillery support, including mortars and some siege guns of exceptionally large calibre.

China After four days' fighting the Chinese are forced to withdraw from Chuhsien.

11 June

North Africa Axis forces take Bir Hacheim, capturing about 100 French soldiers, many of them wounded.

Malta Double Operations *Harpoon* and *Vigorous* to get supplies through to Malta have begun.

☐ The conclusion of a new mutual assistance pact with the Russians is announced in London and Washington. Under it the Russians will be able to repay in kind the loans made to them under the Lend–Lease Act.

12 June

North Africa Tank battles continue in the area of El Adem and 'Knightsbridge'; Germans now within 15 miles of Tobruk.

Eastern Front Having checked the Russian offensive in the Kharkov area, the Germans go over to the counter-offensive. In the course of three days they crush three Russian

Italian troops in action during Rommel's June offensive.

armies.

□ Rumania. The Ploesti oilfields are bombed by American aircraft from bases in Egypt. On their way home several of the B-24s have to make emergency landings in Turkey, and their aircrews are interned.

13 June

North Africa Axis armour inflicts a heavy defeat on the British, forcing them to withdraw from El Adem and 'Knightsbridge', so that the supply lines of XIII Corps are threatened. The force defending 'Knightsbridge' falls back on Acroma.

14 June

Pacific Ocean The Japanese Imperial General Staff determines to invade New Caledonia, Samoa and Fiji.

North Africa General Ritchie orders the most advanced divisions of XIII Corps, the South African 1st and British 50th, to fall back: with the loss of El Adem and of so many tanks their position has become too exposed. The two divisions retire to the Egyptian frontier, the first along the coast road, the second inland. The Germans and Italians attack towards Acroma, but make little progress in spite of the numerical

superiority of their armour. 'Although', says General Auchinleck, 'I have made it clear to you that Tobruk must not be invested, I realize that its garrison may be isolated for short periods until our winter-offensive can be launched.' It may be that General Headquarters at Cairo do not know the true position of the 8th Army.

General Auchinleck tells Churchill that General Ritchie, GOC 8th Army, foresees the possibility that the British may have to withdraw to the 'old frontier', the Egyptian border. Churchill is alarmed and telegraphs Auchinleck: 'Presume

THE BATTLE OF MIDWAY

27 May

The Japanese I Naval Squadron, commanded by Vice-Admiral Chuichi Nagumo, leaves the base of Hashirajima in the island of the same name, between Honshu and Shikoku islands, bound for Midway. The 21 ships comprise 4 aircraft carriers (*Akagi*, *Kaga*, *Soryu* and *Hiryu*) with the battleship *Kirishima*, and cruisers *Mikuma*, *Chikuma*, *Tone* and *Haruna* and a number of smaller ships. The object is to capture Midway Island, an American base from which their bombers control a vast area of the Pacific. At the same time an invasion force of 5,000 men, on board 12 transports escorted by 2 battleships, 4 heavy cruisers and other ships, under the command of Vice-Admiral Kurita, sails from Saipan and Guam and from metropolitan bases; and there are two more support groups commanded by Vice-Admirals Tanaka and Kondo. Six hundred miles – 24 hours' sailing time – behind Nagumo's squadron, the main fleet sails under the command of Admiral Isoroku Yamamoto, including among others the most powerful battleship in the world, the *Yamato* 72,800 tons fully laden, with nine 18-in guns, twelve 6-in and twelve 5-in guns and a top speed of 27.5 knots (the armament was later modified) and two other battleships, the *Nagato* and *Mutsu*, together with an escort of 1 light cruiser and 9 destroyers, with auxiliaries.

28 May

The Americans are in possession of the Japanese secret code and are aware of their intentions – not merely the capture of Midway Island, but also to draw Admiral Nimitz's Pacific Fleet, weaker

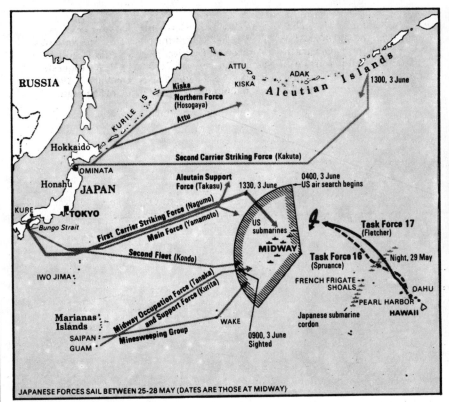

Admiral Isoroku Yamamoto, commander of the main Japanese fleet at Midway, and the man who masterminded the attack on Pearl Harbour.

CV 6 Enterprise (United States 1938). The first aircraft carrier of this name (also given to the first nuclear-powered aircraft carrier *CVAN 65* in 1960). She had a rectangular flight deck, supported by pillars fore and aft, and a large island to starboard that had quadruple 1.1 in (28 mm) anti-aircraft machine gun emplacements abaft and before it. She also had eight 5 in (127 mm) anti-aircraft guns on four platforms at the sides of the flight deck. She belonged to a class of three units which included *Yorktown* and *Hornet*, and was stricken in 1956.

than the Japanese fleet, into a trap. Nimitz accordingly orders Task Force 16, under Rear-Admiral R. A. Spruance, to sail for Midway; his force comprises the aircraft carriers *Enterprise* and *Hornet*, the heavy cruisers *Pensacola*, *Northampton*, *New Orleans*, *Minneapolis* and *Vincennes*, the light cruiser *Atlanta*, 11 destroyers, 2 tankers and 19 submarines.

30 May
Task Force 17, under Rear-Admiral F. J. Fletcher, also sails from Pearl Harbour. It consists of the aircraft carrier *Yorktown*, the heavy cruisers *Portland* and *Astoria* and six destroyers.

Yamato (Japan 1941). The *Yamato* class was to have included four units, but only *Yamato* and *Musashi* were completed One of the other two, *Shinano*, was converted during construction to an aircraft carrier. They were the largest battleships in the world with their displacement of 71,748 ft 872,900 tonnes), double the 30,000 tons allowed by the Washington Treaty. On April 7, 1945, under attack from torpedo planes and bombers, she was sunk off Kyushu.

Above: a Japanese Nikojima hit by anti-aircraft fire from the *Yorktown*.
Below: a Japanese torpedo plane attacks the *Yorktown*.

31 May

The Japanese intercept at least 180 radio messages, many of them 'urgent', and suspect that the enemy knows of their presence. Nagumo's squadron, ahead of the main body of the fleet, has to observe radio silence for fear of being discovered.

2 June

Nagumo has to carry out an unexpected change of course, of which Admiral Yamamoto must be informed. He decides to send a signal on his internal communications system, which is very low-powered. The *Yamato* receives the signal but the Americans, although they are actually nearer to the Japanese squadron, fail to intercept it.

Spruance and Fletcher's task forces rendezvous about 350 miles north-east of Midway. Fletcher takes overall command of the operation and moves the two squadrons to some 200 miles north of Midway.

4 June

At 4.30 a.m. local time reconnaissance aircraft and bombers take off from the aircraft carriers *Akagi* and *Kaga* and the cruisers *Tone*, *Chikuma* and *Haruna*. The first wave, 108 fighters and dive-bombers, makes for Midway. But they fail to surprise the Americans. When still 150 miles from their target they are spotted by a US seaplane, which quickly turns round and gets to the island ahead of them, firing a rocket to warn the fighters already alerted, that an attack is imminent. The Japanese come off better in their engagement with the American aircraft, but they fail to achieve the object of their mission, the neutralization of the aircraft on Midway. At 7.00 a.m. a second attack is ordered. Five minutes later the alarm sounds on board Nagumo's ship; a destroyer has sighted enemy aircraft, a squadron of bombers. Their attack is driven

An aircraft in flames on the aircraft carrier *Hornet*.

Above: US airmen are picked up by a submarine.
Below: the *Soryu* tries to escape. Bottom: the *Akagi* dodges the bombs.

off by anti-aircraft fire from the destroyers, the cruisers, the battleship *Kirishima* and the *Akagi* herself, the Americans' main target. At this point the aircraft in the Japanese second wave have to replace the torpedoes – with which they had been armed for an attack on the American aircraft carriers – with bombs for another attack on Midway, which has not been neutralized.

Between 7.02 and 9.00 a.m., while the flight decks of the Japanese carriers are still cluttered with torpedoes and bombs and aircraft waiting to take off, 131 dive-bombers and torpedo-planes from the aircraft carriers *Hornet*, *Enterprise* and *Yorktown* appear over Nagumo's squadron in successive waves. Many of the American aircraft are destroyed, and the Japanese suffer no damage.

At 9.30 a.m. more American aircraft attack the Japanese fleet. Meanwhile the American submarine *Nautilas* attacks the Japanese carriers with torpedoes. At 10.20 a.m. Vice-Admiral Nagumo orders the aircraft to take off. Hardly four minutes later American dive-bombers attack the Japanese carriers. The *Akagi*,

Above: the *Yorktown*, already burning, puts up an anti-aircraft barrage.
Below: the *Mikuma* collides with the *Mogami*. Below right: The *Yorktown* goes down.

Soryu and *Kaga* are all hit. Serious fires break out and there are explosions among the aircraft and bombs on the flight decks. Only the *Hiryu* manages to escape the enemy bombers.

2.45 p.m.: The American aircraft carrier *Yorktown* is hit by aircraft from the *Hiryu*.

5 June

3.30 p.m.: Yamamoto has the wreck of the *Akagi* torpedoed. The crew are safely taken on board the cruiser *Nagara*.

6.00 p.m.: After another attack by aircraft from the *Enterprise* the aircraft carrier *Hiryu* sinks.

7.00 p.m.: The aircraft carrier *Soryu*, badly damaged the previous day, sinks with her whole complement of 728 men, including the captain.

7.25 p.m.: The aircraft carrier *Kaga*, also hit the day before, sinks.

6 June

2.15 a.m.: The cruisers *Mogami* and *Mikuma* collide.

3.00 a.m.: Admiral Yamamoto orders a general withdrawal. During the next few hours the *Mogami* and *Mikuma*, though damaged, manage to get away; but during the night American aircraft manage to locate the *Mikuma* and attack and sink her. A Japanese submarine torpedoes and sinks the American destroyer *Hammam*. With their aircraft back on board, the Americans lose contact with the retreating enemy.

7 June

A Japanese submarine torpedoes and sinks the American aircraft carrier *Yorktown*; already hit on the 4th, she has been withdrawing at reduced speed.

So ends one of the most important naval battles in history. The Japanese have lost 3,500 men, 4 aircraft carriers and a cruiser, besides 332 aircraft. But worst of all is the loss of a high proportion of their bravest and most experienced aircraft carrier pilots. Moreover they have failed in their object of seizing Midway. The Americans have lost 307 men, 1 aircraft carrier, 1 destroyer and 150 aircraft. But they can celebrate a great victory. The Battle of Midway marks the turning-point in the Pacific war.

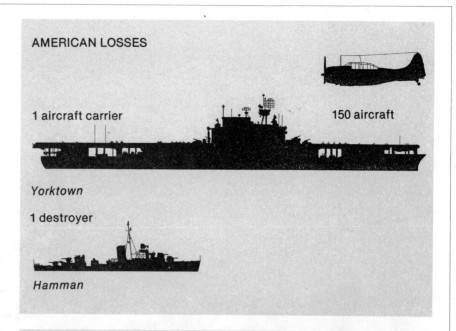

AMERICAN LOSSES

1 aircraft carrier   150 aircraft

Yorktown

1 destroyer

Hamman

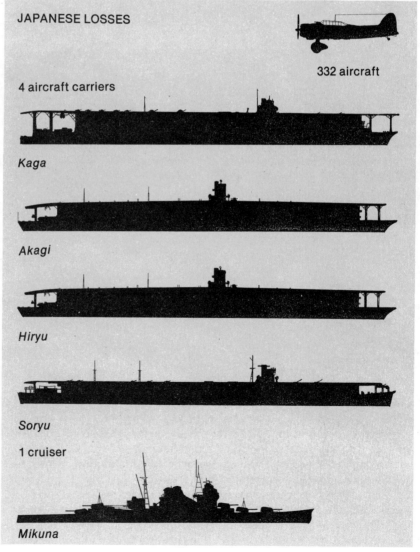

JAPANESE LOSSES

332 aircraft

4 aircraft carriers

Kaga

Akagi

Hiryu

Soryu

1 cruiser

Mikuna

Italian *Bersaglieri* clearing British minefields south-east of Mersa Matruh as Rommel pursues the retreating British army towards El Alamein.

there is no question in any case of giving up Tobruk.' The reply from the Commander-in-Chief of British forces in the Middle East is reassuring: 'War Cabinet interpretation is correct. General Ritchie is putting into Tobruk what he considers an adequate force to hold it, even should it become temporarily iso-lated by enemy. Basis of garrison is four brigade groups, with adequate stocks of ammunition, food, fuel, and water.'

Meanwhile, in the Gazala sector, the Axis forces have by-passed Acroma and the Via Balbia and reached the coast west of the Tobruk perimeter.

15 June
North Africa Rommel reports that he has won the battle against the British 8th Army; it only remains to take Tobruk.

The 29th Brigade of the 5th Indian Division drives off attacks by German and Italian troops with tank and air support in the area of El Adem.

Major-General Klopper, GOC 2nd South African Division, is given the command of the Tobruk fortress, with the task of defending it to the last man.
Mediterranean Air–naval battle off Pantelleria. The Italians lose the cruiser *Trento*, the British 1 cruiser, 3 destroyers and 6 merchant ships,

part of a convoy bound for Malta.

16 June
North Africa The British send four infantry brigades, with artillery and armoured units, to man the Tobruk fortress. The rest of the British 8th Army continues its action against heavy Axis pressure. A German–Italian armoured column makes for Sidi Rezegh and creates a diversion against El Adem. British troops withdraw from El Adem during the night.
☐ Evidently reassured by General Auchinleck's optimistic despatch, Winston Churchill leaves for Washington to review the military situation on the various fronts with President Roosevelt.

17 June
North Africa Axis forces move on to the coast from inland and secure control of the road to Bardia, so that Tobruk is cut off.
Eastern Front In the Crimea the Germans and Rumanians attacking Sevastopol storm the 'Siberia' fortress, an important strongpoint in the defensive perimeter.

18 June
North Africa Axis troops occupy the area of Gambut, outside Tobruk, site of the landing-strips that should have been used for supplying the fortress. Rommel thus completes his manœuvre to surround the fortress.
Eastern Front The Germans at Sevastopol take the 'Maxim Gorki' fort after eleven days' bloody fighting: Germans now two miles from the harbour.
☐ General Spaatz takes command of the US VIII Air Force, stationed in Britain.
☐ The Supreme Soviet meets in Moscow to ratify the Anglo-Soviet alliance.

19 June
North Africa The British withdraw beyond Bardia, on the Libyan–Egyptian frontier.

20 June
North Africa The attack on the

Tobruk fortress, preceded by a violent air bombardment starting at 5.30 a.m., is in the hands of the *Afrikakorps* and the Italian XX Corps. The tanks go into action at 7.00 a.m., penetrating over a mile inside the perimeter. The Italian XX Corps attack towards the south-west. The British tanks and artillery are wiped out. General Klopper is authorized to leave the fortress, but he cannot do this since the Axis forces have succeeded in cutting him off from the harbour. The British 7th Armoured Division tries to break through to the troops cut off, but is unable to reach them in time. At 7.00 p.m. the tanks of the German 21st *Panzerdivision* enter Tobruk.
Eastern Front The Germans and Rumanians attacking Sevastopol take the 'Lenin' fort and reach the southern bank of the harbour after violent fighting.

21 June
North Africa 2.00 a.m.: The South African General Klopper, commander of the Tobruk fortress, tells General Ritchie, that he will fight 'to the last man and the last round'.
6.00 a.m.: General Klopper asks General Ritchie for authority to surrender.
8.00 a.m.: Klopper sends officers forward with a white flag to ask Rommel for surrender terms. Together with Klopper the Germans take five other generals and brigadiers and 30,000 men of, among others, the 2nd South African Division, the 29th Indian Brigade and two battalions of the Guards.
General Ritchie decides to fall back on Mersa Matruh, in Egypt, and orders XIII Corps to slow down the enemy advance while XXX Corps organize the defence of Mersa Matruh.
In the evening Hitler personally sends a telegram to Rommel awarding him a Field-Marshal's baton. 'It would be bettter if he had sent me another division,' comments Rommel.
Along with Tobruk Rommel captures 2,000 tons of petrol, 5,000 tons of rations, vast quantities of ammuni-

tion and 2,000 vehicles in working order, plus the harbour and a big water distillation plant. The victory has cost him, since 26 May, 3,360 men, including at least 300 officers, 70% of all the officers in the *Afrikakorps*. The Italians have lost about 3,000 of all ranks.

Mussolini now writes to Hitler to ask for a decision on the invasion of Malta: 'It is my opinion, and surely yours too, that we must consolidate and build up on the successes achieved. Central to our strategic picture lies the problem of Malta, on which we have in the past taken decisions of which you are aware. To maintain the positions we have gained in Marmarica, and to provide for future requirements, we must be able to provide the necessary transport. The occupation of Malta would not only solve the problem of sea traffic in the Mediterranean but also make our air forces available in other fields.' Together with this message Mussolini submits to his ally a problem that

the Italian command has been studying for a long time, and for which they have been making operational preparations – the project (Operation C3) for a landing in Malta. Behind this project are the Italian Chief of Staff, General Ugo Cavallero, and the German Field-Marshal Albert Kesselring. These two senior officers have recognized how important the island can be in the overall picture of the Mediterranean war, not least in its contribution to Rommel's African campaign. Their plan has been worked out down to the minutest details, and now the troops of the invasion force, after a meticulous rehearsal on the cliffs south of Leghorn (which are similar in form to those in Malta) have been transferred to Sicily and, since April, have been waiting for the order to go. But Rommel wants priority. He asks for (and gets) authority from Hitler to attack Tobruk first (the Italians have to be content with a formal undertaking that, once the African

fortress is taken, Rommel will stop and consider the possibility of carrying out the landing); then, when the town is taken, he declares (and tells Hitler) that he has no intention of stopping. 'I am going on to Suez,' he declares, 'and I hope the Italians will follow me.' To settle the matter at once Rommel applies directly to Hitler, holding up to him the dazzling prospect of an incredible advance to Suez and an (impossible) occupation of the Persian Gulf oilfields. Hitler, always susceptible to the fascination of Rommel, and carried away by the grandeur of the plan, finally opts in Rommel's favour.

22 June

Eastern Front On the anniversary of the German invasion the *Sovinformbureau* publishes a *Review of the First Year of the War*, drawing up the following balance-sheet of losses suffered by the two sides:

Dead, wounded and prisoners: Germany about 10 million, USSR 4·5 million. Guns lost: Germany 30,500, USSR 22,000. Tanks: Germany over 24,000, USSR 15,000. Aircraft: Germany over 20,000, USSR 9,000.

These highly improbable figures have not been repeated in the histories of the Second World War since published by the Russians. The official figures given by the Germans for their losses during the same period are just as improbable: 271,612 dead and 63,730 missing. More convincing are the figures for German losses quoted in General Halder's *Diary*, which give the following statistics for dead, wounded and prisoners, not counting the sick: up to 15 February 1942, 946,000; to 10 May, 1,183,000; to 20 May, 1,215,000; to 10 June, 1,268,000; to 30 June 1942, 1,362,000. By 10 September 1942 German losses in dead, wounded and prisoners are to jump to 1,637,000 as a result of the campaign preceding the battle of Stalingrad.

Russian figures for human losses must certainly be greater; those for material losses may have been 'inflated' to stimulate the war industries

Axis troops advance through British artillery fire at Tobruk.

to maximum production and perhaps also to get more substantial help from the Western Allies.

In his Directive No. 41 Hitler lays down the following objectives for the summer campaign: liquidation of the Russians in the Crimea, capture of Voronezh so as to threaten both the central sector of the front and also Stalingrad; encirclement and elimination of the Soviet forces in the great bend of the Don, attacking from Voronezh in the north and Taganrog in the south. With the road to Stalingrad open, the capture or destruction of that city; a wheel south to the Caucasus to capture the Maykop, Grozny and Baku oilfields, bringing the Germans to the Turkish frontier, which may induce the Turks to line up with the Axis. A new effort to liquidate Leningrad is also planned.

But the campaign does not work out exactly as planned. The Russians hold up the Germans at Voronezh, but giving way quickly at Rostov. Hitler is induced to make some far-reaching changes in his strategy. He wants, for example, to carry out the taking of Stalingrad and the conquest of the Caucasus at the same time. As Zhukov said later, this was a monstrous error, pregnant with disastrous consequences for the Wehrmacht.

North Africa The British 8th Army withdraws to Mersa Matruh. Axis forces reach Bardia, near the Egyptian border.

General Auchinleck visits 8th Army headquarters for discussions with General Ritchie.

Eastern Front Army Group South opens a limited offensive in the Izyum sector to improve German positions east of the Donetz in preparation for the great offensive that is to be launched as soon as Sevastopol is taken. The struggle for Sevastopol grows fiercer.

☐ USA. A Japanese submarine shells the military depot at Fort Stevens, Oregon, on the river Columbia estuary. The damage is trivial. This is the first attack on a military installation in the USA since the war of 1812, and is to be the only one in this war.

☐ France. Laval broadcasts his hopes for a German victory.

23 June

North Africa The Axis forces are ready for another drive forward. Their advance guards encounter the 7th Armoured Division of the British XIII Corps near Sollum, already in Egyptian territory. In view of the critical situation in this theatre of operations 24 American B-17 bombers on the way to China are diverted to Khartoum.

Hitler writes to Mussolini about the projected invasion of Malta. 'Fate, Duce, has offered us an opportunity that will never be repeated in the same theatre of war ... The British 8th Army has been virtually destroyed, the port installations at Tobruk are almost intact. If we do not now follow up the remnants of the 8th Army without an instant's delay, the same thing will happen that happened to the British when they stopped, almost at the gates of the port of Tripoli, to send reinforcements to Greece. This time, in the right conditions, Egypt can be seized from the British ... My advice is this: order the operations to be followed up until the British forces are completely wiped out ... The goddess of fortune in battle passes by her captains but once; he who does not seize her now may never overtake her.' Hitler's letter appeals to Mussolini's vanity and the Italian leader decides to postpone Operation C3, and orders that all the men and equipment of the landing force should be put at Rommel's disposal. In the evening the Italian supreme command signals the Italian commander in Africa, General Bastico: 'The Duce is in full agreement with the proposal to exploit success to the full.' Malta is safe.

24 June

North Africa Rommel launches his

Rommel, the 'Desert Fox', marks up another success with the capture of Tobruk on 21 June.

THE FALL OF SEVASTOPOL

7 June

After an aerial and artillery bombardment lasting five days, seven German and two Rumanian divisions of the Army Group South, commanded by von Manstein, attack the Sevastopol fortress, which has been cut off for many months despite Russian efforts to relieve it with their counter-offensives against Kerch and Feodosiya and the Crimea. The fortress is manned by more than 100,000 Soviet troops. Sevastopol is the biggest port on the Black Sea, and is surrounded by a triple defence line, the first of trenches and minefields, the second of a series of forts between the Belbak valley and the Gulf of Severnaia – forts which the Germans have given names to, 'Stalin', 'Molotov', 'Volga', 'Gepeu', 'Siberia' and so on, biggest of all are 'Maxim Gorki I' and 'Maxim Gorki II' armed with batteries of 305-mm guns and protected by immense reinforced concrete walls. The third defensive line is just outside the city, and consists of trenches, gun positions and machine-gun nests. There are at least 600 guns and 2,000 mortars defending the fortress, and against them the Germans have brought up some quite extraordinary weapons to reinforce their normal artillery and dive-bombers. One of them is the 'Gamma' mortar, an up-to-date version of the First World War 'Big Bertha', which had a calibre of 420 mm. The 'Gamma's' calibre is 427 mm; its range is 8.7 miles, its projectile weighs over 2,000 lb, the barrel is 22 feet long and it needs a crew of 235 men. Besides the 'Gamma' there is also 'Karl', which has already been used against Brest Litovsk. It is specially designed for use against reinforced concrete

Sevastopol: a decapitated statue of Lenin (top) and above: the harbour area.

German sappers before the giant guns of fort 'Maxim Gorki', one of the chain of forts defending the city.

fortifications: its calibre is 615 mm, length of its barrel 16·4 feet, weight of the projectile 4,850 lb. Then there is 'Dora' (also called 'Big Gustav'), a gun that can fire three projectiles an hour, a real monster of artillery which no reinforced concrete can resist. 'Dora' has a calibre of 800 mm, a barrel 106 feet long and a shell 25.6 feet long with its shell-case; it weighs 9,920 lb and has a maximum range of 28 miles. There are at least 4,120 men concerned with 'Dora's' operation; just to aim, load and fire the weapon takes a crew of 1,500 men, commanded by a brigadier and a colonel. But a single shell from 'Dora' at Sevastopol, in the Gulf of Severnaia, has destroyed an ammunition depot 100 feet underground.

The German and Rumanian in-fantry go into the attack at 3.50 a.m. on 7 June and are met by a tremendous barrage from the Russians.

13 June
Fort 'Stalin' falls after a day's savage fighting by attackers and defenders.

14–17 June
The Germans and Rumanians continue with fierce attacks on the second line of fortifications. The defenders are winkled out of Fort 'Siberia' with flamethrowers, or burnt to death.

18 June
The Germans take Forts 'Gepeu', 'Molotov', 'Cheka', 'Volga' and 'Urals', and after a long struggle marked by superhuman tenacity and heroism on both sides they capture the dreaded 'Maxim Gorki I', one of the biggest of the forts.

20 June
The Germans take Fort 'Lenin'. Every yard of ground is fiercely contended. The Rumanians are no less courageous than the Germans. The Russians in their desperate defence put all available personnel in the front line, including reservists and boys.

27 June
After three weeks of slaughter Sevastopol has virtually fallen, though some small pockets of resistance continue to hold out until 3 July before they are finally wiped out.

assault on Egypt, sending his armoured columns east and north-east, 50 miles into Egypt, and throwing the British rearguards into confusion in the area of Sidi Barrani. The X Corps, which has only just arrived in Egypt from Syria, relieves XIII Corps, which is sent to El Alamein to take over a new defence line.

Eastern Front Army Group South reaches the line of the river Oskol, the objective set for it by the headquarters in the Izyum area. The battle still rages at Sevastopol, but the end is in sight.

□ Major-General Dwight D. Eisenhower assumes command of US forces in Britain.

25 June

Eastern Front Now that the threat from Sevastopol to their right flank is virtually eliminated, the Germans attack all along the southern sector with 35 divisions, moving from the Kursk sector in the direction of Voronezh. Russians evacuate Kupyansk, south-east of Kharkov.

North Africa The Axis forces, pounded by the RAF, advance into Egyptian territory towards Mersa Matruh. General Auchinleck assumes personal command of the 8th Army in place of General Ritchie. After a thorough examination of the situation he decides to

proceed with the withdrawal of his divisions from Mersa Matruh to El Alamein, 96 miles to the east.

□ Churchill attends Pacific War Council in Washington.

26 June

Eastern Front Major victory by the German 6th Army (General von Paulus) at Kharkov, on the Donetz. Further south the Army Group South retakes Rostov-on-Don.

North Africa In the late evening the Axis troops attack in the sector south of Mersa Matruh. Axis forces include the German 90th Light Division and 15th and 21st Armoured Divisions and the Italian *Littorio*, *Ariete* and *Trieste* Divisions.

27 June

North Africa Heavy fighting at Mersa Matruh. At 7.00 p.m. the 90th Light Division reaches the coast at the Ras Hawala height, 25 miles east of Mersa Matruh.

South-West Pacific Supreme Commander General MacArthur reveals his plan (*Tulsa II*) for the recapture of New Britain, New Ireland and the Admiralty Islands.

Eastern Front The Germans establish several bridgeheads over the Don. A gap is being opened in the Russian lines in the central sector. In the northern sector too the Germans have regained the initiative, so long held by the Russians.

28 June

Eastern Front The Germans step up their offensive in all sectors. They launch an offensive at Kursk and in the northern sector they gain an important victory, crossing the river Volkhov and eliminating the Soviet salient.

North Africa Axis forces break through the 29th Brigade of the 5th Indian Division, which is covering the withdrawal of X Corps to the Fuka area. The X Corps withdraws to El Alamein. Advance guards of the German 90th Light Division reach Fuka, about 45 miles east of Mersa Matruh.

Youthful German troops receive a rapturous send off in the Unter den Linden, Berlin, as they set off for the Eastern Front, which is taking an increasing toll on German military resources.

Top: German light tank with Finnish infantry. Above: an Italian 'Alpino' in Russia shows how lucky he has been.

29 June

North Africa Axis troops enter Mersa Matruh.

Pushing on eastwards, the German 90th Light Division reaches Sidi Abd el Rahman, only about 20 miles from El Alamein, where General Auchinleck is preparing the 8th Army's defence line. The front to be defended is about 30 miles broad, and the only routes by which the enemy can advance are at the extreme northern and southern ends of the front itself, one along the coast and the other along the 'Barrel Track' which leads straight to Cairo. Mussolini leaves for Cyrenaica, piloting his own aeroplane. It is said that there is a white horse on board which the Duce wants to ride when he makes his entrance into Cairo, which he believes will be a matter of days, if not hours. 'Within 15 days,' he declares, 'we shall instal an Italian High Commission.'

China Chiang Kai-shek has a meeting with General Stilwell and asks for an American guarantee to despatch three divisions and 500 aircraft, with 5,000 tons of supplies every month.

Mediterranean The British submarine support ship *Medway*, on the way to Haifa carrying 90 torpedoes, is sunk by the German submarine U-372. The central Mediterranean is now completely dominated by the Italian navy and the Axis air forces.

□ London. World Jewish Conference reviews sufferings of Jews under the Nazis.

30 June

North Africa The Axis forces maintain their pressure, while the British XXX Corps takes up positions at the north end of the Alamein line; XIII Corps is deployed in the south, while X Corps headquarters organizes Delta Force to defend Alexandria and the Nile delta. In his order of the day circulated to the troops, General Auchinleck, Commander-in-Chief of British forces in the Middle East, says 'The enemy is making his final effort and thinks of us as a defeated army . . . He hopes to take Egypt by bluffing. Your job is to show that he is mistaken.'

Eastern Front The Germans step up their offensive in the southern sector. The German 2nd Army and IV *Panzergruppe* attack towards Voronezh, while the 6th Army pushes on eastwards in the region south-east of Belgorod. In the Crimea the battle for Sevastopol is virtually over. The Army Group North eliminates the Russian pocket of resistance west of the river Volkhov.

New Guinea An Australian unit carries out a raid on the Japanese base at Salamaua. A few days later a similar raid is made on another important Japanese strategic and supply base, at Lae.

1 July

North Africa The German 90th Light Division reaches the El Alamein defensive perimeter following up the British 4th Armoured Brigade, which is moving towards Alam el Onsol.

6.00 p.m.: The two armoured divisions of the *Afrikakorps* (the 15th and 21st) attack the area of Deir el Shein, but the attack is contained by the 18th Indian Brigade, supported after a time by the British 1st Armoured Division.

Eastern Front Hitler's headquarters announces Sevastopol in German hands. Army Group Centre continues its advance in the Don basin.

2 July

Indian Ocean British forces occupy Mayotte Island, north of the Mozambique Channel, to establish an air base.

New Guinea The Australian 7th Brigade is ordered to embark from its home base for Milne Bay.

South-West Pacific Instructions are issued for the occupation of the New Britain–New Ireland–New Guinea area. Starting on 1 August, the Allied forces are to occupy the Solomon Islands, then the north-east coast of New Guinea, finally Rabaul in New Britain and neighbouring areas in New Guinea and New Ireland. Later the date for the operation is put back by a week.

□ A Conservative Member of Parliament, Sir John Wardlaw-Milne, moves a vote of censure on the Prime Minister, Winston Churchill, in the House of Commons. The disasters in Africa have put Churchill in a very difficult position and he returned at once from Washington on hearing of the fall of Tobruk. Now even his close friends (like Admiral Keyes and Hore-Belisha) join in the attack on him, arguing that the conduct of the war ought to be in the hands of someone not directly involved in the business of government. In his reply to the motion Churchill displays all his aggressiveness and brilliant oratory. He says: 'The will of the House should be made manifest upon important occasions. It is important that not only those who speak but that those who listen, watch and judge should count as a factor in world affairs. We are still fighting for our lives and for causes dearer than life itself . . . Sober and constructive criticism has its place, but the duty of the House is to sustain the Government or change the Government. If it cannot change, it should sustain. There is no middle course in wartime.'

The censure motion is defeated by 476 votes to 25.

3 July

Eastern Front According to an estimate put out by the 'Foreign Armies East Branch' of the German information service the Russians have lost 7,300,000 men, killed, wounded, permanently sick and missing, up to 1 May 1942. Since, according to this report, the total forces that the USSR can mobilize add up to 17 million men, it is concluded that the potential manpower still available to the Russians is about 9,700,000 men. 7.8 million of these have already been called up (6 million in the army, 1.5 million in the air force, 300,000 in the navy); 4.5 million are front-line troops. Reserves still available for mobilization are thus about 2 million men. By the same date, says the report, the Russians have lost 60% of their production of coke, with consequent repercussions in their steel

'L'ETRANGER'

A young French writer of Algerian origin, Albert Camus, published *L'Etranger*.

Written between 1939 and 1940, *L'Etranger* (translated under the title of *The Outsider* in the UK and *The Stranger* in the USA) was an extremely harsh novel in which a humble clerk is involved in an absurd sequence of events and having committed a crime without any obvious reason, allows himself, consciously and impassively, to be condemned to death without defending himself, exemplifying the growing cult of existentialism.

German Army Group South resumes the offensive east of Kharkov, but the thaw holds up the advance.

output. However, in compensation for this reduced domestic production Russia is receiving considerable help from the Allies. During July 1942 at least 2,800 tanks and thousands of aircraft, trucks and locomotives reached Murmansk by the Arctic route.

North Africa The Italian *Ariete* Division, which has been attacking towards Alam Nayil, is held up by New Zealand artillery and suffers heavy losses. By midday the *Ariete* has only five tanks and two guns left – a calamity for Rommel.

4 July

North Africa The XXX Corps of the British 8th Army is reinforced by the Australian 9th Division, which has been moved up to El Alamein. XIII Corps continues its attacks on the southern flank of the Axis positions.

☐ For the first time, six American aircraft join a British bomber formation in a raid on airfields in Holland.

5 July

Eastern Front All organized Russian resistance in the Crimea has ceased. The IV *Panzergruppe* reaches the Don in the area of Voronezh, meeting with bitter resistance from the enemy. In the central sector the Germans move to better positions in the Smolensk area.

6 July

Eastern Front The German 6th Army and IV *Panzergruppe* move towards Voronezh from the west and south-west.

North Africa Fighting continues around El Alamein. RAF aircraft attack Tobruk and Benghazi.

7 July

Eastern Front The German 6th Army and IV *Panzergruppe* join up north-east of Valuyki. Germans take Voronezh, but the Russians hold up the Germans by a violent counter-attack just east of the town. Meanwhile the other units of Army Group South continue with the destruction of the Russian forces in the Don basin.

Pacific The aircraft carriers *Saratoga* and *Enterprise* sail from Pearl Harbour for the South Pacific.

☐ Sicily. British aircraft raid Messina and Reggio Calabria.

8 July

Pacific Admiral Nimitz issues his operational plans. The American South Pacific naval forces are to take the Santa Cruz Islands and the islands of Tulagi and Guadalcanal in the Solomon Islands.

China General Chennault takes over command of American air forces in China. The bravery of his pilots

earns them the nickname 'the flying tigers'.

Eastern Front The evacuation of Oskol, south-east of Kursk announced by the Russians. Unable to push on beyond Voronezh, the Germans detach the 6th Army from this sector and send it south, along the right bank of the Don, to attack Stalingrad.

Malta Continued heavy Axis air raids.

☐ Cardinal Hinsley, in a broadcast to Europe, declares that in Poland alone over 700,000 Jews have been massacred by the Nazis.

9 July

Eastern Front The Army Group South is divided into two groups. Army Group A, in the south, is made up of the 1st Armoured Army and the 11th and 17th Armies, and Army Group B, in the north, of the German 2nd Army, the Hungarian 2nd Army, the 4th Armoured Army (formerly IV *Panzergruppe*) and the 6th Army. Army Group A is to retake Rostov-on-Don, where the largest enemy forces are thought to be concentrated, and then to advance south towards the Caucasus. Army Group B is to advance along the Don as far as Stalingrad, and then along the Volga towards Astrakhan.

North Africa Rommel's efforts to

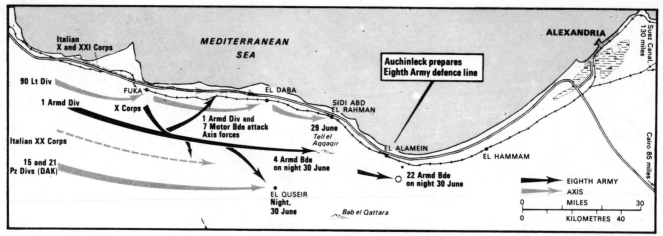

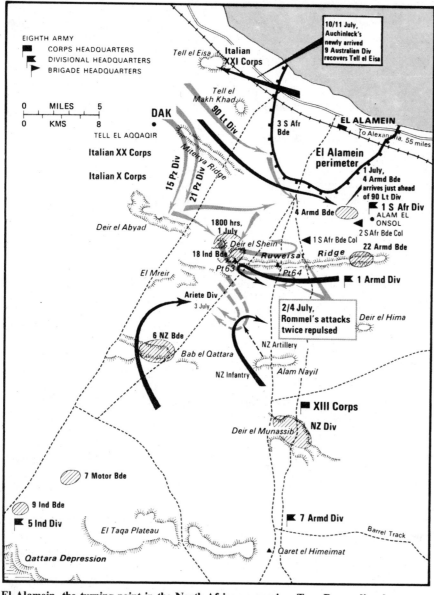

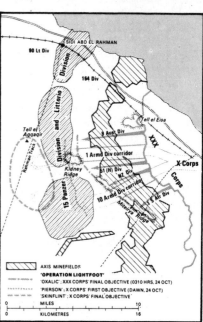

El Alamein, the turning point in the North African campaign. Top: Rommel's advance to the final British line of defence running from El Alamein to the Qattara Depression. Above: the first battle of El Alamein, July 1942. Right: Montgomery's plan of attack for the second decisive battle of El Alamein, which began on 23 October 1942.

break through the El Alamein defences break down against the stubborn resistance of the British.
South-West Pacific More Australian troops embark for New Guinea.

10 July
North Africa In a series of limited attacks the Australian 9th Division of the British XXX Corps takes the high ground at Tellel Eisa, west of the Alamein line. The *Afrikakorps* tries unsuccessfully to reduce the salient established by the enemy.
Mussolini returns to Rome from North Africa, putting off for the time being his plan to make a triumphal entry into Cairo.
Eastern Front The German 4th Armoured Army joins up with the 6th Army advancing along the Don

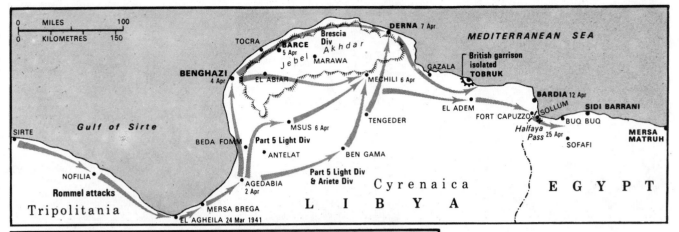

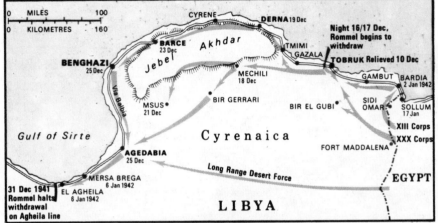

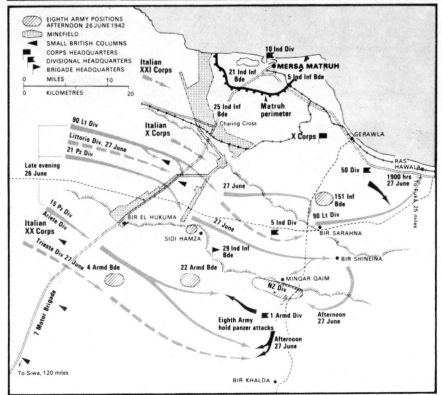

Top: Rommel's first offensive which took him to the Egyptian frontier by the end of April 1941. Centre: Operation *Crusader*, the British counter-offensive in November 1941. Above: the Axis break-through at Mersa Matruh, June 1942.

towards Stalingrad, while the 1st Armoured Army and 17th Army of Army Group A press on in the direction of Rostov. The Russians admit the loss of Rossosh and also admit considerable German forces on the east bank of the Don.

11 July
Eastern Front The *Oberkommando der Wehrmacht* announces that between 28 June and 9 July Reich troops have broken through the enemy lines beyond Kharkov and Kursk. Pushing on towards Rostov, Army Group A takes Lisichensk on the Donetz.

12 July
Eastern Front The Russians establish the 'Stalingrad Front' under the command of Marshal Timoshenko. Moscow sources state that the Don is 'running with blood'.
New Guinea Australian force from Port Moresby arrives at Kokoda.

13 July
Pacific The operational plans for *Tulsa II* are slightly modified, and the relevant troop movements begin in Australia.

14 July
Eastern Front Army Groups B and A make swift progress, the one towards Stalingrad, and the other towards Rostov. The 4th Armoured Army is transferred from Army Group B to Army Group A to join in the operations south of Rostov.
Pacific General Harmon appointed to the command of the Ameri-

The Allied convoy PQ-17 in the Arctic.
Below: a Heinkel attacks the convoy.

can armed forces in the South Pacific area. In preparation for the invasion of the Solomon Islands the ships of Task Force 44 leave Brisbane for New Zealand, where they join the combined operations force for the Solomon Islands. Task Force 42, a submarine force, is to harry Japanese communications in the area of Rabaul. The 7th Marine Regiment, stationed in Samoa, is ordered to stand ready to leave for the Solomons at four days' notice.

North Africa The British attack along and south of Ruweisat Ridge, not gaining much ground but inflicting heavy losses on the enemy. Rommel's dream of capturing Alexandria and Suez within a few days is rapidly fading.

15 July

South-West Pacific Plans are prepared for Operation *Providence*, the occupation by the Allies of Buna, on the north coast of New Guinea.

China The air lift from India to China, operated by General Chennault's daring pilots, starts to function.

North Africa Axis troops twice counter-attack with tanks, and win back a small part of the ground lost on the Ruweisat Ridge, about 5 miles south of the El Alamein perimeter. The fire from the British artillery is outstandingly effective.

Eastern Front Russian news bulletins admit the loss of Boguchar and Millerovo. While the German Army Group A pushes on quickly towards Rostov, the 1st Armoured Army and 4th Armoured Army reach Kamensk, on the Donetz.

16 July

North Africa The British counter-attack. They widen the salient opened west of El Alamein by the capture of some rocky ground 3 miles from the railway station. The British XIII Corps launches more attacks on the southern flank of the Axis line.

17 July

Eastern Front The Russians put up a desperate resistance on the Don in the Stalingrad area to give themselves time to prepare the defences of the city.

North Africa The Italian *Trieste* and *Pavia* Divisions, supported by the *Afrikakorps*, succeed in checking a counter-attack by British troops in the Miteirya Ridge sector, southwest of the Alamein perimeter, which might have broken the Axis line. But Axis losses are heavy. Rommel sums up the situation: 'On that day the last German reserves were thrown into the battle. Our forces were already so small compared with the British, who were continually being reinforced, that we were beginning to think ourselves lucky when we succeeded in holding on to our positions. Our front was manned sparsely because of the enormous losses suffered by the Italians ... We were left practically without reserves.' The supply problem is the worst headache for the Axis. Rommel demands more men and materials. At a meeting with Cavallero and Kesselring he makes the realistic suggestion that the Axis troops should withdraw from El Alamein to Sollum, but is sharply silenced. 'Withdrawal', says Cavallero, 'is a word that must be erased from the military vocabulary in this sector.' The British, unlike the Axis forces, are able to receive supplies and reinforcements regularly and continually, so that they can stand up to the siege of El Alamein with confidence.

South-West Pacific Troop movements for the occupation of Buna, New Guinea, get under way. The operation is planned to take place between 10 and 12 August.

18 July

Eastern Front Continuing their advance southwards on a broad front, the Germans take Voroshilovgrad, a mining and industrial centre in the Donetz basin. To the south-east, they reach the river Don at the Tsimlyansky height.

19 July

Eastern Front The Russians concentrate their forces on the Don to defend Stalingrad. The Germans are still advancing on Rostov.

South-West Pacific A Japanese contingent about 1,800 strong embarks at Rabaul (New Britain) to capture Buna and Gona, in New Guinea.

China General Stilwell asks Generalissimo Chiang Kai-shek for Chinese help in the recapture of Burma as a condition for increased American aid to China.

20 July

Pacific Tactical directions are issued for the Allied invasion of the Solomon Islands.

21 July

Pacific The Solomons expeditionary force (Task Force 61) is ordered to rendezvous south-east of the Fiji Islands on 26 July.

Allied aircraft sight and attack a Japanese convoy headed for New Guinea. This is the contingent that left Rabaul on the 19th. During the night of 21/22 July it lands at Gona and Buna, so forestalling the Allies' projected Operation *Providence*. Japanese naval forces stationed at Lae carry out diversionary actions, attacking Mubo and Komiatum. This operation by the Japanese brings the Empire of the Rising Sun to its maximum territorial expansion.

North Africa The British attack the central sector of the Axis line, sending sappers forward to make gaps in the enemy minefields to enable the tanks to get through.

Rommel sends the *Oberkommando der Wehrmacht* a detailed report on the state of the German army in Africa. In this paper the Field-Marshal says that the German units have to record extremely heavy losses, that the front can hold, but that the situation will remain critical for his troops until the whole of the 164th Division becomes available; his formations are reduced to 40% of their strength. As for the Italians, says Rommel, they have shown themselves so unreliable that they should be split up and incorporated in German formations.

☐ Heavy RAF raids over Belgium and Northern France.

German tanks and infantry in Russia in July on the southern front near Cherkovo.

22 July

Pacific The Solomons invasion force, including the US 1st Marine Division, sails from Wellington, New Zealand, for the rendezvous near Fiji, where it will be joined by a battalion from Pearl Harbour.

New Guinea Allied aircraft attack enemy transports north of the island. The Japanese who landed at Buna and Gona thrust south as far as Giruwa and penetrate inland as far as the Soputa area to reconnoitre the track that leads across the mountains to Port Moresby. MacArthur orders General Morris, Allied commander in New Guinea, to arrange urgently for the reinforcement of Kokoda.

North Africa The British 23rd Armoured Brigade, which only reached the front a few days earlier, passes through the Axis minefields but makes very little progress and loses a great number of tanks. The

Axis forces counter-attack vigorously, wiping out the New Zealand 6th Brigade and one battalion of the 161st Indian Brigade.

Losses to the German and Italian forces have also been heavy. Rommel decides for the time being to abandon his original plan of breaking through the British line and by-passing El Alamein to get to the Nile. Just now it is more urgent for him to rebuild and reorganize his units before undertaking any new operations or working out any new plans.

Eastern Front The German Army Group A opens the final offensive against Rostov-on-Don.

☐ The British turn down an American proposal for a landing in Europe in 1942.

23 July

Eastern Front The Germans are at

the gates of Rostov. The Russians still fight back desperately west of Stalingrad.

New Guinea The Japanese advance along the track across the mountains and run into Australian units near Awala, forcing them to fall back towards Wairopi.

23–27 July

North Africa Fierce fighting continues between Axis and British troops on the El Alamein front, but the overall tactical picture remains unchanged. General Auchinleck, like Rommel, is mainly concerned with the 'reconstruction' of his forces.

Malta The hammering of the island by Axis bombers goes on.

24 July

Eastern Front Army Group A takes Rostov and Novocherkassk. Large

Russian forces are wiped out or completely surrounded.

New Guinea The Australians have to retire to Kokoda after blowing up the bridge over the river Kumusi at Wairopi.

25 July

New Guinea The Japanese advance further inland.

Eastern Front The Germans consolidate their positions at Rostov and Novocherkassk. Further south there is a growing threat to Stalingrad, but the Russians still hold several bridgeheads west of the Don.

☐ Roosevelt and Churchill have been continually asked by Stalin to open a second front. They are not ready yet to invade Europe, but decide on a large-scale landing in Africa. This is Operation *Torch*, the new name for Operation *Gymnast*.

26 July

Pacific The Allies' Solomon Islands expeditionary force reaches its rendezvous point south-east of the Fiji Islands.

North Africa Late in the evening the XXX Corps of the British 8th Army delivers an attack on the left wing of the Axis positions.

☐ Large-scale RAF night attack on Hamburg.

27 July

Eastern Front The Germans capture Bataysk and continue mopping up the remains of the Soviet forces in the great bend of the Don. Von Paulus' 6th Army launches a powerful offensive to eliminate the Soviet bridgehead at Kalach, west of Stalingrad.

New Guinea The Australians yield the important strategic position of Kokoda, which is occupied by the Japanese.

28 July

New Guinea The Australians retake Kokoda, but Japanese reinforcements on the way from the Buna bridgehead make their position precarious. The Japanese Imperial General Staff orders an immediate general offensive for the capture of eastern New Guinea, and plans are

**Above: British infantry at El Alamein.
Below: an Italian counter-attack.**

Two Russian T-34 tanks put out of action before Rostov.

Rostov: fighting in a railway station.

made for amphibious operations in Milne Bay and land and sea attacks on Port Moresby.

China The Japanese offensive in the province of Chekiang, apparently launched in retaliation for the raids on Tokyo and other towns by Doolittle's aircraft, comes to an end.

Eastern Front Russian news bulletins announce the fall of Rostov and Novocherkassk. Now the ordinary Russian citizen realizes that the Germans are poised to invade the Kuban and the Caucasus. The enemy has attacked Rostov not from the west, as in 1941, but from the north and north-east, the least strongly defended area. The Russians are seized by panic; whole units have been disbanded, men and officers of all ranks have been shot for desertion. The announcement of the fall of Rostov spreads terror in the Soviet Union. Three days later Stalin declares: 'Not one more backward step!' In fact there will be further withdrawals, but people know that there is little room for them. If the Germans are not stopped at Stalingrad and the foothills of the Caucasus, the war is lost. After the fall of Rostov an iron discipline is introduced in the Red Army. Deserters are executed on the spot. More authority is given back to the officers, and the political commissars are subordinated to them. Officers are given more of a professional status –

among other things the gold stripes are restored to their uniforms, and new decorations are created for officers only, inspired by patriotism, not politics – the Order of Kutuzov, of Suvorov, of Alexander Nevsky, the great predecessors. And a few months later the role of the political commissars is still further reduced.

29 July

Eastern Front The Germans take the town of Proletarskaya and establish a bridgehead over the river Manych in the Caucasus.

New Guinea The Japanese retake Kokoda and consolidate their positions. Allied aircraft prevent two Japanese transports from landing reinforcements on the north coast of the island.

30 July

Eastern Front In the southern sector Army Group A consolidates its bridgehead over the river Manych, while Army Group B concentrates on reducing the Russian bridgehead at Kalach, in the Don estuary west of Stalingrad. In the central sector the Russians attack in the Rzhev area.

Dutch East Indies The Japanese occupy the strategic islands of Aru, Kei and Tanimbar between Timor and New Guinea.

North Africa General Auchinleck decides to remain on the defensive

until reinforcements arrive. Since 26 May, when their offensive opened, the Axis in this theatre of operations have taken 60,000 prisoners, British, South African, Indian, French, Australian and New Zealanders, and destroyed over 2,000 tanks and motor vehicles.

31 July

Pacific The amphibious force for the Solomon Islands operation, escorted by the aircraft and ships of Task Force 63 (Admiral McCain), leaves Fiji for the Solomons. Liberators from the task force begin a series of raids on Guadalcanal and Tulagi in preparation for the landing.

☐ Heavy night bombing raid by RAF on Düsseldorf.

1 August

North Africa Patrol activity and artillery exchanges. Both sides are getting ready for a major action.

Churchill decides to go to Cairo. Alarmed by a telegram he has received from the British Commander-in-Chief in the Middle East, General Auchinleck, he wants to examine the situation in person. The telegram says: 'Owing to lack of resources and enemy's effective consolidation of his positions we reluctantly concluded that in present circumstances it is not feasible to renew our efforts to break enemy front or turn his southern flank. It is unlikely that an opportunity will arise for resumption of offensive operations before mid-September.'

Atlantic A new phase in the Battle of the Atlantic now begins and lasts until May 1943. During this period the activities of groups of U-boats, the so-called 'wolf packs', rise to a climax. An average of 108 submarines operate at a time. The successes logged by the German submarines add up to a formidable total: 3,857,705 tons of shipping sunk for the loss of 123 U-boats. However, as time goes by the German success grows less and less striking; by the early months of 1943 the Allies have got long-range aircraft specially adapted for submarine-hunting, they have improved radar, Asdic (Sonar), got more escort ships and submarine-hunters, particularly active in the Bay of Biscay, equipped with powerful depth charges. By this time the price the German craft have to pay for their successes is out of all proportion to the results achieved.

Eastern Front In the southern sector Army Group A (once more including the 1st Armoured Army) fans out south of Rostov, cutting the railway between Novorossiysk and Stalingrad and taking the town of Salsk. Advance guards reach the Kuban river. In the Army Group B sector bitter fighting continues in the bend of the Don opposite Stalingrad, where the Germans are trying to cut off the defenders. In the central sector the Russians renew their attacks in the Rzhev area.

China Chiang Kai-shek accepts General Stilwell's proposal that he should assist in the recapture of Burma, and modifies the requests he put forward on 29 June.

2 August
Malta Attacks by Axis bombers continue against harbours, airfields and other military installations on the island.

3 August
Eastern Front The German Army Group A advances swiftly into the Kuban area, capturing the town of Voroshilovsk (now Stavropol). The

Street fighting in Rostov-on-Don. It finally falls to German Army Group A on 24 June 1942.

Germans cross the Don and establish a bridgehead at Tsimlyansky, then push on to Kotelnikovo, advancing more slowly from there towards Stalingrad until 18 August. However, the Russians succeed in holding the region north of the great bend of the Don, with a certain number of bridgeheads across the river, for instance at Kletskaya, barring the way to the German Army Group B. In the central sector the Russians continue to attack in the area of Rzhev.

4 August
Churchill arrives in Cairo.

5 August
Eastern Front The German Army

Group A establishes a bridgehead over the river Kuban in the area of Armavir–Nevinnomyssk, a short way away from the northern foothills of the Caucasus and the Maykop oilfields. They also take the town of Kropotkin. The Red Army continues its courageous but apparently vain defence of the great bend of the Don in front of Stalingrad.

North Africa Churchill visits the front. In the evening he sends a telegram to Clement Attlee, Secretary of State for the Dominions: 'Wherever the fault may lie for the serious situation which exists, it is certainly not with the troops, and only to a minor extent with their equipment.' The British Prime Minister is of the opinion that there must be an immediate change in the command of the war in the Middle East. He has lost faith in General Auchinleck.

6 August

Eastern Front The Russians admit the loss of Kotelnikovo. The Germans take Tikhoretsk in the Kuban area, south of Rostov and north of Krasnodar, and seize Armavir on the river Kuban with Army Group A, while Soviet resistance to Army Group B in the bend of the Don near Stalingrad is weakening.

Pacific The Allied landing force heading for the Solomons draws near its objective without being spotted by the Japanese.

New Guinea No change. All Australian and American forces in Australian New Guinea (Papua and northern New Guinea) are combined in 'New Guinea Force'.

7 August

Solomon Islands After massive air and naval bombardment of the areas selected for the landings, the US 1st Marine Division, commanded by General Vandegrift, lands on the islands of Florida, Tulagi, Gavutu, Tanambogo and Guadalcanal. With close support from naval guns and carrier-based aircraft under the command of Vice-Admiral F. J. Fletcher, the Marines land at 7.40 a.m. on Florida and at 8.00 a.m. on the south coast of Tulagi. On this latter island

A Japanese transport, hit by Allied aircraft, in flames off the coast of New Guinea, in the Buna-Gona area.

THE BIRTH OF BE-BOP

A number of black jazz musicians, then poor and unknown (Charlie Parker, Dizzy Gillespie, Thelonius Monk, etc.), deeply frustrated by the limitations of swing, began to experiment with revolutionary instrumental techniques: and from the jam sessions in the smoky bars of Harlem a new movement was born. It was known, from a distinctive rhythmic device, as 'be-bop' and it paved the way for modern jazz. Bored with the then-fashionable themes of older jazz forms, the 'boppers' introduced bold new melodic ideas as well as astonishing harmonic innovations.

they meet with strong resistance from the Japanese, who halt them about half a mile from the south-east point. At 9.10 a.m. a Marine regiment lands without opposition on the north coast of Guadalcanal, about 4 miles from Lunga Point, establishing a bridgehead between the mouths of the rivers Tenaru and Tenavatu and advancing south-west towards Mount Austen. By evening the landing force has penetrated about a mile into the island. At mid-

day a parachute battalion lands on the twin islands (joined by a dyke) of Gavutu and Tanambogo, east of Tulagi, and occupies them almost completely despite enemy fire.

The Japanese air force attacks the landing force and damages an American destroyer, the *Mugford*.

Aleutian Islands A task force of American cruisers and destroyers commanded by Rear-Admiral W. W. Smith shells the island of Kiska, held by the Japanese, and damages military installations.

North Africa The aircraft carrying the British General W. H. E. Gott to Cairo from the front is intercepted and shot down by two German Messerschmidts. General Gott, the GOC XIII Corps, had been chosen by Churchill to take over the command of the 8th Army. He and all on board the aircraft are killed. General Sir Bernard Law Montgomery is appointed in his place.

8 August

North Africa Churchill appoints General Alexander to succeed General Auchinleck as Commander-in-Chief, Middle East. Auchinleck is sent to command the Iraq–Persia sector.

Eastern Front Army Group B takes Surovikino, west of Stalingrad. Army Group A approaches nearer to Maykop and Krasnodar.

Solomon Islands Waves of Japanese aircraft attack the American naval forces carrying the landing force, sinking the transport *George F. Elliott* and damaging the transport *Barnett* and the destroyer *Jarvis*, which sinks next day trying to reach Noumea.

On Guadalcanal the Americans seize the village of Kukum and an airfield in course of construction, which they immediately re-name Henderson Field. The capture of Tulagi, Gavutu and Tanambogo is completed.

The Battle of Savo Island. On learning of the American landings in the Solomons the Japanese despatch a squadron from Rabaul (New Britain) on the night of 8/9 August, consisting of five heavy cruisers (*Chokai*, *Aoba*,

Kako, *Kinugasa* and *Furutaka*), two light cruisers (*Tenryu* and *Yubari*) and the destroyer *Yunagi*, under the command of Vice-Admiral Gunichi Mikawa, to take the Allied fleet protecting the transports for the Solomons landing by surprise off Savo Island. The Allied squadron, commanded by the Australian Admiral Crutchley, is composed of six heavy cruisers (*Chicago*, *Astoria*, *Quincy*, *Vincennes* and the Australian ships *Australia* and *Canberra*), two light cruisers (*San Juan* and *Hobart*, the latter Australian) and eight destroyers. During a hard-fought night battle the heavy cruisers *Astoria*, *Quincy*, *Vincennes* and *Canberra* are sunk and the heavy cruiser *Chicago* and two destroyers are severely damaged. The Japanese get away almost unharmed; the cruisers *Kinugasa*, *Chokai* and *Aoba* are slightly damaged, and they have 58 dead and 53 wounded. Allied losses are 1,023 dead and 709 wounded.

□ Churchill and Roosevelt agree that General Eisenhower should be given command of Operation *Torch*, the landing on French North Africa.

□ The Indian Congress asks for independence from Britain.

9 August

Solomon Islands After their heavy defeat in the night battle the Americans hastily withdraw their amphibious and air support groups, taking with them about 2,000 men and more than half the supplies for 60 days for the landing force. The 17,000 Marines already landed are left to fend for themselves on the various islands. The 11,000 Marines on Guadalcanal consolidate their bridgehead and get to work to complete the runway on the airfield. Other parties occupy the small islands of Mbangai, Kokomtambu and Makambo.

New Guinea The Australian General Sydney F. Rowell takes over command of Allied forces in New Guinea.

Eastern Front German Army Group A captures the oilfields at Maykop and Krasnodar in the Caucasus.

Top: a German U-boat takes in fuel from another of the United States coast. Above: a depth charge explodes.

Malta: a 40-mm Bofors gun.

☐ Mahatma Gandhi and all members of the Congress Working Committee arrested.

10 August

North Africa Churchill tells Alexander what his object must be: the destruction of Italian and German forces in Egypt and Libya.

Mediterranean The start of Operation *Pedestal*, the despatch of a big supply convoy to Malta.

Pacific An American submarine sinks the Japanese heavy cruiser *Kako* off Kavieng (New Ireland) on her way back from the battle of Savo Island.

☐ Riots in Bombay and Delhi; police fire on crowds.

11 August

New Guinea The Americans set up a big supply and communications centre at Port Moresby. Australian and native troops are forced to evacuate the airfield at Kokoda, which can no longer be defended.

Eastern Front The German threat to Stalingrad increases as Army Group B eliminates the Soviet bridgehead at Kalach in the bend of the Don.

There is disagreement between Hitler and Halder. Halder still insists that priority should be given to the capture of Moscow, while Hitler's first objective is the Caucasian oilfields. Hitler is wrong; Germany is able to wage war for two and a half years more without oil from the Caucasus.

12 August

Eastern Front Russian attacks in the Rzhev area reach their greatest intensity but still bring no clear result. In the southern sector advance guards of the German Army Group A reach Slavyansk in the Kuban area, only a little way from the east coast of the Sea of Azov.

North Africa General Montgomery, the new GOC British 8th Army, reaches Egypt from Britain.

Solomon Islands 1,400 Marines who should have been landed on Guadalcanal land instead on Espiritu Santo, which is to be the supply base for the forces in the Solomons. The

first aircraft with supplies lands on Henderson Field, Guadalcanal, which has just been completed.

☐ First Moscow Conference. Stalin, Churchill, Averell Harriman (representing Roosevelt) and emissaries from General de Gaulle meet in Moscow between 12 and 15 August to discuss the opening of a second front in Europe.

13 August

Eastern Front The Germans take Elista, in the Kalmyk district, south of Stalingrad and south-east of Kotelnikovo, towards the Caspian Sea.

New Guinea A Japanese convoy lands 3,000 engineers at Basabua, near Gona. The Japanese mount a powerful attack against the Australian and native troops in the area of Deniki, forcing them back five miles. With their hold on the Buna–Kokoda track secured by this successful action, they confine themselves to consolidating their positions.

New Britain The Japanese Imperial General Staff gives the 17th Army, stationed at Rabaul, the task of driving the Americans out of Guadalcanal and the other islands in the Solomons where they have landed. General Maruyama makes the necessary preparations.

14 August

Eastern Front A large part of the German 6th Army (von Paulus), supported by General Hoth's armoured army, completes the capture of the whole of the region within the bend of the Don (apart from a few minor Soviet bridgeheads in the north) and advances on Stalingrad from south, west and north-west.

15 August

Eastern Front The Germans take Georgievsk, near Pyatigorsk, in the foothills of the Caucasus.

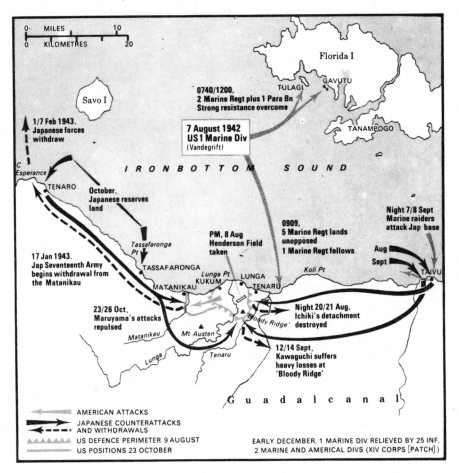

Solomon Islands: operations on Guadalcanal following the US landings on 7 August 1942.

Solomon Islands The first destroyers used for rapid transport of supplies arrive at Guadalcanal.

North Africa General Montgomery, newly arrived from England, starts at once on the strengthening and re-organization of the British 8th Army. The X Corps is held in reserve. The 44th Division and 10th Armoured Division are brought up from the Delta zone to man the Alam el Halfa Ridge behind the El Alamein line, which Montgomery regards as a position of vital importance for the defence of Alexandria. One brigade of the 44th Division is attached to the New Zealand 2nd Division at El Alamein.

Middle East General Alexander takes over from General Auchinleck as Commander-in-Chief, Middle East.

16 August
North Africa For the first time, American medium bombers attack the Axis positions at El Alamein.

Eastern Front Russians evacuate Maykop.

17 August
Gilbert Islands A formation of US Marines land on Makin Island from two submarines and carry out a two days' raid on the Japanese garrison, destroying a radio station.

Guadalcanal Task Force 62 (Admiral Turner) is given the task of securing communications with the troops landed on Guadalcanal. Henderson Field becomes fully operational. During the night the Japanese land reinforcements on Taivu Point and in the area of Kukumbona, 900 men in all, brought in by four destroyers.

Eastern Front The Germans establish a bridgehead over the river Kuban, in the Caucasus, and capture the thermal stations of Pyatigorsk, Essentuki and Kislodovsk in the Caucasian foothills. Units of the German 1st and 4th Mountain Divisions get ready to climb the

Elbrus, the highest peak in the Caucasus, over 18,000 ft. But this is more an athletic than a military undertaking for, given the nature of the terrain, the Russians will always have an advantage over the attacking forces.

18 August
New Guinea Three Japanese transports with naval escort land a strong contingent of troops at Basabua without being observed.

19 August
Eastern Front While the Germans advance on a wide front in the Don basin, a Russian counter-attack opens a gap between the Italian army and the German 6th Army.

In the northern sector, from this period until the end of September, the Russians in the Leningrad and Volkhov sector launch a series of attacks to try to cut the corridor between Tosno, south of Leningrad,

The US motor torpedo-boat PT-109 in action at Guadalcanal. In 1943 she was commanded by the future President Kennedy.

and Lake Ladoga, in order to relieve Leningrad, but are repulsed by the German 18th Army.

North Africa General, Alexander impresses on Montgomery that he must hold the El Alamein positions at all costs while preparations are made for the counter-offensive.

Guadalcanal The 5th Marine Regiment, part of the 11,000 US forces landed on the island, takes the villages of Matanikau and Kokumbona; but the perimeter round the zone occupied by the Americans, taking in Lunga Point and Henderson Field, is still very narrow. Meanwhile from Rabaul, in New Britain, the Japanese despatch 1,500 more men to Guadalcanal in four transports escorted by destroyers.

New Guinea Units of the Australian 7th Division arrive in Port Moresby and move off at once towards Isurava to help 'Maroubra Force', which is in trouble.

France Dieppe raided by Allied force consisting of 5,000 Canadians, 1,057 British, about 50 American Rangers and a handful of Free French.

3.00 a.m.: The ships carrying the landing party arrive about eight miles off Dieppe without being spotted.

3.30 a.m.: The LSIs (Landing Ships Infantry) used for transporting the infantry launch the landing craft. But things go wrong almost at once. The flotilla of landing craft with the Royal Regiment of Canada ends up a long way from the prescribed route and so is unable to be at the right sector of the beach at the right time. Then at 3.47 the gunboat leading the way for No. 3 Commando runs into a group of German armed trawlers. A fierce exchange of fire begins, and the British craft gets the worst of it. The 20 landing craft carrying No. 3 Commando have to scatter for safety.

When the Canadians manage to reach the areas allotted to them they are pinned down on the narrow beach by a murderous, accurate fire. 27 light tanks are landed from special Royal Navy craft, but are destroyed as soon as they come on shore, and the attackers are blown to pieces.

After the defeat at Savo, the 17,000 Marines landed are left to fend for themselves.

Guadalcanal: a Marine prepares to throw a hand-grenade at the Japanese.

OPERATION *PEDESTAL*

Churchill regards the security of Malta as basic to British strategy in the Mediterranean. Following the unhappy failure of Operations *Harpoon* and *Vigorous* to deliver any substantial supplies to the island in June, the British government decides early in August to send another big supply convoy to Malta. The operation, code-named *Pedestal*, calls for exceptional forces: to escort 13 merchant ships and 3 tankers the British assemble a squadron of 4 aircraft carriers (*Eagle*, *Furious*, *Indomitable* and *Victorious*), the 2 battleships *Nelson* and *Rodney*, 7 cruisers, 34 destroyers, 8 submarines and 20-odd smaller craft. The 90 vessels making up this powerful force sail from Gibraltar on 10 August, headed straight for the Sicilian Channel.

Obviously the movement of such large forces does not go unnoticed by the enemy. Being short of fuel, they decide to take on the convoy with submarines, coastal motor-boats, motor torpedo-boats and aircraft. The Axis attacks begin on 11 August. At 1.00 p.m. the aircraft carrier *Eagle* is sunk by the German submarine U-73, and next day it is the turn of another aircraft carrier to be seriously damaged as the result of direct hits from the air. Aircraft from the *Eagle* which had taken off cannot land on their flight deck; they have to land on the *Victorious*, which has to jettison its own fighters to make room for them. The destroyer *Foresight* is also hit and sinks during the raid.

When evening comes the British battleships and aircraft carriers and three of the cruisers leave the convoy and return to Gibraltar. The British think the battle is over, but they are wrong. At 8.00 p.m. the Italian submarine *Axum*, which has picked up the convoy off Cape Blanc, fires four torpedoes 'fanwise', and they hit the cruisers *Nigeria* (Admiral Burrough's flagship) and *Cairo* and the tanker *Ohio*; the *Cairo* sinks and the tanker and *Nigeria* are severely damaged. A little later Axis aircraft attack and sink two more of the convoy's steamships, and later again the submarines *Alagi* and *Bronzo* sink two more steamships and damage the cruiser *Kenya*. Just after midnight the Axis motor torpedo boats go into action, sinking the cruiser *Manchester* and three more merchantmen.

At dawn on 13 August the British position is desperate. Admiral Burrough counts his forces, reduced now to two cruisers and about ten destroyers, while of the sixteen ships that sailed with the convoy only seven are left. At this juncture the Italian cruisers should have gone into action, on the understanding that they would be given effective air cover against the fighters and bombers which would be sure to take off from Malta. But the Germans, who were due to provide the air umbrella, are not interested (perhaps they have no faith in the capacity of the Italian navy), and the Italian cruisers have to return to port; on the way the British submarine *Safari* scores hits on the cruisers *Bolzano* and *Attendolo*. However, what is left of the British convoy has by now been able to reach Malta with no further trouble – just five ships, which are able to land 30,000 tons of war materials on the island.

Furious **(Great Britain). Designed as a cruiser, in 1917 she was given a long forward take-off deck. In 1939 a small island was added to the starboard side of the flight deck. She was taken out of operational service in 1944 and broken up in 1948.**

9.00 a.m.: The operation has clearly failed, and the troops are ordered to re-embark at once. Some 3,000 of those engaged, at least half of them, are left behind, killed or captured; all the vehicles, the equipment and a good number of the weapons are left on the beach. (Hitler comments: 'This is the first time the British have had the courtesy to cross the sea to offer the enemy a complete sample of their new weapons.')

4.00 p.m.: In Dieppe there is no sign of the morning's encounter on the beach; life is quite normal, all the shops are open...

20 August

Eastern Front The German advance south-east of Stalingrad is held up by the rivers Aksai and Myshkova.

Guadalcanal With the arrival of 30 American aircraft Henderson Field is ready for action. Units of the US 1st Marine Division are involved in the evening with Japanese units advancing from the east, on the river Ilu.

Moscow: Stalin and Churchill take part in the four-power talks which discuss the Second Front.

New Guinea A Japanese contingent of 1,500 men from Buna and New Ireland prepares to land at Milne Bay, at the eastern end of the island.

Heinrich Himmler comforts a homeless Russian orphan boy near Minsk.

21 August

Eastern Front Elements of the German Army Group A take Krymsk, on the north coast of the Black Sea not far from Novorossiysk.

Guadalcanal The Japanese attack

The German 6th Army in action before Stalingrad, where violent tank battles rage. On the left, a destroyed German Pz-III, with a dead soldier between the track wheels.

Canadian troops land at Dieppe on 19 August. The operation goes disastrously.

before dawn in an attempt to seize the west bank of the Ilu, but are driven back and counter-attacked from the rear, losing about 800 men. *New Guinea* The Japanese convoy reported on 20 August lands reinforcements at Salamaua, completing the force which is to attack and capture Port Moresby. The Australian 18th Brigade reaches Milne Bay and joins up with the Australian 7th Brigade, which has been in position there since July.

22 August

Solomon Islands On Guadalcanal, a battalion of US Marines arrives from Tulagi to reinforce the garrison at Lunga. More Marines from the New Hebrides arrive at Tulagi.
New Guinea The Japanese forces, 11,000 men commanded by General Tomitaro Horii, prepare for the

offensive; they will be opposed by an equal number of Australian, American, British and native troops.
☐ Brazil declares war on Italy and Germany.

23 August

Eastern Front The German Army Group B breaks through north of Stalingrad in the direction of the Volga, capturing a salient 5 miles wide between Rynok and Erzovka. 600 Luftwaffe bombers attack Stalingrad, killing 40,000 and destroying three-quarters of the great industrial city. But the Russians do not panic, and the salient is 'stabilized'. To avoid encirclement, most of the Russian troops fall back on the city. At Izbushensky, in the great bend of the Don, 600 men of the Italian 'Savoy Cavalry' under the command of Colonel Bettoni charge against 2,000

Russians armed with mortars and machine-guns in a last desperate attempt to close a breach opened by the Russians between the German 6th Army and the Italian army. The Italians, in the last cavalry charge in history, put the enemy to flight. Sabres and hand-grenades against mortars and machine-guns – the victory is important locally, but the price is very high.
The Swastika flag flies at the summit of the Elbrus, planted there by German Alpine units.

24 August

Pacific: Eastern Solomons Three combined American task forces under the command of Vice-Admiral Frank J. Fletcher, comprising 3 aircraft carriers (*Saratoga, Enterprise* and *Wasp*, with a total of 254 aircraft), the battleship *North Carolina*, 5 heavy cruisers (*Minneapolis, New Orleans, Portland, San Francisco* and *Salt Lake City*), 2 light cruisers (*Atlanta* and *San Juan*) and 18 destroyers, intercept a group of Japanese squadrons east of Guadalcanal. The Japanese ships are commanded by Vice-Admiral Nobutake Kondo, but under the strategic direction of the Commander-in-Chief of the Imperial Fleet, Admiral Yamamoto, now on board the battleship *Yamato* at anchor in Truk. The Japanese forces consist of 3 aircraft carriers (*Shokaku, Zuikaku* and *Ryujo*), with a total of 168 aircraft, 3 battleships (*Mutsu, Hiei* and *Kirishima*), 13 heavy cruisers (*Ataqa, Maya, Takao, Myoko, Aguro, Suzuya, Kumano, Chikuma, Tone, Chokai, Aoba, Kinugasa* and *Furutaka*), 3 light cruisers, 1 seaplane transporter, 31 destroyers and 12 submarines. One squadron is escorting 4 transport ships with reinforcements for Guadalcanal. A tremendous air and sea battle breaks out, in which the Japanese lose 90 aircraft against 20 by the Americans. Before they withdraw the Japanese also lose the aircraft carrier *Ryujo*, hit by bombs and torpedoes, the light cruiser *Jintsu*, one destroyer and one troop transport, with the loss of many lives. On the American side, the aircraft carrier *Enterprise* is damaged by dive-bombers.

Guadalcanal Japanese air strikes on Henderson Field are intensified. Eleven dive-bombers have been detached from the aircraft carrier *Enterprise* to operate from the airfield.

New Guinea General Horii gives orders for a general offensive. Two amphibious forces, from Buna and from New Ireland, sail for Milne Bay. The one coming from Buna – seven big lighters – is sighted by the Australians.

☐ Prime Minister Churchill returns from Moscow.

25 August

Pacific Battle of the Eastern Solomons. US army and navy bombers attack Japanese transports carrying reinforcements to Guadalcanal and force them to turn back. One transport and one destroyer are sunk, and a cruiser is damaged.

Gilbert Islands The Japanese occupy Nauru.

New Guinea The Japanese occupy Goodenough Island, in the D'Entrecasteaux Islands, near the south-east coast of New Guinea. Their seven lighters were actually headed for Milne Bay, but lost their way; they are destroyed by American aircraft. During the night of 25/26 the Japanese land without opposition east of Rabi, on Milne Bay, and are engaged by the Australians as they advance westwards.

Eastern Front The German Army Group A repulses a Russian counter-attack at Mozdok and heads for Grozny and Baku, in the Crimea.

26 August

Guadalcanal The American Marines prepare a limited offensive to eliminate Japanese pressure on the western flank of their beachhead.

The Japanese occupy Ocean Island, west of the Gilbert Islands.

New Guinea Allied aircraft attack the Japanese in Milne Bay, at the eastern end of the island, destroying supply and ammunition depots and damaging some transport ships. In the evening a Japanese convoy from New Ireland lands a new contingent of troops in the bay. In the area of Isurava the Japanese advancing on Port Moresby across the mountains force the Australian units to withdraw.

27 August

Guadalcanal A battalion of US Marines lands west of Kokumbona, while another unit moves inland from Kukum to cut off the enemy's retreat. The manœuvre is frustrated by the resistance of the Japanese about three-quarters of a mile from Kokumbona. A fighter squadron arrives to reinforce the American air units.

New Guinea The Japanese advance both along the coast and along the path that links Port Moresby with the south coast. An Australian brigade is sent to reinforce the troops inland.

Eastern Front Army Group B exerts continued pressure on Stalingrad where bitter fighting is taking place. Army Group A approaches Grozny, taking Prochladnii and establishing a bridgehead over the river Terek.

German mountain troops of the 1st and 4th Division climb Mt Elbrus, the highest peak in the Caucasus.

The last cavalry charge in history. On 23 August 1942, at Izbushensky in the bend of the Don, 600 mounted men of the Savoy Cavalry charge and rout 2,000 Russians armed with mortars and machine-guns.

28 August
Eastern Front The German Army Group A begins the assault on Novorossiysk, on the Black Sea.
New Guinea The Australians at Milne Bay stand firm against violent frontal attacks by the Japanese. Fighting continues inland on the Owen Stanley range, connecting Port Moresby and the south coast.

29 August
New Guinea More Japanese reinforcements, about 750 men, land at Milne Bay. Fighting continues along the track over the Owen Stanley Range.

30 August
North Africa 11.00 p.m.: Rommel launches an attack along the whole of the El Alamein front. The Battle of Alam el Halfa has begun, so called because the main fighting is around the ridge of that name south-east of El Alamein. Rommel's plan is for diversionary attacks against the enemy XXX Corps on the left, towards El Alamein, by the German 164th Division and the Italian *Trento* and *Bologna* Divisions; the main attack will then be delivered against the British XIII Corps in the southern sector of the German line, by the 90th Light Division, the Italian motorized corps (with the *Ariete* and *Littorio* Divisions), the *Folgore* Division and the reconnaissance group. Rommel's intention is to turn the British positions from the south, then move east from Alam el Halfa Ridge and surround the whole of the British 8th Army.

What makes Rommel's offensive necessary at this moment is the realization that the rebuilding and redeployment of General Alexander's forces can only improve with time. Rommel declares: 'The decision to attack today is the most serious I have taken in my life. Either we reach the Suez Canal now, or else . . .'
Guadalcanal Twelve dive-bombers and 18 fighters arrive to strengthen the American air force on Henderson Field. Japanese dive-bombers attack and sink the fast American transport *Colhoun* off the coast.
New Guinea In the evening the Japanese attack at Milne Bay and seize a landing strip. Next morning they are driven back after bloody fighting. Inland they are still advancing towards Port Moresby.

31 August
North Africa Rommel fails to break the British defences at Alam el Halfa. He is held up by RAF mastery of the skies, by the British 7th Armoured Division on his right flank

(preventing him from surrounding Alam el Halfa Ridge), by a shortage of fuel, and the minefields.

Solomon Islands The American aircraft carrier *Saratoga* is damaged by torpedoes from a Japanese submarine 260 miles south-east of Guadalcanal, near Santa Cruz, and has to stay in dry dock at Pearl Harbour until November.

New Guinea The Australians take the initiative at Milne Bay. General Horii is ordered by the Japanese headquarters to go on the defensive inland as well, on the Owen Stanley mountains.

Eastern Front Despite increased Russian resistance on the river Terek, the forces of Army Group A strengthen their bridgehead over the river in the area of Mozdok. The Russians claim to be within 15 miles of Stalingrad on the south-west front.

1 September

North Africa The German 15th Armoured Division tries again to take Alam el Halfa, but is driven back on the slopes by the British 22nd Armoured Brigade. The British are preparing a counter-attack to close the gap opened by the enemy on the southern flank of XIII Corps line. The XIII Corps' losses are made good by units of XXX Corps. The X Corps is brought up from the rear area to the battlefield.

Eastern Front Desperate fighting is taking place in the Stalingrad area, where the German 6th Army continues its pressure. The Germans have reached the suburbs of the city and threaten to cut off the Soviet 62nd Army. Army Group A takes the port of Anapa on the Black Sea.

New Guinea The Australians are still making a little progress at Milne Bay, though they lose ground in the Owen Stanley mountains. Japanese units sent from Salamaua attack the Australians garrisoning the valley of Bulolo, and take Mubo.

☐ The Japanese Foreign Minister, Shigenori Togo, resigns. His portfolio is taken over by the Prime Minister, Hideki Tojo.

2 September

Eastern Front The German Army Group A fights its way to Novorossiysk and Grozny. Other German and Rumanian troops cross the Kerch strait from the Crimea, so that Novorossiysk is threatened from the west as well as from the north.

North Africa The Axis forces fall back to their start lines (El Taqa–Bab el Qattara), expecting a British counter-offensive which does not in fact take place.

New Guinea The Australian advance in the southern part of Milne Bay, at the eastern end of the island, but inland they are unable to withstand Japanese pressure in the direction of Port Moresby. During the night of 2/3 September 1,000 more Japanese from Rabaul land at Basabua.

3 September

Eastern Front The threat to Stalingrad becomes graver as the Germans break through to the Volga south of the city and penetrate into the western suburbs. The Luftwaffe makes incessant dive-bombing attacks. The Germans continue to advance on Novorossiysk and Grozny. Russian resistance everywhere is intense.

North Africa The New Zealand 2nd Division, XIII Corps, attacks during the night of 3/4 September to close the gap in the minefields opened by the Axis forces, but is hurled back to its starting point. The British aircraft concentrate their attacks on the trucks bringing supplies to the Axis forces, who are short of rations, ammunition and above all of fuel. It is the lack of fuel that has prevented Rommel from launching a new offensive.

4 September

Eastern Front The Stalingrad battle rages without pause. Over 1,000 German planes make continual attacks on the city.

New Guinea The Australians continue to advance eastwards at Milne Bay, and take Goroni.

Pacific During the night of 4/5 September two fast American transports are sunk by the Japanese in the Solomons Sea as they take reinforcements and supplies to Guadalcanal.

5 September

North Africa The British XIII Corps continues its attacks against Axis positions at El Alamein.

New Guinea The Japanese take off about 1,300 men from Milne Bay,

Guadalcanal: US marines man a 75-mm gun emplacement near Lunga.

leaving only 600 to oppose the Australians.

☐ The Allied Supreme Command has decided that the main landing points for Operation *Torch* shall be Algiers and Oran in Algeria and Casablanca in Morocco.

6 September

Eastern Front The Germans take the major Black Sea port of Novorossiysk. Battle of Stalingrad, the 'Red Verdun', reaches critical phase as both sides throw in reinforcements.

North Africa The British XIII Corps makes slow progress southwards, but at the cost of heavy losses in men and materials.

New Guinea The Australians mop up the last centres of Japanese resistance at Milne Bay but in the Owen Stanley mountains they have to retreat further towards Port Moresby.

Pacific The American battleship *South Dakota* strikes a coral reef off Tonga and is seriously damaged.

7 September

Eastern Front The Russians manage to contain German pressure both at Stalingrad and east of Novorossiysk.

North Africa General Montgomery calls off the XIII Corps's attacks in the El Alamein–Alam el Halfa area, leaving the enemy with a strip about 5 miles deep on the southern flank of the 8th Army. Meanwhile preparations for the offensive are intensified.

New Guinea All Japanese resistance ceases at Milne Bay. But the Australians still cannot hold up the enemy advance across the Owen Stanley mountains towards Port Moresby.

8 September

Guadalcanal American units leave Lunga Point in small boats and land at Tasimboko, near Taivu Point, where a great part of the Japanese reinforcements which have reached the island recently is concentrated. After a brief action, in which aircraft based on Henderson Field take part, the Americans re-embark.

New Guinea General Horii attacks the Australian 21st Brigade near the Efogi spur in the Owen Stanley

Russian tank crews collect new tanks from a Stalingrad factory to take them direct to

mountains, surrounding two battalions.

North Africa British aircraft step up their bombing attacks on Tobruk.

9 September

Madagascar The British make a new landing on the island and occupy Majunga, on the west coast. The object is to ensure the safe passage of the Mozambique Channel.

☐ A very heavy bombing raid

by the RAF on Düsseldorf, in which the two-ton bombs nicknamed 'block-busters' are used.

☐ USA. A small Japanese aircraft launched from a submarine drops incendiary bombs near Brookings, Oregon, setting a forest on fire. This is the only air attack on US metropolitan territory during the war.

10 September

New Guinea Allied aircraft sink the Japanese destroyer *Yaoi* near Nor-

the front.

manby Island in the D'Entrecasteaux Islands, near New Guinea. Fighting taking place only 50 miles from Port Moresby.

11 September
Guadalcanal Six thousand Japanese have reached the island since 29 August in fast transports escorted by warships, landing by night. The Americans call these the 'Tokyo Night Express'.
Aleutian Islands Now that an air-strip has been completed at Adak, the Americans begin a series of raids on Kiska Island, 250 miles away, which is occupied by the Japanese.
Madagascar The British advance along the coast towards Tananarive, capital of the island.
New Guinea The Australians retire again in the Owen Stanley mountains sector. MacArthur makes known a plan for the use of a US regiment beside the Australians to drive the enemy off the island.

12 September
Eastern Front The German 6th Army continues its intense pressure on the outskirts of Stalingrad from south and north. The command of the Russian 62nd Army, the backbone of Stalingrad's defence, is given to General Zhukov. (The Communist Party is represented by Nikita Krushchev.)
Russians report the first winter snows in the Caucasus.
Arctic Ocean U-boats and Luftwaffe begin a series of attacks, which lasts for ten days, against two important Allied convoys, PQ19 and QP14, carrying supplies to Russia. Seventeen ships, totalling 94,791 tons are sunk. The Germans lose four submarines and 41 aircraft.
Guadalcanal After furious fighting which goes on for the whole of the next night the Japanese succeed in infiltrating into the American defensive perimeter near Lunga. Fatigue, rain and tropical diseases combine with the incessant artillery and rifle fire of the Japanese to exhaust the Americans.

13 September
Eastern Front The great battle for Stalingrad enters its fourth week. The German 6th Army penetrates into the city. By 18 November the Germans will have taken almost all the city, with the Russians holding no more than three bridgeheads across the Volga. But the mass of the Russian artillery is dug in on the other side of the Volga and is relatively protected from German air attacks.
To avoid the sufferings endured by German troops the previous winter, Hitler appoints Generals Halder, Jacob and Wietersheim to look after military requirements and supplies.
Guadalcanal The Japanese launch air and land attacks against the defensive perimeter at Lunga in an attempt to re-take Henderson Field, where the forces have been strengthened by the arrival of 18 more aircraft, mostly dive-bombers. The Americans try to counter-attack along a line of low hills called Bloody Ridge, but only succeed in advancing a few

Japanese reinforcements prepare to sail for Guadalcanal.

hundred yards. Then they have to go on to the defensive, and it is only thanks to intensive artillery support that they manage to hold out against the assaults carried out by the Japanese during the night. The Japanese also attack along the river Ilu but do not manage to break through.

North Africa During the night of 13/14 August, after a heavy aerial bombardment, the British carry out a raid on Tobruk by land and by sea, supported at sea by six cruisers and destroyers, in an attempt to destroy the Axis depots and port installations. A motorized column starting from Kufra Oasis, about 500 miles away, tries a similar operation against Benghazi. Both attempts fail with heavy losses to the attacking forces. About 9.00 a.m. the Tobruk landing forces have to re-embark.

☐ Heavy night attack by RAF on Bremen, which has its hundredth raid.

14 September

Eastern Front Von Paulus' infantry overcome desperate Russian resistance and penetrate into the centre of Stalingrad, reaching the banks of the Volga. The Battle of Stalingrad approaches its epic climax.

Guadalcanal The Japanese break off their assaults on Bloody Ridge at dawn and withdraw, leaving 600 dead on the field. The Marines have lost 150 men. There are skirmishes along the river Ilu. In the afternoon the Japanese attack an American battalion on the hills overlooking the coast road in the western sector of

the US bridgehead, but are driven off. A battalion of the 2nd Marine Regiment arrives to reinforce the island.

New Guinea The Japanese drive the Australians back on to Imita Ridge, the last peak in the mountain range, only 32 miles from Port Moresby. But Allied counter-attacks stop them from advancing any further.

15 September

Eastern Front The Germans attack powerfully in the centre of Stalingrad. Hundreds of dive-bombers assault the city. But the Russian defenders, holed up in the factories, hold out.

Pacific Ocean An American task force commanded by Rear-Admiral Noyes, escorting a convoy taking reinforcements to Guadalcanal from Espiritu Santo, in the New Hebrides, is attacked by two Japanese submarines which sink the aircraft carrier *Wasp* and damage the battleship *North Carolina* and a destroyer.

Guadalcanal The 5th Marine Regiment extends its defensive perimeter from Lunga to south of Henderson Field, beyond the crest of Bloody Ridge. The Japanese fire intermittently on the enemy positions, which are also hit by shells from a Japanese battleship.

New Guinea The first American infantry units arrive at Port Moresby from Australia.

16 September

New Guinea The Japanese advance across the mountains is halted at Ioribaiwa. Further south the Austra-

lians, firmly established on Imita Ridge, prepare a counter-attack.

Madagascar Governor-General of the island asks for armistice terms.

China General Chennault suggests that the prime task of his aircraft should be the defence of the air-lift between India and China.

Aleutian Islands The Japanese have evacuated Attu Island, transferring the garrison to Kiska.

☐ USA protests to the Vichy government against the mass deportation of Jews.

17 September

Eastern Front Fierce hand-to-hand street fighting rages in north-west outskirts of Stalingrad.

New Guinea While the Australians and Americans prepare to counter-attack, the Japanese are in a precarious position at Ioribaiwa. Almost in sight of Port Moresby, they cannot attack the Australian positions for lack of supplies and reinforcements.

Madagascar Vichy government rejects British armistice conditions.

18 September

Guadalcanal The Americans receive reinforcements (over 4,000 men of the 7th Marine Regiment), with vehicles, arms, ammunition, supplies and petrol. Their rations are restored to the normal level. There are minor encounters with the Japanese along the defensive perimeter.

New Guinea The Japanese Imperial General Staff orders the expeditionary force to hold its positions and to reinforce the Buna–Gona bridgehead. General Horii begins to thin out the ranks, sending men back to the Buna–Gona sector. New American reinforcements embark for New Guinea at Brisbane.

Madagascar The British 29th East African Brigade lands on the east coast, at Tamatave, without opposition, and pushes on inland towards Tananarive. The 22nd Brigade is also marching on the capital from the west coast.

19 September

Guadalcanal General Vandegrift has divided his bridgehead into ten parti-

WOMEN AND THE WAR

As the war went on, civilian life became increasingly difficult: air raids, restrictions on personal freedom and food shortages made simple day-to-day living very hard.

This was a testing time for everyone, not least for women; running a household was quite a challenge. Subject to rationing right from the start of the war, even basic foodstuffs became rarer and rarer, and some actually disappeared altogether to be replaced by a range of substitute items. Chicory was used instead of coffee, margarine instead of butter, powdered eggs, instead of real eggs and so on.

Difficulty in finding fabrics made clothing equally scarce. Fashion was scarcely the major concern of women at this time, and yet, by using a little ingenuity and a lot of skill, discarded uniforms

A curious hat dating from 1940.

could be altered to provide military-style suits with economically tapered waistlines for the jackets, and skirts to just below the knee. For practical reasons the close-cropped hairstyle became fashionable. Economical materials, such as cork, were used for the soles of shoes, thus setting the fashion for orthopaedic styles.

Although women had been part of the working world of many countries for some time before the war, they now became a major source of labour throughout industry. In some countries the levels of female employment almost doubled. Female labour was also used to the full in the health services, communication systems and in public transport; furthermore women played an important role in almost all the forces.

Applying a little imagination and skill, women re-model old military uniforms.

A unit of the *San Marco* Division marching through the ruins of Tobruk after repelling an attempted landing by British Commandos.

ally independent sectors, and established a continuous defensive line.
☐ Sicily. British air raids on the island begin again. Catania and Licata are hit.

20 September

Eastern Front The bitter house-to-house fighting continues in Stalingrad, where, as in Leningrad, Russian women fight side by side with the men. Army Group A takes the town of Terek, on the south bank of the river of the same name, in the centre of the Caucasus.
☐ Stalin again presses Eden and Wendell Wilkie to open a second front.
☐ Operational plans for Operation *Torch* are issued; the landing in North Africa is to take place on 8 November.

21 September

Eastern Front Russians continue to hold German forces in north-west suburbs of Stalingrad.

22 September

Eastern Front Bitter fighting in Stalingrad as Luftwaffe continues to pound the city.

23 September

Eastern Front The Russians launch a counter-attack in north-west sub-

urbs of Stalingrad.
German Army Group A sends an assault group to take the port of Tuapse on the Black Sea north-west of Sochi.
Guadalcanal The Americans begin a limited operation to drive the enemy back to a safe distance from Henderson Field.
New Guinea The 128th Regiment of the US 32nd Division is air-lifted to Port Moresby. General Blamey takes personal control of Allied forces on the island.
Madagascar The 22nd East African Brigade enters Tananarive, which is declared an open city.

24 September

Guadalcanal The Americans go over to the attack on Mount Austen and in the area of Matanikau-Kokumbona.
☐ General Franz Halder, who has disagreed with Hitler about the conduct of the war in Russia, is dismissed from the post of Chief of Staff of the *Wehrmacht*. He is replaced by General Kurt Zeitzler, with responsibility limited to the Eastern Front.

25 September

Eastern Front The Russian counter-attack to north-west of Stalingrad continues to make progress. Ger-

mans report bitter hand-to-hand fighting.
New Guinea The Australians open their counter-offensive in the mountains along the Port Moresby–Kokoda track, attacking Ioribaiwa in force.
Madagascar The British now control the central part of the island.

26 September

Madagascar General Platt, commanding the British forces, moves his headquarters from Majunga to Tananarive.

27 September

Guadalcanal The Americans carry out local, unsuccessful attacks in an attempt to widen their bridgehead.
New Guinea Overwhelmed by the Australians, the Japanese withdraw rapidly along the path over the Owen Stanley mountains.
Gilbert Islands The Japanese take Kuria Island, having taken Maiana on the 24th, Beru on the 25th.

28 September

Eastern Front In Rzhev sector the Russians cross the Volga and capture 25 villages. Heavy fighting continues around Leningrad. At Stalingrad, the Germans throw in fresh reinforcements.

29 September

Guadalcanal American forces on the island now number more than 19,000, with another 3,260 manning Tulagi. The Seabees (construction battalions) are turning Henderson Field into a fully operational airport, though the runway is often broken up by Japanese bombs.
Madagascar British troops advancing south from Tananarive take Fianarantsoa. Other units which sailed from Diego Suarez land at Tuléar on the south-west coast and occupy the harbour, airfield and seaplane base, which enables them to reconnoitre the Mozambique Channel.

30 September

Aleutian Islands The Japanese carry out the first of a series of 'nuisance

The US aircraft carrier *Wasp* enveloped in smoke after being torpedoed by a Japanese submarine of Guadalcanal.

raids' on Adak Island.

☐ Hitler speaks to Nazi Party rally: 'I said that if Jewry started this war in order to overcome the Aryan people, then it would not be the Aryans but the Jews who would be exterminated. The Jews laughed at my prophecies . . . I doubt if they are laughing now.'

1 October

Eastern Front The impetus of the German thrust is becoming exhausted. Bloody fighting continues in Stalingrad, where the German 6th Army pays dearly for every yard of ground gained. The Russians try in

vain to bring help to the ruined city. Army Group A, charged with the task of conquering the Caucasus with its rich oilfields, is halted by Russian resistance. The Germans do not succeed in taking Grozny. Bitter fighting continues between Novorossiysk and Tuapse on the Black Sea. Heavy losses in men and material, shortage of supplies (especially fuel), and the nature of the terrain are beginning to tell on the armies of the Reich.

2 October

Ellice Islands American unit from Espiritu Santo occupies the Funafuti

atoll, near the Gilbert Islands, South Pacific.

Madagascar The British proceed with the occupation of the southern part of the island.

3 October

Eastern Front In the Caucasus German Army Group A makes some progress towards Grozny.

The battle for Stalingrad continues, but the Russian position is gradually, but at immense cost, improving.

4 October

New Guinea The Australians continue to advance along the Port

A detachment of German soldiers in Stalingrad after storming a Russian pocket of resistance.

Panzer grenadiers and a Pz-III attacking   near Terek, in the Caucasus.

Moresby–Kokoda track. American patrols carry out a reconnaissance on another inland track, near Jaure.

5 October
Pacific American carrier-borne aircraft bomb Japanese installations in Bougainville Island, in the Solomons.

6 October
North Africa Montgomery issues his first directives for the offensive being prepared by the 8th Army.
Eastern Front Army Group A takes Malgobek, an important oil-producing centre in the Caucasus, west of Grozny.
☐ A second agreement on American aid to the USSR is signed in Washington. Between this date and 1 July 1943 it is proposed to send 4,400,000 tons of supplies to Russia, three-

quarters of it by sea and the remainder through Iran.

7 October
Guadalcanal Still aiming to put Henderson Field out of range of the Japanese guns, the 1st Marine Division puts in an attack with artillery and air support west of the defensive perimeter, reaching the mouth of the river Matanikau. Two columns advancing south-west dig in on Height 65, overlooking the river itself. There is little Japanese resistance.
New Guinea Allied troop movements in readiness for the counter-offensive which is to lead to the complete destruction of the enemy.

8 October
Guadalcanal Torrential rains force the Marines to break off their attacks

on the enemy beyond the river Matanikau. However, some units manage to reduce the bridgehead which the Japanese still hold east of the river, after some bloody fighting. American intelligence reports that the Japanese are preparing a counter-attack in force, and the Marines are ordered to carry out a thrust against the Japanese units at Cruz Point and then to return within the Lunga perimeter.

9 October
Guadalcanal The Marines return from the action on the river Matanikau. During the fighting the Japanese have lost about 700 men, the Americans 190 dead and wounded.
Eastern Front Single command is restored in the Soviet army. The military commander now has the respon-

sibilities given to commanding officers in all other armies. The political commissar is to be designated 'vice-commandant in the political field' in army units, but all responsible decisions of a military nature are now reserved solely to the commanding officer.

☐ A force of 100 bombers of the American Air Force carry out a daylight raid on industrial plants at Lille. (Americans and British share the bombing, the Americans taking on the daylight raids, the British those by night.) Of the German aircraft which take off to intercept the raiders, 100 are destroyed or damaged.

10 October
Guadalcanal In readiness for the Japanese counter-offensive, the Marines set up defensive positions on the east bank of the river Matanikau.

11 October
Eastern Front After 51 days continuous fighting, no German infantry or tank assaults take place at Stalingrad.
Madagascar General Platt hands over command in this theatre to General Smallwood.

11–12 October
Guadalcanal Air battle of Cape Esperance. An American squadron commanded by Rear-Admiral Norman Scott (the heavy cruisers *San Francisco* and *Salt Lake City*, light cruisers *Boise* and *Helena* and five destroyers), patrolling Solomons waters to prevent the arrival of reinforcements and supplies by the famous 'Tokyo Night Express', intercepts a Japanese squadron east of Savo Island escorting transports with reinforcements, heavy artillery and tanks to be used in the final offensive against the Americans on Guadalcanal. The Japanese squadron, commanded by Rear-Admiral Aritomo Goto, is made up of three heavy cruisers (*Aoba*, *Kinugasa* and *Furutaka*), two seaplane carriers and eight destroyers. During the battle, which begins during the night of 11/12 October and lasts for the whole of

the next day, with Japanese aircraft from Rabaul and American aircraft from Guadalcanal taking part, the Japanese heavy cruiser *Furutaka* and three destroyers are sunk, as well as one American destroyer. Two American cruisers (*Salt Lake City* and *Boise*) and two destroyers are damaged. Rear-Admiral Goto is killed during the battle, which may be regarded as the US Navy's revenge for the defeat of Savo. However, the Japanese transports succeed in landing some 800 men and heavy material at Guadalcanal. The Japanese suffer heavy casualties at Cape Esperance. Many of the seamen whose ships are sunk refuse to be picked up by American ships, preferring to be devoured by the sharks that infest these waters.
Big Japanese air formations put Henderson Field out of action, destroying the runway, aircraft and stocks of precious fuel.

13 October
Guadalcanal The 1st Marine Division is reinforced by a regiment of infantry. The newly landed long-range Japanese guns, and groups of Japanese bombers, pound Henderson Field.

14 October
Eastern Front Russian relief force reported to be within sight of Stalingrad.
Guadalcanal Shortly after 1.00 a.m. the Japanese battleships *Kongo* and *Haruna*, of the 3rd Division of the line commanded by Vice-Admiral Takeo Kurita and including also the cruiser *Isuku* and nine destroyers, shell the American positions near Lunga Point, and Henderson Field in particular. The 'Tokyo Night Express' is still bringing regular supplies and reinforcements to the Japanese contingent, landing about 4,000 men at Tassafaronga, west of Lunga. Forty-eight of the 90 American aircraft on Henderson Field are destroyed.
New Guinea Australian and American reinforcements reach Wanigela by air: one regiment of US Marines and one Australian battalion.

In the mountains the Japanese resist the Australian attacks at Templeton's Crossing.

15 October
Guadalcanal Six Japanese transports put their loads ashore at Tassafaronga in broad daylight, in the certainty that no American aircraft can take off from Henderson Field. But some dive-bombers take off from a roughly repaired runway and sink or strand three enemy transports.
The seaplane support ship *MacFarland* and transport aircraft from the base on Espiritu Santo supply the Americans with aviation fuel. The headquarters of the Japanese 17th Army draws up the dispositions for the great offensive against the American perimeter at Lunga. The operation is to be launched on 18 October. The American destroyer *Meredith* is sunk by an enemy torpedo plane near San Cristobal Island. During the night of 15/16 October the Japanese cruisers *Maya* and *Myoko* fire 1,500

Two Russian snipers in action at Stalingrad.

The Battle of Stalingrad: Red Army soldiers reply to German fire amid the ruins of the 'Red October' tank factory.

shells into the American defensive perimeter, concentrating on Henderson Field.

16 October

Solomon Islands Aircraft taking off from the aircraft carrier *Hornet*, which is patrolling the waters south of Guadalcanal, carry out a raid on Rekata Bay, Santa Isabel, destroying Japanese arms and ammunition depots near Tassafaronga. The Japanese deploy their forces in readiness for the offensive. Japanese artillery fire against the American defensive perimeter grows more and more intense and precise.
Aleutian Islands American aircraft sink a Japanese destroyer.

17 October

New Guinea Hard fighting between Australians and Japanese on the Port Moresby–Kokoda track near Eora Creek.
□ The convoy of vessels for Operation *Torch*, the landing in North Africa, begins to assemble in the Firth of Clyde.

18 October

Eastern Front Renewed German assaults on Stalingrad. Tanks and infantry advance in several areas. Desperate Russian resistance continues.
Pacific Vice-Admiral W. F. Halsey replaces Vice-Admiral R. L. Ghormley as commander of the southern Pacific sector.
New Guinea Savage fighting continues in the area of Eora Creek, along the Kokoda pass.

19 October

Madagascar The British continue with the occupation of the southern part of the island. They seize the town of Andriamanalina by a pincer movement.
Guadalcanal The Japanese attack planned for the 18th is postponed until the 22nd, since their deployment is still not complete.
□ The US War Department undertakes to arm and equip 30 more Chinese divisions.

20 October

Guadalcanal At General Vandegrift's request Vice-Admiral Halsey sends another infantry regiment, the 147th, to the island.
North Africa The RAF steps up its attacks against the positions, lines of communication and, most of all, the airfields of the Axis forces, in order to guarantee air supremacy during the coming offensive, which Montgomery plans to launch on the 24th.

21 October

Eastern Front Stalingrad: violent fighting continues in heavy rain.
Guadalcanal Japanese units supported by artillery and by nine tanks try, without success, to force the American line on the river Matanikau.

22 October

Eastern Front First winter snows falling on hills outside Stalingrad.
Guadalcanal The Japanese have still not managed to get all their units into position and put off the start of their offensive against the Lunga perimeter for 24 hours.
New Guinea To ensure control of the southern part of Milne Bay, the Australians send a battalion of the 18th Brigade in two destroyers to occupy Goodenough Island, manned by about 300 Japanese.
North Africa In complete secrecy, moving at night, the troops of the British 8th Army take up their positions for the imminent offensive.
□ US General Mark W. Clark,

'MRS MINIVER'

Greer Garson, the star of *Mrs Miniver*.

The melodramatic adventures of a courageous English family during the early war years gripped and moved American cinema audiences. Directed by William Wyler, and clearly intended as a condemnation of Nazi Germany, *Mrs Miniver*, although primarily a family story, was quickly adopted by Hollywood as an instrument of war propaganda.

Enjoyed in particular by President Roosevelt (and also, apparently, by Goebbels), the film made a powerful impact on public opinion and was a huge box-office success, winning five Oscar awards.

A contingent of US Marines on the march through the jungle on Guadalcanal.

Eisenhower's deputy, with some of his staff, arrives in Algeria by night on board a submarine for discussions with General Charles Mast, leader of the French officers who support the Allies. Mast assures Clark and the American Consul-General, Robert Murphy, that the French units commanded by General Henri Giraud are ready to support the Allied action. Meanwhile the first convoy for Operation *Torch* sails from Britain.

23 October

North Africa 9.30 p.m.: The second battle of El Alamein begins with a crescendo of artillery fire from a thousand guns onto the Italian and German positions. The attack completely surprises the Axis forces. To make things worse, Rommel has been in Germany for some weeks and has been temporarily replaced by General Georg Stumme. The Axis forces have been ordered not to reply to the British artillery fire, to save ammunition. This is a very delicate moment for the British. Some days earlier, Churchill telegraphed Alexander, the Commander-in-Chief of British armed forces in the Middle East, that 'all our hopes' rested on the outcome of the battle.

The British are markedly superior to the Axis in manpower and materials. They can deploy 195,000 men (against the Axis' 105,000), 1,029 tanks, including American Shermans, against the Axis' 490, more than 1,000 guns against their enemy's 480, 530 aircraft against 350, and 1,400 anti-tank guns against only 744. Montgomery has under him the XXX, X and XIII Corps, deployed respectively at the north, centre and south of the line. On the other side the German 15th Armoured Division and 164th Division have taken position at the north of the line with the Italian *Littorio* Division, the Italian *Trento*, *Bologna* and *Brescia* Divisions in the centre and the German 21st Armoured Division and two more Italian divisions, the *Ariete* and *Folgore*, in the south. The Italians' task is to hold their positions,

A US light machine-gun crew in position to cover a patrol crossing a river in the New Guinea jungle.

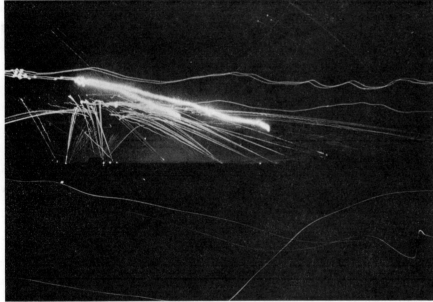

Top: General Montgomery observes the progress of the battle of El Alamein from a Grant tank. Above: Night-time barrage by British artillery at El Alamein.

while any possible attack will be carried out by the German armour, which is handicapped by having to be spread widely along the front and so losing in striking power.

The British plan is for the decisive attack to be delivered in the north by the infantry of the XXX Corps and the armoured divisions of X Corps; the XIII Corps is to carry out diversionary actions.

10.00 p.m.: The three British corps launch their attack; the Axis forces are taken by surprise at this unexpected offensive, but react swiftly.

Guadalcanal At 6.00 p.m. Japanese artillery starts to put down a tremendous barrage on the American positions on the river Matanikau. Then the infantry and tanks attack, but fail to cross the river and suffer heavy casualties: 600 men and at least eight tanks. The mass of the Japanese force should have launched an attack on the southern flank of the American perimeter at the same time, but logistic difficulties prevent it.

24 October

North Africa The British XXX Corps reaches its objective (the 'Oxalic' line) at dawn, in the rear of the German 15th Armoured Division and the Italian *Littorio* Division, but the X Corps' armour has not yet succeeded in crossing the minefields and reaching their first objective ('Pierson').

On the south flank the XIII Corps engages the German 21st Armoured Division.

In the afternoon General Stumme, acting commander in place of Rommel, is stricken by a heart attack when his armoured car is hit by an enemy shell. The general, who was holding on to the turret of his vehicle, falls to the ground without his driver realizing what has happened, and at first is reported missing; his body is not found until many hours later.

By nightfall the British 1st Armoured Division has managed to get its units through the minefields, but the 10th is still working its way through the corridor between the mines.

Guadalcanal During the night of 24/25 October a Japanese regiment launches a powerful attack on the southern flank of the American defensive perimeter. The Americans call up reinforcements from other sectors and contain the Japanese pressure, and at dawn the Japanese withdraw to their original position.

New Guinea The Japanese evacuate Goodenough Island. The garrison is embarked on two destroyers, which make for Rabaul, New Britain.

☐ USA. A gigantic convoy sails for the Mediterranean under Rear-Admiral Hewitt, carrying American troops under General Patton, for the landing in North Africa (*Operation Torch*).

☐ Britain. Two Anglo-American convoys sail for the Mediterranean to take part in Operation *Torch*.

☐ British aircraft raid northern Italy again, mainly striking at Milan, Monza and Novara.

25 October

North Africa The situation of the 10th Armoured Division in the corridor through the minefields has become very difficult by the early hours of the morning, but at 3.30 a.m. Montgomery confirms that the attempt to break through must go on, cost what it may.

Midday: the British commander decides to modify his plan of attack, shifting the pivot of the offensive to the north. The main attack is given to the Australian 9th Division, supported by the 1st Armoured Division. Particularly violent fighting is reported around Kidney Ridge. The German 15th Armoured Division suffers heavy losses; the 119 tanks it started with in the morning being reduced to 39. Rommel hurries back to Africa.

The tankers *Proserpina* and *Luisiano*, loaded with petrol for the nearly empty tanks of Rommel's vehicles, are sunk in Tobruk Harbour.

Guadalcanal After considerable activity by the Japanese air force and artillery during the day, there is a resumption of ground operations during the night of 25/26, when two Japanese regiments attack the American positions on the southern flank of the Lunga perimeter and other units attack the river Matanikau line. There are considerable losses on both sides. Ground activity stops next morning.

☐ Bermuda. A squadron of American aircraft carriers sails for North Africa for Operation *Torch*.

26 October

North Africa Fighting continues all along the front, especially severe in the gap opened in the enemy line by

El Alamein: a British gunner goes to the help of a wounded comrade during the decisive battle at the end of October 1942.

the British around Kidney Ridge. The Australian 9th Division launches its attack in the north; the switch forces the Germans to move their reserves some way to the north. However, the British action has slowed considerably compared with the first days. Montgomery summons his generals and urges them to resume the advance with the determination of the first few hours. In London they are waiting for decisive news, which does not arrive; Churchill is furious, and is said to have exclaimed: 'Is it really impossible to find a general who can win a battle?' Rommel gets back to his headquarters. He sees at once how serious the situation is and prepares countermeasures. The first priority is to move the 21st Armoured Division from the southern sector to the northern.

Eastern Front The battle for Stalingrad still rages. In the Caucasus, Army Group A takes Nalchik.

Guadalcanal The Japanese troops, commanded by General Kawaguchi, renew their attacks but once again are driven off. Their guns are silenced to a great extent by accurate fire from American batteries. Up to this time the Japanese have lost over 4,000 men on Guadalcanal; American losses are much lower. The Japanese air force, too, has lost over 100 aircraft in the last few days against about 15 by the Americans. Japanese naval units have also taken part in the battle, and American aircraft from Henderson Field have seriously damaged the light cruiser *Yura*.

☐ Britain. Another convoy sails for North Africa (*Operation Torch*).

Churchill tanks returning to their lines at the end of an engagement in the course of the battle of El Alamein.

A dramatic picture from the African war: a parachutist from the Italian *Folgore* Division throws himself between the tracks of a

27 October
North Africa Rommel launches a series of counter-attacks against the British line, mainly against the 1st Armoured Division. These attacks result in a further reduction in the number of his own tanks; at the end of the day 61 of the 15th Armoured Division's tanks and 56 of the *Lit-* *torio* Division's have been destroyed or captured by the Allies. The fighting at Tell el Aqqaqir is exceptionally fierce.

The British 7th Armoured Division is detached from the XIII Corps and moved to the northern sector of the front.

28 October
North Africa RAF formations allow no rest to the Axis armoured units, which are trying to re-group for a new counter-attack. By evening Rommel can count on 148 German tanks and 187 Italian, a miserable number compared with the 800 tanks still available to the British. Rommel

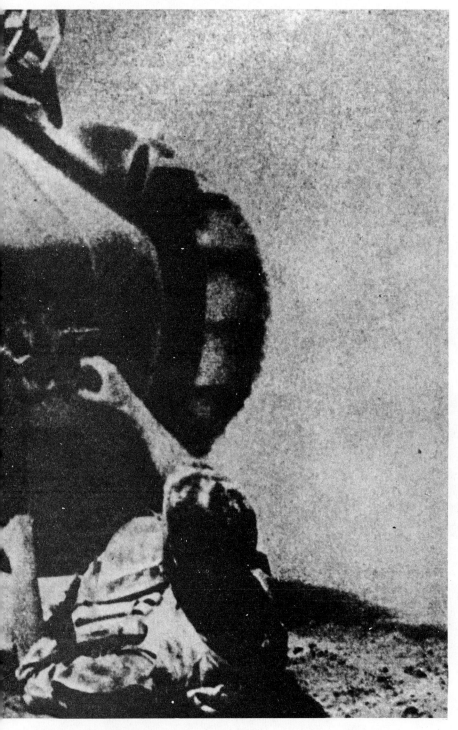

British Sherman tank to blow it up with a mine.

exploits all his tactical and strategic skill, but he knows quite well that the battle is lost. In the north the Australian 9th Division continues to attack and by the evening is near the coast road after driving a wedge into the enemy line. Rommel quickly brings up the 90th Light Division and 21st Armoured Division; the latter's place in the line is taken over by the Italian *Trieste* Division, kept in reserve until now. The Axis forces try to re-group for a new attack on the British positions, but they are hampered by the incessant pounding of the RAF. During the night of 28/29 October the British attack towards the sea to eliminate the salient that the Axis still hold on the coast and to cut the coastal road and railway. They almost reach the road, but are held up by the defenders of the strongpoint 'Thompson'.

Eastern Front German troops take two streets in north Stalingrad at immense cost.

29 October

North Africa New counter-attacks by the Axis in the northern sector of the British XXX Corps. Montgomery, knowing that the mass of the German forces are concentrated in the north, decides to try to break through, not westwards along the coast, but southwards, in the sector manned by the already exhausted Italian infantry.

Guadalcanal In view of the heavy losses they have suffered in recent engagements, the Japanese begin a general retirement on Koli Point and Kokumbona. Meanwhile the Americans, reinforced by two battalions of Marines transferred from Tulagi, build foot-bridges over the river Matanikau and prepare an offensive to be launched on 1 November.

New Guinea The Japanese on the Owen Stanley mountains withdraw.

30 October

North Africa The Australian 9th Division attacks again in the coastal sector, reaching the sea during the night of 30/31 October and quickly turning west so as to enclose huge enemy forces in a pocket; but the Axis forces are freed by an armoured thrust and are able to withdraw towards Cyrenaica.

Solomon Islands American cruisers and destroyers shell Japanese positions on Santa Cruz.

On Guadalcanal the Marines complete the preparations for their offensive and build more improvised bridges over the river Matanikau.

31 October

North Africa General Alexander, Commander-in-Chief of the British armed forces in the Middle East, telegraphs to Churchill as follows: 'Enemy is fighting desperately, but we are hitting him hard and continu-

American ships engaged in the Battle of Santa Cruz. Above: the aircraft carrier *Enterprise* (on the left). Opposite: the aircraft carrier *Hornet* under attack by Japanese dive-bombers.

THE BATTLE OF SANTA CRUZ

26 October

East of the Solomons four US task forces under the Commander-in-Chief of air and naval forces in the South Pacific, Admiral William F. Halsey, commanded at sea by Rear-Admirals Kinkaid, Murray and Lee (the fourth task force is the aerial force, No. 63, based on Guadalcanal), are involved in an air and naval engagement with numerically superior Japanese forces. The Americans have 2 aircraft carriers (*Enterprise* and *Hornet*), 2 battleships (*South Dakota* and *Washington*), 4 heavy cruisers (*Portland, Northampton, Pensacola, San Francisco*), 5 light cruisers (*San Juan, San Diego, Juneau, Helena, Atlanta*), 19

destroyers, 161 carrier-based aircraft and 251 based on Guadalcanal, Espiritu Santo and New Caledonia. The Japanese forces under Admiral Yamamoto, on board the battleship *Yamato*, at anchor at Truk, and operationally commanded by Vice-Admiral Nobutake Kondo, comprise 4 aircraft carriers (*Shokaku, Zuikaku, Zuiho, Junyo*), 4 battleships (*Hiei, Kirishima, Kongo, Haruna*), 9 heavy cruisers (*Kumano, Tone, Chikuma, Suzuya, Atago, Takao, Myoko, Maya, Chokai*), 4 light cruisers (*Nagara, Isuzu, Katori, Yura*), 31 destroyers, 12 submarines, and 412 aircraft, 212 of them carrier-borne.

The battle is fought entirely by air-

craft. The two fleets never come within range of each other. The Americans lose the aircraft carrier *Hornet*, hit by dive-bombers on the 26th and finished off by torpedo aircraft on the 27th. There is serious damage to the aircraft carrier *Enterprise*, the battleship *South Dakota*, the light cruiser *San Juan* and three destroyers, as well as the heavy cruiser *Portland*. The Japanese lose about 100 aircraft, the Americans 74.

The result of the battle is a substantial success for the Japanese. But the Americans have succeeded in temporarily paralysing Japanese movements by sea, including the despatch of reinforcements to Guadalcanal.

A platoon of British infantry attacks in the El Alamein sector, October 1942.

An Axis sapper defuses a British mine.

ously, and boring into him without mercy. Have high hopes he will crack soon.'

1 November

Eastern Front The fighting at Stalingrad between the Soviet 62nd and 64th Armies and the German 6th Army and 4th Armoured Army continues as fiercely as ever. But the German dream of capturing the entire city is beginning to fade before the enemy's indomitable resistance.

In the Caucasus the Red Army has succeeded in frustrating every effort by Army Group A to take Grozny. But the Germans succeed in taking Alagir, in the centre of the Caucasus, an important road junction southeast of Nalchik.

Guadalcanal The 1st Marine Division launches its planned attack westwards towards the river Poha, with powerful support from the air, and artillery and naval guns. Crossing the river Matanikau on the bridges thrown over it the previous days, the 5th Marine Regiment advances to within a short distance of Cruz Point, a Japanese strongpoint. East of the defensive perimeter, other units advance towards the river Metapona to stop the Japanese from landing fresh forces at Koli Point.

2 November

North Africa At 1.00 a.m. the XXX Corps of the British 8th Army launches the opening attacks of Operation *Supercharge* – code-name for the breakthrough offensive. Under cover of a tremendous artillery barrage the New Zealand 2nd Division opens a new corridor through the enemy minefields, allowing the 9th Armoured Brigade to pass through and establish a bridgehead beyond a track that goes south from Rahman. Axis anti-tank batteries wreak havoc among the British brigade's tanks at dawn, destroying 75% of them, but they cannot drive the enemy back behind the minefields. The X Corps sends its tanks to help, while the British 1st Armoured Division is engaged in fierce fighting near Tell el Aqqaqir, west of Kidney Ridge. By the evening Rommel has only 32 tanks in action in the front line.

Guadalcanal The 5th Marine Regiment surrounds the Japanese forces at Cruz Point. Supplies, ammunition and two batteries of 155-mm guns are landed on the island, enabling the Americans to return the Japanese fire effectively. To the east of the defensive perimeter a battalion of the 7th Marine Regiment crosses the mouth of the river Metapona and

establishes itself near the village of Tetere. During the night the Japanese 17th Army lands supplies and 1,500 men east of Koli Point, where the Japanese plan to build an airfield.

New Guinea The Australian 25th Brigade, after their long campaign in the Owen Stanley mountains, reach Kokoda and the nearby airport, which will enable the troops in the area to be supplied by air. The Allies are preparing for action. MacArthur intends to open the attack on the Japanese beachhead in the Buna-Gona area on 15 November.

3 November

North Africa The Axis anti-tank guns are still holding up the Allies' armoured thrust. During the night of 3/4 November the 51st Division and a brigade of the 4th Indian Division seize the Rahman track south of Tell el Aqqaqir and break through the Axis anti-tank defences. However, during the night Rommel has already given the order to withdraw. Some Italian divisions, including the *Folgore* Parachute Division, stay behind to sacrifice themselves while the main body retreats. Much RAF activity.

At 10.30 a.m. Rommel receives a telegram from Hitler in which it is impressed on him that he must hold his positions: 'In the situation in which you find yourself there can be no thought other than to resist, not to yield a single step, to throw into the battle every man and every weapon still available ... Despite their superiority, the enemy too are at the limit of their resources. It would not be the first time in history that the stronger will triumphed over the stronger enemy battalions. You can show your troops no other road than that which leads to victory or to death.'

Guadalcanal The 5th Marine Regiment eliminates the Japanese pocket at Cruz Point. East of the defensive perimeter, however, the Americans are forced back. Reinforcements are sent to them when headquarters learns of imminent Japanese landings at Koli Point.

☐ Generalissimo Chiang Kai-shek promises 15 Chinese divisions, to be put under the command of General Stilwell, for the recapture of Burma, for which the British are concentrating forces in India.

4 November

North Africa Desperate but hopeless defence by Italians: the *Ariete* Armoured Division, the *Littorio* Division and the *Trieste* Motorized Division are wiped out. Faced with this disaster, Rommel once more gives the order to withdraw, despite Hitler's message. During the day, thanks to intervention by Kesselring (Commander-in-Chief of the southern operational sector) Hitler authorizes Rommel to retire.

A communique from Cairo states the Axis forces 'are now in full retreat'.

Eastern Front While desperate fighting continues at Stalingrad, the Russians launch attacks in all the other sectors of the front to discover the weak points in the Germans' winter line.

Guadalcanal West of the defensive perimeter the Americans dig in about just over a mile from Cruz Point. To the east they have to contain powerful Japanese attacks. The Japanese positions near Koli Point are attacked by US cruisers, destroyers and aircraft. The Americans too

receive reinforcements: units of the 8th Marine Regiment land in Aola Bay.

New Guinea The Australian 16th Brigade attacks Japanese positions near Oivi but are held off.

Madagascar The French Governor-General again asks the British for armistice terms and now accepts the same conditions that he rejected on 17 September.

5 November

North Africa Axis forces are still retiring and British and Dominion troops advance on a broad front. The Germans have managed to withdraw 70,000 of the 90,000 men who made up their expeditionary force. The

A wounded German despatch rider is given first aid on return to the lines at Stalingrad.

Allies have taken 20,000 Italian prisoners and 10,000 German. The *Folgore* Division has already reached the end of its powers of resistance. The British XXX Corps takes Fuka, half-way between El Alamein and Mersa Matruh.

Guadalcanal An American infantry regiment pushes forward two miles inland, south of Koli Point, in an effort to surround the Japanese forces concentrated in the area.

Madagascar Hostilities between the British and the Vichy French forces cease officially at 2.00 p.m.

□ As the convoys that have sailed from Britain and the United States, headed for North-West Africa, draw near to their objective, General Eisenhower flies to Gibraltar and sets up the Allied headquarters there. The British Admiral Sir Andrew Cunningham will direct the Allied naval forces; the American General James H. Doolittle and the British Air-Marshal Sir William Welsh will command their two countries' air forces; Lieutenant-General K. A. N. Anderson will be in command of the British land forces.

6 November

North Africa In heavy rain, the British X Corps follows hard on the heels of the Germans and Italians in the area around Mersa Matruh. By 2.35 p.m. the *Folgore* Division, which left its base in Italy with 5,000 men, now numbers '32 officers, 262 other ranks'.

Eastern Front In the Caucasus the Red Army firmly repulses enemy efforts to take Ordzhonikidze, southwest of Grozny.

Guadalcanal The US 164th Infantry Regiment reaches Koli Point without opposition. American reinforcements continue to land at Aola Bay.

□ Genoa is attacked by RAF bombers during the night. The eastern central part of the city is devastated, with many killed and wounded. The city is again heavily raided on the night following.

7 November

North Africa Heavy rains hold up the British pursuit in the Mersa Matruh area. Rommel takes advantage of this to rescue as many as possible of his divisions from the threat of encirclement.

Guadalcanal Aircraft from Henderson Field attack and damage two Japanese destroyers off the island. The Americans advance east of the defensive perimeter to about a mile from the river Metapona without opposition.

Stalingrad, November 1942: under incessant enemy fire, Russian troops attack German positions.

'YANKEE DOODLE DANDY'

George N. Cohan, one of Broadway's greatest stars, died in New York on 5 November. Born in 1878, Cohan grew up in a family of vaudeville actors and in 1901 produced his first musical, *The Governor's Son*. Within a few years he had gained a reputation as one of the major author-actors of the Broadway stage and also as a prolific and successful song-writer. His composition *Over There* became a battle-song of American troops during the First World War. In the 1930s Cohan also appeared successfully on the stage, including a memorable performance in Eugene O'Neill's *Ah, Wilderness*.

His glittering career was celebrated in the film *Yankee Doodle Dandy*, produced and acted by James Cagney and directed by Michael Curtiz. Departing from his more usual gangster roles, the famous actor, who was also brought up in vaudeville, gave a stunning display of tap-dancing.

James Cagney (centre) in a scene from the film.

□ General Henri Giraud, who has escaped from southern France by submarine, has talks with General Eisenhower at his headquarters in Gibraltar. Giraud believes that he has been called on to take over the command of the Allied forces landing in Africa, but Eisenhower has to disillusion him. The Frenchman stalks out indignantly, but next day he accepts the task of civil administration of the French North African territories when they are liberated.

□ American General Wheeler is allotted the task of studying the question of supplies for the offensive which the Chinese propose to launch in the spring of 1943.

8 November
North-West Africa During the night of 7/8 November the Allied Expeditionary Force that left Britain and the United States appears off the ports of Algiers, Oran and Casablanca. Operation *Torch* is under way. There are 500 warships and 350 transports, divided into three main groups: Western Naval Task Force (Rear-Admiral Hewitt, USA), which lands troops under General Patton, USA, at Casablanca in Morocco; Central Naval Task Force (Commodore Troubridge of the Royal Navy), which lands its troops at Oran in Algeria under the command of the American General Fredendall, and Eastern Naval Task Force (Rear-Admiral Burrough of the Royal Navy), which lands its troops, commanded by the American General Ryder, at Algiers. Overall command of the naval forces is entrusted to the British Admiral Cunningham, and the Commander-in-Chief of the operation is General Dwight D. Eisenhower. Agreement on the operation was reached by Churchill and Roosevelt on 25 July. The landing at Algiers takes place at 1.00 a.m. and is carried out by two US regiments, two British brigades, two battalions of British Commandos, plus one US regiment which penetrates into Algiers harbour at 5.30 a.m. The city surrenders at 7.00 p.m.

The central group lands at 1.30 a.m., on the outskirts of Oran: one division, one armoured battalion, one battalion of Rangers, and also a parachute battalion. The whole contingent is American. The British ships *Walney* and *Hartland* are sunk trying to take the harbour intact.

The western group lands at 5.00 a.m. near Casablanca, all US troops, comprising one division and two regiments of infantry, three armoured battalions and special units. As a consequence of the invasion the Vichy government breaks off diplomatic relations with Washington.

By 6.30 a.m. U-boat Command in Paris realizes what is happening off the African coasts and orders 15 submarines to rendezvous off the coast of Morocco to intercept the Allied ships carrying out Operation *Torch*. But by the time they get there the Allied convoy has passed.

POLITICAL BACKGROUND TO OPERATION *TORCH*

For some months the Allies have been preparing men and materials to enable them to open a new front in North-West Africa. The decision has been a difficult one. When Roosevelt and Churchill first discussed it in Washington in June 1942 the Allies were under pressure on all fronts. In Africa Rommel was marching towards Suez; on the Russian front German troops were threatening Georgia and the Caspian; U-boats were inflicting catastrophic losses on British shipping. Stalin was persistently demanding the opening of a second front in Europe, but neither Roosevelt nor Churchill could seriously consider giving the Russians what they asked. Churchill for his part maintained that it would be far more useful to carry out a diversionary operation (still on the Western Front) with the aim of seizing a 'base' in the Mediterranean for an invasion of the Balkans, where it would be possible to open the second front Stalin was so anxious for. A landing in North-West Africa would also make it possible to take Rommel's *Afrikakorps* from the rear while the British 8th Army engaged them from the east. It would also provide the Allies with a bridgehead from which they could threaten Italy.

Despite opposition from many of his colleagues Roosevelt finally came round to Churchill's way of thinking. A victory in the west, even if only a limited one, would provide a salutary injection of confidence to American public opinion, severely shaken by the defeats in the Pacific. The two statesmen signed the definite agreement on 25 July and Stalin gave the plan enthusiastic approval. The British and American staffs worked out detailed times and modes of operation for what was first code-named *Gymnast*, then *Torch*. Militarily, the operation

General Patton (helmet with two stars) on the launch bringing him ashore.

was scrupulously prepared with nothing left to chance. The troops were specially trained for desert warfare. But the political side was more complicated. Particularly important was to find a Frenchman able to persuade the French, both military and civilians, to support the Allied landing (or at any rate not to oppose it). Clearly such a person could not be found among the supporters of the Vichy government, nor among the followers of General de Gaulle, to whom the Americans had not yet granted diplomatic recognition. So where were the Allies to look? Roosevelt decided to send Robert Murphy, his counsellor, and Admiral William Leahy (who was US ambassador to the Vichy government from 5 January 1941 to May 1942) to North Africa to see if they could find someone

there who would be disposed to help the Western Allies. It is no easy task. Edouard Herriot, a politician of consummate experience, is in prison because the collaborationist government does not trust him. Alexis Léger, former Secretary-General of the Quai d'Orsay, refuses to help. Roosevelt's colleagues suggest General Henri-Honoré Giraud, who had escaped some months before from Königstein castle in Germany, where he had been a prisoner of war since 1940, and had been in hiding in Vichy France. On 16 September 1942 Roosevelt decides on Giraud, keeping de Gaulle completely in the dark, 'even if it does give him a reason for getting annoyed, or for annoying us', as the President says. The Allies are counting on Giraud's attracting the support of both Gaullists and Pétainists in North Africa. A few weeks before the date fixed for Operation *Torch* to begin, the US General Mark Clark lands clandestinely in Africa (at Cherchell) from the submarine *Seraph* to meet Giraud's supporters and make arrangements for the general to cross from France to North Africa.

In the evening of 7 November Eisenhower meets Giraud in Gibraltar. The French general thinks he has been invited to take overall command of the operation. Eisenhower explains that the Allies' intention is rather to offer him command of the French territories in Africa liberated after the landing, and Giraud's reaction is to refuse co-operation. But the night brings counsel. Next day Giraud agrees to take over the civil administration of the liberated French territories in North Africa and two days later he and General Clark fly to Algiers to accept the cessation of resistance in the whole of French North Africa. But Giraud is received with great coolness, if not actually ignored. Only now do Giraud and Clark learn that Darlan, Commander-in-Chief of French armed forces in Africa, is in Algiers. He is the one who could legitimately give the order to cease resistance, and it is even possible that, through him, the Allies might get hold of the valuable French fleet at anchor in Toulon. Darlan is ready to co-operate. Well aware that the French fleet will neither go over to the Allies nor let itself be taken by the Germans, he orders a cease-fire in Africa. Marshal Pétain repudiates him at once. Darlan cancels the order. But then, on learning that the Germans have occupied Vichy France, he confirms the order again and declares himself ready to collaborate with the Americans. Finally on 13 November in Algiers, he signs an agreement with Eisenhower by which it is confirmed that the French will cease all resistance provided they remain under French authority.

Admirals Eisenhower and Darlan at the monument to the dead in Algiers.

7.00 a.m.: A personal letter from Roosevelt is delivered to Pétain informing him of the Allied landing in North Africa. Pétain's reply seems to leave no doubt about the Vichy government's intention: 'I have always declared that we shall defend our empire if attacked ... We are attacked, and we defend ourselves. This is the order that I give.' Officially, of course, Pétain wants to keep the Germans happy by declaring that he will oppose the Anglo-American landing. In practice, a few hours later he sends a secret telegram to the High Commissioner in Algiers, Admiral François Darlan, leaving him free to negotiate with the Allies. However, Pétain has no intention of lining up with the British and Americans, although this is urged on him by General Weygand, whom the President has called to Paris.

8–9 November

Pierre Laval, Prime Minister of the Vichy government, agrees to German demand that French airports in Tunisia shall be opened to German aircraft.

9 November

Eastern Front 'Foreign Armies East Branch' of the German information service reports that Russian forces are concentrating in the Stalingrad area and opposite the 3rd Rumanian Army. The German services are not able at this stage to say whether these concentrations suggest a big general offensive or simply a local action.

North Africa As the bad weather improves the British 8th Army renews its pursuit of the enemy, whose resistance is broken by the New Zealand 2nd Division at Sidi Barrani.

Tunisia Airborne German troops land on El Aouina airport, near Tunis, meeting no opposition from the French.

Algeria General Anderson assumes command of the British 1st Army. He immediately sends motorized columns towards Tunis and Bizerta to prevent those two important centres from being captured by the Axis forces. Axis submarines, dive-bombers and torpedo planes attack the Allied convoys and sink an American transport off Algeria. They also damage the US battleship *Massachusetts*, two cruisers, two destroyers and other ships. Vichy French forces still hold out at Oran, while the Americans take La Senia airport.

Morocco General Patton's troops attack Port Lyautey and the airport, meeting with unexpected resistance from the French. The US 3rd Division slows down its advance on Casablanca, waiting for heavy equipment and artillery which has still to be landed.

Guadalcanal The 7th Marine Regiment succeeds in almost completely surrounding Japanese units near the Gavaga torrent and repulses enemy attempts to break out of the encirclement. The Americans are preparing

Operation *Torch*: American Marines of General Ryder's force (Eastern Task Force) land on the beach in Algeria a little way from Algiers.

to attack again at Kokumbona.

New Guinea One regiment and one battalion of American infantry are air-lifted from Port Moresby to Natunga.

10 November

Algeria Admiral François Darlan reads over the radio a proclamation in which he orders French forces in Algeria and Morocco to cease all resistance to the Allies. American infantry and armour converge on Oran, and the city surrenders at 12.30 p.m.

North Africa Troops of the British 8th Army take Halfaya Pass.

Morocco French resistance in the Port Lyautey area ceases. The airport is repaired at once and American fighter squadrons from the aircraft carrier *Chenango* land there. Armoured columns resume the advance on Casablanca, while a battalion of the 2nd Armoured Division heads for Marrakech. US naval forces engage French ships at Casablanca.

Guadalcanal While the 7th Marines Regiment proceeds to destroy the Japanese whom they have almost completely surrounded in the area of the Gavaga torrent, the 2nd Marines and one battalion of the 164th Infantry Regiment renew their attacks west of Cruz Point with the object of taking Kokumbona.

New Guinea The Australian 16th Brigade forces the Japanese back from Oivi towards the mouth of the river Kumusi.

☐ Marshal Pétain announces that he has taken command of French sea, land and air forces.

11 November

North Africa The X Corps of the British 8th Army, still following up the retreating Axis forces, enters Libya and occupies Bardia without a shot fired. The 1st and 7th Armoured Divisions are on the heels of the Axis rearguards in Libya. The New Zealand 2nd Division halts on the Libyan–Egyptian border to reorganize.

North-West Africa The resident French authorities sign an armistice

The Japanese merchant ship *Yusyu Maru*, beached on Guadalcanal.

Mopping up: a British patrol collects arms abandoned by the enemy. In the foreground, a dead *Afrikakorps* soldier.

The French battleship *Jean Bart* damaged during the Allied bombardment of Casablanca.

Left: wounded American soldiers returning to base through the New Guinea jungle.
Below: American camp on Guadalcanal, showing conditions in the rainy season.

with the Allies, and all resistance by Vichy troops ceases at 7.00 a.m. Half an hour later the American 3rd Division, which would have had to take Casablanca by assault, enters the city amid popular enthusiasm. The various military installations are taken over by Allied troops. In Algeria units of the 36th Brigade of the British 1st Army land at Bougie, 110 miles east of Algiers, without meeting any resistance. The 11th Brigade of the 78th Division moves from Algiers towards Bône.

Guadalcanal The Americans break off their offensive against Kokumbona and begin to withdraw across the river Matanikau, since there are many signs that the Japanese are preparing a large-scale offensive against the Lunga perimeter. East of the perimeter the Americans proceed with the wiping out of the remaining surrounded Japanese both sides of the Gavaga torrent.

A convoy arrives from the New Hebrides and begins to unload supplies and ammunition, but after three transports have been damaged by Japanese aircraft the operations are broken off and the convoy puts to sea, making for a naval squadron on its way from New Caledonia.

☐ German troops enter Unoccupied France, taking possession of Vichy, Limoges, Lyons and several other places. Pétain broadcasts on the radio his official protest against the German invasion of Vichy France: 'I have tonight received a letter from the Führer telling me that, on necessary military grounds, he is forced to take certain steps which will result in the suppression of the agreements and the actual fundamental terms of the armistice. I protest formally against these decisions, which are incompatible with the terms of the armistice.'

12 November

Algeria Units of the British 1st Army take Bône, 150 miles east of Algiers; Commando units land near the harbour and seize it. Axis aircraft attack repeatedly during the day, hitting military and civil objectives. Two companies of American parachutists are dropped on Duzerville airport, 6 miles south-east of Bône, and occupy it. (The American parachutists are attached to the British 1st Army.)

Tunisia German units of General von Arnim's army land at Tunis and Bizerta.

Morocco Axis submarines sink two American transports off the coast of Morocco.

Guadalcanal The enemy troops trapped at Gavaga torrent are liquidated by the Americans. A convoy from the New Hebrides and New Caledonia lands over 6,000 men and considerable amounts of supplies at Lunga Point, but has to break off operations and put back to sea under the escort of a squadron of destroyers when a powerful Japanese naval squadron, including two battleships, is sighted approaching the island from the north.

Battle of Guadalcanal. During the night of 12/13 November the Japanese naval squadron is reported by the radar stations between Savo Island and Cape Esperance. In Iron Bottom Sound (so called because so many ships have been sunk there) between Savo and Guadalcanal a furious battle breaks out. The US forces include the aircraft carrier *Enterprise*, the battleships *Washington* and *South Dakota*, the cruisers *San Francisco*, *Pensacola*, *Portland*, *Helena*, *Juneau*, *Atlanta*, *Northampton* and *San Diego*, 22 destroyers and 7 transports, with 79 aircraft on board the *Enterprise* and 194 more based on Guadalcanal and the New Hebrides. The Japanese force includes the aircraft carriers *Junyo* and *Hiyo*, with 95 aircraft, the battleships *Hiei*, *Kirishima*, *Kongo* and *Haruna*, the cruisers *Atago*, *Takao*, *Sendai*, *Nagara*, *Tone*, *Chokai*, *Kinugasa*, *Suzuya*, *Maya* and *Tenryu*, 30 destroyers, 14 submarines and 11 transports. This fleet is supported by 215 aircraft from bases on New Britain. The battlo is fought out both by the naval and the air forces, with the following outcome: the Americans lose the light cruisers *Atlanta* and *Juneau* and 7 destroyers, while the cruisers *San Francisco*, *Portland* and *Helena*, the battleship *South Dakota* and 4 destroyers are damaged. The Japanese have to record the sinking of the battleships *Hiei* and *Kirishima*, the heavy cruiser *Kinugasa*, 2 destroyers and 7 of the 11 transports that should have landed over 10,000 men as reinforcements on Guadalcanal. Only 4,000 men and a few tons of supplies are later able to be unloaded at Tassafaronga.

New Guinea The Australian 25th Brigade takes Gorari, while the Japanese manage to withdraw behind the river Kumusi without loss.

□ German troops take over Marseilles and reach the fortified area of Toulon, which the Germans announce will not be occupied.

13 November

North Africa The X Corps of the 8th Army takes Tobruk.

Tunisia Italian units from Libya join up with Germans. The Axis forces occupy the Mareth Line, a fortified line somewhat boastfully called the 'African Maginot', built by the French for the protection of the eastern border of their colony. A few days later Axis forces occupy Tunisia.

Algeria General Eisenhower flies to Algiers to meet Admiral Darlan, who pledges that French Africa will be on the side of the Allies. An Allied convoy lands a parachute brigade at Bône, together with an infantry regiment and the advanced headquarters of the British 1st Army. The 36th Brigade advances as far as Djidjelli, 40 miles east of Bougie.

Solomon Islands The Japanese battleship *Hiei*, damaged the previous night, is attacked repeatedly by American torpedo aircraft and dive-bombers near Savo Island. Damaged beyond repair, she is sunk by the Japanese themselves.

New Guinea The Australians eliminate Japanese rearguards near the Kumusi river.

□ A succession of RAF night raids on Genoa cause many casualties and severe damage to the city centre.

14 November

Eastern Front Further bitter fighting in Stalingrad after a comparative lull.

On the Caucasian fronts Berlin admits the initiative is in Russian hands.

Guadalcanal Japanese ships shell Henderson Field heavily to neutralize it while they land reinforcements. Aircraft from the *Enterprise* and from land bases inflict severe losses

Fire from the guns of American ships during the naval battle off Guadalcanal on the night of 12 November 1942.

Top: wrecked tanks on the battlefield at El Alamein bear witness to the violence of the fighting.
Above: German soldiers take a rest during the long retreat from El Alamein.

on the enemy. This is the sequel to the Battle of Guadalcanal, begun on the 12th and described under that date.

New Guinea The Allies prepare to attack the Japanese beachhead in the area of Buna and Gona. American troops consolidate their positions at Natunga, and Australians and Americans take up positions in the area of Embogu–Embi–Oro Bay. The Australian 25th Brigade puts up a pontoon bridge on the Kokoda track, at Wairopi.

☐ Axis forces surround the naval base at Toulon, where the French fleet is concentrated. Despite official denials, they are preparing a military coup.

15 November

North Africa The British X Corps occupies Martuba airfield.

Algeria The British 1st Army crosses the Tunisian frontier and takes Tabarka, on the coast about 75 miles from Tunis. A battalion of American parachutists takes Youks-les-Bains, near Tebessa in Algeria, about 95 miles south of Bône.

Guadalcanal The last four of the eleven Japanese transports which should have landed reinforcements and materials on Guadalcanal are sighted at Tassafaronga, west of the American perimeter, and attacked by American aircraft and naval and land-based guns. No more than 2,000 men are able to land; 2,000 more are killed on the beach, or trying to reach it. The four transports are sunk. This is the last time the Japanese try to re-inforce the island on any consider-able scale. Japanese effectives on Guadalcanal at this date number about 20,000, though many of them are seriously ill with beri-beri and various forms of dysentery; there are about 23,000 Americans on the island.

☐ Church bells ring through-out Britain to celebrate the vic-tory in Egypt.

16 November

Tunisia The whole country is now occupied by Axis troops. The British 1st Army makes slight progress

'OSSESSIONE'

Directed by Luchino Visconti, in collaboration with Jean Renoir, this powerful film about the passionate affair between an innkeeper's wife and her young lover that leads to the pair murdering the husband, marked a dramatic turning point in the Italian cinema.

A dark and naturalistic drama set in the foggy Po valley in northern Italy, *Ossessione* heralded the cinematic genre of neorealism. In it Visconti blends elements of French realism with elements of the American *film noir*, his depiction of pessimism, crime, social and moral poverty and deprivation refuting the official image of Fascist Italy.

Massimo Girotti and Clara Calamai, the lovers in *Ossessione*.

along the coast. Another battalion of American parachutists is dropped at Souk el Arba, 30 miles south of Tabarka. The first engagements between French and German troops take place at Oued Zarga, Mateur and the road between Beja and Djebel Abiod.

New Britain The Japanese set up at Rabaul the headquarters of the 8th Army under General Hitoshi Ima-mura, who has under him the 17th Army operating in the Solomons and the 18th, in New Guinea.

New Guinea The Australians and Americans begin operations against the Japanese beachhead at Buna–Gona. The American 32nd Division advances on Buna, the Australian 7th Division on Gona and Sanananda. The Allies had expected to find the Japanese disorganized and demoralized, but instead they are quite ready to put up a vigorous defence, favoured by the broken ter-rain and by a line of strongpoints. The Japanese troops are commanded by Colonel Yokoyama, west of the river Girua (General Horii has dis-appeared during the retreat from the Kokoda track); those to the east of the river are under Captain Yasuda. Japanese aircraft hold up the Ameri-can landing south of Buna.

17 November

Tunisia The British make contact with the Germans west of Djebel Abiod, about 60 miles west of Tunis. Further south the American parachutists take Gafsa airport.

New Guinea The Australians and Americans move closer to the Buna–Gona beachhead. The Japanese receive reinforcements, landed from destroyers at Basabua in the evening.

18 November

Eastern Front The Russians are about to launch a huge offensive against the German forces at Stalingrad. In Stalingrad itself are the German 6th Army and part of the 4th Armoured Army. South-west of the city is Army Group B (von Weichs), with part of the 4th Armoured Army and the Rumanian 4th Army. Further north, in the great bend of the Don, are the Italian 8th and Rumanian 3rd Armies. On the Russian side, north of the Don and as far as the bridgehead at Kletskaya, beyond the river, is the South-West Front commanded by General Vatutin and comprising the 1st Army, 5th Tank Army and 21st Army. Between Kletskaya and Stalingrad is deployed the Don Front under the command of Rokossovsky, made up of the 65th, 24th and 66th Armies. From Stalingrad to the south is the Stalingrad Front, commanded by Eremenko and comprising part of the 62nd Army (General Zhukov), the 64th Army, 57th Army (Tolbukhin) and the 51st Army (Trufanov).

Tunisia A brigade of the British 78th Division drives off an attack by the Germans at Djebel Abiod, but east of this position another brigade is cut off. The Germans also attack the French XIX Corps at Medjez el Bab, 35 miles south-west of Tunis and south of Mateur.

Guadalcanal The Americans advance south of Cruz Point in the western sector, in readiness for a new offensive.

New Guinea The Australian 16th Brigade takes Popondetta, where orders are given for the immediate construction of a landing strip, and

pushes on towards Soputa without making contact with the enemy.

□ British bombers attack Turin during the night.

19 November

Eastern Front At 8.50 a.m., after a murderous artillery preparation the Russians launch their great counter-offensive at Stalingrad. For the Germans this is the beginning of a colossal disaster. Six corps of the Don Front move from the Kletskaya bridgehead beyond the Don, 75 miles north-west of Stalingrad. Further north the armies of the South-West Front are advancing from Serafimovich on the Don, about 95 miles north-west of Stalingrad. A pincer movement is beginning (the other line is positioned in the south on the Stalingrad front), which will develop during the next days. The Germans and Rumanians hold out fairly well everywhere, except that a powerful Russian penetration is immediately reported in the Kletskaya area. The commander, von Weichs, of Army Group B, consisting of part of the 4th *Panzerarmee* and the Rumanian 4th Army, orders immediate counter-attacks. But all that results is temporary containment of the enemy.

Tunisia The French XIX Corps rejects the German ultimatum demanding that they abandon Medjez el Bab. During the day British and American infantry and artillery units arrive and force the German tanks and infantry to retire.

Guadalcanal During the night of 19/20 November the Japanese launch an attack from Kukombona against American positions in the sector west of the river Matanikau.

20 November

Eastern Front While fighting rages in and north of Stalingrad, a new large-scale attack by the Russians gets under way from Beketovka and Plodovitoye, south of the city. Three armies are engaged, the 64th, 57th and 51st, with several armoured and mechanized corps. The Russian forces are subdivided into the 'Don' group, attacking from the north and

'Volga', attacking from the south-east.

North Africa In Libya, the 8th Army takes Benghazi. Rommel continues his withdrawal westwards. In Tunisia, renewed German pressure forces the French XIX Corps to retire some ten miles in the area of Medjez el Bab.

Guadalcanal Japanese attacks in the Cruz Point sector. The Americans retire, but later recover the lost ground by artillery and air action.

New Guinea The Australians succeed in entering Gona, but are driven out again by a Japanese counter-attack after sunset. However, the Japanese are dislodged from Soputa and withdraw as far as Cape Killerton, where they put up a firm resistance.

□ Laval broadcasts on the necessity of collaborating more closely with Germany.

21 November

Eastern Front North-west of Kletskaya the Rumanian 3rd Army shows signs of giving way to the assaults of the Russian 5th Tank Army. Fighting continues on the whole front. To the south, the Russians advance towards the Don; the 64th Army carry out a turning movement and threaten to cut off the Germans in Stalingrad. The armour, which opened the Serafimovich offensive, now advances on Golubaya and Kalach. Hitler rejects a proposal by von Paulus to retreat to the Don.

North Africa In Libya British and American aircraft carry out a heavy raid on the harbour at Tripoli. No major operations in Tunisia, where both the Allies and Axis are reorganizing.

Guadalcanal The Americans succeed in driving the Japanese out of Cruz Point, but make no further progress.

New Guinea The Australian 16th Brigade, reinforced by the American 126th Infantry Regiment, make slight and very costly progress towards Sanananda. Units of the American 32nd Division move from Dobodura towards Buna, but are held up by the Japanese, whose positions in the area called 'The Triangle' are well fortified, and whose defence is helped by the marshy nature of the ground.

22 November

Eastern Front The two branches of the Soviet pincer close at Kalach, trapping the German 6th Army and part of the 4th Armoured Army, besides some smaller formations – 250,000 crack troops, 100 tanks, 1,800 guns and over 10,000 vehicles.

North Africa Thrusts by strong British columns in the Agedabia area, in Libya, are temporarily checked by the enemy. In Tunisia the 36th Brigade and the British 78th Division repel a German attack at Djebel Abiod.

Guadalcanal Unsuccessful attacks by the Americans against Japanese positions west of the Lunga perimeter.

New Guinea While the Australian 25th Brigade pushes on in the direction of Gona, the US 126th Regiment attacks in the Sanananda sector.

Other American units advancing from Soputa cross to the east bank of the river Girua on pontoon bridges.

23 November

Eastern Front Five of the Rumanian divisions, part of the 3rd Army, surrounded by units of the Soviet 5th Tank Army and 21st Army south of Serafimovich, surrender. The Germans trapped at Stalingrad are attacked in the rear by the Soviet 65th and 64th Armies. The Commander of Army Group B, von Weichs, urges von Paulus, Commander of the 6th Army, to break out of the encirclement before the Russians can bring up new forces round the besieged city. But Hitler has assumed personal command of the army. When Field-Marshal Goering assures him that the Luftwaffe will be able to get supplies, ammunition and material into Stalingrad at a rate of 700 tons per day, he orders von Paulus to hold out where he is, in the expectation that Army Group B will resume the offensive to relieve him.

ALASKA HIGHWAY

On 21 November the Alcan International Highway (Alaska Highway) was opened. The road, 1,523 miles long, linked Dawson Creek, British Columbia, to Fairbanks in Yukon Territory.

Work had begun in March and was quickly carried out by US Army engineers in conjunction with other US government agencies and with the assistance of the Canadian government.

The highway was built for military purposes by the US War Department which considered it essential to have a rapid and safe link between its army bases in Alaska and the rest of the United States.

The cost of the operation was in the region of 115 million dollars.

A Russian patrol in action amid the ruins of Stalingrad.

Hitler goes on to order the setting up of 'Fortress Stalingrad', and insists that not a yard of ground shall be given up. Meanwhile Field-Marshal von Manstein is recalled from the Leningrad front and assumes command of the Don Army Group, consisting of the 4th *Panzerarmee* (except for the contingent which stayed with the 6th Army), part of the 6th Army and several armoured and mechanized groups. He is given the task of relieving Stalingrad and restoring the original front. Von

Manstein organizes his forces in two big operational groups, the Hoth Group south of the Don and the Hollidh Group north of it. The plan, largely dictated by Hitler, is to attack General Eremenko's Stalingrad Front group, then, unexpectedly, to withdraw to attack Rokossovsky's Don Front in concert with von Paulus' army, which will by then have broken through the Soviet ring round Stalingrad.

The Russians are faced with a very important decision on strategy –

whether they should concentrate their forces from the southern front on liquidating the German troops trapped at Stalingrad, or whether they should isolate Stalingrad and launch a massive attack to cut off the German forces falling back from the Caucasus.

The first alternative prevails – the immediate liquidation of the Germans' left in Stalingrad – because the Russians are convinced that the elimination of von Paulus' 6th Army will only require a few days. The German forces are tightly encircled and a further 'external' ring (with a circumference of about 285 miles) is thrown round the city to resist any attempt by the besieged forces to break out. This decision (which, in fact, permits the Germans to withdraw their forces from the Caucasus) is based on an almost incredible error in estimating the strength of the beleaguered German army. The Russians surround Stalingrad with a relatively small force of 480,000 men, thinking that there are approximately 90,000 Germans in Stalingrad. Not until 26 January (confirms Rokossovsky) do the Russians realize that 330,000 German soldiers are trapped in the city (German sources quote 284,000).

North Africa In Libya the retreating Axis forces, taken in the flank by the 7th Armoured Division of the British X Corps, withdraw from Agedabia to Al Agheila, where Rommel hopes he can hold up the enemy advance.

Algeria The Allied general headquarters is transferred from Gibraltar to Algiers. In Tunisia, British and French commands determine their respective spheres of command: all troops north of a line from Le Kef to Zaghouan will be under British command, those south of the line under French command.

West Africa In Senegal, Dakar is occupied by the Allies without bloodshed.

Guadalcanal After intensive artillery preparation the US 164th Infantry Regiment goes into action west of the perimeter, in the area of Cruz Point, but fails to overcome Japanese resist-

ance. American losses in this sector have been heavy, and are heavy again in this attack. The offensive is called off until reinforcements can be brought up.

New Guinea The Australian 25th Brigade has regrouped and attacks the enemy positions at Gona, but makes little headway against firm resistance. A US battalion continues to move towards Sanananda. A battery of field-guns is air-lifted to the airport at Popondetta, already functioning, and goes into action in the Soputa sector. Attacks against Japanese fortifications in the 'Triangle' fail completely.

24 November

Eastern Front In the Stalingrad sector the Russians exploit their breakthrough. The German High Command admits that the Red Army has 'broken into our defensive front on the Don'. And in the central sector they launch local offensives near Velikiye Luki and Rzhev.

North Africa In Libya, Rommel has reached El Agheila. All he has left is 35 tanks and the tattered remnants of two divisions. Yet Montgomery, now at Agedabia, less than 62 miles away, takes time – more than three weeks – to reorganize the 8th Army and resume the offensive. By 13 December, when the decision to attack finally comes, Rommel will already have slipped away brilliantly. Even the 8th Army GHQ admits 'The enemy has escaped with a clever withdrawal.'

Tunisia The British 1st Army is ordered to advance on Tunis, with Tebourba and Mateur as their first objectives. Some American armoured units have crossed into Tunisia.

New Guinea The Japanese drive off attacks against Gona by the Australian 25th Brigade. Units of the US 32nd Division push on towards Sanananda (near Gona, to the west). A co-ordinated attack is launched in the afternoon against the 'Triangle' after a brief preparation by aircraft and mortars, but the Japanese repulse it easily. Little action in the other areas of the island.

Solomon Islands The Japanese land special units at Munda in New Georgia, west of Guadalcanal, where they intend to construct airfields. Notwithstanding the close patrolling activities of the American navy the Japanese manage to bring supplies to Guadalcanal by sea. Fast destroyers operating at night drop floating drums tied together with cord, near the coast, and the infantry picks them up in boats or by swimming.

☐ General Stilwell is informed by the US War Department that the United States will not be able to supply men and materials, over and above those they are already supplying, for the projected offensive for the recapture of Burma.

25 November

Tunisia The 36th Brigade of the British 1st Army advances north of Djebel Abiod in the direction of Mateur. In the centre, other British troops penetrate the enemy positions between Mateur and Tebourba. A contingent of the American 1st Armoured Division carries out a raid on the airport at Djedeida, 5 miles from Tebourba, destroying 30 enemy aircraft on the ground. The British 78th Division retakes Medjez el Bab.

Guadalcanal An American destroyer surprises and shells a group of 40 Japanese motorized lighters at Tassafaronga. Enemy movements are reported on the islands of New Georgia and Santa Isabel.

26 November

Eastern Front Russians make important advances in the north-west Stalingrad sector and in the area of the Don bend.

Tunisia Armoured encounters south of Mateur.

New Guinea At Gona the Australians and Japanese face each other without either side taking the initiative. The American 32nd Division tries again to capture Sanananda by frontal and flanking attacks, but without success, gaining only a few hundred yards. The Allies get to within 700 yards of the Killerton track and capture a supply depot, stubbornly defended by the Japanese. A powerful attack prefaced by a long air and artillery bombardment is launched on the west flank of the 'Triangle', where the Japanese defences are least strong. The enemy shelters in bunkers during the bombardment and emerges to repel the attack with no great difficulty. The 127th Infantry Regiment of the 32nd Division reaches Port Moresby from Australia.

27 November

Tunisia The British 78th Division takes Tebourba, 22 miles from Tunis, but is driven out again by the Germans, supported by armour and Stukas. The bulk of the American 1st Armoured Division is transferred from the Oran sector to the British 1st Army.

☐ Toulon. At dawn the SS take over the naval base. The Commander of the French fleet, Admiral Jean de Laborde, gives orders for the ships to be scuttled. Two battleships, one battle-cruiser, seven cruisers, one aircraft transport, 29 destroyers, two submarines and other minor craft are lost. Four submarines are able to put to sea and reach freedom.

28 November

Eastern Front The tragedy of Stalingrad unfolds. Von Manstein, unknown to Hitler and in direct contradiction of the Führer's plans, works out Operation *Winter Storm*, aimed at breaking the Russian encirclement and relieving the 6th Army.

Russians announce that they have launched an offensive on the central front.

Tunisia The 11th Brigade of the British 78th Division and armoured units of the American 1st Armoured Division reach the outskirts of Djedeida, 14 miles from Tunis. This is as close as the Allies get to Tunis before the final phase of the campaign. To the south the Germans evacuate Pont du Fahs, 35 miles south-east of Tunis. Two British regiments are in danger of being surrounded south of Djedeida as the result of a brilliant turning movement by German armoured groups from St Cyprien towards Tebourba.

Pacific Admiral William F. Halsey, promoted from Vice-Admiral two days before, replaces Rear-Admiral Kinkaid with Rear-Admiral C. H. Wright in command of Task Force 67, which is responsible for patrolling Iron Bottom Sound between Savo and Guadalcanal to prevent the arrival of Japanese supplies. Task

Cossack cavalry, protected by a smoke screen, counter-attack north of Stalingrad.

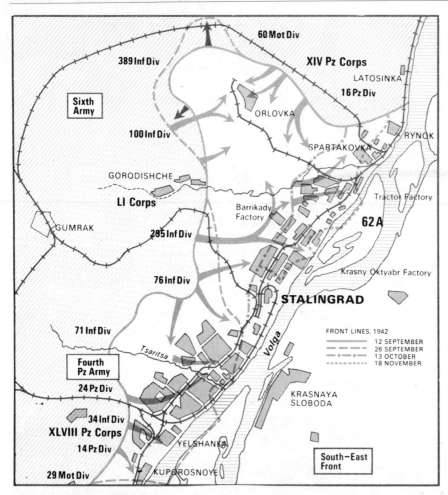

The final abortive German assault on Stalingrad, mid-September to mid-November 1942.

Force 67 comprises five cruisers (*Minneapolis, Honolulu, Northampton, Pensacola* and *New Orleans*) and four destroyers. The Japanese, who have lost their air and naval superiority in this sector, are trying to set up firm positions on the islands of New Georgia and Santa Isabel as jumping-off places for Guadalcanal. ☐ French Somaliland. A third of the garrison of Djibouti, until now loyal to the Vichy government, crosses into British Somaliland and adheres to the Allied cause.

29 November

Eastern Front The Russians continue to gain ground in the Stalingrad sector, and von Manstein begins to see the danger into which his own army is falling. Fighting flares up again in the Caucasus, where the Russians begin a series of attacks in the Terek sector.

Tunisia The 11th Brigade of the British 78th Division is held up at Djedeida by firm German resistance. Two battalions of the British 1st Parachute Brigade are dropped at Depienne, 10 miles north-east of Pont du Fahs, with the task of capturing Oudna airport, but they are repulsed and forced to retreat.

Guadalcanal Three incomplete battalions of infantry and Marines and another contingent of Seabees are landed in the Koli Point area, where the Americans want to build a new

airfield. The Americans examine the possiblity of withdrawing the Marines from Guadalcanal and giving operational responsibility to the army; more and more army units have reached the island in the last month or so. General Alexander M. Patch would succeed General Vandegrift, who has directed operations up to now.

New Guinea Allied bombers intercept four Japanese destroyers in the Vitiaz Strait and attack, forcing them to change course. The four ships were transporting reinforcements from Rabaul, New Britain, to the Gona beachhead. Japanese troops who have withdrawn towards positions north of Gona along the west bank of the river Kumusi reach Giruwa on board a lighter.

30 November

Tunisia The Germans and Italians have managed to land in Tunisia up to this date about 15,500 combatant troops, who without too much effort are containing the offensive thrusts of the British 1st Army and the American and French divisions. The 11th Brigade of the British 78th Division fights off German attacks near Djedeida.

Guadalcanal Naval battle of Tassafaronga. Rear-Admiral Wright's Task Force 67 intercepts and engages a squadron of eight Japanese destroyers, commanded by Rear-Admiral Tanaka, transporting troops and materials to Guadalcanal. During the night battle one Japanese destroyer is sunk and another damaged. The squadron has to withdraw without carrying out the landing, but inflicts serious damage on the American ships, torpedoing the heavy cruisers *Pensacola, New Orleans, Minneapolis* and *Northampton*. The *Northampton* sinks at 3.04 a.m. next day as a result of major leaks in the hull.

New Guinea The Australian 21st Brigade, after a period of rest and reorganization following the campaign in the Owen Stanley mountains, replaces the 25th on the Gona front. In the Sanananda sector, turning the enemy positions, units of the 126th

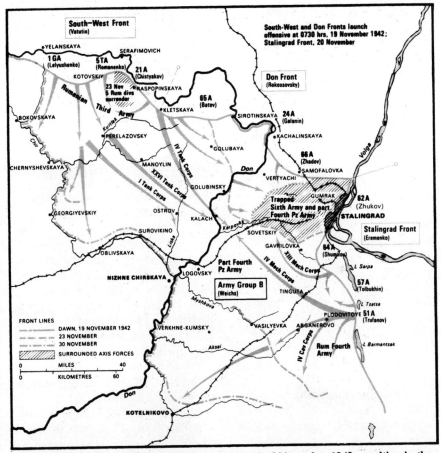

The Russian counter-attack at Stalingrad at the end of November 1942, resulting in the encirclement of the German 6th Army.

BOSTON NIGHTCLUB FIRE

A sudden and terrible fire which broke out in the Coconut Grove Nightclub in Boston on the evening of 29 November caused the death of some 300 people and injured over 150 others. The causes of the disaster were unknown. The only certain fact is that around ten o' clock that evening, while the band was getting ready to play, flames from the basement swept swiftly through the club. The customers, mainly sailors and marines in Boston for the weekend, rushed for the exits but the speed with which the fire took hold made escape virtually impossible.

Regiment of the US 32nd Division block the Soputa–Sanananda track, but frontal attacks on Sanananda itself are unsuccessful. The Japanese 'Triangle' is still impregnable.

1–2 December
Mediterranean Brief naval battle off the Tunisian coast between an Italian formation composed of three destroyers and two torpedo-boats and a British group formed of two cruisers and four destroyers. The Italians lose a destroyer, but succeed in hitting an enemy cruiser.

1 December
Tunisia Attempting to forestall the Allied attack expected next day, von Arnim's Germans attack towards Tebourba, a little way west of Djedeida, with infantry and armour supported from the air. The British lose a great number of tanks and are forced to withdraw. The US 1st Armoured Division is attached to the British 78th Division to hold the Germans in the Tebourba area. Axis aircraft bomb port installations at Bône and Algiers.
Guadalcanal The 8th Regiment of the 2nd Marine Division is withdrawn from the advance positions west of the river Matanikau, which are taken over by infantry of the US Army.
New Guinea The Australian 21st Brigade captures Gona. The Japanese retire to Gona Mission to carry on their resistance. Elsewhere they show no sign of giving way; they press very vigorously on the roadblock set up on the Soputa–Sanananda track by units of the US 32nd Division, repelling American counter-attacks. Allied attacks on Buna and Cape Esperance are unsuccessful.
Burma After a period of rest and re-equipment the Japanese man a line Tengchung–Myitkyina–Kamaing–Kalewa–Akyab.

☐ Responsibility for the India–China air lift is transferred from General Stilwell to Air Transport Command, based in India.

☐ General Spaatz hands over command of the US 8th Air Force, based in Britain, to General Ira C. Eaker and takes command of Allied air forces in North-West Africa.

☐ London. Sydney Silverman, MP, reports that more than 2,000,000 Jews have been exterminated by the Nazis up to the end of September.

2 December

Tunisia The British 1st Army beats off another German attack on Tebourba, losing about 40 tanks. An American parachute regiment and two American battalions, together with French units, attack Faïd Pass, 62 miles north-east of Gafsa in eastern central Tunisia.

New Guinea The Japanese, with four destroyers, try to land 800 men at Basabua at dawn, but are stopped by Allied air action. However, they manage to carry out the operation near the mouth of the river Kumusi, some 12 miles north of Gona. Japanese units attack the road-block on the Soputa–Sanananda track and succeed in reducing its perimeter, but not in breaking through it. Allied attacks against Buna collapse a little way from their objective. General Harding, commanding US 32nd Division, is relieved of his command and replaced by General Waldron. So far, 15,000 Australians and 15,000 Americans, despite their complete mastery of the air, and consequently largely of the sea as well, have not been able to overcome 12,000 Japanese.

3 December

Tunisia Von Arnim's German forces attack again and succeed in taking Tebourba during the night of 3/4 December. The British 78th Division, which has had heavy losses, withdraws north of Medjez el Bab. In the south, French and American forces take Faïd Pass.

New Guinea The road-block set up by the US 126th Infantry on the Soputa–Sanananda track is now threatened by unceasing Japanese assaults. MacArthur has ordered the troops to prepare a large-scale offensive, to begin on 5 December.

New Georgia American bombers based on Henderson Field begin an almost daily series of raids on

Munda Point to prevent the Japanese from constructing an airfield.

4 December

Libya Artillery action only.

Tunisia In Tebourba area the Germans destroy 25 British tanks, 7 armoured cars, 41 guns, 300 vehicles and large amounts of ammunition, capturing 400 prisoners.

New Guinea American advance elements reach Dobodura.

☐ RAF Liberators from Egypt raid Naples. The light cruiser *Muzio Attendolo* is sunk. Two other cruisers, the *Eugenio di Savoia* and *Raimondo Montecuccoli*, are badly damaged. Italian sources state 159 dead and 358 wounded in the raid.

5 December

Tunisia Activity by the air forces of both sides; 14 British and 10 Axis planes are shot down. Eisenhower fixes 9 December as the date for the general offensive. But the British 1st Army is in trouble through lack of advanced airfields and because its supply lines have become too long.

New Guinea The Australian 21st Brigade is still in action in the Gona area. A reinforced Australian battalion tries to prevent the landing of enemy supplies near Basabua, while another battalion advances westwards to hold up the Japanese who have landed at the mouth of the river Kumusi. The road-block on the Soputa–Sanananda track is surrounded by the Japanese and cannot be supplied. Combat groups called Urbana and Warren Forces are thrown into the attack on the village of Buna and get within 50 yards of the houses. General Waldron is wounded and the command of the US 32nd Division is taken over by General Clovis.

6 December

Tunisia German troops penetrate the positions of the American 1st Armoured Division in the El Guessa heights sector. The battle of Tebourba causes heavy Allied losses: 72 tanks and 1,100 prisoners, according to an Italian bulletin, not the 25

tanks and 400 prisoners originally claimed.

New Guinea The troops manning the road-block on the Soputa–Sanananda track, surrounded by the Japanese, are almost out of rations and ammunition. At Buna they are waiting for tanks to arrive to renew the attack on the Japanese.

7 December

North Africa Local encounters. Axis aircraft bomb Philippeville harbour and the RAF bomb Tripoli.

Guadalcanal Two Japanese destroyers bringing reinforcements to the island's garrison are attacked and damaged by American aircraft taking off from Henderson Field.

New Guinea The Australian 30th Brigade takes the place of the 16th on the Sanananda front (the 16th has seen a lengthy period of action and a large number of troops are sick with malaria). Australian efforts to relieve the Americans cut off in the road-block between Soputa and Sanananda fail. The other American front-line troops are replaced by Australian units. South of Buna the Japanese are dislodged from a line of trenches.

7–8 December

Mediterranean During the night an attempt by three Italian 'pigs' (mini-submarines) to enter Gibraltar harbour fails. Of the six men who compose the crews, three are killed in action, two are taken prisoner and only one succeeds in returning with his craft to the support ship *Olterra*.

8 December

Tunisia Eisenhower agrees that General Anderson should strengthen the line of the British 1st Army in readiness for the offensive. Rain holds up hostilities.

New Guinea Allied aircraft intercept a formation of six Japanese destroyers bringing reinforcements and supplies to the Buna beachhead and force them to turn back. The road-block between Soputa and Sanananda is finally reached by Australian units after violent fighting. The Japanese who are trying to get to Giruwa after escaping from

Gona are annihilated by the Australians. Urbana Force persists in its attack on Buna village, using flame-throwers, which prove ineffectual.

Guadalcanal American motor torpedo boats attack Japanese destroyers approaching the island and prevent them from landing men and materials.

☐ Turin is again heavily bombed by RAF aircraft.

9 December

Tunisia A sudden thrust by British armoured cars in the Tebourba area is driven off by the enemy.

Algeria Italian torpedo aircraft attack enemy shipping at anchor in the Algiers roadsteads and hit two merchant ships.

Guadalcanal General Patch of the US Army assumes command of American forces on the island in place of General Vandegrift, Commander of the 1st Marine Division, which is gradually withdrawn from Guadalcanal during December.

New Guinea After bombardment by aircraft and artillery the Australian 21st Brigade finally overcomes the desperate resistance of the last Japanese units in the Gona area. The battle ends at 4.30 p.m. The Japanese leave hundreds of dead on the field. A battalion of the American 32nd Division is air-lifted into the Buna sector in readiness for the final attack on Buna village.

10 December

Tunisia Columns of German tanks and infantry carry out a thrust on Medjez el Bab from the north-east and east, but are driven off by the four French battalions and the British 1st Guards Brigade. The 11th Brigade of the British 78th Division and units of the US 1st Armoured Division attached to it withdraw to Bedja to regroup. As they retire the American units abandon much of their equipment.

New Guinea The Japanese left in the area north-west of Gona, battered ceaselessly by Allied aircraft, are ordered to prepare a defensive perimeter in the area of Napapo and await reinforcements. The few re-

THE ATOMIC PILE

On 2 December a group of scientists led by Enrico Fermi obtained the first nuclear chain reaction in controlled form.

This extremely important result was achieved by means of an atomic pile (or nuclear reactor) consisting of layers of graphite and uranium, built by Italian scientists on the football field of the University of Chicago.

Bombardment with a neutron of a uranium nucleus resulted in its splitting into two lighter nuclei, simultaneously releasing a powerful charge of nuclear energy and producing free neutrons capable of provoking other similar reactions.

To guard against any possible accident, special precautions had been taken when the reactor was built whereby it would cease functioning in the event of reaching a critical phase.

An integral part of the DSM Project, Fermi's work marked a fundamental stage in the development of the atomic bomb.

Enrico Fermi in Chicago.

inforcements that the Japanese do receive come by air.

☐ Turin is again heavily bombed by the RAF.

11 December

Eastern Front The Red Army retains the initiative everywhere. The Russians make progress in the Stalingrad sector, in the great bend of the Don and in the Caucasus. Von Manstein's 4th Army is under heavy pressure east of Stalingrad. In the Caucasus, Army Group A establishes a defensive line further back, near the river Terek.

Libya Montgomery gives the order for the resumption of the offensive. The British are to attack El Agheila

on the 14th. RAF activity over Axis logistic centres is intensified in preparation for the attack.

New Guinea A lull in operations. During the night of 11/12 December ships begin to arrive in Oro Bay bringing supplies for the Allies; the first convoy brings the first tanks to the island.

11–12 December

Algeria During the night three 'pigs' of the Italian navy enter Algiers harbour and sink four ships in an Allied convoy.

12 December

Eastern Front Operation *Winter Storm*, planned by the Commander

Russian soldiers join their companions barricaded in the ruins of Stalingrad.

of the Don Army Group, von Manstein, contrary to Hitler's orders, gets under way in the area of Kotelnikovo. General Hoth's armoured group, made up of the 17th, 6th and 23rd Armoured Divisions supported by the Rumanian 4th Army and part of the 3rd Army, break through the lines of the Russian 51st Army south of the Don. The rest of von Manstein's forces, the Hollidt operational group, attacks north of the river. The Germans make rapid progress on the first two days, but then the Russians receive reinforcements and their resistance becomes more effective.

Libya Montgomery throws in the New Zealand 2nd Division (from Agedabia) against Mersa Brega, a few miles from the German defensive line at El Agheila.

Tunisia Encounters between German and British armour east and south-east of Medjez el Bab.

Guadalcanal A Japanese unit carries out a raid on Henderson Field under cover of darkness, damaging one of the runways reserved for fighters.

New Guinea The light tanks landed at Oro Bay are moved in the utmost secrecy to Hariko. Some corvettes with Australian units on board begin landing operations opposite Plantation Soena, but break off and take refuge in Porlock Harbour when news arrives that a Japanese naval formation is approaching from Buna.

13 December

Eastern Front Heavy fighting continues in Stalingrad and central sectors.

Libya The New Zealand 2nd Division of the 8th Army takes

Mersa Brega, a little way east of El Agheila. Rommel begins to evacuate the position, leaving a rearguard and a number of minefields to slow down the enemy advance. The RAF harries the retreating Germans and Italians relentlessly.

Tunisia The V Corps of the British 1st Army is ordered to get ready for a new offensive against Tunis. A lull follows.

New Guinea Allied aircraft attack a squadron of five enemy destroyers carrying supplies and 800 men, but with no result. Among those on board is General Kensaku Oda, successor to General Horii as Commander of the 'South Seas Detachment'; the convoy is taking reinforcements to the greatly reduced Japanese garrison on the island. The roadblock between

Buna, New Guinea, December 1942: American soldiers approach a Japanese hideout.

Soputa and Sanananda is cut off by the Japanese again. The Australians direct a heavy artillery barrage on Buna village, and at night the last of the Japanese defenders, now only a hundred strong, evacuate the village and swim to the village of Giruwa.

14 December

Libya The British 7th Armoured Division attacks the Axis forces dug in behind the minefields at El Agheila. The New Zealand 2nd Division begins a diversion to the south-west, in the desert, to by-pass El Agheila.

New Guinea The Japanese convoy already signalled reaches the mouth of the river Mambare in the morning and carries out landing operations. They are not sighted by Allied recon-naissance until the afternoon. Then fighters and fighter-bombers attack the boats, which are still landing men, supplies and ammunition, causing some damage. Two companies of the US 127th Infantry Regiment penetrate cautiously into Buna village, from which the Japanese escaped the night before. In a single day 178 tons of material arrive by air from Australia.

15 December

Libya The New Zealand 2nd Division, after their detour through the desert, advances quickly towards the coast in the area of Merduma to trap the defenders of El Agheila, who are engaged by the 7th Armoured Division from the east.

Tunisia The British 1st Army is slowly preparing its deployment. The US 9th Airborne Division begins a series of raids on Tunisian ports where Italian troops and materials are being landed, attacking Sfax and damaging port installations there.

New Guinea In Oro Bay a Dutch cargo ship lands war materials including tanks. The new tanks are taken to Hariko, where an Australian tank regiment is being formed.

16 December

Eastern Front As von Manstein's forces approach Stalingrad, moving increasingly slowly, the Russians unleash a violent offensive on the middle Don on a front of over 60 miles. The Red Army wipes out the Italian 8th Army and part of the Rumanian 3rd Army. Manstein is forced to detach some of the armoured divisions engaged in Operation *Winter Storm* to plug the gap and re-establish the front line.

Libya The Axis forces withdraw from El Agheila, moving in small groups to avoid the threat from the New Zealand 2nd Division. They make for Buerat, where they intend to establish a new defensive line. In the course of their rearguard action they lose 20 tanks and 500 men killed, wounded and prisoners.

Guadalcanal General Patch orders the 132nd Infantry to take Mount Austen, which dominates the whole island, as prelude to the great offensive planned for January.

New Guinea After fierce fighting an American battalion takes Coconut Grove and establishes a bridgehead over Entrance Creek, which is then bridged. At last it will be possible to attack the 'Triangle' with a good chance of success.

Burma In the coastal Arakan region, on the Gulf of Bengal, the 14th Indian Division advances into Burmese territory with the aim of taking Akyab Island, at the end of the Mayu peninsula. Advance units take the town of Maungdaw without opposition.

17 December

Eastern Front Faced with the *fait accompli*, Hitler has confirmed von

Units of the German 4th Army make an unsuccessful attempt to break through the Russian forces encircling Stalingrad and relieve von Paulus' beleaguered 6th Army.

Manstein's decisions for the liberation of von Paulus' 6th Army from Stalingrad. But the progress of Hoth's armoured group towards the river Myshkova (a tributary of the Don), where the Russians have prepared a fortified line, grows ever slower. Meanwhile von Paulus' 6th Army, surrounded in Stalingrad with part of the 4th Armoured Army, is holding out against pressure by seven Russian armies, the 24th, 66th, 62nd, 64th, 57th, 21st and 65th.

Libya The British break through at El Agheila and pursue the enemy towards Sirte. Rommel deploys several units at Sirte to slow down the advance while the new line is established at Buerat.

Guadalcanal The American 132nd Infantry Regiment begins the occupation of Mount Austen, meeting no opposition.

New Guinea Costly and useless attacks against the 'Triangle'. A large-scale attack against the Buna Mission is planned for the next day. Tanks are brought up to the start line, the sound of their tracks being covered by intense mortar fire.

Burma The 14th Indian Division continues its advance on Akyab and occupies Buthidaung unopposed.

18 December

Libya Hard fighting between the Axis rearguards and the New Zealand 2nd Division at Nofilia, half way between El Agheila and Sirte. Montgomery, his supply lines seriously extended, orders pursuit of the enemy to be halted in case of possible surprise counter-attack by Rommel.

Guadalcanal The American 132nd Infantry meet the first Japanese resistance as they advance up the north-west slopes of Mount Austen. The Japanese cruiser *Tenryu* is sunk by an American submarine in the Bismarck Sea.

New Guinea On the Sanananda front the Australians inflict heavy losses on the Japanese manning Napapo and, with support from American artillery, begin a concerted attack against Sanananda. The resistance of the Japanese surrounding the road-block on the Soputa track is partially broken. Elements of the US 127th Infantry try to take the islet of Musita, but have to fall back in face of the dogged Japanese resistance. An Australian battalion with tank support attacks the Japanese positions at Cape Endaiadere. They are able to destroy the Japanese pill-

The bodies of Japanese soldiers killed near Gona, New Guinea, during the fierce battles of December 1942. Despite their numerical superiority, Allied troops make little headway against fanatical Japanese resistance.

boxes with the tank guns, and drive the enemy out of their positions. They follow up westwards as far as Strip Point, where they are halted by another line of bunkers. In this successful action the Australians lose three tanks.

19 December

Eastern Front The Russians continue to gain ground in the southern sector. Assault groups coming from the middle course of the Don take Kantemirovka, cutting the Voronezh–Rostov railway line north of Millerovo. The retreat of the remnants of the Italian 8th Army, hopelessly ill-equipped to withstand the

rigours of a Russian winter, become a rout. The Germans make a little progress towards Stalingrad.

Guadalcanal Even with artillery and air support the Americans are unable to overcome Japanese resistance on Mount Austen.

New Guinea The Australians attack again in the Sanananda sector. Some enemy positions are captured, while the units on the left flank of the action approach the road-block on the Soputa track. They meet enemy units about 300 yards from the block itself, put them to flight and establish a new entrenched perimeter in the area, called Kano. Other troops attack the 'Triangle', but suffer heavy losses.

20 December

Guadalcanal The Japanese harass the Americans advancing up the north-west side of Mount Austen, while Americans sappers begin to build a road from the Lunga perimeter to the foothills of the mountain.

21 December

Eastern Front Advance Red Army forces now more than half-way between the Don and the Donetz.

Libya Advance units of the British 8th Army reach Sirte, where they are held up by Axis rearguards.

New Guinea General Oda, the commander of the Japanese troops, reaches Giruwa from Napapo.

Tunisian front, December 1942: a US instructor demonstrates to French troops the working of American weapons.

Australian rifleman in Jahore (Malaya).

Fighting begins again in all sectors, starting at Sanananda and the road block. The Japanese in the 'Triangle' suffer considerable losses as the result of a feint attack in a nearby area which brings the defenders out of their bunkers. After mopping up the area east of Simemi Creek the Americans cross the stream and dig in in a favourable position about three-quarters of a mile from the mouth.

Aleutian Islands The American supreme command orders the capture of Amchitka Island from which it will be easier to bomb Kiska Island, which is occupied by the Japanese. □ Munich heavily bombed in RAF night raid.

22 December

Eastern Front Recognizing that his Army Group B may be cut off from the rest of the German army if the Russians defeat von Manstein on the Don front, von Kleist begins the withdrawal from his most advanced positions in the Caucasus, where the Russians, six armies strong and completely reorganized, are attacking vigorously south-east of Nalchik. They are gaining ground on the Don front, and at any moment may surround not only von Paulus' 6th Army but also the whole of von Manstein's Don Army Group in the Stalingrad sector. In the central sector the Russians launch a powerful attack towards Velikiye Luki.

Tunisia The V Corps of the British 1st Army reopens the offensive against Tunis during the night of 22/23 December. The 2nd Coldstream Guards attack and partly occupy Djebel el Ahmera, 6 miles north-east of Medjez el Bab.

New Guinea General Oda takes over direct command of Japanese operations on the Sanananda front. Japanese units hold up the Australian advance along the Soputa-Sanananda track. Units of the US 127th Infantry reinforce the bridgehead across Entrance Creek, while other elements of the same regiment begin mopping up on Musita islet after engineers have repaired the bridge linking it with the coast.

23 December

Eastern Front The Hoth armoured group has reached a point less than 30 miles from the troops besieged in Stalingrad. This is the moment for von Paulus to order a sortie from his desperate position, but he has not enough fuel even to cover that short distance. He himself is undecided what to do (although the Führer has finally given his blessing to the attempted sortie). Von Manstein, whose own forces are in a critical situation and who cannot guarantee the success of the operation, advises him not to attempt a sortie. In the evening von Paulus, tortured by indecision, declares that he will not leave Stalingrad without a direct order from Hitler. So the costly advance of Hoth's group to the river Myshkova has been in vain. Moreover the airborne supplies so optimistically promised by Goering are getting increasingly scarce. The defenders of Stalingrad have to start slaughtering their horses to survive.

Tunisia Torrential rains begin, and hold up operations for three days. A regiment of the US 1st Division which has replaced the Coldstream Guards on the Djebel el Ahmera, has to withdraw when counter-attacked by the Germans.

FRANZ BOAS

The death occurred on 21 December of Franz Boas, one of the founding fathers of American anthropology. Born in Minden, Germany, in 1858, Boas began to be interested in primitive cultures when observing the Eskimos during a scientific expedition to Baffin Island in 1883-4. In 1885 he began his journeys to the regions of the north-west Pacific to study the Kwakiutl and other tribes of British Columbia. A tireless researcher, he collected a wealth of vitally significant data concerning the languages, religions and cultures of North American Indian tribes, always placing emphasis upon the empirical importance of facts. Appointed professor of anthropology at Columbia University in 1899 (a chair he held until his death), Boas also took on the job, from 1901 to 1905, of curator of the departments of anthropology and ethnology at the American Museum of Natural History.

24 December

Algeria Admiral Darlan is assassinated. Darlan, once Marshal Pétain's right-hand man, and on 13 November appointed French governor in Africa by the British and Americans after crossing over to their side at the time of the landing in Algeria, is shot in Algiers by a young student. The assassin, Fernand Bonnier de la Chapelle, is executed by firing squad two days later.

Tunisia British units recapture the positions lost the previous day by the Americans on the Djebel el Ahmera. General Eisenhower and the Commander of the British 1st Army,

Guadalcanal The Americans trying to take Mount Austen are halted by 500 Japanese in a strongpoint called Gifu, between hills 31 and 27.

Dauntless bombers hammer the coastline at Safi in support of Allied operations in French Morocco.

December 1942: American soldiers struggle through the mud in the Guadalcanal jungle.

'WHITE CHRISTMAS'

Bing Crosby and Fred Astaire were the stars of *Holiday Inn*, a modest musical comedy directed for Paramount by Mark Sandrich. Crosby, the world famous 'crooner' sang a number in this film, 'White Christmas' which became a great all-time hit. Written by the Russian-born composer Irving Berlin, 'White Christmas' won an Oscar and made musical history as the most popular of all secular songs associated with the festive season.

Bing Crosby, at the peak of his success in the 1940s.

25 December

Libya Sirte, on the coast, which the British armour has already by-passed inland, is evacuated. The Axis forces are preparing another defensive line, between Homs and Tarhuna, to the west of their Buerat line.

Tunisia For the second time the Germans recapture the Djebel el Ahmera, a strategic centre dominating the roads leaving Medjez el Bab. The British 1st Guards Brigade is dislodged from this position.

Guadalcanal On Mount Austen, the Japanese strongpoint of Gifu holds out against American attacks supported by artillery and aircraft.

New Guinea Japanese submarines supply the Buna bridgehead. Australians and Americans persist in their attacks against the 'Triangle' and at one point drive the Japanese back on to the beaches.

☐ King George VI makes his Christmas broadcast: 'Let us welcome the future in a spirit of brotherhood, and thus make a world in which, please God, all may dwell together in justice and in peace.'

26 December

Eastern Front A special Moscow communiqué announces important gains for the Red Army in the Middle Don sector.

Guadalcanal The Gifu strongpoint held by the Japanese on Mount Austen holds out against further American attacks.

New Guinea Japanese aircraft from Rabaul raid Dobodura but are soon driven off by Allied aircraft. During the night of 26/27 December American and Australian reinforcements and tanks are landed at Oro Bay. The Allies make very little progress in an attempt to cut in two the troops deployed by the Japanese in the Buna area.

French Somaliland French units which recently crossed over to the Allied camp enter the French colony from British Somaliland and capture two railway bridges on the line from Djibouti to Addis Ababa without opposition.

27 December

Guadalcanal Stalemate on Mount Austen, where new American units try to converge on the flanks of the Gifu strongpoint.

New Guinea The Japanese at Napapo are ordered to evacuate the area by sea and move to Giruwa. Fifty-two Japanese aircraft carry out a raid on Allied positions in the Buna area; 14 shot down by Allied fighters. More tanks are landed by night in Oro Bay. A regimental group of the American 41st Division arrives at Port Moresby from Australia.

Burma The 14th Indian Division continues its advance on Akyab without opposition, crossing the river Mayu and the range of hills of the same name. Along the coast the 47th Indian Brigade reaches Indin and sends out patrols as far as Foul Point, at the end of the Mayu peninsula. The advance then has to be halted for logistic reasons.

☐ General Giraud is elected by the Conseil National in Algiers to be High Commissioner for French Africa.

28 December

Libya Advance guards of the British 8th Army reach Wadi el Kebir, not far from Buerat, without opposition.

Tunisia Thrusts by elements of the British 1st Army are repulsed.

Guadalcanal American patrols try to pick out the weak points in the Japanese Gifu strongpoint on Mount Austen. The attacking force's fighting strength has fallen to just over 1,500 and the unit is integrated with another battalion.

New Guinea The Japanese troops in Buna are ordered to retire to Giruwa, protected by units which will attack the Americans from the flank. Patrols of volunteers penetrate into the 'Triangle' in the evening and find the bunkers already deserted.

☐ Chiang Kai-shek sends a message to President Roosevelt, assuring him that the Chinese army will be ready to launch a big offensive from Yunnan in the spring, but asking as an essential condition that Allied naval forces in the Bay of Bengal be substantially reinforced.

29 December

Eastern Front After bitter street fighting the Russians retake Kotelnikovo, south-west of Stalingrad. The town was the starting point of the German attack to relieve the 6th Army and part of the 4th Armoured Army which are now surrounded in Stalingrad.

British tank damaged by Italo-German troops.

A Russian patrol carrying supplies to Stalingrad over the frozen waters of the Volga.

An Italian unit in Russia rests during the tragic retreat from the Don.

Libya Advance elements of the British 8th Army (armoured cars of the 4th Armoured Brigade) arrive outside Buerat and find it already evacuated by the Axis troops. Italian aircraft carry out repeated raids on French columns advancing on Tripoli across the Sahara from Chad.

New Georgia Despite the Allies' continual air attacks the Japanese complete the building of an airfield at Munda.

Guadalcanal The American attack on Mount Austen continues.

New Guinea General Yamagata, given the task of directing the with-drawal from Buna to Giruwa, arrives at Giruwa. The Americans reach the sea south-east of Buna Mission, cutting the only road by which the Japanese still there can retreat overland. Warren Force attacks northwards towards the coast in the area between the Simemi stream and Giropa Point with tank support, but makes little progress in the face of firm Japanese resistance.

30 December

Tunisia A regimental combat group of the American 1st Division reaches the Medjez el Bab positions.

New Guinea Australians and Americans maintain their pressure on Buna Mission and prepare to surround it by attacking from Buna village and the Musita islet.

31 December

Guadalcanal The Americans get ready to renew their attacks on the Gifu strongpoint on Mount Austen with larger forces.

New Guinea Fighting continues round Buna Mission, where the Allies are trying to surround the Japanese defenders.

1943

1943

JANUARY	**14 January** *North Africa*: The Casablanca Conference opens.	**31 January** Hitler appoints von Paulus field-marshal who is forced to seek surrender terms the same day.
FEBRUARY		
MARCH	**3-5 March** Battle of the Bismarck Sea.	**12-15 March** The Pacific Military conference is held in Washington.
APRIL	**19 April** Massacre of the Jews in the Warsaw ghetto.	**23 April** Joint Anglo-American command set up to plan a European landing.
MAY	**12 May** *Tunisia*: General von Arnim, commander of the troops in Africa, surrenders to the Allies.	**25 May** *USA*: Close of the Trident Conference, opened in Washington on 12 May.
JUNE	**30 June** *Pacific*: Operation Cartwheel begins.	
JULY	**10 July** *Sicily*: Operation *Husky* begins. **25 July** *Italy*: The Fascist Grand Council passes a vote of no confidence in	Mussolini, who is jailed. Marshal Badoglio is invited to form a new government.
AUGUST	**17 August** *Sicily*: General Patton's troops enter Messina. The capture of the whole island has taken only 39 days.	
SEPTEMBER	**3 September** *Sicily*: General Giuseppe Castellano signs the three copies of the 'short armistice' on behalf of Marshal Badoglio.	**10 September** *Italy*: The Germans occupy Rome.
OCTOBER	**13 October** Italy declares war on Germany and acquires the hybrid status among the Allies of 'co-belligerent'.	
NOVEMBER	**20 November** Start of Operation Galvanic. **28 November** Roosevelt and Churchill meet Stalin at Teheran. The conference	(code-named 'Eureka') begins.
DECEMBER	**7 December** The supreme command in the Mediterranean is unified. Eisenhower, already selected by Roosevelt as Commander-in-Chief	for *Overlord*, will be responsible for all operations in the Mediterranean theatre.

Anti-aircraft battery on board an American ship.

1 January

Eastern Front Six Russian armies keep up their pressure on the German forces surrounded at Stalingrad. The area defended by the Germans is reduced to approximately 25 by 40 miles. The efforts of the Luftwaffe to bring in supplies and to evacuate the more seriously wounded cost them an ever increasing number of aircraft. In order to escape the threat of encirclement themselves, the Hoth armoured group, reinforced by troops recalled from France, retreats to 120 miles south-west of Stalingrad.

In the northern sector the Russians re-take Velikiye Luki, an important railway junction north of Vitebsk, after a fierce struggle. Acting on Hitler's orders, the German commander, General Scherer, orders his troops to resist to the death. The Russians, fighting for every house and street, annihilate the Germans.

Guadalcanal The Japanese High Command decide to evacuate Guadalcanal. The convoy carrying the main body of the 28th Division (commanded by General Sano) has been almost totally destroyed. Out of eleven transports, six have been sunk, one seriously damaged and four have had to be grounded in shallow waters off the coast to avoid sinking. The decision means losing the Solomons, and with them the mastery of the north-east approaches to Australia and New Zealand. But such huge sacrifices can no longer be borne. Since 7 August 1942, the day the Marines landed, the Japanese have lost 65 naval vessels and over 800 aircraft, in addition to the human losses. Emperor Hirohito approves the decision. The evacuation is to be carried out gradually, and the task is entrusted to the destroyers of the 'Tokyo Night Express' under the brilliant Rear-Admiral Tanaka. Meanwhile, General Vandegrift's Marines on the island have been almost completely replaced by fresh forces – the 2nd Marine Division, the Americal Division and the 25th Infantry of the army, forming the XIV Corps under the command of General Patch. In

readiness for the final offensive activity is concentrated on the Gifu strongpoint, on Mount Austen, still obstinately defended by 500 Japanese.

New Guinea After a heavy artillery preparation, Urbana Force attacks Buna Mission, but makes little progress. In the evening Japanese soldiers are seen leaving the Mission by swimming. At Giropa Point a Japanese unit is surrounded, while an Australian battalion with armoured support moves east from Giropa Point mopping up the Japanese along the coast as far as the Simemi river.

2 January

Eastern Front Von Kleist realizes that if the Russians break through the German lines on the Stalingrad front they will be well placed to press on towards Rostov (at the mouth of the Don), so cutting off Army Group A in the Caucasus from the rest of the Wehrmacht. In view also of the offensive launched against that Army Group by the Russian Trans-Caucasus Front armies (44th, 58th, 9th and 37th) on the river Terek line, von Kleist orders his 1st Armoured Army to withdraw slowly northwards, so that they can attack the left flank of the Russian armies should they advance towards Rostov, and so prevent the complete isolation of Army Group A in the Caucasus.

Guadalcanal The American 132nd Infantry, with the usual artillery support, once more attacks the Gifu strongpoint on Mount Austen. The Americans manage to take Hill 27, just south of the strongpoint, and drive off repeated strong Japanese counter-attacks. The Americans also seize positions north and east of the strongpoint, but their lines are not continuous. General Patch takes over command of the XIV Corps (made up as described under 1 January).

New Guinea At last, with a final combined attack, Australian and American troops succeed in seizing Buna Mission, and all organized resistance by the Japanese ceases there in the afternoon. The Japanese

colonel commanding the garrison and some others of his officers commit harakiri rather than bear the disgrace of surrender. The Allies move on towards Giropa Point, east of which the enemy has been mopped up. The Japanese despatch units from Giruwa to help their comrades escaping from Buna. On this bridgehead alone the Japanese have lost at least 1,400 dead since the fighting began; Australian and American casualties amount to 2,800 dead, wounded and missing. The artillery employed at Buna is gradually transferred to the Sanananda front, where operations are getting bogged down. It should be remembered that during this period both the Allies and the Japanese have concentrated the greater part of their forces and the majority of their air and naval forces in the southern Pacific sector, at Guadalcanal.

3 January

Eastern Front While four Russian army groups (those of Bryansk and Voronezh, the south-western and the southern) prepare to unleash a powerful offensive, the agony of von Paulus' forces continues at Stalingrad.

In the Caucasus von Kleist contains the Russian thrust by withdrawing to a series of defensive lines. In this sector the Russians recapture Mozdok (held by the Germans since 27 August 1942) and Malgobek. Von Kleist stands between the rivers Terek and Kuma. The Don Army Group of von Manstein fights bravely to keep the road to Rostov open for the withdrawal of the 1st Armoured Army and all other units of the Army Group A.

New Guinea Mopping-up operations in the Buna area and east of Giropa Point.

4 January

Eastern Front The destruction of the German forces at Stalingrad continues. The Don Army Group continues its rearguard action, threatened always by a possible enemy breakthrough in the direction of Rostov.

Guadalcanal Although the headquarters of the Japanese 17th Army has received the order to evacuate Guadalcanal gradually, transferring the remaining forces to the island of New Georgia, the Japanese soldiers continue to fight valiantly, despite the increasing shortage of rations and ammunition. The Gifu strong-point continues to hold up the American advance on Mount Austen. The Japanese have so far lost 500 men in this sector, the Americans 383 dead and wounded.

New Georgia During the night of 4/5 January a squadron of American cruisers and destroyers under the command of Rear-Admiral Ains-worth subjects the airfield and other military installations at Munda to a massive bombardment.

New Guinea In a surprise attack the Japanese seize an Allied advanced post near Tarakena, which enables them to rescue a part of the remainder of the Buna garrison. Allied commanders discuss a plan to elimi-nate the enemy west of the river Girua.

5 January
Eastern Front Neutral Swiss reports state that the Germans regard the situation on this front as very serious.

In the Caucasus the Russians recapture Nalchik, east of the upper Terek. Von Kleist swiftly moves his troops to the west, leaving large formations as rearguard to slow down the enemy advance. An armoured column of the Russian Stalingrad Front, advancing along the Don, recaptures Chinliansk.

Guadalcanal General Patch orders the relief of the 132nd Infantry Regi-ment on Mount Austen by units of the 25th Division. Meanwhile the Americans are still receiving large re-inforcements and are preparing for a big offensive.

New Guinea Advance elements of the Australian 18th Brigade, with four tanks, reach Soputa. In prepara-tion for an offensive on a vast scale against Sanananda the American 127th Infantry Regiment moves north-west along the coast towards Tarakena.

6 January
South-West Pacific Allied recon-naissance aircraft sight a Japanese convoy carrying reinforcements and supplies for New Guinea. The convoy is repeatedly attacked by US fighters and dive-bombers.

Burma The 14th Indian Division renews the offensive in the Arakan region – an offensive undertaken more for psychological than for stra-tegic reasons. The advance is firmly checked by Japanese dug in at Don-baik and Rathedaung. Skirmishing in this sector goes on for many weeks with no definite outcome.

7 January
Eastern Front Savage bayonet fight-

Night bombardment by Russian multiple rocket-launchers on the Bryansk front.

ing has now been going on in Stalingrad for many days. Every square yard of the ruins is contested. The German defensive perimeter shrinks every day, but it still encloses two runways where the aircraft land with such supplies as can be brought in. The Hoth Armoured Division defends the Rostov corridor against the attacks of the 51st, 2nd and 20th Russian Armies. A Russian vanguard assembles 25 miles from Rostov and just fails to capture von Manstein's headquarters.

Guadalcanal An American infantry regiment leaves the Lunga perimeter and joins in the attack on Mount Austen. A special unit embarks at Kukum for Beaufort Bay to block the path leading inland from Kokumbona, along which the Japanese who will be attacked in the forthcoming American offensive are expected to pass. American forces in the Guadalcanal sector now number 50,000 men, 24,000 of them actually fighting on land, as against 11,000 Japanese.

New Guinea While Australians and Americans concentrate in the Sanananda sector, the Japanese convoy attacked the previous day by American aircraft reaches Lae and lands men and materials.

8 January

Eastern Front The commander of the Russian Don Front, Rokossovsky, sends an ultimatum to von Paulus with terms for a surrender. The German general knows that the fate of the Germans at Stalingrad is sealed. But he dare not disobey the Führer's orders which refuse to consider the possibility of surrender. Meanwhile the Russians re-take Zimovniki, on the railway line from Stalingrad to Novorossiysk, so that the threat of isolation becomes more real for von Kleist's Army Group A in the Caucasus.

China Chiang Kai-shek sends a message to Roosevelt turning down the suggestion that he should launch a big offensive in the coming spring.

Madagascar General Platt passes over responsibility for the whole island, except the area of Diego Suarez which has been made into a very important air and naval base for the British, to General Legentil-homme, High Commissioner for the French possessions in the Indian Ocean, which are loyal to the Free French.

Guadalcanal The US 35th Infantry Regiment is moved secretly to the Mount Austen sector in readiness for the offensive.

New Guinea Units of the American 127th Infantry Regiment take the village of Tarakena, while the 163rd Infantry open the offensive aimed at dislodging the enemy from the Sanananda road. Meanwhile, despite Allied air raids, the enemy land about 4,000 men and materials at Lae.

9 January

Guadalcanal The Americans take up positions on the river Matanikau and in the sector of the Gifu strongpoint in readiness for the next day's great offensive.

New Guinea The Allies try to take a bridgehead over the Konombi river in the Tarakena sector, but are driven back by intense Japanese fire. The convoy that brought reinforcements and supplies to Lae leaves again, still under Allied air attack. Two Japanese transports are sunk and about 80 aircraft destroyed.

☐ Essen is heavily bombed in night raid.

10 January

Eastern Front Since von Paulus has ignored his ultimatum of the 8th, Rokossovsky launches a great new offensive against the perimeter of the German 6th Army and the other German forces surrounded at Stalingrad. The Russian attacks are preceded and accompanied by tremendous artillery and mortar barrages. Although von Paulus knows that the struggle is hopeless, he still fights on. He holds out, not only in obedience to orders, but for strategic reasons. By keeping the greatest possible number of Russian divisions engaged he will relieve pressure on the Don Army Group and von Kle-ist's Army Group A, which is in danger of being trapped in the Caucasus.

Guadalcanal The Americans begin their great offensive to clear all the Japanese from the island. The immediate objectives are the enemy positions known as Sea Horse and Galloping Horse, and above all the Gifu strongpoint. There is intensive air and artillery preparation. The attacking forces make very limited progress in face of immensely strong Japanese resistance.

New Guinea Units of the US 127th Infantry Regiment succeed in establishing a bridgehead over the Konombi, near Tarakena. Other units, from the US 163rd Infantry Regiment, advance in the area of Kano and Musket, where the Japanese have already evacuated some of their positions.

11 January

Eastern Front Siege of Leningrad at last broken. In the northern sector the Russian armies of the Leningrad and Volkhov fronts (the 42nd, 55th, Neva Assault Group, 8th, 2nd Assault, 54th and 67th) succeed in breaking through the German lines and opening a small corridor south of Lake Ladoga, through which supplies can reach the besieged city. At the opposite end of the immense front, in the Caucasus, von Kleist's Army Group A falls back from the line of the rivers Terek and Kuma, and the Russians reoccupy Pyatigorsk, Georgievsk and Mineralnye Vodi.

Fighting continues at Stalingrad.

Guadalcanal The Americans succeed in taking Sea Horse, but not Galloping Horse. The Gifu strongpoint is virtually surrounded, but the volume and accuracy of the defensive fire holds the Americans off. A tactical group of the American 147th Infantry moves towards Vurai, southwest of Kokumbona, to cut the enemy's retreat.

☐ Naples is heavily bombed by Allied aircraft.

12 January

Eastern Front In the northern sector, the Russian Leningrad and Volkhov forces consolidate the corridor opened south of Lake Ladoga. The narrow strip, which will not be widened for another year, is pounded by German artillery so murderously that it becomes known as 'death corridor'.

Guadalcanal Limited American progress against the position called Galloping Horse. Everywhere else the Japanese check the American thrusts, especially in the Gifu area.

Aleutian Islands A small American contingent commanded by General Lloyd E. Jones occupies Kamchitka Island without opposition. During the operation a destroyer runs on the rocks and is lost.

New Guinea Two battalions of the Australian 18th Brigade, with tank support, attack the enemy positions north-west of Gona. Japanese anti-tank guns knock out the Australian tanks, but the infantry press the attack, though with heavy losses. During the night of 12/13 January the Japanese commander orders a withdrawal.

13 January
Eastern Front The Russian 24th, 65th and 21st Armies of the Don Front, commanded by Rokossovsky, advance from the west as far as the river Rossoshka. The 64th Army is advancing from the south, the 66th from the north, while from east of the Volga the German positions are battered by the guns of the 62nd Army. A fifth of the defensive perimeter of the German 6th Army (with a part of the 4th Armoured Army) is now in Russian hands.

Guadalcanal The American offensive is broadened by the 2nd Marine Division's advance westward along the coast from Cruz Point. Further inland the 25th Division tries in vain to break through the Japanese lines on a 5,000-yard front. The Japanese Gifu strongpoint on Mount Austen still holds out heroically against American attacks. It seems that, although the Japanese have already decided to evacuate the island, they want to postpone it to the last possible moment and to inflict all the

THE OX-BOW INCIDENT

Three cowboys accused of stealing cattle are hanged by the enraged inhabitants of a small town in Nevada. After their death they are found to have been completely innocent.

The *Ox-Bow Incident*, William Wellman's masterpiece, was one of the first examples of the 'psychological Western'. The director handled the theme of lynching with great realism and understated drama; he deliberately played down the obvious sensationalism of the plot, favouring instead the use of long, anguished silences and emphasizing the long interval before the execution. Arthur Miller's terse photography contributed to the film's success, as did the outstanding performances of the stars: Henry Fonda, Dana Andrews and Anthony Quinn.

losses they can on the Americans before withdrawal.

New Guinea General Eichelberger takes command of the advanced Australian and American forces on the island.

14 January
Eastern Front In the northern sector fighting goes on south of Lake Ladoga. The Germans are trying to drive the Russians out of the corridor through which the siege of Leningrad has been partially relieved.

In the huge Stalingrad pocket the Russian armies seize Pitomnik airport, the biggest in the German defensive perimeter. Further east the Red Army breaks through the lines of the Hungarian 2nd Army on the Don. The position of von Manstein's and von Kleist's armies grows graver.

Guadalcanal The Americans still have no success with their attacks either along the coast west of the Lunga perimeter or on Mount Austen, where the Gifu strongpoint remains impregnable. The Japanese land 600 men near Cape Esperance, west of Lunga, to protect their retirement when the time for that comes. Aircraft taking off from Henderson Field attack a formation of Japanese destroyers off the island, and damage two of them.

New Guinea Small actions in the Sanananda sector and on the Killerton track. The Japanese begin to retire slowly towards Lae.

□ The history-making Casablanca Conference opens, attended by Roosevelt and Churchill, with their respective Chiefs of Staff. The third of the 'Big Three', Stalin, cannot attend as military operations keep him in Moscow. They discuss the strategy to be followed when one of the critical moments of the war arrives: i.e. when the Germans lose the impetus of their first offensive thrust and begin to show signs of yielding. Also they discuss Allied strategy for the immediate future. Stalin has sent a message giving his opinion. He maintains that there is only one important issue, the opening of a second front in Europe. This is what Stalin has been saying for months, and now he is more insistent than ever. To open a new front in the West would mean that the Germans have to defend themselves on two fronts, and so split up their forces. The Allies agree with Stalin on the need to open a second front in the West. The question is when. Roosevelt and his staff are in favour of carrying out a landing in France within a few months, Churchill argues for a surprise landing in Italy, the 'soft under-belly of Europe', followed by a linking up with the Russian armies in the Balkans to attack Hitler's empire from the south. When Churchill gives his word to the Americans that he is ready to support the American plan for a landing in France (now planned for 1944), Roosevelt agrees to the preparations for the landing in Italy (in Sicily). At the Casablanca Conference it is also agreed that day and night bombing of Germany on a huge scale should be intensified and 'rationalized', with the object of destroying centres of industrial production and cutting communications. The directive is passed for action to Air Marshal Sir Arthur ('Bomber') Harris, head of the British Bomber Command. Finally it is agreed to demand unconditional surrender by Germany, Italy and Japan at the end of the war.

15 January

Eastern Front The battles continue south of Lake Ladoga and in and around Stalingrad where the Germans' situation is desperate. The Russian Voronezh Army goes over to the offensive and reaches a point near Rossosh, on the railway line from Voronezh to Rostov.
Guadalcanal The Americans use loudspeakers to call on the Japanese to surrender, but their repeated calls are ignored. Japanese resistance is as stubborn as ever. The Gifu strongpoint, which has been attacked again by units of the 35th Infantry Regiment, shows no sign of giving way.
New Guinea The Allies prepare a major offensive to drive the Japanese out of the Sanananda area.

16 January

Eastern Front In the Stalingrad sector Rokossovsky's armies continue their furious attempts to wipe out the enemy. More than half the German defensive perimeter has now been captured by the Russians. Advancing from the west, they are only 6 miles from the centre of the city at some points.
Guadalcanal Three American regiments launch a co-ordinated attack westwards to extend the positions beyond Kokumbona as far as the

river Poha, while a combined division of infantry and Marines advances along the coast and the 25th Division attacks inland, to the southwest, so as to turn the enemy's flank. An important position dominating the river Matanikau is captured. Other units begin a manœuvre to surround the Gifu strongpoint on Mount Austen.
New Guinea After the usual air and artillery preparation Australian and American troops open the offensive in the Sanananda sector. The Australian 18th Brigade opens the road to the coast and engages the enemy along a wide coastal strip from Cape Killerton almost to Sanananda village. Americans of the 163rd Infantry advance to cut the road between Sanananda and Soputa and penetrate for over half a mile to the rear of the Japanese positions, finally linking up with the Australian 18th Brigade.
□ During the night of 16/17 January there is a heavy RAF raid on Berlin, the first since 7 November 1941. The British use their new 'target indicators', bombs which mark the targets for the bombers.

17 January

Eastern Front Violent fighting continues south of Lake Ladoga, at Stalingrad, on the Don front (where the Red Army captures Millerovo, thus increasing the threat to the Don Army Group and to Rostov), and in the Caucasus.
The entire southern front sees movement. From Novosil to the Caucasus no fewer than thirteen Russian armies (not counting the seven engaged in the liquidation of Stalingrad) are on the move. The weakest sector is that on the Don, held by the Hungarian 2nd Army (against which the Russians have thrown in the 40th Army and the 2nd Armoured Army), the Italian 8th Army (in danger of encirclement by the Russian 6th Army and 1st Assault Group) and the Rumanian 3rd Army, faced by the 3rd Assault Group and the 5th Armoured Army.
Guadalcanal After four days' fighting the Americans have succeeded in

advancing about three-quarters of a mile beyond Cruz Point. Loudspeakers are again used to invite the Japanese to surrender. The strong point Gifu is heavily shelled by American artillery.
New Guinea The Australians take the village of Sanananda, but the Japanese dig in in new positions to the west and south. The Americans advance slowly towards Giruwa against stubborn Japanese resistance (favoured by the nature of the terrain).
□ London has its first night raid since May 1941.

18 January

Eastern Front Siege of Leningrad finally raised. After seven days intense fighting, the Russians of the Leningrad and Volkhov Fronts consolidate their control of 'death corridor', the strip of ground 10 miles wide south of Lake Ladoga. Leningrad, cut off since the autumn of 1941, can at last receive more supplies, German gunners permitting.
In the Caucasus von Kleist's Army Group A is resisting the powerful pressure by the Russians to avoid being cut off south of the Sea of Azov, while as many divisions as possible are withdrawn across the Rostov corridor, which is still open. The defensive line extends along the rivers Kuban and Manyon and, in the north, along the lower Donetz. The Russians recapture Cherkessk, on the Kuban, and Divnoye along the Manych.
Guadalcanal The Japanese in the Sanananda sector, though they know they will be defeated, hold out to the bitter end. They contest every yard of ground with the Australians both at Sanananda and at Giruwa. The Americans attack a strongly fortified enemy position straddling the Soputa–Sanananda road. Other units advance westwards along the coast, taking a narrow strip just over 300 yards wide.
Burma The 47th Indian Brigade attacks Japanese positions at Donbaik, but without success. The 123rd Brigade is still dug in near Rathedaung, but is threatened by the enemy

from the east, by an offensive thrust in the Kaladan valley.

19 January
Eastern Front The Russian armies re-take Kamensk Shakhtinsky on the northern Donetz, north of Rostov (on the railway line to Voronezh), and Valuiki, a railway junction east of Kharkov. Von Manstein and his Don Army Group perform miraculously against Soviet forces seven times superior in numbers, as does von Weichs with his Army Group B east of Kharkov. Near the Don, west of Pavlovsk, the Hungarian 2nd Army is caught in two pockets by the Russians, and the same happens to the German 2nd Army further north, at Kastornoye.
Guadalcanal The Americans bring up more troops to the Cruz Point sector to try to break the Japanese resistance.
New Guinea General Yamagata leaves the Sanananda front by sea after ordering his troops to retire westwards the next day, filtering through the Allied lines. General Oda and a colonel are killed directing their units' disengagement. Yet the Australians still cannot break down the final Japanese resistance along the coast west of Sanananda and on the outskirts of Giruwa. The

Japanese manning the fortified line along the Soputa–Sanananda road are surrounded in three separate pockets, but still will not surrender to the American 163rd Infantry Regiment.

20 January
Eastern Front Troops of the Southern Front (hitherto called the Stalingrad Front) under General Eremenko capture Proletarskaya, along the Stalingrad–Novorossiysk railway east of the river Manych, and press on from east-south-east towards Rostov. Von Kleist's forces are still fighting a rearguard action in the Caucasus.
Guadalcanal Local activity west and south of the Lunga perimeter. On Mount Austen the Gifu strongpoint begins to show signs of weakening; the Japanese troops manning it have been decimated by the almost daily assaults and air and artillery bombardment.
New Guinea The Australians mop up the coastal area west of Sanananda and the northern part of the Soputa–Sanananda road, from which the Japanese are retreating. The Americans begin the liquidation of the three enemy pockets straddling the road from Soputa to Sananda. An American regiment

advancing to the west comes in sight of Giruwa.
☐ The Luftwaffe makes heavy raids over South-East England, including London. Thirty-nine children killed when a school in Lewisham is hit.
☐ Chile breaks off diplomatic relations with the Tripartite Pact countries.

21 January
Eastern Front In the Caucasus the Russians recapture Voroshilovsk, east of Armavir.
Guadalcanal The Americans get ready for a new offensive, while Japanese resistance continues in all sectors.
New Guinea Americans and Australians join up east of Sanananda. An American column coming from the east penetrates into the village of Giruwa, meeting little Japanese resistance, and joins up with Australian units west of the village.

22 January
Eastern Front A German communiqué admits for the first time that the Russians, attacking from the west, have considerably reduced the defensive perimeter of the 6th Army at Stalingrad. The Russian Voronezh Front, commanded by General Golikov and consisting of three

January 1943: a German tank advances through the smoke of a burning Russian village in the course of a desperate counter-attack north of the city of Stalingrad.

armies, one armoured army and two assault groups, launches the offensive against Voronezh, one of the 'hedgehogs' of the German line. In the extreme south the Russians retake Salsk, on the Stalingrad–Novorossiysk railway line. Salsk has been an important Luftwaffe base and a main German supply centre for the Caucasus. The German hold on Rostov and the entire Caucasus is imperilled.

Guadalcanal At 6.30 a.m. the units of the American XIV Corps open their offensive, with the river Poha as their objective. The attack is supported by artillery and aircraft and by gunfire from cruisers and destroyers. A division formed from infantry and Marines advances on the heights south-east of Kokumbona to assault the Japanese positions. Although short of rations and ammunition, the Japanese show great skill and courage in the defensive battle in the jungle. They halt the Marines on the coast while retiring in good order from some positions inland. At 5.00 p.m. the American 27th Infantry is in possession of the hills south and east of Kokumbona. On Mount Austen the Americans succeed in opening up a gap of about 200 yards in the Gifu strongpoint and, during the following night, repulse a last desperate enemy counter-attack.

New Guinea The Allies have won their first victory over the Japanese on land during the war, putting an end to the long battle for Papua, the south-eastern part of the island. The Australian 18th Brigade mops up the last centres of resistance on the coast west of Sanananda, while the American 163rd Infantry finally clears the Soputa–Sanananda road, mopping up the last defenders. It is estimated that the Japanese have deployed 12,000 to 16,000 men in the campaign and that they have lost 7,000 killed; there are scarcely 350 prisoners, and most of these are Chinese or Koreans attached to the Japanese. Australians and Americans, whose effectives at the beginning of the campaign amounted to something under 30,000, have lost about 8,500 men, including over 3,000 killed.

23 January

North Africa Continuing their westward advance, the British 8th Army enters Tripoli at 5.00 a.m.

Eastern Front The Russians enter Voronezh after hard fighting. German resistance continues inside the town.

The tragedy of the 6th Army at Stalingrad goes on. Rations have by now been reduced to $1\frac{3}{4}$ oz of bread and $1\frac{1}{4}$ pints of vegetable soup per day. After nearly a month on this diet, introduced on 26 December 1942, the physical condition of the defenders is wretched. Supplies dropped by the Luftwaffe are increasingly inadequate; often they are useless – one day they brought five tons of sweets, and on another they actually delivered 200,000 propaganda leaflets.

In the Caucasus, where von Kleist is rapidly withdrawing, the Russians reoccupy Armavir, a railway junction on the Rostov–Baku line.

Guadalcanal The Americans at last make substantial progress, by-passing Kokumbona and encircling the Japanese still east of the river Poha. Kokumbona itself is captured after hard fighting. The Gifu strongpoint on Mount Austen is finally taken by a battalion of the 35th Infantry Regiment.

New Guinea Japanese troops on the coast in the Buna–Gona area and at Sanananda and inland have been eliminated, and MacArthur now prepares the second phase of the offensive to drive the enemy from Lae and from the rest of the island.

An American submarine sinks the Japanese destroyer *Hakaze* off New Ireland.

A Russian armoured car unit, preceded by a motor-cycle patrol, advances in the sector north of Voronezh in readiness for an offensive.

☐ The ten-day-long Casablanca Conference ends. The Allies have agreed on the following: the principle of 'unconditional surrender'; completion of the Tunisian campaign; a landing in Sicily (Operation *Husky*) in July, or if possible in June; an air offensive against European countries under German control; advance in Pacific to recapture the Philippines; offensives in Burma and China.

24 January

Eastern Front Savage fighting continues at Stalingrad and Voronezh. Von Paulus asks Hitler for permission to surrender. The Führer replies 'The 6th Army will hold its positions to the last man and the last round.'

Guadalcanal The US 25th Division advances west of Kokumbona towards the river Poha. The Japanese contest every yard of ground while they prepare to re-embark. A squadron of US aircraft carriers, cruisers and destroyers commanded by Rear-Admirals Ainsworth and Ramsey carries out heavy bombing and shelling of the Vila-Stanmore area, Kolombangara Island, the Solomons.

25 January

Eastern Front The Red Army completes the capture of Voronezh.

North Africa General Giovanni Messe is appointed to take over from Field-Marshal Rommel in overall command of Axis forces in Africa.

Guadalcanal The Americans reach the river Poha, while the Japanese confine themselves to rearguard actions to cover their withdrawal.

New Guinea The American General Horace Fuller takes over operational control of all Allied troops in the Gona and Oro Bay areas. The Australian 7th Division and American 32nd Division are gradually withdrawn and transferred to Port Moresby.

Pipers lead a march through the streets of Tripoli by men of the 51st Highland Division. Behind them is a tall column bearing the Roman wolf, the symbol of Fascism.

26 January
Eastern Front The Soviets reduce the German defensive perimeter at Stalingrad still further. Von Paulus, faithful to his oath of loyalty, resigns himself to the crucifixion of his soldiers and his staff. Berlin radio announces 'Every Stalingrad defender considers his life has ended, but the will to resist remains unbroken.'
The Italian *Tridentina* Alpine Division, engaged by superior forces as it continues to retreat in the great bend of the Don, suffers heavy losses at Nikolayevka.
Guadalcanal Fearing the Japanese may mount a surprise attack against the Lunga perimeter, the Americans withdraw one division from the river Poha front to reinforce the defences of their base. In fact, the Japanese are in no position to launch any attacks.

27 January
□ The US 8th Air Force, based in Britain, carries out its first raid over Germany, bombing warehouses and industrial plant at Wilhelmshaven.
Eastern Front The fighting at Stalingrad goes on.
Part of Army Group A has succeeded in getting back to the Ukraine thanks to von Kleist's tactical skill; but the Russians are already pushing on towards Rostov, and von Kleist has to withdraw the rest of his forces in the Kuban and prepare to hold a bridgehead in the Novorossiysk area.
North Africa The British 8th Army is on the frontier between Libya and Tunisia.

28 January
Eastern Front The Russian 38th Army takes Kastornoye, west of Voronezh.
Guadalcanal The American advance towards Cape Esperance continues against weak Japanese resistance.
New Guinea The Japanese make a last effort to reach Port Moresby across the inland mountains, attacking the Australian garrison at Wau. Brave defence gives the Allied commander time to bring up reinforcements by air.
□ Germany. A new decree announces the mobilization of men between the ages of 16 and 65 and women aged 17 to 45 for war work.

29 January
Eastern Front The Russian 37th Army in the Kuban takes Kropotkin, a railway junction on the Rostov–Baku line.

29–30 January
Solomon Islands Naval and air battle of Rennell Island. A squadron of American cruisers and destroyers escorting a convoy making for Guadalcanal is attacked by Japanese aircraft. On the 30th the American ships are again attacked by the Japanese. Large formations of American aircraft take off from Guadalcanal and from carriers to engage the enemy. The Americans come off worst in this engagement, the heavy cruiser *Chicago* is sunk by an aerial torpedo, and a destroyer is damaged.

30 January
Eastern Front In the Kuban the Russians recapture Tikhoretsk, northwest of Kropotkin and south-east of Rostov, thus cutting off von Kleist's Army Group A from their main line of withdrawal from Novorossiysk. Troops of the Russian Trans-Caucasus Front, advancing from the south in the same area, retake the Maykop oilfields. Von Manstein's Don Army Group is forced to retire northwards and so can no longer give any support to Army Group A.
Guadalcanal The US 147th Infantry, continuing their advance towards Cape Esperance, reach the mouth of the river Bonegi, but are halted there by the ferocity of the Japanese fire.
New Guinea The defenders of Wau, reinforced by the Australian 18th Brigade, beat off the Japanese attacks and put the Japanese to flight.

A dramatic scene during the terrible retreat of the Italian Army in Russia; the *Tridentina* Division, together with troops picked up from other scattered units, trudges back to Nikolayevka.

☐ Admiral Karl Doenitz appointed Commander-in-Chief of German navy, replacing Admiral Raeder.

☐ RAF makes first daylight raids on Berlin, timed to coincide with broadcasts by Goering and Goebbels. Goering says: 'A thousand years hence every German will speak with awe of Stalingrad and remember that it was there that Germany put the seal on her victory.'

Saturation attack on Hamburg by RAF bombers.

☐ Sicily. Messina heavily bombed by US aircraft.

☐ France. The *Milice* (French Militia) is formed, a political police force intended for use against the members of the Resistance. Its Commander in Chief is Joseph Darnand, a supporter of Pétain and a fervent collaborationist.

31 January

Eastern Front The Russians have now reduced the defenders of Stalingrad to two pockets crowded with starving, desperate men. Hitler appoints von Paulus field-marshal, but this very day the newly promoted commander is forced to seek surrender terms. Hitler is furious that von Paulus should prefer surrender to suicide. Flying into a rage, he swears that he will not create any more field-marshals. Two days later the last nucleus of resistance in Stalingrad, made up of men of the XI Corps commanded by General Strecker in the Alexandrovka quarter, lays down its arms. Of the 284,000 men surrounded at Stalingrad approximately 160,000 have died in action and about 34,000 have been evacuated by air. The Luftwaffe has lost about 500 transport aircraft. The survivors, numbering little more than 90,000, are sent to Siberia on foot, and many of them die of starvation and exhaustion during that terrible march. Much later in the year, on 7 November, Stalin announces that 146,300 bodies have been found and buried.

Stalingrad is the first terrible check to the hitherto invincible Wehrmacht, a disaster that signalizes a military and psychological turning-point in the war.

Guadalcanal US 147th Infantry again tries to cross the river Bonegi, but is held up by enemy fire. One battalion does manage to cross the river further upstream about a mile and a half from Tassafaronga Point. The Americans are winning the battle for Guadalcanal, but they do not succeed in upsetting the timetable that the Japanese have laid down for the withdrawal and re-embarkation operations.

☐ Sicily. Heavy Allied air raids on the island, particularly against Catania, Trapani and Augusta.

1 February

Eastern Front The Russians follow up the offensive opened on 12 January by the Bryansk, Voronezh, south-western and southern armies against Army Group B (von Weichs) and the Don Army Group (von Manstein). The Russian 3rd Armoured Army takes Svatovo, south-east of Kharkov, cutting the railway joining this city with the Don basin.

Guadalcanal Yet another American attempt to cross the mouth of the river Bonegi is repulsed by the Japanese. A battalion of the 132nd Infantry lands at Verahue, in the rear of the Japanese in the Cape Esperance area. During the night of 1/2 February the Japanese start to re-embark what remains of their 17th Army at Cape Esperance, giving the task to 20 destroyers. During the day they have been sighted and attacked by aircraft from Henderson Field and by motor torpedo boats. One Japanese destroyer hits a mine and is blown up, and an American destroyer is sunk by Japanese dive-bombers.

Burma The 55th Indian Brigade, which has replaced the 47th, attacks the Japanese positions at Donbaik, but without success. Japanese anti-tank guns knock out some tanks supporting the action.

FRANK SINATRA

The main attractions at Paramount's traditional New Year's Day concert were the singer Peggy Lee and Benny Goodman, the king of swing, and his sextet. But the surprise hit of the occasion was a young singer who had already appeared with the Harry James and Tommy Dorsey orchestras but who was hardly known yet as a soloist – Frank Sinatra. Although he may have lacked theoretical knowledge, Sinatra was blessed with an innate musical 'ear' and a keen sense of rhythm, impressing audiences with his originality of interpretation which combined the techniques of the Italian *bel canto* singer, the crooner and the great jazz instrumentalists.

The New Year's Day concert heralded the first of many golden years for Sinatra. An eight-week job with Paramount, radio programmes, record hits, a spectacularly successful tour and a contract with RKO for his first film, *Higher and Higher* signalled the rise of a new star.

The blue eyes and the warm, sensuously romantic voice of the singer sent his audiences of young girls wild, as the phenomenon of *Swoonatra* swept the country. *Time* magazine noted that not since the days of Rudolph Valentino had American women so publicly expressed their love for an artist.

Stalingrad: a jubilant Russian soldier waves the red flag over the ruins of a building in the shattered city centre.

New Guinea Small American detachments advance west along the north coast towards the mouth of the river Kumusi.

2 February

Eastern Front With the surrender of the XI Corps, all German resistance at Stalingrad is at an end. Kharkov, Rostov and Kursk are the next objectives that the Red Army plans to reach before the spring thaw holds up operations.

Guadalcanal The Americans succeed in forcing the passage of the river Bonegi at its mouth, and join up with the battalion that crossed the river further upstream on 31 January.

Mediterranean The British submarine *Turbulent* sinks the German tanker *Utilitas* off Palermo, with 5,000 tons of fuel, the entire reserve fuel for the Italian naval squadron in Sicily.

3 February

Eastern Front The Russian troops advancing on Rostov take Kushchevskaya. Further north they seize Kupyansk, on the river Oskol, southeast of Kharkov.

A special communiqué from Hitler's GHQ announces the 'end of the battle of Stalingrad'. German radio announces that all theatres, cinemas, etc., will be closed from 4–6 February which will be a period of national mourning for the 'Stalingrad disaster'.

Guadalcanal The US 147th Infantry establish a line running inland south from Tassafaronga Point. Patrols of the 132nd Infantry get as far as Kamimbo Bay, near Cape Esperance.

New Guinea Australian troops with strong artillery support drive off the Japanese in the Wau sector in the direction of Mubo.

Burma In the Arakan area the 123rd Indian Brigade attacks Rathedaung but is easily repulsed by the Japanese.

4 February

Eastern Front Russian armoured columns make relentless progress to-

wards Rostov, Kharkov and Kursk. Assault troops are landed in a combined operation on the Black Sea coast in the Novorossiysk area, where they are engaged in hard fighting with units of von Kleist's Army Group A. These units are now completely isolated within a fortified line (the 'blue line') in the area between Novorossiysk and Krasnodar, between the Black Sea and the Sea of Azov.

Guadalcanal The US 147th Infantry advance in the Tassafaronga area towards the river Umasani, slowed down by the Japanese rearguards. The usual "Tokyo Night Express', consisting of 22 Japanese destroyers, is spotted and bombed by aircraft from Henderson Field, and four destroyers are damaged. However, during the night the warships take off another considerable proportion of the Japanese troops on Guadalcanal.

New Guinea The Japanese continue to retreat in the Wau area, harassed all the time by Allied aircraft. The first Allied sections to reach Mubo are decimated by the Japanese.

☐ Concentrated air attack on Turin.

☐ A conference of army chiefs in New Delhi, attended by Field-Marshal Wavell, Field-Marshal Sir John Dill and General Stilwell, with the British Generals Arnold and Somervell, comes to an end. Decisions are taken to reoccupy Burma and then to attack the Japanese forces in China. The plan is to be submitted to Chiang Kai-shek.

5 February

Eastern Front Stary Oskol, on the river Oskol south-east of Voronezh and north-west of Kharkov, is reached by units of the Russian 13th Army and the 3rd Tank Army, after a converging manœuvre, Izyum, south-east of Kharkov, also falls to the Russians.

6 February

Eastern Front In the Kuban the Russians take Yeysk on the Sea of Azov, cutting the last links that von Kleist's remaining troops in the Kuban had with the rest of the German army.

These troops are now concentrated in the triangle Yeysk–Novorossiysk–Krasnodar. At the mouth of the Don a Russian advance column is already only five miles from Rostov. The Kharkov 'hedgehog' (von Weichs' Army Group B) holds firm, but is already by-passed by the Russians both north and south. To the north the Red Army is near Belgorod, to the south it takes Lisichansk, on the Donetz.

Guadalcanal The 161st Regiment of the US 25th Division goes ahead of the 147th Regiment in pursuit of the enemy and reaches the river Umasani. The Americans receive new reinforcements from Fiji, while the Japanese await a new 'Tokyo Night Express' convoy to complete the re-embarkation of the forces.

New Guinea Japanese aircraft raid Wau airfield, but they come too late, for the airborne Australian reinforcements arrived some time before. Anti-aircraft batteries and fighters shoot down 24 of the raiders.

7 February

Eastern Front Not even the heroic defence put up by Manstein and Weichs can halt the Russian thrust. The Russians take Azov, on the Sea of Azov, and so move nearer to Rostov. In the Ukraine they take Kramatorsk, north of Donetsk, and cut the main road linking Kursk with Orel.

Guadalcanal The US 161st Infantry cross the river Umasani and advance towards the north-west, to Bunina Point. Other American units move from Titi and reach Marovovo. Aircraft from Henderston Field attack and damage two of the eighteen destroyers making up the new 'Tokyo Night Express', in which the rest of the Japanese contingent is leaving the island after six months of bitter struggle.

☐ Generalissimo Chiang Kai-shek, in a message to President Roosevelt, agrees to the employment of his forces in the campaign for the re-conquest of Burma, but asks for a big increase in American aid.

8 February

Eastern Front The Russian armoured

One of the massive raids by Allied bombers over Germany.

about 1,000 sailors and marines (of the 20,000 who made up the force) have been successfully evacuated to Buin and Rabaul. The Japanese have lost more than 9,000 killed, the Americans 2,000 out of a combatant force of 23,000 men (in fact, allowing for the system of relieving troops, more than 60,000 have fought in the campaign). At sea and in the air, losses have been about equal. Now the Americans are masters of what is for practical purposes a huge, unsinkable aircraft carrier for the protection of Australia, the recapture of the Solomons and the following thrust north across the Pacific. Well satisfied, General Patch is at last able to send the following message to Admiral Halsey: 'Total and complete defeat of Japanese forces on Guadalcanal effected 16.25 today ... Am happy to report this kind of compliance with your orders ..."Tokyo Express" no longer has terminus on Guadalcanal.' The sufferings have been tremendous but they have brought a priceless reward.

☐ In a letter to Stalin, Churchill, with characteristic optimism, foresees the end of the campaign in Africa by April, the conquest of the Italian peninsula by July and the landing in France not later than August (1943, that is).

10 February
Eastern Front North of Rostov Russian forces reach the Rostov-Novocherkassk railway line. Further north, two armoured columns which have been converging on Kharkov take Chukuyev and Volchansk.
New Guinea While other forces are assembled for a big new offensive aimed at the complete expulsion of the Japanese from the island, small American units reach the mouth of the river Kumusi and establish a fortified position there.

11 February
Eastern Front South of Kharkov the Germans have to abandon Lozovaya, a major railway junction.
☐ The RAF makes a heavy concentrated night attack on Wilhelmshaven.

armies, which for some time have had part of the German 2nd Army trapped in a pocket, spread out westwards and take Kursk, one of the strongpoints of the German winter line. This loss still further endangers the whole German position in South Russia.
Guadalcanal Japanese rearguards still contrive to slow down the American advance towards Tenaro and Cape Esperance.
Burma The 77th Indian Brigade (nicknamed the 'Chindits'), under command of Major-General Orde Charles Wingate, moves out from Imphal (India) and penetrates into the Arakan region of Burma. The brigade is sub-divided into two groups, a southern group which has to cross the river Chindwin first in order to distract Japanese attention from the second, northern, group, commanded by Wingate himself. The object of this special unit is to carry out guerrilla activities behind the enemy lines, making surprise attacks and damaging the communications system as much as possible. The Chindits' first objective is the railway, vital to the enemy, that links Mandalay with Myitkyina. It could be called an extended, large-scale patrol action, for once they have crossed the Irrawaddy the Chindits find themselves in increasing difficulties with Japanese forces and are ordered to return to India.

9 February
Eastern Front Russian armoured columns take Belgorod, north of Kharkov on the railway line to Kursk.
Guadalcanal All organized resistance by the Japanese on the island ceases at 4.25 p.m. when the US 161st and 132nd infantry, moving from the east and south-west, link up in the village of Tenaro. Most of the survivors of the campaign, about 11,000 men of the Japanese 17th Army and

Top: airborne supplies arrive for besieged Stalingrad.

12 February

Eastern Front Krasnodar, one of the three points of the triangle held by the remains of Army Group A (von Kleist) in the Kuban, is taken by the Russian Trans-Caucasus Front, which pushes on towards Novorossiysk. On the Don front the Russians cut the railway leading west from Rostov towards Krasnoarmeysk, narrowing that corridor still free for the German withdrawal. They also take Shakhty, west of the Donetz, on the railway between Rostov and Voronezh.

North Africa The British 8th Army spreads out into Tunisia.

South-West Pacific Allied headquarters issues directives for the 'capture and occupation of the area

New Britain–New Guinea–New Ireland'. Code-name for the Operation is *Elkton*.

14 February

Eastern Front The Russian forces occupy Rostov. This has been a vital position for the Germans through which they have been able to evacuate a part of Army Group A from the Caucasus. The great industrial city of Voroshilovgrad also falls to the Red Army, whose advance thrusts have already by-passed it and are moving towards Stalino. The Germans undertake a re-grouping of their forces: the remains of the Don Army Group and Army Group B are combined to form – or actually to re-form – Army Group South (*Heeresgruppe*

'LE CORBEAU'

In this film, a series of cruel and vulgar anonymous letters, signed 'le corbeau' ('the crow'), disturbs the tranquil existence of a provincial French town until one of the victims, Dr. Germain, finally manages to discover who is responsible.

Directed by Henri Clouzot, *Le Corbeau* was one of the first examples in France of the 'film noir'. The pessimistic and sceptical depiction of French provincial life immediately provoked bitter reactions from the clandestine press, linked with the Resistance movement, which accused the director of collaboration. The film was produced by Continental, a subsidiary of UFA, which had been set up specifically to control French wartime cinema production.

Apart from its moral implications, *Le Corbeau* was a well made film with plenty of atmosphere, credible characters and excellent photography.

US marines on a mopping up operation in the Guadalcanal jungle. Airborne supplies arrive for besieged Stalingrad.

Sud), under the command on von Manstein. The 2nd Army, or that part of it not cut off in the pocket north-west of Voronezh, is transferred to Army Group Centre. Berlin admits the evacuation of Rostov and Voroshilovgrad according to plan.

Tunisia 4.00 a.m.: General Jürgen von Arnim's forces launch a violent attack on Allied troops of the 1st Army, which are moving into Tunisia from the west. The plan of attack is Rommel's: it provides for a break through the Allied line in the direction of Kasserine and Tebéssa, followed if successful by an advance on Bône and Constantine. General

Anderson, commanding the Allied army, has at his disposal the British V Corps in the north, the French XIX Corps in the centre and the American II Corps in the south. The Axis forces consist of a part of von Arnim's 5th Army and, in the south, a part of Rommel's *Afrikakorps*.

Von Arnim's action is successful. Axis forces take Sidi Bou Zid and cut off the Americans holding Djebel Lessouda to the north and Djebel Ksaira to the south.

☐ Italy. More than 100 RAF four-engined bombers attack Milan. This is the first of a long series of raids.

15 February

Tunisia Units of the *Afrikakorps* attack in the southern sector of the line and takes Gafsa. An American counter-attack by the US 1st Armoured Division in the Sidi Bou Zid sector is repulsed, but during the night the Americans manage to withdraw from Djebel Lessouda unharmed.

16 February

Eastern Front After five days of bitter fighting, the Russians enter the suburbs of Kharkov, another crucial strongpoint in the Wehrmacht's winter line. The Germans fall back towards Poltava.

Tunisia Axis forces push on towards Fériana and Sbeïtla, south-west and north-east of Kasserine.

Montgomery's 8th Army arrives at Medenine, a few miles south of Mareth, where Rommel is established on the so-called 'Mareth Line'. The line was built by the French between 1934 and 1939, stretching from Djebel Dahar to the sea near Mareth itself, as a defence against a possible Italian attack from Tripolitania. The Mareth defensive line, the 'Desert Maginot' as it is rather pretentiously called, actually consists only of a few dozen pillboxes in the coastal area and some strong fortified positions in the mountainous zone.

Guadalcanal Part of the American 43rd Assault Division is transferred to Guadalcanal as part of the con-

centration of forces for Operation *Cleanslate*, the invasion of the Russell Islands in the Solomons.

South-West Pacific On the initiative of the Commander-in-Chief of the South-West Pacific Area, the US 6th Army is created under the command of Lieutenant-General Walter Krueger. It consists of the I Corps (General Eichelberger), the 2nd Special Engineers Brigade and the 503rd Parachute Infantry Regiment. Attached to this formation of the army is the 1st Division of the US Marines.

Aleutian Islands Japanese aircraft attack Amchitka Island, where the Americans have built a runway for their fighters.

17 February

Eastern Front The inexorable Russian advance continues. The Red Army captures Slavyansk, north of Kramatorsk. The OKW can now foresee the collapse of the whole southern front and issues directives

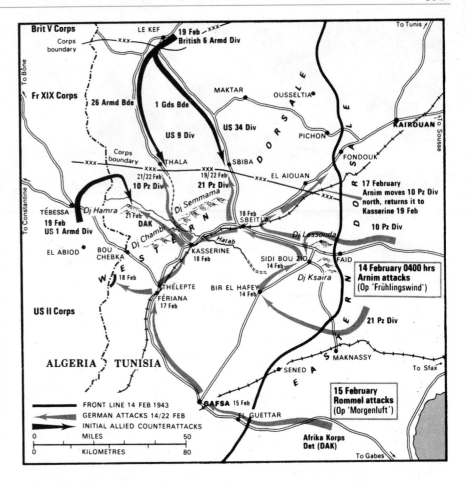

The battle of Kasserine, 14-25 February, a short-lived success for Rommel, in an attempt to relieve Allied pressure on Tunisia.

for the launching of a vigorous counter-offensive.

Tunisia The *Afrikakorps* advance reaches Fériana and goes on towards Kasserine.

Burma The 55th Indian Brigade on the Arakan front attacks Japanese positions at Donbaik, but without success.

18 February

Tunisia Von Arnim enters Sbeïtla and makes for Kasserine.

Guadalcanal Still more forces are brought into the island in readiness for the invasion of the Russell Islands.

A group of American officers sent to reconnoitre the Russells returns with the information that they have already been evacuated by the Japanese.

Aleutian Islands Two cruisers and four destroyers commanded by Rear-Admiral McMorris shell Japanese installations on Attu Island.

Burma The 77th Indian Brigade (the 'Chindits') crosses the Chindwin but without encountering the Japanese and cut the railway line between Mandalay and Myitkyina.

19 February

Eastern Front Russian armies advance south and south-west of Kharkov. The road and railway between Kharkov and Kursk have been entirely cleared of the enemy.

Tunisia Rommel sends his 21st Armoured Division northwards towards Le Kef, occupied by the British 6th Armoured Division. The final objective is still Tebéssa.

20–21 February

Eastern Front In the region south and south-west of Kharkov the Russians re-take Pavlograd and Krasnograd. They continue to close in on Orel from the east, south and southwest, repulsing fierce German counter-attacks.

Tunisia The Axis forces are regrouped, and General Messe takes command of the Italian 1st Army.

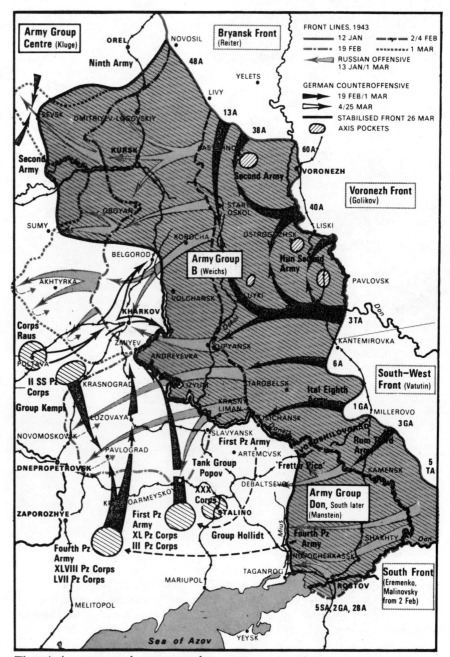

The Axis armoured army under Rommel ceases to exist though Rommel stays in command in Africa for a few weeks more.

☐ The 25th anniversary of the creation of the Red Army is celebrated throughout Britain and the Empire by demonstrations, public meetings and military parades during the weekend. George VI sends a personal message to President Kalinin. A Sword of Honour is to be presented to the city of Stalingrad.

21 February

Eastern Front Von Manstein's Army

The massive Russian advance towards Kharkov between 12 January and the end of March 1943.

The end of a Russian T-34 tank and its crew.

Group South launches a counter-offensive against the left flank of the Russian South-West Army Front (General Vatutin) and against the Voronezh Front under General Golikov. The German XXX Corps advances towards Krasnoarmeyskoye from the area of Stalino. The 1st Armoured Army, with the XL and III Armoured Corps, make for Andreyevka and Izyum; the 4th Armoured Army, with the XLVIII and LVII Armoured Corps, attacks towards Pavlograd and Lozovaya. From the north the SS II Armoured Corps and the Kempf Operational Group converge on Pavlograd, while the Raus Armoured Corps advances from Poltava eastwards and north-eastwards, towards Kharkov and Belgorod.

Tunisia German 10th Armoured Division advances in direction of Thala, about 40 miles north-west of Tebéssa. At the same time, east of Tebéssa, the American 1st Armoured Division repulses a diversionary attack by the *Afrikakorps*.
Solomon Islands The American 43rd Division occupies Banika and Pavuvu Islands in the Russells with no opposition from the Japanese, who have already left. By the end of the month 9,000 men are transferred there from Guadalcanal.

22 February
Eastern Front While the German counter-offensive continues in the south, the Russians open a new offensive in the Orel–Bryansk area and increase their pressure on Rzhev, in the central sector of the front.
Tunisia Rommel breaks off the attacks on Sbiba (21st Armoured Division) and Thala (10th Armoured Division) when reinforcements sent by General Alexander begin to arrive from the British 6th Armoured Division.

23 February
Eastern Front The Russian forces recapture Sumy, in the Ukraine, north-west of Kharkov and south-west of Kursk. Heavy fighting for Orel takes place in violent snow storms. Further south, however, the German counter-offensive makes progress, while in the Caucasus units of Army Group A under von Kleist hold a small bridgehead near Novorossiysk and contain the pressure of the Russian Black Sea Army Group and the northern group of the Trans-Caucasus Front.

24 February
Eastern Front Violent armoured engagements continue in the sector of the German Army Group South and in the Orel area, defended by von Kluge's Army Group Centre.
☐ A declaration by the Führer is read on German radio: 'We shall break and smash the might of the Jewish world coalition, and mankind struggling for its freedom will win the final victory in this struggle.' Following the Stalingrad collapse, German propaganda against the Bolshevik

and Jewish menace has been at fever pitch, urging the Germans to renewed efforts and preparing them for greater hardships.

25 February

Pacific The South-West Pacific and South Pacific headquarters draft the plans for Operation *Reno*, the advance to the Philippines.

Tunisia The battle of Kasserine ends with the city's occupation by the Allies. But the Axis attack has caused 10,000 casualties among the Allies, more than half of them American, against 2,000 Axis dead.

☐ The RAF begin a new, 'round-the-clock' air offensive over Europe. Soon the Allies divide their tasks: the British carry out night raids while the Americans undertake daylight raids. Nuremberg, in Bavaria, heavily bombed at night.

26 February

Burma The 'nuisance raids' of the Chindits, under General Wingate, continue. Ships of the Indian navy sink a lighter loaded with Japanese soldiers and damage another north of the mouth of the river Ramree.

27 February

Eastern Front The Donetz Basin continues to see some of the fiercest fighting of the war. The counter-attacks by the Germans of Army Group South (von Manstein) win a major success with the recapture of Lozovaya. The Germans are also threatening Kramatorsk. The object of von Manstein's counter-offensive is to improve as much as possible the lines held by the Wehrmacht on the Donetz before the spring thaw.

New Guinea As part of the arrangements for the relief and reinforcement of the Allied forces in preparation for the final attack to drive the Japanese out of the island, the American 162nd Regiment of the 41st Division lands at Milne Bay.

☐ It is announced by Bomber Command that Allied air forces have made 2,000 sorties in the last 48 hours.

Soldiers of the German 6th Army captured at Stalingrad, wearing any clothing they can get, start on the long march to prison camp.

German unit advancing across the snow during a counter-attack in the Lake Ilmen area near Novgorod.

THE PARICUTÍN VOLCANO

On the morning of 20 February, Dionisio Pulido, a farmer from Paricutín, a Mexican village in Michoacán, was peacefully ploughing his cornfield when a huge column of smoke suddenly erupted from a furrow, throwing up ashes and stones. The terrified farmer fled headlong from the scene.

By the following morning a hill about 25 feet high had already formed; a week later it measured 250 feet and by the end of the year 1,500 feet in height. In the course of its growth it completely buried the village of Paricutín and partially submerged the town of Parangaricutiro.

28 February

Eastern Front The struggle rages in the Orel–Bryansk area, and further south German armour re-takes Kramatorsk. The beginnings of the spring thaw hold up Russian operations against von Kleist's bridgehead in the Kuban and on the line of the river Mius north of Taganrog.

On the Soviet western front Timoshenko's armies are heavily engaged in the Demyansk sector.

1 March

Eastern Front Timoshenko's forces re-take the towns of Demyansk, Lychkovo and Zaluchie, west of the Valdai Hills and south-east of Staraya Russa.

Burma The construction of the Burma Road, the new route by which Allied supplies are to reach China, is completed. It runs from Ledo in India into Burma.

The Japanese re-group their forces to trap and eliminate the Indian 77th Chindit Brigade. The Chindits continue to move east towards the Irrawaddy, skirmishing here and there with small Japanese garrisons.

Pacific An American B-24 spots a Japanese convoy on its way from Rabaul to the Gulf of Huon in New Guinea.

□ The Reich capital has its heaviest raids so far, which cause considerable damage and loss of life.

2 March

Eastern Front Army Group Centre (von Kluge) evacuates Rzhev.

3 March

Eastern Front The Russians take Rzhev after several days of bitter fighting. They also take Lgov and Dmitriev-Logovskiy on the Kharkov-Bryansk railway. The 1st Armoured Army of von Manstein's Army Group South manages to reach the Donetz and re-takes Slavyansk and Lisichansk.

Burma The Chindits of General Orde Wingate's 77th Indian Brigade cut the Mandalay–Myitkyina railway at another point. Wingate's column crosses the river Mu and, skirting the village of Tongmauw, tackle the Mingin Mountains, east of which the railway runs and the river Irrawaddy flows.

□ Heavy RAF night raid on Hamburg.

□ London. 173 people killed in a Tube shelter when entering after an alert had sounded. Deaths are caused by suffocation as hundreds stumble on the steep steps. No bombs fall in the vicinity.

4 March

Eastern Front The Russians take Sevsk, south of Bryansk and west of Kursk.

5 March

Eastern Front In the central-northern sector of the front the Russians attack towards Staraya Russa. German armour of von Manstein's Army Group South advances in the face of strong resistance in the direction of Kharkov and Belgorod.

In a speech at Kiev the Nazi Commissioner for the Ukraine, Erich Koch, says: 'We belong to the superior race, and we must govern with firmness and justice ... I shall exploit these lands to the absolute limit. I have not come here to make people happy ... The population will have to work, and work, and go on working ... We are a superior race, and we must remember that, on the racial and biological plane, the least of the German workers is worth more than any one of the population of these lands.'

□ A heavy and concentrated raid on Essen. In 40 minutes 150 4,000 lb bombs are dropped. 442 planes take part in the attack. This

THE BATTLE OF THE BISMARCK SEA

3–5 March

Eight Japanese transports making for Lae and Salamaua, in New Guinea, are intercepted by American aircraft. The transports carry the Japanese 51st Division and a cargo of fuel and spare parts for aircraft. They have an escort of eight destroyers commanded by Rear-Admiral Masatomi Kimura. The Japanese commander is relying on an 'air umbrella' from the Japanese air force based in New Guinea. But MacArthur's headquarters orders immediate raids on the Japanese airfields in New Guinea, paralysing all action by enemy aircraft.

On the morning of the 3rd 137 American aircraft, Flying Fortresses and Liberators, supported by American and Australian fighters, attack the enemy convoy and score direct hits both on the transports and the escort vessels. The attacks are successfully repeated next day, while during the night five American motor torpedo boats from a secret base on the north coast of New Guinea intercept the remains of the Japanese squadron, by now about 60 miles from Salamaua. Next day the aerial hammering is renewed. The outcome is disastrous for the Japanese. All the transports and four of the destroyers are sunk, and the other four destroyers, with the remaining infantry on board, are seriously damaged. At least 3,500 men have lost their lives, and the precious cargoes for Lae and Salamaua have been destroyed. The Japanese have also lost ten fighters. For MacArthur it is an important tactical success. He has deprived the enemy of reinforcements and supplies essential to them if they are to hold the next Allied offensive. The Japanese High Command decides that all future supplies for the Lae and Salamaua garrisons must be carried by submarine.

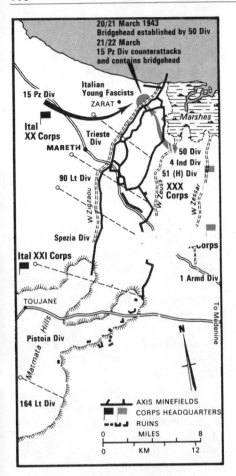

20/21 March 1943
Bridgehead established by 50 Div
21/22 March
15 Pz Div counterattacks
and contains bridgehead

Italian
Young Fascists
ZARAT
15 Pz Div

Ital
XX Corps
MARETH
Trieste
Div

Marshes

90 Lt Div

50 Div
4 Ind Div
51 (H) Div
XXX
Corps

Spezia Div

Ital XXI Corps

1 Armd Div

TOUJANE

Pistoia Div

164 Lt Div

AXIS MINEFIELDS
CORPS HEADQUARTERS
RUINS

MILES
0   8
0   12
KM

The Allied attempt to establish a bridgehead across the German defensive positions on the Mareth line 20–22 March 1943.

is the first full-scale use of 'Oboe' navigational radar equipment.

6 March

Tunisia 9.00 a.m.: Rommel's *Afrikakorps* attacks the 8th Army east of the Mareth Line. Following the battle of Kasserine, Rommel realizes that efforts to relieve the pressure in the west are useless. He makes a sudden about-turn and prepares to face the inevitable offensive by the British 8th Army, which is getting ready to assault the Mareth Line. Advance elements of the Allied troops are established round Medenine, while the main body is safely behind minefields and anti-tank defences.

12.00 midday, the Axis forces fall back before the fire of the British anti-tank guns.

Eastern Front The Russians retake Gzhatsk (which is now renamed Gagarin), on the railway line from Moscow to Smolensk.

Pacific Japanese aircraft bomb the Russell Islands, which the Americans occupied on 21 February.

Three American cruisers and seven destroyers, under the command of Rear-Admiral A. S. Merrill, shell Vila and Munda, important Japanese bases in the Solomons. Attacked by inferior enemy forces, they sink two destroyers.

8 March

Eastern Front In the central sector the Russians retake Sychevka, north of Vyazma, and bring pressure to bear on von Kluge's forces towards Smolensk.

China Japanese forces cross the Yangtze between Yichang and Yoyang. This is one of the many 'rice offensives' which are carried out in the course of the year, raids aimed at securing food supplies which are as essential to the occupying troops as they are to Chiang Kai-shek's army.

9 March

Eastern Front The Russians contain the pressure of von Manstein's armoured armies towards Kharkov and Belgorod, and continue to advance on Smolensk in the central sector.

New Guinea Japanese aircraft attack Wau in force. This is the first of a series of raids carried out on the most important strategic positions of the Allies, including Oro Bay and Milne Bay, Port Moresby, Dobodura and Porlock Harbour.

Solomon Islands The Americans begin a series of air raids against Japanese installations at Munda in New Georgia, an important enemy base.

North Africa Field-Marshal Rommel, called home after the Battle of Medenine stops off in Rome for a meeting with Mussolini. He does not hide the gravity of the Axis position, but Mussolini solemnly announces: 'Tunisia must be saved at all costs ... I agree with the Führer; we must save Tunisia.' Command of the German forces in Tunisia passes to General Jürgen von Arnim, while overall command of the Axis troops goes to General Giovanni Messe.

10 March

Eastern Front After savage fighting von Manstein's armour recaptures Kharkov, so reversing one of the Red Army's biggest recent successes. Russian units continue to hold out in part of the town.

☐ Sicily. Allied bombers make heavy attack on Palermo.

12 March

Tunisia The New Zealand Corps (formed from the 2nd Division and

ALEXANDRE YERSIN

On 2 March the death occurred in Nha-trang (Vietnam) of the Swiss bacteriologist Alexandre Yersin, discoverer of the plague bacillus.

Born in 1863, Yersin studied in Lausanne, Marburg and Paris. Influenced by Pierre Roux, he then devoted himself to bacteriology, carrying out research on rabies and the properties of the diphtheria bacillus. Continuing his work in the Far East, he was commissioned by the French government, during an outbreak of bubonic plague originating in China, to conduct investigations into the dread epidemic. In 1894 Yersin, in his small laboratory in Hong Kong, discovered (almost at the same time as S. Kitasato) the plague bacillus, and after some ten years of study developed a vaccine.

Founder and director of various branches of the Pasteur Institute in the Far East, Yersin spent the last years of his life studying the flora and fauna of Indochina.

Scenes from the partisan war. Top: Yugoslav partisans are blindfolded before being shot. Centre: Polish women lined up to be shot. Above: Yugoslav partisans withdraw into Serbia. Opposite. a detachment of the Todt organization.

the 8th Armoured Brigade) begins to carry out Montgomery's plan to encircle the Axis forces on the left (southern) flank. The plan is for the New Zealanders, after crossing the Matmata Hills, to push on northwards towards Tebaga Gap and take the Italians and Germans in the rear on the El Hamma plain, having by-passed the Mareth Line. Air attacks on Sousse and Tunis cause heavy damage to residential areas in both cities.

Eastern Front Furious fighting in the streets of Kharkov. The Germans in the central sector now give up one position after another to avoid surprise attack from the Russian advance in the south.

Vyazma is occupied by the Russians without a shot fired.

Burma General Stilwell, Chiang Kai-shek's adviser and Chief of Staff, worried by Japanese troop movements in northern Burma, sends Chinese reinforcements to Ledo, in Assam. In the Arakan sector the Japanese try to cut off the Indian units one by one by a series of encircling movements.

☐ Washington. The Pacific Military Conference, to decide on strategy against the Japanese in 1943, opens and lasts until the 15th. General Sutherland, MacArthur's Chief of Staff, submits a revised version of the *Elkton* plan for the capture of New Britain, and especially the vital Japanese base of Rabaul. The plan is for a co-ordinated effort by the South-Western Pacific forces (under MacArthur) and the South Pacific forces (under Vice-Admiral Halsey). MacArthur's forces would invade New Britain from bases in New Guinea, Halsey's would tackle the Solomon Islands. The navy is much concerned with the stortage of shipping, which is holding up the transfer of new forces to the Far East. Once again there are evident differences between MacArthur's strategic ideas and those of Admiral Nimitz, Commander-in-Chief of the Pacific Fleet.

☐ Italy. In Turin 100,000 workers strike. Strikes follow immediately in Lombardy and Genoa. These are the first demonstrations against the

In the German bridgehead in the Kuban, a cook chops wood for cooking the rations.

regime, and bring war production to a halt. The feeble reaction of the Italian authorities infuriates Hitler, who bursts out, in the presence of his staff: 'It is inconceivable to me that work can be stopped ... that anyone can have dared to hold it up ... If you show the least weakness in cases like this, you are finished!'

13 March

Eastern Front Violent fighting continues as the Germans attack the Russian defenders holding Kharkov.

14 March

Eastern Front German armour and infantry eradicate the last resistance in Kharkov.
New Guinea Australians and Americans attack again, forcing the Japanese to retreat slowly north of Guadagasel.

15 March

Burma Almost all the columns making up 77th Indian Brigade's Chindits have crossed the Irrawaddy, having cut the strategic Burma Railway in a dozen places. They continue with their bold guerrilla activities. But their logistic situation is getting precarious, since they have to depend very largely on supplies dropped by aircraft at points fixed from one day to the other. The Japanese are making plans to eliminate the menace presented by the Chindits.
New Guinea A battalion of the 162nd Infantry of the US 41st Division occupies some positions at the mouth of the river Mambare without opposition.

16 March

In a letter to Roosevelt, Stalin, who has taken at face value Churchill's forecasts in his letter of 9 February, complains in blunt language about the 'treachery' (as he describes the delay to the operations in Africa and the preparations for the landing in Sicily) of the Western Allies. 'Your far from clear reply to the question of the opening of a second front in France has aroused here an uneasiness that cannot be hidden.' And he has some justification for his bluntness.

17 March

Germany Berlin admits that, as a result of recent RAF raids, over 20,000 are homeless in Munich, and over 100,000 in Essen, Duisburg, Bottrop and Stuttgart.
Burma The 55th Indian Brigade, which has relieved the 123rd east of the river Mayu, is attacked and surrounded by Japanese at Rathedaung. With the aid of reinforcements it manages to fight clear of encirclement and to withdraw to Buthidaung, but that leaves the eastern flank of the troops west of the Mayu exposed.

18 March

Tunisia The Allies liberate Gafsa.
Burma The 6th Brigade of the British 2nd Division and the 71st Indian Brigade make a last effort to drive the Japanese out of Donbaik. Then they have to withdraw north on account of enemy infiltration.
☐ India. A group of B-24 bombers arrives to reinforce the American 14th Air Force.
☐ French Guyana declares for the Free French.

19 March

Eastern Front After the recapturing of Kharkov the Raus Corps of the German Army Group South also re-takes Belgorod. The Army Group South is now practically back to the winter positions of 1941. Immediately north of Belgorod the Russians have opened up a wide salient in the German front west of Kursk. The elimination of this salient (Operation *Citadel*) is to be for several months the object of one of the most epic battles in history.

Italian infrantry under fire attack the positions of the British 8th Army near the Mareth Line, in Tunisia.

Tunisia The New Zealand Corps advances inexorably towards the Tebaga Gap.

20 March
Tunisia Towards evening the New Zealanders succeed in blocking the Tebaga Pass. During the night divisions of the British XXX Corps launch a frontal attack against the Mareth Line, assaulting the positions held by divisions of the Italian 1st Army.

21 March
Eastern Front The Germans mop up remaining pockets of resistance in Belgorod. Holding the Russian thrust in the Kursk salient, they succeed in restoring communications with Army Group Centre (von Kluge) in the Orel area, which had been cut. The Russians take Durovo,

56 miles north-east of Smolensk. The thaw brings operations to a temporary and almost total halt; no vehicles can move. The German losses during the winter campaign have been terrible; a reliable estimate puts it at over a million dead. The Russians claim the destruction or capture of 9,000 tanks, 20,000 guns and 5,000 aircraft, as well as thousands of trucks. But Russian losses too have been serious. However, the Russian war potential is rising, while the German is in decline.
Tunisia In the small hours of the morning the British 50th Division succeeds in establishing a bridgehead beyond the German defensive line.

22 March
Tunisia The German 164th Light Division leaves the Mareth Line to hold up the New Zealanders at the

Tebaga Gap. The 21st Armoured Division also makes for the pass from the north.
The British 50th Division is driven back from its bridgehead, and Montgomery changes his strategy and decides to attack from the south.
☐ *Sicily.* Further raids on Palermo by American heavy bombers.

22–23 March
Tunisia A counter-offensive by the Italians leads to the recapture of the positions taken by the Allies on the Mareth Line on a 1¼-mile-front.

23 March
Tunisia Bitter and bloody fighting continues for the Mareth bridgehead. The British X Corps, which includes the 1st Armoured Division, moves west over the Matmata Hills.

24 March

Eastern Front Russians make gains on the central front, and penetrate the outer defences of Smolensk.

☐ USA. The Chief of Staffs Committee approves the plan for the recapture of Attu Island, in the Aleutians.

24–25 March

Tunisia The 4th Indian Division overruns the Mareth Line and heads for Beni Zelten.

25 March

Tunisia The British 1st Armoured Division has concentrated a few miles from the Tebaga Gap.
Pacific American aircraft launch a heavy attack on the island of Nauru, occupied by the Japanese.

26 March

Burma General Wavell orders General Wingate to break up his Chindit groups and to pull them back into India. The guerrillas make for India in small groups, pursued by the Japanese. The mass of them manage to get back to India, apart from one group which reaches safety at the beginning of April in China. The Chindits' activities have been more than mere demonstrations, for they have been able seriously to interfere with the Japanese communications system. They have cut the Mandalay–Myitkina railway in at least 25 places.
Bering Sea Battle of the Komandorskiye Islands. A small American naval squadron, consisting of two cruisers, the *Salt Lake City* and the *Richmond*, and four destroyers, commanded by Rear-Admiral C. H. McMorris, patrolling the waters south of the Russian Komandorskiye Islands archipelago, intercepts a Japanese squadron commanded by Vice-Admiral Moshiro Hosogaya. The Japanese force comprises one heavy cruiser (the *Nachi*), two light cruisers and eight destroyers, and is escorting a supply convoy for the Japanese garrisons in the islands of Kiska and Attu, in the Aleutians. The American squadron courageously engages the enemy, and at 8.40 a.m.

a shell from the *Richmond* hits the *Nachi*, starting a fire. About 9.00 a.m. several other hits are scored on the *Nachi*, which is seriously damaged. The Japanese commander responds quickly, and about 9.30 a.m. concentrates his fire on the *Salt Lake City*, which takes avoiding action, but has to slow down when one engine breaks down. At 10.10 a.m. the *Salt Lake City* receives a direct hit which starts a major fire. A second hit opens a leak in the hull. While the Japanese ships bear down on the American vessel to finish her off, the US destroyers take on the Japanese formation and drive them off. Short of fuel, and fearing that more substantial American forces may join in and quite possibly US aircraft from the base at Amchitka also, Vice-Admiral Hosogaya calls

off the engagement and withdraws. The Japanese transports made for home as soon as the battle began, and from now on the Aleutian garrisons will be supplied only by submarine. Although the last great naval battle fought with the naval guns ends with honours even (*Salt Lake City* and *Nachi* both badly damaged), it is a strategy victory for the Americans, whose blockade of the Aleutians is never again forced by surface vessels. Hosogaya's conduct of the battle is considered irresolute and timid and he is relieved of his command.

☐ France. Pierre Laval re-forms Vichy cabinet, gaining more control for himself.

26–27 March

Tunisia The British 1st Armoured

Tunisian front: German troops take cover during a raid by British aircraft.

Division and New Zealand Corps penetrate deep into Tebaga Gap and force the Axis defenders to retire to El Hamma, where they improvise a new defence line.

27 March
Germany. RAF makes heaviest yet night attack on Berlin, dropping more than twice biggest bomb-load dropped on London (18 April, 1941).
☐ Admiral Sir Henry Harwood, victor of the Battle of the River Plate (12–13 December 1939) and Commander-in-Chief of the eastern sector of the Mediterranean, is obliged to retire from the service on health grounds.

28 March
Tunisia The British 1st Army goes over to the the offensive. Troops of

The US cruiser *Salt Lake City* during the battle of the Komandorskiye Islands.

THE MANHATTAN PROJECT

Around mid March a hundred or so scientists and technicians were assembled in laboratories built at Los Alamos, a remote spot in New Mexico situated on a mesa some 6,500 ft (2,000 m) above sea level. In an atmosphere of excitement and absolute secrecy, this team was charged with the construction of the first atomic bomb in history. The scientific director of the project was J. Robert Oppenheimer, the brilliant head of physics at Berkeley University, responsible for coordinating the work of scientists of various nationalities under the strict security conditions imposed by the US military. Scientists of the calibre of Fermi, Szilard, Bohr, Teller and Lawrence were from then on employed at Los Alamos.

The Danish physicist Niels Bohr, recently arrived in the United States, revealed in the early part of 1939 that his German counterparts Hahn and Stressmann had in the previous year succeeded in splitting the uranium atom and as a result paved the way for a controlled chain reaction and release of an enormous quantity of energy. American scientific circles expressed the fear that Germany might within a few years manage to build an atomic bomb of devastating power. After a series of warnings and demands had fallen on deaf ears, a group of Hungarian scientists sent a letter, which was also signed by Albert Einstein, to President Roosevelt, and finally convinced him of the need for the government to embark on a programme of nuclear research and to work towards the construction of an atomic bomb. After several years of inadequate financing and disappointing results, the government decided, in December 1941, to speed up the programme and entrusted Vannevar Bush, director of the Office of Scientific Research and Development, with the task of utilizing all available resources for nuclear research. In March 1942 Bush submitted a report on the situation, in which he urged Roosevelt to implement a programme immediately for the mass production of fissile material to be used for building the atomic bomb, the explosive power of which was ascertainable only in theory. The appeal was heeded and the body of research in this field became known as the Manhattan Project.

The scientists already knew that the derivatives of uranium – the isotope U235 and plutonium – could be subjected to rapid fission, thus producing a chain reaction. But three fundamental problems had still to be resolved: how to control the chain reaction, how to produce sufficient fissile material and how, in practice, to construct an atomic device.

The first problem was solved by Enrico Fermi in December 1942 in Chicago; working out the answers to the other two was the responsibility of Brig. Gen. Leslie R. Groves, military chief of the Manhattan Project. With his customary energy and efficiency, Groves obtained the necessary finances, recruited thousands of scientists and technicians from universities and industry, and set up the secret establishments for production of the fissile material.

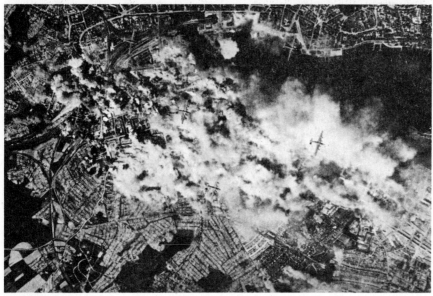

Top: German anti-aircraft guns in action on the Channel coast.
Above: American B-24 bombers, specialists in daylight raids, in action over Kiel.

the Italian 1st Army fall back on the Akarit line (north-west of Gabes, on the road to Sfax), to which a part of the Axis troops have been moved.
New Guinea A battalion of the US 162nd Infantry is given the task of occupying Morobe harbour and the mouth of the river Waria. The action is part of the measures taken to prepare for a new series of operations against the Japanese, who still control the area of Lae and Salamaua. The Chief of Staffs Committee approve new directives for General MacArthur and Admiral Halsey,

resolving the conflict between them in favour of MacArthur, who in addition to the command of the forces in the South-Western Pacific area will also have operational responsibility for the South Pacific forces under Admiral Halsey in the Solomons.

29 March
Tunisia British 8th Army units occupy Gabes and El Hamma after fierce resistance. New Zealand forces play a major role in the capture of both places.
□ The Reich capital is again heavily

bombed by RAF in night attack.

30 March
Tunisia 8th Army takes Sejenane after bitter fighting.

31 March
New Guinea MacKechnie Force – mostly consisting of the 1st Battalion of the US 162nd Infantry and called after the name of the officer commanding the regiment, is taken by sea to the mouth of the river Waria to occupy that position and a neighbouring airfield.
Solomon Islands Japanese aircraft carry out several raids on the Russell Islands.
Aleutian Islands The American Pacific Commands issue a directive for the invasion of the island of Attu. The operation is to take place on 7 May and will be directed by Admiral Kinkaid, Commander of Task Force 16 of the Northern Pacific. Under him will be Rear-Admiral Rockwell, who will command the combined operations landing force, and General Albert E. Brown, heading the US 7th Division – an unexpected task for this division, which has been trained for months in desert warfare.
China The Americans open training centres for Chinese infantry and artillery officers.
□ Iran. The American air force takes over responsibility, hitherto left to a private company, for a big factory at Abadan that assembles the aircraft supplied by the USA to the USSR.
□ Sardinia. Large US bombing force (nearly 100 Fortresses) attacks Cagliari, the relay post for Axis shipments to Tunisia and an important air base.

1 April
Tunisia El Maou airfield, near Sfax, is bombed by British, American and South African aircraft.

2 April
Decree issued by Goering makes air raid patrol duty compulsory for every able-bodied German.

3 April
Eastern Front Heavy fighting and

major air battles are taking place on the Leningrad front.

Tunisia Axis forces begin to withdraw northwards on the so-called Enfidaville line.

New Guinea Units of MacKechnie Force land near Morobe harbour and begin to prepare defensive positions.

4 April

Naples, Palermo, Syracuse (Sicily) and Carloforte (Sardinia) heavily bombed. Official sources put the dead in Naples alone at 221, with 387 injured.

5 April

Burma The Japanese extend their control of the Mayu peninsula northwards as far as Indin, on the Arakan coast, only a little way from the Indian frontier; they overrun the headquarters of the 6th Indian Brigade. Meanwhile the 26th Indian Division has replaced the 14th on the Burma front.

☐ US bombers make heavy raid on Antwerp, causing great damage.

5–6 April

Tunisia During the night General Montgomery's 8th Army launches a heavy attack on the Akarit line. At midnight the 4th Indian Division reaches Hill 275, so turning the line from the south. But the line is not broken, and the Axis troops are able to retire further north, towards the new Enfidaville defence line – a series of heights that reaches as far as Djebel Mansour, and which represents the final protective line in front of Tunis. Axis losses are enormous. The Italian *Centauro* Division has been smashed, less than 50% of the fighting force survives.

6 April

South Pacific After the disastrous Battle of the Bismarck Sea (3–5 March), Yamamoto feels that some action on a huge scale is necessary to halt the American pressure in every sector. In view of Japanese losses in warships and transports there can be no question of a naval operation, nor of an operation on land. The

Troops at the Tunisian front, April 1943.

SERGEI RACHMANINOFF

The great Russian composer and pianist Sergei Rachmaninoff died on 29 March at his villa in Beverly Hills, California.

Rachmaninoff was born at Onega, Novgorod, on 1 April 1873. After some unprofitable studies at the St Petersburg Conservatory, he moved in 1895 to Moscow in order to study the piano and composition with Zverev. Within a few years he had developed into an extraordinary virtuoso and had also made his mark as a composer. His first opera, *Aleko*, gained him first prize in the competition for composers at the Moscow Conservatory.

He then embarked successfully on a threefold career as pianist, composer and orchestral conductor, achieving international fame.

Emigrating to the United States in 1918, Rachmaninoff pursued his musical activities to the end, giving an astonishing number of concerts in many parts of the world and establishing a reputation as one of the greatest instrumentalists of the time.

only possible answer is a great air attack 'which will weaken the claws of the American eagle'. The Japanese bases in New Guinea and the Solomons are under threat. It is clear that the Americans are aiming at the capture of the northern Solomons and important base of Rabaul, in New Britain. The fall of Rabaul would give the enemy a jumping-off place for an attack on the Philippines and might allow them to cut off Truk, the key point of the Japanese imperial forces in the Pacific, their 'Pearl Harbour'. Since there are

many signs that the American offensive is to be launched soon, Yamamoto decides to act at once. He concentrates all available air formations at Rabaul, at Kavieng in New Ireland and at Biun in the south of Bougainville. Even the aircraft from the aircraft carriers are transferred to land bases to take part in Operation *A*. 350 aircraft are assembled and regrouped, ready for action.

7 April

Tunisia The British 8th Army joins up with the American 1st Army not

'OKLAHOMA!'

A love story set in the Wild West at the end of the nineteenth century, *Oklahoma!* had its Broadway première at the St James Theater on 31 March. The authors, Richard Rodgers and Oscar Hammerstein, had written an absolutely original work, defying the traditional precepts of the musical and establishing a genuine folk atmosphere and character. Considerable doubts were voiced, for the show appeared to possess all the ingredients of failure. Based on a stage comedy by Lynn Riggs, *Green Grow the Lilacs*, which had been a notable flop, the musical had no stars in the cast, featured dance numbers that seemed rather too intellectualized for popular acceptance and made few concessions to humour. Furthermore, composer Richard Rodgers was working for the first time in a quarter of a century without his regular partner Larry Hart, librettist Oscar Hammerstein had a long succession of flops behind him, and it was only the second theatrical venture for director Rouben Mamoulian.

Yet from the very start *Oklahoma!* proved a resounding success with critics and public alike. In the course of 2,248 performances on Broadway, the show earned more than 7 million dollars at the box office, shattering all previous records for takings.

A scene from the musical.

Japanese bombers await the signal to take off for action over the Solomons.

far from Graiba, in the Gulf of Gabes.

The Axis forces continue to withdraw towards Enfidaville.

Solomon Islands 188 Japanese aircraft (71 bombers and 117 fighters) carry out a violent raid on airfields and shipping in the area of Guadalcanal, especially at Tulagi. A savage air battle develops, in which the Americans lose seven fighters and the Japanese considerably more (though the number is unknown). However, the attackers succeed in dealing an effective blow, sinking the US destroyer *Aaron Ward* and the tanker *Kanawha*, besides a New Zealand corvette, the *Moa*.

Eastern Front The whole front has come to a halt with the thaw, But Hitler demands that preparations should be hastened for a big offensive to start the moment conditions permit. He plans to break through the great Russian salient at Kursk at its base and wipe out the huge forces concentrated there. The Russians, foreseeing this obvious move by the Germans, are fortifying the salient with at least eight concentric defensive lines and hundreds of thousands of mines, preparing methodically for what may well be the biggest battle of the whole war.

□ The Duce meets Hitler at Salzburg. They discuss the military situation in the light of the severe defeat of Axis troops on every front. Mussolini wants Hitler to sue for a separate peace with Russia so as to be able to reinforce the south European front. But the Führer will have none of it. He enchants Mussolini with fantastic stories of future victories, even in Africa. 'Duce,' he tells him, 'I guarantee you that Africa will be defended. Verdun stood out against the attack of the best German regiments. I do not see why we should not stand out as well in Africa. With your help, Duce, my troops will make Tunis the Verdun of the Medi-

terranean.' Mussolini allows himself to be persuaded. The conference lasts for four days.

8 April
Tunisia Axis forces continue their withdrawal towards the Enfidaville line.

9 April
Tunisia The 8th Army pushes rapidly towards Sfax, with the enemy in full retreat.

10 April
Tunisia The 8th Army occupies Sfax. General Montgomery tells his troops, 'Forward to Tunis and drive the enemy into the sea.'

11 April
New Guinea In line with Yamamoto's directive, the Japanese air force continues its offensive, this time attacking Allied naval concentrations in the south-eastern part of New Guinea, in Oro and Harvey Bays. Two Allied merchant ships are sunk in Oro Bay.

12 April
Tunisia By the afternoon the Axis troops have dug in on the Enfidaville line. The attacks by the 8th Army continue, and the Allies occupy Sousse. Now only Enfidaville separates the 8th Army from Tunis.
Eastern Front The German radio

A Papuan in New Guinea helps a wounded Australian soldier back from the front.

announces the discovery of eight communal graves in the Katyn forest near Smolensk, containing the remains of 4,150 Polish officers deported by the Russians in 1940 and murdered. The USSR denies the accusation. The truth has never been established.

New Guinea The Japanese air offensive continues with attacks on Port Moresby, where the port installations are damaged, but not seriously.

13 April
Allied air raids continue without pause on the Italian mainland and the larger islands.

14 April
Tunisia Allied pressure on the Enfidaville line increases, especially on the strongpoints of Takrouna and Garci, a sign that the final offensive is imminent.

New Guinea Another raid on Allied shipping in Milne Bay brings the air offensive ordered by Yamamoto to an end with no great tactical or strategic results. Against the small bag of ships, plus the destruction of 25 American aircraft, the Japanese have lost 50 aircraft, largely those from aircraft carriers, whose expert pilots have already become scarce and irreplaceable. As for slowing down the American project, if anything Yamamoto has achieved just the opposite, inducing the Americans to accelerate their preparations for the offensive.

☐ Exceptionally heavy night bombing raid on Stuttgart by RAF.

15 April
Russell Islands On Banika Island the Americans complete the first of the two airfields they have decided to build there.

Aleutian Islands Infantry units of the US 7th Division begin the combined operations for the capture of Attu Island. They are to be taken to Adak and Dutch Harbour, then embarked in a destroyer and two submarines for the final phase of the operation.

16 April
China The Japanese 11th Army concentrates in readiness for an offen-

sive in the western province of Hupeh, with the object of extending Japanese control to the upper Yangtze.

☐ Carrying out the policy of massive bombing attacks, the RAF makes heavy raids on Mannheim and on the Skoda works at Pilsen.

☐ Palermo and Catania, in Sicily, are again heavily bombed by US planes.

☐ Vichy announces the evacuation of children and 'non-essential' persons from several major Channel ports.

17 April
Another devastating raid by American bombers on Palermo, Catania and Syracuse.

18 April
Bougainville American aircraft shoot down Admiral Yamamoto's aeroplane, and the admiral is killed.

19 April
Eastern Front Heavy fighting is taking place in the Kuban region. Elsewhere activity is slight.

20 April
Tunisia The British 8th Army launches a night attack against Enfidaville in an effort to break through

the enemy line. Three days of bitter fighting follow, but General Messe's soldiers succeed in holding the British attack, though the Takrouna strongpoint is lost.

Aleutian Islands Rear-Admiral Kinkaid, commanding Task Force 16, issues operation orders for the landing on Attu Island.

☐ Heavy RAF night raid on Stettin, east Prussia.

☐ The massacre of Jews in the Warsaw ghetto begins. Under orders from Himmler 56,000 at least will be killed by 16 May.

21 April
Tunisia Germans counter-attack in the sector between Medjez el Bab and Goubellat, at the centre of the Allied line, but are driven back with heavy losses.

Pacific Admiral Koga replaces the late Admiral Yamamoto as Commander-in-Chief of the Japanese Combined Fleet.

☐ Churchill warns the Germans of reprisals if they use poison gas against the Russians.

22 April
Tunisia Montgomery suspends the 8th Army's attack on the Enfidaville

Tunisian front, March 1943: an American Rangers unit advances in hilly terrain.

WAR PRODUCTION

Considerable economic efforts were required of the countries directly involved in the war. All sectors of industry were geared to war production, with one main purpose in mind, to do everything possible to augment the quantity and quality of weapons.

In Germany, despite the ever more frequent and devastating aerial bombardments, armaments production was practically tripled. Shortage of manpower was remedied by the use, often forced, of foreign labour.

The Soviet Union, although invaded, managed to maintain its productive capacity unchanged by transferring industries to eastern regions. There, safe from the threat of the German armies, new factories were built and the Soviet armies were thus kept continuously supplied.

Among the Allies, the principal burden was naturally sustained by the United States, which had boosted the British economy with the Lend Lease Act. American shipyards achieved remarkable levels of productivity as warships and merchant ships were turned out at a steady rate, many of them, thanks to new technology, of considerable size.

Equally important contributions were made by the steel and aeronautical industries. It was because of the enormously increased production of the latter that the Allies gradually won control of the skies and stepped up their air raids on German cities.

line. At the same time the British 1st Army (commanded by General Sir Kenneth Anderson) launches a series of attacks on the heights south-west of Tunis. The British V Corps heads for Longstop Hill and Peter's Corner, which dominate the valley of the river Medjerda, intending to advance on Tunis by way of Massicault. General Bradley's US II Corps attacks towards Mateur, concentrating particularly on 'Hill 609', which dominates the valley known as the 'Mousetrap' through which it will be easy to get to the plain, while in the south the British IX Corps advances towards the Goubellat plain.

Pacific Japanese aircraft bomb the airfield on Funafuti, in the Ellice Islands.

23 April

Tunisia A Scottish battalion storms Longstop Hill in 3 hours' violent fighting.

New Guinea The Australian 3rd Division takes up positions in the Mubo area. No significant activity is reported from the area, where the Australians man a broken line from Mubo to Komiatum and Bobdubi.

☐ It is decided to set up a joint Anglo-American command to prepare the plans for a European landing. The British Lieutenant-General Sir Frederick E. Morgan is appointed to head the new command, with the designation COS-SAC (Chief of Staff Supreme Allied Commander).

April 1943: the thaw holds up operations in Russia.
Above: German motor-cyclist struggles through the mud.

THE HUNTING OF THE 'PEACOCK'

17 April

Aleutian Islands Dutch Harbour: at 6.36 a.m. an American listening post picks up a radio message in Japanese cypher from Yamamoto's flagship, the battleship *Yamato*, at anchor in Truk. Recognizing the name of the *Yamato* even in cypher, the operators realize even before decyphering that the message is very important and retransmit it to Washington top priority.

In Washington the special information services, who possess the Japanese codes, decypher the message in a few hours and pass its content to the Secretary for the Navy, Frank Knox. The message reveals that Admiral Yamamoto is about to undertake an inspection of Japanese advanced bases in the Solomons; it gives the timetable for his movements, which are to be by air, with the flight plan and even the number of fighters that will be escorting the aircraft carrying the commander-in-chief of the Japanese naval forces.

11.00 a.m.: Realizing the significance of this information, Knox sends for General Arnold, Chief of Staff of the US Air Force, the famous first trans-Atlantic flier Charles Lindbergh and the chief engineer of the Lockheed company, whose P-38 Lightning is the only long-range fighter among the aircraft stationed on Guadal-

canal. Knox weighs up the advantages and disadvantages of mounting an operation to shoot down Yamamoto's aircraft; on the one hand, the danger of letting the Japanese know that the Americans have their secret code; on the other, the possibility of getting rid of one of the most brilliant enemy strategists, a man of legendary charisma able to inspire his men to acts of fanatical heroism, and who symbolises Japanese courage and power. Knox determines that the admiral's aircraft is to be intercepted and shot down. The experts confirm that the operation is feasible, as long as the P-38s used for the mission are fitted with additional fuel tanks to increase their range.

3.35 a.m.: Two urgent messages are sent from Washington, the first to General Kenney ordering that the supplementary fuel tanks for fitting under the wings of the P-38s should be sent to Guadalcanal immediately, the second to Henderson Field on Guadalcanal ordering No. 339 Squadron to shoot Yamamoto down and giving all the necessary details for carrying out the task. The pilots will be able to choose whether they will intercept Yamamoto on his first flight, bringing him to Bougainville Island, or attack the small ship in which he will be embarking to carry out his inspection.

5.10 p.m.: The message is received and carefully considered, and the senior officers on Henderson Field send for the officers picked for the mission. The plan is discussed in every detail and it is decided to launch the attack while Yamamoto is in his aircraft, at 9.35 a.m. next day, just before he is due to land at Ballale. Operation *Peacock* (Admiral Halsey sent a message to Mitscher, Commander of the US Air Force in the Solomons, inviting him to 'grab the peacock' – the code-name for the commander-in-chief of the Japanese navy – 'by the tail') is to begin at 7.20 a.m. on the 18th. The squadron responsible for the operation, commanded by Major John W. Mitchell, will consist of six aircraft to attack Yamamoto's

Yamato (Japan 1941)

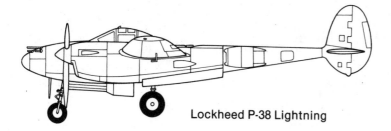

Lockheed P-38 Lightning

Admiral Yamamoto speaks to a group of Japanese pilots only a few days before he is shot down by an American fighter plane.

aircraft and twelve others to give them cover, attacking the fighter escort.

9.00 p.m.: Four B-24 Liberator heavy bombers arrive at Henderson Field with the supplementary fuel tanks for fitting to the eighteen P-38 Lightnings. The entire night is spent preparing the aircraft.

18 April

Pacific 6.00 a.m.: Two Mitsubishi-1 twin-engined aircraft take off from Rabaul in New Britain. In one of them is Admiral Yamamoto, in the other his chief of staff, Vice-Admiral Matome Ugaki. There is an escort of six fighters. The formation climbs to 5,000 ft and flies towards Bougainville.

6.20 a.m.: The P-38s take off from Guadalcanal to intercept Yamamoto.

9.34 a.m.: Precisely on time, the Americans sight the enemy formation flying over Empress Augusta Bay, at the south-west of Bougainville; they drop their spare tanks and go into the attack. Four minutes earlier the radio operator in the Mitsubishi in which Yamamoto's chief of staff is travelling had told the officer that they would land at Ballale, as arranged, at 9.45. Now Americans and Japanese are flying over the jungle.

9.35 a.m.: The twelve escorting fighters draw off the Zeros of Yamamoto's escort to a greater height, where there are furious air duels. Then two of the P-38s responsible for the principal mission climb unexpectedly from the very low level at which they have been flying and attack and shoot down both Mitsubishi bombers. Yamamoto's aircraft crashes in the jungle and the admiral is killed on the spot; the other comes down in the sea after trying to make a forced landing. Vice-Admiral Ugaki is rescued by a Japanese launch that instantly puts to sea. The engagement is finished, and Mitchell immediately orders his fighters to return to base. The Americans have lost only one P-38, with six others damaged; the Japanese have lost the two bombers and all six of the escorting Zeros. Above all, they have lost the most illustrious of their war leaders.

19 April

Japanese soldiers recover the bodies of the admiral and his staff officers. They are taken in complete secrecy to Truk, on board the *Yamato*.

The Americans make no mention of their success so that the Japanese do not realize their codes are known. The Japanese keep silent too, for quite different reasons. On 21 April Admiral Mineichi Koga takes over as commander-in-chief of the Japanese air and naval forces, and two days later he hoists his flag in the *Musashi*, a giant new battleship just arrived at Truk. It is the *Musashi* that returns to Tokyo on 21 May bearing the ashes of Yamamoto, and it is only then that an official communiqué announces that he has been killed in action.

5 June

At a solemn ceremony attended by over a million citizens of Tokyo, a part of the national hero's ashes are buried in Hibiya park. Two days later the rest of his ashes are interred at a similar ceremony at Nagaoka, the home of Yamamoto's sister.

Jews in the Warsaw ghetto are lined up against a wall, after being stripped of every object of value they were carrying with them. This photograph was taken by a member of the German SS.
End of the ghetto: the SS set up a deportation camp for 2000 prisoners on its ruins.

24 April

The main body of the American 7th Division, given the task of capturing Attu (Aleutian Islands), embarks at San Francisco for Cold Harbour, Alaska.

26 April

Tunisia Longstop Hill is taken by troops of the British V Corps, who reach Djebel Bou Aoukaz.
Aleutian Islands A squadron of three American cruisers and six destroyers commanded by Rear-Admiral C. H. McMorris shells the Japanese installations on Attu, concentrating on those in Chicagof Harbour and Holtz Bay.
South Pacific MacArthur's headquarters drafts a new *Elkton* plan to co-ordinate the activities of MacArthur's forces and those of Admiral Halsey for the capture of Rabaul. The operation is code-named *Cartwheel*.
☐ Continuing the now almost nightly raids the RAF bombs railway centres in north-west Germany and the Rhineland. At night Duisburg is bombed in one of the heaviest attacks of the war, the bomb-load being almost equal to that of the 1,000-bomber raid on Cologne.
☐ The Soviet Union breaks off diplomatic relations with the Polish government in London in response to Polish demands for a Red Cross inquiry into the mass graves at Katyn.

27 April

Hitler receives Pavelić, head of the Croatian puppet government, at his headquarters. This is one of a long series of meetings Hitler has had with leaders of Germany's allies, commencing with Mussolini on 7 April. As a result of these meetings, Axis propaganda increasingly stresses the importance of an anti-Bolshevik crusade to save European civilization, rather than the earlier emphasis on the 'New Order'. At the same time Hitler demands even more men and materials from his allies.

28 April

During the night Bomber Command carries out its biggest mine-laying operation of the war, particularly in the Baltic.

28–29 April

Tunisia While a desperate counter-attack by Axis troops allows them temporarily to recapture Djebel Bou Aoukaz, the forces of the American II Corps reach Hill 609 after fierce fighting.

30 April

Tunisia General Alexander sends the 4th Indian Division and 6th and 7th Armoured Divisions to support the British 1st Army. Meanwhile General von Arnim, who has replaced Rommel, has concentrated his forces round Tunis on the heights surrounding the city. This strongpoint is where the next Allied attack takes place. Meanwhile, to the north towards the coast, the American 9th Division breaks through and threatens the German positions in the 'Mousetrap'.
During the month of April the Axis forces have been reinforced and supplied only in driblets. At least 200 Italian and German transport aircraft have been shot down by US fighters between Sicily and Tunisia. If the Axis forces in Africa, faced by immensely superior Allied forces, manage to put up any substantial resistance it will be little short of a miracle.
Aleutian Islands The convoy transporting the main body of the US 7th Division for the Attu landing reaches Cold Harbour, Alaska.
☐ The US Atlantic Fleet transfers to the British and Canadian navies responsibility for protecting convoys between Halifax, Nova Scotia and Great Britain.

1 May

Tunisia The Americans take 'Hill 609' but cannot advance further against the dogged German resistance. The American 1st Armoured Division especially is held up by enemy rearguards in the 'Mousetrap'; the mass of the German army withdraws towards Mateur and organizes a new defence line there.

2 May

Eastern Front Heavy fighting continues in the Kuban.
Tunisia The Americans still cannot break through in the 'Mousetrap'.

3 May

Tunisia Finally the American 1st Armoured Division overcomes the German resistance and succeeds in breaking through the enemy positions in the direction of Mateur. Meanwhile there is also activity on the central and southern sectors of the front, scene of what must be the final attack.
☐ General Marshall, Chief of Staff of the US Army, sends a message to General Stilwell, Chiang Kai-shek's Chief of Staff, that the President has decided to provide substantial air forces to take part in the Chinese war effort. The President also asks for a revision of the plan code-named *Anakim* (the recapture of Burma).

4 May

Tunisia The Germans put up a more stubborn defence than ever on the defensive line at Mateur.
Aleutian Islands After a day's delay due to bad weather, the convoy sails for the landing on Attu. Strong unfavourable winds on the voyage make it necessary to put back Day X by three more days, i.e. to 11 May.
Burma The Japanese, with their technique of infiltrating in small groups, have succeeded in establishing themselves on the line of the Buthidaung–Maungdaw road. The British attacks to dislodge them are easily repulsed.
☐ Italy. After a four days' lull the Allied bombing raids on the peninsula begin again.

5 May

Eastern Front After an intense battle the Russians capture Krymskaya. The Red Army also captures Neberjaisk, 10 miles from Novorossiysk.
Tunisia Towards evening the British 1st Division infantry take Djebel Bou Aoukaz. Following behind them is the IX Corps of General Horrocks, who has taken the place of

General Crocker, wounded a few days before. To the south General Juin's French XIX Corps attacks towards Pont du Fahs, the last line of defence before Tunis.

6 May

Tunisia British 1st Army begins final assault on Tunis. At dawn, protected by a tremendous artillery barrage, the 6th and 7th Armoured Divisions of the British IX Corps succeed in reaching the plain behind Djebel Bou Aoukaz, throwing Axis communications and supply lines into disorder. The two armoured divisions manage to reach Massicault.

To the south French troops continue to advance in the direction of Pont du Fahs, while to the north the American 9th Division heads for Bizerta and the American 1st Armoured Division, by-passing Mateur, is making for Ferryville (to the north) and Protville (to the east).

South-West Pacific Allied headquarters sends out further instructions for the preparation of Operation *Cartwheel*, the plan for the recapture of Rabaul.

□ The heavy Allied attacks on Sicilian harbours continue. Reggio Calabria, the mainland terminal of the ferry system to Sicily, is devastated in severe raids.

7 May

Tunisia Tunis and Bizerta captured. At 3.40 p.m. British forces enter Tunis, while at 4.15 p.m. forward elements of the US 2nd Corps enter Bizerta. Further south, French forces with the 1st Army enter Pont du Fahs.

Burma The Japanese go over to the attack in the Buthidaung area, forcing the 26th Indian Division to retire north-westwards.

South Pacific American minelayers lay a minefield across the Blackett Straits in Kula Gulf, in the Solomons.

8 May

Tunisia The Allied advance to the sea continues, while the Axis troops withdraw into the Cape Bon peninsula. An Axis convoy of three steamships succeeds in reaching the waters off Tunisia, but are then attacked by British units and sunk before they can unload. During the morning the commander of the Axis army group in North Africa signals that none of his units can move for lack of fuel.

9 May

Tunisia Fighting ends in north-east Tunisia at 11.00 a.m. as the Germans accept unconditional surrender. Meanwhile the Allies advance towards the Cape Bon peninsula. The British arrive near Hammam Lif, where they are fiercely engaged by the Germans.

Mediterranean A violent bombardment heralds the Allies' operation for the capture of the island of Pantelleria (Operation *Corkscrew*).

Far East The US General Wheeler is given the task of co-ordinating and speeding up the construction of a big airfield in Assam, in India, to support the Burma front and increase

7 May 1943: patrol of British soldiers engaged in a mopping-up operation in Bizerta.

the Allies' capacity to send supplies to China.

☐ Allied air raids on towns in southern Italy and Sicily continue without respite.

10 May

Tunisia The 6th Armoured Division takes Hammam Lif and now goes for Hammamet and Korba, on the east coast of the Cape Bon peninsula. The plan is to join up with the units of Montgomery's 8th Army advancing from Enfidaville.

Aleutian Islands Japanese troops on Attu Island, alerted a week before against the danger of an American landing by reports from the Japanese intelligence service, are stood down, convinced the Americans have cancelled the operation in view of adverse weather conditions.

11 May

Tunisia Allied forces rout the remaining Axis forces. Organized resistance ceases, and the Allies control the whole country.

Aleutian Islands The US 7th Division lands at several points on Attu Island, which the Japanese have occupied since the Battle of Midway. Thick mist severely limits the barrage provided by Rear-Admiral Kinkaid's Task Force 16, and also prevents air support, but does favour surprise. The units land in the afternoon in Massacre Bay, at Alexai Point, west of Holtz Bay in the northern part of the island. More landings are carried out during the night. The landing forces advance towards the Jarmin Pass, but about 7.00 p.m. they are held up by intense fire from defending troops on the heights on either side of the pass. Mud paralyses trucks and tractors. The divisional commander, General Brown, plans an assault on the pass the following day.

☐ Sicily. Continuing heavy Allied raids on Catania, Marsala and Trapani.

☐ The monsoon rains make it impossible to proceed with work on the construction of the new Burma Road, which is to lead from Ledo, in Assam, to China. The roadway has

been completed up to 45 miles east of Ledo, in Burmese territory.

12 May

Tunisia General von Arnim, commander of the German troops in Africa, surrenders to the Allies.

Aleutian Islands: Attu Supported by aircraft and naval guns, the 7th Division converges on Jarmin Pass from two directions. A frontal attack carried out from Massacre Bay has no result.

Solomon Islands A squadron of American cruisers and destroyers commanded by Rear-Admiral W. L. Ainsworth shells Japanese positions on Munda and Vila during the night of 12/13 May, while a group of minelayers returns to mine the Gulf of Kula, a narrow arm of the sea between Kolombangara and New Georgia.

Burma The first Arakan campaign ends in a stalemate. The 26th Indian Division evacuates Maungdaw and withdraws to defensive positions further north. It has been a useless sacrifice of men and materials. Most important of the reasons for its failure is the absence of any intervention by Chinese units from Yunnan province.

☐ The Trident Conference meets in Washington, attended by Roosevelt, Churchill and the heads of the Combined Staffs. The object of the meeting is to determine Anglo-American strategy in the light of recent developments in Africa, on the Eastern Front and in the Aleutians.

13 May

Tunisia General Messe, notified on this very day of his promotion to Field-Marshal, surrenders to the 8th Army. Some 250,000 Germans and Italians have laid down their arms. General Alexander sends the following message to Churchill: 'It is my duty to report that the Tunis campaign is over. All enemy resistance has ceased. We are masters of the North African shores.'

Aleutian Islands: Attu In spite of repeated assaults the Americans are still more or less pinned to the posi-

tions they occupied immediately after their landing. The Japanese have recovered from their surprise and are putting up a vigorous, well co-ordinated defence. In the northern part of the island they have gone over to the attack, trying, but without success, to dislodge the invaders from a hilltop called Hill X. Naval and air support is limited by bad weather.

New Guinea Japanese aircraft begin another series of raids on Allied positions.

☐ Washington. The Trident Conference approves the final version of the plans for the landing in Sicily (Operation *Husky*), including the date (10 July) and the areas chosen for the landings.

☐ RAF continues heavy bombing attacks on targets in northern France, Germany, and Italy. Particularly violent raids are carried out in the central Ruhr; at Bochum over 1,000 tons of bombs are dropped in 45 minutes.

14 May

In Italy the Under-Secretaries for War, Air and Navy announce anti-invasion measures. RAF bombers continue to pound strategic bases in southern Italy.

15 May

Aleutian Islands: Attu The Americans attack at Massacre Bay (in the south) is renewed, but even with the help of naval guns the Americans make no progress. The attack in Holtz Bay (in the north) is deferred until the 11th on account of fog, but then the Americans find that the Japanese have given up the positions they held on the first evening to take up more favourable positions further back. As the Americans advance they suffer severe losses not only from enemy fire but also from bombing by their own aircraft.

China In order to repulse the 'rice offensive' launched by the Japanese in the centre of the country, Chiang Kai-shek orders General Cheng to come back with his army and defend Yichang, on the Yangtze.

The Combined Chiefs of Staff decide to give absolute priority to the construction of the airfield in Assam, In-

Japanese infrantry storm a British position in the Arakan region, in Burma.

A Russian patrol carrying out mopping-up operations in a cane-break in the Novorrossiysk sector. Some of the troops are equipped with large life-belts.

The dam on the river Möhne shattered by 'bouncing bombs' dropped by British Lancasters during the night of 16 May 1943, in the course of Operation *Chastise*.

dia; the quantity of war materials to be supplied to China is to be increased to 7,000 tons a month by 1 June.

16 May
Aleutian Islands: Attu More American attacks in the Holtz Bay area. The Japanese, numerically greatly inferior (2,380 men against 11,000 Americans) and in danger of being taken in the rear if the Americans succeed in breaking through from Massacre Bay, retire during the night of 16/17 to Chicagof Harbour to put up their final resistance.

☐ During the night a squadron of RAF Lancasters specially adapted to carry their purpose-designed bombs weighing 4.5 tons attack the dams on the rivers Möhne, Eder and Sorpe, in the Ruhr. The first two provide drinking water for 4 million people and supply 75% of the electric power required by the industries of the Ruhr basin. Both dams are damaged, causing many deaths and widespread flooding. But they are repaired with astonishing speed so that British hopes of paralysing the war production of Germany's main in-

dustrial area are disappointed. The third dam, on the Sorpe, is not damaged.

17 May
Aleutian Islands: Attu The units from Holtz Bay advance and occupy the positions evacuated by the enemy during the night. The units at Massacre Bay also discover that the Japanese have gone, and occupy the Jarmin Pass.

18 May
Mediterranean Allied attacks on Pantelleria are intensified, and the island is virtually cut off by a naval blockade.

Aleutian Islands: Attu US forces coming from the north (Holtz Bay) and those from the south (Massacre Bay) join up. In the northern sector new units and supplies are immediately landed. The next phase of the operation, against Chicagof Harbour, is prepared.

19 May
Aleutian Islands: Attu The Americans attack before dawn to open a pass which would clear a way to the

Sarana valley. Fighting continues until sunset, with the Japanese forces apparently dislodged.

20 May
Aleutian Islands: Attu The Americans are still held up at the pass (later called Clevesy Pass) by the Japanese, who have taken up positions during the night on the peaks that overlook it. Men trained in desert warfare have to turn themselves into mountaineers to get behind the enemy. After hard fighting the attackers succeed in advancing into the Sarana valley. Some progress is also made in the northern part of the island.
Burma It is officially announced that the three-month commando operations carried out by the Chindits commanded by General Wingate have ended. In their guerrilla actions behind the enemy lines the Chindits have lost a third of their effectives.

21 May
Aleutian Islands: Attu On the southern front the Americans succeed in eliminating the only remaining Japanese strongpoint on one of the peaks overlooking Clevesy Pass and

advance towards a crest near another pass leading from the Sarana valley to Chicagof Harbour. The troops landed at Holtz Bay advance more slowly on account of the greater difficulty of the mountainous terrain.

☐ Tokyo announces death in action of Admiral Yamamoto.

☐ The First American-built airfield in Britain officially taken over by 8th US Army Air Force.

22 May

Aleutian Islands: Attu Troops on the southern front succeed in penetrating into the valley that leads to Chicagof, while those in the north stay in their positions. Whenever the weather permits, an important contribution is made by fire from the ships of Task Force 51, which, under cover from Task Force 16, was responsible for the landing operation. Task Force 51, commanded by Rear-Admiral Rockwell, consists of the old battleships *Pennsylvania* and *Idaho*, 1 escort aircraft carrier, 6 cruisers and 19 destroyers.

☐ India. Urgent messages are sent to all headquarters concerned with the building of new airfields in Assam to get the work completed more quickly.

☐ Italy. Allied bombers pound Sicily and Sardinia.

☐ Moscow announces the dissolution of the Comintern. This is an act of goodwill intended to placate the very large sections of public opinion in the West that are still nervous of dealings with Soviet Russia. The decision was taken on 15 May.

23 May

Aleutian Islands: Attu The units from the southern front attack the important Fish Hook Ridge but are held up by intense enemy fire. The mountains of Attu Island seem to present an insurmountable obstacle to the American forces, despite their large numbers and better equipment. After the day's unsuccessful efforts it is decided that Fish Hook Ridge must be the objective of a co-ordinated attack by units from both southern and northern fronts. This begins the final phase of the Attu Island battle.

☐ Germany. In the heaviest RAF raid of the war so far, 2,000 tons of bombs are dropped on Dortmund.

☐ Yugoslavia. German news agency reports heavy fighting in South Croatia between German troops and Yugoslav guerillas.

24 May

Eastern Front Battles continue over much of the front. There is fierce fighting in the Sevsk sector, on the Kuban front, and in the Central Don area.

Aleutian Islands: Attu Renewed American attacks on Fish Hook Ridge are repulsed by the Japanese.

The Japanese are resisting with fanatical determination.

The Chief of Staffs Conference approve a plan for the capture of Kiska Island.

25 May

Aleutian Islands: Attu American troops coming up from the south manage to reach the top of Fish Hook Ridge after hand-to-hand fighting in a complex system of trenches and tunnels dug by the Japanese. The units from the northern sector also make some progress from the other end of the ridge.

A Yugoslav partisan unit during the retreat to Mount Sutjeska in Croatia, May 1943. The partisans on the stretchers are suffering from typhus.

Tunisia Sousse is chosen as the site for the headquarters for the invasion of Pantelleria. The tactical method chosen is to be saturation bombing.

☐ USA. The Trident Conference, begun in Washington on 12 May, comes to an end. It has been decided that the invasion of north-west Europe (Operation *Overlord*) will start early in May 1944. The invasion will be preceded by a gigantic air offensive. In Italy, after the landing in Sicily (Operation *Husky*), whatever actions are necessary will be taken to eliminate the country from the war. Systematic bombing of the Ploesti oilfields in Rumania, vital to the Germans, will be undertaken from bases in the Mediterranean. The strategy to be adopted in the Pacific was also approved in outline.

26 May

Aleutian Islands: Attu The Americans improve their positions both on the southern slope and on the north side of Fish Hook Ridge.

☐ Italy. The Allied air offensive on Sicily, Sardinia and Pantellaria is maintained.

27 May

Aleutian Islands: Attu Forces of the US 7th Division finally seize Fish Hook Ridge. The construction of a fighter runway near Alexai Point is begun.

☐ USA. The Joint Committee for War Planning is asked to work out the requirements in men and materials, and to suggest possible dates, for the invasion of the Marshall Islands in the Pacific.

☐ France. In Paris the Council of National Resistance is founded.

☐ Yugoslavia. First parachute landings of British liaison officers to join Yugoslav partisans.

☐ Germany. Violent night raid by RAF on Essen. Over 1,000 tons of bombs dropped. In the last six mass raids on the Ruhr the RAF has now dropped 8,800 tons of bombs.

28 May

Aleutian Islands: Attu The Japanese, already squeezed into the Chicagof Harbour area, take refuge in the sur-rounding mountains. The Americans drop leaflets inviting them to sur-render.

☐ Italy. Over 100 US Fortress bombers made devastating daylight raid on Leghorn. Other heavy attacks on Italian targets continue.

29 May

Aleutian Islands: Attu Before dawn the Japanese come down from the mountains round Chicagof Harbour in absolute silence and deliver a violent counter-attack which takes them into the American positions. Savage fighting continues all day and during the following night.

☐ Germany. RAF drop over 1,500 tons of bombs on Wuppertal.

30 May

Aleutian Islands: Attu After their last, desperate effort, all organized resistance by the Japanese on the island is exhausted. The Americans have paid dearly for their conquest. In the fighting on the 29th alone they lost 550 dead and 1,140 wounded and some of their men went mad with fright before the shrieking fury of their assailants. As for the Japanese, apart from 28 wounded men who have fallen into American hands, the whole garrison has sacrificed itself. There are 2,352 dead, 500 of whom committed suicide with hand grenades.

On the same day, an American detachment occupies the island of Shemya without opposition.

☐ Algeria. General de Gaulle arrives at Algiers to make contact with Giraud, now Supreme Commander of French forces in North Africa. Talks take place to establish a central authority for the unified conduct of the French war effort.

☐ Italy. The sixtieth air raid on Naples. Round the-clock bombing of Pantelleria continues.

THE NEW PROPAGANDA WEAPONS

Aware that the final outcome of the war would also be determined by the attitudes and levels of active support of the civilian populations, all the governments of the belligerent powers set great store on the dissemination of propaganda, designed to promote ideological consensus, patriotic fervour and fighting spirit. In addition to the old, tested methods of moulding popular opinion, two modern techniques of mass communication were used to great effect: the radio and the cinema.

Wireless or radio had already proved capable of influencing millions of listeners and was used by all governments as a basic means of manipulating public opinion. The messages that went out over the air were intended both to arouse enthusiasm and combat defeatism. Radio stations also engaged in preparing special programmes to be transmitted abroad, to encourage the people of occupied countries, to link up with resistance groups and to sow doubt and uncertainty in the enemy camp.

Film also played a significant role in war propaganda. Almost all the cinema industries were urged to contribute with manpower and materials to the war effort. Government agencies were set up to promote and to coordinate film production and to censor its ideological content.

LESLIE HOWARD

In June an aeroplane travelling from Lisbon to London was attacked and shot down by a squadron of German fighters, acting on the mistaken assumption that Churchill was on board. Among the passengers on the plane, which crashed in flames in the Bay of Biscay, was the English actor Leslie Howard, returning from a propaganda tour.

Born in London in 1893, to a family of Hungarian origin, Howard made his theatrical debut in the 1920s, immediately proving a success at home and even more so on Broadway. With the arrival of sound he also made his first appearance in the cinema, and after a series of supporting roles gained international recognition in 1934 when he starred alongside Bette Davis in *Of Human Bondage*. From then on he concentrated on romantic parts, making the most of his elegant English looks and his splendid voice. In 1939 he played the sensitive and long-suffering Ashley Wilkes in *Gone With the Wind*. When war came he returned to England to direct and act in a few propaganda films and to work for the British Council.

Leslie Howard (right) in *Pygmalion*.

31 May
Aleutian Islands: Attu The Americans reconnoitre the whole of island in search of Japanese survivors. They find only corpses.
☐ Relays of Allied bombers continue to attack Italian targets.

1 June
Eastern Front In the Kuban, major air battles are taking place.
Mediterranean The round-the-clock Allied air offensive against Pantelleria continues.
☐ New forces are assembled and begin training in California to join the forces now on Attu in an operation to seize Kiska Island, also occupied by the Japanese.
☐ Germany. Air raid by the RAF on the Zeppelin factories at Friedrichshafen, where German radar equipment is manufactured.

2 June
Eastern Front The day brings some of the most violent air fighting yet seen in Russia. The Luftwaffe makes ferocious attacks on Kursk. Major air battles also continue over the Kuban.

3 June
Eastern Front Russian air force makes mass attack on enemy base at Orel.

Solomon Islands Admiral Halsey's H.Q. issues general instructions for the invasion of New Georgia, in the central Solomons. The main objective is to be Munda airfield, a jumping-off place for a series of 'hops' towards the northern Solomons. The landing force will be commanded by Rear-Admiral Turner, the occupation forces by General Hester at the head of the army's 43rd Division reinforced by two battalions of Raiders from the US Marines.
China The Japanese end their 'rice offensive' in the west of Hupeh province, in the Yichang area, and begin to withdraw. They have seized quantities of rice and captured many boats on the upper Yangtze.
Algeria In Algiers the Free French announce the formation of the *Comité Français de Libération Nationale* (CFLN), a provisional government of the French Empire under Generals de Gaulle and Giraud.

4 June
Mediterranean Attacks on Pantelleria and other Italian targets continue.
☐ Algiers. General de Gaulle and General Giraud both broadcast to the French people.

5 June
London. Churchill arrives back by air from North Africa, which he had visited after the Washington Conference.

6 June
Mediterranean The Allied bombers press home their attacks on Pantelleria.

7 June
Solomon Islands Japanese aircraft begin a series of heavy raids on Guadalcanal, the assembly and communications centre of the American troops preparing for the offensive. Allied fighters intercept and destroy 23 aircraft, losing 9 themselves.

8 June
Aleutian Islands The Japanese Supreme Command orders the evacuation of Kiska Island. The island is being shelled every day by American destroyers which prevent the arrival of any supplies except those that can be brought in by submarine.
Mediterranean British naval units, including three torpedo-boats, shell the harbours and coastal batteries on Pantelleria. Leaflets demanding unconditional surrender are dropped on the island.

Bunkers for ocean-going submarines built by the Todt organization on the French Atlantic coast.

9 June

Eastern Front Hundreds of Russian bombers make mass night raid on the German positions at Yaroslavl.

Mediterranean Allied Headquarters North Africa, state that bombardment of Pantelleria will continue as no reply has been received to surrender demands.

10 June

Eastern Front Hitler is pressing for the launching of Operation *Citadel*, the penetration of the Kursk salient and annihilation of the Russian forces in it. The attack is to be delivered by the 9th Army from the north and the 4th Armoured Army from the south. Both armies will be equipped with the greatest possible number of tanks, if necessary taking them from other sectors of the front.

11 June

Mediterranean After ten days of intense attacks by air and sea, during which 45 Allied aircraft have been shot down, the defence of Pantelleria ends and its garrison surrenders at 12 noon. The British 1st Division lands on the island. Over 5,000 tons of bombs have been dropped on the island since 8 May. The fall of Pantelleria allows the Allies to concentrate the activities of the Mediterranean air forces on Operation *Husky*, the invasion of Sicily.

During the night the Allies carry out an intensive air and naval bombardment of Lampedusa.

☐ Germany. Fortresses of the American 8th Air Force, unescorted, attack Wilhelmshaven in the evening, damaging shipyards where U-boats are built. But it becomes clear that, without adequate fighter escort, precision bombing is prevented by enemy interceptor aircraft.

The greatest force yet of RAF bombers attack Düsseldorf, dropping over 2,000 tons of bombs. Münster is struck by a smaller force.

12 June

Solomon Islands Allied fighter planes attack big formations of Japanese bombers and fighters making for Guadalcanal, shooting down 31 aircraft and losing 6 of their own.

Mediterranean After intense bombing and naval bombardment Lampedusa surrenders unconditionally to the Allied forces at 5.30 p.m.

Sicily. Allied bombing continues without respite; raids on Catania and Palermo cause many casualties and serious damage.

☐ King George VI visits fighting forces in North Africa.

13 June

Mediterranean The garrison on the small island of Linosa, surrenders unconditionally to the Allies.

New Guinea The Americans and Australians, preparing for the new offensive, reorganize by forming new 'Forces' consisting of a pair of infantry battalions supported by groups of gunners. These formations will be more suitable to the kind of warfare conducted on the island.

☐ Germany. Sixty B-17 bombers of

The British bomb the port of La Spezia, where the battleship *Littorio* is at anchor (partly visible on the right).

the US 8th Air Force attack the submarine shipyards at Kiel. During the aerial battle that follows at least 22 American aircraft are brought down.

14 June
Mediterranean A ship of the Royal Navy takes the uninhabited island of Lampione. The Allies now control all the islands in the Sicilian Channel.
China The headquarters of the US 14th Air Force is set up at Kweilin, in southern China, in Kwangsi Chuang province.

16 June
Solomon Islands American headquarters decide on the first objectives to be taken in the central Solomons as a preliminary to the attack on the main objective, which is Munda airfield on New Georgia. The operation is to begin on 30 June.
About 120 Japanese aircraft attack Guadalcanal and shipping in the waters off the island, damaging two warships and a transport which has to be grounded to prevent it sinking. But they pay dearly for this comparatively successful operation, losing nearly a hundred of their aircraft in combat with swarms of American fighters which have taken off from Henderson Field.
☐ Naples. Night attack by RAF.

17 June
China. General Stilwell informs Chiang Kai-shek about the decisions taken at the Trident Conference relating to the proposed Far East strategy.
☐ BBC broadcasts to French not to stay near factories working for Nazis.

18 June
Solomon Islands The headquarters of the US 43rd Division issue detailed instructions for the complex troop movements connected with the invasion of New Georgia.
☐ Sicily. The British and Americans step up their air attacks on Messina in preparation for Operation *Husky*, the invasion of Sicily.
☐ Australia. Mr John Curtin, the Prime Minister, announces that Australia is no longer threatened by invasion.
☐ India. Churchill announces that General Auchinleck is to replace General Wavell as Commander-in-Chief of British forces in India.

General Wavell is to become Viceroy of India.

19 June
The authorities give the populations of Naples and towns in Sicily matter of weeks to evacuate their cities.

20 June
New Guinea The headquarters of the US 6th Army (General Krueger) are set up at Milne Bay. The Japanese put in powerful attacks on the positions of the 17th Brigade of the Australian 3rd Division in the hilly area between Mubo and Lababia, but are driven off.
☐ India. General Auchinleck takes over as Commander-in-Chief of British forces in the Far East.
☐ Germany. RAF Lancasters attack the Zeppelin works at Friedrichshafen, where the German radar equipment is made, and instead of returning to Britain fly on to North Africa, inaugurating the 'shuttle' technique. On their return flight from Africa to Britain on the night of 23/24 June they bomb the Italian naval base at La Spezia.

21 June

Solomon Islands A battalion of American Raiders from Guadalcanal take Segi Point, at the extreme southern tip of New Georgia, which the Japanese have not bothered to garrison.

☐ Germany. In two raids on Wuppertal the RAF cause immense destruction and 5,000 deaths. Production is held up for 52 days. The famous German raid on Coventry killed 380 and stopped production for a month. Even the British protest when London newspapers compare photographs of the two bombed cities.

☐ Belgium. BBC warns Belgians to stay away from industrial plants working for Germany.

22 June

Solomon Islands Infantry units of the US 43rd Division reinforce the Raiders of the US Marines who have landed at Segi Point in New Georgia.
Trobriand Islands An American regimental group starts to land on Woodlark Island (95 miles southeast of New Guinea) without meeting any opposition.

☐ Germany. In their first big daylight raid bombers of the US 8th Air Force make a successful attack on a synthetic rubber factory at Hüls, in the Ruhr, putting it temporarily out of action.

23 June

Trobriand Islands During the night of 23/24 June American units land on Kiriwina Island, the biggest island in the group.
New Guinea In the area between Mubo and Lababia the Japanese slowly ease their pressure on the Australian 17th Brigade.

24 June

Allied air forces continue their intense attacks on industrial targets in Germany and Occupied Europe. Particularly heavy attacks are made on Elberfeld, the western half of Wuppertal.

☐ Italy. Mussolini speaks in Rome to Fascist Party Directorate on the threat of invasion.

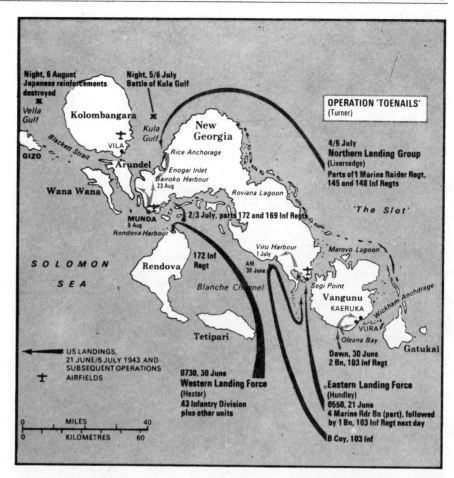

Solomon Islands: the US landings in New Georgia, launched on 21 June 1943.

25 June

Sicily. Allied bombing continues in preparation for the invasion of the island. 300 tons of bombs are dropped on Messina.

26 June

New Guinea MacKechnie Force, assembled at Morobe, where a supply depot has been established, embarks in light craft for Mageri Point, 15 miles to the north, to prepare a combined operation in Nassau Bay.

27 June

Solomon Islands From Segi, in New Georgia, the Marines of the 4th Raider battalion move by sea near to the plantation at Lambeti.

28 June

Solomon Islands In New Georgia, after having been landed without opposition near Lambeti, the

Marines begin the march across the jungle towards the port of Viru.

☐ Germany. Cologne is the target of a heavy night attack, described in Berlin as 'a terror raid'.

☐ Italy. Allied bombers maintain their intensive raids; Leghorn and Messina heavily attacked.

29 June

Solomon Islands During the night of 29/30 June, while American landing parties sail towards the central Solomons, four cruisers and four destroyers commanded by Rear-Admiral Merrill shell the Vila–Stanmore area on the island of Kolombangara, and the Biun–Shortland area on Bougainville. The waters off Shortland are also mined to stop the Japanese bringing in any reinforcements.

30 June

South Pacific Operation *Cartwheel*

Top: Marines unload ammunition on Rendova Island. Above: American units leave Guadalcanal for another part of the Pacific.

begins according to plan with a series of assaults and amphibious operations carried out by the South Pacific and South-West Pacific forces, with the object of capturing Rabaul, New Britain, advance post of the Japanese Empire. The forces of the US army and navy act in co-ordination under the overall command of General MacArthur.

Solomon Islands The amphibious force of the US 3rd Fleet, organized as Task Force 51 under the command of Rear-Admiral R. K. Turner and with land-based air support commanded by Vice-Admiral A. W. Fitch, lands the New Georgia occupation force (made up of the US 43rd Division and contingents of Marines and commanded by General Hester) in several of the central Solomon Islands.

The main landing is on Rendova Island. The troops landed here are to occupy the island and then cross to New Georgia to take Munda airfield. The landing on Rendova takes place with no difficulty; the units from the 43rd Division press on inland for over half a mile before they meet any resistance from the few Japanese patrols.

In New Georgia units of the 103rd Infantry, not getting the signal agreed with the Raiders that they have already occupied Viru habour, are put ashore at Segi Point. The Raiders occupy Viru in the evening. Other landings are made on smaller islands: Sasavele, Baraulu and Vangunu. Here the Japanese, while not holding up the landing (as they generally have elsewhere), put up a strenuous resistance to the Marines' penetration from Oleana, where they land, towards Wickham Anchorage. The Japanese air force is very active, sinking the transport *McCawley* and damaging other ships.

Trobriand Islands The main body of the occupation forces of the US 6th Division lands on Woodlark and Kriwina Islands, together with a contingent of Seabees who are to build two airfields.

New Guinea MacKechnie Force, commanded by the American Colonel MacKechnie and including

American and Australian units, lands without opposition in Nassau Bay and immediately pushes northwards towards the river Bitoi and southwards towards the river Tabali; but not without stern resistance by the Japanese.

The enemy salient at Mubo is held despite constant pressure by the Australian 17th Brigade.

1 July

Solomon Islands The troops landed on Rendova consolidate their bridgehead, and those on New Georgia their bridgehead in the port of Viru.

New Guinea Allied troops reinforce their positions along the southern branch of the river Bitoi in Nassau Bay, where US troops are landed.

2 July

Solomon Islands The US 43rd Division begins to assemble the units which are to be transported from Rendova to New Georgia to capture Munda airfield. Japanese bombers attack Rendova with great violence, and during the night the island is shelled by an enemy cruiser and several destroyers.

New Guinea MacKechnie Force holds firm in its bridgehead against light Japanese attacks, and makes contact with the Australian 3rd Division.

Trobriand Islands The Seabees start on the construction of an airfield.

☐ Major ports in central and southern Italy, Sicily and Sardinia continue to be the targets for heavy Allied air raids. Between 12 June and this date the Allies have dropped more than 2,000 tons of bombs on Italian territory, causing immense damage and shattering the morale of the troops who will have to face the Allied landing.

3 July

Eastern Front Operation *Citadel*, the offensive for the elimination of the Russian Kursk salient, is delayed by preventive bombing by the Russians which holds up the deployment of the German forces.

Solomon Islands The first contin-

KARL LANDSTEINER

The death occurred on 26 June of the Austrian scientist Karl Landsteiner, discoverer of human blood groups and winner of the Nobel Prize for Medicine and Physiology in 1930.

Born on 14 June 1868 in Vienna, Landsteiner studied at various European universities and in 1891 graduated in medicine from Vienna University. Engaged until the early years of the present century in haematological work, he made the fundamental discovery, published in 1909, that human blood comprises three distinct groups, A, B and C (subsequently O). Two of his colleagues, De Castello and Sturli, later discovered the AB group.

Landsteiner was also the first to determine the viral etiology of poliomyelitis, following an experiment with a rhesus monkey in 1908. In 1919 he went to Holland for three years and later accepted an invitation from the Rockefeller Institute for Medical Research to work in New York.

gents of the force detailed to take Munda airfield on New Georgia land on the beach at Zanana, about 6 miles east of Munda, and meet with no resistance from the Japanese. The beachhead is quickly consolidated in the next few days. On Vangunu Island the Americans occupy Wickham Anchorage.

4 July

Solomon Islands The Raiders manning Viru harbour are replaced by infantry of the 43rd Division. The units

landed at Zanana advance westwards towards the river Barike, the starting line for the assault on Munda.

The transports carrying the landing force for Rice Anchorage sail during the night escorted by Rear-Admiral Ainsworth's squadron, whose ships shell Vila and Bairoko.

☐ General Sikorski, the leader of the Polish Government in exile, is killed when his plane crashes near Gibraltar.

5 July

Eastern Front The Germans launch their great offensive against the Kursk salient in the Orel, Kursk, and Belgorod sectors. The battle takes place on a 200-mile front. From the north, from the Orel area, the attack is delivered by the 9th Army. From the south the 4th Armoured Army and Kempf Operation Group advance from the Belgorod area. The forces north of the salient are commanded by General Model, those to the south by General Hoth. At the sides of the salient the Germans have concentrated 2,000 tanks (Russian sources say 3,000), including many of the new Panthers and Tigers and the new Ferdinand self-propelled gun. Over 2,000 aircraft will support the ground operations, in which a million men will be taking part.

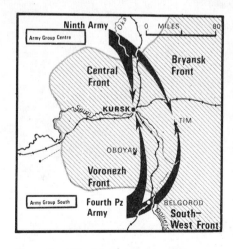

Operation *Citadel*, the unsuccessful German attempt to eliminate the salient at Kursk, launched on 5 July 1943.

The Russians are just as strong. Under the overall command of Zhukov and Vasilevsky they have concentrated inside the highly fortified salient the forces of the Central Front (Rokossovsky) and the Voronezh Front (Vatutin): in all nine armies, including two armoured armies and two assault groups. They have 20,000 guns and mortars, 920 'Katyusha' flame-throwers, ten armoured trains and two airborne divisions. The density of the minefields in the most important sectors is 1,500 anti-tank mines and 1,700 anti-personnel mines to every square kilometre (3,900 and 4,400 per square mile).

The Germans manage to make small penetrations in the Russian positions both to the north and south, but at a stupendous cost. In the north, the gain of 6 miles of ground on a front of 12 miles costs them 25,000 dead and the loss of 200 tanks and as many aircraft. In the south an advance of about 25 miles on a front of 30 miles is paid for with 10,000 dead and the destruction of 350 tanks. On the very first day the Russians announce that they have destroyed 586 tanks and 203 aircraft. This is certainly an exaggeration, but it gives an idea of the scale of this gigantic battle, in which some 6,000 tanks, 4,000 aircraft and over 2 million men are engaged, the biggest tank battle in history, and one of the most important aerial battles which is to see the Luftwaffe lose its dominance in the Russian skies for the first time.

Solomon Islands The main body of the American troops is concentrated on Rendova, where there is a Japanese garrison 6,000 strong. Four battalions land at Rice Anchorage in New Georgia, not far from Bairoko, and advance elements reach the river Giza Giza. The troops landed at Zanana move towards Munda, but the track they follow is barred by Japanese units.

Three groups of Japanese destroyers, ten ships in all, land reinforcements (850 men) at Kolombangara from the Shortlands. As soon as the operation is completed the 'Tokyo Night Express' (which has never been out of action, even if it has ceased to be the main supply line to Guadalcanal) leaves immediately, but is intercepted at once in the Gulf of Kula by three American cruisers and four destroyers under command of Rear-Admiral Ainsworth. A battle flares up and the Americans get the worst of the engagement. They lose the light cruiser *Helena* and the destroyer *Strong*, sunk by a submarine, while the Japanese lose two destroyers, the *Niizuki* and *Nagatsuki*, the latter grounded and finished off at dawn by American aircraft.

6 July
Eastern Front The battle of the Kursk salient develops. Model's 9th

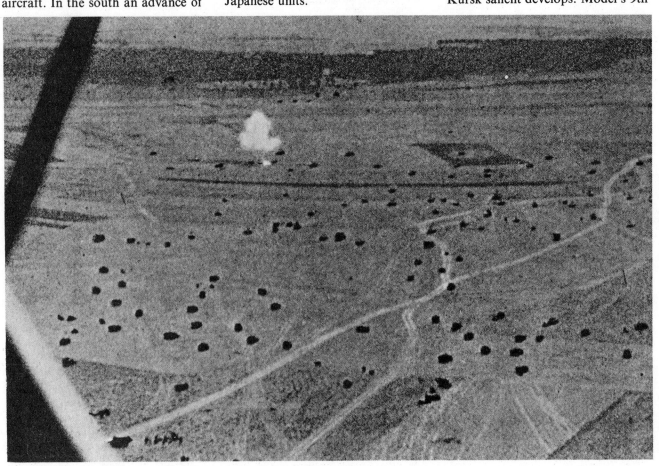

Aerial view of a concentration of German tanks on the Kursk plain, ready for Operation *Citadel*.

Army (part of von Kluge's Army Group Centre) makes slight progress, while the 4th Armoured Army under Hoth and the Kempf Operational Group (from von Manstein's Army Group South) drive the Russians back about 12 miles to the north. The Russian bulletin speaks of the destruction of 433 tanks and 111 aircraft. German losses (and Russian losses cannot be smaller) are not as great as the day before, but still very high.

Solomon Islands American aircraft begin a series of heavy raids on airports on the island of Bougainville, a future objective of the invasion forces. The raids gradually grow stronger; medium bombers often accompany the heavy bombers to hit more and more often the enemy shipping operating in the area. Two regiments of the 43rd Division are already established on New Georgia, concentrated near the river Barike.

Some battalions are trying without success to force the Japanese block on the track from Zanana to Munda.

Aleutian Islands An American squadron of cruisers and destroyers (Rear-Admiral Giffen) shells Kiska Island.

China Bombers of the US 14th Air Force attack ships in ports in western China held by the Japanese.

7 July

Eastern Front While the Germans make more progress on the south flank of the Kursk salient, in the north the Russian armies halt them. The Russians carry out local counter-attacks while preparing a general counter-offensive. Russian sources speak of 520 tanks destroyed and 111 aircraft shot down; reports also mention the recklessness of German tank crews in driving straight through Russian minefields and suffering severely as a result.

Solomon Islands Fighting continues

on the Zanana–Munda track on New Georgia, north of the river Barike. Further south, new American units reach the Bairoko–Munda track. More forces sail from Guadalcanal for Rendova.

New Guinea Allied aircraft drop more than 100 tons of bombs on Japanese positions in the Mubo sector. MacKechnie Force, after moving to Napier from the coast, is deployed for an attack on Nitoi Ridge. The Australians take Observation Hill, a feature of particular strategic value about a mile from Mubo.

☐ General Giraud arrives in Washington to confer with President Roosevelt and other senior military officers about the role of the Free French in the war's coming stages.

8 July

Eastern Front The battle of Kursk continues with undiminished vio-

A Russian anti-tank gun fires on an advancing German tank in the course of the great battle fought out in the Orlov–Kursk sector.

lence. The losses attributed to the Germans by the Russians today are 304 tanks and 161 aircraft. The Germans claim the loss of 400 tanks and 193 aircraft by the Russians. There can be no question about the outcome of the battle. From the start the attackers have been outnumbered by the defenders, and Russia's intelligence network has always kept them minutely informed about the plans of the Wehrmacht.

Solomon Islands In New Georgia the US 43rd Division finally succeeds in driving off the Japanese troops that were blocking the Zanana–Munda track, and takes up positions on the river Barike. On Kolombangara Island US aircraft bomb Vila.

9 July
Sicily While the attacks on the island by Allied bombers are stepped up, the landing force – the US 7th Army under General Patton and the British 8th Army under General Montgomery, the two armies forming part of the XV Army Group commanded by General Alexander – sails from harbours in Tunisia in some 3,000 craft and heads for Sicily. The defence of Sicily is in the hands of General Alfredo Guzzoni's Italian 6th Army of 230,000 men, who include some 40,000 highly trained German troops.

During the night airborne troops are dropped on the south-east coast of the island, where the Allied landing is due to take place. But a gusty wind, sometimes reaching Force 7, poor visibility and lack of previous experience in night drops make this first attempt at an airborne attack practi-cally useless. The 3,400 parachutists of the 82nd Airborne Division under the American Colonel Gavin are scattered over a vast area and their intervention is of little or no value. Meanwhile the vessels transporting the landing forces are in serious difficulties; the strong wind and rough sea impose a great strain on the Allied infantrymen.

Eastern Front The Russians launch a counter-attack in the area of Oboyan, south of Kursk, in the southern part of the salient, and bring the German advance to a halt here too. There is bitter fighting. The Russian press speaks of the 'slaughter of the Germans' and compares the battle with the historic battle of Kulikovo, in which Prince Dmitri Donskoi saved his country by defeating the Tartars in 1380.

July 1943: a platoon of American Marines in the Solomon Islands.

The Allied landing in Siciliy, 10 July 1943: as well as tanks and guns, trucks and other
logistic material, dozens of mules bought in Tunisia are landed on the island. They prove
themselves an invaluable means of transport in the more inaccessible parts of the
peninsula during the Italian campaign.

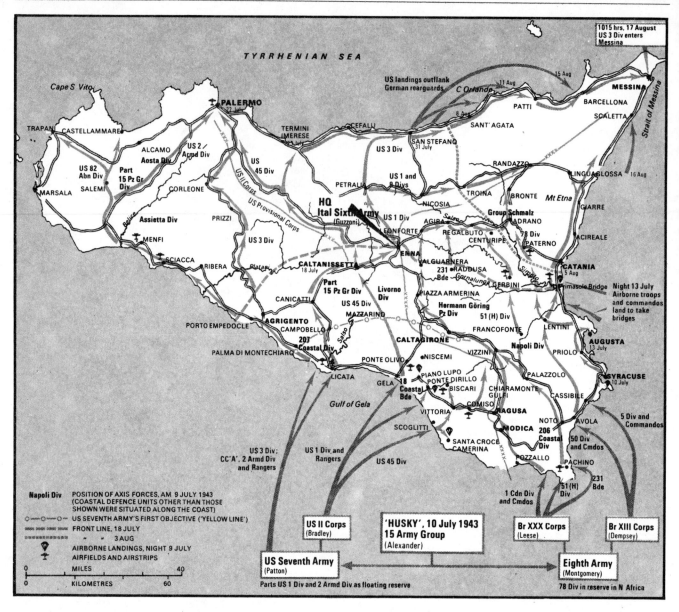

TYRRHENIAN SEA

1015 hrs, 17 August
US 3 Div enters
Messina

US landings outflank
German rearguards

Cape S Vito

MESSINA

PALERMO
27 July

BARCELLONA

PATTI

SCALETTA

TRAPANI

CEFALU

Strait of Messina

CASTELLAMMARE

TERMINI
IMERESE

SANT' AGATA

US 3 Div

SAN STEFANO
31 July

LINGUAGLOSSA
16 Aug

ALCAMO

Aosta Div

US 2
Armd Div

US
45 Div

RANDAZZO

US 82
Abn Div

Part
15 Pz Gr
Div

CORLEONE

US 1 and
9 Divs

TROINA

BRONTE

Mt Etna

GIARRE

SALEMI

PETRALIA

NICOSIA

ACIREALE

MARSALA

HQ
Ital Sixth Army
(Guzzoni)

US 1 Div

AGIRA

REGALBUTO
CENTURIPE

Group Schmalz

78 Div

PRIZZI

ADRANO

PATERNO

Assietta Div

US 3 Div

LEONFORTE

CATANIA
5 Aug

MENFI

ENNA

SCIACCA

RIBERA

CALTANISSETTA
18 July

VALGUARNERA
231
Bde

RADDUSA

Primasole Bridge

Night 13 July
Airborne troops
and commandos
land to take
bridges

Part
15 Pz Gr Div

CANICATTI

Livorno
Div

PIAZZA ARMERINA

Hermann Göring
Pz Div

GERBINI

US 45 Div

51 (H) Div

PORTO EMPEDOCLE

AGRIGENTO

MAZZARINO

FRANCOFONTE

LENTINI

CAMPOBELLO

AUGUSTA
13 July

207
Coastal Div

CALTAGIRONE

Napoli Div

PRIOLO

PALMA DI MONTECHIARO

PONTE OLIVO

VIZZINI

PALAZZOLO

SYRACUSE
10 July

LICATA

GELA

18
Coastal
Bde

NISCEMI

PIANO LUPO
PONTE DIRILLO
BISCARI

CHIARAMONTE
GULFI

CASSIBILE

Gulf of Gela

COMISO

RAGUSA

5 Div and
Commandos

VITTORIA

AVOLA

SCOGLITTI

NOTO

206
Coastal
Div

50 Div
and Cmdos

SANTA CROCE
CAMERINA

MODICA

US 3 Div;
CC 'A', 2 Armd Div
and Rangers

US 1 Div and
Rangers

POZZALLO

PACHINO

US 45 Div

1 Cdn Div
and Cmdos

51 (H)
Div

231
Bde

Napoli Div — POSITION OF AXIS FORCES, AM 9 JULY 1943
(COASTAL DEFENCE UNITS OTHER THAN THOSE
SHOWN WERE SITUATED ALONG THE COAST)
US SEVENTH ARMY'S FIRST OBJECTIVE ('YELLOW LINE')
FRONT LINE, 18 JULY
" " 3 AUG
AIRBORNE LANDINGS, NIGHT 9 JULY
AIRFIELDS AND AIRSTRIPS

MILES 0 ... 40
KILOMETRES 0 ... 60

| US II Corps (Bradley) | 'HUSKY', 10 July 1943 15 Army Group (Alexander) | Br XXX Corps (Leese) | Br XIII Corps (Dempsey) |

US Seventh Army (Patton)

Eighth Army (Montgomery)

Parts US 1 Div and 2 Armd Div as floating reserve

78 Div in reserve in N Africa

According to Russian sources the Germans have lost nearly 2,000 tanks since 5 July.

Solomon Islands Supported by artillery and naval guns as well as by the air force, two regiments of the US 43rd Division open the attack on Munda from the river Barike line. The regiment attacking inland succeeds in advancing more than half a mile, but the one on the coast makes no progress worth mentioning. A third battalion approaching Munda from Triri is held up by the Japanese at Enogai Point. US destroyers shell Munda.

New American units reach Rendova from Guadalcanal, while on Kolombangara the Japanese land 1,200 men

brought from the Shortland Islands.

10 July

Sicily Operation *Husky*, the Allied landing on Sicily, begins at first light. 160,000 men with 600 tanks set foot on the south-east coast of Sicily, the Americans of the 7th Army in the Gulf of Gela, between Licata and Scoglitti, and the British of Montgomery's 8th Army in the Gulf of Syracuse, between the capital and Pachino. The landings are carried out without much difficulty, thanks to the accurate and intense fire of the warships, and because the defending forces did not expect a landing in such bad weather (and in fact no fewer than 200 landing craft are put out of action by the rough sea). Dur-

ing the operation British and American fighters from bases in Malta and Pantelleria fly in formation over the landing places to deal with any possible Axis counter-attacks. While the British 8th Army meets little resistance, and its units enter Syracuse during the night, Americans of the 1st Division and the Rangers, once they have taken Gela at about 8.00 a.m., encounter powerful counter-attacks by the German *Hermann Goering* and Italian *Livorno* Divisions.

In the south, where the American 45th Division is in action, Vittoria and Santa Croce Camerina are taken. To the north the US 3rd Division, 2nd Armoured Division and Rangers take Licata, including the harbour and airfield, and consolidate their positions, keeping an eye on the movements of the German 15th Armoured Division, whom they have identified between Canicatti and Caltanissetta, and who are reported by American reconnaissance to be moving east.

Solomon Islands In New Georgia the American advance across the river Barike is greatly slowed down both by Japanese resistance and by the thick jungle, which among other things makes close air support impossible. The battalion pinned down at Enogai Point manages to wipe out the Japanese resistance, but is short of rations and drinking water. Supplies have to be dropped by parachute.

Eastern Front Two armies and an assault group from the Steppe Front, commanded by General Konev, are brought up from reserve and thrown in against Hoth's 4th Armoured Army in the southern sector of the Kursk salient.

New Guinea American forces from Nassau Bay manage to join up with units of the Australian 3rd Division on the Buigap stream, cutting Japanese communications between Mubo and Salamaua.

11 July

Eastern Front The 4th Armoured Army (Hoth) and Kempf Operational Group, in the southern sector of the Kursk salient, throw in all the forces at their command in a desperate attack on enemy positions at Prokhorovka. They succeed in taking several miles of territory, but lose 400 tanks. However, the northern and southern points of the German forces are still very far apart, and they never get any closer. Von Manstein and von Kluge beg the Führer to call off the terrible costly Operation *Citadel*, already doomed to failure. But they receive refusals.

Sicily The Axis counter-attack towards Gela is stepped up. The action is supported by Italian and German aircraft, which bomb the beaches at Gela and the warships off the coast. The units of the *Livorno* Division,

UFA

Universum Film Aktiengesellschaft (UFA), the biggest production, control and propaganda organization of the Nazi film industry, celebrated the twenty-fifth anniversary of its foundation with J. von Baky's film *Münchhausen*. UFA was established at the express wish of the German government in December 1917, during wartime, with clear propagandist and educational intentions, to unite the numerous production companies, many of them small and often dependent upon outside subsidy, into a single entity.

Remaining active even after the German military defeat, UFA was associated with the great period of Weimar cinema, producing and distributing at home and abroad films directed by such men as Pabst, Murnau, Lubitsch and Lang. After the 1923 crisis and rigid financial restructuring, UFA re-emerged at the beginning of the 1930s, taking fullest advantage of the advent of sound.

With the rise of the Nazis and the resultant policy of centralization and state control, UFA reinforced its monopoly and became one of the pillars of the regime's propaganda campaigns.

After war broke out, UFA followed in the wake of the advancing German armies to extend its monopoly to all the countries under military occupation. It was a time of considerable productive activity: between 1940 and 1944 UFA and its subsidiaries made more than 200 films.

from the north, and of the *Herman Goering* Division, from the east, converge on Gela. The Italian units' attack is repulsed almost at once by fire from the Rangers and from naval guns, but the German tanks east of Gela reach the coast road only a mile from the sea. Here, however, they are pinned down by fire from American field guns and from the guns of the cruisers off the coast.

On the 8th Army front the British XXX Corps (General Leese) reaches Palazzolo and makes for Caltagirone, while in the XIII Corps sector (General Dempsey) the 5th Division, after taking Syracuse, continues to advance along the coast road towards Augusta, hardly seeming to halt at all. However, in the evening, at Priolo (about half way between Augusta and Syracuse), advance patrols meet the armoured cars of the German Schmalz Group, which has hurried up from Catania, and are forced to retire.

Solomon Islands Stalemate in New Georgia. The Americans' supply situation is becoming critical. A runway for fighter aircraft has been prepared at Segi Point. Admiral Halsey names General Vandegrift, just promoted to command the I Amphibious Corps of the US Marines, to direct the land operations for the capture of Bougainville, the last Japanese bulwark between New Georgia and New Britain, where the Japanese have their vital base at Rabaul.

12 July

Eastern Front The Russians open a huge counter-offensive from the northern sector of the Kursk salient and the Kirov and Novosil sectors. The eight armies of the Central Front (Rokossovsky), Bryansk Front (Popov) and Western Front (Sokolovsky) are engaged. Hitler finally yields to pressure and calls off the operation. But he insists that his armies must not retire from the positions they have gained.

Sicily 2.00 p.m.: The remaining tanks of the German *Hermann*

Goering Armoured Division call off the attack and withdraw northwards, leaving a third of their tanks behind. The forces of the American 7th Army's central sector, the main targets of the Italian and German attacks, are safe.

The American 7th Army has reached its immediate objectives, and is now digging in on the so-called 'yellow line' which starts from Palma di Montechiaro (on the coast) and passes through Campobello, Mazzarino, Caltagirone and Grammichele. On the left of the American line the 3rd Division takes Canicatti. The 45th Division presses on beyond Comiso and finally takes Chiaramonte Gulfi. All the airfields in this field of operations are firmly in Allied hands. The Americans have taken 18,000 prisoners and lost about a thousand men killed and wounded.

In the British sector of the front the 5th Division (XIII Corps) repulses attacks by the Schmalz Group and the Italian *Napoli* Division with the help of dive-bombers and support from naval guns, and advances on

Augusta. The British 50th Division pushes on towards Lentini.

Solomon Islands In the battle for Munda, in New Georgia, the Americans make slight progress against the very resourceful enemy. They are in severe difficulties with supplies.

Naval Battle of Kolombangara. During the night of 12/13 July the 'Tokyo Night Express' bringing 1,200 men to Kolombangara is intercepted in the Gulf of Kula (between Kolombangara and New Georgia) by an American naval formation consisting of three light cruisers and ten destroyers. The landing takes place while the Japanese escort to the four destroyers carrying the troops is already engaged with the enemy. The escort includes one light cruiser and five destroyers under the command of Vice-Admiral Izaki. There is a violent exchange of fire, and the Japanese especially fire a great many torpedoes. The American formation loses the destroyer *Gwin*, while the cruisers *Saint Louis*, *Honolulu* and *Leander* (this last a New Zealand ship) are damaged by torpedoes. Two other American destroyers are

badly damaged as the result of a collision. The Japanese lose the cruiser *Jintsu*, which sinks with the commander Admiral Izaki, and 482 officers and ratings.

New Guinea Allied forces advance on Mubo, wiping out several Japanese strongholds.

China Chiang Kai-shek accepts the proposal put forward at the Trident Conference for a limited offensive, code-named *Saucy*, to re-establish communications by land across Burma.

13 July

Sicily Troops of the British 5th Division take Augusta. The 51st Division of XXX Corps is engaged near Vizzini by the German *Hermann Goering* Armoured Division and the remains of the Italian *Napoli* Division, which are withdrawing on Catania. The British units are obliged to hold up their advance.

Solomon Islands The Americans in New Georgia succeed in capturing a hill that overlooks the Zanana-Munda track and establish a salient into the positions of the Japanese,

A dramatic scene from the battle of Kursk: a German soldier watches a Mark IV tank outlined behind him against the light from blazing fires.

who defend themselves with their usual fanaticism. Nearly 30,000 men of the US army and Marines have now landed on New Georgia, Rendova and the smaller islands.

New Guinea The enemy is completely eliminated from the Mubo area. The Australian 3rd Division completes the mopping-up of Lababia ridge.

☐ The French West Indies adhere to the *Comité Français de Libération Nationale*.

13–14 July

Sicily During the night General Dempsey's British XIII Corps opens an offensive against the Schmalz Group's positions in an effort to penetrate on to the Catania plain. At the same time British and American airborne troops are parachuted south of Catania to guarantee the crossing on two very important bridges, the Ponte dei Malati on the river Lentini, about 3 miles north of the town of that name, and the Ponte Primasole on the river Simeto, which gives the easiest and most convenient access to the Catania plain. The Ponte dei Malati is captured by a Commando force landed on the coast from British ships. The operation to take the Ponte Primasole starts disastrously since the Allied transport aircraft, under heavy anti-aircraft fire, drop the parachutists a bit off target. Only 200 of the 1,900 men dropped manage to reach the bridge, with three anti-tank guns. Despite this disastrous beginning they succeed in capturing it.

14 July

Eastern Front Now the Voronezh Front (Vatutin) also goes over to the offensive, in the southern sector of the Kursk salient opposite the 4th Armoured Army and Kempf Operational Group.

Sicily The American 1st Division enters Mazzarino and Niscemi, while on the outskirts of Vizzini the British 51st Division (XXX Corps), supported by the American 45th Division, overcomes forceful resistance by the Axis troops. While the US division is shifted out on to the

left sector, the village is taken by a brigade of the 51st Division. The Canadian 1st Division now moves north-west towards Enna. Near Lentini, in the British XIII Corps sector, an attack by the 5th and 51st Divisions is contained by the Axis forces. The parachutists at Ponte Primasole hold out all day. As the evening falls they run out of ammunition and withdraw over a hill south of the river, where they are joined by the men of the Durham brigade of the 50th Division.

Allied bombing is intensified on the lines of communication leading from the north to the south of the peninsula and the main southern towns. Naples is the principal target.

Solomon Islands Heavy fighting in the New Georgia jungle. New reinforcements and tanks are landed at Laiana.

Trobriand Islands The Americans complete the construction of the airfield begun by the Seabees immediately after the landing.

15 July

Eastern Front The Russian supreme command announces that since the start of the counter-offensive in the direction of Orel the Red Army has taken 15–30 miles of territory.

Sicily General Patton, commanding the US 7th Army, forms a provisional corps which he makes responsible for the western part of the island. It is commanded by General Geoffrey Keyes and is made up of the 3rd Division reinforced by the 3rd Battalion of Rangers and the 82nd Division reinforced by a regiment from the 9th Division and by airborne troops.

The Canadian 1st Division takes Caltagirone and Grammichele. In the British sector, the battle continues in the area of Lentini and at the Ponte Primasole; Colonel Schmalz, fearing an attack from his eastern flank, withdraws north of the river Gomalunga, and then across the Simeto.

Solomon Islands The Japanese carry out a big raid on American troop and shipping concentrations in the central Solomons. 45 of the 75 air-

craft taking part are shot down by American fighters. After this defeat the Japanese air force confines itself to night operations.

Seeing that the situation is not going according to plan, the American headquarters replace General Hester by General Griswold as head of the New Georgia occupation force. Rear-Admiral Turner, commander of the South Pacific amphibious force and of Task Force 31, is also replaced.

15–16 July

Sicily During the night two companies of the Durham brigade of the 50th Division ford the river Simeto west of Ponte Primasole.

16 July

Eastern Front In the Kursk salient sector the Germans withdraw as they try to hold the powerful Russian thrust. Hitler justifies the abandonment of Operation *Citadel* by the possible need to send substantial forces to deal with the situation in Italy. In the Kuban the Russians are preparing an offensive to liquidate the enemy bridgehead between the Black Sea and the Sea of Azov.

Sicily The American 3rd Division attacks in the direction of Agrigento, while the American 2nd Armoured Division is sent in by General Patton against Palermo.

During the night the Canadian 1st Division (British XXX Corps) takes Caltagirone and goes on into Piazza Armerina after a hard battle with a battalion of the German 15th Armoured Division.

South of Catania, where the British divisions are operating, men of the Durham brigade supported by artillery and armoured cars try to capture Ponte Primasole and establish a bridgehead on the opposite bank. The operation is defeated by the quick reaction of the German parachute battalion defending the bridge, but during the night units of the brigade succeed in crossing the stream. At dawn a certain number of tanks and anti-tank guns are also able to cross the bridge. The Germans retire.

Solomon Islands In New Georgia the

Russian infantry attacking German defensive positions on the river Donetz.

US 172nd Infantry Regiment gradually extends the Laiana beachhead; the 169th take a hill but are still exposed to strong Japanese pressure.
Trobriand Islands The airfield constructed on Woodlark Island comes into service.
Kuril Islands A US submarine shells Matsuwa Island, in the Kuriles. This group of islands is already within range of American bombers based in the Aleutians.
☐ Churchill and Roosevelt direct a joint appeal to the Italians to decide 'whether they want to die for Mussolini and Hitler or live for Italy and civilization'.

17 July

Eastern Front While the Western, Bryansk and Central Fronts continue their counter-offensive north of the Kursk salient, other Russian armies attack in the area south of Izyum and south-west of Voroshilovgrad. Moscow announces that Russian troops have completely recaptured the positions they held before 5 July south of Orel.
Sicily The American 3rd Division enters Agrigento. In line with General Alexander's directives, General Patton's II Corps makes for the north coast of the island.
In the eastern sector the troops of the British XIII Corps reinforce the bridgehead over the Simeto, in the coastal area. During the night two brigades of the 50th Division begin to attack northwards towards Catania; the *Hermann Goering* Armoured Division and the Schmalz Group, putting up a lively resistance to the attacking forces, block the coast road in defence of the city.
Solomon Islands During the night of 17/18 July the Japanese garrison on New Georgia launches the only coordinated counter-offensive of the whole campaign, penetrating into the American positions at some points.

New Guinea The Australian 3rd Division and two battalions of the American 41st Division begin to advance on Salamaua. This is a diversionary action; the Allies' real objectives are the valley of the river Markham and the Huon peninsula, from which it will be possible to control the Vitiaz and Dampier Straits.

18 July

Sicily The US 45th Division takes Caltanissetta and pushes on to the north to cut highway 121 which joins Palermo with Enna. After two days of strenuous fighting with the German 15th Armoured Division the Canadian 1st Division (XXX Corps) takes Valguarnera, a few miles south-east of Enna, by-passes the city and heads for Leonforte. From there their orders are to turn east, towards Agira and Regalbuto, to get to Adrano, a key point of the German defence on Etna, north-west of Catania.

Rome, 19 July 1943: Pope Pius XII among survivors from the American air raid on the San Lorenzo district. The raid claimed about 2,000 victims and caused considerable damage, including a hit on the San Lorenzo basilica.

In the eastern sector the advance of the British 5th and 51st Divisions is halted before Catania, where the Germans have set up an effective defence line. Montgomery then tries to pass round the obstacle to the west; the Germans do their utmost to hold the Catania sector, which is the pivot on which the line of the Axis troops retiring to north-east Sicily hinges.

2nd Brigade of the Canadian 1st Division, the British 51st Division and 231st Brigade are given the task of turning the German defences round Catania.

Eastern Front Fierce fighting to the north and south of the Kursk salient continues.

Solomon Islands In New Guinea the Americans get ready for another attack on Munda, and drive off some Japanese units that have infiltrated into their lines. A Japanese destroyer is sunk by American aircraft near Bougainville Island, where it was to

have landed reinforcements and supplies. American air formations attack enemy installations at Buin, on the same island.

19 July

Sicily The advance of the Allied troops northwards continues. The 231st Brigade reaches the outskirts of Agira, while the Canadian 2nd Brigade (1st Division) attacks towards Leonforte. Near Catania the British XIII Corps is held up by the firm resistance of the Germans. The progress of the American 7th Army towards Trapani and Palermo is faster and the enemy's resistance is negligible.

Hitler and Mussolini meet at Feltre, northern Italy. The talks last from 11.00 a.m. to 6.00 p.m., and the Führer endeavours to revive the Duce's morale, which has slumped in the wake of the military disasters in Africa and Sicily and of the changed political situation at home. Hitler is

aware of proposals put forward by some senior officers and political leaders that Italy should seek a separate peace with the Allies. Hitler dazzles Mussolini with his usual long-winded eloquence. He tells him of secret weapons being built in Germany which will guarantee an Axis victory, and he offers to send German troops to Italy. At the same time he *demands* from his 'colleague', giving the suggestion the form of an ultimatum, that Mussolini should wield the iron fist and purge his party and his country of those who oppose him. The Allies bomb Rome for the first time. Some 700 American bombers drop 800 tons of bombs on the Littorio and Ciampino airport and the railway junction that crosses the San Lorenzo district. The attack, carried out in two phases, one in the morning and one in the afternoon, kills about 2,000 people and causes immense damage, casualties include the basilica of San Lorenzo, built by the

Emperor Constantine in the fourth century and containing the graves of many popes. The historic centre of the city is not bombed, but there is great distress in the city and throughout the country.

Eastern Front The Russians are on the offensive everywhere now that the German effort against the Kursk salient has been all but crushed. From north to south, attacks are mounted by the Kalinin Front (Eremenko), Western Front (Sokolovsky), Bryansk Front (Popov), Central or Belorussia Front (Rokossovsky), Voronezh Front (Vatutin), otherwise called the 1st Ukrainian Front, the Steppe or 2nd Ukrainian Front (Konev), the South-Western or 3rd Ukrainian Front (Malinovsky), the South or 4th Ukrainian Front (Tolbukhin) and finally the North Caucasus Front (Petrov).

Aleutian Islands Rear-Admiral Kinkaid confirms the plan for the invasion of Kiska Island. The island is bombed and shelled from sea and air a number of times. During the past month the aircraft of the US 2nd Air Force have dropped over 1,200 tons of bombs.

20 July

Sicily In the western part of the island the US 82nd Division takes Sciacca and Menfi and pushes on towards Trapani and Palermo. The US II Corps occupies Enna. In the east the Canadian II Brigade (1st Division), presses on to within a few miles of Leonforte, while the British 5th Division attacks Gerbini airport, north-west of Catania.

General Montgomery brings the 78th Division over from Africa, where it has been in reserve. He has given up the idea of a frontal attack on Catania and now proposes to carry out a turning manœuvre to break through the enemy positions on Etna, using XXX Corps and the 78th Division.

With their forces apparently well on the way to complete victory in Sicily, the Allies cancel the plans for Operation *Brimstone*, the invasion of Sardinia, and concentrate their attention on Naples, with its big harbour and relative proximity to Rome.

Eastern Front The Germans retreat in both the northern and southern sectors of the Kursk front. Von Manstein orders withdrawal despite Hitler's instructions.

Solomon Islands In New Georgia the experienced 169th Infantry is re-

placed at Munda by the 145th Infantry. The 148th Infantry breaks through the enemy positions and mans the positions formerly held by the 145th. A road through the jungle between Laiana and the Munda Track is completed, allowing the combatant troops to receive more supplies.

New Guinea American units begin a series of operations to take a line of hills that dominate Tambu Bay and Dot Inlet, a small creek.

21 July

Sicily The Americans enter Castelvetrano and Corleone. In the British sector the Canadian 1st Division enters Leonforte during the night where fighting goes on in the village streets until the morning.

Solomon Islands An American reconnaissance group lands during the night of 21/22 July near Barakoma, on Vella Lavella Island, north-west of Kolombangara, to examine prospects for a landing. If they could take the island the Americans would neutralize the Japanese base at Vila, also on Kolombangara, and would be nearer to Bougainville, where the Japanese have eight airfields and an important base at Biun. Local operations on New Georgia. Two Japanese destroyers bringing reinforcements are sunk by US aircraft south of Choiseul.

☐ Germany. Rommel leaves his new headquarters in Bavaria to inspect Axis defences in Greece and the Aegean. This is the sector where the Axis fear a new Allied landing.

22 July

Sicily The American troops enter Palermo. It now only remains to take the extreme western strip of the island before turning the American forces east, towards Messina.

General Vittorio Ambrosio, Chief of the Italian General Staff, following the directives put out from the meeting at Feltre on 19 July, asks for two German divisions to be sent to Italy and for the German 29th Motorized Division to be transferred from Calabria to Sicily. But he requires – and he makes the point specifically

A Sicilian shepherd shows an American soldier where the Germans are.

– 'that the Italian Supreme Command should be able to dispose freely of the troops put at its disposition.'

Solomon Islands: New Georgia General Griswold, the new commander of the occupation force, plans an offensive on a huge scale against the Munda air base for the 25th. Units of the 25th Division reach the island; they will be attached to the 37th Division, which will carry out the operation with the 43rd Division. American land forces on New Georgia, Rendova and the smaller islands now amount to 32,000 army personnel and 1,700 Marines.

Eastern Front The Russians take Mtsensk and Bolkhov and in the northern sector launch a limited offensive south of Lake Ladoga.

Aleutian Islands Two battleships, five cruisers and nine destroyers again bombard Japanese installation on Kiska Island, which the Japanese Imperial Staff has already decided to evacuate.

Solomon Islands In the Bougainville sector the small Japanese seaplane carrier *Nisshin*, escorted by three destroyers, tries to reach New Georgia but is intercepted and sunk by American aircraft near Bougainville.

23 July

Sicily The American Provisional Corps occupies the ports of Trapani and Marsala, while units of the US 45th Division reach the north coast east of Termini Imerese.

The whole of western Sicily is now under Allied control, and General Patton can now turn east towards the final target, Messina. He sends his II Corps with all available artillery along two roads, the northern coast road and highway 120, from Petralia to Randazzo.

Eastern Front The Russians complete the expulsion of German forces from the southern sector of the Kursk salient and advance in the Orel area.

24 July

Eastern Front Stalin sends a message to Generals Rokossovsky, Vatutin and Popov praising the 'final liquida-

tion of the German summer offensive' and recalling that in the Orel–Kursk and Belgorod sectors the Germans concentrated 37 divisions, 17 armoured, 2 motorized and 18 infantry. They have lost 70,000 dead, and 2,900 tanks, 195 Ferdinand self-propelled guns, 844 guns, 5,000 trucks and 1,392 German aircraft have been destroyed.

The figures for tanks and aircraft destroyed are exaggerations, but after the war the German generals do in fact admit that they sacrificed the best of their armour and lost their air superiority over the Russians as a result of the ill-fated Operation *Citadel*.

Sicily The American Provisional Corps mops up the western part of the island, capturing, according to American sources, 'a record number of prisoners'.

The American 45th Division takes Cefalu and the 1st attacks Nicosia.

The Fascist Grand Council meets for ten hours to hear and discuss a statement by Mussolini. The Council passes a resolution inviting the King of Italy to assume command of the armed forces, contrary to Mussolini's proposals.

Solomon Islands In New Georgia the Japanese put up a stubborn resistance against the 161st Infantry on the Munda pass. The Americans are taking up their positions for the attack on Munda.

☐ Germany. The RAF makes a massive night raid on Hamburg. Huge formations of heavy bombers drop 2,300 tons of bombs (as much as the combined tonnage of the five heaviest German raids on London). At 8.00 a.m. Berlin radio reports: 'All Hamburg seems to be in flames.' 20,000 people are killed and 60,000 taken to hospital. But this is just the first of a long series of raids on the city.

☐ Norway. 167 bombers of the US 8th Air Force drop 400 tons of bombs on industrial targets at Heroya, while 41 other B-17s bomb naval installations at Trondheim.

25 July

In the early hours of the morning

the Fascist Grand Council passes a vote of no confidence in Mussolini, and Mussolini is arrested. The king invites Marshal Badoglio to form a new government. The new government insists 'the war goes on'.

The news of the fall of Mussolini reaches Hitler at his headquarters at Rastenburg (now called Ketrzyn, in Poland) in the afternoon. The Führer immediately discusses the position with his generals and makes a lightning decision to send the eight German divisions in southern Germany and France to occupy all the Italian Alpine passes. Every pass between Italy and France, Italy and Switzerland, Italy and Austria, is in German hands before Badoglio even has time to think of a countermeasure.

Hitler tells his generals: 'I shall send someone to Rome tomorrow with orders for the Commander of the 3rd Division to arrest everyone in the government – the king and the crown prince and all that crew at once, and then Badoglio and his friends.'

Sicily General Patton's US troops

Crowds at the end of an anti-Fascist demonstration in Milan.

THE FALL OF MUSSOLINI

The Allied landing in Sicily on 10 July and the speed with which the British and Americans advanced over the island shocked the whole of Italy and caused disillusion and uneasiness within the government and increased dissatisfaction among the senior members of the Fascist Party and the armed forces. The news reached Mussolini at his home in Villa Torlonia, but the military authorities told him the defences were 'holding'. However, when he returned to the Palazzo Venezia in the afternoon he was given the news that the base at Augusta had already fallen to British troops. This was a severe blow. And between the 11th and the 14th the situation of the Axis troops on the island grew far graver.

On 16 July a group of Fascist leaders asked Mussolini for an audience. Besides Scorza (the Party Secretary) the delegation included Acerbo, Bottai, De Bono, De Cicco, De Vecchi, Farinacci, Giurati and Teruzzi. As Scorza later explained, what prompted the request for an audience was the fact that, while the leaders were being urged to raise the people's morale by making propaganda speeches, they were given no directions and were kept in the dark about what was really happening in Sicily.

Finally, in reply to a straight question by Mussolini ('Well, what is it you want?'), Scorza replied timidly that they wanted a meeting of the Fascist Grand Council, the supreme organ of the regime. Some of the other leaders (Bottai, Farinacci and Giurati) supported Scorza, trying in various ways to convince the Duce that the Grand Council would be the most appropriate place for a problem so vital to the fate of the country to be discussed. (Bottai reminded him among other things that the Grand Council had not met since 7 December 1939.) However, Mussolini dodged the request by postponing it, pointing out that he had to prepare for his meeting with Hitler (fixed for the 19th, at Feltre) and undertaking to look into the question when he came back to Rome. The audience was finished.

The question of convening the Grand Council was raised again after the Feltre meeting and again after the first bombing of Rome on the same day, 19 July.

On the morning of the 21st Scorza, told Grandi that the Duce had ordered him to convene the supreme organ of the regime. The meeting was fixed for 5 p.m. on 24 July. During the afternoon, Grandi drafted a provisional agenda which he proposed to lay before the Grand Council with the object of getting a clear understanding with the Duce. Grandi sent one copy directly to Scorza, and later he submitted the draft to Federzoni and Bottai and found them fully in agreement with him. On 22 July the paper drafted by Grandi found its way on to Mussolini's desk. Scorza had placed it there himself, troubled by his loyalty to the Duce. Scorza tells us that Mussolini reacted violently. 'The Duce', he wrote, 'was absolutely furious . . . and said that it was time we all put our cards on the table.' It was decided that an agenda in direct opposition to Grandi's should be laid before the Grand Council.

On 24 July, early in the afternoon, Grandi dictated the definitive text of his agenda. Most important was the item that declared: 'The functions and responsibilities in all affairs of state of the Crown, the Grand Council, the Government, Parliament and the Cor-porations, as established by our statutory and constitutional law, should be immediately restored.' The Fascist Grand Council should also ask the government to request the king 'that he should be pleased . . . to assume, with the effective command of the land, sea and air forces . . . that supreme initiative of decision that our institutions attribute to him.' This was nothing less than a rebellion against Mussolini.

Grandi sent a copy of his document to the king, with a note in which among other things he asked Victor Emmanuel, 'at this grave and decisive hour for the fate of the nation and of the monarchy', not to leave the country.

The meeting began at 5.00 p.m. on 24 July. In addition to the two members of the Quadrumvirate, De Bono and De Vecchi, the Party Secretary, Scorza, and the President of the Senate, Suardo, those present were Grandi, Acerbo, Ciano, Galbiati, Pareschi, Polverelli, Farinacci, Albini, Frattari, Gottardi, Rossoni, De Marsico, Biggini, Federzoni, Bastianini, Bottai, Cianetti, Tringali-Casanova, Alfieri, De Stefani, Balella, Buffarini-Guidi, Bignardi and Marinelli.

Mussolini began with a long, defensive preamble in which he recalled the events leading up to the convocation of the Grand Council, reviewed the military situation on the different fronts, and declared that it was not by his own wish that he had taken over supreme command of the armed forces, but that the responsibility had been entrusted to him by the king on 16 June 1940. He then outlined the most important events of the war from the British and American landing in Africa to the evacuation of Tunisia by the Axis forces, the fall of Pantelleria and the landing in Sicily, and ended with a tedious sermon on the popularity or unpopularity of wars: 'A war that goes badly is one man's war, but they are the people's wars when . . . they end in victory.'

And then the debate began. It was Grandi that everyone was waiting to hear. He spoke to his agenda clearly and unequivocally, as Mussolini did at the beginning of his speech, and his words implied one shocking truth: Fascism was in rebellion against its own leader. When he spoke, Ciano, the former Foreign Minister (and the Duce's son-in-law) accused Germany of having gone back on her agreements with Italy. In any case, he said, the position was now so serious that not even the greatest sacrifices could rekindle any hope of victory. He was followed by De Marsico, Federzoni and others.

Towards midnight Scorza proposed that the session be adjourned until next day. Grandi was firmly against this, and the Duce supported him, but suspended the sitting for half an hour. While Mussolini conferred with Scorza and others of the faithful, Grandi collected the signatures of those who supported his agenda. De Bono was the first to sign, followed by De Vecchio and Ciano, then Acerbo, De Stefani, Cianetti, De Marsico, Pareschi, Gottardi, Balella, Bignardi, Rossoni, Albini and Marinelli.

When the sitting was resumed Grandi placed the signed copy of his agenda on Mussolini's desk. Various members of the Grand Council now made their personal positions clear. When Mussolini replied it seemed that he had swung the balance of feeling in his favour – as when he exclaimed that, if the document meant that the regime should be dissolved, it would be better to say so outright. But Grandi parried the blow when he declared that the person of the Duce himself was not in question. Between accusations and personal attacks, acid replies and second thoughts, the proceedings dragged on until three in the morning, and then Mussolini called for a vote on the two agendas before the Council – Grandi's which they have been discussing, and Scorza's with its unconditional support of the Duce. Grandi's paper was approved by 19 votes to 8, with one abstention. 'Grandi's agenda is approved,' said Mussolini, and then: 'Gentlemen, with this document you have precipitated a government crisis.' Next day, 25 July, Mussolini was summoned to a meeting with the king at five o'clock in the afternoon. The king had already decided that he must get rid of him once and for all, and the Grand Council's 'vote of no confidence' made it very much easier for him. When Mussolini told him that in law the vote of the Grand Council had no more than advisory force, Victor Emmanuel III answered drily: 'No, my dear Duce, the Grand Council's vote is absolutely substantial, make no mistake.' Mussolini appeared to accept his fate. He wondered: 'What will become of me? And my family?' The king reasured him, and at 5.20 p.m. went with him to the door. Half an hour later Marshal Pietro Badoglio was entrusted by his sovereign with the formation of a new government. One of his first steps was to prohibit any leak of information about the night of the Grand Council.

Marshal of Italy, Pietro Badoglio, the new head of government following the fall of Mussolini.

Solomon Islands: artillery ammunition is unloaded on Arundel Island.

face increasing difficulties as they advance towards Messina. In the British sector the Canadian 1st Division, supported by the 231st Brigade, attacks Agira, east of Leonforte, where it meets with strong resistance.

Solomon Islands General Twining replaces Rear-Admiral Mitscher in command of the air force in the Solomons, which now has 539 aircraft available and since 30 June has shot down 316 Japanese aircraft for the loss of only 71.

New Georgia The 43rd and 37th Divisions open the offensive against Munda. In spite of massive air and naval support they are only able to overcome the tenacious Japanese resistance in a few sectors. Some units get behind a dominant position called Bartley Ridge, while others on the right flank reach the coast near Terere. But progress in general is disappointing.

26 July

Martial law declared throughout Italy. Badoglio forms new cabinet omitting all Fascist leaders.

The Führer wants to withdraw the SS armoured divisions from the Russian front and send them to Italy to restore the Fascist regime, but Kluge declares that he cannot spare a single man from the front. However, Hitler does succeed shortly after in sending the SS *Leibstandarte* Armoured Division to Italy, though it is sent back to the Eastern Front in October.

Solomon Islands In New Georgia the two American divisions attack again after an intensive artillery barrage and with the support of tanks and flamethrowers.

One regiment of the 43rd Division seizes the village of Ilangana and reaches the coast at Kia, but the 37th Division does not succeed in defeating the defenders of Bartley Ridge.

Aleutian Islands In a single raid American bombers drop 104 tons of bombs on Japanese positions on Kiska. At 6.40 p.m. three light cruisers and eight destroyers of the Japanese navy, making clever use of the Arctic fog that has enveloped the

Sicily: a patrol sent out by the American 1st Division advances towards Troina in the southern foothills of the Nebrodi mountains, which are held by a strong Axis force.

An American B-24 Liberator bomber during a raid on the Ploesti oil refineries, Rumania.

island, take off in one hour almost all the 6,100 men in the garrison and leave without being spotted by the enemy. Some submarines also take part in the operation.

27 July
At a conference called to decide a plan of action in Italy, Hitler and his staff work out the order of the steps to be taken: one, liberation of Mussolini (Operation *Oak-tree*); two, occupation of Rome and restoration of Mussolini in the government (Operation *Student*); three, military occupation of the whole of Italy; and four, capture or destruction of the Italian fleet. Mussolini in fact is to become another 'Quisling' puppet leader.
In the evening Mussolini is transferred from Rome to the island of Ponza.

Sicily Units of the 45th Division advancing along the coast road towards Messina reach Tusa, a few miles west of Santo Stefano. They cross the river of the same name but are driven back.
They later cross the river Tusa again and succeed in establishing a small bridgehead in the direction of Santo Stefano. After three days' hard fighting Nicosia falls to the American 1st Division. In the British sector the Canadian 1st Division takes Agira after a tough battle. Meanwhile the 231st Brigade resumes its advance eastwards along highway 121, but is held up a few miles west of Regalbuto.
General Alexander, the commander of the XV Army Group, moves his headquarters from Africa to Sicily.

The headquarters of Allied forces in the Mediterranean asks for consideration to be given to a plan for the capture of Naples and the neighbouring airports as a base for the support of future operations. The date for the landing is fixed, purely provisionally, as 7 September.
Solomon Islands: New Georgia The Americans call off the attack on Bartley Ridge and concentrate their efforts on a hill called Horseshoe Hill, silencing several machine gun nests.
Aleutian Islands During the night of 27/28 July the last Japanese leave Kiska. Again the Americans do not spot them; they are preparing for their own landing.
☐ India. A Chinese-American squadron is formed within the US 14th Air Force, with American-

trained Chinese pilots.

28 July

Solomon Islands In New Georgia General Griswold asks for reinforcements to follow up the attack on Munda. The Americans are advancing extremely slowly, and the Japanese exact a high price for every yard of ground gained.

The reconnaissance group sent to Vella Lavella returns from Barakoma and reports favourably on the possibilities of a landing.

29 July

Sicily The British 78th Division, just arrived to reinforce the British XXX Corps, attacks the line from Catenanuova to Adrano, north-west of Catania.

Solomon Islands Heavy fighting continues in the New Georgia jungle.

Eastern Front Von Kleist's Army Group A makes several counterattacks to try to improve its positions on the river Mius, north of Taganrog on the Black Sea.

30 July

Sicily On highway 120 the American 1st Division advances towards Troina, while on the coast road the US 45th Division is heavily engaged by the German rearguards covering Santo Stefano. In the British sector, at first light, the British 78th Division makes a successful assault on Catenanuova against strong resistance.

Solomon Islands In New Georgia the Americans take Bartley Ridge and repulse violent Japanese counterattacks.

Eastern Front After their initial attacks, von Kleist's Army Group A loses the initiative, which passes to the troops under Tolbukhin and Malinovsky.

31 July

Sicily The American 45th Division takes Santo Stefano. The British 231st Brigade fails in an attempt to occupy Regalbuto; the 78th Division attacks Centuripe, held by large German forces.

Sicily, 5 August 1943: a British 8th Army patrol advances among the ruins of Catania.

A German anti-tank gun in action in the Orel sector. German resistance there is finally coming to an end.

Solomon Islands: New Georgia Two American battalions mop up on Bartley Ridge. The Japanese drive off new attacks on Horseshoe Hill.

Algeria General Henri Giraud is appointed Commander-in-Chief of Free French forces.

1 August

Sicily The American 1st Division attacks Troina, doggedly defended by Axis forces, and one of the hardest, bloodiest battles of the campaign flares up. In the British sector the 231st Brigade, supported by units of the Canadian 1st Division, succeeds in penetrating into Regalbuto. But Axis resistance round Centuripe continues, taking advantage of the terrain – the town lies at the top of a high, flat-topped hill and there is only one approach road.

Solomon Islands In New Georgia the Americans advance to the edge of the Munda airfield without resistance. The Japanese Imperial Staff realizing that New Georgia is no longer defensible, has decided to concentrate all available men and materials on Kolombangara Island, north-east of New Georgia. However, the units left in New Georgia are ordered to defend the airfield to the last man.

☐ *Rumania.* 177 American B-24 Liberator bombers commanded by General Brereton, commander of the US 9th Air Force, drop 311 tons of bombs on the oil refineries at Ploesti, centre of the Rumanian oil-fields (Operation *Tidalwave*). The attack puts 40% of the refining plant out of action, but it costs the Americans dearly, for they lose 54 bombers and

532 aircrew.

☐ Burma declares itself independent of Great Britain. A nationalist government takes over, which has the backing of the Japanese and directed by U Ba Maw. In Indonesia a party of national unity has recently been founded under Japanese aegis and has set up a central council which is collaborating in the creation of the sphere of common prosperity in Asia to which the Japanese look forward. As for Thailand, it has been an ally of Japan since 1942 under its regent, Marshal Pibul Songgram. At this period the Japanese Empire has about 500 million people under its control. It controls 95% of the world production of rubber, 70% of the production of rice and of tin, and almost the whole world production of quinine. The Allies have found several substitutes for quinine, and have increased – as the Germans have also – the production of synthetic rubber.

2 August

Sicily The American 1st Division continues its attacks on Troina which is resolutely defended by the Axis troops. The advance of the US 3rd Division along the coast road is slowed down a good deal by minefields, the destruction of bridges and similar obstacles.

In the British area the Allied columns move on from Regalbuto towards the east, where the 78th Division is attacking Centuripe.

☐ A message from the Allies to the people of Italy, broadcast from Algiers, announces the imminent invasion of the peninsula by the British and Americans.

Eastern Front The Russian offensive continues on all fronts. The deepest penetrations are made north of the Kursk salient, in the direction of Orel.

Solomon Islands In New Georgia the battle for Munda airfield continues. Another American infantry division, the 37th, has landed on the island.

Aleutian Islands Two big American naval formations (two battleships, five cruisers and nine destroyers) shell Kiska Island, which is also heavily bombed from the air every day. Between 2 August and 15 August, the date of the landing, the island is to be shelled from the sea ten more times. Meanwhile the Japanese have evacuated their garrison.

3 August

Sicily In the north the US 1st Division continues its assault on Troina. In the British sector the 78th Division takes Centuripe, forcing the enemy northwards over the river Salso. During the night the British

5th Division, operating in the coastal sector south of Catania, carries out a series of attacks on the town. Meanwhile the remaining Italian forces begin to evacuate the island, leaving the Germans to cover their withdrawal with rearguard actions.

Eastern Front The Russian offensive is further stepped up by the armies of the Voronezh and Steppe Fronts in the direction of Kharkov, while three other Russian Fronts, the Western, Bryansk and Central, converge on Orel.

Solomon Islands The Americans continue to make progress against Munda airfield in New Georgia. Some units advance from the Bairoko sector to cut off the enemy's retreat towards the southern part of the island.

4 August

Eastern Front The Russians, continuing their advance, break into Orel where bitter street fighting takes place. Berlin reports: 'continuous Russian attacks with unabated fury'. The Red Army closes in on Belgorod.

Sicily The Americans make powerful attacks on Troina, but fail to take it. The 9th Division, whose units are concentrated at Nicosia, is attached to the American II Corps.

In the British sector the 5th Division

Russian and German armour during the battle for Orel. The fighting results in the virtual annihilation of the German 2nd Panzer Army.

continues its attacks in the Catania plain and advances to within a short distance of Catania. The 50th Division is ordered to be ready for a move towards Catania.

☐ Naples is attacked by US planes. This raid is denounced in Rome as 'the most barbarous and merciless of the 96 raids made on the city'.

Solomon Islands In New Georgia the Americans mop up the airfield area at Munda, which is still not entirely under their control.

Aleutian Islands The pre-invasion softening-up reaches its peak – at least 152 tons of bombs are dropped during the day on the deserted island of Kiska.

5 August

Eastern Front The Red Army captures Belgorod – a key position on the north side of the German salient at Kharkov. In the battle for Orel the German 2nd Armoured Army has been virtually wiped out; what is left of it is incorporated in the 9th Army, in von Kluge's Army Group Centre. Besides holding their own salient at Kursk the Russians are eliminating the German salient at Orel, to the north of Kursk. But the Germans have prepared a fortified line, called the Hagen line, at the base of the salient, based on Bryansk and covering almost the whole of a line running from Sevsk in the south to Kirov in the north.

Sicily British troops enter Catania at 8.30 a.m. In the American sector the battle round Troina continues, but during the night the Axis troops withdraw. On the coast the American 3rd Division's advance is held up by German defences on the crest of San Fratello hill, between Sant' Agata and the sea.

Solomon Islands In New Georgia, after twelve days of savage jungle warfare, the Americans finally take their main objective, Munda airfield, and begin the mopping-up of the whole island.

6 August

Sicily At first light the 16th Regiment of the American 1st Division enters Troina, and during the night the British 78th Division takes Adrano.

☐ Representatives of Italy and Germany meet at Tarvisio, on the border between Italy and Austria, to clarify relations between the two countries. The Germans have requested the meeting, which is attended by the two Foreign Ministers, Guariglia and Ribbentrop, and the two Chiefs of Staff, Ambrosio and Keitel. The Italians try to reassure their ally about rumours that the new government is preparing to enter into secret negotiations with the Allies.

Eastern Front In Moscow 120 guns fire 12 salvos in honour of the forces that liberated Orel and Belgorod. The daily bulletin announces that Kromy (25 miles south-west of Orel) and 70 other places have been liberated, and that the great offensive in the direction of Kharkov is developing favourably.

Solomon Islands Battle of the Gulf of Vella. Four Japanese destroyers sail from Rabaul in the early morning with 820 men and 50 tons of supplies for Kolombangara (the 'Tokyo Night Express' had carried out a similar mission three nights before with complete success). The ships are intercepted just before midnight by six American destroyers commanded by Commodore F. Moosbrugger,

Motorcyclists of the *Bersaglieri* in action near Djebel Garci.

between the islands of Vella Lavella and Kolombangara. The engagement lasts until a little after midnight and ends in a brilliant victory for the Americans, who sink three Japanese destroyers with torpedoes without themselves incurring the least damage. About 300 Japanese manage to reach Vella Lavella in the one remaining destroyer, and are later transferred to Kolombangara; 1,500 others, soldiers and seamen, lose their lives.

There are now 12,400 Japanese man-

'VREDENS DAG'

It is 1623. In a gloomy atmosphere of religious obscurantism and witch-hunting, the tale unfolds of Anne, young wife of an elderly pastor. Drawn to the magic arts, Anne falls in love with her stepson, is accused of witchcraft and is denounced by her sister-in-law. The young woman defends herself, but when her husband dies and her lover abandons her she is arraigned for criminal acts and condemned to be burned at the stake.

A parable on the subjects of intolerance and superstition, *Vredens Dag* (entitled *Day of Wrath* for foreign distribution) was made in Nazi-occupied Denmark and marked the return to the screen of Carl Dreyer, the great master of Scandinavian cinema. Based on the play *Anne Pedersdotter* by Hans Wier Jensen, *Vredens Dag* was a film of great chromatic richness and psychological complexity: all the characters, in fact, had ambiguous, contradictory personalities. Dreyer here handled one of his favourite themes with starkly expressive mastery: the conflict of good and evil, reason and unreason, and the impossible search for happiness.

Above: a bombed street in Nantes, France.
Below: the Palais de Justice at Rouen.

ning Kolombangara, and hundreds more are transferred from New Georgia every night across the Gulf of Kula.

7 August
Eastern Front The Red Army advances rapidly on the Bryansk and Kharkov fronts.
Sicily Finding that their attacks on San Fratello hill are having no success, the Americans by-pass the obstacle by means of an amphibious landing east of Sant' Agata. The operation is successfully carried out overnight and allows the Americans to move forward again towards Messina.

8 August
Sicily In the north the Americans enter Sant' Agata, and in the British sector the 78th Division takes Bronte.
☐ A week of hell begins for the big cities in the north of Italy. Milan is bombed four times by a total of 916 RAF aircraft, which drop 4,000 tons of bombs on the city, completely destroying 11,700 buildings and seriously damaging 15,000 others. British bombers, 380 strong, carry out three violent raids on Turin, causing tremendous damage and many deaths, and Genoa is laid waste by an attack by 73 aircraft, again with many casualties.
☐ Benito Mussolini is imprisoned on Maddalena Island, off the north-east coast of Sardinia.
☐ Berlin radio announces that over 1,000,000 women, children, and elderly and infirm persons are being evacuated from Berlin.

9 August
Eastern Front The Russians continue to advance on the Bryansk and Kharkov fronts.
Sicily Axis forces continue to withdraw along the whole front, making for Messina. The main effort during this phase of the campaign is made by the British XIII Corps, whose divisions are engaged south and east of Etna in particularly difficult country.
Solomon Islands In New Georgia the Americans are still mopping up Japanese troops hidden in the jungle. The 35th Infantry Regiment is ordered to be ready to embark for Vella Lavella Island.

10 August
Sicily During the night US forces make a second amphibious landing behind the enemy's lines east of Cape Orlando.
Solomon Islands The Americans on New Georgia deploy one or two battalions to intercept the Japanese escaping from Munda, trying to reach the north coast and cross to Kolombangara Island.
☐ Swiss newspaper *Neue Züricher Zeitung* states: 'The accumulation of bad news is shaking even the firmest believers in Hitler... German hopes of victory are completely dwindling. They have been replaced by a deep anxiety, as the people are convinced that the party will not give in, even if more towns like Hamburg are erased.'

11 August
Eastern Front The Russian

Voronezh Front (Vatutin), Steppe Front (Konev) and South-Western Front (Malinovsky) continue to close on Kharkov, which has already been by-passed in the north-west by the capture of Akhtyrka. The Russians also reach the Kharkov–Poltava railway. Von Manstein stands up to the enemy manœuvres with considerable skill, but skill is not enough to repulse troops who are numerous, well armed, and – since Stalingrad and Kursk – convinced of their ability to win.

Solomon Islands Admiral Halsey issues instructions for the next stage of operations in the central Solomons. Task Force 31, under command of Rear-Admiral Theodore S. Wilkinson (who replaced Rear-Admiral Turner on 15 July), is to land units of the 25th Division on Vella Lavella with the task of occupying the Japanese air and naval bases. This will neutralize and by-pass the Japanese garrison at present on Kolombangara. This is the first application of the 'island-hopping' tactics which the Americans are often to use in future operations. In New Georgia long-range guns are to be sited along the north-west coast to shell the Japanese positions on Kolombangara.

12 August
Eastern Front Chuguyev, a short distance south-east of Kharkov, is taken by the Russians. The Red Army advance on the Bryansk front continues.

Sicily Reports come in of large-scale German evacuation. In the American sector, the divisions of the II Corps push on eastwards; the 9th Division reaches Floresta, north of Randazzo, the last stronghold along the II Corps line of advance.

☐ Milan. During the night of 12/13 August at least 504 British bombers drop 1,252 tons of high explosive and incendiary bombs on Milan in the heaviest raid yet suffered by an Italian city. Among the buildings hit are the Castello Sforzesco, the Palazzo

On the eve of the landings. Top: Bordeaux harbour. Above: Saint-Etienne (May 1944).

Reale and almost all the buildings in the centre of the city.
☐ Rome. General Giuseppe Castellano leaves by train for Madrid. He is to meet the British ambassador to Spain, explain the Italian military situation to him, learn what are the Allies' intentions (if they have any) and, above all, say that Italy cannot drop her German ally without help

from the Western Allies.

Solomon Islands Advance guards of the invasion forces leave Rendova and land near Barakoma, on Vella Lavella, during the night of 12/13 August to prepare the ground for the main body. They find only a few Japanese. One company lands on the islet of Baanga to establish a bridgehead there, but is driven back into

American infantry mopping up in a district of Messina at the end of the campaign in Sicily.

the sea with heavy losses by the little Japanese garrison.

Aleutian Islands Five US cruisers and five destroyers carry out the last pre-invasion bombardment of Kiska Island, firing over 60 tons of shells.

13 August

Sicily The Germans abandon Randazzo, which is occupied by the 39th Regiment of the American 9th Division. In the north, on the coast road, units of the US 3rd Division push on eastwards towards Patti.

☐ Rome. To try to force the Badoglio government to surrender, the US 12th Air Force carries out a second heavy raid on Rome using 106 B-17s, 102 B-26s and 66 B-25s. About 500 tons of bombs are dropped, causing serious damage.

Eastern Front The Kalinin Front (Eremenko) and the West Front (Sokolovsky), pressing on towards Smolensk, force von Kluge's Army Group Centre to retire. They re-take Spas-Demensk, east of Smolensk.

Dutch East Indies B-24s of the US 380th Heavy Bomber Group, taking off from Australia, carry out a raid on the Balikpapan oilfield in Borneo.

Solomon Islands The first American aircraft land on Munda airfield, New Georgia, which the occupation forces have quickly got back into use.

☐ Austria. US planes bomb Wiener Neustadt, 27 miles from Vienna. This is the first Allied attack on an Austrian city.

14 August

Eastern Front Fierce fighting for Karachev, on the Bryansk front, as the Germans try desperately to halt the Russian advance.

New Guinea American troops take a ridge called Roosevelt, but the Japanese hold on to a row of hills overlooking Dot Inlet.

Mediterranean The Allied Supreme Command issues the naval plan for Operation *Avalanche* (the landing at Salerno).

☐ The Italian government declares Rome an 'Open City' to avoid further destruction by bombing.

15 August

Eastern Front The Russians capture

Karachev. Further south, bitter fighting takes place around Kharkov.

Sicily The Allies are nearing Messina. On the north coast the Americans reach Barcellona, on the east the British are marching on Linguaglossa.

☐ Urgent meeting between German and Italian military representatives is held at Bologna to discuss the two countries' strategies on the Italian peninsula. The delegations are led by Field-Marshal Rommel and General Roatta, Chief of Staff of the Italian army. The talks take place in a very tense atmosphere. The Germans are suspicious about Italian troop movements from the south of Italy to the north, and both sides make veiled suggestions that the others are pursuing ends which are not strictly those of both allies.

The meeting ends with no new resolutions and the discussions are deferred. And now the Italian General Giuseppe Castellano, working in close collaboration with the Chief of the General Staff, General Ambrosio, begins his laborious negotiations with the Allies for an armistice. The first stage is Madrid, where Castellano is to meet the British ambassador to Spain, Sir Samuel Hoare.

Solomon Islands At dawn the 3rd Amphibious Force begins to land 6,000 men of the 25th Division at Biloa, near Barakama, on the southeast coast of Vella Lavella Island. The landing, with strong aerial support, is carried out without difficulty, and the Japanese forces are very thin on the ground. In New Georgia, units of the US 25th Infantry Regiment take Zieta.

New Guinea Japanese aircraft carry out the first raid on the new Allied airfield at Tsili Tsili.

Aleutian Islands 29,000 American and 5,300 Canadian soldiers who sailed from Adak on the 13th in about a hundred special transports – LSTs (landing ships, tanks: ships of 1,500 tons specially designed for the transport of armoured fighting vehicles), LCIs (landing craft, infantry) and LCTs (landing craft, tanks: able to carry three medium tanks) – escorted by huge naval forces, land at dawn on the western beaches of Kiska Island. They discover for the first time that the Japanese have gone. Everything that the Japanese have not destroyed on

A German paratrooper opens fire with his MP-38 machine-pistol during the bitter fighting at Kharkov.

Above: The Quebec conference. From left to right, in the foreground: Mackenzie King, prime minister of Canada, Franklin D. Roosevelt, and Winston Churchill.

leaving has been destroyed before or after by American bombs and shells.
Burma Work on the construction of the new 'Burma Road' east of Ledo makes slow progress; the roadway has only advanced 3 miles since the end of March.

16 August
Sicily The Germans continue to retire on Messina as quickly as possible. By evening advanced US forces reach the outskirts of the town.
Mediterranean The Allied Supreme Command issues the final directives for the landing in Italy: between 1 and 4 September the British XIII Corps, with two divisions (the 1st Canadian and 5th British) will be put down on the coast of Calabria. This operation, code-named *Baytown*, will be followed on 9 September (or not more than 48 hours later) by the landing of the American 5th Army at Salerno (Operation *Avalanche*).
Solomon Islands Two American regiments are despatched to take Baanga island, from which Japanese guns have been shelling Munda airport.

17 August
Sicily General Patton's troops enter Messina at 10.15 a.m. The capture of the whole island has taken only 39 days. However, the Germans have managed to transfer a good part of their forces (60,000 men out of 90,000) back to the mainland, together with their equipment.
□ General Giuseppe Castellano is received in Lisbon by the British ambassador Sir Ronald Campbell, but talks cannot proceed until the Allies send military spokesmen to take part in them.
Solomon Islands The Americans land more forces on Vella Lavella against powerful opposition by the enemy air force. In Baanga Island they make little progress although their two infantry regiments receive support from dive-bombers and artillery.
New Guinea Allied aircraft carry out a series of heavy raids against the enemy airfields at But, Dagua, Wewak and Boram, in preparation

for a land offensive against Lae.
□ Germany. 315 American bombers carry out a daylight raid on aircraft factories at Schweinfurt and Regensburg; 60 aircraft are brought down, but the industrial areas of the two towns are severely damaged.
□ First Quebec Conference. Roosevelt and Churchill commence conference which will, among other things, approve plans for a cross-Channel invasion.

18 August
Sicily All German resistance on the island ceases.
Mediterranean Plans for the air support of Operation *Avalanche* (the Allied landing at Salerno) are issued.
Solomon Islands The Americans land new forces on Baanga Island. A Japanese convoy of 20 motorized lighters carrying 400 men and escorted by 4 destroyers is intercepted on its way to Vella Lavella, first by aircraft, then by 4 American destroyers. The Japanese lose some of their lighters, but manage to land their reinforcements on Vella Lavella, in Kokolope Bay, and escape from the American pursuit.
□ Germany. During he night of 17/18 August 570 British four-engined bombers pound the 'V1' and 'V2' factories at Peenemünde, on the Baltic coast.

The catastrophic effect of the Allies' deadly bombing of the V1 and V2 factories at Pennemünde, on the Baltic coast on the night of 17/18 August.

☐ Roosevelt and Churchill (in Quebec) authorize General Eisenhower to send two representatives to Lisbon to negotiate with the Italian emissaries about an armistice.

19 August

Solomon Islands The big guns that have been firing on Munda airfield from Baanga Island are captured by American troops.

New Guinea Under pressure by Australians and Americans, the Japanese abandon Mount Tambu and the Komiatum Ridge, the last natural obstacles of any size in front of Salamaua, and fall back on new defensive positions.

☐ Italy. Heavy Allied air raids on Avellino, Salerno and Foggia.

☐ Lisbon. US General Walter Bedell Smith, Eisenhower's Chief of Staff, and General Kenneth Strong, head of the intelligence service at the Allies' Mediterranean headquarters, arrive in Lisbon as the official Allied military spokesmen to negotiate with General Castellano, the semi-official emissary of the Badoglio government. Castellano must still refer to Rome about the Allies' reaction to the Italian wish for an armistice.

☐ In a special report to the Führer, Georg von Mackensen, the German ambassador in Rome, looks optimistically at the Italian situation: 'There is a widespread desire for peace among the Italian people, but the present government wants to fight on, because they are aware that they cannot obtain peace without turning the whole of Italy into a battlefield.'

20 August

Eastern Front Russians occupy Lebedin in the Kharkov sector.

Solomon Islands In New Georgia the Americans are still mopping up the last pockets of enemy resistance in the Bairoko area. The Japanese evacuate the southern part of Baanga Island.

☐ Lisbon. The talks between General Castellano and Generals Bedell Smith and Strong finish. The Allies insist on Italy's unconditional surrender. General Castellano is given ten days to inform his government of the decisions.

☐ Italy. Further heavy air raids on Naples, Avellino and Salerno provinces.

21 August

Eastern Front The Red Army vice tightens around Kharkov.

New Guinea Australian forces enter Komiatum.

22 August

Eastern Front After violent fighting the Germans evacuate Kharkov, and the city changes hands for the fourth time. The battle extends south of Izyum and along the river Mius, where the Germans have a hard task holding up the Russian attacks. Near the Mius the Russians reach the Taganrog–Stalino railway.

☐ Italy. Allied aircraft attack Salerno and cause serious damage.

23 August

Eastern Front At 9.00 p.m. 20 salvoes are fired from 224 guns in Moscow to salute the troops who have taken Kharkov. Bells peal throughout the city.

Solomon Islands Three Japanese destroyers making for Rekata Bay in Santa Isabel Island to take off the local garrison are spotted and attacked by American aircraft, and forced to return to their base. In view of the American pressure and the wide dispersion of their forces, the Japanese Imperial Headquarters has decided to evacuate the central Solomons and concentrate men and materials in the southern islands, especially in Bougainville.

A partisan hanged at Belgrade.

Editors of the Croatian resistance newspaper *Vjesnik* at work in a wood in the Petrova Mountains.

24 August

New Guinea The Australian 3rd Division is replaced by the 5th Division in the final phase of the operations against Salamaua. But the attack on Salamaua is really a feint; the true objective is Lae, and the main body of the Australian forces are approaching it from the interior of the island. The Americans carry on with their operations for the capture of Dot Inlet.

□ The eight-day Quebec Conference comes to an end. Roosevelt and Churchill, with their Chiefs of Staff, have taken or confirmed the following decisions: precedence in operations against Germany will be given to Operation *Pointblank*, the Anglo-American air offensive aimed at destroying Germany's industrial potential as a prelude to *Overlord*, the invasion of north-west Europe, still fixed for 1 May 1944. The plans for the invasion of the Italian mainland are approved, but the forces at present engaged must suffice. The big offensive against Japan will be carried out along two centre-lines, one for the Central Pacific and one for the South-West Pacific. In the Central Pacific precedence will be given to the capture of the Gilbert Islands and Marshall Islands. In the South-West Pacific Rabaul will have to be neutralized without being captured, and New Guinea will have to be neutralized in a westward direction as far as the air base at Wewak. Manus, on the other hand, and the base at Kavieng in New Ireland, will have to be captured and used as jumping-off places for further leaps forward. Supreme command of the South-East Asia front will be assumed by Admiral Lord Louis Mountbatten, with General Stilwell as his deputy; but both of these will still be under Chiang Kai-shek where the Chinese front is concerned. The offensive for the recapture of Burma will be launched in February 1944.

□ Heinrich Himmler, head of the SS, is appointed Minister for the Interior in the Third Reich.

25 August

Solomon Islands The Americans wipe out the last pocket of Japanese resistance at Bairoko in New Georgia. Those Japanese who have managed to get away have been taken off to Kolombangara or to Arundel, an island between New Georgia and Kolombangara, which the Americans are preparing to occupy in part.

26 August

Devastating raids on centres in southern Italy continue without respite.

□ The British, United States and Canadian governments recognize De Gaulle's Committee of National Liberation as the *de facto* French authority. The Russian and Chinese governments follow suit on 27 August.

27 August

Eastern Front The Russian advance continues. On the Bryansk front Sevsk is captured, as is Kotelva, 60 miles west of Kharkov.

Solomon Islands An American infantry regiment lands on the Nauro peninsula, in the south-east of Arundel Island, and occupies the whole peninsula without opposition.

□ France. 187 B-17 'Flying Fortresses' of the US 8th Air Force carry out their first mission over Europe, bombing Watten.

□ Mussolini is moved from Maddalena Island (off Sardinia) to the Gran Sasso d'Italia, in the Abruzzi.

28 August

Ellice Islands Marines and Seabees land on Nanomea and Nukufetau in the Ellice Islands and begin to construct an airfield.

□ Bulgaria. Death of King Boris III. His six-year-old son, Prince Simeon, succeeds to the throne.

29 August

Solomon Islands The Americans extend the ground held by them in the islands of Arundel and Vella Lavella. Meanwhile the destroyers of the 'Tokyo Night Express' run the gauntlet of the American air and naval forces to take off about 3,400 men from the Japanese garrison of Santa Isabel and transfer them to Bougainville or New Britain. The Japanese airfield at Vila, on Kolombangara Island, is the target of continual attacks by American aircraft.

30 August

Eastern Front Stalin, in a special Order of the Day, announces two major successes. The West Front under Sokolovsky, in its advance on Smolensk, re-takes Yelnya. In the south, Tolbukhin's armies recapture Taganrog, on the Sea of Azov.

The Russian advance following the counter-offensives in the Kursk salient has been spectacular, particularly in the southern sector of the front. The Germans now face the prospect of having to evacuate their forces from a great part of the Ukraine.

□ The period laid down at the Lisbon talks for the acceptance by Italy of unconditional surrender is about to expire, but the Italian government has not yet come to a decision. General Castellano is summoned to Sicily by the Allies through the British ambassador to the Vatican, D'Arcy Osborne.

Meantime General Keitel issues instructions for the occupation of Italy when the time comes. 'The most important task', he declares, 'will be to disarm the Italian army as quickly as possible ... The pacification of North Italy will be carried out through the Fascist organizations.'

31 August

Eastern Front The Russians make further important gains. In the Svesk area the Red Army advances 40 miles and recaptures Glukhov and Rylsk, south of Bryansk. Four days of fighting in this region have brought the recapture of some 200 villages.

□ General Castellano flies to Termini Imerese (Sicily) and is taken from here to Cassibile, near Syracuse. The talks begin. The Italians ask for guarantees against German reactions as soon as the armistice is signed. The Allies stick to the basic point in their demands: the armistice must be proclaimed at the same time as the Allies make their principal landing on the Italian mainland. In the evening Castellano returns to

American Marines of I Amphibious Corps advance through the mud on Bougainville Island.

Rome and reports: 'If the Italian Government insists on refusing to announce the cease-fire on the same day that the Allies land, contrary to what General Eisenhower has laid down with the approval of London and Washington, it will have no opportunity in the future to negotiate with the military for the conclusion of an armistice. Should that happen it will be necessary to convene a conference of diplomats from the Allied nations, who may well look on us less favourably than do the military and would impose far more severe conditions on us.'

□ A large force of British four-engined bombers makes a severe night attack on Berlin.

1 September

The Italian government dispatches a telegram to Allied Headquarters implicitly accepting the armistice: 'The answer is affirmative repeat affirmative. Known person will arrive Thursday morning 2 September time and place arranged. Stop. Please confirm.'

Pacific American units land on Baker Island (east of the Gilberts, a little north of the Equator), which is to be transformed into a base for future operations in the Central Pacific. The landing party builds a landing strip there in the course of a single week. The Americans now have five bases in the Central Pacific from which their bombers can reach the Gilberts: Funafuti, Nanomea and Nukufetau in the Ellice Islands, Canton Island and now Baker Island.

Aircraft taking off from a US aircraft carrier bomb Marcus Island, causing severe damage to Japanese military installations.

Solomon Islands Advance elements of the force landed on Vella Lavella reach the area of Orete Cove, some 15 miles from the Barakoma beachhead.

New Guinea The air offensive in advance of the attack on Lae is stepped up. Allied aircraft concentrate their attacks on Japanese stores, airfields and transports in New Guinea and New Britain.

2 September

Eastern Front The Russians press on towards the Dniepr, advancing on a huge front that runs from the area of Smolensk in the north to the Sea of Azov in the south. They reach the Bryansk–Konotop railway, and the important Ukrainian town of Sumy (between Konotop and Kharkov). A series of gains on the Donetz means that the Russians are directly threatening Stalino.

☐ American air attacks throughout Calabria continue in preparation for the Allied invasion. Every airport in southern Italy except that at Foggia is now neutralized.

☐ General Castellano returns from Rome to Termini Imerese and goes on from there to Cassibile.

3 September

Italian Front 4.30 a.m.: Under air and naval cover General Montgomery's 8th Army lands on the Calabrian coast between Reggio and Villa San Giovanni, and the Allied troops' long and devastating advance along the peninsula begins.

This attack is actually a diversion, with the object of attracting the German troops south, away from the Salerno area. But Kesselring, commander of the German forces in southern Italy, does not take the bait. In fact there is no resistance at all as the only German regiment defending the Calabrian coast withdraws northwards into the mountains.

☐ 5.00 p.m.: at Cassibile, Sicily, in the big General Staff mess tent, General Giuseppe Castellano signs the three copies of the 'short armistice', 'on

behalf of Marshal Badoglio'. The American General Bedell Smith signs on behalf of the Allies. General Eisenhower is present. The armistice is to come into effect on 8 September.

Solomon Islands The Americans occupy more of Arundel Island and consolidate their beachhead in the area of Barakoma, on Vella Lavella.

New Guinea The Allied command decides that, to protect future movements towards Cape Gloucester (at the western end of New Britain), it is necessary to secure the line from Dumpu to Saidor, north of Lae. As the air offensive in preparation for the landing at Lae continues, the assault force is already embarked in its transports off Buna.

4 September

Eastern Front With no halt in their relentless advance the troops of Konev and Malinovsky take Merefa, a railway junction south of Kharkov. The last escape route left to the Germans in this sector is thus closed.

Hitler (yielding to the evidence, for once) authorizes the evacuation of the remaining German forces holding the bridgehead in the Kuban, the powerfully fortified and mined 'blue line'.

The Germans execute a fighting withdrawal from the vital mining region in the Don basin.

New Guinea The diversionary action against Salamaua carried out by the Australian 5th Division and American 162nd Infantry Regiment comes to an end and the big offensive against Lae, the biggest Japanese base in New Guinea, opens. After a short naval bombardment two Australian brigades and some special American units land at two different points, 14 and 18 miles east of Lae. The only Japanese opposition to the landing comes from their air force, which damages several landing craft, but is then driven off by Allied aircraft, which enjoy great numerical superiority. While one Australian brigade moves off westwards towards Lae, other units thrust to the east towards Hopoi, the capture of which will protect the eastern flank of the beachhead.

5 September

Eastern Front Russians make further advances in the Donetz and Bryansk sectors.

Italian Front The forces for Operation *Avalanche*, the landing at Salerno, sail from North Africa for Italy.

Solomon Islands On Arundel Island, the Americans find themselves up against unexpected resistance by the Japanese.

New Guinea The American 503rd

3 September: General Giuseppe Castellano signs the armistice between Italy and the Allies at Cassibile, near Syracuse, Sicily.

American parachute troops land in force in the Lae sector, New Guinea, protected by a heavy smoke-screen.

Parachute Regiment and an Australian detachment, flown from Port Moresby in aircraft of the US 5th Air Force, are dropped at Nazdab, near the Markham river north-west of Lae, after fighter-bombers have 'cleaned up' the area of the drop. A few hours later the parachutists are joined by Australian units from Tsili Tsili. Work immediately starts on the construction of a landing strip for the Australian 7th Division, which is to be airborne. Nazdab airfield quickly becomes one of the main Allied air bases in the sector.

During the night of 5/6 September two more Australian brigades land on the coast east of Lae.

6 September

Italian Front 8th Army captures Palmi and Delianuova.

Eastern Front The Russian Central Front (under Rokossovsky), following up its thrust to the west, seizes Konotop, an important railway centre on the lines from Kursk to Kiev and from Moscow to Odessa. The Germans withdraw from the Don Basin leaving 'scorched earth' in front of the Russians and destroying the equipment of the coal mines.

Solomon Islands The Americans on Arundel Island advance in the Bomboe and Stima peninsulas against strong opposition by the Japanese garrison. On the island of Vella Lavella a New Zealand contingent is engaged in mopping-up operations against the Japanese.

New Guinea The Australian 26th and 24th Brigades advancing towards Lae meet with strong resistance by the Japanese for the first time on the river Bunga.

China General Stilwell suggests to Chiang Kai-shek that the Nationalist forces should collaborate with the Communist forces to anticipate the Japanese offensive to be expected as a reprisal for the raids on southern Chinese ports by the US 14th Air Force.

7 September

Italian Front Troops of the British 8th Army advance into Calabria on the Nicastro–Catanzaro road and in the north towards Pizzo.

Eastern Front The Germans evacuate Stalino. The remnants of Army Group A, withdrawn from the Caucasus through the tactical skill of von Kleist, is grouped with von Manstein's Army Group South.

Ellice Islands The airfield on Nanomea, just completed by the Americans, is bombed by Japanese aircraft.

8 September

Italian Front Italy surrenders. At 5.30 p.m., with Operation *Avalanche* in full swing and the Allied convoys already in sight of Salerno (the coast of Campagna has been intensively attacked from the air for the past week in preparation for the landing), General Eisenhower announces the unconditional surrender of Italy: 'The Italian government has surrendered its forces unconditionally ... Hostilities between the armed forces of the United Nations and those of Italy terminate at once. All Italians who now act to help eject the German aggressor from Italian soil will have the assistance and support of the United Nations.'

The head of the Italian government, Marshal Badoglio, makes a similar announcement on Italian radio at 7.45 p.m.

The Germans continue to concentrate their forces from the south of the peninsula in the Salerno sector.

Eastern Front The Russians occupy Stalino, which the Germans have evacuated. Berlin admits the evacuation of Stalino as 'shortening of the front'. Stalin's Order of the Day congratulates the army on the recapture of the entire Donetz Basin.

Central Pacific A landing strip suitable for use by fighters is ready on Baker Island.

Solomon Islands The American 172nd Infantry Regiment is reinforced by a battalion of the 169th Regiment to speed up the elimination of the Japanese from Arundel Island. The Japanese also transfer a battalion from Kolombangara to Arundel, with a view to staging a possible counter-attack against New Georgia.

New Guinea The units of the Australian 9th Division advancing towards Lae are held up by the river Busu. The Japanese headquarters orders the troops left at Salamaua to withdraw to Lae.

Meanwhile the Australian 5th Division, advancing on Salamaua, reaches the river Francisco, near the Japanese airfield at Salamaua.

Lae is shelled by four US destroyers.

9 September

Italian Front At 3.30 a.m. General Mark Clark launches Operation *Avalanche*, the landing of Allied troops on the Italian coast near Salerno.

The British 1st Airborne Division

A 'bouncing bomb' slung underneath a Lancaster bomber – the specially designed bomb used during the raid on the Möhne and Eder dams in the Ruhr.

seizes Taranto without opposition (Operation *Slapstick*).

☐ The Italian Royal Family and some representatives of the Italian government, with the Chiefs of Staff of the three armed forces, leave Rome for Pescara, from which they later sail to Brindisi.

In Rome the anti-Fascist parties set up the Committee of National Liberation.

The Italian battle fleet leaves Spezia; the battleship *Roma* is sunk by German bombers.

Corsica The Italian *Cremona* and *Friuli* Divisions drive off the Germans at Bastia.

Eastern Front The Russians push on west from Konotop. They cross the river Seym and take Bakhmach (on the railway line to Kiev), by storm. Further north they reach the river Desna south of Bryansk.

Solomon Islands Admiral Halsey suggests occupation of the Treasury Islands and part of Choiseul, which could serve as bases to neutralize the Japanese bases in the Shortland Islands and the southern part of Bougainville. MacArthur turns the suggestion down – another example of the conflict of strategy between the American army and navy.

On Arundel Island the Americans hold up the activities of their infantry, but pound the enemy positions with their guns.

New Guinea The Australian 9th Division succeeds in crossing the river Busu and establishing a bridgehead on the opposite bank. Japanese counter-attacks are repulsed.

☐ The Germans take over direct control of Croatia, Greece and the coasts and islands of Yugoslavia.

☐ Iran declares war on Germany.

10 September

Italian Front The Germans occupy Rome after brief skirmishes with Italian troops.

In Calabria the XIII Corps of Montgomery's 8th Army reaches a line from Catanzaro to Nicastro, while the Germans speed up their withdrawal towards Salerno to strengthen the defences of the sector where the Allied landing is taking place.

☐ King Victor Emmanuel III, his family and following, meet in Brindisi on the corvette *Baionetta*. Meanwhile Hitler broadcasts to the German people on the Italian surrender.

Malta The Italian fleet formally surrenders to Admiral Cunningham, Commander-in-Chief of the British Mediterranean Fleet.

Eastern Front Units of Tolbukhin's and Malinovsky's armies carry out a landing west of Mariupol on the Sea of Azov and succeed in capturing it. The German 17th Army begins to withdraw over the Kerch Strait into the Crimea from its bridgehead at Novorossysk. In this sector the North Caucasus Front is operating under General Petrov, supported by the Black Sea naval forces under the command of Vice-Admiral Vladimirsky.

Solomon Islands The task of capturing Arundel Island proves much harder than was foreseen, and the American troops are reinforced by two infantry battalions.

New Guinea The Australian 7th Division, after reorganization, takes the place of the US 503rd Parachute Regiment at Nazdab and begins to move west, towards Lae. The big Japanese base is thus threatened both from the west and from the east.

11 September

Italian Front The British 1st Airborne Division takes Brindisi without resistance.

The German garrison on Sardinia embarks for Corsica.

Solomon Islands On Arundel Island the 27th Infantry Regiment, of the US 25th Division, lands on the western point of the Bomboe peninsula and advances eastwards to where the 172nd Infantry are deployed. For the first time in the Pacific the Americans employ their new 105-mm mortars against the Japanese positions.

New Guinea The Australian 5th

'THE OUTLAW'

Doc Holliday and Billy the Kid, those legendary Western gunslingers, have become friends and rivals for the same girl, the beautiful Rio. Meanwhile Pat Garrett is after both of them. Doc dies in a gun duel and Billy and Rio go off together.

A somewhat untypical and pretentious Western, *The Outlaw*, directed and produced by Howard Hughes, concealed behind its erotic façade a theme rather unusual for the genre, namely homosexuality. The film emphasized the sexual jealousy of the three protagonists.

The huge close-ups of the ample bosom of Jane Russell, Hughes's last discovery, aroused the wrath of the censors who immediately banned the film. Not until 1950 did it get another showing, and then in a cut version.

AN ARMY BREAKS UP

The curtain went up on the drama of the Italian army at 7.45 p.m. on 8 September 1943. Italian radio carried Marshal Badoglio's message that Italy 'had asked General Eisenhower, Commander-in-Chief of the Allied forces for an armistice' and that the request had been granted. Within a few hours the drama became a tragedy for the hundreds of thousands of soldiers abandoned in perhaps the most bitter moment since the start of the war. For at this moment their German allies suddenly became their enemies.

On the eve of the capitulation Italy's forces present on the peninsula and in Sardinia added up to a total of about 1,090,00 men (ten divisions in northern Italy, seven in the centre and four in the south of the peninsula, with four more in Sardinia), as against some 400,000 soldiers in the German units now opposing them. But the Germans were as highly efficient and well equipped as the Italians were poorly equipped and demoralized. Even the Italian General Staff expected automatic defeat when their troops fought. A good half of the Italian divisions were completely ineffectual and desperately short of arms. Italian forces abroad numbered 230,000 men in France (and Corsica), about 300,000 in Slovenia, Dalmatia, Croatia, Montenegro and Kotor, more than 100,000 in Albania and about 260,000 men in Greece and the Aegean Islands, a total of about 900,000 men – in theory a formidable force. But only in theory. In practice the army was absolutely unfitted to modern conditions.

If we add to the situation on that fateful 8 September the complete absence of any instructions from Italy's war leaders (from Badoglio, head of the government, who was after all a soldier, from General Ambrosio, Chief of the General Staff, and from the Chief of the Army Staff, General Mario Roatta), and the recklessness with which they approached the inevitable moment when accounts would have to be settled with the Germans, it is easy enough to understand the complete collapse of the Italian army the day after the armistice was announced. At the critical moment many commanding officers were away from their units, or if they were present had received no instructions. Amid the chaos there were indeed some courageous, albeit useless, attempts to oppose the German aggression. In Trentino Alto-Adige and in France Alpine troops resisted, but these were momentary episodes. The centres of resistance were stamped out with ruthless ferocity. In Greece, amid the dreary spectacle of the unopposed disarming of Italian units by the Germans, the bravery of the *Acqui* Division shines out. At Cephalonia they chose the path of struggle and self-destruction – 9,646 men were killed in a savage bloodbath.

On 7 November 1943, in his report to Hitler on the strategic situation, General Jodl, Chief of Staff of the Wehrmacht, summed up in figures what had happened in Italy since 8 September. He spoke of 51 divisions 'certainly disarmed', 29 divisions 'probably disarmed' and 3 divisions 'not disarmed'. Prisoners numbered more than half a million, the loot in arms and materials enormous. He said nothing in his report about the number of dead, and not even a rough figure can ever be known. The air force and navy deserve separate consideration. Of the thousand or so aircraft – bombers, fighters, reconnaissance aircraft and the rest – theoretically available, not more than one half were fit for action. After 8 September,

246 aircraft succeeded in taking off for territories not directly under German control. 203 reached their destinations; the other 43 were either shot down or forced down in neutral territory. All the others were taken.

Most efficient of the three services was certainly the navy, which counted at the time 5 battleships, 8 cruisers, 7 auxiliary cruisers, 23 submarines, 70 or so MAS (coastal motor-boats) and 37 destroyers and torpedo-boats. On 8 September this considerable naval force was dispersed as follows: at La Spezia and Genoa, under the command of Admiral Bergamini, were the battleships *Roma*, *Vittorio Veneto* and *Italia* (formerly the *Littorio*); the cruisers *Eugenio di Savoia*, *Duca degli Abruzzi*, *Montecuccoli*, *Duca d'Aosta*, *Garibaldi* and *Regolo*, with two flotillas of destroyers. At anchor in Taranto harbour were the battleships *Doria* and *Duilio* and the cruisers *Cadorna*, *Pompeo Magno* and *Scipione*, under the command of Admiral Da Zara.

Smaller craft were in Corsica and Albania and in other Italian ports, while there were 2 submarines at Bordeaux and 9 at Danzig. Finally there were 4 submarines, 2 gunboats and the auxiliary cruiser *Calitea* in Japanese ports.

When news of the signing of the armistice reached Genoa and La Spezia, the first idea was to sink the ships, but after a telephone conversation between Admiral Bergamini, commander of the squadron, and the Chief of Naval Staff, Admiral De Courten, the naval squadron put to sea at dawn on 9 September at De Courten's suggestion and headed for Maddalena Island, near the north-east coast of Sardinia. Very early in the afternoon, as the squadron was about to enter the estuary in which the island lies, Admiral Bergamini received an urgent message from

Supermarina with the order to change course and make for Bône, in Algeria. During the morning the Germans had occupied Maddalena and arranged to capture the Italian ships.

The order was carried out at once. The squadron made for the African coast and the Germans, cheated of their opportunity to capture the Italian warships, put into effect their plan to sink them. A little after 3.00 p.m. a formation of Junkers attacked Admiral Bergamini's squadron, but without doing any substantial damage. Towards 4.00 p.m. another group of German bombers arrived over the Italian ships. The flagship, the battleship *Roma*, was hit by two rocket-bombs and sank within a few minutes. Of the complement of about 2,000 men, 1,552 lost their lives, among them the commander of the squadron, Admiral Bergamini, and the whole of his staff. The command passed to the next senior officer, Admiral Oliva, flying his flag on the cruiser *Eugenio di Savoia*. The squadron steamed south and during the morning of 10 September entered Valletta harbour in Malta, where the ships of the fleet based at Taranto had already taken refuge. Next day they were joined by the battleship *Giulio Cesare*. For the Italian navy the war thus went on, but now on the side of the Allies. Since 10 June 1940 Italy had lost in the Mediterranean about 3,000,000 tons of merchant shipping (which means more than 80% of the whole merchant fleet) and almost 300,000 tons of warships with 28,937 seamen.

Rome, 8 September 1943: an Italian field-gun in position on the courtyard of the Ostiense Station, ready to resist a German attack.

Division crosses the river Francisco, near Salamaua airfield. The Japanese garrison is in retreat towards Lae.

Aleutian Islands General Davenport Johnson takes over command of the US 11th Air Force, which has begun an air offensive against the Kuril Islands from bases in the Aleutians. Japanese fighters and anti-aircraft guns have been causing heavy losses.

12 September

Eastern Front The Russians advance on all sectors, and capture over 240 villages and towns.

New Guinea The Australian 9th and 7th Divisions advance on Lae, from east and west. The 5th Division occupies Salamaua town and airfield and the isthmus of Salamaua, while the Japanese continue to fall back on Lae.

☐ Mussolini is rescued from his prison on the Gran Sasso by a German commando unit under Captain Otto Skorzeny.

All the representatives of the Italian Government have already left Rome.

13 September

Italian Front The German General Heinrich von Vietinghoff, Commander of the German 10th Army,

launches a counter-attack against the Allied bridgehead at Salerno and threatens to cut the Allied forces in two. The US 5th Army has a plan ready for evacuation in case of emergency.

New troops begin to arrive during the night to reinforce the bridgehead, and it is stabilized. German attacks are repulsed with increasing effectiveness.

The resistance of the Italian *Cremona* and *Friuli* Divisions at Bastia (Corsica) is crushed by German forces.

☐ In Cephalonia, Greece, the Italian *Acqui* Division, commanded by General Antonio Gandin, refuses to hand over its arms and determines to hold out against attack by the German troops.

☐ Mussolini arrives in Munich, Upper Bavaria.

Solomon Islands An American battalion is moved from Arundel Island to the neighbouring island of Sagekarasa, north-east of the Bomboe peninsula.

Aegean Sea British troops occupy the island of Kos and immediately establish an RAF base there.

MUSSOLINI IS RESCUED

Hitler's first thought on hearing news of Mussolini's arrest on the evening of 25 July is to make plans for a rescue. Twenty-four hours later, on the evening of the 26th, Captain Otto Skorzeny of the 'special troops', a burly 35-year-old officer with a deep scar on his left cheek, who specializes in commando actions, arrives at Hitler's headquarters at Rastenburg. To him Hitler entrusts the task of rescuing his 'friend Mussolini' as quickly as possible, before the new Italian government hands him over to the Allies. Skorzeny will be operating, Hitler tells him, directly under General Kurt Student of the Luftwaffe; he is immediately appointed ADC to Student.

Early in the afternoon of the 27th Skorzeny and Student land at Rome airport and go off at once to Frascati, the headquarters of Field-Marshal Kesselring, Commander-in-Chief of the group of German armies in Italy. The first thing is to find out where the Italians are holding Mussolini – not difficult, since the Duce is still in Rome. By the evening, with the help of two SS officers, Kappler and Dollmann, Skorzeny has discovered that Mussolini is kept prisoner in a 'police barracks: but the discovery is of no use, for that same evening the suspicious Badoglio has his prisoner moved to a safer place. In great secrecy, the Duce is taken to the island of Ponza.

Skorzeny has to start again. Doggedly, he gets on the trail once more.

After some weeks of laborious – and slightly lucky – detective work Skorzeny is able to identify the island in the Tyrrhenian as Mussolini's new prison. But just as he is working out his rescue plan, his prey escapes again. The Italian government – it may have been warned of, or guessed, the object of Skorzeny's mission in Italy – transfers Mussolini to the island of Maddalena, near the northeast coast of Sardinia. Skorzeny begins his investigations again – not such a difficult task in Italy, where secrets are not easily kept. Flights by a German reconnaissance aircraft over Maddalena confirm Skorzeny's suspicions, and special attention is concentrated on the Villa Weber, where the captain believes that Mussolini is being held. Skorzeny is proved right by a stratagem carried out by a fellow-officer, Lieutenant Warger. Warger lands on Maddalena disguised as a sailor. He goes to an inn, and during a conversation with the locals he says: 'I bet the Duce is dead!' That induces a fruit and vegetable seller (who delivers to the Villa Weber every day) to take him to see the Duce. The pseudo-sailor loses his bet (gladly enough, we may suppose), but now Skorzeny is able to work out his plan. The operation for the liberation of Mussolini, approved personally by Hitler, is to be a full-scale attack on the island by German forces on 28 August, but once more the Germans find that the bird has flown. The authorities on the island, especially those directly in charge of Mussolini, have been suspicious of the flights over the Villa Weber by German reconnaissance aircraft. So yet another transfer is arranged. On 27 August, the very day before Skorzeny's assault to liberate the Duce is due to take place, a Red Cross seaplane takes off from the waters by Maddalena with the prisoner on board, destination – obviously – unknown. At the very last moment Lieutenant Warger learns that Mussolini is no longer on the island, and the operation is cancelled. (Skorzeny is actually present himself on the island at the time, studying some of the details of his plan on the spot).

Still Skorzeny does not give up and he starts to lay another trap. This time fortune smiles on him in the guise of Herbert Kappler, a senior SS officer, who has found out that security measures are being greatly tightened on the mainland in the area of the Gran Sasso in Abruzzi. This is something that may interest Skorzeny. He follows up the clue, and it proves fruitful. In the area of the Gran Sasso there is a big plateau, the Campo Imperatore, which has been made into a popular skiing centre, with a hotel that can only be reached by cable-car starting from Assergi – clearly a place hard to get at and easy to defend, just the sort of place to keep a prisoner as important as Mussolini. This is the theory, but it is essential to be absolutely certain about it. One unsuccessful effort, one error of judgment, and the Germans' intentions would be betrayed and the Italians put on the alert, and the prisoner would be much more closely guarded. Confirmation of Skorzeny's and Student's hypothesis comes from a German medical officer, Lieutenant Leo Krutoff, who has had orders to look into the possibility of using Campo Imperatore as a convalescent centre for German troops suffering from malaria (at least, that is what the innocent medical officer has been told). Krutoff is unable to carry out his mission. When he goes to take the cable-car from the village of Assergi he is roughly turned back by Italian *carabinieri* – the Gran Sasso has been declared a 'military zone' and he cannot go up. Skorzeny has learnt enough.

His plan is a bold one. A number of gliders and a hundred airborne troops are to land on the plateau behind the hotel, an undertaking of considerable danger given the broken nature of the ground and the shortness of the strip for take-off after the rescue. The experts think the operation, if not impossible, certainly too dangerous, and advise against it, but nevertheless Skorzeny is given permission to try. And on 12 September, about 1.00 p.m., 12 German aircraft take off from the airfield at Pratica di Mare, a hamlet near Pomezia, in Rome province. The landing on Campo Imperatore is adventurous, but satisfactory on the whole. Skorzeny and his parachutists at once make for the hotel, taking everyone there by surprise. To confuse the *carabinieri* on guard at the hotel still more, Skorzeny has brought with him Soleti, General of the *carabinieri*. Mussolini's innocent jailers are completely at a loss, and Skorzeny exhorts the colonel in command not to resist, to avoid useless bloodshed. The German officer's advice is followed all too meticulously. Mussolini and Skorzeny take their seats in a small, highly manoeuvrable aircraft called a 'Storch', sent to Campo Imperatore specially because there would be too much risk of detection if they left the plateau by any other means; it is piloted by Captain Gerlach, personal pilot to General Student, the German flying ace. Gerlach does not really want to take Skorzeny as well as Mussolini. He is not sure that his aircraft will be able to take off, and they have to carry out a hair-raising manoeuvre. The parachutists hold the aircraft back by the tail, and the pilot opens the throttle to maximum revolutions; he gives a signal, the parachutists release the tail and the little aircraft leaps forward over the edge of the plateau. For a moment it disappears into the abyss; then it appears in the distance, rising steadily. At Pratica di Mare it comes down and the Duce is transferred to a Heinkel 111, which flies him to Vienna and on to Munich. There Mussolini meets his wife; and on the 14th, at Rastenburg, meets the Führer.

Allied landing at Salerno: British troops bring a barrage balloon ashore as protection against German air attacks.

14 September
Eastern Front The Red Army occupies part of Bryansk, while in the Kuban bitter house-to-house fighting rages in Novorossiysk.
Italian Front Units of the British 1st Airborne Division take Bari. The British 5th Division (XIII Corps) continues to push northwards on the Tyrrhenian coast and arrives south of Sapri.
☐ Meanwhile Mussolini reaches Rastenburg, the 'wolf's lair', Hitler's headquarters. Vittorio Mussolini, the Duce's son, describes the scene: 'Deeply moved, the two men clasped each other by the hand for a long time.'
Solomon Islands On Vella Lavella, after an intense artillery barrage, the Americans advance in Kokolope Bay and occupy Horaniu, which the enemy have already left.
On the islet of Sagekarasa, near Arundel, the Japanese put in a strong counter-attack against the American battalion landed the previous day. The Americans send reinforcements to Sagekarasa, while the Japanese complete the despatch of a regiment from Kolombangara to Arundel.

A New Zealand brigade, on the way to a landing on the Treasury Islands (Admiral Halsey having persuaded General MacArthur to accept his plan), reaches Guadalcanal.
New Guinea The Australians erect a bridge over the river Busu and send their 26th Brigade over to the other side. The 25th Brigade occupies Heath Plantation in its advance on Lae.
Aegean Sea British forces take the island of Leros.

15 September
Eastern Front In the central sector the Russians go over to the offensive towards Smolensk. The Central Front led by Rokossovsky, making for Kiev, takes Nezhin.
Italian Front The British 5th Division reaches Sapri in an effort to join up with the US VI Corps, which has landed south of Salerno.
General Alexander orders the US 5th Army to continue its advance across the Volturno.
☐ Mussolini issues a proclamation. He resumes supreme direction of Fascism in Italy.
New Guinea The Australians are

still advancing on Lae. General MacArthur orders an operation with special air support to take Kaiapit and Dumpu.

16 September

Eastern Front General Petrov's troops capture the ruins of Novorossiysk. A large part of the German 17th Army has already managed to reach the Crimea across the Kerch Strait. This is the end of the Germans' venture into the Caucasus. South-west of Bryansk the Russians take Novgorod Severskiy. In the region east of Kiev they take Romnyi and, south of Kharkov, Lozovaya. The Germans announce the evacuation of Bryansk.

Italian Front Forward units from the American 5th Army and the British 8th Army join up near Vallo di Lucania. Field-Marshal Kesselring, commanding the southern group of armies, begins a cautious withdrawal northwards towards the Gustav Line, along the rivers Garigliano and Sangro.

Aegean British forces occupy Samos.

Solomon Islands More reinforcements, including an infantry battalion and some Marines with light tanks, are landed on Arundel Island to wipe out the last Japanese resistance.

New Guinea Under attack from the air and the sea and cut off from supplies by the Allied blockade, the Japanese in Lae (7,500 men plus the remnants of the garrison of Salamaua, decimated in earlier fighting) furtively leave the position and retire to the north-west. It takes them a whole month before they reach Sio, on the north coast of the island opposite New Britain. The Australians of the 7th and 9th Divisions converge on the abandoned base and occupy it.

17 September

Eastern Front The Russians enter Bryansk, overcoming ferocious German resistance. The OKW is already resigned to the loss of huge areas of ground, and considers it essential that the Wehrmacht should hold the line of the Dniepr.

Italian Front The British XIII Corps advances towards the Potenza–Auletta line. American units of the US VI Corps continue their attacks against Altavilla.

Solomon Islands Fighting continues on Arundel Island and the near-by islet of Sagekarasa, with intensive artillery activity. At a conference of Allied commanders at Port Moresby in New Guinea, General MacArthur maintains that it is necessary to establish a beachhead on Bougainville as quickly as possible and build up a big base there which would give the Allies control over the whole South-West Pacific and enable them to break out towards the Central Pacific.

New Guinea The Australian 9th Division is to be employed for a landing in force at Finschhafen on the 22nd, in accordance with decisions taken by the South-West Pacific Area Headquarters. Finschhafen, at the tip of the peninsula that encloses the northern part of the Gulf of Huon, will be used as an advanced air base and for light naval units.

18 September

Eastern Front The railway junction of Pavlograd, south of Lozovaya, is re-taken by the Russians.

Italian Front The Americans enter Altavilla, while the US 45th Division (VI Corps) enters Persano without opposition.

Solomon Islands The New Zealand General Barrowclough takes over from the American General McClure in command of operations in Vella Lavella. The New Zealand 14th Brigade tries to cut off the retreating enemy, but the Japanese finally succeed in escaping and leaving the island. On Arundel the Americans deploy fresh forces at the base of the Stima peninsula.

Central Pacific US carrier-borne aircraft bomb Tarawa, Makin and Abemama in the Gilbert Islands.

19 September

Eastern Front Further great victories announced by Stalin. The Kalinin Front (Eremenko) and West Front (Sokolovsky), con-

tinuing their attacks against von Kluge's Army Group Centre, liberate Yartsevo and Dukhovschina, already threatening Smolensk, west of Moscow. In the southern sector the Germans withdraw on to the Dniepr, giving up Priluki, Piryatin, Lubny, Khorol and Krasnograd to the Russians.

Italian Front Troops of the British XXIII Corps reach the Auletta–Potenza line.

Above: the people of Poltava acclaim the arrival of Red Army units on 23 September 1943.

☐ The Germans, in one of their reprisal measures, burn down Boves, in Cuneo province, and kill 32 civilians. This episode sparks off the partisan struggle in Italy.

New Guinea After some hard fighting the Australians take Kaiapit and drive off repeated Japanese counterattacks.

20 September
Eastern Front Russian troops of the Kalinin Front re-take Velizh, northwest of Smolensk. They also take Kholm and many other towns.
Italian Front General Lucas takes over command of the US VI Corps (5th Army).
Yugoslavia Very heavy fighting is

taking place at Split, which is held by Mihailovitch's patriot army. The Germans have made repeated attacks, using waves of divebombers, for the last seven days.
Solomon Islands The units deployed on Sagekarasa, near Arundel, discover that the Japanese have abandoned their positions in the night.

A train-load of Italian soldiers (left), captured by the Germans after the armistice, stands in the station at Saranjovo, Yugoslavia. They are en route to a prisoner-of-war camp in Germany.

Russians on the attack in the Smolensk sector (centre) and the Bryansk sector (above).

21 September

Eastern Front Rokossovsky's forces liberate Chernigov, between Gomel and Kiev, completely destroyed by the Luftwaffe in 1941. The town is taken after three days of bitter fighting.

Italian Front General Alexander draws up his plan for future operations. There will be four phases: first, consolidation of the positions on the Salerno–Bari line; second, capture of Naples and Foggia; third, capture of Rome; and fourth, possible attacks on Florence and Arezzo.

The Germans complete evacuation of Sardinia and move to Corsica.

Solomon Islands On Arundel Island, too, the Americans discover that the Japanese, having lost 600 men in defence of the island, have abandoned it as well as Sagekarasa and the other neighbouring islets. Japanese troops are leaving the Central Solomons and concentrating in the southern islands.

New Guinea An Australian brigade sails from Lae to occupy Finschhafen; a second moves from Lae towards Langemak Bay, and two others are air-lifted from Nazdab to Kaiapit to follow up the Japanese garrison from Lae, which is withdrawing along the valley of the river Markham.

22 September

Eastern Front The Germans admit to the evacuation of Poltava, west of Kharkov, which can no longer be defended against the advance of Konev's Steppe Front. Before leaving, the Germans have laid much of the city waste.

Italian Front The British X Corps (US 5th Army) is ordered to advance on Naples, while the US VI Corps makes for the Avellino–Teora line, preparing to push on towards Benevento. In the 8th Army sector the 8th Indian Division arrives from Africa. Elements of the 78th Division and 4th Armoured Brigade land near Bari, and later move up to Foggia.

☐ In Cephalonia, Greece, troops of the Italian *Acqui* Division lay down their arms, and the Germans take revenge by killing 5,000 officers and

France, September 1943: two members of the resistance are about to be summarily executed by members of the SS as they kneel on the edge of their grave.

men (added to the 1,200 men and 446 officers killed in action and 3,000 who died when the ships taking them to prisoner-of-war camps in Germany were sunk, this figure brought up to 9,646 the total number who died resisting the Germans. The *Acqui* Division has been literally wiped out.)

Pacific Admiral Halsey asks Rear-Admiral Wilkinson (who is to command the landing forces) to prepare detailed plans for the invasion of the northern Solomons. After that it will be decided to occupy the Treasury Islands and Empress Augusta Bay in Bougainville Island.

South-West Pacific From the headquarters of this sector, which is under MacArthur, comes instructions for Operation *Dexterity*, the landing at Cape Gloucester, at the western tip of New Britain. (Rabaul, the highly important Japanese base, is at the other end of the island.) Parachutists and airborne troops will take part in the operation, which is to start on 20 November but put off to 26 December.

New Guinea An amphibious force of destroyers and landing craft under the command of the American Rear-Admiral Barbey, lands the 20th Brigade of the Australian 9th Division

American infantry columns on the march towards the interior of New Guinea.

at the mouth of the river Song, 6 miles north of Finschhafen, in the early hours of the morning, after a brief barrage by naval guns. Japanese aircraft which tried to attack the convoy as it approached were driven off by Allied aircraft, which cover both the landing and the advance on Finschhafen.

23 September

Italian Front The US 5th Army begins a general advance north. The British X Corps attacks towards the Nocera–Pagani Pass and on the road between Salerno and San Severino, but firm German resistance considerably slows down the Allied advance. The troops of Montgomery's 8th Army occupy Altamura and drive out the Germans.

☐ Mussolini, now no more than a puppet manipulated by Hitler, proclaims the 'Italian Social Republic', and he forms a new government with authority over the part of the peninsula occupied by the Germans. However, Italy has to yield Trieste, Istria and the Trentino–Alto Adige to direct administration by Germany.

Eastern Front Konev's troops enter the important Ukrainian city of Poltava. The battle has lasted three days. On other fronts, too, the Russians continue to advance, and Konev's troops now push on towards Kremenchug.

New Guinea The Australian 20th Brigade, landed the previous day near Finschhafen, advances towards the town, taking an airfield and reaching the river Bumi, where the Japanese have set up a powerful defensive line.

24 September

Eastern Front Bitter fighting rages near Smolensk and Roslavl. The Germans are forced to withdraw from both cities.

Solomon Islands The first Allied aircraft land on Vella Lavella airfield.

New Guinea Japanese aircraft attack Allied ships carrying supplies to the Finschhafen bridgehead, but with only moderate success. The Australian 20th Brigade breaks through the Japanese line on the river Bumi, north of Finschhafen.

25 September

Eastern Front Stalin announces the greatest victory of the summer campaign, the recapture of Smolensk. Troops of the Russian West Front (Sokolonsky) occupy both Smolensk and Roslavl. Smolensk, with its vast network of defences constructed by the Germans over two years and claimed by Berlin to be impregnable, was the keystone to the entire German defence system in Russia. The German 4th Army, which has been withdrawn west of Smolensk, withstands the powerful Russian thrust in the direction of the river Orsha. In the southern sector the Russians have reached the Dniepr (which the Germans look on as the line that must be held at all costs) from Kremenchug to Dnepropetrovsk.

New Guinea The Australian 20th Brigade advances slowly towards Finschhafen.

26 September

Italian Front The British X Corps continues a series of attacks aimed at breaking into the Naples plain.

Patrols from the British XIII Corps take Canosa.

New Guinea The Japanese launch violent counter-attacks against the Australians in the Finschhafen area, but are nowhere able to drive them back.

27 September

Eastern Front The Russians occupy the north bank of the Kuban river and take Temruk, the last German-held port in the Kuban. The German 17th Army's bridgehead is reduced to a very small size.

Italian Front Troops of Montgomery's 8th Army enter Foggia and occupy the airport, one of the Allied forces' first objectives.

☐ At Brindisi the Allied Generals Bedell Smith, Macmillan and Murphy meet the Italian delegates, Badoglio, Ambrosio and Acquarone to make final arrangements for the meeting of Badoglio and Eisenhower at which the final text of the armistice will be signed.

☐ The people of Naples rise against the Germans, who have made the city into one of their 'game preserves', plundering shops, requisitioning public transport and rounding up thousands of citizens to be sent to forced labour. The rising begins in the afternoon, when German soldiers try yet again to plunder a large shop in the main street in the city centre, the Via Roma, and some men there are driven to resist, forming a line and shooting at the Germans. The Germans retreat and fire back, shooting at random and killing a youth walking by. The fighting quickly spreads through the whole city. Through the streets, from the windows, from the roofs of houses, hundreds of improvised resistance

A stretcher party brings a wounded Canadian back from the front near Termoli, Campobasso.

Armed civilians in a Naples street during the rising against the Germans in the last few days of September.

fighters start shooting at the Germans.

☐ Germany. The US 8th Air Force bombs Emden.

28 September

Italian Front In the sector in which the US 5th Army is operating the British X Corps and US VI Corps are able to resume their attacks, one towards Naples, the other towards Avellino. The 23rd Armoured Brigade advances in the direction of Castellammare di Stabia, while US Rangers take Sala Consilina.

☐ The Naples rising has not subsided. Colonel Scholl, the German area commander, sends tanks in against the insurgents, but the rebels, at heavy cost to themselves, immobilize eight of the tanks and set them on fire, so that they hold up the others behind them. Barricades are erected, and the struggle grows.

Yugoslavia The battle for Split continues; the Germans step up their attacks.

Solomon Islands During the night of 28/29 September the Japanese begin to evacuate Kolombangara Island, where their bases have become useless as a result of the Americans' 'island-hopping' strategy.

29 September

Eastern Front After three days bitter fighting Konev's troops (the Steppe Front) cross the Dniepr at Kremenchug and capture the town. Even the vital 'Dniepr Line' looks like crumbling. Now Rokossovsky and Vatutin advance towards Kiev.

Italian Front General Alexander issues instructions for future operations. They fall into two phases: first, the capture of Naples and the advance of the front to the line Sessa Aurunca – Venafro – Isernia – Castropignano – the river Biferno – Termoli; second, advance to the line Civitavecchia–Terni–Visso–San Benedetto del Tronto.

In the operational area of the US VI Corps, units of the 3rd Division converge on Avellino, and during the night begin the assault on the city.

☐ Eisenhower and Badoglio sign full armistice terms.

'FOUR QUARTETS'

The complete edition of the English poet Thomas Stearns Eliot, was published. Regarded by many as the greatest work of poetry written during the war, *Four Quartets* is a collection of four short poems (*Burnt Norton*, *East Coker*, *The Dry Salvages* and *Little Gidding*), written by Eliot between 1935 and 1942 and already published separately.

Inspired by the musical structure of certain Beethoven quartets, the poems are small masterpieces of mysticism and subjective meditation on the apparent contradictions of time and eternity, immobility and movement, and the antagonism of politics and religion.

All four poems, additionally, have associations with the seasons and the natural elements: spring and air, summer and earth, autumn and water, winter and fire.

T.S. Eliot (right) with L. Torrey.

☐ Furious engagements continue in Naples between the insurgents and the German troops. Finally, after the Germans have again used tanks, a truce comes into force at 7.00 a.m. on 30 September.

China General Stilwell announces a 'programme for China'. He recommends the re-establishment, with American aid, of 60 divisions of the Nationalist Army.

30 September

Eastern Front The Soviet government announces that the Red Army is advancing on Kiev in the Ukraine and on Vitebsk, Gomel and Mogilev in Belorussia. September has seen the liberation of large regions. October will see the crossing of the Dniepr, but also much more determined resistance by the Germans.

Italian Front Despite the truce heavy fighting continues in Naples. About 11.00 a.m. comes the news that the Allies are at the gates in the southern part of the city.

The British V Corps (US 5th Army) has surrounded Vesuvius. Avellino has been taken by troops of the US VI Corps (US 5th Army).

1 October

Eastern Front During the first week in October the armies of the Central Front, Steppe Front and South-West Front exert intensive pressure on the Army Groups Centre and South along the great bend of the Dniepr, and succeed in crossing the river and establishing small bridgeheads near Kiev, Kremenchug and Dnepropetrovsk.

Italian Front During the morning the King's Dragoon Guards, of the British X Corps, enter Naples without opposition.

The British XIII Corps (8th Army) pushes on towards the line Vinchiaturo–Termoli, the 78th Division along the coast and the Canadian 1st Division inland across the mountains.

Solomon Islands Admiral Halsey tells General MacArthur that he has

Devastation in the docks at Naples caused by bombs dropped by the Allies in the days immediately preceding their occupation of the city.

decided to carry out a landing in Empress Augusta Bay, Bougainville. MacArthur assures him that he will get the maximum air support from the South-West Pacific Area forces.
New Guinea The Australians resume their attacks on Finschhafen, inflicting heavy losses on the Japanese.

☐ Austria. Allied bombers drop 187 tons of bombs on Vienna.

2 October

Italian Front In the US VI Corps sector, while the 3rd Division on the left of the line makes for the Volturno river, the 34th and 45th Divisions move by separate routes towards Benevento, an important road junction.

During the night Allied Commandos

land near Termoli and seize the harbour and the town, and the British 78th Division links up with them, advancing northwards along the coast and stabilizing a bridgehead over the river Biferno.
Central Pacific The US 27th Division, which was to have been getting ready for a landing on Nauru, is ordered to prepare plans for the capture of a new objective, suggested by Vice-Admiral Spruance to Admiral Nimitz – Makin atoll, in the Gilbert Islands.
Solomon Islands During the night of 2/3 October the Japanese 'Tokyo Night Express' completes the evacuation of the garrison, some 9,400 men, of Kolombangara. US naval and air forces intervene, but to no effect.

New Guinea The Australian 20th Brigade captures the village and harbour of Finschhafen after hard fighting and joins up with the 23rd Brigade, which has advanced in the meantime from Lae. However, the Japanese still hold two strongpoints overlooking the harbour.

3 October

Italian Front In the VI Corps sector the 34th Division and the 133rd Infantry Regiment take Benevento and establish a bridgehead across the river Calore.

In the Termoli sector the Germans despatch reinforcements (the 16th *Panzerdivision*, which was operating on the Volturno) in an attempt to drive the British back across the river Biferno, and a fierce battle begins.

During the night a brigade of the 78th Division lands in the sector in which the British have captured their bridgehead. Meanwhile the Canadian 1st Division, held up by the terrain, is about 12 miles from Vinchiaturo.

The 3rd *Panzergrenadier* Division takes the place of the 16th Armoured Division on the Volturno.

Mediterranean The Germans land on the island of Kos, used by the British as an RAF base.

☐ Germany. Heavy night attack on Kassel; 1,500 tons of bombs dropped in 30 minutes.

4 October

Italian Front In Corsica Italian and French troops recapture Bastia. The whole island is under the control of the Allied forces.

Eisenhower and Alexander forecast that Allied troops will be able to enter Rome by the end of the month. So, having decided to transfer GHQ from Algiers to Naples, Eisenhower now decides to wait so that he can establish himself in Rome.

Mediterranean The German forces landed on Kos overcome the British garrison. The loss of this island, the only Allied air base in the Aegean, endangers the Allied hold on Leros and Samos.

5 October

Italian Front On the Adriatic coast, where the XIII Corps of the British 8th Army is operating, fighting continues around the Biferno bridgehead near Termoli. For a time the Germans are able to enter Termoli.

Pacific An American Task Force consisting of 6 aircraft carriers, 7 cruisers, 24 destroyers and auxiliary craft, commanded by Rear-Admiral A. E. Montgomery, shells and bombs Wake Island (the island that Admiral Kajioka rechristened 'Island of Birds' when he officially took possession of it in the name of the Japanese Emperor on 23 December 1941). The attack causes great damage, and is repeated the following day.

The Commander-in-Chief in the Pacific, Nimitz, issues the directives for the coming offensive in the Central Pacific. Vice-Admiral Spruance is to direct the landings on Makin, Tarawa and Abemama Islands in the Gilberts, protecting the landing forces by all available means and neutralizing the Japanese bases on the Marshall Islands and Nauru during the operation, which is timed to start on the 19th, later put back to the 20th.

6 October

Italian Front The American 5th Army reaches the south bank of the Volturno, bringing another phase of the advance up the Italian peninsula to a successful conclusion. Troops of the British 10th Division, attached to the US 5th Army, seize Capua.

Solomon Islands The capture of the Central Solomons by the Americans can be regarded as a *fait accompli* with the unopposed landing of units of the 25th Division on Kolombangara, already evacuated by the Japanese. Excluding Vella Lavella, the occupation of which is not yet complete, the campaign has cost the Americans 1,100 dead and about 4,000 wounded; Japanese dead, counted by the Americans, number 2,483. The Allies now have four airfields (Munda, Barakoma, Segi and Ondonga) from which their aircraft can attack the next objective, Bougainville.

Battle of Vella Lavella. During the night of 6/7 October three US destroyers commanded by Captain Walker intercept a 'Tokyo Night Express' – nine Japanese destroyers under the command of Rear-Admiral Matsuji Ijuin, evacuating 600 men from Vella Lavella. A violent engagement develops, fought mostly with torpedoes; the Japanese lose a destroyer, but succeed in carrying out their mission. The Americans also lose a destroyer, and two others are damaged, one in a collision, the other by a torpedo.

New Guinea Elements of the Australian 7th Division take Dumpu unexpectedly easily. A landing strip for fighters is begun.

New Britain US patrol parties landed secretly near Cape Gloucester carry out a thorough reconnaissance of the area chosen for the forthcoming landing.

7 October

Eastern Front In the central sector the Russians take Nevel, a railway centre north of Vitebsk. The Dniepr is crossed at three places. But German resistance is stiffening along the whole front, and the Russian advance is becoming much less spectacular.

Italian Front The American 5th Army gets ready to attack the Volturno line. The date for the operation is fixed for the night of 9/10 October, then put off to the night of 12/13. Meanwhile the troops strengthen their positions on the south bank of the river.

In the eastern sector, where the British XIII Corps is operating, a second brigade of the 78th Division lands in the Biferno bridgehead, while the Germans withdraw across the Trigno.

8 October

Germany. 357 bombers of the American 8th Air Force carry out a massive raid on Bremen and Vegesack, but incur heavy losses.

9 October

Eastern Front The North Caucasus Front (Petrov) wipes out all remaining resistance by the Germans in the Taman peninsula, between the Black Sea and the Sea of Azov. The German 17th Army has crossed into the Crimea in small parties.

11 October

Eastern Front The armies of the Bryansk Front (Popov) tighten their hold round Gomel and manage to capture one of its suburbs. But German resistance is tenacious.

Italian Front In the eastern sector of the Allied line, where Montgomery's 8th Army is operating, the V Corps (78th Division and 8th Indian Division) is deployed on the right flank while XIII Corps mans the central sector.

12 October

Italian Front During the night

troops of the US 5th Army begin the assault on the Germans on the Volturno on a front of about 40 miles.
New Britain The US 5th Air Force, with its new airfields such as Munda and Barakoma, is now able to start a big strategic offensive aimed at isolating and neutralizing the whole of the Bismarck Archipelago, and in particular the Japanese base at Rabaul. 349 aircraft systematically raid the roadstead, airfields and military installations, causing considerable damage, sinking four transports and a patrol boat and damaging three destroyers, three submarines, one tanker and one auxiliary craft. The Japanese headquarters are completely taken by surprise.

☐ Churchill makes known that the Portuguese government has agreed to give the UK naval facilities in the Azores. These will help in the protection of merchant shipping.

13 October

Italian Front During the night of 12/13 troops of the 5th Army begin the bridgeheads on the north bank of the Volturno, but troop movements are made difficult by the terrain, which torrential rain has turned into a quagmire. Moreover the three German formations given the task of defending the Volturno line – the 15th Armoured Division, *Hermann Goering* Armoured Division and 3rd Division, making up General Hans Hube's XIV Armoured Corps – put up stiff resistance to General Clark's Allied units.

In British X Corps sector, on the left of the Anglo-American front, while the 46th Division tries to break through towards Cancello, the 7th Armoured Division and the 56th Division, on the centre and the right, carry out some diversionary activities in the direction of Grazzanise and Capua. The 46th Division succeeds in establishing a bridgehead in the coastal sector, and the 7th Armoured Division takes several places on the way to Grazzanise, but the 56th Division is pinned down and cannot push on beyond Capua.
The US 3rd and 34th Divisions of the

Allied soldiers on the beach of a newly captured island in the Solomons.

VI Corps succeed in crossing the Volturno on the right of the front. The first takes Mounts Majulo and Caruso and the Caiazzo plain, while the other establishes a bridgehead from the Caiazzo plain to where the river Calore flows into the Volturno. On the extreme right the American 45th Division takes Monte Acero when units of the German 26th Armoured Division retire.
Italy declares war on Germany at at 3.00 p.m. Italy has the somewhat hybrid status among the Allies of 'cobelligerent'.

14 October

Eastern Front After intense and bitter fighting Malinovsky's troops (the Russian South-West Front) take Zaporozhye, an important Ukrainian industrial centre south of Dnepropetrovsk. Further south the troops of Tolbukhin's South Front are fighting in the suburbs of Melitopol. The Russian aim is to cut off the German 17th Army, just evacuated from the Taman peninsula, in the Crimea. They have cut the Melitopol–Crimea railway in two places.
Italian Front General Clark, Commander of the US 5th Army, shifts eastwards the line between his two

corps, the British X and American VI, so altering his plan of attack. The operation is made necessary by the failure of the British 56th Division to break through towards Capua. Clark's move enables the 56th Division to use one of the bridges built over the Volturno by the American 3rd Division and so cross the river upstream of Monte Triflisco. Meanwhile the American 3rd Division, which has secured a bridgehead nearly $4\frac{1}{2}$ miles deep during the morning, directs its attacks on Dragoni, together with the 34th Division. The American V Corps advances astride the Volturno towards the Venafro–Isernia sector, taking the upper Volturno valley. In the British XIII Corps sector the Canadian 1st Division takes Campobasso.

☐ Germany. About 300 bombers of the American 8th Air Force attack factories at Schweinfurt. The damage they cause is relatively slight, while at least 60 of the attacking aircraft are shot down and 138 more or less seriously damaged.

15 October

Italian Front The British 56th Division (X Corps), having crossed the Volturno, joins up with the other

Top: natives help American troops to land equipment in New Guinea.
Above: a church south of Naples is used by the Allies as a hospital.

units of the 5th Army which are trying to advance on to the ridge that divides them from the rivers Rapido and Garigliano. North of the Volturno General Hans Hube's German XIV Armoured Corps has established three fortified defensive lines: the so-called *Barbara* line which goes from Monte Massico to the Matese hills by way of Teano and Presenzano; the *Bernhard* (*Reinhard*) line, much longer and stronger, consisting of a broad strip of fortified strongholds, from the mouth of the Garigliano to Castel di Sangro, relying on the natural defences of the mountains, Difensa, Maggiore and Camino in the area between Presenzano and Sant' Ambrogio, and Monte Sammucro west of Venafro; and lastly, further north, the *Gustav* line, the most solid of the three defensive lines, which follows the rivers Garigliano and Rapido and takes in the natural fortification provided by Monte Cassino, then turning north through Roccaraso and Casoli to finish on the Adriatic coast south of San Vito. Behind these lines stands General Vietinghoff's 10th Army, with General Hube's XIV Armoured Corps to the south and General Trangott Herr's LXXI Armoured Corps to the north.

After crossing the Volturno the American 3rd Division (VI Corps) takes Cisterna.

In the northern sector the Canadian 1st Division takes Vinchiaturo.

Pacific The headquarters of the US I Marine Corps issues directives for the invasion of the Northern Solomons. The attacking force, Task Force 31 under the command of Rear-Admiral Wilkinson, will land the Marines on 27 October on the Treasury Islands, where the enemy bases must be taken or neutralized in readiness for the main landing on Bougainville, which will take place on 1 November.

16 October

New Guinea A captured enemy sary steps to repulse a series of fierce counter-attacks launched by the Japanese from their strongpoint of Sattelberg, which overlooks Finschhafen.

China Admiral Lord Mountbatten, Supreme Allied Commander for South-East Asia, arrives in Chungking, the provisional capital of Nationalist China, for a conference with Generalissimo Chiang Kai-shek.

☐ *Britain.* General Brereton assumes command of the newly formed US 9th Air Force.

17 October

Eastern Front In the southern sector the Red Army breaks the German lines at Kremenchug and presses on towards Krivoy Rog, further south. The objective is still to cut off the Crimea. In the Gomel sector troops of the Soviet Central Front (Rokossovsky) succeed in crossing the Dniepr and taking Loyev.

Italian Front Units of the American 3rd Division, after some skirmishes, take Liberi and Villa, evacuated by the German troops.

Elements of the American 34th Division occupy Alvignano.

18 October

Italian Front The US 3rd and 34th Divisions continue to advance towards Dragoni. After taking Roccaromana the two units of the American VI Corps prepare for the decisive attack to capture Dragoni and the bridges over the Volturno beyond it.

Solomon Islands Big American air forces carry out a heavy raid on the Japanese base at Buin, on Bougainville. They also resume their attacks on Rabaul with considerable effect. General Hyakutake, in command of the Japanese 17th Army, deploys his forces (about 33,000 men) for the defence of Bougainville. Twenty-five thousand are concentrated in the south of the island, near Buin and Kahili airfields, 5,000 on the north coast, about 3,000 on the east coast (where the mouths of several rivers might favour possible landings).

19 October

Italian Front Units of the US 34th Division (VI Corps) open the attack on Dragoni at dawn, only to find that the Germans have withdrawn during

Flying Fortresses of the US 8th Air Force release their bomb load on Bremen, 15 October 1943.

A Russian patrol crawls forward towards the German defences on the Lower Dniepr.

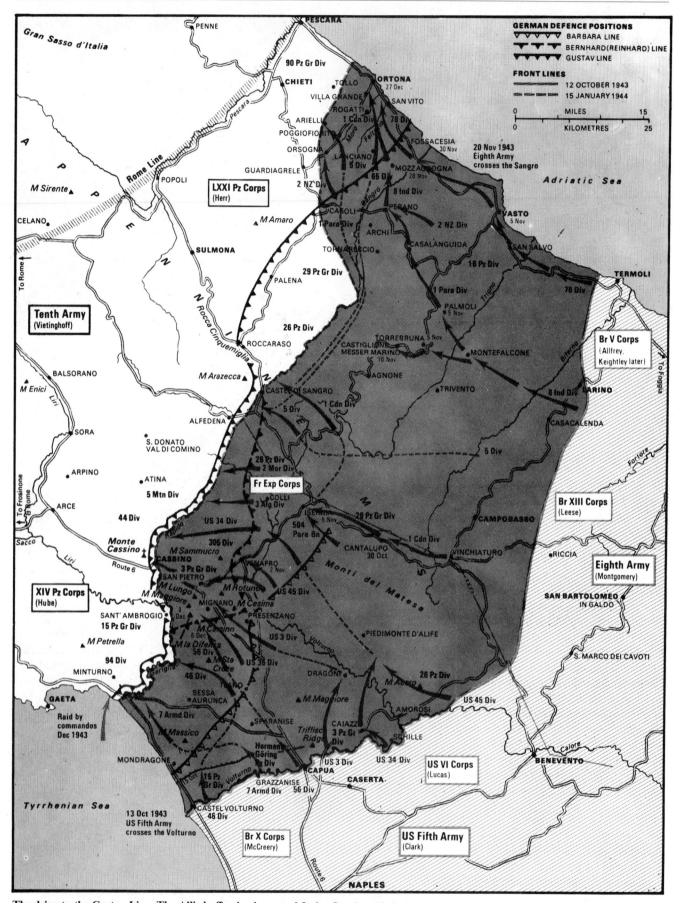

GERMAN DEFENCE POSITIONS
BARBARA LINE
BERNHARD (REINHARD) LINE
GUSTAV LINE

FRONT LINES
12 OCTOBER 1943
15 JANUARY 1944

MILES 15
KILOMETRES 25

Gran Sasso d'Italia

PENNE

PESCARA

90 Pz Gr Div

CHIETI

TOLLO

ORTONA
27 Dec

VILLA GRANDE

SAN VITO

ROGATTI

ARIELLI

1 Cdn Div

78 Div

POGGIOFIORITO

FOSSACESIA
30 Nov

ORSOGNA

LANCIANO
5 Div

MOZZAGROGNA
28 Nov

GUARDIAGRELE

65 Div

8 Ind Div

**20 Nov 1943
Eighth Army
crosses the Sangro**

Adriatic Sea

2 NZ Div

CASOLI

PERANO

VASTO
5 Nov

Rome Line

POPOLI

LXXI Pz Corps
(Herr)

M Sirente

M Amaro

1 Para Div

ARCHI

2 NZ Div

SAN SALVO

TERMOLI

CELANO

SULMONA

TORNARECCIO

CASALANGUIDA

16 Pz Div

29 Pz Gr Div

1 Para Div
5 Nov

78 Div

Tenth Army
(Vietinghoff)

PALENA

PALMOLI
5 Nov

Br V Corps
(Allfrey,
Keightley later)

M Enici

BALSORANO

26 Pz Div

ROCCARASO

TORREBRUNA 5 Nov

CASTIGLIONE
MESSER MARINO
10 Nov

MONTEFALCONE

SORA

M Arazecca

AGNONE

TRIVENTO

8 Ind Div

LARINO

CASTEL DI SANGRO

5 Div

1 Cdn Div

CASACALENDA

S. DONATO
VAL DI COMINO

ALFEDENA

5 Div

ARPINO

ATINA

Fr Exp Corps

26 Pz Div
2 Mor Div

COLLI
3 Alg Div

ISERNIA
5 Nov

29 Pz Gr Div

Br XIII Corps
(Leese)

ARCE

5 Mtn Div

44 Div

US 34 Div

504
Para Bn

CAMPOBASSO

RICCIA

305 Div

CANTALUPO
30 Oct

1 Cdn Div

VINCHIATURO

Eighth Army
(Montgomery)

Monte
Cassino

M Sammucro

VENAFRO
2 Nov

US 45 Div

XIV Pz Corps
(Hube)

CASSINO

3 Pz Gr Div

SAN PIETRO

M Lungo

M Rotundo

SAN BARTOLOMEO
IN GALDO

M Maggiore

MIGNANO

M Cesima

US 3 Div

15 Pz Gr Div

SANT' AMBROGIO

M Camino
6 Dec

PRESENZANO

PIEDIMONTE D'ALIFE

M Petrella

M la Difensa
56 Div

M Sta
Croce

US 36 Div

US 45 Div

S. MARCO DEI CAVOTI

94 Div

M Abate

26 Pz Div

MINTURNO

46 Div

DRAGONI

M Maggiore

AMOROSI

US 45 Div

SESSA
AURUNCA

GAETA

Raid by
commandos
Dec 1943

7 Armd Div

SPARANISE

CAIAZZO
3 Pz Gr
Div

Triflisco
Ridge

SCHILLE

BENEVENTO

M Massico

Hermann
Göring Div

US VI Corps
(Lucas)

MONDRAGONE

15 Pz
Gr Div

US 3 Div

US 34 Div

CAPUA

GRAZZANISE
7 Armd Div

56 Div

CASERTA

Tyrrhenian Sea

**13 Oct 1943
US Fifth Army
crosses the Volturno**

CASTEL VOLTURNO
46 Div

Br X Corps
(McCreery)

US Fifth Army
(Clark)

Route 6

NAPLES

The drive to the Gustav Line. The Allied offensive in central Italy, October 1943–January 1944.

Italian Front: Allied bombardment of German defensive positions in the river Sangro sector, November 1943.

the night.

New Guinea More fierce attacks by the Japanese in the Finschhafen area, contained by the Australian 9th Division with artillery support.

☐ The Foreign Ministers of the USSR (Molotov), USA (Cordell Hull) and Great Britain (Eden) meet in Moscow. Chinese representatives are admitted as and when the conference considers matters of specific interest to China.

☐ The 3rd London Protocol is signed in Washington, extending American aid to the USSR until 30 June 1944. The United States will provide the Soviet Union with 2,700,000 tons of supplies through Russian ports on the Pacific and a further 2,400,000 tons through the Persian Gulf.

20 October

Italian Front In the VI Corps (US 5th Army) sector the 34th Division takes Alife and the 45th Division Piedimonte d'Alife. While the US 3rd Division continues its march northwards against Mignano, west of the Volturno, the 34th makes for Capriati on the Volturno, east of the river.

New Guinea The Australian 26th Brigade arrives by sea to reinforce the 9th Division, severely held up by the enemy at Finschhafen.

Pacific The Japanese Imperial Headquarters had decided to send powerful air reinforcements to Rabaul to slow up the American advance, while the Japanese 'second line' of defence in the Central Pacific is reinforced. Admiral Koga, successor to Yama-

moto, decides to send naval forces (not enough, however) to the Solomons and New Britain.

In the American camp Admiral Halsey has agreed with General MacArthur's view that it would be impossible to 'skip' Bougainville as was done with Kolombangara, and in fact the Americans are preparing to invade the big island, from which it will be much easier to capture or neutralize New Britain.

22 October

Italian Front During the night a battalion of the 78th Division (British 8th Army) crosses the river Trigno. This is the first time the 8th Army has been in action since General Montgomery's reorganization of the sector.

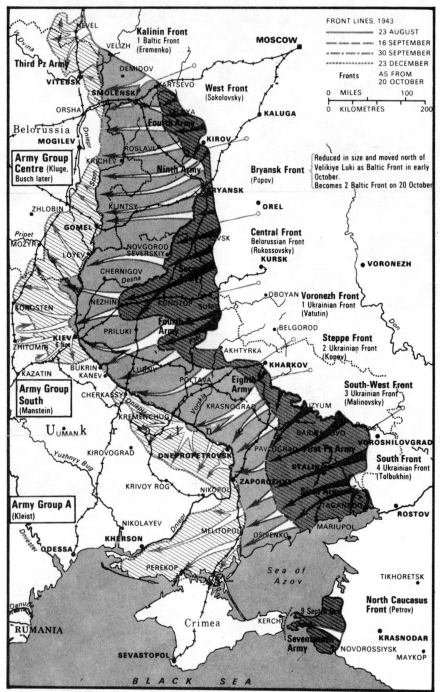

FRONT LINES, 1943

	23 AUGUST
	16 SEPTEMBER
	30 SEPTEMBER
	23 DECEMBER

Fronts AS FROM 20 OCTOBER

0 MILES 100

0 KILOMETRES 200

The Russian offensive towards the Dniepr along the whole length of the Eastern Front from Smolensk in the north to Rostov in the south, August–December 1943.

Units of the US 34th Division begin the attack on Sant'Angelo d'Alife, but are driven back.

Pacific The Americans decide to drop a parachute battalion at Voza, in Choiseul Island, south-east of Bougainville, on the night of 27 October. Minimum objective: diversionary attack; maximum: to establish a base for use against Bougainville.

□ Germany. Two-thirds of Kassel, an important tank- and locomotive-manufacturing town, is destroyed by Allied bombers. Industrial production is paralysed for three months. During the same raid serious damage is done to the towns of Ludwigshafen and Mannheim.

23 October

Eastern Front The violent struggle for Melitopol ends in victory for General Tolbukhin's forces. But the Russians do not achieve their aim, the isolation of the Crimea, during the course of the month.

□ Churchill sends Admiral Mountbatten clear directives about the limits and the objectives of his mandate as Supreme Allied Commander for South-East Asia.

24 October

Italian Front Units of the American 34th Division enter Sant' Angelo. But this is one of the few successful actions in this phase of the battle. The Germans continue to slow down the Allies' progress.

25 October

Eastern Front Malinovsky launches a carefully planned surprise attack and succeeds in crossing the lower Dniepr at Dnepropetrovsk, and takes the city. To the north-west, his troops also occupy Dneprodzerzhinsk. Berlin admits the German position in Russia to be 'extremely grave'.

Pacific US Vice-Admiral Spruance issues his first plan for Operation *Galvanic*, the invasion of the Gilbert Islands.

New Guinea The Japanese have no more forces to throw into the attack, and begin to withdraw to their strongpoint of Sattelberg, north of Finschhafen.

26 October

Pacific The Treasury Islands assault group, part of Rear-Admiral Wilkinsons' Task Force 31, sails for its objective.

27 October

Eastern Front German Army Group

A (subordinate operationally to Army Group South) counter-attacks in the Melitopol area to establish positions in front of Nikopol and Krivoy Rog and allow the German (and Rumanian) 17th Army to escape from the Crimea. The evacuation is to begin on 1 November.

Pacific A brigade of the New Zealand 3rd Division captures Stirling and Mono Islands, in the Treasury Islands. The first is entirely undefended but the Japanese garrison on the second resists strongly. The operation is supported by aircraft based in New Georgia.

During the night of 27/28 October the 2nd Parachute Battalion of the US Marines lands on Choiseul and during the next few days carries out a number of demonstrations with the idea of appearing far more numerous than they are. The Japanese are not deceived for more than a day or two; actually Radio Tokyo at first announces that 20,000 Americans have landed on Choiseul, but the surprise action very soon turns into a war of attrition.

28 October

Eastern Front As Russian advances continue, Berlin radio admits 'the main German defences have been broken'.

29 October

Eastern Front Army Group Centre, now commanded by Field-Marshal Busch in succession to von Kluge, fights with great vigour to hold up the enemy near the river Orsha (with the 4th Army) and in front of Vitebsk (with the 3rd Armoured Army).

30 October

Italian Front The American 34th Division (US VI Corps) continues its difficult march northwards.

□ The Moscow Conference between the Foreign Ministers of the Soviet Union, Great Britain and the United States ends. The principle of 'unconditional surrender' for Germany is confirmed, as is the wish to found an international organization for the preservation of peace. It is also decided to set up in London a consultative European commission

MAX REINHARDT

Max Reinhardt, one of the most brilliant and innovative figures of the contemporary theatre, died in New York on 21 October.

Born in Baden, a city near Vienna, on 9 September 1873, Reinhardt studied acting with Otto Brahm. He began his career as an actor and, more importantly, as a director with small avant-garde companies, and his productions soon created a sensation. He then went on to direct Berlin's Deutsches Theater and emerged as one of the leading lights of the European theatrical scene. His productions, influenced by Expressionism, were brilliant combinations of spectacle and fantasy. Ranging from the classics to contemporary authors, Reinhardt smashed the barriers of the proscenium stage, putting on his plays in circuses, in cathedrals, on the steps of churches and in amphitheatres.

Despite some rather unhappy directing experiences, Reinhardt's contributions during the 1920s and 1930s to German cinema were likewise considerable. He attracted many famous actors and directors, and his staging, with its violent contrasts of light and shade, was a hallmark of the Expressionist cinema.

Leaving for the United States in 1933, Reinhardt made one unhappy Shakespearean film, *A Midsummer Night's Dream*, for Hollywood; after that he opened a school of acting and directing.

A scene from *A Midsummer Night's Dream*, **Max Reinhardt's ill-fated Hollywood film.**

to study the problems that will arise on the continent when the war ends.

31 October

Italian Front In the sector in which the 7th Armoured Division and 46th Division of infantry (British X Corps) are operating, attacks against Monte Massico and Monte Santa Croce continue. On the right flank of the X Corps, the 56th Division takes Teano.

In the east, where the British 8th Army is operating, the 5th Division (XIII Corps) captures Cantalupo.

Solomon Islands Task Force 31 sails for Bougainville, having taken on board in the Central Solomons the 20,000-odd men of the I Amphibious Corps of the US Marines, made up of the 37th Infantry Division and 3rd Marine Division, under the com-

Admiral Sparzani, reviewing the Italian troops on their way to the front, stops to talk to a boy soldier.

mand of General Alexander Vande-grift. The Americans are well aware that they are outnumbered, but rely on support by their powerful navy and air force, which in the course of the last weeks has put every enemy airfield in the south of Bougainville out of action.

1 November
Eastern Front In the Crimea, the Russians achieve their object of iso-lating the German forces when they capture Armyansk, at the base of the peninsula. They also land more troops east of Kerch. In the Krivoy Rog area the Germans make heavy counter-attacks, and Berlin claims 'great successes'.

Italian Front Field-Marshal Kes-selring, Commander-in-Chief of the German forces in southern Italy, issues a 'directive for the conduct of the campaign', in which he lays down that General Vietinghoff's 10th Army can disregard the danger of Allied combined operations on the Tyrrhenian and Adriatic coasts, but should concentrate all its efforts on the defence of the *Bernhard* (*Rein-hard*) line to gain time and fortify the *Gustav* line even more. On the left flank of the US 5th Army, the attack by the British X Corps continues against the line between Monte Mas-sico and Monte Santa Croce. Mean-while the 56th Division (British X Corps) enters Roccamonfina and units of the American 34th Division (US VI Corps) reach Capriati on the Volturno.

Solomon Islands After a forceful air and naval preparation the northern group of Task Force 31, commanded by Rear-Admiral Wilkinson, begins at 7.30 a.m. to put the 3rd Marine Division ashore in the area of Cape Torokina (Empress Augusta Bay) on the central southern coast of Bou-gainville. The little Japanese garrison of 207 men puts up a lively resistance, but the landing party is able to estab-lish a solid beachhead within a few hours. Task Force 39, and carrier-borne aircraft from Task Force 38 bomb the airfields on Buka Island, north-west of Bougainville, and Shortland. But although many of

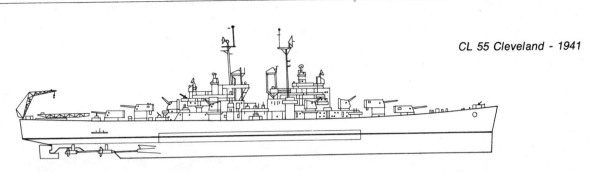

CL 55 Cleveland - 1941

THE BATTLE OF EMPRESS AUGUSTA BAY

The Japanese 8th Fleet, commanded by Rear-Admiral Sentaro Omori and consisting of the heavy cruisers *Myoko* and *Haguro*, the light cruisers *Sendai* and *Agano*, 11 destroyers and 5 transports, sails from Rabaul at 5.20 p.m. on 1 November with the task of harassing the Torokina beachhead on Bougainville and trying to make a landing in opposition. At 9.45 p.m. the Japanese formation is sighted and bombed, without effect, by an American four-engined bomber. Japanese headquarters at Rabaul is at once informed and, since a counter-landing is already impossible, orders the transports to change course; but the rest of the formation is to carry out its mission against the enemy's warships and transports.

2 November

1.39 a.m.: A Japanese flying-boat reports the presence, 50 miles off, of one enemy cruiser and three destroyers. Omori proceeds, ordering his ships to change formation.
Task Force 39, commanded by Rear-Admiral Stanton Merrill and made up of the light cruisers *Montpelier, Cleveland, Columbia*

and *Denver* and 8 destroyers, told of the approach of the enemy squadron, steams north, determined to deny the enemy access to Empress Augusta Bay. At 2.30 a.m. the enemy ships appear on the Americans' radar screens. At 2.45 a.m., now within range, the destroyers fire the first torpedoes against the enemy squadron. Meanwhile, as the Japanese ships in close formation manœuvre to launch their attack, there is a collision that puts the guns and torpedo-tubes of one destroyer out of action and damages the cruiser *Sendai*. At 2.52 a.m. the Americans open fire and with their first salvo hit the cruiser *Sendai*, already damaged. Immediately afterwards three more salvos land on the cruiser, and an enormous fire breaks out.
There follows an artillery duel between the American cruisers and Japanese heavy cruisers. Destroyers and light cruisers, at closer range, rely more on the use of torpedoes.
At 3.00 a.m., in the confusion of the battle, there is another collision, this time between the heavy cruiser *Myoko* (Omori's flagship) and the destroyer *Hatsukaze*. The

Americans concentrate their fire on these two ships, which are almost immobilized.
At 3.20 a.m. Japanese aircraft join the battle, flying over the American ships and dropping powerful flares, enabling the Japanese to aim correctly and score three hits on the cruiser *Denver*.
At 3.34 a.m. the Japanese squadron receives orders to break off the fight and return to Rabaul at full speed.
The Americans begin to follow them, but stop after a little while, foreseeing an attack by Japanese aircraft at first light. And in fact – but not until eight o'clock – a hundred enemy aircraft attack the American ships, which shoot down 25 of them without suffering any damage themselves.
During the night engagement the Japanese have lost the cruiser *Sendai* and the destroyer *Hatsukaze*, and almost every one of their ships returns to base with some heavy damage. The Americans have had two cruisers, *Denver* and *Montpelier*, and two destroyers damaged; none of their ships has been sunk.

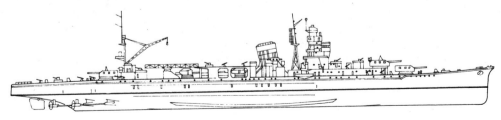

Agano - 1941

American B-25 and Lightning bombers attack the Japanese air and naval base at Rabaul in force, 2 November 1943 but meet with strong resistance.

their aircraft are unserviceable the Japanese manage to concentrate a considerable number of planes against the landing force, and damage a destroyer and several American transports. All the same, they lose about 100 of their 104 fighters and 16 bombers.

Vandegrift has chosen the landing point skilfully, foreseeing that Hyakutake would concentrate his forces near the airfields. And the difficult nature of the terrain means that the Japanese will take a long time to bring up reinforcements to Cape Torokina.

A small contingent of Raiders lands on the small islet of Puruata, less than about half a mile from the Cape

Torokina beachhead, and there meets with savage resistance from a platoon of Japanese. By the evening of the 1st the Task Force has landed 14,000 men and 6,000 tons of materials. Rear-Admiral Wilkinson sends off his transport ships and has four minesweepers lay a minefield off the coast covering the beachhead.

2 November

Italian Front In the British X Corps (US 5th Army) sector patrols from the 7th Armoured Division and 46th Division reach the river Garigliano. During the night the 78th Division and 8th Indian Division (8th Army) make repeated attacks across the river Trigno, where the German 16th

Armoured Division is positioned. The 78th Division's operations are supported, not only by a tremendous barrage from field guns, but also by effective shelling by warships cruising along the Adriatic coast.

Eastern Front Russians capture Kakhovka on the lower Dniepr.

Solomon Islands The Americans gradually extend their beachhead on Bougainville and mop up the remaining resistance by the Japanese on the islet of Puruata.

New Britain 75 B-25 US bombers escorted by 80 P-38 Lightning fighters attack the Japanese installations at Rabaul to good effect, but meet with very strong resistance by Japanese aircraft and anti-aircraft batteries. They sink two merchant ships and one submarine-hunter, and destroy 18 Japanese aircraft on the ground, but they lose 8 bombers and 9 fighters.

Burma On the river Tarung the Japanese drive off attacks by a regiment of the Chinese 38th Division.

☐ Austria. Allied heavy bombers carry out a major attack on Vienna's airports.

3 November

Italian Front On the San Salvo hills the British V Corps meets with forceful resistance from the German 16th Armoured Division.

Solomon Islands The US Marines continue to extend their beachhead at Cape Torokina, on Bougainville. A patrol lands on the island off the coast, also called Torokina, but finds it deserted.

EIGHTH SYMPHONY OF SHOSTAKOVICH

A very lengthy adagio, intense and profound, with overtones reminiscent of Beethoven, opens Shostakovich's Eighth Symphony, probably his most finished and mature work. Composed during the counter-offensive of the Soviet armed forces, it is pervaded by a feeling of expectation and meditation.

A typical exponent of Russian realism, even if frequently accused by orthodox critics of abstractionism and formalism, Shostakovich had in 1942 received the Stalin Prize for his Seventh Symphony, composed while he was sharing with his fellow citizens the horrors of the long siege of Leningrad.

German infantry surrender to the Russians just outside Kiev. By 6 November they have been forced to withdraw from the city completely.

A British 8th Army Sherman tank in Torino di Sangro, south of Ortona and Pescara, has to slow down and wait for the pack-mules in front of it.

☐ **Germany.** A daylight raid by 500 aircraft of the US 8th Air Force devastates Wilhelmshafen harbour.

4 November

Eastern Front The Russians bring pressure to bear on Kherson, at the mouth of the Dniepr, and force the Germans to give ground. The armies of the Central and Voronezh Fronts, spreading out from their bridgehead over the Dniepr, threaten to surround Kiev.

Italian Front In the US 5th Army sector the British X Corps, which already controls Monte Massico and Monte Santa Croce, prepares to send in the 56th Division against Monte Camino. Units of the US 34th Division also advance; elements of the 45th Division take Venafro, while troops from the 34th Division enter Santa Maria Oliveto and Roccavirondola.

General Lesse's British XIII Corps (8th Army) enters Isernia, an important road junction, without opposition, and on the right of Montgomery's line the V Corps takes San Salvo after the German LXXVI Armoured Corps has retired throughout the sector.

Solomon Islands The Americans withdraw their parachutists from Choiseul. The arrival at Rabaul of a strong Japanese naval squadron, comprising 7 heavy cruisers and 173 aircraft, brings a threat to the Cape Torokina bridgehead on Bougainville. Task Force 38 is ordered to attack Rabaul with carrier-borne and land-based aircraft.

Burma Local activity. The regiment of the Chinese 38th Division that was attacking the Japanese lines on the river Tarung is making no progress and retires northwards, but one battalion is surrounded by the Japanese.

5 November

Eastern Front Threat of encirclement for German troops in Kiev grows.

Italian Front The US 5th Army launches a series of attacks in an attempt to break through the *Bernhard* (*Reinhard*) line, the last bastion before the Germans' final defensive line, the *Gustav* line. The attacks go on for ten days, during which the Allied troops have to battle with adverse weather conditions as well as with the dogged resistance of General Hube's XIV Armoured Corps. The British 56th Division (X Corps), with support from units of the US VI Corps, begins the battle for Monte Camino; on its right, 3rd Division (US VI Corps) attacks to turn the enemy position at Mignano. In the British 8th Army sector the 78th Division takes Vasto on the Adriatic coast against strenuous defence by General Herr's tanks. The 8th Indian Division penetrates into Palmoli.

Solomon Islands On Bougainville the Americans repulse a Japanese counter-attack on the Mission track. Later they advance to the point where this track crosses the Numa Numa track. These two tracks are the main lines of communication in the area of Cape Torokina.

New Britain Exposing his aircraft carriers *Saratoga* and *Princeton* to grave danger, Admiral Halsey sends them as close as possible to New Britain so as to be able to launch a big attack on the powerful naval squadron of Admiral Takeo Kurita, which has just arrived at Rabaul. At 11.15 a.m. over 100 American aircraft, torpedo-planes, dive-bombers and fighters, appear over the Japanese base and, although attacked by 70 Zero fighters (to which the new American Grumman F6F Wildcat fighters prove

Nikita Khrushchev talks with a group of soldiers and civilians the day after the liberation of Kiev.

superior), surprise Kurita's squadron, causing serious damage to seven cruisers, the *Atago*, *Maya*, *Takao*, *Mogami*, *Chikuma*, *Agano* and *Noshiro*, and two destroyers. The only heavy cruiser undamaged is the *Suzuya*, which nurses the damaged ships back to Truk, except for the heavy cruiser *Maya* and the light cruiser *Agano*, which have been too badly hit. It is a major disaster for the Japanese; whose whole squadron has been wiped out without firing a shot. The threat that it might have posed for the American beachhead on Bougainville has vanished.

6 November
Eastern Front Kiev, the third largest city in the USSR is captured by the Russians. Before withdrawing the Germans destroy most of Kiev's ancient buildings. The few surviving Jews tell how the Germans have massacred tens of thousands of Kiev's Jewish men, women and children.
Italian Front The 56th Division (British X Corps and units of the US 3rd Division (VI Corps) continue their attacks against Monte Camino and Monte la Difensa. Further east the batteries of the 45th and 34th Divisions fire on the positions of the Germans on Monte Rotundo and Monte Lungo, but to no effect.

7 November
Eastern Front The Russians exploit the withdrawal of the Germans from Kiev to pursue the enemy as far as Fastov, a railway junction southwest of Kiev. They are held up there by fierce enemy resistance.
Italian Front Units of the US 5th Army continue their attacks on the *Bernhard* (*Reinhard*) line, with little or no success.
Solomon Islands A swarm of 100 Japanese bombers and fighters locate the two American aircraft carriers *Saratoga* and *Princeton* 235 miles south-east of Rabaul and attack them, with no success (though Tokyo radio says that two carriers, three cruisers and a destroyer have been sunk). Later a convoy of Japanese destroyers – (the usual 'Tokyo

8 November 1943: Canadian infantry in action during house-to-house fighting in a village in the Upper Sangro sector.

Night Express' – lands about 500 men north of the American beachhead on Bougainville, near the Koromokina marsh, while other ships land 700 men and 25 tons of materials on Buka Island, north of Bougainville. Very hard fighting goes on all day at the northern end of the beachhead; 377 Japanese are killed, against only 17 US Marines.

8 November
Italian Front In the British X Corps (US 5th Army) sector the 56th Division drives off a series of fierce counter-attacks by German armoured units under General Hube near Calabritto.
Units of the US VI Corps reach the summit of Monte Rotundo, and further north the 45th Division continues its efforts to take the hills north of Venafro and Pozzilli.
To the east, where Montgomery's 8th Army units are operating, the 78th Division reaches the upper

Above: Russian infantry in action on the outskirts of Kiev.

A landing ship loaded with American soldiers and vehicles draws onto a beachhead on Bougainville Island.

reaches of the river Sangro. General Herr, commander of the German LXXVI Armoured Corps, has withdrawn his regiments behind the north bank of the river. The weather is still very bad, and the state of the ground imposes a new lull in the operations.

General Alexander, Commander-in-Chief of the XV Army Group, operating in Italy, prepares plans for an amphibious landing on the Tyrrhenian coast behind the *Gustav* line.

9 November

Solomon Islands At Bougainville two American regiments begin their advance into the interior, widening the tracks to allow the passage of their mortars. They suddenly come face to ace with the Japanese 23rd Infantry Regiment. A bloody battle continues over three days, culminating in the extermination of the Japanese force, though with grave losses to the Americans.

☐ In Algiers the French National

Liberation Committee is reorganized under the leadership of General de Gaulle.

☐ Lebanon proclaims the end of the mandate with France.

10 November

Italian Front Units of the US 45th Division reach the hills between Pozzilli and Filignano without opposition. The units of the 45th Division on Monte Corno are relieved by the 1st Battalion Rangers.

Meanwhile there have been important changes in the deployment of the German troops. General Joachim Lemelsen, who has recently replaced General Vietinghoff in command of the 10th Army, expecting an imminent Allied break through the *Bernhard* (*Reinhard*) line on the road to Cassino, decides to move the 26th *Panzerdivision* and 29th *Panzergrenadiere* to that sector to reinforce the units of General Hube's XIV Armoured Corps. The battered 16th Armoured Division has been sent back to refit, so the German LXXVI Corps now has the 65th Infantry Division (on the lower Sangro) and the 1st Parachute Division (in the central sector) in the front line.

Yugoslavia It is reported from Cairo that British representatives of Middle East Command are serving with the forces, both of General Mihailovitch ('Chetniks') and General Tito ('Partisans'). Since the surrender of Italy on 8 September the Yugoslav forces have scored many successes against the Germans, but there are wide internal differences between Tito (who looks more to Moscow) and Mihailovitch (who has closer links with Britain).

Pacific The main body of the Gilbert Islands invasion force (Operation *Galvanic*) sails from Pearl Harbour.

11 November

Eastern Front The Russian armies strengthen their positions west of Kiev, taking a small bridgehead on the river Teterev. But in the Fastov area, where the Germans have again seized the initiative, they are under heavy pressure. The Russian

Life in France under the occupation. Top: queueing for food rationing cards. Above left: the bicycle became the main means of transport. Above right: German signs in Paris, for the benefit of the occupying troops.

The crew of one of the American 82nd Airborne Division's mortars eating their rations in the area of the river Volturno.

Central Front, west of Gomel, advances northwards.

Solomon Islands On Bougainville, Japanese resistance in the entrenched line blocking the Mission track is exhausted. About 550 Japanese have been killed. The Americans move forward in all directions to widen their perimeter and find a place where they can construct an airfield.

New Britain Two task forces of aircraft carriers including the *Saratoga* and the *Princeton*, under the command of Rear-Admiral Sherman, and the *Essex*, *Bunker Hill* and *Independence*, under the command of Rear-Admiral Montgomery, send 185 aircraft over Rabaul. 68 Zero fighters are destroyed, the destroyer *Suzunami* is sunk and the cruiser *Agano* and the destroyer *Naganami*, already badly damaged, are reduced to smoking hulks. The Japanese send 120 aircraft out to attack the aircraft carriers. They succeed in locating and attacking Rear-Admiral Montgomery's squadron, but do no serious damage to it and lose 41 aircraft against 11 lost by the Americans.

Italian Front Units of the 8th Indian Division (British V Corps) occupy Casalanguida and push on towards

UNRRA

On 9 November, in Washington DC, during a ceremony presided over by Roosevelt, the representatives of forty-four nations signed the act that created the United Relief and Rehabilitation Administration (UNRRA), an organization formed by the United Nations to furnish civil and economic assistance to the people hardest hit by the war. The thirty-two member states which had been spared military invasion were called upon to contribute to the operating expenses on the basis of 1 per cent of their national income, calculated for the fiscal year 1942-3. Herbert H. Lehman, former governor of the state of New York, was appointed director-general.

UNRRA, which remained in operation until 1947, represented the most massive postwar assistance programme in history, in quantity, value of goods and donated services. The goods provided amounted to about 26 million tonnes, valued at some 4,000 million dollars. The principal financing nations were the United States (2,700 million dollars), Britain, Canada and Australia.

More than 40 per cent of UNRRA funds were used to purchase foodstuffs; the rest went to buy various types of merchandise (motor fuel, medicine and clothing) in addition to all the equipment and raw materials necessary to revitalize the industries and agriculture of the assisted countries.

UNRRA also did much to help war refugees, political refugees and displaced persons: between 1946 and 1947 over 800,000 refugees owed their survival to the assistance provided by the organization.

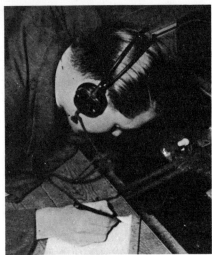

The resistance in France. Top: partisans in the Pyrenees. Left: two partisans in the Jura. Above: a Maquis radio operator.

the Sangro.

12 November
Eastern Front The Red Army continues its advance west of Kiev, taking the important railway junction of Zhitomir, only 75 miles from the 1939 Polish frontier.
Italian Front The 56th Division (British X Corps), after long and fruitless attacks, is forced to retire from the Monte Camino positions.

In the US VI Corps sector, too, very little progress is made. Units of the 45th Division make unsuccessful attempts to reach Acquafondata. In fact the whole Allied line is in difficulties in front of the *Bernhard* (*Reinhard*) line.
Solomon Islands In the Treasury Islands the 8th Brigade of the New Zealand 3rd Division wipes out all enemy resistance in the island of Mono. The Japanese lose 205 dead,

the New Zealanders and Americans 52.
New Britain The Japanese withdraw the carrier-based aircraft reinforcements from Rabaul. The Japanese base no longer represents any serious danger to the Allies.

13 November
Italian Front General Clark, Commander of the US 5th Army, tells Alexander that any further attempts

by the Allies to advance in the prevailing conditions can only lead to the pointless sacrifice of his divisions, particularly of the British 56th and American 3rd Divisions.

☐ The Allies officially recognize the 'status' of Italy as a 'co-belligerent nation'.

Pacific The southern group for the invasion of the Gilbert Islands sails from the New Hebrides. American Flying Fortresses taking off from Funafuti bomb Tarawa atoll. There is little resistance from fighters but a powerful anti-aircraft barrage.

Solomon Islands On Bougainville the Americans attack Japanese positions at the crossing between the Numa Numa track and the track running east to west. The cruiser *Denver* is damaged off Bougainville by a torpedo from a Japanese aircraft.

14 November

Eastern Front The Germans launch a counter-offensive to re-take Zhitomir. On the Kerch peninsula, in the Crimea, violent battles are taking place.

Italian Front During the night the British 56th Division begins to leave its advance positions on Monte Camino.

In the eastern sector units of the 8th Indian Division (British V Corps), supported by tanks of the New Zealand 2nd Division, take Perano and force the Germans to retire northwards towards Archi and Tornareccio.

Solomon Islands The Americans on Bougainville resume their attacks on the crossroads manned by the Japanese, this time supported by five tanks, and succeed in taking it. Their defensive perimeter is thus widened and the safety of the airfield that they are to build is guaranteed.

15 November

Eastern Front In the coastal sector, on the Bryansk front, Russian forces cut the important Gomel–Pinsk railway. German radio reports 'bloody battles' in the Krivoy Rog area.

Italian Front Alexander suspends the Allied offensive. He considers

German soldiers attack positions held by the British and Italians on the Greek island of Leros. The recapture of the island on 16 November is one of Germany's few successes at this time.

that his men have been tried too hard during the past two weeks, especially in the western sector. Meanwhile he orders a regrouping of his forces in readiness for a new attempt to break through the German lines.

In the Adriatic sector a number of patrols of the British 78th Division (8th Army) have succeeded in crossing the river Sangro and establishing small bridgeheads on the north side which serve as reference points for

reconnaissance groups and Royal Engineer units looking for more suitable places for tanks to cross the water and for the construction of Bailey bridges.

Burma On the northern Burma front the Chinese 38th Division sends reinforcements to the 112th Regiment, which is being hard pressed by the Japanese. In the Japanese 14th Army sector, Japanese troops occupy Fort White after driving out the British garrison.

16 November

Eastern Front In the Kiev area Russian advance guards reach Korosten, but some units are threatened with encirclement at Zhitomir, where the German counter-offensive is developing. In the central sector the Russians advance on Gomel.

Greece The Germans complete the occupation of the island of Leros.

Italian Front The bridgeheads established by the British 78th Division on the north bank of the river Sangro are consolidated.

Pacific Since 13 November, US heavy bombers have been attacking the Gilbert and Marshall Islands every day, dropping 173 tons of bombs on military installations.

New Guinea The Australian 9th Division, with support from the air, heavy artillery and tanks, begins operations to eliminate the Sattelberg strongpoint, north of Finschhafen, where the nature of the terrain favours defence.

17 November

Eastern Front Von Manstein's forces counter-attack forcefully in the Zhitomir–Fastov sector and gain some ground.

18 November

Eastern Front South-east of Kiev the Russians break through the German defences on the Dniepr near Cherkassy and re-take Ovruch, northwest of that town. In the Zhitomir sector, however, German pressure forces them to withdraw. In the central sector the Germans are in danger of being surrounded at Gomel, where the salient at Rezhitsa, west of the town, has been rapidly broadened.

☐ Germany. Berlin suffers immense damage as the result of a night raid by 444 RAF bombers.

19 November

Eastern Front The Russians evacuate Zhitomir to avoid being surrounded.

Italian Front In the British V Corps (8th Army) sector, where the 8th Indian Division is operating on the lower Sangro, the Germans complete their withdrawal to the north bank of the river.

Pacific Carrier-borne aircraft pound the Gilbert Islands, Marshall Islands and Nauru in preparation for the coming invasion.

20 November

Pacific Start of Operation *Galvanic*. More than 100 warships, transports and landing craft of all kinds

approach the atolls of Tarawa and Makin, in the Gilbert Islands, during the night. For some time the Japanese have been building up the fortifications of these two islets, especially Tarawa, where Rear-Admiral Keichi Shibasaki has 5,000 men, as well as 400 specialists, on the airfield and a certain number of Korean labourers turned into auxiliary riflemen. Guns of all calibres, from 37-mm to 203-mm, light tanks dug in, well-camouflaged pillboxes, beach obstacles and huge bunkers covered in earth and sand many feet deep make the atoll an extremely difficult objective, and its capture costs the Americans dear.

At 5.07 a.m. landing craft of Task Force 53, carrying the 2nd Marine Regiment plus one battalion of the 8th and auxiliary units, arrive a little way off Betio Island, the south-western point of the atoll and the most strongly manned by enemy troops. The Japanese open fire on them. A few minutes later the big guns of the battleships *Maryland* and *Mississipi* and the other American warships attack the island, raining shells on it and blowing up ammunition and fuel stores. At 5.42 a.m., in accordance with plans, the ships cease fire and give way to aircraft. But the aircraft do not appear, and the defenders are able to reopen fire on the landing

Gilbert Islands: US landing parties advance towards the shore of Makin atoll.

A Japanese soldier captured on Tarawa.

craft with their 203-mm and 140-mm guns. The landing has to be put back from 8.30 to 9.00 a.m., since it is not until 6.30 a.m. that the bombers arrive to carry out their short but deadly attacks on the island.

At 8.25 a.m. the first wave of landing craft and amphibians finally moves in. They have to cover 10 miles before they reach the shore; they must pass enemy obstacles, and before those they must cross the coral reef. But the water over the reef is very shallow, and many of the landing craft fail to get past it. However, the amphibians cross it, and just at that moment the Japanese open fire with every gun they have. There are heavy casualties among the attacking troops, and the few who succeed in approaching the anti-landing obstacles are mown down by fire from automatics.

A second wave manages to reach the coral reef in landing craft, and from there, in tracked amphibians, to get to the beach, where there is bloody hand-to-hand fighting. The Marines succeed in getting ashore but can go

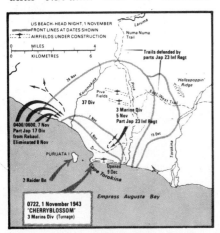

US operations on Bougainville, Solomon Islands, November 1943.

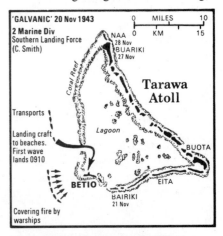

US landing on Tarawa atoll, Gilbert Islands, 20 November 1943.

Bougainville, Solomon Islands: the crew of an American battery inspect their gun following a raid by Japanese bombers.

no further. The Sherman tanks which should be supporting the attack reach the reef in their landing craft, and some of them cross the lagoon where the water is particularly shallow and reach the shore. In the evening the few forces that have landed and survived the deadly enemy fire prepare themselves for a night counter-attack, following the technique so often used by the Japanese on Guadalcanal. But the attack does not take place, and at least the Marines have an opportunity to dig fox-holes for themselves while they await reinforcements.

On Makin atoll things go much more smoothly for the infantry of the 165th Regiment and the tanks supporting them. The landing begins according to plan at 8.30 a.m. and in the course of a few hours the landing forces establish sound beachheads on Butaritari Island, the main island of the atoll, after occupying Kotabu islet without opposition.

Solomon Islands On Bougainville the 3rd Marine Division extends its positions near the river Piva after overcoming the last enemy resistance. The 37th Division broadens the defensive perimeter of the beachhead without coming in contact with the enemy.

Italian Front In the eastern sector of the front, where the 8th Army is operating, the 36th Brigade of the 78th Division succeeds in crossing the river Sangro. The crossing is made in torrential rain, which turns the ground into a quagmire and slows the operation down. The units that have crossed the river are cut off.

21 November

Gilbert Islands At dawn, with new waves of Marines approaching the Betio beaches in Tarawa, all hell breaks loose again. Vice-Admiral Spruance, commander of the operation, has heard reports from several unit commanders during the night. Some of them have suggested that the operation be called off and the forces re-embarked, but in view of the great strategic importance of the objective Spruance is determined to proceed.

Japanese boats sunk by the U.S. air force in the area of Guadalcanal.

A district of Cagliari, Sardinia, destroyed by Allied bombardment.

On the North Burma front, the Burmese pack up 20,000 parachutes used for building trenches against the Japanese.

American carrier-borne aircraft give effective support to the troops on the island, who are able to deploy field guns and shell the Japanese positions all day and to make a little progress. During the day small American units land on other islets in the Tarawa atoll.

On Makin atoll, again with support from aircraft, artillery and naval guns, the 165th Infantry launch an assault on Butaritari Island and seize several Japanese fortified positions. Small units land on the islet of Kuma, carry out reconnaissance, and withdraw.

22 November

Gilbert Islands Another day of furious fighting on Betio Island, in Tarawa atoll. Aircraft, naval guns and artillery hammer the Japanese pillboxes, and they fall one after another, but not until all the men in them are dead, after blowing themselves up with hand-grenades held against their chests rather than be taken prisoner. (The word 'surrender' does not exist in the army of the Rising Sun; and Japanese propaganda has often told of the torture inflicted by the Americans on their prisoners.)

The only fortified strongpoint on the islet of Bairiki is destroyed by aircraft action. In the evening the attacking forces are reinforced, and there appears to be a slight diminution in the strength of the Japanese fire. In fact, the defenders are running out of ammunition, and Rear-Admiral Shibasaki is cut off in a heavily fortified redoubt of reinforced concrete and unable to communicate with the rest of his garrison.

A desperate counter-attack by the Japanese during the night is driven off.

The American advance on Makin atoll continues and here too they have impressive supporting fire. The last centres of Japanese resistance seem to have been overcome, and before evening falls the capture of the main island, Butaritari, is announced. But during the night the last remaining Japanese units, who

have been withdrawn from the eastern end of the island, launch a counter-attack. They are virtually wiped out.

New Guinea The Australian 9th Division is still engaged in the operation for the capture of the Japanese strongpoint of Sattelberg, north of Finschhafen.

Italian Front Five battalions of the British 78th Division (V Corps) have secured possession of a broad bridgehead on the north bank of the river Sangro. The swollen river washes their Bailey bridges away, so isolating the bridgehead, but the Germans do not take advantage of this.

☐ First Cairo Conference opens, attended by Roosevelt, Churchill and Chiang Kai-shek.

☐ Germany. At night, hundreds of British and Canadian Lancasters, Stirlings, Halifaxes make heaviest raid of the war on Berlin. 2,300 tons of bombs dropped in 30 minutes.

23 November

Gilbert Islands Tarawa and Makin atolls finally fall to the Americans, the defenders' ammunition is exhausted, their forces almost exterminated. During the battle Japanese aircraft based on Nauru have attacked the American invasion fleet with great courage, suffering heavy losses and achieving very small results, except for torpedo damage to the aircraft carrier *Independence*.

During the capture of Makin the Americans have lost only 64 dead and 154 wounded, the Japanese about 450 dead and 105 prisoners. On Tarawa the American losses are much greater, about 3,500 killed and wounded; the Japanese have lost about 5,000 killed, while 17 wounded have been captured and 129 Koreans have surrendered.

Bougainville The 3rd Marine Division still faces determined resistance by the Japanese in the river Piva area. The 1st Parachute Battalion of the Marines reaches the island.

Burma The Japanese overrun the Chinese 112th Regiment and capture their headquarters.

☐ Germany. Berlin again attacked in force in huge night raid.

24 November

Gilbert Islands A Japanese submarine torpedoes and sinks the American escort carrier *Liscome Bay* off Makin atoll. The 700 dead must be added to the price paid for the capture of Tarawa and Makin.

New Britain During the night near Cape St George (New Britain), five Japanese destroyers en route for Buka Island with reinforcements and materials are intercepted by five Allied destroyers. In the course of the battle the Japanese lose three destroyers; the Allies suffer no damage. This is the last of the night battles that have characterized the Solomons campaign.

Bougainville In the river Piva sector the Marines drive off a Japanese attack. Work on the construction of a runway is almost finished, and an aircraft manages to make an emergency landing there.

Eastern Front German communiqué announces that their troops have advanced in the Korosten area.

Italian Front The headquarters of the US 5th Army draws up the final plan of attack, the first phase of which is to be launched about 2 December. This phase is to consist of the capture of the Monte Camino–Monte la Difensa–Monte Maggiore sector, preceded on 1 December by the capture of Calabritto. The second and third phases comprise the taking of Monte Sammucro and an attack on the Liri valley.

25 November

Eastern Front In a new offensive in the central sector the Russian armies succeed in breaking through the German lines on a broad front in the area of Propoisk, north of Gomel, reaching the Gomel–Mogilev road and threatening to surround enormous enemy forces.

Italian Front Allied Supreme Command approves the plan for Operation *Shingle*, a landing at Anzio on the west coast behind the enemy's *Gustav* line.

The headquarters of the French Expeditionary Force, which is to be attached to the American 5th Army, arrives in Italy from Africa.

New Guinea The Australian 9th Division finally concludes its long series of attacks by taking the Japanese strongpoint of Sattelberg, north of Finschhafen.

Burma Allied aircraft begin a series of co-ordinated attacks against Japanese installations in the Rangoon area.

☐ Formosa. The American 14th Air Force carries out a raid on the airport at Shinchiku, destroying 42 Japanese aircraft in combat or on the ground.

26 November

Eastern Front The Russians capture Gomel.

Gilbert Islands American units land on the atoll of Abemama and begin to fortify it.

☐ Germany. 663 bombers of the US 8th Air Force attack Bremen. But the weather is adverse and the results modest.

☐ The first part of the Cairo Conference comes to an end without any definite decisions having been reached about Operation *Overlord* (the invasion of northern France). In the spring of 1944, with the help of Chiang Kai-shek's forces, communications are to be re-established between India and China by recapturing northern Burma.

☐ Roosevelt and Churchill leave for Teheran, where they are to meet Stalin.

27 November

Italian Front The British 4th Armoured Brigade (V Corps) succeeds in making a crossing to the north bank of the river Sangro with 100 tanks.

28 November

Eastern Front Army Group South (von Manstein) surrounds huge Russian forces in the Korosten area, north-west of Kiev, inflicting heavy losses on them.

Italian Front At 9.30 p.m., in the eastern sector of the front, the British V Corps launches its offensive against the Sangro line. During the night the 8th Indian Division reaches Mozzagrogna, north of the river, against effective opposition by the German 65th Infantry Division. The New Zealand 2nd Division also begins to cross the Sangro.

☐ Roosevelt and Churchill meet Stalin at Teheran. The conference (codenamed 'Eureka') begins.

29 November

Italian Front The US VI Corps begins a limited operation on its right flank.

In the eastern sector the British 4th Armoured Brigade (V Corps), with effective air support, begins the attack on the hills north of the Sangro.

New Guinea The Australians pursue the enemy along the coast of the Huon peninsula, taking Bonga, once an important Japanese supply base, and Gusika.

30 November

Eastern Front The Russians announce the withdrawal of their forces from Korosten.

Italian Front In preparation for the start of Operation *Raincoat* (attack on the enemy positions on Monte Camino), units of the American 5th Army begin a series of diversionary attacks against San Pietro and the lower Garigliano, to deceive the Germans.

In the eastern sector the British 4th Armoured Brigade and the 34th Division move towards the coast and take Fossacesia. On the left of the line the New Zealand 2nd Division is now also across the Sangro.

Pacific General Krueger orders the setting up of a special force to invade the Arawe peninsula, on the south coast of New Britain, on 15 December, before the main landing in the Cape Gloucester area.

☐ The Teheran Conference ends. In response to Stalin's pressing requests, absolute priority is given to *Overlord* (the invasion of northern France) and *Anvil* (landing in southern France). Stalin promises that Russia will join the struggle against the Japanese after they have beaten the Germans. From Teheran Roosevelt and Churchill go back to Cairo, where their advisers pick up the threads of the Cairo Conference.

1 December

Italian Front In the US 5th Army sector there is intensive air activity in advance of the attack on the *Bernhard* (*Reinhard*) line. At dusk the 139th Brigade (46th Division) begins a diversionary attack against Calabritto, but find it protected by obstacles and minefields. In the US VI Corps sector, too, the resistance put up by the retiring Germans is very effective.

Teheran Conference, 28 November: Stalin kisses the Sword of Honour sent to him by George VI. Facing him is Churchill, and Molotov is on his left.

2 December

Eastern Front Following up their advance in the area of the lower Dniepr, the Russians cross the river Ingulech and get within 6 miles of Znamenka, south-west of Kremenchug.

Italian Front During the night about 30 German bombers attack Bari, with outstanding results. Several ships loaded with ammunition are blown up, causing huge fires, and damage to the harbour sets back operational possibilities by some three weeks. Allied aircraft and artillery attack the German positions in preparation for Operation *Raincoat*, the assault on Monte Camino.

While the attack on Calabritto fails, the British 56th Division (X Corps) launches its attack on Monte Camino from the south at nightfall, and II Corps moves in on Monte Camino from the north-east. In the US VI Corps sector the 45th Division pushes on towards La Bandita and the 34th towards Monte Pantano; both encounter stubborn resistance. In the east New Zealand troops of V Corps (British 8th Army) capture Castelfrentano.

3 December

Eastern Front The Russians improve their positions north-west of Gomel and capture the town of Dovsk.

Italian Front The 56th Division (X Corps) advances up Monte Camino as far as height 819; units of the US 36th Division seize Monte Maggiore. In the British V Corps (8th Army) sector, the 8th Indian Division and British 78th Division reach the river Moro, by-passing San Vito Chietino and Lanciano. The 78th Division is relieved by the Canadian 1st Division, which is transferred from the XIII to the V Corps.

Pacific The dates for the landings on Arawe peninsula and Cape Gloucester, in New Britain, are confirmed for 15 December and 26 December.

□ Germany. Operation *Crossbow* directed against secret weapons bases in Germany is accorded absolute priority for the Allied air forces in the West.

4 December

Solomon Islands: Bougainville 1st Parachute Battalion of the US Marines arrives on Bougainville and is sent into the line immediately to extend the defensive perimeter.

Marshall Islands An American task force commanded by Rear-Admiral

Refugees from Chang-te after the capture of the town by the Japanese 11th Army during one of the periodic 'rice offensives'. These serve not only to obtain supplies, but also to disrupt attempts by the Chinese to concentrate their forces.

Infantry of the Italian Motorized Group in action on Monte Lungo. This is the first formation of the Italian Royal Army to fight with the Allies and it suffers heavy losses.

Pownall and consisting of six aircraft carriers carries out a heavy air attack on the atolls of Kwajalein and Wotje. The aircraft carrier *Lexington* is damaged by a torpedo from a Japanese aircraft, and the light cruiser *Mobile* suffers severe damage from an accidental explosion.

Yugoslavia General Tito becomes chairman of Committee for National Defence in the newly formed provisional government in liberated territories.

China The Japanese 11th Army, in the course of one of its periodic 'rice offensives', takes the town of Changte, in the Lake Tung-ting area. The object of this offensive is not only to ransack the rice stores but also to prevent the concentration of Chinese troops. The Japanese withdraw soon

after taking Chang-te.

☐ Japan. South-east of Honshu island an American submarine torpedoes and sinks the Japanese escort carrier *Chuyo*.

☐ Second Cairo Conference begins. Churchill and Roosevelt meet President Inönü of Turkey. They discuss prospects of bringing Allied troops to Turkey.

5 December

Italian Front In the western sector units of the US 5th Army hold on to their positions with heavy losses.

In the British 8th Army sector the V Corps pushes on to Ortona, where there is a harbour that can be used for supplies. The 8th Indian Division crosses the river Moro.

Solomon Islands American destroyer

force shells enemy installations in Choiseul Bay, on Choiseul Island.

India A big formation of Japanese bombers attacks Calcutta harbour.

☐ Germany. The US 9th Air Force opens Operation *Crossbow* against the bases where the Germans are experimenting with secret weapons.

6 December

Eastern Front The Russians advance slowly in the Znamenka area and cut the railway line between that town and Smela, south-west of Kremenchug.

Italian Front The British 56th Division (X·Corps) reaches the top of Monte Camino. Fierce fighting begins for Monte la Difensa.

In the eastern sector of the front the Canadian 1st Division (V Corps) crosses the river Moro.

☐ Netherlands. Mussert, leader of the Dutch Nazis, admits situation in Holland very difficult. About 100 Dutch Nazis have been killed. He says that 150,000 Dutch Jews have been expelled.

7 December

Italian Front The US 5th Army begins the second phase of the operations to break through the *Bernhard* (*Reinhard*) line. Allied units move towards the San Pietro positions, towards Monte Sammucro in the north. After very hard fighting the Germans begin to withdraw from Monte la Difensa, the defence of which has become doubtful now that the British have seized Monte Camino.

In the British V Corps (8th Army) sector, units of the New Zealand 2nd Division attack Orsogna, but are driven back. Further north, the 5th Division captures Poggiofiorito.

Mediterranean The supreme command in the Mediterranean is unified. Eisenhower, already selected by Roosevelt as Commander-in-Chief for *Overlord*, will be responsible for all operations in the Mediterranean theatre except strategic bombing.

☐ The Second Cairo Conference is concluded. The Allied military chiefs in the West have determined the new strategic directives in the light of the political talks at Teheran between Stalin, Churchill and Roosevelt. The proposed operations for the recapture of Burma across the Bay of Bengal are cancelled to make the amphibious craft available for Operation *Anvil*, the landing in the south of France. All decisions are deferred for northern Burma, which must be liberated to re-establish land communication between India and China, largely on account of Chiang Kai-shek's insistence that he cannot take part without more substantial aid.

The following timetable is provisionally fixed for the offensive against Japan: January 1944, capture of the Marshall Islands and New Britain; April, invasion of Manus and the Admiralty Islands; June, capture of Hollandia in New Guinea; October, invasion of the Mariana Islands.

8 December
Italian Front The II Corps is still fighting to take the positions around San Pietro. The Italian 1st Motorized Group, incorporated in the Allied formations, attacks Monte Lungo but is driven off with very heavy losses.

On Monte Sammucro units of the

'CASABLANCA'

Casablanca, a French protectorate in Morocco, is the final staging post for European exiles attempting to reach America. Rick, the cynical owner of a night club frequented by soldiers of fortune, spies, Nazis and refugees, meets an old flame, Ilse, who has in the meantime married a Hungarian resistance leader hunted by the Nazis. While Sam, the pianist, sings *As Time Goes By*, their former love is rekindled; but Rick, who has acquired two exit permits, sacrifices his own happiness and tricks Ilse and her husband into leaving. Then, along with the ambiguous figure of Renault, a French captain, he goes off to enlist in the resistance.

A splendid example of the wartime propaganda film, full of noble sentiments and devotion to democracy, *Casablanca* assembled a peerless cast. Bogart played to perfection one of his favourite roles of tough guy given to romantic, selfless impulses; Bergman was memorable.

Winner of three Oscars, *Casablanca* became a cult film after the war and also scored a great commercial success.

Ingrid Bergman and Humphrey Bogart in *Casablanca*.

US 36th Division (VI Corps) have to face a powerful German counter-attack. The American 34th Division is relieved by the Moroccan 2nd Infantry Division.

New Guinea The Australians occupy Wareo and push on towards Sio, north-west of Finschhafen, to which the Japanese garrison of Lae has retired.

India Japanese aircraft bomb Tinsukia airfield in Assam, in expectation of an early offensive in Burma.

9 December

Eastern Front The Red Army retakes Znamenka.

Italian Front The capture of Rocca d'Evandro by the American 36th Division brings the operation in the Monte Camino sector to an end. The German counter-offensive against Monte Sammucro is firmly repulsed.

Solomon Islands: Bougainville The airfield at Cape Torokina comes into use. The 3rd Marine Division begins a series of attacks which go on until the end of the month, to take the hills that dominate the beachhead.

China Chiang Kai-shek, in response to a message from Roosevelt, insists on greater financial aid and on a strengthening of the Allied air force in China.

10 December

Eastern Front After a lull the 2nd Ukraine Front (formerly the Steppe Front) under Konev resumes the offensive, attacking Cherkassy on the lower Dniepr and Kirovo.

Italian Front Around San Pietro and on Monte Sammucro there is much less activity while the Americans are consolidating.

In the Adriatic sector (British 8th Army) the V Corps continues its advance northwards along the coast with the Canadian 1st Division and the 8th Indian Division. With the support of an intensive naval and air barrage the Canadian 1st Division attacks Ortona.

Solomon Islands American fighters arrive at Bougainville to operate from the Torokina airfield. This new air base is only 220 miles from Rabaul.

11 December

Far East Admiral Lord Louis Mountbatten decides to integrate the US 10th Air Force and the RAF 'Bengal Command' in a single Eastern Air Command. All Allied air forces in the sector are put under the command of Air Chief-Marshal Sir Richard Peirse.

12 December

Italian Front The 36th Division (II Corps) prepares for the final attack on the German positions on Monte Lungo and occupies San Giacomo hill, between Monte Lungo and Monte Maggiore. Units of VI Corps are also getting ready for a general attack planned for 15 December.

13 December

Pacific The Task Force detailed for the invasion of Arawe peninsula, New Britain, sails from Goodenough Island for Buna, New Guinea, from which they will go on to their objective.

☐ Germany. 710 bombers of the US 8th Air Force attack Kiel.

14 December

Eastern Front The Russians launch the first phase of their winter offensive (though in fact there has been no break in continuity between the autumn and winter offensives). From the Nevel salient, in the central sector, the Kalinin Front (or 1st Baltic Front) under Eremenko advances on Vitebsk. The 2nd Ukraine Front (Konev) takes Cherkassy.

Continuing the counter-offensive which brought them the recapture of Korosten, the Germans take Radomyshl, east of Zhitomir.

Italian Front Units of the US 5th Army complete their preparations for the offensive of the 15th. The first troop movements are carried out during the night.

15 December

Italian Front The US 5th Army attacks the *Bernhard* (*Reinhard*) line with all its major units. There is a particularly fierce battle for San Pietro, where the II Corps is engaged. In the US 45th Division (VI Corps)

sector, the attack begins on the left against the hills overlooking the stream called La Rava and on the right against Lagone. On the north side of the VI Corps, units of the Moroccan 2nd Division take Monte Castelnuovo and the San Michele Pass. The Germans resist forcefully.

New Britain According to plan, Task Force 76, commanded by Rear-Admiral Daniel E. Barbey, lands the US 112th Cavalry Regiment, with reinforcements, on the west coast of Arawe peninsula.

The landing, preceded by air and naval bombardment, is carried out at 7.00 a.m., and the thin Japanese defence is overcome with no difficulty. A surprise landing is attempted, but with no success, on the east coast of the peninsula at Umtingalu, and also on the islet of Pilelo. This latter is captured during the day. The Japanese oppose the operation with fighters and bombers, attacking the American troops and ships, but to no great effect.

☐ A public trial of four German war criminals has opened in Kharkov. The Germans tell the court of the methods used for mass killings of Soviet citizens such as the use of 'gas vans'. The four are executed publicly on 19 December.

16 December

Italian Front The US 36th Division (II Corps) takes Monte Lungo, and attacks continue on San Pietro, where the positions are not easy to defend now that Monte Lungo has fallen. To cover their withdrawal the Germans launch powerful counter-attacks, lasting for the whole of the night. In the VI Corps sector patrols sent out by the 45th Division enter Lagone, which the retreating Germans have abandoned.

17 December

Italian Front The Germans withdraw from San Pietro pursued by units of the American II Corps, which enters the ruined village at dawn.

On the right of the line, the US VI Corps sector, the Germans have withdrawn a little in the centre.

At 7.46 a.m. on 26 November 1943, after tremendous air and naval preparation, advance guards of the US 1st Marine Division land in Borgen Bay, north-east of Cape Gloucester, on New Britain.

After sunset units of the 45th Division take Monte la Posta, meeting with no opposition. The Germans also begin to withdraw from Monte Pantano.

Pacific General MacArthur orders General Krueger to prepare plans and detail forces for the capture of Saidor, in New Guinea, for use as an air and naval base against the Japanese forces both in New Guinea and in New Britain.

China Chiang Kai-shek again asks President Roosevelt for substantial financial aid and for more aircraft.

18 December

Italian Front The VI Corps advances in the centre of the line, while the Germans continue to withdraw.

New Britain The American air force steps up its operations against targets in New Britain in preparation for the landing at Cape Gloucester.

China Chiang Kai-shek gives General Stilwell command of all Chinese troops in India and the Hukawng valley in northern Burma. Japanese aircraft bomb Kunming, in Yunnan. This action fits into the plan for campaign of strategic bombing aimed at disrupting the Allies' vital centres as a preliminary to an offensive against India.

20 December

Mediterranean A unified air command for the Mediterranean is set up under the title of Allied Air Force, Mediterranean. It covers the RAF units, including those stationed in the Middle East, all American air formations stationed in North Africa and occupied Italy and the French and Italian air forces operating in the theatre. Commander-in-Chief is Air Chief Marshal Sir Arthur Tedder, with the American General Spaatz as his deputy.

Italian Front The plans for a combined operation on the Tyrrhenian coast are cancelled on account of the slow progress being made against the Germans and a shortage of landing craft.

Units of the II Corps continue their attacks to clear the western slope of Monte Sammucro.

In the British V Corps sector, on the Adriatic coast, the Canadian 1st Division reaches the outskirts of Ortona, where they are engaged in heavy fighting.

Pacific Intensive air and naval activity in advance of the landing on Cape Gloucester, New Britain. Meanwhile the Americans find no great difficulty in consolidating their beachhead on the Arawe peninsula, though it proves useless both as a naval and as an air base.

American air formations are transferred from New Caledonia to Stirling Island and the Russell Islands to support the coming landing.

China In reply to Chiang Kai-shek's message of the 17th, President Roosevelt confirms that the USA are giving consideration to the grant of a loan to China, and invites his ally to play his part in the struggle for the recapture of Burma. The United States will do everything in its power to reopen the Burma Road, which among other things would give greater security to the American pilots who are at present flying between India and China over enemy territory. Chiang Kai-shek replies that the Chinese will go over to the attack only if the British and Americans succeed in recapturing the Andaman Islands, Rangoon or Moulmein. If Mandalay or Lashio can be retaken, the Chinese will take part in the Burma campaign without insisting, as they have previously, that the Allies mount a big combined operation across the Bay of Bengal.

21 December

Eastern Front Army Group Centre presses with great force on the Russian salient west of Zhlobin (northwest of Gomel), beyond the Dniepr. The Germans are making supreme efforts to hold at least part of the vital Dniepr line.

India General Stilwell arrives at Ledo, in Assam, to take over personal direction of the preparations for the coming campaign in northern Burma.

□ US bombers based on Attu, in the Aleutians, bomb military targets in the Kuril Islands, on Japan's

doorstep.

22 December

Italian Front The battle for Ortona goes on, with the Germans resisting from house to house and units of the Canadian 1st Division compelled to fight a sort of urban guerrilla war which they are not used to.

China The Japanese bomb Kunming, in Yunnan, again as part of their preparations for the offensive against India.

23 December

Italian Front The British 5th Division (XIII Corps) takes Arielli, north of Orsogna; fighting continues at Ortona.

24 December

Eastern Front From their big bridgehead over the Dniepr in the area of Kiev the 1st Ukraine Front (Vatutin) throws in six armies and three assault groups against von Manstein's Army Group South along a centre line between Kiev and Zhitomir. The German 4th Armoured Army, spread over too wide a front, does all it can to hold the forceful enemy thrust. In the Vitebsk sector the Russians take Gorodok causing the collapse of a whole line of German strongpoints hinged on that position.

Italian Front The New Zealand 2nd Division (British XIII Corps), bypassing Orsogna, captures the hills that overlook the town from the north-east.

□ Roosevelt and Churchill jointly announce the appointment of General Eisenhower as Commander-in-Chief of the Allied liberation forces in Europe. Churchill also announces that Montgomery has been appointed to command the 21st Army Group in place of General Sir Bernard Paget. General Sir Oliver Leese, commanding the British XIII Corps, operating in Italy, is named as Montgomery's successor in command of the 8th Army.

New Britain Large American bomber formations carry out at least 280 missions against airfields and other military installations of the Japanese in New Britain.

A Marine carries a wounded comrade back to the first aid post during fighting on Cape Gloucester.

Canadian infantrymen of Princess Patricia's Light Infantry mop up a street in Ortona on the Adriatic coast. There has been bitter fighting in the small town, which, like Cassino, has been destroyed.

Burma In the Hukawng valley units of the Chinese 38th Division succeed in rescuing a battalion of the 112th Regiment surrounded by the Japanese in the Yupbang Ga area. But the enemy hold their positions west of the river.

25 December

Eastern Front The Russians cut the Vitebsk–Polotsk railway line.

Pacific A task force of aircraft carriers commanded by Rear-Admiral Sherman sends 86 bombers to attack port installations at Kavieng, the biggest Japanese base in New Ireland. The raid proves to be fairly ineffective.

In New Britain the Japanese attack the enemy beachhead on the Arawe peninsula, forcing the Americans to withdraw slightly on to the periphery of the defensive perimeter. Meanwhile the Cape Gloucester invasion fleet sails from New Guinea.

India Japanese bombers raid Chittagong.

26 December

Eastern Front Russians announce new offensive in the Kiev salient. Over 150 places taken, including Radomysl.

New Britain At 6.00 a.m. two American cruisers and eight destroyers open fire on the Japanese positions on Cape Gloucester, finishing off the work of destruction begun some weeks earlier by B-24 Liberator bombers, which have dropped at least 2,000 tons of bombs on the area. At 7.46 a.m. the first units of the 1st Marine Division, with reinforcements, land in Borgen Bay, northeast of the Cape, where they meet negligible Japanese opposition, partly on account of the surprise effected, partly owing to the terrible nature of the marshy ground, which the Americans later called the 'green

hell' and the 'slimy sewer'. The Division is commanded by General Rupertus. Two units land in Borgen Bay, others at Tauali, south-west of the Japanese airfield on Cape Gloucester, and a brigade of engineers goes ashore on Long Island. The Japanese make a number of counter-attacks during the night, but are driven off. Only the Japanese air force makes an effective effort to oppose the landing, sinking one US destroyer and damaging three others, besides one landing craft.

Italian Front The Sammucro hills are finally taken by Allied troops.

☐ The legendary German battleship *Scharnhorst*, 38,900 tons, is sunk by the British Navy off the North Cape as she seeks to attack a convoy to Russia. Only 36 men of the complement of 1,800 are saved.

27 December

Eastern Front In the Vitebsk sector troops of the Western Front (Sokolovsky) reach the Vitebsk-Polotsk railway.

The 1st Ukraine Front (Vatutin) pushes on, re-taking from the enemy the positions lost in the Korosten area.

New Britain The 1st Marine Division extends its beachhead, held up by the rain more than the enemy. The Japanese General Iwao Matsuda, in command of the western New Britain sector, can call on about 10,000 men, partly deployed along the coast, particularly in defence of the airfield, and partly concentrated inland near Nakarop.

New American reinforcements reach the Arawe peninsula, where the Japanese counter-attacks are beginning to die down.

28 December

Eastern Front The 1st Ukraine Front takes Korostishev, an important position east of Zhitomir.

Italian Front Units of the British V Corps complete the capture of Ortona.

New Britain General Krueger makes his reserve forces available to General Rupertus, consisting of the 5th Marine Regiment reinforced by

December 1943: the Marines capture an atoll on Tarawa (Gilbert Islands), after fierce fighting against Japanese troops.

The *Scharnhorst*, which was sunk off the North Cape.

army units. The Americans attack the defences of Cape Gloucester airfield.

New Japanese counter-attacks are repulsed by the troops manning the beachhead on the Arawe peninsula.

Burma The Chinese 38th Division takes a number of Japanese strongpoints in the valley of the river Tarung.

29 December

Eastern Front The Russians overcome German resistance at Korosten and seize a large part of the railway connecting it with Zhitomir, advancing as far as Chernakov.

Italian Front An Allied Commando unit carries out a raid on the Tyrrhenian coast north of the mouth of the Garigliano.

New Britain The Marines seize the Japanese airfield at Cape Gloucester with unexpected ease.

Fresh Japanese attacks against the Arawe beachhead have no more success than the earlier ones.

New Guinea The operation for the occupation of Saidor is provisionally fixed for 2 January 1944.

□ France. Reprisals against 'terrorists' continue. The Vichy government announces that more than 20,000 people have been arrested in the last three months.

30 December

Eastern Front The Russians take Kazatin, south-west of Kiev and south of Zhitomir.

New Guinea The operation against Saidor is now fixed for 2 January.

31 December

Eastern Front Zhitomir falls to the Red Army and in the central sector Vitebsk is virtually surrounded by the Russians, but fierce defence by the Wehrmacht prevents them from capturing it.

Italian Front On the western front, the US 5th Army sector, the American 6th Infantry Regiment replaces the 15th on Monte Lungo. Other units try unsuccessfully to dislodge the Germans from their positions east of Acquafondata. On the British

American and New Zealand troops and supplies land in New Britain.

8th Army front there is fighting in the Adriatic coast area around Ortona and Orsogna.

Casualties resulting from Allied air raids on the Italian peninsula and islands over the past three months amount to 6,500 dead, about 11,000 wounded, with 3,500 buildings destroyed and 10,000 damaged.

New Guinea The Allied troops for the occupation of Saidor embark at Goodenough Island, north-east of New Guinea.

Burma There is continued fighting between the Chinese 38th Division and Japanese forces in the Hukawng valley, north of Yupbang Ga in northern Burma.

So ends a year of global struggle, from Africa to Italy, from Russia to the Pacific and from the Atlantic to the Indian Ocean. The balance has shifted decisively and irrevocably in favour of the Allies. The terrible climax of Stalingrad and the gigantic battle of Kursk marked the turning-point in Europe; the massive air and naval battle of Midway in 1942 marked the turning-point in the Pacific. Italy, after its capitulation and subsequent declaration of war against Nazi Germany, has become a battlefield absorbing an ever-increasing number of German divisions which the OKW desperately needs on the Eastern Front. And more German forces

have to be employed against the ever more active resistance movements all over occupied Europe; the partisans have gone into battle in Russia, destroying thousands of the enemy's military trains and disrupting their communications. In Yugoslavia, France, Norway, Holland, Belgium, Greece and now also in Italy, liberation movements are becoming more aggressive and need many of the Reich's divisions to oppose them.

Over a front of 1,300 miles, between November 1942 and the end of 1943, the Russians have recaptured from the enemy a large part of the territory lost since the day of the invasion, advancing in the southern sector of the front at least 800 miles and destroying thousands of tanks, aircraft and guns. The German war potential, notwithstanding the forced labour of millions of people deported from occupied countries, can no longer keep pace with the material losses. Nor can the human losses be replaced. The brilliant divisions of the best army in the world are now mostly undermanned. Reinforcements consist of boys (whose fanaticism cannot make up for their inexperience), or of disheartened middle-aged men. Hitler now pins his faith on his 'secret weapons', which are taking a long time to materialize. Most of them are imaginary.

U-boat anchored at a base in northern Germany.

1944

1944

JANUARY	**27 January** The Russians announce the complete lifting of the Leningrad blockade.	**31 January** *Pacific*: Start of the invasion of the Marshall islands.
FEBRUARY	**15 February** B-17 Flying Fortresses in a first wave and B-25s in a second wave drop bombs on Monte Cassino.	
MARCH	**20 March** The Germans complete their occupation of Hungary.	**27 March** German troops occupy Rumania by agreement with the Rumanian government.
APRIL	**12 April** *Italy*: Abdication of King Victor Emmanuel III in favour of his son Umberto.	**17 April** *China*: The Japanese launch their last big offensive against Nationalist China.
JUNE	**3 June** *France*: The French Committee of National Liberation proclaims itself the provisional government of the Republic. **5 June** *Italian front*: Triumphant entry into Rome by the Allied troops.	**6 June** *France*: In the early hours of the morning the Allies land in Normandy. The gigantic operation Overlord is underway. **20 June** Battle of the Philippine Sea.
JULY	**20 July** Failure of the attempt on Hitler's life in Rastenburg in East Prussia.	
AUGUST	**15 August** The convoys for Operation *Dragoon* leave for the south coast of France.	**25 August** Paris is liberated.
SEPTEMBER	**4 September** *Eastern front*: The Finns cease fire on all fronts.	**17 September** Operation *Market Garden* is launched.
OCTOBER	**2 October** Surrender of Warsaw insurgents. **9-18 October** Stalin, Churchill and Eden meet in Moscow.	**23-26 October** Air and naval battle of the Gulf of Leyte.
NOVEMBER	**7 November** Roosevelt is re-elected for a fourth term as President of the United States.	
DECEMBER	**16 December** Battle of the Ardennes.	

466

Two G.I.s help a wounded American officer during the Normandy landings.

The events of 1943 have decided the ultimate outcome of the war. The initiative has passed to the Allies both in Europe and in the Pacific. For Germany and Japan, the two remaining members of the Tripartite Pact, disaster has followed disaster. The generals at the front realized it (Admiral Yamamoto, killed during the year, had foreseen it: 'We shall be invincible for six months and then . . .'). But fanatical leaders in Hitler's dictatorship still lived in a world of illusions. Hitler trusted in the 'secret weapons' still to come, and in the miracles foretold by the astrologers whom he liked to have around him. But reality was very different. The Russians had survived the previous year's crisis and were now growing stronger and stronger. Their factories beyond the Urals were producing at a feverish rate. As for America, that great country was making the weight of its inexhaustible industrial potential felt in a massive way. In 1943 it produced 85,000 aircraft (against 47,000 in 1942); since the beginning of 1942 its factories and shipyards had turned out 148,000 tanks, 1,200,000 trucks, 42,000 guns of various calibres and 27 million tons of merchant shipping and warships, more than enough to replace the gaps opened in the Allied fleets by the enemy's submarines and air and naval forces. The United States were the free world's arsenal. Up to the end of 1943 they had given aid worth 3·5 thousand million dollars to the USSR, 6 thousand million dollars to Great Britain, 1·5 thousand million dollars to China, India, Australia and New Zealand, while another 2 thousand million dollars had gone to the African, Middle East and Mediterranean sectors. The USSR had received 7,000 aircraft, 3,500 tanks, 195,000 vehicles (especially trucks, which the Russian troops particularly valued), 5·5 million pairs of boots specially designed for the hard Russian winter, as well as entire chemical plants, railway engines and other war material. Add to these the human and material resources, also enormous, of the Soviet Union itself and the combined potential of Great

Britain and the Empire (Canada, India, Australia, New Zealand and South Africa), together with the colonies in Africa and it becomes clear just how colossal were the forces ranged against the dictatorships.

1 January

Mediterranean General Patton hands over command of the US 7th Army to General Clark. Clark retains command of the 5th Army and is given the task of planning Operation *Anvil*, the Allied landing on the south coast of France.

New Britain The headquarters of the force landed on 26 December at Cape Gloucester decides to launch a powerful attack on 2 January in the direction of Borgen Bay.

New Ireland Carrier-borne aircraft from Rear-Admiral F. C. Sherman's task force carry out a successful attack on a Japanese convoy, escorted by cruisers and destroyers, off the enemy base of Kavieng.

New Guinea The fleet carrying the troops of the 32nd Division, US 6th Army, on their way to occupy Saidor, north of the Huon peninsula, leaves Oro Bay and joins its escort of destroyers and cruisers commanded by the American Rear-Admiral Barbey.

Far East General Stilwell sets up the operative headquarters of 'Zebra

Force', a Chinese division armed and trained by the Americans.

☐ Germany. The RAF begins a wave of massive bombing attacks on Berlin. 1000 tons of bombs are dropped tonight. Tomorrow will bring a similar load, while on the night of 20 January no fewer than 2,300 tons will be dropped on the German capital.

☐ Hitler gives his usual New Year's message to the German people. He attacks the 'Jewish-Bolshevist' alliance fighting against Germany. Germany is determined to continue the struggle. However long it may last, it is infinitely preferable to the fate that the German people would suffer in the event of defeat.

☐ The Russian government has rejected the proposal of the Yugoslav government in exile that the two should draw up a treaty of friendship and collaboration, implicitly guaranteeing the sovereignty and independence of Yugoslavia after the war. Moscow's attitude has to be considered in relation to the support given by the Russians to Marshal Tito in opposition to General Mihailovitch, head of the Chetnik movement and supporter of the monarchy. London, too, after supporting Mihailovitch for a long time, has recently changed its attitude, giving political and material support to the pro-Communist partisans, who are indeed the

German soldiers advance under an artillery barrage in the Olevsk sector on the central Russian front, January 1944.

main military and political force in the country.

2 January

Eastern Front The Russian Southern Fronts continue with their attacks, driving back the German troops in the area north-west of Kiev. The Russians capture Radovel, just 18 miles from the 1939 Polish frontier.

Italian Front General Alexander, commanding the XV Army Group in Italy, decides that Operation *Shingle* (the combined operation on the coast of the Tyrrhenian Sea near Anzio) should take place between 20 and 31 January. Some days before the operation the 5th Army is to launch a strong attack against Cassino and Frosinone to keep as many as possible of the German forces occupied.

New Britain In the Cape Gloucester area the 7th Marine Regiment launches the planned attack against Borgen Bay, but is prevented from reaching its objective by a Japanese strongpoint which, although almost surrounded, puts up a furious resistance.

New Guinea Protected by fire from Rear-Admiral Barbey's cruisers and destroyers and by a thick smoke-screen (adverse weather conditions make air support of the operation impossible), units of the 32nd Division of the US 6th Army land on Saidor, occupy the harbour and take the airfield. The US aircraft attack other Japanese positions in association with the landing to prevent the despatch of reinforcements. Australian troops advance along the north coast of the Huon peninsula from Finschhafen and take the village of Sialum.

3 January

Eastern Front The Russians have recaptured Olevsk, north-west of Kiev, only ten miles from the 1939 Polish frontier. South of Olevsk the city of Novograd-Volynsky falls into Russian hands, together with the whole of the railway line leading from this area to Korosten.

Italian Front General Juin's French Expeditionary Force takes up positions on the north flank of the 5th Army, while the US VI Corps under General Lucas is withdrawn from the front line to prepare to carry out Operation *Shingle* against Anzio.

Pacific The headquarters of the US joint expeditionary force (Task Force 51, commanded by Vice-Admiral R. K. Turner) issues the operational plan for the invasion of the Marshall Islands, detailing the units to take part and laying down a 'calendar' of preliminary bombing for the air forces.

New Britain A battalion of US engineers begins work on the reactivation of Cape Gloucester airfield. American attacks continue with the aim of joining up with the units landed in Borgen Bay. The Japanese resist and counter-attack, preventing the Americans from building a bridge over a stream required to allow their tanks to cross.

Burma In the extreme north of the country the Chinese 38th Division resumes its encounters with the Japanese in the area of Taihpa Ga.

4 January

Eastern Front The reconquest of the Ukraine continues. After a violent four-day battle the Russians occupy the German strongpoint of Belaya-Tserkov, railway town south of Kiev, and push on in the direction of Uman.

☐ American and RAF aircraft start dropping arms and supplies to French, Belgian, Dutch and Italian partisan formations. The operation goes under the name of *Carpetbagger*.

New Britain After a powerful artillery preparation the American units succeed in getting their tanks over the Suicide Stream on an improvised dam. They destroy many Japanese positions and advance south from the Cape Gloucester beachhead to reach the line of the Aogiri stream.

New Ireland US carrier-borne aircraft under Rear-Admiral Sherman make a new attack on Japanese shipping in Kavieng harbour.

New Guinea Patrol activity by the American units landed on Saidor. The Australians advancing from Finschhafen reach Cape King William, 15 miles from Sio, where the Japanese survivors from Lae have taken refuge.

4–5 January

Italian Front During the night, in preparation for the attack on Monte Cedro, units of the British 46th Division (X Corps) establish a bridgehead on the north bank of the river Peccia.

5 January

Eastern Front The Russian armies recapture Berdichev, a rail and road junction south of Zhitomir and south-west of Kiev.

German infantry protected by tanks advance in the Uman sector, on the Ukraine Front, January 1944.

Italian Front The attacks by the British X Corps beyond the river Peccia against Monte Cedro and Monte Porchia are held by the German forces of Vietinghoff's 10th Army.

□ The headquarters of the American strategic air force is moved to Britain; General Spaatz is appointed Commander-in-Chief, to co-ordinate the operations of the US 8th and 15th Air Forces.

New Guinea American units on reconnaissance west of the Saidor beachhead meet with the first Japanese resistance. The Australians advancing along the north coast of the Huon peninsula reach Kelanoa, bringing them within 62 miles of the Americans on Saidor.

Burma The Chinese 38th Division tries without success to capture the last Japanese strongpoint keeping them from the river Tarung.

□ The Japanese Government imposes major increases in taxation to meet the costs of the war.

6 January
Eastern Front The Russians take Rokitno, 12 miles inside the 1939 Polish Frontier.
Pacific The operational plans for the occupation of the Marshall Islands are set out in more detail, and forces are detailed for the landing on the important atoll of Kwajalein. General Harmon takes over command of the US 13th Air Force.
New Britain American units from the Cape Gloucester bridgehead make slight progress to the south. The Japanese bring in fresh forces near the perimeter of the Arawe bridgehead.
New Guinea American engineer units arrive on Saidor.
Far East Since all available landing

craft in the sector are to be transferred to the Mediterranean, Admiral Lord Mountbatten, Commander-in Chief of Allied forces in South-East Asia, officially cancels the project for a landing in central Burma across the Bay of Bengal. There is talk of giving up all offensive action in Burma until Germany is defeated. When General Stilwell, hears this he decides to send a mission to Washington to argue against Mountbatten's decision.

7 January
Eastern Front The Russian Southern Fronts break through von Manstein's positions on a 60-mile front in the area of Kirovograd, south-east of Cherkassy. The town is practically encircled.
Italian Front Units of the US II Corps and the British X Corps take Monte Porchia and Monte La

Napalm bombs dropped by US aircraft shower a burning rain on the Japanese air and naval base of Rabaul.

Chiaia.

Far East Admiral Lord Mountbatten gives up the project for an offensive in Burma in the coastal sector of Arakan.

☐ Japanese Imperial Headquarters orders the Southern Army to commence operations for the capture of strategic positions in the area of Imphal, in India, in readiness for a large-scale offensive.

8 January

Eastern Front The Russians have taken another important road and rail junction – Kirovograd, south of the great bend of the Dniepr. Further north the German Army Group Centre launches a counter-offensive in the Zhlobin area, north-west of Gomel, on the Dniepr.

Italian Front The 139th Brigade of the 46th Division (British X Corps) takes Monte Cedro without meeting with any resistance. In the Tyrrhenian sector, where the American II Corps is engaged, a task force surrounds and takes Height 1109.

☐ The Italian Socialist Republic puts the 19 members of the Fascist Grand Council held responsible for the fall of Mussolini on 25 July 1943 on trial at Verona. Only six of them are actually in custody, including Count Ciano, Mussolini's son-in-law.

Solomon Islands An American task force of cruisers and destroyers commanded by Rear-Admiral Ainsworth shells Japanese coastal installations at Faisi and Poporan and in the Shortlands.

☐ The operations division of the US War Department asks for the Allies to maintain the initiative in Burma and China and for US Air Force effectives in this theatre to be increased. Strengthening of this Far Eastern sector would help the American offensive in the Pacific by drawing off Japanese forces.

9 January

Italian Front The 10th and 34th Divisions (US II Corps) make the final attacks to take Cervara and Monte Trocchio. The last units of the American 45th Division are relieved

EDVARD MUNCH

The Norwegian painter and engraver Edward Munch, one of the leading exponents of Expressionism, died on 23 January at Ekely, near Oslo. Munch was born on 12 December 1863 at Löten; virtually self-taught, he came to painting under the influence of naturalism, producing a series of pictures poetically intimist in tone.

As he matured artistically, Munch's work took on predominant and unmistakable characteristics: violent expressivity, deep emotionalism and accentuated symbolism – some of the principal formative influences of Expressionism.

The uninhibited nature of his work shocked the public and sometimes provoked powerful and contradictory reactions: one of his Berlin exhibitions in 1892 was closed the day after it opened, an occurrence that led some hundred German artists to protest violently and eventually resulted in their seceding from the Künstlerverein.

Afflicted by serious mental illness, Munch spent his last years in solitude, bravely refusing to collaborate with the Quisling government during the German occupation of Norway.

The Scream **(1895), one of Edvard Munch's most famous paintings.**

by the Algerian 3rd Division (French Expeditionary Corps).

Solomon Islands A second airfield is completed in the Piva area, which will help to strengthen the air offensive against targets in New Britain.

New Britain The Americans secure some positions on the Aogiri Ridge, which have been stubbornly defended by the Japanese.

Burma Two regiments of the Chinese 38th Division converge on the small town of Taihpa Ga, in the Hukawng valley, while other units of the division try to eliminate some Japanese infiltration. On the Arakan front the XV Corps of the British 11th Army takes Maungdaw.

10 January

Eastern Front North of Kirovograd the Russians mop up a pocket in which several enemy divisions have been trapped. Meanwhile the Red Army resumes the offensive in the centre, in the Mozyr area, west of the Dniepr and south-west of Gomel.

Italian Front A powerful German counter-attack is launched near Cervara and Monte La Chiaia.

☐ The trial of Fascist hierarchs at Verona ends with death sentences on 18 of the 19 accused.

New Britain The Americans on the Aogiri Ridge make some small progress after driving off fierce Japanese counter-attacks launched at 1.00 a.m. Following the report that the Japanese have brought in fresh troops round the Arawe defensive perimeter, reinforcements are sent to this second bridgehead.

New Guinea Japanese concentrations give warning of a coming attack on the beachhead on Saidor, and it is decided to send reinforcements (a regimental combat group, with additional troops).

11 January

Eastern Front The Red Army offensive in the central sector of the front continues in the Mozyr area. Hitler refuses to allow any rectification of the front and any strategic withdrawal, thus sacrificing men and materials in the vain hope of being able to regain the Dniepr line.

The execution of the Italian Fascist leaders De Bono, Gottardi, Pareshi, Ciano and Marinelli at Verona on 11 January.

☐ Five Fascist leaders, including former Foreign Minister Ciano and Marshal De Bono, are executed.

Marshall Islands US naval aircraft based in the Gilbert and Ellice Islands attack Japanese shipping and installations on Kwajalein atoll, Marshall Islands. The task of destroying enemy installations and lines of communication is taking shape in readiness for the invasion.

New Britain Fighting continues in the jungle round the Cape Gloucester beachhead.

New Guinea The airfield on Saidor, reactivated by the Americans, comes into operation.

12 January

Eastern Front The Russians take Sarny after violent fighting.

The German Army Group South counter-attacks in the area of Vinnitsa, south-west of Kiev.

Italian Front The Allied air offensive in preparation for the Anzio landing begins. General Lucas's VI Corps receives orders to carry out the landing in the Anzio–Nettuno sector at 2.00 a.m. on 22 January. Units of the 34th Division advance beyond Cervara and seize the surrounding hills. In the French Expeditionary Corps sector the 3rd Algerian Division on the left of the line and the 2nd Moroccan Division on the right

launch attacks towards Sant'Elia Fiumerapido.

☐ Operation *Pointblank* gets under way, a strategic air offensive against the German aeronautical industry. About 650 bombers of the US 8th Air Force attack factories in Halberstadt, Brunswick and Ochersleben. While the bombing may have have had the desired effect, the price paid by the American air formations is very high; 60 aircraft are shot down in the course of the raid.

☐ The operations division of the US War Department rejects the proposed Operation *Culverin* (landing on Sumatra) and supports General Stilwell's point of view that priority should be given to operations in Burma that will allow land communications to be reopened between India and China. This means an offensive in Burma and strengthening of the US air forces in the Far East, with the object of collaborating with the operations in the Pacific.

13 January

Italian Front The US II Corps is near Monte Trocchio, the last bulwark barring the road to the river Rapido.

New Britain Skirmishing continues round the Cape Gloucester beachhead. The US air force and artillery give unusually strong support to the units on the ground, but they still cannot take the day's objective, Hill 660. A unit of specialist engineers arrives on the beachhead to reopen the airfield captured from the Japanese.

Pacific The plans for the next campaign in the Pacific, code-named *Granite*, are completed. Around 24 March, aircraft from a task force still to be detailed are to attack the big Japanese base on Truk Island (the enemy's Pearl Harbour) in support of the landing on the Admiralty Islands and New Ireland. The invasion of the atolls of Eniwetok and Ujelang in the Marshall Islands is fixed for 1 May, the capture of Mortlock and Truk in the Carolines for 1 August and the landing in the Marianas (Operation *Forager*) for 1 November. If the operations go well enough to allow Truk Island to be 'skipped', a landing could be made on the Palau Islands on 1 August.

Burma In the Hukawng valley the Chinese 38th Division succeeds in eliminating a Japanese strongpoint in the Yupgang Ga area, so that they now control the whole of the river Tarung area. Some units cross the Tarung and thrust north as far as Tabawng.

14 January

Eastern Front In the central sector the Russians break through the German lines on a broad front and take Mozyr and Kalinkovichi, south-west of Gomel, forming a salient in the enemy line. In the northern sector, too, the Red Army resumes the offensive. There are advances by the Leningrad Front (Govorov) and the Volkhov Front (Meretskov) with the 42nd Army and the 2nd Assault Army, which are making for Oranienbaum, and the 59th Army, which is attacking in the direction of Novgorod. The German Army Group North, under Küchler, is hard pressed to hold the vigorous Russian thrust.

□ In a letter to Chiang Kai-shek, President Roosevelt asks him to use his forces in Yunnan against the Japanese occupying Burma, at the same time as the British launch an offensive from India. He makes it clear to the Generalissimo that, if he does not agree, the United States may review its policy of aid to China.

15 January

Eastern Front New offensives are opened on the Novgorod and Leningrad fronts. Units of the Soviet 59th Army make a surprise crossing of the frozen Lake Ilmen and make for the southern flank of the German strongpoint at Novgorod. This sector is defended by the German 18th Army. Further north the armies of the Leningrad Front push forward vigorously in the direction of Krasnoye Selo.

Italian Front Supported on the right flank by the French Expeditionary Corps, General Geoffrey Keyes's American II Corps launches an attack towards the river Rapido, taking Monte Trocchio, the last barrier before they reach the river. The moment has come for the Americans to try to break through the *Gustav* line and reach the valley of the Liri.

New Guinea Units of the Australian 9th Division, still advancing along the north coast of the Huon peninsula, take Sio, already evacuated by the Japanese who retreated there from Lae.

Burma Local actions are reported in Upper Burma between Japanese contingents and small units of the Chinese 38th Division.

16 January

Eastern Front While the chief thrust of the Russian offensive is in the north, south of Leningrad, in the central sector the Red Army deepens the Sarny salient beyond the pre-war Polish frontier.

New Britain In the Cape Gloucester area the Japanese launch their last and bloodiest, but useless, counter-attack against the Americans in the Hill 660 sector. Moving from the perimeter of the Arawe beachhead, American units with armoured support assault the enemy positions and advance one mile.

Burma Units of the Chinese 38th Division cross the river Sanip, but are held up by an enemy strongpoint near the confluence of the rivers Tanai and Tarung. The Chinese 112th Regiment seizes Gum Ga and advances as far as Warang, where it halts.

January 1944: a unit of Moroccan troops engaged in the Cassino sector, one of the most bitterly contested sectors of the Italian front.

Far East Chiang Kai-shek, in reply to the recent message from Roosevelt, threatens to cut off supplies from the American forces in China and to turn them out of their quarters with effect from 1 March 1944 unless the United States grant China a credit of a thousand million dollars. This blackmail arouses violent criticism in Washington. Admiral Mountbatten suggests that the Chinese army in India should be put under command of the British, but General Stilwell refuses the offer, preferring to retain operational control of such large units himself.

17 January

Italian Front The US VI Corps ends its brief but intensive training for the amphibious landing at Anzio-Nettuno.

Towards evening the artillery of the British X Corps opens fire on the enemy positions on the north bank of the Garigliano, while the Allied fleet off Gaeta shells the lines of communication between the German units in the front line and their rear areas. While on the right flank of the start line the British 46th Division, supported by a part of the artillery of the American II Corps, tries to secure control of the Sant'Ambrogio sector (the confluence of three rivers, the Liri, Rapido and Garigliano), two brigades of the British 56th Division attack in the centre. On the left, the British 5th Division attacks towards Minturno and Tufo, also carrying out a turning manœuvre by sea, using landing craft across the mouth of the Garigliano.

At 9.00 a.m. Operation *Panther* begins, the full-scale assaults by the British 5th, 46th and 56th Divisions across the Garigliano. The efforts of the 46th Division near Sant'Ambro-gio fail, but those of the other two are crowned with success.

New Britain The Americans continue with the mopping up of the territory captured from the enemy on the edge of the Arawe beachhead.

Burma The 113th Regiment of the Chinese 38th Division, by-passing a Japanese strongpoint on the Brangbram stream, advances on Taihpa Ga.

18 January

Italian Front By dawn all the units of the 5th and 56th Divisions (General McCreery's British X Corps) have established bridgeheads on the north bank of the Garigliano and two brigades have already advanced a mile beyond the river and occupied the first of the foothills, from which they have prised several companies of the German 94th Infantry Division.

General von Vietinghoff, command-

The 'green devils', a select German unit of the 1st Parachute Division, counter-attacking through the ruins of the town of Cassino, at the end of January 1944.

ing the German 10th Army, cancels the order to send the *Hermann Goering* Armoured Division to France and transfers the 90th *Panzergrenadiere* from the Adriatic sector to the Aurunci mountains to hold up the attack by the British X Corps. He also moves the 29th Armoured Division from Rome to reinforce the sector. Meanwhile, further north, the US II Corps is engaged in clearing the minefields along the tracks leading to the Rapido.

19 January

Eastern Front The Russian 2nd Assault Army takes Ropsha, and the 42nd takes Krasnoye Selo. The advance units of the two armies join up at Russko-Vysotskoye, a place south-west of Krasnoye Selo and Leningrad, thus cutting off the Germans from the Gulf of Finland.
Italian Front The British 5th and 56th Divisions further widen their bridgeheads over the Garigliano; the 5th takes Minturno, the 56th approaches Castelforte.
New Britain In the Cape Gloucester area American troops try to maintain contact with the Japanese as they retreat, and at the same time to extend the occupied area in the western part of the island as far as a line Borgen Bay–river Itni.

20 January

Eastern Front Novgorod taken by storm by the Soviet 59th Army. The German 18th Army is forced to retire to avoid being surrounded. Meanwhile the 2nd Baltic Front (Popov) also goes into action, vigorously engaging the German 16th Army to prevent it from sending reinforcements towards Novgorod and Leningrad.
Italian Front The British 5th and 56th Divisions expand the bridgeheads thrown across the river Garigliano. In the American II Corps sector, the 36th Division occupies the south bank of the Rapido without much difficulty, but when it tries to cross the river at Sant'Angelo in Theodice height it meets with violent resistance from German artillery. Meanwhile the 34th Division

Salerno, January 1944: landing craft of the American VII Corps are loaded on to ships of the Allied fleet for use in the Anzio landings.

(American II Corps) carries out diversionary actions towards Cassino.
☐ Germany. The 'Battle of Berlin' continues with the heaviest and most concentrated bombing attack yet unleashed on Berlin. Hundreds of Lancasters and Halifaxes drop over 2,300 tons of bombs. This is Berlin's 11th massive attack since 18 November, 1943.
☐ General Carl Spaatz takes over supreme command of the American air forces in the European theatre of war.

21 January

Eastern Front Troops of the Soviet 8th Army (Volkhov Front) occupy Mga, 25 miles south-east of Leningrad. In the Ukraine, troops of Vatutin's 1st Ukraine Front and Konev's 2nd Ukraine Front have the 1st Armoured Army trapped in a pocket in the area of Korsun-Shevchenkosky, west of Cherkassy and south of Kiev; the Germans are supplied by an improvised air lift as they try to fight their way out.
Italian Front The ships carrying the American VI Corps to land on the beaches of Anzio and Nettuno sail

from Naples.
Meanwhile the 36th Division's attack on the German positions on the river Rapido meet with stubborn German resistance. South of Sant'Angelo in Theodice the 143rd Regiment succeeds in crossing the river but is forced back on to the south bank almost at once. North of Sant'Angelo some units of the 141st Infantry Regiment have managed to establish a bridgehead, but it remains isolated.
In the afternoon a new attack by the 143rd Regiment allows five companies to stabilize another bridgehead, but during the night it is wiped out by the Germans.
☐ In London, General Eisenhower has his first meeting with his commanders about Operation *Overlord*, the landing of Allied troops in France.
Burma General Stilwell decides to attack towards Walawbum. The 113th Regiment of the Chinese 38th Division digs in at Ningru Ga, a little more than three-quarters of a mile from Taihpa Ga.
☐ For the third successive night American aircraft based on Attu, in the Aleutians, bomb targets in the

After a particularly heavy bombardment, a woman from Anzio wanders distractedly round the ruins.

area of Paramushiru-Shimushu, in the Kuril Islands.

22 January

Italian Front Anzio landing: Operation *Shingle* is launched in the small hours of the morning. Taking part, under the command of US General Lucas, are the American VI Corps, which includes the British 1st Division under General Penney, the US 45th Infantry Division under General Eagles, the US 1st Armoured Division, the US 3rd Infantry Division and a number of American Ranger and British Commando units. They are supported by 4 cruisers, 24 destroyers and 6 transports, with numerous landing craft and amphibians. The Germans have only two battalions of the 29th *Panzergrenadier* Division deployed in the sector, and these inadequate forces are completely taken by surprise. The Allies very quickly succeed in taking Anzio and Nettuno harbours. Within 24 hours they have more than 36,000 men landed at Anzio and Nettuno. North of Anzio they land part of the British 1st Division, with some Commando units; between Anzio and Nettuno, two American parachute battalions; finally, south of Nettuno, the US 3rd Division. The American 1st Armoured Division and 45th Infantry Division are in reserve, with the rest of the British 1st Division as 'flying reserve'.

☐ Allied aircraft drop two million leaflets on Rome announcing the imminent arrival of the liberation forces.

Eastern Front The Germans announce that they have repulsed the attacks of the Russian armies of the 1st Baltic Front (Eremenko) against Vitebsk, north-west of Smolensk. But Vitebsk, a crucial German strongpoint, is now completely surrounded by the Russians.

Pacific The main body of the invasion force for the Marshall Islands sails for its objectives.

Admiralty Islands Relays of American bombers begin the 'softening-up' offensive in advance of the invasion, attacking Japanese shipping in the area. Photographic reconnaissance missions are carried out over Lorengau and Momote.

New Britain Squadrons of Zero fighters drawn from the Japanese 2nd Fleet's aircraft carriers arrive to reinforce the defences of Rabaul, bringing the total to 92 fighters.

23 January

Italian Front The Allied troops ashore on the Anzio bridgehead now number 50,000. Despite the advantage of surprise and numerical superiority, General Lucas acts cautiously. He waits for tanks and heavy artillery to arrive instead of launching immediate attacks inland against the undefended roads and railways which carry supplies for the defenders of the *Gustav* line. This caution helps the Germans, who are quick to reorganize themselves. On the *Gustav* line, while units of the French Expeditionary Corps under General Juin re-take Monte Santa Croce, north of the German defensive line, the American 34th Division (II US Corps) prepares to put in an attack towards the Rapido, north of Cassino, so as to encircle the town from the north and reach highway No. 6, Via Casilina.

Eastern Front Moscow announces that adverse weather conditions and difficult terrain have held up the Russian forces in the Vitebsk sector.

New Guinea Australian troops of the 18th Brigade (7th Division) drive the Japanese from Shaggy Ridge, about six miles north of Dumpu, in the Ramu valley. Their success is made easier by air attacks made shortly before by the 3rd Task Force. As a result of this victory and of the occupation of Saidor the Allies now control the Huon peninsula completely. The Japanese garrisons, target of frequent air raids, withdraw north-west towards Madang.

24 January

Eastern Front In the Korsun-Shevchenkosky area, west of Cherkassy and the Dniepr, the 1st and 2nd Ukraine Fronts throw in powerful forces (seven armies, three of them armoured) against the pocket in which the German XLII and XI Corps have been trapped. The Germans have nine infantry divisions, the *SS Viking* Armoured Division and *SS Valonja* Motor Brigade, the 8th Army and the 1st Armoured Army. From the south a number of German armoured divisions try to penetrate the Russian lines to open a gap for the surrounded forces. A little further south, other troops of Konev's 2nd Ukraine Front mount an offensive in the Kirovograd area.

Italian Front An Order of the Day from Hitler instructs German troops

JEAN GIRAUDOUX

On 31 January the French essayist, novelist and playwright Jean Giraudoux died in Paris.

Born at Bellac on 29 October 1882, Giraudoux studied at the École Normale Supérieure in Paris. After publishing a collection of short stories, *Provinciales* (1909), he held numerous diplomatic posts throughout his life, which did not impede his literary activities. Soon he brought out a series of novels, notable for their originality, fantasy and psychological subtlety (*Simon le pathétique*, *Suzanne et le Pacifique*, etc.).

In due course he also gained success as a playwright, adapting the drama *Siegfried* for Louis Jouvet and producing an interesting series of works that played to full houses in French theatres. Giraudoux cleverly reworked the principal themes of classical mythology, adding his very personal type of ironic symbolism.

His play *La folle de Chaillot* (*The Madwoman of Chaillot*), staged after his death, was highly successful.

to hold the *Gustav* line at all costs. In the Anzio sector the divisions of the US VI Corps extend the line of their beachhead to the left, advancing towards the river Moletta with General Penney's British 1st Division, and to the right, where the US 3rd Division reaches the Mussolini Canal.

On the *Gustav* line, the Germans counter-attack in the southern sector, driving the divisions of the British X Corps back and recapturing Castelforte and Monte Rotondo, but at the cost of heavy losses. Further north, during the night, the American 34th Division opens its attack on the river Rapido to secure a bridgehead over the river north of Cassino.

25 January

Eastern Front South-west of Leningrad, Russian troops take the railway junction of Krasnogvardeisk by storm.

The 1st and 2nd Ukraine Fronts continue their offensive west of Cherkassy and Kirovograd against the opposition of von Manstein's Army Group South. Further south the 3rd and 4th Ukraine Fronts under Malinovsky and Tolbukhin, keep up the pressure on von Kleist's Army Group A.

Italian Front On the *Gustav* line, the regiments of the 34th Division (US

II Corps) still cannot establish a bridgehead across the river Rapido. Further north, on the American division's right flank, the French Expeditionary Corps moves to the west and reaches Belvedere Hill.

26 January

Eastern Front Fighting in the northern sector continues from the Gulf of Finland to Lake Ilmen. In the Ukraine the battle of Korsun-Shevchenkosky also rages.

Italian Front On the *Gustav* line the 3rd Algerian Division, after taking Belvedere Hill, pushes on westwards and seizes Monte Abate.

During the night the 3rd Division (US II Corps) launches another attack towards the river Rapido, and this time some units succeed in establishing a small bridgehead a little north of Cassino.

Marshall Islands US B-25 bombers, escorted by fighters for the first time, carry out a raid on Maloelap and destroy a number of Japanese aircraft.

New Britain More than 200 American fighters and bombers attack the Japanese base of Rabaul, destroying military installations and a great number of the Zero fighters that have recently arrived to strengthen the island's defences. Since the beginning of the air offensive the US air force is reckoned to have brought

down or destroyed on the ground a total of 863 enemy aircraft. At this point the second phase of the battle begins – the destruction of Rabaul in conditions of complete impunity. For the Japanese base, from the point of view of the air offensive, has ceased to pose any threat to MacArthur's forces in the Solomons and New Guinea.

China President Roosevelt tells Chiang Kai-shek that, while the question of a loan to China is still under discussion, from the beginning of March the United States will limit its monthly supply of aid to a value of 25 million dollars.

☐ General Chennault, head of the US Air Force in China, submits to President Roosevelt a major plan for air action. First, to gain air supremacy in China; then an offensive against enemy maritime traffic; next attacks against major industrial tar-

The siege of Leningrad: top, left: a supply column struggles through the 'corridor of death' to the stricken city. Top, right: the agony of starvation on the face of a Leningrad citizen. Above: a Russian policeman gazes at the bodies of civilians who have died of starvation.

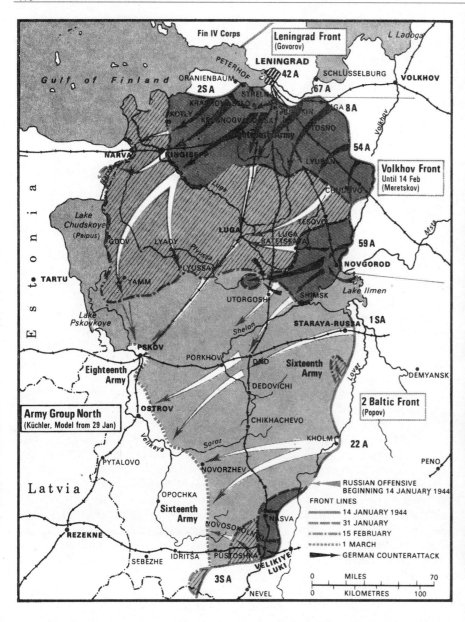

Map legend:
- Leningrad Front (Govorov)
- Volkhov Front — Until 14 Feb (Meretskov)
- 2 Baltic Front (Popov)
- Army Group North (Küchler, Model from 29 Jan)

RUSSIAN OFFENSIVE BEGINNING 14 JANUARY 1944
FRONT LINES
- ———— 14 JANUARY 1944
- —·—·— 31 JANUARY
- —×—×— 15 FEBRUARY
- ·········· 1 MARCH
- ➤ GERMAN COUNTERATTACK

MILES 0 – 70
KILOMETRES 0 – 100

Above: British 25-pounder gun used by the Australians in New Guinea. Below: Russian soldiers welcomed when the siege of Leningrad is finally lifted.

gets in Japan; finally, offensives against enemy military installations in China, Formosa and Hainan.

Burma From Taro units of the Chinese 22nd Division try to penetrate into the Hukawng valley.

27 January

Eastern Front In a special Order of the Day the Russians announce the complete lifting of the Leningrad blockade. The Russians capture Tosno and the railway line from Tosno to Lyuban, and so restore at long last communications between Leningrad and Moscow.

Italian Front In the southern sector of the *Gustav* line the divisions of the British X Corps try again to reinforce the bridgehead on the right bank of the Garigliano. Under an intensive German barrage the 46th Division makes for Monte Juga and the 5th Division for Monte Natale (west of the village of Santa Maria Infante). Further north the regiments of the 34th Division (US II Corps) take Height 771 and Maiola Hill, north of Cassino, advancing very slowly on account of the Germans' effective defence. The 168th regiment of the 34th Division, having taken Caira, pushes on towards Monte Cairo.

The 3rd Algerian Division, French Expeditionary Corps, is driven from Monte Abate by German counterattacks.

28 January

Eastern Front Violent fighting takes place in the area of Korsun-Shevchenkosky between the 1st and 2nd Ukraine Fronts and the re-grouped German forces, including the 1st Armoured Army. The surrounded Germans themselves manage to encircle two Russian armoured corps, the XX and XXIX, but the Russians succeed in breaking out.

In the north the armies of Meretskov's Volkhov Front push on from Lyuban towards Chudovo.

Italian Front In the southern sector of the *Gustav* line the British X Corps continues its efforts to broaden the bridgehead on the right bank of the Garigliano.

☐ Foreign Secretary Eden makes a statement in the House of Commons, giving details of Japanese atrocities against prisoners of war.

29 Januray

Eastern Front In the northern sector the Russian 59th Army and the 2nd Guards Army liberate Chudovo and mop up the whole area between Tosno and Chudovo, south-east of Leningrad. The railway line to Moscow is now completely safe.

Küchler is replaced by Model in command of the German Army Group North. The 18th Army continues to withdraw towards the river Luga.

South of Cherkassy the German 8th Army evacuates the town of Smela, in the area where the battle of Korsun-Shevchenkosky is raging.

Italian Front In the Monte Cassino sector the 168th Regiment of the US 34th Division, with appropriate tank and artillery reinforcements, advances swiftly towards Heights 56 and 213.

At Anzio General Lucas decides to go over to the attack and break out of his bridgehead. He has about 70,000 men available, with 500 guns, about 250 tanks and 5,000 vehicles of various types. But instead of the scattered units of the German 29th *Panzergrenadiere* Division that manned the area when they landed, the Allies now face an improvised but none the less efficient, 14th Army

– a total of eight divisions – under the command of General von Mackensen. The US 3rd Division and British 1st Division attack towards Cisterna and Campoleone, but are held up before they reach their objectives. However, the front has advanced slightly.

☐ Germany. 800 bombers of the US 8th Air Force make a massive attack on the industrial centre of Frankfurt-on-Main.

Marshall Islands As the invasion force approaches, aircraft from the fast aircraft carriers of Task Force 58 (Rear-Admiral Mitscher) start on the final 'neutralization' phase, bombing enemy airfields and other military installations on Kwajalein atoll, on Taroa airfield in Maloelap atoll and the airfield on Wotje atoll. Aerial bombardment is followed by naval shelling. Aircraft from bases in the Gilbert and Ellice Islands also take part in the offensive, attacking the islands of Roi-Namur and Kwajalein as well as Jaluit and Mille.

30 January

Eastern Front In the northern sector the Russian 42nd Army and 2nd Assault Army occupy a long stretch of the east bank of the lower Luga river.

Savage fighting continues in the Korsun-Shevchenkosky area.

Italian Front Units from the 5th Division break through the *Gustav* line and capture Monte Natale. Further north the 168th Regiment of the 34th Division repulses a powerful counter-attack by the Germans on the west bank of the river Rapido.

Marshall Islands Task Force 58 continues its intensive attacks. US aircraft carry out 400 bombing missions, and the seven battleships of the task force shell the primary objectives, Kwajalein and Roi-Namur island, for four hours. Eniwetok atoll is also attacked and 19 Japanese aircraft destroyed on the ground.

☐ A conference of the governors of the French colonies and the representatives of the Consultative Assembly is opened at Brazzaville. The main subject discussed is the new French strategy towards the peoples

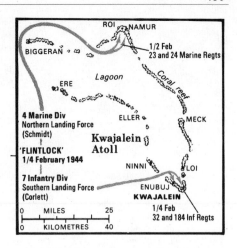

of the overseas territories, the first step towards the creation of the Union Française. General de Gaulle is present.

31 January

Marshall Islands Start of the invasion of the Marshall Islands. Admiral Nimitz has assembled the biggest force so far employed in a single operation in the Pacific – 40,000 men of the Marines and army, against Rear-Admiral Monzo Akiyama's forces of about 8,000. The archipelago, made up of 36 atolls comprising at least 2,000 islands and islets, is about 620 miles long and cannot be 'skipped' in any attack from the South Pacific towards Japan. The Japanese, well aware of this, have strengthened their defences, especially those of the major atolls, on which they have built a number of airfields. For some time, however, the 750 aircraft of Task Force 58 and hundreds more from bases in the Gilbert and Ellice Islands have been hammering the military installations and sea traffic. In overall command of the operation is Vice-Admiral Spruance, who has under him the landing force (General H. M. Smith), the southern attack force (Rear-Admiral Turner), the northern attack force (Rear-Admiral Conolly), the Majuro attack group and the reserve force (Rear-Admiral Hill).

During the night the Majuro attack force lands units of the 106th Regiment of the 27th Infantry Division on Majuro atoll. By the evening the atoll is firmly in their hands. At the

American infantry, with tank support, advance on Kwajalein atoll, in the Marshall Islands. A thick cloud of smoke rises in the background, a result of US air bombardment.

same time a large number of US torpedo-boats attack the twin islands of Roi and Namur, the first of which consists almost entirely of the airfield. Starting at first light, Marines and army troops land on undefended islets a short way from Roi-Namur and Kwajalein (the southernmost island in the atoll of that name) and locate guns there so that they can direct fire on the bigger islands, which are then subjected to an intense barrage of fire from B-24 Liberator bombers, carrier-based aircraft and the battleships *Tennessee*, *Colorado* and *Maryland*. Never before has a landing been preceded by such a heavy barrage. The islands of Roi and Namur disappear under a cloud of smoke and dust, and many

of the defenders are killed. At 12.15 p.m. the Marines of the 23rd and 24th Regiments launch their assault. They advance fairly quickly on Roi, but on Namur they are held up by some Japanese pillboxes which have escaped destruction. The explosion of a big dump of torpedoes and of two ammunition depots blown up by the Japanese causes numerous casualties among the attacking troops. During that night the Japanese put in furious counter-attacks, which are driven off with the support of tanks.

Italian Front In the southern sector of the *Gustav* line the 138th Brigade of the 46th Division (British X Corps) reaches Monte Purgatorio. North of Cassino the 168th Regi-

ment of the US 34th Division captures the village of Caira and repulses vigorous enemy counter-attacks. Further north the French retake Monte Abate.

1 February

Eastern Front In the northern sector the Russians force the crossing of the river Luga. During the advance the town of Kingisepp is taken and the Russians reach within a mile of the Estonian frontier. Further south the German 18th Army counter-attacks near the town of Luga and near Peredel they surround two Russian divisions and a regiment of partisans.

Italian Front On the Cassino front the 135th Regiment of the American 34th Division (II Corps) launches an attack on Castellone and Monte Maiola, supported by the artillery of the 168th Regiment (US 34th Division) from Heights 56 and 213. Both objectives are reached.

Marshall Islands After a preliminary barrage comparable to the one that pulverized Roi and Namur, the Americans land on the west end of Kwajalein, near the airfield, with 11,000 men of the 7th Infantry Division. The landing begins at 9.30 a.m. and is carried out in record time. The Japanese garrison puts up a stubborn resistance despite their heavy losses during the bombardment, but by the evening the Americans occupy nearly a third of the island, including the western part of the airfield. Japanese resistance has ceased on Roi and the Americans have only to mop up, but on Namur they still hold out desperately, and during the night they resume unsuccessful counter-attacks.

Burma Units of the Chinese 38th Division attack a Japanese strongpoint in the Taihpa Ga area. Engineers begin the construction of a military road in the Hukawng valley to support the proposed offensive against central-northern Burma. But the Japanese too have for some time been concentrating forces for an offensive against India.

2 February

Eastern Front In the southern sector the 3rd Ukraine Front (Malinkovsky) and 4th Ukraine Front (Tolbukhin) open a powerful offensive on a front of six miles against von Kleist's 6th Army (Army Group A). Near Peredel the two Soviet Divisions and the partisan regiment succeed in breaking out of their encirclement.

Italian Front General Lucas is ordered to reinforce his Anzio beachhead and prepare for defence. The attacks of the American II and British X Corps continue on the *Gustav* line, but are contained by the German forces of the XIV Armoured Corps.

Marshall Islands The capture of Roi and Namur is completed in the afternoon. The Americans have lost 737 dead and wounded, the Japanese

3,742 dead (including many suicides) and 99 prisoners (mostly wounded or in a state of shock from the bombardment). But 165 Korean labourers attached to the Japanese (the Americans call them 'termites') have given themselves up. Fighting continues on Kwajalein, while small units begin the occupation of all the islets in the atoll.

New Guinea The headquarters of the US 6th Army is transferred from Australia to the Cape Cretin area in New Guinea.

China Chiang Kai-shek replies to Roosevelt's recent message, confirming his request for a substantial loan and his own readiness to send the Chinese Yunnan armies into Burma on the understanding that the Allies undertake a big amphibious operation in the sector.

3 February

Eastern Front The greatest Russian victory since Stalingrad is saluted by 20 salvoes from 224 of Moscow's guns. After five days of ferocious fighting in the Korsun-Shevchenkosky area, troops of the 1st and 2nd Ukraine Fronts link up and converge south of the town to encircle two corps (10 divisions) of the German 8th Army. Desperate efforts are made by the Germans to save their forces, and to enable reinforcements to be sent every other initiative in the sector is reduced to a minimum.

South of Leningrad Army Group North is still heavily engaged with the forces of the Leningrad and Volkhov Fronts and the 2nd Baltic Front.

Italian Front During the night units of General von Mackensen's German 14th Army launch the first major counter-attack against the salient created by the American 1st Division in the area of Campoleone, in the Anzio sector.

General Alexander, Commander-in-Chief of the XV Army Group, orders the New Zealand 2nd Division and the 4th Indian Division to be placed under the command of General Bernard Freyberg as commander of a New Zealand Corps. This new corps then joins General Clark's US 5th Army.

Marshall Islands Admiral Nimitz, seeing that the operations on Kwajalein and the other islands are going to be completed sooner, and with smaller forces, than expected, decides to bring forward the invasion of Eniwetok. Meanwhile the American advance continues on Kwajalein. Japanese night counter-attacks are repulsed, and they are prevented from taking the Americans by surprise by powerful searchlights set up in front of the American positions. Units of the 7th Division, after the usual barrage, land on Burton Island, where they meet with tenacious resistance, and on two other islets which are occupied without trouble.

4 February

Eastern Front In the northern sector the Russian 2nd Assault Army occupies Gdov, which partisans have already liberated. The Russians have now reached the mouth of the River Narva and the shores of Lake Peipus. The Leningrad–Novgorod railway has been completely cleared.

Italian Front On the Monte Cassino front the 135th Regiment of the US 34th Division (II Corps) takes Height 593, the highest point on what the Americans call the 'snake's head ridge', and Height 445. The abbey of Monte Cassino is only 1,000 yards away. Further north the 168th Regiment takes Sant'Angelo hill, but a strong German counter-attack drives the Americans out of their positions.

Marshall Islands By the late afternoon all organized resistance by the Japanese has ceased on Kwajalein, the capture of which has cost the Americans 177 dead and 1,000 wounded, against 4,800 dead and missing and 41 prisoners lost by the Japanese, plus 125 Korean prisoners. However, operations are still proceeding on Burton Island and the smaller islands in the southern part of the atoll; the occupation of the northern part of the islands is already complete.

Burma The Japanese secretly withdraw from the Taihpa Ga area. At the same time they go over to the

PIET MONDRIAN

Piet Mondrian, the most renowned contemporary Dutch painter, died in New York on 1 February.

Mondrian was born at Amersfoort on 7 March 1872. He received his artistic training at the Amsterdam Academy of Fine Arts, being influenced by the Dutch romantic school. Leaving for Paris in 1910, he met Picasso and Braque and was fascinated by Cubism. He then began to experiment in this style, gradually eliminating from his work all formal elements and emphasizing the structural function of colour and line.

His career development took a decisive turn when, after returning to Holland and making the acquaintance of Theo Van Doesburg, he concentrated increasingly on spatial characteristics and began to break up his paintings into geometrically rectangular sections.

Together with Van Doesburg he founded the art periodical *De Stijl*, destined to become the theoretical mouthpiece of the Neoplastic movement, which was formally established in 1920. Thanks to contacts with the Bauhaus, the new movement exerted considerable influence and Mondrian was regarded as a key figure by the avant-garde artists of the period.

Piet Mondrian: *Still Life with Gingerpot.*

offensive on the Arakan front, in the coastal area of northern Burma, attacking the 7th Indian Division frontally and seeking to get behind it past its left flank.

5 February
Eastern Front Another great Russian victory: troops of the 1st Ukraine Front occupy Rovno and Lutsk. These attacks bring the Russians to within 50 miles of the 'Curzon Line' at Brest Litovsk from where the Germans launched their attack against the USSR.

Italian Front The II Corps continues the battle for Cassino with day and night attacks. But they bring no substantial results even though some units do succeed for a short time in digging in on the edge of the valley overlooked by the abbey.

Marshall Islands The occupation and mopping up of the smaller islands in the south part of Kwajalein atoll goes on. Most are found to be deserted, but some small Japanese units are found on a few, and these as usual fight to the death.

☐ Argentina breaks off diplomatic relations with Vichy France, Bulgaria, Hungary and Rumania.

6 February
Eastern Front The 3rd Ukraine Front (Malinovsky) opens a wide breach in the German lines in the area north-east of Krivoy Rog and Nikopol, capturing Apostolovo, a railway junction between the two towns, reaching the Dniepr near Nikopol and trapping considerable enemy forces (5 divisions) belonging to the 6th Army.

In the northern sector the Germans are driven back across the river Narva. The coast of the Gulf of Finland is now firmly in Russian hands.

Italian Front On the Cassino front American troops of the 135th Regiment (US 34th Division) try again to take Height 593.

Marshall Islands The occupation of the smaller islands of Kwajalein atoll continues.

Burma The Japanese look like surrounding the 7th Indian Division. From Ledo, in Assam, the advance guards of the 'Special Force' under General Wingate (the brilliant commander of the Chindits) move into Burma; they comprise two Indian brigades, the 77th and 111th, and three independent brigades of the British 70th Division, the 14th, 16th and 23rd, supported by a US air force group. Wingate's columns have the task of dislodging Japanese troops from the area of Myitkyina and so facilitating the despatch of General Stilwell's Chinese troops from Yunnan, while inflicting the greatest possible losses on the Japanese in northern Burma.

7 February
Eastern Front Troops of the 3rd Ukraine Front reach the outskirts of Nikopol (an important centre for manganese production).

Italian Front In the Anzio sector the Germans launch a fresh counter-attack against the positions of the British 1st Division (US VI Corps) in the direction of Carroceto and Aprilia. During the night of 7/8 February, in the southern sector of the *Gustav* line, the British X Corps puts in a limited attack towards Monte Faito in a vain attempt to seize the mountains behind Castelforte and open the road to the Liri valley.

Marshall Islands Mopping-up operations on the smaller islands of the Kwajalein atoll have been completed. The Americans prepare for the occupation of Eniwetok, the most westward atoll of the Marshalls, in the direction of the Caroline Islands.

China Another message from President Roosevelt to Chiang Kai-shek about the American loan to China. The General expects, in Chinese money, the sums required for the pay and maintenance of US military personnel in China for the next three months, plus another 500 million Chinese dollars for the construction of Cheng-tu airfields, west of Chungking, as a base for B-29 'Super-Fortresses'. The US 14th Air Force, under the command of General Chennault, is operating from Liuchow, Kweilin, Lingling, Hengyang and Chihkiang airports, in southeast China, inflicting serious damage on Japanese maritime traffic and military installations in China and Formosa (now Taiwan).

8 February

Eastern Front The 3rd Ukrainian Front captures Nikopol and wipes out a German bridgehead over the Dniepr.

Italian Front In the Anzio sector the German attacks on the Carroceto and Aprilia salients continue, opposed by the British 1st Division. In the southern sector of the *Gustav* line the bridgehead established by units of the British X Corps north of the river Garigliano reaches its maximum depth, with the 46th Division dug in on a huge area northeast of Castelforte. The US II Corps begins a powerful new attack to reach highway No. 6, the Via Casilina.

☐ France. During the night the RAF bomb military targets in Limoges, using a 12,000 lb bomb.

Far East Marshal Terauchi, the Japanese Supreme Commander in Burma, foreseeing the Allied offensive, prepares to attack in force

against the Indian province of Assam.

9 February

Eastern Front Bloody battles in the Kirovograd region, west of the Dniepr, are bringing about the annihilation of the German 8th Army. The Russian forces involved are the 3rd Ukrainian Front (Malinovsky) and 2nd Ukrainian Front (Konev).

Italian Front At Anzio the German LXXVI Armoured Corps and 1st Parachute Corps capture the Carroceto and Aprilia salients, driving out the British 1st Division under General Penney.

In the Cassino sector the US II Corp's effort to reach the Via Casilina fails.

10 February

New Guinea The US 6th Army and their Australian allies complete Operation *Dexterity* (the capture of the western part of New Britain and the Huon peninsula in New Guinea). The American units that landed on Saidor and the 5th Division of Australians advancing along the north coast from the Huon peninsula join up a few miles east of Saidor.

Burma The Japanese occupy the Ngakyedauk Pass, thus cutting off

A German 280-mm gun mounted on a railway gun-carriage fires on the Allied lines in the Anzio sector.

Anzio sector, February 1944: German parachutists during a lull in the fighting as they counter-attack against the Allied salients at Carroceto and Aprilia.

the 7th Indian Division (British XV Corps) at Sinzweya. The 26th Indian Division (14th Army), sent to re-establish communications, liberates Taung Bazaar. But the 7th Indian Division is still cut off and now has to be supplied by air. In the mountainous eastern part of upper Burma, on the border with China, the Japanese confine themselves to controlling the river Salween area, a possible route for the passage of any Chinese reinforcements from Yunnan.

11 February

Eastern Front The 1st Ukrainian Front (Vatutin), maintaining its pressure on von Manstein's Army Group South, takes Shepetovka.

Italian Front President Roosevelt describes the situation of the Anzio beach-head as 'very tense'. A new attempt by units of the US II Corps to reach the Via Casilina is still unsuccessful.

North of Cassino the 168th Regiment of the US 34th Division tries without success to seize the abbey of Monte Cassino.

12 February

Eastern Front In the northern sector, the troops of the Volkhov Front (Meretskov) take the important railway junction of Batetskaya and reach the suburbs of Luga.

Italian Front General Freyberg's New Zealand Corps replaces the US II Corps on the Cassino front. The sector of the US 34th Division, north of Cassino, goes to General Tuker's 4th Indian Division, while south of Cassino the 2nd New Zealand Division takes the place of the American 34th Division. General Freyberg announces that, before any other attack is made on Monte Cassino, the abbey will have to be bombed.

Marshall Islands Marines land on Arno atoll, beginning the occupation of the smaller atolls in the archipelago. The powerful Task Force 58 sails from its anchorage off Majuro for the biggest Japanese base in the Pacific, Truk atoll in the centre of the Carolines. Vice-Admiral Spruance is hoping to surprise the

backbone of the Japanese fleet at Truk; he does not know that, a few days earlier, Imperial Headquarters have ordered Vice-Admiral Hitoshi Kobayashi, Governor of Truk, to withdraw the fleet to Palau Island. All the same, the 'neutralization' of Truk could be regarded as a great strategic victory.

Burma In the Arakan the 26th and 5th Indian Divisions converge from north and south to free the 7th Indian Division from its encirclement by the Japanese. This unexpected step by the enemy surprises Terauchi, who has been expecting to launch the bulk of his own forces about this time in an attack against India which might prove decisive.

13 February

Eastern Front The Russians capture Luga and push on towards Pskov. To the north, the troops of the Leningrad Front (Govorov) reach the river Narva and, after five day's fighting, the east bank of Lake Peipus. The Russians are now meeting stiffer resistance from the German Army Group North (Model), which is preventing them from entering Estonia and Latvia.

Italian Front While the Allies suspend their attacks on Cassino, the 4th Indian Regiment (New Zealand Corps) takes over the positions of the US 168th Regiment (34th Division).

Pacific General MacArthur decides on the beginning of April for the invasion of Manus, the Admiralty Islands and the Japanese base at Kavieng in New Ireland, with the object of extending American control to the Bismarck Archipelago and cutting off and neutralizing the base at Rabaul.

15 February

Eastern Front In the northern sector units of the Russian 2nd Assault Army and 42nd and 67th Armies cross the river Narva and capture several Estonian villages.

Italian Front 147 B-17 Flying Fortresses in a first wave and 82 B-25s in a second wave drop some 400 tons of bombs on Monte Cassino. The abbey, one of the shrines of western Christian culture, is completely de-

stroyed, and the bishop and several of the monks are killed. The decision to bomb the Benedictine abbey was taken in response to the request made by General Freyberg, commander of the New Zealand Corps, on 12 February. He maintained that the historic edifice had been transformed by the Germans into a sort of fortress from which the enemy could overlook every movement made by the Allied forces in the sector, so frustrating every attack.

Freyberg's conviction received strong support from evidence given by the British General Sir Henry Maitland Wilson, who declared that when he flew over the abbey at a low altitude he saw German soldiers in the courtyard. The truth was quite otherwise, but this does not emerge until after the war. There were no German soldiers in the abbey; Marshal Kesselring had formally assured the Vatican that the abbey would not be occupied and that none of his soldiers would set foot in it. To make certain of that a kind of 'free zone' was established for a radius of 300 metres round the abbey and all soldiers forbidden to enter it. Moreover, as an extra precaution, the Germans themselves took the priceless ancient documents kept in the abbey to the Vatican for safekeeping.

Freyberg's request aroused fierce argument in the Allied camp. Many were firmly against bombing the monastery and the air force commander, Ryder, for instance, queried Wilson's evidence. General Keyes, Commander of the US II Corps, who was actually responsible for operations in the Monte Cassino sector, stated categorically that none of his soldiers had ever seen a single shot fired from the abbey. At this point in the argument General Clark, Commander-in-Chief of the US 5th Army, of which Freyberg's Corps forms part, who was expected to give the final decision, passed the buck to his direct superior, the Commander-in-Chief of the XV Army Group, General Alexander, and he, relying on General Wilson's evidence, ordered the bombardment to go ahead.

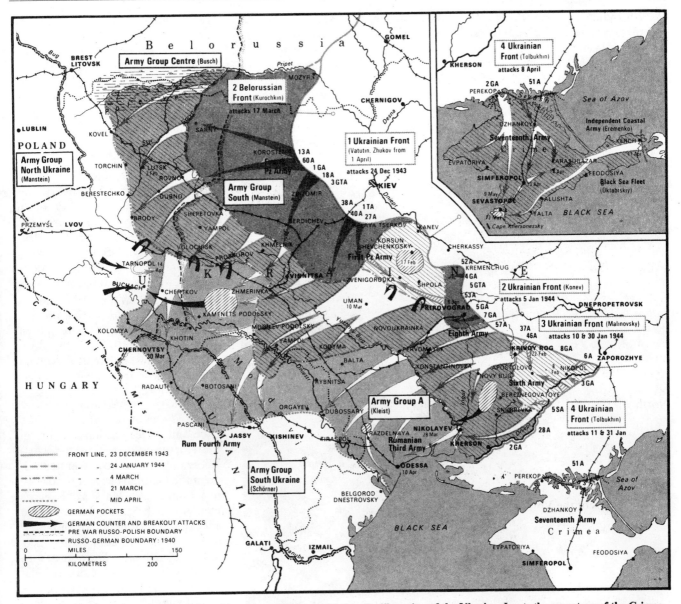

The Soviet offensive in southern Russia, January–April 1944, which led to the liberation of the Ukraine. Inset: the recapture of the Crimea, April–May 1944.

After the raid nothing is left of the abbey but smoking ruins, but the Allies have gained nothing; in fact the 3rd Parachute Regiment under Colonel Heillmann, a unit of picked men belonging to General Heidrich's 1st Parachute Division, is sent to occupy the ruins and sites its own guns there, now really turning the ruins of Monte Cassino into a kind of fortress. From it the Germans can now observe unseen the slightest movement on the part of the enemy. Moreover the Allies have not co-ordinated the bombing of the abbey and operations by other formations,

so that, for example, General Tuker, Commander of the 4th Indian Division, does not know the exact time fixed for the bombardment and his own troops go into action too soon and achieve little or nothing (some of the Allied bombs land on his own positions). What is more he directs his attack not at Monte Cassino but at Monte Calvario, three-quarters of a mile away.

☐ Germany. During the night more than 800 British bombers carry out yet another massive raid on Berlin, causing serious destruction in the city's industrial areas.

Pacific The US 3rd Amphibious Force, escorted by cruisers and destroyers and protected by aircraft from bases in the Solomon Islands, lands New Zealand contingents (the 3rd Division under General Barrow-clough) in the Green Islands, off New Ireland. Japanese resistance is limited to air action, and the great Allied superiority renders it ineffective.

Marshall Islands The invasion force for Eniwetok sails from Kwajalein.
Gilbert Islands Aircraft of the US Navy, taking off from Abemama Island, bombard the Japanese base

at Wake.

□ In Argentina a 'group of six officers' (including Peron) occupies the Foreign Ministry to prevent the declaration of war on the Tripartite Pact countries.

16 February

Eastern Front In the northern sector the Russian offensive thrust is resumed after some slackening due both to German defence and to ground conditions.

In the Ukraine, west of Cherkassy, seven German divisions manage to escape from encirclement in the

Red Army soldiers in action with light machine guns during the offensive in the Ukraine.

Korsun-Shevchenkosky area. The 1st Armoured Army is largely responsible for the successful operation, thanks to which the Germans succeed in bringing 30,000 of the 50,000 men in the pocket back to safety.

Italian Front In the Anzio sector General von Mackensen's 14th Army carries out a second massive assault on the Anglo-American beachhead. The action pushes the Allies back almost to the line of 29 January. But German losses are too heavy for an exhausted army, and Kesselring orders the offensive to be suspended.

Marshall Islands US aircraft taking off from Rear-Admiral Ginder's carrier group bomb Eniwetok atoll, destroying a few batteries and 14 enemy aircraft, and putting the airfield on the islet of Engebi out of action.

Burma Skirmishing in the Arakan area and near the Chinese border.

17 February

Eastern Front A special Order of the Day announces the liquidation of the Korsun-Shevchenkosky pocket. According to the Soviet announcement the Germans have lost 100,000 men although Marshal Konev's memoirs give 55,000 German dead and 18,200 prisoners. A substantial haul of arms and ammunition falls into Russian hands. The next day, in Moscow, the great victory is celebrated by the firing of twelve salvos of 224 guns.

Italian Front The remaining monks at Monte Cassino are evacuated by the German military authorities and taken to Rome.

During the night units of the 4th Indian Division make an assault on Height 593, north of Monte Cassino.

Caroline Islands Vice-Admiral Spruance's formidable Task Force 58, which, although incomplete (the group engaged on the Eniwetok landing has been detached), still counts nine aircraft carriers and six battleships, attacks installations and shipping at Truk. American bombers and torpedo-planes cause tremendous damage; 265 Japanese aircraft are destroyed on the ground or in combat (among them 200 aircraft

which were to go to reinforce the base at Rabaul), and the light cruiser *Naka*, three auxiliary cruisers, two destroyers and some thirty other ships, including five tankers, are sunk; the airfields and port installations are disrupted. The Americans lose only 25 aircraft, and the aircraft carrier *Intrepid* is damaged during the night by an enemy torpedo-plane. In their night counter-attack the Japanese lose another 31 aircraft. The battleships *Iowa* and *New Jersey* intercept the light cruiser *Katori* and a destroyer which escaped from the first attack on Truk, and sink them.
Marshall Islands The Eniwetok landing force, commanded by Rear-Admiral Hill and including the battleships *Pennsylvania*, *Colorado* and *Tennessee*, lands army troops and Marines on some of the islets of Eniwetok atoll after a powerful preparation by aircraft and naval gunfire. The tactics are the same as those so successful at Kwajalein: the occupation of objectives smaller and less strongly defended than the main objective and the landing on them of guns which can hammer the main objective and support operations on it. The atoll is defended by 2,600 Japanese under the command of General Yoshima Nishida, nearly all concentrated on Eniwetok and the neighbouring islet of Engebi.
Having cited their guns on the islets of Rujoru and Aitsu, the Americans begin to bombard Engebi from the air, sea and land. During the night groups trained in the demolition of under-water obstacles approach the beaches chosen for the landing.
Green Islands The New Zealanders continue 'cleaning up' the islands, while a base for US motor torpedo-boats is made effective.

18 February
Eastern Front In the northern sector Soviet forces retake Staraya Russa, an important town south of Lake Ilmen and Novgorod. In the southern sector the 3rd and 4th Ukraine Fronts (Malinovsky and Tolbukhin) have almost completed the annihilation of the German 8th Army.
Italian Front During the night mas-

STREPTO-MYCIN

After several years of unremitting research into antibiotics produced by soil micro-organisms, a team of scientists led by Selman A. Waksman and working in the laboratories of the Department of Microbiology at the New Jersey Agricultural Station, Rutgers University, identified and isolated streptomycin, an antibiotic produced by *Streptomyces griseus*.

Second in importance and practical application only to penicillin, streptomycin, which proved active against gram-positive, gram-negative and acid-resisting bacteria, was used successfully to cure many diseases of humans, animals and plants, and was particularly effective against tuberculosis.

Streptomycin acting against *Bacterium Coli*.

sive air bombing and artillery fire slow down the German attacks on the Anzio beachhead.
Caroline Islands Task Force 58 fulfils its mission to the letter, completing the destruction of the Japanese base at Truk. During the operation, begun the previous day, about 200,000 tons of enemy shipping have been destroyed. As an exception to its usual practice, Radio Tokyo admits the serious blow suffered by Japan.
Marshall Islands Beginning at dawn,

the guns of the American warships and those sited on the islets surrounding Engebi open up on that island, and at 8.42 a.m. two battalions of the 22nd Marine Regiment land. The Japanese only put up any organized resistance at the south end of the island; the area is captured by the Marines in the first afternoon. During the night Japanese counter-attacks are driven off.
Meanwhile other American units begin the occupation and mopping up of the smaller islets.
Bismarck Archipelago Allied destroyers open up on the Japanese bases at Rabaul in New Britain and Kavieng in New Ireland.
New Guinea Local encounters only between the Americans and Japanese who have infiltrated into the Saidor area.
Burma In the Chinese 22nd Division sector Japanese units retire several miles to avoid being surrounded.

19 February
Italian Front In the Anzio sector the British 1st Division manages to stem the German advance. The situation is stabilized, the Germans desisting from any further counter-attacks and the Allies regarding the mere retention of their beachhead as a success. The German attack is suspended following a message from General Westphal, Marshal Kesselring's Chief of Staff, at 2.30 p.m. in which he admits that the firm resistance of the Allies, their superiority in the air and the intense bombardment from their ships will not allow the Germans to throw them back in the sea.
Marshall Islands Fighting flares up again on Engebi at dawn. The Japanese resist doggedly, moving from one position to another across a system of tunnels made from old petrol tins. At 9.55 a.m. another Marine battalion lands and by systematically destroying the enemy's ingenious trench system, puts an end to Japanese resistance during the course of the morning.
At 9.15 a.m., after an intensive artillery barrage, two battalions of the US 106th Infantry Regiment land on Eniwetok Island, at the south of the

Cassino and, in the distance, the abbey of Monte Cassino, after the horrifying bombardment by Allied aircraft on 15 February. The tragic and unnecessary destruction of this ancient centre of western Christian culture was the result of a blunder

by the Allied command, who thought, mistakenly, that German forces were operating from inside the abbey.

atoll of that name. Japanese resistance is better organized than on Engebi, and at 1.30 p.m. the Americans think it wiser to land another battalion, this time of Marines. Forceful enemy counter-attacks slow down the advance of the invading forces.

20 February

Eastern Front In the northern sector the 22nd Army of the 2nd Baltic Front (Popov) breaks through the German defences near Kholm.

Italian Front The German 1st Parachute Division under General Heidrich begins to replace the 90th *Panzergrenadiere* in the Monte Cassino sector. The German 71st Infantry Division is also withdrawn from the front to be deployed in a sector of the Aurunci mountains to the north of the 94th Division.

☐ Germany. The US strategic air force begins a series of heavy attacks against German aircraft factories (Operation *Argument*).

☐ Norway. Allied sabateurs damage a ferry-boat carrying heavy water to German laboratories. Heavy water is an essential element in the manufacture of atomic bombs.

Marshall Islands Slow American advance in the northern part of Eniwetok Island, while a landing is being prepared on Japtan and Parry, this last one of the three biggest islands in the atoll.

A group of aircraft carriers commanded by Rear-Admiral J. W. Reeves take part in the bombardment of Japanese positions on Jaluit atoll.

Green Islands New Zealand contingents crush the last resistance of the Japanese garrison on the islands (which are situated opposite New Ireland).

21 February

Eastern Front The Russians re-take Kholm, south of Leningrad. In the Ukraine they reach the outskirts of Krivoy Rog, defended, like Nikopol, to the bitter end by the Germans because of the vital manganese and iron deposits.

Italian Front General Freyberg issues

French soldiers in an abandoned village near Monte Cassino, Italy.

a new plan of attack against Cassino.

Marshall Islands Japanese resistance ceases on Eniwetok Island. Artillery units are landed on Japtan Island, which has been cleared of the enemy, and fire directed on to Parry Island from there. The pre-invasion bombardment of Parry Island begins.

New Guinea The 5th Marine Regiment advances along the north coast of the island from Natamo towards the Iboki Plantation. A battalion of the same regiment carries out an amphibious operation to take Karaiai, near Cape Raoult, where there is a Japanese supply depot.

☐ General Hideki Tojo, the Japanese Prime Minister, becomes Chief of Japanese Army General Staff, replacing Field-Marshal Sugiyama.

22 February

Eastern Front The Germans lose Krivoy Rog. The southern wing of the German front, where von Kleist's Army Group A is operating, is forced back on to the southern Bug near Uman.

Marshall Islands After three days of preliminary bombardment by aircraft, ships, and finally by land-based guns, the 22nd Marine Regiment begins the landing on Parry Island at 9.00 a.m. 100 tons of bombs, 245 tons of artillery shells and 944 tons of shells from naval guns have fallen on the island, yet still the Japanese put up a desperate resistance.

☐ Churchill makes a statement in the House of Commons about relations between Russia and Poland. He declares that the USSR desires a strong, independent Poland and that, if the eastern frontier of Poland has to be adjusted at the end of the war, territorial compensation will be made at the expense of Germany both in the north and the west. Four days later the Polish government in exile in London protests against the Premier's statement, declaring that Poland cannot accept the 'Curzon line' as its future frontier, which would deprive the country of almost half its territory and about 11 million of its citizens.

During the same speech Churchill also pledges support for Marshal Tito in Yugoslavia.

23 February

Eastern Front Russian troops penetrate into the suburbs of Dno, south-west of Lake Ilmen.

Italian Front Anzio sector: General Lucas is replaced as Commander of the US VI Corps by General Lucius

Truscott, previously in command of the US 3rd Division.

Marshall Islands Japanese resistance on Parry Island ceases during the morning. The capture of the Marshall Islands may be said to be complete. In the operation against Eniwetok the Americans have lost 300 dead and 766 wounded. The Japanese garrison of 2,600 men has been wiped out except for 66 infantrymen taken prisoner.

Mariana Islands Aircraft of Rear-Admiral Mitscher's task force of fast aircraft carriers bomb Saipan, Tinian, Rota and Guam. This is the first heavy blow struck by Mitscher's aircraft but there are to be many more. A great number of enemy aircraft are destroyed on the ground or in combat.

New Britain More American fighter squadrons arrive at Cape Gloucester.

Burma Two regiments of the Chinese 22nd Division occupy Yawngbang, from which the Japanese have already retired. In the British 14th Army sector, after trying hard but in vain to overcome the resistance of the 7th Indian Division at Sinzweya, the Japanese withdraw.

24 February

Eastern Front Troops of the Leningrad Front and the 2nd Baltic Front occupy Dno. In the central sector the 1st Belorussian Front reduces the German bridgehead on the left bank of the Dniepr south of Vitebsk and liberates Rogachev, north of Zhlobin.

Admiralty Islands General MacArthur orders a reconnaissance in force of the Admiralty groups of islands.

New Guinea US advance units from Saidor reach Biliau on Cape Iris.

Burma From Ningbyen, in the north-eastern part of the country, the US 5307th 'provisional unit' (Marauders) sets off on its march to the Hukawng valley. The final objective of this minor campaign is the capture, with Chinese collaboration, of Myitkyina airfield. In the Arakan sector elements of the 7th Indian Division cross Ngakyedauk Pass and make contact with the 5th Indian

Division.

25 February

Burma In the north-east of the country the American units have their first skirmish with Japanese patrols. In the Arakan the 81st (West African) Division takes Kyauktaw in the Kaladan valley.

☐ Churchill assures Roosevelt that the campaign in northern Burma will not be given up in favour of an amphibious operation in central Burma or the opening up of another front in the Dutch East Indies.

New Britain A battalion of the 5th Marine Regiment lands at Iboki Plantation. US destroyers shell the Japanese bases at Rabaul, New Britain, and Kavieng, New Ireland, both already almost completely blockaded and neutralized by the long air and naval offensive.

26 February

Eastern Front In the northern sector, the Leningrad Front and 2nd Baltic Front occupy Porkhov, east of Pskov. The railway line between Dno (west of Staraya Russa) and Novosokolniki (west of Velikiye Luki) is completely cleared of Germans.

Italian Front General Heidrich takes over command of the Cassino sector, defended by the 1st Parachute Division. The task of garrisoning the town of Monte Cassino is given to the 3rd Parachute Regiment under Colonel Heillmann.

South-West Pacific The Americans prepare to launch Operation *Brewer*, the invasion of the Admiralty Islands. A task force of destroyers under the command of Rear-Admiral Fechteler will land the invasion force, whose nucleus is the US 1st Cavalry Division under General Swift, in the area of Momote airfield. The pre-invasion aerial bombardment, carried out by the US 5th Air Force, has to be scaled down on account of bad weather conditions.

27 February

Eastern Front Von Manstein's Army Group South (to be renamed Army Group North Ukraine in March) launches powerful counter-attacks against Russian positions west of the

Marshall Islands: a Japanese soldier burnt by a US flame-thrower, a horrifying reminder of the barbaric fighting in the Pacific.

river Styr (in pre-war Poland).

Admiralty Islands US aircraft bomb Momote and Lorengau in the Admiralty Islands, as well as Wewak in New Guinea. The forces for the landing in the Admiralty Islands embark in Oro Bay, New Guinea.

28 February

Admiralty Islands The first units of the US landing force sail for Los Negros. Bombing of targets in the Admiralty Islands and New Guinea continues.

29 February

Italian Front The third and last attack in force by the Germans against the Anzio beachhead begins. But it is hampered by appalling weather. German vehicles sink into the mud and poor visibility makes their artillery fire ineffective.

Admiralty Islands 8.17 a.m.: After preparatory air and naval bombardment the first units begin to land on Los Negros Island to carry out Operation *Brewer*. Momote airfield, defended by a small Japanese garrison, is taken by 9.50 a.m., but the landing force is not strong enough to hold it, so the defensive perimeter is reduced overnight. MacArthur visits the field in person to inspect the forces, and gives orders that the beachhead must be held at all costs against the expected Japanese counter-attacks by night. The attacks come, but are held without difficulty. The Japanese, though numerically superior to the Americans, are poorly co-ordinated tactically. US air forces carry out several attacks by air and sea against the base at Lorengau, in Manus Island, the biggest island in the archipelago. US destroyers also shell the Rabaul base, in New Britain.

Burma In the Arakan sector British and Indian troops succeed in completely clearing the Ngakyedauk Pass of Japanese.

1 March

Italian Front The German offensive against the Anzio beachhead is contained. On the right flank of the Allied line an attempted break-through in the Ponte Rotto sector is thwarted by the American 3rd Division.

☐ Political strike in Turin: over 100,000 workers cease work, paralysing what little war production the factories are still able to turn out for the German occupation forces and the small army of the Italian Socialist Republic.

Admiralty Islands On Los Negros Island the American landing force wipes out the Japanese who have infiltrated the defensive perimeter during the night counter-attack, and take steps to strengthen the perimeter while waiting for reinforcements. In the evening the Japanese attack again but are unable to break the American lines. Their efforts go on all night.

General Krueger, commanding the US 6th Army, orders General Swift, commander of the 1st Cavalry Division, to proceed with the occupation of the whole archipelago, to secure sites for air and naval bases.

2 March

Admiralty Islands On Los Negros Island units of the 5th Cavalry arrive to reinforce the force already landed. After preliminary air bombing the Americans occupy Momote airfield without difficulty.

Burma In the north-east the units of the American 'provisional unit' regroup south-west of the Tanai river. British forces moving from Ledo, in Assam, cross the river Chindwin near Singkaling Hkamti on boats dropped by parachute.

In the Arakan the 81st West African Division takes Apaukwa, but is driven out again by violent Japanese counter-attacks.

3 March

Italian Front In what are to be the last battles in the Anzio sector for

some weeks, the American 3rd Division halts a fresh German attack near Ponte Rotto and a counter-attack by the American division in the afternoon re-takes some positions.

New Guinea Allied strategists are at work on the first draft of a plan for the invasion of Hollandia, in New Guinea. Since the Japanese bases are out of range of land-based aircraft it will be necessary to call on the aircraft carriers. The nearest air bases that the Japanese have to Hollandia are about 120 miles away, in the Sarmi area and Wadke Island.

Admiralty Islands The Japanese on Los Negros launch a very powerful counter-attack at night against the American beachhead. They are driven back and suffer such heavy losses that they are never able to mount operations on so big a scale again.

Burma In the north-eastern area the American 5307th 'provisional unit' occupies Lagang Ga and clears an open space for the dropping of supplies by air. The Japanese retire towards Walawbum, where they think they will find the Americans. A Chinese-American armoured group, supported by units of the Chinese 22nd Division, occupies Ngam Ga, near Maingkwan, and repulses night counter-attacks by the Japanese.

4 March

Eastern Front In the Ukraine the Russians unleash another big offensive, driving the German forces back over the Bug (though they still have forces in Uman, between Kiev and Odessa) and surrounding some enemy divisions in the area of Tarnopol. Apart from brief lulls the Russian offensive goes on without a break for over three months.

☐ Germany. About 600 Flying Fortresses and Liberators of the US 8th Air Force carry out the first daylight raid on Berlin. They meet with powerful resistance by fighters and anti-aircraft guns and lose nearly 80 aircraft.

Green Islands A landing strip for Allied fighters is operational, and a runway for bombers almost com-

pleted.

Far East General Stilwell, Chiang Kai-shek's Chief of Staff, meets Admiral Lord Mountbatten, Allied Supreme Commander in South-East Asia. During their discussions some of their differences over the conduct of operations in the Far East are smoothed out.

Burma In the north-east the Americans occupy a part of the road leading from Walawbum to Kamaing, and begin to shell Walawbum. The Japanese try unsuccessfully to attack the Americans on the flank, and launch a violent attack against the units manning Lagang Ga. The attack is contained.

The Chinese-American armoured group advances from Ngam Ga to Tsamat Ga, near Maingkwan, and the Japanese evacuate Tsamat Ga.

5 March

Eastern Front The Ukrainian Fronts continue their offensive with the object of destroying the German forces in the great southern bend of the Dniepr.

New Guinea The US 126th Infantry Regiment, from the 32nd Division, with support units, lands without trouble at Yalau Plantation, about 30 miles west of Saidor. Australian forces converge on the north coast west of Saidor from inland. The Japanese avoid encirclement by withdrawing towards Madang.

General MacArthur, hoping to isolate the Japanese forces in New Guinea, presses on with plans for the invasion of Hollandia, New Guinea and of Kavieng, New Ireland.

Admiralty Islands The US 7th Cavalry starts operations to capture the northern part of Los Negros. General Swift takes personal command of the new phase.

Burma In the north-east, the 66th Regiment of the Chinese 22nd Division surrounds and captures Maingkwan.

Admiral Mountbatten asks for Chinese and American reinforcements for the Arakan sector, where he believes a big Japanese offensive is imminent.

In central Burma British and Indian

Allied troops moving up through the streets of Anzio after the landings.

brigades from the Chindits begin parachute drops on the main Japanese lines of communication. The first drops are carried out on a previously prepared landing space about 50 miles north-east of Indaw, code-named 'Broadway'.

In the Arakan the British XV Corps begins an offensive movement against the Maungdaw–Buthidaung road and towards the mouth of the river Naaf.

6 March
New Britain Units of the 1st Marine Division carry out a landing on the west coast of Willaumex peninsula, near Volupai, aiming for the Japanese base at Talasea. Marshy ground and firm defence by the enemy slow down their advance, but they succeed in penetrating a few miles inland.

Bougainville Big Japanese forces are located near a hill overlooking the Cape Torokina beachhead in Empress Augusta Bay. Expecting a counter-attack, the Americans try to extend and strengthen their perimeter, but they are not able to dislodge the Japanese from any of the positions that constitute a danger to the beachhead.

Admiralty Islands Another American regiment lands on Los Negros and joins up with the units pursuing the retreating Japanese. The beachhead is widened to take in the villages of Salami and Porlaka.

Burma Chiang Kai-shek orders General Stilwell to hold up the offensive in the north-east of the country for a time in view of the Japanese Arakan offensive. However, during the day there are violent encounters between Chinese and American forces and the Japanese, who carry out a number of fierce counter-attacks and suffer heavy losses. The

Japanese withdraw from Walawbum.

☐ In Argentina the Foreign Ministry repudiates the breaking off of relations with the Tripartite Pact countries.

7 March

Admiralty Islands American advance guards capture Papitalai and the eastern part of Seeadler Harbour in Los Negros Island. B-25 aircraft are able to make emergency landings on Momote airfield.

Burma The Chinese and Americans concentrate for the occupation of Walawbum where there are still substantial Japanese forces in the vicinity.

8 March

Germany 600 US bombers carry out another raid on Berlin, with the Erkner ball-bearing factory as their main target.

South-West Pacific The US 41st Division begins to move from Australia to Cape Cretin, New Guinea, where it is to concentrate for the attack on Hollandia.

Admiralty Islands The capture of Los Negros is virtually complete. The first American ships tie up in Seeadler Harbour without the Japanese guns being able to fire on them.

Bougainville The Japanese surprise the Americans by opening a tremendous artillery fire on the beachhead and the Piva runways, destroying one bomber and three fighters and damaging 19 more. The American bombers are immediately evacuated and transferred to New Georgia. American field guns, supported by fire from a number of destroyers and by bombers, try to locate and silence the enemy artillery. During the night of 8/9 March two Japanese companies attack the American positions in the 37th Division's defensive sector.

New Britain The 5th Marine Regiment continues its advance on Talasea, meeting with very little resistance.

Burma In the north-east a Chinese-American attack on Japanese units surrounded in the Walawbum area fails for lack of co-ordination. The Chinese-American armoured group enters Walawbum but does not get the expected infantry support and has to withdraw. On the Indian frontier the Japanese carry out a massive attack northwards towards Tiddim and Tamu. A week earlier than the British had expected, the offensive against Imphal and India has opened. The first shots are fired by three of the four divisions of the Japanese 15th Army under General Mutaguchi.

9 March

Eastern Front Troops of the 1st Ukraine front (Vatutin) reach Tarnopol, where a fierce house-to-house battle begins against von Manstein's Army Group South.

Bougainville The Japanese resume their attacks along the perimeter of the Cape Torokina beachhead and succeed in making a small break in the lines of the American 37th Division. Counter-attacks to eliminate the salient are unsuccessful. The Japanese switch their artillery fire from the Piva runways to the Torokina airfield.

Admiralty Islands An American brigade lands at Salami Plantation, Los Negros, and a squadron of US fighters arrives at Momote airfield.

Burma The Chinese-American 1st Armoured Group, with units of the Chinese 22nd and 38th Divisions, occupy Walawbum, from which the Japanese have withdrawn in good order. The occupation of Walawbum gives the Chinese control of the Hukawng valley.

10 March

Eastern Front After violent fighting the 2nd Ukraine Front takes Uman, south-west of Cherkassy, previously an important Luftwaffe base.

Bougainville The Japanese take an important feature on the perimeter of the Cape Torokina beachhead, Hill 260, and drive off repeated American counter-attacks. Elsewhere on the perimeter the Americans manage to reduce, but not to eliminate, the salient that the Japanese have won in their line.

Admiralty Islands New American aircraft arrive at Momote airfield, Los Negros. Other aircraft begin a series of attacks against Manus Island, the biggest island in the archipelago, in preparation for the landing.

☐ The Allied Joint Chiefs of Staff determine the timetable for the Pacific: 15 April, invasion of Hollandia, New Guinea; 15 June, invasion of the Marianas; 15 September, invasion of the Palau Islands; 15 November, landing on Mindanao in the Philippines; 15 February 1945, invasion of Formosa.

Burma The Japanese bomb the Chowringee landing strip in central Burma (built by the Chindits and valuable for supplying the columns operating in the enemy's rear).

11 March

Eastern Front The Russians occupy Berislav, east of Kherson.

Italian Front In the Anzio sector units of the US VI Corps begin preparations for a new offensive around the Albano road.

Bougainville Attacking the Cape Torokina beachhead the Japanese gain a little ground in the direction of the Piva airfield.

Admiralty Islands American patrols land on Manus Island to reconnoitre certain points chosen for the landing. On an islet north of Manus they fall into an ambush laid by the Japanese and only just succeed in re-embarking, after suffering heavy losses.

Burma The 7th Indian Division takes Buthidaung in the Arakan. Strong contingents of British and Indian Chindits are air-lifted into central Burma.

12 March

Bougainville The Japanese are unable to exploit the small penetration made the previous day in the direction of the Piva airfield, and have to give ground in face of the Americans' determined counter-attacks.

Admiralty Islands After a violent preliminary air bombardment, a squadron of the US 7th Cavalry goes ashore on Hauwei Island, north of Manus, and manages to establish a small beachhead there. They meet strong Japanese opposition.

Allied offensive activity is stepped up in the Far East. American bombers in action against the Japanese lines of communication in Burma.

☐ The Allied Joint Chiefs of Staff issue a directive for General MacArthur and Admiral Nimitz laying down the principles of collaboration between the two commanders, and setting as their objectives February 1945 the invasion of Luzon and Formosa. The projected invasion of Kavieng is cancelled. Instead, Emira in the St Matthias Islands will be occupied. The need to invade Hollandia, in New Guinea, is confirmed. Kavieng and Rabaul are to be neutralized and isolated with the least possible expenditure of forces.

Burma In the north-east of the country the Chinese and Americans try to surround the Japanese 18th Division, cutting the Kamaing road south of Jambu Bum Pass. In the Arakan sector the 15th Indian Division advances towards Razabil.

☐ Pope Pius XII appeals to the belligerents to spare Rome from destruction.

13 March

Eastern Front The 3rd Ukraine Front advances swiftly across the lower Dniepr. Kherson is captured and the Red Army advances towards Nikolayev.

Bougainville In an attack supported by tanks the Americans succeed in recapturing almost all the positions occupied by the Japanese since their offensive began, apart from a few which still constitute a threat to the beachhead.

Admiralty Islands The squadron of the US 7th Cavalry landed on Hauwei receives tank support and completes the capture of the island, on which a number of guns are immediately landed to shell Manus Island.

Burma The Japanese attack the 'Broadway' airstrip, used for supplying the Chindit units. Admiral Mountbatten orders aircraft to be detached from the India-China airlift to transport the 5th Indian Division to the central sector of the Arakan front, which is giving way under Japanese pressure.

14 March

Eastern Front The Russians trap a large German force near Nikolayev. 10,000 Germans are killed, and 4,000 taken prisoner.

☐ The pro-Allied Italian government (in the south) establishes diplomatic relations with the Soviet Union.

South-West Pacific Admiral Nimitz proposes to General MacArthur that aerial attacks should be carried out by his aircraft carriers on Hollandia and nearby Japanese strongpoints in New Guinea in preparation for the invasion, and promises air support for the landing and – for a limited period – also for the land operations. Rear-Admiral Wilkinson is given the task of directing operations for the capture of Emira in the St Matthias Islands.

Bougainville The Americans take steps to consolidate the positions retaken around the defensive perimeter of the Cape Torokina beachhead.

Burma The 17th Indian Division is authorized to withdraw to avoid being surrounded, but finds the road to Imphal already blocked by the Japanese.

15 March

Eastern Front The 1st Ukraine Front (Vatutin) and 2nd Ukraine Front (Konev) break through the German positions on the river Bug on a broad front to the west of Uman.

At this date the very long German front in the Soviet Union stretches from the Barents Sea, across Finland to Karelia; from the south shore of the Gulf of Finland, along the Narva and Lake Peipus, to the south, west of Vitebsk and Mogilev; then south, buttressed by the Pripet marshes, enters Poland and turns south-eastwards, following the line of the Bug (except for the salient recently opened by the Russians west of Uman) and down to the Black Sea west of Kherson. The German 17th Army has for some time been cut off in the Crimea. Thus the Wehrmacht has been driven back all the way to the line it held at the beginning of 1941, a few days after the invasion.

Italian Front In the Anzio sector the Allies have landed some 90,000 Americans and 35,000 British.

After a massive aerial bombardment of Cassino, where the Allies drop 1,400 tons of bombs, and after a violent artillery barrage, the Allies advance on the town. The New Zealand 2nd Division of General Freyberg's New Zealand Corps goes into action at 3.30 p.m., and finds that German resistance is extremely tenacious. After a short advance in which the Allies capture Height 193 the attackers are brought to a halt by the brilliant resistance of the German parachutists of the 1st Division. Towards evening the 4th Indian Division takes Height 165.

Meanwhile the Allies are preparing Operation *Strangle*, aimed at 'strangling', enemy movements in their rear areas so as to prevent supplies from reaching the front. With the return of fine weather British and American aircraft bomb and machine-gun streets, bridges, railways and stations and every form of transport used by the enemy behind the lines; all this in addition to the normal bombing of towns and factories in central north Italy. The Germans are only able to move by night, so that very few reinforcements and supplies can reach the front line.

☐ Germany. RAF bombers carry out a heavy night raid on Stuttgart.

Bougainville The Japanese renew their attacks against the American lines near the Piva runways, make a little progress, and then are driven back by an American counter-attack with tank support. The Cape Torokina beachhead in Empress Augusta Bay is not endangered, but it is certainly less secure than it was a week after the landing.

Admiralty Islands After the usual bombardment by aircraft, ships and artillery, the US 8th Cavalry Regiment of the 1st Cavalry Division, lands on the north coast of Manus Island, the largest island in the group, near Lugos Mission. The Americans take this village and converge on Lorengau airfield from two directions, along the coast and inland. On Los Negros Island units of the 5th Cavalry advance to the west in the southern part of the island.

Burma–India While in the north-east the Chinese and Americans advance to within three miles of Jambu Bum Ridge, in the north-west the Japanese 15th and 31st Divisions cross the river Chindwin in force at several points north of Tamu. The Indian Army forces are at a disadvantage.

16 March

Eastern Front In the central sector the two Belorussian Fronts attack with force, breaking through the lines of Busch's Army Group Centre north of the Pripet marshes.

Italian Front While General Freyberg's New Zealanders make determined but largely unsuccessful efforts to take Cassino and Monte Cassino, a powerful counter-attack by German parachutists of the 1st Division drives them back on to the positions they held on 14 March. Faced with this new blow, Churchill complains to Alexander, asking him if he does not think it would be better to break off the attacks against the valley in front of the abbey of Monte Cassino and concentrate on a move to get behind the enemy. 'About five of six divisions have been worn out going into these jaws,' comments the British premier sourly. In his reply Alexander attributes the Allies' lack of success entirely to the courage of the German soldiers: 'The tenacity of these German paratroops is quite remarkable ... I doubt if there are any other troops in the world who could have stood up to it and then gone on fighting with the ferocity they have.'

Admiralty Islands On Manus Island the US 8th Cavalry, with tank support, continues its advance on two centre-lines towards Lorengau airfield. As the Japanese resistance stiffens the Americans launch a heavy bombing attack during the night.

In Los Negros Island US units land without opposition at Chaporowan Point, and elsewhere the advance proceeds.

New Britain The Marines reach

A wounded New Zealander is helped back to the Allied lines after another attack on German positions at Cassino.

A partisan unit operating behind the German lines in Lithuania attends a Mass outside their barracks.

Kilu, on the east coast of the Willaumez peninsula, where they meet the Japanese defenders for the last time.

New Guinea Squadrons of the US 5th Air Force, continuing the blockade of the Japanese base at Wewak, attack a supply convoy on its way there. The Japanese withdraw all their fighters from Wewak and transfer them to Hollandia.

17 March

Eastern Front Troops of the 1st Ukraine Front advance to the south-west of Rovno, in Poland, taking the important road and rail junction of Dubno.

☐ Finland. The Finnish Government, which has recently been approached by Moscow about signing a separate peace, fails to get the guarantees from London that it asks for, and formerly rejects the proposal.

Italian Front Units of the New Zealand Corps penetrate into the eastern part of Cassino and capture the railway station, but the resistance of the German parachutists prevents them from advancing further.

Bougainville The Japanese carry out more attacks on the defensive perimeter of the Cape Torokina beachhead in the area held by the US 129th Infantry. They succeed in making a few small breaks in the American positions, but are then driven back.

Admiralty Islands On Manus Island the US 7th and 8th Cavalry take Lorengau airfield, the landing force's main objective. The airfield is considered too small for use by US aircraft and they have to build another. The Americans are engaged with the Japanese defenders on Los Negros and take some of their positions.

Burma Lord Mountbatten presses Churchill and Roosevelt to urge Chiang Kai-shek to send Chinese reinforcements into Burma.

18 March

Eastern Front Advancing into Bessarabia, the Russians reach the Rumanian frontier at Yampol, on the east bank of the Dniestr. After bitter fighting, troops of the 1st Ukraine Front capture Zhmerinka, south-west of Vinnitsa.

☐ Admiral Horthy, Regent of Hungary, is summoned to the Führer's headquarters at Rastenburg. He is arrested. The Germans are preparing to occupy Hungary.

☐ Germany. 1000 RAF bombers make devastating night raid on Frankfurt, dropping 3000 tons of bombs. A similar attack takes place four nights later.

Pacific The directives for the occupation of Hollandia, New Guinea, are issued. The American amphibian force, commanded by Commodore Reifsnider, which is to land on Emira Island (north of New Ireland, in the St Matthias group)

sails from Guadalcanal.

Admiralty Islands On Manus the Americans take the village of Lorengau with unexpected ease. On Los Negros American units advancing from the perimeter of the Papitalai Mission beachhead come up against Japanese units, which put up a determined opposition.

New Guinea The Japanese convoy attacked by American aircraft the previous day succeeds in reaching Wewak, avoiding a naval bombardment carried out against the base by a flotilla of US destroyers.

Marshall Islands A US naval squadron under command of Rear-Admiral Lee and including one aircraft carrier, two battleships and a flotilla of destroyers bombs and shells Japanese installations on the islet of Mili in the Marshall Islands.

Burma General Stilwell orders the US 5307th 'provisional unit' to block the southern entries to the Tanai valley, in the north-eastern sector.

19 March

Eastern Front In the central sector big German forces are surrounded by the Russians north of the Pripet marshes.

Troops of the 2nd Ukraine Front (Konev) reach the Dniestr on a broad front and begin to cross. North-west of Konev's forces the German strongpoint of Mogilev-Podolsky is taken by assault by Soviet divisions converging from north-east and south-east. In the Dubno region the Germans are forced to evacuate Kremenech.

☐ Hungary. German troops cross the Hungarian frontier. The surprise operation, code-named *Margarete I*, is to ensure Hungary's continued allegiance and exploit its resources, including the small oilfields.

It also looks as if Rumania is about to collapse in the face of the Russian advance and the BBC warns the Rumanian people that the hour of defeat is about to strike.

Italian Front In the Monte Cassino sector a German counter-attack fails to recapture Height 193, but the Allied advance slows down. The fighting is ferocious, although dur-

ing one episode, reminiscent of ancient chivalry, both sides agree to a two hours' truce to allow the dead and wounded to be carried off the battlefield. The Allies lend their stretchers to the Germans and give chocolate to wounded men and stretcher-bearers.

Admiralty Islands The US 8th Cavalry begins to mop up the eastern part of Manus Island.

New Guinea US destroyers repeat their shelling of the Japanese base at Wewak. After putting in at Wewak the Japanese supply convoy has put to sea again for Hollandia, but is surprised and destroyed by bombers and torpedo-aircraft of the US 5th Air Force.

Burma In the north-east sector, a detachment sent from the British and Chinese strongpoint at Fort Hertz occupies the village of Sumprabum. The US 5307th unit is ordered to block the road to Kamaing near Inkangahtawng.

In the central sector the 5th Indian Division moves, partly by train and partly by air, into the area where the Japanese pressure is strongest.

20 March

Eastern Front The Russians re-take Vinnitsa in the Ukraine. Having crossed the Dniestr north of Kishinev they push on towards the Prut, which they reach on the 28th north of Jassy.

☐ The Germans complete their occupation of Hungary.

Pacific: St Matthias Islands The 4th Marine Regiment, commanded by General Noble, lands on Emira Island, north of New Ireland. There is no Japanese garrison, and they occupy the island to turn it into a base for aircraft and small ships. This completes the series of operations called *Cartwheel*, directed towards the capture of Rabaul.

New Ireland In support of the occupation of Emira a task force commanded by Rear-Admiral Griffin and comprising four battleships, two escort carriers, and destroyers brings heavy air and naval bombardment to bear on the Japanese base at Kavieng.

Sticks of bombs rain down from Allied bombers on to the German lines facing the Anglo-American beachhead at Anzio.

21 March
Italian Front General Alexander, Commander-in-Chief of the XV Army Group, calls a conference of the commanders engaged on the *Gustav* line to consider the possibility of suspending operations immediately. General Freyberg opposes the suggestion, still convinced that his troops can break through the front at Cassino.

Admiralty Islands On Los Negros Island the US 5th and 12th Cavalry try to join up their two beachheads so that they can mop up the Japanese forces still holding out.

New Guinea Advance units of the US 32nd Division and Australian 7th Division make contact for the first time about eight miles from Yalau Plantation.

22 March
Eastern Front Units of the 3rd Ukraine Front capture Pervomaysk, north of Odessa. Despite the skill of their commanders, Army Group South (von Manstein) and Army Group A (Kleist) have suffered catastrophic losses in men and materials and have been forced to yield a lot of ground under Russian pressure.

Italian Front Further violent attacks

by the New Zealand Corps in the direction of Monte Cassino prove completely fruitless, while the price paid in casualties is very high.

Burma–India The Japanese offensive against India looks as if it may succeed. The British IV Corps, deployed west of the Chindwin to defend the Indian town of Imphal, shows signs of giving way.

The Chindits continue to carry out nuisance actions and sabotage against the Japanese in central Burma, and new units reach them by air.

23 March
Eastern Front The 1st Ukraine Front breaks through the German positions east of Tarnopol, southeast of Lvov.

Italian Front General Alexander decides to call off frontal attacks on the *Gustav* line. A new lull follows on the Cassino front while the combatants wait for better weather. Meanwhile Operation *Strangle* is launched, the air action on a huge scale to disrupt the lines of communication between central northern Italy and the front.

Pacific Allied headquarters details the US I Corps, under General

Eichelberger, to carry out the land operations against Hollandia, in New Guinea.

Bougainville The Japanese make a general attack against the Cape Torokina beachhead, but make only minimal progress in the face of the heavy barrages laid down by the American artillery.

St Matthias Islands US destroyers shell Elouae, an islet south-west of Mussau Island, where an American patrol from Emira has discovered that the Japanese have a small seaplane base.

24 March
The Germans execute 335 civilians (including many Jews) at the Ardeatine caves, near Rome, as a reprisal for an attack by partisans that resulted in the death of 32 German soldiers.

Bougainville The Japanese try to extend their penetration into the American Cape Torokina beachhead, but an American counterattack drives them back with heavy losses. This is to be the last large-scale action by the Japanese in the Solomon Islands, though sporadic skirmishes go on until May. The perimeter of the beachhead will be slightly extended.

Admiralty Islands Following a short artillery preparation a squadron of the US 5th Cavalry and one of the 12th Cavalry advance westwards, taking several hills on Los Negros Island. Here, too, this is the last engagement of any size, though the mopping up operations continue for a long time. The Japanese Imperial Headquarters has already realized that it is only possible to carry out rearguard actions along the furthest defensive perimeter of their South Pacific empire, and that the Allied threat is now to the central Pacific, where they will have to concentrate all their available forces.

Burma–India The British begin to assemble forces (the XXXIII Corps, preceded by the British 2nd Division) in the area of Kohima, north of Imphal, in India, in case the IV Corps, deployed in defence of Imphal, should give way.

A group of civilians arrested during the German round-up in Rome that followed the partisan attack in Via Rasella on 23 March 1944.

Major-General Wingate, the legendary leader of the Chindits is killed in an air crash. Brigadier Lentaigne is chosen to succeed him.

25 March

Eastern Front The 1st Ukraine Front takes Proskurov (now Khmelnitski) on the southern Bug, north-west of Vinnitsa. The Red Army has already penetrated into Galicia.

Admiralty Islands On Manus Island a massive attack by US Cavalry units supported by aircraft, artillery, tanks, bazookas and flame-throwers puts an end to resistance by the Japanese, who are virtually exterminated. Only scattered groups remain to be located and eliminated.

New Guinea Japanese air force headquarters in New Guinea are transferred from Wewak to Hollandia.

26 March

Eastern Front A large German force is surrounded by the 1st Ukraine Front (Vatutin) in the area of Tarnopol and Kamenets-Podolsky, on the northern frontier of Rumania. Russian troops reach the Prut on a 56-mile front.

Italian Front The British 8th Army takes over the sectors previously held by the French Expeditionary Corps and the New Zealand Corps. The New Zealand Corps is broken up, while the British V Corps is brought in to man the sector between Palena and the Adriatic coast.

27 March

Eastern Front The 1st Ukraine Front takes Kamenets-Podolsky. In the southern Ukraine the Russians are on the point of taking Nikolayev, only a little way from Odessa.

☐ German troops occupy Rumania by agreement with the Rumanian government.

☐ Churchill broadcasts on BBC on the war situation. He speaks of 'the panic and frenzy which prevail in Hungary, Rumania and Bulgaria' and of 'the heroic struggles of the partisans in Yugoslavia under the leadership of Marshal Tito'.

Bougainville The Japanese begin to withdraw their forces from Empress Augusta Bay.

Burma–India Local activity in the north-eastern sector. In the sector opposite Imphal two brigades of the 5th Indian Division are brought back to reinforce the British IV Corps.

28 March

Eastern Front The Germans evacuate Nikolayev, east of Odessa, which is occupied by the 3rd Ukraine Front.

Italian Front In the Anzio sector the American 34th Division replaces the 3rd Division at Cisterna.

Admiralty Islands On Los Negros Island the Americans occupy the village of Loniu. There is intensive patrol activity both on Los Negros and on Manus, with negligible Japanese opposition.

Burma In the north-eastern sector the Chinese and Americans block the Kamaing road below Shaduzup and drive off five Japanese counter-attacks.

29 March

Eastern Front The Russians capture Kolomya in Rumania, in the north-east foothills of the Carpathians.

Italian Front In the Garigliano river sector General McCreery's British X Corps is relieved by the French Expeditionary Corps under General Juin and the US II Corps, which takes up positions at the extreme left of the Allied line, on the Tyrrhenian coast.

Burma–India At General Stilwell's request Chiang Kai-shek promises to send a division to reinforce the Chinese and American troops fighting in north-east Burma. In India, in the area defended by the British IV Corps, the Japanese cut the Imphal–Kohima road near Kohima. Reinforcements are sent to the Kohima garrison.

30 March

Eastern Front In Bessarabia the divisions of the 1st Ukraine Front capture Cernauti (now Chernovtsy), in Rumania (now in the USSR).

Livid at the heavy defeats suffered by the Germans and the huge territory they have lost, the Führer replaces Field Marshal von Manstein, Commander of Army Group South (now called Army Group North Ukraine) by Field Marshal Model. Field Marshal von Kleist, Commander of Army Group A (now Army Group South Ukraine) is replaced by General Schörner. Model's position as Commander of Army Group North is taken by General Lindemann.

Admiralty Islands While mopping-up operations continue on Manus and Los Negros, operations against

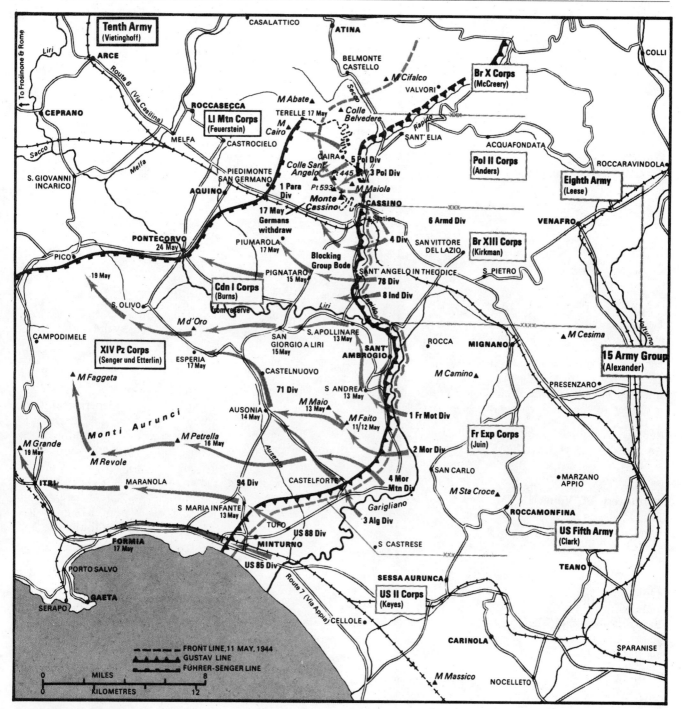

The position on the Italian Front before the Allied offensive against Cassino of 11 May 1944.

the adjacent islands begin. After a preliminary bombardment a squadron of the US 7th Cavalry lands on Pityilu, three miles north of Lugos Mission, meeting no resistance and wiping out the small Japanese garrison.

Caroline Islands Eleven aircraft carriers with appropriate escort, belonging to Task Force 58 under Admiral R. A. Spruance, (recently

promoted and appointed Commander-in-Chief of the US 5th Fleet), make a three-day attack on airfields, shipping, and military and port installations on the islands of Palau, Yap, Ulithi and Woleai in the Caroline Islands. For the first time carrier-based aircraft drop mines during a battle. Over 104,000 tons of Japanese shipping are sunk. The object of the action is not only to de-

stroy the enemy, but to protect the coming invasion of Hollandia.

New Guinea Bombers of the US 5th Air Force, escorted by long-range fighters carry out their first daylight mission over Hollandia.

Burma–India In the north-east the Chinese and Americans are under heavy pressure from the Japanese, who are determined to prevent Chinese forces from being sent

A unit of US Marines, in action on Beleu Island (Palau Islands), take up defensive positions on a newly established beachhead on the island.

across the Salween river to the Burma theatre. The Allied situation is particularly serious in the Arakan sector and before Imphal, in India, where the Japanese 15th, 31st and 33rd Divisions under General Mutaguchi are threatening both Imphal and Chittagong. The evacuation of civilians from New Delhi has begun. Some people fear that the British and Indian line may give way so that the Japanese can overrun the whole of the eastern part of the country. Mutaguchi has a contingent of nationalist Hindus serving under him, firmly on the Japanese side, with their creed of 'Asia for the Asians'.

31 March

Eastern Front The 4th Ukraine Front (Tolbukhin), pressing on Odessa, takes part of the town of Ochakov, south-west of Nikolayev.

□ Germany. During the night 800 bombers attack Nuremberg. But while the damage they do is not particularly serious, they lose at least 95 bombers and have another 71 damaged.

Admiralty Islands The squadron of the US 7th Cavalry landed on Pityilu completes mopping-up operations on the island.

New Guinea Renewed and telling bombing of Hollandia by the US 5th Air Force.

□ During a flight from Palau Island in the Caroline Islands to Davao in Mindanao Island (Philippines), the aircraft carrying Admiral Mineichi Koga, Commander-in-Chief of the Japanese air and naval forces in succession to Yamamoto, crashes on the coast of Mindanao; the Admiral is killed. Disagreements in the inner cabinet and the Imperial General Staff prevent the appointment of his successor; the announcement of the death is not made until early in May.

Burma–India Some American units are cut off by the Japanese in northeast Burma. In India, the Japanese under General Mutaguchi block the Ukhrul–Imphal road and surround the garrison at Imphal, which has to be supplied by air. The defending force is made up of three Indian divisions of the British IV Corps. In the Arakan, in the Mayu peninsula, the British 36th Division takes some tunnels on the Maungdaw–Buthidaung road, but does not manage to clear the highway completely.

1 April

Eastern Front At Skala, just northwest of Kamenets-Podolsky, the 1st Ukrainian front surrounds a large German force. By 10 April, 26,000 of the German force will be killed.

Caroline Islands Task Force 58 concludes its highly successful mission. Besides 104,000 tons of merchant shipping, the Americans have sunk two destroyers and four escort vessels and destroyed 150 aircraft in combat or on the ground, against their own losses of only 20 aircraft.

Admiralty Islands The US 12th Cavalry goes on to occupy more of the small islands in the archipelago not occupied by the Japanese.

Burma–India General Stilwell asks Chiang Kai-shek for two Chinese divisions, the 50th and the 14th, to be air-lifted to Burma. The situation in the north-east is increasingly unfavourable to the Americans and Chinese and the British and Indian troops are in increasing difficulty in the Arakan and on the Imphal plain in India.

2 April

Eastern Front The Russians cross the Prut east of Cernauti (Chernovtsy) and enter Rumania. They occupy the village of Gerca. Molotov has offered a separate peace to the Rumanians, but the occupation of their country by the Germans has made it impossible for the Rumanian government to sign such a treaty.

Burma–India A battalion of the US 5307th unit is attacked and cut off by the Japanese at Nhpum Ga. Efforts by other detachments of the unit to free it are ineffective.

Japanese troops cross the Imphal–Kohima road, isolating Imphal.

3 April

New Guinea Aircraft of the US 5th Air Force carries out the heaviest raid on the Japanese base at Hol-

landia since the offensive began. Since 30 March at least 300 Japanese aircraft have been destroyed, either on the ground or in the air. By now enemy resistance in this sector has become insignificant.

Burma–India Mountbatten urges Stilwell to go on with local offensives against the Japanese in the northeast, in spite of the serious situation in the Imphal–Kohima and Arakan areas, The capture of Myitkyina, in the north, would actually be of the first importance for the reopening, sooner or later, of the road between India and China. The Chindits will send two brigades to assist the Chinese and Americans in their offensive against Myitkyina.

Efforts by the US 5307th unit, supported by aircraft and artillery, to free the battalion surrounded by the Japanese in the Nhpum Ga area are abortive.

4 April

Eastern Front Units of the Army Group Centre (Busch), including the 4th Armoured Army, counter-attack powerfully in the central sector east of Kovel. They succeed in freeing the German forces surrounded since 19 March in the area north of the Pripet marshes by the 2nd Belorussian Front. Further south, the North Ukraine Army Group (Model) launches a number of counter-attacks in the area south-west of Tarnopol.

The German 17th Army (containing five German and seven Rumanian divisions), cut off for some time in the Crimea, prepares to withstand the thrust of the greatly superior forces of the 4th Ukraine Front (Tolbukhin). The Russians can muster about 470,000 men with 6,000 guns and mortars and 772 anti-aircraft guns, 559 tanks and self-propelled guns, and the support of 1,250 aircraft.

Burma–India The Japanese attack in force against the British IV Corps at Kohima. The British send in the few reserves they have. In the northeast sector the Japanese attack the battalion surrounded at Nhpum Ga. The Chinese 114th Regiment takes

over the task, previously assigned to the 112th Regiment, of blocking the road to the Kamaing valley.

☐ The French National Assembly and Committee of National Liberation, in special session, appoint General de Gaulle Commander-in-Chief of the French armed forces.

5 April

Rumania. The US 15th Air Force begins a series of systematic attacks against the Ploesti oilfields, dropping 588 tons of bombs. Later, on 12 May, the US 8th Air Force will join in the offensive, which is to be extended to all German oil refineries. Shortage of fuel is endangering both the Wehrmacht's mobility and the country's war production. The Germans begin to build underground factories, step up the production of synthetic fuel and split up war contracts among a great number of small firms to reduce the risk. But from the middle of 1944 war production fails to keep pace with requirements or balancing losses.

☐ US sources announce that between October 1941 and the beginning of April, 1944, the United States have supplied the USSR with 9·5 million tons of war material, including 8,800 aircraft, 5,500 tanks and armoured cars, 160,000 other vehicles and 19,000 railway trucks.

6 April

Burma–India In the north-east of Burma the 5307th unit makes slight progress in the Nhpum Ga area. On the Indian front the 7th Indian Division is air-lifted from the Arakan to the Kohima–Dimapur area to reinforce the British IV Corps.

New Guinea As a result of the tremendous air offensive of the US 5th Air Force, the air defences of the Japanese base at Hollandia can now only rely on 25 planes.

7 April

Burma–India The Japanese tighten the circle round the town of Kohima, seizing the town's main waterworks. The 17th Indian Division is deployed north of Imphal.

8 April

Eastern Front At 9.00 a.m. Tolbukhin launches the attack of the 2nd Guards Army and 51st Army against the Crimea, defended by the German 17th Army (Colonel-General Jaenicke), under the South Ukraine Army Group (Schörner). Tolbukhin strikes, with forces enormously superior to the enemy's (which number about 170,000 Germans and Rumanians), from the Perekop isthmus. The 17th Army is split in two. Troops of 1st Ukranian Front reach the Czechoslovak frontier. Soon the line will be stabilized on account of the spring thaw, while the Russian offensive in northern Bessarabia and on the Moldau will be halted and a front will be established between Stanislav and Kovel.

9 April

Admiralty Islands The Americans land on Pak Island without meeting any resistance. The last Japanese are rounded up on Manus Island.

Burma–India In north-east Burma the US 5307th unit occupies Nhpum Ga, which has been evacuated by the Japanese.

In India the Japanese complete the encirclement of the British IV Corps in the Imphal area. Its divisions can now only be supplied by air, a difficult task because of the approaching monsoon rains.

10 April

Eastern Front Odessa recaptured by the 3rd Ukraine Front. Savage fighting continues in the Crimea, where the Germans and Rumanians still manage to contain Tolbukhin's tremendous thrust.

New Guinea The embarkation of men and materials for the operation against Hollandia begins.

11 April

Eastern Front The Russians capture Kerch and Zhankoi in the Crimea.

12 April

Eastern Front Colonel-General Jaenicke, commanding the German–Rumanian 17th Army, asks Hitler, with the agreement of the Commander of the South Ukraine Army Group, General Schörner, for authority to evacuate the whole of the Crimea. His forces are now in an in-

A Russian look-out during the Red Army's counter-attack in the Crimea against the German 17th Army, April 1944.

defensible position which must end in their being wiped out. But the Führer refuses, and orders resistance to the last man. The German armies, he declares, are going to take the initiative again. Moreover, German occupation of the Crimea is an important political weapon which helps him to bring pressure on Turkey and prevent it from joining the Allies.

□ Italy. King Victor Emmanuel abdicates and his son Umberto becomes Regent. The effective transfer of power will take place when Rome is liberated.

Admiralty Islands The Americans complete the occupation of Pak Island and the mopping up of Manus Island.

Burma–India While the British try to reinforce the XXXIII and IV Corps in the Kohima–Imphal sector by airlifting troops to them from the Arakan, and from within India, the Chindits are reinforced by a new brigade from central Burma.

13 April

France The US Tactical Air Force begins to attack the German heavy guns in Normandy.

14 April

China Chiang Kai-shek, pressed by the Americans, decides to order Chinese troops to open an offensive

in Burma across the Salween river. Mountbatten recommends that the Chinese and Americans operating in the north of Burma should confine themselves to taking on as many of the enemy units as possible, their only major objective being the capture of Myitkyina. The vital issue in this sector is the reopening of the road from India to China.

15 April

Eastern Front After a siege of two months the Russians capture Tarnopol south-east of Lvov.

Italian Front The British X Corps replaces the II Polish Corps in the sector north of the *Gustav* line.

Burma–India The air lift of the Chinese 50th Division to Maingkwan is almost completed. This division will be followed by the 14th. Chiang Kai-shek orders General Stilwell to move his troops cautiously into the Mogaung valley. General Chennault warns Chiang Kai-shek against the danger, which he believes to be imminent, of a huge Japanese air offensive against China. Mountbatten's headquarters are moved from New Delhi to Kandy, in Ceylon, a precaution which shows the danger threatening India.

16 April

Eastern Front The Russians capture

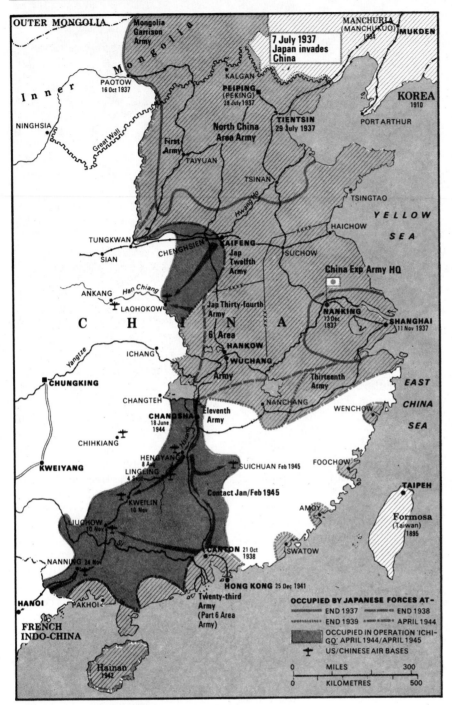

Japanese operations in China from 1937 to 1945.

Burma–India In the north-eastern sector the Chinese troops make progress along the Mogaung valley, where the Japanese have evacuated the town of Wazarup. Stilwell does not have enough forces to launch an offensive against the efficient Japanese 18th Division manning this sector. For the Allies, assuming that the situation in India does not collapse, it would be important to gain possession of Myitkyina and Mogaung. Both are on the line of the Burma Road between India and China, and the first could act as a staging-point for aircraft on the airlift between India and China, as well as being the terminus of the railway to the south of the country.

In the Imphal area the reinforced British IV Corps begins a counter-offensive against the Japanese.

18 April

Eastern Front Tolbukhin's troops occupy Balaklava, a short distance from Sevastopol.

Caroline Islands The US 13th Air Force sends the B-24 Liberators of its V Bomber Group against the Japanese base at Woleai. This is the first of a series of attacks intended to prevent any interference by Japanese aircraft with troops landing in the area of Hollandia, in New Guinea. This action shows that the Japanese bases in the southern Pacific (Solomons, New Britain, New Ireland, New Guinea) have been completely neutralized.

19 April

Indian Ocean An Allied naval squadron commanded by Admiral Somerville of the Royal Navy, consisting mostly of British ships, but also including the American aircraft carrier *Saratoga* and three US destroyers, as well as the Free French battleship *Richelieu*, bombards Japanese positions at Sabang, north of Sumatra (Dutch East Indies). This alarms the Japanese Imperial Headquarters, which thought it had eliminated the Allied naval presence from the Indian Ocean.

☐ Germany. The Allied air offensive continues. The RAF is now using the 5-ton Tallboy bomb. Sir Arthur

Yalta. The German 17th Army retreats towards Sevastopol, the fortress whose capture cost them so much blood. The 17th army leaves behind vast quantities of arms and supplies in its retreat.

Tolbukhin hurls the huge forces at his command (2nd Guards Army, 51st Army, Independent Maritime Army) against the city. Two years ago the Germans were besieging

Sevastopol, now they are the besieged.

17 April

Admiralty Islands The mopping up of the islands may be regarded as finished.

China The Japanese launch their last big offensive against Nationalist China, penetrating into the province of Honan across the Yellow River.

'GOING MY WAY'

A young priest brings a breath of fresh air to a poor neighbourhood in New York. After many clashes he even manages to win over his crusty predecessor.

Having already starred in the successful *Road to ...* series, together with Bob Hope and Dorothy Lamour, Bing Crosby gained extraordinary popularity with this film, directed for Paramount by Leo McCarey. An unctuously sentimental comedy, *Going My Way* nevertheless won a number of Oscars and launched the character of Father O'Malley, who reappeared in two other films.

Bing Crosby as Father O'Malley.

US landing craft, under fire from the Japanese, approach the beaches of Hollandia, New Guinea.

Tedder has command of all the Allied bomber forces.

20 April
Italian Front The Free French 1st Motorized Division begins to land in Naples; it is to be followed by other French forces early in May.

☐ Under persistent pressure by the Allies, Turkey stops the despatch of chrome to Germany. There exists an alliance between Britain and Turkey; seeing how the war is going, Turkey decides to respect it.

Burma–India In the north-eastern sector the Chinese 38th Division advances southwards in the Mogaung valley, towards Kamaing. It occupies Height 1725, previously held most tenaciously by rearguards of the Japanese 18th Division, which has the task of protecting the retirement of the main body on to the Wala–Malakawng line.

In India, in the XXXIII Corps sector, the British and Indian formations besieged by the Japanese at Kohima are reached by the British 2nd Division advancing from Dimapur. However, the Japanese hold on to the village and are still blocking the road to Imphal.

21 April
New Guinea A US task force commanded by Vice-Admiral Mitscher and including aircraft carriers, battleships, cruisers and destroyers brings aerial and naval bombardment to bear on the Japanese airfields and defence installations in the Hollandia area, Wadke Island, Sawar and Sarmi, destroying many enemy aircraft on the ground and meeting no air opposition worth mentioning. The attack, in preparation for the landing, goes on until the 22nd.

Burma–India The Chinese–American forces re-group to prepare an offensive against Myitkyina.

☐ General Henri Giraud resigns his post as Commander-in-Chief of French forces in North Africa.

☐ Italy. At Salerno, Marshal Pietro Badoglio sets up the first Government of National Unity, which is made up of all the parties of the Committee of National Liberation.

22 April
New Britain The last engagement of the 1st Marine Division with the Japanese.

New Guinea The 7th Amphibious Force under the American Rear-Admiral Barbey, carrying 84,000 men, supported by the aircraft and naval guns of Task Force 58 under Vice-Admiral Mitscher, puts ashore the units that will be taking part in the operation against Hollandia. The Japanese garrison in the area numbers 11,000 men of the 18th Army, under General Hatazo Adachi. The landings begin at 7.00 a.m. One regiment goes ashore at Aitape, east of Hollandia, two divisions land in Humboldt Bay and Tanahmerah Bay, south and north of

Hollandia. Stunned by the bombardment, and in line with a technique already tried out against a numerically superior enemy, the Japanese withdraw into the nearby mountains, leaving a few troops to harass the enemy during the landing phase. The Americans immediately penetrate inland as far as Pim and Jangkena (the latter about eight miles from the coast), meeting resistance only near the airfields at Sentani and Cyclops (so called by the Americans). The Japanese counter-attack by night, but to no effect.

23 April

New Guinea The Americans occupy Hollandia without opposition. They advance inland along a centre-line Pim–Lake Sentani. The beaches at Tanahmerah Bay are so congested that a convoy due the next day is redirected to Humboldt Bay. One regiment reaches the village of Sabron, and beyond that, near a stream, they meet the first organized Japanese resistance. The American commander withdraws his regiment on Sabron.

The troops landed in the Aitape area occupy Tadji airfield and push on towards Hollandia to join up with the main body.

Burma Units of the Chinese 38th Division replace the American units in the Manpin area, in the north of the country. The final attack on this place is entrusted to the Chinese 22nd Division.

24 April

Eastern Front Desperate fighting continues in the Crimea.

□ Finland rejects the peace offer recently put forward by the Russians, which demands: rupture with Germany and the expulsion of German troops; withdrawal to the 1940 frontier; the demobilization of the Finnish army; reparations of 600 million dollars, to be paid in goods over a period of five years; and the restoration of the base at Petsamo.

New Guinea Australian troops advancing west from Huon peninsula occupy Madang, which the Japanese have evacuated. In the Hol-landia area the US 186th Infantry advance as far as the shore of Lake Sentani. In the Aitape sector the landing party occupies the village of Aitape and Rohn Point.

25 April

New Guinea Reinforcements and supplies are landed in Humboldt Bay. The US 186th Infantry Regiment advances in this sector as far as Nefaar, beyond Lake Sentani. In the Aitape sector, American patrols carry out thrusts both to the east towards Wewak and to the west towards Hollandia (now called Jayapura or Sukarnapura).

26 April

New Guinea Units of the Australian 5th Division occupy Alexishafen. In the Hollandia area the US 21st Infantry, moving from Tanahmerah Bay, occupy Cyclops airfield and join up with the units that landed at Humboldt Bay.

27 April

Italian Front The Polish II Corps takes over the Monte Cassino sector from the British XIII Corps.

New Guinea In the Hollandia area the Americans consolidate their beachhead. MacArthur has already decided on new objectives for the invasion force: an offensive against Sarmi and Wadke Island on 15 May, landing on Biak Island towards the middle of June. The object is not to occupy territory but to wipe out the Japanese 18th Army.

Burma–India In upper Burma the last preparations are made for the offensive against Myitkyina and for the despatch from China, across the river Salween, of two Chinese divisions from Force Y (Yunnan Force), trained by the Americans.

In India the British IV Corps puts up a desperate resistance against the Japanese forces, waiting for the monsoon rains to come and paralyse all operations in the region. The 17th and 20th Indian Divisions, concentrated north of Imphal, are moved south of the town to block the enemy advance.

28 April

New Guinea In the Aitape area the first encounters take place between American troops and the small Japanese garrison. Some American units are transferred in an amphibious operation to Nyaparake, near the river Nigia, to hold up the advance of Japanese reinforcements sent to Aitape from Wewak.

China The Japanese offensive in Honan is stepped up. The US 14th Air Force bombs bridges over the Yellow River. The Chinese and Americans strengthen the defences of the Cheng-tu airfields, the bases from which the giant B-29 Superfortress bombers deliver their attacks against the bases in east and south China occupied by the Japanese.

Burma The Chinese and Americans open their offensive for the capture of Myitkyina. The Chinese 38th Division, attacking frontally and in turning movements, force the Japanese to withdraw slowly towards Wala.

□ Frank Knox, Secretary of State for the US Navy and one of the most powerful figures in the rebuilding of the US Navy after the catastrophe at Pearl Harbour, dies.

29 April

New Guinea American engineers reopen Hollandia and Aitape airfields with great speed.

Caroline Islands A part of Task Force 58 including 12 aircraft carriers and commanded by Vice-Admiral Mitscher, launches a series of air attacks on Truk, lasting for two days. The big Japanese base suffers a complete knock-out. Shipping, fuel and ammunition depots, airfields and other military installations are destroyed. Of the 104 Japanese aircraft on the atoll before the attack, at least 93 are shot down or destroyed on the ground. With this blow Nimitz obliterates any possible danger to the New Guinea operations.

30 April

Eastern Front While Tolbukhin still exerts pressure on Sevastopol, local

Russian offensives are reported in the area of Ostrov, south of Pskov, near the Lithuanian border.

Caroline Islands While the main attack on Truk continues, a squadron of US cruisers and destroyers under the command of Rear-Admiral Oldendorf shells enemy positions on Satawan Island, in the central Carolines.

Burma–India The Chinese-American advance on Myitkyina, in upper Burma, continues.

On the Indian front the 20th Indian Division contains the Japanese in front of Palel, a village south of Imphal, while the 5th and 23rd Indian Divisions push northwards towards Ukhrul.

1 May

Caroline Islands A detachment of battleships and aircraft carriers from Task Force 58, under the command of Vice-Admiral Lee, bombs and shells military targets on the fortified atoll of Ponape, in the eastern Carolines.

New Guinea In the Aitape beachhead the Americans occupy the village of Kamti, which the Japanese have evacuated.

2 May

Spain changes its pro-Axis political attitude, withdrawing its volunteers from the *Azul* Division on the Russian front and cutting down its monthly export of wolfram (required for hollow-charge shells) to 40 tons.

3 May

Burma In the northern sector the Chinese 22nd Division advances along the Kamaing road towards Inkangahtawng. The 64th Regiment of the same division cuts the Kamaing road a short way from the Hwelon stream.

☐ After an astonishing delay, caused by disagreement in the inner cabinet and the Imperial General Staff, Admiral Soemu Toyoda is appointed Commander-in-Chief of Japanese air and naval forces. He succeeds Admiral Mineichi Koga, who died in an air crash on Mindanao, in the Philippine Islands, on 31 March. The appointment is made public on 5 May, and Admiral Koga's death is announced at the same time. The loss of a man of such great prestige as Koga is another psychological blow for the entire Japanese armed forces following the death of the national hero, Yamamoto. Moreover Toyoda does not inspire confidence in the Japanese officers and he has had no experience of command at sea.

4 May

New Guinea No action in the Aitape sector. Since 22 April, the date of the landing, the Japanese have lost 525 dead and 25 prisoners in fighting around Aitape, the Americans about 20 dead and 40 wounded.

The famous Burma Road, built to facilitate access to the firing lines.

5 May

Eastern Front Tolbukhin launches the final attack against Sevastopol, throwing in the 51st Army, the 2nd Guards Army, and the Independent Maritime Army. Russian forces enormously outnumber the Germans and Rumanians of the 17th Army. The *Katyusha* rocket-launcher, which the Germans call the 'black death', has its customary devastating and terrifying effect on the defenders.

Admiralty Islands The US 8th Cavalry Regiment begins the last phase of the mopping up of Manus Island.

Burma–India While the Kohima–Imphal front is stabilized, in upper Burma the Chinese and Americans are fighting in the jungle against the Japanese in the area of Myitkyina.

6 May

New Guinea Rear-Admiral Barbey has advised that the start of the operation to land at Sarmi and on Wadke Island, in the north-west of New Guinea, be put back from 15 May to 21 May. MacArthur counters with a change to the original plan.

The operation against Wadke Island, from which the air forces will be able to cover the future landing on Biak Island, will take place on the original date, but the landing at Sarmi can be temporarily postponed.

Burma The Chinese and Americans attack the village of Ritpong, northeast of Kamaing, without success.

7 May

Burma The Chinese and Americans block all the ways out of Ritpong, halting an attempt by the Japanese to withdraw during the night.

New Britain Units of the US 40th Division occupy the airfield at Cape Hopkins without opposition.

8 May

Eastern Front The defences of Sevastopol crumble under the sledgehammer blows of the Russians. General Schörner, Commander of the South Ukraine Army Group, in defiance of Hitler's orders, takes responsibility for ordering naval and air forces to evacuate his forces. In fact the evacuation of the Germans and Rumanians has already begun, in secret, on the previous day. German and Rumanian naval craft succeed in taking at least 130,000 men across the Black Sea to Rumania.

☐ General Eisenhower fixes 5 June as D-Day, the date for the invasion of Normandy. Later the date has to be put back one day.

New Guinea The Americans reinforce the perimeter of their beachhead at Aitape.

Burma The Chinese and Americans shell the village of Ritpong and send in a regiment of the Chinese 30th Division to take it by assault. But the attack is repulsed. Units of the Chinese 38th Division advance on Kamaing, and others from the same division prepare to attack Warong.

9 May

Eastern Front Moscow fires 24 salvoes from 324 guns as Tolbukhin's troops capture the fortress of Sevastopol. German rearguards hold out for three days in defence of the points at which the remains of the army are embarking. The whole of the Crimea is now once more in Russian hands. There is now another lull on the Russian front. German Army Group North (Lindemann) still holds Narva and the west bank of Lake Peipus, covering the Baltic countries. Army Group Centre still occupies Vitebsk, with salients on both sides of the Dvina, and is still east of the Dniepr in the Orsha and Mogilev areas. The Germans are still 60 miles from Smolensk, as if they intended to attack Moscow. But in the south their front has collapsed. The Russians have liberated the Ukraine and penetrated into Rumania and Poland, and are now only 30 miles from Brest Litovsk. And they have reached the frontier of Czechoslovakia. They are at the foothills of the Carpathians, they have crossed the Dniestr and the Prut, they have invaded Bukovina and Bessarabia. And behind the German lines the partisans – at least 250,000 of them – are operating, supplied at night by some 200 aircraft. Hitler calls for increased war production. Boys of 18 are being drafted into the armed forces.

☐ France–Belgium. The US 8th Air Force begins a large-scale attack on French airfields, particularly those at Laon, Florennes, Thionville, St-Dizier, Juvincourt, Orléans, Bourges and Avord.

New Guinea The date for the invasion of Wadke is fixed for the 17th, the Sarmi landing for 27 May.

Burma The Japanese partly succeed in breaking out of their encirclement at Ritpong. The Chinese troops stay in the area to mop up. The 114th Regiment of the Chinese 38th Division occupies Hlagyi and Wala and prepares to join up with the 112th Regiment of the same division north of Manpin.

10 May

Italian Front Allied military commanders at Caserta put the finishing touches to the plan for the next day's offensive at Cassino. The operation is based on breaking through the enemy front on the right wing of the German 10th Army so as to be able to reach the Via Casilina. The Allies are deploying the US 5th Army on the left, with the American II Corps in the south and the French Expeditionary Corps further north covering the Tyrrhenian coast sector at the confluence of the Liri and Gari rivers. (The US 36th Division is in reserve.) On the right of the Allied line (British 8th Army) there are deployed, from south to north, the British XIII Corps (with the Canadian I Corps further to the rear), the Polish II Corps, the British X Corps and lastly, on the Adriatic coast, the British V Corps. A total of 16 Allied divisions are drawn up on the Cassino front opposite seven German divisions. Kesselring has completed the construction of a series of defensive positions along the Italian peninsula. Behind the *Gustav* line they include the *Hitler* line (later re-named the 'Senger Bolt'), the *Caesar* line (protecting Rome) and finally the *Gothic* line, the final defence to hold up the Allied advance to Florence.

Eastern Front The German High Command announces: 'The ruins of Sevastopol were evacuated in the course of a disengaging move.'

New Guinea After bombing, carried out by Australian aircraft, the American units at Nyaparake advance on the village of Marubian and take it without opposition.

Burma–India On the river Salween front, Force Y (the Yunnan Force, consisting of the Chinese 116th and 190th Divisions with American stiffening) begins to cross the river at Mengta Ferry.

On the Indian front the British IV Corps re-groups. The 23rd Indian Division is given the task of manning the Palel–Tamu road, the 20th Indian Division moves towards Ukhrul in two columns.

☐ James Forrestal succeeds the late Frank Knox as Secretary of State for the US Navy.

11 May

Italian Front At 9.05 a.m. General von Vietinghoff, Commander of the German 10th Army, reports to Field-Marshal Kesselring that all is quiet on his front, and that nothing of any consequence is happening. His corps commanders have told him that they have no reason to believe that anything special is going on. Towards evening Vietinghoff leaves Italy for Hitler's headquarters at Rastenburg, where he is given a decoration.

During the morning Churchill telegraphs to General Alexander, Commander-in-Chief of the XV Army Group: 'All our thoughts and our hopes are with you in what I trust and believe will be a decisive battle ...having for its object the destruction and ruin of the armed force of the enemy south of Rome.'

11.00 p.m.: 2,000 guns open fire simultaneously on a line from the mountains east of Cassino to the sea, pounding the German lines. At 11.45 p.m. the infantry go into the attack.

12 May

Italian Front General Juin's French Expeditionary Corps launches a weighty attack against the positions of the German 71st Infantry Division south of Sant'Ambrogio, on the upper Garigliano. At 3.00 a.m. the 4th Moroccan Sharpshooter Regiment (2nd Moroccan Division) captures Monte Faito.

Meanwhile General Anders' Polish units reach positions below the ruins of the abbey, but are driven back by the swift reaction of the German parachutists, who wreak havoc on the attacking forces. In consequence of the heavy losses suffered by his men, General Anders (Polish II Corps) is forced to withdraw his 5th Division to its start line, and Sant'Angelo hill, north of Monte Cassino, remains firmly in German hands.

New Guinea Heavy fighting continues around the American beachheads at Hollandia and Aitape. The persistent counter-attacks, carried out by men with no supplies and many of them weakened by tropical diseases, bring the Japanese no success.

Burma One of the Chinese–American units finds its advance halted when engaged by numerically superior forces near Tingkrukawng. The 113th Regiment of the Chinese 38th Division advances towards West Wala and Maran. On the river

The secret hide-out of Marshal Tito, head of the Yugoslav resistance, above the Drvar caves in Croatia.

Salween front the Chinese 198th Regiment attacks the Japanese forces manning Mamien Pass. The Chinese 36th Division attacks Japanese positions east of Tatangtzu Pass and is driven back to the river Salween by a night counter-attack.

☐ The Swedish Defence Staff announces an investigation is being made into a mysterious 'flying torpedo' which has crashed at Brösarp, flying from Bornholm (40 miles away) where the Germans are conducting 'secret weapon' experiments.

Italy, May 1944. From left to right: Generals de Gaulle, de Monsabert, Juin and de Lattre de Tassigny confer with one another.

13 May

Italian Front The 4th Division (British XIII Corps) succeeds in broadening its bridgehead on the north bank of the river Rapido in the face of bitter enemy resistance.

In the sector of General Juin's French Expeditionary Corps, the 2nd Moroccan Division captures Monte Girofano and Monte Maio, destroying the southern hinge of the Cassino line and opening the road to Rome. By the evening the 1st Moroccan Division reaches the Liri (to the north). In the sector of Sant'Apollinare village the left wing German 71st Division suddenly gives way, and the French also gain some ground in the south.

The 4th Moroccan Division and 3rd Algerian Division have broken through the *Gustav* line, taking Castelforte and Damiano and, later on, Monte Ceschito.

In the southern sector the American 88th Division (US II Corps) captures Santa Maria Infante.

Repeated attacks against Monte Cassino by General Anders' Polish forces during the night are skilfully repulsed by the 2nd Battalion of the 3rd Regiment of the German 1st Parachute Division.

Burma Having unsuccessfully tried to take Tingkrukawng by a frontal attack and an attack on the flank, the Chinese and Americans push on to by-pass the Japanese positions. On the river Salween front the Japanese succeed in almost wiping out a Chinese battalion, but the situation is restored when reinforcements are despatched, and the Japanese have to withdraw. Fresh Chinese regiments cross the Salween and recapture the positions lost on Tatangtzu Pass.

14 May

Italian Front The 78th Division (British XIII Corps) succeeds in crossing the river Rapido near Sant'Angelo in Theodice and in establishing and consolidating a bridgehead across the river.

12,000 men, Moroccans and elements of the 4th Mountain Division under command of General Guillaume (French Corps) attack towards Monte Petrella, in the Aurunci mountains.

New Guinea The Americans evacuate by sea some units which the Japanese have managed to cut off.

New Britain The Japanese, after holding up the American efforts to extend their beachheads for so long, retire on Rabaul. 5,000 men of the 65th Brigade are dead and 500 (an enormous figure in view of the Japanese standards and their code of honour) have been taken prisoner.

15 May

Italian Front The British 78th Division (XIII Corps) reaches the Cassino-Pignataro road, while further south the French 1st Motorized Division enters San Giorgio on the Liri.

Burma The Chinese and Americans reach the upper reaches of the river Namkwi, 15 miles from Myitkyina.

☐ France. The Consultative Assembly asks the French National Liberation Committee to become the government of the Republic.

☐ German measures against Jews reach a crescendo. During the next 12 days 62 railway trucks, laden with Jewish children, are sent from Hungary to death-camps in Poland. Atrocities against Jews take place in every German-held territory throughout Europe.

16 May

Italian Front In the southern sector of the *Gustav* line the American 88th and 85th Divisions (US II Corps) pursue the units of the German 94th Division, retiring north-west; the regiments of the 85th Division advance along the coast in the direction of Formia, along Highway No. 7, while the units of the 88th Division move towards Itri.

On the right of the II Corps sector, the French Moroccan units under General Guillaume occupy in rapid succession Monte Petrella and Monte Revole in the Aurunci mountains. South of Cassino General Burns' I Canadian Corps, brought up out of reserve, attacks towards Pontecorvo on the *Senger* line. A little further north, the British 78th

Division (XIII Corps) advances in the direction of Piumarola. The Polish II Corps renews its attacks towards Monte Cassino after re-grouping and reinforcement.

New Guinea Task Force *Tornado* sails from the area of Hollandia for the occupation of Wadke Island. The consolidation of the beachheads goes on. The new leap forward has cost the Allies 1,060 dead and 4,000 wounded. 9,000 Japanese have been killed and at least 650 taken prisoner.

Burma The Chinese-American force operating in upper Burma crosses the river Namkwi. All the inhabitants of the village of the same name have been temporarily sent to an internment camp to ensure the maximum possible security. On the river Salween front a regiment of the Chinese 190th Division reaches the Shweli valley near Laokai after crossing a ridge of mountains. The rest of the division is still held up by Japanese strongpoints on the Mamien Pass. Further south, in a sector which the Japanese have left undefended in order to reinforce their garrisons in the Shweli valley, units of the Chinese 76th and 88th Divisions approach Pingka after occupying 13 places to the north-east of it.

Burmese guerrillas occupy Washang for a time, a town about 30 miles east of Myitkyina.

Bougainville Skirmishing between the rearguards of the retiring Japanese and American advance units. What remains of the Japanese 18th Army, under General Yakutake drag themselves back across the jungle in the hope of finding refuge on Buka Island, north of Bougainville.

17 May

Italian Front The US 85th Division (American II Corps) has got as far as Formia, while on the right some units of the 88th Division approach Maranola and others move towards Monte Grande.

In the French sector the Algerians of the French Expeditionary Corps take Esperia, which the Germans have abandoned, but suddenly run into fierce resistance on the road that runs from Esperia towards Sant' Olivo. Some French units push on towards Monte Oro, a little north of Esperia, which overlooks the *Senger* line. The French 1st Motorized Division continues its advance along the south bank of the river Liri, but is halted by fire from the enemy dug in on Monte Oro, and by mines. With the capture of Monte Faggeta by the Moroccan 4th Motorized Division, the French Expeditionary Corps controls the Itri–Pico road, the highway used by the German XIV Armoured Corps for supplies. Kesselring, fearing that communication with his rear areas may be cut, orders a withdrawal.

In the Cassino sector the divisions of the Polish II Corps take Sant' Angelo hill, north of Monte Cassino. During the night the German parachutists begin to withdraw from Monte Cassino; the many breaches in the *Gustav* line by the Allied forces south of Cassino have made their position indefensible.

New Guinea Task Force *Tornado* begins the preliminary phases of the operations against Wadke Island, landing a regiment of infantry near Arare, on the coast of Dutch New Guinea, opposite the island. The landing has been preceded by a powerful naval bombardment. Following a technique already tried out on many occasions, guns have been landed and carry out a systematic hammering of the main objectives. Other units occupy the islet of Insumanai, not manned by the Japanese.

Burma The Chinese and American forces take Myitkyina airfield in a surprise attack. A battalion of Marauders occupies the village of Pamati, a crossing-place on the Irrawaddy river. A number of Chinese units are sent by air from Ledo, in India, to take part in the attack on Myitkyina town.

Dutch East Indies Carrier-based aircraft of the British Far Eastern Fleet bomb the Japanese base at Surabaya, in Java. During the night B-24 Liberator bombers carry on the attack from bases in the South-West

JEAN-PAUL SARTRE

Jean-Paul Sartre, one of the major exponents of French existentialism, wrote that war leaves men stripped of their illusions, abandoned to their own devices and more than ever persuaded that they can rely only on themselves.

During the war years, with the publication of his philosophical essay *L'Être et le Néant* (1943) and the plays *Les Mouches* (1943) and *Huis Clos* (1944), Sartre outlined the fundamental aspects of his thinking, destined to influence the post-war generation.

War sweeps away all myths, all transcendent criteria, yet the anguish it causes should not be allowed to sink into desperation: man must become master of his destiny in order to attain freedom.

Pacific, devastating the base depots.

18 May

Italian Front In the Monte Cassino sector the Polish 12th *Podolski* Regiment takes the ruins of the abbey by assault. At 10.30 a.m. the Polish flag flies from what remains of the Benedictine monastery.

South-West of Monte Cassino itself General Burns' I Canadian Corps stands before the *Senger* line, or 'Senger Bolt' (formerly the *Hitler* line), a series of fortified positions on the line Piedimonte–Aquino–Pontecorvo. The French advance in the direction of Pico is meeting with strong opposition.

Admiralty Islands The headquarters of the 6th Army officially announces the end of the campaign for the capture of the islands. The figures for men lost in the fighting supplied by the American authorities are as follows: Japanese, 3,820 dead and 75 prisoners; Americans, 326 dead, 1,189 wounded, 4 missing.

New Guinea After a powerful air and artillery preparation, units of the US 163rd Infantry land on Insoemoar Island, where Wadke airfield is sited, taking the greater part of it before evening and driving off the Japanese counter-attacks during the following night.

Burma In the Myitkyina area the Chinese and Americans defend the airfield against Japanese counter-attacks, while units of the Chinese 30th and 50th Divisions begin the assault on the city and capture the railway station.

19 May

Italian Front In the extreme southern sector of the front, on the Tyrrhenian coast, units of the US 85th Division (II Corps) reach Gaeta, abandoned by the Germans; not much more than 45 miles now separate the forces of the US II Corps from the perimeter of the Anzio beachhead.

Further north, still opposite the *Gustav* line, the 88th Division – the other formation in the US II Corps – reaches Monte Grande. The French Expeditionary Corps are near Pico after having reached and by-passed Campodimele.

New Guinea Japanese resistance on Insoemoar weakens. The last defenders retire to the north-eastern end of the island, and the occupying forces begin work on re-opening the airfield.

Burma The Japanese garrison in

Myitkyina is partly surrounded by the Chinese and Americans, who occupy several positions south and north of the town. The Chinese 38th Division, having obtained Chiang Kai-shek's authority, advances towards Kamaing and Mogaung, important road junctions.

20 May

Italian Front Units of the American 88th Division (II Corps) pass Fondi and make for Monte Passignano. While the French reach Pico, the Polish II Corps opens the battle for Piedimonte San Germano.

General von Senger und Etterlin, commanding the German XIV Armoured Corps, replaces the 71st Infantry Division, already decimated by the attacks of the French Corps, by a fresh formation, the 26th Armoured Division.

New Guinea Task Force *Tornado* completes the occupation of Wadke Island, the near-by islets and the tract of the coast of New Guinea opposite. The 800 men of the Japanese garrison have been wiped out; the American losses amount to 53 dead and 139 wounded. On the mainland the Japanese try a counter-attack against the beachhead, but are driven off.

Marcus Island A task force of aircraft carriers from the 5th Fleet, under the command of Rear-Admiral Montgomery, attacks military targets for the second day running.

21 May

Italian Front An infantry battalion of the US 85th Division (II Corps) embarks at Gaeta for a landing further up the coast, at Sperlonga meeting no opposition. The American 88th Division captures Monte Calvo and Cima del Monte, while the French positions have to withstand fierce German pressure.

General Clark, Commander of the US 5th Army, orders General Truscott, commanding the US VI Corps, dug in on the Anzio beachhead, to launch his attack against the German positions at 6.30 a.m. on 23 May. The British 8th Army will attack in force simultaneously from the north to breach the *Senger* line and pene-

trate into the valley of the river Liri.

☐ *France–Germany.* Operation *Chattanooga Choo-Choo* begins, the systematic attack by Allied aircraft on trains in Germany and France.

New Guinea The airfield at Wadke is re-opened. A regimental combat group drawn from the reserve is landed on the mainland near Arare.

Burma The Japanese counterattack; a battalion of American Marauders repulses enemy attacks along the Mogaung road, but is then halted by the Japanese when it tries to advance.

22 May

Italian Front In the Anzio and 8th Army sectors there is preliminary activity in advance of the general attack of 23 May. Meanwhile, as the *Senger* line crumbles in the French Corps sector, Kesselring makes systematic plans for the withdrawal of General Vietinghoff's 10th Army from the Liri valley across Valmontone and Palestrina.

New Guinea In view of the ease with which Wadke and the coast opposite have been occupied, General Krueger, Commander of the US 6th Army, orders Task Force *Tornado* to extend its objectives, and advance along the coast towards Sarmi, the Japanese base whose capture had been postponed. In the Aitape sector

the landing force, trying to extend its perimeter, meets unexpected resistance.

India The Japanese offensive against Imphal and Kohima slows down, while the British and Indian forces are reinforced daily.

23 May

Italian Front The general offensive in the Anzio area and against the *Senger* line opens. In the Anzio perimeter at first light more than 500 Allied guns open fire on the units of Mackensen's 14th Army, while 60 light bombers raid Cisterna to prepare the ground for the attack by the American divisions of the VI Corps. At the end of the bombardment the 45th, 3rd and 1st Armoured Divisions of the VI Corps go forward from north to south. Despite the violence of the Allied attack and the simultaneous attack from the north, the German line holds firm. The Americans reach the Cisterna–Rome railway line and take about 1,500 prisoners, but their losses are extremely high (the 3rd Division alone has 950 dead, wounded and missing). Meanwhile, on the Tyrrhenian coast, the units of the American 85th Division (II Corps) advance as far as the suburbs of Terracina.

In the British 8th Army sector under General Leese, the Canadian I Corps

Northern Burma: two scouts of a Chinese armoured column advance towards Ledo, to join up with the American forces.

pushes forward to the Aquino–Pontecorvo road, breaching the *Senger* line. The Canadian 5th Armoured Division bursts through the corridor.

New Guinea American units advance from the Tor estuary towards Sarmi but are halted by the Japanese defenders only a short way from their start line, and heavily engaged. In the Aitape beachhead sector the Japanese succeed in forcing some US units back to Tadji, where the airfield is situated.

24 May

Italian Front Heavy fighting around the Anzio beachhead continues and also along the length of the *Senger* line. In the Anzio sector the Germans retain possession of Cisterna but the American 1st Armoured Division succeeds in reaching Highway No. 7 north of Latina. The Allies thus have a salient between the German 10th and 14th Armies. Hitler authorizes Kesselring to withdraw his armies (Group C) on to the *Caesar* line, a defensive line which starts from the Tyrrhenian coast about half-way between Anzio and the Ostia lido and reaches the Adriatic in the area of Pescara, touching Albano, Popoli and Chieti. To slow down the Allies' movement as much as possible (though it is already cautious enough) the Germans carry out effective rearguard actions, in which the *Hermann Goering* Armoured Division plays a major part, enabling von Vietinghoff's forces to withdraw successfully.

On the Tyrrhenian coast the American 85th Division (II Corps) captures Terracina, from which the Germans have already retired.

In the northern sector of the front (British 8th Army), units of the Canadian I Corps take Pontecorvo in the morning, putting pressure on the Germans in the fortified positions north of Aquino. Meanwhile the Canadian 5th Armoured Division reaches the Melfa river and establishes a bridgehead on the north bank during the night.

Pacific Aircraft taking off from a group of aircraft carriers under the orders of Rear-Admiral Montgomery bomb Japanese installations on Wake Island. The day before a squadron of US destroyers had shelled the enemy fortifications on Wotje atoll. By now the Americans have mastery of the Pacific. Not a day passes in which their air and naval forces do not strike some point of the 'sphere of common prosperity'. Admiral Toyoda, inexperienced in battle but a good administrator, is planning to reorganize the Japanese naval air forces very much on the lines of the American task forces, and is getting ready to parry the next American move, which will almost certainly be the capture of the Marianas. If the Americans are successful in this new task they will have opened the way to the Philippines, and indeed to the very home islands of Japan. To avoid this danger he works out a plan, code-named *A-Go*, with the following objects: to attract the American fleet into the Marianas–Palau–Carolines sector and destroy it there by joint action by the whole fleet and all available land-based and carrier-based aircraft. If in spite of this action the enemy succeeds in carrying out the landing in the Marianas, they will find themselves facing very large Japanese forces. The big group of task forces, including almost the whole of the Imperial Fleet, is put under command of Vice-Admiral Ozawa. Nine aircraft carriers, with a powerful escort of battleships, cruisers and destroyers, are assembled in the roadstead at Tawi-Tawi in the Sulu Islands, the southernmost of the Philippines. The 1st Air Fleet, which completes the line-up, deploys its 540 aircraft on many different islands, from Chichi Jima in the north to Biak, off the north coast of Dutch New Guinea, in the south. 172 aircraft are stationed on the Marianas.

New Guinea Employing armoured cars and flamethrowers, the US 158th Combat Group gradually opens up a road west from the Arare beachhead towards Sarmi, and reaches the river Tirfoam.

In the Aitape beachhead the Americans in the Nyaparake sector withdraw to a new line.

Burma–China The Japanese 18th Division counter-attacks strongly and drives the Chinese–American forces out of Charpate to open the road north to Myitkyina.

On the river Salween front the Chinese carry out an ineffective frontal attack against a ridge enclosing the Pingka valley to the south-east.

25 May

Italian Front The US II Corps, going up the Tyrrhenian coast, joins up with the US VI Corps, which has

German soldiers surrender in the Anzio sector after the decisive Allied offensive of 23 May 1944.

Top: a flotilla of German motor torpedo-boats patrols the Atlantic coast of France in readiness for the Allied landing.

meanwhile broken through the German ring closing in the Allied forces in the Anzio beachhead. (The VI Corps is deployed in the coastal sector, taking the place of the II Corps, which remains on the left flank of the French.) The 3rd Division captures Cisterna and Cori, while the American 1st Armoured Division pushes on towards Velletri. With a front so broad and so firmly held, there are two things that General Clark, commander of the US 5th Army, can do: make straight for Rome and reap the glory and prestige of capturing the city, which would have outstanding propaganda value, or else move all his forces east as quickly as possible to trap Vietinghoff's German 10th Army. From the military and strategic aspect the second alternative would probably mean the end of the war in Italy. But Clark finds the attraction of Rome irresistible.

In the 8th Army sector the Allied advance progresses swiftly, since the Germans are falling back. While the British 78th Division takes Aquino, units of the British X Corps capture Monte Cairo and the divisions of General Anders' Polish II Corps enter Piedimonte San Germano. The British XIII Corps reaches the river Melfa.

New Guinea The Americans, after

hard fighting, succeed in crossing the river Tirfoam. Meanwhile the huge Tast Force *Hurricane*, with 12,000 men for the operations against Biak, sails from Humboldt Bay.

Burma–China In the northern sector the 3rd Indian Division begins to withdraw, abandoning some road and rail blocks. General Stilwell protests, for he wants the supply routes from the south to Myitkyina blocked. The Chinese 38th Division succeeds in cutting the Kamaing road at Seton, arousing furious Japanese reaction. On the river Salween front, the Chinese succeed in forcing the Japanese from the Tatangtzu Pass.

26 May

Italian Front The Allied advance continues on the whole front despite growing German resistance. While the 45th and 34th Divisions (American VI Corps) on the left flank advance along the line from Campoleone station to Lanuvio, the 1st Armoured Division tries unsuccessfully to get to Velletri over impossible terrain. In the US II Corps sector the 85th Division strengthens its positions west of Priverno. During the night advance units of the 88th Division (US II Corps) advance from the Roccasecca sector to cross the

Amaseno valley, only about twenty miles from Frosinone.

Burma In the northern sector the Japanese 18th Division recaptures the village of Namkwi in the Myitkyina area.

On the Salween front the Chinese troops of 'Force Y' are short of supplies.

27 May

Italian Front The US 3rd Division (VI Corps) takes Artena and drives off several German counter-attacks. While units of the 88th Division (US II Corps) reach Roccagorga, further north the French capture Amaseno, Castro dei Volsci and Monte Siserno.

In the 8th Army sector units of the Canadian I Corps cross the river Liri and occupy Ceprano. The 6th Armoured Division (General Kirkman's British XIII Corps), supported by the 8th Indian Division, continues its attacks to reach Arce.

New Guinea An invasion force of 12,000 men, mostly made up of the US 41st Infantry Division and escorted by a squadron of cruisers under Rear-Admiral Fechteler, goes ashore after a preliminary air and naval bombardment on Biak Island, 150 miles north-west of Wadke in the big Geelvink Bay. The first units land in the area of Bosnek. Command of the land operations is assumed by General Fuller, the divisional commander. The Japanese garrison puts up very little resistance and the reaction from the air is no greater. The Americans therefore feel optimistic – but they are wrong; the Japanese have an experienced garrison of 11,000 men on the island.

In the Wadke–Sarmi area the US 158th Infantry (formerly called the combat group) progresses very slowly, winning a few positions. The Japanese launch a series of attacks against the perimeter of the beachhead during the night. They attack at least 200 times along the whole perimeter, but are repulsed.

Burma–China In the Myitkyina area two Chinese-American battalions are engaged in hard fighting with Japanese units south of Charpate, trying to get to Radhapur. They do not reach their objective and suffer heavy losses.

On the river Salween front Chinese troops get within five miles of Hongmoshu. The monsoon rains limit operations by both sides.

The Japanese advance with two divisions in the region east of the Hsiang river, in south China.

28 May

Italian Front Bitter fighting continues along the whole front. In the southern sector the VI Corps meets with growing resistance by the German forces. However, the advance of the French Corps over the Monti Lepini continues.

During the night the Germans withdraw from Arce, leaving it to the British XIII Corps.

New Guinea While the US 186th Infantry extends the beachhead, the 162nd advances westwards towards the Biak Island airfields. West of the village of Mokmer, which has an airfield nearby, the Japanese counterattack with great force, cutting one American battalion in two and inflicting heavy losses. Recognizing that the position cannot be held, General Fuller orders the unit to withdraw and wait for reinforcements.

In the zone of Wadke-Sarmi, too, the American advance points have to retire because of Japanese pressure.

Burma–China On the river Salween front General Wei decides to send the Chinese 71st Army (which includes the 88th Division, already west of the Salween) across the river, already swollen by the monsoon rains, to capture the town of Lungling.

29 May

Italian Front The US 1st Armoured Division (VI Corps) attacks on the Albano road and about midday takes Campoleone station. But it is then slowed down by the determined opposition of the German 1st Parachute Corps. German resistance also continues to be firm where the American 34th Division is operating in the Lanuvio sector.

Above: German infantry training at La Rochelle to meet the expected Allied invasion.

In the British 8th Army sector the Canadian I Corps begins to advance from Ceprano towards Frosinone.

New Guinea On Biak a tank battle develops – the first in the Pacific. The Japanese force the 162nd Infantry back almost as far as their landing point near Bosnek. General Krueger orders two battalions of the 163rd Infantry to be transported to Biak, even though the Arare-Toem beachhead on the mainland is still threatened by the Japanese.

Burma–China The Chinese supply situation on the Salween front improves with the repair of a small bridge over the river. It is soon found that the volume of traffic that can cross by this bridge is insufficient, and the Chinese have to ask for supplies to be air-lifted.

General Chennault asks for an increase in supplies for the US 14th Air Force to oppose the Japanese threat to vital Chinese positions in eastern China.

30 May

Eastern Front A long lull on the whole front is broken by powerful German attacks on Konev's Front in Rumania.

Italian Front In the US 5th Army sector the Germans hold their positions between Albano and Velletri in spite of repeated attacks by the numerically superior Allied forces. Further north the Canadian I Corps continues its advance towards Frosinone.

New Guinea Minor skirmishes on Biak, where the Americans are regrouping. In the Wadke–Sarmi area the US 158th Infantry establishes a new defensive line along the river Tirfoam. Japanese night attacks along the perimeter of the Arare mainland beachhead, opposite Biak.

31 May

Eastern Front The Germans continue their attacks in Rumania, throwing in strong tank, infantry and air forces.

Italian Front The American VI and II Corps receive orders to mount an offensive against the Alban Hills. Albano still holds out against attacks by units of the US VI Corps. The 85th Division (II Corps) captures Lariano and reaches positions across the road linking Velletri with Artena. In the 8th Army sector, the Canadian I Corps enters Frosinone, while the X Corps takes Sora.

New Guinea In the Wadke-Sarmi area the Americans reduce their defensive perimeter to have a greater concentration of fire, but still keep a small bridgehead over the river Tor. In the Hollandia-Aitape area there is considerable patrol activity by the

Japanese.
Burma–China Air drops of supplies begin to the Chinese divisions across the river Salween.

1 June

Italian Front Allied troops continue to put pressure on the German 14th Army, which holds out both in the Albano sector and near Lanuvio. South of the Alban Hills the 141st Regiment of the US 36th Division takes Velletri after a hard struggle, and the II Corps opens the final offensive towards Rome, making for Highway 6; on the left flank the 85th Division attacks Monte Ceraso, meeting strong resistance.

On the right flank of the US II Corps, the American 3rd Division launches an offensive towards the north, in the direction of Valmontone.

With the *Gustav* line breached, Field-Marshal Kesselring, Commander-in-Chief of the Army Group C, orders the 10th and 14th Armies to carry out a fighting withdrawal to the *Gothic* line. This fortified line crosses Italy from the Ligurian Sea (between La Spezia and Viareggio) as far as the Adriatic, just above Pesaro, passing north of Lucca and Pistoia and then turning south of San Marino before finally continuing northwards to Pesaro.

New Guinea On Biak Island the Americans resume the offensive to break out of their beleaguered beachhead. The 163rd Infantry Regiment remains to man the beachhead, while the 186th, supported by artillery and tanks, moves north towards the plateau in the centre of the island, repulsing several vigorous Japanese counter-attacks from north and south. Units of the 162nd Infantry move out from another small beachhead across the jungle towards the central plateau to join up with the 186th Regiment. The Japanese cut the main coast road.

In the Aitape area the Japanese force the 1st battalion of the US 126th Infantry back slightly.

Burma–China On the northern front the Chinese 22nd Division overcomes Japanese resistance and cuts the Kamaing road, in the Mogaung valley, at several places south-east of Nanyaseik, above Kamaing. Since the Chinese 38th Division is already blocking the road at Seton, below Kamaing, there is a serious threat to the Japanese garrison in that town. American reinforcements are sent urgently to the Myitkyina area.

The monsoon slows down operations. The Allied supply situation in the area is difficult for the Americans have rations for only 24 hours, the Chinese for two days.

On the Salween front units of two Chinese divisions reach the Shweli valley from Tatangtzu Pass and join up with a regiment of the Chinese 198th Division coming from Mamien Pass. The Japanese withdraw some units from the upper Shweli valley to reinforce the line at Lungling, further south. Two regiments of the Chinese 9th Division cross the Salween. After hesitating so long, Chiang Kai-shek has finally decided to send adequate forces to Burma.

2 June

Italian Front As the German forces gradually disengage, the Allies advance on the whole front from the Albano sector to the Lanuvio, from the heights east of the Monti Cavi to Highway 7 (US VI Corps).

In the US II Corps sector, units of the 85th Division capture Maschio d'Ariano, Monte Fiore and Monte Ceraso, pushing on as far as Highway 6, though this is 'cut' beyond San Cesareo by troops of the 88th Division. The 7th and 30th Regiments (US 3rd Division) continue to advance in the Palestrina and Valmontone areas – the latter recently abandoned by the Germans.

South-East Asia The British and American Chiefs of Staff reach a compromise agreement on the strategy to be followed in South-East Asia. The airlift between India and China is to be further strengthened so as to play a part in the Pacific operations as well as in China. Land operations are to be undertaken and maintained to the extent that they can help to increase the volume of supplies from India to China; to this end the capture of the Myitkyina area in northern Burma and the reopening of the land route from India to Burma, including the construction of an oil pipeline into China, are of the first importance.

New Guinea On Biak the 186th In-

A heavy artillery emplacement erected by the Todt organization on the Atlantic coast in anticipation of the Allied invasion.

fantry attacks westward along the edge of the internal plateau towards the airfields. The capture of the airfields is considered essential, not only for their future use as bases but because Japanese aircraft can use them to make strikes on Wadke airfield, where a number of American aircraft have already been destroyed. The battalion of the US 162nd Infantry that has succeeded in joining up with the 186th Regiment is integrated in the latter. In the coastal sector the other battalions of the 162nd block a track that leads to the interior and force the Japanese out of one of their positions.

Burma–China–India The final siege of the Japanese garrison in Myitkyina begins. The Chinese dig tunnels to get inside the enemy lines. On the Salween river front the Chinese 36th Division captures the village of Kaitou and surrounds Chiaotou, in the valley of the Shweli. On the Arakan front the Indian divisions have re-established contact and resumed the initiative against the Japanese, advancing towards Akyab. On the Indian front, where there is bloody fighting around Imphal, the British–Indian forces can now call on 100,000 effectives. The 7th Indian Division, brought back from the Arakan, succeeds in breaking through the lines of the Japanese 31st Division north of Kohima. The Japanese begin to withdraw slowly.

3 June

Eastern Front Heavy fighting continues to rage on the Rumanian front, but the Germans can make little headway against fierce Russian resistance.

Italian Front The Allied advance continues along the whole front. Albano, Lanuvio and Frascati are among towns to fall, while units of the American 3rd Division and the French Expeditionary Corps advance along Highway 6. In the British 8th Army sector the Canadian I Corps reaches Anagni. Hitler authorizes Kesselring to withdraw from Rome. The disengagement operation has already been in progress for some time;

according to Kesselring's plan, fighting south and south-east of Rome must be kept up as long as possible to allow the troops stationed in the city to be evacuated, and particularly to let the 14th Army retire beyond the Tiber. The operation is successful. Moreover, respecting the status of 'open city' proclaimed for Rome since 13 August 1943, and also in accord with an agreement made with the Resistance, the troops on leaving the city do not blow up the bridges over the Tiber nor any other buildings. In exchange, the partisans do not harass the retiring troops.

☐ France. The French Committee of National Liberation proclaims itself the provisional government of the Republic.

New Guinea The US 186th Infantry Regiment continues to move west on a broad front, held up more by the nature of the terrain than by the enemy. The 162nd Regiment, also advancing westwards, is halted by the Japanese manning the Ibdi area. The Americans decide that they must eliminate this pocket before continuing the advance.

Burma The Chinese and American forces of the 42nd, 150th and 89th Regiments launch an assault on the

Japanese positions, but are driven back with heavy losses, especially to the Americans.

4 June

Italian Front The US 9th Army captures Rome. As the last German rearguards are leaving the capital, General Clark's first units enter the suburbs in the south. At 7.15 p.m. the American 88th Division reaches the Piazza Venezia.

New Guinea Preparations begin for the invasion of Noemfoor, or Numfoor Island, west of Biak, between Biak and the peninsula that forms the north-west extremity of New Guinea. There are three airfields on Numfoor that can be used as jumping-off places against the central Pacific and also to control the sea routes west of Biak.

Burma–China–India On the river Salween front, Chinese artillery silences the Japanese batteries shelling Huei-jen bridge. The Chinese 87th and 88th Divisions converge on Lungling. The Chinese 28th Division, only recently formed, occupies the village of Lameng and engages the Japanese garrison of Sung Shan. In the Imphal area the 20th Indian Division advances north

Units of American infantry go ashore on an island in the Philippines; in the background a dense column of smoke shows how fires are spreading over the island.

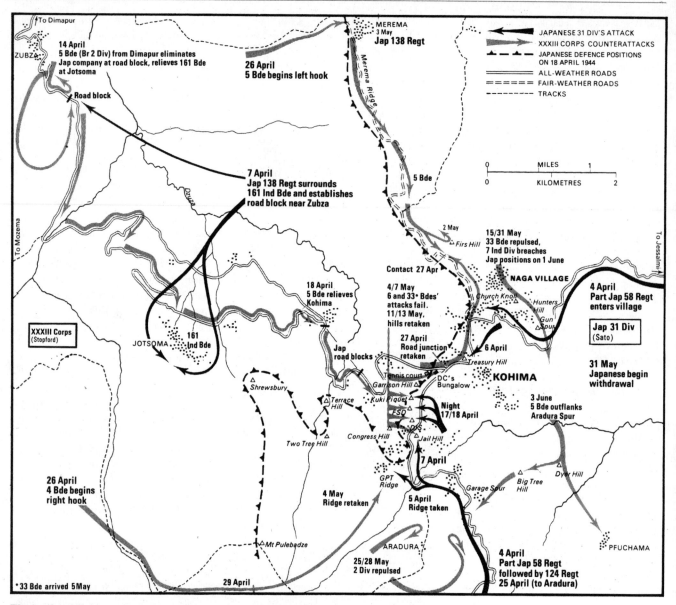

To Dimapur

14 April
5 Bde (Br 2 Div) from Dimapur eliminates
Jap company at road block, relieves 161 Bde
at Jotsoma

ZUBZA

Road block

To Mozema

7 April
Jap 138 Regt surrounds
161 Ind Bde and establishes
road block near Zubza

MEREMA
3 May
Jap 138 Regt

26 April
5 Bde begins left hook

JAPANESE 31 DIV'S ATTACK
XXXIII CORPS COUNTERATTACKS
JAPANESE DEFENCE POSITIONS
ON 18 APRIL 1944
ALL-WEATHER ROADS
FAIR-WEATHER ROADS
TRACKS

Merema Ridge

5 Bde

0   MILES   1
0   KILOMETRES   2

2 May
Firs Hill

15/31 May
33 Bde repulsed,
7 Ind Div breaches
Jap positions on 1 June

Contact 27 Apr

NAGA VILLAGE

4 April
Part Jap 58 Regt
enters village

XXXIII Corps
(Stopford)

18 April
5 Bde relieves
Kohima

JOTSOMA

161
Ind Bde

Jap
road blocks

4/7 May
6 and 33* Bdes'
attacks fail.
11/13 May,
hills retaken

Church Knoll
Hunters
Hill
Gun
Spur

27 April
Road junction
retaken

6 April

Jap 31 Div
(Sato)

Shrewsbury

Terrace
Hill

Tennis court
Garrison Hill
Kuki Piquet
FSD
DIS

DC's
Bungalow

Treasury Hill

KOHIMA

31 May
Japanese begin
withdrawal

Night
17/18 April

3 June
5 Bde outflanks
Aradura Spur

Two Tree Hill

Congress Hill

Jail Hill

26 April
4 Bde begins
right hook

Mt Pulebadze

4 May
Ridge retaken

GPT
Ridge

7 April

5 April
Ridge taken

Garage Spur

Big Tree
Hill

Dyer Hill

ARADURA

25/28 May
2 Div repulsed

29 April

4 April
Part Jap 58 Regt
followed by 124 Regt
25 April (to Aradura)

PFUCHAMA

*33 Bde arrived 5 May

To Jessami

The battle of Kohima, April–May 1944.

towards Ukhrul to join up with the
7th Indian Division, which is coming
south from Kohima. The Japanese
15th Division is in danger of being
trapped north-east of Imphal.

5 June
Italian Front Triumphal entry into
Rome by the Allied troops, who are
given a rapturous welcome by the
population.
Having passed through the 'open
city' the Allies take up the pursuit of
the German 14th Army, the command of which is being taken over by
General Lemelsen.
□ King Victor Emmanuel III, in
accordance with his undertaking,

leaves his kingdom in the hands of
his son, Umberto of Savoy.
New Guinea General Krueger, commander of the US 6th Army, urges
the invasion force on Biak to capture
the airfields quickly, since the
Japanese are still able to use them for
attacks against the American beachheads at Hollandia and Aitape. The
186th Infantry Regiment advances as
far as the biggest hill on the island,
north-east of Mokmer airfield. In the
Ibdi area the 162nd Infantry Regiment succeeds in wiping out the
Japanese on the track leading to
the interior of the island and making
contact with the 186th Regiment, but
although naval ships give supporting

fire the Japanese resistance is unbroken.
In the Aitape area the Americans are
forced to take off the units occupying
the Yakamul area by sea. Other units
are sent inland from Aitape so as to
get behind the Japanese advancing
from the east and take them in the
rear. The beachhead cannot be considered secure, but the Japanese are
paying dearly for any progress they
succeed in making.
Burma–China–India 20,000 men of
the Chinese 71st Army have now
crossed the river Salween.
On the Indian front, in the XXXIII
Corps sector, the battle of Kohima
ends in an Allied victory; the British

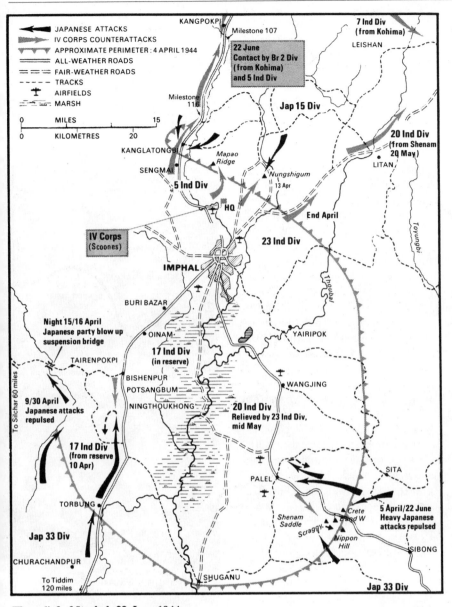

Key:
- JAPANESE ATTACKS
- IV CORPS COUNTERATTACKS
- APPROXIMATE PERIMETER: 4 APRIL 1944
- ALL-WEATHER ROADS
- FAIR-WEATHER ROADS
- TRACKS
- AIRFIELDS
- MARSH

MILES 0 — 15
KILOMETRES 0 — 20

KANGPOKPI
Milestone 107
LEISHAN
7 Ind Div (from Kohima)
22 June Contact by Br 2 Div (from Kohima) and 5 Ind Div
Milestone 116
Jap 15 Div
20 Ind Div (from Shenam 20 May)
KANGLATONGBI
Mapao Ridge
LITAN
SENGMAI
Nungshigum 13 Apr
Toyungbi
5 Ind Div
HQ
End April
IV Corps (Scoones)
23 Ind Div
IMPHAL
Tinoubal
BURI BAZAR
Night 15/16 April Japanese party blow up suspension bridge
OINAM
YAIRIPOK
TAIRENPOKPI
9/30 April Japanese attacks repulsed
17 Ind Div (in reserve)
BISHENPUR
POTSANGBUM
WANGJING
NINGTHOUKHONG
20 Ind Div Relieved by 23 Ind Div, mid May
17 Ind Div (from reserve 10 Apr)
To Silchar 60 miles
SITA
PALEL
TORBUNG
Crete E and W
5 April/22 June Heavy Japanese attacks repulsed
Shenam Saddle
Scraggy
Nippon Hill
Jap 33 Div
SIBONG
CHURACHANDPUR
To Tiddim 120 miles
SHUGANU
Jap 33 Div

The relief of Imphal, 22 June 1944.

2nd Division finishes off the Japanese resistance on the Aradura spur, south of Kohima, but the road from here to Imphal has still to be reopened. From the south, from Imphal, the 20th Indian Division and the remaining divisions of the IV Corps are still moving north.

☐ Thailand. B-29 Superfortresses of the US XX Bomber Group carry out their first bombing mission against Bangkok.

6 June

France In the early hours of the morning the Allies land in Normandy, on the north coast of France. The gigantic Operation *Overlord* is under way. The Second Front has arrived at last.

☐ Pétain broadcasts from Paris radio: 'The trend of the battle may lead the German army to take special measures in the battle areas. Accept this necessity.'

Italian Front The US VI Corps (5th Army) speeds northwards and units of the US 1st Armoured Division reach positions about 25 miles north of Rome. In the British 8th Army sector, the XIII Corps advances rapidly east of the Tiber, and its South African 6th Armoured Division reaches Civita Castellana in a swift surprise action. On the right flank the British 8th Division (X

Corps) pursues the Germans in the direction of Subiaco. General Lemelsen replaces General von Mackensen in command of the German 14th Army, which is reinforced on its right flank by the 2nd Division of the Luftwaffe, in an infantry role.

☐ 104 B-17 Flying Fortresses and 42 P-51 fighters of the US 15th Air Force, taking off from bases in the USSR, carry out a raid on Galati airport in Rumania.

New Guinea Ordered by the divisional commander, General Fuller, to capture Mokmer airfield immediately and then push on to the south coast of Biak, the US 186th Infantry Regiment leaves the commanding heights it has captured and gets ready to attack the airfield. But then the operation is put off until the next day, while the regiment waits for the necessary supplies of rations and ammunition, and above all of water, to come up from the beachhead. In the area of Ibdi the 162nd Infantry Regiment is unable to overcome the stubborn Japanese resistance.

China Supplies of ammunition from India for the US 14th Air Force are substantially increased in view of its heavy liabilities resulting from the Japanese offensive in eastern China.

7 June

Italian Front General Alexander instructs General Leese, commander of the British 8th Army, to step up attacks in the direction of the Arezzo–Florence line (while leaving the V Corps to man the Adriatic coast), while General Clark's American 5th Army is to proceed along the Tyrrhenian coast towards Pisa, Lucca and Pistoia. The advance in both sectors is to be as fast as possible. Meanwhile units of the US 43rd Division occupy Civitavecchia. Damaged as they are the dockyards there can serve as a supply point for the troops in the front line. In the evening General Clark withdraws General Keyes's American II Corps (85th and 88th Divisions) from the front and sends in the French Expeditionary Corps. The South African 6th Armoured Division, followed by the 78th Division (British XIII

(continued on page 530)

THE NORMANDY LANDINGS

At 9.35 a.m. on 6 June 1944 the following message is broadcast to the world by Supreme Headquarters Allied Expeditionary Force: 'Under the command of General Eisenhower, Allied naval forces, supported by strong air forces, began landing Allied armies this morning on the northern coast of France.' The news of Operation *Overlord* reaches Field-Marshal Rommel, Commander of the German forces on the Channel (Army Group B) at 10.15 a.m. on 6 June while he is on a brief visit to his family in Germany. It is brought to him by his Chief of Staff, General Hans Speidler and it gives him a most unpleasant shock. What the Field-Marshal has often called 'the longest day' is half over and he, the great strategist, has played no part in it.

The Allies have been preparing for this operation, the decisive turning-point of the war, for many months. The British, indeed, have been considering it for years, ever since they were driven from the Continent at Dunkirk in 1940. The men and equipment for the landing have been building up in the south of England for a long time. The gathering has been truly astonishing, as men and equipment for *Overlord* arrive in force from overseas. The Americans, alone of the different fighting services, number 1,700,000 by 6 June. More and more airfields have been constructed (in addition to those that already exist, another 163 have been built) and the ports are filled with warships. By the spring of 1944, 2,000,000 tons of war materials have been assembled; more than 50,000 tanks, armoured cars, half-tracks, jeeps and trucks are concealed in the woods and moorlands of southern England.

Early in May this spectacular mass of men and materials begins to move towards the embarkation points in readiness for the day of the operation, the fateful 'D-Day', as it is called.

Allied bombers have been literally 'flattening' the French coasts for months, especially the areas selected for the landing, cutting lines of communication and neutralizing the Luftwaffe. In the days immediately before the landings the air offensive becomes more crushing than ever and the radar stations between Caen and Cherbourg are almost totally destroyed.

There are over half a million German soldiers deployed along the 800 miles of coast from Holland to Brittany. The greatest concentration of these forces, the 15th Army, is on the Channel coast, the shortest distance from England, and it is there that the Allies are generally expected to land. Rommel, who has been in France since the end of 1943, has devoted all his great energies to building up the defences of the Atlantic Wall. But notwithstanding German propaganda the defences are still incomplete. To compensate for the lack of reinforced concrete emplacements Rommel has devised innumerable obstacles and has had millions of mines laid on every beach that could possibly be used by invading armies. His plan of defence also depends on his being able to call up at least five armoured divisions to whatever point on the coast the enemy lands, within two or three hours, to drive the Allies back into the sea. But Hitler has laid it down that the armoured divisions are to be kept in reserve, too far from the sea, and they may not be moved without the Führer's express permis-

sion. To win Hitler over (he has often said: 'With Hitler, whoever is speaking last wins'), Rommel decides at the end of May, when the period during which the meteorological conditions for a landing are favourable is over, to return to Germany and talk with him personally. Exhausted and

Men and vehicles embark at a base in the south of England ready to take part in the Normandy landings.

strained, Rommel is anxious to spend a few days with his family. Tuesday, 6 June, is his wife's birthday. Rommel believed there was nothing to fear before the latter half of June for he took it for granted that the landing would be timed to coincide with the end of the thaw in Poland and the con-

sequent resumption of Russian activity in the east.

1 June
9.00 p.m.: The radio monitoring post at the headquarters of the German 15th Army picks up, after the BBC news bulletin, a 'personal message' – the first verse of the

Chanson d'Automne by the French poet Paul Verlaine: '*Les sanglots longs / Des violons / De l'automne*'... ('The long sighing of the violins of autumn ...'). Canaris, head of the German secret service, has told headquarters that this verse is the first part of a message that will be transmitted on the first and fifteenth days of the month to give the French Resistance advance warning of the invasion. The second part of the message, the second half of Verlaine's verse, will be transmitted within 48 hours of the start of the landing. On 2 June, therefore, following the interception of this famous verse, the 15th Army is alerted. But by an omission due to a misunderstanding between the Army Supreme Command (the OKW, Jodl), Western General Headquarters (Rundstedt) and the headquarters of Army Group B (Rommel), the 7th Army, which guards the Normandy coast, never gets the warning.

2–3 June

The first part of the radio message is repeated after the usual English news bulletin, which the experts of the German intelligence service find rather disconcerting, since according to their information it should only be transmitted once. Meanwhile Rommel prepares to leave for Germany.

In England, from a caravan in a wood near Portsmouth, General Eisenhower issues orders for the invasion. He has under him three million men – 1,700,000 Americans, 1,000,000 British and Canadians and 300,000 Free French, Poles, Belgians, Dutch, Norwegians and Czechs.

The date for Operation *Overlord* (the landing in Normandy, where the enemy least expect it) was fixed by Eisenhower on 8 May, and confirmed on 17 May, as 5 or 6 June, or at the very latest 7 June. These are the only dates on which he can rely on two conditions essential to success: first, the moon will rise late and help the landing by the parachutists and airborne troops – about 22,000 men of the American 101st and 82nd Divisions and the British 6th Division; second, low tide will be at dawn and will uncover all the obstacles and mines that Rommel has had put down, so that they can be most easily neutralized by specialists going ashore ahead of the first wave, blowing up the mines and destroying the obstructions. The next low tide will come just before sunset, and then the second wave will land. These three days are the only ones in the whole month when the meteorological requirements will be right. Although the tides will be favourable again on 19 June, by then the moon will be wrong and the airborne forces would have to attack in complete darkness. If the June dates are missed it will be necessary to wait until July, but so long a delay, as Eisenhower says later, is 'too painful to contemplate'. Eisenhower decides first that the landing shall take place on 5 June, but on 4 June (a Sunday, the day on which Rommel leaves for Germany) he orders a 24 hours' delay on account of bad weather.

4 June

Gigantic convoys have already sailed from British harbours and anchorages, and now they have to turn about in a sea that grows more menacing every hour.

About 10 p.m. on the 4th, after consulting the Allied Joint Chiefs of Staff and receiving the weather report from the meteorologists (headed by Air-Marshal I. N. Stagg of the RAF), Eisenhower confirms the irrevocable decision. The landing will take place on 6 June. 'I don't like it,' he says, 'but I don't see what else I can do. I am absolutely convinced that the order must be given.'

At midnight on 4/5 June the convoys re-form and set off again for France. Among the Germans, also lulled by the bad weather, and especially in the 7th Army, which has not even received the alert, complete calm reigns. Ironically enough, a number of senior German officers are expected at Rennes, in Brittany, on 6 June to take part in a tactical exercise (without troops) based on a hypothetical landing in Normandy.

The forces available to the two sides at the time of the invasion are as follows. The Germans have 59 Divisions, including 10 armoured divisions with Tiger and Panther tanks. The Luftwaffe can contribute only 165 bombers and 183 fighters (of which only 160 are battle-worthy. Several squadrons have been withdrawn

Panzerkampfwagen V Panther

Panzerkampfwagen VI Tiger

from northern France only a few days earlier, though Hitler has promised his generals that there will be 1,000 aircraft ready to support the land forces on the day France is invaded. Commander-in-Chief of the German forces in the west is Field-Marshal Gerd von Rundstedt, with headquarters at St Germain, and the commander of the forces facing the Channel (Army Group B) is Field-Marshal Rommel, with headquarters at La Roche-Guyon. Army Group B comprises the LXXXVIII Corps (stationed in Holland), the 15th Army, between Antwerp and the river Orne, and the 7th Army manning the sector between the Orne and the Loire. Against these the Allies can call on 86 divisions (including 25 armoured divisions equipped with Churchill and Sherman tanks and 55 motorized divisions), 3,100 bombers and 5,000 fighters. In overall command of the Allied forces is General Eisenhower, with the British Air Chief-Marshal Sir Arthur Tedder as his deputy. General Montgomery commands all the Allied land forces, the British Admiral Sir Bertram Ramsay and Air Chief-Marshal Sir Trafford Leigh-Mallory command the naval and air forces. The strategic air force is under the American General Spaatz.

5 June

10.15 p.m.: The German 15th Army's radio monitor intercepts the second half of Verlaine's verse, the second part of the message to the Resistance, which according to Canaris is to be given not more than 48 hours before the invasion: '*Blessent mon cœur/D'une langeur/Monotone.*' ('Wound my heart with a monotonous langour.') The 15th Army – but still only the 15th – is put on a state of maximum alert.

Just after 10.00 p.m. the parachutists and glider-borne infantry take off. A little after midnight the sky over Normandy, bright as day with the flares, is filled with the rumble of aircraft and of German anti-aircraft guns, as Allied night bombers open the assault.

Night of 5/6 June

A vast fleet approaches the French coast. 2,727 ships of every kind (merchant ships, cross-Channel steamers, hospital ships, small Transatlantic liners, tugs, petrol tankers) carry or tow more than 2,500 landing craft. They are escorted by over 700 warships, including 23 cruisers, 5 battleships (the British *Ramillies* and *Warspite* and the American *Texas*, *Arkansas* and *Nevada*, back in action after being sunk in the shallow waters of Pearl Harbour) and 104 destroyers. To oppose this armada, the equal of which has never been seen on the seas, the Germans have a total of 3 destroyers, 36 motor torpedo-boats and 34 submarines.

There are 21 American convoys and 38 British and Canadian. Sailing from almost the entire south coast of England, they carry men and equipment for the first wave of the invasion on the Normandy coasts; the Americans are heading for the beaches code-named 'Utah' (at the base of the Cotentin peninsula) and 'Omaha' (between Vierville sur mer and Ste Honorine) and the British and Canadians for 'Gold' and 'Juno' (between Arromanches and St Aubin) and 'Sword' (between Lion and the mouth of the Orne.

6 June

For the British and American parachutists H-Hour is midnight. It is then that the invaders' first parachutes open in the Normandy skies. There are three airborne divisions, the American 82nd and 101st and the British 6th, a total of about 20,000 men. They are to be dropped inland between Ste Mère Église and Carentan (82nd and 101st divisions) in support of the landings on 'Utah' beach, and east of the river Orne, in the Caen sector (6th Division), in support of the 'Sword' landings. They land without meeting any organized German resistance. Many of the parachutists (no one will ever know how many) are drowned in the swamps round the rivers Douve and Merderet and in the areas flooded by Rommel as an anti-invasion obstacle (e.g. the Dives valley), weighed down by

Infantry Tank Mk IV Churchill V   *Medium Tank Sherman V C Firefly*

their awkward equipment. Some of the gliders crash on landing, killing the occupants. But the bulk of both Americans and British, about 18,000 men, succeed in joining up and carrying out their missions – to disrupt the enemy's communications, cause the maximum confusion, and capture vital bridges before the Germans can blow them up. At dawn American parachutists enter Ste Mère Église, the first village in France to be liberated, and in the eastern sector the British hold Caen bridge and one of the bridges over the river Orne.

Just after 1.00 a.m. the headquarters of the German LXXXIV Corps at St Lô begins to get messages that 'enemy parachutists' have landed in the region of Ranville–Bréville and on the north side of Barent Wood, northeast of Caen near Ste Marie-du-Mont and St Germain de Varreville.

All goes reasonably well for the British 6th Division in their sector. By 3.30 a.m. when the Divisional Commander, General Richard Gale lands with the third wave, a great part of its objectives have been achieved. The Ranville bridgehead has been consolidated, the coastal batteries at Merville have been destroyed, the bridges over the river Dives blown up. But of the 5,000 men in the British division, something like half are missing.

The Americans have the same trouble, for the floods, the mud and the darkness make it hard to keep in touch and the plans so long studied all too easily go awry. Of the 13,200 men in the two American divisions, only a few thousands manage to concentrate immediately after the landing, and only a very few units are where they ought to be by dawn. However, the 101st Division (501st, 502nd and 506th Parachute Regiments, commanded by General Maxwell Taylor) succeeds in winning con-

trol of the area between St Martin de Varreville and Pouppeville, and there gets ready to support the landing of the 4th American Division at 'Utah'. Further inland, the 82nd Airborne Division (505th, 507th and 508th Parachute Regiments, under the command of General Matthew Ridgway) have captured Ste Mère Église, but fail to carry out two important tasks – to cross the rivers Merderet and Douve and to join up with the 101st Division. As the parachutists were landing in enemy territory, the vast and complex armada of 5,300 ships and craft moved towards the Normandy coast. Five Allied divisions (two American, one Canadian and two British), all part of Montgomery's 21st Army Group, are to invade the Normandy coast between Caen in the east and the Cherbourg Peninsula in the west. The American divisions – part of General Bradley's 1st US Army – are assigned the westerly points of attack at two areas code-named 'Utah' and 'Omaha'. The British-Canadian divisions – part of General Dempsey's 2nd British Army – are to land at beaches code-named 'Gold', 'Juno' and 'Sword'.

The landings have been preceded by intensive bombing of the beaches and the landings themselves are given tremendous air cover and deadly supporting fire from the warships. The convoys are preceded by minesweepers and are protected from enemy air attack by barrage balloons. A fleet of tugs tows across the Channel the huge floating reinforced concrete caissons for the construction of Mulberry Harbour, an artificial harbour that can take ships of up to 10,000 tons (including Liberty ships), and the elements of the prefabricated pipeline, code-named Pluto (Pipe Line Under the Ocean), which will keep the forces supplied with fuel.

The first landings of the Allied in-

vasion force from the sea occur at 6.30 a.m. on the 'Utah' sector. The first amphibious unsinkable tanks arrive with the infantry and take the Germans by surprise. In the British sectors the first landings are at 7.25 a.m.

When, many hours later, the Germans are fully convinced that this is the real landing and not a diversion (the news reaches Berchtesgaden at 5.00 a.m. on 6 June, but no one wants to wake Hitler from his drugged sleep), Rundstedt orders the 12th SS Armoured Division and the *Panzerlehr* Division to move to the coast with all speed to hold up the Allies.

On 'Utah' the first troops to land are the VII Corps under General Collins. At 'Omaha' the first troops ashore are the V Corps under General Gerow. At 'Utah' the operation proceeds quite smoothly and by midday advance guards of the US 4th Division are on the road to Pouppeville and Ste Marie in an effort to link up with General Taylor's parachutists. But at 'Omaha' the rough sea and surf and the deadly defence of units of the German 352nd Division make the situation of General Gerow's men extremely critical; the landing craft are hard to control in the waves, while a number of the amphibious tanks launched at sea are engulfed by the water, complete with crews.

On 'Gold', 'Juno' and 'Sword' beaches, too, where the units of General Dempsey's British 2nd Army land, the sea makes things difficult, though not to the same extent as at 'Omaha'. By midday the 50th Division has pushed on from 'Gold' beach, the objective of General Bucknall's British XXX Corps, towards Arromanches and Ver-sur-Mer. On 'Juno' beach the Canadians of the 3rd Division (General Crocker's British I Corps) by-pass the defences of Courseulles and dig in on the hills behind it, and in the 'Sword' sector the 3rd Infantry

American infantry attack under enemy fire during the landings on the Normandy coast.

Division and three groups of Commandos advance to Biéville, about 2½ miles from Caen.

Winston Churchill gives the House of Commons news of the Normandy landings: 'During the night and the early hours of this morning the first of a series of landings in force upon the European Continent has taken place. In this case the liberating assault fell on France.'

By afternoon the German defences are able to put up an effective resistance, especially in the Caen sector, where the 22nd *Panzer* Regiment holds up the British advance on the city, while the 192nd *Panzergrenadiere* reach the sea between 'Juno' and 'Gold' beaches. However, in the 'Gold'

sector the 50th Division, reinforced by the 8th Armoured Brigade (British XXX Corps), is approaching Bayeux.

At 'Utah', in the American sector, the 101st Airborne Division joins up with units of the American VII Corps between 12.15 and 12.30 p.m., while on 'Omaha' beach units of the US V Corps advance, very slowly, to the hills behind the beach, held up by the firm resistance of the German 352nd Infantry Division. But by sunset the American penetration is nowhere more than a mile deep. In the late afternoon Rommel, Commander of Army Group B, and so directly responsible for the Normandy beaches, reaches his headquarters at La Roche-

Guyon. Although still not fully convinced that this is really the Allies' main landing on French soil, he prepares to launch counterattacks against the British and American beachheads as instructed by Hitler, who has told him to drive the invaders back into the sea 'during the night'. He has available the 7th Army under Dollmann, consisting of the LXXXIV Corps and XLVII Armoured Corps, whose 21st Armoured Division is among the first to go into action against the British in the 'Juno' and 'Sword' areas. But he cannot rely on the 15th Army, deployed east of the invasion front. Hitler himself has forbidden its use for operations in Normandy, for the Führer is still firmly convinced that the real invasion is still to come, and will certainly not come in Normandy. At sundown fighting dies down on the whole front. The Allies are too exhausted to think of following up their offensive, while the Germans have neither the equipment nor the men to mount a large-scale counter-attack. Even though, from the tactical point of view, the Allies have not reached any of the targets set for 6 June on any of their beaches, D-Day has still been a great success for the British and Americans. They have landed 155,000 men on French soil, a colossal force for the enemy to drive back into the sea. Rommel has always maintained that the loss of the first battle, on the beaches, will mean leaving the European continent open to invasion. And he is proved right.

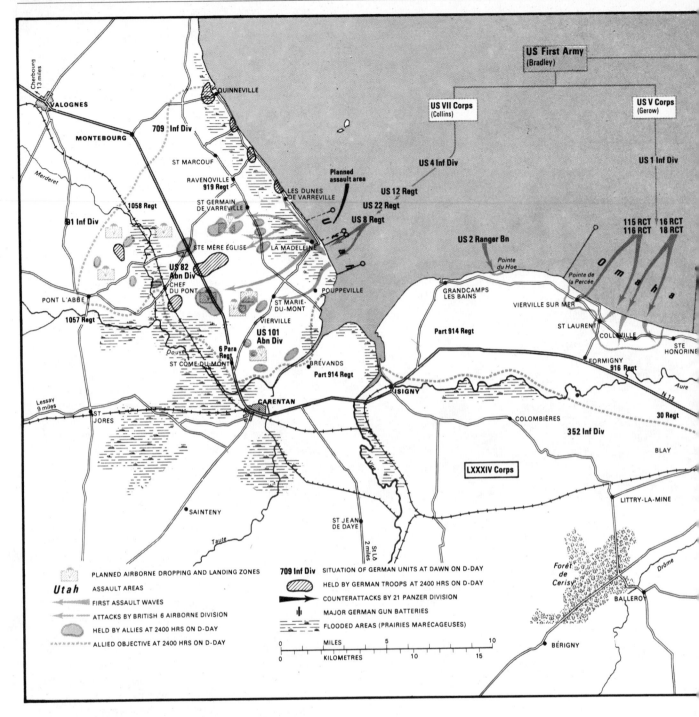

D-Day, the Allied landings in Normandy, 6 June 1944.

Corps), moves towards Orvieto, an important road junction.

France Although the Allies have not reached the targets set for them in the *Overlord* plan during the first day, all the landings except that on 'Omaha' beach have been reasonably successful and now the British and Americans have established wide beachheads.

When the sun rises, fighting flares up again. The Allies' most urgent problem is to consolidate the beachheads and reach the line planned for them for the previous day as quickly as they can. For the Germans it is a matter of life or death to drive their enemies back before they can widen the breach they have made in the coastal defences.

General Eisenhower, visiting the front, orders the US V and VII Corps to converge as soon as the one has taken Isigny (29th Division) and the other Carentan (101st Assault Division). The 4th Division (VII Corps) advances north in the direction of the line Quineville–Montebourg, but is halted by firm German resistance on the line of fortifications from Crisbecq to Azeville. Meanwhile columns from the 8th Regiment converge on Ste Mère Église to

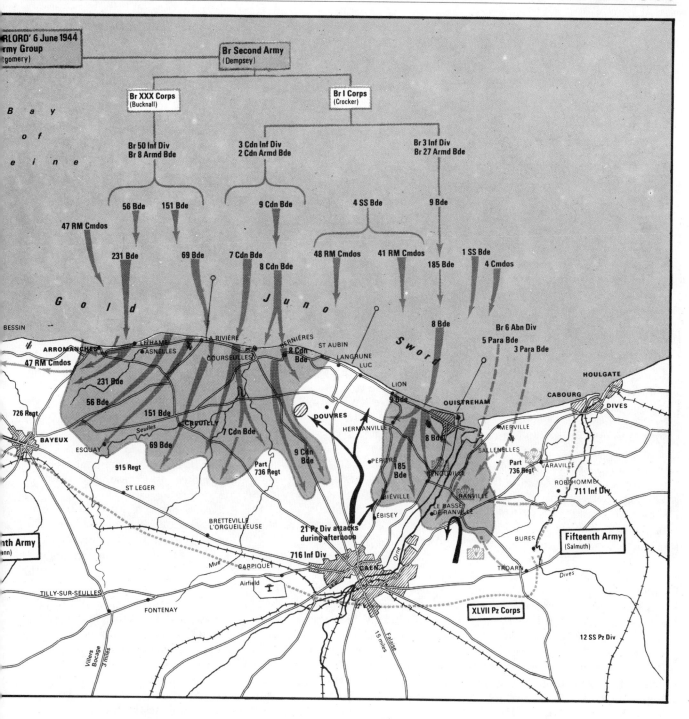

support the units of the 82nd Airborne Division against a dangerous German counter-attack from the north. Other units from the 82nd Division reach the east bank of the river Merderet, but meet with violent opposition at the La Fière bridge. South of Ste Mère Église units of the 101st Airborne Division on the north bank of the river Douve hold up their attacks to establish a bridgehead across the water. The German detachments at Le Port and La Barquette surrender to them. The US V Corps, with the 29th Division on its right flank and the 1st Division on its left, advances towards Isigny and Bayeux.

Units of the 29th Division reach the St Laurent region and press on to the south-west towards Louvières and Montigny. On the right of the sector where the US 1st Division is in action elements of the 26th Regiment fail to capture Formigny. In the centre the 18th Regiment pushes on towards Engranville, Manderville and Mosles. The 16th Regiment, on the left, captures Huppain.

The Germans keep a solid grip on the narrow corridor dividing the British and American forces, along the river Drôme as far as its con-

5 June 1944: units of the American 5th Army enter Rome, passing through the Porta Maggiore.

fluence with the Aure. In the evening troops of the US 2nd Division begin to come ashore.

In the British 2nd Army sector the 50th Division (British XXX Corps) takes Bayeux (which is miraculously taken intact) and some of its units press on southwards towards Route 13, which links Bayeux and Caen. A similar operation is carried out further east, near Caen, by a brigade of the Canadian 3rd Division (II Corps).

New Guinea On Biak the US 186th Infantry Regiment, with air and artillery support, captures Mokmer airfield and reaches the south coast without opposition, but later the whole area is subjected to intense fire from Japanese artillery and machine-guns. The 162nd Infantry Regiment begins to transfer the bulk of its forces by sea to the coastal sector south of Mokmer airfield so as to be able to attack the Japanese positions from the south and, after taking the southern positions, to eliminate the threat from the Japanese batteries to the supply lines between the island and the mainland. There is also fighting round the Ibdi pocket. American artillery begins to neutralize the enemy fortifications in caves in the eastern part of the island, east of Mokmer airfield. Fighting goes on in

the areas round the Hollandia and Aitape beachheads.

Burma–China The Chinese and Americans prepare to mount a fresh attack against Myitkyina on the 10th.

On the Salween front the Chinese 88th Division reaches the eastern outskirts of Lungling. The Chinese 87th Division, advancing along the Burma Road, is also approaching the town.

8 June

France Contact between the American 1st Army and the British 2nd Army is made near Port-en-Bessin. Units of the 82nd Airborne Division (US VII Corps) and the US 4th Division begin to advance towards Cherbourg. Efforts by the 22nd Regiment (4th Division) to cross the line of fortifications from Azeville to Crisbecq are fruitless. Along the bank of the river Merderet the 82nd Airborne Division is severely engaged with the German 243rd Division. On the southern flank of the VII Corps sector the 101st Airborne Division begins the battle for Carentan, trying to link up with the American V Corps as quickly as possible. The V Corps reaches the target set for it on Day 1 and the following night, Isigny, in complete

calm; its 115th Regiment pushes on south of the river Aure, passing across Longueville. In the sector where the 1st Division is operating the 26th Regiment, trying to trap the enemy between the American and British beachheads, takes Tour-en-Bessin and, during the night, Ste Anne. The 16th Regiment tries to cut off the Germans retreating from Port-en-Bessin, but they manage to keep a corridor open and during the night they get most of their forces away. In the British XXX Corps (2nd Army) sector, the 47th Regiment Royal Marines enters Port-en-Bessin in the early hours of the morning.

Italian Front The advance of the US VI Corps (5th Army) is slowed down south of Tarquinia by German resistance. The US II Corps comes within 6 miles of Viterbo. In the British sector the British V Corps, manning the Adriatic coast, continues its march north as the German troops retire. In the centre of the Allied line the South African 6th Armoured Division (XIII Corps) makes rapid progress in the direction of Orvieto.

The British 6th Armoured Division is halted at Corese Pass, west of Monte Maggiore.

Eastern Front As a prelude to the big summer offensive the Russian 23rd and 21st Armies of the Leningrad Front (Govorov), after a three-hour-long artillery preparation, attack the Finnish positions in the Mannerheim line in the isthmus of Karelia, between Lake Ladoga to the east and the Gulf of Finland to the west. Russian diplomacy has tried to get Finland out of the war with a negotiated peace, but the conditions demanded by Moscow have so far been unacceptable to the Finns.

New Guinea The islets south of Biak have all been occupied by the Americans, and today a motor torpedo-boat base on one of them is activated. On Biak the US 186th Infantry consolidates its positions in the Mokmer airfield area. The US 162nd Infantry Regiment, whose forces are spread out between the east coast and the west coast of the island, runs into strong opposition by the enemy in the area of the 'eastern caves', the

D-Day, 6 June 1944: under fire from the German defences, men and vehicles from the American contingent go ashore on the 'Omaha' beachhead.

fortifications in caves east of Mokmer airfield. In the area of the Parai Defile the Japanese put up a strong resistance to the combined forces of the US 163rd, 186th and 162nd Regiments. From Parai advance guards of the 162nd Regiment reach the outskirts of the village of Mokmer, near the airfield.

Near the Aitape beachhead the Americans go over to the counter-attack and succeed in getting within a mile of the river Tirfoam, from which they had been forced to retire. During the night an Allied naval squadron commanded by the British Rear-Admiral Crutchley intercepts five Japanese destroyers off the Schouten Islands (the group to which Biak belongs), carrying reinforce-ments and supplies for the Biak garrison, and puts them to flight. Another destroyer has been sunk by an American bomber the previous day.

Burma–China On the Salween front the Chinese 88th Division achieves a limited penetration into the defences of Lungling. The Chinese 87th Division reaches the north gate of the town and cuts the Japanese supply route between Lungling and Teng-chung.

9 June

France The American 4th Division (VII Corps) makes significant pro-gress in its advance on Cherbourg. The 22nd Regiment forces the 169 men defending the Azeville fortifica-tions (four reinforced concrete case-mates camouflaged as civilian dwell-ing-houses, linked by covered trenches, armed with 150-mm guns and machine-guns) to surrender. A task force is then sent through the breach opened at Azeville, with Quineville as its objective. The 82nd and 101st Airborne Divisions mount attacks, the first on the river Mer-deret, the second, to the south, against Carentan.

In the central sector of the US V Corps, the 38th Regiment (2nd Division) enters Trévières, while the 9th Regiment, from the east, pushes on towards Rubercy. Troops on the left flank of the 1st Division reach Agy and Dodigny. The landing of the US 2nd Armoured Division begins.

In the British 2nd Army sector, the I Corps encounters strong resistance in the Caen area.

Italian Front Tarquinia is taken by units of the 34th Division, in the US VI Corps sector. In the early hours of the morning Viterbo also falls, without a shot fired, to the US 1st Armoured Division. In the British 8th Army sector a new line of battle between the XIII and the X Corps is fixed along the Tiber, so that some units of the XIII Corps (the British 6th Armoured Division and 4th Division) pass to the X Corps. In the XIII Corps sector the South African 6th Armoured Division makes contact at Viterbo wiith units of the American 1st Armoured Division (5th Army) and pushes on in the direction of Orvieto, while the British 6th Armoured Division (X Corps) continues its advance towards Terni.

The US 1st Armoured Division, as well as the 85th and 88th Divisions, is withdrawn from the front, while the US IV Corps takes over responsibility for the sector occupied by the US VI Corps (whose headquarters is moved to Naples) and the 36th Division (General Crittenberger).

☐ Rome. The President of the Italian Council of Ministers, Marshal Badoglio, resigns. Ivanoe Bonomi is charged with forming a new grouping to act as a provisional government.

New Guinea In the area of the Hollandia–Aitape beachhead the Americans break the Japanese resistance and get back to the Tirfoam river, but they are held up there because one infantry regiment has to be taken out of the line for the landing on Numfoor Island. An Australian fighter squadron reaches Tadji airfield in the Aitape area.

Burma–India Admiral Mountbatten sends an instruction to General Giffard, Commander of the British-Indian 11th Army Group: the area of Dimapur-Kohima-Imphal road must be cleared of the enemy by 15 July, so as to go on to the liberation of the Imphal plain and the area between Yuwa and Tamanthi and then to an offensive across the Chindwin after the end of the monsoon rains.

10 June

France The V and VII Corps of the US 1st Army join up at Auville-sur-le-Vey, but the town of Carentan remains firmly in the hands of the German 17th Armoured Division. In the US VII Corps sector units of the 4th Division take some positions below the Montebourg–Quineville road and objectives along the road from Montebourg to Le Ham. The 101st Airborne Division begins to surround Carentan.

The American 9th Division, latest to arrive, begins to land. By the end of the day the Allies have put ashore

325,000 men.

On the left flank of the US V Corps units of the 1st Division reach the road linking Bayeux to St Lô.

In the British 2nd Army sector the I and XXX Corps keep up their pressure on Caen, Montgomery's plan is for a double attack, from the east by the I Corps advancing as far as Cagny from the right bank of the Orne, south-east of the city, and from the west by the 7th Armoured Division (XXX Corps), which will move from the Bayeux region and after taking Tilly-sur-Seulles, Villers-Bocage and Noyers-Bocage will occupy the heights at Evrecy, south-west of Caen. The 7th Armoured Division begins the offensive in the direction of Tilly-sur-Seulles, meeting stubborn resistance from the German *Panzerlehr* Division.

Italian Front The divisions of the British V Corps continue their advance up the Adriatic coast to reach Chieti and Pescara. On the outskirts of Bagnoregio German rearguards slow down the advance of the South African 6th Armoured Division (XIII Corps). The X Corps also meets with strong resistance before Terni, while the New Zealand 2nd Division captures Avezzano.

New Guinea Fighting continues on Biak, where the Americans meet a more and more obstinate resistance. But Japanese activity in the Hollandia–Aitape area grows less.

Burma Chinese–American attacks

Normandy, June 1944: camouflaged German soldiers emerge from cover and launch a fierce attack.

A seductive blonde persuades her husband to take out a life insurance policy prior to a business trip; then, to cash in on the double indemnity under the policy, she compels the insurance salesman with whom she is having an affair to kill him. After the crime, the intervention of an investigator and the guilty feelings of her accomplice combine to foil her plans.

Incisively directed by Billy Wilder and scripted by Raymond Chandler from the novel *Double Indemnity* by James Cain, this was one of the best films of the 1940s. Set in a Los Angeles of opulent decadence, the film starred Barbara Stanwyck as the cold-blooded *femme fatale*, Fred MacMurray as the greedy, infatuated salesman, and Edward G. Robinson as the insurance company investigator.

'DOUBLE INDEMNITY'

Fred MacMurray and Barbara Stanwyck in a scene from the film.

---

against Myitkyina meet with no success. In the Mogaung valley Chinese forces besiege Kamaing. On the Salween front the Chinese 87th and 88th Divisions attack Lungling.
China The Japanese advance along the river Liu-yang with five divisions and threaten the important town of Changsha, north of Canton.

11 June
France While the US 90th Division

A column of American infantry reinforcements in the salient north of the Ardennes.

continues its slow advance west of the river Merderet, the 101st Airborne Division mounts the decisive attack on Carentan. During the night, under deadly fire from the American artillery, the Germans leave the town. Carentan is occupied, but it is not long before the enemy endeavours to re-take it.
In the US V Corps sector units of the 2nd Armoured Division are ordered to reinforce the bridgehead at

Auville-sur-le-Vey as long as the 101st Airborne Division (VII Corps) continues to be engaged at Carentan. Lull on the rest of the US V Corps front.
The 7th Armoured Division (XXX Corps of the British 2nd Army) encounters fierce resistance round Tilly-sur-Seulles from the German *Panzerlehr* Division, which takes advantage of the vegetation and the nature of the terrain to adopt guerrilla tactics, lying concealed, advancing rapidly, then retiring unexpectedly. The British manage to take Tilly, but then a sudden German counter-attack drives them from the village. East of Caen, too, where the British I Corps is operating, the Allied situation is difficult; counter-attacks here by the German LXXXVI Corps have halted their advance.
Italian Front In the French Expeditionary Corps sector the 1st Motorized Division captures Montefiascone and the 3rd Algerian Division enters Valentano. The South African 6th Armoured Division (British XIII Corps) fails to overcome German resistance

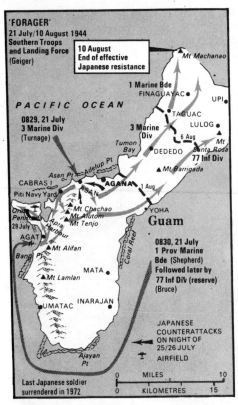

'FORAGER'
21 July/10 August 1944
Southern Troops
and Landing Force
(Geiger)

10 August
End of effective
Japanese resistance

PACIFIC OCEAN

Mt Machanao

1 Marine Bde
FINAGUAYAC
UPI
TAGUAC
LULOG

0829, 21 July
3 Marine Div
(Turnage)

3 Marine
Div
6 Aug
Mt
Santa Rosa

Tumon
Bay
DEDEDO
77 Inf Div

Mt Barrigada

Asan Pt
Adelup Pt
AGANA
1 Aug

CABRAS I
ASAN
Piti Navy Yard

Mt Chachao
Mt Alutom
Mt Tenjo

YOHA

Guam

Orote
Peninsula
29 July
AGAT

Apra Harbour

0830, 21 July
1 Prov Marine
Bde (Shepherd)
Followed later by
77 Inf Div (reserve)
(Bruce)

Bangi Pt
Mt Alifan

MATA

Mt Lamlan

Coral Reef

INARAJAN
UMATAC

JAPANESE
COUNTERATTACKS
ON NIGHT OF
25/26 JULY

AIRFIELD

Ajayan
Pt

Last Japanese soldier
surrendered in 1972

MILES   10
0
0   KILOMETRES   15

The US occupation of the Marianas, 15 June–1 August 1944.

below Bagnoregio. Another armoured division, the British 6th, crosses the river Galantina and reaches Cantalupo, which the Germans have already abandoned.

Eastern Front Following up their offensive against the Mannerheim line, the Leningrad Front armies penetrate 15 miles into the Finnish lines on a front of 30 miles.

☐ Aircraft of the US 15th Air Force bomb the Rumanian airfield at Focsani in the first of their 'shuttle raids' between the USSR and Italy.

New Guinea The US 186th and 162nd Infantry Regiments go over to the attack and reach a point a little more than 1,000 yards from the west side of the runway on Mokmer airfield. Captured Javanese labourers speak of Japanese positions in caves about three-quarters of a mile northwest of units of the US 162nd Regiment.

Molucca Islands Vice-Admiral Matome Ugaki, commander of the Japanese fleet at sea, orders the two giant battleships *Yamato* and *Musashi* (72,800 tons fully laden)

with cruiser and destroyer escort to Bacan to strike a decisive blow at MacArthur's 7th Amphibious Force. But just as this powerful force is about to sail it receives orders to head for the Marianas.

Mariana Islands Aircraft taking off from 15 aircraft carriers of Task Force 58 (Vice-Admiral Mitscher) begin a three-day bombardment of Japanese shipping and installations on the islands of Saipan (against which an American landing force is sailing from the Marshall Islands), Tinian, Guam, Pagan and Rota, in the Mariana archipelago. Two Japanese convoys are attacked and seriously damaged. The Americans win complete air superiority, bringing down or destroying on the ground between 150 and 200 Japanese aircraft.

China The Japanese penetrate in force across the river Liu-yang, meeting little resistance from the Chinese forces in the 11th war zone.

12 June

France The US VII Corps (1st Army) has still not reached the line it was meant to occupy on the first day of landing. However its units advance both in the Cotentin peninsula and south in the direction of St Lô. On the east coast of the peninsula the 4th Division and elements of the 9th enter Crisbecq, from which the enemy has been forced to withdraw. Azeville is captured by the American 22nd Regiment after a massive barrage from land and sea. The 8th Regiment tries several attacks against Montebourg but is repulsed by units of the German 243rd Division. Equally unsuccessful is a new attempt by two regiments of the 9th Division to continue their advance west of the river Merderet.

Units of the 82nd Airborne Division, reinforced and regrouped, cross the river Douve near Benzeville-la-Bastille, trying to link up with the 101st Airborne Division at Baupte.

In the American V Corps sector the 29th Division crosses the rivers Vire and Taute but are held up in the area of Monmartin-en-Graignes by determined German defence. The

divisions of the V Corps begin the assault towards St Lô; on the left the 1st Division reaches Caumont, the St Lô–Caen road.

Italian Front The American IV Corps continues to advance up the Tyrrhenian coast, though now slowed down by growing opposition from motorized units of the German 14th Army. A special group is set up under General Ramey to protect the IV Corps's right flank and maintain contact with units of the French Expeditionary Corps; it is composed of the 9th Squadron of the Reconnaissance Cavalry, the 14th Regiment of the US 36th Division and other units.

New Guinea The Japanese still resist doggedly on Biak.

Mariana Islands Aircraft from Task Force 58's carriers continue their attacks on military targets on Saipan and other islands in the Marianas, destroying several airfields. They attack an escaping enemy convoy and sink about ten ships.

13 June

At 3.30 a.m. the first German V1 flying bombs (the 'V' stands for *Vergeltung*, the German for 'reprisal') are directed towards England from launching pads on the Channel coast. Hitler's secret weapon, developed in the base at Peenemünde, is very much like a small aircraft, 26 feet long with a wing span of 16 feet; the total weight is two tons, including about 1,800 lb of explosive. Launched from slightly sloping ramps (and also from specially adapted aircraft), the V1 flies at a height of about 3,000 feet at a maximum speed of about 375 m.p.h. Of the ten V1s launched on this occasion, only four reach British soil, and only one lands in London, where it kills six people.

Between this date and 6 September about 8,000 of these flying bombs are launched (and, later, over 1,200 are launched from ramps built on the North Sea coast).

France In the American VII Corps sector the 4th Division continues to advance slowly along the east coast of the Cotentin peninsula and the

90th Division makes slow progress westwards across the river Merderet. A violent counter-attack by the German 17th Armoured Division to recapture Carentan carries the attacking troops to the outskirts of the town but swift intervention by the 101st Airborne Division and units of the US 2nd Armoured Division halts the Germans. In the US V Corps sector the 1st Division captures Caumont, while the 38th Regiment of the 2nd Division, with decisive artillery support, reaches a point about 2 miles from the river Elle in the direction of St Lô. As evening falls General Bradley, Commander of the US 1st Army, holds up the advance of the V Corps, ordering the formation to maintain its positions, waiting for the attempt by VII Corps to cut off the Cotentin peninsula and capture Cherbourg. In the British XXX Corps sector (British 2nd Army), the 7th Armoured Division captures Villers-Bocage, an important road junction between Caen and St Lô, and moves on towards Caen as far as Height 213, north-west of the town, where it is held up by lively resistance by the German 2nd Armoured Division, which has just arrived from the Beauvais area. The German counter-attack takes the British by surprise, and they withdraw to the west, abandoning Villers-Bocage. The British division's position is critical.
Italian Front In the British 8th Army sector the South African 6th Armoured Division breaches the enemy front at Bagnoregio and pushes on towards Orvieto. The British 6th Armoured Division (X Corps) advances towards Terni.
New Guinea The Mokmer airfield is repaired sufficiently to take American fighters. Enemy fire from cave positions in the east of the island is neutralized sufficiently to allow supply columns to drive up the south coast road without too much danger.
Mariana Islands US intelligence sources report that Japanese forces on Saipan amount to about 17,000 men, and those on Tinian to around 10,500. Actually the Japanese garrisons are bigger, 30,000 men. A squad-

American infantry, with tank support, try to wipe out pockets of German resistance after the Normandy landings.

ron of 7 battleships and 11 destroyers under Vice-Admiral Lee bombards the Japanese installations on Saipan and Tinian. Japanese air defence is non-existent.
Burma Severe fighting occurs in the Myitkyina area, where Japanese counter-attacks win them small penetrations in the Chinese and American lines.
China A train load of arms and ammunition is sent to the Chinese 11th war zone, at Hengyang, south of Chang-sha, where the Japanese threat is greatest.

14 June
France The divisions of the US VII Corps continue to advance in the

north and west of the Cotentin peninsula, the 4th Division proceeding along the east coast of the peninsula, the 82nd Airborne, 9th and 90th west of the river Merderet, in an attempt to cut off Cherbourg. On 'Utah' beach, the 79th Division is landed. The newly formed US XIX Corps enters the line between the V and VII Corps. The XIX Corps is made up of the 29th Division (transferred from the V Corps) and the 30th, which occupies the sector between Carentan and Isigny.
In the British sector, intervention by the American 1st Division allows the 7th Armoured Division (British XXX Corps), which is being pushed south by the German armour, to disengage from the enemy and seek

safety in the area of Parfourn–l'Eclin. The offensive against Caen is held up for a time both east and west of the river Orne.

Italian Front While the German 14th Army under General Lemelsen slowly withdraws, maintaining contact with the enemy with its rear-guards, the advance of the American IV Corps (US 5th Army) in the Tyrrhenian sector of the front continues, north and north-east towards Leghorn and Florence. At the centre of the Allied line the South African 6th Armoured Division (XIII Corps) takes Orvieto without opposition.

Eastern Front The Russian 23rd and 21st Armies, Leningrad Front, advance into the Karelian Isthmus after breaching the outer defences of the Mannerheim line.

New Guinea Fighting continues on Biak. The Americans manage to get nearer to the Japanese strongpoint based on caves in the west of the island. General Fuller is replaced by General Eichelberger, Commander of the US I Corps, as Commander of Task Force *Hurricane*, (i.e. the regiments engaged on Biak).

Mariana Islands As the invasion convoy for the Marianas (Operation *Forager*) approaches its objectives, two US squadrons with 7 battleships, 11 cruisers and 26 destroyers, commanded by Rear-Admirals Oldendorf and Ainsworth, bombard Japanese installations on Saipan and Tinian. The Japanese coastal batteries hit the battleship *California* and a destroyer, causing some damage and a number of casualties. The Americans begin the operations of minesweeping and clearing the under-water obstacles.

Burma The Chinese and American forces continue to attack Myitkyina. The Japanese counter-attack, taking advantage of the gaps they have opened between the enemy units to create little pockets, but they do not succeed in wiping these out. A part of the 3rd Indian (Chindit) Division is ordered to reinforce the Sino–American force, but cannot reach them because of the flooded condition of the ground and exhaustion of the men; also, the approaches to the

A column of Chinese soldiers crosses the river Salween by temporary bridge on its way to the front.

area are strongly defended by the Japanese. In the Mogaung valley the Chinese tighten the ring round Kamaing.

On the Salween front the Japanese reinforce their positions and mount vigorous counter-attacks on the outskirts of Lungling, retaking an important bridge.

China The Japanese capture Liuyang, increasing the threat to Changsha.

15 June

France The American VIII Corps is set up under command of General Middleton, and takes over the sector on the west side of the Cotentin peninsula. General Collins, Commander of the US VII Corps, maintains that his units' principal efforts must be directed towards cutting the Cotentin peninsula in two so as to capture Cherbourg as quickly as possible.

Italian Front The IV Corps of the US 5th Army reaches the river Ombrone which it begins to cross at sundown. Patrols are sent towards Grosseto.

The VI Corps, withdrawn from the front a little time earlier, is assigned to the US 7th Army for Operation *Anvil*, the Allied landing in the south of France.

In the British sector, while the advance of the V Corps along the Adriatic coast continues, the British 3rd Division replaces the 4th Indian Division in the front line.

☐ The launching of V1s against England is resumed during the night; 244 bombs are launched, of which 144 cross the Channel and 73 of these reach London, causing severe damage. Churchill comments: 'The impersonal nature of the new weapon has a depressing effect.'

New Guinea On Biak Island the Japanese counter-attack with tanks from their strongpoint in the western caves on the island. The counter-attack is held. Mokmer airfield cannot be used to support operations against the Marianas, since it is still under enemy fire.

Mariana Islands The huge amphibious fleet carrying the 2nd and 4th Marine Divisions and one reserve regiment appears off Saipan. This island, Tinian, and the rest of the Marianas are defended by 30,000 men, partly marine infantry (commanded by Vice-Admiral Chuichi Nagumo), partly from the 31st Army, comprising the 43rd Division and 47th Composite Brigade (commanded by General Yoshitsugo Saito). On Saipan the Japanese have little more than 60 guns. The amphibious force is commanded by Vice-Admiral Turner and the Marine divisions by General H. Smith.

The bombardment begins at 5.45 a.m with covering fire from the battleships and cruisers, and after violent bombing by aircraft the first of the 700 amphibious craft of the Marines go ashore at 8.40 a.m. on the west coast of Saipan. The 2nd Division lands north of Point Afetna, the 4th Division south of it. The accurate Japanese fire opens large gaps among the men who have just reached the beaches. The distance between the two divisions is bigger than had been planned, since by an error, part of the 2nd Division has been landed farther north than was ordered. At the end of the day the Marines have established a beachhead 5½ miles wide and three-quarters of a mile deep, but its flanks are not really secure and Point Afetna is still in Japanese hands.

As usual, the Japanese counter-attack during the night and suffer heavy losses, but are not able to drive the Americans back into the sea. The Marines' defence is made easier by the continual firing of flares. The reserve regiment has made a landing to the north at the same time as the main landing, to draw off the enemy forces. Meanwhile another division, the 27th Infantry, is arriving. The battleship *Tennessee* is damaged by fire from the Japanese coast defence guns.

At 9.30 a.m. Vice-Admiral Jisaburo Ozawa, in command of the Japanese naval air forces for Operation *A-Go*, the project conceived by Admiral Toyoda for the destruction of Task Force 58, receives an order from Toyoda that echoes the famous order given by Admiral Togo before the historic naval battle of Tsushima against the Russians in 1905: 'The fate of the Empire depends on this

MARC BLOCH

The French historian Marc Bloch, founder of the *Annales*, was shot by the Germans on 16 June at Les Roussilles (Lyon). After the occupation of France he became an influential member of the Resistance. He had been arrested in March and was repeatedly tortured prior to his execution.

Bloch was born at Lyon in 1886. He studied in Paris, Leipzig and Berlin, fought in the First World War and in 1919 became professor of medieval history at Strasbourg University. In 1936 he was invited to teach economic history at the Sorbonne and held this post until 1940.

His book *Les Rois thaumaturges*, published in 1924, virtually marked the birth of a new form of historiography, a revolutionary approach that subsequently came to fruition in *Annales d'histoire économique et sociale*, a review founded by Bloch together with Lucien Febvre in 1929. Bloch and the historians of the *Annales* inaugurated a new method of historiographic research, making fullest use of other disciplines such as psychology, sociology and economics, which until then had played only peripheral roles.

battle. Everyone must give all he has.'

Volcano and Bonin Islands Airfields, barracks and fuel dumps in the islands of Iwo Jima (Volcano Islands) and Chichi Jima and Haha Jima (Bonin Islands) are attacked by aircraft taking off from two groups of US aircraft carriers commanded by Rear-Admirals Clark and Harrill. Iwo Jima is attacked again the next day.

Burma Fighting continues in the Myitkyina area. On the Salween front the Chinese succeed in capturing part of a mountainous feature dominating some 40 miles of the Burma Road, where it crosses the Salween valley.

☐ Japan. B-29 Superfortresses of the US 20th Bomber Command, taking off from China, carry out their first raid on Japan, They drop over 200 tons of bombs on steelworks at Yawata, on Kyushu Island.

16 June

France The American VII Corps reaches the river Douve and succeeds in establishing a bridgehead across it. After formidable German opposi-

tion and bitter street fighting units of the 82nd Airborne Division enter St Sauveur-le-Vicomte, on the west bank of the Douve. The Germans withdraw in disarray. In the American XIX Corps sector, while some units man the canal linking the rivers Taute and Vire, the 29th Division, with the V Corps' 2nd Division, advances in the direction of St Lô.

Italian Front Units of the British X Corps approach Perugia, while the Germans are still completing the withdrawal of their 10th and 14th Armies behind the *Gothic* line.

New Guinea Fighting continues in the area of the western caves on Biak Island.

Mariana Islands A squadron of American battleships, cruisers and destroyers under the command of Rear-Admiral Ainsworth bombards enemy installations on the island of Guam. Meanwhile Vice-Admiral R. A. Spruance puts back the date for the invasion of Guam, in the knowledge that a big fleet under the command of Vice-Admiral Ozawa is about to arrive there.

At Saipan, on the north flank of the

beachhead, the US 2nd Marine Division consolidates its own positions, capturing Point Afetna and the village of Charan Kanoa and joining up with the 4th Marine Division south of Point Afetna. The 4th Marine Division advances inland against strong resistance. In the previous night's fighting the Japanese have lost more than 1,000 men. American guns try to silence the Japanese batteries which are firing very effectively on the beachheads from the interior of the island.

Burma Units of the Chinese 50th Division capture Kamaing in the Mogaung valley. Beyond Kamaing the Chinese 38th Division links up with the Chindits of the Indian 3rd Division at Gurkhaywa.

On the Salween front the Japanese counter-attack, driving the Chinese 87th Division back 3 miles. Farther north, the Chinese 2nd and 36th Divisions capture Chiaotou.

China The Japanese open their offensive against Changsha, and the garrison there, units of the Chinese 4th Army, withdraws to Paoching.

17 June
France The 9th Division, US VII Corps, launches a powerful offensive in the direction of Carteret, on the west coast of the Cotentin peninsula. During the night a column reaches Carteret, cutting off Cherbourg and the northern part of the peninsula. Rommel wants to evacuate the peninsula, but Hitler refuses even to discuss abandoning it. Rommel has no alternative but to order the divisions in the north (709th, 243rd, 91st, 77th) to sacrifice themselves for Cherbourg. The rest of the German LXXXIV Corps (General Dollmann's 7th Army) is deployed in defence of the base of the Cotentin peninsula. Hitler brusquely summons Marshals Rundstedt and Rommel to Margival, near Soissons, and flies into one of his usual rages. He says the army in the West has 'let itself be caught in its sleep' and accuses the soldiers of cowardice. Rommel tries to argue, pointing out the disproportion between the Allies' numbers and those of the Germans, and again suggests evacuating the Cotentin peninsula. But Hitler will not give way. At the same time as the capture of Carteret, the 82nd Airborne Division, now under the command of the VIII Corps, is ordered to establish a bridgehead on the right bank of the river Douve at Pont-l'Abbé.

In the XIX Corps sector the 29th Division, advancing on St Lô, is engaged in a hard battle by the German 3rd Parachute Division.

Italian Front In the eastern sector of the Allied line (British 8th Army) the British V Corps is relieved by the Polish II Corps. Sudden violent rain slows down the movements of the British X Corps; however, when a bridge has been completed over the Tiber about 3 miles north of Todi, the advance on Perugia continues along both banks of the river. Southeast of Perugia the 8th Division meets stiff resistance by the Germans.

Units of the French Expeditionary Corps land on the island of Elba and proceed to occupy it (Operation *Brassard*).

New Guinea On Biak the US 186th and 162nd Regiments occupy a hill overlooking the Japanese strongpoint in the island's western caves.

Mariana Islands The US 27th Division reaches Saipan. The Marine divisions make some progress to both north and south, but cannot advance into the interior against the tenacious Japanese resistance. The aircraft of Task Force 58 do not give their usual support to the operations for they are engaged in the neutralization of Guam and in looking for the Japanese fleet.

Burma–China–India On the Salween front the Chinese 87th and 88th Divisions are ordered to withdraw in the area of Lungling.

In India where the British and Indians have resumed the offensive, the British have had 2,700 dead and 10,000 wounded since 4 March, the Japanese about 30,000 dead.

18 June
France The Commander-in-Chief of the 21st Army Group, General Montgomery, issues his first written instructions since the landing in Normandy. He calls for the capture of Caen and Cherbourg. On the Cherbourg front the American VII Corps begins its advance on the city with the 9th, 79th and 4th Divisions

Infantry of the American VIII Corps advance in the La Haye-du-Puits sector in the Contentin peninsula.

operating left, centre and right respectively of the line.

The situation in the St Lô sector is unchanged, with the XIX Corps held up north of the town.

Italian Front Units of the 1st Motorized Division of the French Expeditionary Corps under General Juin reach Radicofani, north-west of Orvieto, overlooking the road from Florence to Rome.

In the British sector the columns converging on Perugia meet with a certain resistance in the outskirts of the city. During the night the Germans abandon Città della Pieve, which is occupied by British XIII Corps units.

Eastern Front The Leningrad Front (Govorov) breaks through the Mannerheim line in the direction of Viipuri and Vuosalmi, in the isthmus of Karelia.

New Guinea A fresh US Regiment is deployed in Biak Island, where the Americans are getting ready to launch a determined attack to liberate the Mokmer airfield area. General Kreuger orders the forces in the Wadke–Sarmi area to resume the offensive to the west of the river Tirfoam line.

Mariana Islands On Saipan, the guns of the navy and the US landing craft prevent the Japanese from bringing reinforcements up against the Tanapag Harbour beachhead, north of the harbour itself. While the 2nd Marine Division maintains its positions, the 4th advances rapidly to the east coast of the island, in Magicienne Bay. The Japanese forces are thus cut in two. The 27th Infantry Division, which has just come into the line, takes Aslito airfield, in the south of the island, and advances almost as far as Magicienne Bay.

An American destroyer is sunk by Japanese coastal batteries on Saipan and two US tankers are sunk by bombers, while the escort carrier *Fanshaw Bay* is hit by bombers off the Marianas.

Taking advantage of the absence of American aircraft, Japanese air forces attack American shipping and beachheads, losing about twenty aircraft by anti-aircraft fire.

China Japanese troops capture Chang-sha,

19 June

France The Americans begin their final attack on Cherbourg. On the

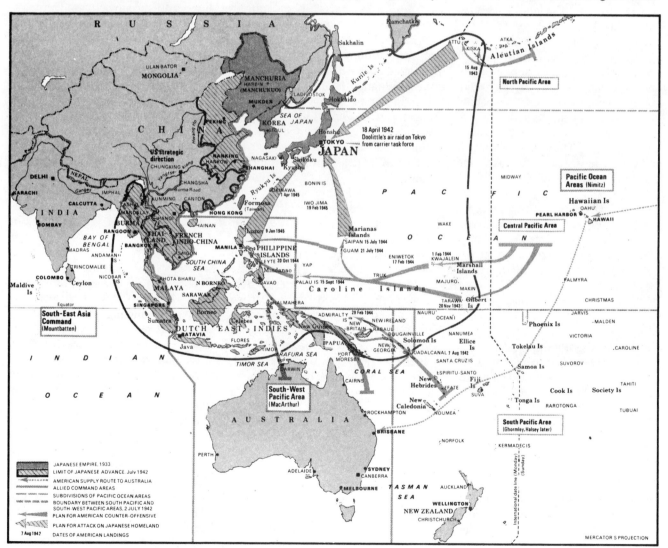

General picture of the Allied counter-offensive in the Pacific.

left the 9th Division advances in the direction of Helleville, St Christophe-du-Foc and Couville, in the centre the 79th Division makes for the line from Golleville to Urville and for Bois-de-la-Brique. On the right of the US line the 4th Division, the farthest advanced, meets with fierce resistance by the German forces defending Cherbourg. The 82nd Airborne Division and the 90th Division are transferred from the VII Corps to the VIII. It is officially announced that the British 7th Armoured Division – the famous 'Desert Rats' of the North African campaign – is fighting in Normandy.

Italian Front The French Expeditionary Corps completes the occupation of Elba.

□ Further V1 'flying bombs' fall on southern England. German propaganda magnifies their effect, saying that 'the roads from London are choked with refugees'.

New Guinea On Biak, after an accurate artillery barrage, the US 186th Infantry succeeds in getting behind the Japanese positions in the western caves, cutting the road that leads to the north. The 34th Infantry occupies the airfields at Borokoe and Sorido.

Mariana Islands On Saipan the 4th Marine Division, having reached Magicienne Bay on the east coast, turns north, leaving the 27th Infantry Division to mop up the Japanese still holding out in the southern part of the island. This is expected to be a straight-forward mopping-up operation, but things turn out very differently.

Battle of the Philippine Sea. The great Japanese fleet commanded by Vice-Admiral Ozawa, with nine aircraft carriers, and Admiral Spruance's Task Force 58, with 15 carriers, are about to meet. Task Force 58 has not yet succeeded in locating the enemy fleet, but furious battles develop in the skies above the Marianas between US carrier-borne aircraft and Japanese aircraft coming both from their aircraft carriers and their land bases. The Japanese lose at least 400 aircraft, the Americans 130. There is slight damage to some US warships.

Burma–China On the Salween front the Chinese capture Kutung and advance towards Teng-chung.

20 June

France While the US VII Corps offensive against Cherbourg continues (the 4th and 79th Divisions are about 5 miles from the town), units of the 29th Division (American XIX Corps) try in vain to advance in the direction of St Lô.

Italian Front Units of the US 5th Army have reached half-way between the Tiber and the Arno. While some units of the French Expeditionary Corps are held up on the river Orcia, a tributary of the Ombrone, the 1st Motorized Division is replaced during the night by the 2nd Moroccan Division so that it can take part in Operation *Anvil*. The 6th Armoured Division (British X Corps) enters Perugia with no opposition from the Germans.

Eastern Front The Russian armies of the Leningrad Front take Viipuri. The safety of Leningrad and the opening of the Gulf of Finland to the Russian fleet are assured. In the central sector the Russians are preparing to launch their great summer offensive.

Battle of the Philippine Sea. Task Force 58, having identified the position of the Japanese fleet, attacks it with high-level bombers, dive-bombers and torpedo-planes, as well as with submarines. The Japanese lose three aircraft carriers (*Shokaku*, *Taiho* and *Hiyo*), two destroyers and one tanker, while three aircraft carriers, one battleship, three cruisers, one destroyer and three tankers are seriously damaged. The Americans lose 130 aircraft, 57 brought down by the enemy and 73 which run out of fuel or lose their way back to the carrier in the dark and have come down in the sea. Two of their aircraft carriers, two battleships, one heavy cruiser and two destroyers are damaged. To save what remains of his fleet, Ozawa orders a rapid retreat.

After this great victory by Spruance and Mitscher the Japanese realize that the outcome of the war is decided.

New Guinea On Biak the US 162nd Infantry attacks the Japanese positions in the western caves, but with no success. The 34th Infantry occupies Borokoe and Sorido airfields and the village of Sorido, easily overcoming the weak Japanese resistance; they then block the road by which the Japanese might despatch reinforcements to the western caves area.

In the Aitape beachhead area the Japanese reinforce their positions and in the area of Wadke and Sarmi the US 6th Division advances to the west across the river Tirfoam.

Mariana Islands On Saipan the 4th Marine Division continues its sweep to the north, linking up with the 2nd Division. The enemy has formed a line across the island from Garapan, in the west, to the north-west end of Magicienne Bay in the east. The 27th Infantry Division makes for the extreme south of the island, Point Nafutan, but its progress is suddenly held up by the Japanese.

Burma–China On the Salween front the Chinese 36th Division takes Watien, in the Shweli valley.

□ The US Vice-President, Henry A. Wallace, arrives in Chungking for discussions with Generalissimo Chiang Kai-shek and General Chennault, Chief of the US air forces in China.

21 June

France The divisions of the American VII Corps (9th, 79th and 4th) prepare for the final attack on Cherbourg. At sundown General Collins, the Corps Commander, invites the Commander of the Cherbourg garrison, General Karl Wilhelm von Schlieben, to surrender. No reply comes from Cherbourg.

Italian Front In the British 8th Army sector, advance guards of the Polish II Corps reach the river Chienti and manage to establish a bridgehead there, despite the enemy's prepared defences. The South African 6th Armoured Division captures the heights overlooking Chiusi but cannot get into the town. The 36th Division (US IV Corps) continues its slow advance along Highway 1 and comes within 8 miles of Grosseto.

Eastern Front The Russian armies of the Karelia Front launch an attack inside Finland on the shores of Lake Onega.

☐ The US 8th Air Force makes its first 'shuttle raid' between Britain and bases in Russia, bombing oil refineries at Ruhland, south of Berlin.

New Guinea Although they attack with tanks and flame-throwers, the Americans are unable to make any progress in the area of the western caves on Biak Island.

In the area of the Sarmi beachhead the advance of the Americans to the west is halted by heavy and accurate enemy fire a little beyond the river Tirfoam. The units of the US 6th Division are forced to retire behind the Snaky River.

Mariana Islands On Saipan, slight progress by the US 27th Division in the south towards Point Nafutan.

22 June

France The final attack on Cherbourg is launched at 12.40 p.m. with an intensive air bombardment. The three divisions of VII Corps (the 9th, 79th and 4th) advance with difficulty over the rough terrain. The opposition they meet is mixed. Some German units resist stubbornly, but others quickly surrender.

Italian Front The Polish II Corps is forced to evacuate its small bridgehead across the river Chienti, in the eastern sector of the front. The units of the US 5th Army continue their slow advance north.

Eastern Front The big Russian offensive begins between the Pripet Marshes and the Dvina river against the positions of the German Army Group Centre (Field-Marshal Busch, to be replaced within six days by Model). Twenty-eight of the 40 divisions making up the army group are in immediate danger of being surrounded by a double pincer movement skilfully carried out by the Russians.

☐ Finland. Ribbentrop, the German Foreign Minister, visits Helsinki to try to persuade the Finnish govern-

ment not to surrender. Despite official announcements to the contrary, surrender seems imminent in view of the desperate military situation.

New Guinea US fighters begin to operate from Mokmer airfield, on Biak. The 162nd Infantry Regiment renews its attacks on the western caves, driving the enemy out with flame-throwers. In the afternoon the area is claimed to be free of enemy forces, but during the night groups of Japanese who have escaped from the mopping-up operations attack the American positions. In the Wadke–Sarmi area, on the mainland, the Japanese counter-attack after dusk in the Snaky River sector and succeed in cutting off two American battalions.

Mariana Islands On Saipan the 2nd Marine Division begins to attack northwards. It takes Mount Tipo Pale and gets to within a little more than three-quarters of a mile of the summit of Mount Tapotchau, which dominates the entire island. Meanwhile the units attacking along the east coast advance rapidly to the north. In the south, the US 27th Infantry Division continues the mopping-up of Point Nafutan.

Burma–China–India Chindits of the 77th Brigade (3rd Indian Division), together with units of the Chinese 38th Division, begin the assault on Mogaung.

On the Salween front the Chinese troops who already control the whole of the Shweli valley prepare to attack Teng-chung.

In India, the British IV and XXXIII Corps link up after reopening the Dimapur–Kohima–Imphal road. The Japanese are forced to speed up their withdrawal in the difficult conditions of the monsoon rains. In the long campaign to penetrate into India they have lost 30,000 men.

23 June

France The divisions of the VII Corps (US 1st Army) penetrate the outer defences of Cherbourg. On the left the 60th Regiment (9th Division) takes the Flottemanville sector while the 47th completes the capture

of Height 171. In the centre of the Allied line the 79th Division advances in the direction of La Mareà-Canards but is unable to take this strongpoint. On the right wing, too, the 4th Division advancing towards Tourlaville is in some difficulty.

To the east, in the British sector, the 5th Division (I Corps) takes Ste Honorine, north-east of Caen.

Italian Front After bitter fighting some units of the British XIII Corps enter Chiusi, but a German counterattack cuts them off. The 4th Division takes over the XIII Corps's central sector, between Vaiano and Lake Chiusi, relieving some units of the 78th Division.

Eastern Front The battle in the central sector, between the Pripet Marshes and the Dvina, develops over a front of 350 miles. The 1st Baltic Front and the three Belorusssian Fronts fall on the German salient at Minsk, exerting intense pressure in the Vitebsk and Bobruysk sectors, north-east and south-east of Minsk. The Red Army has massive air and artillery support. The German troops are too thin on the ground to hold such a huge front, and a large part of their air support has been transferred to the West.

New Guinea Mopping-up of the western caves on Biak continues; the Japanese will fight to the death. In the Sarmi area, on the mainland, the Japanese attack the American lines west of the beachhead, inflicting heavy losses on the Americans, who are only just able to hold them off. The two American battalions cut off in the Snaky River sector are unable to reopen the way back to their lines.

Mariana Islands On Saipan unsuccessful attacks by the Americans on Mount Tapotchau, on the slopes of which the Japanese have set up strongpoints in caves. However, the Marines manage to take some heights near the mountain and to make some small progress in what has already been christened 'Death Valley'. The Japanese counterattack along this valley with tanks during the night, but are driven back. In the south of the island the 105th Infantry Regiment is still not able to

wipe out the 500 or so Japanese defending the Point Nafutan area.
China By agreement between the American Vice-President Wallace and Chiang Kai-shek a group of American observers is to be sent to the Chinese Communist army in the north of the country.

24 June
France Fighting continues round Cherbourg, where the Germans continue to fight with what Allied correspondents call 'the courage of despair'. Elements of the 9th Division press on the city from the north-west while in the centre the regiments of the 79th Division reach and capture La Mare-à-Canards and Hameau-Gringer and advance towards Forte-du-Roule.
The garrison commander in Cherbourg, General Schlieben, reports to his superiors that the ability of his troops to hold out is rapidly diminishing. He is doubtful whether another attack can be repulsed.
Italian Front The 1st Motorized Division of the French Expeditionary Corps leaves Italy to take part in Operation *Anvil*, the landing projected for the south of France.
In the US 5th Army sector, the IV Corps continues its advance north, meeting firm opposition from the German rearguards.
The *Groupe Guillaume* (French Expeditionary Corps) crosses the river Omborne and advances northwards to meet the 1st Armoured Division of the US IV Corps.
Eastern Front The Leningrad Front continues its offensive in the isthmus of Karelia. In the central sector the Army Group Centre is breaking up under the Russian thrust.
New Guinea On Biak the 186th and 163rd Regiments of US infantry cut off considerable Japanese forces in the central sector of the island, north of the western caves.
In the area of the Sarmi beachhead, the Americans land small units west of the Snaky River and try to get round to the rear of the Japanese forces which have cut off the two American battalions in the sector.
Mariana Islands On Saipan the 27th

Infantry Division (less some units still engaged at Point Nafutan) joins the forces in the centre of the island, where the Americans are meeting tenacious resistance from the Japanese. Fighting is particularly intense on Mount Tapotchau and in Death Valley. General Smith, Commander of the 27th Infantry Division, is accused of inefficiency and replaced by General Jarman.

25 June
France The battle for Cherbourg has reached its last act. Naval and air bombardments are crippling the resistance of the Germans. After a day of furious fighting, General Schlieben sends a despairing message to Rommel's headquarters: 'The troops are worn out ... the loss of the town is inevitable and must come very shortly ... Among the troops defending the town there are 2,000 wounded who cannot be treated. Is the sacrifice of the others still necessary?' Rommel replies drily: 'In accordance with the Führer's orders you are to hold out to the last round.' Units of the American VII Corps are already in the suburbs of Cherbourg. The 9th Division is penetrating into the town from the west, while units of the 79th Division, coming up from the south, reach and capture Forte-du-Roule, only just outside Cherbourg, and penetrate into the suburbs of the town. To the east it falls to the 12th Regiment (4th Division) to be first into the city.
In the sector where the corps of the British 2nd Army are operating, the 49th Division (XXX Corps) opens an offensive directed at Rauray, about 10 miles west of Caen. The Germans have a number of divisions deployed in defence of the town from the LXXXVI Corps and I and II *Panzer SS* Corps.
Italian Front The 36th Division of the American IV Corps takes Piombino harbour without resistance. This is the last action in Italy of this division, which leaves to take part in Operation *Anvil*. The French Expeditionary Corps begins the crossing of the Orcia in force, and German resistance weakens. The 78th Division

(British XIII Corps) succeeds with great difficulty in widening its bridgehead near Pescia. The 4th Division succeeds in driving the German rearguards out of Vaiano. At nightfall, after fierce fighting lasting all day, the Germans withdraw from Chiusi.
Eastern Front In the central sector, where the battle rages with increasing ferocity, the Russians surround Vitebsk, trapping five German divisions and cutting the Smolensk–Minsk road.
In Germany, Nazi propaganda spreads stories of treachery in high military circles rather than admit that the Wehrmacht has insufficient forces in the sector where the Russians have broken through.
New Guinea During the night the Japanese evacuate the area in the centre of Biak Island where they have been cut off by the Americans.
American patrols find some more underground positions in the western caves.
American attacks in the Sarmi area force the Japanese to withdraw westwards.
Mariana Islands On Saipan marines of the 8th and 29th Regiments reach the summit of Mount Tapotchau. The 27th Infantry Division puts pressure on enemy positions in Death Valley, but to no effect. The 4th Marine Division seizes the Kagman peninsula. In the south of the island the 105th Infantry Regiment succeeds in breaking through the enemy positions near Point Nafutan, which they are already certain to capture despite the desperate resistance of the Japanese.
Burma–China On the Salween front the Japanese inflict a bloody defeat on the 261st Regiment of the Chinese 87th Division in the Lungling area. 1,500 Japanese have sufficed to get the better of at least 10,000 Chinese. Chiang Kai-shek sends the Chinese 8th Army up from Indo-China towards Teng-chung (in China, southeast of Myitkyina) and orders them to resume the offensive against Lungling.

26 June
France The American VII Corps

tightens the circle round Cherbourg. The advance of units of the 9th Division from the west is halted before the dockyard. Meanwhile the 39th Regiment reaches Octeville and the outer suburb of St Sauveur-le-Vicomte, where 1,000 Germans are taken prisoner, including the garrison commander, General Schlieben and Admiral Hennecke, naval commandant of the city. Hennecke has had the harbour completely destroyed so that the Allies will not be able to use it – a gesture for which Hitler decorates him with a knighthood of the Iron Cross. But the battle is not over.

Italian Front In the Tyrrhenian sector the 34th Division of the IV Corps, replacing the 36th Division, advances across the river Cecina. The French Expeditionary Corps, having crossed the Orcia at the cost of heavy losses, advances on Siena. In the centre of the Allied line the South African 6th Armoured Division (British XIII Corps) enters Chiusi.

Eastern Front In the central sector the Russians capture Vitebsk by storm, after heavy bombing by 700 aircraft. Six thousand German bodies are found in the streets. Vitebsk is one of the most famous of the 'hedgehog' strongpoints which Hitler has ordered to be defended at all costs in order to avoid the fall of Minsk to the west.

The important railway centre of Zhlobin also falls to the Russians.

Mariana Islands Off Saipan American amphibian craft attack a convoy of Japanese lighters carrying troops from Tanapag harbour (west coast) to the south. One lighter is sunk and the Japanese effort is thwarted. In the interior of the island the 2nd Marine Division takes an important position north of Mount Tipo Pale; the 27th Infantry Division is still held up in Death Valley, and the 4th Marine Division, on the American right, is mopping up the Kagman peninsula. In the south the 105th Infantry Regiment comes nearer to Point Nafutan, repulsing a night counter-attack by the Japanese.

Burma–China The Chinese 38th Division and Chindit units

Italian front, June 1944: a British 40-mm Bofors gun in action near Arezzo.

of the 77th Brigade, 3rd Indian Division, take Mogaung, an important position on the Burma Road and the Myitkyina–Mandalay railway. Just over the Chinese border, American B-25s attack Teng-chung.
China Japanese troops take Hengyang airfield, a major American base north of Canton in Hunan province.
Kuril Islands A US naval squadron commanded by Rear-Admiral Small bombards Paramushiro Island.

27 June
France The Cherbourg dockyard surrenders, while units of the 4th and 9th Divisions advance towards Cap-Lévy (east of the town) and Cap de la Hague (the extreme north-west point of the Cotentin peninsula).
In the British 2nd Army sector the attack of the 49th Division (XXX Corps) west of Caen continues with the capture of Rauray. A counter-attack by the 9th *Panzer SS* Division is repulsed. East of the 49th Division the British VIII Corps succeeds in establishing a small bridgehead over the Odon, adding to the threat to the enemy in the area of Grainville (this is the start of Operation *Epsom*,

which aims at taking Caen from the south).
Italian Front The British X Corps advances in the sector contained between the east bank of Lake Trasimene and the river Tiber, following the general retreat of the German 10th Army from the *Albert* line.
Eastern Front Troops of the three Belorussian Fronts (commanded by Marshal Zhukov, Deputy Supreme Commander of the Red Army) capture Orsha, in the central sector, and surround huge enemy forces at Bobruysk. Orsha was one of the main bastions of the German line, and is on the direct rail and highway to Minsk.
New Guinea On Biak the Americans complete the mopping up of the western caves so putting an end to surprise attacks. Minor skirmishes occur in the sectors of the other beachheads, Sarmi and Aitape.
Mariana Islands On Saipan the Americans capture some positions in the Purple Heart Peak sector, west of Mount Tapotchau. In the south, all Japanese resistance comes to an end at Point Nafutan where more than 500 Japanese bodies are counted.

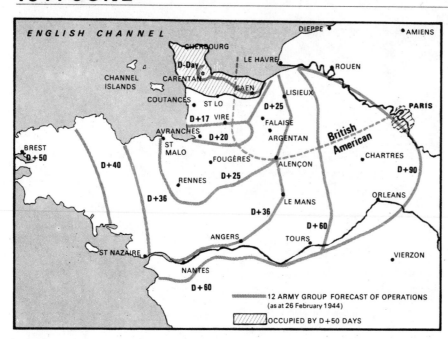

Forecast of Allied progress in the first 50 days following D-Day, and the ground actually occupied.

Map labels: ENGLISH CHANNEL · DIEPPE · AMIENS · CHERBOURG · D-Day · LE HAVRE · ROUEN · CHANNEL ISLANDS · CARENTAN · CAEN · LISIEUX · PARIS · COUTANCES · ST LO · D+25 · FALAISE · D+17 · VIRE · ARGENTAN · British · American · AVRANCHES · D+20 · CHARTRES · BREST · D+50 · ST MALO · D+40 · FOUGÈRES · ALENÇON · D+90 · RENNES · D+25 · ORLEANS · D+36 · LE MANS · D+36 · D+60 · ANGERS · TOURS · VIERZON · ST NAZAIRE · NANTES · D+60

12 ARMY GROUP FORECAST OF OPERATIONS (as at 26 February 1944)

OCCUPIED BY D+50 DAYS

28 June

France The American 79th Division (VII Corps) leaves the Cherbourg sector for the area where the US VIII Corps is operating, south-west of the Cotentin peninsula. The 9th Division continues preparations for the final attack at Cap de la Hague.

Italian Front The American IV Corps, with the 34th Division on the left and the 1st Armoured Division on the right, advances along Highway 68, which runs parallel with the river Cecina. The South African 6th Armoured Division (British XIII Corps) reaches Chianciano without engaging the enemy. The positions of the 8th Indian Division are taken over by the 10th Indian Division.

Eastern Front The 7th Army of the Karelia Front (Meretskov) takes Petrozavodsk, on the west bank of Lake Onega, cutting the railway to Murmansk. The same railway line is also cut north of the lake by the 32nd Army. The Finnish II and VI Corps still resist stubbornly. Hitler replaces Busch by Model in command of the German Army Group Centre.

☐ Finland. Keitel, Chief of Staff of the OKH, the supreme command of the German army, goes to Helsinki and promises to send reinforcements from Estonia. This meeting follows in the wake of Ribbentrop's visit. The Germans are trying desperately to avoid the separate peace that seems imminent.

New Guinea General Eichelberger hands over command of Task Force *Hurricane* to General Doe. The Japanese begin to withdraw from the eastern caves towards the north, preparing to go over to guerrilla warfare in the absence of reinforcements and supplies.

Mariana Islands On Saipan fighting continues along the line crossing the island from just south of Garapan, on the west coast, across the features of Mount Tipo Pàle, Mount Tapotchau and Purple Heart Peak, to the east coast north of the Kagman peninsula. The 27th Infantry Division suffers considerable losses in Death Valley, near Mount Tapotchau, and on Purple Heart Peak.

China The Japanese move in to take Hengyang (they have already captured the airfield there) and for the first time they run into stern resistance from the Chinese.

Burma In the north of the country units of the Chinese 14th Division advance towards Sitapur with the object of cutting off the Japanese units north of Myitkyina. On the Salween front Japanese aircraft appear for the first time, dropping supplies to the garrison of Sung Shan.

29 June

France The last of the German strongpoints in the Cherbourg harbour area surrenders. The VIII Corps sends the 101st Airborne Division to Cherbourg.

Italian Front In the western sector of the front (American IV Corps) units of the US 34th Division are heavily engaged by the 16th *Panzergrenadiere SS* not far from Cecina. To the east, on the British 8th Army front, Vietinghoff's German 10th Army is in general retreat. The South African 6th Armoured Division reaches Acquaviva and Montepulciano, and the 78th Division Castiglion del Lago.

Eastern Front The armies of the 1st Belorussian Front (Rokossovsky) capture Bobruysk. The Russians threaten Minsk.

New Guinea American mopping up continues on Biak. The Japanese shell the American positions from the eastern caves, which in turn are shelled by tanks and mortars.

Mariana Islands On Saipan the 106th Regiment, US 27th Infantry Division, advances about three-quarters of a mile in Death Valley.

30 June

France The last German resistance at Cap de la Hague gives way under attacks by the 9th Division (US VII Corps). The 101st Airborne Division replaces the 4th Division in front of Cherbourg.

In the US XIX Corps sector the slow advance of the 3rd Armoured Division continues in the area south of St Lô. Before evening this division is replaced by the 29th.

Italian Front The 34th Division continues the battle for Cecina.

New Guinea The main phase of the operations on Biak Island is finished. Part of the landing force is withdrawn into the beachhead, while the rest undertake the mopping up of the island.

On the mainland, in the Wadke–Sarmi area, mopping up operations are in progress.

An improvised field hospital in a street in Teng-chung, China.

Mariana Islands On Saipan the 2nd Marine Division advances north of Mount Tipo Pale and Mount Tapotchau. The 27th Infantry Division, in the centre of the line, captures Death Valley and Purple Heart Peak, making firm contact with the 2nd Marines on their right and the 4th Marines on their left. This completes the mopping up of the Kagman peninsula, and marks the end too of the battle in the central strip of Saipan.

American headquarters decide to carry out the landing on Guam on 21 July. The operation is to be undertaken by the troops at present engaged on Saipan, plus the 77th Infantry Division from Hawaii.

1 July

France The headquarters of the US 1st Army issues to its divisions directives for a general offensive. This is to begin on 3 July with the US VIII Corps, west of the Cotentin peninsula, and extend progressively eastwards to all the other formations in the army. In the extreme north of the Cotentin peninsula all organized German resistance ends with the capture of Cap de la Hague by the American 9th Division (VII Corps). In the British 2nd Army sector the VIII and XXX Corps, with heavy

artillery support, repulse powerful counter-attacks by the I *Panzer SS* Group in the area of Tilly-sur-Seulles and Caen, with wholesale destruction of German tanks.

Since D-Day on 6 June, the Allies have landed in Normandy 920,000 men, nearly 600,000 tons of equipment and 177,000 vehicles. Each of the two Allied armies, the 1st American and 2nd British, can put 15 or 16 divisions in the line, while 15 more (9 US and 6 British and Canadian) are in reserve in the south of England, ready to embark. In 24 days' fighting the Allies have lost nearly 62,000 men killed and wounded.

Italian Front While some of the units of the 34th Division (US IV Corps) take Cecina town, others advance towards the Cecina river. East of the town, despite resistance by the Germans, the 135th Regiment succeeds in holding the bridgehead captured the previous day. On the right of the American corps, the 1st Armoured Division advances on Siena.

On the right of the Allied line the British X Corps (8th Army) which has not yet made contact with the enemy, replaces the British 6th Armoured Division in the front line.

Eastern Front Troops of the 3rd Belorussian Front (Chernyakovsky)

take Borisov, a major centre on the Orsha–Minsk railway line, by storm.

New Guinea Task Force 77 under Rear-Admiral Fechteler, with the US 158th Infantry Regiment and Australian units, sails for Numfoor Island, between Biak and the northwest point of New Guinea. The Japanese 18th Army has to split up its slender forces to try to defend an impossible number of Allied targets. On Biak the Americans try to prevent the Japanese from re-grouping. In the Wadke-Sarmi area, on the mainland, to ensure the safety of Maffin Bay, American troops advance as far as the mouth of the river Woske and then move inland.

Mariana Islands On Saipan the attacking forces make little progress towards the north of the island.

☐ USA. An important international conference opens at Bretton Woods to create post-war financial institutions and economic rehabilitation. Forty-four countries take part (all of them enemies of Germany and Japan). As a result of this conference the International Monetary Fund and the International Bank for Reconstruction and Development will be established.

2 July

France The divisions of the American 1st Army are reorganized. The VII Corps, now consisting of the 4th, 9th and 83rd Divisions, is moved between the VIII and XIX Corps, on the west and east. The VIII Corps now comprises four divisions, the 8th, 79th, 90th and 82nd Airborne, while the 29th and 30th Divisions stay in the XIX Corps. The 2nd Armoured Division and the 1st and 2nd Infantry Divisions make up the V Corps.

Italian Front Cecina Marina is captured by the 133rd Regiment, US 34th Division, thus bringing to an end a bloody battle on the left of the American line. The 135th consolidates and reinforces its bridgehead beyond the river Cecina. Efforts by the 1st Armoured Division to take Casole d'Elsa, an agricultural town some 25 miles from Siena, are unsuccessful, and the US formation has heavy losses in men and tanks. The

French Expeditionary Corps captures Sovicille and continues its advance towards Siena.

In the British sector of the front the South African 6th Armoured Division (XIII Corps) makes for Sinalunga, from which the enemy has withdrawn. The 4th Division takes Foiano, about 20 miles from Arezzo and then presses on towards Arezzo. The XIII Corps has thus completely breached the *Albert* line.

Eastern Front Both the 1st and 3rd Belorussian Fronts converge on Minsk. The 1st Belorussian Front cuts the railway line between Minsk and Baranovichi.

□ Marshal Karl von Rundstedt asks to be relieved of the command of German forces in the West. Hitler accepts.

New Guinea After an intense and highly effective 80-minute bombardment of the landing zone from air and sea, the US 158th Regiment, reinforced by Australian units, lands on the north coast of Numfoor Island, near Kamiri airfield. It meets no resistance. General Patrick, taking command of the operations, asks for the 503rd Parachute Regiment, held in reserve, to be dropped on Kamiri airfield. As the Americans advance cautiously inland they meet the first opposition from the Japanese. They establish a beachhead about two miles wide and half a mile deep. Artillery units are landed and begin to shell Kamiri airfield.

Mariana Islands: Saipan On the left of the American line the 2nd Marine Division captures the ruins of Garapan. The whole front advances an average of half a mile. The Japanese withdraw to a new defensive line running from the north of Tanapag harbour to the east coast of the island.

Burma–China The Chinese divisions reinforce the north flank of the Myitkyina area, fearing a Japanese counter-offensive from the north. On the Salween front the Chinese 116th Division advances on Teng-chung in spite of the violent monsoon rain.

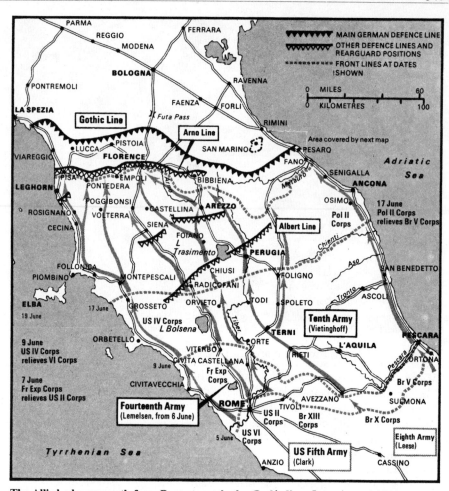

The Allied advance north from Rome towards the *Gothic* line, June–August 1944.

3 July

France At 5.30 a.m. in a blinding rainstorm the American 1st Army launches the so-called 'Battle of the Hedges', a general offensive beginning from the western flank of the Allied line, in the Cotentin peninsula. Starting here, General Middleton's US VIII Corps attacks south against the divisions of the German LXXXIV Corps. The Americans deploy three divisions, the 79th, 82nd Airborne and 90th, but they make very little progress on account of the rain and generally bad weather (which does not allow proper air cover and makes the terrain almost impassable), and of the determined opposition of the German 243rd, 353rd and 91st Divisions. Units of the 82nd Airborne Division report a small advance, taking Height 131, north-east of La Haye-du-Puits, on the road to Coutances.

Italian Front The 34th Division (US IV Corps) begins its push to Leghorn, in the teeth of stubborn and effective German resistance. Units of the US 135th Infantry Regiment advance as far as the vicinity of the Rosignano fortress (south-east of Leghorn) after a fierce battle with units of the 16th *SS Panzergrenadiere* Division. Further east the 3rd Algerian Division of the French Expeditionary Corps enters Siena.

In the British 8th Army sector the 78th Division (XIII Corps) reaches Cortona, which the Germans have evacuated.

Eastern Front Minsk falls to the 1st and 3rd Belorussian Fronts. The German Army Group Centre has been torn asunder and 28 of its 40 divisions are encircled. The Russians claim 400,000 German dead and 158,000 taken prisoner and the capture of 2,000 enemy tanks and 10,000 guns. This overwhelming victory brings a grave threat to the Army Group North, stationed in the Baltic states, which is in danger of being cut off. The 1st Baltic Front (Bagramyan) is about to unleash a powerful offensive against it. The Russians have superiority in every respect and during the attack against Army Group Centre could muster at least 320 guns to every mile of the front in the most vital sectors.

☐ General Gunther von Kluge takes over the command in the Western Front in place of von Rundstedt.

New Guinea On Numfoor Island the US 158th Infantry Regiment extends the perimeter of its beachhead eastwards over a mile in the direction of Kornasoren airfield. A battalion of the 503rd Parachute Regiment drops on Kamiri airfield and occupies it. Many of the parachutists are killed during the drop.

On Biak the Americans occupy the eastern caves without difficulty and begin mopping up operations.

On the mainland the headquarters of the Japanese 18th Army issues a directive for the preparation of an attack in force against the Americans' Aitape beachhead.

Mariana Islands: Saipan The Americans, advancing north, capture a height overlooking Tanapag on the west coast. They are held up on the east coast by an enemy strongpoint, which they bombard heavily during the following night.

Volcano Islands–Bonin Islands Two task forces of American aircraft carriers and escort vessels commanded by Rear-Admirals Clark and Davison bomb and shell Japanese installations in the Volcano Islands and on Chichi Jima and Haha Jima in the Bonin Islands. Four enemy ships are sunk.

Burma–India On the Assam front the 7th Indian Division, XXXIII Corps, captures Ukhrul. But the Japanese dig in close to this important road junction.

4 July

France On the right flank of the American 1st Army the VIII Corps continues its slow advance southwards. To the east, the VII Corps's offensive begins.

In the British sector, in preparation

American soldiers in Normandy, July 1944.

for the general offensive against Caen, the Canadian 3rd Division (British I Corps) takes Carpiquet (a few miles west of Caen), but is halted a little way from the local airfield by the German defences.

Italian Front In the Tyrrhenian sector the 34th Division (US IV Corps) drives on towards Rosignano. On the right flank of the IV Corps, units of the 361st Regiment of the 1st Armoured Division penetrate into Casole d'Elsa before dawn. They are now only about 25 miles south of Siena. There are some troop movements both in the American and the French formations. The 361st Regiment, after taking Casole d'Elsa (abandoned by the German garrison), is moved from the 1st Armoured to the 91st Division, and the 3rd Algerian Division hands over its positions to the 4th Mountain Division and is sent to Naples for a rest period.

The 8th Army continues its advance in the central-eastern sector of the front. The XIII Corps, with the South African 6th Armoured Division on the left, the British 4th Division in the centre and the British 6th Armoured Division on the right, makes rapid progress towards

Arezzo meeting negligible enemy resistance. The 6th Armoured Division takes Castiglion Fiorentino.

Eastern Front In the northern sector the 1st Baltic Front goes into the attack towards Riga with six armies, taking Polotsk, north-west of Vitebsk. Army Group North, after the Russians' huge breakthrough in the centre, is now in a highly critical position.

New Guinea On Numfoor the Americans take Kornasoren airfield and the village of Kamiri. Another battalion of the 503rd Parachute Regiment is dropped on Kamiri airport. They lose one in every twelve of their men, due to inexperience and the difficult terrain rather than to enemy fire. The losses are so high that it is decided that the rest of the regiment must be air-lifted instead of being dropped by parachute. Kamiri airfield is quickly reactivated to meet this requirement.

On the mainland, in the Wadke–Sarmi area, the US 63rd Infantry makes a little progress westwards.

Mariana Islands: Saipan The US 27th Infantry Division, after a skirmish with the retreating enemy, reaches the Tanapag plain. A regiment of the same division reaches a seaplane base at Point Flores and, with a Marines regiment, wipes out a Japanese cave strongpoint. About 100 Japanese who have infiltrated into the American lines are eliminated.

☐ The Allied Joint Chiefs of Staff send a message to Roosevelt suggesting that he should put pressure on Chiang Kai-shek to give General Stilwell command of all the Chinese armed forces and that General Sultan should be put at the head of the Chinese forces in Burma in succession to General Stilwell. Sultan's position as Deputy Supreme Commander in South-East Asia, under Admiral Mountbatten, should go to General Wheeler.

5 July

France Heavy fighting continues over the whole Normandy front. The US VIII Corps captures La Haye-du-Puits railway station. The US VII Corps continues its slow advance to the south towards Périers, on the road leading from St Lô to Lessay on the west coast of the Cotentin peninsula.

Italian Front The battle for Rosignano continues. The Americans of the 34th Division (IV Corps) make very slow progress against the tenacious German resistance.

The resistance of Vietinghoff's German 10th Army stiffens in the area in which the British XIII Corps is advancing.

New Guinea On Numfoor Island the Japanese launch the only attack in force since the landing. The attacking troops, about 400 strong, are exterminated.

Mariana Islands: Saipan The Americans begin the last stage of the capture of the south of the island. The 4th Marine Division makes headway, but the 105th Regiment of the 27th Infantry Division, is held up by the enemy, dug in on the north side of a ravine called Harakiri Gulch.

Burma–China On the Salween front the Chinese 8th Army attacks Sung Shan from east and south but such ground as they are able to take is recaptured by the Japanese in a

Saipan, Mariana Islands, 7 July 1944: Japanese soldiers who have committed suicide after the failure of their assault on American lines on the Tanapag plain.

powerful counter-attack.

6 July

France The American VII and VIII Corps continue their slow advance to the south in the direction of Lessay and Périers against exceptionally fierce German resistance.

☐ De Gaulle begins a visit to the United States and Canada.

Italian Front In the British 8th Army sector, the 3rd (*Carpatica*) Division (Polish II Corps) captures Osimo, about 20 miles south of Ancona.

Eastern Front Troops of the 1st Belorussian Front occupy Kovel, in Poland, south-east of Brest-Litovsk, which the Germans have evacuated the previous day.

New Guinea On Numfoor, units of the US 158th Infantry occupy Namber airport in an amphibious operation, following an air and naval barrage. Squadrons of Australian P-40 fighters land on Kamiri airfield to support the land operations.

On Biak the Americans use loudspeakers to call on the Japanese in the eastern caves to lay down their arms.

Mariana Islands: Saipan The US units make some progress on the west coast towards the village of Makunsha, but are still held up by the desperate Japanese defence in the

Harakiri Gulch area. On the east coast the 24th Marine Regiment advances rapidly as far as Mount Petosukara, meeting only sporadic resistance. At dawn General Saito calls his officers together and, after exacting from them a promise that they will not fall into enemy hands alive, kills himself in accordance with the Japanese code of honour. At almost the same time, Admiral Nagumo commits harakiri. The remaining Japanese plan a final Banzai assault (a fierce suicide attack) to salve Japanese honour.

Guam–Rota Aircraft from US carriers begin a series of daily bombing raids on the islands of Guam and Rota, in the Marianas, in preparation for the landing.

☐ Roosevelt forwards to Chiang Kai-shek the proposals made by the Joint Chiefs of Staff.

7 July

France RAF bombers carry out a heavy night raid on Caen, dropping more than 2,500 tons of bombs, in preparation for the final assault on the city.

In the west the 79th and 90th Divisions (American VIII Corps) continue their efforts to break through the defensive line between

La Haye-du-Puits and Mont-Castre-Forest, but have to withstand violent counter-attacks. Units of the American VII Corps move slowly along the Carentan–Périers road against growing opposition by two SS divisions, the 2nd and the 17th Armoured. East of the American VII Corps, the US 30th Division (XIX Corps) establishes a bridgehead near the village of St Jean-de-Daye, which they capture, and then push on towards the river Vire.

□ De Gaulle has a meeting with President Roosevelt in Washington.

Italian Front Rosignano is captured by the 135th Regiment of the 34th Division. But the German rearguards have not yet yielded and they take up positions just outside the town. The 4th Mountain Division (French Expeditionary Corps) takes Val d'Alsa hill.

New Guinea On Biak some units of the Japanese are still holding out in the Ibdi area, which is heavily bombarded.

Mariana Islands: Saipan At first light about 3,000 Japanese (all that is left of the garrison of Saipan) hurl themselves in a furious assault against the American lines in the Tanapag plain, sweeping through one regiment of the 27th Infantry Division and the guns of the 3rd Battalion of the 10th Marines. There is bitter hand-to-hand fighting. Towards the end of the morning an American counter-attack drives the Japanese back and they are pursued northwards and massacred.

Pacific Admiral Nimitz orders his commanders in the field to prepare forces for an invasion of the southern Palau Islands (Angaur, Peleliu and Ngesebus) on 15 September and of Yap and Ulithi, north-east of the Palaus, on 5 October.

Burma–China Fresh attacks by the Chinese 8th Army against Sung Shan are repulsed by the Japanese with considerable losses.

□ A second raid on the Japanese metropolitan islands by US Superfortresses. The B-29s concentrate their attack on naval installations at Sasebo, in Kyushu Island.

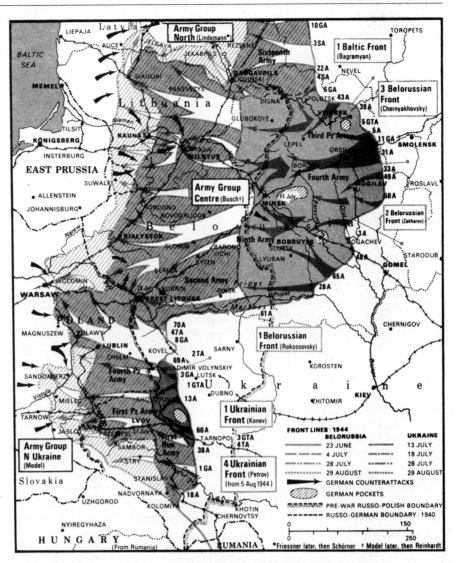

The Russian advance into Poland 23 June–29 August 1944.

8 July

France In the course of an attack from the west by the 78th Division, the Americans of VIII Corps overrun La Haye-du-Puits. The 8th Division, only just arrived from England, goes into the line in the sector between the 79th and 90th Divisions. Units of the VII Corps continue their difficult advance along the Carentan–Périers road, while the XIX Corps (reinforced by the newly landed 35th Division) continues to advance on St Lô.

In the eastern sector, at 4.20 a.m., the British I Corps launches its offensive against Caen with, from left to right of the line, the 59th and 3rd British and 3rd Canadian Divisions. The first Allied troops enter the city from the north-east.

Italian Front With the capture of Rosignano the American 34th Division (IV Corps) are able to speed up their advance on Leghorn. The 88th Division occupies Volterra and the heights north and east of the town. Units of the French Expeditionary Corps mount an offensive in the direction of San Gimignano, west of Poggibonsi, and capture Height 380, about two miles north of Highway 68.

Eastern Front The 1st Belorussian Front, advancing north of the Pripet Marshes, captures Baranovichi, north-east of Brest-Litovsk.

Mariana Islands: Saipan Having overcome Japanese resistance in Harakiri Gulch, the Americans advance all along the line towards the north of the island.

Guam A squadron of US carriers and destroyers under the command of Rear-Admiral Joy begins a series of daily bombardments of the defences of Guam. On the 14th several battleships will join in this work of demolition.

Burma–China On the Salween front five Chinese divisions surround Teng-chung.

□ Chiang Kai-shek agrees in principle with Roosevelt's request that Stilwell should have operational command of the Chinese army. But he asks for a personal representative of the President to be sent to China.

9 July

France The American 5th Division lands in France. The US VIII Corps, trying to push on beyond La Haye-du-Puits, is pinned down by the difficult terrain and by the stiff resistance of the divisions of the German LXXXIV Corps. The American 4th and 83rd Divisions (VII Corps) advance towards Périers under a violent German barrage. The 9th Division, brought up from Cherbourg, is sent into the sector east of the river Taute. In the XIX Corps sector the 30th Division's offensive towards the road linking St Lô and Lessay continues.

In the British 2nd Army sector, units of the British I Corps begin to enter the suburbs of Caen from the west (Canadian 3rd Division) and north (British 1st Division), driving out the 12th *Panzer SS* Division.

Italian Front On the left flank of the American 34th Division the northward advance beyond Rosignano continues, while on the right the 88th Division has to face the determined opposition of the German units. The British 8th Army prepares an attack against Arezzo.

Eastern Front In the central northern sector, troops of the 3rd Belorussian Front capture Lida, east of Minsk and south of Vilna in Lithuania. The Army Group North is isolated in the Baltic states as a direct result of Hitler's reckless orders.

Mariana Islands: Saipan The Americans reach Point Marpi, the final

objective of their advance. Apart from the completion of normal mopping-up operations, the capture of the island is now completed, and officially announced by Vice-Admiral Turner at 4.15 p.m. It has cost the Americans over 14,000 killed and wounded. The Japanese have had nearly 30,000 dead, their entire garrison apart from some hundred or so wounded taken prisoner. At Point Marpi hundreds of civilians, possibly collaborators with the Japanese, are found smashed to death at the foot of a high cliff.

10 July

France General Montgomery, Commander-in-Chief of the 21st Army Group, issues directives for Operation *Cobra*, the American 1st Army's offensive to penetrate the defences of the Germans west of St Lô and take Coutances.

In the VIII Corps sector the American troops advance south of La Haye-du-Puits. The three divisions of the VII Corps, the 4th, 9th and 83rd, continue their offensive from the west.

The British VIII Corps (2nd Army) opens an offensive south-west of Caen in the area between the rivers Odon and Orne. The 43rd Division captures Eterville and Height 112 on the road to Evrecy. In the Caen sector the Canadian II Corps under General Simonds, grouped with the British 2nd Army, goes into action.

Italian Front In the Tyrrhenian sector the divisions of the American IV Corps make negligible progress northwards towards Leghorn.

Eastern Front Field-Marshal Model, Commander of the German Group Centre, requests Hitler to have the Army Group North withdrawn across the Dvina to help with the defensive operations in the central sector. As usual, Hitler refuses. Army Group Centre has lost almost the whole of the 9th and 4th Armies. The 3rd Belorussian Front, under Chernyakhovsky, surrounds Vilna in Lithuania.

New Guinea During the night the Japanese attack in force over the river Driniumor, inflicting heavy

losses on the US 128th Infantry Regiment.

Burma–China–India On the Salween front the Chinese persevere with their costly efforts to dislodge the Japanese from Sung Shan.

On the Assam front, in India, the British XXXIII Corps has succeeded in driving the Japanese out of the immediate vicinity of the road junction at Ukhrul.

11 July

France The US 1st Army's offensive is now being carried out by all four corps at once, the VIII, VII, XIX and V, deployed on a front from the west coast of the Cotentin peninsula to Caumont, about 13 miles east of St Lô.

While the units of the VIII Corps make considerable progress south of La Haye-du-Puits, a counter-attack by the *Panzerlehr* Division succeeds in breaking through the lines of the 9th Division in the Le-Désert sector. A combined infantry and artillery action, with air support, drives the Germans back with the loss of a number of tanks.

The XIX Corps opens its offensive against St Lô with its 30th Division west of the river Vire and the 35th and 29th Divisions on the east. The units in the V Corps renew their attacks in the direction of Height 192, north-east of St Lô.

In the British sector, the 50th Division (XXX Corps) improves its positions near Hottot-les-Bagues, some 13 miles west of Caen. Meanwhile the British 43rd Division (VIII Corps) captures Height 112.

□ The government of the United States recognizes as *de facto* the hitherto provisional government of the French Republic headed by General de Gaulle.

Italian Front Orders are issued for Operation *Mallory Major*, the destruction of bridges over the river Po. The American IV Corps makes limited progress northwards. In the British XIII Corps (8th Army) sector the New Zealand 2nd Division gets ready to support the final attack on Arezzo.

New Guinea On Numfoor the US

158th Infantry and 503rd Parachute Regiments begin the systematic mopping up of the island, the infantry in the north and the parachutists in the south. In the Aitape beachhead sector on the mainland, the Americans withdraw from the river Driniumor river line. General Krueger orders that the line should be recaptured as quickly as possible.
China In central east China the Japanese 11th Army renews the attack against Hengyang but is repulsed by the Chinese with effective air support.

12 July
France The US 1st Army sends the 101st Airborne Division back to England for a period of rest and to train new recruits. While the VIII Corps makes considerable progress southwards, towards the rivers Ay and Sèves, the VII is in difficulties along the Carentan–Périers road. The US XIX Corps' offensive against St Lô goes on, but at a reduced pace, as the 30th Division is in trouble in the Pont-Hébert sector, as is the 116th Regiment (29th Division) west of that town. All the objectives on the features called Height 192, north-east of St Lô, are captured by the 2nd Division (US V Corps).
Italian Front The Us IV Corps (5th Army), advancing on Leghorn, takes Castiglioncello. On the right of the line the 34th Division runs into serious difficulties, while the 88th, supported by effective artillery fire, takes Laiatico.
Operation *Mallory Major* is launched by the US Tactical Air Force in perfect weather.
Eastern Front The great Russian offensive grows in scale and intensity. Moscow announces that the 2nd Baltic Front has launched a series of attacks between Nevel and Ostrov, south of Lake Peipus, capturing Idrica, west of Velikiye Luki along the railway line to Riga.
New Guinea In the Aitape area the Americans re-group for the recapture of the positions lost on the river Driniumor.
Burma–China The Chinese and

A Russian SU-76 self-propelled gun drives past a German gun disabled during the battle for Vilna.

Americans, with strong air support, launch an attack in force against Myitkyina but are repulsed. Some of the aircraft bomb their own troops through a communications error.
On the Salween front the Japanese in the Sung Shan garrison continue to repulse the attacks of two Chinese divisions. The Chinese offensive is suspended.

13 July
France The American 4th Armoured Division lands in northern France. General Headquarters of the US 1st Army approves plans for Operation *Cobra*, the attack on St Lô.
The American VIII Corps continues to push south, but in the VII Corps sector only the 9th Division, on the left flank, makes headway, while action on the rest of the line is virtually suspended. The US XIX Corps continues the hard struggle for St Lô. Finally, in the V Corps sector, the 5th Division goes into the line to replace the 1st Division, which is moved to Colombières, some six miles south-east of Isigny, before going over to the VII Corps sector.
Italian Front The American 34th Division (IV Corps) advances about

three miles towards Leghorn. The other two divisions in the American IV Corps, the 88th and the 9th, are engaged in the central and right sectors. The 4th Mountain Division of the French Expeditionary Corps captures San Gimignano, while another French division, the 2nd Moroccan, gets nearly as far as Poggibonsi and the suburbs of Castellina in Chianti, about half way between Arezzo and Leghorn.
In the centre of the Allied line the New Zealand 2nd Division captures the summit of Monte Castiglione Maggiore.
Eastern Front After fierce street fighting the 3rd Belorussian Front captures Vilna, the capital of Lithuania. The German Army Group North is in still greater danger of being completely cut off.
New Guinea On Numfoor Island the American parachutists make contact with the main body of Japanese who are still holding out about three miles north-east of Namber airfield. On the mainland, in Aitape sector, US units counter-attack and succeed in reaching the river Driniumor at two points. The 128th Infantry routs the Japanese coastal attack group,

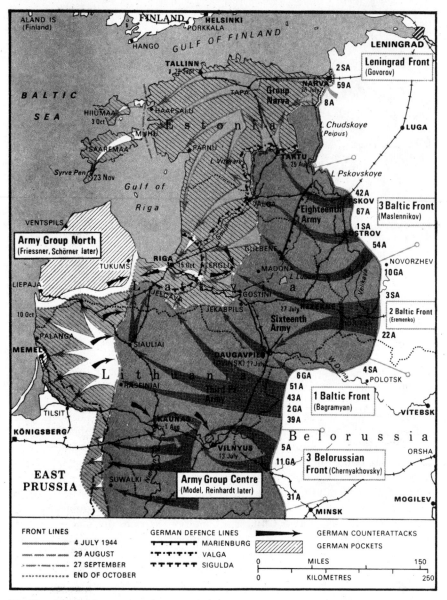

FRONT LINES

~~~~~~~~~~ 4 JULY 1944
─ ─ ─ ─ ─ 29 AUGUST
─ ·· ─ ·· ─ 27 SEPTEMBER
─ ··· ─ ··· END OF OCTOBER

GERMAN DEFENCE LINES

ꞱꞱꞱꞱ MARIENBURG
·Ʇ·Ʇ·Ʇ·Ʇ VALGA
ꞱꞱꞱꞱꞱ SIGULDA

➤ GERMAN COUNTERATTACKS
▨ GERMAN POCKETS

MILES
0 ——————————— 150
0 ——————————— 250
KILOMETRES

The Russian advance into Latvia and Lithuania.

destroying most of its guns.

☐ Before leaving for Hawaii for discussions with Nimitz and MacArthur on the Pacific war strategy, Roosevelt replies to Chiang Kai-shek's letter of 8th July, agreeing to send him a personal political representative and asking him in the meanwhile to entrust the command of the Chinese army to General Stilwell.

14 July

France The four corps of the US 1st Army (VIII, VII, XIX and V) still advance south, meeting firm resistance all the time from the German 7th Army. In particular, units of the 30th Division (XIX Corps) capture Pont-Hébert after a bitter struggle, while the 35th Division reaches the road joining Pont-Hébert and St Lô.

Italian Front The 34th Division continues its advance towards Leghorn, with the 442nd Regiment taking San Pieve di Luce and the 133rd approaching Usigliano. Units of the American 9th Division seize Chianni, meeting with no resistance. The Germans have also abandoned Terricciola. Units of the French Expeditionary Corps capture Poggibonsi and push on towards Certaldo.

Eastern Front The central and southern Fronts of the Red Army are once more on the move. The 1st

Ukraine Front (Konev) goes over to the offensive in Poland, north and south of Brody, in the region east of Lvov. Further north, forces of the 1st Belorussian Front capture Pinsk, east of Brest-Litovsk.

New Guinea Japanese counterattacks on the river Driniumor, in the Aitape area, are driven off.

Burma–India General Lentaigne asks for the few platoons of Chindits in Morris Force (from the 3rd Indian Division) to be withdrawn west of the Irrawaddy, but the British headquarters refuses to give the necessary authority.

In India, the British XXXIII Corps completes the encirclement and elimination of enemy forces along the Ukhrul–Imphal road. The IV Corps, whose advance on Tiddim (over the Burma frontier) has been firmly held up by the Japanese, manages to weaken the enemy's resistance through a series of attacks by the 5th and 17th Indian Divisions.

15 July

France The offensive by the American 1st Army comes to a halt west of the river Taute while the operational plans for Operation *Cobra* against St Lô and Coutances are prepared. The offensive of the 9th Division (VII Corps) continues, while the 30th and 1st Infantry Divisions and 2nd and 3rd Armoured Divisions are regrouped under VII Corps. The 35th and 29th Divisions (XIX Corps), supported by artillery and bombers, continue their advance towards St Lô; on the left of the 35th Division the 134th Regiment reaches Height 122, nearly a mile and a quarter beyond St Lô, but the division as a whole fails to keep up the momentum. Units of the 29th Division reach the Bayeux–St Lô road near La Madeleine, but are immediately cut off by the Germans.

In the British 2nd Army sector the British XII Corps attacks during the night along a line Bougy–Evrecy–Maizet, south-west of Caen between the Orne and the Odon.

Italian Front Units of the 34th Division are now advancing rapidly on Leghorn. Two regiments, the

168th and 133rd, press on towards Pisa. In the centre of IV Corps sector, the 363rd Regiment (9th Division) captures Bagni di Casciana without opposition, but then has to help to support the 34th Division's attack on Leghorn. The 88th Division's offensive on the right flank of IV Corps continues. In the French Expeditionary Corps sector the 8th Moroccan Regiment captures Castellina in Chianti.

In the centre of the front the British XIII Corps (8th Army) mounts an attack against Arezzo. The attack is preceded by an aerial bombardment at dawn, and is carried out by two divisions, the 6th Armoured on the left and the New Zealand 2nd Division on the right. The German positions are held by units of the LXXVI *Panzerkorps*, 1st Parachute Division, by two infantry divisions (the 334th and 719th) and some units of the 15th *Panzergrenadiere*. After sunset the Germans begin to withdraw along the whole front.

☐ The Italian government returns to Rome.

Eastern Front The 2nd Baltic Front captures Opochka, south of Ostrov and Lake Peipus.

Burma The commander of the Japanese forces in Myitkyina considers the possibility of breaking out through the surrounding forces and withdrawing. The garrison has already had 800 dead and 1,180 wounded, and the Japanese positions have been gradually eroded by the limited but incessant attacks of the past weeks.

16 July

France The American VI Corps (US 1st Army) continues to push on with two divisions, the 9th on the right and the 30th on the left, in the direction of the road linking Périers and St Lô. They are opposed in this sector by the German 5th Parachute Division and the *Panzerlehr* Division. In the vicinity of La Madeleine, on the Bayeux–St Lô road, the 29th Division tries without success to reach the units cut off after the attack of the 15th.

'TO HAVE AND HAVE NOT'

Harry, an American mercenary who earns his living by renting out his boat to wealthy fishing enthusiasts in the warm waters of Martinique, becomes involved unwillingly in the fight against the Nazis.

Based on the novel by Ernest Hemingway, *To Have and Have Not*, in spite of the direction of Howard Hawks and the person of William Faulkner among the scriptwriters, was a fairly unoriginal film which, in the wake of *Casablanca*, joined the roster of adventure films made with propagandist intent.

Humphrey Bogart was, as usual, impeccable in the role of the renegade who can be relied on to pick the right side at the right moment; with him, for the first time, was the young Lauren Bacall, passionate, sensual and bitterly ironic.

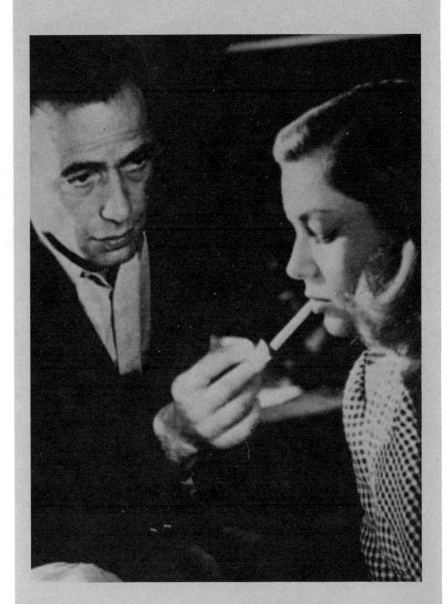

Humphrey Bogart and Lauren Bacall starring together for the first time in *To Have and Have Not*.

A French woman offers a British soldier a drink during street fighting in Caen.

An American patrol advancing cautiously through the ruins of St Lô.

On the right of the British 2nd Army, the 59th Division (XXX Corps) attacks in the direction of Noyers, while the 50th strengthens its positions near Hottot-les-Bagues. Further east, the 15th Division (British XII Corps) captures Gavrus, Bougy and Esquay, the latter above Evrecy.

In a report sent to the general headquarters of Army Group West Rommel emphasizes that since 6 June his units have lost nearly 100,000 men killed, wounded and missing, including 2,360 officers, of whom only one-tenth have been replaced. He warns that his troops are being steadily and inexorably exhausted. His message ends on a pessimistic note: 'The enemy is on the point of smashing our weak front line and penetrating deep into the interior of France.'

Italian Front The 135th Regiment, 34th Division (American IV Corps) captures Height 232 and Monte Maggiore (Heights 449 and 413), south-east of Leghorn. Units of the 133rd Regiment seize Usigliano and penetrate several miles into the valley of the Arno. The 9th Division is advancing at the centre of the US formations, with the 88th Division on the right.

In the British sector the 6th Armoured Division (British XIII Corps) takes Arezzo. The stubborn and tenacious German resistance in this sector has not only held up the Allied advance in a remarkable way (and, all things considered, with only slight damage), but has also allowed the units of Vietinghoff's 10th Army and Lemelsen's 14th to strengthen and improve the defensive positions on the *Gothic* line. Some units of the British XIII Corps press on as far as the Arno, seize a bridge and establish a bridgehead on the opposite bank. The next target is Florence.

Eastern Front Armoured columns from the 3rd Belorussian Front and the 1st Belorussian Front converge from north and south to capture Grodno, south-west of Vilna and north-east of Bialystok. The Russian southern fronts in southern Poland and Galicia clash with the German

North Ukraine Army Group, commanded now by General Harpe in place of Model, who has left this very day to take over command of the Army Group Centre.

New Guinea Minor actions on the river Driniumor line in the Aitape sector. On Numfoor Island the parachutists lose contact with the main body of the Japanese forces. Kamiri airfield is ready to accommodate an entire fighter group.

17 July

France Returning to his headquarters at La Roche-Guyon after inspecting the I *Panzer SS* Corps, south of Caen, Field-Marshal Rommel is severely wounded in the head during an air attack near Vimontiers. Rommel is replaced temporarily in command of Army Group B by Field-Marshal von Kluge, who has been Commander-in-Chief of the Western Front since 3 July, after Rundstedt's resignation. In the American sector the 4th Armoured Division is put under command of the VIII Corps. The US 9th Division (VII Corps) overcomes German resistance and advances rapidly along the Périers–St Lô road. The units of XIX Corps succeed in penetrating the enemy lines along the river Vire, near Rampan. In the centre of the Allied line, in the British 2nd Army sector, the XXX Corps continues to advance slowly towards Noyers, but the XII Corps units fail to reach Evrecy.

Italian Front The units of the American 34th Division make only slight progress towards Leghorn. Units of the 91st Division take Prusacco and head for Pontedera.

In the British 8th Army sector the XIII Corps pursues the Germans as they withdraw towards Florence. The Polish II Corps begins its attack on Ancona with air support.

General Leese, Commander of the British 8th Army, decides to attack the *Gothic* line with two corps on two centre-lines, Florence–Fiorenzuola and Florence–Bologna.

New Guinea In the Aitape area the Americans succeed in making a continuous line along the river

Winston Churchill visits the Allied lines in northern Italy. Accompanied by General Alexander, he looks out from a Polish Corps observation post towards the Germans' last main fortified positions, the *Gothic* line.

Driniumor, but the Japanese break it again with a night attack. Other Japanese forces are concentrating in readiness for an attack against Afua, along the American perimeter.

18 July

France The Americans of the XIX Corps (US 1st Army) enter St Lô. In the eastern sector of the Allied line the British divisions open an offensive (Operation *Goodwood*) in the Caen area, with the object of drawing as many of the German forces as possible into that sector and so reduce German strength in the western sector, where the American divisions are preparing for Operation *Cobra* (fixed for 24 July), the attempt to break through the enemy lines west of St Lô and capture Coutances.

The Canadian II Corps crosses the

Orne south-west of Caen and its 3rd Division captures Colombelles and Giberville, north-east of the city. The British VII Corps attacks in force from the west and after a strenuous battle with the divisions of the I *Panzer SS* Group reaches the line Hubert–Folie–La Hogne–Cagny, south of Caen.

Italian Front The 34th Division opens its final attack against Leghorn. Some units reach the suburbs of the town but the Germans manage to preserve a good part of the garrison. The 9th Division reaches the Arno at Pontedera, and the French Expeditionary Corps advances all along the line.

In the British 8th Army sector, the South African 6th Armoured Division (XIII Corps) reaches and passes Radda in Chianti, while in the Arno valley the 4th Division and

British 6th Armoured Division are almost brought to a halt by the first of a series of defensive lines which the Germans have prepared north of Arezzo. However, the 4th Division reaches Montevarchi, on Highway 69.

The Germans defend Città di Castello desperately against attacks by the British X Corps. The Polish II Corps takes Ancona.

Eastern Front Troops of the 1st Ukraine Front capture Brody, east of Lvov, in Poland. In the sector immediately to the north, armoured columns from the 1st Belorussian Front advance from Kovel towards Lublin. The 3rd Baltic Front, on the offensive south of Lake Peipus, threatens Ostrov and Pskov, advanced strongpoints which until now the Germans have maintained at a high cost.

West of Grodno the Russians have already nearly reached the East Prussian border, but they are halted by a violent counter-attack by Model's armies near Augustow.

New Guinea In the Aitape area the Americans capture the west bank of the river Driniumor from the mouth to the village of Afua.

☐ Japan. The Tojo government falls. General Koiso forms a new government.

19 July

France After capturing St Lô the US XIX Corps (1st Army) pushes on southwards. In the British sector the Canadian 2nd Division (II Corps) captures Louvigny and Fleury, on the north and south banks of the river Orne. East of Caen the battle for Troarn, between the British I Corps and German LXXXVI Corps, is raging.

Italian Front The 34th Division takes Leghorn. In the sector where the French Expeditionary Corps is advancing the 4th Mountain Division reaches Certaldo, north-west of Castellina. The South African 6th Armoured Division begins to advance between the Chianti hills, but is greatly slowed down by German fire. Units of the British 6th Armoured Division secure a new

The Soviet Marshal Georgii Zhukov.

crossing of the Arno near Laterina. *Eastern Front* The Russian 1st Ukraine Front surrounds five German divisions west of Brody. *New Guinea* Fighting continues near Afua, in the Aitape beachhead area.

20 July

France The US 1st Army continues its preparations for Operation *Cobra*.

In the Caen sector the Canadian 2nd Division (II Corps) captures St André-sur-Orne after some very hard fighting.

Italian Front Units of the American 34th Division (IV Corps) succeed in establishing an advance post along Highway 67 south-east of Pisa. The French 4th Mountain Division reaches the line Santo Stefano–Castelfiorentino–Certaldo, on the left flank of the line.

The British XIII Corps has to modify its plan of attack to allow it to cover a wider front with its divisions, so as to take in the sector at present held by the French Expeditionary Corps (which is being withdrawn from the front). The region between the Chianti hills and Highway 2 offers few defences, and the greatest efforts will be concentrated on the left flank,

where the New Zealand 2nd Division and 8th Indian Division are getting ready to attack.

The South African 6th Armoured Division captures Monte San Michele and Monte Querciabella, allowing the 4th Division and British 6th Armoured Division to advance into the Arno valley.

Eastern Front South-west of Kovel, in the central sector, the forces of the 1st Belorussian Front reach the river Bug on a front of 40 miles.

☐ Attempt to assassinate Hitler fails (see pages 557–9). The planned military *Putsch* to get rid of Nazism and make peace with the Allies is stillborn.

Mariana Islands As the American fleet approaches its objective, the air and naval bombardment of Guam, which has been almost ceaseless since 7 July, is stepped up to an unprecedented pitch. The bombing of Tinian is only slightly less intensive.

21 July

Italian Front At the US 5th Army headquarters plans are drawn up for the attack on the *Gothic* line. In the British 8th Army sector elements of the New Zealand 2nd Division and the South African 6th Armoured Division replace units of the French Expeditionary Corps, which is beginning to be withdrawn from the line. After sunset the German troops begin to withdraw from the Città di Castello salient, leaving the field open to the British X Corps.

Eastern Front Ostrov, south of Lake Peipus, falls to the 3rd Baltic Front. In the central sector the 1st Belorussian Front, after crossing the Bug south-west of Kovel, is split into two columns, one advancing towards Brest-Litovsk, the other towards Lublin.

☐ General Kurt von Zeitzler, Chief of Staff of the German army, tenders his resignation, which is immediately accepted by Hitler. General Heinz Guderian, the genius of tank warfare, is appointed in his place.

New Guinea In the Aitape sector the Americans reinforce their positions on the river Driniumor. In a violent

THE ATTEMPT ON HITLER'S LIFE

20 July

At 12.42 p.m. the *Wolfsschanze* (Wolf's Lair), Hitler's headquarters at Rastenburg, in a forest in East Prussia, is suddenly shaken by a violent explosion. Flames and smoke rise from the hut where Hitler and his Chiefs of Staff began their daily meeting only a few minutes earlier. The screams of the wounded – some have been hurled through the open windows – and calls for help ring out. Others lie dead. But Hitler is almost untouched. Apart from shock (his first reaction is 'Oh my new boots ... !'), a blackened face, ruffled hair and the burns and scratches on his boots, Hitler escapes completely. Indeed, a few hours later he is able to receive Mussolini.

It is at once clear that someone has attempted to assassinate Hitler and the hunt for those responsible begins. The assassin (or assassins) cannot be far away – indeed, must have been present at the meeting. Apart from those killed, only one person is missing, a young colonel, 37-year-old Count Claus Schenk von Stauffenberg, who was first thought to be among the wounded taken to hospital. The suspicions of the investigators fall on him when it is learned that he left the meeting only a minute or two before the explosion. After hearing evidence from some of the officers and soldiers of the SS guard at Rastenburg, their suspicions become a certainty.

But who is von Stauffenberg? Was he acting on his own, or was he just the agent of a much larger group planning to get rid of Hitler? To learn the answers we must take a step back to 7 April 1943. On this date Colonel von Stauffenberg, a member of a noble South German family, was

seriously wounded in Tunisia. His car hit a mine and was blown up. Von Stauffenberg lost his left eye, his right hand and two fingers of his left hand, and during his long convalescence he had time to reflect on the critical situation of his country. He came to some serious and fundamental conclusions. He wrote to his wife: 'I must do something to save Germany.' And in another letter he declared more specifically: 'Even if the effort is bound to fail, it must be made. The important thing is to show the world, to show history, that the German resistance movement existed and dared to take action, even at the cost of life.' From this time onwards he formed part of an opposition group which aimed at getting rid of the dictator and bringing the war to an end, salvaging all that could be saved of Germany. Among the members of the group were the former mayor of Leipzig, Carl Gördeler, General Ludwig Beck (the military leader of the plot), the former ambassador in Rome, Ulrich von Hassel, General Friedrich Olbricht, Field-Marshal Erwin von Witzleben, General Hans Henning von Tresckow, Chief of Staff of the Army Group Centre on the Russian front, General Erich Fellgiebel, Chief of Signals at Rastenburg, the former ambassador in Moscow, Friedrich Werner von der Schulenburg. General Edward Wagner, Pastor Dietrich Bonhoeffer and the Jesuit priest Alfred Delp, the Social Democrat politician Julius Leber, the young Count Helmuth James von Moltke and other young men of good Prussian families (Stauffenberg himself was a grand-nephew of Count August von Gneisenau, the national hero of the Napo-

leonic wars). There are others who knew about the plot, although they took no active part in it: Rommel, von Kluge, and even the head of the *Abwehr* (the military intelligence service) Admiral Hans Wilhelm Canaris. General Fromm, Commander-in-Chief of the home forces is also aware of the plot, though his role is ambiguous.

During the afternoon of 19 July von Stauffenberg was summoned to Rastenburg by Hitler to take part, in his capacity as chief of staff to General Fromm, in a conference of all the military leaders of the Reich, arranged for 1.00 p.m. the next day. This is the chance Stauffenberg has been waiting for, and he tells the other conspirators. The plan (called Operation *Valkyrie*) must not fail. Preparations have been meticulous, the alliance between the plotters tried and trusted.

On the morning of 20 July, then, von Stauffenberg leaves Rangsdorf, one of the Berlin airports, by air, carrying with him a brief-case containing, hidden among the papers, a bomb manufactured by General Helmut Stieff from a special British explosive with a delayed-action fuse. A little after 10.00 a.m. the aircraft lands at Rastenburg. The meeting, put forward half an hour because Hitler is expecting a visit from Mussolini, begins punctually at 12.30 p.m. Stauffenberg comes into the room at 12.36 p.m., together with Keitel. He has already broken the capsule of the detonator and in six minutes' time, unless something goes wrong, the bomb will go off. The room is about 30 feet by 15 feet and contains a big oval table. Seated at the table, in addition to Hitler (who is sitting at one of the long sides of the table

THE ATTEMPT ON HITLER'S LIFE

20 July 1944: Hitler, Mussolini, and the interpreter, Paul Schmidt, among the ruins of the building at Rastenburg where the bomb exploded a few hours earlier.

with his back to the door), there are some 22 officers of the three armed services and the SS. Keitel sits down on Hitler's left and Stauffenberg on his right, between Generals Korten and Brandt, the Chiefs of Staff of the Luftwaffe and of the operations branch. As soon as he sits down Stauffenberg puts his brief-case down about six feet from Hitler's legs, inside the framework that holds up the right-hand end of the table.

General Hensinger, Adjutant-General of the army, speaks, illustrating the situation on the Russian front and making frequent references to a map spread out on the table. It is 12.37 p.m.; the minutes tick by. Von Stauffenberg, unnoticed, leaves the room. Everyone is listening closely to what Hensinger is telling them. Particularly interested is General Brandt, who, leaning over the table to see the map better, kicks against Stauffenberg's brief-case. He tries to shift it with his foot, then he leans down and moves it to the extreme end of the frame holding up the right end of the table. It is probably this movement that saves Hitler's life. At 12.42 p.m. the bomb goes off.

Stauffenberg, already about 200 yards away, sees the hut literally blown up into the air. Convinced that the attempt has gone according to plan, he leaves Rastenburg. At 1.00 p.m. he takes off in his aircraft in the direction of Berlin to receive the rewards of his action. He does not know yet that the attempt has failed, and General Fellgiebel, Chief of Signals at Rastenburg, does not carry out the order to transmit the news instantly to the conspirators in Berlin, nor the far more important order to cut off communications between Hitler's headquarters and the capital. Consequently the conspirators waiting in Berlin remain in complete ignorance for several hours, uncertain what to do. Meanwhile the plot has been discovered and Himmler has already left for Berlin with orders to crush a possible revolt.

Stauffenberg reaches the German capital at 4.30 p.m., when the news that the Führer has escaped from the attempt on his life has already reached the military commanders in the city.

General Fromm, who had only given formal allegiance to the plot, learning that Hitler is not dead, rushes into the office of General Friedrich Olbricht (chief of the supply branch of the home forces), where he also finds Stauffenberg telephoning all the German headquarters in Europe. He tells him to commit suicide. The response by Stauffenberg and Olbricht is to arrest Fromm.

Goebbels, Minister of Propaganda, has remained calmly in his office in the Wilhelmstrasse. Von Hase, Berlin fortress commander, another of the conspirators, orders the *Wachtbataillon Grossdeutschland*, commanded by Major Otto Ernst Remer, to surround the ministries. But Goebbels manages to contact Remer and gets him to speak directly to Hitler. The battalion hastens to Bendlerstrasse, where the conspirators have their headquarters. But the astute Fromm (who has now been released), to ensure that no one will give damaging evidence against him, has already had Stauffenberg, Olbricht, and Staff Colonel Mertz von Quirnheim shot in the courtyard of the Supreme Command of the Army in Berlin by the light of a lorry's headlamps. Only General Beck escapes with his life. Fromm too, despite his zeal, is also shot. During the following months some 5,000 people are tried and executed. Among them are Field-Marshal von Witzleben, Generals Hase and Stieff and many other officers and senior officials, former diplomats like von Hassel and von der Schulenburg, ambassadors as well as the legation counsellor Adam von Trott zu Solz, politicians like Gördeler, the former Prussian finance minister Johannes Popitz, the Social Democrat politicians Wilhelm Leuschner and Julius Leber and the clerics Alfred Delp and Dietrich Bonhoeffer.

Many, too, commit suicide, including von Kluge (18 August) and Rommel (14 October). Summary trials and death sentences go on until April 1945. The victims include Generals Wagner, von Tresckow, Fellgiebel and Hans Oster and Admiral Hans Wilhelm Canaris. Some only escape because their trials are not held before the end of the war; among them are two ministers, Andreas Hermes and Hjalmar Schacht, and Generals Halder and von Falkenhausen.

Hitler visits General Scherf, wounded in the assassination attempt of 20 July 1944 at Rastenburg, in East Prussia.

The US battleship *Pennsylvania* firing with its big guns on Japanese positions on Guam, the largest of the Mariana Islands.

attack lasting till the morning of the 22nd July, the Japanese succeed in surrounding some units of the US 112th Cavalry near the village of Afua.

Mariana Islands A US amphibious force under the command of Rear-Admiral Conolly, after a preliminary air and naval bombardment, lands the 3rd Marine Division and part of the 77th Infantry Division at 8.30 a.m. on the west coast of the island of Guam, on the southern border of the Marianas. The Marines go ashore near Asan and Agat and after overcoming a moderate Japanese resistance establish a beachhead more than two miles wide and one mile deep. The infantry land near Agat to reinforce the southern beachhead. The Japanese garrison, some 12,000 strong, is commanded by General Takashima. The island was seized from the Americans on 23 December 1941 and rechristened by the Japanese 'Bird Island'.

22 July

France The advance of the American 90th Division (US 1st Army) towards St Germain-sur-Sèves is halted by strong resistance from units of the German 7th Army.

Italian Front In the British X Corps sector the 10th Indian Division enters Città di Castello. The troops of the New Zealand 2nd Division (British XIII Corps) take Tavernelle. The South African 6th Armoured Division advances on the heights near Greve capturing the summits of Monte Domini and Monte Fili. The 4th Division reaches San Giovanni.

Eastern Front The Leningrad Front (Govorov) and Karelia Front (Meretskov) reach the 1940 Russo-Finnish frontier. In Poland the 1st Belorussian Front, pushing on towards Lublin, takes Chelm.

New Guinea Minor skirmishes in the area of the Aitape beachhead. The American units surrounded by the Japanese near Afua can still not free themselves.

Mariana Islands: Guam The US Marines repulse several Japanese counter-attacks against their beachhead and advance inland for about three-quarters of a mile towards Mount Chachao. In the southern sector Marines and infantry reach Mount Alifan. Units of the 3rd Marine Division make determined efforts to dislodge the enemy from the Orote peninsula.

23 July

Eastern Front The 3rd Baltic Front

captures Pskov, a vital German strongpoint south of Lake Peipus, the first town within the 1939 Soviet borders to be captured by the Germans.

☐ General Hans Friessner, who replaced Lindemann in command of the German Army Group North on 3 July, is in turn replaced by Field-Marshal Schörner. He had made the mistake, in Hitler's eyes, of insisting on authority to withdraw his army group in the face of possible encirclement in the Baltic states.

New Guinea Local fighting in the Aitape area. On Biak Island the final mopping up of the Japanese positions in the Ibdi area begins. On Numfoor Island, patrols of American parachutists re-establish contact with the main body of the Japanese defenders near the village of Inasi, on the east coast.

Mariana Islands: Guam The 3rd Marine Division, after bitter fighting, extends its southern beachhead beyond the steep Chonito bluffs in the direction of Point Adelup.

Burma–China On the Salween front the 8th Chinese army makes good progress towards Sung Shan.

Mountbatten proposes two operations to be carried out as soon as possible: Operation *Capital*, an offensive across the river Chindwin, and Operation *Dracula*, an attack in the Rangoon area to be carried out by amphibious and airborne troops.

☐ Generalissimo Chiang Kai-shek sends a message to Roosevelt confirming that he is prepared to give General Stilwell command of the Chinese forces. His conditions are that the Chinese Communist army, before coming under General Stilwell's command, should recognize the authority of the Nationalist government; that General Stilwell's responsibilities are clearly specified; and that the Chinese should have complete right to aid received under the Lend-Lease Act.

24 July

France The 28th Division (US) lands in France. Allied air bombardment begins in preparation for Operation *Cobra*, but very bad weather makes it necessary to postpone the operation.

Eastern Front Lublin, in Poland, falls to the 1st Belorussian Front. The right flank of the 1st Ukraine Front, advancing on the left of the 1st Belorussian Front, forces the passage of the river San north-west of Lvov.

☐ As a display of loyalty the German armed forces are ordered to replace the normal military salute with the Nazi salute, to be accompanied by the words 'Heil Hitler'.

Mariana Islands: Guam The Americans are ordered to join up their two beachheads and eliminate the enemy from the Orote peninsula by the 26th. The 3rd Marine Division, attacking the heights overlooking the northern beachhead, meet with obstinate Japanese resistance.

Tinian At 8.30 a.m., after a prepara-tory bombardment by naval guns and by aircraft, some carrier-borne and some taking off from Saipan, an amphibious group under the command of Rear-Admiral Hill lands the 2nd and 4th Marine Divisions on the north-west coast of Tinian Island, with additional support from 156 heavy guns sited on neighbouring Saipan. The Japanese garrison, commanded by Colonel Ogata, is drawn off to the south-west by a clever manœuvre by the 2nd Marine Division, making a dummy landing opposite the little town of Tinian. Japanese artillery hits the battleship *Colorado* and the destroyer *Norman Scott*.

During the afternoon Ogata's troops try to reach the north of the island, where the landing has been securely carried out, but suffer severe losses from a hail of napalm bombs dropped by US aircraft. During the night, 600 Japanese attack the beach-head, but are wiped out. Later attacks, in which they use tanks, are beaten off with heavy losses. At dawn the Marines advance; they count 1,241 Japanese bodies.

China The garrison of the town of Hengyang, although cut off and un-able to receive any supplies for a week owing to the bad weather con-ditions, continues to hold out bravely against the Japanese attacks.

New Guinea In the Aitape area the Americans repulse yet another attempt by the Japanese to cross the river Driniumor during the night. Near Afua about 2,000 Japanese are still surrounding units of the US 112th Cavalry and stopping the 127th Infantry Regiment from com-

Tinian, Mariana Islands, 24 July 1944: after the usual series of 'softening-up' operations and a murderous preliminary bombardment by warships and aircraft, the US pioneers – first to land – organize the beach for the landing of the Marines.

ing to their rescue.

25 July

France After an effective air bombardment the American 1st Army launches Operation *Cobra*, aiming at an advance by the American troops towards Coutances, south-west of St Lô.

Italian Front The British XIII Corps continues to advance in the direction of Florence.

Eastern Front Troops of the 2nd Baltic Front cut the road between Dvinsk and Riga, in Latvia. The 1st Ukraine Front surrounds Lvov, while four Russian armoured columns converge on Brest-Litovsk.

Dutch East Indies Admiral Somerville's British Far Eastern Fleet bombards the Japanese naval base of Sabang, an island off the north coast of Sumatra, causing severe damage. Carrier-borne aircraft hit airfields in the area.

Mariana Islands: Guam At least seven attacks by the Japanese prevent the Americans from joining up their two beachheads. Some 3,500 Japanese soldiers are killed during the furious fighting, which is at its fiercest before the northern beachhead. Other attacks are driven off among the marshes of the Orote peninsula.

Tinian The 2nd and 4th Marine Divisions follow closely after the Japanese as they retire southwards towards the centre of the island. They occupy two of the island's four airfields.

New Guinea A vigorous counter-attack enables the troops of the US 127th Infantry to open a gap for the surrounded units of the 112th Cavalry to return to the American lines.

A German soldier in despair amidst the wreckage of a field battery as Wehrmacht resistance collapses on the Eastern Front.

26 July

France In the American VIII Corps sector the 8th Division cuts the road linking Lessay (on the west coast of the Cotentin peninsula) with Périers and the 90th Division establishes a bridgehead across the river Sèves. The 1st Division (VII Corps) captures Marigny and the 2nd Armoured Division takes St Gilles and Canisy. East of St Lô the V Corps' offensive gets under way.

Eastern Front Troops of the Leningrad Front, detached from the relatively quiet Finnish front, are concentrated against the positions of the German Army Group North and take the town of Narva, in Estonia. Units of the 1st Belorussian Front reach the Vistula, east of Radom.

☐ Fighter-bombers of the US 5th Air Force, on the shuttle between USSR and Italy, make a successful attack on enemy installations in the area between Ploesti and Bucharest, in Rumania.

☐ Goebbels makes radio announcement on the attempted assassination of Hitler: 'Never again will the Almighty reveal Himself to us as He has just done in saving the Führer. His intention was to let us know that it is for us now to work for victory. Let us go to it.'

New Guinea The American forces in the Aitape area re-group in readiness for future Japanese attacks expected in the Afua area.

Guam Supported by eight battalions of artillery, the US Marines and infantry begin mopping up on the Orote peninsula, advancing a mile through very difficult marshy jungle. Strong Japanese attacks on the northern beachhead are driven off by the 3rd Marine Division.

Tinian The 4th and 2nd Marine Divisions, who have now completed their landing, advance towards the south of the island meeting slight resistance.

☐ Hawaii. President Roosevelt has a conference with Admiral Halsey and General MacArthur about the strategy of the Pacific war. Halsey maintains that it will be possible to 'skip' the Philippines for a direct attack on Formosa. MacArthur does not agree. This difference of opinion is to last a long time.

Burma–China Preceded by aerial bombing, the Chinese forces attack Teng-chung, east of the Salween, and take the Lai-feng, a rocky peak that overlooks the access roads to the town. They also mount an assault from the south-east, but are driven off.

27 July

France US troops break through west of St Lô. In the western sector of the front (VIII Corps, US 1st Army) the 79th Division overruns Lessay, the 80th pushes southwards between Lessay and Périers and the 90th Division occupies Périers and crosses the river Taute. Units of the VII Corps also continue to advance south.

Italian Front The Germans withdraw towards Florence, while the New Zealand 2nd Division captures San Casciano.

Eastern Front In the northern sector units of the 2nd Baltic Front capture Daugavpils on the river Daugava, in southern Latvia. The 2nd Belorussian Front, after a week of bloody fighting, seizes Bialystok, while armoured columns from the 1st Ukraine Front take Lvov and Stanislav. The German North Ukraine Army Group also has to fall back after sustaining severe losses.

Guam The Marines slowly proceed with the mopping up of the Orote peninsula. They succeed in extending their northern beachhead in some sectors, but are held up just past the edge of the plateau that spreads inland from the Chonito bluffs. To speed up the linking of the two beachheads the 77th Division is ordered to take Mount Tenjo by assault; this important position lies between the two bridgeheads.

Tinian The northern third of the island is in American hands; they start to reactivate the airfield at Point Ushi.

Burma–China The Chinese and Americans capture the airfield north of Myitkyina, where the garrison is beginning to show signs of weariness. On the Salween front the Chinese mop up the area of Lai-feng Peak, captured the previous day, counting 400 Japanese dead. The Chinese have lost 1,200 killed.

28 July

France At 5.00 p.m. the American 4th Armoured Division (US 1st Army) enters Coutances, and the objective of Operation *Cobra* is achieved. East of St Lô the 30th Division continues the advance southwards on the west bank of the river Vire.

Eastern Front The Russians capture Brest-Litovsk. Units of the 1st Ukraine Front are on the river San.

New Guinea With the liquidation of the Ibdi pocket, all organized Japanese resistance on Biak Island ceases. Mopping up continues. On the mainland, in the Aitape area, the Americans shorten their lines, withdrawing in the Afua area.

Guam While mopping up continues in the Orote peninsula, where the Marines reach the edge of the airfield, the 77th Infantry Division succeeds in joining up the two beachheads. Infantry and Marines take Mount Chachao and Mount Alutom and advance on Mount Tenjo from Point Adelup. General Takashima, the Japanese garrison commander, is killed during the day; General Obata takes his place.

Tinian The Marines advance rapidly southwards.

29 July

France The 4th and 6th Armoured Divisions (VIII Corps, American 1st Army) continues to advance south, towards Avranches. Units of the US VII Corps reach Percy, while Hausser's German 7th Army retires. On the right sector of the front, where the XIX Corps is operating, the 29th Division reaches the area east of Percy and the 30th, despite heavy enemy fire, continues to push on southwards along the west bank of the river Vire in the direction of Tessy-sur-Vire. The V Corps is rapidly approaching Torigny-sur-Vire, south-east of St Lô.

Italian Front The 8th Division, British XIII Corps, reaches the Arno in the vicinity of Empoli.

New Guinea In the Aitape area, near

Afua, the Americans are forced back a little way.

Guam The Marines take the airfield on the Orote peninsula, and have occupied the entire peninsula by the end of the day.

Tinian The progress of the 2nd and 4th Marine Divisions to the south is halted by strong Japanese resistance.

30 July

France The Units of the US VIII Corps (6th and 4th Armoured Divisions) advance rapidly towards Avranches and Granville. Units of the 4th Armoured Division press on into the outskirts of Avranches and capture the bridges over the river Sée. The other corps of the US 1st Army also continue their march south, but while units of the VII Corps quickly approach Villedieu-les-Poêtes, on the road between Granville and Vire, the XIX Corps has to face violent German counter-attacks near Percy.

New Guinea Without the usual preliminary bombardment, and without air support, the Americans carry out a surprise landing by two infantry divisions and an amphibious force of cavalry and infantry in the Vogelkop peninsula, near Sansapor on the north-west point of New Guinea, and on some coastal islets. The landing takes place at 7.00 a.m. and the divisions establish a beachhead about a mile and a half wide and half a mile deep.

In the Aitape area the Americans regroup their forces to go over to the counter-attack on the river Driniumor line.

Tinian Despite stiff Japanese resistance the 2nd and 4th Marine Divisions push on southwards, taking the town of Tinian and squeezing the Japanese into a little strip at the extreme south of the island.

Burma The commander of the Japanese forces in the Myitkyina area orders his troops to withdraw, then takes his own life.

31 July

France The 6th Armoured Division (US VIII Corps), after taking Granville on the coast, advances quickly

Western Front: General Patton (left) in conversation with General Bradley (centre) and General Montgomery.

south-east towards Avranches, where it takes over from the 4th Armoured Division, which moves on south of the city, crossing the Selune near Pontaubault. The units of the VII Corps advance towards Brecey, while in the area of Tessy the Germans still hold up the advance of the XIX Corps.

Since 6 June the Allies have lost 122,000 men killed, wounded and missing, against German losses of 114,000 (to which must be added some 40,000 prisoners).

Eastern Front In Latvia the 1st Baltic Front takes Jelgava, near the Gulf of Riga. If they reach the Gulf the Russians will cut off the German Army Group North. Forces of the 3rd Belorussian Front press on towards East Prussia and fight in the streets of Kaunas (Kovno), capital of Lithuania. The 2nd Belorussian Front is also approaching East Prussia, while the 1st, making for Warsaw, captures Siedlce.

New Guinea With scarcely any opposition, the Americans extend their beachhead on Cape Sansapor, in the Vogelkop peninsula. In the Aitape sector, four American battalions cross the river Driniumor and reach the Niumen stream, engaged

by Japanese rearguard actions. There is also fighting near the village of Afua, where it is believed that at least 500 Japanese have been killed in the past two weeks.

Guam The 3rd Marine Division and 77th Infantry Division follow up the enemy to the north, reaching a line running from Agana on the west coast to Yona on the east. The installations and the big airport built by the Americans are recaptured.

Tinian The Marines continue their drive to liquidate the last enemy forces in the extreme south of the island. The American actions are supported by the usual fire from artillery, aircraft and warships.

Burma–India The Japanese are in retreat along the Tiddim road, closely pursued by the divisions of the British IV Corps, which has been given the task of driving the enemy back across the Chindwin.

On the Arakan front the British XV Corps has during this period been engaged in actions designed to hinder Japanese troop movements into India.

1 August

France The US 3rd Army is formed under General George Smith Patton, who has four corps – the VIII, XII, XV and XX – under his command. The new formation is given the sector on the right of the 1st Army, so that it forms the extreme right flank of the Allied line. The 3rd Army's objective is Brittany. The VIII Corps, transferred from the 1st Army, is commanded by General Middleton, and consists of four divisions (4th, 6th, 8th and 79th), the first two being armoured.

The XV Corps, under General Haislip, consists of two infantry divisions (the 83rd and 90th) and the 5th Armoured Division. The other two corps in the 3rd Army, the XII and XX, still being formed, are commanded by General Eddy and General Walker.

In the 1st US Army sector (now commanded by General Hodges, General Bradley having been appointed to command the 12th Army Group), the VII and XIX

Corps continue their advance in the area of Vire, north-east of Avranches, which has been taken.

In the British sector (2nd Army of Montgomery's 21st Army Group) the XXX Corps is advancing in the direction of Villers-Bocage.

Eastern Front The 3rd Belorussian Front, which is heading for Königsberg in East Prussia, captures Kaunas, the capital of Lithuania. Elements of the 1st Baltic Front reach the Gulf of Riga about 25 miles west of the city. However, the Russians are unable to consolidate so as to capture Riga and isolate the German Army Group North from the rest of the German army.

In Poland patriots, knowing that the Russians are so near, rise against the occupying forces in Warsaw. They reason that, when the Russians arrive – and they are already on the Vistula – they will find a liberated capital, a solid basis for a free, independent Poland. For reasons never made clear (military reasons according to the Russians, essentially political according to the Western powers), the Russian advance halts suddenly at the suburb of Praga, the other side of the Vistula. The insurgents are surrounded and virtually annihilated by the Germans. The remnants of the patriot forces surrender on 2 October.

□ The Finnish President Risto Ryti resigns. His place is taken by Marshal Karl Gustav Mannerheim.

New Guinea Operations on Biak and on the Vogelkop peninsula continue on a small scale.

In the Aitape sector the Americans advance as far as the Niumen stream, stabilizing their advanced lines.

Guam US Marines and infantry pursue the enemy northwards, reaching a line that goes from the west coast north of Agana to Pago Bay on the east coast. They have taken more than half of the island.

Tinian All organized resistance by the Japanese comes to an end after the failure of their last counterattack. The Marines begin mopping up.

China The Japanese still besiege Hengyang, frustrating attempts by

SAINT-EXUPÉRY

The French writer and aviator Antoine de Saint-Exupéry died on 31 July when he was shot down in a reconnaissance mission over occupied France.

Born in Lyon on 29 June 1900, Saint-Exupéry joined the air force and in 1926 became a pilot for the Compagnie Latécoère which specialized in commercial flights, helping to pioneer the airmail services in France, North Africa and South America. His varied experiences furnished the inspiration for his first books, featuring the type of ideal hero who was to appear in all his later works. The novel *Vol de nuit* (*Night Flight*), published with a preface by Gide, won him the Prix Fémina in 1931.

Continuing to fly and to write of his exploits, Saint-Exupéry joined the French air force when war broke out. After France fell he went to America where he published two highly successful novels, *Pilot de guerre* (*Flight to Arras*) and *Le petit prince* (*The Little Prince*), which became a classic of children's literature. After the Allied landing in North Africa, Saint-Exupéry rejoined

his old unit, now reformed under American command, and despite his age took part in a number of reconnaissance missions, the last of which proved fatal.

Antoine de Saint-Exupéry in his aviator's uniform (above); an illustration by the author for *The Little Prince*.

Warsaw, August 1944: a German soldier
surrenders to a patrol of Polish patriots
during the rising against the occupying
forces.

the Chinese garrison to open a gap through the enemy lines.

The US 14th Air Force has carried out 4,454 missions since 26 May in support of the Chinese forces engaged in central east China.

2 August

France In the British 2nd Army sector the VIII and XXX Corps continue to advance in the direction of the road that links Vire and Argentan. The US VIII Corps (3rd Army) heads strongly for Brittany. The 6th Armoured Division reaches the outskirts of Dinan and the 4th gains further positions around Rennes.

The VII Corps (US 1st Army) advances rapidly with the 1st Division plus elements of the 3rd Armoured Division towards Mortain, some twenty-five miles east of Avranches. On the left flank of the VII Corps, the XIX Corps is making a determined advance south-east of the area of Tessy.

Hitler orders a counter-attack between Mortain and Avranches to cut off the American forces in Brittany.

New Guinea In the Aitape area the Japanese renew their attacks without success. Both sides have high losses.

Guam On the left flank the 3rd Marine Division advances northwards almost unopposed, and occupies Tiyan airfield; on the right flank the 77th Infantry Division is held up near the village of Barrigada by Japanese units deployed in the jungle in perfectly camouflaged positions.

Burma–China On the Salween front the aircraft supporting the Chinese attacks on Teng-chung bomb the town walls and open at least five breaches.

3 August

France In the US 3rd Army sector, units of the VIII Corps press on to the west. The assault on Rennes is opened by units of the 8th Division, while the 4th Armoured Division moves on south of the city.

The VII Corps of the US 1st Army

takes Mortain, while further north the XIX and V Corps of the same army advance south-eastwards in the river Vire area.

In the British sector the 50th and 53rd Divisions of the VII Corps take positions along the road between Villers-Bocage and Caen.

Eastern Front Troops of the 1st Ukraine Front cross the Vistula at Sandomierz, establishing a bridgehead over the river.

New Guinea In the Aitape area the Americans attack along the Niumen stream towards the Torricelli Mountains.

Offensive activity by the Japanese near the village of Afua dies down.

Guam The US 77th Infantry Division advances on the right flank, but the Japanese have evacuated their fortified positions in the jungle and retired northwards. The Americans take the village of Barrigada. On the left flank, the 3rd Marine Division goes ahead quickly, occupying Finegayan and pushing on towards Tumon Bay. American naval vessels shell Mount Santa Rosa, which overlooks the northern part of the island and on which the Japanese have concentrated.

Burma–China Units of the Chinese 50th Division take Myitkyina, capturing 187 Japanese, almost all sick or wounded. The rest of the garrison has either escaped or been killed. The long struggle, which has cost the Chinese and Americans more than 6,500 killed and wounded is a most valuable victory for the Allies, since it reopens land communications between India and China.

On the Salween front the Chinese 8th Army attacks Teng-chung and Sung Shan.

4 August

France In Brittany, while the 6th Armoured Division (US 3rd Army) advances on Brest, the 4th moves north-west towards Vannes. The German troops (General Farmbacher's XXV Corps) withdraw to the ports (St Malo, Brest, Lorient, St Nazaire). Rennes is captured by the 13th Regiment, US 8th Division. In the US 1st Army sector, the VII

Corps reinforces its positions at Mortain, and some of its units move southwards towards Mayenne.

The XIX Corps has to face a new German counter-offensive, while the V Corps reaches its objectives in the Vire sector. In the British sector General Montgomery orders the Canadian 1st Army under General Crerar to advance in the direction of Falaise as quickly as possible. The XXX Corps, British 2nd Army, captures Hermilly (43rd Division) and Villers-Bocage (50th Division).

Italian Front Indian and New Zealand troops of the British XIII Corps reach the south bank of the Arno near Florence. Advance guards of the South African 6th Armoured Division penetrate into the southern suburbs of the city, from which the Germans have withdrawn after destroying all the bridges over the Arno except the Ponte Vecchio.

Eastern Front The German Army Group North pushes back the troops of the 1st Baltic Front which have reached the Gulf of Riga and reopens the Estonia–Latvia corridor between Riga and the Russian salient north of Jelgava.

□ For the first time, at the request of the Russians, fighter-bombers of the US 15th Air Force carry out a huge raid on a number of Rumanian airfields, and land on Russian bases.

New Guinea After a last, desperate

Engineers of the US 5th Army blow up unexploded German mines among the ruins of the Santa Trinità bridge in Florence.

attack in the Afua area (Aitape bridgehead) the Japanese withdraw to the south. The Americans prepare to advance across the river Driniumor.

Guam The US 77th Infantry Division takes Mount Barrigada and links up with the 3rd Marine Division, advancing on its left. American progress is slowed down more by the terrain than by Japanese resistance. The bombardment of Mount Santa Rosa by American warships continues day and night.

Burma–China On the Salween front the Chinese succeed in penetrating the town of Teng-chung, where bitter house-to-house fighting takes place. The British 2nd Division, XXXIII Corps, coming up from the area of Imphal, occupies Tamu, across the Burmese frontier.

5 August

France In Brittany General Middleton's VIII Corps attacks simultaneously to the west, south-west and south. While the 6th Armoured Division continues to advance westwards towards Brest and the 83rd Division attacks the outer defences of the fortress of St Malo, units of the 4th Armoured Division reach Vannes. Further east the 90th Division (General Haislip's XV Corps) seizes Mayenne and the 79th Division approaches Laval.

In the US 1st Army sector, the advance of the VII Corps south-east of Mortain continues, while the 29th Division (XIX Corps) pushes on towards Vire and the V Corps prepares to seize the region between Tinchebray and St Jean-du-Bois.

Eastern Front In Poland the Russians send the 4th Ukraine Front, under the command of General Petrov, into the line south of the 1st Ukraine Front.

Pacific Two squadrons of US aircraft carriers (Rear-Admiral Clark and Rear-Admiral Montgomery), with a squadron of cruisers and destroyers (Rear-Admiral DuBose) bomb and shell military installations on Chichi Jima and Haha Jima, in the Bonin Islands. The day before, Montgomery's squadron has

attacked airfields on Iwo Jima, and DuBose's squadron has intercepted a Japanese convoy near Chichi Jima, sinking a destroyer and two transports.

6 August

France In the American 3rd Army sector units of the VIII Corps continue their offensive into the heart of Brittany. On the north coast of the peninsula Dinard, to the west of St Malo, comes under attack by units of the 8th Division, and the 83rd Division. The 4th Armoured Division advances on Lorient. To the east, the XV Corps is making swift progress towards Le Mans and the 79th Division captures Laval, south of Mayenne. The 3rd Armoured Division of the US VII Corps (1st Army) also reaches Mayenne from the north. Vire is taken by the 29th Division.

Italian Front Instructions are issued for the preliminary operations for an offensive against the *Gothic* line.

New Guinea In the area of Aitape hard-fought encounters between the Americans and Japanese rearguards.

Guam US Marines and infantry have by now occupied two-thirds of the island. On the right flank of the 77th Infantry Division the Japanese send in tanks against the 305th Regiment sector, inflicting serious losses on the Americans, then suddenly retire before the latter can mount a counter-attack.

Burma General Slim orders the British and Indian XXXIII Corps to advance to the Chindwin and occupy Sittaung and Kalewa. It is at this point that they will have to cross the Chindwin.

7 August

France The Germans open their powerful counter-offensive ordered by Hitler in the Avranches area. German armoured divisions penetrate into the American positions between the VII and XIX Corps (US 1st Army), recapturing Mortain and reaching Le Mesnil-Tôve, where they are halted with the help of American aircraft. The VII and XIX Corps, duly reinforced, prepare to counter-

attack.
The 6th Armoured Division (US VIII Corps, 3rd Army) reaches Brest in the evening, but it is too late for an assault on the city, and anyway the Americans do not have the equipment necessary for an operation on that scale. The Germans are thus allowed to reinforce their garrison and complete their defence works. The 83rd Division continues the battle for St Malo, while on the south coast the 4th Armoured Division attacks Lorient.

During the night the Canadian II Corps (Canadian 1st Army) launches an offensive south of Caen in the direction of Falaise, after violent bombing from the air.

Eastern Front The Russians are contained by the Wehrmacht almost everywhere. In any case the Russians have to suspend their summer offensive for a time after advancing nearly 450 miles in order to reorganize their over-stretched supply lines.

New Guinea On Biak Island the US 162nd Regiment advances along the track from Sorido to Korim Bay to link up with the 163rd Regiment, which has been operating against the Japanese in the north of the island.

Guam The 3rd Marine Division, the 77th Infantry Division and the 1st Marine Brigade, following a heavy barrage, launch a heavy attack against Yigo and Mount Santa Rosa. They succeed in taking Yigo, but their advance to the peaks of Mount Santa Rosa is slowed by fierce Japanese resistance and by the extremely dense vegetation in the jungle. During the night the Japanese counter-attack with tanks, but are driven back.

8 August

France The German garrison of Brest, in Brittany, rejects the surrender ultimatum of the commander of the American 6th Armoured Division (VIII Corps of the 3rd Army). Fierce actions continue round the outskirts of St Malo between the US 8th Division and the German garrison. The 79th Division (US XV Corps) reaches and takes Le Mans, while units of the 5th Division advance swiftly towards Nantes and Angers. In this sector the Germans deploy several detachments from the LVIII Armoured Corps, the 9th Armoured Division and 708th Infantry Division, brought up from the south of France.

In the Avranches sector the German 2nd and 116th Armoured Divisions are still trying to penetrate more deeply into the American lines between the American VII and XIX Corps (1st Army).

The Canadian II Corps does not succeed in reaching Falaise, 30 miles south-east of Caen.

☐ Aircraft of the US 8th Air Force, taking off from airfields in Russia and heading for Italy, attack Rumanian airfields. From Italy they will fly on to Britain, bombing north Italy and Germany. This is an elaboration of the 'shuttle'.

Guam Organized resistance by the Japanese ceases. The US 77th Infantry Division takes Mount Santa Rosa and virtually clears the whole area of the enemy. The last Japanese take refuge in the extreme north of the island.

China The Japanese capture Hengyang. This is the prelude to the launching of the *Ichi-Go* plan, which is to lead to the capture of all the American airfields in the south-east of China, and of a huge expanse of territory.

9 August

France The Canadian II Corps continues to advance along the road that leads from Caen to Falaise.

The offensive by the divisions of the American VIII Corps (3rd Army) continues throughout Brittany – the 6th Armoured Division at Brest, the 83rd Division at St Malo (where German resistance is by now confined to the citadel) and the 4th Armoured Division at Lorient. From Le Mans the divisions of the XV Corps move south towards Alençon.

In the Avranches sector the German counter-offensive loses some of its impetus, though there is still violent fighting.

New Guinea All Japanese action

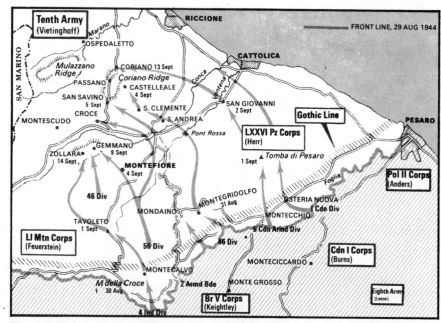

The Allied break-through of the eastern section of the *Gothic* line, end of August 1944.

ceases in the Aitape area.

Guam The Americans continue mopping up in the northern part of the island. The Japanese units isolated in the extreme north will fight to the death rather than surrender.

Burma–China On the Salween front the Japanese carry out a successful raid against artillery emplacements and supply dumps in the Chinese 8th Army sector of Sung Shan.

In China, following the defeat at Hengyang, Marshal Li Chi-shen, President of the Military Consultative Committee, tells an American consul that the Eastern Chinese 'war lords' are about to set up a provisional government of national unity to drive out the Japanese invader. The new government will demand Chiang Kai-shek's resignation. The American reaction to this is anxiously awaited.

10 August

France In the Canadian 1st Army sector, the 49th Division (British I Corps) and the Canadian II Corps advance towards Vimont, meeting with tough resistance.

In Brittany units of the American VIII Corps continue their operations against Dinard and St Malo, Brest and Lorient. To the south, units of the 4th Armoured Division enter

Nantes and reach the Loire. In the US XV Corps sector, armoured columns continue the advance towards Alencon.

In the Avranches–Mortain sector the US VII Corps now takes the initiative and the German divisions begin slowly to withdraw to the east.

Mediterranean The Allies open the first phase of the air operations in preparation for Operation *Dragoon* (formerly *Anvil*), the landing of Allied forces in the south of France.

Eastern Front A lull along a great part of the front. The Polish patriots in Warsaw still have to bear the weight of German repression by themselves. The Russians ignore their request to give them at least some support from the air. The patriots now ask London for help.

Troops of the 2nd Belorussian Front force the crossing of the river Narew near Bialystok.

New Guinea On Numfoor Island parachutists of the 503rd Regiment make contact again with the Japanese south-south-west of Inasi, and try to surround them.

Guam Several hundred Japanese have been killed during the mopping up operations. In the fierce fighting for the capture of the island the Americans have lost 1,400 killed. The Japanese have lost over 10,000 according to official figures, though since the number of troops manning the island was over 15,000, their losses may have been even higher.

11 August

France In Brittany the German garrisons at Dinard and St Malo hold out resolutely against the attacks of the units of the 83rd Division (US VIII Corps). In the American VII Corps (1st Army) sector, the 30th and 35th Divisions close in on Mortain, and the German forces there are in difficulties. Field-Marshal von Kluge, Commander-in-Chief in the Western Front, puts the suggestion to Hitler that three armoured divisions be withdrawn from the Mortain salient to put in a counter-attack from west to east on the flank of the US XV Corps. The Führer agrees in principle, but he is anxious not to give up the offensive against Avranches and so authorizes only a partial withdrawal of troops from the Mortain area.

Italian Front The first convoys carrying the assault forces for Operation *Dragoon* sail from Naples.

Eastern Front Suddenly resuming the offensive in the northern sector, the 3rd Baltic Front breaches the German lines south of Lake Peipus over a front of about 45 miles, and spreads out northwards. Hitler's obstinacy has now ensured that his Army Group North will be virtually isolated from the main body of the German army.

12 August

France While units of the US 1st Army have completely wiped out the enemy forces in the Avranches area, some German armoured divisions begin to leave the Mortain salient for the planned attack towards the east against the flank of the XV Corps. The situation is unchanged in Brittany, where the 83rd Division is still held up outside St Malo and Dinard.

After reaching Alençon the US XV Corps under General Haislip advances rapidly northwards towards Argentan, defended by the German 116th Armoured Division.

China Chiang Kai-shek accepts

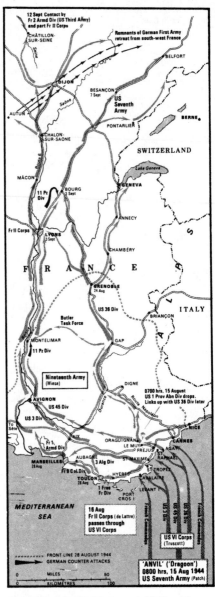

Operation *Anvil*, 15 August 1944, and the rapid Allied advance through southern France.

Roosevelt's proposal to send General Hurley and his economic adviser, Donald M. Nelson, to China as his personal representatives.

13 August

France The US XV Corps (3rd Army) reaches the Argentan sector, where it halts on the orders of General Bradley, Commander-in-Chief of the 12th Army Group. The US XX Corps advances simultaneously from the Le Mans sector towards the north-east, reaching the outskirts of Chartres still in German hands.

South-west of Le Mans, meanwhile, the American 4th Armoured Division and 35th Division (the first from the US VIII Corps, the second from the VII Corps) are concentrated under the command of General Eddy (XII Corps); their first mission is to advance east in the direction of Orléans.

After reaching the Mayenne, the VII Corps moves north towards the road connecting Vire with Argentan.

China General Chennault sends a number of reconnaissance aircraft of the US 14th Air Force on a mission over Manila, in the Philippines. His action is immediately criticized by Stilwell and MacArthur, who insist, on political grounds, that the Philippines must not be bombed.

14 August

France The Canadian 2nd Division (II Corps of the Canadian 1st Army) gets within 4½ miles of Falaise, which has been so heavily bombed by the British that it is not even possible to trace the streets.

In Brittany, the resistance of the German garrisons in St Malo and Dinard persists. The American XV Corps (3rd Army) moves east from Argentan towards Dreux.

The 7th Armoured Division and the 5th Division (US XX Corps) move in the direction of Chartres, and the XII Corps continues its advance towards Orléans.

Mediterranean The convoys for Operation *Dragoon*, after a stop-over in Corsica, leave for the south coast of France.

□ RAF aircraft have begun dropping supplies and ammunition for the Polish insurgents in Warsaw.

15 August

Southern France Allied forces land on the south coast of France; Operation *Dragoon* is under way. General Patch's US 7th Army lands in Provence, between Toulon and Cannes, to be followed the next day by the French II Corps under General De Lattre de Tassigny.

Northern France In the vicinity of Tinchebray, about 12 miles north-east of Mortain, the British VIII Corps (2nd Army) joins up with the

American V Corps. In the Canadian 1st Army sector, the 4th Armoured Division (II Corps) advances in the direction of Falaise, east of the road between Falaise and Caen. Northeast of Falaise the Polish 1st Armoured Division manages to secure a bridgehead on the east bank of the river Dives. In the Avranches–Mortain sector the Germans have evacuated the Mortain salient and it is immediately reoccupied by the American VII Corps. The German armoured divisions of the XLVIII Armoured Corps, which carried out the counter-attack on Avranches, now withdraw eastwards towards Falaise. They occupy a long, narrow strip about 30 miles by 12 miles and are in danger of being cut off and encircled as a result of the simultaneous pressure of the Allies towards Falaise from the north (British 1st and 2nd Armies) and from the south towards the Tinchebray–Argentan road (US XV and VII Corps). As if their situation were not critical enough, it is made still more serious by the inexplicable disappearance of General von Kluge, the Commander-in-Chief in the Western Front. The news sends Hitler into a frenzy, for he has no doubt that von Kluge has gone over to the enemy. But the facts are quite different. Von Kluge left at dawn for the headquarters of General Heinrich Eberbach, Commander of the 5th Army. Near Falaise his car and the escorting vehicle were destroyed by enemy aircraft. Von Kluge escaped death. He waits until twilight hidden in a cornfield, then manages to return to headquarters. In Brittany, units of the 83rd Division (US VIII Corps) enter Dinard, while the position of the German garrison at St Malo grows increasingly critical.

In the US 1st Army sector, units of the V Corps reach the hills that dominate Tinchebray from the south.

South-West Pacific The Allied High Command issues directives for the invasion of Morotai Island in the northern Moluccas, north-west of New Guinea and south of the Philippines. The island can be made into

an ideal jumping-off place for operations against the Philippines themselves. Two divisions and a regimental combat group under the command of General Hall will carry out the operation.

OPERATION *ANVIL*

15 August

Towards dawn an awesome convoy approaches the south coast of France, consisting of some 2,000 transports and landing craft escorted by 300 warships. It includes some veterans of Normandy landing, such as the American battleships *Nevada*, *Texas* and *Oklahoma* and the British *Ramillies*. At first light the troops of General Patch's American 7th Army are to land from the convoy vessels on the coast between Toulon and Cannes, so launching Operation *Anvil–Dragoon*, the invasion of southern France. They are to link up with the Allied forces landed in Normandy on 6 June, and, if possible, isolate the frontier between France and Italy.

Postponed several times during 1944 on account of opposition from Churchill, who (rightly, perhaps) sees no strategic military need for an attack in this region, the operation is planned and brought to its operational phase by the Americans. supported by Franco-Moroccan commando groups and the French II Corps under General De Lattre de Tassigny. Singularly trouble-free, the convoy has sailed partly from Naples (US 7th Army) and partly from North Africa (French II Corps). It arrives off the French coast without meeting any opposition, except from a single German patrol-boat, the *Escarburt*. The patrol-boat appears at 3.14 a.m., approaches the Allied fleet off the Ile-du-Levant, near Toulon, and fires a salvo which sinks the destroyer *Somers*. But the presence of the patrol-boat is quite fortuitous.

At dawn the American 1st Parachute Division is dropped in the region between Draguignan and Le Muy, about 20 miles west of Cannes, while the American special troops (Sitka Force) and the French and Moroccans (Romeo Force and Rosie Force) land on the islets east of Port Cros, at Cap Nègre and at Point Esquillon. At 8.00 a.m., after a violent naval and air bombardment, the first units of the US VI Corps (infantry) under General Truscott come ashore, the 36th Division opposite St Raphaël on the right of the line, the 45 Division in the centre in the vicinity of Ste Maxime and the 3rd Division on the left between Cavalaire Bay and Pampelonne. There is hardly any resistance from General Wiese's 19th Army, and while at least 94,000 men land during the course of the single day and quickly establish a solid beachhead, the Allies lose only 183 men.

Starting on 16 August the French and Americans move off to capture Toulon and Marseilles to the west and Cannes and Nice to the east. Before the end of August all the French coast from the mouth of the Rhône to Nice are to be firmly in the hands of the Allies (who have by then taken nearly 48,000 prisoners), while inland a pincer movement on Montélimar by Butler's task force and two divisions from the south (the US 3rd and 45th) only just fails to trap the whole of Wiese's 19th Army. The action is frustrated by the skilful tactics of the German commander, but he loses 15,000 men and 4,000 vehicles to the Allied forces.

The US 3rd Amphibious Force, having completed its operations in the Marianas earlier than expected, is ordered to get ready for the invasion of the Palau Islands.

New Guinea On Numfoor Island the

main Japanese garrison manages to break off contact with the American parachutists and takes refuge in the area of Pakriki, on the central south coast.

16 August
Northern France The Canadians of the II Corps enter Falaise; there is bitter street fighting. To the north, in the coastal sector, the British I Corps (2nd Army) moves in strength westwards towards the Seine. The US XV and XX Corps (3rd Army), advancing on Paris, reach Dreux and Chartres.
Southern France While units of the American VI Corps (7th Army) under General Truscott consolidate the beachhead in Provence, General De Lattre de Tassigny's French II Corps passes through the American units to lead the advance.

17 August
Northern France The Canadian 2nd Division (II Corps) completes the capture of Falaise. The corridor through which the units of the German 5th Armoured Army and 7th Army can escape encirclement is reduced to a minimum. But during the previous night, without asking Hitler's authority, von Kluge orders the withdrawal of the units of those two armies which are in the pocket between Falaise and Argentan.
In Brittany, the garrison of the St Malo citadel surrenders to the Americans of the 83rd Division (VIII Corps). Fighting continues in the other pockets of resistance.
Hitler replaces von Kluge, Commander-in-Chief in the West, with Field-Marshal Model.
Italian Front Plans for the offensive against the *Gothic* line are finalised.
Eastern Front The German Army Group North counter-attacks strongly in the area of Siauliai, in Lithuania, to cut off the Russian salient towards Riga and eliminate the threat to its armies still in Estonia. Further south, the 3rd Belorussian Front reaches the border of East Prussia along the river Sesupe.
New Guinea The Aitape beachhead

is extended. Units of the US 43rd Division advance in all directions, meeting with enemy resistance only near the mouth of the river Dandriwad.
On Numfoor Island, after a long pursuit, the US 503rd Parachute Regiment finally succeeds in engaging and destroying the greater part of the tiny Japanese garrison. On Biak Island, too, Japanese resistance is almost exhausted.

18 August
Northern France Allied troops continue to advance westwards towards the Seine. During the night the rearguards of General Hausser's 7th Army manage to withdraw to the east bank of the river Orne.
At Chambois, between Falaise and Argentan, units of the Canadian II Corps coming from the north join up with advance guards of the US XV Corps, closing the so-called Falaise gap, through which the German 7th Army and some units of the 5th Armoured Army have been withdrawing.
□ Field-Marshal von Kluge commits suicide. Once the architect of so many German victories, but now deprived of his command and involved in the attempt on Hitler's life, von Kluge takes his own life at Metz rather than be hauled before a People's Court. He leaves a letter for Hitler, in which he writes among other things: 'I do not know whether Field-Marshal Model will be able to restore the position. I hope so with all my heart. But if not, and if your new weapons, in which such burning faith is placed, do not bring success, then, *mein Führer*, take the decision to end the war. The German people have suffered such unspeakable ills that the time has come to put an end to these horrors.'
Southern France While the American VI Corps heads for Aix-en-Provence, the French 1st Division advances westwards towards Toulon and Marseilles.
Eastern Front The Germans maintain their powerful counter-attack in the area of Siauliai, in Lithuania. The 1st Baltic Front is only just able to

resist the German onslaught. Sandomierz, on the west bank of the Vistula, in southern Poland, is captured by the armies of the 1st Ukraine Front.

19 August
Eastern Front During the night the 2nd Ukraine Front (now commanded by Malinovsky) opens a powerful offensive in the area of Jassy, in which the 3rd Ukraine Front (now under command of Tolbukhin) also takes part, attacking in the area of Tiraspol, in Rumania. Their aim is to destroy the German–Rumanian 6th Army, part of the South Ukraine Army Group (Friessner). This army consists of 23 Rumanian and 21 German divisions. Marshal Antonescu can foresee his own political downfall coming with the end of the big expeditionary force he sent into Russia, where it has fought valiantly in the Ukraine, the Caucasus and the Crimea.

20 August
Northern France During the night the last units of the German 7th and 5th Armies succeed in crossing the Dives opposite St Lambert to avoid encirclement by the Allies. The US XV Corps establishes a bridgehead across the Seine at Mantes-Gassicourt, about 30 miles north-west of Paris. The Americans also reach the Seine south of Paris, where the 7th Armoured Division and the 5th Division (US XX Corps) try to establish a bridgehead over the river at Melun and at Montereau. Other Allied troops reach the outskirts of Fontainebleau.
□ At Vichy the Germans arrest Marshal Pétain, who refuses to leave the seat of government, and transfer him to Belfort.
Southern France The 3rd Division of the US VI Corps (7th Army) reaches the outskirts of Aix-en-Provence. The French troops of the II Corps continue their advance towards Toulon and Marseilles.
New Guinea General Krueger announces officially that operations on Biak Island are at an end. Since 27 May, Task Force *Hurricane*,

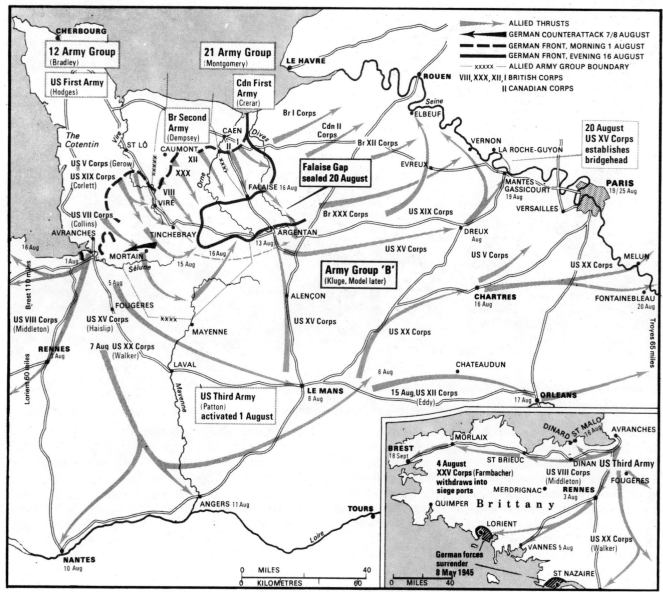

The collapse of the German defences in Normandy, August 1944. Inset: the advance through Brittany.

given the task of conquering the island, has lost 2,555 men, killed, wounded and missing. The Japanese have lost 4,700 dead, and 220 more have been taken prisoner.

Burma–China On the Salween front, the Chinese blow up the Japanese fortifications at Sung Shan with mines, and after a bloody assault with flame-throwers and with bayonets, succeed at last in seizing the position.

21 August

Northern France The whole Allied line is advancing towards the Seine, the Canadian II Corps in the north towards Rouen, the British XIX and XXX Corps and American XV Corps in the centre to the north of

Paris and the American V, XX and XII Corps south of the French capital. In the area of Mantes–Gassicourt the US 79th Division (XV Corps) widens its bridgehead across the Seine. In the south the US 4th Armoured Division enters Sens.

Southern France Units of the 3rd Division (US VI Corps, 7th Army) capture Aix-en-Provence. Columns from the 45th Division advance in the direction of Avignon, and the 36th Division makes for Grenoble. In the French sector, on the left of the Allied line, the units of the French II Corps make progress towards Toulon and Marseilles, and other units of the 1st Division and of the 3rd Algerian Division reach Aubagne, a little east of Marseilles.

Eastern Front: the forces of the Red Army continue their westward advance: a Russian patrol goes into action in East Prussia.

Eastern Front The German Army Group North continues its counter-offensive in the area of Siauliai, in Lithuania, and also counter-attacks in Estonia. In Rumania the pincer formed by the 2nd and 3rd Ukraine Fronts is about to close on the German–Rumanian 6th Army in the area of Kishinev, between Jassy and Tiraspol.

22 August

Northern France While the bridge-head established by the 79th Division (US XV Corps) at Mantes–Gassicourt stands up to counter-attacks by the Germans, the XX Corps advances rapidly towards Melun and Montereau and its 5th Division threatens Fontainebleau. The 4th Armoured Division, after taking Sens, pushes on towards Villeneuve.
Southern France The 36th Division (US VI Corps) reaches and takes Grenoble without meeting any resistance. To the west, in the Toulon and Marseilles sectors, the 3rd Algerian Division and 1st Armoured Division of the French II Corps continue to advance along the coast against strong German resistance.

Italian Front The Polish II Corps (British 8th Army) reaches and occupies the south bank of the river Metauro from Sant' Ippolito to the Adriatic coast south of Fano.
Eastern Front The 2nd Ukraine Front captures Jassy, in Rumania.
Burma–China On the Salween front, Japanese counter-attacks around the town of Sung Shan have no success.

23 August

Northern France Paris is liberated. The French Forces of the Interior (FFI) under General Koenig and Paris civilians free the French capital. Since 19 August when Koenig announced a general uprising against the Germans in Paris, there has been bitter fighting in the city, finally leaving it in the hands of the patriots.
The French 2nd Armoured Division (American V Corps) begins to move towards Paris along two centre-lines in support of the final assault on the city by the FFI. The US 4th Division captures Arpajon, south of Paris.
The 30th Division (US XIX Corps) enters Evreux, while further north units of the 2nd Armoured Division capture Le Neubourg and press on

towards Elbeuf.
In the American 3rd Army sector the 79th Division (XV Corps) maintains firm control of its bridgehead at Mantes–Gassicourt, north of Paris, while the 5th Division (XX Corps) takes Fontainebleau and the 7th Armoured Division approaches Melun.
Southern France The French 9th Colonial Division and 1st Division (II Corps) penetrate into the suburbs of Toulon and advance resolutely towards the city centre. Units of the 3rd Algerian Division and the 1st Armoured Division break into the outskirts of Marseilles from north and east. The German garrison there rejects a demand to surrender by the French headquarters.
Eastern Front South-west of Jassy the pincer formed by the 2nd and 3rd Ukrainian Fronts closes, surrounding the German and Rumanian 6th Army; about 130,000 men are caught in the pocket. The few troops that escape encirclement, mostly Germans, retire hurredly towards the Carpathian passes.
☐ Rumania. *Coup d'etat* in Bucharest. The pro-German premier, Jon

The collapse of the German defences in the Balkans.

Antonescu, *conductor* of Rumania since 1940, is deposed and arrested. King Michael I asks the moderate Sanatescu to form a government, and on the same day he orders the cessation of hostilities against the Red Army and accepts the unconditional surrender demanded by Moscow. At the same time he allows the Germans to leave his country unmolested.

New Guinea The US 503rd Parachute Regiment leaves Numfoor Island, now cleared of Japanese.

Mariana Islands US destroyers shell Aguijan.

Burma–China General Stilwell receives orders to construct a highway from the India–Burma frontier to Myitkyina and to improve the miserable track that leads from Myitkyina to China. The Americans

are still asking for Stilwell to be appointed Commander-in-Chief of the Chinese army.

On the Salween front the Japanese defending Lung-ling ask for reinforcements.

24 August

Northern France In Paris the Germans return to the attack and desperate fighting rages. The French 2nd

Paris is liberated, 25 August 1944: a German soldier surrounded by civilians.

Armoured Division under General Leclerc nears the south-western suburbs of Paris, running into heavy opposition. On General Bradley's personal orders as Commander-in-Chief of the 12th Army Group, the US 4th Division prepares to attack Paris from the south.

In the south, the XX Corps (US 3rd Army) establishes two bridgeheads over the Seine at Melun and Montereau. Units of the US XII Corps advance eastwards.

Southern France Parachutists of the US 1st Airborne Task Force enter Cannes without opposition and head for Antibes. Units of the US 3rd Division reach the Rhône at Arles. The battle for Toulon continues.

Eastern Front In Rumania the German South Ukraine Army Group, hotly pursued by the 2nd and 3rd Ukraine Fronts, withdraws speedily over the Danube. The Russians, after surrounding the German–Rumanian 6th Army, now overrun the Rumanian 3rd Army, many of whose units lay down their arms. The two armies formed part of the Dumitrescu Army Group. The Russians occupy Kishinev.

☐ German aircraft raid Bucharest as a reprisal for Rumania's defection.

Burma–China On the Salween front the Japanese send reinforcements to Lung-ling from Mangshih.

25 August

Northern France At 7.00 a.m. the French 2nd Armoured Division enters Paris from south-west, and half an hour later the US 4th Division moves towards the centre of the city from the south. The fortress commander, General Deitrich von Choltitz, defying Hitler's orders, refuses to mine the public buildings, museums and bridges of Paris. Rather than engage in a protracted but useless resistance, at 3.15 p.m. he surrenders to the French General Leclerc. While the 15th Division of the British XII Corps (2nd Army) prepares to cross the Seine opposite Louviers, south of Rouen, the British 43rd Division establishes a bridgehead across the river at Vernon.

At 1.00 p.m., three divisions of the American VIII Corps (3rd Army), the 2nd, 80th and 90th, begin the offensive against Brest, in Brittany, after an hour-long aerial bombardment. The garrison, formed from units of the XXV Corps, is not giving up without a fight.

Southern France The American 3rd Division (VI Corps) enters Avignon. While fighting continues for Toulon and Marseilles, the units of General Wiese's 19th Army withdraw to the north along the Rhône valley.

Italian Front During the night the British 8th Army (British V Corps, Canadian I Corps and Polish II Corps) goes into the attack against the *Gothic* line from the river Metauro. Caught by surprise, General Herr's German LXXVI Armoured Corps only puts up a patchy defence.

Eastern Front In the northern sector the troops of the 3rd Baltic Front capture Tartu, in Estonia, a strong-point on a fortified line called the *Valga* line, prepared by the Germans between the river Velikaya in the east and the stronger *Sigulda* line prepared round Riga.

☐ Rumania declares war on Germany.

☐ The German forces in Greece and the Aegean are regrouped as Army Group E (General Löhr), with headquarters at Thessaloniki. But operationally they are under the south-eastern sector commanded by Field-Marshal von Weichs, the Commander-in-Chief of Army Group F, with headquarters at Belgrade. Following the defection of Rumania and the fall of Bulgaria, now seen as inevitable, the Aegean islands are going to lose some of their strategic and political value as a guarantee against Turkish hostility. Hitler, yielding for once to pressure from the military, agrees to their evacuation. The withdrawal is to take place on 2 September. The Peloponnese is to be evacuated at the same time, except for Athens and the port of Piraeus, the possession of which is necessary until the evacuation of the Aegean islands is over.

New Guinea General Krueger announces officially that operations in the Aitape beachhead area are completed. In the course of the bitter fighting the Allies have lost 3,000 killed, wounded and missing. The Japanese have lost 8,821 dead and 98 prisoners. The Japanese 18th Army has thus lost more than two divisions in their efforts to recapture the beachhead, and by now it is no longer a serious threat to the Americans and Australians.

In the north-west of the Vogelkop peninsula (now called Djazirah Doberai), the Japanese carry out their first daylight air raid since the day of the landing.

26 August

Northern France After crossing the lower Seine the Canadian 1st Army moves off north towards Calais, and the British 2nd Army towards Belgium. In support of the British, the American 1st Army moves along the axis Paris–Brussels. The Allied divisions resume their advance to the east from their bridgeheads on the right bank of the Seine. The 7th Armoured Division of the American XX Corps thrusts swiftly north-east in the direction of Château-Thierry and the river Marne.

In Brittany the attacks by the American VIII Corps against Brest are still unsuccessful.

Southern France As the Germans retire north, the resistance by the Toulon and Marseilles garrisons is visibly weakening. A large part of both cities has been captured by units of the French II Corps.

Italian Front The divisions of the 8th Army establish bridgeheads over the river Metauro.

Eastern Front The 3rd Ukraine Front, advancing into Rumania along the river Prut towards Galati, reaches the lower course of the Danube. The 2nd Ukraine Front breaks through the gap opened in the enemy lines between Galati and Focsani.

27 August

Northern France The British I Corps reaches the mouth of the Seine, while units of the Canadian II Corps begin to cross the Seine between Elbeuf and Pont-de-l'Arche. Further south,

in the XII Corps sector, the 15th Division crosses the Seine east of Louviers, while in the Mantes–Gassicourt sector the 30th and 79th Divisions of the XV Corps (US 1st Army) attack across the river.

The US XX Corps (3rd Army), with the 7th Armoured Division in the lead, reaches the Marne at Château-Thierry as it advances towards Rheims. The US XII Corps advances from Troyes north-eastwards, towards Châlons-sur-Marne.

In Brittany the VIII Corps (3rd Army) completes the encirclement of Brest.

☐ General Eisenhower, the Allied Commander-in-Chief, with General Bradley, Commander of the 12th Army Group, visits Paris and confers with General de Gaulle.

Southern France The US 3rd Division, moving north along the Rhône valley, nears Montélimar. The American 45th Division pushes on from Grenoble towards Lyons. At Marseilles the German garrison asks for talks on surrender terms.

Italian Front The British 8th Army continues to advance towards the *Gothic* line.

Eastern Front In Rumania, the 2nd Ukraine Front takes Focsani and advances towards Ploesti, while the 3rd Ukraine Front occupies Galati, Rumania's third city and the main river port on the Danube.

Burma The 36th Division, British XXXIII Corps, advances along the Mogaung–Mandalay road and captures Pinbaw.

28 August

Northern France In the northern sector of the Allied line the Canadian II Corps expands its bridgehead towards Rouen and the British XXX Corps (2nd Army) crosses the Seine in force, while further south the American XV Corps further widens the Mantes–Gassicourt bridgehead. The French 2nd Armoured Division and American 4th Division, having entered Paris, continue to advance towards the north-east. The XX Corps (3rd Army) is approaching Rheims and in Brittany the VIII Corps continues the siege of Brest.

Southern France The French II Corps advances northwards along the west bank of the Rhône, while the American VI Corps, aiming at linking up with the *Overlord* forces, also goes north along a line Lyons–Beaume–Dijon. The German 19th Army manages to get most of its troops out of the trap at Montélimar. Units of the American 45th Division advance towards Lyons.

The battle at Toulon ends when the last German troops surrender to the French 9th Colonial Division. The German garrison at Marseilles also surrenders.

Italian Front Units of the 8th Indian Division (British XII Corps, US 5th Army) capture Tigliano, north of Pontassieve. The British 8th Army continues its advance towards the *Gothic* line.

Eastern Front In Rumania troops of the 2nd Ukraine Front penetrate into Transylvania across the Oituz Pass in the Carpathians. Now Hungary is threatened.

Faced by the imminent breakthrough by the Russians, General Lakatos forms a new government which declares itself ready to negotiate Hungary's surrender.

29 August

Northern France General Eisenhower's orders are to push on northwards. Units of the British XXX Corps lead the Allied columns in the northern sector, making for Amiens with the object of crossing the Somme. To the south-east the US 3rd Armoured Division (VII Corps, 1st Army) crosses the river Aisne east of Soissons on the way to Laon. The American 5th Division (XX Corps, 3rd Army) enters Rheims. Southeast of Rheims units of the XII Corps capture Châlons-sur-Marne.

In Brittany, resolute defence by the German troops still holds up the efforts of the American VIII Corps to take Brest.

Southern France While the American 3rd Division (VI Corps) concentrates at Voiron, north-west of Grenoble, the 36th and 45th Divisions continue their advance on Lyons.

WAR HELICOPTERS

Having made its appearance in an experimental capacity only in the preceding decade, the helicopter was used in the later stages of the war, especially by Germany and the United States, for military purposes, for communication, for reconnaissance, for tactical observation of artillery fire and for rescue operations in places otherwise inaccessible.

Although the helicopter was not designed for such functions at the outbreak of war, technical advances in Germany persuaded the government to build an underground factory near Berlin to mass produce the Fa 233, a powerful military version of the famous Focke-Achgelis Fa 61, a singleseater which had set impressive records in this class towards the end of the 1930s.

However, the real link between the autogiro and the modern helicopter was the Flettner FI 282, better known as the Kolibri, an aircraft with an enclosed plexiglass cabin used for reconnaissance on German warships from 1942 onwards. The Kolibri qualifies as the first military helicopter in history.

The American armed forces displayed interest in helicopters after 1941, when, having observed the excellent results achieved by the VS-300, built by the Russian-born engineer Igor Sikorsky, one of the pioneers of vertical flight, it commissioned Vought-Sikorsky to construct the R-4, an experimental helicopter comprising a steel-plated fuselage and glass cockpit. This highly successful model (130 machines were built during the war) was the prototype for the later R-5 and R-6.

VS 300

FLETTNER FI 282

Italian Front The infantry of the British 8th Army reach the river Foglia, just north of Pesaro.

Eastern Front In Rumania, the 3rd Ukraine Front captures Constanta, a port on the Black Sea.

China The Japanese 11th Division, re-grouping after the capture of Hengyang in south-east China, advances towards Kweilin and Liuchow, the sites of two of the US 14th Air Force's major airfields.

30 August

Northern France The 7th Armoured Division (XX Corps, US 3rd Army) is rapidly approaching Verdun, while further south, on the road to Nancy, the XII Corps reaches the St Didier sector.

Southern France Units of the American 36th Division (VI Corps) and French II Corps advance in force towards Lyons, the first along the east road, the second along the west bank of the Rhône.

Italian Front The British 8th Army starts its offensive against the *Gothic* line and the Canadian I and British V Corps cross the river Foglia.

Eastern Front Troops of the 2nd Ukraine Front occupy Ploesti, the vital Rumanian oil centre.

31 August

Northern France The British XXX Corps (2nd Army) reaches Amiens and crosses the river Somme. In the American XX Corps (3rd Army) sector the 7th Armoured Division succeeds in establishing a bridgehead across the Meuse near Verdun. In Brittany the operations of the VIII Corps against Brest are temporarily suspended. The Meuse is also crossed by units of the 4th Armoured Division (XII Corps, US 3rd Army), which establish a bridgehead in the vicinity of Commercy.

☐ The provisional government of France is transferred to Paris.

Italian Front As the Germans retire, patrols of the American IV Corps (US 5th Army) cross the Arno during the night.

In the eastern sector (British 8th Army), while the Polish II Corps continues the battle for Pesaro, elements of the Canadian I and British

V Corps penetrate into the defences of the *Gothic* line.

☐ General Montgomery is promoted to field-marshal.

Eastern Front Bucharest, capital of Rumania, is taken by troops of the 2nd Ukraine Front. An enormous gap has now been opened in the German front, from the Carpathians to the mouth of the Danube. The Wehrmacht has insufficient forces to be able to close it, so the Red Army occupies Walachia without opposition.

Pacific Aircraft from a carrier squadron of Task Force 38 (a new number allocated to Task Force 58), under the command of Rear-Admiral Davison, begin an attack lasting three days against the Japanese installations on Iwo Jima and the Bonin Islands. During the next two days a naval bombardment carried out by cruisers and destroyers makes life even more unpleasant for the Japanese defenders.

New Guinea Operations on Numfoor and the Sansapor area in the Vogelkop peninsula are officially declared closed. On Numfoor the American casualties have been 63 killed, 343 wounded and three missing, while they have killed 1,730 Japanese and captured 186. At Sansapor the American losses have been minute, 14 dead, whereas the Japanese (including some units from Formosa) have lost 385 killed and 215 taken prisoner.

1 September

Northern France Verdun, scene of the heroic French stand under Marshal Pétain in the last war, is liberated by General Patton's 3rd US army. The British I Corps, having crossed the Seine, thrusts westwards towards Le Havre. Units of the Canadian II Corps reach Dieppe, while two divisions of the XXX Corps (British 2nd Army), the 11th Armoured and the Guards Division, reach Arras. In the sector where the US XIX and V Corps are operating, the Americans advance rapidly towards St Quentin and Cambrai. On the east of the Allied line the US XX

Corps (3rd Army) advances from Verdun in the direction of Metz.

Southern France Units of the VI Corps are rapidly approaching Lyons.

Italian Front The IV Corps of the US 5th Army begins the pursuit of the Germans across the Arno. In the eastern sector (British 8th Army) the Canadian I and the British V Corps throw all their forces into an attack on the *Gothic* line and reach Tomba di Pesaro.

Eastern Front The Red Army reaches the Bulgarian frontier at Giurgiu, on the Danube. Since its adhesion to the Tripartite Pact (1 March 1941) Bulgaria has occupied Yugoslav and Greek territory (in Greece as far as Thessaloniki) and is consequently at war with Great Britain and the United States, though it has declared its own neutrality in its relations with Russia. It has had little experience of war until the beginning of 1944, since when – especially Sofia, the capital – it has become a target for Allied air raids. Now, faced with the threat of Russian occupation, the Prime Minister, Muraviev, asks for support from the British and Americans. But he does not get it.

☐ Balkans. While the Germans prepare to evacuate the Aegean and Ionian islands, as well as part of Greece, British and American air forces pound the main railway line that will be used in the withdrawal.

2 September

Northern France The Allied advance continues all along the front, in the west towards Le Havre (British I Corps) and in the east towards the Belgian frontier (US 1st Army).

In Brittany the German garrison at Brest still holds out.

Southern France Having reached the outskirts of Lyons, the American 36th Division (VI Corps) halts to allow the French II Corps to enter the city first.

Italian Front In the British 8th Army sector the advance towards Rimini makes progress. The Poles of General Anders' II Corps occupy Pesaro, while Canadian units reach

the Conca river during the night and establish a bridgehead on the north bank about 3 miles west of Cattolica.

☐ Strength of the German armed forces at the beginning of September 1944: 10,163,303, including 7,536,946 in the Wehrmacht and *Waffen-SS*, 1,925,291 in the Luftwaffe and 703,066 in the *Kriegsmarine*. But few of these are troops comparable with those serving at the beginning of the war; many of them are elderly men and boys.

☐ Finland. Following the collapse of Rumania, Antti Hackzell, who has been Prime Minister for only a few days, decides to break off diplomatic relations with Germany.

☐ Field-Marshal Erwin von Witzleben, condemned to death by a People's Court for his part in the conspiracy against Hitler, is barbarously executed, hung on a butcher's hook.

New Guinea Operations in the area of the Wadke–Sarmi beachhead are officially declared closed. Although there are no published figures for casualties, losses must have been high on both sides.

3 September

Western Europe Brussels is liberated by the Guards Armoured Division (XXX Corps, British 2nd Army).

At this point the Allied front in the north runs from the mouth of the Somme in the north to Troyes in the south, following the line Lille–Brussels–Mons–Sedan–Verdun–Commercy.

In the south the French 1st Infantry Division (General De Lattre de Tassigny's II Corps) enters Lyons. Wiese has managed to withdraw most of the German 19th Army. The German 1st Army under General von der Chevallerie, manning the Bay of Biscay, has also withdrawn from south-west France. 130,000 German soldiers succeed in rejoining Army Group B, but 80,000 others are taken prisoner.

4 September

Western Europe General Eisenhower lays down the general objectives of his armies: the 21st Army Group (Canadian 1st Army and British 2nd Army) and US 1st Army are given the task of following up the advance towards the Ruhr area, and the final objective of General Patton's US 3rd Army is the Saar.

The 11th Armoured Division (XXX Corps, British 2nd Army) enters Antwerp. The city's harbour, one of the biggest on the North Sea, is intact, but the Germans still control the Scheldt estuary, through which Antwerp communicates with the sea. In southern France, after capturing Lyons, the American VI Corps and French II Corps continue to advance north, on Besançon and Dijon.

Hitler restores command of the German forces in the Western Front to the ageing Field-Marshal von Runstedt.

Italian Front In the western sector, divisions of the British V Corps advance towards the hills of Gemmano and Coriano, two key enemy defence positions manned by General Feuerstein's LI Mountain Corps and General Herr's LXXVI Armoured Corps.

Eastern Front The Finns cease fire on all fronts. An armistice is agreed between the Finnish and Russian governments as a preliminary to peace negotiations.

Pacific The first units of the III Amphibious Corps of the US Marines leave the Solomons for the invasion of the Palau Islands, between the Caroline Islands and the Philippines. In New Guinea troops are being trained for the invasion of Morotai in the Moluccas, north of Halmahera and east of the Celebes.

Burma General Slim, Commander of the British 14th Army, directs the XV Corps to engage the enemy in the Arakan sector, while the XXXIII Corps will launch a big offensive across the Chindwin at the beginning of December.

In the XXXIII Corps sector the 11th East African Division (which has replaced the 23rd Indian Division in the pursuit of the enemy forces beyond Tamu), occupies Sittaung without opposition and sends several

units forward to Kalemyo.

5 September

Western Europe Major successes for the Allied armies on the whole front: in the north, units of the Canadian II Corps (General Crerar's Canadian 1st Army) take Boulogne and approach the Calais area; Hodges's divisions (US 1st Army) approach Liège and cross the Meuse at Sedan; in the south, the 3rd Army crosses the Moselle near Nancy.

Italian Front Units of the American 1st Armoured Division (IV Corps, 5th Army) enter Lucca. In the eastern sector the battle begins for the capture of the hills of Coriano and Gemmano, west and south-west of Cattolica.

Eastern Front The Red Army captures Brasov, in the middle of the Carpathians, and starts to penetrate the so-called 'Carpathian Trench'.
□ Russia declares war on Bulgaria. Russian forces invade and within a few hours Bulgaria is forced to capitulate.

6 September

Western Europe Units of the 3rd Army cross the Moselle. The US VII Corps (1st Army) pushes on towards Liège.

In southern France the French II Corps enters Chalons-sur-Saône. The American VI Corps moves rapidly towards Besançon.

Italian Front Units of the British V

Rumanian civilians fraternize with a Russian tank crew in a street in Bucharest.

Corps (8th Army) prepare an offensive on a huge scale to capture Coriano. Patrols from the Canadian I Corps reach the river Marano.

Eastern Front Troops of the 3rd Ukraine Front reach the Rumanian–Yugoslav frontier at Turnu Severin, near the Iron Gate on the Danube. There they make contact with Tito's partisans.

The loss of Rumania and its oilfields has the most serious consequences for Germany. Any attempt to hold the Carpathian–Hungarian line must now fail for the lack of fuel, manpower and equipment.

☐ In Serbia the German-backed government under Milan Neditch is still in power. The government was set up by the Germans on 30 August 1941. But Neditch has been in secret contact with Mihailovitch, leader of the Serbian monarchists, the 'Chetniks'. However, both Neditch and Mihailovitch have steadily lost influence, as the initiative in a long and courageous struggle against the Germans has been taken by the Communist partisans led by Tito, Secretary-General of the Croat Communist party.

☐ A Finnish delegation flies to Moscow to negotiate an armistice.

Pacific Aircraft from sixteen carriers of Vice-Admiral Mitscher's fast carrier squadron, escorted by cruisers and destroyers, carry out attacks against Japanese airfields and other installations in the Palau Islands and in Yap and Ulithi Islands in the western Carolines. The attacks are to go on for three days, causing tremendous damage. The targets are also shelled from the sea.

Burma–China On the Salween front the commander of the Japanese forces in the Sung Shan sector is killed in action.

7 September

Western Europe The British 2nd Army and American 1st Army reach the Albert Canal in Belgium; the 113th Cavalry Group (US XIX Corps) cross the canal near Hasselt. The 3rd Armoured Division (VII Corps, US 1st Army) reaches Liège. The American VI Corps enters Besançon.

General de Lattre de Tassigny.

Italian Front During the night the Germans withdraw from their positions on the hills north and north-east of Florence.

Eastern Front The Russians have penetrated into the eastern Carpathians, almost up to the Hungarian border.

☐ Bulgaria declares war on Germany, as occupation by part of the 3rd Ukraine Front continues.

Burma–China On the Salween front the Chinese 8th Army completes the mopping up of the Sung Shan zone. The battle for the capture of this important staging point on the Burma Road has cost the Chinese nearly 8,000 dead. The Japanese garrison of 2,000 odd has been wiped out.

8 September

The first of the V2s falls on London. These are quite different and a great deal more deadly than the slow V1s, which the British fighters could pursue and shoot down. The construction of the main launching bases near St Omer, south of Dunkirk, has been halted by the massive Allied bombing raids. More easily constructed ramps are then put up on the

Dutch islands. The range of the V2s is about 230 miles and their accuracy is remarkable. The main target is England, and particularly London, but after the Germans lose Antwerp that city also becomes a constant target for the new weapon in order to prevent the Allies from making use of the harbour. Hitler's objective, the breaking down of the morale of the British, is not achieved. Instead, the *V-Waffen* increase Britain's determination to crush Germany. The last V2 lands on London on 27 March 1945. By that date some 1,115 have been launched at Britain, resulting in 2,724 dead and 6,467 seriously wounded. By the end of the war, the total number of British civilians killed in air raids amounts to 60,000. Up to 5 April 1945, more than 2,050 V2s are fired at Antwerp, Brussels and Liège.

Western Europe In the northern sector of the front (Canadian 1st Army) the 2nd Division (II Corps) attacks Dunkirk, while the 4th Division reaches the outskirts of Bruges.

In Brittany, after a heavy bombardment, the VIII Corps begins a general offensive against Brest.

Liège is occupied by units of the American VII Corps (1st Army). The Albert Canal is crossed opposite Gheel (XXX Corps, British 2nd Army) and at Maastricht (XIX Corps, US 1st Army).

French troops of the II Corps enter Beaune and Autun, south-west of Dijon.

☐ The Belgian government of premier Hubert Pierlot, which took refuge in London when Belgium capitulated in May 1940, returns to Brussels.

Italian Front Units of the British V Corps and I Canadian Corps are still held up by stubborn German resistance on the Coriano and Gemmano hills. Consequently the Allied advance on Rimini is stalled.

Eastern Front The Russians complete the occupation of Bulgaria and continue their advance into the eastern Carpathians. The German South Ukraine Army Group (Friessner), after the loss of the German–Rumanian 6th Army and the

Rumanian 3rd Army (Dumitrescu Group) now consists of no more than the German 8th Army, the Rumanian 4th Army and the German XVII Corps. It is quite unable to stand up to the eight armies, including one armoured and one air army, that make up Malinovsky's 2nd Ukraine Front, which is supported by a large part of Tolbukhin's 3rd Ukraine Front with its four armies, one motorized corps and one air army. With these two Fronts the Russians have 929,000 men in the line, the Germans only half that number.

Burma–China On the Salween front the Japanese have received substantial reinforcements and open an offensive against the Chinese positions north of Lung-ling.

In China, the Japanese advance from Hengyang towards the south and occupy Ling-ling from which the US 14th Air Force has withdrawn.

The US air bases at Kweilin and Liuchow are also threatened by two divisions and one brigade of the Japanese 23rd Army, advancing northwards from Canton.

9 September

Western Europe Units of the American XIX Corps cross the borders of Belgium and Holland in the area of Maastricht.

The French II Corps continues to advance on Dijon.

☐ The Allies estimate they have captured about 300 flying-bomb sites in northern France.

Italian Front The British V Corps and Canadian I Corps step up their attacks on the Coriano and Gemmano hills. In Val d'Ossola and Val Cannobina, held by the partisans, a provisional government is set up.

Eastern Front It is announced by Moscow radio that Russian troops have ceased operations in Bulgaria. The Allies prepare peace terms.

The Germans concentrate forces in Hungary for a counter-attack against the 2nd Ukraine Front.

Pacific Aircraft from Vice-Admiral Mitscher's fast carrier task force, made up of 16 aircraft carriers escorted by cruisers and destroyers,

bombard Japanese installations on Mindanao, in the Philippines.

10 September

Western Europe General Eisenhower decides to postpone the operation to liberate the port of Antwerp. On the suggestion of Montgomery he decides instead on Operation *Market Garden*, a landing by airborne troops at Arnhem, Grave and Eindhoven to secure a bridgehead over the Rhine. After a heavy air raid by Allied bombers, the British I Corps (Canadian 1st Army) launches a general offensive against Le Havre, and succeeds in piercing the German defences. The Canadians of II Corps occupy Ostend.

The American 5th Armoured Division (V Corps, 1st Army) reaches the city of Luxembourg.

The French II Corps enters Dijon. At Sombernon the 1st Division makes contact with the French 2nd Armoured Division (XV Corps, American 3rd Army).

Italian Front The Allied offensive to reduce the *Gothic* line continues. In the US 5th Army sector the Allies cross the river Serchio at Vecchiano, capture Villa Basilica and cross the Sieve. But in the east, units of the German 10th Army keep up their powerful resistance on the summits of the Gemmano and Coriano hills.

Palau Islands Aircraft from a fast US carrier task force under Rear-Admiral Davison carry out a heavy raid, repeated the next day, against Japanese defences on the islands of Peleliu and Angaur, in preparation for the invasion.

11 September

Western Europe Apart from the ports of Boulogne, Calais and Dunkirk, the whole of the French Channel coast is now in Allied hands. The advance of the Allied divisions continues along the whole front. American patrols from the 1st Army cross the German border near Aachen, creating panic among the defenders, but the action is not followed up.

Italian Front Units of the American IV Corps (5th Army) reach the

suburbs of Viareggio, while the South African 6th Armoured Division enters Pistoia.

Eastern Front The initial armistice between the USSR and Bulgaria is confirmed. Bulgaria begins to evacuate its troops from the occupied provinces of Yugoslavia.

☐ The US 8th Air Force carries out the last of its 'shuttle' raids. 139 aircraft attack an arms factory at Chemnitz, in Germany, and go on to land at bases in the Soviet Union.

Pacific In New Guinea forces are assembled for the invasion of Morotai Island, in the Moluccas.

☐ Canada. The *Octagon* Conference between the British and American chiefs of staff opens at Quebec, and goes on until the 16th. Guidelines are laid down for the war in the Pacific and the occupation of Germany after the Allied victory. The conclusive operations in the Pacific are to be the invasion of Kyushu Island in October 1945 and Honshu Island (on which Tokyo is) in December. Admiral Mountbatten's task will be the recapture of Burma and re-opening of the road from India to China, objectives to be achieved by 15 March 1945.

12 September

Western Europe The German garrison of Le Havre surrenders and 12,000 men are taken prisoner.

Italian Front At 11.00 p.m. the second battle for the capture of the Coriano hill-top begins.

Eastern Front A lull on the various fronts while the Russians consolidate, and overhaul their supply system.

☐ The armistice between Rumania and the Soviet Union, Great Britain and the United States is signed in Moscow. Rumania will take part in the war against Germany and Hungary and will pay reparations. The frontier between the USSR and Rumania will be that fixed by the Rumanian–Soviet agreement of 28 June 1940. The USSR promises that Transylvania will be restored to Rumania.

During fighting in Hungary, Czechoslovakia and Germany, the

Above: a V1 falls on London. Right: V2s on the launching ramps at Peenemünde.

Rumanian army is to lose a further 170,000 men killed, wounded and missing by April 1945.

Pacific The 16 aircraft carriers of the Mitscher group begin a three-day attack against the central Philippines, meeting very little resistance from the Japanese air force and navy. No resistance forthcoming from Leyte, one of the objectives of the next landing.

Palau Islands The US battleships, cruisers and aircraft carriers under the command of Rear-Admirals Oldendorf and Ford begin an intensive bombardment of the Palaus in advance of the landing. The Americans undertake the necessary mine-lifting and the destruction of under-water obstacles protecting the beaches.

13 September

Western Europe The German garrison at Brest refuses to surrender. Units of the US 3rd Army continue their offensive along the line of the Moselle from Thionville to Épinal.

Italian Front In the British 8th Army sector the 5th Armoured Division (Canadian I Corps) and the 1st Division (British V Corps) take the Coriano and Gemmano hill positions and the Germans are forced to retire to the north, leaving the road to Rimini open.

Eastern Front In response to insistent requests by the Allies, the Russians at last begin dropping supplies to the Warsaw insurgents (the 'Underground Army'), fighting a desperate battle against German tanks.

Lomza, west of Bialystok, a German strongpoint for the defence of East Prussia and Warsaw, is taken by the 2nd Belorussian front.

☐ The US 8th Air Force, on its return flight to Italy, bombs the great Diosgyoer steelworks in Hungary.

Moluccas The US invasion force for Morotai is on its way.

China General Stilwell has a meeting with emissaries from the Chinese Communist army, and also inspects the Chinese positions at Kweilin.

14 September

Western Europe Field-Marshal Montgomery issues instructions for the British 2nd Army's offensive towards the Rhine and the Meuse (Operation *Market Garden*) and for a possible attack by the Canadian 1st Army to liberate the port of Antwerp and capture Boulogne and Calais.

Italian Front The units of the British 8th Army that captured Gemmano and Coriano now reinforce their positions and advance towards the river Marano, which is crossed by several patrols. In the western sector the American 5th Army continues to pound the defences of the *Gothic* line.

Eastern Front The 1st Belorussian Front, with the support of Polish forces, captures Praga, a suburb of Warsaw, but makes no attempt to cross the Narew and the Vistula, strongly defended by the Germans.

Burma–China The Chinese complete the capture of Teng-chung, the town they first managed to enter on 4 August. With the loss of Teng-chung and increasingly strong Chinese resistance in the Lung-ling sector, the Japanese break off their counter-offensive on the Salween front.

15 September

Western Europe The Allied armies enter Germany. From Aachen to Luxembourg, units of the US VII and V Corps have reached the south-western frontiers of the Reich. Since D-Day 6 June, the Allies have landed more than 2,000,000 men in France, 40,000 of whom have fallen in battle. In the same period German losses have been catastrophic – the ranks of the Wehrmacht have been depleted by 700,000.

Apart from a strip of land on the German border, Belgium and Luxembourg are completely liberated. The new front runs from near Ostend to Épinal (west of Colmar) by way of Antwerp, Maastricht, Thionville, Metz and Nancy. The Germans deploy General Model's Army Group B in the north and General Blaskowitz's Army Group G in the south. The first consists of the 15th Army

under General Zengen and the 1st Parachute Army under General Student (stationed in Holland) and General Brandenberger's 7th Army defending the German border between the Ruhr and the Saar. The second Group deploys, between Metz and Epinal, General Knobelsdorff's 1st Army and General Manteuffel's 5th Armoured Army.

Eastern Front The German South Ukraine Army Group succeeds in concentrating 27 divisions and brigades, including six armoured divisions, before Cluj in Transylvania. These forces block the advance of the 2nd Ukraine Front.

☐ Greece. Between 12 and 15 September the Germans evacuate Mitilini and the Ionian Islands.

Palau Islands At 8.30 a.m. the US 1st Marine Division (1st, 5th and 7th Regiments), under the command of General Rupertus, lands on the south-west coast of Peleliu Island, in the Palau group, east of the southern Philippines. The Japanese fire, slight at the start of the landing, becomes intense as the Marines proceed inland, and is especially deadly on the division's flanks. At the end of the day the perimeter of the beachhead measures $1\frac{1}{2}$ miles from north to south, but is only a few hundred yards deep. The Palau Islands, which have been made into a strategic centre for the concentration of Japanese air and naval forces since the destruction of Truk, are defended by over 30,000 soldiers, crack troops under the command of General Sadao Inoue. The Japanese have 20,000 men on Babelthuap, the biggest of the islands, 11,000 men on Peleliu and 1,400 men on Angaur, an islet about 10 miles south of Peleliu. There is an excellent airfield on Peleliu and another on the islet of Ngesebus, joined to Peleliu by a narrow embankment. Peleliu has been strongly fortified, with over 500 strongpoints in caves connected by tunnels.

Moluccas: Morotai At 8.30 a.m. the US 31st Division under General Persons lands on the south-west coast of Morotai Island, on Gila peninsula. The landing has been preceded by an intense two-hour bombardment from a US amphibious fleet under the command of Rear-Admiral Barbey. There is little opposition from the Japanese, but the conditions of the terrain are terrible. Within the day the division occupies the whole of Gila peninsula.

China–Burma Chiang Kai-shek threatens to withdraw his troops from the Salween if the Chinese and American forces in the Myitkyina sector do not carry out an offensive to the south within a week.

In Burma, in the British XXXIII Corps sector, the 5th Indian Division continues its advance on Tiddim, establishing a bridgehead across the river Manipur near Tuitum.

□ The Joint Chiefs of Staff, examining the situation in the Pacific in the light of the limited resistance by the Japanese in the central Philippines, decide to bring forward the invasion of Leyte from 20 December to 20 October, and to cancel the planned operations against the islands of Yap (east of the Palaus), Talaud (south of Mindanao) and Mindanao in the southern Philippines.

16 September

Western Europe Hitler outlines his plans for an offensive in the Ardennes to his generals.

Italian Front The headquarters of the British 8th Army issues instructions for the advance on Rimini. The British V Corps will follow Highway 9 in the direction of Bologna and the Canadian I Corps will make for Ravenna and Ferrara.

Eastern Front Troops of the Leningrad Front and the three Baltic Fronts open a new offensive towards the Baltic in the direction of Tallinn in Estonia and Riga in Lithuania.

In Bulgaria the 3rd Ukraine Front, resuming its westward offensive to block the routes by which the German Army Groups F (von Weichs) and E (Löhr) can withdraw from Greece and Yugoslavia, enters Sofia. In Rumania fighting continues between the South Ukraine Army Group and the 2nd Ukraine Front.

Greece British commandos land on Kithira Island, south of the Peloponnese.

Palau Islands On Peleliu the 7th Marine Regiment occupies the south point of the island and begins mopping up. The beachhead reaches a depth of about 1¼ miles, despite strong fire by the Japanese. The 5th Marines capture a good part of the island's airfield. General Rupertus takes over command on land now that the amphibious phase of the operation, under naval command, is completed.

Morotai The US 31st Division extends the depth of its beachhead by an average of 4 miles, while the Japanese begin a series of not very powerful air raids.

17 September

Western Europe 1st Allied Airborne Army lands in Holland. Under Operation *Market Garden* the landings by three airborne divisions, British and American, are on Arnhem, Grave (south of Nijmegen), Veghel and Eindhoven.

After a violent bombardment by aircraft and artillery, the Canadian 3rd Division (Canadian 1st Army) launches a general offensive against Boulogne.

Italian Front In the western sector the American IV Corps (5th Army) opens a general attack on the left flank.

Palau Islands Groups of Japanese attack during the night at the north end of the American beachhead, but are repulsed by mortar fire and by fire from American warships. During the morning, with all the south of the island captured, including Peleliu airfield, the 1st and 5th Marines mount attacks from south-west and south-east on the southern spurs of the highly fortified Mount Umurbrogol in the centre of the island, but are halted with heavy losses after taking one or two pill-boxes. The heavy guns of the battleship *Mississippi* are brought into action, successfully bombarding the Japanese positions. At 8.30 a.m. a regiment of the US 322nd Infantry Division lands on the east coast of the little island of Angaur, south of Peleliu. Japanese

resistance is not great and the landing force makes good progress. Japanese counter-attacks during the night fail.

Morotai The US 31st Division begins mopping up the island and occupies the islets off the coast.

Burma On the British XXXIII Corps front, the 5th Indian Division captures Tuitum.

18 September

Palau Islands: Peleliu The Marines, with perhaps inadequate preparation, go into the attack against all the enemy positions on Mount Umurbrogol. They make very little progress and suffer heavy losses from the resistance of the seasoned Japanese defenders.

Angaur The American infantry advance in wedge formation to the centre of the island; in some sectors they are mistakenly attacked by their own aircraft. Units advancing in the north are partly cut off by the Japanese.

Morotai On the south coast, east of Gila peninsula, surveying begins for the construction of an airfield able to accommodate heavy bombers. The Pitoe airfield only takes fighters.

19 September

Western Europe The capture of Brest is completed when the American 8th Division (VIII Corps) takes the Crozon peninsula and takes General Hermann Bernhard Ramcke, the garrison commander, prisoner.

Eastern Front Bitter fighting rages near Cluj, between the 2nd Ukraine Front and the North Ukraine Army Group. In Estonia troops of the 3rd Baltic Front capture Valga, on the frontier between Estonia and Latvia. Other forces push on towards Tallinn and Riga.

□ The armistice between the Finns and the Allies is signed in Moscow. Finland retains its independence within the 1940 frontiers. But Finland has to cede Viipuri to the USSR because of its proximity to Leningrad, also the Petsamo district in the north of the country, and control, but not sovereignty, over the Porkkala peninsula south of Helsinki, important for the control of communi-

Eisenhower's plans for a broadly based Allied offensive towards the Rhine.

Two American NCOs in conversation with a Florentine in medieval dress.

cations between the Gulf of Finland (and Leningrad) and the Baltic. The Russians restore Hanko, or rather do not press their claim to that town. The Finns will have to pay reparations and the Allies will have the right to use the country's airfields.

Palau Islands: Peleliu Extremely bloody fighting rages on Mount Umurbrogol, where the Japanese have the 1st and 7th Marines pinned down. Elements of the latter regiment, advancing from the east, capture the village of Asias. Because of Mount Umurbrogol, the American U-shaped advance is held up at both extremities.

Angaur The small Japanese garrison puts up a stubborn resistance.

Morotai The enormous superiority of MacArthur's 7th Amphibious Force (28,000 men) gives the Ameri-

cans an easy victory over the few hundred Japanese manning this little island, which is soon turned into a big air base less than 400 miles from Mindanao in the Philippines.

China Roosevelt and Churchill send a message to Chiang Kai-shek telling him of the decisions of the Quebec Conference. The message is accompanied by a letter from Roosevelt which, in far from diplomatic terms, demands that the Generalissimo stop vacillating and make good his words. Chiang Kai-shek is furious.

20 September
Italian Front The 4th Indian Division (British V Corps) enters San Marino.

Palau Islands The Marines are held up on Peleliu, but Japanese resistance on Angaur is dying out; the few

remaining units take refuge in the north-west of the island, where they prepare to hold out to the bitter end in a wide depression near Lake Salome.

21 September
Italian Front The Canadians of the I Corps and the Greek 3rd Mountain Brigade enter Rimini which the Germans have evacuated. Since the beginning of operations against the *Gothic* line, the British 8th Army has lost 14,000 men killed, wounded and missing.

Pacific General MacArthur tells the US Chiefs of Staff that he is in a position to launch a big operation against Luzon, in the Philippines, following the advanced deadline for the landing on Leyte. He also declares that there will be no point in a landing on Formosa once Luzon has been captured.

Palau Islands: Peleliu Stalemate for the US Marines in the face of the powerful Japanese defence from the caves on Mount Umurbrogol.

Philippines Twelve US aircraft carriers of Task Force 38, commanded by Vice-Admiral Mitscher, begin three days of heavy attacks on the Japanese airfields and shipping on Luzon and the islands in the Visaya Sea in the Philippines archipelago. One Japanese destroyer, one tanker and seven other ships are sunk.

22 September

Western Europe In the Canadian 1st Army sector, the garrison at Boulogne surrenders to the Canadian 3rd Infantry Division (II Corps). On the rest of the front, the Allied advance continues. General Eisenhower decides to give absolute priority to the operations for the liberation of the Scheldt estuary so as to be able to use the port of Antwerp.

Italian Front All the units of the US 5th Army are now past the *Gothic* line; only one little strip on the Tyrrhenian coast, between Leghorn and La Spezia, remains in German hands.

Eastern Front The armies of the Leningrad Front capture Tallinn, capital of Estonia.

□ Croatia. Pavelić decrees general mobilization. Since the changed allegiance of Rumania and Bulgaria, Pavelitch has been receiving more help from the Germans. But despite mobilization and German aid, Tito's forces become more and more threatening, and the Croat units armed by the Germans collapse the first time they encounter the partisans.

Palau Islands: Peleliu General Geiger decides to replace the 1st Marine Regiment, exhausted by the fighting on Mount Umurbrogol, with the 321st Infantry Regiment (US 81st Division), which is landed and sent into the line. The Japanese are still solidly dug in in their 'termite nests' and still hold the attackers at bay.

Angaur Units of the 323rd Regiment

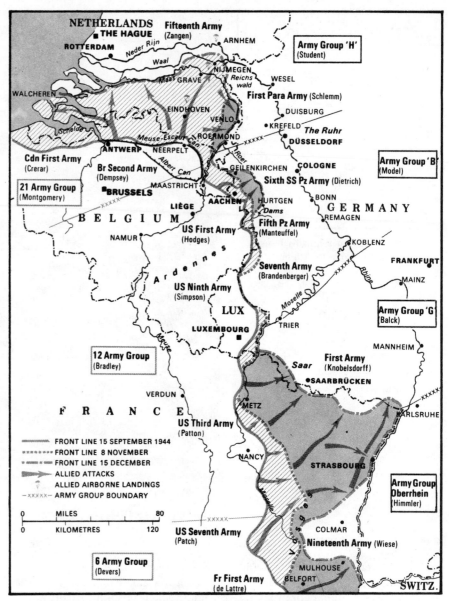

Progress on the Western Front 15 September–15 December 1944.

of the 81st Division press on into the Lake Salome area, but withdraw at nightfall.

Ulithi A regimental combat group from the US 81st Division lands on Ulithi atoll, in the north-west Carolines, the same group that includes the Palau Islands.

23 September

Eastern Front In the northern sector, troops of the 3rd Baltic Front reach the Gulf of Riga at Pärnu, in southern Estonia. The German Army Group North can do no more than try to slow down the Russian advance.

Greece A specially picked British

unit is parachuted on to Araxos (north-west coast of the Peloponnese) to occupy the local airfield. From here the Allies will be able to strike at the Germans as they retreat from Greece, and possibly advance and occupy Patras. The Germans have abandoned the whole of the Peloponnese 48 hours ago and are now carrying out the evacuation of 60,000 men from Crete, as well as the small garrisons in the Aegean islands.

Palau Islands On Peleliu the 321st Infantry Regiment, only just arrived in the line, advances along the west coast as far as the village of Garekoru. But efforts to advance along

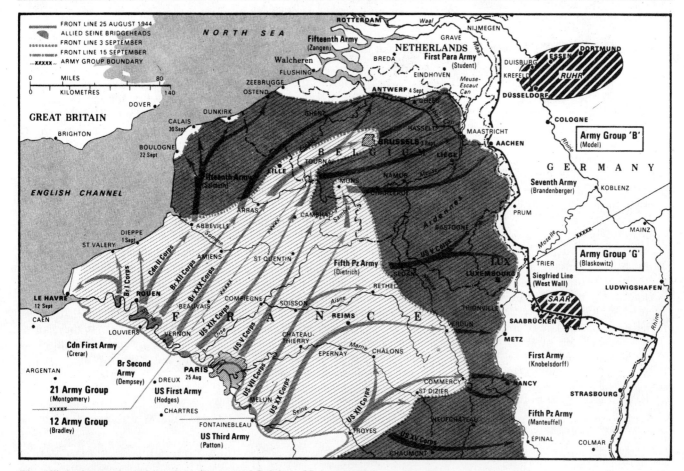

The Allied advance through northern France and Belgium, 25 August–15 September 1944.

the whole line fail in face of the solid resistance of the Japanese on Mount Umurbrogol and on another position in the eastern part of the island which the Americans call 'Bloody Hill'.

Angaur Another raid by the US 322nd Infantry into the Lake Salome area, and another withdrawal in the evening.

Burma–China On the Salween front the Japanese despatch a column with supplies for the garrison at Pingka, which the Chinese are attacking.

24 September

Western Europe The Canadian 2nd Division (I Corps) establishes a bridgehead over the Antwerp–Turnhout canal.

Italian Front The Allies steadily continue their advance north of the *Gothic* line.

Eastern Front After nine days of bitter fighting, the 2nd Ukraine Front succeeds in repelling the 27 German

and Hungarian divisions and brigades holding them up in the Cluj area, in northern Rumania. Rumaina is by now almost entirely in Russian hands, and the Red Army reaches the Rumanian–Hungarian frontier in the area of Mako.

Palau Islands: Peleliu After a bombardment by aircraft, ships and field guns, the US 321st Infantry Regiment advances beyond Garekoru, on the American left flank. Infantry and Marines try to take the enemy positions on Mount Umurbrogol in the rear, but the attempt is frustrated by a powerful Japanese counter-attack.

Angaur The Americans invite the Japanese still holding out in the Lake Salome area to surrender, but only two men come forward. The artillery thereupon begins a murderous bombardment which lasts until the next day.

Burma In the north, the British 36th Division, advancing cautiously southwards in the area of Namma, runs into considerable enemy forces

and the advance is held up.

25 September

Western Europe The Canadian 3rd Division (II Corps) attacks the Calais defences after an intensive artillery bombardment.

Operation *Market Garden* ends in failure.

Italian Front Although forced back to the north by the massive, unrelenting Allied offensive, the German units of Lemelsen's 14th Army and Vietinghoff's 10th Army continue to fight back determinedly against the American divisions of General Clark (on the west of the front) and Leese's British division (in the east). But the position of Vietinghoff's divisions is becoming more and more critical. He has now no more than 90 battalions of infantry, only 10 of which are more than 400 men strong, while at least 38 of them can only deploy some 200 men.

Palau Islands: Peleliu The 7th Marines and 321st Infantry attack on

OPERATION *MARKET GARDEN* (ARNHEM)

17 September

Sunday, 17 September, Operation *Market Garden* is launched, the landing of Allied parachute and airborne troops in Holland, near Arnhem, Nijmegen and Eindhoven. The plan has been conceived by Montgomery in the hope of forcing Eisenhower to give up his strategy of a fan-shaped advance, in favour of a concentrated, determined blow which would among other things ensure the continuity of the advance to the north. The objective, clearly defined, is penetration into the Ruhr basin. The operation is to be carried out by the 1st Airborne Army. 1068 aircraft carrying parachutists and 478 towing gliders will drop or land the British 1st Airborne Division on Arnhem, with the task of captur-

ing the bridges over the lower Rhine; the US 101st Parachute Division (General Maxwell Taylor) will attack north of Eindhoven and the US 82nd Parachute Division near Grave, south of Nijmegen, with the task of taking the town and the two big bridges over the Meuse and the Waal. If successful, the operation will create a corridor along the line Eindhoven–Nijmegen–Arnhem and allow the XXX Corps (British 2nd Army) to advance north from Belgium into the heart of Holland. The US 101st Division lands without trouble, occupies Eindhoven and takes the bridges over the Wilhelmina and Zuiter Willemsvaart canals. The 82nd captures the bridge over the Meuse at Grave, but not that over the Waal at Nijmegen, owing to a violent German

counter-attack. But the British parachutists find the road to Arnhem blocked by powerful German forces; only one battalion, the 2nd, manages to reach the bridge over the Rhine, and there it is halted and cut off.

18 September

The British XXX Corps joins up with the American 101st Airborne Division north of Eindhoven. There is bitter fighting on the front of the British 1st Airborne Division. Aware of the extreme danger now facing the Reich, the Germans send every man they can raise into the line, even a battalion of wounded.

19 September

At 8.30 a.m. the British XXX Corps joins up with the parachut-

Parachutists of the American 82nd Division land near Arnhem.

ists of the US 82nd Airborne Division, who have captured the bridge over the Meuse at Grave. At Arnhem all the British efforts to break through the German defences and get to the bridge over the Rhine fail.

20 September
At Nijmegen a combined attack by the American 82nd Airborne Division and the British XXX Corps ends in the capture of the bridge.

21 September
At Arnhem the British troops defending the bridge are overwhelmed. The rest of the British 1st Airborne Division form a defensive perimeter on the north bank of the Rhine, west of Oosterbeek, and get ready to hold out there.

22 September
German resistance slows down the advance of the XXX Corps, while a brigade of Polish parachutists moves in south of the Rhine and of Arnhem. Together with advance units of the XXX Corps, the Poles try to cross the river, but are driven back.

26 September
After three days of violent fighting about 2,200 of the 1st Airborne's more than 10,000 men succeed in recrossing the Rhine to safety.
On the whole the operation has proved a failure, and Montgomery gives up trying to impose his own strategy on Eisenhower and agrees to work loyally under him. Not the least of Montgomery's objects was that of cutting Holland in two so as to eliminate the V2 launching ramps which the Germans have been using to bombard Britain since 8 September. The ramps are on Walcheren Island and on the outskirts of The

Top: American paratroops in action at Arnhem. Above: a German soldier killed on the Nijmegen birdge, which the Allied forces capture intact.

Hague. Although the V2 attacks were broken off on the 17th, the day of the airborne landing, they were resumed and stepped up on the 25th. These rocket-sites are a further powerful inducement to Hitler to defend German frontiers in Holland.

the left flank to dislodge the Japanese from the north-west part of the island. The 5th Marines also attack, along the coast on the right flank.

Angaur Finding that their raids and their shelling are equally ineffective in the Lake Salome area, the 322nd Infantry and the engineers begin to build a road so that they can get at the enemy pocket from the north-east.

China After so much hesitation, and stung by Roosevelt's candid message, Chiang Kai-shek refuses to entrust the operational command of the Chinese Nationalist army to General Stilwell.

26 September

Palau Islands: Peleliu After repelling three furious Japanese counterattacks, the Marines reach the point at which the western and eastern roads meet, at the foot of Mount Amiangal in the north of the island. A special unit attacks the Japanese positions towards the south with flame-throwers and tanks, blocking up the pill-boxes with earth and stones and directing flames through the slots. By evening the important Hill 120 is in American hands. The Japanese are by now cut off in a number of pockets on Mount Umurbrogol and 'Bloody Hill', in the centre of the island, and Mount Amiangal in the north.

Angaur The US 322nd Infantry succeeds in making a small penetration into the northern part of the Lake Salome basin.

27 September

Western Europe Field-Marshal Montgomery presses General Crerar, Commander of the Canadian 1st Army, to free the Scheldt estuary as quickly as possible.

The American XX Corps (3rd Army) begins to attack the forts at Metz.

Eastern Front The 13 armies of the Leningrad Front and the three Baltic Fronts force the German Army Group North back into the defensive perimeter round Riga, which is powerfully fortified. The Germans still retain a narrow corridor back into East Prussia.

German resistance grows stronger

Palau Islands: US amphibious tanks approach the beaches of Angaur.

west of the Carpathians, in the area north of Cluj. The Russian 57th and 46th Armies prepare to advance on Belgrade from Bulgaria and Rumania.

Palau Islands: Peleliu The 321st Infantry, supported by the 7th Marines, attacks the enemy pocket on Mount Umurbrogol. The fire from the defenders, experienced veterans of the 14th Japanese Infantry Division, which distinguished itself in Manchuria, opens wide gaps in the attackers' ranks. Units of the 5th Marines mop up on Mount Amiangal, while others reach the north point of the island, where they come under fire from enemy artillery in the islets of Ngesebus and Kongauru.

Angaur The US 322nd Infantry begins the methodical liquidation of the Japanese in the Lake Salome area.

28 September

Western Europe The Canadian 3rd Division (II Corps, 1st Army) succeeds in penetrating into the defences of Calais.

Eastern Front The Russian 57th Army, with nine divisions, moves from Vidin in Bulgaria into Yugoslavia, heading for Belgrade.

Palau Islands At 9.00 a.m. units of the 5th Marines, supported by artillery, tanks and fighter-bombers taking off from Peleliu airfield (quickly reactivated by the 'Seabees') land on the islet of Ngesebus and on Kongauru and begin to clear them of the enemy. The Ngesebus airfield is almost entirely captured by 3.00 p.m. On Peleliu, where bad weather has set in, a war of attrition starts against the Japanese positions in the central northern area of the island.

Angaur Mopping up continues in the Lake Salome area.

Burma–India The British XV Corps receives orders to go over to the offensive on the Arakan front to drive the Japanese from the area of Chittagong and from the estuary of the river Naaf.

29 September

Italian Front At Marzabotto, in Bologna province in the foothills of the Apennines, two SS regiments begin a reprisal operation against the partisans. Within a few days the Germans, commanded by Major Walter Reder, have murdered 1,836 civilians.

Palau Islands On Peleliu the 7th Marines are replaced by units of the 321st Infantry in the attack on the Japanese positions in the Mount

Umurbrogol pocket. The reduction of the Mount Amiangal pocket also goes ahead.

Angaur The Americans succeed in driving the Japanese out of the centre of the Lake Salome area, forcing them to withdraw to the extreme north-west of the island. The islets of Ngesebus and Kongauru are reported clear.

Burma–China Chinese engineers and civilians, assisted by American technicians, begin the construction of a military road between Myitkyina, Teng-chung and Kunming.

30 September

Western Europe Calais surrenders to the Canadian 3rd Division.

In the Antwerp sector the Polish 1st Division captures Merxplas, north-west of Turnhout.

In the American XII Corps (3rd Army) sector, a powerful counter-attack by the Germans to recapture the forest of Gremlécey is only contained with the help of the American 6th Armoured Division.

Eastern Front Following the 57th Army, the 47th Army of the 3rd Ukraine Front now crosses the Danube in force upstream of Turnu Severin (on the frontier between Rumania and Yugoslavia), advancing on Belgrade.

Palau Islands Command of the western Carolines sector passes from Rear-Admiral Wilkinson, Commander of Task Force 31, to Rear-Admiral Fort, Commander of the Western Attack Force (Task Force 32). Fort announces officially that the capture of Peleliu, Angaur, Ngesebus and Kongauru has been completed. In fact, operations against the pockets of Japanese resistance are to go on for a long time.

1 October

Western Europe The Canadian 3rd Division (II Corps) completes the occupation of Calais.

In the Antwerp sector the Canadian 2nd Division (I Corps) begins to cross the Antwerp–Turnhout canal and makes for the Beveland peninsula, passing through the northern suburbs of the city of Antwerp. The

'GASLIGHT'

In Victorian London the killer of a wealthy, elderly singer marries the latter's niece in order to inherit the family jewels. He attempts by trickery to persuade his wife she is going mad but she, suspecting deception, eventually unmasks him with the help of a young Scotland Yard detective.

Strongly directed by George Cukor, *Gaslight* was a film steeped in Gothic atmosphere. The mystery, intrigue and suffering that permeated the mansion where most of the action was set form the backdrop to a penetrating analysis of the couple's married life.

Oscars went to the designers, Gibbons and Ferrari, and to Ingrid Bergman.

US 1st Army begins operations for the surrounding of Aachen.

☐ Marshal Pétain and Pierre Laval are taken from Belfort to Sigmaringen in Germany.

Italian Front In the western sector (US 5th Army), at dawn, the American II Corps begins the offensive against Bologna, meeting with extremely strong resistance from the Germans.

At British 8th Army headquarters General Sir Oliver Leese, who is to go to the Asian front, hands over to General McCreery.

Greece British Commandos, coming from Kithira, land on the Island of Poros. Greek forces incorporated in the British 8th Army land at Mitilini, Lemnos and Levita.

2 October

Western Europe In the American XIX Corps (1st Army) sector, the 30th Division, after a violent air and artillery preparation, opens the attack on the West Wall (the Siegfried Line) between Aachen and Geilenkirchen, north-west of Aachen.

Italian Front The American II and IV Corps (5th Army) are almost entirely held up at Monte Catarelto and

Monte Galletto.

Eastern Front General Tadeo Bor, leader of the insurrection in Warsaw, signs the surrender of his forces to the Germans. The city is a pile of rubble and more than 250,000 Polish patriots have lost their lives in this gallant, though ill-starred venture.

Yugoslavia. In the area of Negotin, south of Turnu Severin, the Russian 57th Army is engaged in a bitter battle with the German *Serbia* Group, part of von Weichs' Army Group F.

Palau Islands On Peleliu the US 321st Infantry Regiment liquidates Japanese resistance on Mount Amiangal. In the Mount Umurbrogol sector the 7th Marines are still held up by the Japanese forces, determined to resist to the very last man.

Angaur The 322nd Infantry breaks off its attacks against the Japanese in the north-west of the island, in an area not more than a few hundred yards square, and begins the systematic shelling of the area.

Burma In accordance with the decisions of the British War Cabinet, Admiral Mountbatten orders that the offensive against Mandalay should be launched as quickly as possible, while the other planned operations are postponed and reduced. Headquarters of the northern Burma sector is to guarantee the security of air communications between India and China and to re-establish land communications between the two countries.

3 October

Western Europe The American 3rd Division (XIX Corps, 1st Army), having penetrated into the Siegfried Line, reaches Übach, where it is overtaken by the 2nd Armoured Division, which has crossed the Wurm at Marienberg.

In the XX Corps (US 3rd Army) sector, attacks are resumed for the capture of Metz. Early in the afternoon 247 bombers of RAF Bomber Command attack the Westkapelle dyke on the island of Walcheren (Holland). The mission is a complete success: over a hundred yards of the dyke are demolished and the sea floods thousands of acres of land.

Eastern Front In Estonia troops of the Leningrad Front land on the island of Hiiumaa, at the entrance to the Gulf of Riga, and begin the destruction of the German garrison. The three Baltic Fronts continue their pressure on the German Army Group North which is being slowly driven back towards Riga.

Palau Islands On Peleliu the US 7th Marine Regiment makes some progress against the Japanese positions on the east side of the Mount Umurbrogol pocket.

☐ The Joint Chiefs of Staff agree with MacArthur in the difference of opinion on strategy between him and Nimitz. The American Pacific forces will give precedence to the capture of bases in the island of Luzon, in the Philippines. The operation will be directed by MacArthur.

4 October

Western Europe The Canadians of the 2nd Division (1st Army) continue to advance north of Antwerp, liberating the Merxerem–Eeckeren sector. North of Aachen, where units of the US XIX Corps have breached

the Siegfried Line, the German 6th Armoured Division launches a counter-attack to close the gap opened in the German defensive system. However, the Americans succeed in retaining the ground they have gained. The American V Corps operating in the Luxembourg sector, is also preparing to attack the Siegfried Line.

Eastern Front In the area of Negotin, in Yugoslavia, the Russian 57th Army surrounds and routs the German divisions of the *Serbia* Group. Units of the Russian 46th Army capture Pančevo, on the east bank of the Danube near Belgrade.

☐ It is reported that German males born in 1928 are to be called up.

Palau Islands In torrential rain the 7th Marine Regiment continues its attacks against the Japanese positions on Mount Umurbrogol, Peleliu, but at the end of the day it has suffered such heavy losses that headquarters orders its relief.

Burma In the British XXXIII Corps sector the 11th East African Division captures Yazagyo, while the 5th Indian Division nears Tiddim.

5 October

Western Europe Units of the US 2nd Army (XIX Corps, 1st Army) advance in the direction of Geilenkirchen, and towards the south reach the road between that town and Aachen. In the American XII Corps sector, bad weather holds up the attack towards Schmidt, an important target on the Rur dykes south of Aachen.

Italian Front West of the American IV Corps (5th Army) attacks are resumed in the direction of La Spezia, while the other units continue to advance north, hill after hill.

Eastern Front In the northern sector the armies of the 1st Baltic Front starting from the area of Siualiai, in Lithuania, open a powerful offensive towards the Baltic and East Prussia, with the aim of bottling up the German Army Group North. It is left to the 2nd and 3rd Fronts to continue the advance towards Riga.

Almost at the other end of this enormous front, Malinovsky's 2nd

Ukraine Front, starting from the area of Arad, in Rumania, begins the offensive against south-east Hungary, aiming for Szeged and Budapest.

Greece British forces land on the Greek mainland and enter Patras.

Palau Islands On Peleliu operations are temporarily slowed down by the rain, and by the relieving of the American units in the Mount Umurbrogol sector.

6 October

Western Europe In the northern sector of the front, Montgomery launches the offensive to clear the estuary of the Scheldt and so make it possible for the Allies to use the port of Antwerp. The extreme west of the Dutch mainland has already been evacuated by the Germans; there is just one division left, manning the small port of Breskens, south of Flushing. And it is against Breskens that the Canadian II Corps opens the first attack of this battle, called the 'battle of the polders', fought in mud and water. North of the Leopold Canal they are able to set up two small bridgeheads. German reaction is extremely violent and forces the Canadians to send substantial reinforcements to the bridgeheads they have won.

The XIX Corps of the US 1st Army continues the battle around Aachen and at Geilenkirchen, on the Siegfried Line.

Eastern Front Units of the Leningrad Front land on Saaremaa Island, south of Hiiumaa Island, in the Gulf of Riga.

Palau Islands Operations on Peleliu come to a standstill again. On Angaur, artillery fire is resumed against the Japanese at the extreme northwest of the island.

China As a result of the breach between Chiang Kai-shek and Roosevelt, General Stilwell is relieved of the post of Chief of Staff to the Generalissimo. He is now only to command the Chinese troops in Burma and those, trained and equipped by the Americans, in the province of Yunnan. Stilwell is also relieved of his responsibility for

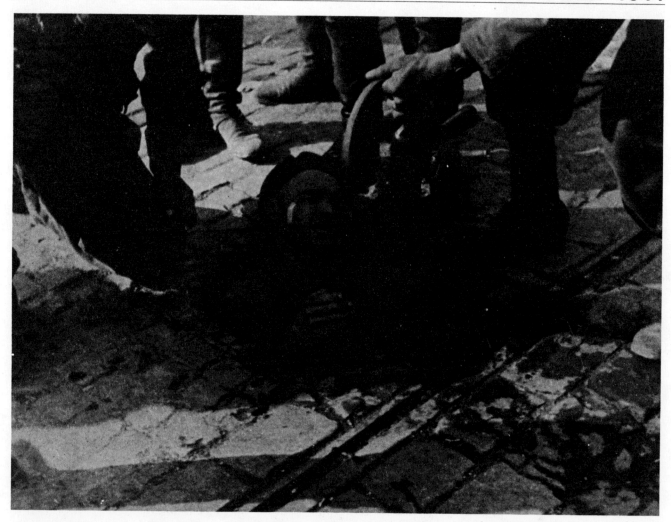

supplies to China under the Lend-Lease Act.

7 October

Western Europe In the northern sector of the front, the battle for the port of Antwerp continues. The Canadian 3rd Division (II Corps) sends reinforcements to the north bank of the Leopold Canal, but they do not arrive on account of powerful German resistance.

Units of the US XX Corps (3rd Army) capture Wormeldange, liberating Luxembourg as far as the Moselle. German counter-attacks in the Maizières-lès-Metz sector, some 6 miles north of Metz, slow down the operations of the 90th Division; during the battle that follows some US units are able to reach the city.

Italian Front In the eastern sector, the V Corps (8th Army) opens an offensive against the Rubicon. On the left of the Allied line, units of the US IV and II Corps advance in the Monte Stanco, Castelnuovo di Bisano and Monte Cavallara sectors. *Pacific* US aircraft based in the Marianas carry out the heaviest raids to date on Iwo Jima.

Palau Islands It is decided to suspend for the time being the operations against the Japanese fortified positions on Mount Umurbrogol, Peleliu, following new unsuccessful efforts carried out with tank support by the 5th Marines.

8 October

Western Europe An attempt by units of the Canadian II Corps to advance from Hoogerheide to Korteven, on the road from Antwerp to Bergen-op-Zoom, is halted by the swift reaction of the Germans of the 15th Army, who drive the attackers back to their starting point. The counter-attack is

The Warsaw rising is ruthlessly crushed. A wounded insurgent emerges from a sewer into the hands of waiting German soldiers.

withstood only with difficulty.

Units of the US XIX Corps advance south along the valley of the Wurm and take Herzogenrat. A violent German counter-attack near Mariadorf holds up the American advance in this sector. The units of the 90th Division that had penetrated into Maizières-lès-Metz have to wrest the town from the Germans house by house. The divisions of the American XII Corps, after a short but intensive barrage, begin to advance along the banks of the river Seille, taking Moivron, Arraye-et-Han, Lixières and Fossieux.

Greece The Germans have evacuated Corinth, which is occupied by British units from Araxos. Elements of the British 9th Commando reach Nauplia, south of Corinth.

9–10 October

Start of third Moscow conference. Churchill and Eden in talks with Stalin. The conference ends on 20 October. The principle subject discussed is the 'Polish problem'. Also Churchill agrees to give Russia complete control in Rumania (with the approval of the Americans, who are much more accommodating to the Russians and less far-seeing than the British statesman). Bulgaria is also recognized as 'belonging one hundred per cent to the Soviet sphere of interest'; Hungary is to be equally under Soviet and Western influence (though the agreement is never respected), while in Greece the 'reserved rule' of Britain is recognized.

9 October

Western Europe In the north, units of the Canadian 3rd Division (II Corps) land at Breskens, on the western arm of the Scheldt south of Flushing. The operations of the American 1st Division (VII Corps) around Aachen continue, and so does the battle in the streets of Maizières-lès-Metz. Further south, in the sector of the American XII Corps, units of the 6th Armoured Division try unsuccessfully to reach Létricourt. The advance of the American 80th Division along the banks of the river Seille is held up, and in this sector of the front activity

ceases for almost a month.

Greece More British troops, under the command of General Scobie, land at Corinth. The Germans retain possession of the port of Piraeus.

Pacific Admiral Nimitz issues the first directives for the invasion of Iwo Jima, fixed provisionally for 20 January 1945. Admiral Spruance is appointed to command the operation, together with Vice-Admiral Turner in charge of the amphibious force and General H. M. Smith, who will command the expeditionary corps. The forces will be assembled in Hawaii and the Marianas.

Marcus Island US cruisers and destroyers commanded by Rear-Admiral A. E. Smith shell the coast defences of Marcus Island (in Japanese, Minami-Torishima), 800 miles east of the Bonin Islands.

China Chiang Kai-shek in a memorandum denounces Allied strategy in South-East Asia. The blame for the loss of south-eastern China (where the Japanese are making rapid progress in the area north-west of Hong Kong, which is where the American airfields are sited) is put on General Stilwell, but indirectly on President Roosevelt.

10 October

Western Europe The US 30th Division (XIX Corps) makes repeated attacks but fails to reach Bardenberg. The US 1st Division tightens its ring round Aachen and issues an ultimatum to the defenders of the city demanding surrender within 24 hours.

Italian Front The American II Corps starts a new phase of attacks in the direction of Bologna, but with little result either in the Monterumicini sector (where the 34th Division has been engaged for some days), or towards Livergnano, or in the vicinity of the Monte delle Formiche. In the eastern sector (British 8th Army) the German defence along the Rubicon comes to an end with the fall of Spaccato to the 10th Indian Division (V Corps); the 46th Division takes Longiano and La Crocetta; and the 1st Division also gets ready to cross the river at Savignano di Romagna.

Eastern Front In the northern sector, the 1st Baltic Front reaches the Baltic in Lithuania, north of Memel, which the Russians then attack. Other armies of the same Front on the left flank push on to the river Niemen, on the north-east frontier of East Prussia. In the southern sector the armies of the 3rd Ukraine Front reach and cut the railway from Nish to Belgrade at Velika Plana, a little south of Belgrade.

Pacific A task force of fast aircraft carriers, comprising 17 carriers, 5 battleships, 14 cruisers and 58 destroyers, commanded by Vice-Admiral Mitscher, bombards coastal defences and shipping at Okinawa and other islands of the Ryukyu group. 110 Japanese aircraft are brought down and some transports are sunk. The war draws nearer to Japan. The US Navy, which commenced the conflict so disastrously at Pearl Harbour, can now deploy at least 1,500 warships, including 80 heavy and light aircraft carriers and 17 battleships. US air forces control the Pacific in every quarter, and the amphibious fleet is immensely powerful.

11 October

Western Europe The 30th Division (US XIX Corps, 1st Army) captures Bardenberg, opening the way north in the direction of Würselen.

At Aachen the last ultimatum sent by the American 1st Division (VII Corps) to the Germans expires, and the besieging forces resume the violent air and artillery bombardment.

Italian Front The Allied advance continues along the whole front, but slowed down by the determined defence of the Germans, who make a strongpoint of every ravine and every hill. It is the same at Livergnone, at Monte delle Tombe, at the Gesso Ridge, at Monte Battaglia, on all the western part of the front, where the divisions of the US 5th Army are engaged.

In the eastern sector (British 8th Army) the 10th Indian Division and the British 46th Division (V Corps) continue to advance towards the

A Hungarian woman talks to a German officer following a successful German counter-attack.

river Savio and Cesena, capturing the heights east of the river Rubicon. The Canadian 1st Division (I Corps) widens its bridgehead across the river and advances along Highway 9 as far as Rigossa. The New Zealand 2nd Division establishes two bridgeheads across the Rubicon, north of Savignano, without meeting any opposition, and during the night they capture Gatteo a Mare.

Eastern Front The armies of the 2nd Ukraine Front force the crossing of the river Tisza on a wide front at Szeged, Hungary's second city.

Further east they besiege Debrecen, another major strongpoint in the German–Hungarian defensive system. In a desperate battle before Cluj, the Rumanians are fighting side by side with the Russians.

Philippines Aircraft from two task forces of US aircraft carriers (commanded by Vice-Admiral Cain and Rear-Admiral Davison) attack the Japanese airfields and other installations in the south of Luzon Island.

China Chiang Kai-shek asks Roosevelt to recall General Stilwell immediately.

12 October

Western Europe In the Aachen sector the Germans mount an air and artillery counter-attack on the Bardenberg–Euchen line. The bombing and shelling of the city by the Allies continue.

The 3rd battalion of the 357th Regiment of the 30th Division (US XX Corps, 3rd Army) advances on Metz to support the 2nd battalion. During the night the last elements of the 5th Division are withdrawn from Fort Driant.

Italian Front Units of the American IV Corps make yet another effort to capture the summit of Monte Cavallara, but once more are repulsed, and attacks in this sector are suspended.

Also repulsed is an attack by the American 91st Division (II Corps) at Livergnano, about 13 miles south of Bologna. The US 88th Division reaches the Gesso Ridge.

In the eastern (British 8th Army) sector the divisions of the V Corps press on from the Rubicon towards the river Savio and Cesena. The 10th Indian Division advances on the V Corps's left flank towards Monte dell'Erta, east of the Savio, and its units cross the Rubicon. Attacking north of the Rubicon, on the right flank of the V Corps front, the 46th Division captures Casale.

Eastern Front The 2nd Ukraine Front captures Oradea, in Transylvania. The battle for Debrecen continues.

In Yugoslavia the Russians capture Subotica on the Belgrade–Budapest railway, near the Hungarian frontier.

Greece The German rearguards evacuate the port of Piraeus, which they were only holding to allow the greatest possible number of men to be taken off the Greek islands. Athens, already practically abandoned, is declared an 'open city' to avoid useless destruction. British troops land at Corfu and in the area of Sarandë in southern Albania.

Pacific In preparation for the invasion of Leyte, in the Philippines, Task Force 38 of the US 3rd Fleet, under command of Admiral Halsey, begins a series of heavy air attacks on Formosa (now Taiwan), where industrial plant and military equipment are destroyed, and on Luzon. The attacks go on for five days and meet with an unexpectedly strong reaction from Japanese aircraft. In the biggest air battle of the war the Japanese lose about 500 aircraft, the Americans 89. Forty Japanese warships and auxiliaries are sunk.

Palau Islands On Peleliu the 1st Marine Division launches a series of attacks against the Japanese pocket on Mount Umurbrogol.

13 October

Western Europe The first German V1s and V2s fall on Antwerp. The Belgian city is to be the main target of the missiles after London. In south-east Holland, where the formations of the British 2nd Army are operating, the 3rd Division (VIII Corps) opens an offensive from Overloon, about 20 miles south of Nijmegen, towards the south-east in the direction of Venray, but runs into strong resistance.

Units of the American 1st Division (VII Corps) continue their final assault on Aachen. While the 2nd Battalion fights in the streets, from house to house, the 3rd Battalion storms Observatory Hill, one of three heights that dominate the city from the north.

Italian Front Units of the 6th Armoured Division (US 5th Army) advance in the Grizzana sector, about 20 miles south-west of Bologna, and after several unsuccessful attacks succeed in capturing Monte Stanco and Bombiana.

The German resistance around Livergnano begins to show signs of giving way under the offensive of the 91st Division (US II Corps) and the land and air bombardment. The Americans capture Height 603 and the village of Casalino, north-west of Livergnano. During the night units of the 88th Division cross the river Sillaro, west of Height 339.

In the eastern sector (British 8th Army), units of the 46th Division (V Corps) enter Carpineta.

Eastern Front The 2nd and 3rd Baltic Fronts break through the strong defensive ring round Riga, capital of Latvia and an important naval base. German forces in northern Latvia are threatened with encirclement.

Greece British Commandos and Greek contingents land near Piraeus and occupy Kalamata airfield. A British parachute battalion is dropped at Megara and captures the airport there.

Formosa US Task Force 38 continues its attacks on targets on the island. The Australian cruiser *Canberra* is seriously damaged by a torpedo from a Japanese aircraft, and the US aircraft carrier *Franklin* is also damaged, though not so seriously, by a Japanese suicide aircraft.

China General Hurley, Roosevelt's personal representative with Chiang Kai-shek, recommends to the President that General Stilwell should be recalled.

14 October

Western Europe The Canadians of the II Corps secure communications with the Breskens pocket from the east. House-to-house fighting continues in the ruins of Aachen.

In the south-eastern sector of the front, where General Devers' 6th Army Group (Patch's US 7th Army and the French 1st Army under De Lattre de Tassigny) is operating, the 3rd Algerian Division reaches Cornimont.

Italian Front The South African 6th Armoured Division (II Corps, US 5th Army) enters Grizzana. In the Livergnano sector the 91st Division advances, taking Querceto and forcing the Germans out of the residential part of Livergnano.

The 78th Division (British XIII Corps, 8th Army) continues to attack towards Monte La Pieve. The Polish II Corps is moved from the British X Corps sector and the forces operating on the left flank of the army, with orders to advance towards Forlì.

The V Corps occupies the hills to the east of the river Savio. During the night elements of the Polish 2nd Division enter Sant'Angelo.

Eastern Front The Russian armies and Tito's partisans converge on Belgrade, capital of Yugoslavia, which is almost completely surrounded. Further south the Germans are forced to evacuate Nish to avoid being cut off from the main body of von Weichs' forces.

Greece The British III Corps, including some Greek units, is about to land at Piraeus. The ships are waiting for the mines to be swept from the waters outside the harbour.

☐ Field-Marshal Erwin Rommel, under suspicion of having been involved, even if only indirectly, in the attempt on Hitler's life, is ordered by Hitler himself to take his own life. Generals Burgdorf and Maisel are chosen to bear news of the death sentence pronounced by the Führer to

Herrlingen, where the Field-Marshal is still convalescing from the wound in the head received in Normandy. The only concession made to this gallant officer is a choice between trial before a People's Court for having plotted against Hitler, and suicide by poison. (In fact, Rommel had agreed to the plot of 20 July in principle but had never taken any practical part in it.) Rommel chooses the second alternative, and the two generals themselves give him the phial of cyanide with which, a few hours later, the Reich's most glorious and best loved soldier kills himself. At Hitler's wish Rommel is given a state funeral, to avoid ugly rumours which would have a demoralizing effect on the people.

Pacific The III Amphibious Force sails from Manus Island for the invasion of Leyte, in the Philippines.

Formosa Task Force 38 carries out more attacks, completing the neutralization of Formosa. The light cruiser *Houston* is damaged by a Japanese aerial torpedo; other ships damaged are the aircraft carrier *Hancock*, the light cruiser *Reno* and two destroyers.

Palau Islands On Peleliu the 81st Division of the US Army replaces the Marines in the arduous task of liquidating the Japanese pocket on Mount Umurbrogol. On Angaur the task of capture and occupation is declared completed, even though the US troops have not yet managed to eliminate the Japanese still resisting in the north-west of the island.

15 October

Western Europe The Canadian 1st Army, operating in the north to liberate the port of Antwerp, is reinforced by the US 104th Division, detached for the occasion from General Simpson's 9th Army (12th Army Group), engaged in Luxembourg. No change at Aachen, where the garrison is still holding out against units of the 29th Division (US XIX Corps) and 1st Division (US VII Corps). A battalion of the 1st Division, the 3rd Battalion of the 26th Regiment, succeeds in taking a good part of Observatory Hill, north

A group of Greek partisans move forward near Athens to join up with the Allied forces. British Commandos begin to land on 13 October.

of the city, but is driven out again by a swift German counter-attack.

In the 7th Army sector the VI Corps begins to move from the north-west and the south towards Bruyères, between Épinal and St Dié.

Italian Front The South African 6th Armoured Division (US 5th Army) continues its advance in the Grizzana sector.

The American 91st Division (II Corps) consolidates its positions north of Livergnano.

The Polish 2nd Division (Canadian I Corps, British 8th Army) liberates Gambettola.

Eastern Front In Finland, the Russians' Karelia Front drives the Germans from the port of Petsamo. The 2nd and 3rd Baltic Fronts take Riga. In northern Rumania the Russians capture Cluj and advance westwards.

Greece The British (General Scobie's III Corps, made up of Greek units) land in force in the harbour of Piraeus and prepare to eliminate 'with bloodshed if necessary', according to Churchill's instructions, the armed wing of the Greek Communist Party, ELAS.

☐ Hungary. Admiral Nicolaus Horthy, the Regent, already faced by a desperate situation (the whole of Transylvania is on the point of being overrun by the Russians), makes a speech on the radio in which he proposes to ask the Russians for an armistice. Under pressure from the Germans, Horthy repudiates his message to the country, but next day he is taken off to Germany. The head of the pro-Nazi movement, Ferenc Szálasi, takes office as Prime Minister. He collaborates fully with the Germans, but enjoys no sort of following among the people. On 21 October Horthy is arrested and interned in a castle in Bavaria.

Philippines A task group from Task Force 38, under the command of Rear-Admiral Davison, deploys aircraft from its carriers against various Japanese targets in the area of Manila, in Luzon Island. The aircraft carrier *Franklin* is hit again, this time by a Japanese high-level bomber. The attacks are repeated on the 16th and 17th, and more heavily on the 18th, when two other task groups and 13 aircraft carriers take part. The 1st Air Fleet of the Japanese navy suffers severe losses.

Burma British and Chinese–American forces go over to the offensive to free the north of the country and re-establish land communications between India and China. The Chinese and Americans move down from south of Myitkyina as far as the line Katha–Shwegu–Bhamo meeting little or no resistance. The British 36th Division advances in the area of Namma along the Myitkyina–Mandalay railway, supported by the Chinese 50th Division. The Chinese 22nd Division moves south-east of Kamaing towards the area between the railway and the Myitkyina–Bhamo road, with the intention of establishing a bridgehead at Shwegu, across the Irrawaddy. The Allied command in north Burma can now call on the Chinese 1st and 6th Armies, newly formed, and two American regiments.

16 October

Western Europe With the fall of Woensdrecht to the Canadian 2nd Division, the isthmus of South Beveland is virtually cut off by the Allies. In the same sector, the Canadian 3rd Division continues its attacks on the Breskens pocket now reduced to half its original size.

In south-east Holland, where the British 2nd Army is operating, the 3rd Division reaches the suburbs of Venray, half-way between Helmond and the German frontier.

The agony of Aachen goes on as bitter street fighting continues. In the afternoon the circle of Allied troops round the city is closed when patrols from the US XIX Corps and VII Corps (1st Army) link up.

In the US 7th Army sector the 45th and 36th Divisions (VI Corps) approach Bruyères, but are heavily engaged by the forces of the German 1st Army. On the right flank of the 7th Army, where the French 1st Army is operating under De Lattre de Tassigny, the 3rd Algerian Division and French 1st Armoured Division launch an offensive to break through enemy lines in the Vosges.

Italian Front In the US 5th Army sector the South African 6th Armoured Division, with support from the II Corps on the right, opens an offensive north-east of Grizzana in the area between the rivers Reno and Setta. The II Corps begins the last stage of the attack towards Bologna.

In the eastern sector of the front, units of the 10th Indian Division (British V Corps) establish a small bridgehead across the river Savio, not far from Borello.

The Canadian 1st Division makes rapid progress towards Cesena.

Eastern Front With the remnants of the German Army Group North cut off in northern Latvia, on the Gulf of Riga, the Soviet High Command sends the 3rd Belorussian Front to attack East Prussia. The Germans prepare to defend the soil of their fatherland.

In Yugoslavia there is bitter street fighting in Belgrade. Further south the Russians occupy Nish, evacuated by the Germans.

Palau Islands On Peleliu the 321st Infantry Regiment, reinforced by units of the 323rd Regiment just arrived from Ulithi, continues its efforts to eliminate Japanese resistance in the area of Mount Umurbrogol.

17 October

Western Europe In Holland, the town of Venray, about 10 miles from the German frontier, is liberated by the 3rd Division of the VIII Corps (British 2nd Army).

In the US 7th Army sector, while the 44th Division (XV Corps) nears the Lunéville region, some 10 miles south-east of Nancy, the 45th and 36th Divisions of the VI Corps approach Bruyères, against strong opposition.

In view of his heavy casualties, General De Lattre de Tassigny, Commander of the French 1st Army, holds up the offensive by the 3rd Algerian and 1st Armoured Divisions towards the Vosges.

Italian Front The II Corps continues to advance north. The 91st Division reaches Lucca, the 34th the slopes of Monte della Vigna, while the 85th continues its advance beyond Monterenzio.

In the British XIII Corps sector, units of the 8th Indian Division begin an attack on Monte Pianoresso. On the right of the front the Polish II Corps attacks towards Forlí.

Greece The last Germans leave the island of Lemnos.

Philippines Small units of American Rangers land on the unmanned islets of Suluan and Dinagat after a preliminary bombardment to secure the approaches to the Gulf of Leyte, about to be entered by the main body of the Leyte invasion force, at present on board the 3rd and 7th Amphibious Forces.

18 October

Western Europe At a generals' conference in Brussels Eisenhower describes his plans for future operations on the Western Front. The efforts of the 21st Army group, and in particular of the Canadian 1st Army, must be concentrated on the liberation of the port of Antwerp. The British 2nd Army is then to advance south-east between the Meuse and the Rhine, starting about 10 November, to support the advance of the American 1st Army across the Rhine in the area of Cologne (an operation planned for between 1 and

5 November). The US 9th Army, after protecting the southern flank of the 1st Army in its advance up to the Rhine, will take part in the capture of the Ruhr.

US XIX Corps, 1st Army: General Corlett is replaced by General McLain.

At Aachen the Americans counter German efforts to break out by renewing their offensive.

In the US 7th Army sector, the 36th Division (VI Corps) captures part of Bruyères.

Italian Front The advance of the II Corps is still slow. In the 8th Army sector, the 5th (*Kresowa*) Division (Polish II Corps) enters Galeata without opposition. The 10th Indian Division (British V Corps) is ordered to attack across the river Savio.

Eastern Front The offensive by the 3rd Belorussian Front against East Prussia continues against bitter German resistance.

Belgrade is on the point of falling into the hands of the Russians and the partisans, while the German Army Group F (von Weichs) hastens the pace of its retreat from the Balkans.

Troops of the 4th Ukraine Front (Petrov) break in from Poland across the Carpathian passes and penetrate into Czechoslovakia from the east, meeting opposition from the German 1st Armoured Army.

Philippines While the three task groups with 13 aircraft carriers of the US 3rd Fleet (Admiral Halsey) hammer the northern part of Luzon and the Manila area, a squadron of cruisers commanded by Rear-Admiral Oldendorf shells the coastal defences of the island of Leyte. The Japanese, already aware of the impending American landing, attack the invasion fleet with all the forces they can muster, sinking one American fast transport.

Japanese Imperial Headquarters orders the putting into effect of Operation *Sho-go* ('Victory'), a decisive action against the American land and naval forces about to invade Leyte.

China Roosevelt recalls General

Laurence Olivier, director and star of *Henry V* (above); Olivier and Vivien Leigh (below).

'HENRY V'

In the course of the Hundred Years' War the English king Henry V, reaffirming the rights of the Plantagenets, invades France with his army and defeats the much more powerful concentration of French troops at the battle of Agincourt (1415). After the treaty of Troyes he marries Catherine, the beautiful daughter of the French king Charles VI.

Remarkable for its period reconstruction, *Henry V* was the first film version of a Shakespearean play to be made by Laurence Olivier. The story opens with an imaginary performance in an Elizabethan theatre, the Globe, but the remainder of the action is translated into pure cinema, with grandiose settings inspired by French miniatures and Italian fifteenth-century painting, all in superb colour.

One of the most memorable moments in the film is the monologue of Olivier, as Henry, on the eve of the fateful battle.

Stilwell to Washington and tells Chiang Kai-shek that, while the Americans do not actually insist on taking over command of the Chinese army, General Wedemeyer would be available to act as Chief of Staff. The proposal is accepted.

Burma On the British XXXIII Corps front, the 5th Indian Division enters Tiddim.

Palau Islands The fighting still goes on in the Mount Umurbrogol area on Peleliu and against the little Japanese pocket on Angaur Island.

19 October

Western Europe In the Antwerp sector, where the II Corps of the Canadian 1st Army is operating, the 52nd Division, just brought up from the rear, takes up a position beyond the bridgehead thrown over the Leopold Canal to the north by the Canadian 3rd Division.

German resistance at Aachen is diminishing perceptibly. Units of the American 1st Division (II Corps, 1st Army) and the 3rd Armoured Division advance towards the city, one taking Salvator Hill and the other the Lousberg heights. Patrols from the armoured division succeed in cutting the Aachen–Laurensberg road.

On the right of the Allied line in the US 7th Army sector, the 36th Division (VI Corps) completes the capture of Bruyères; the 3rd Division assembles behind the 45th Division in readiness for the attack towards St Dié.

Italian Front Units of the South African 6th Armoured Division advance on to the slopes of Monte Salvaro, while others, on the right, are in sight of Monte Alcino, south-east of Monte Salvaro. In the 34th Division (II Corps) sector an attack in force is unleashed on the right flank in the direction of Monte Grande and Monte Cerere. The 88th Division, after an effective bombardment, takes Monte Cerere without difficulty and reaches the top of Monte Grande. On the western flank of the II Corps, the positions of the 91st Division are unchanged.

In the British 8th Army sector, the 5th (*Kresowa*) Division (Polish II

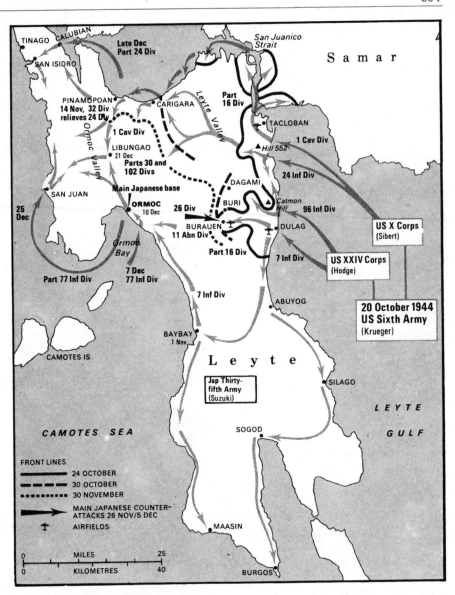

Philippines: operations on Leyte Island, 20 October–5 December 1944.

Corps) enters Civitella di Romagna, meeting no resistance. On its left, where the British V Corps is operating, the 46th Division nears Cesena, and its patrols penetrate into the town from the south. At the same time the 4th Division takes the place of the 46th, but the troops that have penetrated into Cesena stay in their positions. Units of the 20th Indian Brigade (10th Indian Division) move across the river Savio in the neighbourhood of Falcino, while others from the 25th Brigade establish a bridgehead over the Savio not far from Roversano.

Philippines While the Leyte invasion force nears its objective under the protection of the US 7th Fleet, the

operation of minesweeping and destroying the under-water obstacles put down by the Japanese is completed. Bombing from the air continues. Japanese reaction is vigorous; the aircraft carrier *Sangamon* is hit by a bomber and two destroyers are damaged, one by a mine, the other by coastal defence batteries.

Burma A brigade of the British 26th Division occupies Mohnyin, where the Japanese have abandoned big ammunition and supply dumps.

20 October

Western Europe The British I Corps (Canadian 1st Army) opens an offensive in the direction of the road joining Bergen-op-Zoom, about 20 miles north-west of Antwerp, with Tilburg, committing all three divisions, the 4th Armoured on the left, the 49th in the centre and the Polish 1st Armoured Division on the right.

The 26th Regiment of infantry, US 1st Division (VII Corps, American 1st Army) presses back the German defenders in the southern suburbs of Aachen.

At Marseilles (US 7th Army sector) two more American divisions land, the 100th and 103rd. The American 3rd Division (VI Corps, 7th Army) makes for St Dié, north-east of Bruyères, with the 7th Infantry Regiment.

Italian Front The South African 6th Armoured Division (US 5th Army) repels a counter-attack by units of the German XIV Armoured Corps against Allied positions on Monte Salvaro, and reaches the slopes of Monte Alcino. On the right flank of the US II Corps the 88th Division advances as far as Farneto. There is a lull in the other sectors.

In the eastern sector of the line (British 8th Army) the 4th Division reaches and fords the river Cesano beside the bridge, which the Germans have blown up. On the Adriatic coast the Allies occupy Cesenatico after the withdrawal of the units of the German LXXVI Armoured Corps.

Eastern Front In Hungary, the 2nd Ukraine Front, supported by Rumanian and Bulgarian troops, drive the Germans out of Debrecen. In Yugoslavia, the 46th and 57th Armies of the 3rd Ukraine Front with Tito's partisan forces complete the liberation of Belgrade. Tito's partisans capture Dubrovnik.

Philippines At 10.05 a.m. the US 6th Army (General Krueger), consisting of four divisions and ancillary troops, totalling over 120,000 men, carried in the 3rd and 7th Amphibious Forces (350 troop and cargo transports and over 400 landing craft of every kind), escorted by the 7th Fleet commanded by Vice-Admiral T.C. Kinkaid (6 battleships, 18 escort carriers, and destroyers and auxiliary vessels), begin to land on

American Marines land on Leyte Island.

the east coast of Leyte Island, near the chief town, Tacloban. General MacArthur himself is in overall command of the operation; Vice-Admiral Kinkaid commands the escort force and General Krueger the operations on land. A deadly naval fire begins at 6.00 a.m. and is broken off at 8.50 a.m. while US aircraft drop hundreds of tons of bombs in the area of Dulag; then the landings take place on a front of 16 miles on two separate beachheads.

After a few hours General MacArthur sets foot once more on Philippine soil (he had promised: 'I shall return'), accompanied by his Chief of Staff General Sutherland and the new President of the Philippines, Sergio Osmena, the successor to the vanished Quezon, with many senior officers. Using a small radio transmitter, MacArthur solemnly addresses the Filipino people, reminding them how he has kept the promise he made two and a half years

before and inviting them to collaborate with the liberators.

To man the whole of the Philippines the Japanese have deployed 260,000 men under the command of Marshal Count Terauchi. On Leyte the defence is in the hands of the 16th, 26th, 30th and 102nd divisions of the 35th Army, commanded by General Tomoyoku Yamashita, the conqueror of Malaysia and Singapore.

The Americans, with continuous air support, capture Tacloban airfield, the Cataisan peninsula and the northern approaches to the Leyte Valley, San José and Dulag. Only in some sectors do the Japanese put up a solid resistance; as usual, they mount infantry counter-attacks during the night, which are repulsed by the Americans. However, the Americans are unable to link up their two beachheads, a mile to a mile and a half deep, which are still 10 miles apart.

☐ Churchill arrives in Cairo to discuss strategy in South-East Asia with Admiral Lord Mountbatten.

21 October

Western Europe At 12.05 p.m. the German garrison of Aachen surrenders. The city is reduced to a pile of rubble, and, especially for the Germans, there can be no justification for the continued sacrifice of human lives, either from the strategic point of view or from that of military prestige.

In the American 7th Army sector, units of the VI Corps enter Brouleveurs (units of the 45th Division), continue to advance towards St Dié (3rd Division) and improve their positions east of Bruyères (36th Division).

Italian Front On the west of the Allied line (US 5th Army),, while the South African 6th Armoured Division completes the capture of Monte Alcino, there is no change in the positions of the II and XIII Corps. In the British 8th Army sector, units of the British V Corps succeed in consolidating and expanding their three bridgeheads over the river Savio in spite of persistent rain and the consequent rapid rise in the level of the water in the river.

The British 4th Division completes the occupation of Cesena.

The Canadian 1st Division (I Corps) also succeeds, with its 2nd Brigade, in establishing a bridgehead over the Savio.

Eastern Front The leading units of Malinovsky's 2nd Ukraine Front push on west of Szeged, reaching the Danube at Baja (southern Hungary, east of Pécs). In Yugoslavia the German Army Groups F (von Weichs) and E (Löhr) abandon one position after another, menaced all the time by the Bulgarian 1st Army on the eastern flank and elsewhere by Yugoslav and Albanian partisans. The Russians, after their thrust against Belgrade, now concentrate on Hungary. In Finland the Karelia Front under Meretskov advances from Petsamo with the 14th Army towards the Norwegian border, driving back

General MacArthur (left) returns to the Philippines. He disembarks from a landing craft a few hours after the start of operations on Leyte Island.

the German 20th Mountain Army (Rendulic).

Philippines: Leyte The Americans on Leyte repel a violent night counter-attack by the Japanese, killing over 600. At first light, with support from the guns and aircraft of the 7th Fleet, they start to advance again, capturing Tacloban, the capital of the island, and Dulag airfield. They also cross the river Labiranan, but are forced back over it at once by powerful Japanese resistance. The two main bridgeheads are still not able to be linked. Meanwhile, aircraft from a squadron of aircraft carriers under the command of Rear-Admiral Bogan attack the islands of Panay, Cebu, Negros and Masbate, to the west and north-west of Leyte.

Palau Islands On Angaur (where an airfield has already been prepared to take US heavy bombers) all organized resistance by the Japanese ceases; they have lost some 1,300 dead and 45 prisoners, against American casualties of 265 dead and 1,355 wounded. The biggest islands in the Palau archipelago are not occupied by the Americans; their garrisons, with no supplies, no longer present any danger to US forces.

22 October

Western Europe The Canadian 3rd Division (II Corps, 1st Army) captures Breskens, while the Canadian 4th Armoured Division (British I Corps) reaches Esschen.

To the east, in the British 2nd Army sector, the XII Corps opens an offensive in the region east of the Meuse. The 15th Division makes for Tilburg, while the 7th Armoured and 53rd Divisions, followed by the 51st, head for 's Hertogenbosch.

Operations leading up to the Allied offensive against the Rhine begin with the drawing up along the Allied front of the three American armies which are to take part, from north to south, the 1st, 9th and 3rd.

☐ The French provisional government under General de Gaulle is recognized *de jure* by Great Britain, the USA and the USSR.

Italian Front Persistent rain hampers Allied movements, but the Allied units continue to advance in the different sectors. On the Adriatic coast, units of the Canadian I Corps seize Cervia and Pisignano.

Eastern Front The armies of the 1st Baltic Front and the 3rd Belorussian Front, which have succeeded in breaking through the advance defences of East Prussia, are halted in front of Insterburg by determined German resistance. The positions in this sector of the front will now remain almost unchanged until the end of January 1945.

In Yugoslavia, with the fall of Sombor (south-west of Subotica), Allied forces control a large part of the east bank of the Danube as far as the Hungarian town of Baja.

Philippines On Leyte the 1st Cavalry Division (US X Corps) mops up the city of Tacloban and captures the hills to the south-west. Units of the 24th Infantry Division, supported by artillery and naval guns, capture the area of Pawing. In the XXIV Corps sector, further south near Dulag, after an intensive all-night barrage, units of the 96th Infantry Division recapture the positions across the river Labiranan lost on the previous day. Other units take the villages of San Roque, Tigbao and Canmangui, pushing on inland towards Burauen. The 7th Infantry Division advances about two miles to the south, towards Abuyog.

23–26 October

Pacific Air and naval battle of the Gulf of Leyte. The Japanese fleet – almost the entire fleet – attempts a huge attack to cripple the invasion of the Philippines and strike a decisive blow at the US 3rd and 7th Fleets. The engagement, which breaks down into three separate battles, ends disastrously for the Imperial Fleet, which loses four aircraft carriers, three battleships, ten cruisers and nine destroyers. Japanese naval power is virtually wiped out. The Americans lose one aircraft carrier, three destroyers and two escort ships, and many other vessels emerge with more or less serious damage.

It is in the Gulf of Leyte that the special assault corps: *kamikaze* – meaning 'divine wind', recalling the storms that in 1274 and 1281 dispersed the Mongol fleets sent by Kublai Khan to invade Japan – first goes into action as an officially recognized unit. Organized by Admiral Arima, this body of voluntary suicides, army and naval pilots, will by

The opening stages of the battle of Leyte Gulf.

the end of the war have sacrificed the lives of over 5,000 of its members, sinking 34 US ships and damaging 290.

23 October

Western Europe On the left flank of the British I Corps (Canadian 1st Army), the 4th Armoured Division moves off westwards towards Bergen-op-Zoom, to close off the isthmus of South Beveland, along which the Canadian 2nd Division (II Corps) is preparing to advance.

The advance towards St Dié by the 3rd Division (VI Corps, US 7th Army) is effectively opposed by units of von Wiese's German 19th Army. On the right flank of the VI Corps, the US 36th Division is advancing east of Bruyères towards Biffontaine.

Italian Front In the western sector

(US 5th Army) the position of the Allied divisions remain substantially unchanged. In the east, where the units of the British 8th Army are operating, the bridgeheads over the river Savio are reinforced.

Philippines: Leyte In a solemn ceremony at Tacloban, on Leyte Island, MacArthur re-installs the legitimate government of the Philippines under the presidency of Sergio Osmena.

North of Tacloban the US 1st Cavalry Division exerts powerful pressure against part of the Japanese 16th Division to drive them out of the north-west part of the island and liberate the San Juanico Strait, between Leyte and the neighbouring island of Samar, so as to hinder enemy movement between the two islands.

(continued on page 614)

THE BATTLE OF LEYTE GULF

The Japanese Imperial Headquarters has been expecting for months that the Americans will try to seize the Philippines, the last Japanese bulwark in the Pacific. The loss of the Philippines would almost certainly cut the Japanese off from access to South-East Asia, the source of so much of their oil and other vital raw materials. Their expectations are confirmed by the powerful attacks launched by Nimitz's fleet on Formosa and on the Philippines themselves, particularly Luzon.

The Americans for their part foresee precisely the reaction they can expect from the Japanese when they attack the Philippines. A few days after the fall of Tojo's cabinet, Admiral Yonai, the new Minister for the Navy, conferred with the other members of the Cabinet to put the finishing touches to a plan called *Sho-go* (Operation *Victory*). When the invasion comes, the troops on land will hold out to the last man, while the navy will face the American amphibious forces and aircraft carriers on a huge scale, in 'a general and decisive battle'.

Admiral Toyoda, Commander-in-Chief of the Fleet, is aware of the impossibility of defeating the American fleet, above all because the Japanese capital ships will lack air cover. He works out a stratagem to divide the enemy: when the Americans invade the Philippines it will be necessary to draw off the powerful Task Force 38 and take the opportunity to send in the Japanese battleships to destroy the invasion fleet. The bait to attract the enemy away from the Philippines will mostly be made up of aircraft carriers. The composition of the fleet that is literally to be sacrificed in order to win the decisive victory has already been decided. It will consist of the heavy aircraft carrier *Zuikaku*, two battleships converted into semi-carriers, but without aircraft, the *Ise* and the *Hyuga*, the light aircraft carriers *Zuiho*, *Chitose* and *Chiyoda*, the light cruisers *Oyodo*, *Tama* and *Isuzu* and 8 destroyers. This tempting bait contains so many aircraft carriers because, while the Japanese still have the ships, they no longer have the aircraft to equip them, nor the crews to man them. While this decoy fleet, commanded by Admiral Ozawa, draws the big fish away from the Philippines, three squadrons will converge on the Philippines and destroy the American amphibious fleet, at the same time halting the invasion and dealing a mortal blow to the enemy's naval power. Apart from the decoy fleet, the three Japanese squadrons, commanded by Vice-Admiral Takeo Kurita, Vice-Admiral Shoji Nishimura and Vice-Admiral Kiyohide Shima, under overall command of Admiral Soemu Toyoda, comprise 7 battleships (the giant *Yamato* and *Musashi* of 72,800 tons plus the *Nagato*, *Kongo*, *Haruna*, *Yamashiro* and *Fuso*), 11 heavy cruisers (*Atago*, *Maya*, *Takao*, *Chokai*, *Myoko*, *Aguro*, *Kumano*, *Suzuya*, *Tone*, *Chikuma* and *Mogami*), 5 light cruisers (*Nashiro*, *Yahagi*, *Nachi*, *Ashigara* and *Abukuma*) and 28 destroyers. In addition to these squadrons there will be a flotilla of submarines with 11 vessels and two land-based air fleets with about 800 aircraft as well as 116 seaborne aircraft.

The Japanese have been certain since 6 October, thanks to a leak (accidental or deliberate) let slip in Moscow, that the Americans' objective is to be the Philippines. On 7 October Toyoda went to Manila to warn the local military commanders to be ready for the American landing between 20 and 30 October. The element of surprise thus disappears for the Americans. Nonetheless, including Task Force 38, commanded by Admiral Halsey with Vice-Admiral Mitscher as his deputy, they can deploy something like 32 heavy, light and escort carriers (*Wasp, Hornet, Hancock, Intrepid, Essex, Lexington, Enterprise, Franklin, Monterey, Cowpens, Cabot, Independence, Langley, Princeton, San Jacinto, Belleau Woods, Marcus Island, Kadashan Bay, Savoy Island, Omanney Bay, Fanshaw Bay, St Lo, White Plains, Kalinin Bay, Kitkun Bay, Gambier Bay, Sangamon, Suwannee, Santee, Petrof Bay, Natoma Bay, Manila Bay*); 6 fast battleships (*New Jersey, Iowa, Massachusetts, South Dakota, Washington, Alabama*); 6 old battleships (*Mississippi, Maryland, West Virginia, Pennsylvania, Tennessee, California*); 9 heavy cruisers (*Chester, Pensacola, Salt Lake City, Boston, Wichita, New Orleans, Louisville, Portland, Minneapolis*); 14 light cruisers (*San Diego, Oakland, Biloxi, Vincennes, Miami, Santa Fe, Birmingham, Mobile, Reno, Denver, Columbia, Phoenix, Boise* and the Australian *Shropshire*); about 100 destroyers, 49 reconnaissance motor-boats and 22 submarines.

17 October
8.09 a.m. the commanders of the Japanese squadrons receive orders to put the plan into effect.

18 October
1.45 a.m. Kurita's squadron, which contains the bulk of the Japanese forces, sails from Lingga (east of Sumatra), heading northeast towards Brunei (Borneo), where it will take on supplies.
11.00 a.m. Kurita receives orders on the tasks allotted to the ships of his 1st Attack Force.

20 October
5.00 p.m. Vice-Admiral Ozawa's

23 October

The decoy force of aircraft carriers under Vice-Admiral Ozawa, despite all its efforts to carry out its function, has still not been spotted by the Americans, and in the evening the commander orders the ships to break radio silence and send out long messages with the sole object of

CV 19 Hancock (USA)

decoy force of aircraft carriers sets a course north-east towards the Philippines.

All squadrons receive Admiral Toyoda's order fixing 25 October as the day of the attack.

21 October

Vice-Admiral Shima's squadron receives orders to support Vice-Admiral Nishimura's squadron. In the afternoon the squadron sails from Bako in the Pescadores, heading for Coron Bay in the Calamian Islands, where it will take on supplies.

22 October

At 8.00 a.m. Kurita's main squadron sails from Brunei heading north-east, to follow a course west of the Palawan Islands and then to turn north of the Calamian Islands and penetrate into the Strait of Mindoro.

3.00 p.m. Nishimura's squadron leaves Brunei and, after a long detour to avoid enemy submarines, enters the Jolo Sea, between Borneo and the Philippines.

having them intercepted.

Meanwhile two American submarines, the *Darter* and the *Dace*, are on the trail of Kurita's battleship squadron; they picked them up on the evening of the 21st and have reported to that effect.

5.32 a.m. the *Darter* hits the heavy cruiser *Atago*, Admiral Kurita's flagship, with three torpedoes, and she sinks. The *Darter* hits another Japanese cruiser, the *Takao*, with two torpedoes; she just manages to get back to Brunei. At 5.54 a.m. the *Dace* scores hits with four torpedoes on the heavy cruiser *Maya*, which explodes and sinks very quickly.

8.27 a.m. following the reports from the submarines, Admiral Halsey orders three task groups from Task Force 38, under Sher-

man, Bogan and Davison, to concentrate at the north, centre and south of the eastern mouth of San Bernardino Strait, east of the Philippine islands of Luzon and Samar.

24 October

Japanese aircraft based in the Philippines attack the American fleet. At 8.30 a.m. 60 aircraft are reported near Admiral Bogan's task group, in front of San Bernardino Strait. Fighters from the American aircraft carriers make mincemeat of them, but at 9.08 a.m. a Suisei dive-bomber succeeds in penetrating the defensive screen and hits the aircraft carrier *Princeton*. The ship is wrecked by the explosions, and in the afternoon the cruiser *Reno* finishes her off.

9.15 a.m. an aircraft from the *Franklin* sights Nishimura's squadron 75 miles south of the Cagayan Islands. A little later a score of US aircraft arrive over the battleship *Fuso* and the destroyer *Shigure* and damage them, but not seriously. Meanwhile Kurita's squadron has arrived south of Mindoro Island and entered the Sibuyan Sea, where it is sighted by a reconnaissance aircraft from the *Intrepid* and attacked, the first wave of 12 American dive-bombers and 12 torpedo-bombers coming in at 10.26 a.m.

10.27 a.m. the super-battleship *Musashi* is hit by a torpedo and a bomb and seriously damaged.

12.35 p.m. a second wave of American aircraft arrives. The *Musashi* is hit by four more torpedoes.

Three more American attacks follow during the day. A little after 3.20 p.m. US aircraft hit the *Musashi* again with at least ten torpedoes and several bombs. By now the ship has been hit by nineteen torpedoes and nineteen bombs; her fate is sealed – out of control, she cannot even be beached. The crew fight the fires that blaze aboard her.

7.35 p.m. the *Musashi* capsizes and sinks. Thirty-nine officers and 984 ratings go down with her; another 1,264 are saved.

2.00 p.m. in order not to expose his squadron to destruction, Kurita gives up for the moment his intention of proceeding towards the Gulf of Leyte, and sets a course north-west to get out of range of the US aircraft.

7.59 p.m. Admiral Toyoda, informed that Kurita has changed course, tells him to stick to the original plan.

8.20 p.m. Nishimura tells Kurita that his squadron (Force C, or South Force) will emerge from the Surigao Strait (between Leyte and Dinagat) on the 25th, at 4.00 a.m. Kurita, who will be converging on Dinagat from the north, agrees to meet him at 9.00 a.m. on the 25th off the Gulf of Leyte.

8.22 p.m. Admiral Halsey decides to attack Ozawa's squadron with the whole of Task Force 38, now that it has finally been spotted by American reconnaissance aircraft. Halsey thus falls into the trap laid by the Japanese, detaching huge forces to pursue the decoy fleet while the three enemy assault squadrons converge on the Gulf of Leyte, now defended only by the 7th Fleet (Kinkaid).

25 October

12.37 a.m. Kurita's main squadron enters the Philippine Sea, heading for San Bernardino Strait. Nishimura's and Shima's squadrons, further south, make for the Surigao Strait. Most of Kinkaid's 7th Fleet is concentrated off Surigao; the battleships of Task Force 34 (Rear-Admiral Lee) are guarding San Bernardino Strait. The defence of the Surigao Strait is in the hands of Rear-Admiral Oldendorf, with six old battleships and six destroyers in the centre, five cruisers and nine destroyers on the left and three cruisers and thirteen destroyers on the right. In addition to these forces there are thirty-nine motor torpedo-boats.

2.40 a.m. the destroyer *MacGowan* reports sighting Nishimura's squadron, led by four destroyers followed by the battleships *Yamashiro* and *Fuso* and the cruiser *Mogami* bringing up the rear.

3.01 a.m. five American destroyers attack the enemy formation with torpedoes, hitting three Japanese destroyers (one of which sinks instantly) and damaging the battleship *Fuso* seriously and the battleship *Yamashiro* less seriously.

3.20 a.m. six more destroyers, five American and one Australian,

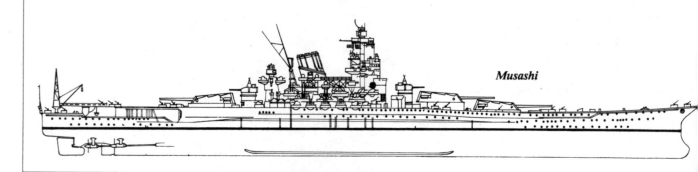

Musashi

Mogami – 1943

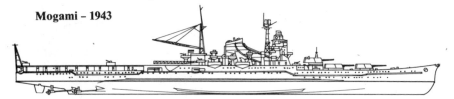

resume the torpedo attack. At 3.25 a.m. the battleship *Yamashiro* is hit directly by a torpedo, and at 3.50 a.m. she explodes, breaking in two. The Japanese destroyer *Michishio* is also sunk, by a torpedo fired by the US destroyer *Hutchins*.

3.51 a.m. the American cruisers open fire on the Japanese, followed immediately by the heavy guns of the battleships. The Japanese, already engaged by the destroyers, now have to return the fire of the bigger ships as well.

4.04 a.m. nine more American destroyers attack the Japanese, firing about fifty torpedoes; but they score only one direct hit, on the battleship *Fuso*.

An American destroyer, the *Albert W. Grant*, is put out of action by Japanese guns, and also, through an error, by American fire. As a result of this serious incident, Rear-Admiral Oldendorf orders the battleships to cease fire at 4.06. Three minutes later the same order is sent to the cruisers. The Japanese battleship *Fuso* is on fire from end to end, but manages to limp away slowly. The cruiser *Mogami* and the destroyer *Shigure* also escape.

4.18 a.m. now sure that he runs no risk of firing on his own ships, Oldendorf orders reopening of fire. A minute later the Japanese battleship *Fuso* sinks. The *Mogami*, also badly damaged, makes her escape preceded by the destroyer *Shigure*, the only ship in Nishimura's squadron still undamaged.

4.20 a.m. Shima's squadron arrives in the Surigao Strait, with the heavy cruisers *Nachi* and *Ashigara* and two destroyers. The light cruiser *Abukuma*, which was included in the squadron, has been hit by an American motor torpedo-boat at 3.21 a.m. and has been left behind, seriously damaged.

4.25 a.m. while the Japanese ships prepare for battle, the cruiser *Nachi* comes into collision with the *Mogami* and receives damage that reduces her speed to 20 knots. Shima orders his ships to go about, and the Americans set off in pursuit.

7.07 a.m. the cruisers *Denver* and *Columbia*, with three destroyers, open fire on the Japanese destroyer *Asagumo*, already damaged, and sink her. At 7.23 a.m. the pursuit is suspended and the Americans head for the north entrance to the Surigao Strait. The Japanese cruiser *Mogami*, hit by US aircraft at 8.45 a.m., is put out of action at 9.10 a.m. and sunk by a Japanese

The US aircraft carrier *St Lo* in flames, following an attack by a *kamikaze* aircraft.

The Japanese battleship *Yamashiro* on the point of sinking, after being hit by American torpedoes.

destroyer at 12.30 p.m.

Kurita's main squadron (the super-battleship *Yamato*, the battleships *Nagato*, *Kongo* and *Haruna*, the heavy cruisers *Caokai*, *Chikuma*, *Tone*, *Kumano*, *Suzuya* and *Haguro*, two light cruisers and eleven destroyers) moves away east of the island of Samar, according to plan, heading for the Gulf of Leyte. In this area Vice-Admiral Kinkaid has sixteen unarmoured escort carriers and twenty-one destroyers. These forces are broken up into three groups: Taffy 1 in the south, towards the island of Mindanao (Rear-Admiral Sprague), Taffy 2 in the centre off the Gulf of Leyte (Rear-Admiral Stump) and Taffy 3 to the north off Samar (Rear-Admiral Clifton A. F. Spruance). It is this last group, with six escort carriers and seven destroyers, which is taken by surprise by Vice-Admiral Kurita's squadron.

7.01 a.m. the *Yamato* opens fire from 37,000 yards, joined at once by the other battleships. The surprise is possible because Kinkaid is under the impression that Task Force 38 is still to the north of Taffy 3, whereas actually Halsey has sent the whole force off to tackle Ozawa's decoy squadron without telling Kinkaid, putting the whole fleet in serious danger. Spruance calls for help and sends his carriers to the east to let every available aircraft take off. The *White Plains* and *St Lo* are badly hit. The Americans put up smoke-screens and are also, fortunately for them, protected by heavy

A cruiser draws alongside the aircraft carrier *Princeton*, which has been hit by a bomb.

cloud cover.

7.20 a.m. the US destroyers *Hoel*, *Heermann* and *Johnston* now launch an audacious attack with torpedoes. The heavy cruiser *Kumano* is hit and catches fire, and takes no further part in the battle. The American destroyer *Johnston* is heavily damaged by three 14-inch shells and a number of 6-inch. The Japanese battleship *Kongo*, attacked with torpedoes by the destroyer *Hoel*, manages to dodge the torpedoes and hits back at her attacker, causing immense damage to her superstructure.

7.50 a.m. the destroyer *Hoel* fires her last torpedoes against the cruiser *Haguro*, without hitting her (and sinks shortly after). At the same time the *Heerman* also fires a torpedo at the *Haguro* and

misses. *Heerman* then attacks the big Japanese battleships, which fire a storm of shells back at her which she avoids by a miracle.

7.54 a.m. The battleship *Yamato* retires to a position behind the rest of the Japanese squadron.

Meanwhile, at 7.50 a.m., the little escort destroyers *Roberts*, *Butler*, *Dennis* and *Raymond* join the *Heerman* and the badly damaged *Johnston* in the battle against the Japanese squadron. And now, too, the aircraft from Taffy 3 and Taffy 2 (the nearest group to Spruance's squadron) arrive over the Japanese ships.

8.00 a.m. while the small American ships cause confusion among the Japanese, a bomb from an aircraft hits the cruiser *Haguro*, putting one of her turrets out of action.

8.30 a.m. the small escort destroyer *Raymond* attacks the cruiser *Tone*, forcing her to break off her fire against the escort

CVE 27 Suwanee (USA).

carrier *Gambier Bay*. The *Raymond* and the *Butler* are badly hit.

9.00 a.m. the *Chokai* and the *Chikuma* are hit from the air and put out of action. A little later, both sink.

9.07 a.m. the escort carrier *Gambier Bay*, hit several times, capsizes and sinks. The *Kalinin Bay* and all seven destroyers are also damaged.

9.15 a.m. the escort carrier *Fanshaw Bay* is hit several times by the Japanese battleships and cruisers; a little later the *St Lo* is hit and the destroyer *Roberts* is put out of action.

10.05 a.m. the *Roberts* sinks.

10.10 a.m. the destroyer *Johnston* also sinks. Already badly hit, she has gone in to attack the Japanese light cruiser *Yahagi* and her escorting destroyers.

Kurita orders a temporary withdrawal to the north to re-group. At 11.47 a.m. he orders the squadron to set a course for the Gulf of

from the destroyer *Whitehurst*. Aircraft from the escort carriers *Kitkun Bay*, *Manila Bay* and *Kadashan Bay* and the heavy carriers *Wasp*, *Hornet* and *Hancock* (from Task Force 38) set off in pursuit of Kurita's squadron and arrive over it between 12.45 p.m. and 1.10 p.m. The carrier-borne aircraft damage several Japanese vessels but sink none.

1.22 p.m. Japanese heavy cruiser *Suzuya* sinks as a result of damaged sustained earlier in the day.

At 9.40 p.m. a reconnaissance aircraft from the carrier *Independence* still has Kurita's squadron in sight as it retires through the San Bernardino Strait.

Chiyoda, already hit several times by bombs, is immobilized by a torpedo. Hits are then scored on the light cruiser *Tama*, proceeding at low speed. Later the *Chiyoda* sinks.

1.00 p.m. a third wave of American aircraft arrives. After a few minutes three torpedoes strike the *Zuikaku* and three bombs hit and damage the *Zuiho*.

1.10 p.m. 40 aircraft attack the *Zuiho*, scoring repeated hits.

1.30 p.m. the *Zuiho*, still under attack, receives a mortal blow.

2.14 p.m. the light aircraft carrier *Zuikaku* capsizes and sinks.

2.45 p.m. the fourth wave of American bombers. They attack the battleship *Ise* without hitting her; the *Zuiho* is hit yet again.

3.26 p.m. the light aircraft carrier *Zuiho* sinks.

Before evening the Americans launch two more attacks against Ozawa's squadron, but without effect.

Zuiho

Leyte, at 12.15 p.m. he has them change course to the north-west, and at 12.36 p.m. he orders a withdrawal to the north.

Japanese aircraft taking off from neighbouring islands have meanwhile attacked the escort carrier *Santee*, and a self-immolating *kamikaze* leaves her severely damaged. The *Suwannee* has also been damaged by a suicide plane.

10.51 a.m. the escort carrier *St Lo*, already damaged, is another *kamikaze* target. She sinks at 11.15.

11.10 a.m. the *Kalinin Bay* is damaged by a suicide plane. In the evening the destroyer *Eversole*, looking for survivors, is sunk by a Japanese submarine, which is sunk in its turn by depth charges

25 October

2.08 a.m. an American night reconnaissance aircraft sights the advance guard of the decoy squadron under Vice-Admiral Ozawa.

7.10 a.m. 180 fighters, bombers and torpedo-aircraft take off from Vice-Admiral Mitscher's aircraft carriers.

8.00 a.m. the American aircraft are over their target and begin the attack, hitting the aircraft carriers *Zuiho*, *Chitose* and *Zuikaku*.

About 9.00 a.m. the Japanese destroyer *Akitsuki* sinks.

9.37 a.m. the aircraft carrier *Chitose* sinks.

9.45 a.m. a new wave of American aircraft arrives.

10.18 a.m. the aircraft carrier

During the follow-up action and in other actions on the 26th and 27th October, American ships and aircraft also sink the light cruisers *Noshiro*, *Abukuma*, *Kinu* and *Tama* (already hit by aircraft, this last is finished off by a submarine), the seaplane support ship *Akitsishima*, and the destroyers *Shiranuhi*, *Yamagumo*, *Hayashimo*, *Hatzusuki*, *Wakaba*, *Nowaki* and *Uranami*.

In the southern sector, where the US XXIV Corps is in action, the 96th Infantry Division is short of supplies. The 7th Division, supported by a tank battalion, continues to advance inland towards Burauen, near to which are San Pablo airport and other landing grounds. The tanks get as far as Burauen; the infantry occupy Julita and San Pablo and take the airport.

24 October
Western Europe On the Dutch coast the Canadian 2nd Division (1st Army) begins to advance along the isthmus of South Beveland. In Brabant, on the British 2nd Army front, the XII Corps (7th Armoured Division and 53rd infantry Division) reach 's Hertogenbosch. There is a sudden lull on the fronts of the three armies of the 12th Army Group (1st, 9th and 3rd), while in the south, in the US 7th Army sector, the 3rd Division (US VI Corps) steps up its thrusts along the road to St Dié.

The 45th Division (US VI Corps) advances rapidly to capture the village of Mortagne after house-to-house fighting. General De Lattre de Tassigny, Commander of the French 1st Army, issues directives for Operation *Independence*, the capture of Belfort in south-east France. Belfort is not far from the Swiss border on the road leading from Strasbourg through Mulhouse to Lyons.

Italian Front The South African 6th Armoured Division captures the Passo del Termine and the 78th Division (British XIII Corps) reinforces its positions on Monte Spadura. Meanwhile the 61st Brigade of the British 6th Armoured Division reaches Monte Orsaro between the Parma and the Magra.

In the British 8th Army sector the 10th Indian Division advances swiftly towards the river Ronco on the left flank of V Corps.

Eastern Front In Rumania, Russian forces complete the occupation of the whole of Transylvania.

Pacific Battle of the Leyte Gulf. The US 7th Fleet attacks and destroys enemy ships heading for Leyte through the Surigao Strait during the night. The US 3rd Fleet, after attack-

Western Front: infantry of the American 7th Army advance through the ruins of Dannemarie.

ing another enemy squadron, steams north in pursuit of a third squadron which deliberately acts as a decoy to draw the American fleet away from Leyte and the San Bernardino Strait (between Luzon and Samar) to allow other Japanese squadrons to penetrate into the waters off Leyte and attack the US landing forces.

Philippines: Leyte A squadron of the US 7th Cavalry (1st Division), starting from Tacloban, crosses the San Juanico Strait and lands on Samar Island, at La Paz, setting up a road block on the road to Basey and repelling a Japanese night counter-attack. The main body of the division advances north along Highway 1 as far as Guintiguian, the northern entrance to the San Juanico Strait, thus achieving its object of preventing the Japanese 16th Division from moving between Leyte and Samar. South of Tacloban, in the US XXIV Corps sector, the 383rd Infantry Regiment, 96th Division, has to confine itself to patrol activity for lack of supplies, while the 17th Infantry, 7th Division, mops up Burauen and advances north towards Dagami. North-west of San Pablo airfield, near Burauen, the Japanese force back part of the US 32nd Infantry.

Burma This theatre of operations, previously unified, is now divided into two: the Indo-Burmese sector

and the Chinese sector. Command of the latter is temporarily assumed by General Chennault, pending the arrival of General Wedemeyer.

25 October
Western Europe In Holland the Canadians continue their slow advance along the isthmus of South Beveland. Further east the US 104th Division (British I Corps) advances towards Zundert, just in Holland on the Antwerp–Breda road.

In the sector of the XV Corps of the US 7th Army, the 44th Division is repeatedly counter-attacked by the forces of the German 19th Army.

General Truscott is replaced in command of the US VI Corps by General Brooks, formerly in command of the V Corps.

Italian Front On the right of the Allied line the British V Corps reaches the river Ronco from the heights in front of Meldola, on Highway 9. Units of the 4th Division capture Forlimpopoli without opposition. During the night the 10th Indian Division succeeds in establishing a bridgehead over the Ronco, south and north of Meldola.

Eastern Front The Karelia Front advances from Petsamo (on the Arctic Ocean) into Norway and takes the important port of Kirkenes on the Barents Sea.

Pacific Battle of Leyte Gulf. Aircraft of the US 3rd and 7th Fleets attack the combined Japanese fleet, which withdraws pursued by the Americans.

Philippines: Leyte In the northern sector, where the US X Corps is operating, units of the 1st Cavalry Division reach Carigara Bay, on the north coast of the island, finding few Japanese troops there.

In the south, in the XXIV Corps sector, units of the US 19th Infantry attack Tabontabon, a small town, but are repulsed by the Japanese. The 382nd Infantry takes Aslom and Kanmonhag. The 17th Infantry takes several villages but does not succeed in advancing towards Dagami, north of Burauen.

Burma Advancing from Upper Burma, the 29th Brigade of the British 36th Division reaches 25 miles past Namma, until held up by a strong Japanese counter-attack in the region of Mawpin.

26 October

Western Europe In Holland, while the Canadian 2nd Division continues to advance westwards along the isthmus of Beveland, the 52nd Division, II Corps (1st Army) carries out a combined operation on the south coast of South Beveland and succeed in establishing a beachhead near Baarland.

In Brabant, the 53rd Division (XII Corps, British 2nd Army) advances beyond s' Hertogenbosch.

In the US 7th Army sector, the 3rd Division continues the battle to reach St Dié, in the teeth of deadly fire from the Germans.

Italian Front Patrol activity along the whole of the US 5th Army front. In the British 8th Army sector, the 10th Indian Division (V Corps) strengthens its bridgehead over the river Ronco, but the swollen river holds up the operations of the 4th Division on its south bank, and incessant rain immobilizes the Canadian I Corps.

Eastern Front In Hungary, the 2nd and 4th Ukraine Fronts join up near Mukachevo, in eastern Hungary. The Hungarian 1st Army and German 1st Armoured Army withdraw in good order. This front is more or less stabilized along the river Tisza, with a Russian salient north of the river near Subotica along the Belgrade–Budapest railway.

Pacific Battle of Leyte Gulf. The great battle, lasting four days, in which the Japanese had gambled such high stakes, comes to an end. The result is disastrous for the Japanese who have lost three battleships (the giant *Musashi*, of 72,800 tons fully laden, the *Fuso* and the *Yamashiro*), four aircraft carriers (the heavy carrier *Zuikaku* and the light carriers *Chitose*, *Chiyoda* and *Zuiho*); six heavy cruisers (*Maya*, *Atago*, *Chikuma*, *Chokai*, *Suzuya*, *Mogami*); four light cruisers (*Tama*, *Abukuma*, *Noshiro*, *Kinu*); ten destroyers (*Asagumo*, *Shiranuhi*, *Wakaba*, *Michishio*, *Yamagumo*, *Akitsuki*, *Hatzusuki*, *Hayashimo*, *Nowaki*, *Uranami*) as well as minor vessels.

The Americans have lost the light aircraft carrier *Princeton*, the escort carriers *St Lo* and *Gambier Bay*, the destroyers *Hoel* and *Johnston* and the escort destroyers *Eversole* and *Samuel B. Roberts*, plus two submarines (one of which sank as a result of a malfunction of its own torpedoes). Many other craft have been more or less seriously damaged (mostly by Japanese suicide pilots), among them seven escort carriers, one light cruiser, eight destroyers, two landing craft and one tanker.

Philippines: Leyte In the northern sector, the Americans advance slowly from the north into Leyte Valley. In the central-southern sector they try to capture Catmon Hill, on the coast north of Dulag, but are repulsed by the Japanese, who then withdraw much of their garrison from this excessively exposed area. Units of the US 7th Infantry Division overcome obstinate Japanese resistance to reach the edge of Buri airfield. The Japanese land 2,000 men at their base at Ormoc.

Palau Islands On Peleliu the determined resistance of the Japanese in the Mount Umurbrogol pocket shows no signs of giving way, although the suicide garrison is already reduced to holding a few cave positions and the whole pocket measures little more than about 550 yards from north to south and about 350–475 yards from east to west. Japanese resistance is favoured by bad weather and difficult terrain.

Burma The Chinese 22nd Division, advancing in the centre of the north Burma front, reaches the airfield 25 miles south-east of Hopin formerly used by the Chindits and known by them as 'Broadway'. The division stays here for several days.

27 October

Western Europe In Holland, the Canadian 52nd Division (II Corps, 1st Army) widens the bridgehead it has established on the south coast of South Beveland, near Baarland, in the direction of Oudelande. The Canadian 2nd Division reaches the Beveland Canal. Further east, in the British I Corps sector, the Canadian 4th Armoured Division enters Bergen-op-Zoom.

On the right of the front, where the Canadian 1st Army is operating, units of the 104th Division, supported by British tanks, take Zundert by storm.

West of Venlo, parachutists of the German 1st Army launch a sudden violent attack towards Asten in the sector held by the American 7th Armoured Division (VIII Corps, British 2nd Army), re-taking the positions captured by the division on the Deurne and Nord Canals. The Germans reach Meijel and also break through the Allied positions at Heitrak, on the road between Deurne and Meijel, and near Nederweert, where the 7th Armoured Division immediately closes the breach.

General De Lattre de Tassigny, commanding the French 1st Army, submits his plans for Operation *Independence* to his immediate superior, the American General Devers, Commander of the 6th Army Group. Devers agrees to them. The French action against Belfort will be carried out in co-operation with the general Allied offensive early in November.

Italian Front The 26th Armoured Brigade, British XII Corps (US 5th Army) takes Rocco San Casciano, on Highway 67. In the British 8th Army sector, units of the Polish 5th (*Kresowa*) Division (II Corps) retake Predappio Nuovo after losing it the previous day to a German counter-attack. Other troops, from the 10th Indian Division, succeed in crossing the river Ronco during the night.

Eastern Front The 4th Ukraine Front takes Uzhgorod on the north-east frontier of Hungary.

□ Goebbels makes a radio broadcast to the German people: 'Hell would yawn before us if we laid down our arms and surrendered to the mercy of our enemies. Germany is firmly determined to hold out to a successful finish.'

Pacific Aircraft from two squadrons of aircraft carriers under command of Rear-Admirals Sherman and Davison attack enemy ships and coastal installations in the waters of the central Philippines and on Luzon Island, sinking two destroyers. The battleship *California* is attacked and damaged by Japanese aircraft.

Philippines: Leyte In the US X Corps sector, units of the 24th Infantry Division, after a night-long artillery barrage capture the village of Pastrana and begin mopping up. In the XXIV Corps sector, the 96th Division attacks Tabontabon again; one battalion penetrates into the town, but is then cut off by a sudden Japanese counter-attack. The 7th Division occupies Buri airfield against slight resistance. The 17th Infantry Regiment continues its advance towards Dagami, getting to within a mile and a quarter of it, to the south.

China The Japanese step up their offensive for the capture of the American air bases in eastern China. Several divisions advance on Kweilin and Liuchow.

28 October

Western Europe Eisenhower's proposed offensive for the beginning of November with General Bradley's 12th Army Group will have three objectives: to eliminate every German strongpoint west of the Rhine, to establish bridgeheads east of the river and to penetrate into the heart of Germany.

The American 104th Division (British I Corps) takes Rijsbergen, half-way between Zundert and Breda. Further east, Tilburg also falls into Allied hands, while between Eindhoven and Venlo the American 7th Armoured Division tries to retake Meijel, lost the previous day to a German counter-attack.

□ The French provisional government dissolves all armed movements which do not belong either to the police or to the army.

Yugoslavia Tito's partisans capture Split, chief town of Dalmatia.

□ The armistice between the Soviet Union and Bulgaria is signed in Moscow. Bulgaria withdraws its troops from Yugoslavian Macedonia and from Greece and puts them under Soviet command (something that, in practice, has already happened) so that they can take part in the operations against the German Army Group E. The question of repatriations will be determined later.

Pacific Aircraft from Rear-Admiral Davison's task group attack Japanese shipping in the waters off Cebu, in the Philippines, sinking two submarines. An American destroyer is sunk by a Japanese submarine, and the light cruiser *Denver* is damaged in a *kamikaze* attack.

Philippines: Leyte In the US X Corps sector there is hard fighting at Carigara, on the north coast of the island. The Americans make slow progress in the Leyte Valley. In the XXIV Corps sector the 382nd Regiment of the 96th Division takes Tabontabon and pushes on towards Kiling. The 17th Infantry, in the Dagami area, advances slowly and suffers heavy losses.

29 October

Western Europe The Canadian II Corps (1st Army) advances rapidly in Beveland, and the 52nd Division reaches Goes. On the army's right flank the I Corps reaches the road between Bergen-op-Zoom and Tilburg, and prepares to advance north.

The Polish 1st Armoured Division takes Breda. In the sector between Eindhoven and Venlo the Germans resume their counter-offensive; units of the American 7th Armoured Division are forced to evacuate Liessel, east of Asten, on the Meijel–Deurne road. In the US 3rd Army sector, units of the 90th Division capture a large part of Maizières-lès-Metz.

Pacific A squadron of American aircraft carriers commanded by Rear-Admiral Bogan attacks targets in the area of Manila, on Luzon Island. In the waters off Leyte the aircraft carrier *Intrepid* is seriously damaged by a *kamikaze* attack.

Philippines: Leyte The American advance in the Valley of Leyte continues. On the coast north of Dulag, Catmon Hill (actually a series of hills), completely abandoned by the Japanese, is occupied by units of the 96th Division. In the centre of the island the Americans continue to attack Dagami. A battalion of the 32nd Infantry advances south from Burauen without meeting any opposition, and reaches the coastal town of Abuyog.

Burma Indo-Burmese sector: in the north of Burma the British 36th Division, after several days' rest at Mawpin, resumes its advance southwards along the Myitkyina–Mandalay railway.

On the Salween front the Chinese troops, supported by aircraft of the US 14th Air Force, resume their offensive against Lung-ling, the Chinese 200th Division, providing the advanced elements.

30 October

Western Europe In the south-eastern sector of the front, where the US 7th Army is operating, units of the 45th Division take St Benoît, on the Rambervillers–Raon-l'Etape road.

Italian Front In the British V Corps sector (8th Army), the 10th Indian Division reaches Meldola, from which the Germans have withdrawn. On the corps' northern flank the 4th Division tries unsuccessfully to cross the river Ronco.

Pacific The Allied command decides on another massive air attack against the Philippines in preparation for a landing on Mindoro. The US 5th Air Force and Australian 13th Air Force are to take part, together with the carrier-borne aircraft of the US 3rd and 7th Fleets and the B29 Superfortresses of the US 20th Air Force.

In the waters around Leyte the US aircraft carrier *Franklin* and the light carrier *Belleau Wood* are damaged in Japanese suicide attacks.

Philippines: Leyte The 17th Infantry, 7th Division, captures Dagami and begins mopping up. The town has been tenaciously defended by the Japanese, whose main forces are now concentrated in the hills in the central northern part of the island. From Abuyog, on the east coast, the American units move south and then turn west towards the west coast.

31 October

Western Europe At Breskens and Ostend, in the Scheldt sector, amphibious assault units of the Canadian II Corps prepare to land on the island of Walcheren. Units of XII Corps (British 2nd Army) overcome German resistance in the Raamsdonk sector.

Italian Front The 10th Indian Division (V Corps, British 8th Army) advances swiftly towards the river Rabbi on the heels of the retiring Germans. The 4th Division establishes two bridgeheads over the river Ronco between Selbagnone and Highway 9.

Eastern Front In Hungary the 2nd Ukraine Front steps up its operations, forcing the passage of the river Tisza near Kecskemet and penetrating into the city, where fierce street fighting develops.

Greece German troops evacuate Thessaloniki.

Philippines: Leyte Units of the US XXIV Corps advance from Abuyog across the centre of the island towards Baybay, on the west coast. In the X Corps sector, to the north, the Americans mop up the area of Jaro, near Tacloban.

Burma In the northern sector the British 36th Division occupies Mawlu. Japanese resistance grows.

China General Wedemeyer takes over command of the American

An American gun emplacement in a village near Aachen.

forces in the Chinese theatre of operations. His main task is to direct air operations in China, Burma and the Pacific.

1 November

Western Europe The Canadian II Corps begins the general attack on the island of Walcheren for the final capture of the Scheldt estuary. The island is defended by the German 70th Division of infantry (nicknamed '*Weissen Brot*' from the special rations provided for its men, all of whom are suffering from a stomach ailment). The Canadian 4th Brigade and the special brigade under command of the 52nd Division cross the estuary onto the south coast near Flushing, which the attacking force storms and partly captures. Commandos of the special brigade, starting from Ostend, land in the island of Walcheren near Westkapelle. Some units advance along the coast to the north-east, others move off south-east towards Flushing. The planned air support by bombers based in Britain for the Canadian II Corps' attack on Walcheren and South Beveland is cancelled owing to the very bad weather, while naval support leads to little or no result on account of the enemy

fire (nine of the twenty-eight craft taking part in the operation on its east flank are sunk and eleven seriously damaged) and of the mines sown thickly off the coasts.

In the US 3rd Army sector, the 5th Division, XX Corps, re-occupies the Arnaville bridgehead south of Metz, relieving the 95th Division. The XII Corps carries out limited attacks with units of the 8th Division to cross the river Seille, capturing Létricourt and Abacourt.

The French 2nd Armoured Division (XV Corps, US 7th Army) enters Bertrichamps. The US 100th Division arrives in the VI Corps sector to replace the 45th Division on the north flank. The 15th Regiment of the 3rd Division occupies La Bourgonce, north-west of St Dié.

Italian Front In the 8th Army sector the 10th Indian Division (British V Corps) crosses the Rabbi near Collina, taking Gusignano. The 4th Division is held up a short way from Forlì airfield.

Eastern Front Troops of the 3rd Ukraine Front complete the capture of Kecskemét, south-east of Budapest.

Greece With the evacuation of Florina the whole of Greece is freed from German occupation, apart from some islands which the Germans have been unable to evacuate; thus the garrisons of Rhodes, western Crete, Milos and some smaller islands (Leros, Kos, Piskopi and Simi), some 20,000 men in all, remain. Eventually these garrisons surrender – Rhodes on 1 May 1945, the others on 9 May 1945.

Philippines: Leyte Fast Japanese transports land reinforcements (2,000 men) and supplies at Ormoc, the main Japanese base on Leyte. The Commander-in-Chief of Japanese troops in the Philippines, General Yamashita, forms the 35th Army on Leyte made up of the 16th, 30th and 102nd Divisions and commanded by General Suzuki.

2 November

Western Europe The Germans still hold out on Walcheren, while the British 157th Brigade (52nd Division) relieves the units of the Canadian 2nd Division (II Corps). Flushing is taken by the I Corps after an intense preparatory bombardment. The 104th Division establishes a bridgehead in the area of Standdaarbuiten.

In the VIII Corps (British 2nd Army) sector, units of the 7th Armoured Division open the offensive to drive the enemy from the Canal du Nord. On the entire front the forces are getting ready for the great offensive planned for the coming days. General de Tassigny, commanding the French 1st Army, prepares to carry out Operation *Independence* against Belfort.

Italian Front The headquarters of the US 5th Army issues directives (in confirmation of verbal orders given on 30 October) for future operations during the unavoidable winter lull, reminding formations of the necessity of consolidating the Bologna salient.

In the British 8th Army sector the 128th Brigade (46th Division) replaces the 10th Indian Division, which is sent into reserve.

Yugoslavia Tito's partisans capture the Dalmatian port of Zadar.

Philippines: Leyte With the occupation of the whole of Leyte Valley in the north-east of the island, the Americans complete the second phase of their campaign. To the north, in the X Corps sector, the 1st Cavalry Division and 24th Infantry Division converge on Carigara, on the north coast, near the northern entrance to the valley leading to the big Japanese base of Ormoc on the west coast. In the central northern sector, where the XXIV Corps is operating, the 382nd Infantry (96th Division) is engaged with the Japanese in lively actions west of Dagami; units of the 7th Infantry Division reach Baybay, on the west coast, late in the evening.

Palau Islands As weather conditions improve, the Americans renew their attacks to eliminate the Japanese pocket on Mount Umurbrogol, Peleliu, but without success.

Burma In the north-west, the 5th Indian Division (British XXXIII Corps) eliminates a Japanese strongpoint known as 'Vital Corner', south of Tiddim.

3 November

Western Europe German resistance ends in the Breskens pocket. The long battle has cost the Canadians 2,077 men (314 killed, the rest missing and wounded), while some 12,500 Germans have been taken prisoner. On Walcheren Island the 52nd Division advances steadily to join up with the assault forces coming from Westkapelle and Flushing. The 104th Division extends its bridgehead, while the Polish 1st Division establishes a bridgehead near Zevenbergen on the right flank of the II Corps and the Canadian 4th Armoured Division improves its positions in the same sector.

Eastern Front The slow retreat of the formations of the German Army Group E in the Balkans continues. The Red Army's southern fronts continue their pressure in Hungary, and in the northern sector the German Army Group North is still cut off in northern Latvia and the island of Saaremaa, and on smaller islands in the Gulf of Riga.

Philippines: Leyte Units of the US 96th Infantry Division (XXIV Corps) are held up by the firm Japanese resistance west of Dagami on a hill known as Bloody Ridge, and forced to withdraw. During the night a violent Japanese counter-attack is repulsed.

Mariana Islands Japanese aircraft begin a series of raids on the US bases on Saipan and Tinian, where the heavy bombers that attack Japan are based.

Burma–China On the Chinese Salween front the Chinese 1st Division retakes Lung-ling after heavy fighting. The Chinese 22nd Division, in the north, reaches the Irrawaddy near Shwegu.

4 November

Western Europe The first Allied minesweeper reaches the port of Antwerp, and from there, with a great many other craft, begins to clear the whole of the Scheldt estuary. The British 52nd Division and groups of Commandos eliminate pockets of resistance on Walcheren Island. In the centre of the British I Corps sector the 49th and 104th Divisions continue to advance northwards towards the Maas; on the right, the Polish 1st Armoured Division takes Geertruidenberg, while on the left Steenbergen is surrounded.

The 3rd Division, VI Corps (US 7th Army) continues to advance west of St Dié, in the Mortagne forest.

Italian Front The South African 6th Armoured Division comes under command of the IV Corps (US 5th Army); until now it has been directly under Army command.

Eastern Front In Hungary, troops of the 2nd Ukraine Front take Cegléd and Szolnok, on the railway between Debrecen and Budapest, a short way from the capital. Heavy rain and growing resistance by the Germans and Hungarians have almost halted the Russians' offensive thrust.

Yugoslavia Sebenico, on the Dalmatian coast, falls to the partisans.

☐ Germany. Allied bombers are now over German cities day and night. During the day over 1,100 American Fortresses and Liberators bomb targets in the areas of Hamburg, Hanover and Saarbrücken. At night the RAF bombs targets in the Ruhr with over 1,000 bombers.

Philippines: Leyte For fear of a Japanese counter-attack by sea, the X Corps is ordered to re-group and take up defensive positions in the Carigara area, in the north of the island. Elements of the X Corps will have to advance towards Ormoc and select positions that can be used as gun emplacements to shell the big enemy base. In the XXIV Corps sector, units of the US 96th Infantry Division renew their attacks at Bloody Ridge, west of Dagami, and succeed in advancing about a thousand yards. More night counter-attacks by the Japanese are repelled by heavy artillery fire, and the Japanese lose 254 men.

Since 1 November one US destroyer has been sunk and four others, plus the light cruiser *Reno*, have been damaged in the waters off Leyte by Japanese bombers, *kamikaze* attacks and submarines.

Burma In the north-west of the country the 5th Indian Division (British XXXIII Corps) occupies Kennedy Peak, another Japanese strongpoint south of Tiddim.

5 November

Western Europe In the Scheldt sector, the II Corps (Canadian 1st Army) continues to advance rapidly in Walcheren Island. While the headquarters of the British I Corps sends forward several units towards the Maas, the US 104th Division, less a certain number of elements of the 414th Infantry Regiment sent to support the Polish 1st Division in their advance on Moerdijk, prepares to advance towards Aachen.

The 5th Division, XII Corps (British 2nd Army), clears the south bank of the Maas. In the VIII Corps sector, the 7th Armoured Division approaches the area of Meijel from the south and the 15th Division from the north. The 3rd Algerian Division (II Corps of the French 1st Army) continues the offensive against Gerardmer, taking Rochesson and Menaurupt.

The formations of the other Allied armies take up their positions for the general offensive against the Rhine.

ALEXIS CARREL

After suffering for some time from heart trouble, Alexis Carrel, the French surgeon and physiologist, died in Paris on 5 November.

Born at Ste-Foy-les-Lyon in 1873, Carrel graduated in medicine at Lyon University in 1900, specializing in blood vessel surgery. Controversy aroused by his experiments led him to leave France for the United States, where he worked for the Rockefeller Institute for Medical Research in New York. There he resumed his experiments on the suturing and grafting of blood vessels, and extended his activities to cardiac surgery and the culture of tissues and organs in test-tubes. For his work he was awarded the Nobel Prize for medicine and physiology in 1912.

During the First World War he served as a military surgeon, successfully using a disinfectant solution (Carrel-Dakin liquid) which saved many soldiers from having limbs amputated.

After the war he managed, thanks to the collaboration of the trans-Atlantic flier Charles Lindbergh, to cultivate various isolated organs, such as the kidney and thyroid gland, in test-tubes, getting them to survive for several days.

His research work in experimental medicine led him to broaden his sphere of interests: one of his treatises, *Man, the Unknown*, was translated into nineteen languages and brought him international fame.

Having returned to France, during the Nazi occupation he accepted the post of director of the Fondation Française pour l'Étude des Problèmes Humains, which caused him to be accused of collaboration after the liberation.

Philippines: Leyte Further attacks by the 382nd Infantry of the US 96th Division against Bloody Ridge, west of Dagami. Tanks and artillery force the Japanese to a limited withdrawal.

Luzon A squadron of US aircraft carriers commanded by Vice Admiral J. S. McCain begins a two-day attack against shipping and airports in the north of Luzon and the surrounding waters. The Japanese heavy cruiser *Nachi*, damaged in a collision with the cruiser *Mogami* at the battle of the Gulf of Leyte, is sunk by US aircraft. The aircraft carrier *Lexington* is hit and damaged by a Japanese suicide plane.

6 November

Western Europe Middelburg, the most important town on Walcheren Island, is captured in a surprise attack by the II Corps of the Canadian 1st Army. General Daser, the garrison commander, surrenders with 2,000 men.

In the British I Corps sector the Polish 1st Armoured Division, supported by units from the US 104th Division, begins the offensive against Moerdijk.

Italian Front The 8th Indian Division (XII Corps, US 5th Army) captures Monte Monsignano.

In the eastern sector (British 8th Army) the Polish II Corps continues its advance, taking Monte Chiodo and Monte Pratello with the 3rd (*Carpathian*) Division and Monte Testa, east of Dovadola, with the 5th (*Kresowa*) Division.

Philippines: Leyte It becomes clear that there is no danger of an amphibious counter-attack by the Japanese, and the X Corps is ordered by General Krueger to advance immediately with the object of taking Ormoc. In the XXIV Corps sector, the 382nd Infantry Regiment, 96th Division, captures Bloody Ridge, west of Dagami, except for a few isolated pockets of resistance.

Burma A regiment of the Chinese 22nd Division crosses the Irrawaddy and overcomes weak Japanese resistance at Shwegugale.

China The Japanese besiege Kunming, capital of Yunnan province.

7 November

Western Europe The headquarters of the Canadian 1st Army takes direct control of the final operations for the occupation of Walcheren

Island.

German resistance continues at Moerdijk on the Hollandsch Diep, some 12 miles from Breda.

In the US 1st Army sector, the 28th Division of the V Corps is withdrawn from the bridgehead over the river Kall after a series of fierce counterattacks by the German 5th Armoured Army.

General Patton (US 3rd Army) decides to launch the offensive on the Rhine on 8 November in spite of the violent rain which at the moment prevents any air force activity.

Italian Front In the 8th Army sector, the V Corps begins the attack against Forlì after a prolonged artillery bombardment. While the 4th Division attacks the city's airport, the 46th Division, on the left, advances towards San Martino in Strada.

Philippines: Leyte The X Corps begins to advance on Ormoc from the north. Units of the 24th and 19th Divisions of infantry attack enemy positions a little south-west of Carigara after a heavy artillery preparation, but are driven back with considerable losses. In the US XXIV Corps sector, the 382nd Infantry of the 96th Division completes the capture of Bloody Ridge, killing about 480 Japanese.

Burma In the north, the Chinese 22nd Division captures Shwegu and while some of the division stays there as garrison, one regiment advances towards Man-tha.

□ Roosevelt is re-elected for a fourth term as President of the United States. Everything possible is done to conceal from world public opinion the fact that he is suffering from a serious illness.

8 November

Western Europe The Canadian 1st Army completes the capture of Walcheren Island. The last defenders surrender, bringing the number of prisoners taken by the Allies during operations in the Scheldt estuary to 8,000.

The US XII Corps under General Gillem goes into the line on the left of the 12th Army Group. It consists of the 102nd Division (except for the 406th Regiment) and the 84th Division.

The US 3rd Army begins its offensive against the Saar.

The XX Corps completes its final preparations for the attack in the Metz area with the 90th, 95th and 1st Armoured Divisions; the XII Corps will attack at dawn towards the river Seille with the 80th, 35th and 26th Divisions.

Italian Front In the eastern sector of the front, the Polish 3rd (*Carpathian*) Division (Polish II Corps, British 8th Army) enters Dovadola, while the 5th (*Kresowa*) Division pushes on towards Castrocaro. The British V Corps makes only limited progress in the Forlì sector.

Philippines: Leyte In the X Corps sector, not even the raging of a typhoon puts an end to the fierce fighting.

Burma On the British XXXIII Corps front, the 5th Indian Division completes the recapture of the area south of Tiddim, occupying Fort White, previously a Japanese strongpoint, without opposition.

9 November

Western Europe In the Canadian 1st Army sector, while the I Corps completes the liberation of the area south of the Maas, the II Corps assumes responsibility for the Nijmegen area (the former battlefield of the British XXX Corps). It has command of the two American airborne divisions, the 82nd and 101st, the 43rd Guards Armoured Brigade and the 50th Division of infantry, as well as the 8th Armoured Brigade, which operates independently. The XII Corps (British 2nd Army) goes into the line along the Maas on the right of the VIII Corps with three divisions, the British 53rd and 51st and the Belgian 1st, and the 8th Brigade. In the US 3rd Army sector, the XX Corps launches a very heavy attack to surround and take Metz, helped by effective air bombing in the area between Metz and Thionville. The Moselle is reached by the 90th Division in the vicinity of Malling and by the 95th at Uckange. In both cases the Americans succeed in establishing firm bridgeheads. South of Metz, the 5th Division crosses the river Seille.

On the right of the line the formations of the US XII Corps advance rapidly. The 35th Division, after reaching the village of Delme, advances towards Château-Salins, about twenty miles north-east of Nancy.

Italian Front The 4th Division (V Corps, 8th Army) forces the Germans out of Forlì.

Philippines: Leyte A Japanese convoy lands reinforcements at Ormoc, but a surprise air attack forces it to withdraw without landing ammunition and supplies. Later the convoy, made up of destroyers adapted for use as fast transports, is destroyed by US aircraft.

In the north-west of the island, the US X Corps continues its slow advance towards Ormoc, but is driven back at several points by Japanese units. Torrential rain hinders the operations.

Burma The British 36th Division resumes its advance after resting in the Mawlu area.

China Chiang Kai-shek, at General Wedemeyer's request, orders the 'Yunnan Force' to attack the Japanese retreating from Lung-ling to Mang-shih (now called Luxi, in western China near the Burmese border). Three Chinese armies move up to this area.

10 November

Western Europe The US XX and XII Corps (3rd Army) continue their offensives in the area of Metz and east of Nancy. The three divisions of XX Corps, the 90th, 95th and 5th, make progress in the Koenigsmacker area, in the Uckange and Malling bridgeheads and south of Metz towards the north-east. At the same time the two divisions of the XII Corps, the 6th Armoured and the 80th, advance rapidly on the northern flank despite the mud, the mines, and the traffic congestion on the centre-lines of the attack. Units of the 6th Armoured Division, together with the 5th Division (XX Corps), advance through Vigny and Buchy, and the 80th Division moves forward about 6 miles. On the right flank of the XII Corps, while the 137th Regi-

An American sentry looks out over anti-tank obstacles erected by the Germans along the Siegfried Line.

ment of the 35th Division reaches Viviers after hard fighting and pushes on past Laneuveville-en-Saulnois, the 320th and 134th Regiments advance into the forest of Château-Salins and to Gerbécourt.

Philippines: Leyte Troops of the US X Corps advance into the central mountains, where the Japanese are dug in. Near Carigara the 24th Division mounts a frontal attack on a series of hills called Breakneck Ridge, defended resolutely by the Japanese. Some units of the same division carry out an amphibious operation, embarking near Carigara and landing 7 miles to the west; from there they thrust inland to a ridge near the village of Belen. In the XXIX Corps sector, the 382nd Infantry completes the liquidation of the last Japanese nests of resistance on Bloody Ridge.

Burma In the Pinwe area, along the Myitkyina–Mandalay railway, the British 36th Division reaches one of the Japanese defensive lines. Further east, the Chinese 38th Division outflanks the Japanese positions along the river Taping in the area of Bhamo (on the Irrawaddy, south of Myitkyina), penetrating into the Bhamo plain.

China The Japanese expeditionary force captures Kweilin and Liuchow without difficulty, depriving the US 14th Air Force of these two bases, and prepares to march on Kweiyang, a major town and road junction south of Chunking.

11 November

Western Europe In readiness for the offensive by the US 9th Army in the Rur valley, north-east of Aachen, the units of the British 2nd Army take up their positions in the southern sector allocated to them.

In the US 3rd Army sector, the offensive by units of XX Corps continues (some units of the 95th Division succeed in establishing a bridgehead over the Moselle near Thionville, and begin the assault on Fort Yutz), and the 6th Armoured Division, with support from the 80th Division (XII Corps) establishes bridgeheads over the river Nied. The 35th Division continues to advance through the forest of Château-Salins. Units of the 4th Armoured Division and the 26th Division push on in the direction of the right flank of the XII Corps, the first towards the area between Conthil and Rodalbe, the second reaching

Rodalbe itself.

The headquarters of the I Corps of the French 1st Army asks for, and obtains, permission to defer the start of Operation *Independence* from 13 November to the following day, as they have still to complete their plan of attack.

Pacific A squadron of US cruisers and destroyers commanded by Rear-Admiral A. E. Smith shells Japanese airfields and coastal installations on the island of Iwo Jima. The bombardment commences at midnight and goes on during the next day, when land-based aircraft also take part. Off Ormoc (Leyte Island), aircraft from three squadrons of carriers commanded by Rear-Admiral Sherman attack the convoy that managed to land reinforcements for the defenders of Leyte on 9 November, sinking the destroyers *Hamanami*, *Naganami*, *Shimakaze* and *Wakatsuki* and a minesweeper.

Burma The British 36th Division is forced to halt after an unsuccessful attempt to outflank the Japanese positions in the important Pinwe area.

China Aircraft of the US 14th Air Force attack Hengyang airfield, captured by the Japanese, so effectively that it is made unusable for the Japanese bombers.

12 November

Western Europe The bridge at Malling, on the Moselle, is destroyed in the course of a counter-attack by units of the German 1st Army. Engaged by the American 90th Division (XX Corps), the Germans are driven back with heavy losses. The 358th Regiment of the same division reaches a line Elzange–Valmestroff, taking those two villages. The building is begun of a bridge over the Moselle at Cattenom.

In the US XII Corps sector, German attempts to hold up the 80th Division in the triangle between the river Nied and a stream called the Rotte collapse when units of the US 6th Armoured Division outflank the enemy to the south and the Rotte is crossed at three points.

Italian Front The Polish II Corps,

The German battleship *Tirpitz* is tracked down and photographed by a British reconnaissance aircraft in a Norwegian fjord north of Trondheim. She is sunk in Tromsö Fjord by RAF bombers on 12 November.

working closely with the British V Corps (8th Army), attacks on the line Castrocarc–Converselle–Santa Lucia, south of Faenza.

Eastern Front In Yugoslavia, troops of the Bulgarian 1st Army capture Kumanovo, on the railway between Skopje and Nish.

☐ Norway. In Tromsö Fjord, in the Arctic, 29 Lancaster bombers of the RAF sink the battleship *Tirpitz*, 42,900 tons, the twin ship of the more famous *Bismarck* sunk on 27 May 1941.

Philippines: Leyte In the X Corps sector, the 21st Infantry of the 24th Division captures the summit of Breakneck Ridge, but fails to push on further south along the road to Ormoc because of stubborn resistance by the enemy.

13 November

Western Europe In the US XX Corps (3rd Army) sector, the bridge over the Moselle at Cattenom is completed and in full use by the 90th Division. On the southern flank of the corps, the 5th Division advances towards Metz from the north.

South-east of Metz, where forces of the US XII Corps are engaged, units of the 6th Armoured Division,

assisted by the 317th Regiment of the 80th Division, advance towards Falquemont, while still further south elements of the 4th Armoured Division, suppported by the 35th Division, make for Morhange, an important road junction.

In the 7th Army sector, the XV Corps opens its offensive north-eastwards towards Sarrebourg with two divisions, the 44th and 79th, one on the left of the advance and the other on the right, with cover on the north flank by the 106th Cavalry Regiment. Faced with the advance by the VI Corps, the Germans prepare to withdraw from St Dié.

Italian Front On the left of the Allied line (US 5th Army), units of the 8th Indian Division (British XII Corps) capture Monte San Bartolo, and on the right (British 8th Army) units of the 46th Division take Varano.

Eastern Front In Yugoslavia, the German garrison evacuates Skopje.

Greece The Greek armed forces are put under the British High Command.

Philippines: Leyte The 21st Infantry, US 24th Division, makes some small headway in the Breakneck Ridge area.

Aircraft from three squadrons of aircraft carriers commanded by Rear-Admiral Sherman begin a series of attacks lasting two days against enemy shipping and installations in the area of Manila and the central strip of Luzon Island. This operation costs the Japanese the light cruiser *Kiso* and the destroyers *Akebono, Akishimo, Hatsuharu* and *Okinami* and an auxiliary vessel.

Burma In the British XXXIII Corps sector, the 5th Indian Division and 11th East African Division make contact with each other at Kalemyo (east of Tiddim and south of Kennedy Peak).

14 November

Western Europe In the British 2nd Army sector, the XII Corps opens the offensive to reduce the German bridgehead west of the Maas between Venlo and Roermond.

On the right of the Allied line, where the US 3rd Army is operating, units of the 90th Division (XX Corps) enter Oudrenne and Distroff, east of Thionville. East of the Moselle, in the same area, units of the 95th Division reach Haute-Yutz and open the assault on Fort d'Illange. In the XII Corps sector, the units of the 4th Armoured Division and 35th Division, advancing on Morhange, capture Destry and Baronville.

On the south of the Allied front the I Corps of the French 1st Army begins the offensive towards Belfort, attacking with the 2nd Moroccan Division supported on the left by the 5th Armoured Division and on the right by the 9th Colonial Division.

Norway The Norwegian government in exile announces that Norwegian units under the command of Colonel Arne Dahl have landed in Norway. They will operate against the Germans on the Arctic front, in conjunction with Russian troops of the Karelia Front. Since 29 October, the German 20th Mountain Army has been dug in on a line west of Kirkenes and west of Lake Inari.

Yugoslavia Bulgarian and Yugoslav troops occupy Skopje, evacuated by the Germans the previous day. The town was the main German strongpoint in Yugoslav Macedonia during the retreat from Greece.

Philippines: Leyte The US 32nd Division, previously under orders to occupy the southern part of Samar Island, next to Leyte, is now sent to relieve the 24th Division, exhausted by the hard fighting on Breakneck Ridge, still not wholly in American hands.

Burma The Chinese 22nd Division occupies Man-tha, blocks the road to Bhamo and advances towards Si-u. Two regiments of the Chinese 38th Division converge on Bhamo; the one meets stiff resistance from the Japanese in the Momauk area, about 7 miles from Bhamo, the other crosses the river Taping and advances east towards Bhamo.

15 November

Western Europe Troops of the 95th Division (XX Corps, US 3rd Army), on the east of the Moselle, are assigned to Colonel Bacon's task force moving south in the direction of Metz.

Further north the 5th Division reinforces its positions and prepares for the final attack against Metz.

In the US II Corps sector units of the 4th Armoured Division reach the Metz–Sarrebourg railway at the same time as the 35th Division, which has arrived by way of Morhange (abandoned by the Germans). In the US 7th Army sector, the 44th Division (XV Corps) advances towards Avricourt and the 79th Division reaches Halloville. The 100th Division (VI Corps) penetrates into the enemy's positions in the region north of Raon-l'Etape, some 6 miles north-west of St Dié, against which the 103rd Division is preparing to advance from the south-west. The French 1st Army under General de Tassigny continues to advance towards Belfort.

Italian Front Patrols from the 8th Indian Division (XIII Corps, US 5th Army) enter Modigliana, where they make contact with units of the Polish II Corps (British 8th Army).

☐ A general strike paralyses the city of Turin, taking the German occupying forces by surprise.

Eastern Front In Hungary, the Russians capture Jaszberény, east of Budapest.

Pacific: Mapia Islands The US 31st Division, 8th Army, supported by gunfire from a British and American squadron commanded by Admiral Lord Ashbourne, lands in the Mapia Islands, 160 sea-miles north-east of the western tip of New Guinea. The occupation goes ahead quickly, since there is little resistance from a tiny Japanese garrison long since isolated.

Burma The Chinese 38th Division blocks all the access roads to Bhamo. The Chinese 22nd Division, its manpower increased by the attachment of the US 475th Infantry, advances on Si-u.

In the western sector, where the British XXXIII Corps is operating, the 5th Indian Division occupies Kalemyo, evacuated by the Japanese.

16 November

Western Europe The US 9th and 1st Armies launch a co-ordinated offensive to seize the flat country north of Aachen, between the rivers Wurm and Rur (Operation *Queen*). Units of the XIX Corps (9th Army) advance north of Aachen towards the Rur, with the 2nd Armoured Division on the left making for Jülich, the 29th Division in the centre moving on Aldenhoven and the 30th Division on the right in the Würselen sector. The divisions of the VII Corps, US 1st Army (the 104th, 3rd Armoured and 4th), move towards Düren (and Cologne), east of Aachen.

In the US 3rd Army sector all the divisions of the XX and XII Corps continue to advance. Units of the 6th Armoured Division and two regiments of the 80th Division (XII Corps) launch an offensive against Faulquemont, overrunning units of the German 1st Army and taking 1,200 prisoners.

Philippines: Leyte Fighting continues in the Breakneck Ridge area. The US 24th Division advances from Jaro, in the east of the island, towards Ormoc on the west coast.

Burma The British 36th Division is still held up by the firm resistance of the Japanese in the Pinwe area.

17 November

Western Europe Operation *Queen* continues. In the southern sector of the XIX Corps, the 30th Division reaches Würselen, 6 miles north of Aachen.

In the southern sector of the front the offensive by General Patton's 3rd Army is developing: the 10th Division (XX Corps) fans out to pursue the Germans across the Saar while the 95th and 5th Divisions continue to advance towards Metz. The units of the XII Corps prepare for the final assault towards the Saar. During the night the Germans begin a general withdrawal.

South-east of Lunéville, the 100th Division (XV Corps, 6th Army) prepares to attack Raon from the north, while during the night patrols from the 103rd Division penetrate into St Dié. The divisions of the French 1st Army, advancing on Belfort, reach Héricourt, Montbéliard and Hérimoncourt.

China The Japanese begin to advance from the area of Kweilin and Liuchow towards Kweiyang. If they can conquer Kweiyang, the road will be open to Kunming, the Chinese 'terminus' of the Burma Road, and to the Nationalist capital, Chungking.

An American submarine sinks the Japanese escort carrier *Jinyo* in the Yellow Sea.

18 November

Western Europe The two divisions of the XXX Corps, British 2nd Army, the 43rd and 84th, launch an offensive for the capture of the Geilenkirchen salient (Operation *Clipper*). In the course of Operation *Queen* the US 2nd Armoured Division (XIX Corps, 9th Army) reaches Apweiler, and the 29th Division reaches Setterich; some units of the latter division penetrate into the outer defences of Jülich.

In the US 1st Army sector, the 4th Division (VII Corps) advances in the forest of Hürtgen, where the 8th Infantry Regiment penetrates into the outer defences of Düren.

In the US 3rd Army sector the 10th Armoured Division, continuing its pursuit of the units of the German 1st Army, captures Launstroff and Schwerdorff and reaches the river Nied near Bouzonville, only a little way from the Franco-German frontier. Task Force 'Bacon' (95th Division) enters Metz from the north-east and the 5th Division from the south. Two divisions of the XII Corps, the 35th and 26th, resume the advance on the Saar after an intensive bombardment; the first reaches Bistroff and the enemy positions east of Vallerange, the other, operating on the right flank, launches an assault on the line from Dieuze to Bénestroff.

In the southern sector of the Allied front the 79th Division (XV Corps, US 7th Army) begins the attack on Fremonville; in the VI Corps sector, the 100th Division attacks Raonl'Etape, about 10 miles north-west of St Dié. The 5th Armoured Division and 2nd Moroccan Division (I Corps, French 1st Army) approach Belfort from the corps' north flank. The French 1st Division, with support from the 9th Colonial Division, advances about 6 miles beyond Belfort between the Rhine Canal and the small town of Delle, on the Swiss border.

Italian Front Headquarters of the British 8th Army fixes 8.00 p.m. as H-hour for the joint attack by the British V Corps and Polish II Corps against Faenza.

Eastern Front The Leningrad Front resumes the offensive against the German forces tenaciously defending the southern point of Saaremaa Island, in the Gulf of Riga. The possession of this tongue of land is important to the Wehrmacht, which has to consider the evacuation of the Army Group North, trapped in Northern Latvia, east of Riga.

Philippines: Leyte In the US X Corps sector there is bitter fighting in the areas of the hills called Kilay and Corkscrew, where the resistance of the Japanese 30th Division is intense.

19 November

Western Europe In the British 2nd Army sector the 84th Division (XXX Corps) continues clearing the Plummern area of the remaining enemy forces. The 51st Division (XII Corps) captures Helden and Panningen and makes contact with the 15th Division (VIII Corps).

Units of the 2nd Armoured Division (US XIX Corps, 9th Army) repel the determined counter-attacks of the German 7th Army under Brandenberger in the direction of Apweiler. Metz is completely surrounded by divisions of the US XX Corps (US 3rd Army). In the XII Corps sector, the 6th Armoured Division reaches Bertring and Gros-Tenquin. The 26th Division throws in all its forces against the line from Dieuze to Bénestroff, meeting stiff opposition from units of the German 1st Army which is giving cover to the general withdrawal.

In the Blamont–Cirey sector the German defensive line along the Vezouse yields and while the 79th Division finishes off the capture of Fremonville, the French 2nd Armoured Division reaches Cirey, some 16 miles east of Lunéville. General Leclerc's French armour breaks through the German line near Saverne and converges on Strasbourg. The VI Corps nears the river Meurthe and prepares to cross over to the east bank; the 100th Division, already east of the river, is still advancing towards the area of Raon. In the south, where the French 1st Army is operating, the 2nd Moroccan Division and 5th Armoured Division (French I Corps) reach the suburbs of Belfort. At 6.30 p.m. a French detachment reaches the Rhine at Rosenau, near Basel. The villages in the area bordering Switzerland are quickly liberated.

Pacific: Asia Islands Units of the US 8th Army land in the Asia Islands, east of the Mapias (north of New Guinea).

Philippines Aircraft from a task force of fast aircraft carriers commanded by Vice-Admiral McCain attack Japanese ships in the Luzon area and the airfields on the island,

Western Front: French soldiers reach the Rhine and bathe their flag in the river.

destroying many aircraft on the ground.

Leyte Fighting continues. The Americans are forced to give a little ground on Kilay Ridge under extremely heavy fire by the Japanese.

Burma The 19th Indian Division (British IV Corps) begins to cross the Chindwin at Sittaung.

20 November

Western Europe The XII Corps, British 2nd Army, pushes on towards the Maas with the 49th and 51st Divisions.

In the US 9th Army sector, the 29th Division, XIX Corps, launches two attacks against Aldenhoven, about 3 miles south-west of Jülich and capture it. In the streets of Metz the 95th and 5th Divisions (XX Corps, US 3rd Army) continue the battle with the German rearguards. The town is the biggest objective reached by General Patton's forces. The commander of the sector, General Kittel, is killed in action after the staff of the German 1st Army has withdrawn the best units from the Metz trap. The 80th Division (XII Corps) reaches the Nied at Falquemont and establishes a bridgehead on the north bank of the river.

In the US 7th Army sector, the 3rd Division VI Corps crosses the Meurthe in the area of Clairefontaine–St-Michel, capturing a large bridgehead taking in the villages of La Paire, Hurbache and La Voivre. The 100th Division opens an offensive eastwards from the Raon-l'Etape area. During the night the 103rd Division crosses the Meurthe in the 3rd Division's area and advances towards St Dié.

The 2nd Moroccan Division and units of the 5th Armoured Division (French 1st Army) enter Belfort, where fighting continues for several days. The divisions of the II Corps, the 3rd Algerian and the 1st, also advance. Some units of the French 1st Armoured Division reach the suburbs of Mulhouse.

Italian Front The 46th Division of the V Corps (British 8th Army) takes Castiglione.

Albania The Germans evacuate Tirana.

Philippines: Leyte The American thrust towards Ormoc is solidly contained by the Japanese.

Burma–China On the Salween front, troops of the Chinese 11th Army Group take Manshih, where the airfield is immediately reactivated.

21 November

Western Europe The 49th and 51st Divisions, two formations of the XII Corps (British 2nd Army) advance swiftly towards Venlo. The American 84th Division (XXX Corps) fails in its attempt to capture the villages of Müllendorf, Wurm and Beeck. In the US 9th Army sector the XIX Corps starts the final phase of the attack on the river Rur.

Units of the 10th Armoured Division (XX Corps, US 3rd Army) open an offensive towards Saarbourg with task forces 'Standish' and 'Chamberlain', on the left and right flanks respectively. Their thrust is halted by the Germans on the Orscholz defensive line.

In the XII Corps sector, the 80th Division widens its bridgehead over the Nied, making contact with units of the XX Corps. The 104th Regiment of the 26th Division takes Albestroff, an important road junction. US 7th Army command orders the XV and VI Corps to attack and capture Strasbourg (originally an objective only of the VI Corps), since the latter's advance is too slow.

Italian Front The Polish 3rd (*Carpathian*) Division (Polish II Corps, 8th Army) opens up an offensive south of Faenza, taking Monte Fortino and pushing on to the north.

Philippines: Leyte While the troops of the US X Corps are held up in the Ormoc Valley, where they are advancing from the north-east, the 7th Infantry, XXIV Corps, begins a slow advance from Baybay, on the south-west coast, towards Ormoc.

Pacific North-west of Formosa, the US submarine *Sealion* sinks the Japanese battleship *Kongo* and the destroyer *Urakaze*.

US cruisers and destroyers shell the air base of the Japanese navy in Matsuwa Island, in the Kurils.

China General Wedemeyer suggests to Chiang Kai-shek that he should concentrate the Chinese forces in the south-west of the area of Kunming, capital of Yunnan, to confront the Japanese threat to the Generalissimo's capital.

22 November

Western Europe Sevenum and Horst, north-west of Venlo, are occupied by the 15th Division, VIII Corps (British 2nd Army).

In the US 3rd Army sector the headquarters of the XX Corps orders an attack on a huge scale towards the river Saar by all three divisions, the 10th Armoured on the left, the 90th in the centre and the 95th on the right.

There is a new plan of attack for the 35th and 26th Divisions of XII Corps along the Maderbach: units of the 35th Division reach Leyviller and St Jean-Rohrbach, with support from the 6th Armoured Division, while the 104th Regiment of the 26th Division tries to surround Alberstroff. The German 1st Army withdraws its units from the town during the night.

In the southern sector of the front, where the US 7th Army is operating, units of the 2nd Armoured Division, advancing from Bouxwiller in the north and Birkenwald in the south, converge on Saverne.

Meanwhile the 100th Division reaches Senones and heads for St Blaise. The 3rd Division accelerates its advance towards enemy positions near St Blaise and Saales and units

Italian Front, November 1944: Polish engineers prepare an explosive charge, while in the foreground a soldier bandages the hand of a wounded comrade.

of this division take St Dié without opposition.

In the French 1st Army sector, the 1st Division, II Corps takes Giromagny, opening a gap in the enemy line along the course of the Savoreuse. The I Corps re-takes the ground lost following the counter-offensive by the forces of Wiese's German 19th Army, and enters Mulhouse, north-east of Belfort, only a little way from the frontier between France and Germany.

Eastern Front In the extreme north, Finnish troops (now, in accordance with the terms of the armistice, fighting the Germans) pursue the enemy and reach the Norwegian border.

In Hungary the Germans take over full powers in Budapest. The Russians have already reached the Danube south of the city.

Philippines: Leyte In the US X Corps sector, the 128th Infantry of the 32nd Division finally wipes out Breakneck Ridge and captures Limon, west of Carigara, not far from the north coast of the island. The small Japanese pockets left behind are liquidated by the middle of December. One battalion of the 34th Infantry, fiercely attacked by the Japanese on Kilay Ridge, has to rectify its line to avoid being surrounded. The Americans are getting

ready to move south towards Ormoc.

23 November

Western Europe General Student (commanding Army Group H on the right of the German front) withdraws General Zangen's 15th Army towards central Holland in view of the rapid Allied advance.

The advance of the XIX Corps (9th Army) towards Merzenhausen (2nd Armoured Division) and Bournheim (29th Division) provokes instant reaction by the divisions of the German 7th Army, whose counter-attack continues for three days.

In the US 3rd Army sector, both the 90th Division (XX Corps) and the 6th Armoured Division (XII Corps) are preparing to advance against the Saar.

The armour of the French 2nd Division (XV Corps, US 7th Army) enters Strasbourg. The 3rd Division of the VI Corps reaches Saulxures and Saales and, supported by the 100th Division, attacks St Blaise.

Eastern Front In Hungary the railway centre of Csap is finally captured by the Russians after several weeks of exceptionally bitter fighting. In the northern sector, the forces of the Leningrad Front crush the last German resistance on Saaremaa Island, so gaining control of the access to the Gulf of Riga.

Philippines: Leyte The Americans consolidate their positions south of Limon.

24 November

Western Europe In the US 3rd Army sector, units of the 90th Division (XX Corps) continue their assault on the Orscholz line, while further south units of the 35th Division (XII Corps), supported by tanks and by an intensive air bombardment, capture Hilsprich. Units of the 4th Armoured Division cross the river Saar in the XV Corps sector near Romelfing and Gosselming and then turn north-east. The I and II Corps, French 1st Army, are ordered to converge on Burnhaupt as quickly as possible to force the German troops in the region to withdraw into Alsace.

Philippines: Leyte In the north, in the US X Corps sector, a Japanese counter-attack on Kilay Ridge is repulsed. The Japanese also mount night counter-attacks in the east and south, in the XXIV Corps sector, notably south of Ormoc.

China In south China the Japanese take Nanning. From there it will be easy for them to link up with their forces manning French Indo-China.

☐ **Japan.** 111 B-29 Superfortresses from bases in the Marianas raid Tokyo, the start of a long series of raids.

25 November

Eastern Front The Germans and Hungarians repel Russian attempts to take Csepel Island (an island between two branches of the Danube just south of Budapest).

Philippines: Leyte In the US X Corps sector north of Ormoc, the Japanese renew their counter-attacks on Kilay Ridge. They also counter-attack east of Ormoc, in the central mountains, in the US XXIV Corps sector. The American troops contain their thrust. The US 511th Parachute Regiment starts on a difficult mountain march west from Burauen, towards Ormoc; their immediate objective is Mahonag, 10 miles from Burauen.

Luzon Two squadrons of US aircraft carriers commanded by Rear-Admirals Bogan and Sherman attack airfields in the centre of Luzon and enemy ships in the waters round the island, sinking the cruisers *Kumano* and *Yasoshima*.

After the naval defeat suffered in the Gulf of Leyte, it seems that the task of completing Operation *Sho-go* has been taken over by the Japanese air force in the absence of the navy. Every aircraft still available is sent against the Americans; many of them are flown by *kamikaze* in day-time attacks on the US ships off Luzon. Damage is caused to the aircraft carriers *Essex*, *Intrepid* and *Hancock* and the light carrier *Cabot*. Another light carrier, the *Independence*, is damaged when an American aircraft explodes as it is coming in to land.

The liberation of Strasbourg: an American tank advances through the crowd as part of a celebratory parade.

Burma General Kimura, commander of the Japanese armed forces in Burma, orders the units that have been pinning down the British 36th Division in the Pinwe area, along the Myitkyina–Mandalay railway, to withdraw towards central Burma.

26 November

Western Europe Port of Antwerp is opened. Germans begin attacks on the port with V1 and V2 rockets.

In the US 1st Army sector the 104th Division (VII Corps) passes through Weiseweiler, about 6 miles north of Aachen, and takes Frenz. The 4th Division consolidates its positions in the Hürtgen forest.

In the southern sector (US 3rd Army) the units of the XX Corps continue to advance north-east; on the right flank the 95th Division penetrates into the Maginot Line.

The 3rd Division of the American VI Corps (7th Army) crosses the Vosges and emerges into the flat country in Alsace.

Italian Front Persistent rain seriously delays operations in the Lamone sector.

Eastern Front Troops of the 2nd Ukraine Front take Hatvan, in Hungary, north-east of the capital. Budapest is already threatened from the south.

☐ Agreement reached with Tito that the Royal Navy and the RAF should have temporary use of certain Yugoslav ports and airfields.

Philippines: Leyte The Japanese launch violent night attacks on various sectors of the front, contained by the Americans largely by the employment of artillery. Over 400 Japanese bodies are counted next morning on a ridge west of Burauen, where the Japanese 26th Division is deployed.

27 November

Western Europe Units of the 2nd Armoured Division (XIX Corps, 9th Army) complete mopping up in the Merzenhausen sector, while the 29th Division completes the same operation towards the river Rur.

Mopping up operations also in the Weiseweiler–Frenz area, which the 104th Division of the VII Corps (US 1st Army) reached the previous day. In the US 3rd Army sector, the 10th Armoured Division breaks off its

Russian soldiers on the outskirts of Budapest firing with their 'parabellum' from cover behind a wooden fence.

action in the direction of Saarburg, in order to dislodge the German forces that had filtered into Tettingen. The 90th Division halts in the vicinity of the Saar and gets ready for the assault to force the passage of the river. The 95th Division makes rapid progress and patrols from the 377th Regiment come within a mile or two of the German frontier. The 80th Division, XII Corps, enters St Avold on the Metz–Saarbrücken road.

General Eisenhower orders General Patch's US 7th Army to turn north to support Patton's 3rd Army in the capture of the Saar basin. While the 100th Division (XV Corps) arrives in the Saarburg sector, the 3rd Division (VI Corps) replaces the French 2nd Armoured Division at Strasbourg.

Pacific: Palau Islands After months of warfare and guerrilla war, hostilities finally end on Peleliu. Some 13,600 Japanese have lost their lives defending the islands – Peleliu, Anguar and the surrounding islets. The Americans of the 81st Infantry Division and the 1st Marines have lost 1,792 killed and over 8,000 wounded.

Philippines: Leyte The Americans counter-attack all along the line. The Japanese are also preparing a powerful offensive with the object of recapturing the airfield in the area of Burauen, in the centre of the island. Japanese suicide aircraft attack American naval forces in the Gulf of Leyte, damaging the battleship *Colorado* and the light cruisers *St Louis* and *Montpelier*.

28 November

Western Europe While the advance of the VII and V Corps (US 1st Army) continues in the Inden river and Hürtgen forest sectors, units of the 95th Division (3rd Army) cross the German frontier. The 101st Division, XII Corps, is despatched to Burbach to reinforce the 4th Armoured Division east of the river Saar, about to advance towards the Saar–Union sector.

The French 2nd Armoured Division (VI Corps, US 7th Army) reaches the Erstein sector, about 10 miles south-west of Strasbourg, where the stubborn resistance of the German 19th Army brings it to a halt.

Italian Front The British XIII Corps, US 5th Army, reaches Casola Valsenio.

In the British 8th Army sector, bad weather hinders the operations of the V Corps. The Canadian I Corps prepares to attack along the Adriatic coast.

Pacific Vice-Admiral Kinkaid issues the operational plan for the landing on Mindoro, the island in the Philippines south of Luzon. Rear-Admiral Struble will be in charge of the amphibious part of the operations.

Philippines: Leyte At night the Japanese attack in force to recapture Kilay Ridge, in the US X Corps sector. They succeed in taking some ground and in cutting off some American units. The US 12th Cavalry Regiment advances very slowly in the area of Mount Badian, about 5 miles north-east of the town of Kananga. As expected, the Japanese also attack towards Buri and Bayug airfields, but are held by the troops of the US XXIV Corps.

China The Japanese 11th Army, acting on its own initiative and against orders, pushes northwards from

Nanning in the province of Kwangsi.
Burma The Chinese 38th Division
puts pressure on the northern
defences of the town of Bhamo but
is not able to breach them.

29 November

Western Europe The advance of the
XIII Corps of the US 9th Army in
the direction of the Rur begins in the
Lindern sector and, on the south
flank of the corps, along the Lindern–Linnich road, north-west of
Jülich. No change in the VII Corps
(US 1st Army) sector, with the 104th
Division engaged in the Inden–Lammersdorf sector and the 4th in the
Hürtgen forest area.
In the US 3rd Army sector the 90th
and 95th Divisions (XX Corps)
launch a joint offensive against the
river Saar. But while some patrols
from the 90th Division succeed in
reaching the river, the 95th Division
runs into fierce resistance in the
hills in front of Saarlautern. The
French 2nd Division (VI Corps, US
7th Army) takes Erstein, 10 miles
south-west of Strasbourg.
Italian Front While the XIII Corps
(US 5th Army) reaches Fontanelice,
in the eastern sector of the front
(British 8th Army) the 7th Armoured
Division leaves Recanati to join the
V Corps in readiness for the coming offensive.
Eastern Front In Hungary, the 2nd
and 3rd Ukraine Fronts, supported
by Yugoslav units, advance south-
west of Budapest, north of the
Drava, driving the Germans and
Hungarians out of Pécs. Mohacs is
also taken.
In Albania the Germans evacuate
Scutari. The troops moved from this
area are eventually (December 18)
able to link up with the German
Army Group E (Löhr), which is
fighting to hold open a withdrawal
route.
Following the evacuation from
Albania and Serbia, and later Bosnia
and Herzegovina, the Germans dig
in on a line from Mostar to Višegrad
to the river Drina. As the Russians
penetrate into Hungary, this line has
to be extended along the Drava.
After a retreat lasting four and a half

months, during which the Army
Group covers 1,000 miles without
suffering catastrophic losses despite
the fierce battles fought with the partisans, the southern front is again
stabilized, albeit temporarily, on 13
January 1945.
Pacific Japanese aircraft flown by
kamikaze again attack American
shipping in the Gulf of Leyte, seriously damaging the battleship *Maryland* and two destroyers. Against
this, the US submarine *Archerfish*
sinks the Japanese aircraft carrier
Shinano south of the Japanese island
of Honshu.
Philippines: Leyte Japanese attacks
continue on Kilay Ridge, but the
Americans repulse them and free the
units cut off the previous day.

30 November

Western Europe In the south-east
Netherlands, the VIII and XII Corps
of the British 2nd Army have almost
wiped out the bridgehead of German
parachutists on the west bank of the
Maas, reducing it to a little pocket
near Blerick.
The US XIII Corps (9th Army) continues to advance in the Linnich sector and the VII Corps (1st Army) in
the area of Lammersdorf and Inden.
In the US 3rd Army sector, the 10th
Armoured Division (XX Corps)
attacks towards the Saar on the
north flank, and the 90th and 95th
Divisions continue the battle for the
Saar. The situation of the XII Corps
is unchanged except on the right
flank, where the 4th Armoured
Division captures the hills dominating Mackwiller in the Saar-Union
sector.
Eastern Front The armies of the 2nd
Ukraine Front, with help from the
Rumanian 4th Army, capture Eger,
north-east of Budapest, and push on
towards Miskolc.
Philippines: Leyte The Americans,
now on the defensive, confine themselves to holding the continual
Japanese counter-attacks.
Burma The British 36th Division
occupies Pinwe, which the Japanese
have already evacuated.
China Chiang Kai-shek decides to
withdraw the Chinese 22nd Division

from Burma and attach it to the 14th
Division to strengthen the defences
of Kunming, threatened by the
Japanese. He promises to despatch a
further 270,000 men by 1 April 1945
for a counter-offensive in southern
China, but refuses to provide the
Communist army with arms.

1 December

Western Europe Linnich, about
three miles north-west of Jülich, is
captured by the units of the 102nd
Division (US 9th Army).
The US VII Corps (1st Army) is in
difficulties in the Hürtgen forest
area.
The XX Corps (US 3rd Army) continues to advance west of the Saar in
readiness for the crossing of the river.
The 90th Division is engaged in the
sector south of Merzig, the 95th in
the direction of Saarlautern and the
5th, brought up from Metz, is preparing an attack in the Warndt
salient.
In Alsace, while the 79th Division
(XV Corps, US 7th Army) liberates
Schweigenhause, a few miles west of
Haguenau, the 44th and 45th
Divisions further north are engaged
in severe fighting with General
Wiese's German 19th Army near
Tieffenbach and Zinswiller.
Italian Front The British 8th Army
continues its preparations for the
attack fixed for 4 December.
Eastern Front In eastern Czechoslovakia, troops of the 4th Ukraine
Front force the crossing of the river
Ondava near Humenné and Trebi-
šov.
In Hungary, the Germans contain
the attacks of the 2nd Ukraine Front,
but the 3rd Ukraine Front, deployed
south-west of Budapest, makes
further progress north and north-
east of Pécs.
Philippines: Leyte The offensive
capacity of the Japanese is already
severely limited by the lack of
supplies and ammunition. However,
there is still hard fighting on Kilay
Ridge and on a line of hills south-east
of Limon, west of Carigara.
China–Burma On the Salween front,
the Chinese take Chefang.

A group of German infantry in positions near the Hungarian border.

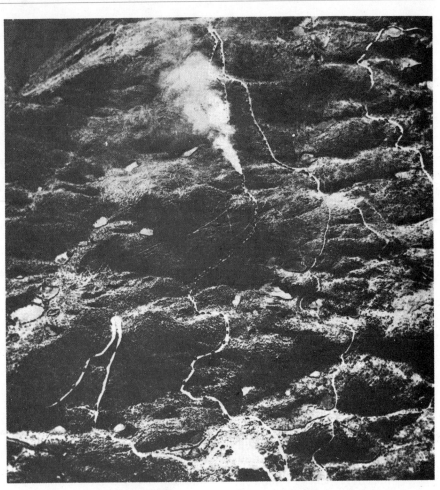

Yugoslavia, December 1944: aerial view of a German mechanized column under attack from Allied aircraft in the mountains near Bioce.

Italian Front, December 1944: a 40-mm gun in position on the US 5th Army front.

2 December

Western Europe The Germans blow up a dyke on the lower Rhine near Arnhem, flooding the region south-west of Arnhem and forcing the Canadian II Corps (1st Army) to withdraw from their bridgeheads over the Waal.

With the fall of Dreisbach, General Patton's US 3rd Army has completed the capture of its sector west of the Saar; during the night, in the XX Corps sector, the 90th Division crosses the river in the area of Dillingen and the 95th opposite Saarlautern, where there is bitter house-to-house fighting, and the 5th Division crosses the western border of the Houve forest. The XII Corps crosses the Saar near Saar-Union. General Devers, Commander of the 6th Army Group, orders the US 7th Army to concentrate and re-group by 5 December, the date for which an important attack to the north is planned. The Colmar sector is entrusted to the only French troops in the 1st Army, joined by the French 2nd Armoured Division, detached from the US 7th Army. The 44th and 45th Divisions (XV Corps, US 7th Army) capture Waldhambach, Engwiller and Meitesheim.

The French 1st Army is reinforced by the US 76th Division; its commander, General De Lattre de Tassigny, orders his troops to converge on the Colmar pocket from north and south simultaneously, to reach the Rhine in the area of Neuf-Brisach, about 6 miles south-east of Colmar.

Eastern Front In Czechoslovakia, the 4th Ukraine Front extends its bridgehead over the Ondava.

In Hungary, the 2nd Ukraine Front attacks the strong enemy fortifications in the Miskolc area, while the 3rd Ukraine Front and formations of partisans force the Germans back on a broad front between the Danube and the Drava, south of Lake Balaton.

Philippines: Leyte Little activity on the ground. Groups of American destroyers shell the Japanese positions at Palompon, on the west coast of Leyte, and in Ormoc Bay. Four destroyers which entered Ormoc Bay by night are engaged by Japanese aircraft, destroyers and coast defence batteries. One American destroyer is sunk and two are damaged, and one Japanese destroyer is sunk.

Burma In the British XXXIII Corps sector, the 11th East African Division reaches the river Chindwin at Kalewa.

China A Japanese column advancing on Kweiyang reaches and occupies Tu-shan.

The Americans suggest to Chiang Kai-shek that he should arm three Communist regiments in Shen-si province, the first region to be administered by the Communists. The three regiments would be employed in Nationalist territory under American officers. The Generalissimo refuses.

3 December

Western Europe In the British 2nd Army sector, with the capture of Blerick (on the west bank of the Maas opposite Venlo) by the XII

Corps, the whole region west of the river has been cleared of Germans. The XIII Corps of the American 9th Army reaches the river Rur, while in the US 1st Army sector Task Force 'Hamberg' of the 5th Armoured Division reaches Brandenberg. Units of the 95th Division (XX Corps, US 3rd Army) capture a large part of the town of Saarlautern, while other elements of the Division head for the river Saar.

While the 44th Division (XV Corps, US 7th Army) is held up near Ratzwiller by fire from units of the German 19th Army, the 45th Division takes Zinswiller.

Italian Front The British 8th Army opens its offensive in the direction of Bologna with three corps, the Polish II Corps on the left, the V Corps in the centre making for Santerno along Highway 9, and the Canadian I Corps on the Adriatic coast.

Eastern Front In Hungary, forces of the 2nd Ukraine Front take Miskolc, north-east of Budapest, a key position in the German defensive line and an important industrial centre.

Greece The Communist guerrillas of ELAS rise in arms in Athens. On Churchill's orders, General Ronald Scobie crushes the revolt. Loyal to the agreement made with Churchill in Moscow on 18 October, Stalin withdraws all support from the Greek Communists.

Philippines: Leyte Fighting in the area south east of Limon, near the north coast.

Burma In the British XXXIII Corps sector, the 11th East African Division establishes a bridgehead over the Chindwin near Kalewa, and the 20th Indian Division also crosses the Chindwin in the area of Mawlaik.

China The Japanese 11th Army, short of reinforcements, breaks off its unauthorized advance towards Kweiyang, in Kweichow province, south of Chungking.

4 December

Western Front The XIII Corps (US 9th Army) breaks off its offensive after taking all its objectives west of the Rur except the villages of Wurm and Müllendorf.

In the American 1st Army sector

(VII Corps) the 104th Division reinforces its bridgehead over the river Inden. To take advantage of the capture of the bridge over the Saar at Saarlautern, north-west of Saarbrücken, the 95th Division of the XX Corps (US 3rd Army) quickly regroups and sends several units across the river, where they begin a hard struggle for the capture of the outskirts of Fraulautern, which forms part of the Siegfried Line (the West Wall).

The XII Corps opens the final assault on the Saar and the Siegfried Line with its four divisions, the 80th, 6th Armoured, 35th and 26th; the 104th Regiment of this latter division eliminates the last centres of resistance at Saar-Union.

Italian Front In the British 8th Army sector the Polish II Corps takes Montecchio, while units of the Canadian I Corps enter Ravenna.

Eastern Front Fighting continues north-east and south-west of Budapest. Mitrovica falls to the Russians.

Philippines The US 7th Air Force begins a series of night raids against Japanese airfields on the island of Luzon. On Leyte, in the US X Corps sector, the 112th Cavalry renews its attacks on Japanese positions southeast of Limon, but without success. Other units, from the 24th Division, withdraw from Kilay Ridge towards Pinamopoan. The XXIV Corps prepares for the offensive against Ormoc; the 7th Division will advance along the coast and the 77th will carry out an amphibious operation, landing in Ormoc Bay.

5 December

Western Front Units of the 95th Division (XX Corps, US 3rd Army) continue their attacks against Saarlautern and Fraulautern. On the southern flank of the attack, the 5th Division enters Lauterbach. Patrols from the 35th Division reach the Saar.

The US 7th Army opens a general attack northwards towards the Maginot Line and the Siegfried Line with two corps.

Eastern Front Units of the 3rd Ukraine Front operating in south-west Hungary, reach the south bank of Lake Balaton. Other units advancing along the Drava take Szigetvar. German headquarters announce that the Russians have crossed the Danube near Vukovar.

Philippines: Leyte The US 6th Army begins the offensive against Ormoc. The advance moves south, while in the north the Americans are still pinned down by the Japanese.

Japanese suicide aircraft seriously damage two US destroyers off Leyte. However, the Japanese are quite unable to break the American air and naval blockade round the island.

Burma The Japanese send a big contingent (3,000 men) to Bhamo to relieve the garrison, which has been besieged for some time. The Chinese 30th Division advances in the same area, moving south towards Namhkam, harassed by small Japanese detachments hidden in the hills.

6 December

Western Front Assault craft of the 90th Division (XX Corps, US 3rd Army) cross the Saar between Rehlingen and Wallerfangen and establish a small bridgehead in the area of Patchen–Dillingen.

The battalions of the 95th Division which have already crossed the Saar continue the battle for Saarlautern and Roden, Fraulautern and Ensdorf, on the Siegfried Line. On the corps' southern flank the 5th Division continues to advance across the river, accepting the surrender of the St Quentin forts.

Two divisions of the XII Corps, the 6th Armoured and the 35th Infantry reach the west bank of the Saar between Grosbliederstraff and Wittrin.

Eastern Front The Russian offensive against Hungary is intensified. Against the advancing Russians the Germans have deployed the Army Group South (Wöhler), supported on the right flank, in Yugoslavia, by Army Group F (von Weichs). The Army Group South, actually defending Hungarian soil, comprises the German 6th and 8th Armies, the Hungarian 3rd Army and the German 2nd Armoured Army (south of Lake Balaton), the Hungarian 9th Cavalry Army (north of Debrecen) and the Hungarian 1st Army.

Against these forces the Russians deploy, from north-east to south-west, the 4th Ukraine Front (Petrov), with three armies; the 2nd Ukraine Front (Malinovsky), with five armies plus a group of mechanized cavalry and the Rumanian 1st Army; the 3rd Ukraine Front (Tolbukhin), with three armies and a group of mechanized cavalry, plus the Bulgarian 1st Army and the Yugoslav 1st and 3rd Armies.

The German Army Group South, the direct descendant of the South Ukraine Army Group, has 550 aircraft, while the Russians have more than 2,000.

On this day the German High Command announces that the 2nd and 3rd Ukraine Fronts have attacked in force both east and west of Budapest, and that some of their units have succeeded in crossing from Csepel Island to the west bank of the Danube, south of Budapest. Rumanian forces are engaged with the Russians in the capture of northeast Hungary, while Bulgarians and Yugoslavs, with part of the 3rd Ukraine Front are mopping up the region between the Danube and the Sava, in northern Yugoslavia, driving back Army Group F (von Weichs) to the north-east. The Russians take the road and rail junction of Sid.

Philippines: Leyte In the north, the renewed efforts by the US 112th Cavalry to drive the Japanese from the line of hills south-east of Limon are still unsuccessful. In the south, the 7th Division pushes on towards Ormoc, taking Balogo and Kang Dakit. The 77th Division, protected by huge air and naval forces, sails for the landing in Ormoc Bay. The Japanese make a surprise attack on Buri airfield.

Burma The Japanese contingent sent to reinforce the troops besieged at Bhamo crosses the river Shweli and advances on Tonk-wa, where part of the Chinese 22nd Division is in position and towards which the US 475th Regiment is making its way.

7 December

Western Front The US 90th and 95th Divisions continue the battle to consolidate their positions, the first in the Patchen–Dillingen sector, the second in the Saarlautern bridgehead. The XII Corps re-groups in readiness for the attack on the Siegfried Line by the 35th and 26th Divisions, between Saarbrücken and Zweibrücken.

On the southern flank of the front, while the I Corps of the French 1st Army opens the attack on the Colmar pocket, the II Corps is engaged in holding the very strong counter-attacks of the German 19th Army in the Ostheim, Guemar and Mittelwihr sectors.

☐ In Britain, as from 9 December, premises need not be blacked out when alerts are sounded.

Eastern Front In Hungary, the 3rd Ukraine Front reaches the south bank of Lake Balaton. As part of the plan to free the area between the lake and the Danube, Adony, about 25 miles south of Budapest, is occupied and also Eyning, some 20 miles from Szekesfehervar. The Russian left wing, operating between Lake Balaton and the Drava, takes Barcs. Moscow announces that the Germans are drawing reinforcements from Italy and the Western Front to defend Budapest, which has become the southern pillar of their Eastern Front.

Yugoslav troops cross the Danube at various points near Vukovar in Slovenia. The German High Command announces that German troops are evacuating Montenegro and western Serbia in accordance with prearranged plans. Actually Montenegro was evacuated some time ago.

Philippines: Leyte Aircraft of the US 5th Air Force, together with army and Marines aircraft, attack a Japanese convoy of six transports and six escort vessels heading for Leyte with reinforcements and provisions. The pilots report that they have sunk all the enemy ships.

At 7.07 a.m., after an intensive preparation by naval gunfire, the US 77th Division (XXIV Corps, under General Hodges) begins the landing at Deposito, in Ormoc Bay. It is exactly three years since Pearl

Harbour. The Japanese put up very little resistance, and the landing force is able to penetrate into the interior very quickly. Some 50 Japanese aircraft carry out sixteen raids on the landing zone; 36 aircraft are brought down, but not before *kamikaze* have sunk one American destroyer and one fast transport, and damaged another destroyer, a fast transport and a tank landing craft.

Meanwhile the US 7th Division continues its advance on Ormoc from the south. Fighting goes on in the Buri airfield area.

8 December

Western Front Plans are prepared for an attack by the VII Corps (US 1st Army) in the region between the rivers Inde and Rur, and on the town of Düren, the final objective of the offensive.

In the sector of Dillingen and Saarlautern, the 90th and 95th Divisions have to face a heavy German counter-attack.

The XII Corps (with the 35th Division) also crosses the Saar.

Eastern Front In Hungary, the Russians widen the breach opened north of Budapest by the 2nd Ukraine Front. South of the city, advanced units of the 3rd Ukraine Front are only 10 miles from Szekesfehervar. The Germans repel enemy efforts to break through between Lake Balaton and the Drava.

Philippines: Leyte In the north, in the US X Corps sector, the Americans try to cut the Japanese supply lines beyond the hills south-east of Limon. In the XXIV Corps sector, a regiment of the 77th Division, with a battalion of tanks and a flame-thrower unit, comes within less than a mile of Ormoc. Japanese attacks on Buri airfield are repelled.

Pacific A squadron of US cruisers and destroyers under Rear-Admiral A. E. Smith, with B-24 and B-29 (Superfortress) bombers, carries out a heavy attack on airfields and coast defences in Iwo Jima Island.

Burma The Japanese contingent on its way to Bhamo takes Tonk-wa, defended by part of the Chinese 22nd Division. To the west, the British IV Corps prepares to advance to the

Irrawaddy in the area of Pakokku, with the intention of crossing to the east of the great river and advancing on Meiktila and Thazi.

China The Japanese of the 11th Army join up with units coming up from Indo-China.

9 December

Western Front In the US 3rd Army sector fighting continues round the bridgeheads at Dillingen (90th Division, XX Corps) and Saarlautern (95th Division). The US 7th Army continues its offensive, attempting to reach the Maginot Line and the Siegfried Line; on the left of its front units of the XV Corps take Singling (12th Armoured Division), Enchenberg (44th Division) and Lemberg (100th Division); on the right, the 45th Division reaches Niederbronn.

The II Corps of the French 1st Army overcomes strong German resistance to capture Mittelwihr.

Eastern Front Moscow announces that the 2nd Ukraine Front has reached the bend of the Danube north of Budapest, at Vac, and has made contact south of the city with the 3rd Ukraine Front on Lake Velencei, between the Danube and Lake Balaton. Budapest is thus two-thirds surrounded. The Bulgarian government announces that the Bulgarian and Yugoslav armies, with the support of the Russian air force, have completed the occupation of Serbia and Macedonia, expelling the last units of German Army Group E.

Philippines: Leyte The Japanese manage to land some reinforcements at Palompon, west of Ormoc. In the north, the Americans are still held up on the hills south-east of Limon. In the west, the 77th Division expands its beachhead near Ormoc. The Japanese carry out night counter-attacks against Buri airfield.

Burma Chinese attacks continue on Bhamo, which the Japanese defend with courage and tenacity.

China The Chinese 5th and 53rd Armies, which should have concentrated in defence of Kunming, have not yet carried out the necessary movements. General Wedemeyer protests to Chiang Kai-shek.

10 December

Western Front The VII Corps (US 1st Army) mounts a co-ordinated offensive to liberate the west bank of the river Rur and the town of Düren, using three divisions of infantry, the 9th, 83rd and 104th, and one armoured division, the 3rd.

A powerful German counter-offensive aims at destroying the Dillingen bridgehead, and is held only with great difficulty.

In the Saarlautern sector units of the 95th Division try to step up their attacks to get through to Fraulautern, but a surprise enemy counter-attack frustrates their efforts.

The 2nd Moroccan Division (I Corps, French 1st Army) completes the capture of Thann, and the 9th Colonial Division eliminates the last German bridgehead west of the Rhine between Kembs and the Swiss frontier.

☐ A treaty of alliance is signed between France and USSR.

Philippines: Leyte The US 77th Division, supported by naval gunfire, takes Ormoc. Japanese units attack Burauen airfield, temporarily forcing the garrison from the US 5th Air Force to withdraw. A counter-attack restores the position. In the waters off Leyte *kamikaze* sink an American destroyer and a motor torpedo-boat.

China General Wedemeyer asks Chiang Kai-shek to order the Yunnan Force to capture Wanting (north-east of the Shweli valley), where the new Burma Road coming from Ledo is to link up with the route of the old Burma Road. When Japanese forces in China link up with their garrisons in Indo-China, Japan reaches the highest point of its expansion into the continent of Asia.

11 December

Western Front At Dillingen the US 90th Division (XX Corps, 3rd Army) re-groups in order to resume the offensive and expand the Saarlautern bridgehead, and the 95th Division succeeds in reaching the centre of Fraulautern.

The 35th Division (XII Corps) takes Sarreguemines and pushes on towards the river Blies.

□ Some 1,600 US Fortresses and Liberators, the biggest American force yet sent over Germany, bomb Frankfurt, Hanau and Giessen.

Philippines: Leyte Bombers of the US 5th Air Force, despatched from the island, begin the pre-invasion hammering of Mindoro Island.

The Americans succeed in outflanking the Japanese positions south-east of Limon and in splitting the enemy forces, isolating those in the Limon area from the main body concentrated north-west of Ormoc. The Japanese try to land reinforcements in Ormoc Bay during the night, but their effort is mostly frustrated.

Another American destroyer is sunk off Leyte by a Japanese suicide aircraft.

Burma In the British IV Corps sector units of the 268th Brigade capture Indaw.

12 December

Western Front In the US 1st Army sector, the 104th Division takes the village of Pier, forcing the 5th *Panzerarmee* to withdraw over the Rur, while units of the 9th Division and 3rd Armoured Division complete the occupation of a good deal of the region west of the Rur, and of the town of Düren.

The advance of the XV Corps of the US 7th Army is halted at Hottvillers-Bitche on the Maginot Line.

Italian Front During the night, the 6th Armoured Division (XIII Corps, US 5th Army) begins the second stage of its offensive, throwing in the units of the 61st Brigade against Tossignano. In the 8th Army sector, the 5th Armoured Division and 1st Division of infantry (Canadian I Corps) advance from Fosso Vecchio to the Canale Naviglio; the 1st Division establishes a bridgehead north of Bagnacavallo.

Philippines: Leyte During the night two task groups from the US 7th Fleet sail from Leyte for Mindoro. Fighting continues south of Limon and in other areas in the north-west of the island. An American destroyer is damaged off Leyte by a Japanese suicide aircraft.

Burma The British XV Corps opens

the offensive to free the coastal sector of the Arakan, where bases will be set up for the recapture of Burma. The 25th Indian Division advances in the Mayu peninsula towards Akyab, the 82nd West African Division penetrates into the Kalapanzin valley near Buthidaung, the 81st attacks near Kyauktaw.

13 December

Western Front Much of the region between the Inde and the Rur is taken by the 30th Division (XIX Corps, 9th Army), and Derichsweiller is captured by the 9th Division. The operations of the VII Corps (American 1st Army) are concluded. Meanwhile the 104th Division has reached the river Rur on a front of some $4\frac{1}{2}$ miles.

The 90th Division of the XX Corps (US 3rd Army) prepares for the general offensive for the capture of Dillingen. In the Saarlautern bridgehead, the 95th Division is halted on the previous day's positions.

Italian Front More units of the 6th Armoured Division (British XII Corps, American 5th Army) are sent against Tossignano.

Eastern Front Advanced elements of the 2nd Ukraine Front are only 6 miles from Budapest to the north-east and 8 miles to the east.

Philippines In the Mindanao Sea the squadrons of the US 7th Fleet en route for the landing on Mindoro are attacked by Japanese aircraft, including many piloted by *kamikaze*. The cruiser *Nashville* and the destroyer *Haraden*, badly damaged, have to abandon the formation.

Leyte Japanese night counter-attacks in the US X Corps sector. In the XXIV Corps sector, the 77th Division is held up in front of a strong Japanese fortified line a little north of Ormoc.

Burma While the 114th Regiment of the Chinese 38th Division finally succeeds in breaking the northern defences of Bhamo, in the Tonk-wa area the US 475th Infantry repel an attack by the Japanese contingent sent to the help of the forces besieged in Bhamo.

14 December

Western Front The capture of the region between the rivers Inde and Rur by the 30th Division (XIX Corps, US 9th Army) is concluded. Units of the US 1st and 3rd Armies are virtually at a standstill on the previous day's positions.

Italian Front In the XIII Corps (US 5th Army) sector, the 6th Armoured Division loses contact with the patrols that have reached Tossignano.

During the night the Polish II Corps resumes its offensive on the left of the Canadian V Corps, and the 5th Armoured Division establishes a bridgehead over the Canale Naviglio.

15 December

Western Front The 90th Division (XX Corps, 3rd Army) moves in to capture Dillingen and the bridge over the river Prims on the road linking Dillingen with Saarlautern. There is then a lull in operations in the sector, and the 90th Division suspends its attack. The 95th Division continues to advance in the Saarlautern bridgehead. Units of the 35th Division capture Habkirchen.

In the southern sector of the front, the French 1st Army attacks the positions of the German 19th Army west of the Rhine in the Colmar area.

Eastern Front Units of the Red Army cross the river Ipely, north of Budapest, and establish a bridgehead in Czechoslovakian territory, at Sahy.

Philippines: Mindoro After the usual barrage from naval guns, the US 24th Division, reinforced by a parachute battalion, lands on Mindoro at 7.35 a.m. The landing is carried out on the south-west coast of the island (which is immediately south of Luzon) in the area of San Agustin. The Americans advance 8 miles inland without meeting any resistance and they man the perimeter of their beachhead and start at once to construct an airfield.

Japanese aircraft attack the transports and escort ships, sinking two motor torpedo-boats and damaging the escort carrier *Marcus Island*, two

WASSILY KANDINSKY

The great Russian painter Wassily Kandinsky, one of the founders of modern abstract art, died on 15 December at Neuilly-sur-Seine , where he had been living in exile since the Nazis came to power.

Kandinsky was born in Moscow on 4 December 1866. After studying law, he abandoned his university career and went to Munich in order to become a painter. He became a pupil of Franz von Stuck and was influenced by the major art movements of the time. Around 1911 he was one of the founders of the *Der blaue Reiter* group. His works gradually lost all contact with apparent realism and he intensified his search for an association between forms, colours and music.

On the outbreak of the First World War he returned to Russia, but in 1921 he went back to Germany; the following year he became professor at the Bauhaus in Weimar.

Wassily Kandinsky: *First Abstract Water-colour* (above) and *Arc and Point* (below).

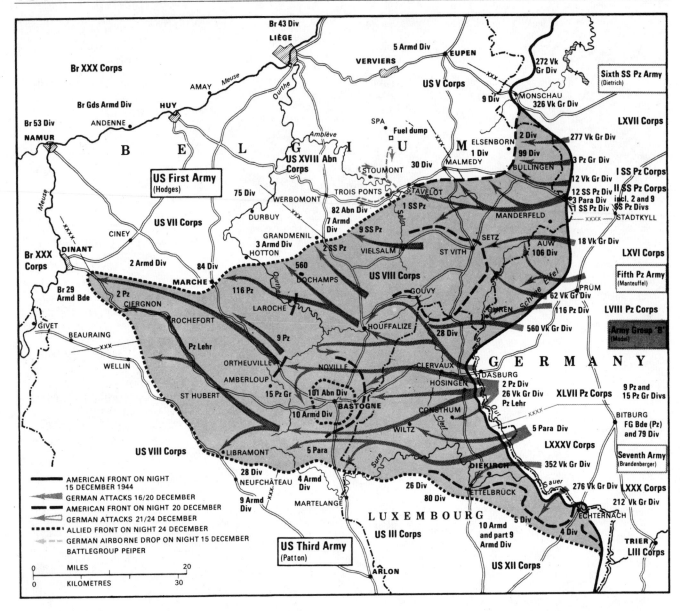

The map shows:
- AMERICAN FRONT ON NIGHT 15 DECEMBER 1944
- GERMAN ATTACKS 16/20 DECEMBER
- AMERICAN FRONT ON NIGHT 20 DECEMBER
- GERMAN ATTACKS 21/24 DECEMBER
- ALLIED FRONT ON NIGHT 24 DECEMBER
- GERMAN AIRBORNE DROP ON NIGHT 15 DECEMBER
- BATTLEGROUP PEIPER

MILES 0–20 / KILOMETRES 0–30

The German counter-offensive in the Ardennes from 15 December to its high point on 24 December.

destroyers and a third motor torpedo-boat, *kamikaze* being responsible in every case.

In the waters of the Philippines, American aircraft and submarines sink one Japanese destroyer and one transport.

Leyte The Americans begin liquidating some pockets of resistance in the Ormoc area, but do not pursue their operations against the main body of the enemy, now concentrated north and north-west of Ormoc.

Burma During the night, the Japanese garrison of Bhamo manages to filter across the Chinese lines. The Chinese 38th Division occupies the town.

In the Arakan, the 82nd West African Division captures Buthidaung.

16 December

Western Front The Germans launch their counter-attack in the Ardennes. The US 3rd Army transfers the 10th Armoured Division to the VIII Corps of the US 1st Army, which has to face the enemy thrust.

The 95th Division continues to extend its bridgehead at Saarlautern; during the night its units begin to be relieved by the 5th Division. The area between the XX and XII Corps is allocated to the II Corps; the XII Corps continues its attacks against the outer defences of the Siegfried Line, but these are suspended when news is received of the German offensive in the Ardennes. In the south, the VI Corps (7th Army) sends its divisions forward towards the German frontier.

Italian Front General Alexander, promoted Field-Marshal, is appointed Supreme Allied Commander, Mediterranean, replacing General Wilson; General Clark is appointed Commander-in-Chief of Allied forces in Italy (15th Army Group) in his place, and command of the US 5th Army passes to General Truscott.

In the 8th Army sector, the British V Corps advances towards Faenza; the New Zealand 2nd Division reaches the river Senio and the 10th Indian Division enters Pergola.

Philippines: Mindoro The Americans confine their activity to patrolling their perimeter and fortifying the area round the airfield they are constructing. The Japanese continue to attack American ships from the air.

Luzon Aircraft of the US 3rd Fleet continue their attacks on military targets in the island.

Leyte The US 77th Division takes Cogon and San Jose, resuming their advance north of Ormoc.

Burma In the British IV Corps sector, the 19th Indian Division occupies Pinlebu and Banmauk. Some units reach Indaw, making contact with the British 36th Division coming from the north.

China The Chinese 57th Division has not yet been transferred to the Kunming area; General Wedemeyer protests to Chiang Kai-shek, who agrees that a part of the army may be air-lifted.

The protracted and difficult negotiations between Chinese Nationalists and Communists (represented by Chou En-lai) over increased co-operation in the struggle against the Japanese are finally concluded.

17 December

Western Front The 82nd and 101st Airborne Divisions (XVIII Corps, Allied 1st Airborne Army) are despatched to the Ardennes front,

GLENN MILLER

Band leader Glenn Miller died on 16 December in an air crash over the English Channel. Born in 1904 at Clarinda, Iowa, Miller formed his first jazz group in the early 1920s and after ten years or so won fame with his enticing and enormously successful song, *Moonlight Serenade*.

On the outbreak of war, Miller enlisted and formed a band which engaged in concert performances for the troops. His song *In the Mood*, broadcast incessantly by radio stations in the United States, became one of the most popular wartime numbers and virtually a signature tune of the American armed forces.

Glenn Miller conducting his big band.

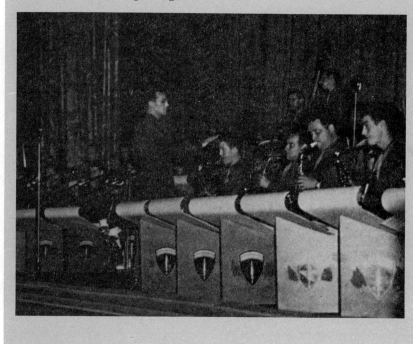

where the German offensive is going ahead.

In the 3rd Army sector, the 5th Division continues relieving the units of the 95th Division (XX Corps) in the Saarlautern bridgehead.

Units of the US 7th Army (XV and VI Corps) are almost completely halted in front of the outer defences of the Siegfried Line.

Italian Front On the Senio, the 5th (*Kresowa*) Division (Polish II Corps, 8th Army) relieves the units of the 3rd (*Carpathian*) Division. The 10th Indian Division establishes several small bridgeheads over the Senio south and north of Tebano.

Eastern Front In Hungary, Malinovsky's troops are only 5 miles from Budapest.

Philippines: Leyte The squadrons of the 7th Fleet that escorted the invasion force to Mindoro return to the Gulf of Leyte after more attacks by Japanese aircraft.

The 32nd Division (US X Corps) advances slowly south of Limon. The 307th Infantry, XXIV Corps, supported by artillery and aircraft, attacks Valencia airfield and reaches the edge of the runway

18 December

Western Front In the US 9th Army

(continued on page 644)

THE BATTLE OF THE ARDENNES

16 December

At 5.30 a.m. on this Sunday morning German artillery opens a deadly fire on the positions of the US 1st Army in the sector of the Western Front running from Monschau in the north to Echternach in the south. The barrage does not last long (between 20 and 90 minutes), but it has a shattering effect on the Americans, who are completely taken by surprise. Until now the initiative has always rested with the Allies. Only the previous day Field-Marshal Montgomery had summed up the Allied view when he told a group of colleagues: 'The enemy is at present fighting a defensive campaign on all fronts; his situation is such that he cannot stage any major offensive operations.' Montgomery's belief was to be totally disproved within a bare 24 hours by one of the biggest operations mounted by the Germans in the last eighteen months of the war.

The idea for an offensive in the Ardennes took shape in Hitler's mind (he actually worked out the plans himself in the face of the growing distrust of his generals and strategists) during September and October. He had in fact begun to think of it late in August, after the Allied landings and their first successes in the south of France, when he exhorted his commanders to 'resume the offensive in November'.

On 24 October Hitler revealed his plan of attack for the first time to Generals Westphal and Krebs

American soldiers observe a squadron of Allied fighter bombers during a pause in the advance on the Ardennes.

Pz. Kw III A   Pz. Kw III Ausf E   Pz. Bef Wg III Ausf H

Continuous improvements made to the basic tank models led to the formation of whole families of great tanks throughout the belligerent armies. A typical example of this development is the Pz. Kw III series which featured 12 variants of the original model.

Variants of the original model

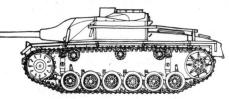

7.5 cm Stu. G. III Ausf G

Pz. Kw III Ausf N

(chiefs of staff respectively to von Rundstedt, Commander of the Western Front and to Field-Marshal Model, Commander of Army Group B). The object of the offensive, Hitler explains, is to break through the Allied front at its weakest point (in the Ardennes, in fact) and occupy Antwerp, which represents the real main objective of the whole Allied campaign. Once Antwerp harbour has been cleaned up and cleared of mines, the Allies will be able to let loose the whole of their deadly military potential on the German front. With the objective clear, these are the means of attaining it: Model's four armies (the 5th and 6th Armoured, the 7th and 15th Infantry), which will be given – this is still Hitler unfolding his plan – substantial reinforcements, including a certain number of armoured divisions transferred from the Eastern Front, and will be able to rely on air cover from 3,000 aircraft (at least, this is what Goering has promised). It goes without saying, concludes Hitler, that the outcome of the operation depends very largely on the element of surprise. It is therefore necessary that the whole of his plan must be kept secret.

General Alfred Jodl, Director of Operations at the Supreme Command of the Wehrmacht, returns to this essential need for secrecy when on 3 November he holds a meeting of the army commanders concerned to explain Hitler's plan in detail. By Hitler's own order, Jodl tells them, the officers present must sign a written undertaking not to reveal to anyone, for any reason, what they are about to hear, under penalty of death. And this is the plan: the offensive will be carried out by Model's Army Group B, four armies deployed on the Ardennes front between Monschau and Echternach. First to attack will be the two armies on the wings, the 15th under General von Zangen on the right and the 7th under General Brandenberger on the left; the main thrust, in the centre, will come from two armoured formations, the 5th *Panzer* Army and the 6th *Panzer SS* Army, the first under von Manteuffel and the second under Dietrich.

The offensive is fixed for 27 November, but as the days pass it is gradually realized that it is impossible to be ready by that date, and Hitler agrees to put the attack back to 16 December. The greatest difficulties are with the transport of materials and the movement of reinforcements to the Western Front, operations which the Allies must not be allowed to observe. Most moves are therefore carried out at night, and in order not to leave tracks, men and vehicles advance on roads covered with straw, which is then removed at first light. The guns are towed by horses instead of mechanized tractors, and the noise of the tanks coming up to their start lines is covered by German fighters flying low up and down the front line for no apparent purpose, to the surprise of the puzzled Americans. With the aid of such stratagems the Germans manage to assemble on the Western Front, along a line of attack of some 80 miles, a force of 30 divisions (a total of about 250,000 men), nearly 2,000 guns, 1,000 tanks and about 1,500 aircraft (of the 3,000 promised by Goering).

During the intensive preparations Hitler several times summons his commanders to discuss the plan and put the finishing touches to the details. Both von Rundstedt and Model are sceptical about the possibility that such an ambitious project can succeed and on 2 December, during another meeting at Hitler's headquarters, they suggest that the plan should be scaled down. But Hitler is unmovable; the plan must be carried out as he has laid down.

Opposite the tremendous attacking force assembled by the Germans there are no more than six Allied divisions, those of General Gerow's V Corps (the 2nd, 99th and 106th) and General Middleton's VIII Corps (the 28th, 4th and 9th Armoured); a total of 80,000 men, completely unprepared to stand up to the unexpected simultaneous attack of four armies.

At 5.30 a.m. on 16 December the shelling of Allied positions begins. Then the German armoured divisions go into action, the divisions on which the hopes of the German commanders rest (though it is hoped also that bad weather and low clouds will prevent the Allied air forces from intervening in the battle for a few days more). The American lines fall like ninepins; the surprise is so complete that four hours after the attack begins news of the German action still has not been received by the XII Corps (deployed on the right flank of the VIII Corps).

Adding to the confusion and disorder that reign among the American divisions caused by the violence of the German tank assault, is another strange element, a highly secret initiative planned by Hitler himself, called by the code-name Operation *Greif* (*Grab*). Groups of English-speaking Commandos, perfectly trained by Colonel Otto Skorzeny (the officer who rescued Mussolini), infiltrate the Allied lines dressed in American uniforms and driving captured American vehicles, spreading panic among the bewildered troops by passing on alarmist rumours, altering the signposts on the roads, blowing up ammunition dumps, cutting telephone wires etc.

The trick is discovered quite quickly, but results in a frenzy of suspicion. Exaggerating the extent of the German sabotage plans, the Americans set up hundreds of rigidly controlled road blocks and stop and interrogate the occupants of every jeep and every other vehicle that passes them, even those of senior officers. They check the drivers by asking them questions about the characters in American comic strips, about the baseball league, about the details of Hollywood film stars' private lives. This is how General Bradley, Commander of the 12th Army Group, remembers those days: 'A half million GIs played cat and mouse with each other each time they met. Neither rank nor credentials nor protests spared the traveller an inquisition at each intersection he passed. Three times I was ordered to prove my identity by cautious GIs. The first time by identifying Springfield as the capital of Illinois (my questioner held out for Chicago); the second by locating the guard between the centre and tackle on a line of scrimmage; the third time by naming the then current spouse of a blonde named Betty Grable. Grable stopped me, but the sentry did not. Pleased at having stumped me, he nevertheless passed me on.'

News of the German attack comes to Eisenhower at Versailles, where he now has his headquarters. The Supreme Commander's first order is to reinforce the sector under attack with all available armoured forces. The 82nd and 101st Parachute Divisions are also mobilized; the first reaches the Houffalize sector, at the very centre of the German line of attack, on which the units of the LVIII and the XLVII Armoured Corps are converging, and the 101st Division moves to Bastogne, the most important road junction in the region, about 12 miles south of Houffalize. The Allies are seriously handicapped by the bad weather, for they cannot call up the air force (which is just what the Germans are relying on).

On the northern flank of the German LXVII Armoured Corps (6th *Panzer SS* Army), the German offensive is fairly well contained in the Monschau sector, while in the south the German I Armoured Corps has reached Trois-Ponts, on the left bank of the river Amblève, by 19 December, pushing on from there to the north in the direction of Spa. However, it does not advance far; nor does the 9th SS Armoured Division (II Armoured Corps), which has to face a counter-attack from the 82nd Parachute Division and is forced to cross back to the right bank of the Amblève, and dig in.

25 December

By 25 December, however, with its initial impetus exhausted, the whole of the 6th *SS Panzer* Army goes on the defensive.

In the central sector, the corps of Manteuffel's 5th Armoured Army advance in depth. The LXVI Corps reaches St Vith (23 December), the LXVIII and XLVII cross the Our and reach Houffalize (116th Armoured Division) and Bastogne (*Panzerlehr* Division). Houffalize is taken, but Bastogne holds out, defended by the 101st Parachute Division and units of the 9th and 10th Divisions, commanded by General McAuliffe. During the days that follow, though completely surrounded by a regiment of the *Panzerlehr* Division and the *Führer Begleit* Brigade, the town resists all attacks by the besieging forces and contemptuously refuses General Kokott's surrender demand. And on 26 December the ring round Bastogne is broken by units of the 4th Armoured Division of Patton's 3rd Army.

Meanwhile the main body of the German armies push on towards the west. In the north the 116th Armoured Division crosses the Ourthe south of Hotton, but is then halted by the American 84th Division, while in the south the *Panzerlehr* thrusts forward as far

as Ciergnon, about 13 miles from Dinant, and the 2nd Armoured Division occupies the small town of Foy-Notre-Dame, barely 4 miles from the Meuse, on 24 December. And here Hitler's great dream collapses; 60 miles from their starting line, the Germans are exhausted. The Allies are now reacting from every side to the offensive that Hitler has unleashed; besides the counter-attack by the 3rd Army in the south and the 1st Army in the north on the flanks of the salient captured by the units of the German 5th and 7th Armies, there is now (starting on 22 December) a massive, devastating intervention by Allied fighter-bombers, at last enabled to take off by a considerable improvement in the weather. The German lines of communication are totally confused by bombing, while the armoured divisions are decimated by enemy fire and paralysed by lack of fuel. The 2nd *Panzer* Division, which has ventured out into a narrow corridor nearly as far as Dinant, is virtually wiped out. For the Germans there begins a slow but inexorable retreat; in fact, as early as 22 December von Rundstedt (with the full agreement of Field-Marshal Model and Guderian, Chief of Staff of the *Oberkommando der Wehrmacht*), has asked Hitler to authorize a withdrawal behind the Siegfried Line. But Hitler has refused. And so, as Manteuffel has written: 'Instead of ordering a timely withdrawal, we were forced to retire, yard by yard, under the pressure of the attacking Allies, suffering useless losses ... For us, the Hitlerian policy of "no retreat" meant ruin, for we could not afford losses on that scale.'

After the failure of the German attempt to re-take Bastogne on 3–4 January 1945, the attacks of the American 1st and 3rd Armies become more incisive, imposing a ruinous rhythm on the German

retreat. By 20 January the German armies are back to their starting point; in 34 days' fighting they have lost about 100,000 men killed, wounded and prisoners, 800 tanks and at least 1,000 aircraft. Allied losses are also heavy: 81,000 American and 1,400 British soldiers out of the 600,000 who took part altogether in the containment of the German offensive, and about 800 armoured fighting vehicles. But while the Americans are in a position to replace their losses in no more than 15 days, the German losses are decisive to the future course of the conflict. As Churchill wrote, the Ardennes offensive forced the Allies to postpone their advance into Germany by three weeks, but gave some unlooked-for advantages.

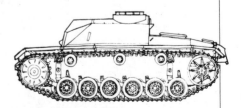

Stu. G III F ammunition carrier.

A formation of American aircraft drops reinforcements and supplies to American troops encircled at Bastogne during the battle of the Ardennes.

sector, the 84th Division reaches its final objectives, Wurm and Müllendorf.

In the Ardennes, the US 1st Army is still being attacked by the Germans. In the Saarlautern bridgehead sector the 5th Division has completed the relief of the US 95th Division.

Eastern Front North of Miskolc, in Hungary, the Red Army reaches the Czechoslovakian frontier on a front of more than 60 miles.

Philippines: Leyte The US 307th Infantry occupies Valencia and its airfield. The south part of the Ormoc Valley, from Ormoc to Valencia, is now firmly in American hands.

☐ East of the Philippines a violent typhoon hits the US 3rd Fleet. Three destroyers sink, and there is serious damage to four light aircraft carriers and four escort carriers, óne cruiser, seven destroyers, three escort destroyers, one tanker and various other ships. The weather forces the Americans to cancel a planned operation for the bombing of Luzon.

China Seventy-seven B-29 Superfortress bombers and 200 other aircraft of the US 14th Air Force carry out a heavy raid on Hankow, an industrial town and Japanese supply base.

19 December

Western Front The Allied commanders, meeting at Verdun, decide to put off the offensive on the Rhine so as to concentrate the greatest possible number of men and equipment in the Ardennes to confront the German advance. On both sides of the German breakthrough, the US 1st and 3rd Armies re-group in readiness for a coordinated attack, cutting at the base of the salient formed by the advance of the German armies.

Italian Front During the night the V Corps (British 8th Army) resumes its offensive, liberating the Faenza sector.

Philippines: Mindoro The Americans, together with Filipino guerrillas, begin a series of patrol actions in several parts of the island.

Leyte The Japanese 35th Army is left to its fate. General Yamashita is told by his headquarters that from

German soldier captured in this sector.

now on he will have to rely on local resources, since they are no longer able to send him reinforcements or supplies. Fighting continues south of Limon. The 77th Division advances towards Libongao and Palompon. Valencia has to be defended from a Japanese counter-attack.

East China Sea An American submarine sinks the Japanese aircraft carrier *Unryu*.

Burma The 19th Indian Division takes Wunthe. In the XXXIII Corps sector the British 2nd Division, coming from Kohima, crosses the river Chindwin at Kalewa and relieves the 11th East African Division.

20 December

Western Front The German armies are still advancing in the Ardennes; Bastogne, with its important road junction, 'the logistic centre of the Ardennes', is completely surrounded.

Italian Front In the British 8th Army sector, the 56th Division (V Corps) starts on the capture of the area between the Canale Naviglio and the river Lamone, north of Faenza. During the night the Canadian 1st

Division and 5th Armoured Division (Canadian I Corps) force the Germans to withdraw across the Senio.

Philippines: Leyte The US artillery brings heavy fire to bear on the Japanese pockets west of Palompon and south of Limon.

Burma In the British IV Corps sector, the 19th Indian Division takes Kawlin.

21 December

Western Front While American armies not directly concerned with the Ardennes break-through detach what formations they can to reinforce the 1st Army sector (the 2nd Armoured Division goes from the XIX Corps, 9th Army, and the 75th Division from the XVI Corps) the Germans advance in a wedge west of Bastogne.

Italian Front The 5th (*Kresowa*) Division (Polish II Corps, 8th Army) completes the capture of the east bank of the Senio, and the Canadian I Corps reaches the river in the Cotignola–Alfonsine sector.

Eastern Front While the Germans proceed with the evacuation of the Balkans, violent fighting rages between the German Army Group South and the 3rd Ukraine Front south-west of Budapest, between the Danube and Lake Balaton.

Philippines: Mindoro The Japanese receive reinforcements from Luzon by air. Japanese aircraft attack an American supply convoy, sinking two tank landing craft and damaging several other ships. A destroyer is sunk by a Japanese suicide aircraft.

Leyte Troops of the X Corps, advancing from the north, link up with troops of XXIV Corps coming up from Ormoc. The whole Ormoc Valley is now cleared of Japanese, apart from some major pockets of resistance that still have to be liquidated.

Burma The British advance in the Arakan is so fast that Admiral Mountbatten calls the senior commanders to Calcutta to discuss the best way of exploiting this unexpected success.

22 December

Western Front The American troops

holding Bastogne under siege conditions refuse an offer of surrender by the Germans. In reply General McAuliffe, commanding the defending forces (101st Airborne Division) sends back a large envelope with a sheet of paper with the single word Nuts!

Italian Front Expecting a German offensive in the western sector of the front (US 5th Army), the 92nd Division, operating in the area of Lucca, is reinforced by units from the 8th Indian Division and 85th Division, and with tanks and guns.

Philippines: Leyte The Americans capture several villages. The problem now is to wipe out the remaining Japanese forces concentrated west of Palompon in two big pockets.

Burma The British 36th Division, advancing from the north along the valley of the Irrawaddy, reaches Tigyaing, which the Japanese have evacuated, and prepares to attack Mongmit.

23 December

Eastern Front The battle of Budapest continues. The city is three-quarters surrounded by the 2nd and 3rd Ukraine Fronts.

Philippines: Leyte The guns of the US 77th Division and aircraft of the 5th Air Force hammer Palompon, on the west coast, in preparation for an imminent landing. The Japanese launch their usual night counterattacks, which are repulsed.

Burma In the British XXXIII Corps sector, the 19th Indian Division occupies Kokoggon.

24 December

Western Front The town of Bastogne, half destroyed by the attacks of German aircraft and artillery, still holds out.

In the French 1st Army sector, the US 3rd Division liberates Bennwihr, thus completing the operations in the Colmar sector.

Eastern Front The Soviet Supreme Command announces that in the course of the past three days the 3rd Ukraine Front, after breaking through the German lines south-west of Budapest in the area between Lake Velencei and the Danube, has

ROMAIN ROLLAND

The French musicologist and writer Romain Rolland, winner of the Nobel Prize for Literature in 1915, died on 30 December at Vézelay.

Rolland was born at Clamecy on 29 January 1866; after being a member of the École Française in Rome, he became professor in history of art at the École Normale Supérieure in 1895, and later teacher in history of music at the Sorbonne. His numerous works on history and music criticism, full of intuitive wisdom, made him one of the most influential musicologists of the age.

A versatile author, engaged over the years with art history, literature, theatre and political essays, Rolland owed his principal fame to the monumental novel *Jean-Christophe*, the imaginary biography of a German musician, published in ten volumes between 1904 and 1912, in which he expounded his social and moral vision of the world.

advanced 25 miles and taken 160 towns and villages, including the important strongholds of Szekesfehervar and Bicske. The Germans' escape route from Budapest is now no more than 18 miles wide.

Volcano Islands: Iwo Jima A US naval squadron commanded by Rear-Admiral A. E. Smith bombards the airfields and other installations on the island. Two Japanese transports are sunk.

Burma In the British XXXIII Corps sector, the British 2nd Division and the 20th Indian Division overcome the dogged Japanese resistance in the Pyingaing area.

25 December

Western Front The XXX Corps (British 2nd Army) takes up positions along the west bank of the Meuse from Givet to Liège. The 51st Division is transferred from the US 9th Army to the 1st Army. Bastogne still holds out, while the German advance slows down and almost comes to a halt through lack of supplies.

Eastern Front The Russians narrow the enemy escape route from Budapest to a mere 10 miles.

Philippines: Luzon Attacks on the island by American aircraft are stepped up in preparation for the landing.

Leyte The US 6th Army, which is to carry out the invasion of Luzon, is gradually replaced by the 8th Army. Units of the 77th Division land north of Palompon without meeting any resistance and begin the liquidation of the Japanese positions in this sector.

26 December

Italian Front The 1st Armoured Division is sent to the Lucca sector. Units of the German 14th Army launch a series of counter-attacks against the positions of the 92nd Division (IV Corps) along the banks of the river Serchio.

Eastern Front Units of the 3rd Ukraine Front virtually close the ring round the defenders of Budapest, and take the fortified town of Esztergom.

Philippines: Mindoro A Japanese naval squadron, escaping American air and naval surveillance, arrives off Mindoro by night and bombards the American beachhead. Later a Japanese destroyer is sunk by US ships and aircraft.

Burma In the coastal Arakan area, the 25th Indian Division reaches Foul Point long before it was expected. The Japanese have decided to withdraw from Akyab.

China General Wedemeyer submits to Chiang Kai-shek his plans for an offensive against Kweilin, Liuchow and Canton.

27 December

Western Front The British XXX Corps halts the advance of the German armour in the Celles sector, some 3 miles south-east of Dinant. Meanwhile the pressure of the US 1st and 3rd Armies on the flanks of the German salient in the Ardennes is increasing.

Eastern Front The final stage of the battle for Budapest begins. The city is now completely encircled.

Philippines: Mindoro Japanese aircraft begin a series of bombardments which go on until the end of December against the American positions on the island and their supply convoys.

Leyte Some American units land at Taglawigan, on the north-west coast of the island, occupying that village and Daha. Others advance on San Isidro. In the Palompon area the Japanese still resist energetically.

Iwo Jima American aircraft and ships bombard the island, which is one of the next invasion targets.

28 December

Western Front General Eisenhower has a meeting with Field-Marshal Montgomery at Hasselt, in Belgium, and studies the counter-measures to be taken in the Ardennes. Meanwhile units of Patton's 3rd Army prepare a counter-offensive between the rivers Sauer and Wiltz, while the XII Corps, which now has the 6th Armoured Division under command, is deployed in defensive positions.

Italian Front In the US 5th Army sector, the units of the 8th Indian Division advance north along the valley of the Serchio, while the German troops begin to withdraw northwards.

29 December

Western Europe All quiet on almost the whole front, with both Germans and Allies on the defensive.

Eastern Front Bitter street fighting rages in Budapest, where the Germans have prepared a large number of fortified positions. The Russians had intended to negotiate the surrender of the city to avoid useless bloodshed, but the emissaries sent to open negotiations are killed, probably by mistake, in front of the German trenches.

30 December

Western Front In the American 3rd Army sector the VIII Corps begins to advance on Houffalize, a small Belgian town 3 miles from the border with Luxembourg. Trying to cut the road south from Bastogne to Arlon, the Germans reach Lutrbois and surround Villers-la-Bonne-Eau, cutting off some units of the US 35th Division.

Eastern Front In Hungary, bloody street fighting continues in the western part of Budapest between the German defenders and the troops of the 3rd Ukraine Front, while the armies of the 2nd Ukraine Front break in from the east.

Philippines: Mindoro A second American supply convoy reaches the island; it has been heavily attacked on the way by Japanese aircraft, losing three merchant ships, three tank landing craft, two vehicle landing craft and two destroyers. Once again, it is the death-defying *kamikaze* who do the damage.

Leyte The Americans attack in force in the Palompon area, and during the night the Japanese withdraw most of their forces from the sector.

Burma In the British XXXIII Corps sector, the British and Indian forces take Kaduma.

31 December

Western Front Units of the 87th Division (VIII Corps, US 3rd Army) reach Remagen.

Italian Front In the Serchio valley the American 5th Army has regained the positions held at the end of October.

☐ Hungary declares war on Germany.

Pacific The headquarters of the US 5th Fleet issues operational plans for the capture of the island of Iwo Jima. The date of the landing is fixed for 19 February 1945.

Philippines: Leyte With the strength born of desperation, the Japanese unleash new counter-attacks in the north-west of the island. The headquarters of the 77th Division calculates that in the last ten days the Japanese have lost at least 5,800 men in action against them, while American losses have been insignificant.

Mindoro More attacks by Japanese suicide aircraft against American supply ships.

Burma In the British XXXIII Corps sector, the British 2nd Division takes Kabo.

1945

JANUARY	**9 January** *Philippines*. Landing of 67,000 men in the Gulf of Lingayen on the central western coast of Luzon begins.	**12 January** Operation *Vistula-Oder* is started by the 1st Ukraine Front.
FEBRUARY	**11 February** The Yalta conference is concluded. **19 February** *Iwo Jima*: The American V Amphibious Corps lands part of the	4th and 5th Marine Divisions on the south-east coast of the island.
APRIL	**1 April** *Okinawa*: The landing of the US 10th Army (General Buckner) on the south-west coast of Okinawa. **12 April** President Roosevelt dies at Warm Springs, Georgia. **23 April** Hitler takes over command of the defence of Berlin. **25 April** At Torgau, on the Elbe south of Berlin, the 5th Guards Army makes the first contact with the Americans of the 1st Army. The whole of Germany is now cut in two.	Opening of the San Francisco conference, to complete a charter for the United Nations Organisation. **29 April** Unconditional surrender of all German troops in Italy. **30 April** At 3.30 p.m. Hitler commits suicide in the Chancellery Bunker.
MAY	**7 May** At Rheims, in Eisenhower's headquarters, German representatives sign the unconditional surrender of all German armed forces to the Allies.	**9 May** At one minute past midnight, hostilities in Europe officially come to an end.
JUNE	**13 June** *Okinawa*: The Japanese in the Oroku peninsula cease all resistance.	
JULY	**16 July** The first atomic bomb is successfully tested.	**17 July** Opening of the Potsdam conference.
AUGUST	**6 August** Operation *Centreboard*: A B-29 named *Enola Gay*, drops the first atomic bomb on Hiroshima.	**8 August** The USSR declares war on Japan.
SEPTEMBER	**2 September** The Japanese Foreign Minister Mamoru Shigemitsu and the Chief of	Staff sign the instrument of capitulation in the presence of General MacArthur.

A section of US Marines hoists the American flag on one of the many hilltops in the blood-soaked island of Okinawa.

The year 1944 has seen a series of triumphs for the Allies, a series of catastrophic defeats for Germany and Japan. The Russians have liberated the whole of their country from the invader, inflicting staggering losses on the Germans, and already they are pressing forward in Poland, in Hungary and in East Prussia. They have forced Rumania, Bulgaria and Finland to capitulate. They have linked up with Tito's forces in Yugoslavia, driving the Germans almost completely from the Balkans. Their war production has made great strides, thanks to the liberation of the Don basin. In 1944 they produced 29,000 tanks and self-propelled guns, 40,300 aircraft and 122,500 guns. Their new IS-2 tank, with a 122-mm gun, has made its appearance. Now they are getting ready to give the Reich that final blow that will lead to the total destruction of Hitler's hopes.

Hitler himself conducts the German war effort in a state bordering increasingly on insanity. The Führer has unveiled some of his secret weapons, but with little effect, either material or psychological. German war production has not diminished as much as might have been expected, but it cannot compete with that of the American colossus. And when it comes to secret weapons, the Americans are preparing a really terrifying one which, in its time, will bring the long years of butchery to an end.

The Allies are poised before Bologna, having liberated almost the whole of peninsula Italy, and are now preparing the final thrust towards the Alps planned for the coming spring. But this front, while it still performs the function of keeping substantial German forces engaged, has become secondary for the British and Americans and their allies since Operation *Overlord* (the invasion of northern France) and Operation *Anvil* (landing in the south of France). *Overlord* was an operation on a gigantic scale, calling for the employment of 4,000 transports and landing craft, more than 350 warships, and 11,000 aircraft, and

deploying over 2,000,000 men on the Western Front who are already on the borders of the Reich that was to last for a thousand years. Although the offensive launched by Model's armies in the Ardennes is still in progress, the end is already in sight. The Allies have the situation firmly under control and are preparing to eliminate the German salient and go on to the final offensive against the Rhine and into the heart of Germany. After some faltering in the last weeks of 1944, the huge Allied war machine is now able to go forward swiftly again. Gaps in the ranks caused by the unexpected German resurgence have been made good and Eisenhower's plan for an offensive against the Ruhr (in the north of the front) and the Saar (in the south) is re-activated. Not even the most desperate defence by German troops will be enough to change a situation that must inevitably lead to the annihilation of Germany.

The Pacific, too, has witnessed a battle of Titans. Japan has lost vast territories it once controlled, the Solomons, the Carolines, the Marshalls, New Guinea and many more. And Japan's military strength is seriously eroded: the navy, for example, has lost 2,242 ships, including 407 warships, among them the super-battleship *Musashi* of 72,800 tons.

America's unlimited industrial potential is making its weight felt more and more. In 1944 the United States produced 134,000 aircraft, 148,000 tanks, 27,000,000 tons of shipping, 1,200,000 vehicles of various types and 42,000 guns.

And on the other side, as the spectre of defeat looms, there remains the fanaticism of the few, the fatalistic resignation of the many.

1 January

Western Europe About 800 Luftwaffe bombers carry out raids on airfields in Belgium, Holland and France, taking the Allied air forces by surprise and destroying or damaging 156 aircraft, mostly on the ground.

Meanwhile the counter-thrust against the Germans by the III and

VIII Corps of Patton's 3rd Army continues in the Ardennes; Moircy, Jenneville and Chenogne are recaptured by the 87th Division of the VIII Corps, while units of the III Corps succeed in containing the German salient south-east of Bastogne. In Alsace, in the southern part of the front, units of the German Army Group G under General Balck (ten divisions, but under strength) launch an offensive against General Patch's 7th Army (Operation *Nordwind*), which is forced to withdraw. On precise orders from General Eisenhower, the formations of the 6th Army Group, and the US 7th Army in particular, are to evacuate Alsace and withdraw westwards to a new front on the crest of the Vosges (on the Maginot Line) and then occupy, on their left, a line Bitche–Strasbourg, and finally, by 5 January, the line from Bitche to Dabo.

Italian Front An almost complete calm reigns over the whole front on the first day of the year, with General McCreery's 8th Army dug in on the banks of the river Senio, in the flat country of Romagna, and Truscott's US 5th Army ten miles from Bologna. The lull in the fighting is to last many weeks, allowing the units of Vietinghoff's Army Group C (the 10th and 14th Armies of Generals Herr and Lemelsen) to strengthen their defences, and General Clark, who has succeeded Alexander in command of the Allied forces in Italy, to perfect his plans for the final offensive.

Eastern Front As a result of the defeats they have suffered, the Germans now have to hold a front against the Russians and their allies reduced from 2,750 miles to 1,400 miles. In the far north it runs from west of Petsamo and Kirkenes, to Lake Inari. South of the Baltic the German Army Group North is faced with the threat of encirclement in northern Latvia. In East Prussia Memel is also isolated, and the rest of the front more or less follows the border of the German province. The line of the Narew, the Vistula and the San marks the front in Poland, with a big Russian salient in the south in the Sandomierz area. The extreme eastern part of Slovakia is in Russian hands, while in Hungary the Red Army is fighting in Budapest and has established itself along a line that, from the Czechoslovakian frontier, runs south as far as the Magyar capital, then turns west as far as Lake Balaton and south again to the Drava, and then penetrates into Yugoslavia, where the front is more fluid; the Germans have partly evacuated the Balkans, but not completely. Such fighting as there is, however, consists of rearguard actions.

Against the Russian forces the Germans can still, at the beginning of 1945, deploy 3,100,000 men (out of a total of 5,350,000 'operational' effectives, besides the reserve) with 28,500 guns and mortars, 4,000 tanks and self-propelled guns and 1,960 combat aircraft.

Russian forces add up to 11,500,000 men, of whom 6,000,000 are combatants, with 108,000 guns and mortars, 12,900 tanks and self-propelled guns and 15,540 aircraft. Their armament has more than doubled since the beginning of 1944, whereas that of the Germans has been reduced in the same period by 26,000 guns, 1,450 tanks and self-propelled guns and 1,113 aircraft.

On New Year's Day the furious fighting in and around Budapest goes on.

Philippines To deceive the Japanese about the Allied plans for the invasion of Luzon, the Americans carry out mopping-up operations in the north-east of Mindoro. After that, nuisance operations will be carried out in the southern part of Luzon.

On Leyte the US 8th Army begins mopping up, which goes on until 8 May.

Caroline Islands Small units from the US 81st Infantry Division land on Fais Island, south-east of Ulithi, and begin a detailed reconnaissance.

2 January

Western Front In the Ardennes sector the divisions of the VIII Corps (US 3rd Army), continuing their ad-

A German ship under attack from a Beaufighter in a Norwegian fjord.

vance to the east, take Gerimont (87th Division), Mande St Etienne (11th Armoured) and Senonchamps (10th Armoured). On the German side General Manteuffel, commanding the 5th *Panzer* Army, asks Model, who commands Army Group B, for authority to withdraw his troops towards Houffalize; Model, who is himself in favour of such a withdrawal, is obliged to pass on the request to Hitler, and Hitler of course refuses. The Führer does not want to give up the Ardennes salient, because that is the only way he can keep the Allies engaged on a greatly extended front, and so prevent them (as he is also preventing them by actions like Operation *Nordwind*) from concentrating troops in the north for a new offensive towards the Ruhr.

In the 7th Army sector, German pressure continues; specially critical is the situation of the US VI Corps, which begins its withdrawal to prepare its defence on the Maginot Line.

Italian Front Limited activity on the east bank of the Senio (British 8th Army sector) to complete the liberation of the sector. The 5th Armoured Division, Canadian I Corps, moving north towards the sea, takes Conventelle.

Eastern Front The German Army Group South mounts a vigorous counter-attack north-west of Budapest in the hope of breaking through the forces surrounding the city.

Philippines The convoys transporting the US troops for the invasion of Luzon assemble in the Gulf of Leyte. On Mindoro Island the Americans begin the construction of two airfields to be used by heavy bombers. The Japanese air force attacks the other airfields on the island, destroying 22 American aircraft on the ground.

3 January

Western Front In the Ardennes sector, the US 1st Army mounts its offensive for the further reduction of the German salient from the north (the attack takes place on the Houffalize flank), and General Manteuffel puts in a last, desperate attack on Bastogne with the aim of cutting the corridor leading to the town. The German offensive does succeed in halting the American advance on Houffalize for 24 hours, but more than that it cannot achieve.

Further south, the VIII and III Corps of Patton's 3rd Army continue to press on towards Houffalize. In the sector held by the VI Corps (US 7th Army), General Balck's forces expand their salient towards Bitche, a place on the river Horn, about 15 miles south-east of Saarbrücken, penetrating into Wingen and Philippsbourg. The units at the centre and on the right of the American VI Corps complete their withdrawal to positions on the Maginot Line.

Eisenhower orders units of the French 1st Army to garrison Strasbourg (at one time the Allied Supreme Headquarters had decided to abandon the city but had reversed the decision under pressure from De Gaulle). General Devers, in command of the 6th Army Group, is ordered to withdraw from the salient in the north-east to the river Moder, about 20 miles west of the front line of 1 January.

Pacific Aircraft of Vice-Admiral Mitscher's fast aircraft carrier task force begin a series of attacks lasting two days against Japanese ships and aircraft in Formosa and the Ryukyu Islands. The American escort carrier *Sargent Bay* is damaged in a collision.

Burma The British XV Corps invades Akyab Island on the Arakan coast. The area is defended by the 53rd Division of the Japanese 28th Army.

In the XXXIII Corps area, the British 2nd Division takes Yeu.

China On the Salween front, the 9th Division of the Chinese 2nd Army succeeds in getting into Wanting, on the frontier between China and Burma, but is driven out again in a night counter-attack by the Japanese.

4 January

Western Front The British XXX Corps (2nd Army) launches its offensive in the western sector of the river Ourthe.

In the US 3rd Army sector, the advance of the divisions of the VIII and III Corps is brought to a halt in the area of Pironpré and in the district between Pinsamont, Rechrival and Hubermont (VIII Corps) and east of Bastogne, in the Mageret-Wardin sector.

On the right flank of the front, where the US 7th Army is operating, the 45th Division (VI Corps) continues its thrusts in the direction of Wingen to eliminate the Bitche salient.

An American soldier approaches a wounded German lying in the snow near Bastogne.

Hitler agrees that General Dietrich's 6th *Panzer* SS Division may be withdrawn from the Eifel area, reinforced and then sent to the Eastern front, where a massive Russian offensive is expected. The sector is handed over to the 5th Armoured and 7th Armies.

Pacific By the time its series of attacks is finished Vice-Admiral Mitscher's squadron, despite unfavourable weather, has sunk 12 ships and damaged 28; it has also shot down 110 Japanese aircraft for the loss of 18 US planes.

Philippines Japanese aircraft attack the American ships on their way to the Gulf of Lingayen, Luzon. The escort carrier *Ommaney Bay* is damaged by a suicide aircraft so seriously that it has to be sunk. A destroyer and a tanker are also badly damaged.

On Leyte Island the X Corps of the US 8th Army completes its operations. Japanese aircraft are active again at Mindoro, where they sink a US ship loaded with ammunition.

Burma The British XV Corps completes the occupation of Akyab, an important air and naval base on the Arakan coast. Further east, the American 475th Infantry Regiment crosses the river Shweli, while the American 124th Cavalry waits for reinforcements to be dropped by para-

chute before carrying out the crossing.

5 January

Western Front The US 1st Army advances towards Consy (VII Corps) and Bergeval (XVIII Corps), while in the 3rd Army sector units of the VIII and III Corps go on to the defensive. Although there is still fierce fighting, it is clear that Bastogne is no longer in danger and that the crisis for the Americans in this sector has now passed.

In the Strasbourg sector, on the southern flank of the Allied line, the French 1st Army is relieving the units of the American 7th Army so that French troops can take over the defence of the city.

The XV Corps (American 7th Army) reaches Frauenberg and Gros Réderchin, but on the right flank of the VI Corps the German 553rd *Volksgrenadieredivision* establishes a bridgehead over the Rhine in the Gambsheim sector, between Kilstett and Drusenheim, about 12 miles north of Strasbourg. Task Force *Linden* (five battalions of the US 42nd Division of infantry) launches an immediate counter-attack, but without success.

Pacific The islands of Chichi Jima and Haha Jima, in the Bonins, are attacked by aircraft of the US 7th Air Force and by cruisers and destroyers under the command of Rear-Admiral A. E. Smith. Another group of US cruisers and destroyers, commanded by Rear-Admiral McCrea, shells Japanese installations in the Kuril Islands.

Philippines About thirty Japanese suicide aircraft, taking off from Luzon, attack the American invasion convoy off the island, damaging the escort carriers *Manila Bay* and *Savo Island*, the heavy cruisers *Louisville* and *Australia*, two destroyers and several smaller ships.

On Mindoro Island several places are occupied by Filipino guerrillas commanded by American officers.

6 January

Western Front Units of the VII Corps of the US 1st Army approach Consy and Dochamps (2nd Armoured Division and 84th Division of infantry), capture Odeigne and join up with the units of the 3rd Armoured Division on the road linking Manhay with Houffalize.

In the 3rd Army sector Bonnerne, defended by the 87th Division (VIII Corps) is attacked by General Manteuffel's armoured group; units of the III Corps (6th and 35th Divisions) suffer heavy losses in counter-attacks in the forests north-east of Lutrebois. However, in the Ardennes the withdrawal of Dietrich's 6th *Panzer SS* Army makes the German position in this sector highly vulnerable. Von Rundstedt, in a memorandum sent to the *Oberkommando der Wehrmacht*, once more suggests that the German armies be withdrawn east of the Rhine. Once more Hitler refuses. In the southern sector of the front, the 45th Division (VI Corps, US 7th Army) continues its efforts to reduce the Bitche salient.

Eastern Front The counter-offensive launched by the Germans to open a gap in the Russian forces surrounding the troops cut off in Budapest does not achieve that object, but does lead to the recapture of Esztergom, an important position north-west of the capital.

Philippines Two American naval squadrons, ahead of the Luzon invasion fleet, enter the Gulf of Lingayen. The aircraft carriers send up their aircraft against the Japanese airfields, while the naval guns shell the coastal defences and minesweepers begin to clear the waters of mines. The Japanese react with a violent attack by suicide aircraft, which damage the battleships *New Mexico* and *California*, the cruisers *Louisville* (damaged already), *Minneapolis* and *Columbia*, six destroyers and smaller craft. Two minesweepers are sunk. Of the 150 Japanese aircraft defending Luzon a week ago, there are now only 35 left.

7 January

Western Front Units of the VII Corps (1st Army) make excellent progress along the road leading from Laroche to Salmchâteau, their last objective before Houffalize. They take Dochamps, three miles north of Laroche.

In the US 3rd Army sector the 87th Division (VIII Corps) continues in action round Bonnerne, trying to reach Tillet. The resistance put up by the German units of the XLVII Armoured Corps is particularly powerful in the sector east of Bastogne.

The American and French units (6th Army Group) on the southern flank are in a difficult situation. A new German counter-offensive in the Strasbourg sector is combined with fighting to the north of the city in the Haguenau forest and to the south of Wissembourg, where the Germans threaten the Maginot Line positions. South of Strasbourg, the German 198th Infantry Division, supported by an SS armoured brigade, falls on the 3rd and 1st Free French Divisions and opens a gap as far as Erstein.

Eastern Front The savage fighting in the north-west of Budapest continues.

Philippines While the air and naval bombardment of Luzon continues, special American units begin to seek and remove the under-water obstacles in the Gulf of Lingayen.

8 January

Western Front The units of the American VII Corps (1st Army) continue to advance on Houffalize. Meanwhile Manteuffel's forces have been ordered to withdraw west of the town to a line based on a series of hills about five miles away.

In the Strasbourg sector to the south the French 1st Army continues its battle in defence of the city. Meanwhile, in the US 7th Army sector, the Germans take Rimling and consolidate their bridgehead at Gambsheim.

Philippines Another American naval squadron, commanded by Vice-Admiral Oldendorf, and a carrier squadron commanded by Rear-Admiral Durgin attack objectives in Luzon, in particular the area chosen for the landing. Two escort carriers and other ships are damaged by Japanese high-level bombers and suicide aircraft. The heavy cruiser *Australia* is hit again.

9 January

Western Front In the central-northern sector of the front the units of the US 1st and 3rd Armies continue to advance, with the aim of eliminating the salient taken by the Germans in the Ardennes counter-offensive. In the 3rd Army sector, the 87th Division and 101st Airborne Division (VIII Corps) make further progress towards Tillet and Noville respectively. Units of the III Corps, three infantry divisions (90th, 26th and 35th) and the 6th Armoured Division, attack the German pocket south-east of Bastogne. On the right of the line German pressure continues on the US 7th Army and French 1st Army.

Philippines At about 9.30 a.m., after a massive air and naval preparation, the Americans begin to land 67,000 men in the Gulf of Lingayen on the central western coast of Luzon. Supreme command of the operation is exercised by General MacArthur, and the naval forces are commanded by Vice-Admiral Kinkaid. The island is defended by 262,000 men of the Japanese 14th Army under General Yamashita. First to land are the I Corps under General Swift, on the left, not far from Damortis, and the XIV Corps under General Griswold on the right, near Lingayen. Yamashita decides not to oppose the landing.

The Japanese air force, still in action, sends up the few aircraft still left on the island against the American ships, damaging the battleship *Mississippi*, the light cruiser *Columbia* and other vessels. For the first time the Japanese navy makes use of explosive boats piloted by the equivalent of the *kamikaze* pilots, and sink a big American transport. The battleship *Colorado* is accidentally hit by fire from other American ships.

Meanwhile, in support of the operation against Luzon, US carrier-borne aircraft and land-based heavy bombers attack airfields and other military targets on Formosa, in the Ryukyu Islands and in the Pescadores. The air attacks on Iwo Jima continue, and a raid is also carried out against the Musashino aircraft factory in Tokyo.

10 January

Western Front The 51st Division, British XXX Corps (2nd Army) takes Laroche, about ten miles north-west of Houffalize.

The units of the US 1st Army (VII and XVIII Corps) prepare to step up the attack on the whole front, towards a line from Houffalize to Bovigny and towards St Vith.

In the US 3rd Army sector, the 87th Division (VIII Corps) takes Tillet, while the III Corps continues to advance on the south flank. Although Althorn on the left flank of the Bitche salient (US 7th Army sector) is taken by the 45th Division, the Germans are still able to maintain their positions.

Philippines: Luzon The Americans continue to land in the Gulf of Lingayen. The beachhead, a mile and a quarter wide and three and a half miles deep the previous day, is now considerably expanded. The main body of the American forces move south, towards Manila, occupying several villages; part of the I Corps advances north and north-east, taking San Jacinto.

The Japanese air attacks continue, and so do the forays of explosive boats; two American destroyers and five other ships are damaged.

Burma In the British XXXIII Corps sector, the British 2nd Division and the 19th Indian Division take Shwebo and the 20th Indian Division captures Budalin after prolonged fighting. In the British IV Corps sector, Allied aircraft attack in force Japanese concentrations in the area of Gangaw.

11 January

Western Front Units of the British 6th Division (XXX Corps, 2nd Army) take St Hubert, making contact with units of the VIII Corps of the US 3rd Army which have also entered the town, from which German troops have been withdrawn. The Americans of the VIII Corps take Bommerne, Pironpré and Vesqueville, while units of the III Corps eliminate the German pocket southeast of Bastogne. The American 45th Division (VI Corps, US 7th Army) continues its pressure on the western flank of the Bitche salient. The Germans launch another offensive against the positions of the 79th Division on the Maginot Line south of Wissembourg.

Philippines: Luzon The US XIV Corps consolidates its own sector of the beachhead. Some units meet with the first co-ordinated Japanese resistance. The village of Aguilar is occupied after liberation by Filipino guerrillas. Further north, in the I Corps sector, the US 6th Division occupies Santa Barbara, also liberated by Filipino guerrillas; the 43rd Division occupies Manoag without opposition, but is then held up in front of a chain of hills by intensive fire from Japanese artillery. The I Corps' front has already been extended to some ten miles.

Two escort destroyers, one assault craft and one landing craft are badly damaged in attacks by *kamikaze*-piloted aircraft.

Burma The divisions of the British IV Corps take Gangaw and advance rapidly towards the river Irrawaddy in the area of Pakokku in readiness for a move on Meiktila.

12 January

Western Front In the US 1st Army sector, the 2nd Armoured Division (VII Corps) opens an offensive in the Houffalize–Laroche sector. Further north, the 106th Division (US XVIII Airborne Corps, establishes a bridgehead over the river Amblève south of Stavelot.

The German divisions of the 5th Armoured Army and the 7th Army continue to retire under pressure from the units of the US 3rd Army; the 87th Division (VIII Corps) takes Amberloup, Lavacherie, Fosset and Sprimont, while further south the 6th Armoured Division (III Corps) enters Wardin.

Italian Front The *Cremona* combat group under General Clemente Primieri, incorporated in the Canadian I Corps (British 8th Army), goes into the line to replace the Canadian 1st Division in the sector between Alfonsine (Ravenna) and the Adriatic coast. This is the first of the six big formations (the others are the *Friuli*, *Legnano*, *Folgore*, *Mantova* and *Piceno*) formed by the Italian army in the second half of 1944 in close collaboration with the Allied military mission in Italy.

Eastern Front As the battle for Budapest goes on, the Russians unexpectedly re-open the offensive against Poland, defended by the German Army Group A under the command of General Josef Harpe (and comprising the 1st Armoured Army (Heinrici), the 17th Army (Schulz), the 4th Armoured Army (Graser), the 9th Army (von Luttwitz), 30 infantry divisions, 5 tank divisions and 50 autonomous battalions). South of Army Group A is Army Group Centre under General Schörner (comprising the 2nd Army (Weiss), the 4th (Hossbach) and the 3rd Armoured Army (Rauss). Seven fortified lines have been prepared between the Vistula and the Oder, that on the Vistula being the most strongly manned.

In total 5·3 million Russians are engaged on the Eastern Front, in 527 infantry divisions, 43 artillery divisions, 302 tank brigades (with 13,500 armoured vehicles and self-propelled guns); 1·8 million German troops are engaged in 164 divisions (of which 38 are in the Army Group South, 99 in Army Groups A and Centre, and 27 in northern Latvia.

Operation *Vistula–Oder* is started by the 1st Ukraine Front, which advances from the Sandomierz bridgehead towards Breslavia, and the 2nd Belorussian Front, which throws in nine armies in a surprise attack against the German 2nd Army on the river Narew north of Warsaw.

The first German defensive line on the Vistula is breached by the 1st Ukraine Front within 24 hours.

Philippines: Luzon In the XIV Corps sector the US 40th Division occupies Port Sual and pushes on westwards towards Alaminos without opposition. In the I Corps sector, the task given to the units is to ensure control of the road from Damortis inland to Rosario.

Mindoro Americans and Filipino guerrillas go ahead with the slow occupation of the island. The Americans concentrate at Pinamalayan to launch an attack in force on Calapan, where the main body of the Japanese garrison is concentrated.

Burma In the British XV Corps sector the 3rd Commando Brigade lands after an air and naval bombardment at Myebon on the Arakan coast, establishing a firm bridgehead which the Japanese try unsuccessfully to destroy with vigorous counter attacks.

13 January

Western Front In the British 2nd Army sector, the XXX Corps finishes its task in the Ardennes when the 51st Division reaches the river Ourthe south of Laroche. The VII Corps (US 1st Army) heads steadily for Houffalize. In the region between Stavelot and Malmédy the XVIII Airborne Corps launches a new offensive with the 106th Division on the right and the 30th on the left. The two American formations reach Hénumont and Hédomont. In the US 3rd sector advance patrols of the

9 January 1945: after a massive air and naval preparation, American troops begin to land on Luzon in the Philippines.

87th Division (VIII Corps) reach the river Ourthe. Units of the 11th Armoured Division reach the Houffalize–St Hubert road near Bastogne, and St Hubert is surrounded. On the right flank of the corps units of the 101st Airborne Division capture Foy, on the Bastogne–Houffalize road.

The US XXI Corps under General Milburn goes into the line on the left flank of the 7th Army.

In the southern sector of the front fighting continues round Strasbourg, where the 3rd Algerian Division of infantry holds off the repeated German attacks.

Eastern Front The 1st Ukraine Front and 2nd Belorussian Front mount heavy and brilliantly executed attacks to continue their advance. The 47th Army of the 2nd Belorussian Front surrounds Warsaw.

Philippines: Luzon General Krueger takes over direct command of the US 6th Army. Troops of the XIV Corps occupy Guagua, while naval forces occupy an area on the coast off which a flying-boat base is to be installed. The I Corps occupies Damortis with-

out firing a shot, but there is fighting inland only a few miles away.

Burma In the Arakan sector the British XV Corps extends and strengthens the bridgehead at Myebon, with a landing by the 25th Indian Division.

14 January

Western Front The VII Corps (US 1st Army) continues its advance; the 84th Division reaches its final objective when it takes Nadrin, Filly, Petite-Mormont and Grande-Mormont, coming in sight of the advance patrols of the 3rd Army, while the 2nd Division and 3rd Armoured Division capture, respectively, Wilbrin, Wilogue and Dinez, and Mont-le-Ban and Baclain. The 106th Division (XVIII Airborne Corps) takes Hénumont and pushes on south.

In the US 3rd Army sector, the 17th Airborne Division (VIII Corps) takes Bastogne, while east of Bastogne the 101st Airborne Division mounts an offensive towards the area between Noville, Rachamps and Bourcy. Further south, where the

XX Corps is operating, the 94th Division puts in a series of attacks to improve the defensive positions of the American forces in the triangle at the confluence of the Saar with the Moselle south of Wasserbillig, one of the fortified positions on the Siegfried Line.

Eastern Front Berlin announces that the Russians of the 1st Baltic Front and the 3rd Belorussian Front (Chernyakhovsky) have gone on the offensive in the area of Schlossberg (Pillkallen), near the north-east of East Prussia.

In Poland, the 1st Belorussian Front attacks with seven armies from the area of Magnuszew in the direction of Poznan and from the Pulawy bridgehead over the Vistula in the direction of Radom and Lodz. The right flank of the Front converges on Warsaw from the south. Meanwhile the 1st Ukraine Front, which went on the offensive on 12 January, advances rapidly towards Kielce, an important railway junction.

In Hungary, bitter fighting continues in Budapest, while the German forces continue the regular withdrawal of their forces from Yugoslavia.

Philippines: Luzon The XIV Corps advances up to the river Agno and crosses it, occupying Bautista. In the I Corps sector, the US 43rd Division is held up by intensive Japanese fire as it advances on Rosario.

Burma In the British XXXIII Corps sector, the 19th Indian Division establishes a bridgehead over the Irrawaddy at Thabeikkyin, arousing a violent response from the Japanese, who send substantial reinforcements to the area. The Japanese envisage a threat to Mandalay.

15 January

Western Front In the British 2nd Army sector units of the 7th Armoured Division (XII Corps) capture Bakenhoven, about a mile and a quarter north-west of Susteren, in advance of Operation *Blackcock*, the elimination of the German salient between the Meuse and the Rur, going south from Roermond. The 2nd Armoured Division (US VII

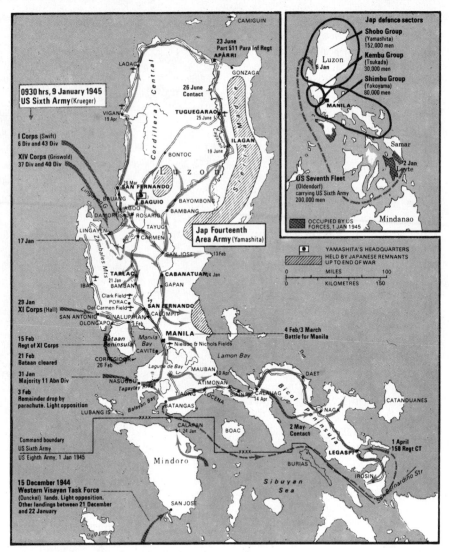

The US offensive in Luzon 9 January–23 June 1945.

Corps, 1st Army), having taken Achouffe, Mont and Tavernaux, sends forward patrols towards the river Ourthe and into Houffalize, which the forces of the German 5th Armoured Army have evacuated. In the XVIII Airborne Corps sector the 75th Division opens an offensive across the Salm, reaching Salmchâteau and Bech, while the 30th Division takes Beaumont, Francheville and Pont.

The units of the US 3rd Army also advance, but while the 11th Armoured Division and the 101st Airborne Division (VIII Corps) push on without opposition, the 35th and 90th Divisions (III Corps) run into violent resistance from the German LXXXV Corps.

The 6th Army Group headquarters

sends the French 1st Army preliminary instructions for the offensive against the Colmar pocket.

Eastern Front The 4th Ukraine Front joins in the fighting in southern Poland, breaking into the Carpathians from the Sanok area, southwest of Krakow. The 1st Ukraine Front seizes Kielce.

Philippines: Luzon While the troops of the US XIV Corps advance cautiously without meeting any opposition, those of the I Corps find themselves faced by stiff enemy resistance in the areas of Urdaneta and Rosario.

Mindoro The Americans withdraw the 503rd Parachute Regiment from the island; up to now it has been giving help and support to the guerrilla operations. The 21st Infantry, mak-

THE NATIONALIZATION OF RENAULT

Without the guidance of its founder Louis Renault, who had been jailed for collaboration at Fresnes and who died on 24 October 1944, the oldest of the French motor companies underwent a radical alteration in structure in the months following liberation.

On 16 January a legislative act signed by General De Gaulle, Pierre Lacoste, Pierre Mendès-France, Alexandre Parodi and René Pleven provided for the nationalization of Renault. Under the new statute the firm became a government corporation with autonomous management under the new name of RNUR (Régie nationale des usines Renault).

From early 1945, under the directorship of Pierre Lefaucheux, Renault production was resumed on a notable scale, with 60 vehicles a day coming off the Billancourt assembly lines, quite an achievement considering the difficulties experienced in obtaining raw materials.

The revolutionary 4 CV, already designed before the war, was introduced, with enormous success, in August 1947.

ing for Calapan, runs into Japanese units which have been ordered to slow down the advance.

Some of the smaller islets in the archipelago, not manned by the Japanese, are occupied by the Americans.

Burma In the British XXXIII Corps sector, the 19th Indian Division establishes another bridgehead over the Irrawaddy, at Kyaukmyaung. In the north, the Chinese 30th Division captures Namhkam, so gaining control of the lower Shweli valley. The first convoy to inaugurate the new Burma road, starting from Ledo, reaches Myitkyina, where it has to wait until the rest of the route is cleared of the enemy.

China In south-east China the Japanese open an offensive to capture the American airfields at Suichuan, south-east of Changsha.

East China Sea A squadron of fast aircraft carriers under the command of Vice-Admiral McCain attacks Japanese airfields and shipping in Formosa and off the Chinese coast from Hong Kong to Amoy. Two Japanese destroyers and a transport are sunk.

16 January
Western Front After preparation by the artillery, the British XII Corps under General Ritchie, with two infantry divisions and one armoured, launches Operation *Blackcock* to eliminate the German salient between the Meuse and the Rur, the so-called 'Roermond triangle'.

Near Houffalize (in the middle of the Germans' Ardennes salient) the 41st Infantry Regiment of the US VII Corps (1st Army) makes contact with the 41st Squadron of cavalry of the US VIII Corps (3rd Army). While the 2nd Armoured Division (VII Corps) occupies the part of the town north of the river Ourthe, units of the German 5th Armoured Army continue to resist on the left flank. The German Ardennes salient has already been reduced to half its former size; starting from Monschau in the north, the front runs west of St Vith to Houffalize, then southeast in the direction of Wiltz and Ettelbruck, where it turns east to Echternach.

In the southern sector of the front, the US 12th Armoured Division (VI Corps, 7th Army) opens an offensive against the Gambsheim bridgehead.

Eastern Front The 69th Army and II Armoured Corps of the 1st Belorussian Front take Radom by storm and push on towards Lodz. The 47th and 61st Armies of the Front attack Warsaw from north and south. The 2nd Armoured Army, with the Polish 1st Army, put pressure on the Germans from the west and the east. Some German units succeed in opening a corridor and escaping from

Warsaw. In the first two days of the offensive the 1st Belorussian Front has advanced an average of 15–25 miles, while the 1st Ukraine Front has advanced 62 miles in four days and is now heading for Czestochowa and Krakow.

East China Sea For the second day, aircraft of the US Task Force 38 attack the south coast of China and Hainan Island. Not much damage is done to Japanese shipping, but there is some success against port installations.

Philippines: Luzon In the US XIV Corps sector, a start is made on the construction of bridges over the river Agno to carry heavy materials across. In the same area, still south of the beachhead, the Americans reach the northern slopes of the Zambales Mountains. In the I Corps sector, the 43rd Division tries to take Rosario, but makes little progress against vigorous resistance.

17 January

Western Front In the course of Operation *Blackcock* units of the 7th Armoured Division (XII Corps, British 2nd Army) advance and capture Echt and Susteren.

Eastern Front In Poland, the Russians give the Polish 1st Army the honour of launching the final offensive and of being the first to enter Warsaw. The city is reduced to a pile of rubble. A few hundred people who have managed to live in shelters and cellars come out to welcome the liberators. After crushing the Warsaw uprising, the Germans deported the whole of the remaining population, about 600,000 people, to concentration camps.

North of Warsaw, the 2nd Belorussian Front takes Ciechanow. In the south, advancing rapidly beyond Kielce, the 1st Ukraine Front overcomes German resistance on the river Warta and occupies Czestochowa.

Following the loss of Warsaw Hitler relieves General Harpe of the command of the Army Group A and replaces him by General Schörner.

Philippines: Luzon The Americans advance slowly in all directions

round their beachhead. MacArthur asks General Krueger for more speed.

Burma In the north, the US 5332nd Brigade and Chinese 38th Division begin mopping up in the area along the Burma Road beyond Myitkyina.

18 January

Western Front Despite firm opposition by the units of the German 1st Parachute Army, Operation *Blackcock* goes ahead with the advance of the XII Corps (British 2nd Army) and the capture of Schilberg and Heide, north-east of Susteren.

In the US 3rd Army sector, the 17th Airborne Division (VIII Corps) advances from Hardigny towards Houffalize. The XII Corps mounts an offensive with the 4th Division and 5th Armoured Division across the Sauer, between Reisdorf and Ettelbruck.

The French 1st Army receives orders to prepare to mount the attack on the Colmar pocket by 20 January; the Allied Supreme Command considers that the pocket must be liquidated to restore the situation in Alsace. It is held by the German 19th Army under General Wiese and comprises two armoured corps, the LXIV and LXIII (in the south), with altogether eight divisions. General de Tassigny also has two corps, I under General Béthouart and the II under General Monsabert.

Eastern Front The 1st Belorussian Front wipes out the last remaining Germans in Warsaw, and the 1st Ukraine Front begins the struggle for Upper Silesia.

In Hungary the last defenders of Pest, south of the Danube, surrender.

Philippines: Luzon The US XIV Corps is ordered to advance in force across the river Agno towards the south, from the present line Bayambang–Urbiztondo–Bogtong. In the US I Corps sector, the 6th Division takes Urdaneta and penetrates in between the Cabaruan hills without making contact with the main body of the enemy. The 43rd Division, near Sison, retains a road block de-

spite heavy Japanese pressure. The 63rd Division opens an attack against a ridge known as Blue Ridge, near Amlang.

Palau Islands Two special Japanese units land at Peleliu and try unsuccessfully to blow up American ammunition dumps and aircraft stores. They do no damage and are wiped out.

Burma In the north, the US 5332nd Brigade, given the job of reopening the Burma Road, digs in on some positions that overlook the road. The Japanese are sending reinforcements to the area of Namhpakka.

19 January

Western Front Fighting continues in the Roermond sector between the Meuse and the Rur, between units of the British XII Corps (General Dempsey's 2nd Army) and the divisions of the German 1st Parachute Army.

With the capture of Rettigny, Brisy and Renglez the US 3rd Armoured Division (VII Corps of the 1st Army) has reached its final objectives. The units of the other two corps of the 1st Army, the XVIII Airborne and the V, continue to advance towards the Our.

In the US 3rd Army sector the 4th and 5th Divisions (XII Corps) take Bettendorf. A series of German counter-attacks from the Bitche salient are halted by units of the 45th Division (VI Corps, US 7th Army). South of Haltern, north-west of Haguenau, and not far from the Rhine and the Franco-German frontier, units of the German 1st Army increase their pressure.

Eastern Front Confirming the German announcement of a new offensive in East Prussia, the Soviet Supreme Command announces that the 3rd Belorussian Front has captured Schlossberg (Pillkallen).

In Poland Operation *Vistula-Oder* continues swiftly. The 1st Belorussian Front captures Lodz, while the 1st Ukraine Front takes Tarnow and its 3rd and 52nd Armies capture Krakow. The 60th Army of the same Front presses forward south and north of Katowice. The 4th Ukraine

Front under Petrov, operating further south, takes Gorlice, south of Tarnow.

Philippines: Luzon The XIV Corps (US 6th Army) begins advancing south, with Clark Airfield as its objective; some of its units reach Carmen and Moncada, and others get to Paniqui. In the north, in the I Corps sector, units of the 43rd Division are repulsed by the Japanese, who drive them out of the positions they had occupied near Sison.

Mindoro The occupation of the island goes ahead. The US 21st Infantry overcomes Japanese resistance at the Gusay stream.

Burma The 25th Indian Division (British XV Corps) takes Kantha, in the Myebon peninsula. In the northern sector the 114th Regiment, Chinese 38th Division, cuts the road between Namhkam and Namhpakka, while the US 5332nd Brigade proceeds with the occupation of the hills dominating the Burma Road.

20 January

Western Front While the German salient in the Ardennes is by now reduced to a minimum and the German armies are preparing to retire to their original positions, in Alsace General Patch's 7th Army has completed its withdrawal, digging in in new positions along the line of the rivers Rothbach–Rau–Moder. The battle has cost the Americans 15,600 men, the Germans 25,000.

General Patton's 3rd Army is advancing on every front, crossing the line Hardigny–Bourcy and the village of Tavigny with the VIII Corps, reaching Chifontaine and Allerborn with the units of the III Corps; the 4th Division (XII Corps) takes the angle formed by the confluence of the rivers Sauer and Our, and the 5th the villages of Kippenhof and Brandenburg. On their right flank, the 95th Division (XX Corps) halts German counter-attacks in the Saarlautern bridgehead.

The French 1st Army begins the first operations against the Colmar pocket, attacking from the south with two Moroccan divisions (the

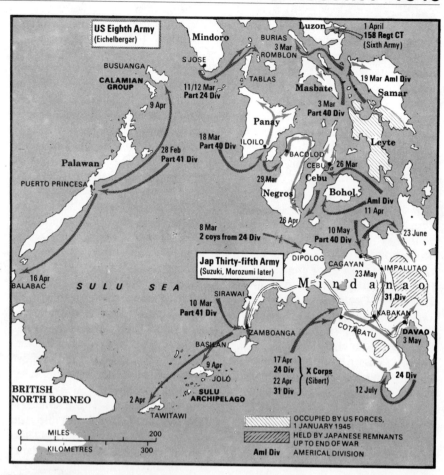

US operations in the southern Philippines February–July 1945.

4th Motorized and 2nd of infantry) of General Béthouart's I Corps, supported by tanks of the 1st Armoured Division, along the Cernay-Ensisheim axis. Bad weather conditions slow down the French advance considerably; they finally reach their objective, Ensisheim, on 1 February. General Monsabert's French II Corps prepares to support the I Corps's offensive from the north with four divisions, including the American 28th Division.

Eastern Front The 3rd Belorussian Front and the 2nd begin to penetrate into East Prussia with the support of the 1st Baltic Front (Bagramian). The 43rd Army of this last Front occupies Tilsit, in the north; the 2nd Belorussian Front, advancing north from Poland, reaches the Tannenberg area with some of its units.

The 1st Belorussian Front and 1st Ukraine Front continue their advance into Poland, the first making for Prussia and the second for Silesia.

In the Carpathian sector the 4th Ukraine Front takes Nowy Sacz in Poland and Bardejov, Presov and Kosice in Czechoslovakia. In Hungary, the Germans offer stiff resistance to the Russians as they try to reach the Danube from the area of Székesfehérvár, south-west of Budapest. Bitter fighting still rages in the capital.

☐ The provisional Hungarian government signs an armistice agreement in Moscow with the Soviet Union, Great Britain and the United States.

Philippines: Luzon In the US XIV Corps sector a regiment of the 40th Division of infantry comes within four miles of Tarlac, while other units of the 37th Division occupy Victoria, evacuated by the Japanese. The US I Corps makes very slow progress in the mountainous country north of the beachhead. The 43rd Division takes Mount Alava.

Burma–China The Chinese 9th Division, on the Salween front, occupies Wanting, which the Japanese have evacuated, while elements of the Chinese 38th Division make contact with the Yunnan Force near Mu-se.

21 January

Western Front The VII Corps (US 1st Army) prepares for an offensive in the Gouvy-Beho region, between Houffalize and St Vith.

The VIII and III Corps of the US 3rd Army increase their pressure. The 17th Airborne Division (VIII Corps) continues to advance north-east of Tavigny, while the divisions of the III Corps take Crendal, Lullange, Hoffelt and Hachiville (6th Armoured Division), Derenbach (90th Division) and Wiltz (26th Division), a town in Luxembourg only a few miles from the Belgian frontier.

Eastern Front In East Prussia the 1st Baltic Front advances in all directions from Tilsit (now Sovetsk); on the right it reaches the stretch of sea enclosed by the long tongue of land stretching almost from Memel (Klaipeda) to the area of Königsberg (Kaliningrad). On the left it occupies Gumbinnen (Gusev). The 2nd Belorussian Front, advancing from the south, captures the historic town of Tannenberg.

In Poland, the 1st Ukraine Front penetrates into the German region of Upper Silesia west of Czestochowa, taking a number of villages.

Formosa–Ryukyu–Pescadores Relays of aircraft from the carrier squadron commanded by Vice-Admiral McCain carry out very heavy raids on the airfields on these islands and on Japanese shipping, destroying about a hundred Japanese aircraft on the ground and sinking a dozen transports and tankers. *Kamikaze* squadrons take off against the American ships, causing serious damage to the aircraft carrier *Ticonderoga* and some damage to the light carrier *Langley* and to a destroyer. The carrier *Hancock* suffers slight damage from an accidental explosion.

Philippines: Luzon In the US XIV Corps sector the 40th Infantry Division occupies Tarlac without

opposition and advances as far as San Miguel. In the US I Corps sector the Americans mop up Blue Ridge, near Amlang, and one or two hills overlooking the village of Rosario. Several Filipino battalions are now deployed among the American units.

Burma After accurate shelling by naval guns, and with substantial air support, a brigade of the 26th Indian Division lands on Ramree Island and takes the town of Kyaukpyu. The 25th Indian Division by now occupies the whole of the Myebon peninsula.

22 January

Western Front The British XII Corps (2nd Army) is still finding it very difficult to advance in the Roermond area, but some progress is reported.

The US 84th Divison, with support from the 3rd Armoured Division, (US VII Corps, 1st Army) takes Gouvy and Beho, between Houffalize and St Vith. Meanwhile the weather has improved allowing the Allies to employ their aircraft again; they wreak havoc among the light vehicles and half-tracks of the retreating Germans as they queue up in long lines waiting their turn to cross the bridges over the river Our. The VIII Corps of the US 3rd Army crosses the Luxembourg frontier with the 11th Armoured Division. In the same sector, the III and XII Corps continue to make progress; units of the 90th Division (III Corps) reach Rumlange and Sassel, while the 4th Division (XII Corps) captures positions along the west bank of the Our and seizes Walsdorf. In the French 1st Army sector, the II Corps (US 3rd Division and 5th Armoured Division and 1st Moroccan Division of Infantry, with support from the French 2nd Armoured Division) begins to advance towards the Colmar pocket; the attack is carried out from the north in the region between Sélestat and Ostheim, while the US 28th Division carries out raids from the west, and complements the offensive launched by the I Corps against the same objective from the south on 20

January.

Italian Front Headquarters, US 5th Army issues the first directives on the training programme for the spring offensive.

Eastern Front In East Prussia the 3rd Belorussian Front captures Insterburg (Chernyakhovsk), west of Gumbinnen; the 2nd Belorussian Front takes Allenstein (Olsztyn) and Deutsch Eylau (Ilawa), south of Königsberg. Two million civilians flee westward.

In Poland, the 1st Belorussian Front is engaged at Bromberg (Bygoszcz) and occupies Gniezno, pushing on towards Poznan. The 1st Ukraine Front, part of which has now entered Upper Silesia, takes the towns of Kronstadt (Wolczyn) and Gross Strehlitz (Strzelce). The Germans defend this important mining and industrial area.

Pacific: Ryukyu Islands The aircraft of Vice-Admiral McCain's fast carrier squadron attack enemy shipping, airfields and other installations.

Philippines: Luzon Fierce fighting between units of the US 43rd Division (I Corps) and Japanese in the area of Hill 355, near Carmen. The Americans call in artillery and tank support but are unable to capture the hill.

Burma In the Arakan coast sector, the 3rd Commando Brigade lands at Kangaw after a preliminary bombardment. The Japanese 54th Division reacts sharply, since the units stationed on the coast south of Kangaw are in danger of being cut off. In the British XXXIII Corps sector, the 20th Indian Division occupies Monywa (the last river port on the Chindwin still in Japanese hands) after hard fighting, and takes Myinmu on the Irrawaddy. In the British IV Corps sector, further east, the 7th Indian Division takes Tilin. In the northern sector, Chinese and Americans continue mopping up the route of the Burma Road.

China The Japanese, advancing from the south, have during the last three days captured several bridges and tunnels on the Canton–Hankow railway.

23 January
Western Front In the American 1st Army sector, St Vith is captured by the 7th Armoured Division (XVIII Airborne Corps). Further south, where the corps of the US 3rd Army are operating, Biwisch, Basbellain, Biensfeld and Fuhren are reached. Wasserbillig, a town at the confluence of the rivers Sauer and Moselle, is occupied by the 346th Regiment of the US 87th Division (XII Corps).

In the southern sector of the front, the 1st Moroccan Division (II Corps, French 1st Army) crosses the river Ill between Illhäusern and Illwald.

Eastern Front In East Prussia, in the north-eastern sector, the 3rd Belorussian Front captures Wehlau, between Insterburg and Königsberg. The 2nd Belorussian Front advances towards Elbing (Elblag) and the Gulf of Danzig, while in northern Poland it occupies the towns of Brodnica and Lipno. The German forces in the eastern province are now cut into three parts.

In Poland, the 1st Belorussian Front continues its battle for the fortified town of Bromberg (Bydgoszcz) and occupies Kalisz, while the 1st Ukraine Front reaches the Oder–Neisse line near Breslau (Wroclaw) on a front of 40 miles.

In Hungary, a powerful counter-attack by the Germans to re-take the Danube line forces the Russians out of Székesfehérvár. North of Miskolc, the 2nd Ukraine Front reopens the offensive northwards and, with assistance from the Rumanian 4th Army, captures a number of places in Slovakia.

The tenacity with which the Germans are fighting in Hungary is due to the oil deposits in the west of the country which are indispensable to the Wehrmacht.

Philippines: Luzon In the US XIV Corps sector, infantry of the 40th Division overcome scattered Japanese resistance and occupy the town and airfield of Bamban (south of Tarlac) and cross the river Bamban not far from the big Clark Airfield. There is fierce fighting in the US I Corps area, east of the beachhead.

24 January
Western Front The British XII Corps (2nd Army) continues to advance in the Roermond triangle and the 7th Armoured Division takes Montfort. The 52nd Division occupies Haaren and the 43rd reaches Schleiden and Uetterath.

The 12th Army Group (US 1st and 3rd Armies) continue their offensive in the Ardennes sector for the elimination of the German salient; in the north, units of the US 7th Armoured Division (XVIII Airborne Corps, 1st Army) capture the area south and south-east of St Vith, while units of the V Corps continue the advance to the south-west towards the road between Büllingen and St Vith. In the US 7th Army sector, the German 1st Army drives the advance guards of the 45th Division (VI Corps) out of Sägmuhl.

On the right flank, the French 1st Army sector, the II Corps launches a new offensive to extend the bridge-head over the river Ill.

Eastern Front The 2nd and 3rd Belorussian Fronts push on in every sector of East Prussia towards Königsberg. The German 3rd Army is the formation that suffers the worst casualties.

In Upper Silesia, the 1st Ukraine Front captures the towns of Oppeln

Identification of American soldiers killed by the Ist *SS Panzerdivision* in the St. Vith sector during the Ardennes counter-offensive.

(on the Oder) and Gleiwitz; north of Breslau some units begin mopping up in Trachenberg (Zmigrod) and Rawicz.

Philippines: Luzon The troops of the US XIV Corps run into stiff Japanese resistance on a line of hills west of Bamban.

Pacific A US task force of battleships, cruisers and destroyers, commanded by Rear-Admiral Badger, bombards Iwo Jima, in the Volcano Islands.

China Negotiations between the Nationalists and the Communists, broken off on 6 December 1944 on account of Chiang Kai-shek's opposition, are resumed.

25 January

Western Front In the British 2nd Army sector, units of the XII Corps press on with Operation *Blackcock*, taking Linne and Putbroeck (7th Armoured Division), Kirckhoven (52nd Division) and positions between Heisenberg and Randerath on the river Wurm (43rd Division). The US 1st and 3rd Armies continue to make progress north and south of the remainder of the German salient in the Ardennes. Units of the V Corps (1st Army) advance on the Büllingen–St Vith road, while the units of the III Corps (many of them already beyond the river Clerf) advance along the road that runs parallel with the river Our and connects Luxembourg with St Vith. A bridgehead over the river Clerf is established by units of the 80th Division (XII Corps, 3rd Army) opposite Willwerwiltz.

Further south the 7th Army again runs into difficulties following a new offensive by Wiese's 19th Army against the sector held by the 103rd Division (VI Corps), which is driven out of Kindwiller. The Germans establish a bridgehead over the Moder between Haguenau and Kaltenhouse.

On the right flank of the front, the French II Corps (1st Army) advances very slowly in the Elsenheim forests. General de Tassigny, commander of the French army, obtains General Milburne's American XXI Corps as

reinforcement, and it enters the line on the right of General Monsabert's French II Corps (in between the two French corps).

Eastern Front The position of the German forces cut off in East Prussia grows increasingly desperate. In Poland, the 1st Ukraine Front takes Ostrow, south-west of Kalisz, and in Upper Silesia occupies Oels (Olesnica). German sources report that the Russians are trying to force the crossing of the Oder at Steinhau and between Gleiwitz and Brieg.

General Reinhardt, commanding the German Army Group Centre, the remnants of which are defending East Prussia, is dismissed. Earlier, he had asked to be allowed to withdraw his forces to the area of the Masuri Lakes, but the Führer would not allow it. General Lothar Rendulic takes his place. It is estimated that the German Army Group Centre has lost 35 divisions.

Philippines: Luzon There is fighting west of Bamban, while the US 37th Infantry Division advances towards the airfields in the middle of the island.

Burma The 81st East African Division (British XV Corps), advancing on Kangaw from the north, occupies Myohaung in the Arakan sector.

In the northern sector, Chinese and Americans attack the last Japanese positions along the Burma Road.

Japanese Imperial General Headquarters orders the expeditionary corps in China to concentrate in the coastal strip, giving up any further thrusts into the interior.

26 January

Western Front Operation *Blackcock* is brought to a close by the XII Corps, British 2nd Army; begun on 16 January, it has led to the elimination of the German salient between the Meuse and the Rur, (the 'Roermond triangle'). The Germans now have only a small bridgehead in the area of Vlodrop.

During the night the 102nd Division of the XIII Corps (US 9th Army) occupies the region between Brachelen, Himmerich and Randerath,

west of the river Rur.

In the US 3rd Army sector the units of the VIII Corps push on north-east, in the Weiswampach area, while the German 7th Army continues to withdraw behind the Siegfried Line. Further south, the 80th Division (XII Corps) widens its bridgehead across the Clerf, while in the area of the Saarlautern bridgehead the 95th Division (XX Corps) improves its positions.

In the US 7th Army sector, the 101st Airborne Division approaches the area of Hochfelden.

The 1st Moroccan Division of the II Corps (French 1st Army) captures the road joining Jebsheim and Illhäusern, which is about six miles north of Colmar.

Eastern Front The 2nd Belorussian Front advances between East Prussia and Danzig, occupying Marienburg (Malbork) and reaching the Baltic north of Elbing (Elblag). Some 500,000 German soldiers are cut off. In Poland the Russians surround Poznan and Thorn.

Troops of the 1st Ukraine Front capture Hindenburg, in Silesia.

In northern Poland the 1st Belorussian Front captures Bromberg (Bydgoszcz).

Philippines: Luzon The Americans make some progress in the XIV Corps sector, where the 37th Division occupies one of the runways on Clark Field, one of the prime objectives.

Burma In the British XV Corps sector Royal Marine units landed from the East Indies Fleet invade the island of Cheduba, south-west of Ramree Island.

27 January

Western Front While units of the US 7th Armoured Division (1st Army) advance from the north in the St Vith forest, the 87th Division of the VIII Corps (US 3rd Army) captures the area to the south. On the right flank of the 3rd Army, the XII and XX Corps continue to advance towards the Siegfried Line.

Eastern Front In East Prussia the Germans launch a surprise counter-attack with six infantry divisions, one motorized and one armoured division, from the west in the direction of Marienburg (Malbork), halting the 48th Army of the 2nd Belorussian Front.

In Poland the Russians complete the encirclement of Poznan and Thorn (Torun) and advance slowly into the German region of Upper Silesia.

In Czechoslovakia, the Rumanian 4th Army captures Dobsina. In Hungary fighting continues in Budapest and in the area of Székesfehérvár.

Philippines: Luzon The US 6th Army is reinforced by two cavalry regiments. In the I Corps sector there is fierce fighting at San Manuel.

□ From Hawaii the American expeditionary force for the invasion of Iwo Jima sails for the Marianas, arriving on 5 February.

Burma The Japanese blockade of China is finally broken; the Chinese 38th Division joins up with the Yunnan Force coming out of China, on the Burma road, now completely liberated. However, the Japanese cut off in the north manage to open a way to the south and join up with the main body of the Japanese 15th Army.

In the British IV Corps sector, the 7th Indian Division occupies Pauk.

China Chiang Kai-shek forbids the Americans to negotiate with the Communists without his express authority.

28 January

Western Front With the German Ardennes salient finally eliminated, the US 1st Army starts the final dash to the Siegfried Line.

A great part of the VIII Corps (US 3rd Army) has reached the river Our.

Eastern Front The 1st Baltic Front captures almost the whole of the German Memel pocket, and Lithuania is completely liberated. In the central part of East Prussia the Russians close in on the Königsberg pocket, capturing Bischofsburg and Sensburg. The Germans hold out at Elbing and exert pressure north-west of Allenstein (Olsztyn).

Pushing on towards Germany on a wide front, the Russians capture the Polish frontier towns of Sepolno,

Czarnkow and Leszno and the German town of Guhrau. In the south, the 1st Ukraine Front completes the capture of the principal industrial towns along the border between Poland and Upper Silesia, taking Beuthen in Silesia and Katowice in Poland. In the Carpathian region, the 4th Ukraine Front takes Poprad in Czechoslovakia.

Burma The first convoy officially despatched from India to China reaches the Chinese border and is received with solemn ceremonies at Mu-se. The Burma Road is re-christened by Chiang Kai-shek the Stilwell Road, in honour of the general who fought so hard for its re-opening and its improvement.

29 January

Western Front Now General Patton's US 3rd Army, protecting the flank of General Hodges' 1st Army, opens an offensive to force a way through the defences of the Siegfried Line. The 90th Division (VIII Corps), covering the right flank of the corps on the east bank of the river Our, crosses the river and the German frontier, taking Walchenhausen and Staupbach.

In the French 1st Army sector, the US XXI Corps crosses the Colmar Canal.

Eastern Front While the fighting continues in East Prussia, where the

A Russian gun-crew hauls its gun across the river Oder, during the advance on Stettin, January 1945.

At its liberation by the Americans on 30 April 1945, Dachau held 32,000 prisoners. In three months 9,000 people had perished. Opposite: Hundreds of emaciated corpses crammed into the train carriages; military doctors look for survivors.

Germans, now on the counter-attack, have advanced about twenty miles towards Marienburg, the 1st Belorussian Front penetrates into Germany in the region of Pomerania, taking the towns of Schönlake and Woldenberg. It is opposed by the recently formed Vistula Army Group which is commanded by Heinrich Himmler.

Philippines: Luzon The US XI Corps, of which two regiments have already landed, lands the rest of its 30,000 men at San Antonio, in the central-western part of Luzon, south-west of Clark and Del Carmen airfields and north-west of the Bataan peninsula.

Burma The Japanese withdrawing from the northern sector inflict heavy losses on Chinese units which try to intercept them in the area north of Lashio.

China The Japanese occupy the US 14th Air Force base at Suichuan.

30 January

Western Front The 78th Division (XIX Corps, US 9th Army) opens its offensive towards the river Rur along the north border of the Monschau forest.

The three divisions of the American V Corps (the 9th, 99th and 2nd), attacking from north to south, open the offensive against the Siegfried Line fortifications. The 3rd Army units also continue their attack against the defences of the line, and Rodgen, Auel and Steinkopf are taken by the US XII Corps.

On the southern flank of the front (French 1st Army sector), while the US XXI Corps advances slowly north of Colmar, the 1st Moroccan Division (French II Corps) liberates the wooded region east of Illhäusern.

Eastern Front In East Prussia, the 3rd Belorussian Front routs the Tilsit Group; the German 3rd Armoured Army, which forms a part of the group, manages to break free and, by-passing Königsberg to the north, to occupy part of the peninsula, which divides it from the sea. The 1st Baltic Front completes the capture of Memel. The German forces in East Prussia are now cut into three: four

divisions are resisting on the peninsula north of Königsberg, five are surrounded in Königsberg and 20 divisions are containing Russian pressure south-west of the city.

North-west of Bydgoszcz, in Poland, the Red Army crosses the German frontier in several places. It also penetrates into Germany west of Poznan, taking Stolzenburg, a little more than 70 miles from Berlin.

☐ In Malta the first stage of the *Argonaut* Conference (code-named *Cricket*) takes place. After preliminary talks between the British and Americans, the main conference will be held at Yalta.

Philippines: Luzon General Krueger issues detailed instructions for the next operations: the XI Corps, which has just landed, will advance on Manila along the base of the Bataan peninsula as far as the line Dinalupihan-Hermosa, where it will link up with the XIV Corps, also advancing on Manila. The I Corps, further north, is to advance south-east with San José as its objective. During the day the XI Corps advances quickly and takes Olongapo, on the west coast, while units of the XIV Corps are engaged by the Japanese in hard fighting north of the river Bamban. Some US patrols thrust further south, coming within little more than 1,000 yards of Calumpit.

Burma In the British V Corps sector, the 25th Indian Division overcomes tenacious Japanese resistance against the Kangaw bridgehead. The 82nd East African Division advances south of Kangaw towards Myohaung. In the north-east sector, the Chinese 38th Division is now at the junction of the Burma Road with the road from Ledo, in Assam, and is preparing to advance on Lashio, north-east of Mandalay.

31 January

Western Front Advance guards of the US 1st and 3rd Armies meet near Widdau. While the V Corps (1st Army) advances in Monschau forest east of Elsenborn, the XVIII Airborne Corps penetrates into Buchholz forest, where it crosses the German frontier.

Units of the VI Corps (US 7th Army) launch an attack along the line Oberhoffen–Drusenheim.

Eastern Front In East Prussia, the Russians occupy Heilsberg (Lidzbark Warminski) and Friedland (Mieroszow), south of Königsberg. In Germany, the 1st Belorussian Front occupies Zehden on the east bank of the Oder, but for some time this is to be the nearest that the Red Army gets to Berlin. East and south-east of Zehden, several Brandenburg towns – Landsberg, Schwiebus, Miedzyrzecz and Züllichau – fall into Russian hands.

In Hungary the German garrison in Budapest holds out doggedly. The violent counter-attack by the German armour north of Lake Balaton has breached the line of the 3rd Ukraine Front. The Russians have had to send huge reinforcements to plug the gap, and now they are pressing hard to restore the position.

Philippines: Luzon The US 6th Army begins the final phase of the attack on Manila. The XVI Corps advances on Calumpit and the XI advances to the base of the Bataan peninsula, coming near to some strong enemy positions in the area of Zigzag Pass, three miles north-east of Olongapo. The strongest Japanese resistance is encountered by the I Corps, in the area of Muñoz.

South of Manila Bay, after the usual preparation by aircraft and warships, the US 8th Army lands most of the 11th Airborne Division (8,000 men) near Nasugbu. The operation is completely successful, and there is little Japanese resistance. The Americans occupy Nasugbu, Guagua and Lian and penetrate quickly into the interior towards Mount Tagaytay.

1 February

Western Front On the northern flank of the Allied front the Canadian 1st and American 9th Armies are putting the finishing touches to their preparations for Operations *Veritable* and *Grenade*, the first for a massive offensive by the Canadians between the Maas and the Rhine, from the north to the south-east, and the second for an offensive by the Americans across the river Rur, north-eastwards towards the Ruhr.

In the US 1st Army sector the divisions of the V Corps press on with their offensive towards the dams on the rivers Rur and Urft. The 9th Division reaches the Hofen-Harperscheid road right in the middle of the Monschau forest, while the 2nd Division moves from Rocherat in Belgium to cross the German frontier and link up with the 9th.

Further south, the VIII Corps (US 3rd Army) continues its offensive to break through the Siegfried Line along the Schneifel hills, capturing among other places Manderfeld (in Belgium) and Auw (87th Division), Mützenich (8th Division), Schweiler and Winterscheid (12th Division). The III Corps reinforces the defensive positions in Luxembourg along the watershed between the rivers Our and Clerf.

On the left flank and in the centre of the US 7th Army, while the XV and XXI Corps reinforce the positions south-east of Saarbrücken, on the right flank the 36th Division (VI Corps) continues to advance towards the Rhine, crossing the river Moder and attacking in the direction of Oberhoffen. The other units of the VI Corps stand firm for the whole month of February, confining themselves to defending their positions and putting in occasional attacks beyond the river Moder.

The French 1st Army continue their operations against the Colmar pocket; the French II Corps completes the capture of the Rhine lowland between Erstein in the north and Artzenheim in the south. In the centre of the French army's front, the American XXI Corps, with support from French armoured units, advances south along the Rhine–Rhone Canal in the direction of Neuf-Brisach, about 5 miles southeast of Colmar. On the French right flank the I Corps continues to advance in the area south of the river Thur between Cernay and Ensisheim, a little to the north of Mulhouse.

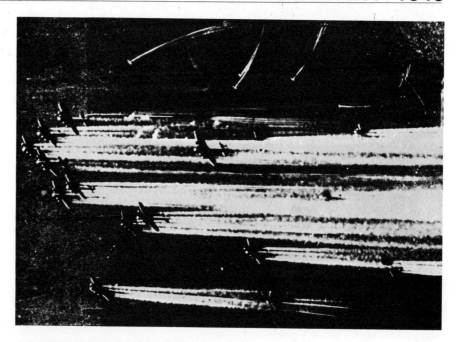

A formation of B-17 Flying Fortresses over Berlin.

Eastern Front In East Prussia the Russians continue their inexorable liquidation of the German pockets of resistance. In Poland the 1st Belorussian Front and 1st Ukraine Front take the town of Thorn (Torun) on the Vistula after a furious assault, and maintain strong pressure on the surrounded town of Poznan. In Germany they continue their advance towards the middle Oder and Berlin, capturing Schneidemühl and putting pressure on Ratzebuhr (Okonek).

In Hungary the elimination of German strongpoints goes ahead in the western part of Budapest.

Philippines: Luzon The units of the XIV Corps advance rapidly towards Manila, occupying Gapan and Santa Rosa. The I Corps is still heavily engaged by the Japanese in front of San Jose, in the middle of the island. On the north flank of the corps the 43rd Division and 158th Regiment consolidate their positions on the hills overlooking the Damortis–Rosario–Pozorrubio road. The XI Corps only manages to advance less than a thousand yards in the Zigzag Pass area, where the Japanese are putting up strenuous resistance.

In the 8th Army sector, the 11th Division meets sharp resistance by the Japanese between Mount Cariliao and Mount Batulao, on the slopes of the Tagaytay Mountains.

2 February

Western Front In the US 1st Army sector, advance guards of the 9th and 2nd Divisions (V Corps) emerge from Monschau forest.

In the XVIII Airborne Corps sector, the 1st and 82nd Divisions open a large-scale offensive against the Siegfried Line. The 1st Division emerges from the Buchholz forest near Ramscheid, while the 82nd passes through the line and takes Udenbreth and Neuhof.

The 36th Division (VI Corps, US 7th Army) continues its offensive in the direction of Oberhoffen.

On the south flank of the front the French 5th Armoured Division enters Colmar and begins mopping up. In the XXI Corps sector, units of the 3rd Division, with armoured support, advance through Artzenheim along the road between the Rhine–Rhone Canal and the river Rhine in the direction of Biesheim, north-east of Neuf-Brisach. The 75th Division is also making for Neuf-Brisach.

☐ In Malta the first part of the *Argonaut* Conference ends.

Philippines: Luzon The XIV Corps pushes on towards Manila after making contact with the I Corps north of Cabanatuan. The I Corps is now in a position to protect the east flank of the XIV from any possible Japanese counter-attacks. In the XI Corps sector, the American advance is held up by the Japanese in front of the Zigzag Pass; further north, the 149th infantry advance towards Dinalupihan without meeting resistance.

In the 8th Army sector, the 11th Division advances slowly to the foothills of the Tagaytay Mountains.

Leyte The Americans withdraw the 77th Division from the island to take part in the landing on Okinawa.

Burma The Japanese force the British 36th Division back over the river Shweli and launch heavy attacks on the US 5332nd Brigade, which nevertheless manages to capture some heights in the Hpa-pen area.

☐ French Indo-China. General Wedemeyer sends a report to Washington on the growing deterioration in the relations between the Japanese occupying forces (100,000 men) and the French administration, headed by the Governor-General, Admiral Decoux, The US 14th Air Force gives some help to the local resistance movement.

3 February

Western Front The American 30th and 83rd Divisions and 2nd Armoured Division (grouped in the XIX Corps) are added to the strength of the US 9th Army, with the 84th (the XIII Corps) and 95th Divisions as reserve formations. In the XVI Corps sector, the 35th Division completes the re-grouping of its units south-east of Maastricht, in Holland.

The 78th Division (V Corps, US 1st Army) crosses the Rur at Dedenborn and takes the village. While some units of the US 7th Armoured Division are attached to the 78th Division in readiness for an advance towards Schwammenauel, site of one of the biggest dams on the Rur, near Hasenfeld, units of the 9th Division take Herhahne Einruhr and Berescheid, and the 2nd Division takes Bronsfeld. The divisions of the XVIII Airborne Corps continue

their battle against the defences of the Siegfried Line; units of the 1st Division enter Ramscheid, which the Germans have already evacuated.

In the US 7th Army sector there is activity by patrols from the 36th Division around Drusenheim, Stainwald and Herrlisheim. On the south flank the three corps of the French 1st Army make further progress south and east following the fall of Colmar. The American 75th and 3rd Divisions (US XXI Corps) continue to advance towards Neuf-Brisach, while the units of the French I Corps complete the first stage of the operation to liberate the south bank of the river Thur between Cernay and Ensisheim, then preparing to move north across the Thur.

Eastern Front In Latvia, the German troops cut off in the north (the 16th Army) repulse powerful attacks by the Russians in the direction of Liepaja (Libau). With help from the German navy, preparations are made for the army to be evacuated. In East Prussia there is fighting north of Heilsberg (Lidzbark Warminski), near Bartenstein, and south and north of Königsberg. German destroyers give supporting fire to their land forces, while transports take off more than 184,000 refugees. The Vistula Army Group under Himmler is deployed in defence of northern Poland, Pomerania and Brandenburg. It contains the pressure of the 2nd Belorussian Front north of Chelmo and Sepolno and also at Küstrin (Kostrzyn), east of the Oder. Elbing is attacked from all sides, as is Pyritz (Pyrzyce), south of Stettin.

The Army Group Centre is engaged near Brieg and Ohlau, at Steinau and along the whole of the middle Oder at Glogau (Glogow), Ratibor (Raciborz) and Pless (Pszczyna). In Hungary, while fighting continues in Budapest, the German forces reach the Danube again east of Lake Velencei, east of Lake Balaton and south-west of Budapest. But the 3rd Ukraine Front, at one time cut in two, has been able to re-establish a continuous line.

Philippines: Luzon The 1st Cavalry

Division (US XIV Corps) reaches the outskirts of Manila and the 37th Division is also near the city. The I Corps advances south and southwest of San Jose. The XI Corps resumes its attacks against Zigzag Pass.

In the US 8th Army sector, a parachute regiment is dropped on the Tagaytay Mountains, where there are no Japanese to oppose them.

China The Japanese capture Namyung.

4 February

Western Front In readiness for the great Allied offensive in the north of the front, the US 1st Army is ordered to attack in the Düren sector in close contact with the 9th Army on its left. During the night the 78th Division (V Corps), attacking east of Kesternich, takes Ruhrberg and the surrounding hills; this action takes place 24 hours before the assault on the fortifications of the Siegfried Line, a first step towards securing the dam at Schwammenauel on the river Rur. A battle develops for the capture of the dams; units of the 9th Division reach Lake Urft, where the Americans secure part of Dam No. 5. In the XVIII Airborne Corps sector, the 1st Division continues the offensive against the West Wall positions, consolidating in the Ramscheid area.

On the Schneifel range, north-east of Brandscheid, the 4th Division (VIII Corps, US 3rd Army) breaches the outer defences of the Siegfried Line. On the south flank of the corps the 90th Division is relieved by units of the 6th and 11th Armoured Divisions and prepares to give support to the 4th Division in the offensive against Brandscheid. The 6th Armoured Division extends its control in the river Our western sector. The XII Corps re-groups its divisions in preparation for the offensive across the Our and the Sauer on the other side of the Siegfried Line.

In the French 1st Army sector, the US 3rd and 75th Divisions (XXI Corps) strengthen their positions around Neuf-Brisach.

Italian Front In the US V Army sec-

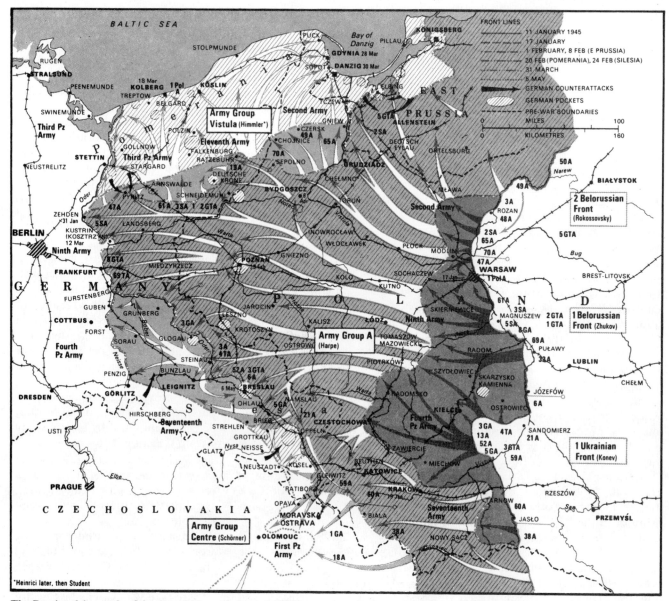

The Russian drive to the Oder launched on 12 January 1945.

tor, the 92nd Division (IV Corps) improves its positions in the Serchio valley.

☐ At Yalta, in the Crimea, the second phase of the *Argonaut* Conference (in code, *Magneto*) begins, attended by the heads of the governments of the United States, the Soviet Union and Great Britain, i.e. Roosevelt, Stalin and Churchill. The Allies discuss common strategy, especially political questions and the 'division' of spheres of influence when the war is over.

Philippines: Luzon The 1st Cavalry Division (US XIV Corps) carries out patrol activity on the outskirts of Manila while waiting for reinforce-

ments. Units from the 37th Division reach it by evening. In the I Corps sector the Americans, with strong air support, take San Jose and block the ways into the Cagayan valley, but are unable to break down the resistance of the Japanese strongpoints at Muñoz. The XI Corps is still held up at Zigzag Pass. Advancing from the south, the parachutists who landed on the Tagaytay Mountains converge on Manila and come within five miles of the city.

Burma–China The first convoy to leave Ledo, in Assam, after a long journey along the re-opened Burma Road, makes its triumphal entry into Kunming, in China.

5 February
Western Front The VII Corps (US 1st Army) begins to move its divisions from Belgium towards the line of the river Rur.

At 3.00 a.m. the American 78th Division (V Corps, 1st Army) opens the attack towards the Schwammenauel dam on the river Rur.

In the US 7th Army sector, the VI Corps re-groups and continues to advance towards the Rhine, while the 79th Division is relieved by the 36th Division and 101st Airborne Division.

On the right of the line, the Colmar pocket is cut in two as units of the American XXI Corps link up with the French I Corps. The German units left on the west bank of the Ill – the bulk of the 19th Army has already been moved back over the Rhine by von Rundstedt, with Hitler's permission – offer almost no resistance and surrender one after the other on successive days. Meanwhile the Allied positions in the sector are reinforced: the XXI Corps along the rivers Ill and Fecht, south and west of Colmar, while the French I Corps takes Ensisheim.

Eastern Front In East Prussia, Elbing is still being attacked from all sides. In the central sector of the front, the Russians reach the Oder only 30 miles from Berlin, pressing on north and south of the fortified city of Küstrin (Kostrzyn) and Frankfurt-on-the-Oder. German bulletins announce that the Russians have forced the crossing of the upper Oder below Breslau, north and south of Brieg. Russian attacks continue on the besieged town of Poznan.

Philippines: Luzon On the northern outskirts of Manila the Japanese withdraw on to the river Pasig, leaving 'scorched earth' in front of the American 37th and 1st Divisions. In the north, the Japanese repel attacks by the I Corps against Lupao and Muñoz. In the XI Corps sector, the 38th Division is engaged in fierce fighting in the Zigzag Pass area, and some units are forced to retire.

The 511th Parachute Regiment of the 11th Division (US 8th Army) reaches the Paranaque bridge, south of Manila.

6 February

Western Front While the offensive to break through the defences of the Siegfried Line continue on the American 1st and 3rd Army fronts, to the south of the line the French 1st Army starts the final stage of the operations to take out the Colmar pocket. In the US XXI Corps sector the 3rd Division takes the old fortress of Neuf-Brisach; some units of the French 2nd Armoured Division advance south between the Rhine–Rhone Canal and the river Rhine towards the French I Corps. The 75th Division reaches the canal south of

Neuf-Brisach and the US 12th Armoured Division, with the French 5th Armoured Division, eliminates the pockets cut off in the Vosges. In the French I Corps sector infantry units of the 2nd Moroccan Division cross the river Ill in the Meyenheim–Reguisheim area and advance east of the Rhine Canal to take Hirtzfelden; the 9th Colonial Division completes the capture of Ensisheim and sends some units in the direction of Baldersheim, north of Mulhouse, and the 4th Moroccan Motorized Division blocks the escape routes from the Vosges, where any kind of organized resistance has come to an end.

Eastern Front Fighting rages in East Prussia and in the cities of Poznan and Budapest, still tenaciously defended by the Germans.

Philippines: Luzon Violent air and artillery bombardment of the Japanese positions at Muñoz, which are surrounded, and of Zigzag Pass, where a regiment of US infantry succeeds in making a small penetration. The US XIV Corps mops up the northern part of Manila, north of the river Pasig, while the 11th Division, advancing from the south, digs in on the outskirts of the city.

7 February

Western Front The 78th Division (V Corps, US 1st Army) continues the offensive against the Schwammenauel dam, taking Kommerscheidt and entering Schmidt and Harscheid.

In the US 3rd Army sector, the VIII Corps' offensive against the Siegfried Line meets with dogged resistance by the units of the German 7th Army, but the advance continues all along the front. The 6th Armoured Division and 17th Airborne Division cross the Our onto the soil of the Fatherland, while the units of the XII Corps put in their offensive across the rivers Our and Sauer between Vianden and Echternach. Finally, the XX Corps takes Sinz and attacks a German pocket between Campholz and Tettingen (94th Division) and with the 26th Division launches a series of thrusts in the sector of the Saarlautern–

Roden bridgehead. In the French 1st Army sector the XXI Corps continues its advance along the Rhine north and south of Balgau and the 1st Armoured Division (French I Corps) crosses the river Ill on a pontoon bridge at Ensisheim.

Eastern Front In Budapest the Russians capture the south railway station. On the Vistula Army Group front, the 1st Ukraine Front throws more troops across the Oder near Fürstenberg and south of Frankfurt. Further north, the 1st Belorussian Front attacks Arnswalde and Deutsch-Krone (now called Choszczno and Walcz). New Russian divisions go into action against the defenders of Poznan. Isolated detachments are still holding out against the Russians at Elbing. In this region there is some slight improvement in the position of the Army Group North in the peninsula, north of Königsberg.

In Yugoslavia the Germans are preparing to leave Višegrad and Mostar, defended until now by Löhr's Army Group E against Tito's partisans.

The Wehrmacht is suffering from an increasing shortage of officers as a result of their high casualty figures. Headquarters orders the suspension of all leave.

Philippines: Luzon Under pressure from MacArthur, the commander of the US 6th Army, General Krueger, orders a speeding-up in the operations to take Manila. The 1st Cavalry Division begins mopping up the eastern part of the city up to the river Pasig, which is crossed by units of the 37th Division in inflatable boats. In the I Corps sector the battle for Muñoz ends in a victory for the Americans; the units of the Japanese 6th Division engaged in the fighting are virtually wiped out when they attempt to escape. But the Japanese at Lupao still hold out vigorously.

China In south-east China the Japanese occupy Kanchow, a base of the US 14th Air Force.

8 February

Western Front The Canadian 1st Army under General Crerar launches the operations for the capture of the region between the rivers Maas and Rhine (Operation *Veritable*). The attack starts at 10.30 a.m. after an intensive air and artillery preparation; taking part are the four divisions of the British XXX Corps (Canadian 3rd Division and British 15th, 43rd and 51st), moving simultaneously along the line Nijmegen–Mook, overrunning the weak resistance of the German 1st Parachute Army and reaching during the day Kranburg, the Reichswald area, Zyfflich and Zandpol. This offensive, part of the more general plan against Germany, has the particular aim of attracting substantial German forces to the northern sector, thus making the tasks of the 12th and 6th Army Groups in the centre and the south easier.

In the US 1st Army sector the 78th Division (V Corps) continues its attacks on Schmidt, which still holds out.

Further south, in the region in which the US 3rd Army is engaged, the 87th and 8th Divisions (VIII Corps) reach Olzheim and Ober Mehlen, while the 90th Division continues its attacks to break through the fortifications of the Siegfried Line. The 6th Armoured Division succeeds in widening and reinforcing the bridgehead over the Our (III Corps).

In the French 1st Army sector, the US XXI Corps completes its local offensive when the 2nd Armoured Division reaches Fessenheim and joins up with the French 1st Armoured Division (I Corps). The 1st Division then moves south along the Rhine towards Chalampé, taking Blodelsheim.

Italian Front The 92nd Division (IV Corps, US 5th Army) opens limited operations in the coastal area of the front.

In the British 8th Army sector the Italian *Friuli* combat group under General Arturo Scattini goes into the line, replacing the Polish *Kresowa* Division, deployed on the river Senio opposite Riolo dei Bagni.

Eastern Front The 3rd Ukraine Front restores the position southwest of Budapest in the Lake Velencei area.

Berliners flee through the smoke following the air raids of 3 February.

The Vistula Army Group contains Russian forces pushing out from the bridgeheads over the Oder.

Philippines: Luzon The US 1st Cavalry Division continues the mopping up of the eastern suburbs of Manila, while the 37th Division reinforces the bridgehead south of the river Pasig. Still in the XIV Corps area, the US 40th Division takes a large part of McSevney Point and repels a series of Japanese counter-attacks. The I Corps succeeds in taking Lupao.

Burma In the north, the XXVI Bri-

gade (British 36th Division) establishes a bridgehead over the river Shweli near Myitson and defends it against Japanese counter-attacks.

9 February

Western Front The British XXX Corps (Canadian 1st Army) continues to advance rapidly, taking Mehr, Niel and Millingen (Canadian 3rd Division), overrunning the defences of the Siegfried Line near Nütterden (which is occupied) and taking the heights near Materborn (15th (Scottish) Division), and sending some units as far as Cleve. In the Cleve sector the Germans begin a counter-offensive with the arrival of the units of the 6th Parachute Division and the XLVII Armoured Corps, the first to consolidate the line together with the 7th Parachute Division, the second to form an armoured reserve in the area and to re-take Materborn.

In the US 1st Army sector, the 9th Division (V Corps) carries out the final assault on the Schwammenauel dam, securing a large part of Hasenfelde and seizing the north bank of Lake Urft. In the centre of the line the units of the VIII Corps (US 3rd Army) take Neuendorf (87th Division) and make substantial progress through the fortifications of the Siegfried Line, while the formations of the III Corps extend and consolidate the bridgehead east of the Our. In the XII Corps sector, too, the bridgeheads over the Our and the Sauer are further strengthened and widened by the forces of the 5th and 80th Divisions.

On the Allied right flank, the French 1st Army completes the elimination of the Colmar pocket. The French I Corps liquidates the last German bridgeheads west of the Rhine in the Chalampé sector. The west bank of the Rhine south of Strasbourg is completely liberated; the battered units of the German 19th Army have been withdrawn across the river, where they dig in for the final battle. The operation in this sector has cost the French and Americans 18,000 casualties, killed, wounded and missing, against German losses of double the number.

Philippines: Luzon Japanese resistance stiffens in Manila south of the river Pasig. In the I Corps sector units of the US 32nd Division repel Japanese night counter-attacks on the Villa Verde track and go on to attack the enemy, but are held up by accurate artillery fire. In the XI Corps sector, the 38th Division makes progress in the Zigzag Pass area. The 11th Division (8th Army) meets strong opposition at Nichols airfield.

Burma The British XV Corps com-

Canadian troop carriers advance along the Nijmegen–Cleve road, flooded with the waters of the Rhine by the retreating Germans, February 1945.

pletes the capture of Ramree Island, in the Arakan sector. In view of the favourable progress of operations in Burma, Admiral Mountbatten decides to speed up the arrangements for the offensive against Mandalay and Rangoon. With Burma liberated, the Allies will go on to recapture Singapore and Malaya.

10 February

Western Front In the Cleve–Materborn sector a German counter-offensive holds up three divisions of the British XXX Corps (the 3rd, 43rd and 15th); during the night the 51st Division comes near to Hekkens, sending patrols across the river Niers in spate, north of the town of Gennep.

The divisions of the VIII Corps (US 3rd Army) advance in the Prüm sec-

tor, while those of the XII Corps continue to extend and strengthen the bridgeheads in the Wallendorf–Dillingen sector (80th Division) and the Weiterbach–Echternach sector in the Siegfried Line fortifications.

Eastern Front In East Prussia, the 3rd Belorussian Front captures the important road junction of Preussisch-Eylau (Ilawa). The 2nd Belorussian Front takes the fortified port of Elbing. On the German Army Group Centre's front, the 21st Armoured Division has to withdraw from Küstrin (Kostrzyn). Arnswalde is surrounded, but rejects Russian surrender terms.

On the front of the Army Group South the 2nd Ukraine Front makes a big breakthrough in the Budapest sector. Fighting continues to rage in the city.

In Yugoslavia there is fighting west of Mostar.

Philippines US General Headquarters, South-West Pacific Area, determines the operational areas for the US 6th and 8th Armies. The 6th Army is to have full responsibility for operations in Luzon, the 8th Army for all islands south of Luzon.

While mopping-up operations continue on Leyte and Samar, on Luzon there is very severe fighting round Manila. The US 37th Division suffers such heavy casualties that it is decided to hold up the operation until aircraft and artillery can soften up the enemy a bit more. Units of the US I Corps reach the east coast of the island, so that the Japanese forces are cut in two; the more numerous, and more aggressive, half is in the northern part of the island.

Burma Units of the British 36th Division take Myitson on the river Shweli. In the British IV Corps sector, the 18th East African Brigade takes Seikpyu.

11 February

Western Front The British XXX Corps (Canadian 1st Army) overcomes German resistance in the area of Cleve and Materborn and the two important road junctions of Hekkens and Gennep.

The VIII Corps (US 3rd Army) continues its offensive in the Prüm sector; Prüm falls to units of the 90th Division. In the XII Corps sector the advance proceeds between the fortifications of the Siegfried Line in the Wallendorf bridgehead. In the vicinity of Metz, in the meantime, the 10th Armoured Division (XX Corps) has been completing the re-grouping of its units.

Eastern Front Moscow announces the breaching of the German line on the Oder north-west of Breslau by the 1st Ukraine Front and the capture of Lüben (Lubin), Haynau (Chojnow), Leignitz (Legnica), Neumarkt (Sroda Slaska) and Kanth (Katy Wroklavskie).

The advance south-east of Breslau means a threat to the chief city of Silesia, while the Russians are now seen to be threatening Dresden also,

75 miles further west. In the northeast sector the Russians take Deutsch-Krone (Walcz). Other Russian forces are preparing to wipe out the German forces at Schneidemühl (Pila) and Poznan.

Forty-five more blocks of buildings in Budapest have fallen into the hands of the Russian forces.

Philippines: Luzon There is fighting south of Manila, where the 11th Division (now part of the XIV Corps, US 6th Army) captures a suburb of the city and part of Nichols airfield. In the I Corps sector, in the north, the 25th Infantry Division advances from San Isidro in the direction of Puncan. The XI Corps makes little progress in the Zigzag Pass area.

☐ The Yalta Conference is concluded, Stalin, Churchill and Roosevelt, assisted by their Foreign Ministers, Molotov, Eden and Stettinius, have reached agreement on future war strategy and on the political order of the post-war world. The USSR confirms its adhesion to the United Nations (an idea very dear to Roosevelt) and agrees to take part in the war against Japan when the war in Europe is over (expected in July) – this request is also made by Roosevelt, though the American military chiefs had warned against it on account of its political implications. In exchange, the Soviet Union is to be given important concessions in the Far East (Dairen, Port Arthur, part of Sakhalin and the Kurils). Churchill has opposed what he considers to be dangerous and unjustified surrenders, particularly with regard to the Soviet sphere of influence in Europe, but he has had to yield to the wishes of his more powerful ally.

12 February

Western Front Further progress by the British XXX Corps in the northern sector of the front, where the Canadian 1st Army is operating. The Canadian 3rd Division reaches Kellen and Warbeyen and relieves the British 15th Division in the Cleve sector; the 15th Division then pushes on north-east towards Calcar, meet-

ing stubborn resistance by the units of the German 1st Parachute Army; the 43rd Division takes Bedburg, an essential objective before going on towards Goch; the 53rd and 51st Divisions carry on with the clearance of the Reichswald.

In the US 3rd Army sector, the VIII and XII Corps advance in the Prüm and Bollendorf sectors.

Philippines: Luzon The Japanese still in Manila are cut off by the American advance, but are determined to fight to a finish. The Americans reach Manila Bay and capture most of Nichols airfield and Neilson airfield. In the XI Corps sector they advance from Dinalupihan towards the Bataan peninsula, which they must take to give them control of Manila Bay.

Burma During the night the 20th Indian Division (British XXXIII Corps) starts to cross the Irrawaddy in the Miynmu–Allagappa sector, west of Mandalay; there is little Japanese resistance.

13 February

Western Front The British XXX Corps (Canadian 1st Army) continues fighting west of the Rhine in the sector between Emmerich, Calcar and Goch. The Canadian 3rd Division heads for Emmerich, the British 15th Division advances towards Calcar and takes Hasselt, and the 53rd Division gets the better of the final efforts of the German 84th Division (1st Parachute Army) in the Reichswald.

A period of reduced activity begins for the III Corps of the US 1st Army. The corps takes up defensive positions on the west bank of the Rur and prepares for the attack on the German positions across the river.

Activity on the US 3rd Army front also lessens, but some units of the XII Corps keep up their advance on Ammeldingen (80th Division) and Ferschweiler (5th Division).

Italian Front The Polish 3rd *Carpathian* Division and the Italian *Friuli* Group come under command of the Polish II Corps (8th Army).

Eastern Front After a month and a half of bitter struggle, Malinovsky's

2nd Ukraine Front finally overcomes the last German defences in Budapest. Pest surrendered on 18 January, and now the defenders of Buda surrender also. The Russians capture 138,000 prisoners. Some units try to fight their way out to the positions of the German 8th Army, but only seven officers and 120 men manage to escape (German sources say several hundred).

In Silesia the Russians advance north-west of Breslau, surrounding Glogau (Glogow) and capturing Beuthen (Bytom Odrzanski).

Philippines: Luzon Fighting continues round Manila. American naval ships begin clearing the mines from the coastal waters and bombarding the Corregidor coasts in preparation for a landing. The 38th Division finally overcomes the Japanese defences in the Zigzag Pass area. The 11th Division completes the capture of Nichols airfield, near Manila.

Burma In the northern sector, the Japanese intensify their pressure on the bridgehead across the Shweli won by the 26th Brigade of the British 36th Division. In the British XXXIII Corps sector, the 20th Indian Division extends its bridgehead over the Irrawaddy. The 7th Indian Division (IV Corps) also begins the crossing of the Irrawaddy, in the Nyaungu area.

14 February

Western Front On the northern flank of the Allied line, the Canadian 3rd Division (British XXX Corps, Canadian 1st Army) captures a village on the Rhine opposite Emmerich, while the British 15th Division continues its advance towards Calcar with considerable difficulty, and the 51st Division takes Kassel during the night, advancing without difficulty.

The XII Corps (US 3rd Army) retains firm control of the bridgehead beyond the Siegfried Line and even reinforces it, getting ready to advance on Prüm.

Eastern Front In Hungary, the Germans counter-attack between Lake Velencei and Lake Balaton. North of

Budapest, the German 8th Army holds attacks by the 3rd Ukraine Front.

In the central sector, the 1st Ukraine Front succeeds in joining up the two bridgeheads established over the Oder west of Breslau and fighting rages on the outskirts of the city. To the south-west, west and north-west of it, troops of the 1st Ukraine Front and 1st Belorussian Front take Striegau (Strzegom), Jauer (Jawor), Goldberg (Zlotoryia) and Sprottau (Szprotowa).

North of Poznan, the 2nd Belorussian Front takes Schneidemühl (Pila). On the front held by Himmler's Vistula Army Group there is fighting south of Frankfurt-on-the-Oder. The Russians advance north-west and south-west of Liegnitz (Legnica).

Philippines: Luzon While fighting continues at Manila, the US I Corps prepares to attack south of the river Pampanga, and the XI Corps to liquidate Japanese resistance at Zigzag Pass and liberate the Bataan peninsula. One regiment of the 38th Division sails from Subic Bay for Mariveles on the tip of the Bataan peninsula.

15 February

Western Front A new corps goes into action in the Canadian 1st Army's Operation *Veritable*, the Canadian II Corps, which takes up positions on the left of the British XXX Corps on the line (south to north) Grave–Groesbeek–Cleve–Emmerich. Until 25 February the new corps carries out limited attacks with the 3rd and 2nd Canadian Divisions in the direction of Calcar (which is the first objective); after that the units are re-grouped for an attack on a huge scale.

Further south, the British XXX Corps' main thrusts are against the German positions that prevent it from reaching Goch, the second important objective.

There is action again on the US 7th Army front where the XV Corps begins limited attacks to straighten up and shorten the line.

Eastern Front The 2nd Belorussian

Front consolidates its positions in north-west Poland, north of Bromberg (Bydgoszcz). In northern Silesia troops of the 1st Ukraine Front take Grünberg (Zielona Gora), south-west of Poznan, and penetrate into Brandenburg.

The Germans are still counter-attacking in Hungary. The Russians announce that in Budapest they have found the bodies of two divisional generals who have committed suicide. They claim to have taken 9,000 prisoners at Schneidemühl (Pila).

Fighting flares up again in East Prussia in the area of Frauenburg–Landsberg–Zinten (Frombork–Górowo–Ilaweckie). In northern Latvia the German 16th and 18th Armies repel Russian attacks, while making arrangements to evacuate their encircled forces.

Philippines: Luzon Fierce fighting in Manila. The US 38th Division (XI Corps) completes the liquidation of the Japanese forces in the Zigzag Pass area. One regiment of the division lands at Mariveles after a preparatory bombardment by a naval squadron under Rear-Admiral Struble. The Japanese do not oppose the landing, but during the night launch a counter-attack which is to be the last action in force by the Japanese on the west coast of the island.

Burma In the British XXXIII Corps sector, the 20th Indian Division meets with increasingly stubborn resistance by the Japanese round the bridgehead over the Irrawaddy. In the British IV Corps sector, the 7th Indian Division extends its bridgehead over the Irrawaddy, while some of its units take Pakokku, west of the river.

16 February

Western Front Further advance by the British XXX Corps (Canadian 1st Army), which takes Asperberg, Asperden and Afferden.

Limited activity in the sector of the XII Corps (US 3rd Army), which concentrates on further strengthening of its positions beyond the Siegfried Line, and in the XX Corps sector, where units of the 26th

THE BOMBING OF DRESDEN

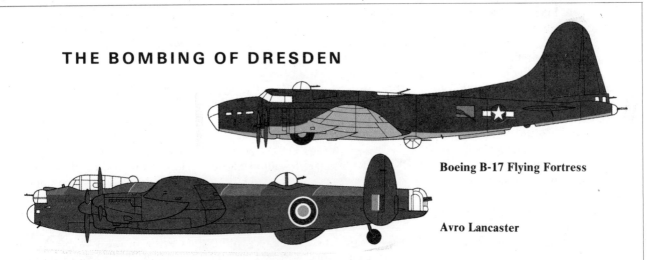

Boeing B-17 Flying Fortress

Avro Lancaster

13–14 February

Dresden, 10.15 p.m. 245 RAF Lancaster bombers begin one of the most ruthless air raids of the whole war, dropping their deadly two-ton bombs and tens of thousands of incendiaries on the undefended city. Dresden, crowded with a flood of refugees from Silesia, fleeing from the Russians, has already been bombed twice, on 7 October 1944 and 16 January 1945, but on both occasions the targets were in the industrial suburbs of the city. The historic residential centre had been spared and the citizens had come to think that the city was the object of a sort of agreement between the belligerents on account of its antiquity and the beauty of its public buildings: the Luftwaffe will spare Oxford if the Allies will spare Dresden. The agreement – if ever there was one – is well and truly broken at 10.15 p.m. on 13 February 1945.

After the merciless bombing of the first wave of Lancasters there follows another, if possible even more tragic, carried out this time by about 550 RAF bombers. The effect of the two raids are terrifying: the bombs and incendiaries destroy the old city – the historic city centre – and the outskirts, while the incendiaries unleash the most catastrophic tempest of fire seen in the whole war. Asphalt melts and burns and a cyclone of fire rages for four days and four nights. To finish off the work of the British bombers, at midday on 14 February 450 B-17 'Flying Fortresses' of the USAF make a further raid (as is well known, the British are specialists in night bombing, the Americans in daylight raids), when the city is already razed to the ground and engulfed in flames. The exact number of the victims of these raids will never be known, but according to current estimates casualties amounted to at least 130,000, while Gestapo estimates put them as high as 200,000. It is certainly the most deadly bombardment of the whole of the Second World War, not excluding the raid on Hiroshima on 6 August 1945, when the first atomic bomb is to claim about 110,000 victims. And it is also the most pitiless raid, and the hardest to justify, of those carried out in the European sector. For Dresden, of no strategic and military importance, is teeming with refugees and is almost undefended, as is shown by the tiny number of bombers – eight – shot down by German anti-aircraft defences.

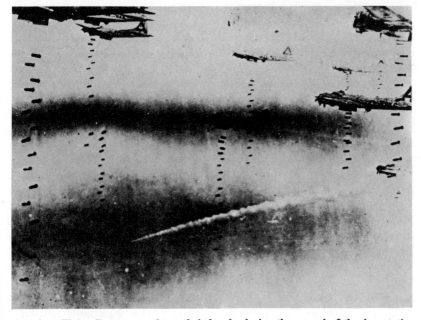

American Flying Fortresses release their bombs during the second of the devastating raids on Dresden.

Division continue with the consolidation of the Saarlautern bridgeheads.

Italian Front Headquarters, US 5th Army, issues directives for limited attacks by the divisions of the IV Corps (to begin on the 20th) to reinforce the positions west of Highway 64.

Eastern Front German headquarters admit for the first time that there are 'gangs' trying with Russian help to penetrate from Slovakia into the Protectorate of Bohemia–Moravia.

The German 8th Army is engaged with the 2nd Ukraine Front in Hungary.

Russian forces complete the encirclement of Breslau. The 1st Belorussian Front takes Sagan (Zagan), from which the Germans manage to withdraw the *Hermann Goering* Corps, which had been almost completely surrounded.

Philippines: Luzon Fighting continues in Manila. In the XI Corps sector, after a powerful preparation by aircraft and naval gunfire, the US 5th Air Force drops a parachute regiment on Corregidor, while a battalion of the 34th Infantry (24th Division) lands on the island from Mariveles. The operation takes place between 8.30 a.m. and 10.30 a.m. The Japanese, taken by surprise, are unable to prevent the Americans from establishing a solid bridgehead.

Volcano Islands: Iwo Jima US carrier-based aircraft and a naval squadron containing battleships, cruisers and destroyers begin the pre-invasion bombardment of the island. The action is repeated next day. There is violent reaction by the Japanese anti-aircraft installations.

□ Japan. In support of the imminent landing on Iwo Jima, a squadron of fast US aircraft carriers commanded by Vice-Admiral Mitscher begins an attack in force, lasting two days, against airfields, aircraft factories and other targets in the area of Tokyo. Shipping in the adjacent sea areas is also attacked.

Mariana Islands Task Force 51, transporting the expeditionary force to Iwo Jima, sails from Saipan.

Burma In the British XV Corps sec-

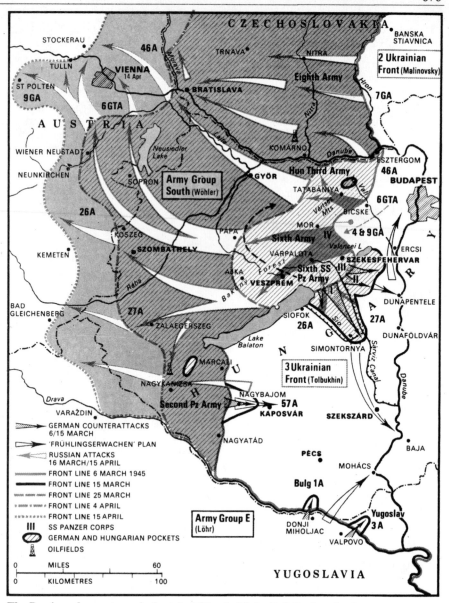

The Russian advance towards Austria 6 March–15 April, following the German counter-attack in Hungary on 6 March.

tor, a brigade of the 25th Indian Division lands on the Arakan coast near Ru-ywa, west of An; with the 82nd East African Division coming down from the north, they will cut the Japanese off from their withdrawal route to Prome. Hard fighting continues between the Japanese and the 20th Indian Division (British XXXIII Corps) on the bridgehead over the Irrawaddy in the Myinmu–Allagappa area.

17 February

Western Front The British XXX Corps (Canadian 1st Army) approaches Goch in the course of Operation *Veritable*. In the US 3rd Army sector, the XII and XX Corps

extend and strengthen their bridgeheads, the one at the confluence of the Saar and the Our, the other at Saarlautern.

The XV Corps of the US 7th Army continues its limited offensive to eliminate the German salients at Gros Réderchin and Wilferding; the 70th Division is now sent in on the left flank of the corps, attacking hills to the south-west of Saarbrücken.

Iwo Jima Air and naval bombardment continues in preparation for the landing. Japanese coast defence guns and a small number of aircraft manage to damage, more or less severely, the battleship *Tennessee*, the heavy cruiser *Pensacola* and three destroyers.

☐ Japan. American bombing of the Tokyo area continues.

Burma In the northern sector the Japanese launch violent counter-attacks against the bridgehead established by the British 36th Division across the river Shweli. The British units are cut off and have to be supplied by air.

China General Wedemeyer warns Chiang Kai-shek against the danger of an imminent attack by the Japanese to capture the airfields at Hsian, Laohokow and Chihchiang. Changting is now the only base left to the American strategic air force in eastern China.

18 February

Western Front The British XXX Corps (Canadian 1st Army) begins the offensive against the town of Goch with three divisions, the 15th (from the north), 51st (from the north-west) and 43rd (from the east). In the US 3rd Army sector the VIII Corps resumes the offensive, attacking southwards towards the XII Corps across the defences of the Siegfried Line, in the area of Prüm. Meanwhile the XII Corps opens an offensive towards the river Prüm, while units of the 26th Division (XX Corps) further consolidate the positions in the Saarlautern bridgehead, repulsing a series of counter-attacks by General Brandenberger's German 7th Army.

Eastern Front In Yugoslavia, the troops of Army Group E are compelled to withdraw three miles from Mostar.

In the area between Lake Velencei and Lake Balaton, in Hungary, three German infantry divisions, supported by two SS armoured divisions, attack the positions of the 3rd Ukraine Front near the Danube. In the central sector, the Russians continue to strengthen their positions on the Oder. The Germans claim that the Russian troops encircling Poznan are suffering heavy losses.

Marshal Ivan Chernyakhovsky, Commander of the 3rd Belorussian Front, dies of wounds received some

days before. In his honour, the name of the town of Insterburg is changed to Chernyakhovsk. Two days later, command of the Front is given to Marshal Vasilevsky.

Philippines: Luzon There is still fighting in Manila, and the occupation of the Bataan peninsula goes ahead.

Burma Fighting continues near the British 36th Division's bridgehead across the river Shweli. Japanese pressure is still strong.

19 February

Western Front Units of the British XXX Corps (Canadian 1st Army) continue the battle for Goch against tenacious opposition by the German 1st Parachute Army.

Units of the 80th Division (XII Corps, US 3rd Army) take Hommerdingen, Nusbaum and Niedergegen, and the 5th Division takes Stockem. After strong artillery preparation the XX Corps goes on to the offensive to liberate the triangle between the rivers Saar and Moselle.

Eastern Front The forces of the German Army Group E are considerably reduced by the transfer of reinforcements from Yugoslavia to Hungary, but the positions are generally maintained.

In Silesia the Russians continue their attacks against the garrison of Breslau and north-west of the city.

The 2nd Belorussian Front in East Prussia puts in vigorous attacks against the Germans crossing the Samland peninsula (the tongue of land that joins Königsberg with Danzig), who are trying to fight their way out to the west. In north-west Poland the Russians surround Grudziadz and press on northwards in the direction of Danzig (Gdansk), opposed by the Vistula Army Group.

Philippines: Luzon Fighting in Manila. Forces of the 25th Division (US I Corps), supported by aircraft and artillery, open operations against the Japanese positions north-west of Lumboy.

Some Japanese counter-attacks at Corregidor are repulsed.

Southern Philippines US 8th Army

(X Corps) begins a series of amphibious operations to clear all the Japanese from the San Bernardino Strait, between the islands of Samar and Luzon.

Leyte The Americans are still engaged in eliminating the last pockets of Japanese resistance.

Iwo Jima At 9.00 a.m., after an extremely powerful preparation in which six battleships add to the firepower, the American V Amphibious Corps, escorted by the 5th Fleet under the command of Admiral Spruance and commanded for the combined operations by Vice-Admiral Turner and for the land operations by General Harris Schmidt, lands part of the 4th and 5th Marine Divisions on the southeast coast of the island, strongly fortified by the Japanese. Japanese resistance at first is negligible, but it increases in ferocity as the Marines begin their move inland from the beaches. The landing force suffers heavy casualties, especially on its right flank. The units on the left flank try to advance southwards towards Mount Suribachi, a feature that dominates the whole island. Tanks and artillery go into action the moment they land.

The landing force consists of 30,000 men. Facing them, in the shelter of a forest of underground fortifications accurately sited and linked by tunnels – a real ants' nest – are 21,500 men, 14,500 of them from the army (109th Infantry Division, 2nd Mixed Brigade from Manchuria, 145th Independent Mixed Regiment, one tank regiment with 30 medium and 10 light tanks, 3 mortar battalions and 5 anti-tank battalions) and 7,000 from the navy, technicians, pilots without aircraft and seamen without ships, hastily trained by the army. The naval troops are commanded by Rear-Admiral Ichimaru; Commander-in-Chief of the garrison is General Tamadichi Kurabayashi. The island, in the Volcano group, covers less than twelve square miles. It has two airfields, with a third under construction. It is dominated by the hill called Mount Suribachi (560 ft), at the south-western extremity. To

Aerial view of the wakes from US landing craft as they approach the beaches of Iwo Jima.

the north is a plateau about 300 feet high, the Motoyama plateau. There is hardly any vegetation; the volcanic nature of the terrain gives the island a lunar appearance. Why have the Americans decided to land here? There is a psychological motive: the loss of Iwo Jima, which is part of metropolitan Japan, could have a serious effect on the enemy's morale. And there is a strategic motive: from Iwo Jima American long-range fighters will be able to reach Japan and escort bombers there, and the bombers too will find it helpful to have a staging-post on the long route they have to cover to carry out their frequent missions against Japan.

In the operations connected with the Iwo Jima landing the heavy cruiser *Chester*, two destroyers and one escort destroyer are damaged.

Burma The Japanese put in a determined counter-attack against the bridgehead opened by the 25th Indian Division at Ru-ywa in the Arakan sector.

20 February

Western Front General Eisenhower, Commander-in-Chief of Allied forces in Europe, lays down in a letter to the commanders of the three army groups – Montgomery (21st), Bradley (12th) and Devers (6th Army Group) – that Montgomery's forces will open the general offensive across the Rhine even if Bradley's and Devers's groups are still engaged in mopping up operations on the west bank in readiness for the crossing. However, once all the armies have reached the east bank, the two main lines of advance will be on the Ruhr and on Frankfurt.

In the British XXX Corps sector (Canadian 1st Army) a Bailey bridge over the Maas is opened to vehicular traffic.

Along the west bank of the Our, the units of the VIII Corps (US 3rd Army), and particularly the 6th Armoured Division, renew their attacks and penetrate the Siegfried Line fortifications north of Dahnen.

Further south, the 80th Division (XII Corps) reaches favourable positions for the attack on the heights south of Mettendorf. In the XX Corps sector (where the objective is the triangle between the rivers Saar and Moselle), the 10th Armoured Division goes into action, supported by units of the 94th Division.

Eastern Front The Germans continue with their counter-attacks in Hungary between Lake Balaton and Lake Velencei. There is bitter fighting between Székesfehérvár and Dunaföldvar. The German divisions also counter-attack from the south across the Drava. The German 8th Army contains Russian pressure in the Esztergom area, on the Danube northwest of Budapest.

There are local actions on the other fronts, in Silesia, East Prussia and northern Latvia.

Philippines: Luzon While the US XIV Corps makes arrangements for the assault on the centre of Manila, the XI Corps takes three of the four enemy strongpoints in the area north-west of Lumboy. The XI Corps reaches the west coast on the Bataan peninsula at Bagac.

Southern Philippines Units of the X Corps (US 8th Army) carry out landings, uncontested by the Japanese, on several islands in the San Bernardino Strait. The occupation of Samar continues.

Iwo Jima The 4th and 5th Marine Divisions, supported by fire from warships, artillery, tanks and flame-throwers, slightly extend their beachhead. The 5th, after repelling a furious night attack by the Japanese, advances slowly to north and south. From Mount Suribachi, which has been made into a fortress, the Japanese direct a murderous volume of fire which causes huge losses among the Americans, and some units are decimated. Tank losses amount to about 30% at the end of the second day of the landing. The cruiser *Biloxi* and a hospital ship are hit.

21 February

Western Front Finally with the capture of Goch by the 51st Division, British XXX Corps (Canadian 1st Army), Operation *Veritable* may be regarded as completed.

In the US 3rd Army sector there is a general advance. The 6th Armoured Division (VIII Corps) advances east of the Our, the 80th Division and 4th Armoured Division (XII Corps) advance south of Mettendorf and into the positions of the Siegfried Line between the rivers Our and Gay (including the capture of Roth), and the 10th Armoured Division (XX Corps) attacks in the direction of Kanzem and Wiltingen bridges, the final objectives of the offensive in the Saar–Moselle triangle.

The XV Corps (US 7th Army) keeps up pressure in preparation for the attack on Saarbrücken.

Philippines: Luzon The US XI Corps completes the occupation of the Bataan peninsula. The operation has been easy and has cost at most fifty men killed or missing. Japanese losses are not much higher. The 40th

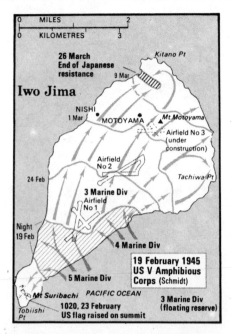

Operations on Iwo Jima, 19 February–26 March 1945.

Division gets ready for mopping up operations in the Zambales Mountains, in the central western part of the island.

Iwo Jima In view of the heavy losses sustained and the little progress made, Schmidt orders the landing of the 3rd Marine Division, until now held in reserve. With powerful supporting fire by artillery, tanks and flame throwers, the Americans resume the attack to the south, towards Mount Suribachi, and to the north, with the island's second airport as objective. The advance is slow and costly and at the end of the day the American armour is down to 50% of its initial strength. But a combat group from the 5th Marines reaches the slopes of Mount Suribachi. During the night the Japanese launch numerous counter-attacks and carry out several efforts to infiltrate.

Although the Americans have complete air superiority, several Japanese suicide aircraft manage to dive on the US ships, sinking the escort carrier *Bismarck Sea* and damaging the aircraft carrier *Saratoga*, the escort carrier *Lunga Point*, one destroyer, one transport and three landing craft.

22 February

Western Front On the way to Calcar the Canadian 2nd Division (II Corps, Canadian 1st Army) takes Moyland. In this sector the German parachutists of the 1st Army retain possession of two wooded hills (Hochwald and Balbergerwald) some six miles from the west bank of the Rhine. Meanwhile Marshal von Rundstedt, Commander-in-Chief of German forces on the Western Front, asks permission to withdraw what little is left of the 1st Parachute Army to the east bank of the river. Hitler replies that every centimetre of Germany must be defended to the last man.

On the northern front of the VIII Corps of the US 3rd Army, the 90th Division sends several patrols towards the river Prüm opposite Lunebach, while the 11th Armoured Division reaches Eschfeld and Reiff, and the 6th Armoured Division captures Irrhausen and Olmscheid, crossing the river Our. Units of the XII Corps consolidate their positions, while the 10th Armoured Division (XX Corps) finishes off the mopping up of the triangle between the rivers Saar and Moselle.

The 70th Division (XV Corps, US 7th Army) comes nearer to Saarbrücken.

Philippines: Luzon The US XIV Corps is still preparing for the final assault against the Japanese garrison in Manila. In the other parts of the island the Americans advance everywhere, but slowly.

Iwo Jima The struggle is still very bitter. The Marines, finding tanks and flamethrowers ineffective, fall back on the method of blowing up with dynamite every rock and every blind corner they encounter. With Mount Suribachi in the south cut off, they advance slowly towards the central part of the island and the second airfield, where they are pinned down by the cross-fire of Japanese skilfully sited on little rises overlooking the two airfields. The enemy perseveres with their night attacks and attempts to infiltrate. But both sides send up flares all through the night to avoid the possibility of surprise attacks.

Burma In the British IV Corps, two mechanized brigades of the 17th Indian Division and one tank brigade advance from the Nyaungu bridgehead towards Meiktila.

23 February

Western Front The US 9th Army launches Operation *Grenade*, the large-scale offensive by the 21st Army Group from the Rur to the Rhine. The attack gets under way at 3.30 a.m. after a heavy artillery barrage lasting 45 minutes, when the divisions of the XIII and XIX Corps cross the Rur. The Germans are taken by surprise. In order to halt the American advance in this delicate sector they despatch the *Panzerlehr* Division and the 15th *Panzergrenadiere* to the area, detaching them from the northern front. The river Rur is crossed by the US XIII Corps opposite Linnich (84th Division) and Roerdorf (102nd Division) and by the XIX Corps in the sector between Broich and Jülich (29th Division) and near Schophven (30th Division). Also at 3.30 a.m. General Hodges' US 1st Army launches a general attack eastwards across the river Rur, crossing it in the neighbourhood of Düren. Further south, the US 3rd Army crosses the Our and the Saar with units of the XII and XX Corps. Facing this new Allied offensive is General Model's Army Group B – from north to south (roughly from Mönchengladbach to Prüm), the 15th Army under General Zangen, the 5th Armoured Army under General Manteuffel and the 7th Army now under General Felber. In the US 7th Army sector, the 70th Division (XV Corps) strengthens its positions near Saarbrücken.

Eastern Front In Poland the Russians finally take Poznan after a long and bloody siege. In Pomerania, German resistance ceases at Arnswalde. Fighting still rages in Breslau.

Philippines: Luzon The US XIV Corps, after a methodical artillery preparation lasting several days, opens the final attack against Manila, where the Japanese have fortified themselves in the In-

Japanese soldier with the bomb he is about to set off under a tank.

tramuros strongpoint. At first, stupefied by the intense bombardment, the Japanese give ground, but later they counter-attack and regain some positions. In the XI Corps sector the Americans are now firmly in occupation of the western part of the island of Corregidor, while the 40th Division, on Luzon, launches an attack to liquidate the last Japanese positions left on the Zambales Mountains. Troops of the I Corps, having occupied Pantabangan, prepare to attack a strong contingent of the Japanese 14th Army identified north-east of the Gulf of Lingayen.

Southern Philippines Troops of the US 8th Army continue their occupation of the islets north-west of Samar.

Iwo Jima There is still very severe fighting in the central part of the island, around Airfield No. 2. The 5th Marine Division, which has surrounded Mount Suribachi, makes very slow progress against the very solid Japanese positions. However, a small group of Marines succeeds in reaching the summit of the mountain and hoisting the American flag there.

24 February

Western Front The 53rd Division of the British XXX Corps (Canadian 1st Army) advances slowly from

Goch towards the south-east in the direction of Weeze.

In the US 9th Army sector the XIII and XIX Corps continue their offensive as laid down in Operation *Grenade*. The 84th Division reaches and takes Doveren, the 29th completes the occupation of Jülich and captures Stetternich, while the 30th enters Hambach and Niederzier in the early hours of the morning.

The VII Corps (US 1st Army) extends its bridgehead over the river Rur.

In the US 3rd Army sector the offensive is followed up by all three corps, the VIII, XII and XX; their divisions take Bellscheid, Ober, Leimbach, Neuerburg, Berscheid and Bauler and begin the crossing of the Prüm during the night.

Eastern Front The 1st Baltic Front is incorporated in the 3rd Belorussian Front. Fighting continues everywhere. In Hungary, the 3rd Ukraine Front firmly repulses efforts to break through made in the last few days by the Germans in the sectors between Lake Balaton and Lake Velencei and near Esztergom.

Philippines: Luzon The Japanese cease to resist at Manila. The Americans now advance east of the city, meeting growing opposition. Montalban and San Isidro are captured by the 6th Division. Almost all the island of Corregidor, except for a strip of about two miles in the east, is firmly occupied by the Americans. Mopping up operations continue in the Zambales Mountains.

Iwo Jima Bitter fighting continues on Mount Suribachi and in the centre of the island near Airport No. 2. On Mount Suribachi, however, Japanese resistance is nearing its end; American sappers have blown up all the caves and many of the Japanese commit suicide. But around Airport No. 2 the Japanese destroy many Sherman tanks with mines and well camouflaged anti-tank guns. Savage hand-to-hand fighting develops.

Storms and collisions cause serious damage to several American ships, including the heavy cruiser *San Francisco*.

Burma In the British XXXIII Corps sector, the British 2nd Division begins to cross the Irrawaddy at Ngazun, west of Mandalay, and meets with immediate powerful resistance by the Japanese. In the IV Corps sector, the 17th Indian Division, advancing on Meiktila, captures the Japanese supply centre of Taungtha.

25 February

Western Front The 53rd Division (British XXX Corps, Canadian 1st Army) comes within about a mile and a quarter of Weeze, and is ordered to halt there.

The 35th Division of the US XVI Corps (9th Army) and armoured units of the 5th Armoured Division of the XIII Corps begin crossing the Rur opposite Linnich and south of Hottorf. On the army's right flank the XIX Corps also continues to advance and its units reach Müntz and Rodingen. In the US 1st Army sector the VII Corps completes the capture of Düren, then reaching the line of the bridgehead, while the 1st Division begins operations for crossing the Rur.

The offensive of the US 3rd Army continues and units of the 4th Armoured Division, after crossing the river Prüm near Hermesdorf, succeed in establishing a bridgehead over the Nims at Rittersdorf. In the XX Corps sector units of the 10th Armoured Division cross the Saar near Taben and advance towards Zerf.

Italian Front In the US 5th Army sector the first stage of the IV Corps' limited offensive west of Highway 64 is concluded.

On the right of the Allied front, the first units of the Italian *Folgore* combat group take up positions in the XIII Corps (British 8th Army) sector; by 3 March the Italian troops will have completed their deployment astride the river Santerno, taking over responsibility for the sector previously held by the British 6th Division.

Eastern Front The Vistula Army Group counter-attacks north-west of Arnswalde (south of Stettin) and

A US patrol hoists the American flag on Mount Suribachi, Iwo Jima.

makes some progress.

Philippines: Luzon The US XIV Corps prepares to liquidate the last nests of Japanese resistance in Manila. Further American progress in the island of Corregidor.

Iwo Jima Bold action by units of the 3rd Marine Division enables them to capture almost the whole of Airfield No. 2. However, the Japanese continue to resist most fiercely from three positions known as Height 382, Amphitheatre and Turkey Ridge. The fighting is ferocious; the Americans have dubbed the area the 'Mincer', and rightly so. During the day and the next night, Japanese fire knocks out 20 Sherman tanks. Mount Surabachi is officially declared captured.

☐ Japan. B-29 Superfortresses of XXI Bomber Command of the US Air Force carry out a heavy raid on Tokyo with incendiary bombs. The Americans pass on from precision bombing of military targets by day to carpet bombing of the big residential centres.

Carrier-borne aircraft from Vice-Admiral Mitscher's squadron of fast carriers also attack targets – airfields and aircraft factories – near Tokyo. These very heavy raids are repeated next day.

Burma The 17th Indian Division (British IV Corps) takes Mahlaing.

26 February

Western Front The Canadian II Corps (Canadian 1st Army) opens

Operation *Blockbuster*, an offensive on a big scale against the towns of Calcar, Udem and Xanten; taking part are two armoured divisions (the Canadian 4th and British 11th), one armoured brigade (the Canadian 2nd), two Canadian infantry divisions (the 2nd and 3rd) and one British (the 43rd Division). On the first day the Allied forces reach the escarpment south of Calcar and positions very near Udem.

Units of the US 9th Army continue to advance; some units of the XVI Corps move on Hückelhoven, while others cross the Rur opposite Hilfarth; the XIII Corps, after reaching and cutting the Erkelenz–Gerderath road, sends in the 102nd Division against Erkelenz, which is taken.

In the US 1st Army sector, the VII Corps advances rapidly from Düren towards Cologne, overrunning the remains of the German 2nd Armoured Division.

While the left flank of the US 3rd Army – the VIII Corps – is relatively calm, in the central sector the XII Corps goes ahead with its offensive, aiming among other things at a crossing of the Moselle at Trier. Further south, where the XX Corps is operating, the 10th Armoured Division and the 94th Division of infantry succeed in joining up their two bridgeheads at Ockfen and Serrig; some units of the 10th Armoured Division cross the Saar in the 94th Division sector and move on towards Irsch.

Eastern Front The 1st and 2nd Ukraine Fronts launch attacks against the frontier of Czechoslovakia. In Yugoslavia, the German Army Group E contains enemy pressure in the Sarajevo area, while Yugoslav and Bulgarian forces concentrate in the Zenica area.

Philippines: Luzon Immediately east and north-east of Manila (where isolated Japanese units still resist) American infantry of the XIV Corps assault Mount Pacawagan and Mount Mataba, but are driven back by intensive enemy artillery and machine-gun fire. The XI Corps winds up operations on the Zambales Mountains and completes the

capture of Corregidor Island, where the usual mopping up still remains to be carried out.

Southern Philippines The divisions of the US 8th Army complete the encirclement of the Japanese forces on the north-west coast of Leyte Island and the occupation of part of Samar and a number of islets in the southern part of the San Bernardino Strait.

Iwo Jima The advance made by the US amphibious V Corps is negligible, despite supporting fire from aircraft, ships and artillery. Japanese resistance is still most resolute. The Americans reach the three hills that overlook Airfield No. 2, but are driven off again.

Burma In the British XXXIII Corps sector, the 19th Indian Division advances firmly southwards, towards Mandalay. In the British IV Corps sector, the 17th Indian Division, still advancing on Meiktila, takes Thabutkon airfield.

27 February

Western Front The Canadian II Corps (Canadian 1st Army) presses on with Operation *Blockbuster*; the British 43rd Division by-passes Calcar, the Canadian 4th Armoured Division penetrates into the Hochwald forest east of Udem, the Canadian 3rd Division reaches Udem and the British 11th Armoured Division advances from Udem towards Kervenheim. After the Canadian II Corps' offensive, the operations of the British XXX Corps are slowed down, though the 3rd Division cuts the road that runs from Udem to Weeze.

While the 35th Division (XVI Corps, US 9th Army) advances swiftly east of the Rur, meeting little opposition from General Zangen's 15th Army, the 8th Armoured Division crosses the Rur opposite Hilfarth. The 2nd Armoured Division (XIX Corps) regroups on the east bank of the Rur in readiness for the final offensive against the Rhine.

The VII Corps (US 1st Army) continues to advance in the flat country round Cologne despite the stout resistance offered here by Zangen's divisions; a number of American

units reach the Erft, and the 3rd Armoured Division succeeds in establishing a bridgehead over it. In the III Corps sector, units of the 9th Division cross the Rur and re-group near Rath.

The 6th Armoured Division (VIII Corps, US 3rd Army) establishes a bridgehead over the Prüm, while the 87th Division advances with some difficulty towards Ormont and Hallschlag. The divisions of the XII Corps also cross the river Prüm. The 76th Division advances from the Wolfsfeld bridgehead south-westwards, towards Trier, and the 10th Armoured Division (XX Corps) also heads for the same city.

Eastern Front Reduced activity in all sectors. Near Sarajevo the Germans re-open communications with the north-west, which has been cut by the Yugoslav and Bulgarian troops.

Philippines: Luzon In the US XIV Corps sector the Americans proceed with the liquidation of the last centres of Japanese resistance in Manila. The 63rd Infantry capture Mount Pacawagan, near Manila, holding off violent Japanese counter-attacks. But the positions captured on Mount Mataba have to be abandoned.

Iwo Jima The very fierce fighting between the Marines and the Japanese is renewed on the three hills which overlook Airfield No. 2. Using bulldozers, flamethrowers and hollow-charge ammunition, the Americans eliminate the pill-boxes, gun emplacements and machine-gun posts one after another. But all their efforts are frustrated by the unexpected and violent enemy counter-attacks, which drive them back to their original positions time after time. The nerve centre of General Kuribayashi's communications is in this area.

A storm causes damage to a number of American ships in the waters off Iwo Jima, including the light aircraft carrier *San Jacinto*, one destroyer, one tanker and several transports.

Burma In the British XXXIII Corps sector, the bridgehead established by the 20th Indian Division across the Irrawaddy is consolidated, after the

Japanese have had to give up their efforts to liquidate it. In the British IV Corps sector, a brigade of the 17th Indian Division is air-lifted to Thabutkon while other units reach the outskirts of Meiktila.

28 February

Western Front Advance units of the Canadian II Corps (Canadian 1st Army) move forward along the Rhine, in the Hochwald and Balberg forests. In the US 9th Army sector the offensive of the 35th Division (XVI Corps), 84th Division (XIII Corps) and 29th Division (XIX Corps) goes on without pause; the 29th Division advances rapidly towards Mönchengladbach. The 2nd Armoured Division, another formation of the XIX Corps, comes within about five miles of Neuss, six miles from the Rhine. The III Corps (US 1st Army) advances along the river Neffel with the 1st Division, while the 9th Division reaches Berg and crosses the Rur at several points. The 9th Armoured Division also crosses the Rur.

In the US 3rd Army sector, the XX Corps pushes on north towards Trier.

Italian Front The US 10th Motorized Division and the 1st Division of the Brazilian Expeditionary Corps (IV Corps, US 5th Army) complete their re-grouping for the second stage of the offensive against the hills west of Highway 64.

Eastern Front Troops of the 2nd Belorussian Front, advancing north in Pomerania, capture Neustettin (Szczecinek), between Danzig and Stettin, and Prechlau. In Silesia fighting continues in Breslau. The Germans are assembling large forces to launch a new counter-offensive in Hungary, north and south of Lake Balaton, against the 3rd Ukraine Front. To this end Hitler has transferred General Dietrich's 6th Armoured Army from the Western Front.

Philippines: Luzon General Krueger orders the US XIV Corps to Balayan and Batangas bays, in the south-west of Luzon south of the Tagaytay Mountains. The XI Corps advances

ANNE FRANK

The young Anne Frank, author of one of the most moving documents on Nazi persecution, died in the German concentration camp of Bergen-Belsen, near Hanover.

Her diary, published in 1947 under the title *Het Achterhuis*, was a dramatic and heart-rending account of two years spent in hiding in an Amsterdam flat, where she, her family and some other Jewish friends had been forced to seek refuge in 1942 from the occupying Nazis.

Showing surprising maturity and sensitivity, the diary in which the young Anne Frank daily recorded every event, including the most commonplace incidents, her own discovery of sexuality and the frequent fears of capture, was later published to international acclaim, a glowing testament to humanity and hope.

in the Ternate area, in the southern part of Manila Bay. In Manila itself the remaining Japanese resistance is confined to two ministerial buildings.

Southern Philippines A combat group from the 41st Division (US 8th Army), after a bombardment by aircraft and ships of Rear-Admiral Fechteler's squadron, lands at Puerto Princesa on Palawan Island and sets up radar stations. On Samar, US and Filipino units begin operations to clear the Mauo area of the enemy.

Iwo Jima The 3rd Marines Division, slowly advancing north, captures the village of Motoyama on the plateau of that name and seizes the hills that dominate Airfield No. 3, under construction further north. There is still bitter fighting in the 'Mincer' area, east and west of Airfield No. 2. Liquidation of the last nests of resistance on Mount Suribachi continues. Japanese bombers and coast defence guns hit two American destroyers in the waters off Iwo Jima and damage them severely.

Burma The 17th Indian Division (British IV Corps) begins the assault on Meiktila, against resistance by General Honda's Japanese 33rd Army.

1 March

Western Front The British XXX

Corps and Canadian II Corps (Canadian 1st Army) continue to advance in the Kervenheim sector and in the Hochwald and Balberg forests. The town of Venlo, in Holland, is taken by units of the 35th Division (XVI Corps, US 9th Army). In the XIII Corps sector the 84th and 102nd Divisions begin a co-ordinated offensive towards Birgen, Dülken, the Niers Canal and Anrath. Units of the 29th Division (XIX Corps) seize Mönchengladbach, the most important town reached by the Allies in Germany so far. The 2nd Armoured Division advances northwards across the Cologne plain, capturing Kleinenbroich, crossing the North Canal and continuing north on the line Willich–Osterath, places which are soon captured.

In the US 1st Army sector, the VII Corps, with the Erft as its start line, continues to attack towards Cologne and the Rhine, with the 3rd Armoured Division operating in the Glesch–Paffendorf region, the 10th engaged on the area of Quadrath and the 8th advancing on the town of Mödrath. The III Corps is also advancing towards the Rhine.

The VIII Corps (US 3rd Army), astride the river Prüm, is still advancing eastwards, but meets with strong resistance from the German 7th Army. The 87th Division reaches

Ormont and the 4th makes some progress in the bridgeheads east of the river Prüm. The 6th Armoured Division reinforces the bridgehead on the right flank of the corps. Between the rivers Prüm and Nims, the 80th Division (XII Corps) makes headway, and between the Prüm and the Kyll the 4th Armoured Division captures Sefferweich and Malbergweich.

Units of the 10th Armoured Division (XX Corps) begin to enter Trier; the bridge over the Moselle was taken intact overnight.

The US 7th Army, with its three corps (XXI, XV and VI) abreast of one another, takes up defensive positions along the rivers Saar, Rotbach and Moder between Emmersweiler (in Germany) and Oberhoffen (in France).

The French 1st Army remains on the defensive along the Rhine, protecting the right flank of the US 7th Army.

Eastern Front In Hungary the Germans still prepare for their counter-offensive. The Vistula Army Group contains the attacks of the 1st and 2nd Belorussian Fronts south-east and south-west of Pyritz, south of Stettin; the German 7th Armoured Division and 4th *SS Panzergrenadiere* Division suffer heavy losses. In Yugoslavia there is fighting in the Sarajevo area.

Philippines: Luzon In the capital, Japanese resistance is now confined to the Ministry of Finance building. East of Manila, the US 6th Division re-groups to attack the Shimbu line, which runs north from Antipolo to Mount Oro and is strongly manned by the Japanese. Filipino guerrillas are carrying out operations against the Japanese in the south of the island. The I Corps takes the initiative again, moving north towards Baguio. The 32nd and 25th Divisions, against strong enemy opposition, move towards the Cagayan Valley and Balete Pass, in the north-east of the island.

Southern Philippines The combat group from the 41st Division (US 8th Army) which landed at Puerto Princesa on 28 February virtually completes the occupation of Palawan Island. Other units of the army land on Lubang Island and take Tilic. Lubang, the biggest of the group of islands of the same name, is occupied in the course of a few days.

Iwo Jima Turkey Crest, one of the three hills near Airfield No. 2 so fiercely contested by the Japanese, finally falls to the assaults of the Marines. The 3rd Division advances east of the village of Motoyama but is held up about half a mile beyond it by the Japanese. The Americans take part of Airfield No. 3 but are then held up by very strong Japanese resistance. The 4th Marine Division fights all day at the base of Height 382, where the enemy shows signs of giving way.

Ryukyu Islands Aircraft from Vice-Admiral Mitscher's fast carrier squadron attack enemy installations in the area of Okinawa. Next day Task Force 58 hits at Okino Daito Island, also in the Ryukyu Islands and only 450 miles from the Japanese island of Kyushu.

☐ Turkey declares war on Germany and Japan.

2 March

Western Front The 53rd Division (British XXX Corps, Canadian 1st Army) captures Weeze and advances south towards Geldern.

From Venlo the 35th Division (XVI Corps, US 9th Army) moves quickly into German territory and reaches Sevelen after passing through Strälen and Nieukerk.

The Niers Canal is crossed by the 84th Division (XIII Corps) near Süchteln and Ödt; the other two divisions of the corps, the 102nd (infantry) and the 5th Armoured, reach Krefeld and Ficheln. The 29th Division reaches its positions at Mönchengladbach, and the 83rd completes the capture of Neuss and reaches the Rhine opposite Düsseldorf, but the retreating Germans have destroyed all the bridges over the rivers.

In the US 1st Army sector, the 99th Division (VII Corps) crosses the Erft in the neighbourhood of Glesch, while further south the 3rd

Armoured Division and 104th Division defend the bridgeheads east of the Erft. The III Corps continues its advance towards the Rhine; its divisions reach Erp, the river Roth at Frieshoim, Mülheim and Wichterich, establishing a bridgehead in the neighbourhood of Friesheim.

In the US 3rd Army sector, units of the 87th and 4th Divisions (VIII Corps) meet with strong resistance near Ormont, and east of Prüm. The XII Corps opens an offensive towards the river Kyll during the night, while the 5th Division tries to establish a bridgehead across the same river between Erdorf and Philippsheim. The 10th Armoured Division (XX Corps) completes the capture of Trier, while the 94th Division continues to extend the bridgehead at Saarsburg (now some six miles deep).

Italian Front In the British 8th Army sector, the Italian *Cremona* combat group (V Corps), supported by partisans of the 28th *Garibaldi* Brigade, opens the offensive against Comacchio.

Eastern Front The Vistula Army Group evacuates the bridgehead over the Oder in the Schwedt area, south-west of Stettin. Fighting flares up again in the whole of East Prussia, where the Russians want to wipe out the German 4th Army before it can be evacuated by sea.

Philippines: Luzon While the XIV Corps clears up the last Japanese resistance in Manila, the US I Corps advances north.

Mopping up of Corregidor is complete, and the island has been inspected by MacArthur. During the operations the Japanese have lost 4,700 dead, and another 500 men have been buried alive in the caverns and tunnels. The Americans have lost 1,000 men killed, wounded and missing.

Southern Philippines On Samar, American units reach the outskirts of Mauo.

Iwo Jima The 3rd Marine Division, in the centre of the line, completes the capture of Airfield No. 3 under intensive Japanese artillery and machine-gun fire. In the area of the 'Mincer' the Americans take another important position, the one called the Amphitheatre. It has been a tremendous struggle, conducted with flame-throwers and explosive charges. The Americans are now in control of two thirds of the island.

Burma The 20th Indian Division and British 2nd Division join up their bridgeheads west of Mandalay.

3 March

Western Front Winston Churchill, during a visit to the Western Front, lunches at Jülich. This is the first time a British Prime Minister has set foot in Germany since Chamberlain went to Munich in 1938.

At Walbeck, south-west of Gelderen, contact is made between the British XXX Corps (Canadian 1st Army) and the American XVI Corps (9th Army).

East of Sevelen, the 35th Division (XVI Corps, 9th Army) has to slow down in the face of severe opposition by the German parachutists of the 1st Army. German resistance makes itself felt also in the XII Corps sector, but the 84th Division still succeeds in taking Rath and advancing towards Homberg.

The units of the VII Corps (US 1st Army) advance rapidly towards the Rhine, taking Sinsteden, Stommeln, Glessen and Dansweiller among other places, and then opening operations against Königsberg (104th Division). In the III Corps sector the 1st Division and 9th Armoured Division reach the Erft. On the south flank of the corps, the 78th Division retains its bridgehead near Hambach. The 2nd Division (V Corps) crosses the Rur at Heimbach and continues south towards Gemund.

There is no improvement in the situations of the 87th and 4th Divisions (VIII Corps, US 3rd Army), virtually pinned down in the vicinity of Ormont and Reuth. Further south, the 11th Armoured Division crosses the river Prüm and attacks towards the river Kyll, taking Fleringen, while the 6th Armoured Division completes its advance from the Prüm to the Nims, which some of its units cross north of Schönecken.

Japanese soldier killed by a flame-thrower.

The 5th Division (XII Corps) manages to secure a small bridgehead east of the Kyll. The 76th Division completes mopping up along the rivers Kyll and Moselle and, during the night begins to cross the Kyll. The 4th Armoured Division concentrates near Bitburg, a short way from the west bank of the Kyll, in readiness for an offensive across the river. In the XX Corps sector, the 10th Armoured Division advances towards Schweich but has to halt at the river Ruwer, near Eitelsbach, where the bridge has been blown up.

Italian Front The IV Corps (US 5th Army) begins the second phase of its limited, local offensive against the hills north-east of Monte Torraccia and Monte Castello.

In the V Corps (British 8th Army) sector, the 56th Division takes a strong position on the east bank of the Senio near San Severo, and the *Cremona* group continues the battle for Comacchio.

Philippines: Luzon All Japanese resistance in Manila is at an end, and with the liquidation of the Japanese units in the Ternate area the whole of Manila Bay is now also clear of the enemy. The 35th Division (US I Corps) captures Digdig and prepares to eliminate some pockets of enemy

resistance in the Puncan area, which part of the division now tackles.

Southern Philippines Units of the US 8th Army land on the islands of Burias and Ticao without opposition. Verde Island is firmly in American hands. On Palawan Island the US 186th Infantry meets sharp resistance from the Japanese.

Iwo Jima The 3rd, 4th and 5th Marine Divisions continue to attack the strong Japanese positions. Height 382, after yet another assault, is finally taken. Once the countless caves and tunnels have been mopped up, the 'Mincer' is securely in American hands; but at the cost of 6,500 American troops. The 5th Marine Division, on the left, attacks Height 362, using flame-throwers against the fortified Japanese positions.

☐ Finland declares war against Germany with retrospective effect from 15 September 1944.

4 March

Western Front In the Canadian 1st Army sector, the 43rd Division (Canadian II Corps) thrusts southeast towards Xanten, while the other two divisions in the corps, the Canadian 2nd and 3rd, complete the capture of the Hochwald and Balberg forests. On the army's right flank, the 53rd Division (British XXX Corps) captures Geldern and makes contact there with the 35th Division of the US XVI Corps (US 9th Army).

Repelen falls to the 5th Armoured Division of the XIII Corps (US 9th Army), which succeeds in cutting the road linking Rheinberg with Mörs. The 2nd Armoured Division captures Kaldenhausen and completes mopping up in the area between Ürdingen and Vietelsheide, bringing operations in the Cologne lowlands to a close.

The 99th Division (VII Corps, US 1st Army) continues to advance north-east along the Erft, but is halted just past the confluence of the Erft and the Rhine, on the line Derikum–Ükrath. The 104th Division forces a way into the outer defences of Cologne. In the III Corps sector, while the 1st Division establishes a bridgehead over the Erft, the 9th Division takes Derikum and Hausweiler on the east bank of the river. The 87th Division and 4th Division (VIII Corps, US 3rd Army) resume their advance, while the XII Corps divisions extend and reinforce their bridgeheads over the river Kyll.

Italian Front The IV Corps (US 5th Army) continues its offensive, reaching Monte Acidola, Monte della Croce and Madonna di Brasa. On the right flank of the Allied line (V Corps of the British 8th Army) the *Cremona* combat group enters Torre di Primaro.

Eastern Front Bitter fighting continues at Breslau where the centre of the city is shelled by Russian 400-mm guns.

Troops of the 1st Belorussian Front force the Vistula Army Group to retire north-east of Stettin (Szczecin), and take Regenwalde (Resko). The X SS Corps suffers heavy losses. Further east the Russians take Rummelsburg (Miastko). In this sector the Germans even send the 600th Russian Division into the line, under the command of General Vlassov, who went over to the Germans after being taken prisoner.

In East Prussia the Russians also attack Königsberg from the north for the first time.

In Norway, the German 7th and 199th Mountain Divisions attempt a retreat south through snowstorms.

Philippines The Americans prepare to attack the Japanese defensive line, the Shimbu line, east of Manila.

Burma In the British IV Corps sector, the 17th Indian Division occupies part of the town of Meiktila, a very important objective on account of its eight airfields.

☐ Japan. 192 B-29 Superfortresses bombers of the US XXI Bomber Command bomb the Musashino aircraft factory in Tokyo. This is the last 'precision bombing' by the Americans, who now go over to carpet bombing.

5 March

Western Front In the US 9th Army sector, the 5th Armoured Division

(XIII Corps) reaches the Rhine at Orsoy, which is taken, together with Rheinkamp. The XIX Corps reaches Rheinhausen and eliminates the pocket near the Adolf Hitler bridge south of Ürdinger, so carrying out the last of the tasks given it in Operation *Grenade*. The 3rd Armoured Division (VII Corps) opens the attack on Cologne from the south in the early hours of the morning, and enters the city during the day. Some units of the 104th Division, continuing their advance eastwards towards Cologne, take Junkersdorf. There is considerable activity in the US 3rd Army sector, where the three corps (VIII, XII and XX, from north to south) cross the Kyll at several points.

Italian Front The limited offensive of the IV Corps (US 5th Army) is concluded.

Eastern Front Troops of the 1st Belorussian Front capture Stargard (Stargard Szczecinski) and Naugard, the south-east bulwarks of the defence of Stettin. The Vistula Army Group announces that it has destroyed 1,800 Russian tanks to date, but has to admit that it has no more news of the German 2nd Army.

Fierce battles continue in East Prussia and in the northern tip of Latvia.

☐ In Germany, boys born in 1929 are to be enrolled in the regular armed forces.

Philippines: Luzon In the US XIV Corps sector, the 11th Division, reinforced by one regiment, begins operations for the occupation of Balayan and Batangas bays, in the south of the island. The Japanese halt the advance near Langanan. In the I Corps sector to the north, Filipino guerrillas now control the north coast west of the mouth of the river Cagayan, and the west coast, except for Vigan, as far as the San Fernando area. The 33rd Division is advancing on San Fernando from the south and the Japanese garrisons in the area are in danger of being encircled. The 25th Division is advancing towards the Cagayan Valley.

Burma In the British XV Corps sector, the 25th Indian Division ad-

vances along the coast from the Arakan and takes Tamandu. In the XXXIII Corps sector, the 19th Indian Division advances at a fair pace towards Mandalay.

6 March

Western Front The British 43rd Division and Canadian 2nd Division (II Corps of Canadian 1st Army) reinforce their positions in the Xanten area, preparing for the final offensive against the city. The Canadian 3rd Division concludes its mission when it takes Sonsbeck; the 4th Armoured Division pushes on from Sonsbeck towards Veen, while in the British XXX Corps sector, the 53rd Division continues to advance slowly towards Alpen, on the road to Wesel.

In the 9th Army sector Operation *Grenade* is brought to a successful conclusion; the XVI, XIII and XIX Corps have moved up from the Rur to the Rhine.

The offensive of the units of the VII Corps (US 1st Army) against Cologne continues, the 3rd Armoured Division attacking from the north and the 104th Division from the south, while south of the city the 8th Division pursues its attacks towards the Rhine. The 9th Armoured Division attacks towards the confluence of the river Ahr with the Rhine. In the 3rd Army sector operations continue along the Kyll.

Eastern Front The 2nd Belorussian Front finishes off the capture of Grudziadz, a key point in the German defensive system on the lower Vistula in Poland, and advances along the Polish Corridor towards Danzig. Enemy forces surrounded in the area of Köslin (Koszalin), in Pomerania, are also destroyed. The 1st Belorussian Front also advances in Pomerania, taking Belgard (Bialogard) and other towns that the Germans had determined to defend to the last.

In Hungary, the German Army Group South, having assembled considerable forces (Dietrich's 6th SS Armoured Army, 6th Army, Hungarian 3rd Army and 8th Cavalry Army, I SS Armoured Corps, 2nd Armoured Army) launches a power-

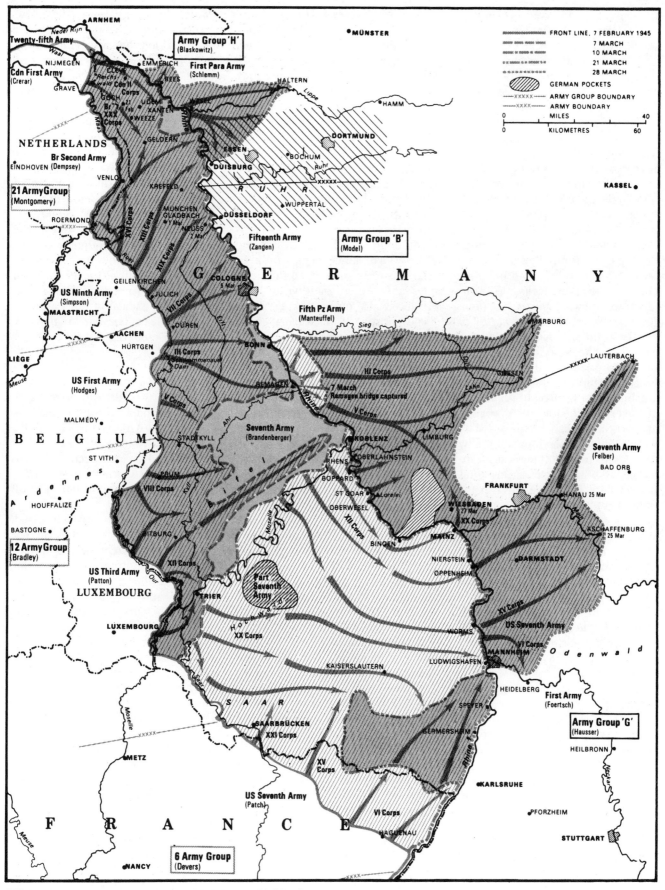

Allied progress to the Rhine and beyond 7 February–28 March.

ful counter-offensive (Operation *Waldteufel*) north and south of Lake Balaton against the armies of the 3rd Ukraine Front. Simultaneously, Army Group E attacks in the south-east on the Drava. The mass of the German forces strike east from Szé-kesfehérvár, towards Pecs from Lake Balaton in the south and towards Tatabanya in the north. The mobile reserves of the 3rd Ukraine Front are quickly sent up to prearranged positions in the Lake Velencei and Sarviz Canal sector, in support of the 27th Army.

Southern Philippines On Palawan the Japanese, firmly dug in, repulse the attacks of the US 186th Infantry. On Burias the Americans make contact with the enemy for the first time.

Iwo Jima After a barrage by artillery and naval guns unprecedented in this campaign, the American V Amphibious Corps renews its attempts to break through the Japanese defensive line in the north of the island, but at the end of the day such progress as it has made can be measured in yards. Moreover the Japanese are by now used to the American technique; as soon as the enemy guns begin to fire, they take cover in the deepest dug-outs, and come out again at once as soon as the barrage stops and the Marines advance to the attack. The scenes of the most bloody struggles are Height 362 B, the area round Airfield No. 3 and that to the east of the village of Motoyama. 28 Mustang fighters and 12 twin-engined P-61s arrive to be stationed on Airfield No. 1, where they can give speedy support to the ground operations.

7 March

Western Front In the Canadian II Corps (1st Army) sector preparations go on for the final attack on Xanten. Apart from some limited activity by the XVI Corps to extend its north flank towards Wesel, the US 9th Army front remains quiet. Cologne, Germany's third city, is captured by the US 3rd Armoured Division and the 104th Division of infantry (VII Corps, US 1st Army). While some units of the 9th

Armoured Division (III Corps) succeed in establishing bridgeheads across the rivers Ahr and Rhine, others at Remagen manage to seize a bridge across the Rhine, the only one that the Germans have not been able to blow up, establishing a small bridgehead on the east bank.

In the US 3rd Army sector, while the 87th Division (VIII Corps) advances swiftly to the north-east towards the river Ahr and the units of the 11th Armoured Division take Dockweiler, Boxberg and Kelberg, the 4th Armoured Division (XII Corps) proceeds along the Ulmen–Kaisersech–Kehrig–Ochtendung axis, south of Andernach. In little more than two days the American division has advanced 45 miles, taking some 5,000 prisoners, capturing huge amounts of equipment and sowing disorder among the units of the German 7th Army, dispersed north of the Moselle and west of the Rhine.

Eastern Front In Hungary and Yugoslavia, along the line Lake Velencei–Balaton–Drava, Operation *Waldteufel* goes ahead. Army Group E crosses the Drava in the area of Donji Miholjac and Valpovo, inflicting heavy losses on the Bulgarian 1st Army and Yugoslav 3rd Army, and heading for Mohacs. South of Lake Balaton, the 2nd Armoured Army breaks through the lines of the Russian 57th Army (3rd Ukraine Front), making for Nagybajom. Between Lale Balaton and Lake Velencei, the Russian 27th Army contains the advance of the 6th SS Armoured Army.

Philippines: Luzon In the I Corps sector, a battalion of the 127th Infantry Regiment occupies the bridge and village of Aringay and advances towards Mount Magabang. Another battalion of the same regiment is held up by strong Japanese resistance on the Villa Verde track.

The XIV Corps begins operations against the Shimbu line, the 158th Infantry occupy Taal, which is undefended, and advance rapidly in the area of Lake Taal.

Iwo Jima Taking the Japanese by surprise by attacking without the usual artillery preparation, a regimental combat group of the 3rd

Marine Division captures Height 362 E on the Motoyama plateau. The 5th Marine Division, attacking on the left of the line, makes limited progress, slowed by the broken nature of the terrain. Supporting fire from ships has to be cut to the minimum because the two sides are so close to one another, something which has already caused several incidents, with losses among the Marines.

Burma In the north, a regiment of the Chinese 38th Division occupies Lashio, north-east of Mandalay.

In the British IV Corps sector, the Japanese launch a counter-offensive to recapture Meiktila, and succeed in cutting off much of the 17th Indian Division in Taungtha. The British threat to Mandalay, from Lashio in the north-east and Meiktila in the south-west, continues to grow.

8 March

Western Front After meticulous preparation, the British 43rd and Canadian 2nd Divisions (Canadian II Corps, 1st Army) launch an attack on Xanten, which they take.

In the US 1st Army sector, the 1st Division (VII Corps) pushes on towards the Rhine opposite the city of Bonn.

At Remagen the III Corps is engaged with every means available in reinforcing and extending the bridgehead over the Rhine; however, the haste with which the operations have to be mounted (the Americans cannot let this unexpected advantage slip) does lead to some lack of co-ordination and to congestion on the routes leading to the bridge. The Germans too are making desperate attempts to plug the leak at Remagen; within two days, more than 300 Luftwaffe aircraft carry out dive-bombing attacks on the bridge in attempts to destroy it, but in vain. The VIII Corps of the US 3rd Army advances rapidly towards the Rhine.

Italian Front The 1st Armoured Division (US II Corps, 5th Army) carries out limited attacks to reinforce the positions of the corps' left flank, taking Carviano, north-east of Vergato.

Eastern Front Fighting goes on

THE REMAGEN BRIDGE

7 March

Late in the morning of 7 March 1945 a detachment of the American 9th Armoured Division (a formation of the III Corps of General Hodges' 1st Army), commanded by Lieutenant Karl Timmermann, emerges from the Eifel woods, overlooking the Rhine opposite the little town of Remagen. When they first catch sight of the river, Timmermann and his men are incredulous, for there stands a bridge over the river still intact, carrying a double railway track. Such a sight is rare, indeed unique, in the German landscape in 1945. Ever since the beginning of the year, officers commanding troops guarding the Rhine crossings have had orders from Hitler to blow up all the bridges the moment the German troops are safely on the east bank of the river. Not a single bridge is to be captured intact by the Allies, under penalty of death for those responsible.

On the east bank, the railway across the Remagen bridge (which is named after Ludendorff) disappears into a tunnel, in which German civilians and troops are concentrated. Why the bridge should still be intact is a mystery. Probably some delay in the operations to evacuate the left bank of the Rhine has left insufficient time for it to be demolished, or perhaps the Americans have come in sight of the bridge before they were expected. However it may be, Timmermann is ordered by the GOC, 9th Armoured Division to attack the bridge and take it intact. The young officer and his men press on towards the Rhine, cross the railway embankment and reach the water. A few minutes later a loud roar shakes the air; German engineers have set off charges to blow up the four pylons that support the bridge's

German prisoners cross the Remagen bridge, carrying their wounded.

steel structure. But when the cloud of smoke clears the bridge is still there, miraculously intact. A few minutes later Timmermann and his troops reach the east bank, while the last German civilians and soldiers disappear into the tunnel. American engineers immediately take steps to defuse a second detonator, disconnecting an unexploded charge of 500lb of dynamite.

The news of the crossing of the Remagen bridge quickly reaches Allied supreme headquarters, arousing great surprise and excitement. Eisenhower is told and, switching his strict plans of attack, he orders General Bradley, Commander of the 12th Army Group (of which the US 1st Army forms part) to 'send forward' all available troops.

With a quite remarkable demonstration of flexibility, the Americans are able to take full advantage of this unexpected opportunity, and by evening they succeed in establishing a firm bridgehead over the Rhine.

The amazing news also reaches the bunker at Hitler's Chancellery, and his rage flares up at once. The most illustrious head to fall is that of Field-Marshal von Rundstedt, who is relieved of the post of Commander-in-Chief of the German forces in the West ('He is finished,' declares Hitler, 'I don't want to hear any more about him.') and replaced by Kesselring, recalled from the Italian Front.

Useful as it was, and particularly effective from the psychological point of view, the capture of the Remagen bridge was not a decisive episode in the course of the Allied offensive. One bridge over the Rhine does not represent a strategic turning-point. It needs several days, and more bridgeheads upstream and downstream of Remagen, before the Allies can cross the Rhine in force and overcome the last natural obstacle to their progress into Germany.

south of Stettin and Danzig as well as in Silesia, while in Hungary and Yugoslavia the German 6th SS Armoured Army presses on from Székesfehérvár towards the Danube and along the Sarviz Canal, and the 2nd Armoured Army, south of Lake Balaton, advances on Nagybajom. The Germans have so far made penetrations of from 6 to 15 miles.

The German Army Group E engages the Bulgarian and Yugoslav forces across the Drava and contains the Yugoslav forces west of Sarajevo.

Philippines: Luzon The US XIV Corps continues its attacks on the Shimbu line with the 6th Division and 1st Cavalry Division and some progress is made towards Antipolo. In the I Corps area the Americans capture Mount Magabang, northeast of Aringay, and the village of Putlan.

Southern Philippines All organized Japanese resistance ceases on Palawan Island. The Americans also occupy the islets of Busuanga, Balabac and Pandanan.

Iwo Jima The three Marine divisions renew their attacks against the Japanese positions with support from artillery and flame-throwers, winning a few hundred yards all along the line. The 4th Marine Division then drives off a violent Japanese counter-attack. The Americans observe that the number of suicides among the enemy dead has greatly increased – an encouraging sign for the Allies.

9 March

Western Front On the northern flank of the Allied line, the Germans abandon their bridgehead in the area of Wesel and destroy the bridges over the river.

In the Canadian 1st Army sector, the 4th Division (Canadian II Corps) takes Veen.

While the German 15th Army abandons the west bank of the Rhine, Bonn is captured by the units of the US 1st Division (American 1st Army).

Control of the bridgehead at Remagen is taken over by the 9th Division (III Corps). The Germans

continue to send aircraft over to try to destroy the bridge. Meanwhile the 7th Armoured Division has taken over the defence of the west bank of the Rhine between Bonn and Remagen.

In the US 3rd Army sector, units of the VIII Corps have reached the Rhine, while the 4th Armoured Division (XII Corps) is ordered to establish a bridgehead at Treis.

Eastern Front In Yugoslavia, the Yugoslav 3rd Army launches a counter-attack against the bridgehead established over the Drava by the German Army Group E. The counter-attack is contained.

In the Vistula Army Group sector, the Russians storm through the defences of Küstrin (Kostrzyn) and bitter house-to-house fighting develops. The 2nd Belorussian Front pushes on in the Danzig area.

Philippines: Luzon Hard fighting continues on the Shimbu line, east of Manila, and in the central eastern part of the island.

Southern Philippines American aircraft and ships bombard the Zamboanga area on the island of Mindanao, in readiness for a landing. American troops are withdrawn from Samar, where the liquidation of the remaining Japanese is left to the Filipino infantry.

Iwo Jima During the night large numbers of Japanese with demolition charges tied to their belts throw themselves against the American positions, achieving some penetration and putting the 4th Marine Division in some difficulty. The suicide attack, which General Kuribayashi had forbidden, is repulsed. In the morning the Americans count 784 enemy dead on the ground.

The three Marine divisions continue their systematic attacks with flame-throwers and explosive charges against the Japanese caves and other strongpoints. Still held up on the right and in the centre, they make good progress along the west coast of the island.

Burma In the British XXXIII Corps sector, the 19th Indian Division penetrates into the outskirts of Mandalay, where bitter fighting develops.

☐ *Japan.* 334 B-29 bombers from Guam, Saipan and Tinian drop incendiary bombs on Tokyo in a massive three-hour raid. Ten square miles, a fifth of the total area of the city, are razed to the ground. A figure of 130,000 dead is confirmed, but some sources put the number as high as 200,000.

French Indo-China The Japanese, fearing an American landing, deprive Admiral Decoux of all authority as Governor-General of the colony, and dismiss the whole French administration. They start on a series of brutal acts which only serve to strengthen the resistance movement. It is in this atmosphere that the Vietminh is born.

10 March

Western Europe The 1st Army finishes off Operation *Veritable* with the capture of the region between the rivers Moselle and Rhine and, with the II Corps, also concludes Operation *Blockbuster*, as a result of which the Allies have control of the Calcar–Uden–Xanten sector. The success of the two operations has cost the 21st Army Group over 23,000 casualties – 7,300 American, about 5,500 Canadian and 10,500 British.

In the US 1st Army sector, the 9th Division (III Corps) extends its bridgehead over the Rhine at Remagen, where the 78th Division also intervenes, while the Germans continue their efforts to destroy the bridge. The 4th Armoured Division (XII Corps, US 3rd Army) completes the occupation west of the Rhine between Andernach and Koblenz and north of the Moselle between Koblenz and Cochem, which last place is reached by units of the 5th Division. On the southern flank of the army the XX Corps is reinforced by the 80th Division in readiness for the attack on the Saarburg bridgehead planned for 13 March. The 10th Armoured Division reaches its objectives in the Wittlich sector and begins to advance towards the Moselle.

Eastern Front The commander of the 3rd Ukraine Front, Tolbukhin, asks the Soviet Supreme Command

'LES ENFANTS DU PARADIS'

Paris, 1840-47. In the popular and picturesque 'Boulevard du Crime', thoroughfare of theatres and homicides, the story unfolds of the love affairs of the beautiful, passionate Garance, mistress and source of contention of four men, the mime Baptiste, the actor Lemaître, the criminal dandy Lacenaire and the wealthy conte de Montray. When Garance realizes that the man she really loves is Baptiste, he is already married with a son. After one night of love, Garance vanishes in the throng of carnival maskers while Baptiste madly but vainly calls out her name.

Screened on the evening of 9 March, *Les Enfants du Paradis* was the first important film to emerge from Paris after the liberation and was warmly received by the public.

Because of the war and the German occupation, the film took more than two years to make and cost over 60 million francs. A lyrical tale about the relationship of life and the theatre, reality and make-believe, and the nature and variety of love, *Les Enfants du Paradis* was Marcel Carné's finest film, thanks in large measure to the script of Jacques Prévert, and represented one of the most sincere tributes to the theatre in the history of cinema.

The excellent cast included Jean Louis Barrault, Arletty and Pierre Brasseur. The original version, lasting 195 minutes, was subsequently cut for commercial reasons.

Maria Casarès and Jean-Louis Barrault in a scene from Carné's film.

for reinforcements in view of the very real threat constituted by the German counter-offensive (Operation *Waldteufel*). But he is denied any. The Germans have to break off their thrust towards the Danube, which is stoutly resisted, but they continue with their penetration along the Sarviz Canal, west of Lake Velencei. They send all their armoured reserves into the battle. The German Army Group Centre is still heavily engaged by the 1st Ukraine Front near Oppeln (Opole), in Breslau, near Grottkau (Grodkow), Striegau (Strzegom) and Lauban (Luban).
Philippines: Luzon Violent aerial and artillery bombardment of the Shimbu line, east of Manila.
Southern Philippines Units of the US 8th Army sail from Mindanao to occupy Romblon and Simara islands. On Mindanao, after a powerful preparation by aircraft and warships, the US 41st Division lands on the Zamboanga peninsula and, overcoming weak Japanese resistance, occupies Wolfe airfield and advances on Mindanao City.
Burma In the northern sector, units of the British 36th Division take Mongmit.

11 March
Western Front With the capture of the Blucher strongpoint, the 35th Division (XVI Corps, US 9th Army) completes its advance on Wesel. American units take up positions round the Remagen bridgehead. The 78th Division (III Corps, 1st Army) is responsible for the northern flank of the bridgehead, while in the centre the 9th Division continues its attacks in the Hargarten area and on the right the 99th Division appears, in an offensive towards the south-east and south that reaches Leubsdorf and Ariendorf. Meanwhile, further south, the 2nd Division (V Corps) strengthens its positions on the Rhine.
The VIII and XII Corps (US 3rd Army) continue mopping-up operations on the West bank of the Rhine and between the Rhine and the Moselle, in preparation for a crossing of the Moselle. The Moselle is also the objective of the XX Corps, whose 10th Armoured Division begins to advance towards the river in the Bullay sector.
Eastern Front Troops of the 2nd Front press from the south towards Danzig and Gdynia. Berlin announces slight penetrations in the area of Küstrin (Kostrzyn). In Hungary, the Germans persist with their offensive, but their losses are getting heavier and heavier, and the Russian resistance is stiffening.
Philippines: Luzon In the US XIV Corps sector, the 43rd Division (infantry) replaces the 1st Cavalry Division in the operations against the Shimbu line. A regiment of the 6th Infantry Division makes considerable progress south of Antipolo and repulses a series of night counter-attacks by the Japanese. In the southern part of Luzon the Americans occupy the Batangas area. In the I Corps sector, the US 33rd Division advances to within ten miles west of Baguio, while on the Villa Verde track the 32nd Division is held up by the Japanese at Salacsac Pass. Units of the 35th Division

occupy Salazar.

Southern Philippines The US 41st Division occupies Zamboanga City on Mindanao Island. The completion of the occupation of the islands of Burias and Ticao is handed over to the Filipino guerrillas. During the night small American units land unopposed on Romblon Island.

Iwo Jima The 4th Marine Division finally overcomes Japanese resistance in its sector on the right flank of the American line. In the centre, the 3rd Marine Division eliminates the remaining Japanese strongpoints one by one, while on the left the 5th Division advances very slowly despite support from close-range fire and the use of tanks armed with flame-throwers.

Burma In the British XXXIII Corps sector, the 19th Indian Division carries on the battle for the capture of Mandalay, occupying a hill that overlooks the north-east part of the city.

12 March

Western Front In the northern part of the Remagen bridgehead, the 78th Division (III Corps, US 1st Army) succeeds in holding off several counter-attacks by the German 7th Army against Honnef, and opens an offensive eastwards towards Kalenborn. In the centre, the 9th Division is heavily engaged in the vicinity of Hargarten, but manages to take the village by the evening, and on the southern flank of the bridgehead the 99th Division succeeds in advancing in the area between Hargarten and Höningen.

In the US 3rd Army sector, the VIII Corps completes the occupation of the west bank of the Rhine, while the XII and XX Corps prepare to cross the Moselle.

Eastern Front Stalin, in his 300th Order of the Day, announces that after violent fighting, the 1st Belorussian Front has taken Küstrin, one of the few bridgeheads on the east bank of the Oder left to the Germans and only about 50 miles from Berlin. The reduction of the other bridgehead east of Stettin continues. The 2nd Belorussian Front continues to press

on towards the Baltic, threatening Danzig and Gdynia. In Hungary, the German thrust between lakes Velencei and Balaton is completely exhausted. There are signs of disaffection among the troops, even among the élite SS armoured corps. Hitler is beside himself with anger, and orders that the division of his personal bodyguard be stripped of their distinctive privileges.

Philippines: Luzon The Americans begin attacks in force on the Shimbu line.

Southern Philippines The occupation of Mindanao continues; there is hard fighting north-east of San Roque, in a village tenaciously held by the Japanese. Small American units land on Simara and meet with no opposition from the Japanese.

Iwo Jima The Americans launch the final attacks against the Japanese fortifications in the centre and east of the island.

Burma The 20th Indian Division captures the road junction of Myotha and mops up the area south-west of Mandalay.

13 March

Western Front On the north flank of the Remagen bridgehead the 78th Division is unable to advance against the firm opposition of the German 7th Army; in the centre the 9th Division, having taken Hargarten, moves on in the region between Kalendorn, Notscheid and Hargarten, while on the southern flank the 99th Division reinforces its positions and succeeds in repulsing a number of counter-attacks. The divisions of the XII Corps (US 3rd Army) complete their preparations for their attack against the Moselle.

Philippines: Luzon The US XIV Corps drives off further Japanese counter-attacks in the area east of Manila.

Iwo Jima The Americans go ahead with the liquidation of the Japanese positions on their left flank. Flame-throwers, bulldozers and tanks are continually in action, as well as field artillery. Naval guns and aircraft cannot intervene because the two sides are at such close quarters.

14 March

Western Front While the Germans continue their air attacks aimed at destroying the Remagen bridge and the pontoon bridges erected by the American sappers in this sector (held by units of the III Corps, US 1st Army), the VII Corps reorganizes its formations in readiness for the attack east of the Rhine. On the northern flank of the Remagen bridgehead, the 78th Division (III Corps) reaches its objectives near Ägidienberg, Rottbiz and Kalenborn.

In the US 3rd Army sector, the 87th Division (VIII Corps) is moved into the Koblenz–Lehmen sector. Meanwhile, in the early hours of the morning, the XII Corps begins to advance from the Moselle to the Rhine, and on the southern flank of the army units of the XX Corps take Heddert (94th Division), Weiskirchen (80th Division), Nieder Felle and Fell (65th Division).

The American 7th Army completes its preparations for the offensive against the Siegfried Line; in the XXI Corps sector, the 101st Cavalry Group and 70th Division penetrate into Germany and patrol the south bank of the river Saar.

Philippines: Luzon The biggest engagements take place north of Antipolo, east of Manila, where the Americans advancing against the Shimbu line find themselves facing a series of strong Japanese defensive positions.

Southern Philippines The Americans attack Japanese positions on Mount Capisan, on Mindanao, while fighting continues north-east of San Roque.

Iwo Jima At 9.30 a.m. the Americans consider that the capture of the island is complete, and hoist their flag. But in the north a number of pockets of resistance have still to be eliminated.

Burma The 19th Indian Division (British XXXIII Corps) takes most of the city of Mandalay, apart from a few enemy strongholds including Fort Dufferin, which is heavily bombarded by Allied artillery and aircraft.

15 March

Western Front In the III Corps sector (US 1st Army), the 9th Division captures Lorscheid and Notscheid, while the 99th Division widens its bridgehead over the Rhine to the east and south-east. The German attacks on the American-built bridges across the Rhine are beginning to slacken. The 87th Division (VIII Corps, US 3rd Army) prepares to cross the Moselle in the Koblenz sector and, with the other formations of the corps, to capture the area between the Moselle and the Rhine. In the centre and on the right of the army, the units of the XII and XX Corps continue to advance.

The US 7th Army launches Operation *Undertone*, with which the Allied headquarters intends to make a clear breach in the Siegfried Line and, working with the 3rd Army to the north, to liberate the Saar–Palatinate triangle between the rivers Rhine, Moselle and Lauter-Saar. Three corps are engaged, the XXI in the Saarbrücken sector, the XV moving towards Zweibrücken, Schorbach, Bitche and Reyersviller and the VI operating on the rivers Rothbach and Moder.

The new Commander-in-Chief of German forces in the west, Field-Marshal Kesselring, reports to Hitler on the situation on the front at the time he took over. In his opinion, although the situation is undoubtedly critical for the German troops, it will almost certainly be possible to halt the Allies if the western armies are reinforced by some picked divisions transferred from the Eastern Front after the defensive success he envisages by the Germans on the Oder.

Eastern Front In East Prussia the 3rd Belorussian Front splits the German forces in two, reaching the Baltic coast south-west of Königsberg. In Hungary and Yugoslavia the Russian forces go over to the offensive.

Philippines: Luzon In the I Corps sector, the 32nd Division is heavily engaged by the Japanese on the Villa Verde track near Imugan, while the 25th Division begins the assault on a rocky crest known as Norton's

Japanese prisoner watches American troops during a landing on the Pacific front, March 1945.

Knob, on which the Japanese hold out for ten days.

Iwo Jima The liquidation of enemy pockets of resistance continues.

Burma In the British IV Corps sector the 17th Indian Division, cut off at Meiktila, holds out against Japanese counter-attacks. A brigade of the 5th Indian Division is air-lifted to the area and the other two brigades of the division advance in that direction from Jorhat.

16 March

Western Europe Units of the VII Corps (US 1st Army) further extend the bridgehead over the Rhine at Remagen; the 78th Division cuts the autobahn between Cologne and Frankfurt.

In the VIII Corps sector (US 3rd Army) the 87th Division launches the offensive for the crossing of the Moselle, sending two regiments over the river in the area between Willingen and Kolber. The units of the XII and XX Corps also cross the Moselle.

In the US 7th Army sector Operation *Undertone* goes on with the three corps trying to break through the Siegfried Line.

Eastern Front The 3rd Ukraine Front goes over to the offensive in the Székesfehérvár area, in Hungary, against the German Army Group South. The final objective is Vienna.

Philippines: Luzon American attacks continue against the Shimbu line and Norton's Knob.

17 March

Western Front The US 1st Division (VII Corps, 1st Army) opens its offensive on the east bank of the Rhine towards the river Sieg. Meanwhile, after the Americans have been able to take thousands of tanks, trucks and guns across it, the Remagen bridge suddenly collapses. But by now the flow of supplies and reinforcements to the Remagen bridgehead is ensured by two further bridges which the Americans have constructed upstream and downstream of the railway bridge.

The 9th and 99th Divisions (III Corps) reach their objectives, the former cutting the railway line near Windhagen, the latter reaching the Wied.

Units of the 87th Division (VIII Corps, US 3rd Army) succeed in crossing the Moselle near Guels and then opening an offensive in the direction of Koblenz. In the XII Corps sector the 90th Division reaches Boppard and St Goar, while the 4th Armoured Division and 89th Division expand their bridgeheads on the Nahe and at Bullay. The Nahe is also crossed at Turkismuhle, by the 10th Armoured Division (XX Corps), and while the 94th Division takes Birkenfeld, its final objective, the 80th establishes a bridgehead over the Prims in the Krettnich area. The 65th Division is preparing to break out of the Saarlautern bridgehead. Some of its units cross the river Saar in the vicinity of Menningen and take the heights south of Merzig in readiness for the offensive against Dillingen. At Lunéville, near the US 7th Army's headquarters, Eisenhower meets General Patton to dis-

cuss co-ordination between the 3rd and 7th Armies for the offensive planned for the end of March. Meanwhile, in the 7th Army sector, the XXI, XV and VI Corps continue their offensive aimed at breaching the Siegfried Line (Operation *Undertone*) and liberating the Saar–Palatinate triangle.

Marshal Kesselring issues a somewhat ambiguous directive which, while ordering 'the maintenance of present positions', adds that 'encirclement, and with it the annihilation of most of the troops' is to be avoided. Hitler's orders against retreat are thus not directly contradicted, but General Hausser, Commander of Army Group G considers this directive is enough to justify the withdrawal of his two most seriously threatened formations, and he orders the retirement of the divisions of the 7th and 1st Armies from the most western positions in the Siegfried Line.

Eastern Front The Führer authorizes the evacuation of the Donij–Miholjac bridgehead over the Drava. The 3rd Ukraine Front, on the offensive in Hungary, makes progress between Lake Velencei and Lake Balaton.

Philippines: Luzon The Americans continue their attacks on the Shimbu line, east of Manila. Powerful Japanese counter-attacks force the US 1st Infantry to withdraw in the San Isidro area.

Southern Philippines On Mindanao, Japanese resistance is mainly concentrated in the area of Masilay and Pasananca.

Iwo Jima The last Japanese units still resisting are confined within an area about 200 to 500 yards wide and 625 yards deep.

Burma Fierce fighting continues in Mandalay, where the Japanese still hold some positions, and at Meiktila, where the British and Indians are defending themselves against Japanese counter-attacks. The British 2nd Division takes Ava Fort, on the bend of the Irrawaddy south of Mandalay.

18 March

Western Front East of the Rhine, in

the 1st Army sector between Bonn and Remagen, the III Corps continues its offensive, reaching Windhaven, strengthening its positions east of Vettelschoss and capturing the hills along the river Wied in the area of Strodt.

Units of the 87th Division (VIII Corps, US 3rd Army) press on with the battle for Koblenz. The units of the XII Corps are ordered to advance towards the Rhine in the region between Mainz and Worms, the 90th Division in the direction of Mainz and the 4th Armoured towards Worms. While units of the 5th Division reach the sector between Gemünden, Mengerschied and Sargenroth, the 89th Division reinforces its positions east of the Moselle and the 76th succeeds in establishing a bridgehead over the river south-east of Wittlich.

All formations of the US 7th Army launch a simultaneous offensive against the Siegfried Line positions, while the finishing touches are put to the plans for the Rhine crossing. Both the XXI and the XV Corps, as well as the VI Corps on the southern flank of the army, succeed in penetrating across the German frontier.

Eastern Front The 1st Belorussian Front captures the town and harbour of Kolberg (Kolobrzeg) in Pomerania, the last German strongpoint on the Baltic between the Polish Corridor and Stettin on the Pomeranian Bay.

Philippines: Luzon In the I Corps sector the Japanese are preparing to withdraw from San Fernando under pressure from the Filipino guerrillas in the north and the Americans from the south. The US 25th Division overcomes Japanese resistance north of Putlan; its next objective is Kapintalan. In the XI Corps sector, east of Manila, the Americans retake ground lost in the Japanese counter-attack and attack towards Mount Baytangan and Mount Tanauan.

Southern Philippines The American forces land on Panay Island in the area of Tigbauan, after a short naval bombardment. The Japanese do not oppose the landing.

Iwo Jima The island is declared

A Russian Katyusha rocket-launcher
on the outskirts of Berlin.

'safe' for American forces. A part of the American force is withdrawn, while the 5th Marine Division proceeds with the liquidation of the last Japanese nests of resistance in the south of the island.

☐ Japan. Aircraft from Vice-Admiral Mitscher's fast carrier squadron concentrate their attacks for two days on the Japanese fleet in the area of Kure–Kobe, and succeed in damaging 16 enemy warships and sinking several transports. Japanese reaction is full-bloodied; for the first time they use piloted flying bombs (*OKA*), and cause serious damage to the aircraft carrier *Franklin* and (less serious) to the carriers *Enterprise*, *Intrepid* and *Wasp*. The Americans also bomb airfields on Kyushu Island.

19 March
Western Front In the US 3rd Army sector Koblenz is taken by units of the 87th Division (VIII Corps). The 90th Division (XII Corps) launches its offensive across the Nahe near Mainz, while the 4th Armoured Division makes rapid progress to reach Wendelsheim and Schim-

sheim. South of the river Nahe the 11th Armoured Division breaks through the last defences of the German 7th Army and starts to pursue the enemy on the east bank of the Rhine. The 76th Division extends its bridgehead across the Moselle so as to allow the engineers to throw a bridge over the river Mühlheim. The XX Corps advances rapidly towards the Rhine; units of the 10th Armoured Division reach the neighbourhood of Kaiserslautern, the 80th Division takes Kusel and St Wendel, and the 65th adds considerably to the Saarlautern bridgehead. In the US 7th Army sector the 70th Division (XXI Corps) crosses the river Saar in the area of Saarbrücken. The army persists in its offensive against the Siegfried Line; in the area in which the XV Corps is operating the village of Webenheim falls to the 45th Division and Zweibrücken to the 3rd Division, while on the south flank the 36th Division (VI Corps) takes Wissembourg.

Hitler orders that in areas of the Reich abandoned by the German army everything must be destroyed –

dykes, power stations, mines, industrial plant, even food and clothing shops; the invaders must find nothing to sustain them. Among those opposed to this insane directive is Albert Speer, in charge of arms production; by arrangement with Guderian, Chief of Staff of the Wehrmacht, he sabotages Hitler's order.

Philippines: Luzon In the US I Corps sector, the 33rd Division occupies the town of Bauang, with its bridge. The offensive against the Shimbu line, east of Manila, continues.

Burma In the British XXXIII Corps sector, the 19th Indian Division follows up its attacks against Fort Dufferin in Mandalay, and a powerful air bombardment succeeds in opening a gap in its walls.

20 March

Western Front Units of the 78th Division (VII Corps, US 1st Army) continue to advance north along the Rhine and reach Geislar, Oberpleis and Bergahausen, cutting the road that runs from Eudenbach to Buchholz.

In the US 3rd Army sector the 4th Armoured Division (XII Corps) blocks the roads leading to Worms. The 94th Division (XX Corps) is still advancing swiftly; some units of the 12th Armoured Division reach the Rhine north of Mannheim. While the 80th Division converges on Kaiserslautern, halting level with Enkenbach and Neukirchen, north-east of Kaiserslautern, the 10th Armoured Division by-passes the town to north and south and makes for the sector between Neukirchen, Enkenbach and Hochspeyer.

The US 7th Army is across the Siegfried Line in the XXI Corps and XV Corps sectors. The 70th Division of XXI Corps occupies Saarbrücken and makes contact with the XX Corps. On the right flank of the army, the divisions of the VI Corps are finding difficulty in penetrating the Siegfried Line.

Eastern Front Troops of the 1st Belorussian Front (Zhukov) take Dabie Aldamm in Pomerania and wipe out the last German bridgehead across the Oder, opposite Stettin. In East Prussia, the 3rd Belorussian Front takes Braunsberg (Braniewo), near the coast north-east of Elbing. The Red Army keeps up strong pressure on Gdynia and Danzig. General Heinrici is appointed to succeed Himmler in command of the Vistula Army Group; until he does, command is temporarily taken over by General Tippelskirch.

Philippines: Luzon In the US I Corps sector the Americans advance from the Bauang area on San Fernando, which the Japanese have evacuated overnight. Fighting continues round Norton's Knob.

Iwo Jima The 5th Marine Division advances slowly north-west towards the sea.

Burma In the British XXXIII Corps sector, the 19th Indian Division takes the last major positions held by the Japanese in Mandalay.

In the northern sector the British 36th Division reaches Mogok and advances in the south-east towards Kyaukme.

21 March

Western Front In the US 1st Army sector, the 78th and 1st Divisions (VII Corps) reach the river Sieg. Units of the XII Corps reach Bingen and extend their control along the Rhine as far as Frei Weinheim. The 90th Division is approaching Mainz and liberates much of the territory west of the Rhine. Units of the 4th Armoured Division advance northwards along the west bank of the Rhine to liberate the region between Worms and Oppenheim. Worms itself is occupied, while south of the city and as far as Mannheim the west bank of the Rhine is occupied by units of the XX Corps. Units of the 12th Armoured Division reach the outskirts of Ludwigshafen. Further south, the 10th Armoured Division captures Neustadt, Darmstadt, Annweiler, Queichhambach and Demsieders.

The US 7th Army continues its offensive towards the Rhine. In the XXI Corps sector, the 63rd Division liberates the region round Neukirchen, while on the right flank of the army the 42nd Division (VI Corps) resumes the offensive towards the West Wall.

Eastern Front German Army Group E holds the attacks by Yugoslavs and Bulgarians against the Valpovo bridgehead across the Drava. The 3rd Ukraine Front takes the industrial district of Tatabanya, in Hungary, and occupies part of Székesfehérvár. The 1st Ukraine Front attacks in Silesia in the Ratibor-Grottkau (Raciborz–Grodkow) area and savage fighting still rages north and south of Breslau. The 2nd Belorussian Front maintains pressure on the Gdynia–Danzig sector.

Philippines: Luzon Troops of the 33rd Division (US I Corps) join up with the Filipino guerrillas organized by the American armed forces in the north of the island at San Fernando, which is occupied without opposition. The Americans now control all the west coast of Luzon. The 161st Infantry (25th Division) attacks the Japanese positions west of Kapintalan, but powerful and accurate Japanese fire holds up the advance until 8 April. The 27th Infantry (25th Division) repels vigorous counterattacks by the enemy in the area of Mount Myoko.

In the XI Corps sector, units of the American 6th Division advance about 650 yards, cutting the track leading from Antipolo northwards by way of Guagua. Units of the 43rd Division occupy Mount Caymayuman, Mount Yabang and other heights; other units reach the top of Mount Tanauan. In the US XIV Corps sector, the 158th Infantry advances rapidly east of Cuenca as far as the foothills of Mount Macolod.

Burma Japanese resistance ceases in Mandalay. The British 2nd Division advances along the Ava–Mandalay road, and the 20th Indian Division puts pressure on Wundwin.

China The Japanese begin to advance against the air base at Laohokow (Guanghua) in the province of Hupeh, north-west of Wuhan.

22 March

Western Front During the night the III Corps (US 1st Army) begins limited attacks across the river Wied.

On the southern flank of the army the V Corps liberates the region between the rivers Wied and Rhine. The XII Corps (US 3rd Army) completes the capture of the west bank of the Rhine and then prepares to cross the river. The 5th Division re-groups near Oppenheim and on the 22nd begins to cross the Rhine near Nierstein. In the XX Corps sector, the 89th Division prepares to cross the Rhine near the bridgehead established by the 5th Division. The 10th Armoured Division (XII Corps) captures Landau.

Units of the US 7th Army continue their advance towards the Rhine. In the VI Corps sector the 103rd Division reaches Klingenmünster and the 36th approaches Bergzabern, while the 14th Armoured Division completes the capture of Steinfeld.

Eastern Front The 3rd Belorussian Front continues its attacks against German pockets in East Prussia, while the 2nd Belorussian Front makes a little progress against the Germans' fortified line in front of Gdynia and Danzig. The 1st Ukraine Front breaches the enemy lines west and south of Oppeln (Opole) in Silesia. In Hungary, the 3rd Ukraine Front steps up its offensive to break through the German lines between Lake Balaton and the Danube. Hard fighting continues at Székesfehérvár.

Philippines: Luzon Units of the US 25th Division (I Corps) advancing along the valley of the river Putlan towards Balete Pass are held up by strong Japanese resistance. In the other sectors mopping up proceeds in the positions taken the previous day.

Southern Philippines The Americal Division prepares to invade the island of Cebu, west of Leyte and east of Los Negros. The US 8th Army (General Eichelberger) continues with its programme for the systematic occupation of the southern Philippines. The islands are defended by 102,000 men of the Japanese 35th Army, mostly concentrated on Mindanao, under command of General Suzuki.

Dutch East Indies The Japanese carry out their last air raid on Moro-

tai Island, in the Moluccas.

Ryukyu Islands Since 18 March in preparation for the landing, Task Force 58 has been carrying out a series of air and naval attacks against the defences of Okinawa and enemy shipping, damaging 16 Japanese warships and transports and destroying over 500 enemy aircraft on the ground or in combat.

Iwo Jima Supported by tanks armed with flame-throwers, the 5th Marine Division continues its slow advance towards the sea in the north-west of the island.

23 March

Western Front The 21st Army Group begins Operation *Plunder*, the offensive across the Rhine north of the Ruhr. At 9 p.m. following a heavy combined artillery and air bombardment, the Canadian 1st Army sends in its divisions north of Emmerich, while the British 2nd Army crosses the Rhine near Rees (British XXX Corps) and Wesel (XII Corps). The two towns are attacked by two British infantry divisions, the 51st and 15th.

In the US 1st Army sector, the 9th and 90th Divisions widen their bridgehead east of the river Wied, through which the units of the V Corps have also passed. The US 3rd Army advances in the Koblenz–Boppard sector (VIII Corps), and in the area of Wallerstädten–Erfelden and Oppenheim–Worms (XII Corps). Units of the 94th Division enter Ludwigshafen, while the 10th Armoured Division, pushing on towards Lauterbourg, makes contact with units of the American 7th Armoured Division.

Italian Front General Heinrich von Vietinghoff succeeds Field-Marshal Kesselring as Commander-in-Chief of German forces in Italy.

Eastern Front In the sector of the German Army Group North, north-west of Zoppot (Sopot), between Gdynia and Danzig, the 2nd Belorussian Front occupies further stretches of the coast and threatens to cut off the retreat of the German forces. The German navy supports operations along the Baltic coast,

bombarding enemy positions and evacuating refugees and troops.

The 3rd Ukraine Front, in Hungary, takes Székésfehérvár.

Philippines: Luzon The US 5th Air Force begins a series of raids in the Legaspi area in preparation for a vast amphibious operation.

Ryukyu Islands The squadron of fast US aircraft carriers under Vice-Admiral Mitscher launches a series of daily raids on Okinawa in preparation for the invasion.

Burma In the British XXXIII Corps sector Wundwin is occupied and a column from the 20th Indian Division moves north towards Kume. In the VI Corps sector the 7th Indian Division, with reinforcements from the 5th Indian Division, occupies Myingan. Fighting continues at Meiktila, which the Japanese are now trying to recapture from the 17th Indian Division.

24 March

Western Front Units of the XII Division (British 2nd Army) capture most of Wesel, while the 15th Division crosses the Rhine north of Xanten.

Some 3,000 aircraft and gliders drop or land north-east of Wesel about 14,000 parachutists of the British 6th Airborne Division and the American 17th Airborne Division (XVIII Corps, Allied 1st Airborne Army), who join up with the British 2nd Army forces. By late evening, the bridgehead established by Montgomery's men has reached a depth of 6 miles. The US 9th Army begins to cross the Rhine with the divisions of the XVI Corps.

In the US 1st Army sector the III and V Corps extend and reinforce their bridgeheads.

On the southern flank of their line, too, the Allies are ready to pass to the offensive, with the units' of the XV Corps (US 7th Army). By nightfall only a few hundred scattered German soldiers are left on the west bank of the Rhine. How many men of Hitler's armies have managed to retreat across the river is not known, but during the past weeks the American 3rd and 7th Armies have taken about 100,000 German prisoners.

Eastern Front The Wehrmacht's front in Hungary is rapidly collapsing. The 8th Army, north of the Danube, and the 6th SS Armoured Army, the 6th Army and the Hungarian 3rd Army, between Esztergom and Lake Balaton (west of Lake Balaton is the Hungarian II Corps) have suffered enormous losses from the attacks of the 3rd Ukraine Front. The 6th SS Armoured Army, almost surrounded near Lake Balaton, succeeds in fighting its way out through a corridor a mile and a half wide. The German 2nd Armoured Army, deployed south of Lake Balaton, retires westwards. Nevertheless the Germans launch powerful counterattacks to save Esztergom. The 3rd Ukraine Front, advancing over 62 miles in a few days on a vast front south-west of Budapest, captures a number of places, including Mor, Veszprém and Kisbér.

In Czechoslovakia, the 4th Ukraine Front has reached the upper Vistula and is exerting pressure on Heinrici's Army Group, on the southern wing of Army Group Centre, with the object of capturing the important industrial district of Moravska-Ostrava. Today the Front captures Sorau (Zary), having broken through the German LIX Corps on a front of 10 miles to a depth of 5 miles. Five German divisions have been surrounded south-west of Oppeln (Opole).

Philippines: Luzon The 1st Cavalry Division (US XIV Corps) advances towards Lipa, north and south of Lake Taal, taking Santo Tomas without difficulty. The 187th Infantry attack Mount Macolod, strongly defended by the Japanese.

Southern Philippines Units of the US 8th Army proceed with the capture and mopping up of Mindanao.

Iwo Jima The Americans are completing the liquidation of the last Japanese pockets, reduced to a few positions on the north coast. General Kuribayashi, said to be still alive, in one of the caves, is never found.

Ryukyu Islands The Americans have begun mine-sweeping operations in the waters round these islands, particularly at Okinawa, which is bombarded by a squadron of battleships under Vice-Admiral Lee.

25 March
Western Front The town of Wesel is liberated by the British XII Corps (2nd Army).

In the US 9th Army sector the XVI Corps maintains pressure on the east bank of the Rhine during the night and the early hours of the morning. The offensive of the VII and III Corps (1st Army) continues in the area roughly between Cologne and Remagen.

The VIII Corps (US 3rd Army) opens an offensive across the Rhine at midnight, sending the 87th Division over to the east bank in the area between Braubach and Boppard. The 6th Division (XII Corps), after crossing the Rhine opposite Oppenheim, heads for the river Main and Frankfurt; units of the 4th Armoured Division reach Aschaffenburg and Hanau.

Eastern Front In East Prussia, the 3rd Belorussian Front takes Heiligenbeil, while the 2nd Front captures Oliva, near Danzig. The 2nd Ukraine Front joins in the advance of the 3rd Ukraine Front towards the Austrian frontier, advancing 30 miles and capturing Esztergom, desperately defended by the Germans, and also Tata and Tatabanya.

In Czechoslovakia the 53rd and 7th Guards Armies, with the Rumanian 1st Army, begin to advance along the left bank of the Danube towards Bratislava, taking Loslaw. The Russian 40th Army and Rumanian 4th Army have meanwhile liquidated the German bridgehead over the river Hron.

Philippines: Luzon The US 1st Cavalry Division moves on from Santo Tomas towards Tanauan; a column from the division occupies Los Baños. The 25th Division, advancing towards Mount Myoko, meets with powerful Japanese resistance.

China The US 14th Air Force abandons Laohokow airfield after destroying the installations. But this is the last airfield that the Americans have to abandon. The continuing Japanese thrusts, towards Sian and Ankang, are halted by Chinese forces a short way from their objectives.

26 March
Western Front Units of the British XXX Corps (2nd Army) succeed in extending their bridgehead over the river Ijssel. The front line of the XVIII Airborne Corps now runs between Ringenberg in the north and the river Lippe near Krudenberg in the south.

The swift advance of the XVI Corps (US 9th Army) continues without a break, with average gains of from two to three miles per day.

In the US 3rd Army sector the 6th Armoured Division (XII Corps) reaches the south bank of the river Main near Frankfurt and attempts to enter the city, under heavy bombardment from the Germans. The other divisions of the XII Corps (5th, 90th, 26th and 4th Armoured) also reach the Main.

The 45th and 3rd Divisions of the XV Corps (US 7th Army) now cross the Rhine, in the early hours of the morning, the first near Hamm and Rhein-Dürkheim, the second near Worms and Mannheim.

Eastern Front In Hungary, the 3rd Ukraine Front takes Papa and Devecser.

Dietrich's 6th SS Armoured Army and the 6th Army try to dig in on the river Raba, where they manage to contain the Russian thrust for two days.

In Czechoslovakia, the 2nd Ukraine Front takes the important road and railway junction of Banská Bystrica. In East Prussia, the 3rd Belorussian Front continues with the liquidation of those German forces that have not been able to save themselves, while the 2nd Belorussian Front crushes the second line of defence in front of Danzig and Gdynia and reaches the third and last line defending these ports in many places.

Philippines: Luzon In the US I Corps sector, units of the 25th Division begin the final attack on Norton's Knob after the enemy positions have been 'softened up' by heavy air and artillery bombardment. In the XI Corps sector, units of the 1st Cavalry

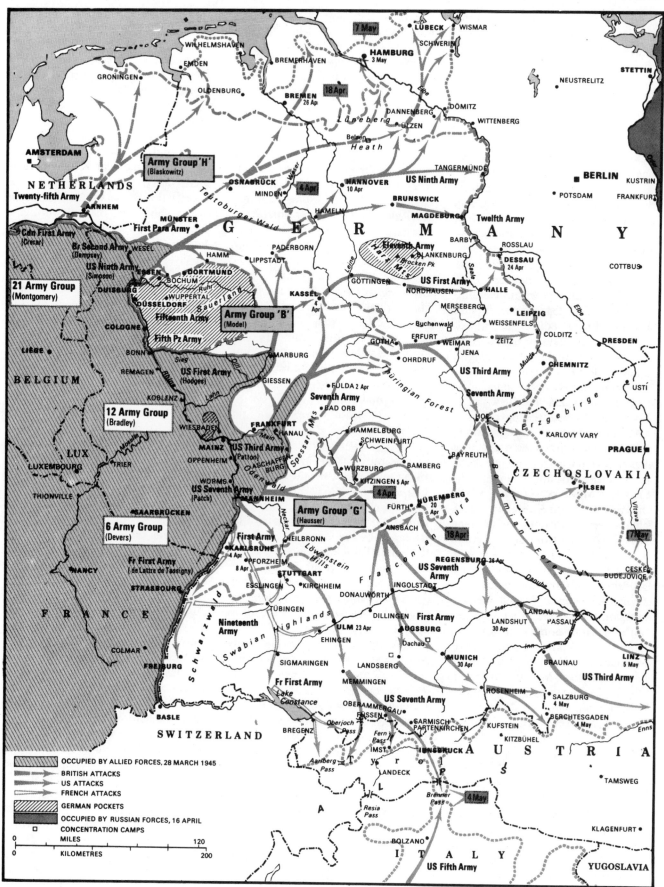

The Allied advance from the Rhine to the Elbe 29 March–7 May.

reach Malvar, while the 11th Division launches unsuccessful attacks on the Japanese positions on Mount Macolod and advances slowly towards Lipa.

Southern Philippines American units come ashore near Talisay on Cebu Island. Overcoming the weak Japanese resistance, they advance on Cebu City, taking the line of the river Mananga before the end of the day.

Iwo Jima At dawn the remaining Japanese troops on the island launch a last desperate attack on the American forces, with no other aim than to kill as many Americans as possible. Of the 200 attackers, 196 are killed. At 8.00 a.m. the Americans declare that the capture of the island has been completed. It has cost them more than 20,000 men killed, wounded and missing (a third of all those taking part in the campaign). The Japanese garrison of 21,500 men has been literally annihilated; the body of General Kuribayashi is never found. The island provides the Americans with a new air base against Japan and serves to enhance the effect of the air and sea blockade of the enemy country.

Ryukyu Islands Forces of the US 77th Division land on Kerama Retto Island and on some near-by islets, in readiness for the main landing on Okinawa. The operations are supported by aircraft and ships of the US 5th Fleet. Japanese reaction is entrusted to a group of suicide aircraft, which manage to damage the battleship *Nevada* (not seriously), the light cruiser *Biloxi* and five destroyers. Another American destroyer is sunk by a mine.

27 March

Western Front The 51st Division (British XXX Corps, 2nd Army) reaches the river Ijssel at Ijsselburg, while the XVIII Airborne Corps advances rapidly some 10 miles across the Wesel forest.

In the US 9th Army sector, the 79th Division of the XVI Corps advances very slowly from the south towards the Ruhr area, where a huge German pocket of resistance is being formed. The VIII Corps (US 3rd Army)

further widens and strengthens its bridgehead across the Rhine, mainly in the sector facing Wiesbaden. Further south, where the XX Corps is operating, the 80th Division completes its preparations for the crossing of the Rhine and the Main in the Mainz sector.

The French 1st Army quickly regroups in readiness for an offensive across the Rhine in the area of Germersheim.

Eastern Front South of the Danube, the Russian 46th Army surrounds and routs huge German forces west of Esztergom. Other forces of the 2nd Ukraine Front advance towards the river Raba, where the enemy forces try to stem their advance.

The 2nd Belorussian Front penetrates into Danzig and Gdynia. The 1st Ukraine Front captures the towns of Strehlen (Strzelin), south of Breslau, and Rybnik, east of Ratibor (Raciborz), while the 4th Ukraine Front, operating south-east of Ratibor, seizes Zary (Sorau) and Wodzislaw.

Philippines: Luzon In the US I Corps sector, units of the 32nd Division open the offensive for the capture of Salacsac Pass No. 2 on the Villa Verde track. The 25th Division takes Norton's Knob and holds it against violent night counter-attacks.

Southern Philippines The units which landed on Cebu break through the weak Japanese resistance and take Cebu City, and advance beyond the town. The Japanese dig in on the surrounding hills.

Ryukyu Islands The Americans proceed with the occupation of Kerama Retto and the neighbouring islands in preparation for the invasion of Okinawa.

Japanese suicide pilots continue to attack American ships, damaging the aircraft carrier *Essex*, one minelayer and one minesweeper.

☐ Japan. B-29 Superfortresses based on Tinian begin a huge mining operation in Japanese waters, while the day and night bombing of the metropolitan Japanese islands is stepped up.

☐ Argentina declares war on Germany; this declaration brings the

number of countries in the anti-German coalition to 53 out of the 70-odd sovereign countries (including Andorra, San Marino, Liechtenstein and Vatican City) existing in the world today.

28 March

Western Front General Eisenhower modifies the plans and the direction of the final assault of his troops. The final objective is no longer Berlin, which the Russians are rapidly approaching from the east, but Leipzig.

The British 2nd Army begins its advance towards the Elbe.

The 15th Army, composed of the XXII and XXIII Corps, is given a double mission: to control the besieged fortresses of Lorient and St Nazaire, on the west coast of France, and to occupy, garrison and administer the Rhineland in Germany. Meanwhile north of Idstein, on the Cologne–Frankfurt autobahn, the US 1st Army links up with the 3rd Army.

In the American 1st Army sector the VII, III and V Corps reach the river Lahn.

The 80th Division (XX Corps, US 3rd Army) attacks simultaneously across the Rhine and the Main, taking a firm bridgehead in the Mainz sector.

The 45th Division (XV Corps, US 7th Army) reaches the Main in the neighbourhood of Obernau and succeeds in establishing a bridgehead across the river. Further south, the 44th Division advances along the Rhine and crosses the Neckar in the direction of Mannheim and Heidelberg.

At this point the general situation on the front is as follows: starting from the Emmerich area in the north, the Allies have formed a huge wedge reaching as far as Haltern, on the river Lippe, then turning back towards Essen, continues southwards passing through Düsseldorf, Cologne and Bonn and then jutting out 60-odd miles to the east as far as Marburg, Giessen and Wiesbaden, before following the course of the Main for a short distance south of

Frankfurt, to reach Lauterbach in the north-east, withdrawing again towards Aschaffenburg and Mannheim, finally following the course of the Rhine as far as Strasbourg. Three German army groups are looking for some way of stemming the Allied advance: on the northern flank General Blaskowitz's Army Group H, with the 25th Army and 1st Parachute Army, in the centre General Model's Army Group B, formed of Zangen's 15th Army and Manteuffel's 5th Armoured Army, and in the south General Hausser's Army Group G, with Felber's 7th Army and General Förtsch's 1st Army.

Heinz Guderian, Chief of the General Staff of the Wehrmacht, is replaced by General Hans Krebs.

Eastern Front Troops of the 2nd Belorussian Front capture Gdynia and the western part of Danzig. The 2nd Ukraine Front, continuing its advance to the west along the south bank of the Danube, takes Györ, reaches the river Raba, and breaches the German defence line on a front of 12 miles, capturing Sarvar.

Philippines: Luzon In the US I Corps sector, the 27th Infantry makes good progress in the Mount Myoko sector. In the XI Corps sector, units of the 20th Infantry reach the summit of Mount Mataba, but Japanese resistance is still powerful. In the XIV Corps sector, the US 1st Cavalry Division reaches the outskirts of Lipa and San Agustin. American attacks on Mount Macolod are still unsuccessful.

29 March

Western Front While the Canadian II Corps (British 2nd Army) continues to meet strong resistance in its advance towards Emmerich, the British VIII Corps advances rapidly towards Osnabrück.

In the US 1st Army sector, the III Corps begins its offensive northwards to cross the Eder. East of Giessen the XX Corps (US 3rd Army) reaches some objectives north-east of Steinbach. Frankfurt is taken finally by the US 5th Division. The 44th Division (XV Corps, US 7th Army) enters Mannheim.

Eastern Front Troops of the 3rd Ukraine Front enter Austria. South of Lake Balaton, the Russian 57th Army and Bulgarian 1st Army concentrate their attacks on the German 2nd Armoured Army. The Russians capture Szombathely, Köszeg and Kapuvar. In East Prussia, the 3rd Belorussian Front is engaged in the liquidation of the trapped German forces south-west of Königsberg. Bitter fighting continues in the eastern part of Danzig.

Philippines: Luzon In the US XIV Corps sector, the 1st Cavalry Division takes Lipa and its airfield.

Southern Philippines Units of the US

A member of the *Hitlerjugend* (Hitler Youth), called up in the last weeks of the war, holding a *Panzerfaust* (anti-tank gun), Berlin, March 1945.

8th Army land at Patik in Negros Island. There is hard fighting on Cebu Island, where the Japanese mine a mountain spur and blow it up, the Americans suffering heavy losses. On Mindanao Japanese resistance in the Zamboanga sector crumbles, but mopping-up operations take some time. Filipino guerrillas with American assistance land on Masbate and take the town of that name.

Ryukyu Islands The US 77th Division completes the capture of Kerama Retto. In the several islands that they have occupied, the Americans prepare flying-boat bases. The waters round Okinawa have already been cleared of mines, so that US naval ships can come in near to the coast and carry out massive bombardments.

Burma The 7th Indian Division, supporting the operations of the 5th Indian Division in the Taungtha–Meiktila area, is placed under command of the British XXXIII Corps.

30 March

Western Front Elements from the Canadian II Corps (British 2nd Army) complete the capture of Emmerich.

In the US 1st Army sector, the III and V Corps reach the river Eder and prepare to cross it. The advance of the units of the VIII Corps (US 3rd Army) continues towards Usingen, Butzbach, Neuhof and Eltville, and the XX Corps pushes on north of Frankfurt in the direction of Kassel, reaching the river Eder in the Zenner–Wader area. The XII Corps advances in the Hersfeld sector, near Hanau, towards Fulda and Michelan-Leisenwald.

Fighting goes on round Mannheim between the XV Corps (US 7th Army) and the German 1st Army.

Eastern Front Rokossovsky's 2nd Belorussian Front completes the capture of Danzig, while in Silesia the 1st Front, under Zhukov, continues the liquidation of the German forces surrounded at Glogau and Breslau. The 2nd Ukraine Front, advancing along the frontier between Czechoslovakia and Hun-

gary, crosses the rivers Hron and Nitra and heads for Bratislava, the capital of Slovakia. Other units of the same Front clear the south bank of the Danube, in Hungary, where the 3rd Ukraine Front, in the west, continues to advance into Austria, having launched its attack from the Hungarian town of Kőszeg, and in the south-west is advancing rapidly towards the Drava beyond Lake Balaton. More than 150,000 men of the German Army Group E, still in Yugoslavia, face a highly critical situation.

Ryukyu Islands American air and naval bombardment in preparation for the invasion of Okinawa continues.

Burma In the north the British 36th Division, which has resumed its advance south-east of Mogok, reaches Kyaukme and links up with the Chinese forces. Operations in this sector come to a halt, since Chiang Kai-shek has obtained an undertaking from Admiral Mountbatten not to employ Chinese forces beyond the line Lashio–Hsipaw–Kyaukme. In the British XXXIII Corps sector, the 20th Indian Division takes Kyaukse after savage fighting. In the British IV Corps sector the 17th Indian Division and the 225th Armoured Brigade consolidate the capture of Meiktila and advance south towards Pyawbwe.

31 March

Western Front Units of the newly formed 15th Army take over responsibility for the French coast and for troops stationed there, with the task of 'controlling' the besieged fortresses of Lorient and St Nazaire.

Units of the 3rd Armoured Division (VII Corps, US 1st Army) continue their offensive against Paderborn.

In the American 3rd Army sector, the XX Corps is heavily engaged by units of the German 7th Army on the line of the rivers Fulda and Eder. The 6th Armoured Division continues to advance towards Kassel, with Mühlhausen as its immediate objective; the 80th Division is also advancing on Kassel, while the XII Corps moves against various objectives in

the area of Eisenach (4th Armoured Division) and advances along the line Nieder Jossa–Kruspis–Grossenmoor.

During the night General De Lattre de Tassigny, Commander of the French 1st Army, opens an offensive across the Rhine in the area of Speyer and Germersheim (French II Corps).

Eastern Front In Upper Silesia Konev's forces (1st Ukraine Front) take Ratibor. The 4th Ukraine Front, pressing against the German Army Group Centre, advances slowly on Moravska-Ostrava (Ostrava). The 2nd Ukraine Front takes Nitra and forces the crossing of the river Vah, seizing Galanta, a little more than 30 miles from Bratislava. The right flank of the 3rd Ukraine Front, under Tolbukhin, is on the point of taking Sopron in Hungary and advances into Austria towards Wiener Neustadt; some units, in the valley of the river Raba, occupy Vasvar, Körmend and Szentgotthard. The Germans counter-attack where they can, but are only able temporarily to slow down the inexorable advance of the Red Army steamroller.

Philippines: Luzon There is fighting near Salacsac Pass No. 2, where the Americans lose ground, and on Mount Myoko. In the US XI Corps sector units of the 43rd Division advance in the Santa Maria valley, making contact with the 1st Cavalry Division.

Ryukyu Islands The 77th Division leaves Kerama Retto, now in American hands. American losses are 31 dead and 81 wounded; Japanese, 530 dead and 121 prisoners. 1,200 enemy civilians are also interned. 350 Japanese 'suicide boats' are captured and destroyed on Kerama and other neighbouring islands.

1 April

Western Front While the Canadian II Corps (British 2nd Army) extends and reinforces the Emmerich bridgehead, the VIII Corps widens its bridgehead over the Dortmund–Ems Canal in the direction of Osnabrück. The US 9th and 1st Armies join up at Lippstadt, closing the circle round the rich industrial region of the Ruhr and cutting off the whole of Model's Army Group B (5th and 15th Armies) and two corps of the 1st Parachute Army (Army Group H). The pocket is about 70 miles long between the Rhine and the source of the Ruhr, and about 50 miles wide between the river Sieg in the south and the river Lippe in the north. While units of the XIX Corps (US 9th Army) reach the Cologne–Berlin autobahn, the XVI Corps pushes on in the sector south of Haltern. The 3rd Division (VII Corps, US 1st Army) seizes Paderborn.

In the US 7th Army sector the XV Corps is in difficulties round Aschaffenburg, while the XXI Corps pushes on north-east towards Würzburg and Königshofen and the VI advances along the river Neckar and makes contact with the French 1st Army.

The French II Corps widens its bridgehead over the Rhine, cutting the Karlsruhe–Frankfurt road near Mingolsheim and Bruchsal and reaching Linkenheim.

Italian Front During the night, in the V Corps (British 8th Army) sector, the 2nd Commando Brigade launches Operation *Roast* to liberate the area of Comacchio.

Eastern Front The 3rd Ukraine Front captures Sopron, a major road junction between Budapest and Vienna, near the Austrian frontier south-west of Lake Neusiedler. The Soviet High Command orders the 2nd Ukraine Front to take Bratislava by 5 or 6 April and go on to the Morava, while the 3rd Ukraine Front marches on Vienna.

There is fierce fighting in the sector defended by the German Army Group Centre, where the Germans claim to have destroyed 1,002 Soviet tanks in the last ten days of March. Savage fighting continues at Breslau. The German garrison at Glogau is ordered to fight its way out to the west.

In East Prussia, the German 2nd Army contains the massive pressure of the 2nd and 3rd Belorussian Fronts. The last remaining ships of the German navy take part in the

operation, the cruisers *Prinz Eugen, Emden, Lützow, Scheer* and *Hipper.* Naval and merchant ships have transported 85,000 men, including 70,000 wounded, to Pomerania in the last 14 days.

Philippines: Luzon In the south of the island, the 158th Regimental Combat Group of the US 6th Army lands, after air and naval bombardment, in the Bicol peninsula. The Japanese do not oppose the landing and the assault forces capture the town, the harbour and the airfield of Legaspi, and Libog. In the US I Corps sector, on the Villa Verde track, the Americans regain some of the ground recaptured by the Japanese the day before. The XI Corps outflanks the Shimbu line to the south.

Ryukyu Island: Okinawa Task Force 51, commanded by Vice-Admiral Turner (under Admiral Spruance, Commander of the US 5th Fleet), begins the landing of the US 10th Army (General Buckner) on the south-west coast of Okinawa, near Hagushi. The landing takes place at 8.30 a.m. The 10th Army is made up of the XXIV Corps of the US Army (General Hodge), with the 7th, 27th, 77th and 96th Divisions of infantry, and the III Amphibious Corps of Marines (General Geiger), with the 1st, 2nd, 5th and 6th Marine Divisions. The 7th and 96th Divisions and 1st and 6th Marine Divisions take part in the first phase. The operation is code-named *Iceberg.*

The operation is carried out by 180,000 combatant troops, 1,320 ships of all types, the 20th Air Force and the Marines tactical air force. These supporting services add another 368,000 men to the 180,000 on the ground, bringing the total to 548,000; it is the biggest amphibious operation so far carried out in the Pacific.

On the Japanese side, under General Mitsuru Ushijima, who has been in command of the Japanese 32nd Army since August 1944, the Ryukyu Islands are garrisoned by a total of 130,000 men. Of these, 85,000 are stationed in Okinawa, made up as follows: the 24th Division of in-

fantry (recently formed and not fully trained), the 62nd Division of infantry (brought over from China, experienced and aggressive), the 44th Independent Mixed Brigade (half-destroyed during its transportation from Japan) and one tank regiment whose tanks have been dug in to act as so many block-houses. In the Motobu and Oroku peninsulas there are 3,500 seamen and 7,000 militarized civilians under command of Admiral Ota, and another 20,000 men form the territorial militia. The Japanese are relying heavily on the navy's explosive boats and *kamikaze* pilots, organized by Vice-Admiral Matome Ugachi, once Yamamoto's chief of staff. But while in the past there have been good pilots available, now Ugachi has to be content with cadets with few hours of active service flying. In the south of the island, the part assigned to General Hodge's XXIV Corps, a formidable defensive line has been prepared, the Shuri line.

In accordance with their accustomed tactics, never abandoned although demonstrated to be wrong, the Japanese do not oppose the first stage of the American landing, so that by the evening the beachhead is 9 miles wide and from 2 to 3 miles deep. Okinawa is 66 miles long and between 3 and 10 miles across, so that the penetration is very substantial. There are also very few air attacks, though the *kamikaze* succeed in hitting the battleship *Virginia,* two destroyers and four landing craft.

The III Amphibious Corps manages to capture Yontan airfield without difficulty, while the XXIV Corps takes the airfield at Kadena and advances towards the south.

Burma British Command Headquarters revises its plans and reorganizes its forces. The IV Corps (15th and 17th Indian Divisions and 255th Tank Brigade) is to move towards Mandalay and Rangoon; the XXXIII Corps (British 2nd Division, 7th and 20th Indian Divisions and 268th Indian Brigade of Infantry) will advance south-west along the Irrawaddy valley towards Prome.

The 19th Indian Division will carry out mopping-up operations in the rear of the IV Corps.

2 April

Western Front The Canadian I Corps (1st Army) moves out from the Nijmegen bridgehead and advances on Arnhem.

In the British 2nd Army sector the XII Corps reaches the Dortmund–Ems canal at Rheine, while the VIII Corps continues its advance on Osnabrück.

While the XIII Corps takes Münster and pushes on towards the Weser, the XIX Corps is engaged in the Teutoburg forest and the XVIth reaches the Dortmund–Ems canal.

The 3rd Armoured Division (VII Corps, US 1st Army) consolidates its positions at Paderborn. The XVIII Airborne Corps takes over responsibility for the sector between the rivers Rhine, Rur, Lenne and Sieg. The 80th Division (XX Corps, US 3rd Army) reaches the suburbs of Kassel.

In the US 7th Army sector the attacks of units of the XV Corps against Aschaffenburg are still unsuccessful; the city is vigorously defended by units of the German 7th Army.

Italian Front Operation *Roast* to liberate Comacchio goes ahead and units of the V Corps (British 8th Army) succeed in establishing a bridgehead in the sector west of Comacchio.

Eastern Front In Hungary, the Russian 57th Army and Bulgarian 1st Army capture Nagykanizsa, centre of the Hungarian oilfields. The 2nd Ukraine Front occupies the industrial town of Mosonmagyarovar and reaches the Austrian border between the Danube and Lake Neusiedler.

There is also hard fighting southwest of Ratibor in the sector of the German Army Group Centre.

Philippines: Luzon The American troops landed at Legaspi dig in to defend their bridgehead, for the Japanese are well trained and determined to deny the Americans access to Highway 1 which runs north from the San Bernardino Strait. In the US

XIV Corps sector, the 1st Cavalry Division reaches San Pablo.

Southern Philippines On Negros Island the US 185th Infantry takes Talisay and its airfield. The 160th Infantry is held up by violent Japanese fire near Concepción.

In Cebu Island intense fighting takes place between the Americans and Japanese on Bolo Ridge.

Okinawa The Americans advance north more easily than they had hoped, and the 6th Marine Division occupies the peninsula north-west of Hagushi. In the east, too, considerable progress, and the 7th Division reaches the east coast in Nagagusuku Bay, cutting the island in two. American losses on the first day have been astonishingly low (28 dead, 27 missing, 104 wounded) – so light that the Americans nickname 1 April, Easter Day, 'Love Day'. Bulldozers shovel the remains of Japanese aircraft off the airfields to make the runways usable; in one hangar they find, intact, one of the new piloted flying bombs (*Oka*). An American convoy with the 77th Division on board is attacked by Japanese aircraft: three destroyers, four assault craft and one tank landing craft are damaged more or less seriously, and there are many casualties.

3 April

Western Front Around Lingen the XXX Corps (British 2nd Army) reaches the Dortmund–Ems canal.

In the US 9th Army sector the XIII Corps, after completing the capture of Münster, goes on to reach the Weser. Further south, the XIX Corps continues its advance to the east and begins to exert pressure on the German pocket in the Ruhr.

The XVIII Airborne Corps and the III Corps (US 1st Army) begin operations against the Ruhr pocket, the first in the area between the river Rur (in the north) and the Rhine (in the west), the second between the rivers Lenne and Rur.

The 80th Division (XX Corps, US 3rd Army) continues the battle for Kassel.

After three days of savage fighting, Aschaffenburg surrenders to the 45th

Division (XV Corps, US 7th Army). The XXI Corps goes into the attack against Würzburg, on the Main, and succeeds in establishing a bridgehead in the western part of the town.

The French 1st Army, engaged in extending its bridgehead on the line Lichtenau–Pforzheim–Ludwigsberg, captures Karlsruhe and prepares to occupy the Black Forest.

Eastern Front Malinovsky's forces (2nd Ukraine Front) reach the open country round Vienna; the German Army Group South (Wöhler) is in danger of disintegrating. The Russian advance has so far maintained a pace of 15–20 miles a day. The Soviet Supreme Command has issued a proclamation to the Austrians, explaining that the aim of the Russians is the destruction of Nazism, not of nations. Meanwhile Hitler's orders are: 'Hold Vienna'. Defending the city is the 6th SS Armoured Army, with eight armoured divisions, and against them are the 46th Army of the 2nd Ukraine Front and the 4th Army, 9th Guards Army and the 6th Armoured Army of the 3rd Ukraine Front. Russian superiority in manpower is enormous.

Between Hungary and Austria the German 2nd Armoured Army continues to fight in the Nagykanizsa area and along the valley of the Raba (Raab). The Russians have breached the German defences between Wiener Neustadt and Lake Neusiedler.

There is also fierce fighting in the other sectors of the front, especially near Bratislava, already besieged by the 2nd Ukraine Front. In Hungary, Russian and Bulgarian troops mop up the area south-west of Lake Balaton and penetrate across the Drava into Yugoslavia.

Southern Philippines Small American units land on Masbate Island to assist the Filipino guerrillas. There is intense fighting on Negros and Cebu, where authority is given for the transfer of the 164th Regimental Combat Group from Leyte.

Okinawa In the III Amphibious Corps sector, north of the beachhead, the 6th Marine Division advances about 5 miles towards the isthmus of Ishikawa and the centre of the island, while the 1st Marine Division moves out along the Katchin peninsula, on the east coast, advancing as far as Hizaonna. The XXIV Corps, south of the bridgehead, makes a converging movement southwards, with the 7th Division on the left and the 96th on the right. The 7th Division comes down the east coast of the island as far as Kuba, while the 96th advances less rapidly inland and on the west coast.

The escort carrier *Wake Island* is seriously damaged by a Japanese suicide aircraft off Okinawa.

☐ The Joint Chiefs of Staff appoint General MacArthur Commander-in-Chief of all American land forces in the Pacific and Admiral Nimitz Commander-in-Chief of all naval forces.

4 April

Western Front In the British 2nd Army sector both the XXX and the XII Corps succeed in establishing bridgeheads over the Dortmund–Ems Canal, one near Lingen, the other near Rheine. Some units of the VIII Corps enter Osnabrück while others press on towards Minden on the river Weser.

The US 9th and 1st Armies continue to press from north and south against the Ruhr pocket, and at the same time to push east in the direction of the river Weser.

The garrison at Kassel surrenders to the troops of the 80th Division (XX Corps, US 3rd Army).

The French 1st Army takes Karlsruhe and then moves south-west towards Freiburg and south-east towards Tübingen.

Eastern Front Advancing from positions south-west of Nowy Targ, in Poland, the 4th Ukraine Front, supported by Czechoslovak units, opens the offensive along the Polish–Czech frontier in the direction of Bohemia; the 2nd Front takes the important road and rail junction of Bratislava. In Austria, advance guards of the 3rd Ukraine Front and Bulgarian troops are now only 2 miles from Vienna. The 2nd and 3rd Ukraine Fronts

have together completely liberated Hungary and the 3rd Ukraine Front is advancing in Yugoslavia. The Germans admit the loss of Baden and announce that they are counterattacking in the area of Moravska-Ostrava and Nitra.

In East Prussia the Germans form the *Silesia* battle group at Swinemünde (Swinoujscie). General Heinrici has taken over command of the Vistula Army Group.

Philippines: Luzon The US 158th Regimental Combat Group, landed on 1 April at Legaspi in the south of the island, advances slowly northwards, doggedly opposed by the Japanese.

Okinawa The situation changes radically. All the American units find themselves facing extremely tenacious resistance carried out from well-sited and well-camouflaged positions both in the north and in the south along the Shuri Line.

Learning that the Japanese intend to launch a huge air attack against the invasion fleet, the Americans decide to attack Kyushu Island, where aircraft of various types have been assembled for the *kamikaze* assault. Eleven US tank landing craft run aground off Okinawa.

5 April

Western Front The I Corps of the Canadian 1st Army completes the liberation of the area between Nijmegen and the lower Rhine, while the II Corps establishes a bridgehead over the Twenthe Canal, east of the Ijssel.

In the British 2nd Army sector, the XII Corps reinforces its bridgehead over the Dortmund-Ems Canal and the VIII Corps, after taking Osnabrück, moves on towards the Weser. While the forces of the XIII Corps prepare to cross the Weser near Minden, the XIX Corps reaches the river south of Hamelin and even manages to send some units over the river. The XVIII Airborne Corps and the III Corps (US 1st Army) are heavily engaged against the Ruhr pocket. The US 3rd Army advances with all its corps (the XX, VIII, V and XII) from the Kassel–Fulda line towards the east, heading for the Weser and the area of Ohrdruf.

In the US 7th Army sector the XV Corps captures Gemünden and the XXI Corps completes the crossing of the Main at Würzburg.

Italian Front In the US 5th Army sector, the 92nd Division launches an attack in the direction of Massa.

Eastern Front While fighting continues on the outskirts of Vienna and

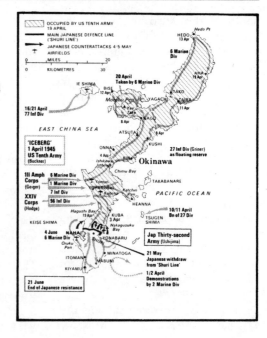

US operations on Okinawa 1 April-21 June 1945. After nearly three months of some of the most savage fighting of the Pacific war, Okinawa falls to the US forces on 22 June. American losses amounted to 50,000 dead, wounded and missing. Japanese losses were 110,000 dead, 7,400 taken prisoner and 7,800 aircraft destroyed.

south of the Austrian capital, the German Army Group Centre launches a series of counter-attacks in Czechoslovakia to relieve Russian pressure on Moravska-Ostrava. In East Prussia, the Russians prepare to launch a massive attack on Königsberg after four days of heavy air and artillery preparation. Taking part in the operation are the 48th, 50th, 11th and 39th Guards Armies, with the Keilsberg group, supported by 2,500 aircraft. The Germans in this sector can put up 200 fighters. Defending the city is the German 4th Army under General Müller, which also holds open the only escape route for the German forces in northern Latvia.

☐ The Soviet Government tells the Japanese ambassador in Moscow that it intends to denounce the five-year non-aggression treaty signed between the USSR and Japan in Moscow on 13 April 1941.

☐ In Tokyo General Kuniaki Koiso's government resigns and a new government is formed by Admiral Kantaro Suzuki.

Philippines: Luzon In the US XI Corps sector, one regiment of the 43rd Division advances along the Bay Lagoon, south of Manila, occupying Lumban and a bridge over the river Pagsanjan. In the Lumban area the 5th Cavalry (US XIV Corps) links up with the 43rd Division as it comes south along the east bank of the Bay Lagoon.

Okinawa The American 10th Army is virtually pinned down by the Japanese resistance. The 22nd Regiment of the 6th Marine Division does manage to make some progress northwards in the area of the Isthmus of Ishikawa, the narrowest part of the island. Meanwhile the Americans carry on with occupying the islets off the coast. The Japanese decide to launch their big *kamikaze* attack the next day, and also to open their desperate Operation *Ten-go*, in which they will deploy every ship in the Japanese navy still effective, i.e. the super-battleship *Yamato*, 72,800 tons, the light cruiser *Yahagi* and eight destroyers. This 2nd Fleet, or 'special surface attack

force', is commanded by Vice-Admiral Seichi Ito. The super-battleship, once the pride of the Japanese navy, is to ground itself off the coast of Okinawa to form a sort of unsinkable fortress. There is to be no return; the ship is given only enough fuel to reach its objective.

6 April

Western Front In the US 9th Army sector, the XIII Corps opens the offensive across the Weser. Units of the XIX Corps cross the Weser near Grohnde and then advance on Burgstemmen.

The XVIII Airborne Corps (US 1st Army) opens an offensive against the Ruhr pocket near the confluence of the rivers Rur and Rhine. While the VII Corps approaches the Weser, the V reaches the river and secures a bridgehead over it.

Elements of the French II Corps (French 1st Army) reach the Neckar in the neighbourhood of Lauffen, the river Enz at Mühlacker and the outskirts of Pforzheim, and take Stein and Königsbach.

Italian Front The US 92nd Division continues its offensive against Massa.

Eastern Front The battle of Vienna begins. The Germans blow up all the bridges across the Danube except one. The German 2nd Armoured Army and 6th SS Armoured Army manage to drive back the Russian forces in the Wiener Wald and counter-attack north-west towards Klosterneuburg. The Russian 46th Army outflanks Vienna from the south. General Rendulic takes over command of the German Army Group South (600,000 men) from General Wöhler.

Army Group Centre renews its attacks against the 4th and 2nd Ukraine Fronts in Czechoslovakia. Breslau still holds out against the Russians.

In the Danzig area the Russians break through the German 2nd Army's line in several places. In East Prussia the 2nd Belorussian Front opens the major attack against Königsberg and penentrates into the city.

Philippines: Luzon The 158th Regimental Combat Group, landed at Legaspi and held up by the Japanese in their advance north, extend their control in the south at the narrowest point of the Bicol peninsula. In the US I Corps sector, a regiment of the 32nd Division captures a hill in the Salacsac Pass area and advances on Kapintalan. In the XI Corps sector, the assault is launched on Mount Mataba, with a manœuvre to approach Mount Oro and Mount Pacawagan.

Okinawa The 6th Marine Division makes little progress northwards in the Isthmus of Ishikawa. There is intense fighting in the southern sector, where the formidable Japanese Shuri line withstands all attacks.

At first light, aircraft from the US 5th Fleet attack Kyushu Island to prevent the planned Japanese attack by suicide aircraft on the US naval forces assembled off Okinawa. Some dozens of aircraft are destroyed, but the Japanese still manage to send about 400 aircraft against the Okinawa invasion fleet; three-quarters of them are destroyed, but they sink two destroyers, one tank landing craft and one fast minesweeper and damage the light aircraft carrier *San Jacinto*, thirteen destroyers and many other ships.

At 4.00 p.m. the Japanese 2nd Fleet sails from Tokuyama Bay, in Honshu Island, heading for Okinawa.

7 April

Western Front The VIII Corps (British 2nd Army) succeeds in establishing a bridgehead over the river Weser in the Minden–Stolzenau area and pushes on from there towards the Leine. In the US 9th Army sector, the 84th Division (XIII Corps) completes the crossing of the Weser and extends its bridgehead. Units of the XVI Corps continue their advance towards the river Rur and south across the Ems and Rhine–Herne canals, between Gelsenkirchen and Essen. The XVIII Airborne Corps continues its offensive against the Ruhr pocket, together with the III Corps (US 1st Army). The VII Corps

Berlin: civilians move about once more in a street that has escaped the worst damage, though a building is still ablaze.

reaches the Weser, over which all the bridges have been destroyed.

In the US 7th Army sector, the 14th Division (XV Corps) captures Neustadt, on the river Saal.

Eastern Front Units of the 3rd Ukraine Front penetrate into the southern districts of Vienna, where there is savage house-to-house fighting. The German 8th Army, now withdrawn from Hungary, is engaged in the defence south of Vienna with the 2nd Armoured Army and the 6th SS Armoured Army; the latter repels a Russian

thrust in the direction of St Pölten. The German Army Group Centre continues its counter-attacks against the 2nd and 4th Ukraine Fronts in Czechoslovakia.

At Königsberg, the German 4th Army has to retire about a mile under Russian pressure; the Russians take 130 scattered posts and strongpoints. Senior German officers suggest that the army should retire to the west by way of the Samland peninsula while it is still possible, but General Müller forbids it.

In Yugoslavia, Army Group E eva-

cuates Sarajevo. There is also fighting in Dalmatia in the Karlopag–Gospic area, from which the Germans manage to fight their way out.

Philippines: Luzon In the US I Corps sector, after air and artillery preparation, units of the 32nd Division launch a heavy attack against the Japanese positions in the Salacsac Pass area. The 25th Division begins the encirclement of Kapintalan. The XIV Corps is ordered to advance on Mauban and Atimonan (on Lamon Bay) and thence into the Bicol peninsula.

Okinawa The 6th Marine Division reaches the line Nago-Taira, at the base of the Motobu peninsula. The XXIV Corps in the south is still severely engaged by the Japanese in front of their positions on the Shuri line.

In the waters off Okinawa Japanese suicide aircraft resume their attacks, damaging the aircraft carrier *Hancock*, the battleship *Maryland*, two destroyers and other ships.

Battle of the East China Sea. Despite Japanese attempts to deceive the Americans by diversions and decoys the Japanese 2nd Fleet is sighted by the American submarine *Hackleback* in the Bungo Strait, which separates Kyushu from Shikoku. Virtually without air cover, the Japanese ships are attacked by hundreds of American aircraft at 12.38 p.m., by a second wave at 1.30 p.m. and by further waves until after 2.00 p.m. The cruiser *Yahagi*, hit by bombs and torpedoes, is the first to sink. At 2.23 p.m., hit by five torpedoes and by countless bombs, the great *Yamato* goes down. Four Japanese destroyers are also sunk and two damaged. Of 376 American aircraft taking part in the operation, only 10 are lost.

8 April

Western Front On the Allies' northern flank, the Canadian II Corps (1st Army), advancing north-east towards Oldenburg, crosses the river Ems in the Meppen–Lathen area.

Units of the British XXX Corps take the defensive positions of the German 1st Parachute Army east of Lingen and push on in the direction of Bremen, and the VIII Corps reaches the river Leine south-east of Nienburg.

The 5th Armoured Division (XIII Corps, US 9th Army) is ordered to cross the river Leine south of Hanover.

While the XVIII Airborne Corps (US 1st Army) extends its bridgehead across the river Sieg, in the Ruhr pocket, the VII Corps establishes a strong bridgehead over the Weser and, further south, the V Corps advances rapidly east of the river.

In the US 7th Army sector the XV Corps advances on the Hohe Rhon hills, while the XXI and VI Corps advance in the areas of Schweinfurt and Heilbronn.

The French 1st Division takes Pforzheim and goes on to reach Dietenhausen and Dietlingen. A bridgehead is established over the river Enz in the neighbourhood of Mühlhausen.

Eastern Front The 3rd Belorussian Front continues the assault against Königsberg and breaks through the German defences from the north-west. At Breslau the Russians continue the systematic liquidation of the encircled German garrison, which holds out gallantly. The 2nd Ukraine Front advances in Czechoslovakia and establishes bridgeheads over the Morava and the Danube east and north-east of Vienna. In Vienna bitter fighting rages and Tolbukhin's forces occupy the southern and eastern districts. Russian troops also advance beyond the city in the direction of Linz, and move south from Wiener Neustadt towards Graz.

General Schörner, Commander of the Army Group Centre, defending Czechoslovakia, is promoted Field-Marshal. He has available to him the most numerous and efficient branch of the Wehrmacht, with about 1,200,000 men, but the forces opposing him are superior in number, armament and morale.

Philippines: Luzon In the I Corps sector, the Americans are still deployed half way between Rosario and Baguio, not far from the place where they landed on 9 January. General Swift is anxious to make a breakthrough. The battle for the Salacsac Pass continues on the Villa Verde track. In the XI Corps sector, Mount Mataba is heavily bombarded by aircraft and artillery in preparation for another attack.

Southern Philippines The capture of Cebu and Negros goes ahead slowly.

Okinawa While the III Amphibious Corps goes into action to capture the Motobu peninsula, the XXIV Corps switches its efforts against the Shuri line, attacking Kakazu Ridge without success.

Two US destroyers and some other ships are damaged by suicide boats and aircraft of the Japanese navy.

China The Japanese test the Chinese positions west of Pao-ching with a view to an offensive against Chihchiang (south-east of Chungking), where there is a US air base.

9 April

Western Front In the British 2nd Army sector, while the XXX Corps advances east and north-east of Lingen, the XII and VIII Corps reach the river Weser (in the Hoya sector) and the river Leine.

The units of the XIII Corps (US 9th Army) launch the assault on Hanover from north, north-west and west.

All the corps of the US 1st Army continue to advance towards the Elbe. The VII Corps makes swiftly for Nordhausen and the river Leine in the Göttingen area.

The US 7th Army pushes on in the area of Schweinfurt, reaching the river Kocher near Weissbach and, further south, a line from Ingelfelden to Weldingsfeld.

Italian Front In the evening General McCreery's British 8th Army launches a big offensive, with General Keightley's V Corps on the right flank and General Anders' Polish II Corps in the Imola sector; they succeed in stablishing bridgeheads over the Senio in the Lugo sector and in the area of San Severo–Felisio. While General Kirkman's British XIII Corps stays on the defensive on the left flank, Hawksworth's British X Corps and the Italian *Friuli* Combat Group launch an offensive across the Senio during the night.

Eastern Front In East Prussia, the 3rd Belorussian Front finishes off the operations against Königsberg. In the evening the fortress commander, General Lasch, orders his troops to surrender. He is condemned to death *in absentia*, and the German High Command also dismisses Müller. The defence of the city has cost the Germans 42,000 dead and 92,000 prisoners, and the Russians have captured 3,675 guns and mortars. Part of the German 4th Army prepares to resist to the last man on the Samland peninsula, north of the city. The battle continues in Vienna, where Tolbukhin's troops take one isolated post after another. The German 6th Army and 6th SS Armoured Army try in vain to stop the Russians from spreading out towards southern and western Austria.

The units of the Army Group E (Löhr), already cut off, still go on fighting against Tito's forces in Yugoslavia.

Philippines: Luzon On the Villa Verde track the 32nd Division (US I Corps) presses its attack against the Salacsac Pass to gain access for the American forces to the valley of the Cagayan, which runs from south to north, west of the Sierra Madre, where the mass of the Japanese forces are concentrated. In the XI Corps sector, aircraft and artillery continue to hammer Mount Mataba.

Southern Philippines Both on Cebu and on Negros the American troops get ready to eliminate the Japanese forces which have taken up positions in the mountains of the interior. In the Sulu archipelago, following two weeks of air bombing and a preliminary naval bombardment, the 163rd Regimental Combat Group lands on Jolo Island without meeting any resistance and proceeds to occupy it.

Okinawa In the XXIV Corps sector, units of the US 96th Division attack Kakazu Ridge, a strongpoint in the Shuri line, but are driven back with heavy losses by artillery fire and counter-attacks by the Japanese infantry. The US 27th Infantry Division lands on the island. In the north, units of the 6th Marine Division begin to penetrate into the Motobu peninsula.

10 April

Western Front On the northern flank of the front, units of the Canadian II Corps advance in the direction of Groningen and Oldenburg. In the British 2nd Army sector, while the XXX Corps pushes on towards Bremen, the XII Corps makes

A Japanese surrenders to the Americans on Okinawa.

for Soltau and the VIII for Celle. The XIII Corps of the US 9th Army takes Hanover. In the XVI Corps sector, the cities reached include Gelsenkirchen, Bochum and Essen.

The XVIII Airborne Corps (US 1st Army) crosses the river Sieg in the Siegburg sector and advances into the German Ruhr pocket. The III Corps is also putting pressure against the same objective, while the VII advances quickly towards Nordhausen. The divisions of the XX Corps (US 3rd Army) are approaching Erfurt. In the US 7th Army sector, the XXI Corps advances north and northwest, towards Schweinfurt and along the east bank of the Main.

Italian Front The 92nd Division (US 5th Army) enters Massa. The British 8th Army continues its offensive on the east flank of the Allied line. The attack in force in this sector takes General Herr's German 10th Army by surprise for they were expecting an offensive in the centre and on the right of their line.

Eastern Front While the battle for Vienna rages, the 6th SS Armoured Army repulses strong attacks in the area of Wiener Neustadt and west of Baden. In the sector of the Army Group Centre, the troops besieged in Breslau are still holding out against continuous attacks. The German communiqués admit that resistance has ended at Königsberg but deny that there has been a capitulation.

Philippines: Luzon The 158th Regimental Combat Group extends its area of control in the Legaspi sector, in the south, and begins reconnaissance of the islands in the Gulf of Albay. In the I Corps sector, the US 37th Division occupies the area of Sablan–Salat, not far from Baguio. Units of the 25th Division proceed with their operations in the Mount Myoko area. The 128th Regiment, 32nd Division, takes Salacsac Pass No. 2, so opening the way into the Cagayan valley. In the XI Corps sector, after the previous day's intensive bombardment, American infantry launch an assault on Mount Mataba, and some units succeed in reaching the top; but the Japanese keep up their resistance in this area for another week. Columns from the XIV Corps advancing southwards, reach Lamon Bay, cutting off the Japanese left in the Bicol peninsula. The 1st Cavalry Division occupies Mauban and the 11th Airborne Division takes Atimonan, northwest of the Bicol peninsula.

Okinawa In the Motobu peninsula the 6th Marine Division begins a flanking manœuvre to get behind the Yae-Take hills, which are strongly manned by the Japanese. On the Shuri line, in the south, the US 96th Division resumes its attacks against Kakazu Ridge and gains some positions, but is unable to drive the enemy out completely.

After the usual air and naval preparation, a battalion of the US 27th Division lands on Tsugen Island, east of Okinawa, and clears it.

11 April

Western Front While the British XXX Corps (2nd Army) advances on Bremen without difficulty, units of the XII and VIII Corps cross the rivers Leine (near Westen) and Aller (at Celle).

The Leine is also reached by the XIII Corps (US 9th Army), south of Hanover, near Pattensen. In the sector where the XIX Corps is operating,

advance guards of the 2nd Armoured Division, with a major leap forward, reach the Elbe south of Magdeburg. The XVI Corps advances into the German Ruhr pocket and reaches the river Rur opposite Witten. Units of the XVIII Airborne Corps continue their crossing of the river Sieg. In the VII Corps sector the towns of Nordhausen, Osterode, Tettenborn and Neuhof are taken.

The XX Corps (US 3rd Army) advances into the Weimar sector, passing the German extermination camp at Buchenwald and Bad Sulza.

Further south, Coburg surrenders to the XII Corps.

The XV Corps (US 7th Army) advances rapidly south of Nuremberg.

Italian Front In the western sector of the Allied line, the 92nd Division (US 5th Army) takes Carrara. On the eastern flank, where the British 8th Army is operating, the Polish II Corps reaches the river Santerno.

Eastern Front The battle for Vienna goes on. The 3rd Ukraine Front puts strong pressure on the left wing of the German 2nd Armoured Army and drives on between the rivers Mur and Raab. The Russians make a deep penentration west of Neuenkirchen. In the capital itself the Russians reach the city centre, and capture the Parliament building and the City Hall.

The German Army Group Centre withdraws under strong enemy pressure along the course of the river Vah in the Low Tatra area. The Russians, says the German communiqué, are marching towards Zilina, south of Moravska-Ostrava.

The Russians announce that, in the period 6–10 April, they have captured 142,000 Germans in East Prussia alone, including 1,819 officers of whom 4 were generals.

☐ A treaty of friendship and collaboration between the USSR and Yugoslavia is signed in Moscow.

Philippines: Luzon Strong Japanese reaction against the US 32nd Division (I Corps) as it penetrates beyond the Salacsac Pass.

In the XI Corps sector, the 38th Division has almost completed mopping up in the area west of Clark

Field; 5,500 Japanese bodies have been counted so far.

Okinawa Savage fighting in the Motobu peninsula, where the Japanese occupy strong positions. Fighting also continues on Kakazu Ridge. There is a virtual stalemate, though the 1st Marine Division, advancing northwards along the east coast, has reached Taira, and units of the 6th Marine Division are even further north on the west coast. General Buckner is undecided whether to persist with the frontal attack on the Shuri line or to try a landing in the rear of it; in the latter case it would be necessary to weaken the forces engaging the line from the north.

Off Okinawa, high-level bombers and *kamikaze* suicide aircraft launch an attack on the ships of the US Task Force 58, seriously damaging the aircraft carrier *Enterprise* (which has to be withdrawn to Ulithi for repairs), the aircraft carrier *Essex*, six destroyers and smaller vessels.

Burma In the British IV Corps sector, the 5th Indian Division, relieving the 17th Indian Division at Pyawbwe, advances, led by armoured units, as far as Yamethin. The armoured advance guard takes the town, but the infantry are held up in the built-up area by strong Japanese resistance.

12 April

President Roosevelt dies at Warm Springs, Georgia. In accordance with the American constitution, he is succeeded by Vice-President Harry S Truman. Hitler drinks the new president's health in champagne.

Western Front In the Canadian 1st Army sector, the I Corps sends in its divisions against Arnhem. The XIII Corps (US 9th Army) reaches the Elbe near Wittenberg and Werben. The XIX Corps succeeds in establishing a bridgehead over the Elbe in the area of Randau, south of Magdeburg.

The penetration by the XVIII Airborne Corps (US 1st Army) into the Ruhr pocket is well under way, and in the XX Corps (US 3rd Army) sector the divisions advance towards the rivers Weisse and Elster. The XII Corps pushes on towards the river Hasslach.

Units of the XV Corps (US 7th Army) are near Bamberg. After nine days' fighting, Heilbronn is taken by the 10th Division of the VI Corps.

The French 1st Army reinforces its positions in the bridgehead over the river Enz after capturing the west bank of the river.

Italian Front The US 5th Army has to postpone the offensive planned for this date by 24 hours on account of bad weather.

The advance of the units of the V Corps (British 8th Army) towards Bastia, on the north bank of the river Reno, continues.

Eastern Front With support from Malinovsky's 2nd Ukraine Front, the 3rd Ukraine Front is overcoming the defenders of Vienna. The Russians advance on Graz and reach the Vienna–Lundenburg road. The battle still continues at Breslau.

The Russians carry out heavy air raids on the Hela peninsula. The German communiqué admits the capitulation of Königsberg and announces the death sentence on the garrison commander, General Lasch.

In Yugoslavia, the Germans are forced to evacuate Zenica. The Yugoslavs and Bulgarians make a deep penetration south of the Drava.

Philippines: Luzon The advance of the US 37th Division (I Corps) on Baguio is held up a little way from Monglo by fire from Japanese dug in on the surrounding hills. Troops of the XIV Corps advance into the Bicol peninsula.

Southern Philippines Fierce fighting on Babay Ridge, Cebu, part of which is captured by the Americal Division.

Okinawa A series of unsuccessful attempts by the Americans to take Kakazu Ridge. In the evening, after a heavy barrage, the Japanese begin a series of counter-attacks, mainly in the sector held by the US 96th Division. The American lines hold, but some enemy elements manage to infiltrate through them.

For the second day running, the Japanese air force launches an attack

in force on American shipping, using suicide aircraft, piloted flying bombs and high-level bombers. They sink one destroyer and one landing craft and damage the battleships *Idaho* and *Tennessee* and eight destroyers.

Burma In the British XXXIII Corps sector, the 7th Indian Division takes Kyaukpadaung, an important communications centre between Chauk and Meiktila.

13 April

Western Front The Canadian I Corps (Canadian 1st Army) continues its attack on Arnhem.

In the British 2nd Army sector the XXX Corps is still advancing towards Bremen and the VIII Corps towards Ülzen.

Operations on the Elbe by the XIII and XIX Corps (US 9th Army) continue, while the XVI Corps captures the sector north of the Ruhr between Witten and Westhofen and completes the capture of Dortmund. The XVIII Airborne Division pursues the enemy retiring from positions in the Ruhr pocket.

The XX Corps (US 3rd Army) throws more troops across the Weisse-Elster, while the VIII Corps continues mopping up on the west bank of the Saal.

Units of the XV Corps (US 7th Army) enter Bamberg.

Italian Front Headquarters of the US 5th Army again has to postpone the start of the offensive on account

An 81-mm mortar in action during the US 7th Army's operations near Nuremberg.

of persistent bad weather.

In the British 8th Army sector, the Polish II Corps extends its bridgehead over the river Santerno.

Eastern Front Following a new breakthrough by the 3rd Ukraine Front west of Vienna, at 2 p.m., after the most savage fighting, the city is in the hands of Tolbukhin's and Malinovsky's troops. The 2nd Front now heads for St Pölten and threatens the Army Group Centre from the south, attacking towards Brno, in Czechoslovakia.

Burma The 20th Indian Division (British XXXIII Corps) takes Taungdwingyi.

China The Japanese open a large-scale offensive against Chihchiang, putting in their main effort along the road leading from Paoching.

□ Japan. 327 B-29 Superfortress bombers carry out a massive raid on Tokyo, razing the north-west part of the city to the ground over an area of 7 square miles.

14 April

Western Front The British 2nd Army presses on towards Bremen, Soltau and Ülzen.

Units of the US 9th Army reach the west bank of the Elbe.

The XVIII Airborne Corps (US 1st Army) starts the final stage of its offensive against the German pocket in the Ruhr. The III Corps sector, between the rivers Rur and Honne, is now firmly in Allied hands. The VII Corps advances rapidly northeast towards the line made by the rivers Elbe and Mulde.

Bamberg is finally taken by units of the XV Corps (US 7th Army).

Italian Front The weather improves and the US 5th Army is at last able to launch its final offensive against the German troops in Italy – in the American sector, the XIV Armoured Corps of Lemelsen's 14th Army. The American IV Corps attacks towards the Lombard plain.

On the right of the Allied line, the offensive by the British 8th Army makes progress.

Eastern Front The German war communiqué reports that the 1st Belorussian Front is putting severe pressure

'A TREE GROWS IN BROOKLYN'

Economic hardships and conjugal misunderstandings plague the lives of the Nolans, an Irish family living in New York at the turn of the century.

Based on the best selling novel of the same name by Betty Smith, *A Tree Grows in Brooklyn* was the first film made by Elia Kazan. The theme of the social integration of immigrants to the United States, close to the director's heart, was handled with optimism, sensitivity and a lightly humorous touch. James Dunn won an Oscar for his portrayal of the alcoholic but spiritually rich head of the family.

on the Vistula Army Group in the areas of Frankfurt-on-the-Oder, Küstrin (Kostrzyn) and Zehden, south of Stettin. In Austria the Russians advance west of Vienna.

Philippines: Luzon Slight progress towards Monglo by the 37th Division in the US I Corps sector. Monglo is one of the last positions before Baguio.

Okinawa In the sector of the III Amphibious Corps, the 29th Marine Division puts in a violent attack against the Yae-Take heights, making some small progress into the foothills. In the XXIV Corps sector, in the south, the Americans repulse further Japanese counter-attacks. Japanese suicide aircraft attack American ships off Okinawa, damaging the battleship *New York* and three destroyers. The *kamikaze* attacks are seriously worrying the

American commanders, for they have put a large number of ships out of action.

China The Japanese Imperial General Staff orders the expeditionary force in China to move four divisions into central and north China. As a result the Japanese abandon the railway linking Hengyang with Kweilin, Liuchow and Yungning, where several American air bases had been sited. The Chinese plan to halt the Japanese advance on Chihchiang by threatening the advancing columns from the flanks. This proves to be an effective strategy.

15 April

Western Front In the Canadian 1st Army sector, the 49th Division (Canadian I Corps) finishes off the capture of Arnhem, while the Canadian II Corps is approaching Groningen.

The advance of the British XXX Corps (2nd Army) towards Bremen, and of the VIII Corps towards Ülzen continues.

The XIII Corps (US 9th Army) begins an offensive on the right bank of the river Saale in an attempt to capture the ground between the Saale and the Rhine. Units of the V Corps reach the bridges over the river Mulde in the area between Colditz and Lastau.

Further south the XX Corps (US 3rd Army) also crosses the river Mulde in the area of Rochlitz and Lunzenau. Units of the 4th Armoured Division advance towards Chemnitz. The XXII Corps (US 15th Army) is made reponsible for the Aachen sector.

The advance of the US 7th Army continues in the sectors of Nuremberg (XV Corps) and Neustadt (XXI Corps).

While the II Corps of the French 1st Army occupies the Black Forest, the I Corps crosses the Rhine north of Kehl.

Italian Front In the US 5th Army sector the IV Corps goes ahead in the sectors of Suzzano and Vergato, and during the night the II Corps launches an attack in the direction of

Bologna, east of Highway 64, after an intensive air bombardment. The Italian *Legnano* Combat Group also takes part in the attack.

On the east of the Allied line, the units of the Polish II Corps (British 8th Army) begin to cross the river Sillaro.

Eastern Front In Austria the 3rd Ukraine Front takes Radkesburg, south-east of Graz. The 2nd Ukraine Front attacks northwards towards Brno. The Führer, in an Order of the Day to the troops fighting on the Eastern Front, declares: 'Berlin is still German, Vienna will return to Germany.'

Meanwhile, the 1st and 2nd Belorussian Fronts are getting ready to unleash the great offensive against Berlin. The three fronts contain 19 armies, 4 armoured armies and 3 air armies, making a total of 1,600,000 men with 3,827 tanks and 2,334 self-propelled guns, 4,520 anti-tank guns, 15,654 field guns and 3,411 anti-aircraft guns, 6,700 aircraft and 96,000 vehicles. To oppose this enormous force the Germans have the 3rd Armoured Army, the 9th Army and the reserve of the Vistula Army Group. plus the 4th Armoured Army of the Army Group Centre, making a total of 47 divisions, of which 3 are armoured and 8 motorized, plus an infantry brigade.

Philippines: Luzon In the south, near Legaspi, the 158th Regimental Combat Group attacks the Cituinan hills without success, while a battalion from the same group attacks and captures the village of San Francisco. Savage and indecisive fighting continues in all sectors.

The Japanese are everywhere resisting with small units, while the bulk of the 14th Army concentrates on the mountains of the Sierra Madre, in the north-east of the island.

Southern Philippines On Cebu, the Americal Division proceeds with the liquidation of the enemy forces in the hills around Cebu City.

Okinawa In the Motobu peninsula the 6th Marine Division is engaged in bloody battles for the capture of the Yae-Take heights.

On the islet of Minna, near Ie Shima

Island, the Americans land strong forces of artillery, which begin to shell the larger island.

⬜ Japan. Aircraft of Vice-Admiral Mitscher's fast aircraft carrier squadron attack airfields in the south of Kyushu to try to prevent the continual attacks on American ships off Okinawa; nonetheless, Japanese suicide aircraft damage two more destroyers, a tanker and a minesweeper.

The B-29 Superfortresses renew their attacks on Tokyo, dropping 754 tons of bombs on the industrial district of Kawasaki, in the south of the city.

16 April

Western Front The II Corps of the Canadian 1st Army takes Groningen.

In the British 2nd Army sector, the XXX Corps is coming close to Bremen, while at Ülzen units of the VIII Corps meet with vigorous resistance from the German 20th Army.

The XVIII Airborne Corps (US 1st Army) pushes on further in the Ruhr

pocket, where German resistance is quickly weakening; many units surrender, and so far the Americans have taken at least 20,000 prisoners. The VII and V Corps extend their bridgeheads on the east bank of the river Mulde; units of the 9th Armoured Division (V Corps) enter Colditz, while the 69th Division advances north-east towards Leipzig.

In the sector in which the units of the US 7th Army are engaged, the XV Corps advances towards Nuremberg and reaches the outskirts of the city.

Italian Front The offensives of the US 5th and British 8th Armies towards the Lombard plain make progress.

Eastern Front At 5.00 a.m. the 1st Ukraine Front opens the offensive against Berlin with a massive bombardment of the positions of the German 4th Armoured Army (Army Group Centre) on the river Neisse in the Triebel area. At 7.00 a.m. the tanks and infantry go in, taking a bridgehead over the river. There are powerful attacks also in the area of

An American armoured car enters a German village in the course of the Allied advance into the heart of the Reich.

Ratibor. At 6.15 a.m. the 1st Belorussian Front attacks the sector held by the Vistula Army Group north and south of Frankfurt-on-the-Oder, advancing from the Küstrin (Kostrzyn) bridgehead over the Oder. The Russian 33rd Army, south of the town, makes the most progress, advancing several miles.

In Austria the 3rd Ukraine Front presses on west of Vienna, taking St Pölten and Fürstenfeld. The 2nd Ukraine Front gains ground in Czechoslovakia south-east of Brno. Hitler sends his last Order of the Day to his Eastern Front armies: 'He who gives the order to retreat is to be shot on the spot.'

Philippines: Luzon The 158th Regimental Combat Group repels several strong Japanese counter-attacks at San Francisco, and occupies the southern point of the Bicol peninsula, making the northern entrance to the San Bernardino Strait safe for American shipping. In the I Corps sector, the US 37th Division overcomes the dogged resistance of the Japanese on the hills north of San Francisco and advances north along the west coast. In the XIV Corps sector, the 511th Infantry of the 11th Airborne Division takes Mount Malepunyo and Mount Dalaga, while the 1st Cavalry Division shuts up some of the Japanese units in a number of pockets north and north-west of Mount Mataasna Bundoc.

After a two-day air and naval preparation, a battalion of the 151st Infantry lands unopposed on Carabao Island, the last objective in Manila Bay not yet secured, and occupies it.

Southern Philippines The Americal Division makes slow progress on Cebu against the Japanese positions on the hills round Cebu City. The Japanese retire during the following night. In the Sulu archipelago units of the US 41st Division eliminate the remaining Japanese resistance.

Okinawa The 6th Marine Division (US III Amphibious Corps) sends in seven battalions to attack the Yae-Take heights in the Motobu peninsula. The fighting is savage and the outcome remains uncertain all day. At 8.00 a.m., after air and naval

bombardment, the US 77th Division begins the landing at Ie Shima, west of the Motobu peninsula. The assault troops advance quickly into the interior, more held up by the mines than by the Japanese, and capture two thirds of the island, including the airfield; Japanese counter-attacks are driven off.

Despite the air raids on Kyushu, renewed again today, *kamikaze* pilots attack American ships off Okinawa in force, sinking the destroyer *Pringle*, seriously damaging the aircraft carrier *Intrepid* and, less seriously, the battleship *Missouri*, three destroyers and other ships.

Burma Advanced guards of the 5th Indian Division (IV Corps) occupy Shwemyo without meeting any resistance, but are held up on the outskirts of the town by intense Japanese fire.

17 April

Western Front The British XXX Corps (2nd Army) is still battling in the suburbs of Bremen, while at Ülzen the VIII Corps is still on the same positions as on the previous day. The XIX Corps (US 9th Army) begins the assault on Magdeburg, on the west bank of the Elbe.

In the Ruhr pocket the XVIII Airborne Corps reaches Duisburg, Solingen, Düsseldorf and Werden, while the III Corps continues to collect the prisoners of war and prepares to be transferred to the US 3rd Army sector. The VII Corps consolidates its positions in the area between the rivers Mulde (in the west) and Elbe (in the north).

The 2nd and 9th Divisions of the V Corps are approaching Leipzig.

The divisions of the XV Corps (US 7th Army) converge on Nuremberg and begin the battle for the city, meeting with fierce resistance.

In the French 1st Army sector the II Corps takes Freudenstadt and cuts the German 19th Army in two.

Italian Front The advance of the Allied forces goes on without pause. In the western sector, the 92nd Division (US 5th Army) makes for Sarzana, while the IV Corps reaches Monte Ferra and Monte Moscoso.

On the eastern flank the Polish II Corps (British 8th Army) pushes on west of Medicina, while the XIII Corps reaches the river Gaiana.

Eastern Front The great battle for Berlin develops. The biggest breakthroughs are made by the 1st Ukraine Front over the Neisse, where three Russian armies are advancing rapidly towards the river Spree, driving back the 4th Armoured Army. The Army Group Centre loses ground in the south, where the Russians advance on Brno, but contains the enemy near Ratibor and Loslaw. On the front held by the Vistula Army Group there are violent clashes south of Frankfurt-on-the-Oder, where the Russian 33rd Army (1st Belorussian Front) is advancing.

In East Prussia, the remains of the German 2nd and 4th Armies have succeeded in retiring west of Königsberg in the area of Pillau, where they suffer heavy casualties from Russian air attacks.

On the Austrian front, the position of the 6th SS Armoured Army grows steadily worse south of St Pölten. Russian troops capture Wilhelmsburg.

Philippines: Luzon In the US I Corps sector, the 37th Division reaches the river Irisan and comes up against the last Japanese defence line before Baguio. The Japanese hold out for several days. The 32nd Division goes on mopping up in the hills round the Salacsac Pass, on the Villa Verde track. The Japanese are still defending the Kapintalan area very vigorously. In the XI Corps sector, the 6th Division eliminates the last Japanese resistance on Mount Mataba. In the XIV Corps sector, the US 1st Cavalry Division makes a little progress on the western slopes of Mount Mataasna Bundoc, the last major enemy position in the central southern part of Luzon.

Southern Philippines Assault units of the 24th Division (US X Corps), supported by aircraft, cruisers and destroyers, land on Mindanao Island, in the area of Cotabatu on the west coast. The landing force makes rapid progress, meeting with no opposition from the Japanese 35th Army (General Morozumi), and takes Parang and the hills overlooking Polloc Harbour. The town of Malabang has already been liberated by guerrillas.

On Cebu, the Americal Division occupies the positions evacuated by the Japanese on the hills round Cebu City. In the Sulu archipelago, Jolo Island is almost wholly liberated from the Japanese except for Mount Daho, which is hammered by aircraft, guns and mortars.

Okinawa The 6th Marine Division (III Amphibious Corps) takes the summit of Yae-Take, in the Motobu peninsula, having finally broken the Japanese. Meanwhile the Americans reinforce their line in the south. Facing the Shuri line there are now the 7th, 96th and 27th Divisions of General Hodges's XIV Corps, and supporting fire is given by 650 Marines aircraft, 27 groups of artillery, 6 battleships, 6 cruisers and 9 destroyers.

On Ie Shima the US 77th Division advances towards Mount Iegusugu, which dominates the whole island, and towards Ie, the chief town, where they reach the outskirts. The Japanese garrison in the north-east of the island puts up a particularly stiff resistance.

18 April

Western Front On the north of the front the Canadian I Corps (1st Army) reaches the Zuider Zee, which completes their mission.

While the XXX Corps (British 2nd Army) gets ready to launch the decisive attack against Bremen, Soltau and Ülzen are taken by units of the XII and VIII Corps.

In the Ruhr pocket, the XVIII Airborne Corps (US 1st Army) finishes off all organized German resistance and begins to mop up the scattered survivors. During the whole of the operation round the Ruhr pocket the Allies have taken 325,000 prisoners, more than twice the number of enemy troops that they believed they had encircled. Much of Halle is captured by the units of the 3rd Division (US VII Corps), while in the V Corps sector the 2nd and 69th

Divisions launch a co-ordinated attack against Leipzig.

The XV Corps steps up its attacks against Nuremberg, at the same time the 42nd Division (XXI Corps) enters Fürth, just west of Nuremberg, closing all the ways out of the town.

Italian Front The 10th Mountain Division (US IV Corps, 5th Army) reaches the Sulmonte–San Chierlo area, taking some 3,000 prisoners from the German XIV Armoured Corps.

On the right of the Allied line the V Corps (British 8th Army) takes Argenta. The Italian *Cremona* Combat Group takes part in the action.

Eastern Front In the north, between Stettin and Schwedt, five armies of the 2nd Belorussian Front begin to put pressure on the Vistula Army Group, crossing the Oder on a wide front.

The 1st Belorussian Front and 1st Ukraine Front make significant progress, overrunning two German defence lines on a wide front. The 4th Armoured Army is cut in two by the 1st Ukraine Front in the area of Forst, east of Cottbus.

The German Army Group Centre has to hold out against the heavy Russian pressure in Czechoslovakia also, in the area of Moravska-Ostrava and south of Brno, a town which has been declared a 'fortress' and will therefore be defended to the last man, even after it has been completely encircled by the enemy.

Philippines: Luzon In the US XIV Corps, the 11th Airborne Division resumes its attacks against Mount Macolod, gaining some ground.

Southern Philippines The troops of the US X Corps, under General Sibert, extend their beachhead on Mindanao; the 24th Division begins a combined amphibious and land operation against Fort Pikit, a first step towards the important crossroads at Kabacan. Other forces cross the Mindanao river and take Tamontaca and Cotabato without difficulty. Some units reach and occupy Lomopog, 20 miles from Cotabato. On Negros the 40th Division, with strong air support, attacks various

Japanese positions but has little success.

Okinawa In the III Amphibious Corps sector, the Marines pursue the Japanese northwards along the Itomi–Manna road, and then reduce the enemy pocket in the northern part of the island. In the south, in the XXIV Corps sector, some units occupy the inlet and village of Machinato, and a pontoon bridge is put up there enabling a number of companies to cross the inlet by night without being spotted by the enemy. There is furious fighting on the island of Ie Shima, where an American battalion manages to penentrate into the chief town, Ie, but has to withdraw to less exposed positions. The 306th Infantry makes good progress northeast, along the coast.

Burma The 5th Indian Division (British IV Corps) overcomes the resistance of the Japanese at Shwemyo and moves south towards Pyinmana.

19 April

Western Front Bremen is attacked by the XXX Corps (British 2nd Army). The XII Corps, advancing swiftly north, cuts the autobahn between Bremen and Hamburg, while the VIII Corps reaches the Elbe in the Lauenburg sector.

The XIX Corps (US 9th Army) reinforces its positions on the Elbe. The XVI Corps is ordered to organize the occupation and military government of the territory occupied by the 9th Army west of the river Weser.

Units of the VII Corps (US 1st Army) complete the capture of Halle, and those of the V Corps that of Leipzig. The XV Corps (US 7th Army) continues the attack on Nuremberg.

In the French 1st Army sector, the II Corps pushes on towards Stuttgart, while the I Corps occupies the western part of the Black Forest, reaching the area of Biberach and Mahlberg.

Italian Front The headquarters of the US 5th Army issues the directives for the imminent Spring offensive towards the Po. The plan is for the 92nd Division to advance in the direction of La Spezia, the IV Corps

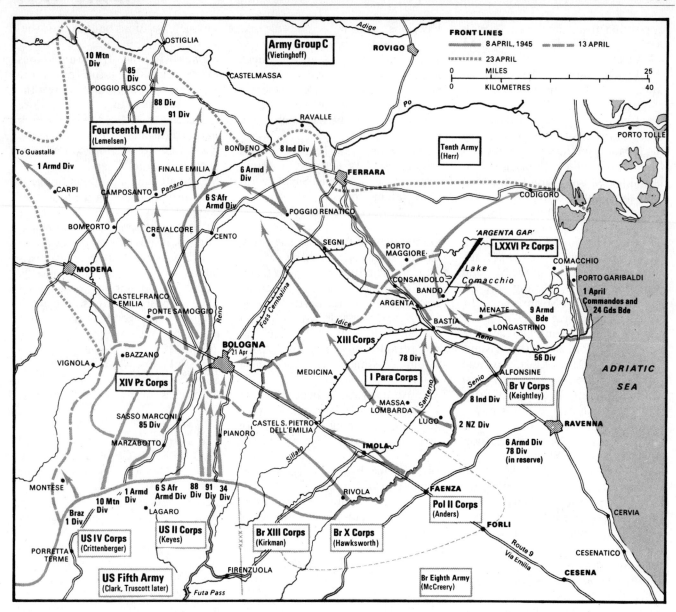

FRONT LINES
8 APRIL, 1945 — 13 APRIL
23 APRIL

0 — MILES — 25
0 — KILOMETRES — 40

Army Group C
(Vietinghoff)

ROVIGO

Fourteenth Army
(Lemelsen)

Tenth Army
(Herr)

10 Mtn Div
85 Div
POGGIO RUSCO
88 Div
91 Div
OSTIGLIA
CASTELMASSA
RAVALLE
Po
PORTO TOLLE

To Guastalla
1 Armd Div
CARPI
FINALE EMILIA
BONDENO
8 Ind Div
FERRARA
CODIGORO

6 Armd Div
CAMPOSANTO
Panaro
6 S Afr Armd Div
BOMPORTO
CREVALCORE
CENTO
POGGIO RENATICO
SEGNI
PORTO MAGGIORE
CONSANDOLO
BANDO
ARGENTA
'ARGENTA GAP'
LXXVI Pz Corps
COMACCHIO
PORTO GARIBALDI
1 April Commandos and 24 Gds Bde

MODENA
CASTELFRANCO EMILIA
PONTE SAMOGGIO
Reno
BOLOGNA
21 Apr
Lake Comacchio

VIGNOLA
BAZZANO
XIV Pz Corps
MEDICINA
XIII Corps
78 Div
MENATE
9 Armd Bde
LONGASTRINO
Reno
56 Div
ADRIATIC SEA
I Para Corps
BASTIA
ALFONSINE
Br V Corps
(Keightley)

SASSO MARCONI
85 Div
PIANORO
MARZABOTTO
CASTEL S. PIETRO DELL'EMILIA
MASSA LOMBARDA
Santerno
Senio
8 Ind Div
LUGO
2 NZ Div
RAVENNA

MONTESE
10 Mtn Div
1 Armd Div
Braz 1 Div
LAGARO
6 S Afr Armd Div
88 Div
91 Div
34 Div
Sillaro
IMOLA
RIVOLA
FAENZA
Pol II Corps
(Anders)
6 Armd Div
78 Div
(in reserve)
CERVIA

US IV Corps
(Crittenberger)
US II Corps
(Keyes)
Br XIII Corps
(Kirkman)
Br X Corps
(Hawksworth)
FORLI
Route 9 Via Emilia
CESENATICO
CESENA

PORRETTA TERME
US Fifth Army
(Clark, Truscott later)
FIRENZUOLA
Futa Pass
Br Eighth Army
(McCreery)

towards the Panaro and then across the Po between Ostiglia and Borgoforte, and the II Corps in the direction of Bologna, crossing the Po between Ostiglia and Sermide.

Eastern Front Moscow confirms that the great offensive against Berlin has begun. A number of bridgeheads over the Oder south of Stettin have been won by the 2nd Belorussian Front; the 1st Belorussian Front and 1st Ukraine Front are across the Neisse. Zhukov's forces are marching on Berlin from the bridgehead at Küstrin, and other forces have crossed the Neisse between Görlitz and Cottbus and are marching on Dresden. North-west of Görlitz the Polish II Army, incorporated in Konev's 1st Ukraine Front, takes Rothenburg. The 2nd Ukraine Front pushes on towards Moravska-Ostrava and, from the south, on Brno, while the 3rd Ukraine Front gains more ground south of Vienna. Bitter fighting continues in the area of Ratibor and Loslaw, and at Troppau and Breslau. The Germans announce that the Russians have crossed the Spree near Spremberg, and admit the loss of Forst, east of Cottbus.

In East Prussia there is hard fighting and heavy artillery fire by the Russians in the area of Pillau (Baltijsk), and the Germans suffer severe losses. Sixteen-year-olds are called up in Germany while fourteen-year-old

The last stages of the campaign in northern Italy, 8-23 April 1945.

boys and elderly men are mobilized in the *Volkssturm*, the People's Militia.

Philippines: Luzon In the Bicol peninsula, the 158th Regimental Combat Group attacks the Cituinan hills from three directions; the operation, with air and artillery support, goes on for a week. In the I Corps sector, the 37th Division takes a number of positions on the hills south and north-west of the crossing of the river Irisan, where a big bridge has been destroyed by the Japanese, who manage to hold on to some heights north-east of the river. The 33rd Division is engaged in fighting for Japanese cave positions in the Asin area. The 32nd Division advances in the Salacsac Pass area, while the 25th Division comes near to Kapintalan. On Mount Myoko, a powerful counter-attack by the Japanese is repulsed by the 27th Infantry. The 11th Airborne Division maintains its pressure on Mount Mataasna Bundoc, in the US XIV Corps sector. On Mount Macolod the Japanese are squeezed into a small pocket.

Okinawa At first light a barrage of steel and fire falls on the Japanese forward positions in the Shuri line. Then three divisions of the US XXIV Corps go into the assault, the 27th Division on the right and the 7th on the left, while the 96th exerts a lesser pressure in the centre. The clear object is to break through the wings so as to outflank the centre.

Burma The 20th Indian Division (British XXXIII Corps) reaches the Irrawaddy, taking Magwe and Myingun.

20 April

Western Front In the US 1st Army sector, the VII Corps prepares to attack the city of Dessau, at the confluence of the rivers Mulde and Elbe. The XX Corps (US 3rd Army) attacks towards the Danube in the area of Regensburg.

Nuremberg falls to the co-ordinated attack of three divisions, the 42nd, 3rd, and 45th (XV Corps, US 7th Army).

Stuttgart is attacked by the French II Corps (French 1st Army) together with the VI Corps of the American 7th Army. The French I Corps moves on towards the Danube in the direction of Sigmaringen.

Italian Front The US 5th Army comes down from the Apennines on to the Lombardy plain; the IV Corps reaches Casalecchio, in the neighbourhood of Bologna, and the II Corps takes the region between Casalecchio and Gesso.

In the British 8th Army sector, the X Corps reaches the river Idice, and the Polish II Corps and British XIII Corps establish bridgeheads over it. General Vietinghoff, Commander of the German Army Group C, orders the German forces (10th and 14th Armies) to withdraw on to the line of the Po. But his decision is too late, for the Allied armoured divisions are already hurling themselves on the German troops all along the line.

Eastern Front Battles rage from the Sudeten Mountains to the Gulf of Stettin. In the area between Stettin and Schwedt Rokossovsky's forces win a wide salient across the Oder, with its point on the river Randow. Further south, Zhukov's troops press on north and south of Spremberg; the Russian 33rd Army inflicts heavy losses on the German 9th Army. South of Cottbus the 1st Ukraine Front breaks through the front of the 4th Armoured Army and advances across the Spree towards Berlin, taking Calau. The Germans launch desperate counter-attacks north and south of Frankfurt-on-the Oder. North-west of Frankfurt there is also furious fighting in the Sternebeck and Prötzel areas. In Czechoslovakia the Russians exert incessant pressure on the industrial district of Moravska-Ostrava (Ostrava) and on Brno.

☐ Hitler celebrates his 56th birthday in the bunker at the Reichs Chancellery in Berlin.

Philippines: Luzon Units of the 37th Division (US I Corps) take the heights north-west of the crossing of the river Irisan. In the XI Corps sector the 145th Infantry, with sustained artillery support, keep up the pressure on Mount Pacawagan. The XIV Corps continues its attacks on Mount Mataasna Bundoc and Mount Macolod, most of which has already been captured.

Okinawa There is still savage fighting in front of the Shuri line, especially on Kakazu Ridge, where the Japanese take heavy toll of the American tanks. The American units manage to make good progress in this sector, but have to withdraw during the night in the face of furious Japanese counter-attacks.

The 6th Marine Division completes the mopping up of the Motobu peninsula.

Fighting continues on Ie Shima, where the 77th Division succeeds in surrounding the 'Pinnacle' in the Mount Iegusugu area, while in the south of the island it seizes a height that the Japanese are defending tenaciously, known to the Americans as 'Bloody Ridge'.

Off Okinawa the battleship *Colorado* is badly damaged by an accidental explosion, and the destroyer *Ammen* by a Japanese bomber.

21 April

Western Front The VII Corps of the US 1st Army begins the offensive against Dessau, sending in the 3rd Division after an intensive air bombardment.

The XV Corps (US 7th Army) advances towards Munich, while the XXI Corps heads for the Danube. The 100th Division, VI Corps, captures the bridges over the river Rems and draws near to Stuttgart.

The 5th Armoured Division of the French II Corps (1st Army) penetrates into Stuttgart from the south and quickly occupies the whole city.

Italian Front Units of the US 5th Army advance towards Bologna, which they enter a few hours after its capture by the Polish II Corps (British 8th Army). The Italian *Legnano* and *Friuli* Combat Groups also enter Bologna.

Eastern Front With the third of the enemy's prepared lines of resistance now broken, the 1st Belorussian Front advances rapidly north and south of Spremberg towards Berlin, where Russian armoured advanced units have already reached the extreme eastern suburbs. North-west of Görlitz, the 4th Armoured Army (already cut in two, puts up a strenuous resistance to the armies of the 1st Ukraine Front. In the north, between Stettin and Schwedt, the Vistula Army Group holds the 2nd Belorussian Front on the river Randow. In the south the Russian advance goes on north-west of Moravska-Ostrava (Ostrava), in Czechoslovakia, and south of St Pölten in Austria.

Philippines: Luzon In the US I Corps sector, the 37th Division takes the river Irisan crossing and goes over the river on a pontoon bridge to advance towards Baguio. Units of the 25th Division finally succeed in capturing the town of Kapintalan, and units of the 27th Division take some heights in the Mount Myoko area. In the XIV Corps sector, the 11th Airborne Division completes the capture of Mount Macolod, wiping out the last pocket of Japanese resistance. Filipino guerrilla units are given the task of garrisoning the region.

Southern Philippines Units of the US X Corps occupy Fort Pikit in Mindanao Island, the Japanese having evacuated it. Operations go ahead also on Negros and other small islands.

Okinawa Fierce fighting still rages between the US XXIV Corps and the experienced Japanese forces defending the Shuri line, in the south of the island. On Ie Shima, the US 77th Division takes the 'Pinnacle' and defends Bloody Ridge against a last Japanese counter-attack. After that, all organized Japanese resistance ceases, and mopping up begins. The savage battle for the capture of the island has lasted six days and cost the Americans the loss of about 1,000 men, killed, wounded and missing. The Japanese have lost 4,706 killed and 149 captured.

Japanese pilots launch yet another *kamikaze* attack against American shipping off Okinawa and sink a minesweeper and damage three destroyers and three minesweepers.

Burma In the British XXXIII Corps

sector, the 7th Indian Division surrounds Yenangyaung, where a strong Japanese rearguard gets ready to put up a determined resistance in order to cover the withdrawal of the main body of the Japanese forces in the sector towards Allanmyo. The 5th Indian Division advances rapidly to the south towards Toungoo, while the 17th is mopping up the Pyinmana area.

China The Japanese continue their advance on Chihchiang, and are engaged by the Chinese in the Keosha–Tungkow area. The Chinese High Command orders the 22nd Division to be air-lifted to Chihchiang, and the 14th Division is sent there in trucks provided by the US 475th Infantry Regiment.

22 April

Heinrich Himmler, who has taken command of the armies of the Rhine and the Vistula, meets Count Bernadette of the Swedish Red Cross in Lübeck. Himmler offers German surrender to the Western Allies, though not to the Russians. Bernadette transmits the verbal message to the Allies on 24 April.

Western Front While those units of the US 9th Army which have not yet reached the Rhine advance rapidly towards the west bank of the river, in the US 1st Army sector the VII Corps is still fighting for the city of Dessau.

The Divisions of the XXI Corps (US 7th Army) reach the Danube at Lauingen and near Dillengen, establishing bridgeheads over the river. Further south, the Danube is also reached and crossed by the VI Corps in the neighbourhood of Ehingen.

In the French 1st Army sector, the II Corps consolidates its positions in the Stuttgart sector and begins to occupy the sector south of Tübingen. The 1st Armoured Division (I Corps) advances swiftly along the Danube in the direction of Ulm.

Italian Front While the IV Corps (US 5th Army) reaches the Panaro, and then takes Modena, the British V Corps (8th Army) reaches Ferrara.

Eastern Front The 1st Belorussian Front, already on the outskirts of

Berlin, reaches the Fürstenwalde–Strausberg–Bernau line. From the south, the 1st Ukraine Front advances north in the direction of Berlin and west in the direction of Dresden. The German headquarters announces that the outer defences of the capital are beginning to be attacked by the enemy. In Czechoslovakia, the 4th Ukraine Front (Petrov) takes the road junction of Troppau (Opava) north-west of Moravska-Ostrava (Ostrava). The 2nd Belorussian Front extends its penetration between Stettin and Greifenhagen. The remaining German forces in East Prussia, regrouped in the Pillau area, are subjected to incessant pressure. There is no change in the situation in Austria and Yugoslavia.

Philippines: Luzon In the US I Corps sector, the 37th Division advances about 3 miles towards Baguio, while one regiment of the 33rd Division reaches the slopes of Mount Mirador, on the western outskirts of Baguio. The 32nd Division drives the Japanese from some hills along the Villa Verde track. In the south, in the XI Corps sector, American attacks persist against Mount Pacawagan and the Cituinan hills. Mount Mataasna Bundoc is virtually surrounded.

Southern Philippines The 31st Division (US X Corps) lands on Mindanao, while units of the 24th Division begin to cross the island, heading for Davao Bay. One battalion advances from Fort Pikit as far as the area of Kabacan. The Japanese forces on Mindanao are thus cut in two.

On Jolo Island units of the US 41st Division take the last Japanese strongpoints on Mount Daho. On Cebu the Americans advance from Cebu City to Toledo and from that town, following the north coast, to Tabuclan.

Okinawa In the south, on the US XXIV Corps front, the 27th Division improves its positions on the western flank of the line, but the Japanese hold on to Kakazu Ridge and other important positions. Units of the 96th Division seize the village of Nis-

APRIL 1945

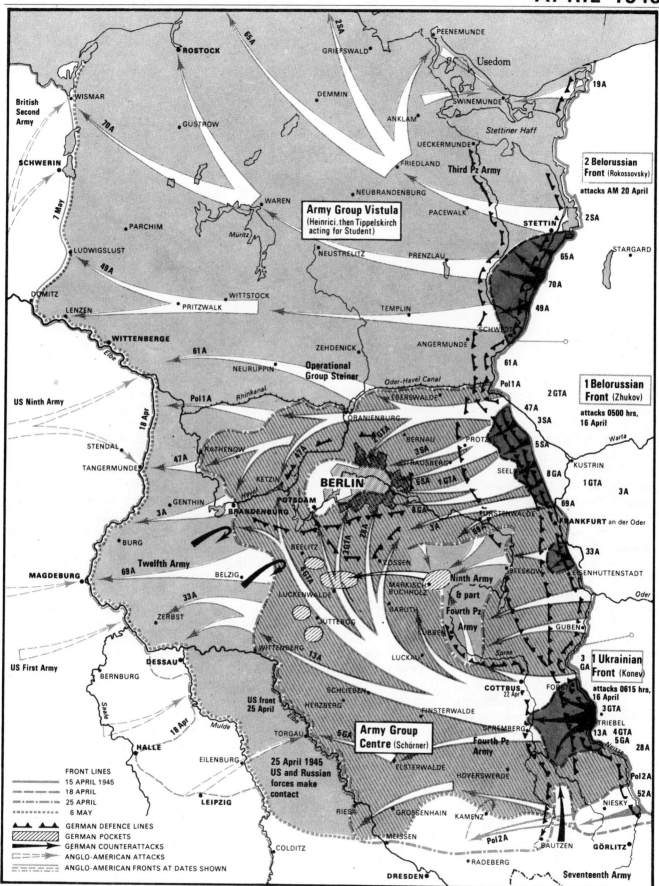

The final stages of the campaign on the Lastern Front.

hibaru but cannot reach the near-by Nishibaru Ridge.

Off Okinawa, Japanese suicide aircraft attack and damage three American destroyers and other ships.

Burma General Kimura, the Commander of the Japanese forces in Burma, orders the withdrawal of the main body of Japanese from Rangoon to the Pegu and Moulmein areas. In the British XXXIII Corps area, the 7th Indian Division takes Yenangyaung, the biggest oilfield in Burma; in the British IV Corps sector the 5th Division, advancing more quickly than had been expected, reaches Toungoo and sends some units south, in the direction of Oktwin.

23 April

Berlin. Hitler officially takes over command of the defence of Berlin. He tells Goebbels to announce that he will never leave the city. This gives the struggle the quality of the supreme defence of European cultural values against Bolshevism, their mortal enemy. The city's garrison, reinforced by troops withdrawn from the Oder, by 32,000 policemen, old men, women and the *Hitlerjugend* armed with the *Panzerfaust* (anti-tank gun), amounts to about 300,000. The defensive perimeter is held in the east by the *Münchberg* Armoured Division and the *Panzergrenadiere Nordland* Division, in the north by the 9th Airborne Division, in the west by the 20th Motorized Division; the 18th Armoured Division is held in reserve. The capital is meant also to be reinforced by the 200,000 men of the Frankfurt–Guben Group (at present south-east of the city and surrounded by the Russians) with their 2,000 guns and 200 tanks; by the Steiner operational group (at present north of the capital); and by General Wenck's 12th Army, which on the 24th is ordered to make for the Brandenburg area, east of the capital. But the expected reinforcements are unable to get through.

☐ Goering sends a telegram to Hitler proposing to assume control as Hitler's deputy. Hitler dismisses

Goering from all his offices and orders his arrest, which is carried out next day.

Western Front The XII Corps (British 2nd Army) reaches the Elbe opposite Hamburg.

The whole of the Dessau sector is in the hands of the 3rd Armoured Division (VII Corps, US 1st Army). The XV and XXI Corps (US 7th Army) push on towards the Danube, while the VI Corps continues its offensive across the river.

Italian Front The IV Corps (US 5th Army) crosses the Po near Guastalla and Luzzara.

In the British 8th Army sector, the XIII Corps establishes several bridgeheads over the Reno, while the 8th Division (V Corps) reaches Ferrara and the Po at Pontelagoscuro.

Eastern Front The armies of the 1st Belorussian Front, advancing from Spremberg, have reached the eastern border of Berlin, while the armies of the 1st Ukraine Front are swarming up from the south. In the south the Germans are resisting on the line Beelitz–Trebbin–Tetlow–Dahlewitz, but the Russians are on the point of closing the circle round the city, reaching the river Havel, west of Potsdam, from north and east.

South-east of Berlin the 1st Ukraine Front takes Cottbus, already by-passed and surrounded since the breakthrough on the Spree.

In Czechoslovakia the struggle goes on south of Brno and northwest of Moravska-Ostrava (Ostrava), with Schörner's Army Group Centre facing the 4th Ukraine Front and 2nd Ukraine Front.

The 5th Guards Army (1st Ukraine Front) advances from Eberswalde and makes firmly for the Elbe. Other forces of the 1st Front take Oranienburg, north of Berlin, and by-pass Frankfurt-on-the-Oder. The 1st Ukraine Front seizes Pulsnitz, northeast of Dresden.

Philippines: Luzon After a violent air bombardment of the area of Mount Mirador, south-west of Baguio, units of the 37th Division (US I Corps) advance as far as the cemetery at Baguio, where they are held up by Japanese fire. In the XI

Corps sector, the 6th Division carries on with the assault on Mount Pacawagan, liquidating the Japanese strongpoints one after another. The XIV Corps keeps up its pressure on enemy positions on Mount Mataasna Bundoc.

Southern Philippines Units of the US 24th Division take Kabacan, on Mindanao Island.

Okinawa In the area between Nishibaru and Tanabaru, the US 96th Division captures several hills; Japanese resistance seems to be weakening.

24 April

Western Front The XXX Corps (British 2nd Army) launches its offensive against Bremen; the VIII Corps approaches the Elbe near Lauenburg.

Units of the US 7th Army press on rapidly towards the Danube; the VI Corps reaches and takes Ulm.

The French II Corps (1st Army) continues its advance in the Black Forest and some of its units reach the Swiss frontier at Basel.

Italian Front In the US 5th Army sector the 92nd Division is ordered to move towards Genoa and the IV Corps heads for Villafranca airport, south of Verona. Units of the 34th Division reach Reggio Emilia. The British XIII and V Corps (8th Army) also succeed in establishing several bridgeheads over the Po, the first at Gaiaba and Stienta, the second west of Pontelagoscuro. The Committee for National Liberation orders general insurrection in northern Italy. The retreating German columns are attacked by the partisans who, on 25 April, take control of Milan.

Eastern Front The Russian 3rd and 28th Armies, 1st Ukraine Front, coming up from the south, penetrate into Berlin and join the forces of the 1st Belorussian Front already fighting inside the city. Savage encounters are reported by the Germans south of Potsdam, south-east of Brandenburg, and on the perimeter east and west of Berlin.

On the lower Oder front, the 2nd Belorussian Front engages the 3rd

Armoured Army (Vistula Army Group), extending its vast bridgehead between Schwedt and Stettin. The German 9th Army and part of the 4th Armoured Army are almost surrounded south of Fürstenwalde.

Philippines: Luzon Fighting less than a mile from Baguio, where the Americans capture the cemetery.

Southern Philippines The US 24th Division advances towards Digos in Davao Bay, on Mindanao Island.

Okinawa The XXIV Corps advances all along the line except on the western flank, occupying the outer strip of the Shuri line, from which the Japanese have retired during the night. The 96th Division occupies the positions on Nishibaru Ridge not captured previously, with some other heights.

Burma The Japanese are in retreat towards Moulmein and Toungoo.

25 April

Western Front The US 3rd Army continues its offensive in the direction of the Czechoslovak frontier and moves south of the Danube with the XX and III Corps. The US 7th Army, engaged along the Danube, crosses the river at several points north and south of the Dillingen bridgehead.

In the French 1st Army sector, the II Corps advances eastwards from the Sigmaringen area; the French I Corps is engaged by the remaining units of the German 19th Army, making a last desperate attempt to escape into the Bavarian Alps and concentrate its forces in the Black Forest before launching an offensive between Villengen and the Swiss frontier.

Italian Front While units of the IV Corps (American 5th Army) take Villafranca airport at Verona (10th Mountain Division) and Parma (3rd Division), the 88th Division (II Corps) liberates Verona. In the British 8th Army sector, the 56th Division and the Italian *Cremona* Combat Group cross the Po at Polesella and near the coast.

Eastern Front At Torgau, on the Elbe south of Berlin, the 5th Guards Army (1st Ukraine Front) makes the

first contact with the Americans of the 1st Army. The whole of Germany is now cut in two.

The 1st Belorussian Front and the 1st Ukraine Front join up north-west of Potsdam, near Ketzin. German headquarters announce that there is fighting in this area and near Nauen. South of the capital the Russians thrust ahead to a line Neubabelsberg–Zehlendorf–Neukölln and in the north there is fighting near Oranienburg.

Meanwhile the Russian troops are engaged in severe fighting with the Guben–Frankfurt group, consisting of the 9th Army and part of the 4th Armoured Army, south of Fürstenwalde. The group is never to get to Berlin nor are the Steiner operational group, or General Wenck's army.

In East Prussia, the 3rd Belorussian Front overcomes the Germans defending Pillau. What is left of the German forces takes refuge in the

Two G.I.s escort one of the first Japanese taken prisoner in the course of the long and bloody campaign for the capture of Okinawa.

narrow strip of land connecting the Samland peninsula to Danzig.

On the Czechoslovak front, forces of the 2nd Ukraine Front reach the outskirts of Brno, an important centre of armaments production.

In north-west Dalmatia, Tito's troops reach the area of Fiume.

The Germans, with a strength born of desperation, still manage to launch the occasional counterattack. Their 17th Army, for instance, succeeds in breaking through the lines of the 1st Ukraine Front in the area of Görlitz–Bautzen–Kamenz (south of Cottbus), inflicting heavy losses on the Russians.

Philippines: Luzon In the US I Corps sector the attack begins on Mount Mirador, near Baguio. Operations continue against Mount Pacawagan, in the XI Corps sector, and Mount Mataasna Bundoc and the Cituinan hills in the XVI Corps sector. During the night the Japanese begin to withdraw from the Cituinan hills.

Okinawa Powerful aerial, naval and artillery bombardment by the Americans against the main positions of the Shuri line.

China On the flanks of the main Japanese column heading for Chihchiang, the Chinese 58th Division is forced to withdraw and yield the town of Wukang.

□ Opening of the San Francisco Conference which is to last for two months to complete a charter for the United Nations Organisation.

26 April

Western Front The XXX Corps (British 2nd Army) completes the capture of Bremen, while the XII Corps is deployed along the west bank of the Elbe opposite Hamburg. Units of the XII Corps (US 3rd Army) penetrate into Austria in the vicinity of Lackenhausen. The XX Corps crosses the Danube southwest of Regensburg and the XX in the neighbourhood of Ingolstadt, after taking the city. Further south, the US 7th Army, having crossed the Danube at several points and established strong bridgeheads on the south bank, pushes on with the XXI Corps in the direction of Augsburg

and with the III towards Memming. The French 1st Army, reaching the frontier area between Basel and Lake Constance, completes the encirclement of the Black Forest.

Italian Front The IV and II Corps of the US 5th Army reach and cross the Adige in the area of Verona and Legnago; the XIII Corps (British 8th Army) west of Badia.

Eastern Front The armies of the 2nd Belorussian Front break through the German defences west of the Oder and capture Stettin.

In Berlin, savage house-to-house fighting continues. Units of the 1st Belorussian Front advance northeast of the capital, while other units continue the liquidation of the Guben–Frankfurt Group.

The 1st Ukraine Front (also engaged in Berlin) captures Torgau and Strehla, on the west bank of the Elbe. In Breslau there is still very severe fighting, and the Russians make progress in the western part of the city. In Czechoslovakia the 2nd Ukraine Front takes Brno and the 4th Ukraine Front puts pressure on Moravska-Ostrava.

In East Prussia, the 3rd Belorussian Front begins the liquidation of the German forces that have taken refuge in the tongue of land running west from Pillau.

Philippines: Luzon In the US I Corps sector the 129th Infantry of the 37th Division takes Mount Mirador, near Baguio.

Southern Philippines On Mindanao the 24th Division advances slowly on Digos.

On Negros a regimental combat group from the Americal Division lands on the south-east coast of East Negros, meeting with no resistance, and occupies the town of Dumaguete and the near-by airfield. Some units advance inland as far as San Antonio and the river Ocoy, where the Japanese offer the first resistance.

Burma In the British IV Corps sector, the 17th Indian Division reaches Dai-ku, on the road to Rangoon.

27 April

Berlin. Count Bernadotte arrives with the Western Allies' reply to

Himmler's offer: the Allies demand unconditional surrender of all fronts.

Western Front The XII Corps (US 3rd Army) reaches the Czechoslovak frontier north of Bischofsreuth. The units of the XX Corps extend their bridgehead in the area of Regensburg and obtain the surrender of the city.

In the US 7th Army sector the 20th Armoured Division (XV Corps) prepares for the attack on Munich. The VI Corps pushes on towards the Austrian frontier.

Italian Front Units of the US 5th Army continue to advance in north Italy; the 92nd Division reaches Genoa.

Eastern Front The 2nd Belorussian Front advances swiftly into Pomerania, taking Prenzlau and Angermünde. In Berlin the struggle for the streets is as bitter as ever. Three-quarters of the city is already in the hands of Zhukov's forces, attacking from the north, and Konev's, attacking from the south. The 1st Belorussian Front captures the suburb of Spandau, in the northwest, Potsdam and Rathenow. From the south-east, the German 9th Army tries in vain to fight its way through to Berlin, counter-attacking in the area of Zossen.

German headquarters admits the loss of Pillau in East Prussia.

Philippines: Luzon In the US I Corps sector, units of the 37th and 33rd Divisions take Baguio. There is still fighting in the area of Mount Myoko. In the XI Corps sector, units of the 6th Division reach the summit of Mount Pacawagan. In the XIV Corps sector, the 11th Airborne Division launches a determined attack against Mount Mataasna Bundoc, the last major Japanese position in southern Luzon.

Southern Philippines On Mindanao, units of the US 34th Division advance in the Digos area against strong Japanese opposition. The Americans try an outflanking manœuvre against Davao City; it is thought that this is the area where the Japanese will put up their final resistance.

Okinawa The Americans continue

After reading a statement, Philippe Pétain lapses into silence.

their attacks against the Japanese Shuri line positions with artillery, tanks and flame-throwers.
The heavy cruiser *Wichita* is damaged off Okinawa by the Japanese coast defence guns. Three destroyers and one fast transport are hit by suicide aircraft.
China The Chinese, with air support from the Americans, hold their posi-

tions in defence of the Ankang and Sian airfields and gradually go over to the counter-offensive.

28 April
Western Front The VIII Corps (British 2nd Army) and the XVIII Airborne Corps (US 1st Army) prepare to cross the Elbe in the Lünenburg and Bleckede sectors.

Further south, units of the XIX Corps (US 9th Army) occupy Zerbst, on the east bank of the Elbe.
Units of the XV and XXI Corps (US 7th Corps) approach Munich.
Italian Front The American 92nd Division (5th Army) reaches Alessandria. The 1st Armoured Division (US IV Corps) reaches Lake Como near the Swiss border, while Vicenza

is liberated by the II Corps.

Units of the XIII and V Corps (British 8th Army) advance towards Padua and Venice.

☐ Mussolini is captured by partisans as he prepares to leave Italy. He is executed at Giulino di Mezzenegra, near Dongo, on Lake Como, together with his mistress Clara Petacci and twelve other Fascist leaders.

Eastern Front In Berlin, Zhukov's forces advance to the river Spree in the Moabit district, while Konev's, coming from the south, reach the Unter den Linden and the Tiergarten. Between these two armies are the Reichstag and the Chancellery Bunker, where Hitler lives in an imaginary world, refusing to face reality. General Heinrici, commander of the Vistula Army Group (or what is left of it) is dismissed for not having followed the 'scorched earth' policy in front of the Russians. He is replaced by the Luftwaffe general Kurt Student; in the interim command is taken over by General Tippelskirch. The 2nd Belorussian Front advances into Pomerania, west of Prenzlau.

In the south, the Russians occupy Ingolstadt and Regensburg. Meanwhile, the 1st Ukraine Front attacks the salient taken by the German 17th Army in the course of counterattacks north of Bautzen.

Philippines: Luzon In the US I Corps sector, the 37th and 33rd Divisions advance north of Baguio. In the XIV Corps sector all organized resistance by the Japanese in the Bicol peninsula ceases.

Southern Philippines On Mindanao, units of the US 24th Division take Digos, cutting the island in two. The 19th Infantry attack towards Davao. On Negros Japanese resistance is virtually at an end.

Okinawa Four American destroyers and some other ships are seriously damaged by Japanese suicide bombers off Okinawa. In the south of the island severe fighting continues along the Shuri line, notably on the Maeda Escarpment, in the area of the Kochi Ridge and in the village of Kuhazu.

Burma The British XV Corps completes the recapture of the Arakan area, occupying Taungup. In the British XXXIII Corps sector the 20th Indian Division captures Allanmyo on the way to Prome.

29 April

Western Front The VIII Corps (British 2nd Army) crosses the Elbe near Lauenburg to begin the army's last action, the Baltic its objective. The advance of the US 3rd Army in the Danube sector continues; units of all corps reach the river Isar.

The XV Corps (US 7th Army) begins the assault on Munich and captures some suburbs of the city. The notorious Dachau concentration camp reveals its horrors.

Italian Front At Caserta, Colonel Schweinitz and his adjutant, Wenner, representing General Vietinghoff, Commander of the German Army Group C in Italy, sign the document for the unconditional surrender of all German troops in Italy with effect from 1.00 p.m. GMT (2.00 p.m. in Italy) on Wednesday 2 May 1945. Besides British and American officers, the Russian General Kislenko is also present at the signing of the surrender.

However, the Allied advance goes on in north Italy; units of the American IV Corps reach Milan, which has already been liberated by the partisans, while the British V Corps reaches Venice and the New Zealand 2nd Division (British XIII Corps), advancing towards Trieste, reaches the Piave.

Eastern Front The 2nd Belorussian Front advances rapidly along the Baltic coast towards Stralsund, taking Anklam and penetrating into Mecklenburg. In Czechoslovakia the 2nd Ukraine Front gains ground east of Brno and south of Olmütz. Southeast of Brno, the Russians capture Austerlitz, while the 4th Ukraine Front, presses on relentlessly northwest of Moravska-Ostrava.

In Berlin the situation reaches its climax. Fierce fighting rages round the Reichstag and the Chancellery, along the Potsdamer Strasse and in the Belle Alliance Platz. South of Cottbus, the Germans hold Russian pressure in the area between Bautzen and Meissen.

☐ Hitler orders that the war must be carried on from the 'Alpine Fortress' in the south of Germany, and appoints Grand Admiral Doenitz his successor as Head of State. Hitler marries Eva Braun.

Okinawa In the centre of the American positions, the 77th Division begins gradually to take over from the 96th Division, weakened by the severe fighting on the Maeda Escarpment Violent Japanese counter-attacks and attempts to infiltrate are held by the Americans in the central sector. The 383rd Infantry captures a salient from which it is possible to bring down artillery fire on the centre of Shuri, the site of the headquarters of the 32nd Army (General Ushijima). On Kochi Ridge, the 7th Division is pinned down by deadly Japanese fire and suffers heavy losses.

The *kamikaze* attacks on American ships off Okinawa continue; today's victims are two destroyers and three minelayers.

Burma In the British IV Corps sector, the 17th Indian Division reaches the outskirts of Pegu.

China The Chinese reinforce the defences of Chihchiang and Ankiang with over 15,000 men of the new 6th Army.

30 April

Western Front In the British 2nd Army sector, while the VIII Corps extends and reinforces the bridgehead over the Elbe at Lauenburg, units of the XVIII Airborne Corps begin to advance from the Elbe towards the Baltic Sea. Munich is taken by the XV Corps (US 7th Army); the XXI and VI Corps push on towards the Austrian frontier in the Garmisch-Partenkirchen and Resenheim sectors.

The French 1st Army enters Austria in the vicinity of Bregenz.

Italian Front The 92nd Division (US 5th Army) reaches Turin, while in the east units of the II Corps reach Treviso. The British XIII Corps presses on towards Trieste.

Eastern Front At 3.30 p.m. Hitler commits suicide in the Chancellery

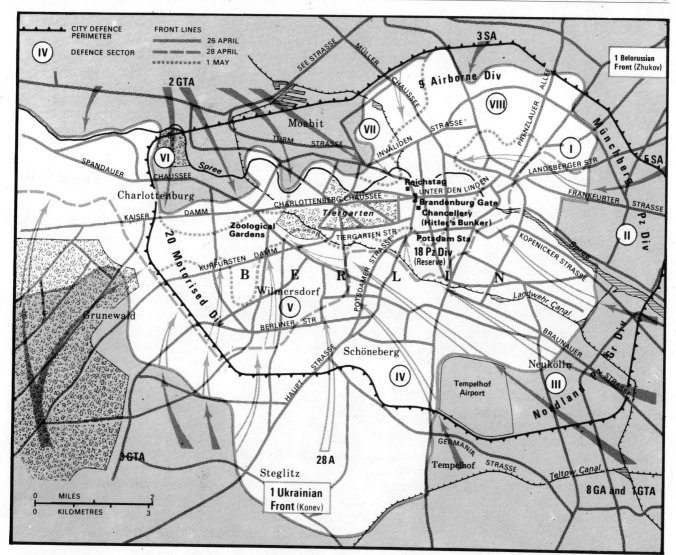

The bitterly-contested battle for central Berlin 26 April-1 May.

Bunker. Eva Braun dies with him. There is no more news of the 9th Army, while all hope is given up of any possibility that Wenck's 12th Army can reach the city. After very severe fighting lasting all day, at 10.50 p.m. three assault battalions of the Russian 150th Infantry Division capture the Reichstag; Lieutenant Berest and two sergeants plant the Soviet flag on the equestrian statue that represents Germany in triumph. During the night General Krebs, Chief of Staff of the Wehrmacht, asks to be allowed to negotiate the surrender of the city to General Zhukov, commander of the army operating in the Chancellery area.

In Czechoslovakia, the Russians take Moravska-Ostrava after a long struggle by the 4th Ukraine Front. The German army is half destroyed;

Army Group South (since 6 April commanded by Rendulic), 600,000 men strong, and Army Group Centre (Schörner), with 1,200,000 men, are still able to fight. Fight they do, but only to clear a way through the enemy armies and make their way back to the west. Army Group South is successful, and a good part of it reaches the American lines.

In the north, in the 2nd Front sector the Russians advance from Anklam on Stralsund, Peenemünde and Ribnitz; from Prenzlau on Neustrelitz and Waren; and from Angermünde on Templin. The struggle for Breslau continues; the German garrison is surrounded but does not surrender. *Philippines: Luzon* In the US XIV Corps sector the Americans take Mount Malepuny, but there are still pockets of Japanese resistance.

**Top: some of the Fascist leaders executed by Italian partisans at Dongo on Lake Como.
Above: bodies of the shot Fascists (including Mussolini) strung up by their feet in Milan.**

Southern Philippines On Mindanao, the US 24th Division (X Corps) advances to within 4 miles of Davao, taking Talomo and the airfield at Daliao.

Okinawa On the western flank of the US XXIV Corps the 1st Marine Division relieves the battle-weary 27th Division. The 77th Division, taking over from the 96th, pursues the costly battle for the Maeda Escarpment. There is no progress on the Kochi Ridge.

Another American destroyer is hit by Japanese suicide aircraft off Okinawa. US Navy losses in this sector since 26 March amount to 20 ships sunk and 157 damaged. Even for such a powerful fleet as the American, this is a disturbing haemorrhage. In the same period the Japanese have lost over 1,100 aircraft, counting only those shot down by the US Navy.

Burma In the British IV Corps sector, the 17th Indian Division penetrates into the town of Pegu and begins mopping up there. Forces from the British XV Corps sail from Rangoon (Operation *Dracula*).

China The Chinese 58th Division is forced to retire on prepared positions in the Wa-wu-tang area, under Japanese pressure.

1 May

It is announced on Hamburg radio that Hitler has died in Berlin, fighting for Germany, and that Admiral Doenitz is his successor.

Western Front In the British 2nd Army sector the units of the VIII Corps advance towards Lübeck and Hamburg. The US 9th Army ends its offensive with its three corps, the XIII, XIX and XVI, firmly dug in along the western banks of the Elbe. In the US 7th Army sector, while the XV Corps proceeds with the mopping up of the Munich area, the VI Corps presses on towards Innsbruck and Imst.

The French 1st Army crosses the Austrian frontier and occupies Bregenz.

Italian Front The II Corps (American 5th Army) begins the liberation of the Piave valley and prepares to advance towards Austria across the Brenner Pass.

Eastern Front General Krebs is received by General Zhukov and asks for a truce. The Russian general demands unconditional surrender, and Krebs returns to the Bunker to report. Bormann and Goebbels want to go on with the struggle, but General Weidling, the Berlin garrison commander, decides on surrender. Goebbels has himself, his wife and his six children killed, Krebs commits suicide, Bormann escapes. After signing the surrender Weidling issues an order to the army and the people of Berlin for the immediate cessation of resistance of any kind. However, there are still a number of fanatical groups who hold out in the heart of the city. In the north the 2nd Belorussian Front spreads out along the Baltic coast and in Mecklenburg, taking Stralsund. Tito's forces, who entered Trieste on the previous day, make contact with the New Zealand 2nd Division on the Isonzo, near Monfalcone. The position of the 150,000 Germans in Löhr's Army Group E, left behind in Yugoslavia, is hopeless.

Okinawa With mountaineers' nets and ladders, units of the 77th Division try to scale the steep east wall of the Maeda Escarpment; some manage to reach the top, but are driven off by a furious night counterattack by the Japanese.

Burma Operation *Dracula* begins: two Gurkha (Nepalese) parachute battalions land at the mouth of the Irrawaddy south of Rangoon.

Dutch East Indies The XXVI Brigade of the Australian 9th Division lands on the island of Tarakan, north-east of Borneo, and begins the occupation of this important oil-bearing district.

2 May

Western Front Near Barow and Abbendorft the XIII Corps (US 9th Army) makes contact with the Red Army. The V Corps of the US 1st Army reinforces its positions along the Czechoslovak frontier.

Units of the XX Corps (US 3rd Army) reach the river Inn near

Passau and Neuhaus. The III Corps also continues to advance towards the Inn.

While the XV Corps (US 7th Army) prepares to advance on Salzburg, the XXI Corps moves along the Inn to the south towards the Degerndorf area. Negotiations for surrender begin between the American VI Corps and the defenders of Innsbruck.

The French I Corps (1st Army) reaches Obersdorf and Goetzis, in Austria.

Italian Front On the strength of the document signed by the Germans at Caserta on 29 April, hostilities cease

A Russian soldier raises the Soviet flag on the Reichstag building in Berlin.

on the whole front and the unconditional surrender of the German forces comes into effect.

Eastern Front In the north, the German forces are driven back to a line running from Rostock to Lake Müritz and Neuruppin.

In Berlin, the 28th Army of the 1st Ukraine Front and the 2nd Army of the 1st Belorussian Front join up on the Charlottenberg Chaussee and carry on with the liquidation of the last nests of resistance. Following the armistice in Italy, the British advance towards the Alpine passes leading to Styria and Carinthia, in the rear of Army Group E. Rendulic takes over command of Army Group South, until now under Wöhler. German resistance continues in Breslau and on the tongue of land near Pillau, Bay of Danzig. In Czechoslovakia, the Russians advance south-west of Moravska-Ostrava and east of Brno.

Philippines: Luzon In the US I Corps sector, the 25th Division continues to attack the Kembu plateau and takes a number of positions. The 145th Infantry (XI Corps) completes the mopping up operation on Mount Pacawagan. The remaining Japanese forces in the Bicol peninsula regroup round Mount Isarog, north-east of Anayan.

Southern Philippines On Mindanao, the 108th Regimental Combat Group lands in Macajalar Bay. The 24th Division runs into determined resistance by the Japanese on the river Davao, but manages to establish a small bridgehead over it.

On Negros, the Americal Division crosses the river Ocoy and takes Badiang, proceeding towards Ticala and Odlumon.

Okinawa While the Americans still vainly hammer away at the Shuri line, the Japanese General Ushijima decides to mount a big counter-offensive on 4 May. He asks Tokyo to step up the *kamikaze* attacks on American ships, which are providing powerful supporting fire to the Americans' land operations.

Burma The 26th Indian Division lands at the mouth of the Rangoon river and advances on Rangoon without meeting any enemy resist-

The battle of Berlin is ended. In much of the city nothing is left but rubble and ruins.

ance, just as the parachutists had done when they were dropped the previous day. The city, heavily bombed by the Allies on 26 April, has been evacuated by the Japanese. In the British XXXIII Corps sector, the 20th Indian Division is at the gates of Prome, on the Irrawaddy, north of Rangoon, cutting off the last route by which the Japanese can

retreat from the Arakan. The 17th Indian Division (British IV Corps) completes the capture of Pegu, north-east of Rangoon.

3 May

Western Front While Field-Marshall Montgomery refuses to accept the surrender of the German forces

Troops and vehicles of the Red Army pause for a rest in front of the Chancellery building.

in the north, including those on the Eastern Front, the British XII Corps (2nd Army) receives the surrender of Hamburg. The VIII Corps follows up the enemy towards the Kiel Canal, while the XVIII Airborne Corps finishes off its offensive operations when it reaches the Baltic west of Klütz. In the US 3rd Army sector, units of the XIII Corps push on in the direction of Linz. The 65th Division (XX Corps) crosses the Inn, while the whole corps moves on eastwards and makes contact with the Red Army. The XV Corps (US 7th Army) advances rapidly towards Salzburg and the XXI Corps crosses the Austrian border and reaches the Reisach area. In the VI Corps sector, negotiations for the surrender of Innsbruck are still going on.

Eastern Front Russian forces wipe out last nests of resistance in Berlin. Advancing into Mecklenburg and Brandenburg on a wide front, Rokossovsky's armies (2nd Belorussian Front) reach the line Wismar–

Wittenberg, linking up with units of the Allied 21st Army Group (Montgomery). South-east of Wittenberg forces of the 1st Belorussian Front are met on the Elbe by units of the US 9th Army. In Czechoslovakia the 2nd and 4th Ukraine Fronts advance north-east of Brno and south-west of Moravska-Ostrava.

Philippines: Luzon The US XIV Corps continues the liquidation of the remaining Japanese forces in the Bicol peninsula. In the US I Corps sector units of the 25th Division prepare to attack Mount Haruna, an important height west of the Balete Pass.
Southern Philippines Units of the US 24th Division occupy the ruins of Davao, on Mindanao Island, and advance as far as Santa Ana, while advanced guards of the 31st Division take Kibawe, with its airfield, and advance along the Talomo track.
On Negros the Americal Division is mainly engaged in the south of the island, where the Japanese have succeeded in cutting its supply lines.
Okinawa The 1st Marine Division, the 77th Division and the 7th Division persist all day in their attacks against the Maeda Escarpment and Kochi Ridge, but are pinned down by murderous Japanese fire. During the night the Japanese launch their only large-scale offensive of the campaign, attempting to land forces behind the American lines both on the east and on the west coast. The amphibious operation fails; almost all the landing craft are destroyed and the small forces that manage to land are wiped out. The effort costs the Japanese about 700 men. As requested by General Ushijima, the counter-offensive is preceded by a violent *kamikaze* attack, in the course of which the Japanese succeed in sinking three American destroyers and damaging the light cruiser *Birmingham*, three destoyers and other ships. One transport is hit by an explosive boat and a minesweeper by a piloted flying bomb.
Burma The 20th Indian Division, coming down the Irrawaddy valley, takes Prome. The 26th Indian Division enters Rangoon and

Meeting of American and Cossack units in Saxony.

Syiram, on the opposite bank of the river; both have been evacuated by the Japanese.

4 May

Western Front At 6.20 p.m. German representatives sign the document of unconditional surrender by the armed forces of the Reich in Holland, north-west Germany and Denmark, to the Commander of the 21st Army Group, Field-Marshal Montgomery.
Units of the V Corps (US 1st Army) prepare to advance into Czechoslovakia, towards Karlsbad (Karlovy Vary) and Pilsen (Plzen).
In the US 3rd Army sector the XX Corps completes the crossing of the river Inn.
Salzburg surrenders to the XV Corps of the US 7th Army, whose units push on towards Berchtesgaden. The VI Corps accepts the surrender of Innsbruck.
Officers of the German 19th Army arrive at the headquarters of the 44th Division (VI Corps, US 7th Army) to discuss arrangements for surrender.

Eastern Front German headquarters admit the end of the struggle for Berlin. Fighting continues (mostly rearguard actions against the Russians, while the bulk of the German units try to reach the British–American lines) in the north between Wismar and Schwerin, in Czechoslovakia, south-east of Moravska-Ostrava and in Austria in the St Pölten sector. In Dalmatia, Tito's forces enter Fiume and threaten Pola.

Philippines: Luzon In the US I Corps sector, units of the 25th Division take Mount Haruna, a few hundred yards west of the Balete Pass. North-west of Manila, in the XI Corps sector, the 145th Infantry attack towards Guagua but are driven back by the Japanese.
Southern Philippines On Mindanao the US 24th Division begins mopping up in the Davao area, while a regiment of the 31st Division carries out patrol activities north of Zibawe. One regiment of the 41st Division reaches Parang, north of Cotabato, from Zamboanga, and other forces land north of Digos, near Santa Cruz, on the east coast.
On Negros the Americal Division tries again to reopen its supply lines, cut by the Japanese, in the eastern part of the island.
Okinawa The *kamikaze* attacks continue in support of the Japanese land offensive. The airfield at Yontan is heavily bombed, while suicide aircraft and piloted flying bombs sink fourteen small ships and damage the escort carrier *Sangamon*, one destroyer and other American ships fairly seriously. 131 Japanese aircraft are brought down.
On land, the Japanese 32nd Army counter-attacks with great vigour all day. The artillery, formerly concealed, is brought out into the open to support the infantry better, but this makes the guns easy targets for the American counter-battery fire. The Japanese concentrate their thrust on the front of the 7th and 77th Divisions, but are unable to break through, and suffer heavy losses. Although not directly involved in the counter-offensive, the 1st Marine Division has very high

casualties when it attacks the Machinato airfield, in the west. Despite the Japanese counter-attacks, the Americans manage to improve their positions on the Maeda Escarpment.

Burma Admiral Mountbatten gets the headquarters of the British Pacific Fleet to promise him, in addition to the ships already allocated to him, the support of three aircraft carriers for Operation *Zipper* (the recapture of Malaya). The advance of the British XV Corps north of Rangoon, and that of the IV and XXXIII Corps coming down from the north, threatens to cut off the Japanese 28th Army (General Sakurai) from the rest of the Japanese forces in Burma (General Kimura). The great Irrawaddy river is between the two armies.

5 May

Eastern Front Grand Admiral Doenitz orders German troops to cease all resistance in north-west Germany, Holland and Denmark, following the signature of the surrender the previous day. But resistance to the Russians continues. There is fierce fighting in Czechoslovakia, near Olmütz, while the Army Group Centre carries out a fighting withdrawal south-east of Moravska-Ostrava. There is a rising in Prague. Fighting is also raging near Trieste, Abbazia and Fiume, and in East Prussia on the Frische Nehrung (Baltijskaya Kosa), the strip of shore between Danzig and Königsberg.

At Haar, in Bavaria, representatives of Army Group G under General Hausser (1st and 19th Armies) sign the unconditional surrender demanded by the Allies.

Philippines: Luzon In the US I Corps sector, the 25th Division continues operations for the capture of Balete Pass. In the XI Corps sector there is a pause in the operations against Guagua.

Southern Philippines On Negros, units of the Americal Division succeed in re-forming the supply lines between the west and east of the island.

Okinawa The Japanese counter-

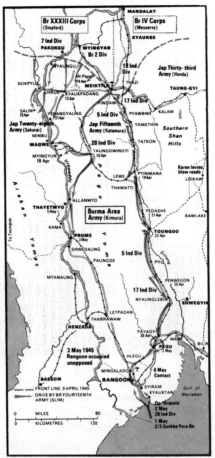

The British offensive for the capture of Rangoon 9 April–3 May 1945.

offensive continues, concentrated on the sector of the American 7th and 77th Divisions. Some units manage to penetrate the American lines, recapturing the town of Tanabaru and Tanabaru Ridge. While one regiment of the US 77th Division holds up the enemy, another captures the south side of the Maeda Escarpment and holds it against the Japanese when they counter-attack during the night.

Two ships are damaged by Japanese suicide aircraft.

Burma With the recapture of Rangoon by the 26th Indian Division, the objectives set by Admiral Mountbatten may be thought to have been achieved. But there are still huge Japanese forces to be eliminated in the middle of the country.

6 May

Western Front Pilsen, in Czechoslovakia, is reached by the 97th Division (V Corps, US 3rd Army). The XII

Corps advances towards Prague.

Eastern Front Fighting continues in Czechoslovakia, near Olmütz, in East Prussia, on the Frische Nehrung, and in Croatia against Tito's troops.

Philippines: Luzon In the US I Corps sector, the 25th Division continues operations towards Balete Pass; one of its regiments finally takes the Kembu plateau. In the XI Corps sector, the 43rd Division advances on Ipo. Aircraft and artillery prevent the Japanese from counter-attacking.

Southern Philippines On Mindanao, the US 24th and 31st Divisions overrun the Japanese positions north of Davao, where the main body of the Japanese 35th Army under General Morozumi is concentrated.

Okinawa The 1st Marine Division, on the right of the American line, is held up by the resolute resistance of the enemy on the heavily fortified Shuri line. One regiment of the 77th Division makes slight progress south of the Maeda Escarpment, in the centre. The units of the 7th Division are gradually eliminating the Japanese units that infiltrated into the Tanabaru area.

Burma The 76th Brigade of the 26th Indian Division (XV Corps), advancing north of Rangoon, makes contact with the 17th Indian Division (IV Corps) at Hlegu. As a result the Japanese 28th Army is cut off from the rest of the Japanese forces in Burma.

Dutch East Indies The Japanese are forced to evacuate the town of Tarakan on the island of that name, near the north-east coast of Borneo.

7 May

At Rheims, at 1.41 a.m. in Eisenhower's headquarters, German representatives sign the unconditional surrender of all German armed forces to the Allies. The surrender will be effective from one minute past midnight on 9 May, but on the Western Front all military action stops immediately.

Eastern Front Troops of the 1st Belorussian Front reach the Elbe north and south-east of Magdeburg.

In Silesia the resolute defence of Breslau finally comes to an end, and the city is taken by the 1st Ukraine Front. In Czechoslovakia fighting still continues north of Olmütz and in the town itself. On the Frische Nehrung, in East Prussia, the remaining German forces still hold out against the Russians near the village of Vogelsang.

Philippines: Luzon In the US XI Corps sector units of the 145th Infantry attack south-east of Mount Pacawagan towards a ridge near Guagua, but are firmly repulsed by the Japanese. The US 43rd Division advances some five miles in the direction of Ipo.

Southern Philippines Fighting continues on Mindanao and Negros.

Okinawa The fruitless American attacks on the Shuri line positions continue; the 1st Marine Division, on the right flank, tries unsuccessfully to seize Height 60.

In the centre, the 77th and 7th Divisions maintain pressure but make scarcely any progress in the direction of Shuri village and Yonabaru. Units of the 7th Division complete the liquidation of Japanese units that infiltrated into the Tanabaru area. South of the town of Kochi a strong Japanese position is holding up the advance of other units of the 7th Division, which confine

themselves to improving their positions on Kochi Ridge.

8 May

President Truman declares 9 May to be 'V-E Day', the day of Victory in Europe.

The German surrender to the Russians is signed at Karlshorst, near Berlin.

Eastern Front The remains of the German 16th and 18th Armies, cut off for months in northern Latvia, surrender to the Leningrad Front. South and south-east of Berlin, Dresden and Görlitz surrender to the armies of the 1st Ukraine Front, some units of which cross the Czechoslovak frontier and advance south towards Prague, where the patriots in revolt are already attacking the Germans. Units of the 4th Ukraine Front take Olmütz and Sternberk, north of Olmütz.

In Croatia the Germans are still fighting against Tito's troops, who liberate Zagreb.

Philippines: Luzon In the US XI Corps sector, the 145th Infantry overcomes Japanese resistance and takes the ridge near Guagua southeast of Mount Pacawagan, coming within 500 metres of Guagua and blocking a track along the river Mariquina.

Southern Philippines On Mindanao, units of the US 24th Division estab-

lish a bridgehead over the river Talomo, north of Mintal, in spite of strong Japanese resistance. The 31st Division clears up the Colgan woods, and some units reach Maramag airfield. American units land on Samar Island.

On Negros the Americans in the south of the island continue their slow progress against strong Japanese opposition.

Okinawa Torrential rain holds up operations by land, sea and air. The 1st Marine Division blows up several enemy positions in caves on Nan Hill which were holding up the advance on Height 60. On the east coast the 7th Division improves its positions.

9 May

Eastern Front At one minute past midnight, hostilities in Europe officially come to an end. But German resistance persists in Czechoslovakia, Austria and Croatia. The 1st Ukraine Front liberates Prague, with the collaboration of the Czechoslovak insurgents. Troops of the 2nd Belorussian Front liberate the island of Bornholm in Denmark. On the northern front, the German troops left in East Prussia and around Danzig surrender to the 2nd and 3rd Belorussian Fronts. The 3rd Ukraine Front, advancing westwards in Austria, reaches Graz and Amstetten and near the latter town makes contact with the American troops.

Philippines: Luzon In the US I Corps sector, Japanese resistance is lessening in the Balete Pass area. In the XI Corps sector, units of the 145th Infantry take Mount Binicayan and send patrols into the Guagua area.

Southern Philippines The 108th Regimental Combat Group leaves Cebu and Leyte for Macajalar Bay, Mindanao Island. Here, units of the 24th Division are defending the bridgehead over the river Talomo against Japanese counter-attacks, but have not succeeded in putting up a bridge. The units of the 31st Division break off their attacks in the Colgan woods, where air attacks and mortar fire are brought to bear on the Japanese positions.

Okinawa General Buckner orders

Rheims, 7 May 1945: General Alfred Jodl (centre) signs the document of unconditional surrender of all the German armed forces.

V-E day in Paris: de Gaulle at the Arc de Triomphe.

the US 10th Army to launch a general offensive against the Shuri line on 11 May. The attack is to be concentrated on the two wings. The 6th Marine Division, on the right flank, prepares to attack on the river Asa. The 1st Marine Division takes Height 60 after wiping out the last Japanese positions on Nan Hill. The 77th Division continues the destruction of Japanese strong-points north of Shuri. The Japanese are now cleared from the Kochi Crest area.

Burma Advancing south from Taungup along the Arakan coast, the 82nd West African Division occupies Sandoway.

10 May

Eastern Front The 1st, 2nd, 3rd and 4th Ukraine Fronts join up when they reach Klagenfurt and Linz in Austria, and also make contact with the Americans.

Philippines: Luzon In the US XI

Corps sector, the advance of the 43rd Division slows down near Ipo.

Southern Philippines On Mindanao, a US naval assault group under command of Rear-Admiral Struble lands the 108th Regimental Combat Group on the coast of Macalajar Bay. With support from Filipino guerrillas, the beachhead is immediately extended and consolidated. Some units advance about 5 miles to the south-east, joining up with units of the 31st Division. Units of the 19th Infantry begin the liquidation of a number of enemy pockets in the Davao area.

Okinawa At 3.00 a.m. the 22nd Regiment of the 6th Marine Division begins the attack against the estuary of the river Asa, occupying a bridgehead about a mile wide and 400 yards deep. During the next night a Bailey bridge is put up to allow tanks and artillery to cross. The 1st Marine Division makes slight progress in the

direction of Shuri under deadly Japanese fire.

Japanese suicide aircraft hit one American destroyer and one minelayer off Okinawa.

11 May

Eastern Front Units of the 1st and 2nd Ukraine Fronts wipe out the last German resistance in Czechoslovakia and make contact with the Americans at Pilsen. In Austria too the Russians force some German units to surrender. In Croatia the German Army Group South-East (formerly Army Group E, under Löhr) continues to hold out against Tito's forces.

Philippines: Luzon In the US I corps sector, units of the 25th and 27th Divisions make contact with each other on Kapintalan Ridge, after blocking up or blowing up over 200 Japanese positions in caves and killing 1,000 enemy troops. The 25th Division advances on Santa Fe.

Southern Philippines On Mindanao, the 108th Regimental Combat Group advances as far as some hills that overlook the airfield at Del Monte. Units of Filipino guerrillas liberate Cagayan.

A reinforced regiment of the 24th Division is ordered to mop up the area north-east of the Talomo river, near Mintal. Small American units landed on Samar Island try to spot the Japanese artillery sites which are still bringing fire down on Davao. Fighting continues on Negros Island, mainly in the mountainous area in the west.

Okinawa After a 30-minute artillery barrage the whole of the US 10th Army, with the III Amphibious Corps on the right and the XXIV Corps on the left, goes into the assault against the Shuri line. The 6th Marine Division advances south of the river Asa; some units reach the outskirts of Amike, taking positions that overlook the island's chief town, Naha. The 7th Marines of the 1st Division, despite intensive fire from the enemy, wins several positions on Dakeshi Ridge. But the 1st Marines cannot advance for the hail of shells falling on them from the Shuri hills, site of the enemy headquarters. The 5th Marines succeed in surrounding some enemy units in the area south of Awacha. The XXIV Corps makes hardly any progress; only the 382nd Infantry, 96th Division, manages to consolidate its positions on Zebra Hill.

Kamikaze aircraft and piloted flying bombs damage the aircraft carrier *Bunker Hill* and two destroyers off Okinawa.

China The Chinese armies hold up the Japanese offensive against Chihchiang, threatening the flanks of the enemy columns and putting up a firm resistance in the Paima Shan area.

New Guinea The 6th Australian Division occupies Wewak, once a big Japanese base and now manned by a meagre, starving garrison.

12 May

Philippines: Luzon In the US XI Corps sector, columns from the 43rd Division converge on Ipo, taking several hills manned by the Japanese.

Southern Philippines On Mindanao, units of the 108th Regimental Combat Group take Del Monte airfield, while others advance south-west of Tankulan. After their long hammering by aircraft and artillery, the Japanese strongpoint in the Colgan woods are attacked and eliminated by the 124th Infantry. US aircraft and artillery attack the places on Samar Island where the Japanese guns are thought to be sited.

Okinawa The bloody battle against the Shuri line continues. At the cost of heavy losses, the 1st Marine Division takes the greater part of Dakeshi Ridge, while the 77th Division advances slowly towards Shuri. The positions most fiercely contested are Sugar Loaf Hill (southeast of Amike) and the 'Conical Hill' in the 96th Division's sector.

Off Okinawa a suicide aircraft explodes on the battleship *New Mexico* causing considerable damage.

South-East Asia Preparations are being made for the invasion of Malaya (Operation Zipper). Force W (amphibious), the XV Corps and the newly formed XXXIV Corps, with the 224th Air Group, are being

reorganized and trained in India. Other assault forces for the operation are being assembled in Burma, in the Rangoon area.

13 May

Eastern Front Tito's forces occupy Trieste. In Yugoslavia most of Löhr's forces surrender, but some units still resist in Upper Slovenia, west of Maribor, near the Austrian frontier. In Czechoslovakia, German units are still trying to escape from the Russians to hand themselves over to the Americans. But all resistance is finished.

Philippines: Luzon The US I Corps completes the occupation of Balete Pass, finally clearing the way into the Cagayan valley. In the XI Corps sector, the 43rd Division comes in sight of the Ipo dam.

Southern Philippines On Mindanao operations go forward in the area north of Davao. The 24th Division advances slowly northwards along the Talomo track and in the valley of the river Talomo.

Okinawa There is still fierce fighting along the Shuri line. The 6th Marine Division suffers heavy losses, but completes the capture of Dakeshi Ridge. In the east coast sector, units of the 96th Division succeed in penetrating into the strip east of the Shuri line and taking part of 'Conical Hill'.

Burma In the Arakan area, the 82nd West African Division takes Gwa unopposed.

☐ *Japan*. Aircraft from Vice-Admiral Mitscher's fast carrier squadron begin a series of attacks lasting two days against airfields on Kyushu Island. Off Honshu Island the aircraft carrier *Enterprise* is hit by a Japanese suicide aircraft.

14 May

Eastern Front At midday, 150,000 men of the *Ostpreussen* Group surrender to the 3rd Army of the 2nd Belorussian Front. The Russians announce that they have taken 180,000 prisoners in northern Latvia. In Yugoslavia, despite the general surrender, the German Army Group South-East still resists.

Philippines: Luzon In the US I Corps sector units of the 25th Division advance north of Balete Pass; in the XI Corps sector units of the 43rd Division reach the Ipoh dam, which the Japanese have fortified.

15 May

The Republic of Austria is proclaimed, restoring the situation which existed before the *Anschluss*.

Eastern Front In Yugoslavia, near Slovenigradesk, 150,000 German soldiers surrender to the Yugoslav and Russian forces. The German Army Group Centre, 1,200,000 men strong, has completely disintegrated. All who can have managed to surrender to the Americans; the rest are in the hands of the Russians.

Philippines: Luzon The US XI Corps prepares to resume the attack against the Ipoh dam, north of Manila.

Southern Philippines Sharp fighting on Mindanao; units of the US 24th Division advance from Davao to the north-east to make contact with the Filipino guerrillas. Mopping up continues in the valley of the river Talomo.

Okinawa In the sector of the III Amphibious Corps, a Marine unit has to withdraw from Sugar Loaf Hill on account of the deadly Japanese fire. In the US XXIV Corps sector, the 305th Infantry of the 77th Division makes some very slight progress, but after the hard fighting of the past days is reduced to a quarter of its effectives. The 1st Marine Division advances along the valley of the river Wana, west of Shuri, ceaselessly battered by enemy gunfire. The Japanese launch many counter-attacks by night, but are driven off.

Burma The 26th Indian Division, advancing from Rangoon towards Prome, joins up with the 20th Indian Division as it comes south.

16 May

Philippines: Luzon In the US XI Corps sector, the 152nd Infantry attack Woodpecker Ridge with strong artillery support, and dig in on the summit. In the XIV Corps sector, the capture of Bicol peninsula is

officially declared to be complete.
Mindanao The Japanese hold the American advance along the course of the river Talomo.
Okinawa The 6th Marine Division attacks the Sugar Loaf with two regiments, but Japanese resistance is more stubborn than ever. In the 1st Marine Division's sector, Japanese anti-tank guns put out of action a number of American tanks which were trying to advance along the valley of the river Wana. The attacks of the 77th Division north of Shuri are still unsuccessful, but the 96th Division succeeds in reaching the edge of the village of Yonabaru. However, the Japanese hold on to Love Hill, west of Conical Hill.

17 May
Philippines: Luzon In the XI Corps sector, the US 152nd Infantry dig in in favourable positions on Woodpecker Ridge, from which the Japanese are retiring. After intensive artillery preparation, the 43rd Division takes the Ipoh dam intact.
Okinawa In the US 10th Army sector, General Buckner takes over command of all land forces, while Admiral Hill replaces Admiral Turner in command of Task Force 51 with all air and naval forces under him. In the sector of the III Amphibious Corps the 6th Marine Division, though by now badly battered, continues the assaults for the capture of the Sugar Loaf after Japanese positions have been heavily bombarded by aircraft, field guns and warships. The 5th Regiment of the 1st Marine Division captures the western part of the valley of the river Wana but is unable to take the ridge that encloses it. Units of the 77th Division (XXIV Corps) carry out a surprise attack on Ishimmi Ridge, west of the village of Ishimmi, but are left dangerously exposed to enemy fire.
Marshall Islands Aircraft taking off from a carrier squadron under Rear-Admiral Sprague attack enemy coastal installations on Taroa Island and Maloelap atoll, causing immense damage.

'THE STORY OF G.I. JOE'

The veteran war correspondent Ernie Pyle follows Lieutenant Walker's company through the North African campaign to Rome, gaining the admiration and confidence of his fellow soldiers.

Based on the memoirs of a war correspondent, *The Story of G.I. Joe* was the film that launched actor Robert Mitchum.

Refusing to indulge in spectacle, director William A. Wellman skilfully explored the psychology of his characters as every day brought new tragedy and new hope.

18 May
Philippines: Luzon Some progress by the American units in the Woodpecker Ridge area.
Okinawa In the US III Amphibious Corps sector, the 6th Marine Division succeeds in capturing the Sugar Loaf and part of two other important positions, the Half Moon and the Horseshoe, which overlook the Sugar Loaf from the south-west. The 1st Marine Division is still battling to take the river Wana valley and Wana Ridge, but not even tanks and flame-throwers can subdue the Japanese resistance.
In the XXIV Corps sector, the 77th and 96th Divisions attack the Japanese positions on the hill called Flat Peak, without success.
China The Chinese forces re-occupy Foochow, in Fukien province. Three

Chinese divisions fighting in Burma are about to return to China.

19 May
Philippines: Luzon In the US I Corps sector, the 25th Division begins mopping up in the area north and west of Santa Fe. In the XI Corps sector there is little activity by the 152nd Infantry against Woodpecker Ridge, while the 43rd Division mops up around the Ipoh dam, where all Japanese resistance has ceased.
Okinawa In the US III Amphibious Corps sector, the 1st Marine Division continues the battle for Wana Ridge. There is also fierce fighting in the XXIV Corps sector where small American units are attacked on Ishimmi Ridge and suffer heavy losses before they are able to withdraw. Units of the US 381st Infantry advance on the Sugar Loaf. Japanese artillery fire has grown intense during the past days. The Japanese commander, General Ushijima, orders Rear-Admiral Ota's seamen to launch a 'special' counter-offensive to re-take the Horseshoe. A number of suicidal attacks are launched, starting at 9.30 p.m. But the 4th Marine Regiment repulses them, killing over 500 Japanese.

20 May
Philippines: Mindanao The 31st Division (US X Corps) advances north in the central eastern part of the island and occupies some positions near the town of Malaybalay. Here they run into powerful resistance by Japanese artillery. Other units advance along the east coast north of Davao, repelling some night counter-attacks.
Okinawa In the US III Amphibious Corps sector, the 4th Regiment of the 6th Marine Division begins mopping up the Japanese cave positions on part of the Horseshoe and the Half Moon. They use flame-throwers and hollow-charge explosives and some of the enemy positions are walled up. The 1st Regiment of the 1st Marine Division takes Wana Ridge after a costly assault. Further east, in the US XXIV Corps sector, the 7th and 96th

Divisions continue the struggle for the capture of Yonabaru. The plan is to surround the Shuri line, defended doggedly by the Japanese.
China The Japanese leave Hochih, in Kwangsi province. The threat hanging over Japan induces the Japanese Imperial General Staff to redistribute the available forces within a defensive perimeter nearer to the homeland.

21 May

Philippines: Luzon The Americans resume their attacks on Woodpecker Ridge. Some patrols reach the area of the Guagua dam.
Mindanao The 155th Regiment of the US 31st Division captures Malaybalay, a Japanese supply base.
Okinawa On the American right the 6th Marine Division goes ahead with operations for the total elimination of Japanese from the Horseshoe and for the capture of the Sugar Loaf. The 1st Marines Division attacks in the direction of Shuri Ridge after taking Wana village and driving off Japanese counter-attacks. Beyond Shuri Ridge is Shuri Castle, site of the Japanese headquarters. Meanwhile the 77th Infantry Division of the XXIV Corps also advances north of Shuri and the 96th Division east of the same village, threatening to surround Shuri. Aware of the danger, the Japanese decide to withdraw from Shuri.

22 May

Philippines: Luzon In the US I Corps sector units of the 25th Division advance to within a mile and a quarter south-east of Santa Fe. In the XI Corps sector, units of the 149th Infantry try to take the Guagua dam but are driven back by the Japanese. The 152nd Infantry, with the help of tanks armed with flame-throwers, take the area where the river Mariquina flows into the Bosoboso.
Mindanao The 155th Infantry of the US 31st Division occupies the town of Kalasungay, abandoned by the Japanese, and during the operation surprises a big enemy contingent, which is cut to pieces. Units of the 24th Division reach Tambongan,

and others gain ground east of the river Talomo.
Okinawa The 7th Division occupies the ruins of the town of Yonabaru, on the left of the American line. On the right, the 6th Marine Division reaches the north bank of the river Asato and sends patrols over to the south bank. The Japanese withdraw all the forces they can from the Shuri line and Shuri village.

23 May

Okinawa The 6th Marine Division crosses the river Asato in force and enters the ruins of the town of Naha without meeting any serious resistance. But when they try to turn east to outflank the Shuri line from the south they run into extremely determined enemy resistance on the fortified hill of Machishi. On the left of the American line the 32nd Infantry of the 7th Division goes on with the outflanking of Shuri. A period of torrential rain begins, which slows operations down, especially in the central sector.

24 May

Okinawa Japanese suicide pilots resume their activity against American shipping. On the 24th and 25th it is particularly intense and leads to the sinking of a fast transport and damage to an escort carrier, five destroyers and other smaller ships. During the night Japanese parachutists are dropped on Yontan airfield. The raiders manage to destroy and damage a great number of American aircraft before being rounded up and wiped out.
Matching the air attacks and Commando activity, the Japanese mount several vigorous counter-attacks on land in the direction of Yonabaru during the night, and make a small penetration into the lines of the US 32nd Infantry.
☐ Japan. 520 US bombers drop 3,646 tons of bombs on central Tokyo and industrial districts in the south of the city.

25 May

The Joint Chiefs of Staff approve the general directives for Operation

Olympic, the invasion of metropolitan Japan; the date fixed for its start is 1 November.
Okinawa After a series of assaults by the 4th Marine Regiment, the Japanese casemates and underground positions on Machishi Hill are eliminated. The 29th Regiment mops up in Naha.

26 May

Philippines: Luzon In the US I Corps sector, units of the 25th Division eliminate Japanese resistance in a gorge north of Balete Pass and enter Santa Fe. In the XI Corps sector, the road to Guagua is completely clear, but the American units approaching the position are driven back by the intense Japanese fire.
Okinawa The Japanese withdrawing from the Shuri line are heavily bombarded from air, land and sea. One

The deck of an American aircraft carrier

regiment of the 7th Division advances south along the east coast as far as a range of hills, but the other units suffer heavy losses in an attempt to take Dick Hill, one of the Japanese strongpoints in the defensive line east of Chan.

Two US destroyers and some smaller ships are damaged by Japanese suicide aircraft off Okinawa.

China In the course of their general withdrawal the Japanese evacuate Nanning, capital of Kwangsi province. They no longer have any land communication with Indo-China. The Chinese re-occupy the city.

☐ *Japan.* US bombers raid Tokyo again, dropping 3,252 tons of bombs and destroying the Ginza district and the surroundings of the Imperial Palace. Over 35 square miles of the city, more than half of it, have now been flattened. Many factories have

been destroyed and the production of some war materials is down by 80 per cent.

27 May
Philippines: Luzon With the capture of Santa Fe, the US I Corps brings to an end the hard struggle in the mountains and the battle for the Villa Verde track. In the XI Corps sector, units of the 38th Division get within about 50 yards of the Guagua dam but are halted by Japanese fire.

Mindanao Operations against the Japanese units concentrating for the final defence of the mountainous central region north of Davao, go ahead slowly.

Okinawa On the left of the American line, the infantry of the 7th Division are still held up in front of Dick Hill and unable to outflank Shuri. On the right, the Marines con-

tinue mopping up in the ruins of Naha, among which some small Japanese units are hidden.

Suicide aircraft sink one US destroyer and damage six other ships.

Admiral Halsey, Commander of the US 3rd Fleet, takes over command of all ships attached to the 5th Fleet. Task Force 58 becomes Task Force 38, and Vice-Admiral McCain takes over command in place of Vice-Admiral Mitscher.

28 May
Philippines: Luzon In the US XI Corps sector, units of the 149th Infantry occupy the Guagua dam, evacuated by the Japanese.

Okinawa In the III Amphibious Corps sector, units of the 6th Marine Division advance through Naha as far as the river Kokuba. They run into violent resistance when they attempt to put a small group on the islet of Ona, in Naha harbour.

The Japanese air force steps up its attacks on American ships, using high-level bombers, dive bombers and *kamikaze* aircraft. Many US ships are damaged, but the Japanese lose about 100 aircraft. This is the last big air offensive mounted by the Japanese in the Okinawa area.

Burma The British undertake a vast reorganization of commands and formations in preparation for the operations against Malaya and the Dutch East Indies. The 12th Army is formed under General Stopford, with two Indian divisions, one West African division and three brigades, of which one is British.

29 May
Philippines: Luzon The US I Corps prepares to move on from Santa Fe to Aritao and take the whole of the Cagayan valley. Filipino guerrillas occupy Cervantes.

Mindanao The US 24th Division advances on Mandog, the last Japanese strongpoint north of the Davao plain, which is attacked from the air.

Okinawa The 6th Marine Division advances from Naha to the east. Units of the 1st Marine Division take Shuri Ridge, south of the Wana val-

following an attack by a *kamikaze* pilot.

ley, and occupy Shuri Castle, which the Japanese have already abandoned. On the left, where the XXIV Corps is in action, the 7th Division continues its attacks against Japanese positions near the village of Karadera.

30 May

Philippines On Negros Island, all organized resistance by the Japanese in the western part of the island ceases.

Okinawa In the US XXIV Corps sector, the 77th Division penetrates among the ruins of the village of Shuri. The 7th Division overcomes Japanese resistance near Karadera. Most of the enemy have already retired further south.

31 May

Philippines: Luzon The Americans form a task force of about 800 men to advance rapidly to Aparri, on the north coast, and operate with the Filipino guerrillas there.

1 June

Philippines In the US I Corps sector, the 37th Division advances rapidly in the Cagayan valley, in Luzon. On Mindanao, operations continue in the area north of Davao.

Okinawa With the fall of the castle and village of Shuri, General Mushijima, who has lost his best men, withdraws the rest of his forces on to the Oroku peninsula, just south of Naha, and on to the hills of Yaeju, Yuza and Mezado, in the extreme south of the island. The conditions are frightful, and there is an extreme shortage of rations; there is even some discontent among the Japanese troops, something unheard-of in the Japanese army. Units of the US 1st Marine Division cross the river Koruba, south of Naha. The divisions of the XXIV Corps, on the left of the American line, pursue the enemy southwards, while some units mop up the area of Shuri.

2 June

Philippines: Luzon In the US XI Corps sector, the 43rd Division finishes the mopping up of the Ipoh

area.

Okinawa Mopping up continues, while the 6th Marine Division gets ready to land two regiments on the Oroku peninsula.

3 June

Philippines: Luzon The US 37th Division overcomes weak Japanese resistance to advance about six miles north of Santa Fe.

4 June

Okinawa General Buckner reduces the sector manned by the III Amphibious Corps, which has suffered the greatest losses, and increases that assigned to the XXIV Corps. The front line goes from the southern suburbs of Naha to the spurs south of Shuri Ridge, reaching the east coast just south of Yonabaru. The 4th and 29th Marines (6th Division), after a heavy preliminary bombardment, land on the north coast of the Oroku peninsula, which is manned by Vice-Admiral Ota's naval infantry, and take about half of the airfield there.

5 June

Philippines: Luzon In the US I Corps sector, units of the 37th Division occupy Aritao and advance beyond this town to the north.

Okinawa The Japanese put up a determined resistance to the 6th Marine Division on the Oroku peninsula, but the Marines manage to capture most of the airfield. The XXIV Corps nears the last Japanese defensive line in the south of the island, which runs from Yuza in the west to Guschichan on the east coast and is based on three hills, Yaeju, Yuza and Mezado.

A sudden typhoon damages a number of American ships off Okinawa; 4 battleships, 8 aircraft carriers, 3 heavy and 4 light cruisers, 14 destroyers, 2 tankers and a transport loaded with ammunition suffer more or less serious damage. The battleship *Mississippi* and the heavy cruiser *Louisville* are hit and seriously damaged by Japanese suicide aircraft.

6 June

Philippines The Americans advance without meeting any strong resistance both in the Cagayan valley, Luzon, and on Mindanao Island, where they are preparing to attack the town of Mandog.

Okinawa The 6th Marine Division completes the capture of the airfield on Oroku peninsula and advances along the coast, but inland the Japanese resist with all their usual determination. In the east, units of the 96th Division (XXIV Corps) reach the lower slopes of Mount Yaeju and are halted there by powerful Japanese fire.

7 June

Okinawa In the Oroku peninsula the Japanese hold up the attacks by the 6th Marine Division, while the 1st Marine Division advances to the south and cuts off the base of the peninsula, so that the Japanese are isolated. On the XXIV Corps front there is considerable artillery activity.

China In Kwangsi province, three Chinese armies prepare to launch an offensive against the Japanese to liberate the Hong Kong–Canton area. In Hunan province the Chinese follow up the retreating Japanese as far as Paoching, which is where the Japanese offensive started from.

8 June

Philippines: Luzon The 145th Infantry (US 37th Division) takes Solano and advances almost as far as Bagabag (both places are north-east of Santa Fe, towards the Cagayan valley). Some patrols push eastwards as far as the river Magat.

Okinawa Severe fighting continues in the Oroku peninsula, while the XXIV Corps prepares a big attack against Mount Yaeju.

9 June

Philippines: Luzon The US 37th Division takes Bagabag. The Americans try to block the routes into the Cagayan valley to cut off the Japanese concentrated on the Sierra Madre, in the north-east of the island.

SIMON LAKE

The American naval engineer Simon Lake died at Bridgeport, Connecticut on 3 June.

Born in 1866 at Pleasantville, New Jersey, Lake built his first submarine, the *Argonaut Junior*, in 1894; it was a wooden ship with three wheels for moving over the seabed. Three years later he completed the *Argonaut*, with a cigar-shaped steel hull, powered by a gasoline engine even when submerged, with an air tube projecting above the surface. Lake's first true submarine, however, was the *Protector*, built for the Russian navy early in the century, which remained in action until 1908. Equipped with an electric motor for underwater navigation and a gasoline engine for surface navigation, *Protector* had a cigar-shaped hull, a large conning tower and armament in the shape of three torpedo tubes.

During the First World War the Lake Torpedo Boat Company built more than 100 submarines in the Bridgeport shipyards.

The inventor, too, of an apparatus for locating sunken ships, Lake lost much of his capital in the 1930s in an unsuccessful attempt to recover a cargo of gold from a vessel that had foundered in the Hudson River in the eighteenth century.

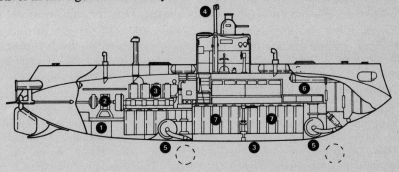

1. water ballast tanks. 2. electric engine. 3. gasoline engine.
4. periscope. 5. wheels (retracted). 6. torpedo tubes. 7. accumulators.

Mindanao Units of the US 24th Division take Mandog, the last major strongpoint in the Japanese defences.
Okinawa The Japanese defending the Oroku peninsula are completely isolated and surrounded by the Marines of the 6th Division. The 1st Marine Division advances south almost as far as Kunishi Ridge, one of the last Japanese strongpoints.

10 June

Philippines: Luzon The Japanese temporarily halt the advance of the American 37th Division near Orioung Pass.
Okinawa Hard fighting continues in the Oroku peninsula, where the units of the 6th Marine Division are in action. The Japanese carry out several night counter-attacks, in

which they lose many men. The 1st Marine Division, at the cost of heavy losses, takes a hill west of the town of Yuza. The XXIV Corps, supported by artillery and naval gunfire, aircraft and tanks armed with flame-throwers, opens a major offensive against the last Japanese defensive line, taking a saddle between Mount Yaeju and Mount Yuza.
Burma Burmese guerrillas led by British officers re-take Loilem, in the Shan Mountains area.
China Chinese forces liberate I-shan and pursue the Japanese towards Liuchow.
Dutch East Indies With support by British and American ships and aircraft, Australian troops land in the Gulf of Brunei and begin the recapture of Borneo. Some contin-

gents also land on the islands of Labuan and Muara.

11 June

Philippines: Luzon There is fighting at Orioung Pass, where the Japanese are still holding up the US 37th Division.
Okinawa In the Oroku peninsula the Japanese are penned into a pocket about a thousand yards deep, but they put up a fanatical resistance. The 1st Marine Division fails to take Kunishi Ridge by assault. In the XXIV Corps sector, one regiment of the 96th Division reaches the town of Yuza, but is driven out again by the violent Japanese fire. The artillery brings down fire on the Japanese cave positions on Mount Yaeju, east of which the Americans manage to take an important height.

12 June

Philippines: Luzon The US 145th Infantry overcomes Japanese resistance at Orioung Pass, occupies the town of Orioung and advances to some positions overlooking the town of Balite.
Okinawa The Japanese infantry (marines) cut off in the Oroku peninsula, hammered by incessant American fire, show signs of giving way. Some give themselves up and many commit suicide. In a night attack the 1st Marine Division captures the west end of Kunishi Ridge. In the XXIV Corps sector the 96th Division attacks Mount Yuza without success, but gains some positions in the Mount Yaeju sector.

13 June

Philippines: Luzon The Americans send an armoured column beyond Orioung Pass to exploit the breakthrough made by the 145th Infantry, but a Japanese counter-attack blocks the road.
Okinawa The Japanese in the Oroku peninsula cease all resistance. The 6th Marine Division takes a record number of prisoners – 169. The 1st Marine Division sends one regiment against Kunishi Ridge; the Americans succeed in taking and holding several positions, but with high

casualties. The XXIV Corps, using armoured flame-throwers, destroys one by one the Japanese cave positions on Mount Yuza and Mount Yaeju and on Hills 153 and 115.

China The Japanese prepare to leave Liuchow and Kweilin and the first stage of the Chinese operation against the Hong Kong–Canton area is made unnecessary.

Dutch East Indies The Australian forces liberate the town of Brunei.

14 June

Philippines: Luzon The Americans dislodge the Japanese blocking the Orioung Pass. Units of the 37th Division, formed into an armoured column, advance as far as Echague. From Santiago other units move on Cabanatuan and Cauayan.

Okinawa While mopping up proceeds on Oroku peninsula, the Marines of the III Corps and infantry of the XXIV Corps continue to wipe out the Japanese fortified caves both on Kunishi Ridge and on Mount Yuza and Mount Yaeju. One regiment of the 96th Division reaches the summit of Mount Yaeju, while the 7th Division extends its control on Hills 153 and 115.

Burma A grand parade held at Rangoon to celebrate the recapture of the city. Admiral Mountbatten has fixed 9 September as the date for the start of Operation *Zipper*, the recapture of the Malayan peninsula.

China After re-taking I-shan, the Chinese pursue the Japanese towards Liuchow.

☐ The Joint Chiefs of Staff order General Douglas MacArthur, General Arnold, and Admiral Nimitz to work out plans for the immediate occupation of the Japanese islands in the event of an unexpected Japanese capitulation. This decision may have been taken in view of progress made in the production of the atomic bomb, but the commanders in the field (not to mention ministers) are not to know this.

15 June

Philippines: Luzon In the north of the island, Filipino guerrillas seize Cervantes. The US 37th Division

pushes on in the Cagayan valley, eliminating a Japanese strongpoint about 3 miles from Santiago, near Cabanatuan.

Okinawa The Marines in action of Kunishi Ridge are unable to advance and suffer heavy casualties. The 1st Division, already short of men, is integrated with the 8th Regiment of the 2nd Marine Division. The elimination of the Japanese positions on Mount Yaeju and Mount Yuza by the XXIV Corps goes on slowly.

Burma The mopping up in the Shan Mountains area ends.

16 June

Okinawa Fighting continues in the south of the island. The 381st Infantry succeeds in taking the summit of Mount Yuza.

The air offensive against American ships in the waters off Okinawa eases off slightly, but the Japanese still sink one destroyer and damage one escort carrier.

17 June

Philippines: Luzon In the US I Corps sector, units of the 37th Division take Naguilian after forcing the passage of the river Cagayan near the town.

Okinawa The arrival of reinforcements in the Kunishi Ridge area enables the Americans to begin to overcome the tenacious Japanese resistance. In the XXIV Corps sector, the last Japanese defence line is crumbling. The 7th Division completes the capture of Hills 153 and 115.

China General Arnold gives order for General Chennault to be replaced by General Stratemeyer as Commander of the US air forces operating in China.

18 June

Philippines: Luzon Units of the US 37th Division, with an armoured column, continue their advance in the Cagayan valley, taking Ilagan airfield and crossing the Ilagan river.

Mindanao The Japanese cease all organized resistance. For some time their 35th Army has been forced to live on roots and the bark of trees. However, small units continue to resist for some time.

Okinawa The remains of the Japanese 32nd Army are still putting up a determined resistance to the attacks of the US III Amphibious Corps and XXIV Corps. General Buckner is killed by an enemy shell while inspecting the lines of the 8th Marines. He is replaced as commander of the US 10th Army by General Geiger, Commander of the 2nd Marine Division.

☐ Japan. US bombers begin a series of violent raids against 23 major Japanese towns, all with populations between 100,000 and 350,000.

☐ On instructions from Emperor Hirohito, Prime Minister Suzuki tells the Japanese Supreme Council of Emperor Hirohito's intention to seek peace with the Allies as soon as possible.

19 June

Okinawa Making use of insistent propaganda by means of leaflets and loudspeakers, the Americans induce as many as 343 Japanese to surrender. The enemy retires in disorder before the III Amphibious Corps, but still offers strong resistance in the XXIV Corps sector.

20 June

Philippines: Luzon Units of Filipino guerrillas come up the Cagayan valley from Aparri, on the north coast, liberate the town of Tuguegarao, half way between Aparri and Ilagan, which is as far as the Americans have reached. The task force sent north by the Americans now enters Aparri, while units of the 37th Division advance 2½ miles north of Ilagan.

Southern Philippines US 8th Army headquarters makes it official that the operations for the recapture of the islands of Panay, Negros, Cebu, Bohol and Palawan and the western part of Mindanao are completed.

Okinawa In the central sector of the XXIV Corps front, Japanese pockets hold out strongly against American pressure. The 32nd Infantry (7th Division) reaches Height 89, near Mabuni, where the Japanese headquarters have been identified. On the wings, the Marines on the right and the infantry on the left advance

A Russian soldier drags a German out of a manhole during the bitter street fighting in Berlin.

almost unopposed, capturing over 1,000 prisoners and reaching the south coast of the island at many points.

China The Allies plan to capture Fort Bayard (now Zhanijang), on the South China Sea, by 1 August to serve as a base area for the campaign against Hong Kong and Canton.

Dutch East Indies The Australian forces extend their occupation of Borneo, landing at Lutong in eastern Sarawak.

21 June

Philippines: Luzon The American advance in the Cagayan valley proceeds with almost no opposition. In the north, units of the task force sent by the Americans make contact with the Filipino guerrillas.

Okinawa Japanese resistance is almost finished. Height 89 is taken by the 32nd Infantry (7th Division). In a cave they find the bodies of General Ushijima, Commander of the Japanese 32nd Army, and his Chief of Staff, both of whom have committed suicide.

22 June

Philippines: Luzon The Americans decide to carry out a parachute drop on the north coast near Aparri. While the 37th Division pushes on northwards taking Tamauini, coming within 6 miles of Cabagan, the Filipino guerrillas who liberated Tuguegarao are driven from it by the Japanese.

Okinawa With the end of all enemy resistance, the Americans hold a ceremony to celebrate the capture of the island. Victory has cost them about 50,000 men dead, wounded and missing. The Japanese have lost 110,000 dead, and 7,400 have been taken prisoner. And they have also lost at least 7,800 aircraft, though these have sunk 36 American ships and damaged 368. The US air offensive continues. The air bases and naval bases on Okinawa bring the Americans considerably nearer to their next objective – Japan itself.

China Chinese forces are at the gates of Liuchow, which the Japanese set on fire before retiring.

Dutch East Indies The Australians

wipe out all Japanese resistance on Tarakan Island, off the north-east coast of Borneo.

23 June

Philippines: Luzon At 9.00 a.m. a battalion of the US 511th Parachute Regiment is dropped on an airfield south of Aparri, on the north coast. The landing takes place without incident and the unit quickly makes contact with the Filipino guerrillas and moves off southwards to join up with the 37th Division.

Okinawa The systematic mopping up of the island begins. General Stilwell takes command of the US 10th Army in place of General Geiger.

25 June

Philippines: Luzon The American parachutists dropped at Aparri advance south, taking Gattaran. Units of the 37th Division recapture Tuguegarao, from which the Japanese had expelled the Filipino guerrillas.

26 June

Philippines: Luzon The parachute battalion dropped near Aparri joins up with the US 37th Division, which takes over command both of the parachute battalion and of the task force sent north earlier and of the guerrillas operating in the area.

Ryukyu Islands Marine units land on Kume Island, where a new radar station is installed.

China Chinese troops take Liuchow airfield.

☐ Japan. B-29 Superfortresses launch a series of night raids against Japanese oil refineries.

☐ The San Francisco Conference of the United Nations comes to an end. The Charter of the United Nations is signed by the representatives of the countries taking part, but is not ratified until 24 October.

27 June

Philippines: Luzon Units of the 37th Division (US I Corps) reach Aparri, on the north coast. The Japanese, mostly gathered on the Sierra Madre in the north-east of the island, are cut off and reduced to a pitiful condition for lack of supplies and medical care. With the occupation by the Americans of the whole of the Cagayan valley, the campaign for the recapture of Luzon is now virtually over.

30 June

Philippines: Luzon The Luzon campaign is officially declared ended. Mopping up of the remaining Japanese forces (there are reckoned to be 23,000 men still in the Sierra Madre and the Kiangan–Bontoc area) will be carried out by the US 8th Army, while the 6th Army is reorganized for its next task, Operation *Olympic*, the invasion of Japan. Mopping up is also still going on on Mindanao, and continues until the end of the war.

Okinawa Mopping up of the island is finished.

1 July

China The Chinese liberate Liuchow.

Dutch East Indies After a series of preparatory air raids and with the support of an American naval attack group, the Australian 7th Division lands at Balikpapan, on the east coast of Borneo. There is hardly any opposition to the landing, but the Japanese have prepared powerful positions inland.

2 July

Dutch East Indies The Australians capture the oil installations on Balikpapan and extend their beachhead.

Ryukyu Islands Operations are officially concluded

4 July

Philippines: Mindanao The US 24th Division organizes an amphibious expeditionary force to liberate Sarangani Bay, in the south of the island, south of Davao.

5 July

Announcement from General MacArthur's headquarters that the liberation of the Philippines is completed.

Dutch East Indies More Australian forces land in Borneo, near Penadjim Point in the Bay of Balikpapan. The Australians quickly extend their control from a number of beachheads along the coast and towards the interior.

6 July

China General Chennault, the legendary commander of the 'Flying Tigers', offers his resignation.

8 July

Philippines: Mindanao Fighting is still going on in the Sarangani Bay area, in which Filipino guerrillas under American leadership take part.

10 July

Japan. American aircraft taking off from a fast carrier squadron commanded by Vice-Admiral McCain attack a number of airfields in the Tokyo area. Industrial targets are also hit. There is little Japanese response; the air force of the Rising Sun has been shattered at Okinawa. What remains of the Japanese navy is also practically immobilized by American attacks and by lack of fuel. The American navy, by contrast, is stronger than ever, in spite of the losses suffered at Okinawa. Its current strength is about 68,000 ships of all types, with a complement of over 4,000,000 men.

11–12 July

Philippines: Luzon Thousands of napalm bombs are dropped on the Japanese in the pockets on the Sierra Madre and in the Kiangan area. The Americans are tightening the screw on the last Japanese forces.

13 July

Italy declares war on Japan.

13–15 July

Philippines: Mindanao The Americans continue to make progress in the Sarangani Bay area.

16 July

At 5.30 p.m. the first atomic bomb is successfully tested at Alamogordo, New Mexico.

17 July

Opening of the Potsdam Conference, which lasts until 2 August. Churchill, Stalin and Truman discuss the problems of peace in Europe and the conditions for the solution of the war against Japan. After July 28, Clement R. Attlee, head of the new British Labour cabinet, replaces Churchill at the Conference.

☐ Japan. Aircraft taking off from ships of US 3rd Fleet and British Pacific Fleet, commanded by Vice-Admiral McCain and Vice-Admiral Rawlings, begin a series of bombardments of military installations and airfields in the Tokyo area. Another American squadron of battleships, cruisers and destroyers, shells the industrial area of Mito-Hitachi, on Honshu Island.

18 July

Dutch East Indies Units of the Australian 7th Division in Borneo occupy the Sambodja oilfield, evacuated by the Japanese.

☐ Japan. Allied air and naval attacks against a number of targets in the Tokyo area meet with almost no opposition from the Japanese. Yokosuka naval base and the surrounding airfields are hit hard.

20 July

Philippines: Mindanao Landing of American units on Balut Island, at the entrance to Sarangani Bay, who wipe out the small Japanese garrison.

25 July

Philippines: Mindanao All organized Japanese resistance ceases in the Sarangani Bay sector. Mopping up begins, but is not completed until 11 August.

☐ *Japan.* For the second day running, aircraft of the US 3rd Fleet attack Kure naval base and the airfields at Nagoya, Osaka and Miho. The battleships *Hyuga*, *Ise* and *Haruna*, the escort carrier *Kaiyo* and the heavy cruisers *Aoba* and *Iwate* are sunk. These air and naval attacks are taking place against a country on the verge of collapse, which no longer offers any resistance.

26 July

The Allies meeting at Potsdam issue a proclamation demanding that Japan should surrender unconditionally on pain of 'complete destruction'. This also refers to the successful atom bomb experiment at Alamogordo (about which Stalin's intelligence service has kept him informed).

27 July

China The first Chinese forces enter Kweilin. Fighting for possession of the town continues until the end of the month.

Other Chinese forces capture Tanchuk airfield.

28 July

Japan. More attacks by the US 3rd Fleet against the naval base at Kure and other targets. This time the American bombers sink the aircraft carrier *Amagi*, the heavy cruiser *Tone*, the old cruiser *Izumo*, the light cruiser *Oyodo* and one destroyer. The Japanese, incapable by now of any reaction in their own country, send yet more *kamikaze* pilots to

THE BOMB

On 16 July, at the Alamogordo airbase in the New Mexico desert, the first plutonium bomb made in the Los Alamos laboratories was exploded. (Confident that it would work, the scientists of the Manhattan Project had decided not to test the U-235 bomb.)

The power of the bomb's explosion, nicknamed 'Fat Man' by reason of its vague resemblance to Churchill's profile, amazed even the scientists and military observers present at Alamogordo.

President Truman, who had been told only in April of latest developments in the Manhattan Project, was informed of the success of the test in a detailed telegram while he was attending the Potsdam Conference.

attack the American ships in the Okinawa area.

29 July

Japan. A squadron of US battleships, cruisers and destroyers commanded by Rear-Admiral Shafroth shells offices, an aircraft factory and other targets at Hamamatsu, on Honshu Island.

On Okinawa, Japanese suicide aircraft damage one American destroyer and one fast transport.

30 July

Japan rejects the Potsdam ultimatum. Nonetheless General Marshall gives instructions to General MacArthur and Admiral Nimitz to co-ordinate plans in readiness for an early surrender by the enemy.

Renewed air bombardment of airfields and industrial plant on Honshu Island by aircraft from the US 3rd Fleet.

Philippines In the Philippine Sea, a Japanese submarine sinks the US heavy cruiser *Indianapolis*. This is the ship which brought the elements of the atomic bomb to Tinian (see 6 August).

31 July–1 August

Japan. The air and naval bombardment continues. One Japanese destroyer and one frigate are sunk.

2 August

The Potsdam Conference ends.

5 August

China The Chinese 13th Army captures the town of Tanchuk. The 58th Division liberates Hsinning.

6 August

Japan. Operation *Centreboard*. At about 9.30 a.m. a B-29 named *Enola Gay* and commanded by the American Colonel Tibbets, which took off from Tinian in the Marianas at 2.10 a.m., drops the first atomic bomb on Hiroshima. The tail-gunner on the aircraft, who sees the explosion, exclaims: 'My God! What have we done!' 92,233 people are killed and 37,425 injured, many of whom die later from the effects of radiation.

7 August

Philippines: Luzon Officers from the headquarters of the US 1st Army meet on Luzon in readiness for the coming invasion of Japan.

8 August

The USSR declares war on Japan.

9 August

Japan. The second atomic bomb is dropped by the US Air Force on Nagasaki. The aircraft is a B-29 christened *Great Artist* and commanded by Major Charles Sweeney. Casualties total 23,753 dead and 43,020 injured, many of whom die later.

Towards midnight Emperor Hirohito calls the Supreme Council together and tries to make the military leaders accept the proposed surrender. But they will not. At 3 a.m. the meeting breaks up with nothing more decided than a cautious sounding of the possibilities of peace through Sweden and Switzerland.

China The Russians open their operations against the Japanese. Their objectives are the occupation of Manchuria and North Korea, the Kuril Islands and Southern Sakhalin, and the destruction of the huge Japanese Kwangtung Army numbering about 1,000,000 men. Against the Japanese forces the Russians deploy 1,158,000 men, grouped into the 1st and 2nd Far East Fronts and the Transbaikal Front, with 26,000 guns and mortars, 5,500 tanks and self-propelled guns and 3,900 aircraft. The Russian troops penetrate into Manchuria and head straight for Mukden.

10 August

Japan informs the Allies that it accepts the surrender terms 'on the understanding that it does not comprise any demand which prejudices the prerogatives of the Emperor as sovereign ruler'.

11 August

Sakhalin Operations are begun by the Russian 2nd Far East Front and the Russian Pacific Fleet for the occupation of the southern part of the island.

12 August

China In view of the imminent capitulation of Japan, the Chinese–American headquarters cancels the operations against Fort Bayard and Hong Kong and Canton.

13 August

The Japanese surrender documents, approved by President Truman, are sent to General MacArthur. American aircraft fly over Tokyo and other

PAUL VALÉRY

The French academician Paul Valéry, one of the greatest poets of his time, died in Paris on 20 July.

Valéry was born at Sète, of a French father and an Italian mother, on 30 October 1871. After studying law at Montpellier, he met Pierre Louÿs who later introduced him to the Parisian literary circle of Stéphane Mallarmé. Under the latter's influence Valéry wrote his first poems, published in Symbolist reviews, and these were followed by some interesting philosophical essays. He then experienced a deep emotional crisis and isolated himself for many years, until in 1917 he brought out, with the encouragement of André Gide, his first major poem, *La Jeune Parque*. After that he wrote the *Odes* and many other lyric poems, collected in 1922 in a volume entitled *Les Charmes*, which extended his fame outside France. A profound thinker as well as a poet, Valéry also wrote a large number of critical essays.

Influenced both by the Parnassians and the Symbolists, Valéry successfully blended classical French traditions and modern *fin-de-siècle* poetic currents to produce lyric poetry of great beauty.

Japanese cities dropping millions of leaflets explaining the position reached in the surrender negotiations and the true state of affairs in Japan. However, the Japanese 'hawks' still refuse to admit defeat.

14 August

Emperor Hirohito assembles the Imperial Council and decides that his rescript shall be transmitted by radio announcing the acceptance of unconditional surrender. At 11.00 p.m. over 1,000 soldiers attack the Imperial Palace to prevent the message being transmitted, but they are driven off by the guard, faithful to the Emperor. On receipt of the news of the surrender, the Americans get ready to occupy Japan.

China The Russians have routed the Japanese Kwangtung Army and penetrated between 100 and 250 miles into Manchuria, occupying a number of towns including Mukden. They also proceed with the occupation of Sakhalin and the Kurils.

15 August

Japan. Aircraft from Vice-Admiral McCain's fast carrier squadron, which has not yet heard the announcement of the cessation of hostilities, attack the airfields in the Tokyo area. Japanese air reaction is unexpectedly violent.

16–18 August

China Russian operations continue. Marshal Vasilevsky proposes that hostilities shall cease at midday on 20 August. There is no reply from the headquarters of the Japanese Kwangtung Army, but from 7.00 p.m. many units begin to surrender.

17 August

General Prince Higashikumi becomes the Prime Minister of Japan and forms a new government.

19 August

A delegation from the Japanese government reaches Manila to agree details of the capitulation.

20 August

The Japanese delegation returns to

Tokyo with the Allied dispositions for the occupation and for the signature of the surrender.

China All operations cease. The Japanese Kwangtung Army has lost 700,000 men killed, wounded and prisoners. However, Russian operations still go on in Sakhalin and the Kurils.

23 August

China The Russians occupy Port Arthur (now Lu-Ta).

24 August

The USSR and China sign a treaty of alliance.

25 August

Southern Sakhalin Operations end as the Russians complete their occupation of the island.

28 August

Japan The first American units (Air Force technicians) arrive in Japan. Their arrival has been delayed for 48 hours by the forecast of a typhoon.

29 August

Singapore Admiral Lord Mountbatten receives the surrender of the Japanese forces in South-East Asia, about 740,000 men. The document is signed by General Itagaki.

30 August

Japan The 11th Airborne Division flies in to Atsugi airfield, while the 4th Marine Regiment of the 6th Division lands in the naval base at Yokosuka. The occupation of Japan in force has begun.

Hong Kong A British naval squadron re-occupies the colony.

31 August

Marcus Island The Japanese garrison surrenders to the American Admiral Whiting.

1 September

Kuril Islands Operations cease with the occupation by Russian troops

2 September

Truk in the *Caroline Islands*, Pagan and Rota in the *Marianas* and the

PIETRO MASCAGNI

On 2 August the Italian composer Pietro Mascagni died in Rome. Born in Leghorn on 7 December 1863, Mascagni began his musical education at the local Schola Cantorum and later transferred to the Milan Conservatory where he studied composition with Amilcare Ponchielli. He was professor of music at Cerignola, a town in Apulia, and in 1890 won a competition run by the publishers Sonzogno with the one-act opera *Cavalleria Rusticana*. Performed at the Teatro Costanzi in Rome on 17 May that year, the opera proved an enormous success and quickly gained Mascagni world renown. Audiences were attracted by the deft, full-blooded, melodious score, by the passionate intensity of the characters, the excitement of the stage action and the skilful blend of naturalism and melodrama. But the expectations aroused by this work were not fulfilled in later operas. For all his attempts at stylistic innovation, Mascagni remained essentially provincial in outlook, virtually impervious to contemporary European musical trends, and never again produced works of importance.

Palau Islands surrender.

Japan A little after 8.00 a.m., on board the battleship *Missouri* at anchor in Tokyo Bay, the Japanese Foreign Minister Mamoru Shigemitsu and the Chief of Staff General Yoshijiro Umezo, representing the Japanese government and armed forces, sign the instrument of capitulation in the presence of General MacArthur. Then MacArthur too, in the name of the Allies, signs the document, which has been prepared in duplicate, with copies in Japanese and English. At MacArthur's wish, the ceremony is attended by the American General Wainwright, the hero of Bataan, and the British General Percival, defeated at Singapore, both of whom have just been freed from prisoner-of-war camps.

The document is countersigned by Admiral Nimitz for the United States, Admiral Sir Bruce Fraser for Great Britain, General Blamey for Australia, General Hsu Yung-chang for China, General Kuzma N. Derebianko for the USSR, Admiral Helfrich for the Netherlands, General Leclerc for France, Colonel M. Moore-Cosgrave for Canada and Air-Marshal Leonard Isitt for New Zealand.

So ends the greatest conflict in history. It has lasted five years and cost the lives of 55 million people. Three million more are missing. The material damage cannot be calculated. The legacy of devastated lands, starving refugees, broken homes, and the wholly new political framework emerging from the rubble of Europe and Asia, must now be faced.

INDEX

NATIONS AT WAR

1 September 1939	Germany invades Poland
3 September 1939	Great Britain declares war on Germany
	France delivers ultimatum to Germany, to expire on 4 September
	Australia, New Zealand and India declare war on Germany
6 September 1939	South Africa declares war on Germany
10 September 1939	Canada declares war on Germany
9 April 1940	Germany invades Denmark and Norway
10 May 1940	Germany invades Belgium, Holland and Luxembourg
10 June 1940	Italy declares herself at war with Great Britain and France from June 11
	Great Britain, France, Australia, Canada, New Zealand, India and South Africa declare war on Italy
28 October 1940	Italy invades Greece after delivery of ultimatum
15 February 1941	Great Britain breaks off relations with Rumania
5 March 1941	Great Britain breaks off relations with Bulgaria
6 April 1941	Germany invades Yugoslavia and Greece
	Italy declares war on Yugoslavia
11 April 1941	Hungary invades Yugoslavia
24 April 1941	Bulgaria invades Greek territory
20 June 1941	Greece breaks off relations with Hungary
22 June 1941	Germany invades USSR
	Italy and Rumania declare war on USSR
24 June 1941	Rumania breaks off relations with Greece
	Hungary breaks off relations with USSR
26 June 1941	Finland declares war on USSR
27 June 1941	Hungary declares war on USSR
28 June 1941	Albania declares war on USSR
2 July 1941	China breaks off diplomatic relations with Axis
28 July 1941	Japanese invade Indo-China
25 August 1941	British and Russian troops enter Iran
5 December 1941	Great Britain, Australia, South Africa, Canada and New Zealand declare war on Finland, Hungary and Rumania
7 December 1941	Japanese attack Pearl Harbour
8 December 1941	USA, Great Britain, Australia, New Zealand, South Africa and Canada declare war on Japan
	China declares war on Axis
	Costa Rica, Salvador, Haiti and Dominican Republic declare war on Japan
9 December 1941	Cuba, Guatamala and Panama declare war on Japan
	Colombia and Egypt break off relations with Japan
11 December 1941	Germany and Italy declare war on USA
	USA declares war on Germany and Italy
	Costa Rica, Cuba, Dominican Republic, Guatamala and Nicaragua declare war on Germany and Italy
12 December 1941	Rumania declares war on USA
	Panama, Salvador, Haiti and Honduras declare war on Germany and Italy
13 December 1941	Bulgaria declares war on Great Britain and USA
	Hungary declares war on USA
15 December 1941	Egypt breaks off relations with Hungary and Rumania
28 December 1941	Great Britain declares war on Bulgaria
29 December 1941	New Zealand declares war on Bulgaria
2 January 1941	South Africa declares war on Bulgaria
12 January 1942	Japan declares war on Dutch East Indies
14 January 1942	Australia declares a state of war with Bulgaria as from 6 January
25 January 1942	Thailand declares war on Great Britain and USA
26 January 1942	Bolivia breaks off relations with Axis
28 January 1942	Brazil breaks off relations with Japan
5 February 1942	USA declares war on Thailand
2 March 1942	Australia declares war on Thailand
22 May 1942	Mexico declares war on Axis
5 June 1942	USA declares war on Bulgaria, Hungary and Rumania
22 August 1942	Brazil declares war on Germany and Italy
1 December 1942	Ethiopia declares war on Axis
16 January 1943	Iraq declares war on Axis
7 April 1943	Bolivia declares a state of war with Japan, Germany and Italy
9 September 1943	Iran declares war on Germany
13 October 1943	Italy (with status of 'co-belligerant') declares war on Germany
4 December 1943	Bolivia declares war on all other Axis countries
26 January 1944	Liberia declares war on Germany and Japan
	Argentina breaks off relations with Germany and Japan
5 February 1944	Argentina breaks off relations with Vichy, France, Bulgaria, Rumania, Hungary and all Occupied Countries
30 June 1944	USA severs relations with Finland
25 August 1944	Rumania declares war on Germany
5 September 1944	USSR declares war on Bulgaria
7 September 1944	Bulgaria declares war on Germany
31 December 1944	Hungary declares war on Germany
2 February 1945	Ecuador declares war on Germany and Japan
8 February 1945	Paraguay declares war on Germany and Japan
13 February 1945	Peru declares war on Gemany and Japan
14 February 1945	Chile declares war on Japan
16 February 1945	Venezuela declares war on Germany and Japan
23 February 1945	Uruguay declares war on Germany and Japan
26 February 1945	Egypt declares war on Germany and Japan
	Syria declares war on Germany and Japan
27 February 1945	Lebanon declares war on Germany and Japan
1 March 1945	Saudi Arabia declares war on Germany and Japan
	Iran declares war on Japan
	Turkey declares war on Germany and Japan
3 March 1945	Finland declares war on Germany as from 15 September 1944
27 March 1945	Argentina declares war on Axis, bringing the number of Anti-Axis countries to 53
6 June 1945	Brazil declares war on Japan
13 July 1945	Italy declares a state of war with Japan
8 August 1945	USSR declares itself at war with Japan from midnight.

LIST OF MAPS

11 Europe in March 1939
22 The Polish campaign
24 The partition of Poland
31 The Finnish campaign
46 The invasion of Norway
48 Military balance in the West
49 The German advance in Holland, Belgium and Luxembourg
62 The fall of France
78 The Italian attack on Greece
114 The invasion of Yugoslavia
116 The invasion of Greece
125 The British offensive in East Africa
130 The attack on Crete
134 The invasion of the USSR
186 The invasion of Malaya
188 The fall of the Philippines
197 The Japanese occupation of the Dutch East Indies
199 The fall of Singapore
202- The conquest of Bataan and
203 Corregidor
208 The Japanese advance into Burma
237 The battle of the Coral Sea
248 The battle of Midway
264 The first battle of El Alamein
264 The second battle of El Alamein
265 Rommel's first offensive
265 Operation *Crusader*
265 Axis break-through at Mersa

Matruh
274 Operation on Guadalcanal
320 The assault on Stalingrad
321 The Russian counter-attack at Stalingrad
350 The battle of Kasserine
351 The Russian advance to Kharkov
355 Breaking the Mareth line
381 The US landings in New Georgia
383 Operation *Citadel*
388 The invasion of Sicily
432 The drive to the Gustav Line
434 The Russian offensive towards the Dniepr
449 US operations on Bougainville
449 US landing on Tarawa atoll
479 The liberation of Leningrad
503 The Italian Front before the Allied offensive against Cassino
508 The war in China
522 The battle of Kohima
523 The relief of Imphal
530 D-Day
536 US occupation of the Marianas
541 Allied counter-offensive in the Pacific
546 Forecast of Allied progress and land occupied in the first 50 days following D-Day
548 The *Gothic* line to the end of August 1944

551 The Russian advance into Poland
554 The Russian advance into Latvia and Lithuania
571 The eastern section of the *Gothic* line to the end of August 1944
572 Operation *Anvil*
575 The collapse of German defences in Normandy
577 The collapse of German defences in the Balkans
589 The drive to the Rhine
590 Operation *Market Garden*
591 The drive to the Rhine to 15 September 1944
604 Operations on Leyte Island
607 The first battle of Leyte Gulf
636 The battle of the Ardennes
656 US offensive in Luzon
659 US operations in the southern Philippines
669 The Russian drive to the Oder
679 Operations on Iwo Jima
676 The invasions of Austria and Hungary
687 Crossing the Rhine
689 The drive into Germany
705 US operations on Okinawa
716 The end in Italy
719 End of the campaign on the Eastern Front
725 The battle of Berlin
731 The capture of Rangoon

The maps are taken from Young, P. and Natkiel, R., *Atlas of the Second World War*, Weidenfeld and Nicolson, London 1973.

Illustration sources: Mondadori Archives, Bildarchiv Preussischer Kulturbesitz (Berlin).